WARREN REEVE DUCHAC

Financial and Managerial Accounting

12e

Carl S. Warren
Professor Emeritus of Accounting
University of Georgia, Athens

James M. Reeve
Professor Emeritus of Accounting
University of Tennessee, Knoxville

Jonathan E. Duchac
Professor of Accounting
Wake Forest University

SOUTH-WESTERN
CENGAGE Learning™

Australia • Brazil • Japan • Korea • Mexico • Singapore • Spain • United Kingdom • United States

SOUTH-WESTERN
CENGAGE Learning™

Financial and Managerial Accounting, 12e

Carl S. Warren
James M. Reeve
Jonathan E. Duchac

Senior Vice President, LRS/Acquisitions & Solutions Planning: Jack W. Calhoun

Editorial Director, Business & Economics: Erin Joyner

Editor-in-Chief: Rob Dewey

Sr. Acquisitions Editor: Matt Filimonov

Supervising Developmental Editor: Aaron Arnsparger

Sr. Developmental Editor: Laura Bofinger Ansara

Editorial Assistant: Ann Loch

Marketing Manager: Natalie Livingston

Sr. Marketing Communications Manager: Sarah Greber

Sr. Content Project Manager: Cliff Kallemeyn

Sr. Media Editor: Scott Fidler

Media Editor: Jessica Robbe

Frontlist Buyer, Manufacturing: Doug Wilke

Sr. Art Director: Stacy Shirley

Sr. Rights Acquisitions Acct. Specialist: Dean Dauphinais

Library of Congress Control Number: 2012949924

Student Edition ISBN 13: 978-1-285-16373-4
Student Edition ISBN 10: 1-285-16373-7

Cover art: Getty Images/Rubberball
© hkeita/Shutterstock

Cengage Learning International Offices

Asia
www.cengageasia.com
tel: (65) 6410 1200

Australia/New Zealand
www.cengage.com.au
tel: (61) 3 9685 4111

Brazil
www.cengage.com.br
tel: (011) 3665 9900

India
www.cengage.co.in
tel: (91) 11 30484837/38

Latin America
www.cengage.com.mx
tel: +52 (55) 1500 6000

UK/Europe/Middle East/Africa
www.cengage.co.uk
tel: (44) 207 067 2500

Represented in Canada by Nelson Education, Ltd.
www.nelson.com
tel: (416) 752 9100 / (800) 668 0671

Cengage Learning is a leading provider of customized learning solutions with office locations around the globe, including Singapore, the United Kingdom, Australia, Mexico, Brazil, and Japan. Locate your local office at: **www.cengage.com/global**

For product information: **www.cengage.com/international**
Visit your local office: **www.cengage.com/global**
Visit our corporate website: **www.cengage.com**

Printed in USA
1 2 3 4 5 6 17 16 15 14 13 12

The Author Team

Terry R. Spray InHisImage Studios

Carl S. Warren

Dr. Carl S. Warren is Professor Emeritus of Accounting at the University of Georgia, Athens. Dr. Warren has taught classes at the University of Georgia, University of Iowa, Michigan State University, and University of Chicago. Professor Warren focused his teaching efforts on principles of accounting and auditing. He received his Ph.D. from Michigan State University and his B.B.A. and M.A. from the University of Iowa. During his career, Dr. Warren published numerous articles in professional journals, including *The Accounting Review, Journal of Accounting Research, Journal of Accountancy, The CPA Journal,* and *Auditing: A Journal of Practice & Theory.* Dr. Warren has served on numerous committees of the American Accounting Association, the American Institute of Certified Public Accountants, and the Institute of Internal Auditors. He has also consulted with numerous companies and public accounting firms. Professor Warren is an avid handball player and has played in the World Handball Championships in Portland, Oregon, and Dublin, Ireland. He enjoys backpacking and recently took an eleven-day, ten-night trip in the Thorofare area of Yellowstone National Park. He has rafted the Grand Canyon and backpacked rim-to-rim. Professor Warren also enjoys fly fishing, skiing, golfing, and motorcycling.

Charles J. Garvey III / Garvey Photography

James M. Reeve

Dr. James M. Reeve is Professor Emeritus of Accounting and Information Management at the University of Tennessee. Professor Reeve taught on the accounting faculty for 25 years, after graduating with his Ph.D. from Oklahoma State University. His teaching efforts focused on undergraduate accounting principles and graduate education in the Master of Accountancy and Senior Executive MBA programs. Beyond this, Professor Reeve is also very active in the Supply Chain Certification program, which is a major executive education and research effort of the College. His research interests are varied and include work in managerial accounting, supply chain management, lean manufacturing, and information management. He has published over 40 articles in academic and professional journals, including the *Journal of Cost Management, Journal of Management Accounting Research, Accounting Review, Management Accounting Quarterly, Supply Chain Management Review,* and *Accounting Horizons.* He has consulted or provided training around the world for a wide variety of organizations, including Boeing, Procter & Gamble, Norfolk Southern, Hershey Foods, Coca-Cola, and Sony. When not writing books, Professor Reeve plays golf and is involved in faith-based activities.

© Ken Bennett

Jonathan Duchac

Dr. Jonathan Duchac is the Merrill Lynch and Co. Professor of Accounting and Director of International Programs at Wake Forest University. He holds a joint appointment at the Vienna University of Business and Economics in Vienna, Austria. Dr. Duchac currently teaches introductory and advanced courses in financial accounting and has received a number of awards during his career, including the Wake Forest University Outstanding Graduate Professor Award, the T.B. Rose Award for Instructional Innovation, and the University of Georgia Outstanding Teaching Assistant Award. In addition to his teaching responsibilities, Dr. Duchac has served as Accounting Advisor to Merrill Lynch Equity Research, where he worked with research analysts in reviewing and evaluating the financial reporting practices of public companies. He has testified before the U.S. House of Representatives, the Financial Accounting Standards Board, and the Securities and Exchange Commission and has worked with a number of major public companies on financial reporting and accounting policy issues. In addition to his professional interests, Dr. Duchac serves on the Board of Directors of The Special Children's School of Winston-Salem, a private, nonprofit developmental day school serving children with special needs. Dr. Duchac is an avid long-distance runner, mountain biker, and snow skier. His recent events include the Grandfather Mountain Marathon, the Black Mountain Marathon, the Shut-In Ridge Trail run, and NO MAAM (Nocturnal Overnight Mountain Bike Assault on Mount Mitchell).

A History of Success

Leading the Way by Activating Learning

Generations of business students have learned accounting from the Warren, Reeve, and Duchac textbook. This tradition of success goes back twenty-five editions. *Financial and Managerial Accounting* is successful because it continues to innovate and respond to changing student learning styles while introducing students to accounting through a variety of learning models and multimedia.

This tradition of innovation continues today. Countless conversations with accounting instructors and the authors' own experiences in the classroom have revealed how much the teaching and learning environment has changed. Today's internet generation has grown up on the computer. The online and digital universe is both a natural learning environment for students and a learning medium they expect beyond the textbook.

In response to changes in student learning, the authors have ensured their text is an integrated print/digital learning experience for students. In crafting the philosophy for this edition, the authors extended the time-tested integrated learning experience of their text to the technology in interactive ways.

For this 12th edition, new online Activation Exercises were created by the authors. These foundational learning activities are the perfect introduction to the major concepts in each chapter. *By using the online environment to demonstrate concepts through activities, the authors have gone beyond what is possible in a printed text.* Students who complete these activities will come to class with a deeper understanding of key terminology, economic events, the accounting system, and the impact on the financial statements. With a better foundational knowledge of accounting concepts, class sessions can be utilized to help students delve even further in their understanding.

These activities are a result of much collaboration with many accounting instructors over the past two years. They reflect the suggestions and feedback we receive from instructors and students on an ongoing basis. We are very happy with the results and think you will be pleased with the new activities as well.

The original author of *Accounting* (the two-semester version of this book), James McKinsey, could not have imagined the success and influence this text has enjoyed over the past 25 editions—or that his original vision would lead the market into the online world through subsequent authors' expertise. As the current authors, we appreciate the responsibility of protecting and enhancing this vision, while continuing to refine it to meet the changing needs of students and instructors. Always in touch with a tradition of excellence, but never satisfied with yesterday's success, this edition enthusiastically embraces a changing environment and continues to proudly lead the way in activating student learning and success. We sincerely thank our many colleagues who have helped to make it happen.

"The teaching of accounting is no longer designed to train professional accountants only. With the growing complexity of business and the constantly increasing difficulty of the problems of management, it has become essential that everyone who aspires to a position of responsibility should have a knowledge of the fundamental principles of accounting."

—James O. McKinsey, Author, first edition, 1929

New to the 12th Edition

NEW

Online Homework Solutions and Student Study Tools

Given the prevalence and expansion of student learning through the use of online tools, the Warren, Reeve, and Duchac team has dedicated significant focus to creating new and valuable homework and teaching solutions for the 12th edition. Designed to work with the typical instructor's workflow in mind, the following online homework solutions offer a number of new and innovative choices for both instructors and students using Cengage Learning's technology platforms: Animated Activities, Activation Exercises, Blueprint Problems, and Blueprint Connections.

Animated Activities

Many instructors struggle to expose students to concepts before class begins. Students who come to class more prepared are more likely to succeed, and **Animated Activities** are the perfect pre-lecture assignment! Animated Activities use illustrations to visually explain and guide students through selected core topics in introductory financial and managerial accounting. Each activity uses a realistic company example to illustrate how the concepts relate to the everyday activities of a business. These activities offer excellent resources for students prior to coming to lecture and will especially appeal to visual learners.

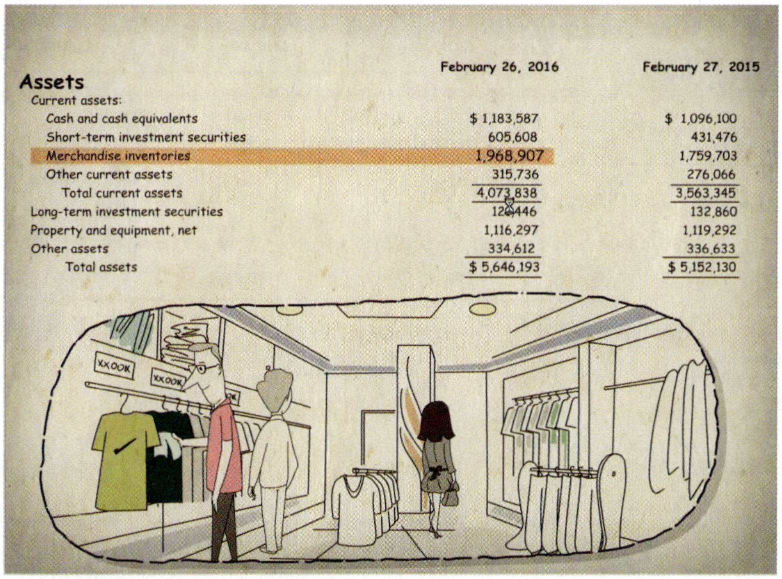

Accounting concepts are brought to life through the use of engaging visuals!

Topics covered include Introduction to the Financial Statements, Transaction Analysis, Adjusting Entries, Receivables, Bank Reconciliations, Inventory, Depreciation, Bonds, Stockholders' Equity, Cost of Goods Sold Model, Job Order Costing, Activity-Based Costing, Mixed Costs, Budgeting, *and more.* Coverage and terminology is consistent with the textbook presentation.

Animated Activities are in CengageNOW as assignable homework items and as assets that populate the Study Tools/Personalized Study Plan. The assignable activities include multiple-choice questions that quiz students on the larger concepts addressed in the animation.

New to the 12th Edition

NEW

Activation Exercises

For most students, a Principles of Accounting course is their first exposure to both *business transactions* and the *accounting system*. While these concepts are already difficult to master individually, their combination and interdependency in the introductory accounting course causes students to struggle. Students often resort to memorization as a way to pass the course, but such surface learning does little to develop the critical thinking skills and deep understanding that are necessary for success in future business courses.

To overcome these challenges, the authors created the **Activation Exercises** to providing a learning system that focuses on developing a better understanding of (1) key terms and definitions, (2) the economics of business transactions, (3) how these transactions are recorded in the accounting system, and where relevant, (4) how these transactions are ultimately reflected in the financial statements.

The Activation Exercise structure builds the critical thinking skills that are necessary for students to succeed in both introductory accounting and future accounting courses. Reviewers have enthusiastically praised the authors' new online activities and indicated that they would be both ideal pre-class activities and after-class assignments. The Activation Exercises are applied to the following financial chapters in this text and available within CengageNOW: Chapters 1–4, 5, 6, and 8–12.

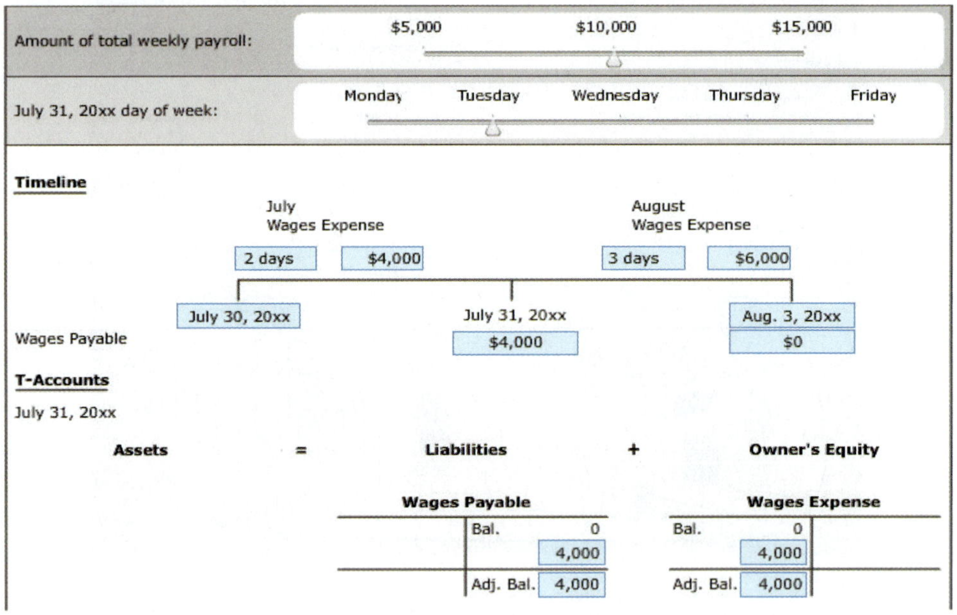

Blueprint Problems

Blueprint Problems provide an opportunity *to teach* more than an opportunity to assess the student's knowledge. Blueprint Problems cover the primary learning objectives and help students understand the fundamental accounting concepts and their associated building blocks, and not just memorize the formulas or journal entries required for a single concept. This means that a Blueprint Problem can include basic concepts from previous chapters, such as account types, the impact on the accounting equation, and other fundamental aspects of the financial statements.

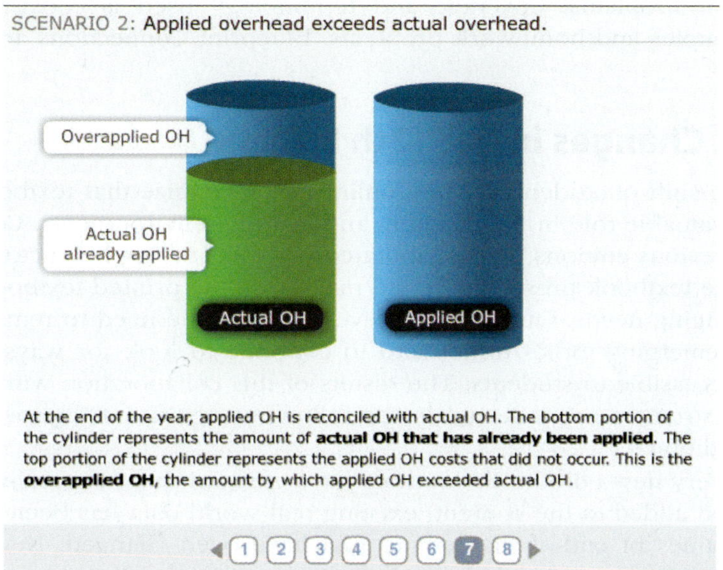

Where applicable, selected Blueprint Problems include dynamic visual elements that help students with difficult concepts.

Blueprint Problems cover most major topics and concepts in financial and managerial accounting and include rich feedback to help students when checking their work. In addition, these problems provide detailed explanations to reinforce the correct solutions, providing students with an excellent learning resource. Coverage and terminology used is consistent with the textbook examples and homework problems. Blueprint Problems are available in CengageNOW and Aplia.

Blueprint Connections

Blueprint Connections are shorter extensions of the Blueprint Problems, created based on market demand for briefer but more focused homework assignments that build upon concepts covered and introduced within the Blueprint Problems.

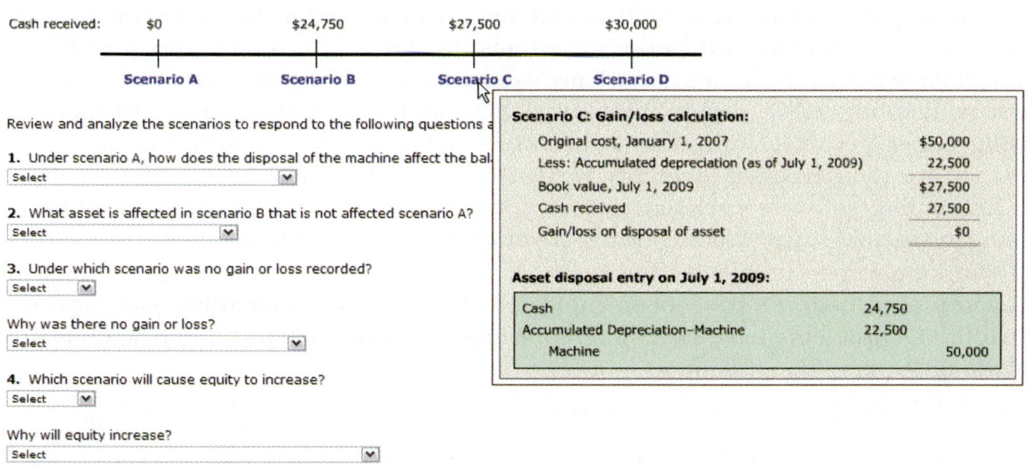

Blueprint Connections extend beyond the foundations covered in the Blueprint Problems. In this example, students are asked to respond to different scenarios related to the disposal of a fixed asset.

Blueprint Connections offer a natural sequence immediately following the completion of a corresponding Blueprint Problem, or completed independently. Blueprint Connections share a similar structure and level of feedback and explanation with Blueprint Problems. Coverage and terminology used is consistent with the textbook examples and homework problems. Blueprint Connections are available in CengageNOW.

Textbook Changes in the 12th Edition

Even with the shift of student learning online, we recognize that textbooks continue to play an invaluable role in the teaching and learning environments. Continuing our focus from previous editions, we collaborated with accounting instructors in an effort to improve the textbook presentation and make sure the printed textbook also meets students' changing needs. Our research revealed to us the need to remain current in the areas of emerging topics/trends and to continue to look for ways to make the book more accessible to students. The results of this collaboration with hundreds of accounting instructors are reflected in the following significant improvements made to the 12th edition.

As with every new edition, the authors have ensured that new real-world companies have been added to the content, existing real world data has been updated, and names and values of end-of-chapter material have been changed. New highlighted chapter opener companies include Twitter (Chapter 1); Apple (Chapter 2); Google, along with updated bylaws and an activity using Google (Chapter 11); and Dick's Sporting Goods (Chapter 12).

"Accounting for Merchandising Businesses" (Chapter 5) was restructured from the prior edition. The discussion of financial statements, including the multiple-step income statement, has been moved to the end of the chapter. The chapter now begins with a brief description of the nature of merchandising operations, followed by the accounting for purchase and sales transactions. The perpetual inventory system is used throughout the chapter to illustrate merchandise transactions. The periodic inventory system is discussed in the end-of-chapter appendix. The homework has been designed so that the instructor can assign the perpetual, periodic, or both systems.

"Inventories" (Chapter 6) has been revised to include coverage of the weighted average inventory cost flow method. The weighted average cost method is now described and illustrated for the perpetual and periodic inventory systems. In doing so, the chapter illustrations were revised and amounts changed to facilitate comparisons between the perpetual and periodic systems, as well as to avoid rounding issues. New homework exercises and problems were added so that instructors can cover the first-in, first-out (FIFO), last-in, first-out (LIFO), and weighted average cost methods using either perpetual or periodic inventory systems. The weighted average cost method for the perpetual inventory system was added because of the increased use of accounting software packages that use it with point-of-sale systems. In addition, many instructors suggested increasing coverage of the weighted average cost method.

Working Paper problems (for series A & B) remaining from prior editions in Chapters 2, 4, and 17 have been moved to the product companion site, and the Chapter 17 problems have been altered within the text to stand alone without the Working Papers requirement.

Hallmark Features

Financial and Managerial Accounting, 12e, is unparalleled in pedagogical innovation. Our constant dialogue with accounting faculty continues to affect how we refine and improve the text to meet the needs of today's students. Our goal is to provide a logical framework and pedagogical system that caters to how students of today study and learn.

Clear Objectives and Key Learning Outcomes To guide students, the authors provide clear chapter objectives and important learning outcomes. All the chapter materials relate back to these key points and outcomes, which keeps students focused on the most important topics and concepts in order to succeed in the course.

Example Exercises Example Exercises reinforce concepts and procedures in a bold, new way. Like a teacher in the classroom, students follow the authors' example to see how to complete accounting applications as they are presented in the text. This feature also provides a list of Practice Exercises that parallel the Example Exercises so students get the practice they need. In addition, the Practice Exercises include references to the chapter Example Exercises so that students can easily cross-reference when completing homework.

See the example of the application being presented.

Follow along as the authors work through the Example Exercise.

Try these corresponding end-of-chapter exercises for practice!

Example Exercise 2-2 Journal Entry for Asset Purchase OBJ 2

Prepare a journal entry for the purchase of a truck on June 3 for $42,500, paying $8,500 cash and the remainder on account.

Follow My Example 2-2

June 3	Truck	42,500	
	Cash		8,500
	Accounts Payable		34,000

Practice Exercises: PE 2-2A, PE 2-2B

"At a Glance" Chapter Summary Students prepare for homework and tests by referring to our end-of-chapter grid, which outlines learning objectives, linking concept coverage to specific examples. Using At a Glance, students can review the chapter's

At a Glance 3

OBJ 1 **Describe the nature of the adjusting process.**

Key Points The accrual basis of accounting requires that revenues are reported in the period in which they are earned and expenses are matched with the revenues they generate. The updating of accounts at the end of the accounting period is called the adjusting process. Each adjusting entry affects an income statement and balance sheet account. The four types of accounts requiring adjusting entries are prepaid expenses, unearned revenues, accrued revenues, and accrued expenses.

Learning Outcomes	Example Exercises	Practice Exercises
• Explain why accrual accounting requires adjusting entries.		
• List accounts that do and do NOT require adjusting entries at the end of the accounting period.	EE3-1	PE3-1A, 3-1B
• Give an example of a prepaid expense, unearned revenue, accrued revenue, and accrued expense.	EE3-2	PE3-2A, 3-2B

Hallmark Features

learning objectives and key learning outcomes. In addition, all the *Example Exercises* and *Practice Exercises* have been indexed so that each learning objective and key outcomes can be viewed. At the end of each chapter, the "At a Glance" summary grid ties everything together and helps students stay on track.

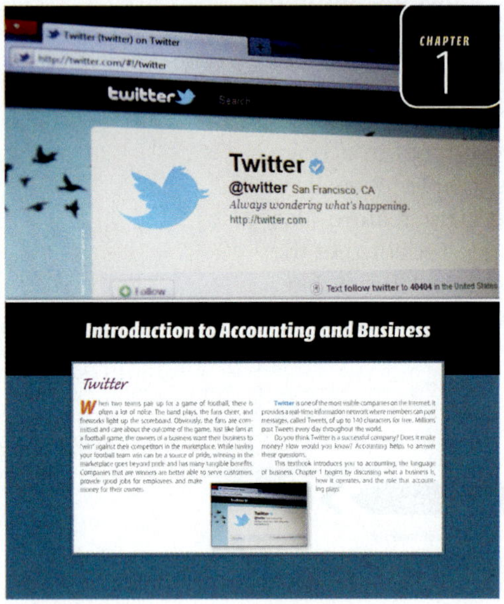

Real-World Chapter Openers Building on the strengths of past editions, these openers continue to relate the accounting and business concepts in the chapter to students' lives. These openers employ examples of real companies and provide invaluable insight into real practice. Several of the openers created especially for this edition focus on interesting companies such as Twitter, Rhapsody, Razor, E.W. Scripps Company, a diverse media concern, and Facebook.

Continuing Case Study Students follow a fictitious company, **NetSolutions**, throughout Chapters 1–5, which demonstrates a variety of transactions. The continuity of using the same company facilitates student learning especially for Chapters 1–4, which cover the accounting cycle. Also, using the same company allows students to follow the transition of the company from a service business in Chapters 1–4 to a merchandising business in Chapter 5.

Illustrative Problem and Solution A solved problem models one or more of the chapter's assignment problems so that students can apply the modeled procedures to end-of-chapter materials.

Integrity, Objectivity, and Ethics in Business In each chapter, these cases help students develop their ethical compass. Often coupled with related end-of-chapter activities, these cases can be discussed in class or students can consider the cases as they read the chapter. Both the section and related end-of-chapter materials are indicated with a unique icon for a consistent presentation.

Integrity, Objectivity, and Ethics in Business

ON BEING GREEN

Process manufacturing often involves significant energy and material resources, which can be harmful to the environment. Thus, many process manufacturing companies, such as chemical, electronic, and metal processors, must address environmental issues. Companies, such as **DuPont**, **Intel**, **Apple**, and **Alcoa**, are at the forefront of providing environmental solutions for their products and processes. For example, Apple provides free recycling programs for Macs®, iPhones®, and iPads®. Apple recovers over 90% by weight of the original product in reusable components, glass, and plastic. You can even receive a free gift card for voluntarily recycling an older Apple product.

Source: Apple Web site.

Business Connection and Comprehensive Real-World Notes Students get a close-up look at how accounting operates in the marketplace through a variety of *Business Connection* boxed features.

Business Connection

AVATAR: THE HIGHEST GROSSING MOVIE OF ALL TIME (BUT NOT THE MOST PROFITABLE)

Prior to the release of the blockbuster *Avatar* in December 2009, many were skeptical if the movie's huge $500 million investment would pay off. After all, just to break even the movie would have to perform as one of the top 50 movies of all time. To provide a return that was double the investment, the movie would have to crack the top 10. Many thought this was a tall order, even though James Cameron, the force behind this movie, already had the number one grossing movie of all time: *Titanic*, at $1.8 billion in worldwide box office revenues. Could he do it again? That was the question.

So, how did the film do? Only eight weeks after its release, *Avatar* had become the number one grossing film of all time, with over $2.5 billion in worldwide box office revenue. However, even though *Avatar* made the most money, was it the most profitable when taking account of the total investment? CNBC analyzed movies by their return on investment (total box office receipts divided by the total movie cost) and found that *Avatar* wasn't even in the top 15 movies by this measure. Number one on this list was *My Big Fat Greek Wedding* with a 6,150% return. To make this list, it helped to have a small denominator.

Sources: Michael Cieply, "A Movie's Budget Pops from the Screen," *New York Times*, November 8, 2009; "Bulk of Avatar Profit Still to Come," *The Age*, February 3, 2010. Daniel Bukszpan, "15 Most Profitable Movies of All Time," cnbc.com, September 10, 2010.

International Financial Reporting Standards (IFRS)

IFRS IFRS

IFRS is on the minds of many accounting educators of today. While the future is still unclear, our research indicates a growing need to provide more basic awareness of these standards within the text. We have continued to incorporate some elements of IFRS throughout the text as appropriate to provide this level of awareness, being careful not to encroach upon the core GAAP principles that remain the hallmark focus of the book. These elements include icons that have been placed throughout the financial chapters which point to specific IFRS-related content, outlined with more detail in Appendix C. This table outlines the IFRS impact on the accounting concept.

Hallmark Features

International Connection *International Connection* features highlight IFRS topics from a real-world perspective and appear in Chapters 1, 4, 6, 9, 11, and 14.

IFRS

International Connection

IFRS FOR STATEMENT OF CASH FLOWS

The statement of cash flows is required under International Financial Reporting Standards (IFRS). The statement of cash flows under IFRS is similar to that reported under U.S. GAAP in that the statement has separate sections for operating, investing, and financing activities. Like U.S. GAAP, IFRS also allow the use of either the indirect or direct method of reporting cash flows from operating activities. IFRS differ from U.S. GAAP in some minor areas, including:

- Interest paid can be reported as either an operating or a financing activity, while interest received can be reported as either an operating or an investing activity. In contrast, U.S. GAAP reports interest paid or received as an operating activity.
- Dividends paid can be reported as either an operating or a financing activity, while dividends received can be reported as either an operating or an investing activity. In contrast, U.S. GAAP reports dividends paid as a financing activity and dividends received as an operating activity.
- Cash flows to pay taxes are reported as a separate line in the operating activities, in contrast to U.S. GAAP, which does not require a separate line disclosure.

* IFRS are further discussed and illustrated on pages 716–723 and in Appendix D.

Mornin' Joe International

Our authors have prepared statements for Mornin' Joe under IFRS guidelines as a basis for comparison with U.S.-prepared statements. This allows students to see how financial reporting differs under IFRS.

The Accounting Equation

We maintain the recently revamped format in Chapter 2 for analyzing transactions. This format includes the following elements: (1) transaction description, (2) analysis, (3) journal entry, and (4) accounting equation impact. This will help students understand that a transaction ultimately affects the accounting equation—*Assets = Liabilities + Owner's Equity.*

Transaction G *Nov. 30 Chris Clark determined that the cost of supplies on hand at November 30 was $550.*

Analysis

NetSolutions purchased $1,350 of supplies on November 10. Thus, $800 ($1,350 – $550) of supplies must have been used during November. This transaction is recorded in the journal as an $800 increase (debit) to Supplies Expense and an $800 decrease (credit) to Supplies.

Journal Entry

Nov.	30	Supplies Expense		800	
		Supplies			800
		Supplies used during November.			

Accounting Equation Impact

Assets = Liabilities + Stockholders' Equity (Expense)

Supplies	
	Nov. 30 800

Supplies Expense	
Nov. 30 800	

Activity-Based Costing

Pulling from our existing appendix coverage, we have placed in Chapter 24 a thorough discussion of activity-based costing (ABC). ABC is framed in the context of product pricing and profit analysis.

A new uniform method for performing differential analysis is employed for all the differential analysis illustrations and end-of-chapter materials. This approach provides the student a consistent solution grid for solving differential analyses.

Financial Analysis and Interpretation

F·A·I

We continute to highlight Financial Analysis and Interpretation learning objectives in the financial chapters and, where appropriate, link to real-world situations. FAI encourages students to go deeper into the material to analyze accounting information and improve critical thinking skills.

Test Bank

Last edition's test bank was completely revamped with the assistance of more than fifteen distinguished professors. We've continued to refresh many of the questions as well as verify for accuracy. The Test Bank delivers more than 3,500 questions overall. Additional tagging has been implemented for increased options in performance outcomes measurement.

Excel Templates

Our enhanced Excel templates allow professors to turn off the "instant feedback" asterisks. Based on the file provided to them, students can complete the spreadsheet and email the file to their instructor. The instructor can then input a code that will automatically grade the student's work. These Excel templates complement end-of-chapter problems. They are located on the companion website at **www.cengagebrain.com** and also within CengageNOW.

Market Leading End-of-Chapter Material Students need to practice accounting so that they can understand and use it. To give students the greatest possible advantage in the real world, *Financial and Managerial Accounting, 12e,* goes beyond presenting theory and procedure with comprehensive, time-tested, end-of-chapter material.

Online Solutions

South-Western, a division of Cengage Learning, offers a vast array of online solutions to suit your course needs. Choose the product that best meets your classroom needs and course goals. Please check with your Cengage representative for more details or for ordering information.

CengageNow

CengageNOW is a powerful course management and online homework tool that provides robust instructor control and customization to optimize the student learning experience and meet desired outcomes. CengageNOW offers:

- Auto-graded homework (static and algorithmic varieties), test bank, Personalized Study Plan, and eBook are all in one resource.
- Easy-to-use course management options offer flexibility and continuity from one semester to another.
- Different levels of feedback and engaging student resources guide students through material and solidify learning.
- The most robust and flexible assignment options in the industry.
- "Smart Entry" helps eliminate common data entry errors and prevents students from guessing their way through the homework.
- The ability to analyze student work from the gradebook and generate reports on learning outcomes. Each problem is tagged in the Solutions Manual and CengageNOW to AICPA, IMA, Business Program (AACSB), ACBSP, and Bloom's Taxonomy outcomes so you can measure student performance.

CengageNOW Upgrades:

- Our General Ledger Software is now being offered in a new online format. Your students can solve selected end-of-chapter assignments in a format that emulates commercial general ledger software.
- For a complete list of CengageNOW upgrades, refer to the introductory brochure at the front of the Instructor's Edition.
- New Design: CengageNOW has been redesigned to enhance your experience.

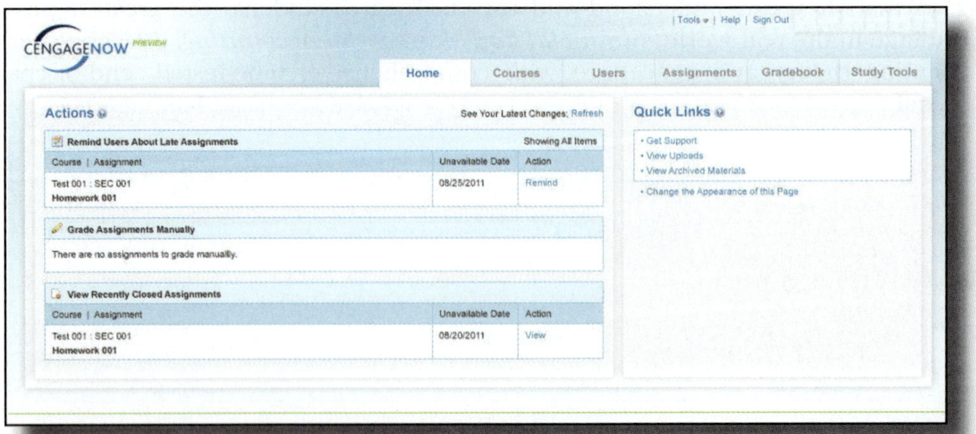

For a CengageNOW demo, visit: www.cengage.com/digital/cnowdemo

Aplia

Aplia is a premier online homework product that successfully engages students and maximizes the amount of effort they put forth, creating more efficient learners. Aplia's advantages are:

- Aplia provides end-of-chapter homework and offers **additional problems sets** that have been authored specifically for the digital environment. These problems sets are available for all chapters and are designed to engage students by providing them with a conceptual, as well as tactical, understanding of accounting.
- Students can receive **unique**, **detailed feedback** and the full solution after each attempt on homework.
- "**Grade It Now**" maximizes student effort on each attempt and ensures that students do their own work. Students have up to three attempts to work each problem and each attempt generates a new randomized version of the problem. The final score is an average of all attempts.
- "**Smart Entry**" helps eliminate common data entry errors and prevents students from guessing their way through the homework.

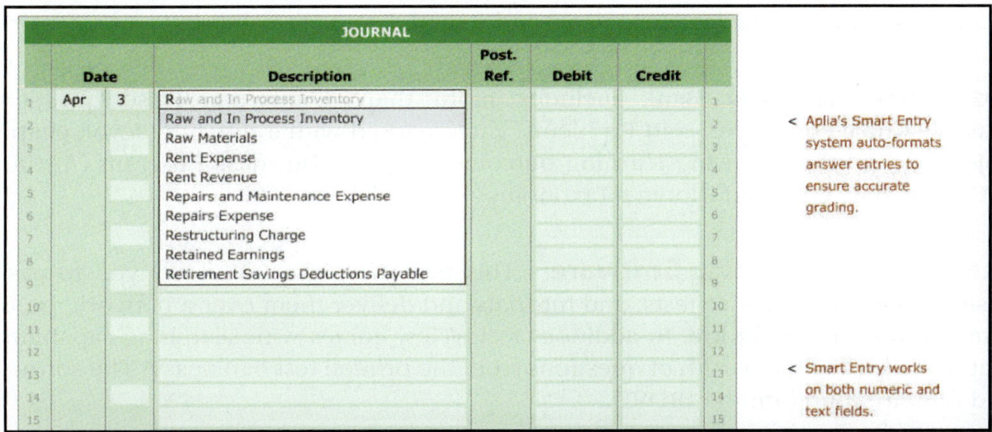

Aplia Upgrades:

- **Blueprint Problems** are a new problem type designed to help students understand fundamental accounting concepts and their associated building blocks. They are structured like a tutorial and stress teaching and learning over assessment. (See pp. vi-vii of this preface for more information.)
- The Warren/Reeve/Duchac titles in Aplia now feature the **MindTap Reader** ebook. This is Cengage's premier ebook format. It is highly interactive, allows for inline note-taking and highlighting, and features a variety of apps to further assist students.

For an Aplia demo, visit: www.aplia.com/accounting

WebTutor™

WebTutor™ on Blackboard® and WebCT®—Improve student grades with online review and test preparation tools in an easy-to-use course cartridge.

Visit www.cengage.com/webtutor for more information.

For the Instructor

When it comes to supporting instructors, South-Western is unsurpassed. *Financial and Managerial Accounting, 12e,* continues the tradition with powerful print and digital ancillaries aimed at facilitating greater course successes.

Instructor's Manual The Instructor's Manual includes: Brief Synopsis, List of Objectives, Key Terms, Ideas for Class Discussion, Lecture Aids, Demonstration Problems, Group Learning Activities, Exercises and Problems for Reinforcement, and Internet Activities. Suggested Approaches incorporate many modern teaching initiatives, including active learning, collaborative learning, critical thinking, and writing across the curriculum.

Solutions Manual The Solutions Manual contains answers to all exercises, problems, and activities in the text. The solutions are author-written and verified multiple times for numerical accuracy and consistency.

Instructor's Resource DVD The Instructor's Resource DVD (IRDVD) includes the PowerPoint® Presentations, Instructor's Manual, Solutions Manual, Test Bank, ExamView®, General Ledger Inspector, and Excel® Template Solutions.

Test Bank The Test Bank includes more than 3,500 True/False questions, Multiple-Choice questions, and Problems, each marked with a difficulty level, chapter objective, and the following learning outcomes tagging: Business Program (AACSB), AICPA, ACBSP, IMA, and Bloom's Taxonomy.

ExamView

ExamView® Pro Testing Software This intuitive software allows you to easily customize exams, practice tests, and tutorials and deliver them over a network, on the Internet, or in printed form. In addition, ExamView comes with searching capabilities that make sorting the wealth of questions from the printed test bank easy. The software and files are found on the IRDVD.

PowerPoint® Each presentation, which is included on the IRDVD and on the product support site, enhances lectures and simplifies class preparation. Each chapter contains objectives followed by a thorough outline of the chapter that easily provides an entire lecture model. Also, exhibits from the chapter, such as the new Example Exercises, have been recreated as colorful PowerPoint slides to create a powerful, customizable tool.

SPREADSHEET

Instructor Excel® Templates These templates provide the solutions for the problems that have Enhanced Excel® templates for students. Through these files, instructors can see the solutions in the same format as the students. All problems with accompanying templates are marked in the book with a spreadsheet icon and are listed in the information grid in the solutions manual. These templates are available for download on the instructor companion site at login.cengage.com or on the IRDVD.

For the Student

Students come to accounting with a variety of learning needs. *Financial and Managerial Accounting, 12e,* offers a broad range of supplements in both printed form and easy-to-use technology. We continue to refine our entire supplement package around the comments instructors have provided about their courses and teaching needs.

Study Guide This author-written guide provides students Quiz and Test Hints, Matching questions, Fill-in-the-Blank questions (Parts A & B), Multiple-Choice questions, True/False questions, Exercises, and Problems for each chapter.

Working Papers for Exercises and Problems The traditional working papers include problem-specific forms for preparing solutions for Exercises, A & B Problems, the Continuing Problem, and the Comprehensive Problems from the textbook. These forms, with preprinted headings, provide a structure for the problems, which helps students get started and saves them time.

Blank Working Papers These Working Papers are available for completing exercises and problems either from the text or prepared by the instructor. They have no preprinted headings. A guide at the front of the Working Papers tells students which form they will need for each problem and are available online in a .pdf, printable format.

Enhanced Excel® Templates These templates are provided for selected long or complicated end-of-chapter problems and provide assistance to the student as they set up and work the problem. Certain cells are coded to display a red asterisk when an incorrect answer is entered, which helps students stay on track. Selected problems that can be solved using these templates are designated by a spreadsheet icon.

SPREADSHEET

General Ledger Software The CLGL software continues to be offered with the choice of an online format or a CD-based version. Students can solve selected end-of-chapter assignments in a format that emulates commercial general ledger software. Students make entries into the general journal or special journals, track the posting of the entries to the general ledger, and create financial statements or reports. This gives students important exposure to commercial accounting software, yet in a manner that is more forgiving of student errors. Assignments are automatically graded online. Problems utilized in CLGL are designated by a General Ledger icon.

GENERAL LEDGER

Practice Sets For more in-depth application of accounting practices, instructors may choose from among six different Practice Sets for long-term assignments. Each Practice Set focuses on one business and can be solved manually or with general ledger software. See the detailed table of contents for business descriptions.

Companion Web Site: www.cengagebrain.com At the home page's search area, type in your book's ISBN (the number located on the back of your text cover) or search by title. Click on "Access" under Related Products and Free Materials. This site provides students with a wealth of introductory accounting resources, including quizzing and supplement downloads and access to the Enhanced Excel® Templates.

Acknowledgments

Many of the enhancements made to *Financial and Managerial Accounting, 12e,* are a direct result of countless conversations we've had with principles of accounting professors and students over the past several years. We want to take this opportunity to thank them for their perspectives and feedback on textbook use and the importance of online homework solutions to activate learning. *12e* represents our finest edition yet!

The following individuals took the time to participate in surveys and content reviews for the 12th edition:

Patrick Borja
Citrus College

Gary Bower
Community College of Rhode Island

Thomas Branton
Alvin Community College

David Candelaria
Mt San Jacinto College

Kelly James Childs
Chippewa Valley Technical College

Gloria Grayless
Sam Houston State University

Jose Hortensi
Miami Dade College

Cathy Larson
Middlesex Community College

Charles Lewis
Houston Community College

Debra Luna
El Paso Community College

Maria Mari
Miami Dade College

Patrick Rogan
Cosumnes River College

Rachel Pernia
Essex County College

Jennifer Schneider
Gainesville State College

Robert Smolin
Citrus College

Paul K. Swanson
Illinois Central College

The following individuals took the time to participate in technology focus groups and online sessions for the purpose of enhancing the online homework experience. Many of these participants also participated in the development review of the new author-created Activation Exercises.

John Ahmad
Northern Virginia Community College

Lizabeth Austen-Jaggard
Dalton State College

Beverly Beatty
Anne Arundel Community College

Lana Becker
East Tennessee State University

B. J. Blackwood
Augusta State University

Susie Bonner
Wilbur Wright College

Patrick Borja
Citrus College

Gary Bower
Community College of Rhode Island

Thomas M. Branton
Alvin Community College

Linda Bressler
University of Houston—Downtown

Carla Cabarle
Minot State University

Roy Carson
Anne Arundel Community College

Xiaoyan Cheng
University of Nebraska—Lincoln

Kelly Childs
Chippewa Valley Technical College

Debra M. Cosgrove
University of Nebraska Lincoln

Mindy Davis
Oklahoma Panhandle State University

Patricia Derrick
Salisbury University

Stephanie Farewell
University of Arkansas at Little Rock

Linda Flaming
Monmouth University

Linda Flowers
Houston Community College

Lori Grady
Bucks County Community College

Marina R. Grau
Houston Community College

John L. Haverty
St. Joseph's University

Travis Holt
University of Tennessee

Michael E. Hopper
University of West Georgia

James B. Johnson
Community College of Philadelphia

Christine Jonick
Gainesville State College

Becky Knickel
Brookhaven College

Pamela Knight
Columbus Tech College

Elida Kraja
St. Louis Community College

Brian Leventhal
University of Illinois at Chicago

Charles Lewis
Houston Community College

James Lock
Northern Virginia Community College—Alexandria

Jennifer Malfitano
Delaware County Community College

Anna C. McAleer
LaSalle University/Arcadia University

Jeffrey McMillan
Clemson University

Michelle Meyer
Joliet Junior College

Kathleen J. Moreno
Abraham Baldwin Agricultural College

Andrea Murowski
Brookdale Community College

Aaron Pennington
York College of Pennsylvania

Rachel Pernia
Essex County College

Kristen Quinn
Northern Essex Community College

Bernadette Rienerth
Owens Community College

Jean Riley-Schultz
University of Nebraska—Lincoln

Sherry K. Ross
Texas State University

Jennifer Schneider
Gainesville State College

Judy Smith
Parkland College

Dawn Stevens
Northwest Mississippi Community College

Paul Swanson
Illinois Central College

Judith A. Toland
Bucks County Community College

Nancy Uddin
Leon Hess Business School

Patricia Walczak
Lansing Community College

Bruce Wampler
University of Tennessee at Chattanooga

Arthur Wharton
Towson University

The following instructors created content for the supplements that accompany the text:

LuAnn Bean
Florida Institute of Technology

Ana Cruz
Miami Dade College

Jose Luis Hortensi
Miami Dade College

Patricia Lopez
Valencia Community College

Kirk Lynch
Sandhills Community College

Blanca Ortega
Miami Dade College

The following individuals took the time to participate in surveys, online sessions, content reviews, and test bank revisions for the 11th edition:

Bridget Anakwe
Delaware State University

Julia L. Angel
North Arkansas College

Leah Arrington
Northwest Mississippi Community College

Donna T. Ascenzi
Bryant and Stratton College—Syracuse Campus

Ed Bagley
Darton College

James Baker
Harford Community College

Lisa Cooley Banks
University of Michigan

LuAnn Bean
Florida Institute of Technology

Judy Beebe
Western Oregon University

Brenda J. Bindschatel
Green River Community College

Eric D. Bostwick
The University of West Florida

Bryan C. Bouchard
Southern New Hampshire University

Thomas M. Branton
Alvin Community College

Celestino Caicoya
Miami Dade College

John Callister
Cornell University

Deborah Chabaud
Louisiana Technical College

Marilyn G. Ciolino
Delgado Community College

Earl Clay
Cape Cod Community College

Lisa M. Cole
Johnson County Community College

Cori Oliver Crews
Waycross College

Julie Daigle
Ft. Range Community College

Julie Dailey
Central Virginia Community College

John M. Daugherty
Pitt Community College

Becky Davis
East Mississippi Community College

Ginger Dennis
West Georgia Technical College

Scott A. Elza
Wisconsin Indianhead Technical College

Patricia Feller
Nashville State Community College

Mike Foland
Southwestern Illinois College—Belleville

Brenda S. Fowler
Alamance Community College

Jeanne Gerard
Franklin Pierce University

Christopher Gilbert
East Los Angeles College, Montery Park, CA

Mark S. Gleason
Metropolitan State University, St. Paul, Minnesota

Marina Grau
Houston Community College

Judith Grenkowicz
Kirtland Community College

Vicki Greshik
Jamestown College

Lillian S. Grose
Our Lady of Holy Cross College

Denise T. Guest
Germanna Community College

Bruce J. Gunning
Kent State University at East Liverpool

Rosie Hale
Southwest Tennessee Community College

Sara Harris
Arapahoe Community College

Matthew P. Helinski
Northeast Lakeview College

Wanda Hudson
Alabama Southern Community College

Todd A. Jensen
Sierra College

Acknowledgments

Paul T. Johnson
Mississippi Gulf Coast Community College

Mary Kline
Black Hawk College

Jan Kraft
Northwest College

David W. Krug
Johnson County Community College

Cathy Xanthaky Larson
Middlesex Community College

Brenda G. Lauer
Northeastern Junior College

Ted Lewis
Marshalltown Community College

Marion Loiola
SUNY—Orange County Community College

Ming Lu
Santa Monica College

Don Lucy
Indian River State College

Debbie Luna
El Paso Community College

Anna L. Lusher
Slippery Rock University

Kirk Lynch
Sandhills Community College

Bridgette Mahan
Harold Washington College

Irene Meares
Western New Mexico University

James B. Meir
Cleveland State Community College

John L. Miller
Metropolitan Community College

Peter Moloney
Cerritos College

Janet Morrow
East Central Community College

Pamela G. Needham
Northeast Mississippi Community College

Jeannie M. Neil
Orange Coast College, Costa Mesa, CA

Carolyn Nelson
Coffeyville Community College

Joseph Malino Nicassio
Westmoreland County Community College

Robert L. Osborne
Ohio Dominican University

Scott Paxton
North Idaho College

Ronald Pearson
Bay College

Rachel Pernia
Essex County College

Erick Pifer
Lake Michigan College

Marianne G. Pindar
Lackawanna College

Kenneth J. Plucinski
State University of New York at Fredonia

Debbie Porter
Tidewater Community College

Shirley J. Powell
Arkansas State University—Beebe

Eric M. Primuth
Cuyahoga Community College

Michael Prindle
Grand View University

Rita Pritchett
Brevard Community College

Judy Ramsay
San Jacinto College—North

Patrick Reihing
Nassau Community College

Richard Rickel
South Mountain Community College

Patricia G. Roshto
University of Louisiana—Monroe

Martin Sabo
Community College of Denver

Tracy M. Schmeltzer
Wayne Community College

Dennis C. Shea
Southern New Hampshire University

Robert W. Smith (retired)
formerly of Briarcliffe College—Patchogue, NY Campus

Kimberly D. Smith
County College of Morris

Richard Snapp
Olympic College—Bremerton

John L. Stancil
Florida Southern College

Barry Stephens
Bemidji State University

Jeff Strawser
Sam Houston State University

Stacie A. Surowiec
Harford Community College

Eric H. Sussman
UCLA Anderson Graduate School of Management

Bill Talbot
Montgomery College

Kenneth J. Tax
Farmingdale State College (SUNY)

Ronald Tidd
Central Washington University

Erol C. Tucker, Jr.
The Victoria College

Henry Velarde
Malcolm X College

Angela Waits
Gadsden State Community College

Dale Walker
Arkansas State University

Shunda Ware
Atlanta Technical College

Cheryl C. Willingham
Wisconsin Indianhead Technical College

Patrick B. Wilson
Tennessee Board of Regents

Jay E. Wright
New River Community College

Brief Contents

Contents

> **Practice Set: Hydro Paddle Boards**
> This set is a manufacturing business operated as a corporation that uses a job order cost system.
> The set can be solved manually or with the General Ledger software.

ANNETTE SHAFF/SHUTTERSTOCK

CHAPTER 1

Introduction to Accounting and Business

Twitter

When two teams pair up for a game of football, there is often a lot of noise. The band plays, the fans cheer, and fireworks light up the scoreboard. Obviously, the fans are committed and care about the outcome of the game. Just like fans at a football game, the owners of a business want their business to "win" against their competitors in the marketplace. While having your football team win can be a source of pride, winning in the marketplace goes beyond pride and has many tangible benefits. Companies that are winners are better able to serve customers, provide good jobs for employees, and make money for their owners.

Twitter is one of the most visible companies on the Internet. It provides a real-time information network where members can post messages, called Tweets, of up to 140 characters for free. Millions post Tweets every day throughout the world.

Do you think Twitter is a successful company? Does it make money? How would you know? Accounting helps to answer these questions.

This textbook introduces you to accounting, the language of business. Chapter 1 begins by discussing what a business is, how it operates, and the role that accounting plays.

Learning Objectives

After studying this chapter, you should be able to: *Example Exercises*

At a Glance 1 Page 22

OBJ 1 Describe the nature of business and the role of accounting and ethics in business.

Nature of Business and Accounting

A **business**[1] is an organization in which basic resources (inputs), such as materials and labor, are assembled and processed to provide goods or services (outputs) to customers. Businesses come in all sizes, from a local coffee house to Starbucks, which sells over $10 billion of coffee and related products each year.

The objective of most businesses is to earn a **profit**. Profit is the difference between the amounts received from customers for goods or services and the amounts paid for the inputs used to provide the goods or services. This text focuses on businesses operating to earn a profit. However, many of the same concepts and principles also apply to not-for-profit organizations such as hospitals, churches, and government agencies.

Types of Businesses

Three types of businesses operating for profit include service, merchandising, and manufacturing businesses. Some examples of each type of business are given below.

Service businesses provide services rather than products to customers.

Delta Air Lines (transportation services)
The Walt Disney Company (entertainment services)

1 A complete glossary of terms appears at the end of the text.

Merchandising businesses sell products they purchase from other businesses to customers.

Walmart (general merchandise)
Amazon.com (Internet books, music, videos)

Manufacturing businesses change basic inputs into products that are sold to customers.

Ford Motor Co. (cars, trucks, vans)
Dell, Inc. (personal computers)

Role of Accounting in Business

The role of accounting in business is to provide information for managers to use in operating the business. In addition, accounting provides information to other users in assessing the economic performance and condition of the business.

Thus, **accounting** can be defined as an information system that provides reports to users about the economic activities and condition of a business. You could think of accounting as the "language of business." This is because accounting is the means by which businesses' financial information is communicated to users.

Note:
Accounting is an information system that provides reports to users about the economic activities and condition of a business.

The process by which accounting provides information to users is as follows:

1. Identify users.
2. Assess users' information needs.
3. Design the accounting information system to meet users' needs.
4. Record economic data about business activities and events.
5. Prepare accounting reports for users.

As illustrated in Exhibit 1, users of accounting information can be divided into two groups: internal users and external users.

EXHIBIT 1

Accounting as an Information System

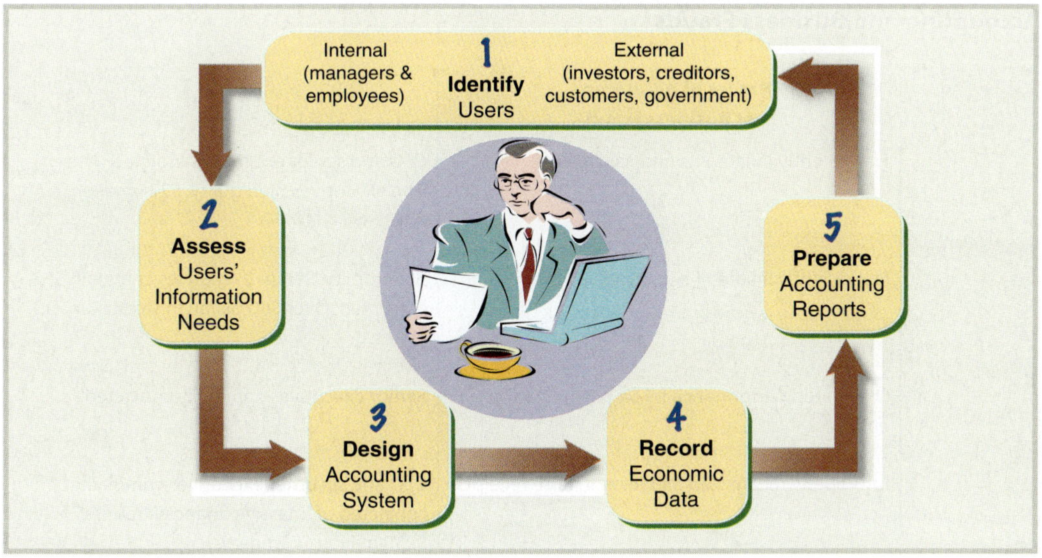

Internal users of accounting information include managers and employees. These users are directly involved in managing and operating the business. The area of accounting that provides internal users with information is called **managerial accounting**, or **management accounting**.

The objective of managerial accounting is to provide relevant and timely information for managers' and employees' decision-making needs. Oftentimes, such information is sensitive and is not distributed outside the business. Examples of sensitive information might include information about customers, prices, and plans to expand the business. Managerial accountants employed by a business are employed in **private accounting**.

External users of accounting information include investors, creditors, customers, and the government. These users are not directly involved in managing and operating the business. The area of accounting that provides external users with information is called **financial accounting**.

The objective of financial accounting is to provide relevant and timely information for the decision-making needs of users outside of the business. For example, financial reports on the operations and condition of the business are useful for banks and other creditors in deciding whether to lend money to the business. **General-purpose financial statements** are one type of financial accounting report that is distributed to external users. The term *general-purpose* refers to the wide range of decision-making needs that these reports are designed to serve. Later in this chapter, general-purpose financial statements are described and illustrated.

Role of Ethics in Accounting and Business

The objective of accounting is to provide relevant, timely information for user decision making. Accountants must behave in an ethical manner so that the information they provide users will be trustworthy and, thus, useful for decision making. Managers and employees must also behave in an ethical manner in managing and operating a business. Otherwise, no one will be willing to invest in or loan money to the business.

Ethics are moral principles that guide the conduct of individuals. Unfortunately, business managers and accountants sometimes behave in an unethical manner. Many of the managers of the companies listed in Exhibit 2 engaged in accounting or business fraud. These ethical violations led to fines, firings, and lawsuits. In some cases, managers were criminally prosecuted, convicted, and sent to prison.

EXHIBIT 2 **Accounting and Business Frauds**

Company	Nature of Accounting or Business Fraud	Result
Computer Associates International, Inc.	Fraudulently inflated its financial results.	CEO and senior executives indicted. Five executives pled guilty. $225 million fine.
Enron	Fraudulently inflated its financial results.	Bankrupcty. Senior executives criminally convicted. Over $60 billion in stock market losses.
HealthSouth	Overstated performance by $4 billion in false entries.	Senior executives criminally convicted.
Qwest Communications International, Inc.	Improperly recognized $3 billion in false receipts.	CEO and six other executives criminally convicted of "massive financial fraud." $250 million SEC fine.
Xerox Corporation	Recognized $3 billion in revenue prior to when it should have been recorded.	$10 million fine to SEC. Six executives forced to pay $22 million.

What went wrong for the managers and companies listed in Exhibit 2? The answer normally involved one or both of the following two factors:

Failure of Individual Character. An ethical manager and accountant is honest and fair. However, managers and accountants often face pressures from supervisors to meet company and investor expectations. In many of the cases in Exhibit 2, managers and accountants justified small ethical violations to avoid such pressures. However, these small violations became big violations as the company's financial problems became worse.

Culture of Greed and Ethical Indifference. By their behavior and attitude, senior managers set the company culture. In most of the companies listed in Exhibit 2, the senior managers created a culture of greed and indifference to the truth.

As a result of the accounting and business frauds shown in Exhibit 2, Congress passed new laws to monitor the behavior of accounting and business. For example, the **Sarbanes-Oxley Act of 2002 (SOX)** was enacted. SOX established a new oversight body for the accounting profession called the **Public Company Accounting Oversight Board (PCAOB)**. In addition, SOX established standards for independence, corporate responsibility, and disclosure.

How does one behave ethically when faced with financial or other types of pressure? Guidelines for behaving ethically are shown in Exhibit 3.[2]

1. Identify an ethical decision by using your personal ethical standards of honesty and fairness.
2. Identify the consequences of the decision and its effect on others.
3. Consider your obligations and responsibilities to those who will be affected by your decision.
4. Make a decision that is ethical and fair to those affected by it.

EXHIBIT 3

Guidelines for Ethical Conduct

Integrity, Objectivity, and Ethics in Business

BERNIE MADOFF

In June 2009, Bernard L. "Bernie" Madoff was sentenced to 150 years in prison for defrauding thousands of investors in one of the biggest frauds in American history. Madoff's fraud started several decades earlier when he began a "Ponzi scheme" in his investment management firm, Bernard L. Madoff Investment Securities LLC.

In a Ponzi scheme, the investment manager uses funds received from new investors to pay a return to existing investors, rather than basing investment returns on the fund's actual performance. As long as the investment manager is able to attract new investors, he or she will have new funds to pay existing investors and continue the fraud. While most Ponzi schemes collapse quickly when the investment manager runs out of new investors, Madoff's reputation, popularity, and personal contacts provided a steady stream of investors, which allowed the fraud to survive for decades.

Opportunities for Accountants

Numerous career opportunities are available for students majoring in accounting. Currently, the demand for accountants exceeds the number of new graduates entering the job market. This is partly due to the increased regulation of business caused by the accounting and business frauds shown in Exhibit 2. Also, more and more businesses have come to recognize the importance and value of accounting information.

As indicated earlier, accountants employed by a business are employed in private accounting. Private accountants have a variety of possible career options within a company. Some of these career options are shown in Exhibit 4 along with their

2 Many companies have ethical standards of conduct for managers and employees. In addition, the Institute of Management Accountants and the American Institute of Certified Public Accountants have professional codes of conduct.

EXHIBIT 4 **Accounting Career Paths and Salaries**

Accounting Career Track	Description	Career Options	Annual Starting Salaries*	Certification
Private Accounting	Accountants employed by companies, government, and not-for-profit entities.	Bookkeeper	$38,500	
		Payroll clerk	$37,000	Certified Payroll Professional (CPP)
		General accountant	$44,625	
		Budget analyst	$47,250	
		Cost accountant	$46,625	Certified Management Accountant (CMA)
		Internal auditor	$51,875	Certified Internal Auditor (CIA)
		Information technology auditor	$60,750	Certified Information Systems Auditor (CISA)
Public Accounting	Accountants employed individually or within a public accounting firm in tax or audit services.	Local firms	$47,313	Certified Public Accountant (CPA)
		National firms	$57,250	Certified Public Accountant (CPA)

Source: Robert Half 2012 U.S. Salary Guide (Finance and Accounting), Robert Half International, Inc. (http://www.rhi.com/salaryguides)
*Mean salaries of a reported range. Private accounting salaries are reported for large companies. Salaries may vary by region.

starting salaries. Accountants who provide audit services, called auditors, verify the accuracy of financial records, accounts, and systems. As shown in Exhibit 4, several private accounting careers have certification options.

Accountants and their staff who provide services on a fee basis are said to be employed in **public accounting**. In public accounting, an accountant may practice as an individual or as a member of a public accounting firm. Public accountants who have met a state's education, experience, and examination requirements may become **Certified Public Accountants (CPAs)**. CPAs typically perform general accounting, audit, or tax services. As can be seen in Exhibit 4, CPAs have slightly better starting salaries than private accountants. Career statistics indicate, however, that these salary differences tend to disappear over time.

Because all functions within a business use accounting information, experience in private or public accounting provides a solid foundation for a career. Many positions in industry and in government agencies are held by individuals with accounting backgrounds.

OBJ 2 Summarize the development of accounting principles and relate them to practice.

Generally Accepted Accounting Principles

If a company's management could record and report financial data as it saw fit, comparisons among companies would be difficult, if not impossible. Thus, financial accountants follow **generally accepted accounting principles (GAAP)** in preparing reports. These reports allow investors and other users to compare one company to another.

Accounting principles and concepts develop from research, accepted accounting practices, and pronouncements of regulators. Within the United States, the **Financial Accounting Standards Board (FASB)** has the primary responsibility for developing accounting principles. The FASB publishes *Statements of Financial Accounting Standards* as well as *Interpretations* of these Standards. In addition, the **Securities and Exchange Commission (SEC),** an agency of the U.S. government, has authority over the accounting and financial disclosures for companies whose shares of ownership (stock) are traded and sold to the public. The SEC normally accepts the accounting principles set forth by the FASB. However, the SEC may issue *Staff Accounting Bulletins* on accounting matters that may not have been addressed by the FASB.

Many countries outside the United States use generally accepted accounting principles adopted by the **International Accounting Standards Board (IASB)**. The IASB issues *International Financial Reporting Standards (IFRSs)*. Differences currently exist between FASB and IASB accounting principles. However, the FASB and IASB are working together to reduce and eliminate these differences into a single set of accounting principles. Such a set of worldwide accounting principles would help facilitate investment and business in an increasingly global economy.

IFRS IFRS

See Appendix C for more information.

In this chapter and text, accounting principles and concepts are emphasized. It is through this emphasis on the "why" as well as the "how" that you will gain an understanding of accounting.

IFRS

International Connection

INTERNATIONAL FINANCIAL REPORTING STANDARDS (IFRS)

IFRS are considered to be more "principles-based" than U.S. GAAP, which is considered to be more "rules-based." For example, U.S. GAAP consists of approximately 17,000 pages, which include numerous industry-specific accounting rules. In contrast, IFRS allow more judgment in deciding how business transactions are recorded. Many believe that the strong regulatory and litigation environment in the United States is the cause for the more rules-based GAAP approach. Regardless, IFRS and GAAP share many common principles.*

*Differences between U.S. GAAP and IFRS are further discussed and illustrated in Appendix C.

Business Entity Concept

The **business entity concept** limits the economic data in an accounting system to data related directly to the activities of the business. In other words, the business is viewed as an entity separate from its owners, creditors, or other businesses. For example, the accountant for a business with one owner would record the activities of the business only and would not record the personal activities, property, or debts of the owner.

Note:
Under the business entity concept, the activities of a business are recorded separately from the activities of its owners, creditors, or other businesses.

A business entity may take the form of a proprietorship, partnership, corporation, or limited liability company (LLC). Each of these forms and their major characteristics are listed below.

Form of Business Entity	Characteristics
Proprietorship is owned by one individual.	• 70% of business entities in the United States. • Easy and cheap to organize. • Resources are limited to those of the owner. • Used by small businesses.
Partnership is owned by two or more individuals.	• 10% of business organizations in the United States (combined with limited liability companies). • Combines the skills and resources of more than one person.
Corporation is organized under state or federal statutes as a separate legal taxable entity.	• Generates 90% of business revenues. • 20% of the business organizations in the United States. • Ownership is divided into shares called *stock*. • Can obtain large amounts of resources by issuing stock. • Used by large businesses.
Limited liability company (LLC) combines the attributes of a partnership and a corporation.	• 10% of business organizations in the United States (combined with partnerships). • Often used as an alternative to a partnership. • Has tax and legal liability advantages for owners.

The three types of businesses discussed earlier—service, merchandising, and manufacturing—may be organized as proprietorships, partnerships, corporations, or limited liability companies. Because of the large amount of resources required to operate a manufacturing business, most manufacturers such as Ford Motor Company are corporations. Most large retailers such as Walmart and Home Depot are also corporations. Companies organized as corporations often include *Inc.* as part of their name to indicate that they are incorporated. For example, Apple's legal name is Apple Inc.

Cost Concept

Under the **cost concept**, amounts are initially recorded in the accounting records at their cost or purchase price. To illustrate, assume that Aaron Publishers purchased the following building on February 20, 2012, for $150,000:

Price listed by seller on January 1, 2012	$160,000
Aaron Publishers' initial offer to buy on January 31, 2012	140,000
Purchase price on February 20, 2012	150,000
Estimated selling price on December 31, 2014	220,000
Assessed value for property taxes, December 31, 2014	190,000

Under the cost concept, Aaron Publishers records the purchase of the building on February 20, 2012, at the purchase price of $150,000. The other amounts listed above have no effect on the accounting records.

The fact that the building has an estimated selling price of $220,000 on December 31, 2014, indicates that the building has increased in value. However, to use the $220,000 in the accounting records would be to record an illusory or unrealized profit. If Aaron Publishers sells the building on January 9, 2016, for $240,000, a profit of $90,000 ($240,000 − $150,000) is then realized and recorded. The new owner would record $240,000 as its cost of the building.

The cost concept also involves the objectivity and unit of measure concepts. The **objectivity concept** requires that the amounts recorded in the accounting records be based on objective evidence. In exchanges between a buyer and a seller, both try to get the best price. Only the final agreed-upon amount is objective enough to be recorded in the accounting records. If amounts in the accounting records were constantly being revised upward or downward based on offers, appraisals, and opinions, accounting reports could become unstable and unreliable.

The **unit of measure concept** requires that economic data be recorded in dollars. Money is a common unit of measurement for reporting financial data and reports.

Example Exercise 1-1 Cost Concept (OBJ 2)

On August 25, Gallatin Repair Service extended an offer of $125,000 for land that had been priced for sale at $150,000. On September 3, Gallatin Repair Service accepted the seller's counteroffer of $137,000. On October 20, the land was assessed at a value of $98,000 for property tax purposes. On December 4, Gallatin Repair Service was offered $160,000 for the land by a national retail chain. At what value should the land be recorded in Gallatin Repair Service's records?

Follow My Example 1-1

$137,000. Under the cost concept, the land should be recorded at the cost to Gallatin Repair Service.

Practice Exercises: **PE 1-1A, PE 1-1B**

OBJ 3 State the accounting equation and define each element of the equation.

The Accounting Equation

The resources owned by a business are its **assets**. Examples of assets include cash, land, buildings, and equipment. The rights or claims to the assets are divided into two types: (1) the rights of creditors and (2) the rights of owners. The rights of creditors are the debts of the business and are called **liabilities**. The rights of the owners are called **stockholders' equity** for a corporation and **owner's equity** for a proprietorship, partnership, or limited liability company. Throughout this text, we use the corporate form of business. However, most of the concepts and principles described and illustrated also apply to proprietorships, partnerships, and limited liability companies.

The following equation shows the relationship among assets, liabilities, and stockholders' equity:

Assets = Liabilities + Stockholders' Equity

This equation is called the **accounting equation**. Liabilities usually are shown before stockholders' equity in the accounting equation because creditors have first rights to the assets.

Given any two amounts, the accounting equation may be solved for the third unknown amount. To illustrate, if the assets owned by a business amount to $100,000 and the liabilities amount to $30,000, the stockholders' equity is equal to $70,000, as shown below.

Assets – Liabilities	=	**Stockholders' Equity**
$100,000 – $30,000	=	$70,000

Example Exercise 1-2 Accounting Equation

OBJ 3

You're A Star is a motivational consulting business. At the end of its accounting period, December 31, 2013, You're A Star has assets of $800,000 and liabilities of $350,000. Using the accounting equation, determine the following amounts:

a. Stockholders' equity as of December 31, 2013.
b. Stockholders' equity as of December 31, 2014, assuming that assets increased by $130,000 and liabilities decreased by $25,000 during 2014.

Follow My Example 1-2

a. Assets = Liabilities + Stockholders' Equity

$800,000 = $350,000 + Stockholders' Equity

Stockholders' Equity = $450,000

b. First, determine the change in stockholders' equity during 2014 as follows:

Assets = Liabilities + Stockholders' Equity

$130,000 = –$25,000 + Stockholders' Equity

Stockholders' Equity = $155,000

Next, add the change in stockholders' equity during 2014 to the stockholders' equity on December 31, 2013 to arrive at stockholders' equity on December 31, 2014, as shown below.

Stockholders' Equity on December 31, 2014 = $450,000 + $155,000 = $605,000

Practice Exercises: **PE 1-2A, PE 1-2B**

Business Transactions and the Accounting Equation

OBJ 4 Describe and illustrate how business transactions can be recorded in terms of the resulting change in the elements of the accounting equation.

Paying a monthly bill, such as a telephone bill of $168, affects a business's financial condition because it now has less cash on hand. Such an economic event or condition that directly changes an entity's financial condition or its results of operations is a **business transaction**. For example, purchasing land for $50,000 is a business transaction. In contrast, a change in a business's credit rating does not directly affect cash or any other asset, liability, or stockholders' equity amount.

Note:
All business transactions can be stated in terms of changes in the elements of the accounting equation.

All business transactions can be stated in terms of changes in the elements of the accounting equation. How business transactions affect the accounting equation can be illustrated by using some typical transactions. As a basis for illustration, a business organized by Chris Clark is used.

Assume that on November 1, 2013, Chris Clark organizes a corporation that will be known as **NetSolutions**. The first phase of Chris's business plan is to operate Net-Solutions as a service business assisting individuals and small businesses in developing Web pages and installing computer software. Chris expects this initial phase of the business to last one to two years. During this period, Chris plans on gathering information on the software and hardware needs of customers. During the second phase of the business plan, Chris plans to expand NetSolutions into a personalized retailer of software and hardware for individuals and small businesses.

Each transaction during NetSolutions' first month of operations is described in the following paragraphs. The effect of each transaction on the accounting equation is then shown.

Transaction A

Nov. 1, 2013 Chris Clark deposited $25,000 in a bank account in the name of NetSolutions in exchange for shares of stock in the corporation.

Stock issued to stockholders' (owners), such as Chris Clark, is referred to as **capital stock**. This transaction increases assets by increasing Cash (on the left side of the equation) by $25,000. To balance the equation, Capital Stock under stockholders' equity (on the right side of the equation) increases by the same amount.

The effect of this transaction on NetSolutions' accounting equation is shown below.

Assets	=	**Stockholders' Equity**
Cash	=	Capital Stock
a. 25,000		25,000

The accounting equation shown above is only for the corporation, NetSolutions. Under the business entity concept, Chris Clark's personal assets, such as a home or personal bank account, and personal liabilities are excluded from the equation.

Transaction B

Nov. 5, 2013 NetSolutions paid $20,000 for the purchase of land as a future building site.

The land is located in a business park with access to transportation facilities. Chris Clark plans to rent office space and equipment during the first phase of the business plan. During the second phase, Chris plans to build an office and a warehouse for NetSolutions on the land.

Business Connection

THE ACCOUNTING EQUATION

The accounting equation serves as the basic foundation for the accounting systems of all companies. From the smallest business, such as the local convenience store, to the largest business, such as Ford Motor Company, companies use the accounting equation. Some examples taken from recent financial reports of well-known companies are shown below.

Company	Assets*	=	Liabilities	+	Stockholders' Equity
The Coca-Cola Company	$72,921	=	$41,918	+	$31,003
Dell, Inc.	$38,599	=	$30,833	+	$7,766
eBay, Inc.	$22,004	=	$6,702	+	$15,302
Google	$57,851	=	$11,610	+	$46,241
McDonald's	$31,975	=	$17,341	+	$14,634
Microsoft Corporation	$86,113	=	$39,938	+	$46,175
Southwest Airlines Co.	$15,463	=	$9,226	+	$6,237
Walmart	$180,663	=	$109,416	+	$71,247

*Amounts are shown in millions of dollars.

The purchase of the land changes the makeup of the assets, but it does not change the total assets. The items in the equation prior to this transaction and the effect of the transaction are shown below. The new amounts are called *balances.*

	Assets		=	**Stockholders' Equity**
	Cash	+ Land		Capital Stock
Bal.	25,000		=	25,000
b.	−20,000	+20,000		
Bal.	5,000	20,000		25,000

Nov. 10, 2013 NetSolutions purchased supplies for $1,350 and agreed to pay the supplier in the near future.

Transaction C

You have probably used a credit card to buy clothing or other merchandise. In this type of transaction, you received clothing for a promise to pay your credit card bill in the future. That is, you received an asset and incurred a liability to pay a future bill. NetSolutions entered into a similar transaction by purchasing supplies for $1,350 and agreeing to pay the supplier in the near future. This type of transaction is called a purchase *on account* and is often described as follows: *Purchased supplies on account, $1,350.*

The liability created by a purchase on account is called an **account payable**. Items such as supplies that will be used in the business in the future are called **prepaid expenses**, which are assets. Thus, the effect of this transaction is to increase assets (Supplies) and liabilities (Accounts Payable) by $1,350, as follows:

	Assets			=	**Liabilities +**	**Stockholders' Equity**
	Cash	+ Supplies +	Land		Accounts Payable +	Capital Stock
Bal.	5,000		20,000	=		25,000
c.		+1,350			+1,350	
Bal.	5,000	1,350	20,000		1,350	25,000

Nov. 18, 2013 NetSolutions received cash of $7,500 for providing services to customers.

Transaction D

You may have earned money by painting houses or mowing lawns. If so, you received money for rendering services to a customer. Likewise, a business earns money by selling goods or services to its customers. This amount is called **revenue**.

During its first month of operations, NetSolutions received cash of $7,500 for providing services to customers. The receipt of cash increases NetSolutions' assets and also increases stockholders' equity in the business. The revenues of $7,500 are recorded in a Fees Earned column to the right of Capital Stock. The effect of this transaction is to increase Cash and Fees Earned by $7,500, as follows.

	Assets			=	**Liabilities +**	**Stockholders' Equity**	
	Cash	+ Supplies +	Land		Accounts Payable +	Capital Stock	+ Fees Earned
Bal.	5,000	1,350	20,000	=	1,350	25,000	
d.	+7,500						+7,500
Bal.	12,500	1,350	20,000		1,350	25,000	7,500

Different terms are used for the various types of revenues. As illustrated above, revenue from providing services is recorded as **fees earned**. Revenue from the sale of merchandise is recorded as **sales**. Other examples of revenue include rent, which is recorded as **rent revenue**, and interest, which is recorded as **interest revenue**.

Instead of receiving cash at the time services are provided or goods are sold, a business may accept payment at a later date. Such revenues are described as *fees earned on account* or *sales on account*. For example, if NetSolutions had provided services on account instead of for cash, transaction (d) would have been described as follows: *Fees earned on account, $7,500.*

In such cases, the firm has an **account receivable**, which is a claim against the customer. An account receivable is an asset, and the revenue is earned and recorded as if cash had been received. When customers pay their accounts, Cash increases and Accounts Receivable decreases.

Transaction E *Nov. 30, 2013 NetSolutions paid the following expenses during the month: wages, $2,125; rent, $800; utilities, $450; and miscellaneous, $275.*

During the month, NetSolutions spent cash or used up other assets in earning revenue. Assets used in this process of earning revenue are called **expenses**. Expenses include supplies used and payments for employee wages, utilities, and other services.

NetSolutions paid the following expenses during the month: wages, $2,125; rent, $800; utilities, $450; and miscellaneous, $275. Miscellaneous expenses include small amounts paid for such items as postage, coffee, and newspapers. The effect of expenses is the opposite of revenues in that expenses reduce assets and stockholders' equity. Like fees earned, the expenses are recorded in columns to the right of Capital Stock. However, since expenses reduce stockholders' equity, the expenses are entered as negative amounts. The effect of this transaction is shown below.

	Assets			=	Liabilities +	Stockholders' Equity					
	Cash	+ Supplies +	Land	=	Accounts Payable +	Capital Stock	+ Fees Earned −	Wages Exp. −	Rent Exp. −	Utilities Exp. −	Misc. Exp.
Bal.	12,500	1,350	20,000		1,350	25,000	7,500				
e.	−3,650							−2,125	−800	−450	−275
Bal.	8,850	1,350	20,000		1,350	25,000	7,500	−2,125	−800	−450	−275

Businesses usually record each revenue and expense transaction as it occurs. However, to simplify, NetSolutions' revenues and expenses are summarized for the month in transactions (d) and (e).

Transaction F *Nov. 30, 2013 NetSolutions paid creditors on account, $950.*

When you pay your monthly credit card bill, you decrease the cash and decrease the amount you owe to the credit card company. Likewise, when NetSolutions pays $950 to creditors during the month, it reduces assets and liabilities, as shown below.

	Assets			=	Liabilities +	Stockholders' Equity					
	Cash	+ Supplies +	Land	=	Accounts Payable +	Capital Stock	+ Fees Earned −	Wages Exp. −	Rent Exp. −	Utilities Exp. −	Misc. Exp.
Bal.	8,850	1,350	20,000		1,350	25,000	7,500	−2,125	−800	−450	−275
f.	−950				−950						
Bal.	7,900	1,350	20,000		400	25,000	7,500	−2,125	−800	−450	−275

Paying an amount on account is different from paying an expense. The paying of an expense reduces stockholders' equity, as illustrated in transaction (e). Paying an amount on account reduces the amount owed on a liability.

Transaction G *Nov. 30, 2013 Chris Clark determined that the cost of supplies on hand at the end of the month was $550.*

The cost of the supplies on hand (not yet used) at the end of the month is $550. Thus, $800 ($1,350 − $550) of supplies must have been used during the month. This decrease in supplies is recorded as an expense, as shown below.

	Assets			=	Liabilities +	Stockholders' Equity						
	Cash	+ Supplies +	Land	=	Accounts Payable +	Capital Stock	+ Fees Earned −	Wages Exp. −	Rent Exp. −	Supplies Exp. −	Utilities Exp. −	Misc. Exp.
Bal.	7,900	1,350	20,000		400	25,000	7,500	−2,125	−800		−450	−275
g.		−800								−800		
Bal.	7,900	550	20,000		400	25,000	7,500	−2,125	−800	−800	−450	−275

Nov. 30, 2013 NetSolutions paid $2,000 to stockholders (Chris Clark) as dividends. **Transaction H**

Dividends are distributions of earnings to stockholders. The payment of dividends decreases cash and stockholders' equity. Like expenses, dividends are recorded in a separate column to the right of Capital Stock as a negative amount. The effect of the payment of dividends of $2,000 is shown below.

	Assets			=	Liabilities +	Stockholders' Equity							
	Cash +	Supp. +	Land	=	Accounts Payable +	Capital Stock	− Dividends +	Fees Earned −	Wages Exp. −	Rent Exp. −	Supplies Exp. −	Utilities Exp. −	Misc. Exp.
Bal.	7,900	550	20,000		400	25,000		7,500	−2,125	−800	−800	−450	−275
h.	−2,000						−2,000						
Bal.	5,900	550	20,000		400	25,000	−2,000	7,500	−2,125	−800	−800	−450	−275

Dividends should not be confused with expenses. Dividends do not represent assets or services used in the process of earning revenues. Instead, dividends are considered a distribution of earnings to stockholders.

Summary

The transactions of NetSolutions are summarized below. Each transaction is identified by letter, and the balance of each accounting equation element is shown after every transaction.

	Assets			= Liabilities +	Stockholders' Equity							
	Cash +	Supp. +	Land =	Accounts Payable +	Capital Stock	− Dividends +	Fees Earned −	Wages Exp. −	Rent Exp. −	Supplies Exp. −	Utilities Exp. −	Misc. Exp.
a.	+25,000				+25,000							
b.	−20,000		+20,000									
Bal.	5,000		20,000		25,000							
c.		+1,350		+1,350								
Bal.	5,000	+1,350	20,000	+1,350	25,000							
d.	+7,500						+7,500					
Bal.	12,500	1,350	20,000	1,350	25,000		7,500					
e.	−3,650							−2,125	−800		−450	−275
Bal.	8,850	1,350	20,000	1,350	25,000		7,500	−2,125	−800		−450	−275
f.	−950			−950								
Bal.	7,900	1,350	20,000	400	25,000		7,500	−2,125	−800		−450	−275
g.		−800								−800		
Bal.	7,900	550	20,000	400	25,000		7,500	−2,125	−800	−800	−450	−275
h.	−2,000					−2,000						
Bal.	5,900	550	20,000	400	25,000	−2,000	7,500	−2,125	−800	−800	−450	−275

You should note the following:

1. The effect of every transaction *is an increase or a decrease in one or more of the accounting equation elements.*
2. The two sides of the accounting equation are *always equal.*
3. The stockholders' equity (owner's equity) is *increased by amounts invested by stockholders (capital stock).*
4. The stockholders' equity (owner's equity) is *increased by revenues and decreased by expenses.*
5. The stockholders' equity (owner's equity) is *decreased by dividends paid to stockholders.*

Stockholders' equity is classified as:

1. Capital Stock
2. Retained Earnings.

Capital stock is shares of ownership distributed to investors of a corporation. It represents the portion of stockholders' equity contributed by investors. For NetSolutions, shares of capital stock of $25,000 were distributed to Chris Clark in exchange for investing in the business.

Retained earnings is the stockholders' equity created from business operations through revenue and expense transactions. For NetSolutions, retained earnings of $3,050 were created by its November operations (revenue and expense transactions), as shown below.

NetSolutions
Retained Earnings
November Operations
(Revenue and Expense Transactions)

	Fees Earned	− Wages Exp.	− Rent Exp.	− Supplies Exp.	− Utilities Exp.	− Misc. Exp.
Trans, d.	+7,500					
Trans, e.		−2,125	−800		−450	−275
Trans, g.				−800		
Balance, Nov. 30	7,500	−2,125	−800	−800	−450	−275

$3,050

Stockholders' equity created by investments by stockholders (capital stock) and by business operations (retained earnings) is reported separately. Since dividends are distributions of earnings to stockholders, dividends reduce retained earnings. NetSolutions paid $2,000 in dividends during November, thus reducing retained earnings to $1,050 ($3,050 − $2,000).

The effects of investments by stockholders, dividends, revenues, and expenses on stockholders' equity are illustrated in Exhibit 5.

EXHIBIT 5

Effects of Transactions on Stockholders' Equity

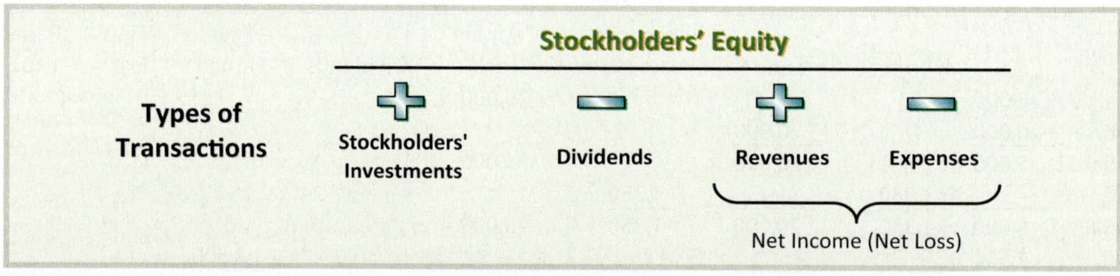

Example Exercise 1-3 Transactions

OBJ 4

Salvo Delivery Service is owned and operated by Joel Salvo. The following selected transactions were completed by Salvo Delivery Service during February:

1. Received cash from owner as additional investment in exchange for capital stock, $35,000.
2. Paid creditors on account, $1,800.
3. Billed customers for delivery services on account, $11,250.
4. Received cash from customers on account, $6,740.
5. Paid dividends, $1,000.

Indicate the effect of each transaction on the accounting equation elements (Assets, Liabilities, Stockholders' Equity Capital Stock, Dividends, Revenue, and Expense). Also indicate the specific item within the accounting equation element that is affected. To illustrate, the answer to (1) is shown below.

(1) Asset (Cash) increases by $35,000; Stockholders' Equity (Capital Stock) increases by $35,000.

Follow My Example 1-3

(2) Asset (Cash) decreases by $1,800; Liability (Accounts Payable) decreases by $1,800.
(3) Asset (Accounts Receivable) increases by $11,250; Revenue (Delivery Service Fees) increases by $11,250.
(4) Asset (Cash) increases by $6,740; Asset (Accounts Receivable) decreases by $6,740.
(5) Asset (Cash) decreases by $1,000; Dividends increases by $1,000.

Practice Exercises: **PE 1-3A, PE 1-3B**

OBJ 5 Describe the financial statements of a corporation and explain how they interrelate.

Financial Statements

After transactions have been recorded and summarized, reports are prepared for users. The accounting reports providing this information are called **financial statements**. The primary financial statements of a corporation are the income statement, the retained earnings statement, the balance sheet, and the statement of cash flows. The order in which the financial statements are prepared and the nature of each statement are described as follows.

Order Prepared	Financial Statement	Description of Statement
1.	**Income statement**	A summary of the revenue and expenses *for a specific period of time*, such as a month or a year.
2.	**Retained earnings statement**	A summary of the changes in retained earnings that have occurred *during a specific period of time*, such as a month or a year.
3.	**Balance sheet**	A list of the assets, liabilities, and stockholders' equity *as of a specific date*, usually at the close of the last day of a month or a year.
4.	**Statement of cash flows**	A summary of the cash receipts and cash payments for a *specific period of time*, such as a month or a year.

The four financial statements and their interrelationships are illustrated in Exhibit 6, on page 17. The data for the statements are taken from the summary of transactions of NetSolutions on page 13.

All financial statements are identified by the name of the business, the title of the statement, and the *date* or *period of time*. The data presented in the income statement, the retained earnings statement, and the statement of cash flows are for a period of time. The data presented in the balance sheet are for a specific date.

Income Statement

The income statement reports the revenues and expenses for a period of time, based on the **matching concept**. This concept is applied by *matching* the expenses incurred during a period with the revenue that those expenses generated. The excess of the revenue over the expenses is called **net income**, net profit, or **earnings**. If the expenses exceed the revenue, the excess is a **net loss**.

Note:
When revenues exceed expenses, it is referred to as *net income, net profit,* or *earnings*. When expenses exceed revenues, it is referred to as *net loss*.

The revenue and expenses for NetSolutions were shown in the equation as separate increases and decreases. Net income for a period increases the stockholders' equity (retained earnings) for the period. A net loss decreases the stockholders' equity (retained earnings) for the period.

The revenue, expenses, and the net income of $3,050 for NetSolutions are reported in the income statement in Exhibit 6. The order in which the expenses are listed in the income statement varies among businesses. Most businesses list expenses in order of size, beginning with the larger items. Miscellaneous expense is usually shown as the last item, regardless of the amount.

Example Exercise 1-4 Income Statement

OBJ 5

The revenues and expenses of Chickadee Travel Service for the year ended April 30, 2014, are listed below.

Fees earned	$263,200
Miscellaneous expense	12,950
Office expense	63,000
Wages expense	131,700

Prepare an income statement for the current year ended April 30, 2014.

Follow My Example 1-4

Chickadee Travel Service
Income Statement
For the Year Ended April 30, 2014

Fees earned		$263,200
Expenses:		
Wages expense	$131,700	
Office expense	63,000	
Miscellaneous expense	12,950	
Total expenses		207,650
Net income		$ 55,550

Practice Exercises: **PE 1-4A, PE 1-4B**

Retained Earnings Statement

The retained earnings statement reports the changes in the retained earnings for a period of time. It is prepared *after* the income statement because the net income or net loss for the period must be reported in this statement. Similarly, it is prepared *before* the balance sheet, since the amount of retained earnings at the end of the period must be reported on the balance sheet. Because of this, the retained earnings statement is often viewed as the connecting link between the income statement and balance sheet.

The following two types of transactions affected NetSolutions' retained earnings during November:

1. Revenues and expenses, which resulted in net income of $3,050.
2. Dividends of $2,000 paid to stockholders (Chris Clark).

These transactions are summarized in the retained earnings statement for NetSolutions shown in Exhibit 6.

Since NetSolutions has been in operation for only one month, it has no retained earnings at the beginning of November. For December, however, there is a beginning balance—the balance at the end of November. This balance of $1,050 is reported on the retained earnings statement.

To illustrate, assume that NetSolutions earned net income of $4,155 and paid dividends of $2,000 during December. The retained earnings statement for NetSolutions for December is shown below.

NetSolutions
Retained Earnings Statement
For the Month Ended December 31, 2013

Retained earnings, December 1, 2013		$1,050
Net income for November	$4,155	
Less dividends	2,000	
Increase in retained earnings		2,155
Retained earnings, December 31, 2013		$3,205

Example Exercise 1-5 Retained Earnings Statement (OBJ 5)

Using the income statement for Chickadee Travel Service shown in Example Exercise 1-4, prepare a retained earnings statement for the year ended April 30, 2014. Adam Cellini, the owner, invested an additional $50,000 in the business in exchange for capital stock, and dividends of $30,000 were paid during the year. Retained earnings were $30,000 on May 1, 2013, the beginning of the current year.

Follow My Example 1-5

Chickadee Travel Service
Retained Earnings Statement
For the Year Ended April 30, 2014

Retained earnings, May 1, 2013		$30,000
Net income for the year	$55,550	
Less dividends	30,000	
Increase in retained earnings		25,550
Retained earnings, April 30, 2014		$55,550

Practice Exercises: **PE 1-5A, PE 1-5B**

Balance Sheet

The balance sheet in Exhibit 6 reports the amounts of NetSolutions' assets, liabilities, and stockholders' equity as of November 30, 2013. The asset and liability amounts are taken from the last line of the summary of transactions on page 13.

EXHIBIT 6

Financial Statements for NetSolutions

NetSolutions
Income Statement
For the Month Ended November 30, 2013

Fees earned		$7,500
Expenses:		
Wages expense	$2,125	
Rent expense	800	
Supplies expense	800	
Utilities expense	450	
Miscellaneous expense	275	
Total expense		4,450
Net income		$3,050

NetSolutions
Retained Earnings Statement
For the Month Ended November 30, 2013

Retained earnings, November 1, 2013		$ 0
Net income for November	$3,050	
Less dividends	2,000	
Increase in retained earnings		1,050
Retained earnings, November 30, 2013		$ 1,050

NetSolutions
Balance Sheet
November 30, 2013

Assets		Liabilities		
Cash	$ 5,900	Accounts payable		$ 400
Supplies	550	**Stockholders' Equity**		
Land	20,000	Capital stock	$25,000	
		Retained earnings	1,050	
		Total stockholders' equity		$26,050
		Total liabilities and		
Total assets	$ 26,450	stockholders' equity		$ 26,450

NetSolutions
Statement of Cash Flows
For the Month Ended November 30, 2013

Cash flows from operating activities:		
Cash received from customers	$ 7,500	
Deduct cash payments for expenses and payments to creditors	(4,600)	
Net cash flow from operating activities		$ 2,900
Cash flows used for investing activities:		
Cash payments for purchase of land		(20,000)
Cash flows from financing activities:		
Cash received from issuing stock	$ 25,000	
Deduct cash dividends	(2,000)	
Net cash flow from financing activities		23,000
Net cash flow and November 30, 2013, cash balance		$ 5,900

Bank loan officers use a business's financial statements in deciding whether to grant a loan to the business. Once the loan is granted, the borrower may be required to maintain a certain level of assets in excess of liabilities. The business's financial statements are used to monitor this level.

Retained earnings as of November 30, 2013, is taken from the retained earnings statement. The form of balance sheet shown in Exhibit 6 is called the **account form**. This is because it resembles the basic format of the accounting equation, with assets on the left side and the liabilities and stockholders' equity sections on the right side.[3]

The assets section of the balance sheet presents assets in the order that they will be converted into cash or used in operations. Cash is presented first, followed by receivables, supplies, prepaid insurance, and other assets. The assets of a more permanent nature are shown next, such as land, buildings, and equipment.

In the liabilities section of the balance sheet in Exhibit 6, accounts payable is the only liability. When there are two or more liabilities, each should be listed and the total amount of liabilities presented as follows:

Liabilities		
Accounts payable	$12,900	
Wages payable	2,570	
Total liabilities		$15,470

Example Exercise 1-6 Balance Sheet

OBJ 5

Using the following data for Chickadee Travel Service as well as the retained earnings statement shown in Example Exercise 1-5, prepare a balance sheet as of April 30, 2014.

Accounts payable	$ 12,200
Accounts receivable	31,350
Capital stock	100,000
Cash	53,050
Land	80,000
Supplies	3,350

Follow My Example 1-6

Chickadee Travel Service
Balance Sheet
April 30, 2014

Assets		**Liabilities**	
Cash	$ 53,050	Accounts payable	$ 12,200
Accounts receivable	31,350		
Supplies	3,350	**Stockholders' Equity**	
Land	80,000	Capital stock	$100,000
		Retained earnings	55,550
		Total stockholders' equity	155,550
Total assets	$167,750	Total liabilities and stockholders' equity	$167,750

Practice Exercises: **PE 1-6A, PE 1-6B**

Statement of Cash Flows

The statement of cash flows consists of the following three sections, as shown in Exhibit 6:

1. operating activities
2. investing activities
3. financing activities

Each of these sections is briefly described below.

Cash Flows from Operating Activities This section reports a summary of cash receipts and cash payments from operations. The net cash flow from operating activities normally differs from the amount of net income for the period. In Exhibit 6, NetSolutions

3 An alternative form of balance sheet, called the *report form,* is illustrated in Chapter 5. It presents the liabilities and stockholders' equity sections below the assets section.

reported net cash flows from operating activities of $2,900 and net income of $3,050. This difference occurs because revenues and expenses may not be recorded at the same time that cash is received from customers or paid to creditors.

Cash Flows from Investing Activities This section reports the cash transactions for the acquisition and sale of relatively permanent assets. Exhibit 6 reports that NetSolutions paid $20,000 for the purchase of land during November.

Cash Flows from Financing Activities This section reports the cash transactions related to cash investments by stockholders, borrowings, and cash dividends. Exhibit 6 shows that Chris Clark invested $25,000 in exchange for capital stock and dividends of $2,000 were paid during November.

Preparing the statement of cash flows requires that each of the November cash transactions for NetSolutions be classified as an operating, investing, or financing activity. Using the summary of transactions shown on page 13, the November cash transactions for NetSolutions are classified as follows:

Transaction	Amount	Cash Flow Activity
a.	$25,000	Financing (Issuance of capital stock)
b.	−20,000	Investing (Purchase of land)
d.	7,500	Operating (Fees earned)
e.	−3,650	Operating (Payment of expenses)
f.	−950	Operating (Payment of account payable)
h.	−2,000	Financing (Paid dividends)

Transactions (c) and (g) are not listed above since they did not involve a cash receipt or payment. In addition, the payment of accounts payable in transaction (f) is classified as an operating activity since the account payable arose from the purchase of supplies, which are used in operations. Using the preceding classifications of November cash transactions, the statement of cash flows is prepared as shown in Exhibit 6.[4]

The ending cash balance shown on the statement of cash flows is also reported on the balance sheet as of the end of the period. To illustrate, the ending cash of $5,900 reported on the November statement of cash flows in Exhibit 6 is also reported as the amount of cash on hand in the November 30, 2013, balance sheet.

Since November is NetSolutions' first period of operations, the net cash flow for November and the November 30, 2013, cash balance are the same amount, $5,900, as shown in Exhibit 6. In later periods, NetSolutions will report in its statement of cash flows a beginning cash balance, an increase or a decrease in cash for the period, and an ending cash balance. For example, assume that for December NetSolutions has a decrease in cash of $3,835. The last three lines of NetSolutions' statement of cash flows for December would be as follows:

Decrease in cash	$(3,835)
Cash as of December 1, 2013	5,900
Cash as of December 31, 2013	$ 2,065

Example Exercise 1-7 Statement of Cash Flows

OBJ 5

A summary of cash flows for Chickadee Travel Service for the year ended April 30, 2014, is shown below.

Cash receipts:	
Cash received from customers	$251,000
Cash received from issuing capital stock	50,000
Cash payments:	
Cash paid for expenses	210,000
Cash paid for land	80,000
Cash paid for dividends	30,000

The cash balance as of May 1, 2013, was $72,050. Prepare a statement of cash flows for Chickadee Travel Service for the year ended April 30, 2014.

(Continued)

4 This method of preparing the statement of cash flows is called the "direct method." This method and the indirect method are discussed further in Chapter 14.

Follow My Example 1-7

Chickadee Travel Service
Statement of Cash Flows
For the Year Ended April 30, 2014

Cash flows from operating activities:		
Cash received from customers	$251,000	
Deduct cash payments for expenses	(210,000)	
Net cash flows from operating activities		$ 41,000
Cash flows used for investing activities:		
Cash payments for purchase of land		(80,000)
Cash flows from financing activities:		
Cash received issuing capital stock	$ 50,000	
Deduct cash dividends	(30,000)	
Net cash flows from financing activities		20,000
Net decrease in cash during year		$(19,000)
Cash as of May 1, 2013		72,050
Cash as of April 30, 2014		$ 53,050

Practice Exercises: **PE 1-7A, PE 1-7B**

Interrelationships Among Financial Statements

Financial statements are prepared in the order of the income statement, retained earnings statement, balance sheet, and statement of cash flows. This order is important because the financial statements are interrelated. These interrelationships for NetSolutions are shown in Exhibit 6 and are described below.[5]

Financial Statements	Interrelationship	NetSolutions Example (Exhibit 6)
Income Statement *and* Retained Earnings Statement	Net income or net loss reported on the income statement is also reported on the retained earnings statement as either an addition (net income) to or deduction (net loss) from the beginning retained earnings.	NetSolutions' net income of $3,050 for November is added to the beginning retained earnings on November 1, 2013, in the retained earnings statement.
Retained Earnings Statement *and* Balance Sheet	Retained earnings at the end of the period reported on the retained earnings statement is also reported on the balance sheet as retained earnings.	NetSolutions' retained earnings of $1,050 as of November 30, 2013, on the retained earnings statement also appears on the November 30, 2013, balance sheet as retained earnings.
Balance Sheet *and* Statement of Cash Flows	The cash reported on the balance sheet is also reported as the end-of-period cash on the statement of cash flows.	Cash of $5,900 reported on the balance sheet as of November 30, 2013, is also reported on the November statement of cash flows as the end-of-period cash.

The preceding interrelationships are important in analyzing financial statements and the impact of transactions on a business. In addition, these interrelationships serve as a check on whether the financial statements are prepared correctly. For example, if the ending cash on the statement of cash flows does not agree with the balance sheet cash, then an error has occurred.

5 Depending on the method of preparing the cash flows from operating activities section of the statement of cash flows, net income (or net loss) may also appear on the statement of cash flows. This interrelationship or method of preparing the statement of cash flows, called the "indirect method," is described and illustrated in Chapter 14.

Financial Analysis and Interpretation: Ratio of Liabilities to Stockholders' Equity

F·A·I

OBJ 6 Describe and illustrate the use of the ratio of liabilities to stockholders' equity in evaluating a company's financial condition.

The basic financial statements illustrated in this chapter are useful to bankers, creditors, stockholders, and others in analyzing and interpreting the financial performance and condition of a company. Throughout this text, various tools and techniques that are often used to analyze and interpret a company's financial performance and condition are described and illustrated. The first such tool that is discussed is useful in analyzing the ability of a company to pay its creditors.

The relationship between liabilities and stockholders' equity, expressed as a **ratio of liabilities to stockholders' equity**, is computed as follows:

$$\text{Ratio of Liabilities to Stockholders' Equity} = \frac{\text{Total Liabilities}}{\text{Total Stockholders' Equity}}$$

NetSolutions' ratio of liabilities to stockholders' equity at the end of November is 0.015, as computed below.

$$\text{Ratio of Liabilities to Stockholders' Equity} = \frac{\$400}{\$26{,}050} = 0.015$$

To illustrate, recent balance sheet data (in millions) for Google Inc. and McDonald's Corporation are shown below.

	Recent Year	Prior Year
Google Inc.		
Total liabilities	$11,610	$ 4,493
Total stockholders' equity	46,241	36,004
McDonald's Corporation		
Total liabilities	$17,341	$16,191
Total stockholders' equity	14,634	14,034

The ratio of liabilities to stockholders' equity for Google and McDonald's for a recent year and the prior year is computed below.

	Recent Year	Prior Year
Google Inc.		
Total liabilities	$11,610	$ 4,493
Total stockholders' equity	46,241	36,004
Ratio of liabilities to stockholders' equity	0.25	0.12
	($11,610/$46,241)	($4,493/$36,004)
McDonald's Corporation		
Total liabilities	$17,341	$16,191
Total stockholders' equity	14,634	14,034
Ratio of liabilities to stockholders' equity	1.18	1.15
	($17,341/$14,634)	($16,191/$14,034)

The rights of creditors to a business's assets come before the rights of the owners or stockholders. Thus, the lower the ratio of liabilities to stockholders' equity, the better able the company is to withstand poor business conditions and to pay its obligations to creditors.

Google is unusual in that it has a very low amount of liabilities; thus, its ratio of liabilities to stockholders' equity of 0.25 in the recent year and 0.12 in the prior year is low. In contrast, McDonald's has more liabilities; its ratio of liabilities to stockholders' equity is 1.18 in the recent year and 1.15 in the prior year. Since McDonald's ratio of liabilities to stockholders' equity increased slightly, its creditors are slightly more at risk at the end of the recent year. Also, McDonald's creditors are more at risk than are Google's creditors. The creditors of both companies are, however, well protected against the risk of nonpayment.

Example Exercise 1-8 Ratio of Liabilities to Stockholders' Equity

OBJ 6

The following data were taken from Hawthorne Company's balance sheet:

	Dec. 31, 2014	Dec. 31, 2013
Total liabilities	$120,000	$105,000
Total stockholders' equity	80,000	75,000

a. Compute the ratio of liabilities to stockholders' equity.

b. Has the creditors' risk increased or decreased from December 31, 2013, to December 31, 2014?

Follow My Example 1-8

a.

	Dec. 31, 2014	Dec. 31, 2013
Total liabilities	$120,000	$105,000
Total stockholders' equity	80,000	75,000
Ratio of liabilities to stockholders' equity	1.50	1.40
	($120,000/$80,000)	($105,000/$75,000)

b. Increased

Practice Exercises: **PE 1-8A, PE 1-8B**

At a Glance 1

OBJ 1

Describe the nature of a business and the role of accounting and ethics in business.

Key Points A business provides goods or services (outputs) to customers with the objective of earning a profit. Three types of businesses include service, merchandising, and manufacturing businesses.

Accounting is an information system that provides reports to users about the economic activities and condition of a business.

Ethics are moral principles that guide the conduct of individuals. Good ethical conduct depends on individual character and firm culture.

Accountants are engaged in private accounting or public accounting.

Learning Outcomes	Example Exercises	Practice Exercises
• Distinguish among service, merchandising, and manufacturing businesses.		
• Describe the role of accounting in business, and explain why accounting is called the "language of business."		
• Define ethics, and list two factors affecting ethical conduct.		
• Differentiate between private and public accounting.		

OBJ 2 Summarize the development of accounting principles and relate them to practice.

Key Points Generally accepted accounting principles (GAAP) are used in preparing financial statements. Accounting principles and concepts develop from research, practice, and pronouncements of authoritative bodies.

The business entity concept views the business as an entity separate from its owners, creditors, or other businesses. Businesses may be organized as proprietorships, partnerships, corporations, and limited liability companies. The cost concept requires that purchases of a business be recorded in terms of actual cost. The objectivity concept requires that the accounting records and reports be based on objective evidence. The unit of measure concept requires that economic data be recorded in dollars.

Learning Outcomes	Example Exercises	Practice Exercises
• Explain what is meant by generally accepted accounting principles.		
• Describe how generally accepted accounting principles are developed.		
• Describe and give an example of what is meant by the business entity concept.		
• Describe the characteristics of a proprietorship, partnership, corporation, and limited liability company.		
• Describe and give an example of what is meant by the cost concept.	**EE1-1**	**PE1-1A, 1-1B**
• Describe and give an example of what is meant by the objectivity concept.		
• Describe and give an example of what is meant by the unit of measure concept.		

OBJ 3 State the accounting equation and define each element of the equation.

Key Points The resources owned by a business and the rights or claims to these resources may be stated in the form of an equation, as follows:

Assets = Liabilities + Stockholders' Equity

Learning Outcomes	Example Exercises	Practice Exercises
• State the accounting equation.		
• Define assets, liabilities, and stockholders' equity.		
• Given two elements of the accounting equation, solve for the third element.	**EE1-2**	**PE1-2A, 1-2B**

OBJ 4 Describe and illustrate how business transactions can be recorded in terms of the resulting change in the elements of the accounting equation.

Key Points All business transactions can be stated in terms of the change in one or more of the three elements of the accounting equation.

Learning Outcomes	Example Exercises	Practice Exercises
• Define a business transaction.		
• Using the accounting equation as a framework, record transactions.	**EE1-3**	**PE1-3A, 1-3B**

OBJ 5

Describe the financial statements of a proprietorship and explain how they interrelate.

Key Points The primary financial statements of a corporation are the income statement, the retained earnings statement, the balance sheet, and the statement of cash flows. The income statement reports a period's net income or net loss, which is also reported on the retained earnings statement. The ending retained earnings reported on the retained earnings statement is also reported on the balance sheet. The ending cash balance is reported on the balance sheet and the statement of cash flows.

Learning Outcomes	Example Exercises	Practice Exercises
• List and describe the financial statements of a corporation.		
• Prepare an income statement.	EE1-4	PE1-4A, 1-4B
• Prepare a retained earnings statement.	EE1-5	PE1-5A, 1-5B
• Prepare a balance sheet.	EE1-6	PE1-6A, 1-6B
• Prepare a statement of cash flows.	EE1-7	PE1-7A, 1-7B
• Explain how the financial statements of a corporation are interrelated.		

OBJ 6

Describe and illustrate the use of the ratio of liabilities to stockholders' equity in evaluating a company's financial condition.

Key Points A ratio useful in analyzing the ability of a business to pay its creditors is the ratio of liabilities to stockholders' equity. The lower the ratio of liabilities to stockholders' equity, the better able the company is to withstand poor business conditions and to pay its obligations to creditors.

Learning Outcomes	Example Exercises	Practice Exercises
• Describe the usefulness of the ratio of liabilities to stockholders' equity.		
• Compute the ratio of liabilities to stockholders' equity.	EE1-8	PE1-8A, 1-8B

Key Terms

account form (18)
account payable (11)
account receivable (12)
accounting (3)
accounting equation (9)
assets (8)
balance sheet (15)
business (2)
business entity concept (7)
business transaction (9)
capital stock (10)
Certified Public Accountant (CPA) (6)
corporation (7)
cost concept (8)
dividends (13)
earnings (15)
ethics (4)
expenses (12)
fees earned (11)
financial accounting (4)
Financial Accounting Standards Board (FASB) (6)
financial statements (14)
generally accepted accounting principles (GAAP) (6)
general-purpose financial statements (4)
income statement (15)
interest revenue (11)
International Accounting Standards Board (IASB) (7)
liabilities (8)
limited liability company (LLC) (7)
management (or managerial) accounting (3)
manufacturing business (3)
matching concept (15)
merchandising business (3)
net income (or net profit) (15)
net loss (15)

Illustrative Problem

Cecil Jameson, Attorney-at-Law, is organized as a corporation and operated by Cecil Jameson. On July 1, 2013, the company has the following assets, liabilities, and capital stock: cash, $1,000; accounts receivable, $3,200; supplies, $850; land, $10,000; accounts payable, $1,530; capital stock, $10,000. Office space and office equipment are currently being rented, pending the construction of an office complex on land purchased last year. Business transactions during July are summarized as follows:

a. Received cash from clients for services, $3,928.

b. Paid creditors on account, $1,055.

c. Received cash from Cecil Jameson as an additional investment in exchange for capital stock, $3,700.

d. Paid office rent for the month, $1,200.

e. Charged clients for legal services on account, $2,025.

f. Purchased supplies on account, $245.

g. Received cash from clients on account, $3,000.

h. Received invoice for paralegal services from Legal Aid Inc. for July (to be paid on August 10), $1,635.

i. Paid the following: wages expense, $850; utilities expense, $325; answering service expense, $250; and miscellaneous expense, $75.

j. Determined that the cost of supplies on hand was $980; therefore, the cost of supplies used during the month was $115.

k. Paid dividends, $1,000.

Instructions

1. Determine the amount of retained earnings as of July 1, 2013.
2. State the assets, liabilities, and stockholders' equity as of July 1 in equation form similar to that shown in this chapter. In tabular form below the equation, indicate the increases and decreases resulting from each transaction and the new balances after each transaction.
3. Prepare an income statement for July, a retained earnings statement for July, and a balance sheet as of July 31, 2013.
4. (Optional). Prepare a statement of cash flows for July.

Solution

1.

Assets – Liabilities = Stockholders' Equity
($1,000 + $3,200 + $850 + $10,000) – $1,530 = Capital Stock + Retained Earnings
$15,050 – $1,530 = $10,000 + Retained Earnings
$3,520 = Retained Earnings

2.

Assets = **Liabilities +** **Stockholders' Equity**

	Cash +	Accts. Rec. +	Supp. +	Land =	Accts Pay. +	Capital Stock +	Retained Earnings −	Dividends +	Fees Earned −	Paralegal Exp. −	Rent Exp. −	Wages Exp. −	Utilities Exp. −	Answering Service Exp. −	Supp. Exp. −	Misc. Exp.
Bal.	1,000	3,200	850	10,000	1,530	10,000	3,520									
a.	+3,928								3,928							
Bal.	4,928	3,200	850	10,000	1,530				3,928							
b.	−1,055				−1,055											
Bal.	3,873	3,200	850	10,000	475				3,928							
c.	+3,700					+3,700										
Bal.	7,573	3,200	850	10,000	475	13,700			3,928							
d.	−1,200										−1,200					
Bal.	6,373	3,200	850	10,000	475				3,928		−1,200					
e.		+ 2,025							+ 2,025							
Bal.	6,373	5,225	850	10,000	475				5,953		−1,200					
f.			+245		+245											
Bal.	6,373	5,225	1,095	10,000	720				5,953		−1,200					
g.	+3,000	−3,000														
Bal.	9,373	2,225	1,095	10,000	720				5,953		−1,200					
h.					+1,635					−1,635						
Bal.	9,373	2,225	1,095	10,000	2,355				5,953	−1,635	−1,200					
i.	−1,500											−850	−325	−250		−75
Bal.	7,873	2,225	1,095	10,000	2,355				5,953	−1,635	−1,200	−850	−325	−250		−75
j.			−115												−115	
Bal.	7,873	2,225	980	10,000	2,355				5,953	−1,635	−1,200	−850	−325	−250	−115	−75
k.	−1,000							−1,000								
Bal.	6,873	2,225	980	10,000	2,355	13,700	3,520	−1,000	5,953	−1,635	−1,200	−850	−325	−250	−115	−75

3.

Cecil Jameson, Attorney-at-Law
Income Statement
For the Month Ended July 31, 2013

Fees earned		$5,953
Expenses:		
Paralegal expense	$1,635	
Rent expense	1,200	
Wages expense	850	
Utilities expense	325	
Answering service expense	250	
Supplies expense	115	
Miscellaneous expense	75	
Total expenses		4,450
Net income		$1,503

Cecil Jameson, Attorney-at-Law
Retained Earnings Statement
For the Month Ended July 31, 2013

Retained earnings, July 1, 2013		$3,520
Net income for the month	$1,503	
Less dividends	1,000	
Increase in retained earnings		503
Retained earnings, July 31, 2013		$4,023

(Continued)

Cecil Jameson, Attorney-at-Law
Balance Sheet
July 31, 2013

Assets		**Liabilities**	
Cash	$ 6,873	Accounts payable	$ 2,355
Accounts receivable	2,225	**Stockholders' Equity**	
Supplies	980	Capital stock	$13,700
Land	10,000	Retained earnings	4,023
Total assets	$20,078	Total stockholders' equity	17,723
		Total liabilities and stockholders' equity	$20,078

4. Optional.

Cecil Jameson, Attorney-at-Law
Statement of Cash Flows
For the Month Ended July 31, 2013

Cash flows from operating activities:		
Cash received from customers	$6,928*	
Deduct cash payments for operating expenses	(3,755)**	
Net cash flows from operating activities		$3,173
Cash flows from investing activities		—
Cash flows from financing activities:		
Cash received from issuing capital stock	$3,700	
Deduct cash dividends	(1,000)	
Net cash flows from financing activities		2,700
Net increase in cash during year		$5,873
Cash as of July 1, 2013		1,000
Cash as of July 31, 2013		$6,873

*$6,928 = $3,928 + $3,000

**$3,755 = $1,055 + $1,200 + $1,500

Discussion Questions

1. Name some users of accounting information.
2. What is the role of accounting in business?
3. Why are most large companies like Microsoft, PepsiCo, Caterpillar, and AutoZone organized as corporations?
4. Josh Reilly is the owner of Dispatch Delivery Service. Recently Josh paid interest of $4,500 on a personal loan of $75,000 that he used to begin the business. Should Dispatch Delivery Service record the interest payment? Explain.
5. On July 12, Reliable Repair Service extended an offer of $150,000 for land that had been priced for sale at $185,000. On September 3, Reliable Repair Service accepted the seller's counteroffer of $167,500. Describe how Reliable Repair Service should record the land.
6. a. Land with an assessed value of $750,000 for property tax purposes is acquired by a business for $900,000. Ten years later, the plot of land has an assessed value of $1,200,000 and the business receives an offer of $2,000,000 for it. Should the monetary amount assigned to the land in the business records now be increased?

   b. Assuming that the land acquired in (a) was sold for $2,125,000, how would the various elements of the accounting equation be affected?

7. Describe the difference between an account receivable and an account payable.
8. A business had revenues of $679,000 and operating expenses of $588,000. Did the business (a) incur a net loss or (b) realize net income?
9. A business had revenues of $640,000 and operating expenses of $715,000. Did the business (a) incur a net loss or (b) realize net income?
10. The financial statements are interrelated. (a) What item of financial or operating data appears on both the income statement and the retained earnings statement? (b) What item appears on both the balance sheet and the retained earnings statement? (c) What item appears on both the balance sheet and the statement of cash flows?

Practice Exercises

Example Exercises

EE 1-1 *p. 8*

PE 1-1A Cost concept

OBJ. 2

On May 19, Integrity Repair Service extended an offer of $335,000 for land that had been priced for sale at $363,000. On June 4, Integrity Repair Service accepted the seller's counteroffer of $345,000. On October 10, the land was assessed at a value of $290,000 for property tax purposes. On February 5 of the next year, Integrity Repair Service was offered $380,000 for the land by a national retail chain. At what value should the land be recorded in Integrity Repair Service's records?

EE 1-1 *p. 8*

PE 1-1B Cost concept

OBJ. 2

On March 31, Higgins Repair Service extended an offer of $415,000 for land that had been priced for sale at $460,000. On April 15, Higgins Repair Service accepted the seller's counteroffer of $437,500. On September 9, the land was assessed at a value of $375,000 for property tax purposes. On December 8, Higgins Repair Service was offered $475,000 for the land by a national retail chain. At what value should the land be recorded in Higgins Repair Service's records?

EE 1-2 *p. 9*

PE 1-2A Accounting equation

OBJ. 3

Ultima is a motivational consulting business. At the end of its accounting period, December 31, 2013, Ultima has assets of $942,000 and liabilities of $584,000. Using the accounting equation, determine the following amounts:

a. Stockholders' equity as of December 31, 2013.
b. Stocholders' equity as of December 31, 2014, assuming that assets increased by $113,000 and liabilities increased by $44,000 during 2014.

EE 1-2 *p. 9*

PE 1-2B Accounting equation

OBJ. 3

Be-The-One is a motivational consulting business. At the end of its accounting period, December 31, 2013, Be-The-One has assets of $395,000 and liabilities of $97,000. Using the accounting equation, determine the following amounts:

a. Stockholders' equity as of December 31, 2013.
b. Stockholders' equity as of December 31, 2014, assuming that assets decreased by $65,000 and liabilities increased by $36,000 during 2014.

EE 1-3 *p. 14*

PE 1-3A Transactions

OBJ. 4

Arrowhead Delivery Service is owned and operated by Gates Deeter. The following selected transactions were completed by Arrowhead Delivery Service during August:

1. Received cash in exchange for capital stock, $25,000.
2. Paid creditors on account, $3,750.

Example Exercises

3. Billed customers for delivery services on account, $22,400.
4. Received cash from customers on account, $11,300.
5. Paid dividends, $6,000.

Indicate the effect of each transaction on the accounting equation elements (Assets, Liabilities, Stockholders' Equity Capital Stock, Dividends, Revenue, and Expense). Also indicate the specific item within the accounting equation element that is affected. To illustrate, the answer to (1) is shown below.

(1) Asset (Cash) increases by $25,000; Stockholders' Equity (Capital Stock) increases by $25,000.

EE 1-3 *p. 14*

PE 1-3B Transactions

OBJ. 4

Interstate Delivery Service is owned and operated by Katie Wyer. The following selected transactions were completed by Interstate Delivery Service during May:

1. Received cash in exchange for capital stock, $18,000.
2. Paid advertising expense, $4,850.
3. Purchased supplies on account, $2,100.
4. Billed customers for delivery services on account, $14,700.
5. Received cash from customers on account, $8,200.

Indicate the effect of each transaction on the accounting equation elements (Assets, Liabilities, Stockholders' Equity Capital Stock, Dividends, Revenue, and Expense). Also indicate the specific item within the accounting equation element that is affected. To illustrate, the answer to (1) is shown below.

(1) Asset (Cash) increases by $18,000; Stockholders' Equity (Capital Stock) increases by $18,000.

EE 1-4 *p. 15*

PE 1-4A Income statement

OBJ. 5

The revenues and expenses of Sunset Travel Service for the year ended April 30, 2014, are listed below.

Fees earned	$1,673,000
Office expense	488,000
Miscellaneous expense	34,000
Wages expense	660,000

Prepare an income statement for the current year ended April 30, 2014.

EE 1-4 *p. 15*

PE 1-4B Income statement

OBJ. 5

The revenues and expenses of Sentinel Travel Service for the year ended August 31, 2014, are listed below.

Fees earned	$750,000
Office expense	295,000
Miscellaneous expense	12,000
Wages expense	450,000

Prepare an income statement for the current year ended August 31, 2014.

EE 1-5 *p. 16*

PE 1-5A Retained earnings statement

OBJ. 5

Using the income statement for Sunset Travel Service shown in Practice Exercise 1-4A, prepare a retained earnings statement for the current year ended April 30, 2014. Craig Daws, the owner, invested an additional $75,000 in the business in exchange for capital stock and cash dividends of $55,000 were paid during the year. Retained earnings as of May 1, 2013, was $250,000.

Example Exercises

EE 1-5 *p. 16*

PE 1-5B Retained earnings statement **OBJ. 5**

Using the income statement for Sentinel Travel Service shown in Practice Exercise 1-4B, prepare a retained earnings statement for the current year ended August 31, 2014. Barb Schroeder, the owner, invested an additional $36,000 in the business in exchange for capital stock and cash dividends of $18,000 were paid during the year. Retained earnings as of September 1, 2013, was $300,000.

EE 1-6 *p. 18*

PE 1-6A Balance sheet **OBJ. 5**

Using the following data for Sunset Travel Service as well as the retained earnings statement shown in Practice Exercise 1-5A, prepare a balance sheet as of April 30, 2014.

Accounts payable	$ 61,000
Accounts receivable	124,000
Capital stock	125,000
Cash	274,000
Land	450,000
Supplies	13,000

EE 1-6 *p. 18*

PE 1-6B Balance sheet **OBJ. 5**

Using the following data for Sentinel Travel Service as well as the retained earnings statement shown in Practice Exercise 1-5B, prepare a balance sheet as of August 31, 2014.

Accounts payable	$ 44,600
Accounts receivable	75,500
Capital stock	116,000
Cash	45,400
Land	310,000
Supplies	4,700

EE 1-7 *p. 19*

PE 1-7A Statement of cash flows **OBJ. 5**

A summary of cash flows for Sunset Travel Service for the year ended April 30, 2014, is shown below.

Cash receipts:	
Cash received from customers	$1,500,000
Cash received from issuing capital stock	75,000
Cash payments:	
Cash paid for operating expenses	1,215,000
Cash paid for land	240,000
Cash paid for dividends	66,000

The cash balance as of May 1, 2013, was $220,000.

Prepare a statement of cash flows for Sunset Travel Service for the year ended April 30, 2014.

EE 1-7 *p. 19*

PE 1-7B Statement of cash flows **OBJ. 5**

A summary of cash flows for Sentinel Travel Service for the year ended August 31, 2014, is shown below.

Cash receipts:	
Cash received from customers	$734,000
Cash received from issuing capital stock	36,000
Cash payments:	
Cash paid for operating expenses	745,600
Cash paid for land	50,000
Cash paid for dividends	18,000

The cash balance as of September 1, 2013, was $89,000.

Example Exercises

Prepare a statement of cash flows for Sentinel Travel Service for the year ended August 31, 2014.

EE 1-8 *p. 22*

F·A·I

PE 1-8A Ratio of liabilities to stockholders' equity

OBJ. 6

The following data were taken from Mesa Company's balance sheet:

	Dec. 31, 2014	Dec. 31, 2013
Total liabilities	$547,800	$518,000
Total stockholders' equity	415,000	370,000

a. Compute the ratio of liabilities to stockholders' equity.

b. Has the creditor's risk increased or decreased from December 31, 2013, to December 31, 2014?

EE 1-8 *p. 22*

F·A·I

PE 1-8B Ratio of liabilities to stockholders' equity

OBJ. 6

The following data were taken from Alvarado Company's balance sheet:

	Dec. 31, 2014	Dec. 31, 2013
Total liabilities	$4,085,000	$2,880,000
Total stockholders' equity	4,300,000	3,600,000

a. Compute the ratio of liabilities to stockholders' equity.

b. Has the creditor's risk increased or decreased from December 31, 2013, to December 31, 2014?

Exercises

EX 1-1 Types of businesses

OBJ. 1

The following is a list of well-known companies.

1. Alcoa Inc.
2. Boeing
3. Caterpillar
4. Citigroup Inc.
5. CVS
6. Dow Chemical Company
7. eBay Inc.
8. FedEx
9. Ford Motor Company
10. Gap Inc.
11. H&R Block
12. Hilton Hospitality, Inc.
13. Procter & Gamble
14. SunTrust
15. Walmart Stores, Inc.

a. Indicate whether each of these companies is primarily a service, merchandise, or manufacturing business. If you are unfamiliar with the company, use the Internet to locate the company's home page or use the finance Web site of **Yahoo** (http://finance.yahoo.com).

b. For which of the preceding companies is the accounting equation relevant?

EX 1-2 Professional ethics

OBJ. 1

A fertilizer manufacturing company wants to relocate to Yellowstone County. A report from a fired researcher at the company indicates the company's product is releasing toxic by-products. The company suppressed that report. A later report commissioned by the company shows there is no problem with the fertilizer.

Should the company's chief executive officer reveal the content of the unfavorable report in discussions with Yellowstone County representatives? Discuss.

EX 1-3 Business entity concept **OBJ. 2**

Ozark Sports sells hunting and fishing equipment and provides guided hunting and fishing trips. Ozark Sports is owned and operated by Eric Griffith, a well-known sports enthusiast and hunter. Eric's wife, Linda, owns and operates Lake Boutique, a women's clothing store. Eric and Linda have established a trust fund to finance their children's college education. The trust fund is maintained by Missouri State Bank in the name of the children, Mark and Steffy.

a. For each of the following transactions, identify which of the entities listed should record the transaction in its records.

Entities	
L	Lake Boutique
M	Missouri State Bank
O	Ozark Sports
X	None of the above

1. Linda authorized the trust fund to purchase mutual fund shares.
2. Linda purchased two dozen spring dresses from a St. Louis designer for a special spring sale.
3. Eric paid a breeder's fee for an English springer spaniel to be used as a hunting guide dog.
4. Linda deposited a $2,000 personal check in the trust fund at Missouri State Bank.
5. Eric paid a local doctor for his annual physical, which was required by the workmen's compensation insurance policy carried by Ozark Sports.
6. Eric received a cash advance from customers for a guided hunting trip.
7. Linda paid her dues to the YWCA.
8. Linda donated several dresses from inventory for a local charity auction for the benefit of a women's abuse shelter.
9. Eric paid for dinner and a movie to celebrate their twelfth wedding anniversary.
10. Eric paid for an advertisement in a hunters' magazine.

b. What is a business transaction?

EX 1-4 Accounting equation **OBJ. 3**

✔ Starbucks, $3,675

The total assets and total liabilities of Peet's Coffee & Tea Inc. and Starbucks Corporation are shown below.

	Peet's Coffee & Tea (in millions)	Starbucks (in millions)
Assets	$209	$6,386
Liabilities	36	2,711

Determine the stockholders' equity of each company.

EX 1-5 Accounting equation **OBJ. 3**

✔ Dollar Tree, $1,459

The total assets and total liabilities of Dollar Tree Inc. and Target Corporation are shown below.

	Dollar Tree (in millions)	Target Corporation (in millions)
Assets	$2,381	$43,705
Liabilities	922	28,218

Determine the stockholders' equity of each company.

EX 1-6 Accounting equation **OBJ. 3**

✔ a. $456,100

Determine the missing amount for each of the following:

	Assets	=	Liabilities	+	Stockholders' Equity
a.	X	=	$118,000	+	$338,100
b.	$766,750	=	X	+	$411,740
c.	$3,250,300	=	$1,178,100	+	X

✔ b. $890,000

EX 1-7 Accounting equation OBJ. 3, 4

Mega Concepts is a motivational consulting business. At the end of its accounting period, December 31, 2013, Mega Concepts has assets of $1,250,000 and liabilities of $475,000. Using the accounting equation and considering each case independently, determine the following amounts:

a. Stockholders' equity as of December 31, 2013.

b. Stockholders' equity as of December 31, 2014, assuming that assets increased by $225,000 and liabilities increased by $110,000 during 2014.

c. Stockholders' equity as of December 31, 2014, assuming that assets decreased by $300,000 and liabilities increased by $90,000 during 2014.

d. Stockholders' equity as of December 31, 2014, assuming that assets increased by $550,000 and liabilities decreased by $135,000 during 2014.

e. Net income (or net loss) during 2014, assuming that as of December 31, 2014, assets were $1,500,000, liabilities were $375,000, and no additional capital stock was issued or dividends paid.

EX 1-8 Asset, liability, and stockholders' equity items OBJ. 3

Indicate whether each of the following is identified with (1) an asset, (2) a liability, or (3) stockholders' equity:

a. accounts payable

b. cash

c. fees earned

d. land

e. supplies

f. wages expense

EX 1-9 Effect of transactions on accounting equation OBJ. 4

Describe how the following business transactions affect the three elements of the accounting equation.

a. Invested cash in business.

b. Paid for utilities used in the business.

c. Purchased supplies for cash.

d. Purchased supplies on account.

e. Received cash for services performed.

✔ a. (1) increase $260,000

EX 1-10 Effect of transactions on accounting equation OBJ. 4

a. A vacant lot acquired for $180,000 is sold for $440,000 in cash. What is the effect of the sale on the total amount of the seller's (1) assets, (2) liabilities, and (3) stockholders' equity?

b. Assume that the seller owes $69,000 on a loan for the land. After receiving the $440,000 cash in (a), the seller pays the $69,000 owed. What is the effect of the payment on the total amount of the seller's (1) assets, (2) liabilities, and (3) stockholders' equity?

c. Is it true that a transaction always affects at least two elements (Assets, Liabilities, or Stockholders' Equity) of the accounting equation? Explain.

EX 1-11 Effect of transactions on stockholders' equity OBJ. 4

Indicate whether each of the following types of transactions will either (a) increase stockholders' equity or (b) decrease stockholders' equity:

1. expenses
2. issuing capital stock in exchange for cash
3. dividends
4. revenues

EX 1-12 Transactions **OBJ. 4**

The following selected transactions were completed by Reuben's Delivery Service during October:

1. Received cash from owner in exchange for capital stock, $20,000.
2. Purchased supplies for cash, $900.
3. Paid rent for October, $3,000.
4. Paid advertising expense, $2,500.
5. Received cash for providing delivery services, $23,100.
6. Billed customers for delivery services on account, $41,750.
7. Paid creditors on account, $4,500.
8. Received cash from customers on account, $36,200.
9. Determined that the cost of supplies on hand was $175 and $725 of supplies had been used during the month.
10. Paid dividends, $1,000.

Indicate the effect of each transaction on the accounting equation by listing the numbers identifying the transactions, (1) through (10), in a column, and inserting at the right of each number the appropriate letter from the following list:

a. Increase in an asset, decrease in another asset.

b. Increase in an asset, increase in a liability.

c. Increase in an asset, increase in stockholders' equity.

d. Decrease in an asset, decrease in a liability.

e. Decrease in an asset, decrease in stockholders' equity.

EX 1-13 Nature of transactions **OBJ. 4**

✔ d. $7,200

Angela Howard operates her own catering service. Summary financial data for July are presented in equation form as follows. Each line designated by a number indicates the effect of a transaction on the equation. Each increase and decrease in stockholders' equity, except transaction (5), affects net income.

	Assets			= Liabilities +	Stockholders' Equity				
	Cash	+ Supplies +	Land	= Accounts Payable	+ Capital Stock	+ Retained Earning	– Dividends	+ Fees Earned	– Expenses
Bal.	30,000	2,000	80,000	12,000	30,000	70,000			
1.	+33,000							+33,000	
2.	−20,000		+20,000						
3.	−24,000								−24,000
4.		+1,000		+1,000					
5.	−3,000						−3,000		
6.	−6,000			−6,000					
7.		−1,800							−1,800
Bal.	10,000	1,200	100,000	7,000	30,000	70,000	−3,000	33,000	−25,800

a. Describe each transaction.

b. What is the amount of the net decrease in cash during the month?

c. What is the amount of the net increase in stockholders' equity during the month?

d. What is the amount of the net income for the month?

e. How much of the net income for the month was retained in the business?

EX 1-14 Net income and dividends **OBJ. 5**

The income statement for the month of February indicates a net income of $17,500. During the same period, $25,500 in cash dividends was paid.

Would it be correct to say that the business incurred a net loss of $8,000 during the month? Discuss.

EX 1-15 Net income and stockholders' equity for four businesses **OBJ. 5**

✔ Kilo: Net income, $230,000

Four different corporations, Juliet, Kilo, Lima, and Mike, show the same balance sheet data at the beginning and end of a year. These data, exclusive of the amount of stockholders' equity, are summarized as follows:

	Total Assets	Total Liabilities
Beginning of the year	$ 600,000	$150,000
End of the year	1,125,000	500,000

On the basis of the above data and the following additional information for the year, determine the net income (or loss) of each company for the year. (*Hint:* First determine the amount of increase or decrease in stockholders' equity during the year.)

Juliet: No additional capital stock was issued, and no dividends were paid.

Kilo: No additional capital stock was issued, but dividends of $55,000 were paid.

Lima: Additional capital stock of $100,000 was issued, but no dividends were paid.

Mike: Additional capital stock of $100,000 was issued, and dividends of $55,000 were paid.

EX 1-16 Balance sheet items **OBJ. 5**

From the following list of selected items taken from the records of Hoosier Appliance Service as of a specific date, identify those that would appear on the balance sheet:

1. Accounts Receivable
2. Cash
3. Fees Earned
4. Land
5. Capital Stock
6. Supplies
7. Supplies Expense
8. Utilities Expense
9. Wages Expense
10. Wages Payable

EX 1-17 Income statement items **OBJ. 5**

Based on the data presented in Exercise 1-16, identify those items that would appear on the income statement.

EX 1-18 Retained earnings statement **OBJ. 5**

✔ Retained earnings, November 30, 2014: $635,000

SPREADSHEET

Financial information related to Infra-Systems Company for the month ended November 30, 2014, is as follows:

Net income for November	$275,000
Dividends paid during November	40,000
Retained earnings, November 1, 2014	400,000

a. Prepare a retained earnngs statement for the month ended November 30, 2014.

b. Why is the retained earnings statement prepared before the November 30, 2014, balance sheet?

EX 1-19 Income statement **OBJ. 5**

✔ Net income: $284,000

SPREADSHEET

Exploration Services was organized on March 1, 2014. A summary of the revenue and expense transactions for March follows:

Fees earned	$1,100,000
Wages expense	715,000
Rent expense	80,000
Supplies expense	9,000
Miscellaneous expense	12,000

Prepare an income statement for the month ended March 31.

EX 1-20 Missing amounts from balance sheet and income statement data **OBJ. 5**

✔ (a) $135,000

One item is omitted in each of the following summaries of balance sheet and income statement data for the following four different corporations:

	Freeman	Heyward	Jones	Ramirez
Beginning of the year:				
Assets	$ 900,000	$490,000	$115,000	(d)
Liabilities	360,000	260,000	81,000	$120,000
End of the year:				
Assets	1,260,000	675,000	100,000	270,000
Liabilities	330,000	220,000	80,000	136,000
During the year:				
Additional issuance of capital stock	(a)	150,000	10,000	55,000
Dividends	75,000	32,000	(c)	39,000
Revenue	570,000	(b)	115,000	115,000
Expenses	240,000	128,000	122,500	128,000

Determine the missing amounts, identifying them by letter. (*Hint:* First determine the amount of increase or decrease in stockholders' equity during the year.)

EX 1-21 Balance sheets, net income **OBJ. 5**

✔ b. $135,000

SPREADSHEET

Financial information related to Ebony Interiors for February and March 2014 is as follows:

	February 28, 2014	March 31, 2014
Accounts payable	$310,000	$400,000
Accounts receivable	800,000	960,000
Capital stock	200,000	200,000
Cash	320,000	380,000
Retained earnings	?	?
Supplies	30,000	35,000

a. Prepare balance sheets for Ebony Interiors as of February 28 and March 31, 2014.

b. Determine the amount of net income for March, assuming that no additional capital stock was issued and no dividends were paid during the month.

c. Determine the amount of net income for March, assuming that no additional capital stock was issued but dividends of $50,000 were paid during the month.

EX 1-22 Financial statements **OBJ. 5**

Each of the following items is shown in the financial statements of Exxon Mobil Corporation.

1. Accounts payable
2. Cash equivalents
3. Crude oil inventory
4. Equipment
5. Exploration expenses
6. Income taxes payable
7. Investments
8. Long-term debt
9. Marketable securities
10. Notes and loans payable
11. Notes receivable
12. Operating expenses
13. Prepaid taxes
14. Sales
15. Selling expenses

a. Identify the financial statement (balance sheet or income statement) in which each item would appear.

b. Can an item appear on more than one financial statement?

c. Is the accounting equation relevant for Exxon Mobil Corporation?

EX 1-23 Statement of cash flows **OBJ. 5**

Indicate whether each of the following activities would be reported on the statement of cash flows as (a) an operating activity, (b) an investing activity, or (c) a financing activity:

1. Cash received from fees earned.
2. Cash paid for expenses.

3. Cash paid for land.
4. Cash paid for dividends.

EX 1-24 Statement of cash flows **OBJ. 5**

A summary of cash flows for Ethos Consulting Group for the year ended May 31, 2014, is shown below.

Cash receipts:	
Cash received from customers	$637,500
Cash received from issuing capital stock	62,500
Cash payments:	
Cash paid for operating expenses	475,000
Cash paid for land	90,000
Cash paid for dividends	17,500

The cash balance as of June 1, 2013, was $58,000.

Prepare a statement of cash flows for Ethos Consulting Group for the year ended May 31, 2014.

EX 1-25 Financial statements **OBJ. 5**

✔ Correct amount of total assets is $51,500.

We-Sell Realty, organized August 1, 2014, is owned and operated by Omar Farah. How many errors can you find in the following statements for We-Sell Realty, prepared after its first month of operations?

We-Sell Realty
Income Statement
August 31, 2014

Sales commissions		$140,000
Expenses:		
Office salaries expense	$87,000	
Rent expense	18,000	
Automobile expense	7,500	
Miscellaneous expense	2,200	
Supplies expense	1,150	
Total expenses		115,850
Net income		$ 25,000

Omar Farah
Retained Earnings Statement
August 31, 2013

Retained earnings, August 1, 2014	$ 0
Less dividends during August	10,000
	$(10,000)
Additional issuance of capital stock on August 1, 2014	15,000
	$ 5,000
Net income for August	25,000
Retained earnings, August 31, 2014	$ 30,000

Balance Sheet
For the Month Ended August 31, 2014

Assets		Liabilities	
Cash	$ 8,900	Accounts receivable	$38,600
Accounts payable	22,350	Supplies	4,000
		Stockholders' Equity	
		Retained earnings	30,000
Total assets	$31,250	Total liabilities and stockholders' equity	$72,600

EX 1-26 Ratio of liabilities to stockholders' equity OBJ. 6

F·A·I

The Home Depot, Inc., is the world's largest home improvement retailer and one of the largest retailers in the United States based on net sales volume. The Home Depot operates over 2,200 Home Depot® stores that sell a wide assortment of building materials and home improvement and lawn and garden products.

The Home Depot recently reported the following balance sheet data (in millions):

	Year 2	Year 1
Total assets	$40,125	$40,877
Total stockholders' equity	18,889	19,393

a. Determine the total liabilities at the end of Years 2 and 1.

b. Determine the ratio of liabilities to stockholders' equity for Year 2 and Year 1. Round to two decimal places.

c. What conclusions regarding the margin of protection to the creditors can you draw from (b)?

EX 1-27 Ratio of liabilities to stockholders' equity OBJ. 6

F·A·I

Lowe's Companies Inc., a major competitor of The Home Depot in the home improvement business, operates over 1,700 stores. Lowe's recently reported the following balance sheet data (in millions):

	Year 2	Year 1
Total assets	$33,699	$33,005
Total liabilities	15,587	13,936

a. Determine the total stockholders' equity as of at the end of Years 2 and 1.

b. Determine the ratio of liabilities to stockholders' equity for Year 2 and Year 1. Round to two decimal places.

c. What conclusions regarding the risk to the creditors can you draw from (b)?

d. Using the balance sheet data for The Home Depot in Exercise 1-26, how does the ratio of liabilities to stockholders' equity of Lowe's compare to that of The Home Depot?

Problems Series A

PR 1-1A Transactions OBJ. 4

✔ Cash bal. at end of June: $29,250

On June 1 of the current year, Bret Eisen established a business to manage rental property. He completed the following transactions during June:

a. Opened a business bank account with a deposit of $30,000 in exchange for capital stock.

b. Purchased office supplies on account, $1,200.

c. Received cash from fees earned for managing rental property, $7,200.

d. Paid rent on office and equipment for the month, $3,000.

e. Paid creditors on account, $750.

f. Billed customers for fees earned for managing rental property, $5,000.

g. Paid automobile expenses (including rental charges) for month, $600, and miscellaneous expenses, $300.

h. Paid office salaries, $1,800.

i. Determined that the cost of supplies on hand was $700; therefore, the cost of supplies used was $500.

j. Paid dividends $1,500.

Instructions

1. Indicate the effect of each transaction and the balances after each transaction, using the following tabular headings:

Assets			= Liabilities +	Stockholders' Equity							
Cash +	Accounts Receivable +	Supplies =	Accounts Payable +	Capital Stock	− Dividends	+ Fees Earned	− Rent Expense	− Salaries Expense	− Supplies Expense	− Auto Expense	− Misc. Expense

2. Briefly explain why issuance of capital stock and revenues increased stockholders' equity, while dividends and expenses decreased stockholders' equity.
3. Determine the net income for June.
4. How much did June's transactions increase or decrease retained earnings?

PR 1-2A Financial statements

OBJ. 5

✔ **1. Net income: $360,000**

SPREADSHEET

Following are the amounts of the assets and liabilities of Oriental Travel Agency at December 31, 2014, the end of the current year, and its revenue and expenses for the year. The retained earnings was $400,000 on January 1, 2014, the beginning of the current year. During the current year, dividends of $25,000 were paid.

Accounts payable	$ 115,000	Miscellaneous expense	$ 7,000
Accounts receivable	370,000	Rent expense	150,000
Capital stock	50,000	Supplies	20,000
Cash	210,000	Supplies expense	14,000
Fees earned	1,100,000	Utilities expense	79,000
Land	300,000	Wages expense	490,000

Instructions

1. Prepare an income statement for the current year ended December 31, 2014.
2. Prepare a retained earnings statement for the current year ended December 31, 2014.
3. Prepare a balance sheet as of December 31, 2014.
4. What item appears on both the retained earnings statement and the balance sheet?

PR 1-3A Financial statements

OBJ. 5

✔ **1. Net income: $31,200**

SPREADSHEET

Seth Feye established Reliance Financial Services on July 1, 2014. Reliance Financial Services offers financial planning advice to its clients. The effect of each transaction and the balances after each transaction for July are shown below.

	Assets			= Liabilities +	Stockholders' Equity							
	Cash +	Accounts Receivable +	Supplies =	Accounts Payable +	Capital Stock	− Dividends +	Fees Earned	− Salaries Expense	− Rent Expense	− Auto Expense	− Supplies Expense	− Misc. Expense
a.	+50,000				+50,000							
b.			+7,000	+7,000								
Bal.	50,000		7,000	7,000	50,000							
c.	−3,600			−3,600								
Bal.	46,400		7,000	3,400	50,000							
d.	+110,000						+110,000					
Bal.	156,400		7,000	3,400	50,000		110,000					
e.	−33,000								−33,000			
Bal.	123,400		7,000	3,400	50,000		110,000		−33,000			
f.	−20,800									−16,000		−4,800
Bal.	102,600		7,000	3,400	50,000		110,000		−33,000	−16,000		−4,800
g.	−55,000							−55,000				
Bal.	47,600		7,000	3,400	50,000		110,000	−55,000	−33,000	−16,000		−4,800
h.			−4,500								−4,500	
Bal.	47,600		2,500	3,400	50,000		110,000	−55,000	−33,000	−16,000	−4,500	−4,800
i.		+34,500					+ 34,500					
Bal.	47,600	34,500	2,500	3,400	50,000		144,500	−55,000	−33,000	−16,000	−4,500	−4,800
j.	−15,000					−15,000						
Bal.	32,600	34,500	2,500	3,400	50,000	−15,000	144,500	−55,000	−33,000	−16,000	−4,500	−4,800

Instructions

1. Prepare an income statement for the month ended July 31, 2014.
2. Prepare a retained earnings statement for the month ended July 31, 2014.
3. Prepare a balance sheet as of July 31, 2014.
4. (Optional). Prepare a statement of cash flows for the month ending July 31, 2014.

PR 1-4A Transactions; financial statements

OBJ. 4, 5

✔ **2. Net income: $23,650**

On October 1, 2014, Kevin Bosley established Sunrise Realty. Kevin completed the following transactions during the month of October:

a. Opened a business bank account with a deposit of $18,000 in exchange for capital stock.

b. Purchased office supplies on account, $3,200.

c. Paid creditor on account, $1,800.

d. Earned sales commissions, receiving cash, $36,750.

e. Paid rent on office and equipment for the month, $4,000.

f. Paid dividends, $3,000.

g. Paid automobile expenses (including rental charge) for month, $2,500, and miscellaneous expenses, $1,200.

h. Paid office salaries, $3,750.

i. Determined that the cost of supplies on hand was $1,550; therefore, the cost of supplies used was $1,650.

Instructions

1. Indicate the effect of each transaction and the balances after each transaction, using the following tabular headings:

Assets		= Liabilities +	Stockholders' Equity							
Cash +	Supplies =	Accounts Payable +	Capital Stock	− Dividends +	Sales Commissions	− Rent Expense	− Salaries Expense	− Auto Expense	− Supplies Expense	− Misc. Expense

2. Prepare an income statement for October, a retained earnings statement for October, and a balance sheet as of October 31.

PR 1-5A Transactions; financial statements

OBJ. 4, 5

✔ **3. Net income: $63,775**

SPREADSHEET

D'Lite Dry Cleaners is owned and operated by Joel Palk. A building and equipment are currently being rented, pending expansion to new facilities. The actual work of dry cleaning is done by another company at wholesale rates. The assets, liabilities, and capital stock of the business on July 1, 2014, are as follows: Cash, $45,000; Accounts Receivable, $93,000; Supplies, $7,000; Land, $75,000; Accounts Payable, $40,000; Capital Stock, $60,000. Business transactions during July are summarized as follows:

a. Joel Palk invested additional cash in exchange for capital stock with a deposit of $35,000 in the business bank account.

b. Paid $50,000 for the purchase of land adjacent to land currently owned by D'Lite Dry Cleaners as a future building site.

c. Received cash from cash customers for dry cleaning revenue, $32,125.

d. Paid rent for the month, $6,000.

e. Purchased supplies on account, $2,500.

f. Paid creditors on account, $22,800.

g. Charged customers for dry cleaning revenue on account, $84,750.

h. Received monthly invoice for dry cleaning expense for July (to be paid on August 10), $29,500.

i. Paid the following: wages expense, $7,500; truck expense, $2,500; utilities expense, $1,300; miscellaneous expense, $2,700.

j. Received cash from customers on account, $88,000.

k. Determined that the cost of supplies on hand was $5,900; therefore, the cost of supplies used during the month was $3,600.

l. Paid dividends, $12,000.

Instructions

1. Determine the amount of retained earnings as of July 1 of the current year.
2. State the assets, liabilities, and stockholders' equity as of July 1 in equation form similar to that shown in this chapter. In tabular form below the equation, indicate increases and decreases resulting from each transaction and the new balances after each transaction.
3. Prepare an income statement for July, a retained earnings statement for July, and a balance sheet as of July 31.
4. (Optional). Prepare a statement of cash flows for July.

PR 1-6A Missing amounts from financial statements **OBJ. 5**

✔ k. $750,000

The financial statements at the end of Wolverine Realty's first month of operations are as follows:

Wolverine Realty
Income Statement
For the Month Ended April 30, 2014

Fees earned		$ (a)
Expenses:		
Wages expense	$300,000	
Rent expense	100,000	
Supplies expense	(b)	
Utilities expense	20,000	
Miscellaneous expense	25,000	
Total expenses		475,000
Net income		$275,000

Wolverine Realty
Retained Earnings Statement
For the Month Ended April 30, 2014

Retained earnings, April 1, 2014		$ (c)
Net income for April	$ (d)	
Less dividends	125,000	
Increase in retained earnings		(e)
Retained earnings, April 30, 2014		$ (f)

Wolverine Realty
Balance Sheet
April 30, 2014

Assets		Liabilities	
Cash	$462,500	Accounts payable	$100,000
Supplies	12,500	**Stockholders' Equity**	
Land	150,000	Capital stock	$375,000
Total assets	$ (g)	Retained earnings	(h)
		Total stockholders' equity	(i)
		Total liabilities and stockholders' equity	$ (j)

Wolverine Realty
Statement of Cash Flows
For the Month Ended April 30, 2014

Cash flows from operating activities:		
Cash received from customers	$ (k)	
Deduct cash payments for expenses and payments to creditors	(387,500)	
Net cash flows from operating activities		$ (l)
Cash flows used for investing activities:		
Cash payments for acquisition of land		(m)
Cash flows from financing activities:		
Cash received from issuing capital stock	$ (n)	
Deduct cash dividends	(o)	
Net cash flows from financing activities		(p)
Net increase (decrease) in cash and April 30, 2014, cash balance		$ (q)

Instructions

By analyzing the interrelationships among the four financial statements, determine the proper amounts for (a) through (q).

Problems Series B

PR 1-1B Transactions

OBJ. 4

✔ **Cash bal. at end of March: $48,650**

Amy Austin established an insurance agency on March 1 of the current year and completed the following transactions during March:

a. Opened a business bank account with a deposit of $50,000 in exchange for capital stock.
b. Purchased supplies on account, $4,000.
c. Paid creditors on account, $2,300.
d. Received cash from fees earned on insurance commissions, $13,800.
e. Paid rent on office and equipment for the month, $5,000.
f. Paid automobile expenses for month, $1,150, and miscellaneous expenses, $300.
g. Paid office salaries, $2,500.
h. Determined that the cost of supplies on hand was $2,700; therefore, the cost of supplies used was $1,300.
i. Billed insurance companies for sales commissions earned, $12,500.
j. Paid dividends, $3,900.

Instructions

1. Indicate the effect of each transaction and the balances after each transaction, using the following tabular headings:

Assets			=	**Liabilities** +	**Stockholders' Equity**							
Cash +	Accounts Receivable +	Supplies	=	Accounts Payable +	Capital Stock −	Dividends +	Fees Earned −	Rent Expense −	Salaries Expense −	Supplies Expense −	Auto Expense −	Misc. Expense

2. Briefly explain why the issuance of capital stock and revenues increased stockholders' equity, while dividends and expenses decreased stockholders' equity.
3. Determine the net income for March.
4. How much did March's transactions increase or decrease retained earnings?

✔ **1. Net income: $200,000**

SPREADSHEET

PR 1-2B Financial statements

OBJ. 5

The amounts of the assets and liabilities of Wilderness Travel Service at April 30, 2014, the end of the current year, and its revenue and expenses for the year are listed below. The retained earnings was $145,000 at May 1, 2013, the beginning of the current year, and dividends of $40,000 were paid during the current year.

Accounts payable	$ 25,000	Rent expense	$ 75,000
Accounts receivable	210,000	Supplies	9,000
Capital stock	35,000	Supplies expense	12,000
Cash	146,000	Taxes expense	10,000
Fees earned	875,000	Utilities expense	38,000
Miscellaneous expense	15,000	Wages expense	525,000

Instructions

1. Prepare an income statement for the current year ended April 30, 2014.
2. Prepare a retained earnings statement for the current year ended April 30, 2014.
3. Prepare a balance sheet as of April 30, 2014.
4. What item appears on both the income statement and retained earnings statement?

✔ **1. Net income: $10,900**

SPREADSHEET

PR 1-3B Financial statements

OBJ. 5

Jose Loder established Bronco Consulting on August 1, 2014. The effect of each transaction and the balances after each transaction for August are shown below.

	Assets			= Liabilities +	Stockholders' Equity							
	Cash +	Accounts Receivable +	Supplies =	Accounts Payable +	Capital Stock	− Dividends +	Fees Earned −	Salaries Expense −	Rent Expense −	Auto Expense −	Supplies Expense −	Misc. Expense
a.	+75,000				+75,000							
b.			+9,000	+9,000								
Bal.	75,000		9,000	9,000	75,000							
c.	+92,000						+92,000					
Bal.	167,000		9,000	9,000	75,000		92,000					
d.	−27,000								−27,000			
Bal.	140,000		9,000	9,000	75,000		92,000		−27,000			
e.	−6,000			−6,000								
Bal.	134,000		9,000	3,000	75,000		92,000		−27,000			
f.		+33,000					+33,000					
Bal.	134,000	33,000	9,000	3,000	75,000		125,000		−27,000			
g.	−23,000									−15,500		−7,500
Bal.	111,000	33,000	9,000	3,000	75,000		125,000		−27,000	−15,500		−7,500
h.	−58,000							−58,000				
Bal.	53,000	33,000	9,000	3,000	75,000		125,000	−58,000	−27,000	−15,500		−7,500
i.			−6,100								−6,100	
Bal.	53,000	33,000	2,900	3,000	75,000		125,000	−58,000	−27,000	−15,500	−6,100	−7,500
j.	−5,000					−5,000						
Bal.	48,000	33,000	2,900	3,000	75,000	−5,000	125,000	−58,000	−27,000	−15,500	−6,100	−7,500

Instructions

1. Prepare an income statement for the month ended August 31, 2014.
2. Prepare a retained earnings statement for the month ended August 31, 2014.
3. Prepare a balance sheet as of August 31, 2014.
4. (Optional). Prepare a statement of cash flows for the month ending August 31, 2014.

✔ **2. Net income: $10,850**

PR 1-4B Transactions; financial statements

OBJ. 4, 5

On April 1, 2014, Maria Adams established Custom Realty. Maria completed the following transactions during the month of April:

a. Opened a business bank account with a deposit of $24,000 in exchange for capital stock.
b. Paid rent on office and equipment for the month, $3,600.
c. Paid automobile expenses (including rental charge) for month, $1,350, and miscellaneous expenses, $600.
d. Purchased office supplies on account, $1,200.
e. Earned sales commissions, receiving cash, $19,800.
f. Paid creditor on account, $750.
g. Paid office salaries, $2,500.
h. Paid dividends, $3,500.
i. Determined that the cost of supplies on hand was $300; therefore, the cost of supplies used was $900.

Instructions

1. Indicate the effect of each transaction and the balances after each transaction, using the following tabular headings:

Assets		= Liabilities +			Stockholders' Equity					
Cash + Supplies	=	Accounts Payable	+	Capital Stock	– Dividends +	Sales Commissions	– Rent Expense	– Salaries Expense	– Auto Expense	– Supplies Expense – Misc. Expense

2. Prepare an income statement for April, a retained earnings statement for April, and a balance sheet as of April 30.

PR 1-5B Transactions; financial statements

OBJ. 4, 5

✔ **3. Net income: $40,150**

SPREADSHEET

Bev's Dry Cleaners is owned and operated by Beverly Zahn. A building and equipment are currently being rented, pending expansion to new facilities. The actual work of dry cleaning is done by another company at wholesale rates. The assets, liabilities, and capital stock of the business on November 1, 2014, are as follows: Cash, $39,000; Accounts Receivable, $80,000; Supplies, $11,000; Land, $50,000; Accounts Payable, $31,500; Capital Stock, $50,000. Business transactions during November are summarized as follows:

a. Beverly Zahn invested additional cash in exchange for capital stock with a deposit of $21,000 in the business bank account.
b. Purchased land adjacent to land currently owned by Bev's Dry Cleaners to use in the future as a parking lot, paying cash of $35,000.
c. Paid rent for the month, $4,000.
d. Charged customers for dry cleaning revenue on account, $72,000.
e. Paid creditors on account, $20,000.
f. Purchased supplies on account, $8,000.
g. Received cash from cash customers for dry cleaning revenue, $38,000.
h. Received cash from customers on account, $77,000.
i. Received monthly invoice for dry cleaning expense for November (to be paid on December 10), $29,450.
j. Paid the following: wages expense, $24,000; truck expense, $2,100; utilities expense, $1,800; miscellaneous expense, $1,300.
k. Determined that the cost of supplies on hand was $11,800; therefore, the cost of supplies used during the month was $7,200.
l. Paid dividends, $5,000.

Instructions

1. Determine the amount of retained earnings as of November 1.
2. State the assets, liabilities, and stockholders' equity as of November 1 in equation form similar to that shown in this chapter. In tabular form below the equation, indicate increases and decreases resulting from each transaction and the new balances after each transaction.

3. Prepare an income statement for November, a retained earnings statement for November, and a balance sheet as of November 30.
4. (Optional). Prepare a statement of cash flows for November.

PR 1-6B Missing amounts from financial statements

OBJ. 5

✔ i. $208,000

The financial statements at the end of Atlas Realty's first month of operations are shown below.

Atlas Realty
Income Statement
For the Month Ended May 31, 2014

Fees earned		$400,000
Expenses:		
Wages expense	$ (a)	
Rent expense	48,000	
Supplies expense	17,600	
Utilities expense	14,400	
Miscellaneous expense	4,800	
Total expenses		288,000
Net income		$ (b)

Atlas Realty
Retained Earnings Statement
For the Month Ended May 31, 2014

Retained earnings, May 1, 2014		$ (c)
Net income	$ (d)	
Less dividends	(e)	
Increase in retained earnings		(f)
Retained earnings, May 31, 2014		$ (g)

Atlas Realty
Balance Sheet
May 31, 2014

Assets		Liabilities	
Cash	$123,200	Accounts payable	$48,000
Supplies	12,800	**Stockholders' Equity**	
Land	(h)	Capital stock	$ (j)
Total assets	$ (i)	Retained earnings	(k)
		Total stockholders' equity	(l)
		Total liabilities and stockholders' equity	$ (m)

Atlas Realty
Statement of Cash Flows
For the Month Ended May 31, 2014

Cash flows from operating activities:		
Cash received from customers	$ (n)	
Deduct cash payments for expenses and payments to creditors	(252,800)	
Net cash flows from operating activities		$ (o)
Cash flows from investing activities:		
Cash payments for acquisition of land		(120,000)
Cash flows from financing activities:		
Cash received from issuing capital stock	$ 160,000	
Deduct cash dividends	(64,000)	
Net cash flows from financing activities		(p)
Net increase (decrease) in cash and May 31, 2014, cash balance		$ (q)

Instructions

By analyzing the interrelationships among the four financial statements, determine the proper amounts for (a) through (q).

Continuing Problem

✔ **2. Net income: $1,340**

Peyton Smith enjoys listening to all types of music and owns countless CDs. Over the years, Peyton has gained a local reputation for knowledge of music from classical to rap and the ability to put together sets of recordings that appeal to all ages.

During the last several months, Peyton served as a guest disc jockey on a local radio station. In addition, Peyton has entertained at several friends' parties as the host deejay.

On June 1, 2014, Peyton established a corporation known as PS Music. Using an extensive collection of music MP3 files, Peyton will serve as a disc jockey on a fee basis for weddings, college parties, and other events. During June, Peyton entered into the following transactions:

June 1. Deposited $4,000 in a checking account in the name of PS Music in exchange for capital stock.
2. Received $3,500 from a local radio station for serving as the guest disc jockey for June.
2. Agreed to share office space with a local real estate agency, Pinnacle Realty. PS Music will pay one-fourth of the rent. In addition, PS Music agreed to pay a portion of the salary of the receptionist and to pay one-fourth of the utilities. Paid $800 for the rent of the office.
4. Purchased supplies from City Office Supply Co. for $350. Agreed to pay $100 within 10 days and the remainder by July 5, 2014.
6. Paid $500 to a local radio station to advertise the services of PS Music twice daily for two weeks.
8. Paid $675 to a local electronics store for renting digital recording equipment.
12. Paid $350 (music expense) to Cool Music for the use of its current music demos to make various music sets.
13. Paid City Office Supply Co. $100 on account.
16. Received $300 from a dentist for providing two music sets for the dentist to play for her patients.
22. Served as disc jockey for a wedding party. The father of the bride agreed to pay $1,000 in July.
25. Received $500 for serving as the disc jockey for a cancer charity ball hosted by the local hospital.
29. Paid $240 (music expense) to Galaxy Music for the use of its library of music demos.
30. Received $900 for serving as PS disc jockey for a local club's monthly dance.
30. Paid Pinnacle Realty $400 for PS Music's share of the receptionist's salary for June.
30. Paid Pinnacle Realty $300 for PS Music's share of the utilities for June.
30. Determined that the cost of supplies on hand is $170. Therefore, the cost of supplies used during the month was $180.
30. Paid for miscellaneous expenses, $415.
30. Paid $1,000 royalties (music expense) to National Music Clearing for use of various artists' music during the month.
30. Paid dividends of $500.

Instructions

1. Indicate the effect of each transaction and the balances after each transaction, using the following tabular headings:

Assets			=	Liabilities +		Stockholders' Equity										
Cash	+ Accts. Rec.	+ Supplies	=	Accounts Payable	+ Capital Stock	− Dividends	+ Fees Earned	− Music Exp.	− Office Rent Exp.	− Equipment Rent Exp.	− Advertising Exp.	− Wages Exp.	− Utilities Exp.	− Supplies Exp.	− Misc. Exp.	

2. Prepare an income statement for PS Music for the month ended June 30, 2014.
3. Prepare a retained earnings statement for PS Music for the month ended June 30, 2014.
4. Prepare a balance sheet for PS Music as of June 30, 2014.

Cases & Projects

CP 1-1 Ethics and professional conduct in business

Group Project

Colleen Fernandez, president of Rhino Enterprises, applied for a $175,000 loan from First Federal Bank. The bank requested financial statements from Rhino Enterprises as a basis for granting the loan. Colleen has told her accountant to provide the bank with a balance sheet. Colleen has decided to omit the other financial statements because there was a net loss during the past year.

In groups of three or four, discuss the following questions:

1. Is Colleen behaving in a professional manner by omitting some of the financial statements?
2. a. What types of information about their businesses would owners be willing to provide bankers? What types of information would owners not be willing to provide?
   b. What types of information about a business would bankers want before extending a loan?
   c. What common interests are shared by bankers and business owners?

CP 1-2 Net income

On January 1, 2013, Dr. Marcie Cousins established Health-Wise Medical, a medical practice organized as a corporation. The following conversation occurred the following August between Dr. Cousins and a former medical school classmate, Dr. Avi Abu, at an American Medical Association convention in Seattle.

Dr. Abu: Marcie, good to see you again. Why didn't you call when you were in Miami? We could have had dinner together.

Dr. Cousins: Actually, I never made it to Miami this year. My husband and kids went up to our Vail condo twice, but I got stuck in Jacksonville. I opened a new consulting practice this January and haven't had any time for myself since.

Dr. Abu: I heard about it . . . Health . . . something . . . right?

Dr. Cousins: Yes, Health-Wise Medical. My husband chose the name.

Dr. Abu: I've thought about doing something like that. Are you making any money? I mean, is it worth your time?

Dr. Cousins: You wouldn't believe it. I started by opening a bank account with $25,000, and my July bank statement has a balance of $80,000. Not bad for six months—all pure profit.

Dr. Abu: Maybe I'll try it in Miami! Let's have breakfast together tomorrow and you can fill me in on the details.

Comment on Dr. Cousins' statement that the difference between the opening bank balance ($25,000) and the July statement balance ($80,000) is pure profit.

CP 1-3 Transactions and financial statements

Lisa Duncan, a junior in college, has been seeking ways to earn extra spending money. As an active sports enthusiast, Lisa plays tennis regularly at the Phoenix Tennis Club, where her family has a membership. The president of the club recently approached Lisa with the proposal that she manage the club's tennis courts. Lisa's primary duty would be to supervise the operation of the club's four indoor and 10 outdoor courts, including court reservations.

In return for her services, the club would pay Lisa $325 per week, plus Lisa could keep whatever she earned from lessons. The club and Lisa agreed to a one-month trial, after which both would consider an arrangement for the remaining two years of Lisa's college career. On this basis, Lisa organized Serve-N-Volley. During September 2014, Lisa managed the tennis courts and entered into the following transactions:

a. Opened a business account by depositing $950.

b. Paid $300 for tennis supplies (practice tennis balls, etc.).

c. Paid $275 for the rental of video equipment to be used in offering lessons during September.

d. Arranged for the rental of two ball machines during September for $250. Paid $100 in advance, with the remaining $150 due October 1.

e. Received $1,750 for lessons given during September.

f. Received $600 in fees from the use of the ball machines during September.

g. Paid $800 for salaries of part-time employees who answered the telephone and took reservations while Lisa was giving lessons.

h. Paid $290 for miscellaneous expenses.

i. Received $1,300 from the club for managing the tennis courts during September.

j. Determined that the cost of supplies on hand at the end of the month totaled $180; therefore, the cost of supplies used was $120.

k. Withdrew $400 for personal use on September 30.

As a friend and accounting student, you have been asked by Lisa to aid her in assessing the venture.

1. Indicate the effect of each transaction and the balances after each transaction, using the following tabular headings:

Assets	=	**Liabilities**	+	**Owner's Equity**													
Cash + Supplies	=	Accounts Payable	+	Lisa Duncan, Capital	−	Lisa Duncan, Drawing	+	Fees Earned	−	Salaries Expense	−	Rent Expense	−	Supplies Expense	−	Misc. Expense	

2. Prepare an income statement for September.
3. Prepare a statement of owner's equity for September. The statement of owner's equity for a proprietorship is similar to the retained earnings statement for a corporation. The balance of the owner's capital as of the beginning of the period is listed first. Any investments made by the owner during the period are then listed and the net income (net loss) is added (subtracted) to determine a subtotal. From this subtotal, the owner's withdrawals are subtracted to determine the increase (decrease) in owner's equity for the period. This increase (decrease) is then added to (subtracted from) the beginning owner's equity to determine the owner's equity as of the end of the period.
4. Prepare a balance sheet as of September 30.
5. a. Assume that Lisa Duncan could earn $10 per hour working 30 hours a week as a waitress. Evaluate which of the two alternatives, working as a waitress or operating Serve-N-Volley, would provide Lisa with the most income per month.

   b. Discuss any other factors that you believe Lisa should consider before discussing a long-term arrangement with the Phoenix Tennis Club.

CP 1-4 Certification requirements for accountants

Internet Project

By satisfying certain specific requirements, accountants may become certified as public accountants (CPAs), management accountants (CMAs), or internal auditors (CIAs). Find the certification requirements for one of these accounting groups by accessing the appropriate Internet site listed below.

Site	**Description**
http://www.ais-cpa.com	This site lists the address and/or Internet link for each state's board of accountancy. Find your state's requirements.
http://www.imanet.org	This site lists the requirements for becoming a CMA.
http://www.theiia.org	This site lists the requirements for becoming a CIA.

CP 1-5 Cash flows

Amazon.com, an Internet retailer, was incorporated and began operation in the mid-90s. On the statement of cash flows, would you expect Amazon.com's net cash flows from operating, investing, and financing activities to be positive or negative for its first three years of operations? Use the following format for your answers, and briefly explain your logic.

	First Year	Second Year	Third Year
Net cash flows from operating activities	negative		
Net cash flows from investing activities			
Net cash flows from financing activities			

CP 1-6 Financial analysis

Internet Project

The now defunct **Enron Corporation**, once headquartered in Houston, Texas, provided products and services for natural gas, electricity, and communications to wholesale and retail customers. Enron's operations were conducted through a variety of subsidiaries and affiliates that involved transporting gas through pipelines, transmitting electricity, and managing energy commodities. The following data were taken from Enron's financial statements:

	In millions
Total revenues	$100,789
Total costs and expenses	98,836
Operating income	1,953
Net income	979
Total assets	65,503
Total liabilities	54,033
Total stockholders' equity	11,470
Net cash flows from operating activities	4,779
Net cash flows from investing activities	(4,264)
Net cash flows from financing activities	571
Net increase in cash	1,086

The market price of Enron's stock was approximately $83 per share when the prior financial statement data were taken. Before it went bankrupt, Enron's stock sold for $0.22 per share.

Review the preceding financial statement data and search the Internet for articles on Enron Corporation. Briefly explain why Enron's stock dropped so dramatically.

YUNUS ARAKON/ISTOCKPHOTO

CHAPTER 2

Analyzing Transactions

Apple Inc.™

Every day it seems like we get an incredible amount of incoming e-mail messages—from friends, relatives, subscribed e-mail lists, and even spammers! But how do you organize all of these messages? You might create folders to sort messages by sender, topic, or project. Perhaps you use keyword search utilities. You might even use filters/rules to automatically delete spam or send messages from your best friend to a special folder. In any case, you are organizing information so that it is simple to retrieve and allows you to understand, respond, or refer to the messages.

In the same way that you organize your e-mail, companies develop an organized method for processing, recording, and summarizing financial transactions. For example, **Apple Inc.** has a huge volume of financial transactions, resulting from sales of its innovative computers, digital media (iTunes), iPods, iPhones, and iPads. When Apple sells an iPad, a customer has the option of paying with credit card, a debit or check card, an Apple gift card, a financing arrangement, or cash. In order to analyze only the information related to Apple's cash transactions, the company must record or summarize all these similar sales using a single category or "cash" account. Similarly, Apple will record credit card payments for iPads and sales from financing arrangements in different accounts (records).

While Chapter 1 used the accounting equation (Assets = Liabilities + Stockholders' Equity) to analyze and record financial transactions, this chapter presents more practical and efficient recording methods that most companies use. In addition, this chapter discusses possible accounting errors that may occur, along with methods to detect and correct them.

Learning Objectives

After studying this chapter, you should be able to: *Example Exercises*

Objective	Example Exercises
OBJ 1 Describe the characteristics of an account and a chart of accounts.	
Using Accounts to Record Transactions	
Chart of Accounts	
OBJ 2 Describe and illustrate journalizing transactions using the double-entry accounting system.	
Double-Entry Accounting System	
Balance Sheet Accounts	
Income Statement Accounts	
Dividends	
Normal Balances	EE 2-1
Journalizing	EE 2-2
OBJ 3 Describe and illustrate the journalizing and posting of transactions to accounts.	
Posting Journal Entries to Accounts	EE 2-3, EE 2-4, EE 2-5
OBJ 4 Prepare an unadjusted trial balance and explain how it can be used to discover errors.	
Trial Balance	
Errors Affecting the Trial Balance	EE 2-6
Errors Not Affecting the Trial Balance	EE 2-7
OBJ 5 Describe and illustrate the use of horizontal analysis in evaluating a company's performance and financial condition.	
Financial Analysis and Interpretation: Horizontal Analysis	EE 2-8

At a Glance 2 Page 75

OBJ 1 Describe the characteristics of an account and a chart of accounts.

Using Accounts to Record Transactions

In Chapter 1, the November transactions for **NetSolutions** were recorded using the accounting equation format shown in Exhibit 1. However, this format is not efficient or practical for companies that have to record thousands or millions of transactions daily. As a result, accounting systems are designed to show the increases and decreases in each accounting equation element as a separate record. This record is called an **account**.

To illustrate, the Cash column of Exhibit 1 records the increases and decreases in cash. Likewise, the other columns in Exhibit 1 record the increases and decreases in the other accounting equation elements. Each of these columns can be organized into a separate account.

An account, in its simplest form, has three parts.

1. A title, which is the name of the accounting equation element recorded in the account.
2. A space for recording increases in the amount of the element.
3. A space for recording decreases in the amount of the element.

The account form presented below is called a **T account** because it resembles the letter T. The left side of the account is called the *debit* side, and the right side is called the *credit* side.[1]

Title	
Left side *debit*	Right side *credit*

1 The terms *debit* and *credit* are derived from the Latin *debere* and *credere*.

EXHIBIT 1 **NetSolutions November Transactions**

	Assets			**= Liabilities +**	**Stockholders' Equity**							
	Cash +	Supp. +	Land =	Accounts Payable +	Capital Stock −	Dividends +	Fees Earned −	Wages Exp. −	Rent Exp. −	Supplies Exp. −	Utilities Exp. −	Misc. Exp.
a.	+25,000				+25,000							
b.	−20,000		+20,000									
Bal.	5,000		20,000		25,000							
c.		+1,350		+1,350								
Bal.	5,000	1,350	20,000	1,350	25,000							
d.	+7,500						+7,500					
Bal.	12,500	1,350	20,000	1,350	25,000		7,500					
e.	−3,650							−2,125	−800		−450	−275
Bal.	8,850	1,350	20,000	1,350	25,000		7,500	−2,125	−800		−450	−275
f.	−950			−950								
Bal.	7,900	1,350	20,000	400	25,000		7,500	−2,125	−800		−450	−275
g.		−800								−800		
Bal.	7,900	550	20,000	400	25,000		7,500	−2,125	−800	−800	−450	−275
h.	−2,000					−2,000						
Bal.	5,900	550	20,000	400	25,000	−2,000	7,500	−2,125	−800	−800	−450	−275

The amounts shown in the Cash column of Exhibit 1 would be recorded in a cash account as follows:

Cash

Debit Side of Account	(a)	25,000	(b)	20,000	Credit Side of Account
	(d)	7,500	(e)	3,650	
			(f)	950	
			(h)	2,000	
	Balance	5,900			

Balance of Account → 5,900

Note:
Amounts entered on the left side of an account are debits, and amounts entered on the right side of an account are credits.

Recording transactions in accounts must follow certain rules. For example, increases in assets are recorded on the **debit** (left side) of an account. Likewise, decreases in assets are recorded on the **credit** (right side) of an account. The excess of the debits of an asset account over its credits is the **balance of the account**.

To illustrate, the receipt (increase in Cash) of $25,000 in transaction (a) is entered on the debit (left) side of the cash account shown above. The letter or date of the transaction is also entered into the account. This is done so if any questions later arise related to the entry, the entry can be traced back to the underlying transaction data. In contrast, the payment (decrease in Cash) of $20,000 to purchase land in transaction (b) is entered on the credit (right) side of the account.

The balance of the cash account of $5,900 is the excess of the debits over the credits as shown below.

Debits ($25,000 + $7,500)	$32,500
Less credits ($20,000 + $3,650 + $950 + $2,000)	26,600
Balance of Cash as of November 30, 2013	$ 5,900

The balance of the cash account is inserted in the account, in the Debit column. In this way, the balance is identified as a debit balance.[2] This balance represents NetSolutions' cash on hand as of November 30, 2013. This balance of $5,900 is reported on the November 30, 2013, balance sheet for NetSolutions as shown in Exhibit 6 of Chapter 1.

2 The totals of the debit and credit columns may be shown separately in an account. When this is done, these amounts should be identified in some way so that they are not mistaken for entries or the ending balance of the account.

In an actual accounting system, a more formal account form replaces the T account. Later in this chapter, a four-column account is illustrated. The T account, however, is a simple way to illustrate the effects of transactions on accounts and financial statements. For this reason, T accounts are often used in business to explain transactions.

Each of the columns in Exhibit 1 can be converted into an account form in a similar manner as was done for the Cash column of Exhibit 1. However, as mentioned earlier, recording increases and decreases in accounts must follow certain rules. These rules are discussed after the chart of accounts is described.

Chart of Accounts

A group of accounts for a business entity is called a **ledger**. A list of the accounts in the ledger is called a **chart of accounts**. The accounts are normally listed in the order in which they appear in the financial statements. The balance sheet accounts are listed first, in the order of assets, liabilities, and stockholders' equity. The income statement accounts are then listed in the order of revenues and expenses.

Assets are resources owned by the business entity. These resources can be physical items, such as cash and supplies, or intangibles that have value. Examples of intangible assets include patent rights, copyrights, and trademarks. Assets also include accounts receivable, prepaid expenses (such as insurance), buildings, equipment, and land.

Liabilities are debts owed to outsiders (creditors). Liabilities are often identified on the balance sheet by titles that include *payable*. Examples of liabilities include accounts payable, notes payable, and wages payable. Cash received before services are delivered creates a liability to perform the services. These future service commitments are called *unearned revenues*. Examples of unearned revenues include magazine subscriptions received by a publisher and tuition received at the beginning of a term by a college.

Stockholders' equity is the stockholders' right to the assets of the business. Stockholders' equity is represented by the balance of the capital stock and retained earnings accounts. A **dividends** account represents distributions of earnings to stockholders.

Revenues are increases in stockholders' equity as a result of selling services or products to customers. Examples of revenues include fees earned, fares earned, commissions revenue, and rent revenue.

Business Connection

THE HIJACKING RECEIVABLE

A company's chart of accounts should reflect the basic nature of its operations. Occasionally, however, transactions take place that give rise to unusual accounts. The following is a story of one such account.

Before strict airport security was implemented across the United States, several airlines experienced hijacking incidents. One such incident occurred when a Southern Airways jet en route from Memphis to Miami was hijacked during a stopover in Birmingham, Alabama. The three hijackers boarded the plane in Birmingham armed with handguns and hand grenades. At gunpoint, the hijackers took the plane, the plane's crew, and the passengers to nine American cities, Toronto, and eventually to Havana, Cuba.

During the long flight, the hijackers demanded a ransom of $10 million. Southern Airways, however, was only able to come up with $2 million. Eventually, the pilot talked the hijackers into settling for the $2 million when the plane landed in Chattanooga for refueling.

Upon landing in Havana, the Cuban authorities arrested the hijackers and, after a brief delay, sent the plane, passengers, and crew back to the United States. The hijackers and $2 million stayed in Cuba.

How did Southern Airways account for and report the hijacking payment in its subsequent financial statements? As you might have analyzed, the initial entry credited Cash for $2 million. The debit was to an account entitled "Hijacking Payment." This account was reported as a type of receivable under "other assets" on Southern Airways' balance sheet. The company maintained that it would be able to collect the cash from the Cuban government and that, therefore, a receivable existed. In fact, Southern Airways was later repaid $2 million by the Cuban government, which was, at that time, attempting to improve relations with the United States.

Expenses result from using up assets or consuming services in the process of generating revenues. Examples of expenses include wages expense, rent expense, utilities expense, supplies expense, and miscellaneous expense.

A chart of accounts should meet the needs of a company's managers and other users of its financial statements. The accounts within the chart of accounts are numbered for use as references. A numbering system is normally used, so that new accounts can be added without affecting other account numbers.

Exhibit 2 is NetSolutions' chart of accounts that is used in this chapter. Additional accounts will be introduced in later chapters. In Exhibit 2, each account number has two digits. The first digit indicates the major account group of the ledger in which the account is located. Accounts beginning with 1 represent assets; 2, liabilities; 3, stockholders' equity; 4, revenue; and 5, expenses. The second digit indicates the location of the account within its group.

Procter & Gamble's account numbers have over 30 digits to reflect P&G's many different operations and regions.

EXHIBIT 2

Chart of Accounts for NetSolutions

Balance Sheet Accounts	Income Statement Accounts
1. Assets	**4. Revenue**
11 Cash	41 Fees Earned
12 Accounts Receivable	**5. Expenses**
14 Supplies	51 Wages Expense
15 Prepaid Insurance	52 Rent Expense
17 Land	54 Utilities Expense
18 Office Equipment	55 Supplies Expense
2. Liabilities	59 Miscellaneous Expense
21 Accounts Payable	
23 Unearned Rent	
3. Stockholders' Equity	
31 Capital Stock	
32 Retained Earnings	
33 Dividends	

Each of the columns in Exhibit 1 has been assigned an account number in the chart of accounts shown in Exhibit 2. In addition, Accounts Receivable, Prepaid Insurance, Office Equipment, and Unearned Rent have been added. These accounts will be used in recording NetSolutions' December transactions.

Double-Entry Accounting System

OBJ 2 Describe and illustrate journalizing transactions using the double-entry accounting system.

All businesses use what is called the **double-entry accounting system**. This system is based on the accounting equation and requires:

1. Every business transaction to be recorded in at least two accounts.
2. The total debits recorded for each transaction to be equal to the total credits recorded.

The double-entry accounting system also has specific **rules of debit and credit** for recording transactions in the accounts.

Balance Sheet Accounts

The debit and credit rules for balance sheet accounts are as follows:

Balance Sheet Accounts

ASSETS Asset Accounts		=	LIABILITIES Liability Accounts		+	STOCKHOLDERS' EQUITY Stockholders' Equity Accounts	
Debit for increases (+)	Credit for decreases (–)		Debit for decreases (–)	Credit for increases (+)		Debit for decreases (–)	Credit for increases (+)

Income Statement Accounts

The debit and credit rules for income statement accounts are based on their relationship with stockholders' equity. As shown on page 55, stockholders' equity accounts are increased by credits. Since revenues increase stockholders' equity (retained earnings), revenue accounts are increased by credits and decreased by debits. Since stockholders' equity (retained earnings) accounts are decreased by debits, expense accounts are increased by debits and decreased by credits. Thus, the rules of debit and credit for revenue and expense accounts are as follows:

Income Statement Accounts

Revenue Accounts		Expense Accounts	
Debit for decreases (–)	Credit for increases (+)	Debit for increases (+)	Credit for decreases (–)

Dividends

The debit and credit rules for recording dividends are based on the effect of dividends on stockholders' equity (retained earnings). Since dividends decrease stockholders' equity (retained earnings), the dividends account is increased by debits. Likewise, the dividends account is decreased by credits. Thus, the rules of debit and credit for the dividends account are as follows:

Dividends Account

Debit for increases (+)	Credit for decreases (–)

Normal Balances

The sum of the increases in an account is usually equal to or greater than the sum of the decreases in the account. Thus, the **normal balance of an account** is either a debit or credit depending on whether increases in the account are recorded as debits or credits. For example, since asset accounts are increased with debits, asset accounts normally have debit balances. Likewise, liability accounts normally have credit balances.

The rules of debit and credit and the normal balances of the various types of accounts are summarized in Exhibit 3. Debits and credits are sometimes abbreviated as Dr. for debit and Cr. for credit.

When an account normally having a debit balance has a credit balance, or vice versa, an error may have occurred or an unusual situation may exist. For example, a credit balance in the office equipment account could result only from an error. This

Example Exercise 2-1 Rules of Debit and Credit and Normal Balances

OBJ 2

State for each account whether it is likely to have (a) debit entries only, (b) credit entries only, or (c) both debit and credit entries. Also, indicate its normal balance.

1. Dividends
2. Accounts Payable
3. Cash
4. Fees Earned
5. Supplies
6. Utilities Expense

Follow My Example 2-1

1. Debit entries only; normal debit balance
2. Debit and credit entries; normal credit balance
3. Debit and credit entries; normal debit balance
4. Credit entries only; normal credit balance
5. Debit and credit entries; normal debit balance
6. Debit entries only; normal debit balance

Practice Exercises: **PE 2-1A, PE 2-1B**

EXHIBIT 3 **Rules of Debit and Credit, Normal Balances of Accounts**

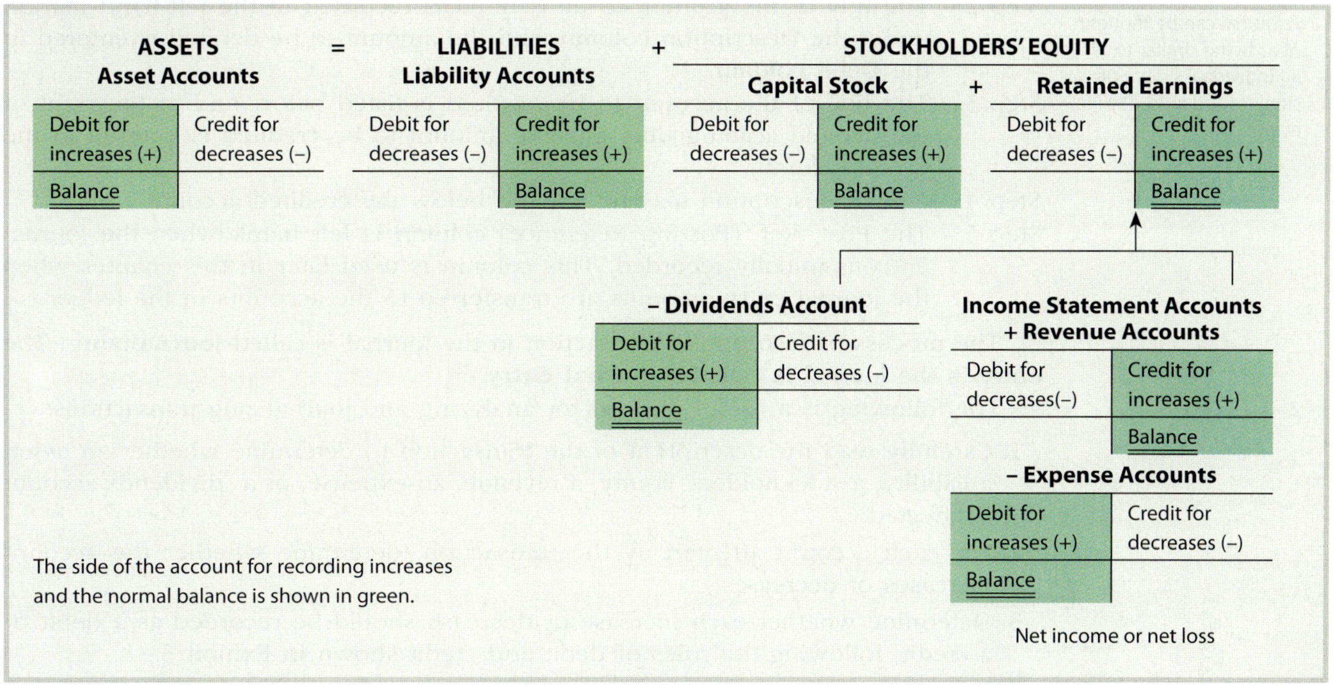

is because a business cannot have more decreases than increases of office equipment. On the other hand, a debit balance in an accounts payable account could result from an overpayment.

Journalizing

Using the rules of debit and credit, transactions are initially entered in a record called a **journal**. In this way, the journal serves as a record of when transactions occurred and were recorded. To illustrate, the November transactions of NetSolutions from Chapter 1 are used.

Nov. 1 Chris Clark deposited $25,000 in a bank account in the name of NetSolutions in exchange for capital stock.

Transaction A

Analysis

This transaction increases an asset account and increases an stockholders' equity account. It is recorded in the journal as an increase (debit) to Cash and an increase (credit) to Capital Stock.

Journal Entry

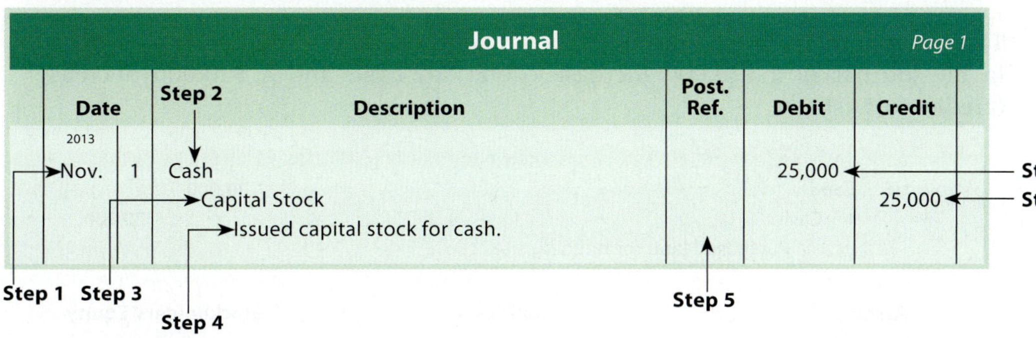

Accounting Equation Impact

Assets = Liabilities + Stockholders' Equity

Cash	
Nov. 1 25,000	

Capital Stock	
	Nov. 1 25,000

A journal can be thought of as being similar to an individual's diary of significant day-to-day life events.

The transaction is recorded in the journal using the following steps:

Step 1. The date of the transaction is entered in the Date column.

Step 2. The title of the account to be debited is recorded in the left-hand margin under the Description column, and the amount to be debited is entered in the Debit column.

Step 3. The title of the account to be credited is listed below and to the right of the debited account title, and the amount to be credited is entered in the Credit column.

Step 4. A brief description may be entered below the credited account.

Step 5. The Post. Ref. (Posting Reference) column is left blank when the journal entry is initially recorded. This column is used later in this chapter when the journal entry amounts are transferred to the accounts in the ledger.

The process of recording a transaction in the journal is called **journalizing**. The entry in the journal is called a **journal entry**.

The following is a useful method for analyzing and journalizing transactions:

1. Carefully read the description of the transaction to determine whether an asset, a liability, a stockholders' equity, a revenue, an expense, or a dividends account is affected.
2. For each account affected by the transaction, determine whether the account increases or decreases.
3. Determine whether each increase or decrease should be recorded as a debit or a credit, following the rules of debit and credit shown in Exhibit 3.
4. Record the transaction using a journal entry.

The following table summarizes terminology that is often used in describing a transaction along with the related accounts that would be debited and credited.

	Journal Entry Account	
Common transaction terminology	**Debit**	**Credit**
Received cash for services provided	Cash	Fees Earned
Services provided on account	Accounts Receivable	Fees Earned
Received cash on account	Cash	Accounts Receivable
Purchased on account	Asset account	Accounts Payable
Paid on account	Accounts Payable	Cash
Paid cash	Asset or expense account	Cash
Issued capital stock	Cash and/or other assets	Capital Stock
Paid dividends	Dividends	Cash

The remaining transactions of NetSolutions for November are analyzed and journalized next.

Transaction B *Nov. 5 NetSolutions paid $20,000 for the purchase of land as a future building site.*

Analysis

This transaction increases one asset account and decreases another. It is recorded in the journal as a $20,000 increase (debit) to Land and a $20,000 decrease (credit) to Cash.

Journal Entry

Nov.	5	Land		20,000		
		Cash			20,000	
		Purchased land for building site.				

Accounting Equation Impact

Assets = **Liabilities** + **Stockholders' Equity**

Land	
Nov. 5 20,000	

Cash	
	Nov. 5 20,000

Nov. 10 NetSolutions purchased supplies on account for $1,350.

Transaction C

Analysis

This transaction increases an asset account and increases a liability account. It is recorded in the journal as a $1,350 increase (debit) to Supplies and a $1,350 increase (credit) to Accounts Payable.

Journal Entry

Nov.	10	Supplies		1,350	
		Accounts Payable			1,350
		Purchased supplies on account.			

Accounting Equation Impact

Assets = **Liabilities** + **Stockholders' Equity**

Supplies	
Nov. 10 1,350	

Accounts Payable	
	Nov. 10 1,350

Nov. 18 NetSolutions received cash of $7,500 from customers for services provided.

Transaction D

Analysis

This transaction increases an asset account and increases a revenue account. It is recorded in the journal as a $7,500 increase (debit) to Cash and a $7,500 increase (credit) to Fees Earned.

Journal Entry

Nov.	18	Cash		7,500	
		Fees Earned			7,500
		Received fees from customers.			

Accounting Equation Impact

Assets = **Liabilities** + **Stockholders' Equity (Revenue)**

Cash	
Nov. 18 7,500	

Fees Earned	
	Nov. 18 7,500

Nov. 30 NetSolutions incurred the following expenses: wages, $2,125; rent, $800; utilities, $450; and miscellaneous, $275.

Transaction E

Analysis

This transaction increases various expense accounts and decreases an asset (Cash) account. You should note that regardless of the number of accounts, *the sum of the debits is always equal to the sum of the credits in a journal entry.* It is recorded in the journal with increases (debits) to the expense accounts (Wages Expense, $2,125; Rent Expense, $800; Utilities Expense, $450; and Miscellaneous Expense, $275) and a decrease (credit) to Cash, $3,650.

Journal Entry

Nov.	30	Wages Expense		2,125	
		Rent Expense		800	
		Utilities Expense		450	
		Miscellaneous Expense		275	
		Cash			3,650
		Paid expenses.			

Accounting Equation Impact

Assets = **Liabilities** + **Stockholders' Equity (Expense)**

Cash	
	Nov. 30 3,650

Wages Expense	
Nov. 30 2,125	

Rent Expense	
Nov. 30 800	

Utilities Expense	
Nov. 30 450	

Miscellaneous Expense	
Nov. 30 275	

Transaction F *Nov. 30 NetSolutions paid creditors on account, $950.*

Analysis

This transaction decreases a liability account and decreases an asset account. It is recorded in the journal as a $950 decrease (debit) to Accounts Payable and a $950 decrease (credit) to Cash.

Journal Entry

Nov.	30	Accounts Payable		950	
		Cash			950
		Paid creditors on account.			

Accounting Equation Impact

Assets = Liabilities + Stockholders' Equity

Cash		=	Accounts Payable	
	Nov. 30 950		Nov. 30 950	

Transaction G *Nov. 30 Chris Clark determined that the cost of supplies on hand at November 30 was $550.*

Analysis

NetSolutions purchased $1,350 of supplies on November 10. Thus, $800 ($1,350 – $550) of supplies must have been used during November. This transaction is recorded in the journal as an $800 increase (debit) to Supplies Expense and an $800 decrease (credit) to Supplies.

Journal Entry

Nov.	30	Supplies Expense		800	
		Supplies			800
		Supplies used during November.			

Accounting Equation Impact

Assets = Liabilities + Stockholders' Equity (Expense)

Supplies		= Liabilities +	Supplies Expense	
	Nov. 30 800		Nov. 30 800	

Transaction H *Nov. 30 NetSolutions paid $2,000 to stockholders (Chris Clark) as dividends.*

Analysis

This transaction decreases assets and stockholders' equity. This transaction is recorded in the journal as a $2,000 increase (debit) to Dividends and a $2,000 decrease (credit) to Cash.

Journal Entry

Journal *Page 2*

Date		Description	Post. Ref.	Debit	Credit
2013					
Nov.	30	Dividends		2,000	
		Cash			2,000
		Paid dividends			

Accounting Equation Impact

Assets = Liabilities + Stockholders' Equity (Dividends)

Cash		= Liabilities +	Dividends	
	Nov. 30 2,000		Nov. 30 2,000	

Integrity, Objectivity, and Ethics in Business

WILL JOURNALIZING PREVENT FRAUD?

While journalizing transactions reduces the possibility of fraud, it by no means eliminates it. For example, embezzlement can be hidden within the double-entry bookkeeping system by creating fictitious suppliers to whom checks are issued.

Example Exercise 2-2 Journal Entry for Asset Purchase

OBJ 2

Prepare a journal entry for the purchase of a truck on June 3 for $42,500, paying $8,500 cash and the remainder on account.

Follow My Example 2-2

June 3	Truck	42,500	
	Cash		8,500
	Accounts Payable		34,000

Practice Exercises: **PE 2-2A, PE 2-2B**

Posting Journal Entries to Accounts

OBJ 3 Describe and illustrate the journalizing and posting of transactions to accounts.

As illustrated, a transaction is first recorded in a journal. Periodically, the journal entries are transferred to the accounts in the ledger. The process of transferring the debits and credits from the journal entries to the accounts is called **posting**.

The December transactions of NetSolutions are used to illustrate posting from the journal to the ledger. By using the December transactions, an additional review of analyzing and journalizing transactions is provided.

Transaction

Dec. 1 NetSolutions paid a premium of $2,400 for an insurance policy for liability, theft, and fire. The policy covers a one-year period.

Analysis

Advance payments of expenses, such as for insurance premiums, are called prepaid expenses. Prepaid expenses are assets. For NetSolutions, the asset purchased is insurance protection for 12 months. This transaction is recorded as a $2,400 increase (debit) to Prepaid Insurance and a $2,400 decrease (credit) to Cash.

Journal Entry

Dec.	1	Prepaid Insurance	15	2,400		
		Cash	11		2,400	
		Paid premium on one-year policy.				

Accounting Equation Impact

Assets = **Liabilities** + **Stockholders' Equity**

Cash 11	
	Dec. 1 2,400

Prepaid Insurance 15	
Dec. 1 2,400	

The posting of the preceding December 1 transaction is shown in Exhibit 4. Notice that the T account form is not used in Exhibit 4. In practice, the T account is usually replaced with a standard account form similar to that shown in Exhibit 4.

EXHIBIT 4 **Diagram of the Recording and Posting of a Debit and a Credit**

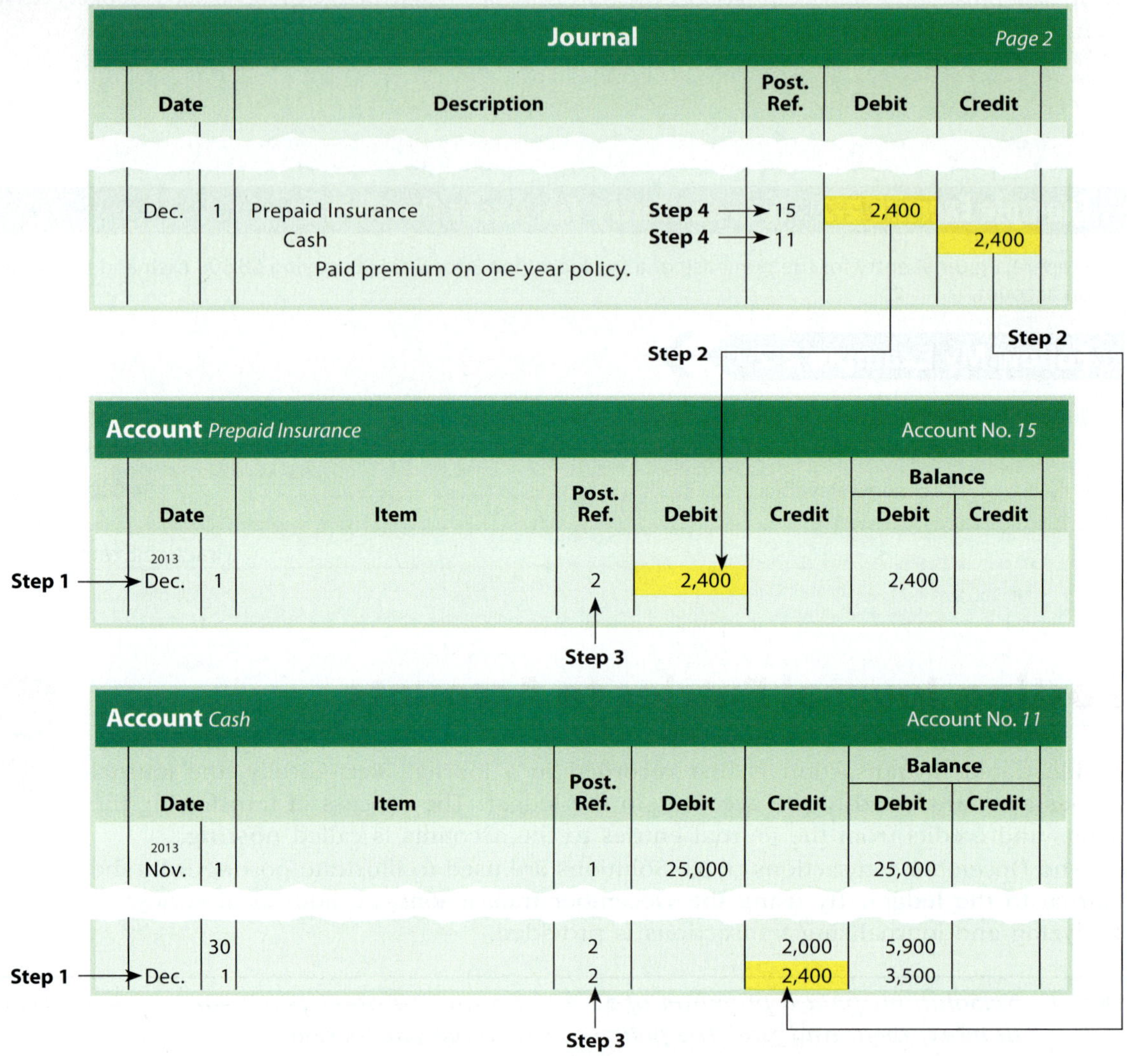

The debits and credits for each journal entry are posted to the accounts in the order in which they occur in the journal. To illustrate, the debit portion of the December 1 journal entry is posted to the prepaid account in Exhibit 4 using the following four steps:

Step 1. The date (Dec. 1) of the journal entry is entered in the Date column of Prepaid Insurance.

Step 2. The amount (2,400) is entered into the Debit column of Prepaid Insurance.

Step 3. The journal page number (2) is entered in the Posting Reference (Post. Ref.) column of Prepaid Insurance.

Step 4. The account number (15) is entered in the Posting Reference (Post. Ref.) column in the journal.

As shown in Exhibit 4, the credit portion of the December 1 journal entry is posted to the cash account in a similar manner.

The remaining December transactions for NetSolutions are analyzed and journalized in the following paragraphs. These transactions are posted to the ledger in Exhibit 5 on pages 69–70. To simplify, some of the December transactions are stated in summary form. For example, cash received for services is normally recorded on a daily basis. However, only summary totals are recorded at the middle and end of the month for NetSolutions.

Dec. 1 *NetSolutions paid rent for December, $800. The company from which NetSolutions is renting its office space now requires the payment of rent on the first of each month, rather than at the end of the month.*

Transaction

The advance payment of rent is an asset, much like the advance payment of the insurance premium in the preceding transaction. However, unlike the insurance premium, this prepaid rent will expire in one month. When an asset is purchased with the expectation that it will be used up in a short period of time, such as a month, it is normal to debit an expense account initially. This avoids having to transfer the balance from an asset account (Prepaid Rent) to an expense account (Rent Expense) at the end of the month. Thus, this transaction is recorded as an $800 increase (debit) to Rent Expense and an $800 decrease (credit) to Cash.

Analysis

		1	Rent Expense	52	800	
			Cash	11		800
			Paid rent for December.			

Journal Entry

Assets	=	Liabilities	+	Stockholders' Equity (Expense)
Cash 11				**Rent Expense** 52
Dec. 1 800 (credit)				Dec. 1 800 (debit)

Accounting Equation Impact

Dec. 1 *NetSolutions received an offer from a local retailer to rent the land purchased on November 5. The retailer plans to use the land as a parking lot for its employees and customers. NetSolutions agreed to rent the land to the retailer for three months, with the rent payable in advance. NetSolutions received $360 for three months' rent beginning December 1.*

Transaction

By agreeing to rent the land and accepting the $360, NetSolutions has incurred an obligation (liability) to the retailer. This obligation is to make the land available for use for three months and not to interfere with its use. The liability created by receiving the cash in advance of providing the service is called **unearned revenue**. As time passes, the unearned rent liability will decrease and will become revenue. Thus, this transaction is recorded as a $360 increase (debit) to Cash and a $360 increase (credit) to Unearned Rent.

Analysis

		1	Cash	11	360	
			Unearned Rent	23		360
			Received advance payment for three months' rent on land.			

Journal Entry

Assets	=	Liabilities	+	Stockholders' Equity
Cash 11		**Unearned Rent** 23		
Dec. 1 360 (debit)		Dec. 1 360 (credit)		

Accounting Equation Impact

Dec. 4 *NetSolutions purchased office equipment on account from Executive Supply Co. for $1,800.*

Transaction

The asset (Office Equipment) and liability accounts (Accounts Payable) increase. This transaction is recorded as an $1,800 increase (debit) to Office Equipment and an $1,800 increase (credit) to Accounts Payable.

Analysis

		4	Office Equipment	18	1,800	
			Accounts Payable	21		1,800
			Purchased office equipment on account.			

Journal Entry

Accounting Equation Impact

Assets		=	Liabilities		+	Stockholders' Equity
Office Equipment 18			**Accounts Payable** 21			
Dec. 4 1,800				Dec. 4 1,800		

Transaction *Dec. 6 NetSolutions paid $180 for a newspaper advertisement.*

Analysis

An expense increases, and an asset (Cash) decreases. Expense items that are expected to be minor in amount are normally included as part of the miscellaneous expense. This transaction is recorded as a $180 increase (debit) to Miscellaneous Expense and a $180 decrease (credit) to Cash.

Journal Entry

	6	Miscellaneous Expense	59	180	
		Cash	11		180
		Paid for newspaper advertisement.			

Accounting Equation Impact

Assets		=	Liabilities	+	Stockholders' Equity (Expense)	
Cash 11					**Miscellaneous Exp.** 59	
	Dec. 6 180				Dec. 6 180	

Transaction *Dec. 11 NetSolutions paid creditors $400.*

Analysis

A liability (Accounts Payable) and an asset (Cash) decrease. This transaction is recorded as a $400 decrease (debit) to Accounts Payable and a $400 decrease (credit) to Cash.

Journal Entry

	11	Accounts Payable	21	400	
		Cash	11		400
		Paid creditors on account.			

Accounting Equation Impact

Assets		=	Liabilities		+	Stockholders' Equity
Cash 11			**Accounts Payable** 21			
	Dec. 11 400		Dec. 11 400			

Transaction *Dec. 13 NetSolutions paid a receptionist and a part-time assistant $950 for two weeks' wages.*

Analysis

This transaction is similar to the December 6 transaction, where an expense account is increased and Cash is decreased. This transaction is recorded as a $950 increase (debit) to Wages Expense and a $950 decrease (credit) to Cash.

Journal Entry

Journal *Page 3*

Date		Description	Post. Ref.	Debit	Credit
2013					
Dec.	13	Wages Expense	51	950	
		Cash	11		950
		Paid two weeks' wages.			

Accounting Equation Impact

Assets		=	Liabilities	+	Stockholders' Equity (Expense)	
Cash 11					**Wages Expense** 51	
	Dec. 13 950				Dec. 13 950	

Business Connection

COMPUTERIZED ACCOUNTING SYSTEMS

Computerized accounting systems are widely used by even the smallest of companies. These systems simplify the record-keeping process in that transactions are recorded in electronic forms. Forms used to bill customers for services provided are often completed using drop-down menus that list services that are normally provided to customers. An auto-complete entry feature may also be used to fill in customer names. For example, type "ca" to display customers with names beginning with "Ca" (Caban, Cahill, Carey, and Caswell). And, to simplify data entry, entries are automatically posted to the ledger accounts when the electronic form is completed.

One popular accounting software package used by small- to medium-sized businesses is QuickBooks®. Some examples of using QuickBooks to record accounting transactions are illustrated and discussed in Chapter 5.

Transaction

Dec. 16 NetSolutions received $3,100 from fees earned for the first half of December.

Analysis

An asset account (Cash) and a revenue account (Fees Earned) increase. This transaction is recorded as a $3,100 increase (debit) to Cash and a $3,100 increase (credit) to Fees Earned.

Journal Entry

	16	Cash	11	3,100	
		Fees Earned	41		3,100
		Received fees from customers.			

Accounting Equation Impact

Assets = Liabilities + Stockholders' Equity (Revenue)

Cash 11	
Dec. 16 3,100	

Fees Earned 41	
	Dec. 16 3,100

Transaction

Dec. 16 Fees earned on account totaled $1,750 for the first half of December.

Analysis

When a business agrees that a customer may pay for services provided at a later date, an **account receivable** is created. An account receivable is a claim against the customer. An account receivable is an asset, and the revenue is earned even though no cash has been received. Thus, this transaction is recorded as a $1,750 increase (debit) to Accounts Receivable and a $1,750 increase (credit) to Fees Earned.

Journal Entry

	16	Accounts Receivable	12	1,750	
		Fees Earned	41		1,750
		Fees earned on account.			

Accounting Equation Impact

Assets = Liabilities + Stockholders' Equity (Revenue)

Accounts Receivable 12	
Dec. 16 1,750	

Fees Earned 41	
	Dec. 16 1,750

Example Exercise 2-3 Journal Entry for Fees Earned (OBJ 3)

Prepare a journal entry on August 7 for the fees earned on account, $115,000.

Follow My Example 2-3

Aug. 7	Accounts Receivable	115,000	
	Fees Earned		115,000

Practice Exercises: **PE 2-3A, PE 2-3B**

Transaction *Dec. 20 NetSolutions paid $900 to Executive Supply Co. on the $1,800 debt owed from the December 4 transaction.*

Analysis

This is similar to the transaction of December 11. This transaction is recorded as a $900 decrease (debit) to Accounts Payable and a $900 decrease (credit) to Cash.

Journal Entry

	20	Accounts Payable	21	900		
		Cash	11		900	
		Paid creditors on account.				

Accounting Equation Impact

Assets = **Liabilities** + **Stockholders' Equity**

Cash	11
	Dec. 20 900

Accounts Payable	21
Dec. 20 900	

Transaction *Dec. 21 NetSolutions received $650 from customers in payment of their accounts.*

Analysis

When customers pay amounts owed for services they have previously received, one asset increases and another asset decreases. This transaction is recorded as a $650 increase (debit) to Cash and a $650 decrease (credit) to Accounts Receivable.

Journal Entry

	21	Cash	11	650		
		Accounts Receivable	12		650	
		Received cash from customers on account.				

Accounting Equation Impact

Assets = **Liabilities** + **Stockholders' Equity**

Cash	11
Dec. 21 650	

Accounts Receivable	12
	Dec. 21 650

Transaction *Dec. 23 NetSolutions paid $1,450 for supplies.*

One asset account (Supplies) increases, and another asset account (Cash) decreases. This transaction is recorded as a $1,450 increase (debit) to Supplies and a $1,450 decrease (credit) to Cash.

Journal Entry

	23	Supplies	14	1,450		
		Cash	11		1,450	
		Purchased supplies.				

Accounting Equation Impact

Assets = **Liabilities** + **Stockholders' Equity**

Cash	11
	Dec. 23 1,450

Supplies	14
Dec. 23 1,450	

Transaction *Dec. 27 NetSolutions paid the receptionist and the part-time assistant $1,200 for two weeks' wages.*

Analysis

This transaction is similar to the transaction of December 13. This transaction is recorded as a $1,200 increase (debit) to Wages Expense and a $1,200 decrease (credit) to Cash.

	27	Wages Expense	51	1,200		
		Cash	11		1,200	
		Paid two weeks' wages.				

Journal Entry

Assets	=	Liabilities	+	Stockholders' Equity (Expense)
Cash 11				**Wages Expense** 51
| Dec. 27 1,200				Dec. 27 1,200 |

Accounting Equation Impact

Dec. 31 NetSolutions paid its $310 telephone bill for the month.

Transaction

This is similar to the transaction of December 6. This transaction is recorded as a $310 increase (debit) to Utilities Expense and a $310 decrease (credit) to Cash.

Analysis

	31	Utilities Expense	54	310		
		Cash	11		310	
		Paid telephone bill.				

Journal Entry

Assets	=	Liabilities	+	Stockholders' Equity (Expense)
Cash 11				**Utilities Expense** 54
| Dec. 31 310				Dec. 31 310 |

Accounting Equation Impact

Dec. 31 NetSolutions paid its $225 electric bill for the month.

Transaction

This is similar to the preceding transaction. This transaction is recorded as a $225 increase (debit) to Utilities Expense and a $225 decrease (credit) to Cash.

Analysis

Journal *Page 4*

Date		Description	Post. Ref.	Debit	Credit
2013					
Dec.	31	Utilities Expense	54	225	
		Cash	11		225
		Paid electric bill.			

Journal Entry

Assets	=	Liabilities	+	Stockholders' Equity (Expense)
Cash 11				**Utilities Expense** 54
| Dec. 31 225				Dec. 31 225 |

Accounting Equation Impact

Dec. 31 NetSolutions received $2,870 from fees earned for the second half of December.

Transaction

This is similar to the transaction of December 16. This transaction is recorded as a $2,870 increase (debit) to Cash and a $2,870 increase (credit) to Fees Earned.

Analysis

	31	Cash	11	2,870		
		Fees Earned	41		2,870	
		Received fees from customers.				

Journal Entry

Assets	=	Liabilities	+	Stockholders' Equity (Revenue)
Cash 11				**Fees Earned** 41
Dec. 31 2,870 |				| Dec. 31 2,870

Accounting Equation Impact

Transaction *Dec. 31 Fees earned on account totaled $1,120 for the second half of December.*

Analysis This is similar to the transaction of December 16. This transaction is recorded as a $1,120 increase (debit) to Accounts Receivable and a $1,120 increase (credit) to Fees Earned.

Journal Entry

	31	Accounts Receivable	12	1,120		
		Fees Earned	41		1,120	
		Fees earned on account.				

Accounting Equation Impact

Assets = **Liabilities** + **Stockholders' Equity (Revenue)**

Accounts Receivable 12	
Dec. 31 1,120	

Fees Earned 41	
	Dec. 31 1,120

Transaction *Dec. 31 Paid dividends of $2,000.*

Analysis This transaction decreases stockholders' equity and assets. This transaction is recorded as a $2,000 increase (debit) to Dividends and a $2,000 decrease (credit) to Cash.

Journal Entry

	31	Dividends	33	2,000		
		Cash	11		2,000	
		Paid dividends.				

Accounting Equation Impact

Assets = **Liabilities** + **Stockholders' Equity (Dividends)**

Cash 11	
	Dec. 31 2,000

Dividends 33	
Dec. 31 2,000	

Example Exercise 2-4 Journal Entry for Dividends

OBJ 3

Prepare a journal entry on December 29 for the payment of dividends of $12,000.

Follow My Example 2-4

Dec. 29	Dividends	12,000	
	Cash		12,000

Practice Exercises: **PE 2-4A, PE 2-4B**

Example Exercise 2-5 Missing Amount from an Account

OBJ 3

On March 1, the cash account balance was $22,350. During March, cash receipts totaled $241,880, and the March 31 balance was $19,125. Determine the cash payments made during March.

Follow My Example 2-5

Using the following T account, solve for the amount of cash payments (indicated by ? below).

Cash

Mar. 1 Bal.	22,350	?	Cash payments
Cash receipts	241,880		
Mar. 31 Bal.	19,125		

$19,125 = $22,350 + $241,880 − Cash payments
Cash payments = $22,350 + $241,880 − $19,125 = $245,105

Practice Exercises: **PE 2-5A, PE 2-5B**

Exhibit 5 shows the ledger for NetSolutions after the transactions for both November and December have been posted.

EXHIBIT 5 **Cash Receipts Journal for a Merchandising Business**

Ledger

Account *Cash* — Account No. *11*

Date	Item	Post. Ref.	Debit	Credit	Balance Debit	Balance Credit
2013						
Nov. 1		1	25,000		25,000	
5		1		20,000	5,000	
18		1	7,500		12,500	
30		1		3,650	8,850	
30		1		950	7,900	
30		2		2,000	5,900	
Dec. 1		2		2,400	3,500	
1		2		800	2,700	
1		2	360		3,060	
6		2		180	2,880	
11		2		400	2,480	
13		3		950	1,530	
16		3	3,100		4,630	
20		3		900	3,730	
21		3	650		4,380	
23		3		1,450	2,930	
27		3		1,200	1,730	
31		3		310	1,420	
31		4		225	1,195	
31		4	2,870		4,065	
31		4		2,000	2,065	

Account *Accounts Receivable* — Account No. *12*

Date	Item	Post. Ref.	Debit	Credit	Balance Debit	Balance Credit
2013						
Dec. 16		3	1,750		1,750	
21		3		650	1,100	
31		4	1,120		2,220	

Account *Supplies* — Account No. *14*

Date	Item	Post. Ref.	Debit	Credit	Balance Debit	Balance Credit
2013						
Nov. 10		1	1,350		1,350	
30		1		800	550	
Dec. 23		3	1,450		2,000	

Account *Prepaid Insurance* — Account No. *15*

Date	Item	Post. Ref.	Debit	Credit	Balance Debit	Balance Credit
2013						
Dec. 1		2	2,400		2,400	

Account *Land* — Account No. *17*

Date	Item	Post. Ref.	Debit	Credit	Balance Debit	Balance Credit
2013						
Nov. 5		1	20,000		20,000	

Account *Office Equipment* — Account No. *18*

Date	Item	Post. Ref.	Debit	Credit	Balance Debit	Balance Credit
2013						
Dec. 4		2	1,800		1,800	

Account *Accounts Payable* — Account No. *21*

Date	Item	Post. Ref.	Debit	Credit	Balance Debit	Balance Credit
2013						
Nov. 10		1		1,350		1,350
30		1	950			400
Dec. 4		2		1,800		2,200
11		2	400			1,800
20		3	900			900

Account *Unearned Rent* — Account No. *23*

Date	Item	Post. Ref.	Debit	Credit	Balance Debit	Balance Credit
2013						
Dec. 1		2		360		360

Account *Capital Stock* — Account No. *31*

Date	Item	Post. Ref.	Debit	Credit	Balance Debit	Balance Credit
2013						
Nov. 1		1		25,000		25,000

Account *Dividends* — Account No. *33*

Date	Item	Post. Ref.	Debit	Credit	Balance Debit	Balance Credit
2013						
Nov. 30		2	2,000		2,000	
Dec. 31		4	2,000		4,000	

(Continued)

EXHIBIT 5 Cash Receipts Journal for a Merchandising Business (concluded)

Account *Fees Earned* — Account No. *41*

Date	Item	Post. Ref.	Debit	Credit	Balance Debit	Balance Credit
2013						
Nov. 18		1		7,500		7,500
Dec. 16		3		3,100		10,600
16		3		1,750		12,350
31		4		2,870		15,220
31		4		1,120		16,340

Account *Wages Expense* — Account No. *51*

Date	Item	Post. Ref.	Debit	Credit	Balance Debit	Balance Credit
2013						
Nov. 30		1	2,125		2,125	
Dec. 13		3	950		3,075	
27		3	1,200		4,275	

Account *Rent Expense* — Account No. *52*

Date	Item	Post. Ref.	Debit	Credit	Balance Debit	Balance Credit
2013						
Nov. 30		1	800		800	
Dec. 1		2	800		1,600	

Account *Utilities Expense* — Account No. *54*

Date	Item	Post. Ref.	Debit	Credit	Balance Debit	Balance Credit
2013						
Nov. 30		1	450		450	
Dec. 31		3	310		760	
31		4	225		985	

Account *Supplies Expense* — Account No. *55*

Date	Item	Post. Ref.	Debit	Credit	Balance Debit	Balance Credit
2013						
Nov. 30		1	800		800	

Account *Miscellaneous Expense* — Account No. *59*

Date	Item	Post. Ref.	Debit	Credit	Balance Debit	Balance Credit
2013						
Nov. 30		1	275		275	
Dec. 6		2	180		455	

OBJ 4 Prepare an unadjusted trial balance and explain how it can be used to discover errors.

Trial Balance

Errors may occur in posting debits and credits from the journal to the ledger. One way to detect such errors is by preparing a **trial balance**. Double-entry accounting requires that debits must always equal credits. The trial balance verifies this equality. The steps in preparing a trial balance are as follows:

Step 1. List the name of the company, the title of the trial balance, and the date the trial balance is prepared.
Step 2. List the accounts from the ledger, and enter their debit or credit balance in the Debit or Credit column of the trial balance.
Step 3. Total the Debit and Credit columns of the trial balance.
Step 4. Verify that the total of the Debit column equals the total of the Credit column.

The trial balance for NetSolutions as of December 31, 2013, is shown in Exhibit 6. The account balances in Exhibit 6 are taken from the ledger shown in Exhibit 5. Before a trial balance is prepared, each account balance in the ledger must be determined. When the standard account form is used as in Exhibit 5, the balance of each account appears in the balance column on the same line as the last posting to the account.

The trial balance shown in Exhibit 6 is titled an **unadjusted trial balance**. This is to distinguish it from other trial balances that will be prepared in later chapters.

EXHIBIT 6

Trial Balance

Step 1

NetSolutions Unadjusted Trial Balance December 31, 2013	Debit Balances	Credit Balances
Cash	2,065	
Accounts Receivable	2,220	
Supplies	2,000	
Prepaid Insurance	2,400	
Land	20,000	
Office Equipment	1,800	
Accounts Payable		900
Unearned Rent		360
Capital Stock		25,000
Dividends	4,000	
Fees Earned		16,340
Wages Expense	4,275	
Rent Expense	1,600	
Utilities Expense	985	
Supplies Expense	800	
Miscellaneous Expense	455	
	42,600	42,600

Step 2

Steps 3–4

These other trial balances include an adjusted trial balance and a post-closing trial balance.[3]

Errors Affecting the Trial Balance

If the trial balance totals are not equal, an error has occurred. In this case, the error must be found and corrected. A method useful in discovering errors is as follows:

1. If the difference between the Debit and Credit column totals is 10, 100, or 1,000, an error in addition may have occurred. In this case, re-add the trial balance column totals. If the error still exists, recompute the account balances.
2. If the difference between the Debit and Credit column totals can be evenly divisible by 2, the error may be due to the entering of a debit balance as a credit balance, or vice versa. In this case, review the trial balance for account balances of one-half the difference that may have been entered in the wrong column. For example, if the Debit column total is $20,640 and the Credit column total is $20,236, the difference of $404 ($20,640 − $20,236) may be due to a credit account balance of $202 that was entered as a debit account balance.
3. If the difference between the Debit and Credit column totals is evenly divisible by 9, trace the account balances back to the ledger to see if an account balance was incorrectly copied from the ledger. Two common types of copying errors are transpositions and slides. A **transposition** occurs when the order of the digits is copied incorrectly, such as writing $542 as $452 or $524. In a **slide**, the entire number is copied incorrectly one or more spaces to the right or the left, such as writing $542.00 as $54.20 or $5,420.00. In both cases, the resulting error will be evenly divisible by 9.
4. If the difference between the Debit and Credit column totals is not evenly divisible by 2 or 9, review the ledger to see if an account balance in the amount of the error has been omitted from the trial balance. If the error is not discovered, review the journal postings to see if a posting of a debit or credit may have been omitted.

3 The adjusted trial balance will be discussed in Chapter 3 and the post-closing trial balance in Chapter 4.

5. If an error is not discovered by the preceding steps, the accounting process must be retraced, beginning with the last journal entry.

The trial balance does not provide complete proof of the accuracy of the ledger. It indicates only that the debits and the credits are equal. This proof is of value, however, because errors often affect the equality of debits and credits.

Example Exercise 2-6 Trial Balance Errors OBJ 4

For each of the following errors, considered individually, indicate whether the error would cause the trial balance totals to be unequal. If the error would cause the trial balance totals to be unequal, indicate whether the debit or credit total is higher and by how much.

a. Payment of dividends of $5,600 was journalized and posted as a debit of $6,500 to Salary Expense and a credit of $6,500 to Cash.

b. A fee of $2,850 earned from a client was debited to Accounts Receivable for $2,580 and credited to Fees Earned for $2,850.

c. A payment of $3,500 to a creditor was posted as a debit of $3,500 to Accounts Payable and a debit of $3,500 to Cash.

Follow My Example 2-6

a. The totals are equal since both the debit and credit entries were journalized and posted for $6,500.

b. The totals are unequal. The credit total is higher by $270 ($2,850 – $2,580).

c. The totals are unequal. The debit total is higher by $7,000 ($3,500 + $3,500).

Practice Exercises: **PE 2-6A, PE 2-6B**

Errors Not Affecting the Trial Balance

An error may occur that does not cause the trial balance totals to be unequal. Such an error may be discovered when preparing the trial balance or may be indicated by an unusual account balance. For example, a credit balance in the supplies account indicates an error has occurred. This is because a business cannot have "negative" supplies. When such errors are discovered, they should be corrected. If the error has already been journalized and posted to the ledger, a **correcting journal entry** is normally prepared.

To illustrate, assume that on May 5 a $12,500 purchase of office equipment on account was incorrectly journalized and posted as a debit to Supplies and a credit to Accounts Payable for $12,500. This posting of the incorrect entry is shown in the following T accounts:

Incorrect:

Supplies (Debit)	Supplies (Credit)	Accounts Payable (Debit)	Accounts Payable (Credit)
12,500			12,500

Before making a correcting journal entry, it is best to determine the debit(s) and credit(s) that should have been recorded. These are shown in the following T accounts:

Correct:

Office Equipment (Debit)	Office Equipment (Credit)	Accounts Payable (Debit)	Accounts Payable (Credit)
12,500			12,500

Comparing the two sets of T accounts shows that the incorrect debit to Supplies may be corrected by debiting Office Equipment for $12,500 and crediting Supplies for $12,500. The following correcting entry is then journalized and posted:

Entry to Correct Error:

May	31	Office Equipment	18	12,500	
		Supplies	14		12,500
		To correct erroneous debit to Supplies on May 5. See invoice from Bell Office Equipment Co.			

Example Exercise 2-7 Correcting Entries

OBJ 4

The following errors took place in journalizing and posting transactions:

a. Dividends of $6,000 were recorded as a debit to Office Salaries Expense and a credit to Cash.

b. Utilities Expense of $4,500 paid for the current month was recorded as a debit to Miscellaneous Expense and a credit to Accounts Payable.

Journalize the entries to correct the errors. Omit explanations.

Follow My Example 2-7

a.	Dividends	6,000	
	Office Salaries Expense		6,000
b.	Accounts Payable	4,500	
	Miscellaneous Expense		4,500
	Utilities Expense	4,500	
	Cash		4,500

Note: The first entry in (b) reverses the incorrect entry, and the second entry records the correct entry. These two entries could also be combined into one entry; however, preparing two entries will make it easier for someone later to understand what had happened and why the entries were necessary.

Practice Exercises: **PE 2-7A, PE 2-7B**

Financial Analysis and Interpretation: Horizontal Analysis

F·A·I

OBJ 5 Describe and illustrate the use of horizontal analysis in evaluating a company's performance and financial condition.

A single item in a financial statement, such as net income, is often useful in interpreting the financial performance of a company. However, a comparison with prior periods often makes the financial information even more useful. For example, comparing net income of the current period with the net income of the prior period will indicate whether the company's operating performance has improved.

In **horizontal analysis**, the amount of each item on a current financial statement is compared with the same item on an earlier statement. The increase or decrease in the *amount* of the item is computed together with the *percent* of increase or decrease. When two statements are being compared, the earlier statement is used as the base for computing the amount and the percent of change.

To illustrate, the horizontal analysis of two income statements for J. Holmes, Attorney-at-Law, is shown on the following page.

J. Holmes, Attorney-at-Law
Income Statements
For the Years Ended December 31

			Increase (Decrease)	
	2014	**2013**	**Amount**	**Percent**
Fees earned	$187,500	$150,000	$37,500	25.0%*
Operating expenses:				
Wages expense	$ 60,000	$ 45,000	$15,000	33.3
Rent expense	15,000	12,000	3,000	25.0
Utilities expense	12,500	9,000	3,500	38.9
Supplies expense	2,700	3,000	(300)	(10.0)
Miscellaneous expense	2,300	1,800	500	27.8
Total operating expenses	$ 92,500	$ 70,800	$21,700	30.6
Net income	$ 95,000	$ 79,200	$15,800	19.9

*$37,500 ÷ $150,000

The horizontal analysis for J. Holmes, Attorney-at-Law, indicates both favorable and unfavorable trends. The increase in fees earned is a favorable trend, as is the decrease in supplies expense. Unfavorable trends include the increase in wages expense, utilities expense, and miscellaneous expense. These expenses increased the same as or faster than the increase in revenues, with total operating expenses increasing by 30.6%. Overall, net income increased by $15,800, or 19.9%, a favorable trend.

The significance of the various increases and decreases in the revenue and expense items should be investigated to see if operations could be further improved. For example, the increase in utilities expense of 38.9% was the result of renting additional office space for use by a part-time law student in performing paralegal services. This explains the increase in rent expense of 25.0% and the increase in wages expense of 33.3%. The increase in revenues of 25.0% reflects the fees generated by the new paralegal.

The preceding example illustrates how horizontal analysis can be useful in interpreting and analyzing the income statement. Horizontal analyses can also be performed for the balance sheet, the retained earnings statement, and the statement of cash flows.

To illustrate, horizontal analysis for two recent years of Apple Inc.'s statements of cash flows (in millions) is shown below.

Apple Inc.
Statements of Cash Flows
For the Years Ended

			Increase (Decrease)	
	Year 2	**Year 1**	**Amount**	**Percent**
Cash flows from operating activities	$ 37,529	$ 18,595	$ 18,934	101.8%
Cash flows used for investing activities	(40,419)	(13,854)	(26,565)	(197.7)
Cash flows from financing activities	1,444	1,257	187	14.9
Net increase (decrease) in cash	$ (1,446)	$ 5,998	$ (7,444)	(124.1)
Beginning of the year balance of cash	11,261	5,263	5,998	114.0
End of the year balance of cash	$ 9,815	$ 11,261	$ (1,446)	(10.2)

The horizontal analysis of cash flows for Apple Inc. indicates an increase in cash flows from operating activities of 101.8%, which is a favorable trend. At the same time, Apple increased the cash used in its investing activities by 197.7% and increased the cash it received from financing activities by 14.9%. Overall, Apple had a 124.1% decrease in cash for the year, which decreased the end-of-the-year cash balance by 10.2%. In contrast, in the prior year Apple decreased its ending cash balance, which is the beginning cash balance of the current year, by 114.0%.

Example Exercise 2-8 Horizontal Analysis

OBJ 5

Two income statements for McCorkle Company are shown below.

McCorkle Company
Income Statements
For the Years Ended December 31

	2014	2013
Fees earned	$210,000	$175,000
Operating expenses	172,500	150,000
Net income	$ 37,500	$ 25,000

Prepare a horizontal analysis of McCorkle Company's income statements.

Follow My Example 2-8

McCorkle Company
Income Statements
For the Years Ended December 31

			Increase (Decrease)	
	2014	**2013**	**Amount**	**Percent**
Fees earned	$210,000	$175,000	$35,000	20%
Operating expenses	172,500	150,000	22,500	15
Net income	$ 37,500	$ 25,000	$12,500	50

Practice Exercises: **PE 2-8A, PE 2-8B**

At a Glance 2

OBJ 1

Describe the characteristics of an account and a chart of accounts.

Key Points The simplest form of an account, a T account, has three parts: (1) a title, which is the name of the item recorded in the account; (2) a left side, called the debit side; and (3) a right side, called the credit side. Periodically, the debits in an account are added, the credits in the account are added, and the balance of the account is determined.

The system of accounts that make up a ledger is called a chart of accounts.

Learning Outcomes	Example Exercises	Practice Exercises
• Record transactions in T accounts.		
• Determine the balance of a T account.		
• Prepare a chart of accounts for a corporation.		

OBJ 2 Describe and illustrate journalizing transactions using the double-entry accounting system.

Key Points Transactions are initially entered in a record called a journal. The rules of debit and credit for recording increases or decreases in accounts are shown in Exhibit 3. Each transaction is recorded so that the sum of the debits is always equal to the sum of the credits. The normal balance of an account is indicated by the side of the account (debit or credit) that receives the increases.

Learning Outcomes	Example Exercises	Practice Exercises
• Indicate the normal balance of an account.	EE2-1	PE2-1A, 2-1B
• Journalize transactions using the rules of debit and credit.	EE2-2	PE2-2A, 2-2B

OBJ 3 Describe and illustrate the journalizing and posting of transactions to accounts.

Key Points Transactions are journalized and posted to the ledger using the rules of debit and credit. The debits and credits for each journal entry are posted to the accounts in the order in which they occur in the journal.

Learning Outcomes	Example Exercises	Practice Exercises
• Journalize transactions using the rules of debit and credit.	EE2-3 EE2-4	PE2-3A, 2-3B PE2-4A, 2-4B
• Given other account data, determine the missing amount of an account entry.	EE2-5	PE2-5A, 2-5B
• Post journal entries to a standard account.		
• Post journal entries to a T account.		

OBJ 4 Prepare an unadjusted trial balance and explain how it can be used to discover errors.

Key Points A trial balance is prepared by listing the accounts from the ledger and their balances. The totals of the Debit column and Credit column of the trial balance must be equal. If the two totals are not equal, an error has occurred. Errors may occur even though the trial balance totals are equal. Such errors may require a correcting journal entry.

Learning Outcomes	Example Exercises	Practice Exercises
• Prepare an unadjusted trial balance.	EE2-6	PE2-6A, 2-6B
• Discover errors that cause unequal totals in the trial balance.	EE2-7	PE2-7A, 2-7B
• Prepare correcting journal entries for various errors.		

OBJ 5

Describe and illustrate the use of horizontal analysis in evaluating a company's performance and financial condition.

Key Points In horizontal analysis, the amount of each item on a current financial statement is compared with the same item on an earlier statement. The increase or decrease in the *amount* of the item is computed, together with the *percent* of increase or decrease. When two statements are being compared, the earlier statement is used as the base for computing the amount and the percent of change.

Learning Outcomes	Example Exercises	Practice Exercises
• Describe horizontal analysis.		
• Prepare a horizontal analysis report of a financial statement.	**EE2-8**	**PE2-8A, 2-8B**

Key Terms

account (52)
account receivable (65)
assets (54)
balance of the account (53)
chart of accounts (54)
correcting journal entry (72)
credit (53)
debit (53)
dividends (54)
double-entry accounting system (55)
expenses (55)
horizontal analysis (73)
journal (57)
journal entry (58)
journalizing (58)
ledger (54)
liabilities (54)
normal balance of an account (56)
posting (61)
revenues (54)
rules of debit and credit (55)
slide (71)
stockholders' equity (54)
T account (52)
transposition (71)
trial balance (70)
unadjusted trial balance (70)
unearned revenue (63)

Illustrative Problem

J. F. Outz, M.D., organized Hearts Inc. three years ago to practice cardiology. During April 2013, Hearts Inc. completed the following transactions:

Apr. 1. Paid office rent for April, $800.

3. Purchased equipment on account, $2,100.

5. Received cash on account from patients, $3,150.

8. Purchased X-ray film and other supplies on account, $245.

9. One of the items of equipment purchased on April 3 was defective. It was returned with the permission of the supplier, who agreed to reduce the account for the amount charged for the item, $325.

12. Paid cash to creditors on account, $1,250.

Apr. 17. Paid cash for renewal of a six-month property insurance policy, \$370.

20. Discovered that the balances of the cash account and the accounts payable account as of April 1 were overstated by \$200. A payment of that amount to a creditor in March had not been recorded. Journalize the \$200 payment as of April 20.

24. Paid cash for laboratory analysis, \$545.

27. Paid dividends, \$1,250.

30. Recorded the cash received in payment of services (on a cash basis) to patients during April, \$1,720.

30. Paid salaries of receptionist and nurses, \$1,725.

30. Paid various utility expenses, \$360.

30. Recorded fees charged to patients on account for services performed in April, \$5,145.

30. Paid miscellaneous expenses, \$132.

Hearts Inc.'s account titles, numbers, and balances as of April 1 (all normal balances) are listed as follows: Cash, 11, \$4,123; Accounts Receivable, 12, \$6,725; Supplies, 13, \$290; Prepaid Insurance, 14, \$465; Equipment, 18, \$19,745; Accounts Payable, 22, \$765; Capital Stock, 31, \$10,000; Retained Earnings, 32, \$20,583; Dividends, 33, \$0; Professional Fees, 41, \$0; Salary Expense, 51, \$0; Rent Expense, 53, \$0; Laboratory Expense, 55, \$0; Utilities Expense, 56, \$0; Miscellaneous Expense, 59, \$0.

Instructions

1. Open a ledger of standard four-column accounts for Hearts Inc. as of April 1. Enter the balances in the appropriate balance columns and place a check mark (✓) in the Posting Reference column. (*Hint:* Verify the equality of the debit and credit balances in the ledger before proceeding with the next instruction.)
2. Journalize each transaction in a two-column journal.
3. Post the journal to the ledger, extending the month-end balances to the appropriate balance columns after each posting.
4. Prepare an unadjusted trial balance as of April 30.

Solution 1., 2., and 3.

Journal Page 27

Date	Description	Post. Ref.	Debit	Credit
2013				
Apr. 1	Rent Expense	53	800	
	Cash	11		800
	Paid office rent for April.			
3	Equipment	18	2,100	
	Accounts Payable	22		2,100
	Purchased equipment on account.			
5	Cash	11	3,150	
	Accounts Receivable	12		3,150
	Received cash on account.			
8	Supplies	13	245	
	Accounts Payable	22		245
	Purchased supplies.			
9	Accounts Payable	22	325	
	Equipment	18		325
	Returned defective equipment.			
12	Accounts Payable	22	1,250	
	Cash	11		1,250
	Paid creditors on account.			
17	Prepaid Insurance	14	370	
	Cash	11		370
	Renewed six-month property policy.			
20	Accounts Payable	22	200	
	Cash	11		200
	Recorded March payment to creditor.			

Journal Page 28

Date	Description	Post. Ref.	Debit	Credit
2013				
Apr. 24	Laboratory Expense	55	545	
	Cash	11		545
	Paid for laboratory analysis.			
27	Dividends	33	1,250	
	Cash	11		1,250
	Paid dividends.			
30	Cash	11	1,720	
	Professional Fees	41		1,720
	Received fees from patients.			
30	Salary Expense	51	1,725	
	Cash	11		1,725
	Paid salaries.			
30	Utilities Expense	56	360	
	Cash	11		360
	Paid utilities.			
30	Accounts Receivable	12	5,145	
	Professional Fees	41		5,145
	Recorded fees earned on account.			
30	Miscellaneous Expense	59	132	
	Cash	11		132
	Paid expenses.			

Account *Cash* Account No. *11*

					Balance	
Date	Item	Post. Ref.	Debit	Credit	Debit	Credit
2013						
Apr. 1	Balance	✓			4,123	
1		27		800	3,323	
5		27	3,150		6,473	
12		27		1,250	5,223	
17		27		370	4,853	
20		27		200	4,653	
24		28		545	4,108	
27		28		1,250	2,858	
30		28	1,720		4,578	
30		28		1,725	2,853	
30		28		360	2,493	
30		28		132	2,361	

Account *Accounts Receivable* Account No. *12*

					Balance	
Date	Item	Post. Ref.	Debit	Credit	Debit	Credit
2013						
Apr. 1	Balance	✓			6,725	
5		27		3,150	3,575	
30		28	5,145		8,720	

Account *Supplies* Account No. *13*

					Balance	
Date	Item	Post. Ref.	Debit	Credit	Debit	Credit
2013						
Apr. 1	Balance	✓			290	
8		27	245		535	

Account *Prepaid Insurance* — Account No. *14*

Date	Item	Post. Ref.	Debit	Credit	Balance Debit	Balance Credit
2013						
Apr. 1	Balance	✓			465	
17		27	370		835	

Account *Equipment* — Account No. *18*

Date	Item	Post. Ref.	Debit	Credit	Balance Debit	Balance Credit
2013						
Apr. 1	Balance	✓			19,745	
3		27	2,100		21,845	
9		27		325	21,520	

Account *Accounts Payable* — Account No. *22*

Date	Item	Post. Ref.	Debit	Credit	Balance Debit	Balance Credit
2013						
Apr. 1	Balance	✓				765
3		27		2,100		2,865
8		27		245		3,110
9		27	325			2,785
12		27	1,250			1,535
20		27	200			1,335

Account *Capital Stock* — Account No. *31*

Date	Item	Post. Ref.	Debit	Credit	Balance Debit	Balance Credit
2013						
Apr. 1	Balance	✓				10,000

Account *Retained Earnings* — Account No. *32*

Date	Item	Post. Ref.	Debit	Credit	Balance Debit	Balance Credit
2013						
Apr. 1	Balance	✓				20,583

Account *Dividends* — Account No. *33*

Date	Item	Post. Ref.	Debit	Credit	Balance Debit	Balance Credit
2013						
Apr. 27		28	1,250		1,250	

Account *Professional Fees* — Account No. *41*

Date	Item	Post. Ref.	Debit	Credit	Balance Debit	Balance Credit
2013						
Apr. 30		28		1,720		1,720
30		28		5,145		6,865

Account *Salary Expense* — Account No. *51*

Date	Item	Post. Ref.	Debit	Credit	Balance Debit	Balance Credit
2013						
Apr. 30		28	1,725		1,725	

Account *Rent Expense* — Account No. *53*

Date	Item	Post. Ref.	Debit	Credit	Balance Debit	Balance Credit
2013						
Apr. 1		27	800		800	

Account *Laboratory Expense* — Account No. *55*

Date	Item	Post. Ref.	Debit	Credit	Balance Debit	Balance Credit
2013						
Apr. 24		28	545		545	

Account *Utilities Expense* — Account No. *56*

Date	Item	Post. Ref.	Debit	Credit	Balance Debit	Balance Credit
2013						
Apr. 30		28	360		360	

Account *Miscellaneous Expense* — Account No. *59*

Date	Item	Post. Ref.	Debit	Credit	Balance Debit	Balance Credit
2013						
Apr. 30		28	132		132	

4.

Hearts Inc. Unadjusted Trial Balance April 30, 2013	Debit Balances	Credit Balances
Cash	2,361	
Accounts Receivable	8,720	
Supplies	535	
Prepaid Insurance	835	
Equipment	21,520	
Accounts Payable		1,335
Capital Stock		10,000
Retained Earnings		20,583
Dividends	1,250	
Professional Fees		6,865
Salary Expense	1,725	
Rent Expense	800	
Laboratory Expense	545	
Utilities Expense	360	
Miscellaneous Expense	132	
	38,783	38,783

Discussion Questions

1. What is the difference between an account and a ledger?
2. Do the terms *debit* and *credit* signify increase or decrease or can they signify either? Explain.
3. McIntyre Company adheres to a policy of depositing all cash receipts in a bank account and making all payments by check. The cash account as of December 31 has a credit balance of $1,850, and there is no undeposited cash on hand. (a) Assuming no errors occurred during journalizing or posting, what caused this unusual balance? (b) Is the $1,850 credit balance in the cash account an asset, a liability, stockholders' equity, a revenue, or an expense?
4. eCatalog Services Company performed services in October for a specific customer, for a fee of $7,890. Payment was received the following November. (a) Was the revenue earned in October or November? (b) What accounts should be debited and credited in (1) October and (2) November?
5. If the two totals of a trial balance are equal, does it mean that there are no errors in the accounting records? Explain.
6. Assume that a trial balance is prepared with an account balance of $8,900 listed as $9,800 and an account balance of $1,000 listed as $100. Identify the transposition and the slide.
7. Assume that when a purchase of supplies of $2,650 for cash was recorded, both the debit and the credit were journalized and posted as $2,560. (a) Would this error cause the trial balance to be out of balance? (b) Would the trial balance be out of balance if the $2,650 entry had been journalized correctly but the credit to Cash had been posted as $2,560?
8. Assume that Muscular Consulting erroneously recorded the payment of $7,500 of dividends as a debit to Salary Expense. (a) How would this error affect the equality of the trial balance? (b) How would this error affect the income statement, retained earnings statement, and balance sheet?
9. Assume that Sunshine Realty Co. borrowed $300,000 from Columbia First Bank and Trust. In recording the transaction, Sunshine erroneously recorded the receipt as a debit to Cash, $300,000, and a credit to Fees Earned, $300,000. (a) How would this error affect the equality of the trial balance? (b) How would this error affect the income statement, retained earnings statement, and balance sheet?
10. Checking accounts are one of the most common forms of deposits for banks. Assume that Surety Storage has a checking account at Ada Savings Bank. What type of account (asset, liability, stockholders' equity, revenue, expense, drawing) does the account balance of $11,375 represent from the viewpoint of (a) Surety Storage and (b) Ada Savings Bank?

Practice Exercises

Example Exercises

EE 2-1 *p. 56*

PE 2-1A Rules of debit and credit and normal balances — OBJ. 2

State for each account whether it is likely to have (a) debit entries only, (b) credit entries only, or (c) both debit and credit entries. Also, indicate its normal balance.

1. Accounts Receivable
2. Commissions Earned
3. Notes Payable
4. Capital Stock
5. Rent Revenue
6. Wages Expense

EE 2-1 *p. 56*

PE 2-1B Rules of debit and credit and normal balances — OBJ. 2

State for each account whether it is likely to have (a) debit entries only, (b) credit entries only, or (c) both debit and credit entries. Also, indicate its normal balance.

1. Accounts Payable
2. Cash
3. Dividends
4. Miscellaneous Expense
5. Insurance Expense
6. Fees Earned

EE 2-2 *p. 61*

PE 2-2A Journal entry for asset purchase — OBJ. 2

Prepare a journal entry for the purchase of office equipment on February 12 for $18,000, paying $7,000 cash and the remainder on account.

EE 2-2 *p. 61*

PE 2-2B Journal entry for asset purchase — OBJ. 2

Prepare a journal entry for the purchase of office supplies on September 30 for $2,500, paying $800 cash and the remainder on account.

EE 2-3 *p. 65*

PE 2-3A Journal entry for fees earned — OBJ. 3

Prepare a journal entry on July 9 for fees earned on account, $12,000.

EE 2-3 *p. 65*

PE 2-3B Journal entry for fees earned — OBJ. 3

Prepare a journal entry on August 13 for cash received for services rendered, $9,000.

EE 2-4 *p. 68*

PE 2-4A Journal entry for dividends — OBJ. 3

Prepare a journal entry on January 25 for the payment of dividends of $16,000.

EE 2-4 *p. 68*

PE 2-4B Journal entry for dividends — OBJ. 3

Prepare a journal entry on June 30 for the payment of dividends of $11,500.

Example Exercises

EE 2-5 *p. 68*

PE 2-5A Missing amount from an account **OBJ. 3**

On February 1, the cash account balance was $14,750. During February, cash payments totaled $93,400, and the February 28 balance was $15,200. Determine the cash receipts during February.

EE 2-5 *p. 68*

PE 2-5B Missing amount from an account **OBJ. 3**

On August 1, the supplies account balance was $1,025. During August, supplies of $3,110 were purchased, and $1,324 of supplies were on hand as of August 31. Determine supplies expense for August.

EE 2-6 *p. 72*

PE 2-6A Trial balance errors **OBJ. 4**

For each of the following errors, considered individually, indicate whether the error would cause the trial balance totals to be unequal. If the error would cause the trial balance totals to be unequal, indicate whether the debit or credit total is higher and by how much.

a. The payment of an insurance premium of $5,400 for a three-year policy was debited to Prepaid Insurance for $5,400 and credited to Cash for $4,500.

b. A payment of $270 on account was debited to Accounts Payable for $720 and credited to Cash for $720.

c. A purchase of supplies on account for $1,600 was debited to Supplies for $1,600 and debited to Accounts Payable for $1,600.

EE 2-6 *p. 72*

PE 2-6B Trial balance errors **OBJ. 4**

For each of the following errors, considered individually, indicate whether the error would cause the trial balance totals to be unequal. If the error would cause the trial balance totals to be unequal, indicate whether the debit or credit total is higher and by how much.

a. The payment of cash for the purchase of office equipment of $12,900 was debited to Land for $12,900 and credited to Cash for $12,900.

b. The payment of $1,840 on account was debited to Accounts Payable for $184 and credited to Cash for $1,840.

c. The receipt of cash on account of $3,800 was recorded as a debit to Cash for $8,300 and a credit to Accounts Receivable for $3,800.

EE 2-7 *p. 73*

PE 2-7A Correcting entries **OBJ. 4**

The following errors took place in journalizing and posting transactions:

a. Utilities expense of $7,300 paid for the current month was recorded as a debit to Miscellaneous Expense and a credit to Utilities Expense.

b. The payment of $6,100 from a customer on account was recorded as a debit to Cash and a credit to Accounts Payable.

Journalize the entries to correct the errors. Omit explanations.

EE 2-7 *p. 73*

PE 2-7B Correcting entries **OBJ. 4**

The following errors took place in journalizing and posting transactions:

a. The receipt of $8,400 for services rendered was recorded as a debit to Accounts Receivable and a credit to Fees Earned.

b. The purchase of supplies of $2,500 on account was recorded as a debit to Office Equipment and a credit to Supplies.

Journalize the entries to correct the errors. Omit explanations.

EE 2-8 *p. 75*

PE 2-8A Horizontal analysis **OBJ. 5**

Two income statements for Fuller Company are shown on the following page.

Example Exercises

Fuller Company
Income Statements
For Years Ended December 31

	2014	**2013**
Fees earned	$680,000	$850,000
Operating expenses	541,875	637,500
Net income	$138,125	$212,500

Prepare a horizontal analysis of Fuller Company's income statements.

EE 2-8 *p. 75*

PE 2-8B Horizontal analysis

OBJ. 5

Two income statements for Paragon Company are shown below.

Paragon Company
Income Statements
For Years Ended December 31

	2014	**2013**
Fees earned	$1,416,000	$1,200,000
Operating expenses	1,044,000	900,000
Net income	$ 372,000	$ 300,000

Prepare a horizontal analysis of Paragon Company's income statements.

Exercises

EX 2-1 Chart of accounts

OBJ. 1

The following accounts appeared in recent financial statements of Continental Airlines:

Accounts Payable	Flight Equipment
Air Traffic Liability	Landing Fees (Expense)
Aircraft Fuel Expense	Passenger Revenue
Cargo and Mail Revenue	Purchase Deposits for Flight Equipment
Commissions (Expense)	Spare Parts and Supplies

Identify each account as either a balance sheet account or an income statement account. For each balance sheet account, identify it as an asset, a liability, or stockholders' equity. For each income statement account, identify it as a revenue or an expense.

EX 2-2 Chart of accounts

OBJ. 1

Innerscape Interiors is owned and operated by Gina Kissel, an interior decorator. In the ledger of Innerscape Interiors, the first digit of the account number indicates its major account classification (1—assets, 2—liabilities, 3—stockholders' equity, 4—revenues, 5—expenses). The second digit of the account number indicates the specific account within each of the preceding major account classifications.

Match each account number with its most likely account in the list below. The account numbers are 11, 12, 13, 21, 31, 32, 33, 41, 51, 52, and 53.

Accounts Payable	Land
Accounts Receivable	Miscellaneous Expense
Capital Stock	Retained Earnings
Cash	Supplies Expense
Dividends	Wages Expense
Fees Earned	

EX 2-3 Chart of accounts

OBJ. 1

LeadCo School is a newly organized business that teaches people how to inspire and influence others. The list of accounts to be opened in the general ledger is as follows:

Accounts Payable	Prepaid Insurance
Accounts Receivable	Rent Expense
Capital Stock	Retained Earnings
Cash	Supplies
Dividends	Supplies Expense
Equipment	Unearned Rent
Fees Earned	Wages Expense
Miscellaneous Expense	

List the accounts in the order in which they should appear in the ledger of LeadCo School and assign account numbers. Each account number is to have two digits: the first digit is to indicate the major classification (1 for assets, etc.), and the second digit is to identify the specific account within each major classification (11 for Cash, etc.).

EX 2-4 Rules of debit and credit **OBJ. 1, 2**

The following table summarizes the rules of debit and credit. For each of the items (a) through (l), indicate whether the proper answer is a debit or a credit.

	Increase	Decrease	Normal Balance
Balance sheet accounts:			
Asset	(a)	(b)	Debit
Liability	(c)	Debit	(d)
Stockholders' equity:			
Capital Stock	Credit	(e)	(f)
Retained Earnings	(g)	(h)	Credit
Dividends	Debit	Credit	(i)
Income statement accounts:			
Revenue	(j)	(k)	Credit
Expense	(l)	Credit	Debit

EX 2-5 Normal entries for accounts **OBJ. 2**

During the month, Gates Labs Co. has a substantial number of transactions affecting each of the following accounts. State for each account whether it is likely to have (a) debit entries only, (b) credit entries only, or (c) both debit and credit entries.

1. Accounts Payable
2. Accounts Receivable
3. Cash
4. Fees Earned
5. Insurance Expense
6. Dividends
7. Utilities Expense

EX 2-6 Normal balances of accounts **OBJ. 1, 2**

Identify each of the following accounts of Kaiser Services Co. as asset, liability, stockholders' equity, revenue, or expense, and state in each case whether the normal balance is a debit or a credit.

a. Accounts Payable
b. Accounts Receivable
c. Capital Stock
d. Cash
e. Dividends
f. Fees Earned
g. Office Equipment
h. Rent Expense
i. Supplies
j. Wages Expense

EX 2-7 Transactions **OBJ. 2**

Value Consulting Co. has the following accounts in its ledger: Cash, Accounts Receivable, Supplies, Office Equipment, Accounts Payable, Capital Stock, Retained Earnings, Dividends, Fees Earned, Rent Expense, Advertising Expense, Utilities Expense, Miscellaneous Expense.

Journalize the following selected transactions for July 2014 in a two-column journal. Journal entry explanations may be omitted.

July 1. Paid rent for the month, $3,200.
3. Paid advertising expense, $750.
5. Paid cash for supplies, $1,300.
6. Purchased office equipment on account, $12,500.
10. Received cash from customers on account, $11,400.
15. Paid creditor on account, $1,175.
27. Paid cash for repairs to office equipment, $600.
30. Paid telephone bill for the month, $180.
31. Fees earned and billed to customers for the month, $33,760.
31. Paid electricity bill for the month, $1,300.
31. Paid dividends, $4,000.

EX 2-8 Journalizing and posting **OBJ. 2, 3**

On May 22, 2014, Hillcrest Co. purchased $6,180 of supplies on account. In Hillcrest Co.'s chart of accounts, the supplies account is No. 15, and the accounts payable account is No. 21.

a. Journalize the May 22, 2014, transaction on page 19 of Hillcrest Co.'s two-column journal. Include an explanation of the entry.
b. Prepare a four-column account for Supplies. Enter a debit balance of $1,500 as of May 1, 2014. Place a check mark (✓) in the Posting Reference column.
c. Prepare a four-column account for Accounts Payable. Enter a credit balance of $16,750 as of May 1, 2014. Place a check mark (✓) in the Posting Reference column.
d. Post the May 22, 2014, transaction to the accounts.
e. Do the rules of debit and credit apply to all companies?

SPREADSHEET

EX 2-9 Transactions and T accounts **OBJ. 2, 3**

The following selected transactions were completed during January of the current year:

1. Billed customers for fees earned, $48,600.
2. Purchased supplies on account, $1,975.
3. Received cash from customers on account, $31,400.
4. Paid creditors on account, $1,350.

a. Journalize the above transactions in a two-column journal, using the appropriate number to identify the transactions. Journal entry explanations may be omitted.
b. Post the entries prepared in (a) to the following T accounts: Cash, Supplies, Accounts Receivable, Accounts Payable, Fees Earned. To the left of each amount posted in the accounts, place the appropriate number to identify the transactions.
c. Assume that the unadjusted trial balance on January 31 shows a credit balance for Accounts Receivable. Does this credit balance mean an error has occurred?

EX 2-10 Cash account balance **OBJ. 1, 2, 3**

During the month, Warwick Co. received $515,000 in cash and paid out $375,000 in cash.

a. Do the data indicate that Warwick Co. had net income of $140,000 during the month? Explain.
b. If the balance of the cash account is $200,000 at the end of the month, what was the cash balance at the beginning of the month?

EX 2-11 Account balances **OBJ. 1, 2, 3**

✔ c. $107,340

a. During March, $276,500 was paid to creditors on account, and purchases on account were $261,000. Assuming the March 31 balance of Accounts Payable was $76,000, determine the account balance on March 1.
b. On July 1, the accounts receivable account balance was $49,000. During July, $525,000 was collected from customers on account. Assuming the July 31 balance was $61,500, determine the fees billed to customers on account during July.

c. On September 1, the cash account balance was $28,440. During September, cash receipts totaled $112,100 and the September 30 balance was $33,200. Determine the cash payments made during September.

EX 2-12 Retained earnings account balance **OBJ. 1, 2**

As of January 1, Retained Earnings had a credit balance of $314,000. During the year, dividends totaled $10,000, and the business incurred a net loss of $320,000.

a. Compute the balance of Retained Earnings as of the end of the year.

b. Assuming that there have been no recording errors, will the balance sheet prepared at December 31 balance? Explain.

EX 2-13 Identifying transactions **OBJ. 1, 2**

Grand Canyon Tours Co. is a travel agency. The nine transactions recorded by Grand Canyon Tours during April 2014, its first month of operations, are indicated in the following T accounts:

Cash

(1)	75,000	(2)	4,000
(7)	11,000	(3)	3,000
		(4)	2,700
		(6)	9,000
		(9)	5,000

Equipment

(3)	25,000		

Dividends

(9)	5,000		

Accounts Receivable

(5)	19,500	(7)	11,000

Accounts Payable

(6)	9,000	(3)	22,000

Service Revenue

		(5)	19,500

Supplies

(2)	4,000	(8)	2,000

Capital Stock

		(1)	75,000

Operating Expenses

(4)	2,700		
(8)	2,000		

Indicate for each debit and each credit: (a) whether an asset, liability, stockholders' equity, dividends, revenue, or expense account was affected and (b) whether the account was increased (+) or decreased (–). Present your answers in the following form, with transaction (1) given as an example:

	Account Debited		Account Credited	
Transaction	**Type**	**Effect**	**Type**	**Effect**
(1)	asset	+	stockholders' equity	+

EX 2-14 Journal entries **OBJ. 1, 2**

Based upon the T accounts in Exercise 2-13, prepare the nine journal entries from which the postings were made. Journal entry explanations may be omitted.

EX 2-15 Trial balance **OBJ. 4**

✔ Total of Debit column: $107,500

SPREADSHEET

Based upon the data presented in Exercise 2-13, (a) prepare an unadjusted trial balance, listing the accounts in their proper order. (b) Based upon the unadjusted trial balance, determine the net income or net loss.

EX 2-16 Trial balance **OBJ. 4**

✔ Total of Credit column: $675,000

The accounts in the ledger of Leaf Co. as of December 31, 2014, are listed in alphabetical order as follows. All accounts have normal balances. The balance of the cash account has been intentionally omitted.

Accounts Payable	$ 23,500	Notes Payable	$ 50,000
Accounts Receivable	38,100	Prepaid Insurance	6,400
Capital Stock	8,000	Rent Expense	36,000
Cash	?	Retained Earnings	42,000
Dividends	16,000	Supplies	3,200
Fees Earned	538,000	Supplies Expense	9,000
Insurance Expense	6,000	Unearned Rent	13,500
Land	40,000	Utilities Expense	18,000
Miscellaneous Expense	12,000	Wages Expense	476,800

Prepare an unadjusted trial balance, listing the accounts in their normal order and inserting the missing figure for cash.

EX 2-17 Effect of errors on trial balance

OBJ. 4

Indicate which of the following errors, each considered individually, would cause the trial balance totals to be unequal:

a. A fee of $21,000 earned and due from a client was not debited to Accounts Receivable or credited to a revenue account, because the cash had not been received.

b. A receipt of $11,300 from an account receivable was journalized and posted as a debit of $11,300 to Cash and a credit of $11,300 to Fees Earned.

c. A payment of $4,950 to a creditor was posted as a debit of $4,950 to Accounts Payable and a debit of $4,950 to Cash.

d. A payment of $5,000 for equipment purchased was posted as a debit of $500 to Equipment and a credit of $500 to Cash.

e. Payment of a cash dividend of $19,000 was journalized and posted as a debit of $1,900 to Salary Expense and a credit of $19,000 to Cash.

Indicate which of the preceding errors would require a correcting entry.

EX 2-18 Errors in trial balance

OBJ. 4

✔ Total of Credit column: $525,000

The following preliminary unadjusted trial balance of Ranger Co., a sports ticket agency, does not balance:

Ranger Co.
Unadjusted Trial Balance
August 31, 2014

	Debit Balances	Credit Balances
Cash	77,600	
Accounts Receivable	37,750	
Prepaid Insurance		12,000
Equipment	19,000	
Accounts Payable		29,100
Unearned Rent		10,800
Capital Stock	40,000	
Retained Earnings	70,000	
Dividends	13,000	
Service Revenue		385,000
Wages Expense		213,000
Advertising Expense	16,350	
Miscellaneous Expense		18,400
	273,700	668,300

When the ledger and other records are reviewed, you discover the following: (1) the debits and credits in the cash account total $77,600 and $62,100, respectively; (2) a billing of $9,000 to a customer on account was not posted to the accounts receivable account; (3) a payment of $4,500 made to a creditor on account was not posted to the accounts payable account; (4) the balance of the unearned rent account is $5,400; (5) the correct balance of the equipment account is $190,000; and (6) each account has a normal balance.

Prepare a corrected unadjusted trial balance.

EX 2-19 Effect of errors on trial balance **OBJ. 4**

The following errors occurred in posting from a two-column journal:

1. A credit of $6,000 to Accounts Payable was not posted.
2. An entry debiting Accounts Receivable and crediting Fees Earned for $5,300 was not posted.
3. A debit of $2,700 to Accounts Payable was posted as a credit.
4. A debit of $480 to Supplies was posted twice.
5. A debit of $3,600 to Cash was posted to Miscellaneous Expense.
6. A credit of $780 to Cash was posted as $870.
7. A debit of $12,620 to Wages Expense was posted as $12,260.

Considering each case individually (i.e., assuming that no other errors had occurred), indicate: (a) by "yes" or "no" whether the trial balance would be out of balance; (b) if answer to (a) is "yes," the amount by which the trial balance totals would differ; and (c) whether the Debit or Credit column of the trial balance would have the larger total. Answers should be presented in the following form, with error (1) given as an example:

Error	(a) Out of Balance	(b) Difference	(c) Larger Total
1.	yes	$6,000	debit

EX 2-20 Errors in trial balance **OBJ. 4**

✔ Total of Credit column: $1,040,000

Identify the errors in the following trial balance. All accounts have normal balances.

Mascot Co.
Unadjusted Trial Balance
For the Month Ending July 31, 2014

	Debit Balances	Credit Balances
Cash	36,000	
Accounts Receivable		112,600
Prepaid Insurance	18,000	
Equipment	375,000	
Accounts Payable	53,300	
Salaries Payable		7,500
Capital Stock		100,000
Retained Earnings		197,200
Dividends		17,000
Service Revenue		682,000
Salary Expense	396,800	
Advertising Expense		73,000
Miscellaneous Expense	11,600	
	1,189,300	1,189,300

EX 2-21 Entries to correct errors **OBJ. 4**

The following errors took place in journalizing and posting transactions:

a. Rent of $13,550 paid for the current month was recorded as a debit to Rent Expense and a credit to Prepaid Rent.

b. Dividends of $14,000 were recorded as a debit to Wages Expense and a credit to Cash.

Journalize the entries to correct the errors. Omit explanations.

EX 2-22 Entries to correct errors **OBJ. 4**

The following errors took place in journalizing and posting transactions:

a. Cash of $8,800 received on account was recorded as a debit to Fees Earned and a credit to Cash.

b. A $1,760 purchase of supplies for cash was recorded as a debit to Supplies Expense and a credit to Accounts Payable.

Journalize the entries to correct the errors. Omit explanations.

EX 2-23 Horizontal analysis of income statement **OBJ. 5**

F·A·I

The following data (in millions) are taken from the financial statements of Target Corporation.

	Recent Year	Prior Year
Revenue	$67,390	$65,357
Operating expenses	62,138	60,684
Operating income	$ 5,252	$ 4,673

a. For Target Corporation, determine the amount of change in millions and the percent of change (round to one decimal place) from the prior year to the recent year for:

1. Revenue
2. Operating expenses
3. Operating income

b. What conclusions can you draw from your analysis of the revenue and the total operating expenses?

EX 2-24 Horizontal analysis of income statement **OBJ. 5**

F·A·I

The following data (in millions) were taken the financial statements of Walmart Stores, Inc.

	Recent Year	Prior Year
Revenue	$421,849	$408,085
Operating expenses	396,307	384,083
Operating income	$ 25,542	$ 24,002

a. For Walmart Stores, Inc., determine the amount of change in millions and the percent of change (round to one decimal place) from the prior year to the recent year for:

1. Revenue
2. Operating expenses
3. Operating income

b. Comment on the results of your horizontal analysis in part (a).

c. Based upon Exercise 2-23, compare and comment on the operating results of Target and Walmart for the recent year.

Problems Series A

PR 2-1A Entries into T accounts and trial balance **OBJ. 1, 2, 3, 4**

✔ 3. Total of Debit column: $85,900

Lynn Cantwell, an architect, organized Cantwell Architects on July 1, 2014. During the month, Cantwell Architects completed the following transactions:

a. Issued capital stock to Lynn Cantwell in exchange for $25,000.

b. Paid July rent for office and workroom, $2,750.

c. Purchased used automobile for $30,000, paying $4,000 cash and giving a note payable for the remainder.

d. Purchased office and computer equipment on account, $9,000.

e. Paid cash for supplies, $1,600.

f. Paid cash for annual insurance policies, $2,400.

g. Received cash from client for plans delivered, $11,150.

h. Paid cash for miscellaneous expenses, $300.

i. Paid cash to creditors on account, $3,500.

j. Paid installment due on note payable, $550.

k. Received invoice for blueprint service, due in August, $1,500.

l. Recorded fee earned on plans delivered, payment to be received in August, $17,300.

m. Paid salary of assistant, $2,200.

n. Paid gas, oil, and repairs on automobile for July, $815.

Instructions

1. Record the above transactions directly in the following T accounts, without journalizing: Cash, Accounts Receivable, Supplies, Prepaid Insurance, Automobiles, Equipment, Notes Payable, Accounts Payable, Capital Stock, Professional Fees, Rent Expense, Salary Expense, Blueprint Expense, Automobile Expense, Miscellaneous Expense. To the left of the amount entered in the accounts, place the appropriate letter to identify the transaction.
2. Determine account balances of the T accounts. Accounts containing a single entry only (such as Prepaid Insurance) do not need a balance.
3. Prepare an unadjusted trial balance for Cantwell Architects, as of July 31, 2014.
4. Determine the net income or net loss for July.

PR 2-2A Journal entries and trial balance

OBJ. 1, 2, 3, 4

✔ 4. c. $7,875

SPREADSHEET

GENERAL LEDGER

On January 1, 2014, Alicia Masingale established Leopard Realty, which completed the following transactions during the month:

a. Alicia Masingale transferred cash from a personal bank account to an account to be used for the business in exchange for capital stock, $23,500.
b. Paid rent on office and equipment for the month, $4,000.
c. Purchased supplies on account, $1,800.
d. Paid creditor on account, $675.
e. Earned sales commissions, receiving cash, $16,750.
f. Paid automobile expenses (including rental charge) for month, $1,000, and miscellaneous expenses, $800.
g. Paid office salaries, $2,150.
h. Determined that the cost of supplies used was $925.
i. Paid dividends, $1,600.

Instructions

1. Journalize entries for transactions (a) through (i), using the following account titles: Cash, Supplies, Accounts Payable, Capital Stock, Dividends, Sales Commissions, Rent Expense, Office Salaries Expense, Automobile Expense, Supplies Expense, Miscellaneous Expense. Explanations may be omitted.
2. Prepare T accounts, using the account titles in (1). Post the journal entries to these accounts, placing the appropriate letter to the left of each amount to identify the transactions. Determine the account balances, after all posting is complete. Accounts containing only a single entry do not need a balance.
3. Prepare an unadjusted trial balance as of January 31, 2014.
4. Determine the following:
   a. Amount of total revenue recorded in the ledger.
   b. Amount of total expenses recorded in the ledger.
   c. Amount of net income for January.
5. Determine the increase or decrease in retained earnings for January.

PR 2-3A Journal entries and trial balance

OBJ. 1, 2, 3, 4

✔ 3. Total of Credit column: $74,375

SPREADSHEET

GENERAL LEDGER

On June 1, 2014, Ellie Hopkins established an interior decorating business, First-Class Designs. During the month, Ellie completed the following transactions related to the business:

June 1. Ellie transferred cash from a personal bank account to an account to be used for the business in exchange for capital stock, $21,500.

1. Paid rent for period of June 1 to end of month, $4,200.

6. Purchased office equipment on account, $8,500.

8. Purchased a used truck for $28,000, paying $3,000 cash and giving a note payable for the remainder.

10. Purchased supplies for cash, $1,800.

12. Received cash for job completed, $9,000.

June 15. Paid annual premiums on property and casualty insurance, $2,700.

23. Recorded jobs completed on account and sent invoices to customers, $13,650.

24. Received an invoice for truck expenses, to be paid in July, $975.

Enter the following transactions on Page 2 of the two-column journal.

29. Paid utilities expense, $2,480.

29. Paid miscellaneous expenses, $750.

30. Received cash from customers on account, $7,800.

30. Paid wages of employees, $5,100.

30. Paid creditor a portion of the amount owed for equipment purchased on June 6, $4,250.

30. Paid dividends, $3,000.

Instructions

1. Journalize each transaction in a two-column journal beginning on Page 1, referring to the following chart of accounts in selecting the accounts to be debited and credited. (Do not insert the account numbers in the journal at this time.) Explanations may be omitted.

11 Cash	31 Capital Stock
12 Accounts Receivable	33 Dividends
13 Supplies	41 Fees Earned
14 Prepaid Insurance	51 Wages Expense
16 Equipment	53 Rent Expense
18 Truck	54 Utilities Expense
21 Notes Payable	55 Truck Expense
22 Accounts Payable	59 Miscellaneous Expense

2. Post the journal to a ledger of four-column accounts, inserting appropriate posting references as each item is posted. Extend the balances to the appropriate balance columns after each transaction is posted.
3. Prepare an unadjusted trial balance for First-Class Designs as of June 30, 2014.
4. Determine the excess of revenues over expenses for June.
5. Can you think of any reason why the amount determined in (4) might not be the net income for June?

PR 2-4A Journal entries and trial balance — OBJ. 1, 2, 3, 4

✔ 4. Total of Debit column: $532,525

GENERAL LEDGER

Elite Realty acts as an agent in buying, selling, renting, and managing real estate. The unadjusted trial balance on March 31, 2014, is shown below.

Elite Realty
Unadjusted Trial Balance
March 31, 2014

		Debit Balances	Credit Balances
11	Cash	26,300	
12	Accounts Receivable	61,500	
13	Prepaid Insurance	3,000	
14	Office Supplies	1,800	
16	Land	—	
21	Accounts Payable		14,000
22	Unearned Rent		—
23	Notes Payable		—
31	Capital Stock		10,000
32	Retained Earnings		36,000
33	Dividends	2,000	
41	Fees Earned		240,000
51	Salary and Commission Expense	148,200	
52	Rent Expense	30,000	
53	Advertising Expense	17,800	
54	Automobile Expense	5,500	
59	Miscellaneous Expense	3,900	
		300,000	300,000

The following business transactions were completed by Elite Realty during April 2014:

Apr. 1. Paid rent on office for month, $6,500.
2. Purchased office supplies on account, $2,300.
5. Paid insurance premiums, $6,000.
10. Received cash from clients on account, $52,300.
15. Purchased land for a future building site for $200,000, paying $30,000 in cash and giving a note payable for the remainder.
17. Paid creditors on account, $6,450.
20. Returned a portion of the office supplies purchased on April 2, receiving full credit for their cost, $325.
23. Paid advertising expense, $4,300.

Enter the following transactions on Page 19 of the two-column journal.

27. Discovered an error in computing a commission; received cash from the salesperson for the overpayment, $2,500.
28. Paid automobile expense (including rental charges for an automobile), $1,500.
29. Paid miscellaneous expenses, $1,400.
30. Recorded revenue earned and billed to clients during the month, $57,000.
30. Paid salaries and commissions for the month, $11,900.
30. Paid dividends, $4,000.
30. Rented land purchased on April 15 to local merchants association for use as a parking lot in May and June, during a street rebuilding program; received advance payment of $10,000.

Instructions

1. Record the April 1, 2014, balance of each account in the appropriate balance column of a four-column account, write *Balance* in the item section, and place a check mark (✓) in the Posting Reference column.
2. Journalize the transactions for April in a two-column journal beginning on Page 18. Journal entry explanations may be omitted.
3. Post to the ledger, extending the account balance to the appropriate balance column after each posting.
4. Prepare an unadjusted trial balance of the ledger as of April 30, 2014.
5. Assume that the April 30 transaction for salaries and commissions should have been $19,100. (a) Why did the unadjusted trial balance in (4) balance? (b) Journalize the correcting entry. (c) Is this error a transposition or slide?

PR 2-5A Corrected trial balance — OBJ. 4

✔ 1. Total of Debit column: $725,000

The Colby Group has the following unadjusted trial balance as of August 31, 2014.

The Colby Group
Unadjusted Trial Balance
August 31, 2014

	Debit Balances	Credit Balances
Cash	17,300	
Accounts Receivable	37,000	
Supplies	7,400	
Prepaid Insurance	1,900	
Equipment	196,000	
Notes Payable		97,600
Accounts Payable		26,000
Capital Stock		35,000
Retained Earnings		94,150
Dividends	56,000	
Fees Earned		454,450
Wages Expense	270,000	
Rent Expense	51,800	
Advertising Expense	25,200	
Miscellaneous Expense	5,100	
	667,700	707,200

The debit and credit totals are not equal as a result of the following errors:

a. The cash entered on the trial balance was understated by $6,000.

b. A cash receipt of $5,600 was posted as a debit to Cash of $6,500.

c. A debit of $11,000 to Accounts Receivable was not posted.

d. A return of $150 of defective supplies was erroneously posted as a $1,500 credit to Supplies.

e. An insurance policy acquired at a cost of $1,200 was posted as a credit to Prepaid Insurance.

f. The balance of Notes Payable was understated by $20,000.

g. A credit of $4,800 in Accounts Payable was overlooked when determining the balance of the account.

h. A debit of $7,000 for dividends was posted as a credit to Retained Earnings.

i. The balance of $58,100 in Rent Expense was entered as $51,800 in the trial balance.

j. Gas, Electricity, and Water Expense, with a balance of $24,150, was omitted from the trial balance.

Instructions

1. Prepare a corrected unadjusted trial balance as of August 31, 2014.
2. Does the fact that the unadjusted trial balance in (1) is balanced mean that there are no errors in the accounts? Explain.

Problems Series B

PR 2-1B Entries into T accounts and trial balance **OBJ. 1, 2, 3, 4**

✔ 3. Total of Debit column: $69,550

Ken Jones, an architect, organized Jones Architects on April 1, 2014. During the month, Jones Architects completed the following transactions:

a. Transferred cash from a personal bank account to an account to be used for the business in exchange for capital stock, $18,000.

b. Purchased used automobile for $19,500, paying $2,500 cash and giving a note payable for the remainder.

c. Paid April rent for office and workroom, $3,150.

d. Paid cash for supplies, $1,450.

e. Purchased office and computer equipment on account, $6,500.

f. Paid cash for annual insurance policies on automobile and equipment, $2,400.

g. Received cash from a client for plans delivered, $12,000.

h. Paid cash to creditors on account, $1,800.

i. Paid cash for miscellaneous expenses, $375.

j. Received invoice for blueprint service, due in May, $2,500.

k. Recorded fee earned on plans delivered, payment to be received in May, $15,650.

l. Paid salary of assistant, $2,800.

m. Paid cash for miscellaneous expenses, $200.

n. Paid installment due on note payable, $300.

o. Paid gas, oil, and repairs on automobile for April, $550.

Instructions

1. Record the above transactions directly in the following T accounts, without journalizing: Cash, Accounts Receivable, Supplies, Prepaid Insurance, Automobiles, Equipment, Notes Payable, Accounts Payable, Capital Stock, Professional Fees, Rent Expense, Salary Expense, Blueprint Expense, Automobile Expense, Miscellaneous Expense. To the left of each amount entered in the accounts, place the appropriate letter to identify the transaction.
2. Determine account balances of the T accounts. Accounts containing a single entry only (such as Prepaid Insurance) do not need a balance.

3. Prepare an unadjusted trial balance for Jones Architects, as of April 30, 2014.
4. Determine the net income or net loss for April.

PR 2-2B Journal entries and trial balance **OBJ. 1, 2, 3, 4**

✔ 4. c. $4,550

SPREADSHEET

GENERAL LEDGER

On August 1, 2014, Rafael Masey established Planet Realty, which completed the following transactions during the month:

a. Rafael Masey transferred cash from a personal bank account to an account to be used for the business in exchange for capital stock, $17,500.
b. Purchased supplies on account, $2,300.
c. Earned sales commissions, receiving cash, $13,300.
d. Paid rent on office and equipment for the month, $3,000.
e. Paid creditor on account, $1,150.
f. Paid dividends, $1,800.
g. Paid automobile expenses (including rental charge) for month, $1,500, and miscellaneous expenses, $400.
h. Paid office salaries, $2,800.
i. Determined that the cost of supplies used was $1,050.

Instructions

1. Journalize entries for transactions (a) through (i), using the following account titles: Cash, Supplies, Accounts Payable, Capital Stock, Dividends, Sales Commissions, Rent Expense, Office Salaries Expense, Automobile Expense, Supplies Expense, Miscellaneous Expense. Journal entry explanations may be omitted.
2. Prepare T accounts, using the account titles in (1). Post the journal entries to these accounts, placing the appropriate letter to the left of each amount to identify the transactions. Determine the account balances, after all posting is complete. Accounts containing only a single entry do not need a balance.
3. Prepare an unadjusted trial balance as of August 31, 2014.
4. Determine the following:
   a. Amount of total revenue recorded in the ledger.
   b. Amount of total expenses recorded in the ledger.
   c. Amount of net income for August.
5. Determine the increase or decrease in retained earnings for August.

PR 2-3B Journal entries and trial balance **OBJ. 1, 2, 3, 4**

✔ 3. Total of Credit column: $70,300

SPREADSHEET

GENERAL LEDGER

On October 1, 2014, Jay Pryor established an interior decorating business, Pioneer Designs. During the month, Jay completed the following transactions related to the business:

Oct. 1. Jay transferred cash from a personal bank account to an account to be used for the business in exchange for capital stock, $18,000.
4. Paid rent for period of October 4 to end of month, $3,000.
10. Purchased a used truck for $23,750, paying $3,750 cash and giving a note payable for the remainder.
13. Purchased equipment on account, $10,500.
14. Purchased supplies for cash, $2,100.
15. Paid annual premiums on property and casualty insurance, $3,600.
15. Received cash for job completed, $8,950.

Enter the following transactions on Page 2 of the two-column journal.

21. Paid creditor a portion of the amount owed for equipment purchased on October 13, $2,000.
24. Recorded jobs completed on account and sent invoices to customers, $14,150.
26. Received an invoice for truck expenses, to be paid in November, $700.
27. Paid utilities expense, $2,240.

Oct. 27. Paid miscellaneous expenses, $1,100.
29. Received cash from customers on account, $7,600.
30. Paid wages of employees, $4,800.
31. Paid dividends, $3,500.

Instructions

1. Journalize each transaction in a two-column journal beginning on Page 1, referring to the following chart of accounts in selecting the accounts to be debited and credited. (Do not insert the account numbers in the journal at this time.) Journal entry explanations may be omitted.

11 Cash	31 Capital Stock
12 Accounts Receivable	33 Dividends
13 Supplies	41 Fees Earned
14 Prepaid Insurance	51 Wages Expense
16 Equipment	53 Rent Expense
18 Truck	54 Utilities Expense
21 Notes Payable	55 Truck Expense
22 Accounts Payable	59 Miscellaneous Expense

2. Post the journal to a ledger of four-column accounts, inserting appropriate posting references as each item is posted. Extend the balances to the appropriate balance columns after each transaction is posted.
3. Prepare an unadjusted trial balance for Pioneer Designs as of October 31, 2014.
4. Determine the excess of revenues over expenses for October.
5. Can you think of any reason why the amount determined in (4) might not be the net income for October?

PR 2-4B Journal entries and trial balance

OBJ. 1, 2, 3, 4

✔ 4. Total of Debit column: $945,000

GENERAL LEDGER

Valley Realty acts as an agent in buying, selling, renting, and managing real estate. The unadjusted trial balance on July 31, 2014, is shown below.

Valley Realty
Unadjusted Trial Balance
July 31, 2014

		Debit Balances	Credit Balances
11	Cash	52,500	
12	Accounts Receivable	100,100	
13	Prepaid Insurance	12,600	
14	Office Supplies	2,800	
16	Land	—	
21	Accounts Payable		21,000
22	Unearned Rent		—
23	Notes Payable		—
31	Capital Stock		17,500
32	Retained Earnings		70,000
33	Dividends	44,800	
41	Fees Earned		591,500
51	Salary and Commission Expense	385,000	
52	Rent Expense	49,000	
53	Advertising Expense	32,200	
54	Automobile Expense	15,750	
59	Miscellaneous Expense	5,250	
		700,000	700,000

The following business transactions were completed by Valley Realty during August 2014:

Aug. 1. Purchased office supplies on account, $3,150.
2. Paid rent on office for month, $7,200.
3. Received cash from clients on account, $83,900.

Aug. 5. Paid insurance premiums, $12,000.

9. Returned a portion of the office supplies purchased on August 1, receiving full credit for their cost, $400.

17. Paid advertising expense, $8,000.

23. Paid creditors on account, $13,750.

Enter the following transactions on Page 19 of the two-column journal.

29. Paid miscellaneous expenses, $1,700.

30. Paid automobile expense (including rental charges for an automobile), $2,500.

31. Discovered an error in computing a commission during July; received cash from the salesperson for the overpayment, $2,000.

31. Paid salaries and commissions for the month, $53,000.

31. Recorded revenue earned and billed to clients during the month, $183,500.

31. Purchased land for a future building site for $75,000, paying $7,500 in cash and giving a note payable for the remainder.

31. Paid dividends, $1,000.

31. Rented land purchased on August 31 to a local university for use as a parking lot during football season (September, October, and November); received advance payment of $5,000.

Instructions

1. Record the August 1 balance of each account in the appropriate balance column of a four-column account, write *Balance* in the item section, and place a check mark (✓) in the Posting Reference column.
2. Journalize the transactions for August in a two-column journal beginning on Page 18. Journal entry explanations may be omitted.
3. Post to the ledger, extending the account balance to the appropriate balance column after each posting.
4. Prepare an unadjusted trial balance of the ledger as of August 31, 2014.
5. Assume that the August 31 transaction for dividends should have been $10,000. (a) Why did the unadjusted trial balance in (4) balance? (b) Journalize the correcting entry. (c) Is this error a transposition or slide?

PR 2-5B Corrected trial balance — OBJ. 4

✓ 1. Total of Debit column: $712,500

Tech Support Services has the following unadjusted trial balance as of January 31, 2014.

Tech Support Services
Unadjusted Trial Balance
January 31, 2014

	Debit Balances	Credit Balances
Cash	25,550	
Accounts Receivable	44,050	
Supplies	6,660	
Prepaid Insurance	3,600	
Equipment	162,000	
Notes Payable		75,000
Accounts Payable		13,200
Capital Stock		18,000
Retained Earnings		83,850
Dividends	33,000	
Fees Earned		534,000
Wages Expense	306,000	
Rent Expense	62,550	
Advertising Expense	23,850	
Gas, Electricity, and Water Expense	17,000	
	684,260	724,050

The debit and credit totals are not equal as a result of the following errors:

a. The cash entered on the trial balance was overstated by $8,000.
b. A cash receipt of $4,100 was posted as a debit to Cash of $1,400.
c. A debit of $12,350 to Accounts Receivable was not posted.
d. A return of $235 of defective supplies was erroneously posted as a $325 credit to Supplies.
e. An insurance policy acquired at a cost of $3,000 was posted as a credit to Prepaid Insurance.
f. The balance of Notes Payable was overstated by $21,000.
g. A credit of $3,450 in Accounts Payable was overlooked when the balance of the account was determined.
h. A debit of $6,000 for dividends was posted as a debit to Retained Earnings.
i. The balance of $28,350 in Advertising Expense was entered as $23,850 in the trial balance.
j. Miscellaneous Expense, with a balance of $4,600, was omitted from the trial balance.

Instructions

1. Prepare a corrected unadjusted trial balance as of January 31, 2014.
2. Does the fact that the unadjusted trial balance in (1) is balanced mean that there are no errors in the accounts? Explain.

Continuing Problem

✔ 4. Total of Debit column: $40,750

GENERAL LEDGER

The transactions completed by PS Music during June 2014 were described at the end of Chapter 1. The following transactions were completed during July, the second month of the business's operations:

July 1. Peyton Smith made an additional investment in PS Music in exchange for capital stock by depositing $5,000 in PS Music's checking account.

1. Instead of continuing to share office space with a local real estate agency, Peyton decided to rent office space near a local music store. Paid rent for July, $1,750.

1. Paid a premium of $2,700 for a comprehensive insurance policy covering liability, theft, and fire. The policy covers a one-year period.

2. Received $1,000 on account.

3. On behalf of PS Music, Peyton signed a contract with a local radio station, KXMD, to provide guest spots for the next three months. The contract requires PS Music to provide a guest disc jockey for 80 hours per month for a monthly fee of $3,600. Any additional hours beyond 80 will be billed to KXMD at $40 per hour. In accordance with the contract, Peyton received $7,200 from KXMD as an advance payment for the first two months.

3. Paid $250 on account.

4. Paid an attorney $900 for reviewing the July 3 contract with KXMD. (Record as Miscellaneous Expense.)

5. Purchased office equipment on account from Office Mart, $7,500.

8. Paid for a newspaper advertisement, $200.

11. Received $1,000 for serving as a disc jockey for a party.

13. Paid $700 to a local audio electronics store for rental of digital recording equipment.

14. Paid wages of $1,200 to receptionist and part-time assistant.

Enter the following transactions on Page 2 of the two-column journal.

July 16. Received $2,000 for serving as a disc jockey for a wedding reception.

18. Purchased supplies on account, $850.

21. Paid $620 to Upload Music for use of its current music demos in making various music sets.

22. Paid $800 to a local radio station to advertise the services of PS Music twice daily for the remainder of July.

23. Served as disc jockey for a party for $2,500. Received $750, with the remainder due August 4, 2014.

27. Paid electric bill, $915.

28. Paid wages of $1,200 to receptionist and part-time assistant.

29. Paid miscellaneous expenses, $540.

30. Served as a disc jockey for a charity ball for $1,500. Received $500, with the remainder due on August 9, 2014.

31. Received $3,000 for serving as a disc jockey for a party.

31. Paid $1,400 royalties (music expense) to National Music Clearing for use of various artists' music during July.

31. Paid dividends of $1,250.

PS Music's chart of accounts and the balance of accounts as of July 1, 2014 (all normal balances), are as follows:

11 Cash	$3,920	41 Fees Earned	$6,200
12 Accounts Receivable	1,000	50 Wages Expense	400
14 Supplies	170	51 Office Rent Expense	800
15 Prepaid Insurance	—	52 Equipment Rent Expense	675
17 Office Equipment	—	53 Utilities Expense	300
21 Accounts Payable	250	54 Music Expense	1,590
23 Unearned Revenue	—	55 Advertising Expense	500
31 Capital Stock	4,000	56 Supplies Expense	180
33 Dividends	500	59 Miscellaneous Expense	415

Instructions

1. Enter the July 1, 2014, account balances in the appropriate balance column of a four-column account. Write *Balance* in the Item column, and place a check mark (✓) in the Posting Reference column. (*Hint:* Verify the equality of the debit and credit balances in the ledger before proceeding with the next instruction.)
2. Analyze and journalize each transaction in a two-column journal beginning on Page 1, omitting journal entry explanations.
3. Post the journal to the ledger, extending the account balance to the appropriate balance column after each posting.
4. Prepare an unadjusted trial balance as of July 31, 2014.

Cases & Projects

CP 2-1 Ethics and professional conduct in business

At the end of the current month, Gil Frank prepared a trial balance for College App Services. The credit side of the trial balance exceeds the debit side by a significant amount. Gil has decided to add the difference to the balance of the miscellaneous expense account in order to complete the preparation of the current month's financial statements by a 5 o'clock deadline. Gil will look for the difference next week when he has more time. Discuss whether Gil is behaving in a professional manner.

CP 2-2 Account for revenue

Bozeman College requires students to pay tuition each term before classes begin. Students who have not paid their tuition are not allowed to enroll or to attend classes.

What journal entry do you think Bozeman College would use to record the receipt of the students' tuition payments? Describe the nature of each account in the entry.

CP 2-3 Record transactions

The following discussion took place between Tony Cork, the office manager of Hallmark Data Company, and a new accountant, Cassie Miles.

Cassie: I've been thinking about our method of recording entries. It seems that it's inefficient.

Tony: In what way?

Cassie: Well—correct me if I'm wrong—it seems like we have unnecessary steps in the process. We could easily develop a trial balance by posting our transactions directly into the ledger and bypassing the journal altogether. In this way, we could combine the recording and posting process into one step and save ourselves a lot of time. What do you think?

Tony: We need to have a talk.

What should Tony say to Cassie?

CP 2-4 Debits and credits

Group Project

The following excerpt is from a conversation between Kate Purvis, the president and chief operating officer of Light House Company, and her neighbor, Dot Evers.

Dot: Kate, I'm taking a course in night school, "Intro to Accounting." I was wondering—could you answer a couple of questions for me?

Kate: Well, I will if I can.

Dot: Okay, our instructor says that it's critical we understand the basic concepts of accounting, or we'll never get beyond the first test. My problem is with those rules of debit and credit . . . you know, assets increase with debits, decrease with credits, etc.

Kate: Yes, pretty basic stuff. You just have to memorize the rules. It shouldn't be too difficult.

Dot: Sure, I can memorize the rules, but my problem is I want to be sure I understand the basic concepts behind the rules. For example, why can't assets be increased with credits and decreased with debits like revenue? As long as everyone did it that way, why not? It would seem easier if we had the same rules for all increases and decreases in accounts. Also, why is the left side of an account called the debit side? Why couldn't it be called something simple . . . like the "LE" for Left Entry? The right side could be called just "RE" for Right Entry. Finally, why are there just two sides to an entry? Why can't there be three or four sides to an entry?

In a group of four or five, select one person to play the role of Kate and one person to play the role of Dot.

1. After listening to the conversation between Kate and Dot, help Kate answer Dot's questions.
2. What information (other than just debit and credit journal entries) could the accounting system gather that might be useful to Kate in managing Light House Company?

CP 2-5 Transactions and income statement

Cory Neece is planning to manage and operate Eagle Caddy Service at Canyon Lake Golf and Country Club during June through August 2014. Cory will rent a small maintenance building from the country club for $500 per month and will offer caddy services, including cart rentals, to golfers. Cory has had no formal training in record keeping.

Cory keeps notes of all receipts and expenses in a shoe box. An examination of Cory's shoe box records for June revealed the following:

June 1. Transferred $2,000 from personal bank account to be used to operate the caddy service.

1. Paid rent expense to Canyon Lake Golf and Country Club, $500.

2. Paid for golf supplies (practice balls, etc.), $750.

3. Arranged for the rental of 40 regular (pulling) golf carts and 20 gasoline-driven carts for $3,000 per month. Paid $600 in advance, with the remaining $2,400 due June 20.

7. Purchased supplies, including gasoline, for the golf carts on account, $1,000. Canyon Lake Golf and Country Club has agreed to allow Cory to store the gasoline in one of its fuel tanks at no cost.

15. Received cash for services from June 1–15, $5,400.

17. Paid cash to creditors on account, $1,000.

20. Paid remaining rental on golf carts, $2,400.

22. Purchased supplies, including gasoline, on account, $850.

25. Accepted IOUs from customers on account, $1,800.

28. Paid miscellaneous expenses, $395.

30. Received cash for services from June 16–30, $4,200.

30. Paid telephone and electricity (utilities) expenses, $340.

30. Paid wages of part-time employees, $850.

30. Received cash in payment of IOUs on account, $1,500.

30. Determined the amount of supplies on hand at the end of June, $675.

Cory has asked you several questions concerning his financial affairs to date, and he has asked you to assist with his record keeping and reporting of financial data.

a. To assist Cory with his record keeping, prepare a chart of accounts that would be appropriate for Eagle Caddy Service. *Note:* Small businesses such as Eagle Caddy Service are often organized as proprietorships. The accounting for proprietorships is similar to that for a corporation, except that the stockholders' equity accounts differ. Specifically, instead of the account for Capital Stock, a capital account entitled Cory Neece, Capital is used to record investments in the business. In addition, instead of a dividends account, withdrawals from the business are debited to Cory Neece, Drawing. A proprietorship has no retained earnings account.

b. Prepare an income statement for June in order to help Cory assess the profitability of Eagle Caddy Service. For this purpose, the use of T accounts may be helpful in analyzing the effects of each June transaction.

c. Based on Cory's records of receipts and payments, compute the amount of cash on hand on June 30. For this purpose, a T account for cash may be useful.

d. A count of the cash on hand on June 30 totaled $6,175. Briefly discuss the possible causes of the difference between the amount of cash computed in (c) and the actual amount of cash on hand.

CP 2-6 Opportunities for accountants

Internet Project

The increasing complexity of the current business and regulatory environment has created an increased demand for accountants who can analyze business transactions and interpret their effects on the financial statements. In addition, a basic ability to analyze the effects of transactions is necessary to be successful in all fields of business as well as in other disciplines, such as law. To better understand the importance of accounting in today's environment, search the Internet or your local newspaper for job opportunities. One possible Internet site is **http://www.careerbuilder.com.** Then do one of the following:

1. Print a listing of one or two ads for accounting jobs. Alternatively, bring to class one or two newspaper ads for accounting jobs.
2. Print a listing of one or two ads for nonaccounting jobs for which some knowledge of accounting is preferred or necessary. Alternatively, bring to class one or two newspaper ads for such jobs.

CHAPTER 3

COURTESY OF RHAPSODY INTERNATIONAL INC.

The Adjusting Process

Rhapsody

Do you subscribe to an Internet-based music service such as **Rhapsody®**? Rhapsody, which was formerly owned by **RealNetworks**, began by providing digital music to its subscribers through Internet audio streaming. You can subscribe to "Rhapsody Premier" for $9.99 per month and listen to music by New Boyz, Coldplay, Flo Rida, or Carrie Underwood.

When should a company such as Rhapsody record revenue from its subscriptions? Subscription revenue is recorded when it is earned. Subscriptions revenue is earned when the service has been delivered to the customer. However, in many cases cash is received before the service is delivered. For example, the subscription to "Rhapsody Premier" is paid at the beginning of the month. In this case, the cash received represents unearned revenue. As time passes and the services are delivered, the unearned revenue becomes earned, and thus becomes revenue.

As a result, companies like Rhapsody must update their accounting records for items such as unearned subscriptions before preparing their financial statements.

This chapter describes and illustrates the process by which companies update their accounting records before preparing financial statements. This discussion includes the adjustments for unearned revenues made at the end of the accounting period.

Learning Objectives

After studying this chapter, you should be able to:

	Example Exercises
OBJ 1 Describe the nature of the adjusting process.	
Nature of the Adjusting Process	
The Adjusting Process	EE 3-1
Types of Accounts Requiring Adjustment	EE 3-2
OBJ 2 Journalize entries for accounts requiring adjustment.	
Adjusting Entries	
Prepaid Expenses	EE 3-3
Unearned Revenues	EE 3-4
Accrued Revenues	EE 3-5
Accrued Expenses	EE 3-6
Depreciation Expense	EE 3-7
OBJ 3 Summarize the adjustment process.	
Summary of Adjustment Process	EE 3-8
OBJ 4 Prepare an adjusted trial balance.	
Adjusted Trial Balance	EE 3-9
OBJ 5 Describe and illustrate the use of vertical analysis in evaluating a company's performance and financial condition.	
Financial Analysis and Interpretation: Vertical Analysis	EE 3-10

At a Glance 3 Page 126

OBJ 1 Describe the nature of the adjusting process.

Nature of the Adjusting Process

When preparing financial statements, the economic life of the business is divided into time periods. This **accounting period concept** requires that revenues and expenses be reported in the proper period. To determine the proper period, accountants use generally accepted accounting principles (GAAP), which requires the **accrual basis of accounting**.

Under the accrual basis of accounting, revenues are reported on the income statement in the period in which they are earned. For example, revenue is reported when the services are provided to customers. Cash may or may not be received from customers during this period. The accounting concept supporting this reporting of revenues is called the **revenue recognition concept**.

Under the accrual basis, expenses are reported in the same period as the revenues to which they relate. For example, utility expenses incurred in December are reported as an expense and matched against December's revenues even though the utility bill may not be paid until January. The accounting concept supporting reporting revenues and related expenses in the same period is called the **matching concept**, or **matching principle**. By matching revenues and expenses, net income or loss for the period is properly reported on the income statement.

American Airlines uses the accrual basis of accounting. Revenues are recognized when passengers take flights, not when the passenger makes the reservation or pays for the ticket.

Although GAAP requires the accrual basis of accounting, some businesses use the **cash basis of accounting**. Under the cash basis of accounting, revenues and expenses are reported on the income statement in the period in which cash is received or paid. For example, fees are recorded when cash is received from clients; likewise, wages are recorded when cash is paid to employees. The net income (or net loss) is the difference between the cash receipts (revenues) and the cash payments (expenses).

Small service businesses may use the cash basis, because they have few receivables and payables. For example, attorneys, physicians, and real estate agents often use the cash basis. For them, the cash basis provides financial statements similar to those of the accrual basis. For most large businesses, however, the cash basis will not provide accurate financial statements for user needs. For this reason, the accrual basis is used in this text.

The Adjusting Process

At the end of the accounting period, many of the account balances in the ledger are reported in the financial statements without change. For example, the balances of the cash and land accounts are normally the amounts reported on the balance sheet.

Some accounts, however, require updating for the following reasons:[1]

1. Some expenses are not recorded daily. For example, the daily use of supplies would require many entries with small amounts. Also, the amount of supplies on hand on a day-to-day basis is normally not needed.
2. Some revenues and expenses are incurred as time passes rather than as separate transactions. For example, rent received in advance (unearned rent) expires and becomes revenue with the passage of time. Likewise, prepaid insurance expires and becomes an expense with the passage of time.
3. Some revenues and expenses may be unrecorded. For example, a company may have provided services to customers that it has not billed or recorded at the end of the accounting period. Likewise, a company may not pay its employees until the next accounting period even though the employees have earned their wages in the current period.

The analysis and updating of accounts at the end of the period before the financial statements are prepared is called the **adjusting process**. The journal entries that bring the accounts up to date at the end of the accounting period are called **adjusting entries**. All adjusting entries affect at least one income statement account and one balance sheet account. Thus, an adjusting entry will *always* involve a revenue or an expense account *and* an asset or a liability account.

Example Exercise 3-1 Accounts Requiring Adjustment

OBJ 1

Indicate with a *Yes* or *No* whether or not each of the following accounts normally requires an adjusting entry.

a. Cash
b. Prepaid Rent
c. Wages Expense
d. Land
e. Accounts Receivable
f. Unearned Rent

Follow My Example 3-1

a. No
b. Yes
c. Yes
d. No
e. Yes
f. Yes

Practice Exercises: **PE 3-1A, PE 3-1B**

Types of Accounts Requiring Adjustment

Four basic types of accounts require adjusting entries as shown below.

1. Prepaid expenses
2. Unearned revenues
3. Accrued revenues
4. Accrued expenses

Prepaid expenses are the advance payment of *future* expenses and are recorded as assets when cash is paid. Prepaid expenses become expenses over time or during normal operations. To illustrate, the following transaction of **NetSolutions** from Chapter 2 is used.

Dec. 1	NetSolutions paid $2,400 as a premium on a one-year insurance policy.

On December 1, the cash payment of $2,400 was recorded as a debit to Prepaid Insurance and credit to Cash for $2,400. At the end of December, only $200 ($2,400 divided

1 Under the cash basis of accounting, accounts do not require adjusting. This is because transactions are recorded only when cash is received or paid. Thus, the matching concept is not used under the cash basis.

by 12 months) of the insurance premium is expired and has become an expense. The remaining $2,200 of prepaid insurance will become an expense in future months. Thus, the $200 is insurance expense of December and should be recorded with an adjusting entry.

Other examples of prepaid expenses include supplies, prepaid advertising, and prepaid interest.

Exhibit 1 summarizes the nature of prepaid expenses.

EXHIBIT 1 **Prepaid Expenses**

Transaction *Cash is paid in advance for an expense.*

Analysis

Advance payments of future expenses are recorded as assets when the cash is paid. The transaction is recorded as a debit to a prepaid expense account and a credit to the cash account.

Journal Entry

		Prepaid Expense		XXX	
		Cash			XXX
		Paid an expense in advance.			

Accounting Equation Impact

Assets = Liabilities + Stockholders' Equity

Cash	
	XXX

Prepaid Expense	
XXX	

Adjustment *An end-of-period adjustment is needed to update the prepaid expense account.*

Analysis

The prepaid expense account is decreased (credited) for the amount of the prepaid expense that has expired or has been used, and the related expense account is increased (debited).

Adjusting Journal Entry

		Expense		XXX	
		Prepaid Expense			XXX
		Adjustment for prepaid expense.			

Accounting Equation Impact

Assets = Liabilities + Stockholders' Equity (Expense)

Prepaid Expense	
	XXX

Expense	
XXX	

Unearned revenues are the advance receipt of *future* revenues and are recorded as liabilities when cash is received. Unearned revenues become earned revenues over time or during normal operations. To illustrate, the following December 1 transaction of NetSolutions is used.

> Dec. 1 NetSolutions received $360 from a local retailer to rent land for three months.

On December 1, the cash receipt of $360 was recorded as a debit to Cash and a credit to Unearned Rent for $360. At the end of December, $120 ($360 divided by 3 months) of the unearned rent has been earned. The remaining $240 will become rent revenue in future months. Thus, the $120 is rent revenue of December and should be recorded with an adjusting entry.

Other examples of unearned revenues include tuition received in advance by a school, an annual retainer fee received by an attorney, premiums received in advance by an insurance company, and magazine subscriptions received in advance by a publisher.

Exhibit 2 summarizes the nature of unearned revenues.

EXHIBIT 2 **Unearned Revenues**

Cash is received for an unearned revenue. — **Transaction**

Analysis

Advance receipts for future services to be provided are recorded as liabilities when the cash is received. The transaction is recorded as a debit to the cash account and a credit to the unearned revenue account.

Journal Entry

	Debit	Credit
Cash	XXX	
Unearned Revenue		XXX
Received cash for unearned revenue.		

Accounting Equation Impact

Assets	=	Liabilities	+	Stockholders' Equity
Cash: XXX (debit)		Unearned Revenue: XXX (credit)		

An end-of-period adjustment is needed to update the unearned revenue account. — **Adjustment**

Analysis

The unearned revenue account is decreased (debited) for the amount of the revenue that has been earned, and the related revenue account is increased (credited).

Adjusting Journal Entry

	Debit	Credit
Unearned Revenue	XXX	
Revenue		XXX
Adjustment for unearned revenue.		

Accounting Equation Impact

Assets	=	Liabilities	+	Stockholders' Equity (Revenue)
		Unearned Revenue: XXX (debit)		Revenue: XXX (credit)

Accrued revenues are unrecorded revenues that have been earned and for which cash has yet to be received. Fees for services that an attorney or a doctor has provided but not yet billed are accrued revenues. To illustrate, the following example involving NetSolutions and one of its customers is used.

Dec. 15 NetSolutions signed an agreement with Dankner Co. under which NetSolutions will bill Dankner Co. on the fifteenth of each month for services rendered at the rate of $20 per hour.

From December 16–31, NetSolutions provided 25 hours of service to Dankner Co. Although the revenue of $500 (25 hours × $20) has been earned, it will not be billed until January 15. Likewise, cash of $500 will not be received until Dankner pays its bill. Thus, the $500 of accrued revenue and the $500 of fees earned should be recorded with an adjusting entry on December 31.

Other examples of accrued revenues include accrued interest on notes receivable and accrued rent on property rented to others.

Exhibit 3 summarizes the nature of accrued revenues.

EXHIBIT 3 **Accrued Revenues**

Transaction *Revenue has been earned but has not been recorded.*

Analysis

Revenues have been earned, but the revenue has not been recorded nor has cash been received. No journal entry has been recorded even though revenues have been earned.

Journal Entry

		No entry has been recorded.				

Accounting Equation Impact

Assets	=	Liabilities	+	Stockholders' Equity

No impact, since the revenue has not been recorded.

Adjustment *An end-of-period adjustment is needed to recognize accrued revenue.*

Analysis

An asset account is increased (debited) for the amount of the revenue that has been earned, and the related revenue account is increased (credited). The type of receivable account that is debited depends upon the type of revenue. For example, Accounts Receivable would be debited for fees earned. Interest Receivable would be debited for interest earned.

Adjusting Journal Entry

		Asset (Receivable)		XXX		
		Revenue			XXX	
		Adjustment for accrued revenue.				

Accounting Equation Impact

Assets	=	Liabilities	+	Stockholders' Equity (Revenue)

______ Receivable	
XXX	

Revenue	
	XXX

Accrued expenses are unrecorded expenses that have been incurred and for which cash has yet to be paid. Wages owed to employees at the end of a period but not yet paid are an accrued expense. To illustrate, the following example involving NetSolutions and its employees is used.

> Dec. 31 NetSolutions owes its employees wages of $250 for Monday and Tuesday, December 30 and 31.

NetSolutions paid wages of $950 on December 13 and $1,200 on December 27, 2013. These payments covered the biweekly pay periods that ended on those days. As of December 31, 2013, NetSolutions owes its employees wages of $250 for Monday and Tuesday, December 30 and 31. The wages of $250 will be paid on January 10, 2014; however, they are an expense of December. Thus, $250 of accrued wages should be recorded with an adjusting entry on December 31.

Other examples of accrued expenses include accrued interest on notes payable and accrued taxes.

Exhibit 4 summarizes the nature of accrued expenses.

EXHIBIT 4 **Accrued Expenses**

An expense has been incurred but has not been recorded. **Transaction**

Analysis

An expense has been incurred, but the expense has not been recorded nor has cash been paid. No journal entry has been recorded even though an expense has been incurred.

Journal Entry

			No entry has been recorded.				

Accounting Equation Impact

Assets = **Liabilities** + **Stockholders' Equity**

No impact, since the expense has not been recorded.

An end-of-period adjustment is needed to recognize the accrued expense. **Adjustment**

Analysis

An expense account is increased (debited) for the amount of the expense that has been incurred, and the related liability account is increased (credited). The liability account that is credited depends upon the type of expense. For example, Wages Payable would be credited for wages expense. Interest Payable would be credited for interest expense.

Adjusting Journal Entry

			Expense		XXX		
			Liability (Payable)			XXX	
			Adjustment for accrued expense.				

Accounting Equation Impact

Assets = **Liabilities** + **Stockholders' Equity (Expense)**

______ Payable	
	XXX

Expense	
XXX	

As illustrated in Exhibits 3 and 4, accrued revenues are earned revenues that are unrecorded. The cash receipts for accrued revenues are normally received in the next accounting period. Accrued expenses are expenses that have been incurred, but are unrecorded. The cash payments for accrued expenses are normally paid in the next accounting period.

Prepaid expenses and unearned revenues are sometimes referred to as *deferrals*. This is because the recording of the related expense or revenue is deferred to a future period. Accrued revenues and accrued expenses are sometimes referred to as *accruals*. This is because the related revenue or expense should be recorded or accrued in the current period.

Example Exercise 3-2 Type of Adjustment

OBJ 1

Classify the following items as (1) prepaid expense, (2) unearned revenue, (3) accrued expense, or (4) accrued revenue.

a. Wages owed but not yet paid.
b. Supplies on hand.
c. Fees received but not yet earned.
d. Fees earned but not yet received.

Follow My Example 3-2

a. Accrued expense
b. Prepaid expense
c. Unearned revenue
d. Accrued revenue

Practice Exercises: **PE 3-2A, PE 3-2B**

OBJ 2 Journalize entries for accounts requiring adjustment.

Adjusting Entries

To illustrate adjusting entries, the December 31, 2013, the unadjusted trial balance of NetSolutions, shown in Exhibit 5 is used. An expanded chart of accounts for NetSolutions is shown in Exhibit 6. The additional accounts used in this chapter are shown in color. The rules of debit and credit shown in Exhibit 3 of Chapter 2 are used to record the adjusting entries.

EXHIBIT 5

Unadjusted Trial Balance for NetSolutions

NetSolutions
Unadjusted Trial Balance
December 31, 2013

	Debit Balances	Credit Balances
Cash	2,065	
Accounts Receivable	2,220	
Supplies	2,000	
Prepaid Insurance	2,400	
Land	20,000	
Office Equipment	1,800	
Accounts Payable		900
Unearned Rent		360
Capital Stock		25,000
Dividends	4,000	
Fees Earned		16,340
Wages Expense	4,275	
Rent Expense	1,600	
Utilities Expense	985	
Supplies Expense	800	
Miscellaneous Expense	455	
	42,600	42,600

EXHIBIT 6

Expanded Chart of Accounts for NetSolutions

Balance Sheet Accounts

1. Assets
11 Cash
12 Accounts Receivable
14 Supplies
15 Prepaid Insurance
17 Land
18 Office Equipment
19 Accumulated Depreciation—Office Equipment

2. Liabilities
21 Accounts Payable
22 Wages Payable
23 Unearned Rent

3. Stockholders' Equity
31 Capital Stock
32 Retained Earnings
33 Dividends

Income Statement Accounts

4. Revenue
41 Fees Earned
42 Rent Revenue

5. Expenses
51 Wages Expense
52 Rent Expense
53 Depreciation Expense
54 Utilities Expense
55 Supplies Expense
56 Insurance Expense
59 Miscellaneous Expense

Prepaid Expenses

Supplies The December 31, 2013, unadjusted trial balance of NetSolutions indicates a balance in the supplies account of $2,000. In addition, the prepaid insurance account has a balance of $2,400. Each of these accounts requires an adjusting entry.

The balance in NetSolutions' supplies account on December 31 is $2,000. Some of these supplies (CDs, paper, envelopes, etc.) were used during December, and some are still on hand (not used). If either amount is known, the other can be determined. It is normally easier to determine the cost of the supplies on hand at the end of the month than to record daily supplies used.

Assuming that on December 31 the amount of supplies on hand is $760, the amount to be transferred from the asset account to the expense account is $1,240, computed as follows:

Supplies available during December (balance of account)	$2,000
Supplies on hand, December 31	760
Supplies used (amount of adjustment)	$1,240

At the end of December, the supplies expense account is increased (debited) for $1,240, and the supplies account is decreased (credited) for $1,240 to record the supplies used during December. The adjusting journal entry and T accounts for Supplies and Supplies Expense are as follows:

Journal *Page 5*

Date		Description	Post. Ref.	Debit	Credit
2013 Dec.	31	Supplies Expense	55	1,240	
		Supplies	14		1,240
		Supplies used ($2,000 – $760).			

Adjusting Journal Entry

Assets = Liabilities + Stockholders' Equity (Expense)

Supplies 14

Bal.	2,000	Dec. 31	1,240
Adj. Bal.	760		

Supplies Expense 55

Bal.	800	
Dec. 31	1,240	
Adj. Bal.	2,040	

Accounting Equation Impact

The adjusting entry is shown in color in the T accounts to separate it from other transactions. After the adjusting entry is recorded and posted, the supplies account has a debit balance of $760. This balance is an asset that will become an expense in a future period.

Prepaid Insurance The debit balance of $2,400 in NetSolutions' prepaid insurance account represents a December 1 prepayment of insurance for 12 months. At the end of December, the insurance expense account is increased (debited), and the prepaid insurance account is decreased (credited) by $200, the insurance for one month. The adjusting journal entry and T accounts for Prepaid Insurance and Insurance Expense are as follows:

	31	Insurance Expense	56	200	
		Prepaid Insurance	15		200
		Insurance expired ($2,400/12).			

Adjusting Journal Entry

Assets = Liabilities + Stockholders' Equity (Expense)

Prepaid Insurance 15

Bal.	2,400	Dec. 31	200
Adj. Bal.	2,200		

Insurance Expense 56

Dec. 31	200	

Accounting Equation Impact

After the adjusting entry is recorded and posted, the prepaid insurance account has a debit balance of $2,200. This balance is an asset that will become an expense in future periods. The insurance expense account has a debit balance of $200, which is an expense of the current period.

If the preceding adjustments for supplies ($1,240) and insurance ($200) are not recorded, the financial statements prepared as of December 31 will be misstated. On the income statement, Supplies Expense and Insurance Expense will be understated by a total of $1,440 ($1,240 + $200), and net income will be overstated by $1,440. On the balance sheet, Supplies and Prepaid Insurance will be overstated by a total of $1,440. Since net income increases retained earnings, stockholders' equity also will be overstated by $1,440 on the balance sheet. The effects of omitting these adjusting entries on the income statement and balance sheet are as follows:

		Amount of Misstatement	
Income Statement			
Revenues correctly stated		$ XXX	
Expenses understated by		(1,440)	
Net income overstated by	(1)	$1,440	
Balance Sheet			
Assets overstated by		$1,440	(2)
Liabilities correctly stated		$ XXX	
Stockholders' equity overstated by		1,440	
Total liabilities and stockholders' equity overstated by		$1,440	

Arrow (1) indicates the effect of the understated expenses on assets. Arrow (2) indicates the effect of the overstated net income on stockholders' equity.

Payments for prepaid expenses are sometimes made at the beginning of the period in which they will be *entirely used or consumed*. To illustrate, the following December 1 transaction of NetSolutions is used.

> Dec. 1 NetSolutions paid rent of $800 for the month.

On December 1, the rent payment of $800 represents Prepaid Rent. However, the Prepaid Rent expires daily, and at the end of December there will be no asset left. In such cases, the payment of $800 is recorded as Rent Expense rather than as Prepaid Rent. In this way, no adjusting entry is needed at the end of the period.[2]

Example Exercise 3-3 Adjustment for Prepaid Expense

OBJ 2

The prepaid insurance account had a beginning balance of $6,400 and was debited for $3,600 of premiums paid during the year. Journalize the adjusting entry required at the end of the year, assuming the amount of unexpired insurance related to future periods is $3,250.

Follow My Example 3-3

Insurance Expense	6,750	
Prepaid Insurance		6,750
Insurance expired ($6,400 + $3,600 – $3,250).		

Practice Exercises: **PE 3-3A, PE 3-3B**

Integrity, Objectivity, and Ethics in Business

FREE ISSUE

Office supplies are often available to employees on a "free issue" basis. This means that employees do not have to "sign" for the release of office supplies but merely obtain the necessary supplies from a local storage area as needed. Just because supplies are easily available, however, doesn't mean they can be taken for personal use. There are many instances where employees have been terminated for taking supplies home for personal use.

2 An alternative treatment of recording the cost of supplies, rent, and other prepayments of expenses is discussed in an appendix that can be downloaded from the book's companion Web site (**www.cengagebrain.com**).

Unearned Revenues

The December 31 unadjusted trial balance of NetSolutions indicates a balance in the unearned rent account of $360. This balance represents the receipt of three months' rent on December 1 for December, January, and February. At the end of December, one month's rent has been earned. Thus, the unearned rent account is decreased (debited) by $120, and the rent revenue account is increased (credited) by $120. The $120 represents the rental revenue for one month ($360/3). The adjusting journal entry and T accounts are shown below.

Adjusting Journal Entry

31	Unearned Rent	23	120	
	Rent Revenue	42		120
	Rent earned ($360/3 months).			

Accounting Equation Impact

Assets = **Liabilities** + **Stockholders' Equity (Revenue)**

Unearned Rent 23

Dec. 31	120	Bal.	360
		Adj. Bal.	240

Rent Revenue 42

		Dec. 31	120

After the adjusting entry is recorded and posted, the unearned rent account has a credit balance of $240. This balance is a liability that will become revenue in a future period. Rent Revenue has a balance of $120, which is revenue of the current period.[3]

If the preceding adjustment of unearned rent and rent revenue is not recorded, the financial statements prepared on December 31 will be misstated. On the income statement, Rent Revenue and the net income will be understated by $120. On the balance sheet, liabilities (Unearned Rent) will be overstated by $120, and stockholders' equity (Retained Earnings) will be understated by $120. The effects of omitting this adjusting entry are shown below.

Best Buy sells extended warranty contracts with terms between 12 and 36 months. The receipts from sales of these contracts are reported as unearned revenue on Best Buy's balance sheet. Revenue is recorded as the contracts expire.

	Amount of Misstatement
Income Statement	
Revenues understated by	$ (120)
Expenses correctly stated	XXX
Net income understated by	$ (120)
Balance Sheet	
Assets correctly stated	$ XXX
Liabilities overstated by	$ 120
Stockholders' equity understated by	(120)
Total liabilities and stockholders' equity correctly stated	$ XXX

Example Exercise 3-4 Adjustment for Unearned Revenue

OBJ 2

The balance in the unearned fees account, before adjustment at the end of the year, is $44,900. Journalize the adjusting entry required if the amount of unearned fees at the end of the year is $22,300.

Follow My Example 3-4

Unearned Fees	22,600	
Fees Earned		22,600
Fees earned ($44,900 – $22,300).		

Practice Exercises: **PE 3-4A, PE 3-4B**

3 An alternative treatment of recording revenues received in advance of their being earned is discussed in an appendix that can be downloaded from the book's companion Web site (**www.cengagebrain.com**).

RadioShack Corporation is engaged in consumer electronics retailing. RadioShack accrues revenue for finance charges and late payment charges related to its credit operations.

Accrued Revenues

During an accounting period, some revenues are recorded only when cash is received. Thus, at the end of an accounting period, there may be revenue that has been earned *but has not been recorded*. In such cases, the revenue is recorded by increasing (debiting) an asset account and increasing (crediting) a revenue account.

To illustrate, assume that NetSolutions signed an agreement with Dankner Co. on December 15. The agreement provides that NetSolutions will answer computer questions and render assistance to Dankner Co.'s employees. The services will be billed to Dankner Co. on the fifteenth of each month at a rate of $20 per hour. As of December 31, NetSolutions had provided 25 hours of assistance to Dankner Co. The revenue of $500 (25 hours × $20) will be billed on January 15. However, NetSolutions earned the revenue in December.

The claim against the customer for payment of the $500 is an account receivable (*an asset*). Thus, the accounts receivable account is increased (debited) by $500, and the fees earned account is increased (credited) by $500. The adjusting journal entry and T accounts are shown below.

Adjusting Journal Entry

	31	Accounts Receivable	12	500	
		Fees Earned	41		500
		Accrued fees (25 hrs. × $20).			

Accounting Equation Impact

Assets = Liabilities + Stockholders' Equity (Revenue)

Accounts Receivable 12

Bal.	2,220	
Dec. 31	500	
Adj. Bal.	2,750	

Fees Earned 41

	Bal.	16,340
	Dec. 31	500
	Adj. Bal.	16,840

If the adjustment for the accrued revenue ($500) is not recorded, Fees Earned and the net income will be understated by $500 on the income statement. On the balance sheet, assets (Accounts Receivable) and stockholders' equity (Retained Earnings) will be understated by $500. The effects of omitting this adjusting entry are shown below.

	Amount of Misstatement
Income Statement	
Revenues understated by	$ (500)
Expenses correctly stated	XXX
Net income understated by	$ (500)
Balance Sheet	
Assets understated by	$ (500)
Liabilities correctly stated	$ XXX
Stockholders' equity understated by	(500)
Total liabilities and stockholders' equity understated by	$ (500)

Example Exercise 3-5 Adjustment for Accrued Revenues (OBJ 2)

At the end of the current year, $13,680 of fees have been earned but have not been billed to clients. Journalize the adjusting entry to record the accrued fees.

Follow My Example 3-5

Accounts Receivable	13,680	
Fees Earned		13,680
Accrued fees.		

Practice Exercises: **PE 3-5A, PE 3-5B**

Accrued Expenses

Some types of services used in earning revenues are paid for *after* the service has been performed. For example, wages expense is used hour by hour, but is paid only daily, weekly, biweekly, or monthly. At the end of the accounting period, the amount of such *accrued* but unpaid items is an expense and a liability.

For example, if the last day of the employees' pay period is not the last day of the accounting period, an accrued expense (wages expense) and the related liability (wages payable) must be recorded by an adjusting entry. This adjusting entry is necessary so that expenses are properly matched to the period in which they were incurred in earning revenue.

To illustrate, NetSolutions pays its employees biweekly. During December, NetSolutions paid wages of $950 on December 13 and $1,200 on December 27. These payments covered pay periods ending on those days as shown in Exhibit 7.

EXHIBIT 7

Accrued Wages

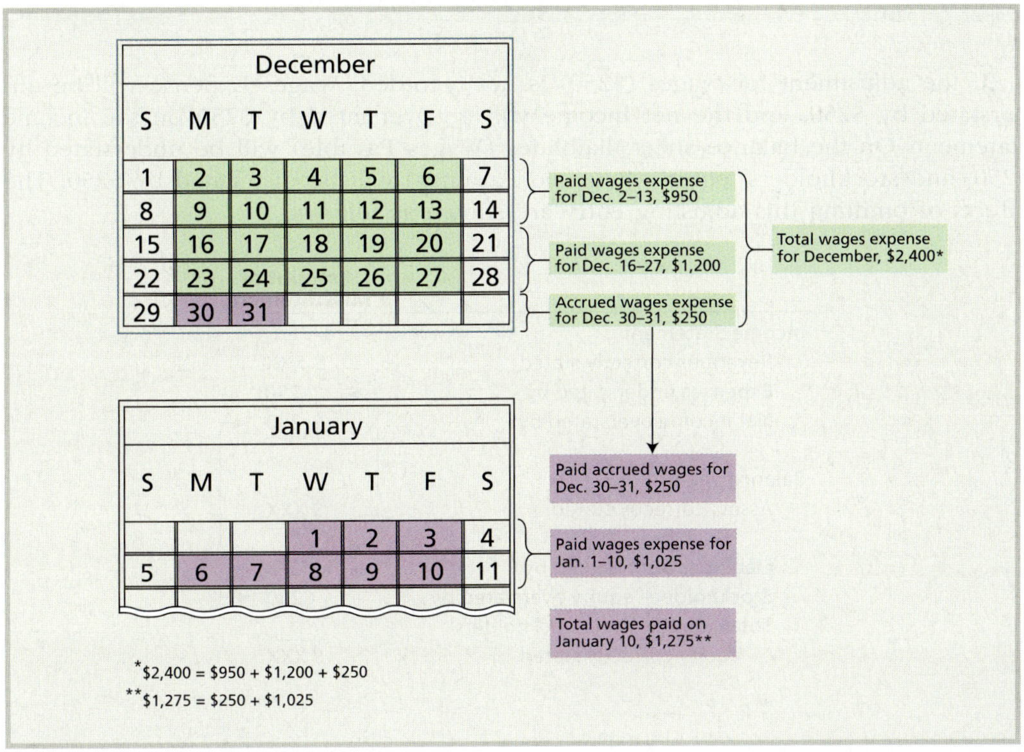

As of December 31, NetSolutions owes $250 of wages to employees for Monday and Tuesday, December 30 and 31. Thus, the wages expense account is increased (debited) by $250 and the wages payable account is increased (credited) by $250. The adjusting journal entry and T accounts are shown below.

Adjusting Journal Entry

	31	Wages Expense	51	250	
		Wages Payable	22		250
		Accrued wages.			

Accounting Equation Impact

Assets = Liabilities + Stockholders' Equity (Expense)

Wages Payable			22
		Dec. 31	250

Wages Expense			51
Bal.	4,275		
Dec. 31	250		
Adj. Bal.	4,525		

Callaway Golf Company, a manufacturer of such innovative golf clubs as the "RAZR Hawk" driver, reports accrued warranty expense on its balance sheet.

After the adjusting entry is recorded and posted, the debit balance of the wages expense account is $4,525. This balance of $4,525 is the wages expense for two months, November and December. The credit balance of $250 in Wages Payable is the liability for wages owed on December 31.

As shown in Exhibit 7, NetSolutions paid wages of $1,275 on January 10. This payment includes the $250 of accrued wages recorded on December 31. Thus, on January 10, the wages payable account is decreased (debited) by $250. Also, the wages expense account is increased (debited) by $1,025 ($1,275 − $250), which is the wages expense for January 1–10. Finally, the cash account is decreased (credited) by $1,275. The journal entry for the payment of wages on January 10 is shown below.[4]

Jan.	10	Wages Expense	51	1,025	
		Wages Payable	22	250	
		Cash	11		1,275

If the adjustment for wages ($250) is not recorded, Wages Expense will be understated by $250, and the net income will be overstated by $250 on the income statement. On the balance sheet, liabilities (Wages Payable) will be understated by $250, and stockholders' equity (Retained Earnings) will be overstated by $250. The effects of omitting this adjusting entry are shown as follows:

	Amount of Misstatement
Income Statement	
Revenues correctly stated	$ XXX
Expenses understated by	(250)
Net income overstated by	$ 250
Balance Sheet	
Assets correctly stated	$ XXX
Liabilities understated by	$ (250)
Stockholders' equity overstated by	250
Total liabilities and stockholders' equity correctly stated	$ XXX

Example Exercise 3-6 Adjustment for Accrued Expense

OBJ 2

Sanregret Realty Co. pays weekly salaries of $12,500 on Friday for a five-day week ending on that day. Journalize the necessary adjusting entry at the end of the accounting period, assuming that the period ends on Thursday.

Follow My Example 3-6

Salaries Expense	10,000	
Salaries Payable		10,000
Accrued salaries [($12,500/5 days) × 4 days].		

Practice Exercises: **PE 3-6A, PE 3-6B**

4 To simplify the subsequent recording of the following period's transactions, some accountants use what is known as reversing entries for certain types of adjustments. Reversing entries are discussed and illustrated in Appendix D, which is available on the product website at www.cengagebrain.com.

Business Connection

FORD MOTOR COMPANY WARRANTIES

Ford Motor Company provides warranties on the vehicles that it sells. For example, Ford offers "bumper-to-bumper" coverage in the United States for five years or 60,000 miles on its Ford brand. A bumper-to-bumper warranty normally implies that every part of a new car will be repaired or replaced if it is defective during the term of the warranty.

When Ford sells a new car, it estimates the future warranty costs that it will incur on the vehicle and accrues a warranty expense. Accruals for estimated warranty costs are based on historical warranty claim experience, which is adjusted for changes such as offering new types of vehicles. For example, Ford adjusted its warranty costs when it began selling its new fuel efficient Ford Escape Hybrid. The Ford Escape Hybrid has a gas-electric engine that automatically shuts off when the vehicle is stopped. The Escape also uses an electric motor to assist in accelerating or when the vehicle is coasting or slowing down.

Ford's warranty cost accruals (in millions) for two recent years are as follows:

	Recent Year	Prior Year
Beginning balance	$ 3,147	$ 3,239
Payments during the year	(2,176)	(2,484)
Warranties issued during year	1,522	1,652
Other	153	740
Ending balance of accrued warranties	$ 2,646	$ 3,147

Depreciation Expense

Fixed assets, or **plant assets**, are physical resources that are owned and used by a business and are permanent or have a long life. Examples of fixed assets include land, buildings, and equipment. In a sense, fixed assets are a type of *long-term* prepaid expense. However, because of their unique nature and long life, they are discussed separately from other prepaid expenses.

Fixed assets, such as office equipment, are used to generate revenue much like supplies are used to generate revenue. Unlike supplies, however, there is no visible reduction in the quantity of the equipment. Instead, as time passes, the equipment loses its ability to provide useful services. This decrease in usefulness is called **depreciation**.

All fixed assets, except land, lose their usefulness and, thus, are said to **depreciate**. As a fixed asset depreciates, a portion of its cost should be recorded as an expense. This periodic expense is called **depreciation expense**.

The adjusting entry to record depreciation expense is similar to the adjusting entry for supplies used. The depreciation expense account is increased (debited) for the amount of depreciation. However, the fixed asset account is not decreased (credited). This is because both the original cost of a fixed asset and the depreciation recorded since its purchase are reported on the balance sheet. Instead, an account entitled **Accumulated Depreciation** is increased (credited).

Accumulated depreciation accounts are called **contra accounts**, or **contra asset accounts**. This is because accumulated depreciation accounts are deducted from their related fixed asset accounts on the balance sheet. The normal balance of a contra account is opposite to the account from which it is deducted. Since the normal balance of a fixed asset account is a debit, the normal balance of an accumulated depreciation account is a credit.

Lowe's Companies, Inc., reported land, buildings, and store equipment at a cost of $33,345 million and accumulated depreciation of $11,256 million.

The normal titles for fixed asset accounts and their related contra asset accounts are as follows:

Fixed Asset Account	Contra Asset Account
Land	None—Land is not depreciated.
Buildings	Accumulated Depreciation—Buildings
Store Equipment	Accumulated Depreciation—Store Equipment
Office Equipment	Accumulated Depreciation—Office Equipment

The December 31, 2013, unadjusted trial balance of NetSolutions (Exhibit 5) indicates that NetSolutions owns two fixed assets: land and office equipment. Land does not depreciate; however, an adjusting entry is recorded for the depreciation of the office equipment for December. Assume that the office equipment depreciates $50 during December. The depreciation expense account is increased (debited) by $50, and the accumulated depreciation—office equipment account is increased (credited) by $50.[5] The adjusting journal entry and T accounts are shown below.

Adjusting Journal Entry

	31	Depreciation Expense	53	50	
		Accumulated Depreciation—Office Equip.	19		50
		Depreciation on office equipment.			

Accounting Equation Impact

Assets = Liabilities + Stockholders' Equity (Expense)

Office Equipment	**18**
Bal. 1,800	

Accumulated Depr.—Office Equip.	**19**
	Dec. 31 50

Depreciation Expense	**53**
Dec. 31 50	

After the adjusting journal entry is recorded and posted, the office equipment account still has a debit balance of $1,800. This is the original cost of the office equipment that was purchased on December 4. The accumulated depreciation—office equipment account has a credit balance of $50. The difference between these two balances is the cost of the office equipment that has not yet been depreciated. This amount, called the **book value of the asset** (or **net book value**), is computed as shown below.

Book Value of Asset = Cost of the Asset – Accumulated Depreciation of Asset
Book Value of Office Equipment = Cost of Office Equipment – Accumulated Depr. of Office Equipment
Book Value of Office Equipment = $1,800 – $50
Book Value of Office Equipment = $1,750

The office equipment and its related accumulated depreciation are reported on the December 31, 2013, balance sheet as follows:

Office equipment	$1,800	
Less accumulated depreciation	50	$1,750

The market value of a fixed asset usually differs from its book value. This is because depreciation is an *allocation* method, not a *valuation* method. That is, depreciation allocates the cost of a fixed asset to expense over its estimated life. Depreciation does not measure changes in market values, which vary from year to year. Thus, on December 31, 2013, the market value of NetSolutions' office equipment could be more or less than $1,750.

If the adjustment for depreciation ($50) is not recorded, Depreciation Expense on the income statement will be understated by $50, and the net income will be overstated by $50. On the balance sheet, assets (the book value of Office Equipment) and stockholders' equity (Retained Earnings) will be overstated by $50. The effects of omitting the adjustment for depreciation are shown on the next page.

5 Methods of computing depreciation expense are described and illustrated in Chapter 9.

	Amount of Misstatement
Income Statement	
Revenues correctly stated	$ XX
Expenses understated by	(50)
Net income overstated by	$ 50
Balance Sheet	
Assets overstated by	$ 50
Liabilities correctly stated	$ XX
Stockholders' equity overstated by	50
Total liabilities and stockholders' equity overstated by	$ 50

***Example Exercise* 3-7 Adjustment for Depreciation** (OBJ 2)

The estimated amount of depreciation on equipment for the current year is $4,250. Journalize the adjusting entry to record the depreciation.

Follow My Example 3-7

Depreciation Expense	4,250	
Accumulated Depreciation—Equipment		4,250
Depreciation on equipment.		

Practice Exercises: **PE 3-7A, PE 3-7B**

Summary of Adjustment Process

OBJ 3 Summarize the adjustment process.

A summary of the basic types of adjusting entries is shown in Exhibit 8 on page 120. The adjusting entries for NetSolutions are shown in Exhibit 9 on page 121. The adjusting entries are dated as of the last day of the period. However, because collecting the adjustment data requires time, the entries are usually recorded at a later date. An explanation is normally included with each adjusting entry.

NetSolutions' adjusting entries are posted to the ledger shown in Exhibit 10 on pages 122–123. The adjustments are shown in color in Exhibit 10 to distinguish them from other transactions.

***Example Exercise* 3-8 Effect of Omitting Adjustments** (OBJ 3)

For the year ending December 31, 2014, Mann Medical Co. mistakenly omitted adjusting entries for (1) $8,600 of unearned revenue that was earned, (2) earned revenue of $12,500 that was not billed, and (3) accrued wages of $2,900. Indicate the combined effect of the errors on (a) revenues, (b) expenses, and (c) net income for the year ended December 31, 2014.

Follow My Example 3-8

a. Revenues were understated by $21,100 ($8,600 + $12,500).
b. Expenses were understated by $2,900.
c. Net income was understated by $18,200 ($8,600 + $12,500 − $2,900).

Practice Exercises: **PE 3-8A, PE 3-8B**

Key Terms

accounting period concept (104)
accrual basis of accounting (104)
accrued expenses (108)
accrued revenues (107)
Accumulated Depreciation (117)
adjusted trial balance (123)
adjusting entries (105)
adjusting process (105)
book value of the asset (or net book value) (118)
cash basis of accounting (104)
contra accounts (or contra asset accounts) (117)
depreciate (117)
depreciation (117)
depreciation expense (117)
fixed assets (or plant assets) (117)
matching concept (or matching principle) (104)
prepaid expenses (105)
revenue recognition concept (104)
unearned revenues (106)
vertical analysis (124)

Illustrative Problem

Three years ago, T. Roderick organized Harbor Realty. At July 31, 2014, the end of the current year, the unadjusted trial balance of Harbor Realty appears as shown below.

Harbor Realty
Unadjusted Trial Balance
July 31, 2014

	Debit Balances	Credit Balances
Cash	3,425	
Accounts Receivable	7,000	
Supplies	1,270	
Prepaid Insurance	620	
Office Equipment	51,650	
Accumulated Depreciation—Office Equipment		9,700
Accounts Payable		925
Wages Payable		0
Unearned Fees		1,250
Capital Stock		5,000
Retained Earnings		24,000
Dividends	5,200	
Fees Earned		59,125
Wages Expense	22,415	
Depreciation Expense	0	
Rent Expense	4,200	
Utilities Expense	2,715	
Supplies Expense	0	
Insurance Expense	0	
Miscellaneous Expense	1,505	
	100,000	100,000

The data needed to determine year-end adjustments are as follows:

a. Supplies on hand at July 31, 2014, $380.

b. Insurance premiums expired during the year, $315.

c. Depreciation of equipment during the year, $4,950.

d. Wages accrued but not paid at July 31, 2014, $440.

e. Accrued fees earned but not recorded at July 31, 2014, $1,000.

f. Unearned fees on July 31, 2014, $750.

Instructions

1. Prepare the necessary adjusting journal entries. Include journal entry explanations.
2. Determine the balance of the accounts affected by the adjusting entries, and prepare an adjusted trial balance.

Solution

1.

Journal

Date		Description	Post. Ref.	Debit	Credit
2014 July	31	Supplies Expense		890	
		Supplies			890
		Supplies used ($1,270 – $380).			
	31	Insurance Expense		315	
		Prepaid Insurance			315
		Insurance expired.			
	31	Depreciation Expense		4,950	
		Accumulated Depreciation—Office Equipment			4,950
		Depreciation expense.			
	31	Wages Expense		440	
		Wages Payable			440
		Accrued wages.			
	31	Accounts Receivable		1,000	
		Fees Earned			1,000
		Accrued fees.			
	31	Unearned Fees		500	
		Fees Earned			500
		Fees earned ($1,250 – $750).			

Solution (concluded)

2.

Harbor Realty
Adjusted Trial Balance
July 31, 2014

	Debit Balances	Credit Balances
Cash	3,425	
Accounts Receivable	8,000	
Supplies	380	
Prepaid Insurance	305	
Office Equipment	51,650	
Accumulated Depreciation—Office Equipment		14,650
Accounts Payable		925
Wages Payable		440
Unearned Fees		750
Capital Stock		5,000
Retained Earnings		24,000
Dividends	5,200	
Fees Earned		60,625
Wages Expense	22,855	
Depreciation Expense	4,950	
Rent Expense	4,200	
Utilities Expense	2,715	
Supplies Expense	890	
Insurance Expense	315	
Miscellaneous Expense	1,505	
	106,390	106,390

Discussion Questions

1. How are revenues and expenses reported on the income statement under (a) the cash basis of accounting and (b) the accrual basis of accounting?
2. Is the matching concept related to (a) the cash basis of accounting or (b) the accrual basis of accounting?
3. Why are adjusting entries needed at the end of an accounting period?
4. What is the difference between *adjusting entries* and *correcting entries*?
5. Identify the four different categories of adjusting entries frequently required at the end of an accounting period.
6. If the effect of the debit portion of an adjusting entry is to increase the balance of an asset account, which of the following statements describes the effect of the credit portion of the entry?
   a. Increases the balance of a revenue account.
   b. Increases the balance of an expense account.
   c. Increases the balance of a liability account.
7. If the effect of the credit portion of an adjusting entry is to increase the balance of a liability account, which of the following statements describes the effect of the debit portion of the entry?
   a. Increases the balance of a revenue account.
   b. Increases the balance of an expense account.
   c. Increases the balance of an asset account.
8. Does every adjusting entry have an effect on determining the amount of net income for a period? Explain.
9. On November 1 of the current year, a business paid the November rent on the building that it occupies. (a) Do the rights acquired at November 1 represent an asset or an expense? (b) What is the justification for debiting Rent Expense at the time of payment?
10. (a) Explain the purpose of the two accounts: Depreciation Expense and Accumulated Depreciation. (b) What is the normal balance of each account? (c) Is it customary for the balances of the two accounts to be equal in amount? (d) In what financial statements, if any, will each account appear?

Practice Exercises

Example Exercises

EE 3-1 *p. 105*

PE 3-1A Accounts requiring adjustment **OBJ. 1**

Indicate with a Yes or No whether or not each of the following accounts normally requires an adjusting entry.

a. Accumulated Depreciation
b. Dividends
c. Land
d. Salaries Payable
e. Supplies
f. Unearned Rent

EE 3-1 *p. 105*

PE 3-1B Accounts requiring adjustment **OBJ. 1**

Indicate with a Yes or No whether or not each of the following accounts normally requires an adjusting entry.

a. Building
b. Cash
c. Interest Expense
d. Miscellaneous Expense
e. Capital Stock
f. Prepaid Insurance

EE 3-2 *p. 109*

PE 3-2A Type of adjustment **OBJ. 1**

Classify the following items as (1) prepaid expense, (2) unearned revenue, (3) accrued revenue, or (4) accrued expense.

a. Cash received for services not yet rendered
b. Insurance paid for the next year
c. Rent revenue earned but not received
d. Salaries owed but not yet paid

EE 3-2 *p. 109*

PE 3-2B Type of adjustment **OBJ. 1**

Classify the following items as (1) prepaid expense, (2) unearned revenue, (3) accrued revenue, or (4) accrued expense.

a. Cash received for use of land next month
b. Fees earned but not received
c. Rent expense owed but not yet paid
d. Supplies on hand

EE 3-3 *p. 112*

PE 3-3A Adjustment for prepaid expense **OBJ. 2**

The supplies account had a beginning balance of $1,975 and was debited for $4,125 for supplies purchased during the year. Journalize the adjusting entry required at the end of the year, assuming the amount of supplies on hand is $1,850.

EE 3-3 *p. 112*

PE 3-3B Adjustment for prepaid expense **OBJ. 2**

The prepaid insurance account had a beginning balance of $9,600 and was debited for $12,900 of premiums paid during the year. Journalize the adjusting entry required at the end of the year, assuming the amount of unexpired insurance related to future periods is $7,360.

EE 3-4 *p. 113*

PE 3-4A Adjustment for unearned revenue **OBJ. 2**

The balance in the unearned fees account, before adjustment at the end of the year, is $78,500. Journalize the adjusting entry required, assuming the amount of unearned fees at the end of the year is $33,675.

EE 3-4 *p. 113*

PE 3-4B Adjustment for unearned revenue **OBJ. 2**

On June 1, 2014, Herbal Co. received $18,900 for the rent of land for 12 months. Journalize the adjusting entry required for unearned rent on December 31, 2014.

EE 3-5 *p. 114*

PE 3-5A Adjustment for accrued revenues **OBJ. 2**

At the end of the current year, $12,840 of fees have been earned but have not been billed to clients. Journalize the adjusting entry to record the accrued fees.

EE 3-5 *p. 114*

PE 3-5B Adjustment for accrued revenues **OBJ. 2**

At the end of the current year, $17,555 of fees have been earned but have not been billed to clients. Journalize the adjusting entry to record the accrued fees.

Example Exercises

EE 3-6 *p. 116*

PE 3-6A Adjustment for accrued expense **OBJ. 2**

Connect Realty Co. pays weekly salaries of $16,250 on Friday for a five-day workweek ending on that day. Journalize the necessary adjusting entry at the end of the accounting period, assuming that the period ends on Wednesday.

EE 3-6 *p. 116*

PE 3-6B Adjustment for accrued expense **OBJ. 2**

Prospect Realty Co. pays weekly salaries of $27,600 on Monday for a six-day workweek ending the preceding Saturday. Journalize the necessary adjusting entry at the end of the accounting period, assuming that the period ends on Friday.

EE 3-7 *p. 119*

PE 3-7A Adjustment for depreciation **OBJ. 2**

The estimated amount of depreciation on equipment for the current year is $9,100. Journalize the adjusting entry to record the depreciation.

EE 3-7 *p. 119*

PE 3-7B Adjustment for depreciation **OBJ. 2**

The estimated amount of depreciation on equipment for the current year is $7,700. Journalize the adjusting entry to record the depreciation.

EE 3-8 *p. 119*

PE 3-8A Effect of omitting adjustments **OBJ. 3**

For the year ending August 31, 2014, Mammalia Medical Co. mistakenly omitted adjusting entries for (1) depreciation of $5,800, (2) fees earned that were not billed of $44,500, and (3) accrued wages of $7,300. Indicate the combined effect of the errors on (a) revenues, (b) expenses, and (c) net income for the year ended August 31, 2014.

EE 3-8 *p. 119*

PE 3-8B Effect of omitting adjustments **OBJ. 3**

For the year ending April 30, 2014, Urology Medical Services Co. mistakenly omitted adjusting entries for (1) $1,400 of supplies that were used, (2) unearned revenue of $6,600 that was earned, and (3) insurance of $9,000 that expired. Indicate the combined effect of the errors on (a) revenues, (b) expenses, and (c) net income for the year ended April 30, 2014.

EE 3-9 *p. 124*

PE 3-9A Effect of errors on adjusted trial balance **OBJ. 4**

For each of the following errors, considered individually, indicate whether the error would cause the adjusted trial balance totals to be unequal. If the error would cause the adjusted trial balance totals to be unequal, indicate whether the debit or credit total is higher and by how much.

a. The adjustment of $9,800 for accrued fees earned was journalized as a debit to Accounts Receivable for $9,800 and a credit to Fees Earned for $8,900.

b. The adjustment of depreciation of $3,600 was omitted from the end-of-period adjusting entries.

EE 3-9 *p. 124*

PE 3-9B Effect of errors on adjusted trial balance **OBJ. 4**

For each of the following errors, considered individually, indicate whether the error would cause the adjusted trial balance totals to be unequal. If the error would cause the adjusted trial balance totals to be unequal, indicate whether the debit or credit total is higher and by how much.

a. The adjustment for accrued wages of $5,200 was journalized as a debit to Wages Expense for $5,200 and a credit to Accounts Payable for $5,200.

b. The entry for $1,125 of supplies used during the period was journalized as a debit to Supplies Expense of $1,125 and a credit to Supplies of $1,152.

Example Exercises

EE 3-10 *p. 126*

F·A·I

PE 3-10A Vertical analysis

OBJ. 5

Two income statements for Hemlock Company are shown below.

Hemlock Company
Income Statements
For Years Ended December 31

	2014	**2013**
Fees earned	$725,000	$615,000
Operating expenses	435,000	356,700
Operating income	$290,000	$258,300

a. Prepare a vertical analysis of Hemlock Company's income statements.

b. Does the vertical analysis indicate a favorable or an unfavorable trend?

EE 3-10 *p. 126*

F·A·I

PE 3-10B Vertical analysis

OBJ. 5

Two income statements for Cornea Company are shown below.

Cornea Company
Income Statements
For Years Ended December 31

	2014	**2013**
Fees earned	$1,640,000	$1,300,000
Operating expenses	869,200	715,000
Operating income	$ 770,800	$ 585,000

a. Prepare a vertical analysis of Cornea Company's income statements.

b. Does the vertical analysis indicate a favorable or an unfavorable trend?

Exercises

EX 3-1 Classifying types of adjustments

OBJ. 1

Classify the following items as (a) prepaid expense, (b) unearned revenue, (c) accrued revenue, or (d) accrued expense.

1. A three-year premium paid on a fire insurance policy.
2. Fees earned but not yet received.
3. Fees received but not yet earned.
4. Salary owed but not yet paid.
5. Subscriptions received in advance by a magazine publisher.
6. Supplies on hand.
7. Taxes owed but payable in the following period.
8. Utilities owed but not yet paid.

EX 3-2 Classifying adjusting entries

OBJ. 1

The following accounts were taken from the unadjusted trial balance of Orion Co., a congressional lobbying firm. Indicate whether or not each account would normally require an adjusting entry. If the account normally requires an adjusting entry, use the following notation to indicate the type of adjustment:

AE—Accrued Expense
AR—Accrued Revenue
PE—Prepaid Expense
UR—Unearned Revenue

(Continued)

To illustrate, the answer for the first account is shown below.

Account	Answer
Accounts Receivable	Normally requires adjustment (AR).
Capital Stock	
Cash	
Interest Expense	
Interest Receivable	
Land	
Office Equipment	
Prepaid Rent	
Supplies	
Unearned Fees	
Wages Expense	

EX 3-3 Adjusting entry for supplies **OBJ. 2**

The balance in the supplies account, before adjustment at the end of the year, is $2,389. Journalize the adjusting entry required if the amount of supplies on hand at the end of the year is $830.

EX 3-4 Determining supplies purchased **OBJ. 2**

The supplies and supplies expense accounts at December 31, after adjusting entries have been posted at the end of the first year of operations, are shown in the following T accounts:

Supplies			Supplies Expense		
Bal.	1,560		Bal.	4,250	

Determine the amount of supplies purchased during the year.

EX 3-5 Effect of omitting adjusting entry **OBJ. 2, 3**

At March 31, the end of the first month of operations, the usual adjusting entry transferring prepaid insurance expired to an expense account is omitted. Which items will be incorrectly stated, because of the error, on (a) the income statement for March and (b) the balance sheet as of March 31? Also indicate whether the items in error will be overstated or understated.

EX 3-6 Adjusting entries for prepaid insurance **OBJ. 2**

The balance in the prepaid insurance account, before adjustment at the end of the year, is $21,700. Journalize the adjusting entry required under each of the following *alternatives* for determining the amount of the adjustment: (a) the amount of insurance expired during the year is $16,450; (b) the amount of unexpired insurance applicable to future periods is $5,250.

EX 3-7 Adjusting entries for prepaid insurance **OBJ. 2**

The prepaid insurance account had a balance of $12,000 at the beginning of the year. The account was debited for $18,000 for premiums on policies purchased during the year. Journalize the adjusting entry required at the end of the year for each of the following situations: (a) the amount of unexpired insurance applicable to future periods is $13,600; (b) the amount of insurance expired during the year is $16,400.

EX 3-8 Adjusting entries for unearned fees **OBJ. 2**

The balance in the unearned fees account, before adjustment at the end of the year, is $37,500. Journalize the adjusting entry required if the amount of unearned fees at the end of the year is $12,300.

EX 3-9 Effect of omitting adjusting entry **OBJ. 2, 3**

At the end of July, the first month of the business year, the usual adjusting entry transferring rent earned to a revenue account from the unearned rent account was omitted. Indicate which items will be incorrectly stated, because of the error, on (a) the income statement for July and (b) the balance sheet as of July 31. Also indicate whether the items in error will be overstated or understated.

EX 3-10 Adjusting entry for accrued fees **OBJ. 2**

At the end of the current year, $8,450 of fees have been earned but have not been billed to clients.

a. Journalize the adjusting entry to record the accrued fees.

b. If the cash basis rather than the accrual basis had been used, would an adjusting entry have been necessary? Explain.

EX 3-11 Adjusting entries for unearned and accrued fees **OBJ. 2**

The balance in the unearned fees account, before adjustment at the end of the year, is $112,000. Of these fees, $71,600 have been earned. In addition, $47,400 of fees have been earned but have not been billed. Journalize the adjusting entries (a) to adjust the unearned fees account and (b) to record the accrued fees.

EX 3-12 Effect of omitting adjusting entry **OBJ. 2, 3**

The adjusting entry for accrued fees was omitted at October 31, the end of the current year. Indicate which items will be in error, because of the omission, on (a) the income statement for the current year and (b) the balance sheet as of October 31. Also indicate whether the items in error will be overstated or understated.

EX 3-13 Adjusting entries for accrued salaries **OBJ. 2**

✔ a. Amount of entry: $7,050

Ocular Realty Co. pays weekly salaries of $11,750 on Friday for a five-day workweek ending on that day. Journalize the necessary adjusting entry at the end of the accounting period, assuming that the period ends (a) on Wednesday and (b) on Thursday.

EX 3-14 Determining wages paid **OBJ. 2**

The wages payable and wages expense accounts at May 31, after adjusting entries have been posted at the end of the first month of operations, are shown in the following T accounts:

Wages Payable			Wages Expense		
	Bal.	7,175	Bal.	73,250	

Determine the amount of wages paid during the month.

EX 3-15 Effect of omitting adjusting entry **OBJ. 2, 3**

Accrued salaries owed to employees for October 30 and 31 are not considered in preparing the financial statements for the year ended October 31. Indicate which items will be erroneously stated, because of the error, on (a) the income statement for the year and (b) the balance sheet as of October 31. Also indicate whether the items in error will be overstated or understated.

EX 3-16 Effect of omitting adjusting entry **OBJ. 2, 3**

Assume that the error in Exercise 3-15 was not corrected and that the accrued salaries were included in the first salary payment in November. Indicate which items will be erroneously stated, because of failure to correct the initial error, on (a) the income statement for the month of November and (b) the balance sheet as of November 30.

EX 3-17 Adjusting entries for prepaid and accrued taxes **OBJ. 2**

✔ b. $71,400

Diamond Services was organized on April 1 of the current year. On April 2, Diamond Services prepaid $28,800 to the city for taxes (license fees) for the *next* 12 months and debited the prepaid taxes account. Diamond Services is also required to pay in January an annual tax (on property) for the *previous* calendar year. The estimated amount of the property tax for the current year (April 1 to December 31) is $49,800.

a. Journalize the two adjusting entries required to bring the accounts affected by the two taxes up to date as of December 31, the end of the current year.

b. What is the amount of tax expense for the current year?

EX 3-18 Adjustment for depreciation **OBJ. 2**

The estimated amount of depreciation on equipment for the current year is $6,760. Journalize the adjusting entry to record the depreciation.

EX 3-19 Determining fixed asset's book value **OBJ. 2**

The balance in the equipment account is $1,375,000, and the balance in the accumulated depreciation—equipment account is $725,000.

a. What is the book value of the equipment?

b. Does the balance in the accumulated depreciation account mean that the equipment's loss of value is $725,000? Explain.

EX 3-20 Book value of fixed assets **OBJ. 2**

In a recent balance sheet, Microsoft Corporation reported *Property, Plant, and Equipment* of $16,259 million and *Accumulated Depreciation* of $8,629 million.

a. What was the book value of the fixed assets?

b. Would the book value of Microsoft Corporation's fixed assets normally approximate their fair market values?

EX 3-21 Effects of errors on financial statements **OBJ. 2, 3**

For a recent period, the balance sheet for Costco Wholesale Corporation reported accrued expenses of $1,893 million. For the same period, Costco reported income before income taxes of $2,054 million. Assume that the adjusting entry for $1,893 million of accrued expenses was not recorded at the end of the current period. What would have been the income (loss) before income taxes?

EX 3-22 Effects of errors on financial statements **OBJ. 2, 3**

For a recent year, the balance sheet for The Campbell Soup Company includes accrued expenses of $560 million. The income before taxes for The Campbell Soup Company for the year was $1,242 million.

a. Assume the adjusting entry for $560 million of accrued expenses was not recorded at the end of the year. By how much would income before taxes have been misstated?

b. What is the percentage of the misstatement in (a) to the reported income of $1,242 million? Round to one decimal place.

EX 3-23 Effects of errors on financial statements **OBJ. 2, 3**

✔ 1. a. Revenue understated, $23,250

The accountant for Astaire Medical Co., a medical services consulting firm, mistakenly omitted adjusting entries for (a) unearned revenue earned during the year ($23,250) and (b) accrued wages ($4,000). Indicate the effect of each error, considered individually, on the income statement for the current year ended August 31. Also indicate the effect of each error on the August 31 balance sheet. Set up a table similar to the following, and record your answers by inserting the dollar amount in the appropriate spaces. Insert a zero if the error does not affect the item.

	Error (a)		Error (b)	
	Over-stated	**Under-stated**	**Over-stated**	**Under-stated**
1. Revenue for the year would be	$ ____	$ ____	$ ____	$ ____
2. Expenses for the year would be	$ ____	$ ____	$ ____	$ ____
3. Net income for the year would be	$ ____	$ ____	$ ____	$ ____
4. Assets at August 31 would be	$ ____	$ ____	$ ____	$ ____
5. Liabilities at August 31 would be	$ ____	$ ____	$ ____	$ ____
6. Stockholders' equity at August 31 would be	$ ____	$ ____	$ ____	$ ____

EX 3-24 Effects of errors on financial statements **OBJ. 2, 3**

If the net income for the current year had been $113,650 in Exercise 3-23, what would have been the correct net income if the proper adjusting entries had been made?

EX 3-25 Adjusting entries for depreciation; effect of error **OBJ. 2, 3**

On December 31, a business estimates depreciation on equipment used during the first year of operations to be $13,900.

a. Journalize the adjusting entry required as of December 31.

b. If the adjusting entry in (a) were omitted, which items would be erroneously stated on (1) the income statement for the year and (2) the balance sheet as of December 31?

EX 3-26 Adjusting entries from trial balances

OBJ. 4

The unadjusted and adjusted trial balances for Editorial Services Co. on March 31, 2014, are shown below.

Editorial Services Co.
Trial Balances
March 31, 2014

	Unadjusted		Adjusted	
	Debit Balances	Credit Balances	Debit Balances	Credit Balances
Cash	8		8	
Accounts Receivable	19		22	
Supplies	6		5	
Prepaid Insurance	10		4	
Land	13		13	
Equipment	20		20	
Accumulated Depreciation—Equipment		4		6
Accounts Payable		13		13
Wages Payable		0		1
Capital Stock		15		15
Retained Earnings		31		31
Dividends	4		4	
Fees Earned		37		40
Wages Expense	12		13	
Rent Expense	4		4	
Insurance Expense	0		6	
Utilities Expense	2		2	
Depreciation Expense	0		2	
Supplies Expense	0		1	
Miscellaneous Expense	2		2	
	100	100	106	106

Journalize the five entries that adjusted the accounts at March 31, 2014. None of the accounts were affected by more than one adjusting entry.

EX 3-27 Adjusting entries from trial balances

OBJ. 4

✔ **Corrected trial balance totals, $369,000**

The accountant for Eva's Laundry prepared the following unadjusted and adjusted trial balances. Assume that all balances in the unadjusted trial balance and the amounts of the adjustments are correct. Identify the errors in the accountant's adjusting entries, assuming that none of the accounts were affected by more than one adjusting entry.

Eva's Laundry
Trial Balances
May 31, 2014

	Unadjusted		Adjusted	
	Debit Balances	Credit Balances	Debit Balances	Credit Balances
Cash	7,500		7,500	
Accounts Receivable	18,250		23,250	
Laundry Supplies	3,750		6,750	
Prepaid Insurance*	5,200		1,600	
Laundry Equipment	190,000		177,000	
Accumulated Depreciation—Laundry Equipment		48,000		48,000
Accounts Payable		9,600		9,600
Wages Payable				1,000
Capital Stock		35,000		35,000
Retained Earnings		75,300		75,300
Dividends	28,775		28,775	
Laundry Revenue		182,100		182,100
Wages Expense	49,200		49,200	
Rent Expense	25,575		25,575	
Utilities Expense	18,500		18,500	
Depreciation Expense			13,000	
Laundry Supplies Expense			3,000	
Insurance Expense			600	
Miscellaneous Expense	3,250		3,250	
	350,000	350,000	358,000	351,000

* $3,600 of insurance expired during the year.

EX 3-28 Vertical analysis of income statement **OBJ. 5**

F·A·I

The following data (in millions) are taken from recent financial statements of Nike Inc.:

	Year 2	Year 1
Net sales (revenues)	$19,014	$19,176
Net income	1,907	1,487

a. Determine the amount of change (in millions) and percent of change in net income for Year 2. Round to one decimal place.

b. Determine the percentage relationship between net income and net sales (net income divided by net sales) for Year 2 and Year 1. Round to one decimal place.

c. What conclusions can you draw from your analysis?

EX 3-29 Vertical analysis of income statement **OBJ. 5**

F·A·I

The following income statement data (in millions) for Dell, Inc., and Hewlett-Packard Company (HP) were taken from their recent annual reports:

	Dell	Hewlett-Packard
Net sales	$61,494	$126,033
Cost of goods sold (expense)	(50,098)	(96,089)
Operating expenses	(7,963)	(18,465)
Operating income (loss)	$ 3,433	$ 11,479

a. Prepare a vertical analysis of the income statement for Dell. Round to one decimal place.

b. Prepare a vertical analysis of the income statement for HP. Round to one decimal place.

c. Based on (a) and (b), how does Dell compare to HP?

Problems Series A

PR 3-1A Adjusting entries **OBJ. 2**

SPREADSHEET

On July 31, 2014, the following data were accumulated to assist the accountant in preparing the adjusting entries for Atrium Realty:

a. The supplies account balance on July 31 is $6,880. The supplies on hand on July 31 are $2,200.

b. The unearned rent account balance on July 31 is $9,200, representing the receipt of an advance payment on July 1 of four months' rent from tenants.

c. Wages accrued but not paid at July 31 are $1,850.

d. Fees accrued but unbilled at July 31 are $11,700.

e. Depreciation of office equipment is $3,500.

Instructions

1. Journalize the adjusting entries required at July 31, 2014.
2. Briefly explain the difference between adjusting entries and entries that would be made to correct errors.

PR 3-2A Adjusting entries **OBJ. 2, 3**

Selected account balances before adjustment for Heartland Realty at August 31, 2014, the end of the current year, are as follows:

	Debits	Credits
Accounts Receivable	$ 80,000	
Equipment	150,000	
Accumulated Depreciation - Equipment		$ 28,000
Prepaid Rent	6,000	
Supplies	3,000	
Wages Payable		—
Unearned Fees		10,500
Fees Earned		410,000
Wages Expense	190,000	
Rent Expense	—	
Depreciation Expense	—	
Supplies Expense	—	

Data needed for year-end adjustments are as follows:

a. Unbilled fees at August 31, $9,150.

b. Supplies on hand at August 31, $675.

c. Rent expired, $5,000.

d. Depreciation of equipment during year, $3,300.

e. Unearned fees at August 31, $3,000.

f. Wages accrued but not paid at August 31, $3,100.

Instructions

1. Journalize the six adjusting entries required at August 31, based on the data presented.
2. What would be the effect on the income statement if adjustments (a) and (f) were omitted at the end of the year?
3. What would be the effect on the balance sheet if adjustments (a) and (f) were omitted at the end of the year?
4. What would be the effect on the "Net increase or decrease in cash" on the statement of cash flows if adjustments (a) and (f) were omitted at the end of the year?

PR 3-3A Adjusting entries

OBJ. 2

GENERAL LEDGER

Electro Repairs & Service, an electronics repair store, prepared the unadjusted trial balance shown below at the end of its first year of operations.

Electro Repairs & Service
Unadjusted Trial Balance
June 30, 2014

	Debit Balances	Credit Balances
Cash	13,800	
Accounts Receivable	90,000	
Supplies	21,600	
Equipment	154,800	
Accounts Payable		21,000
Unearned Fees		24,000
Capital Stock		40,000
Retained Earnings		122,000
Dividends	18,000	
Fees Earned		393,000
Wages Expense	126,000	
Rent Expense	96,000	
Utilities Expense	69,000	
Miscellaneous Expense	10,800	
	600,000	600,000

(Continued)

For preparing the adjusting entries, the following data were assembled:

a. Fees earned but unbilled on June 30 were $12,700.

b. Supplies on hand on June 30 were $4,175.

c. Depreciation of equipment was estimated to be $7,400 for the year.

d. The balance in unearned fees represented the June 1 receipt in advance for services to be provided. Only $14,200 of the services was provided between June 1 and June 30.

e. Unpaid wages accrued on June 30 were $1,100.

Instructions

1. Journalize the adjusting entries necessary on June 30, 2014.
2. Determine the revenues, expenses, and net income of Electro Service & Repairs before the adjusting entries.
3. Determine the revenues, expense, and net income of Electro Service & Repairs after the adjusting entries.
4. Determine the effect of the adjusting entries on Retained Earnings.

PR 3-4A Adjusting entries

OBJ. 2, 3, 4

GENERAL LEDGER

Good Note Company specializes in the repair of music equipment and is owned and operated by Robin Stahl. On November 30, 2014, the end of the current year, the accountant for Good Note Company prepared the following trial balances:

Good Note Company
Trial Balances
November 30, 2014

	Unadjusted		Adjusted	
	Debit Balances	Credit Balances	Debit Balances	Credit Balances
Cash	38,250		38,250	
Accounts Receivable	89,500		89,500	
Supplies	11,250		2,400	
Prepaid Insurance	14,250		3,850	
Equipment	290,450		290,450	
Accumulated Depreciation—Equipment		94,500		106,100
Automobiles	129,500		129,500	
Accumulated Depreciation—Automobiles		54,750		62,050
Accounts Payable		24,930		26,130
Salaries Payable		—		8,100
Unearned Service Fees		18,000		9,000
Capital Stock		100,000		100,000
Retained Earnings		224,020		224,020
Dividends	75,000		75,000	
Service Fees Earned		733,800		742,800
Salary Expense	516,900		525,000	
Rent Expense	54,000		54,000	
Supplies Expense	—		8,850	
Depreciation Expense—Equipment	—		11,600	
Depreciation Expense—Automobiles	—		7,300	
Utilities Expense	12,900		14,100	
Taxes Expense	8,175		8,175	
Insurance Expense	—		10,400	
Miscellaneous Expense	9,825		9,825	
	1,250,000	1,250,000	1,278,200	1,278,200

Instructions

Journalize the seven entries that adjusted the accounts at November 30. None of the accounts were affected by more than one adjusting entry.

✔ 2. Total of Debit column: $780,500

SPREADSHEET

GENERAL LEDGER

PR 3-5A Adjusting entries and adjusted trial balances

OBJ. 2, 3, 4

Dickens Company is a small editorial services company owned and operated by Monica Baker. On October 31, 2014, the end of the current year, Dickens Company's accounting clerk prepared the unadjusted trial balance shown below.

Dickens Company
Unadjusted Trial Balance
October 31, 2014

	Debit Balances	Credit Balances
Cash	7,500	
Accounts Receivable	38,400	
Prepaid Insurance	7,200	
Supplies	1,980	
Land	112,500	
Building	150,250	
Accumulated Depreciation—Building		87,550
Equipment	135,300	
Accumulated Depreciation—Equipment		97,950
Accounts Payable		12,150
Unearned Rent		6,750
Capital Stock		75,000
Retained Earnings		146,000
Dividends	15,000	
Fees Earned		324,600
Salaries and Wages Expense	193,370	
Utilities Expense	42,375	
Advertising Expense	22,800	
Repairs Expense	17,250	
Miscellaneous Expense	6,075	
	750,000	750,000

The data needed to determine year-end adjustments are as follows:

a. Unexpired insurance at October 31, $5,400.
b. Supplies on hand at October 31, $375.
c. Depreciation of building for the year, $6,000.
d. Depreciation of equipment for the year, $3,000.
e. Rent unearned at October 31, $1,350.
f. Accrued salaries and wages at October 31, $2,900.
g. Fees earned but unbilled on October 31, $18,600.

Instructions

1. Journalize the adjusting entries using the following additional accounts: Salaries and Wages Payable; Rent Revenue; Insurance Expense; Depreciation Expense—Building; Depreciation Expense—Equipment; and Supplies Expense.
2. Determine the balances of the accounts affected by the adjusting entries, and prepare an adjusted trial balance.

✔ 2. Corrected net income: $137,750

SPREADSHEET

PR 3-6A Adjusting entries and errors

OBJ. 2, 3

At the end of April, the first month of operations, the following selected data were taken from the financial statements of Shelby Crawford, an attorney:

Net income for April	$120,000
Total assets at April 30	750,000
Total liabilities at April 30	300,000
Total stockholders' equity at April 30	450,000

In preparing the financial statements, adjustments for the following data were overlooked:

a. Supplies used during April, $2,750.
b. Unbilled fees earned at April 30, $23,700.

(Continued)

c. Depreciation of equipment for April, $1,800.

d. Accrued wages at April 30, $1,400.

Instructions

1. Journalize the entries to record the omitted adjustments.
2. Determine the correct amount of net income for April and the total assets, liabilities, and stockholders' equity at April 30. In addition to indicating the corrected amounts, indicate the effect of each omitted adjustment by setting up and completing a columnar table similar to the following. Adjustment (a) is presented as an example.

	Net Income	Total Assets	= Total Liabilities	+ Total Stockholders' Equity
Reported amounts	$120,000	$750,000	$300,000	$450,000
Corrections:				
Adjustment (a)	–2,750	–2,750	0	–2,750
Adjustment (b)	______	______	______	______
Adjustment (c)	______	______	______	______
Adjustment (d)	______	______	______	______
Corrected amounts	______	______	______	______

Problems Series B

PR 3-1B Adjusting entries

OBJ. 2

SPREADSHEET

On May 31, 2014, the following data were accumulated to assist the accountant in preparing the adjusting entries for Oceanside Realty:

a. Fees accrued but unbilled at May 31 are $19,750.

b. The supplies account balance on May 31 is $12,300. The supplies on hand at May 31 are $4,150.

c. Wages accrued but not paid at May 31 are $2,700.

d. The unearned rent account balance at May 31 is $9,000, representing the receipt of an advance payment on May 1 of three months' rent from tenants.

e. Depreciation of office equipment is $3,200.

Instructions

1. Journalize the adjusting entries required at May 31, 2014.
2. Briefly explain the difference between adjusting entries and entries that would be made to correct errors.

PR 3-2B Adjusting entries

OBJ. 2, 3

Selected account balances before adjustment for Intuit Realty at November 30, 2014, the end of the current year, are shown below.

	Debits	Credits
Accounts Receivable	$ 75,000	
Equipment	250,000	
Accumulated Depreciation—Equipment		$ 12,000
Prepaid Rent	12,000	
Supplies	3,170	
Wages Payable		—
Unearned Fees		10,000
Fees Earned		400,000
Wages Expense	140,000	
Rent Expense	—	
Depreciation Expense	—	
Supplies Expense	—	

Data needed for year-end adjustments are as follows:

a. Supplies on hand at November 30, $550.

b. Depreciation of equipment during year, $1,675.

c. Rent expired during year, $8,500.

d. Wages accrued but not paid at November 30, $2,000.

e. Unearned fees at November 30, $4,000.

f. Unbilled fees at November 30, $5,380.

Instructions

1. Journalize the six adjusting entries required at November 30, based on the data presented.
2. What would be the effect on the income statement if adjustments (b) and (e) were omitted at the end of the year?
3. What would be the effect on the balance sheet if adjustments (b) and (e) were omitted at the end of the year?
4. What would be the effect on the "Net increase or decrease in cash" on the statement of cash flows if adjustments (b) and (e) were omitted at the end of the year?

PR 3-3B Adjusting entries

OBJ. 2

GENERAL LEDGER

Crazy Mountain Outfitters Co., an outfitter store for fishing treks, prepared the following unadjusted trial balance at the end of its first year of operations:

Crazy Mountain Outfitters Co.
Unadjusted Trial Balance
April 30, 2014

	Debit Balances	Credit Balances
Cash	11,400	
Accounts Receivable	72,600	
Supplies	7,200	
Equipment	112,000	
Accounts Payable		12,200
Unearned Fees		19,200
Capital Stock		20,000
Retained Earnings		117,800
Dividends	10,000	
Fees Earned		305,800
Wages Expense	157,800	
Rent Expense	55,000	
Utilities Expense	42,000	
Miscellaneous Expense	7,000	
	475,000	475,000

For preparing the adjusting entries, the following data were assembled:

a. Supplies on hand on April 30 were $1,380.

b. Fees earned but unbilled on April 30 were $3,900.

c. Depreciation of equipment was estimated to be $3,000 for the year.

d. Unpaid wages accrued on April 30 were $2,475.

e. The balance in unearned fees represented the April 1 receipt in advance for services to be provided. Only $14,140 of the services was provided between April 1 and April 30.

Instructions

1. Journalize the adjusting entries necessary on April 30, 2014.
2. Determine the revenues, expenses, and net income of Crazy Mountain Outfitters Co. before the adjusting entries.
3. Determine the revenues, expense, and net income of Crazy Mountain Outfitters Co. after the adjusting entries.
4. Determine the effect of the adjusting entries on Retained Earnings.

PR 3-4B Adjusting entries

OBJ. 2, 3, 4

GENERAL LEDGER

The Signage Company specializes in the maintenance and repair of signs, such as billboards. On March 31, 2014, the accountant for The Signage Company prepared the following trial balances:

(Continued)

The Signage Company
Trial Balances
March 31, 2014

	Unadjusted Debit Balances	Unadjusted Credit Balances	Adjusted Debit Balances	Adjusted Credit Balances
Cash	4,750		4,750	
Accounts Receivable	17,400		17,400	
Supplies	6,200		2,175	
Prepaid Insurance	9,000		1,150	
Land	100,000		100,000	
Buildings	170,000		170,000	
Accumulated Depreciation—Buildings		51,500		61,000
Trucks	75,000		75,000	
Accumulated Depreciation—Trucks		12,000		17,000
Accounts Payable		6,920		8,750
Salaries Payable		—		1,400
Unearned Service Fees		10,500		3,850
Capital Stock		50,000		50,000
Retained Earnings		206,400		206,400
Dividends	7,500		7,500	
Service Fees Earned		162,680		169,330
Salary Expense	80,000		81,400	
Depreciation Expense—Trucks	—		5,000	
Rent Expense	11,900		11,900	
Supplies Expense	—		4,025	
Utilities Expense	6,200		8,030	
Depreciation Expense—Buildings	—		9,500	
Taxes Expense	2,900		2,900	
Insurance Expense	—		7,850	
Miscellaneous Expense	9,150		9,150	
	500,000	500,000	517,730	517,730

Instructions

Journalize the seven entries that adjusted the accounts at March 31. None of the accounts were affected by more than one adjusting entry.

PR 3-5B Adjusting entries and adjusted trial balances

OBJ. 2, 3, 4

✔ **2. Total of Debit column: $420,300**

SPREADSHEET

GENERAL LEDGER

Reece Financial Services Co., which specializes in appliance repair services, is owned and operated by Joni Reece. Reece Financial Services Co.'s accounting clerk prepared the unadjusted trial balance at July 31, 2014, shown below.

Reece Financial Services Co.
Unadjusted Trial Balance
July 31, 2014

	Debit Balances	Credit Balances
Cash	10,200	
Accounts Receivable	34,750	
Prepaid Insurance	6,000	
Supplies	1,725	
Land	50,000	
Building	155,750	
Accumulated Depreciation—Building		62,850
Equipment	45,000	
Accumulated Depreciation—Equipment		17,650
Accounts Payable		3,750
Unearned Rent		3,600
Capital Stock		60,000
Retained Earnings		93,550
Dividends	8,000	
Fees Earned		158,600
Salaries and Wages Expense	56,850	
Utilities Expense	14,100	
Advertising Expense	7,500	
Repairs Expense	6,100	
Miscellaneous Expense	4,025	
	400,000	400,000

The data needed to determine year-end adjustments are as follows:

a. Depreciation of building for the year, $6,400.

b. Depreciation of equipment for the year, $2,800.

c. Accrued salaries and wages at July 31, $900.

d. Unexpired insurance at July 31, $1,500.

e. Fees earned but unbilled on July 31, $10,200.

f. Supplies on hand at July 31, $615.

g. Rent unearned at July 31, $300.

Instructions

1. Journalize the adjusting entries using the following additional accounts: Salaries and Wages Payable; Rent Revenue; Insurance Expense; Depreciation Expense—Building; Depreciation Expense—Equipment; and Supplies Expense.
2. Determine the balances of the accounts affected by the adjusting entries and prepare an adjusted trial balance.

PR 3-6B Adjusting entries and errors

OBJ. 2, 3

✔ **2. Corrected net income: $128,700**

SPREADSHEET

At the end of August, the first month of operations, the following selected data were taken from the financial statements of Tucker Jacobs, an attorney:

Net income for August	$112,500
Total assets at August 31	650,000
Total liabilities at August 31	225,000
Total stockholders' equity at August 31	425,000

In preparing the financial statements, adjustments for the following data were overlooked:

a. Unbilled fees earned at August 31, $31,900.

b. Depreciation of equipment for August, $7,500.

c. Accrued wages at August 31, $5,200.

d. Supplies used during August, $3,000.

Instructions

1. Journalize the entries to record the omitted adjustments.
2. Determine the correct amount of net income for August and the total assets, liabilities, and stockholders' equity at August 31. In addition to indicating the corrected amounts, indicate the effect of each omitted adjustment by setting up and completing a columnar table similar to the following. Adjustment (a) is presented as an example.

	Net Income	Total Assets	= Total Liabilities	+ Total Stockholders' Equity
Reported amounts	$112,500	$650,000	$225,000	$425,000
Corrections:				
Adjustment (a)	+31,900	+31,900	0	+31,900
Adjustment (b)	________	________	________	________
Adjustment (c)	________	________	________	________
Adjustment (d)	________	________	________	________
Corrected amounts	________	________	________	________

Continuing Problem

✔ **3. Total of Debit column: $42,340**

GENERAL LEDGER

The unadjusted trial balance that you prepared for PS Music at the end of Chapter 2 should appear as shown on the following page.

(Continued)

PS Music

Learning Objectives

After studying this chapter, you should be able to: *Example Exercises*

OBJ 1 **Describe the flow of accounting information from the unadjusted trial balance into the adjusted trial balance and financial statements.**
Flow of Accounting Information — EE 4-1

OBJ 2 **Prepare financial statements from adjusted account balances.**
Financial Statements
- Income Statement
- Retained Earnings Statement — EE 4-2
- Balance Sheet — EE 4-3

OBJ 3 **Prepare closing entries.**
Closing Entries
- Journalizing and Posting Closing Entries — EE 4-4
- Post-Closing Trial Balance

OBJ 4 **Describe the accounting cycle.**
Accounting Cycle — EE 4-5

OBJ 5 **Illustrate the accounting cycle for one period.**
Illustration of the Accounting Cycle

OBJ 6 **Explain what is meant by the fiscal year and the natural business year.**
Fiscal Year

OBJ 7 **Describe and illustrate the use of working capital and the current ratio in evaluating a company's financial condition.**
Financial Analysis and Interpretation: Working Capital and Current Ratio — EE 4-6

At a Glance 4 Page 182

Cases and

OBJ 1 Describe the flow of accounting information from the unadjusted trial balance into the adjusted trial balance and financial statements.

Flow of Accounting Information

The process of adjusting the accounts and preparing financial statements is one of the most important in accounting. Using the **NetSolutions** illustration from Chapters 1–3 and an end-of-period spreadsheet, the flow of accounting data in adjusting accounts and preparing financial statements are summarized in Exhibit 1.

The end-of-period spreadsheet in Exhibit 1 begins with the unadjusted trial balance. The unadjusted trial balance verifies that the total of the debit balances equals the total of the credit balances. If the trial balance totals are unequal, an error has occurred. Any errors must be found and corrected before the end-of-period process can continue.

Many companies use Microsoft's Excel® software to prepare end-of-period spreadsheets.

The adjustments for NetSolutions from Chapter 3 are shown in the Adjustments columns of the spreadsheet. Cross-referencing (by letters) the debit and credit of each adjustment is useful in reviewing the effect of the adjustments on the unadjusted account balances. The adjustments are normally entered in the order in which the data are assembled. If the titles of the accounts to be adjusted do not appear in the unadjusted trial balance, the accounts are inserted in their proper order in the Account Title column. The total of the Adjustments columns verifies that the total debits equal the total credits for the adjusting entries. The total of the Debit column must equal the total of the Credit column.

The adjustments in the spreadsheet are added to or subtracted from the amounts in the Unadjusted Trial Balance columns to arrive at the amounts inserted in the Adjusted Trial Balance columns. In this way, the Adjusted Trial Balance columns of the spreadsheet illustrate the effect of the adjusting entries on the unadjusted accounts. The totals of the Adjusted Trial Balance columns verify that the totals of the debit and credit balances are equal after adjustment.

EXHIBIT 1

End-of-Period Spreadsheet and Flow of Accounting Data—NetSolutions

	A	B	C	D	E	F	G
1				NetSolutions			
2				End-of-Period Spreadsheet			
3				For the Two Months Ended December 31, 2013			
4		Unadjusted				Adjusted	
5		Trial Balance		Adjustments		Trial Balance	
6	Account Title	Dr.	Cr.	Dr.	Cr.	Dr.	Cr.
7							
8	Cash	2,065				2,065	
9	Accounts Receivable	2,220		(d) 500		2,720	
10	Supplies	2,000			(a) 1,240	760	
11	Prepaid Insurance	2,400			(b) 200	2,200	
12	Land	20,000				20,000	
13	Office Equipment	1,800				1,800	
14	Accumulated Depreciation				(f) 50		50
15	Accounts Payable		900				900
16	Wages Payable				(e) 250		250
17	Unearned Rent		360	(c) 120			240
18	Capital Stock		25,000				25,000
19	Dividends	4,000				4,000	
20	Fees Earned		16,340		(d) 500		16,840
21	Rent Revenue				(c) 120		120
22	Wages Expense	4,275		(e) 250		4,525	
23	Supplies Expense	800		(a) 1,240		2,040	
24	Rent Expense	1,600				1,600	
25	Utilities Expense	985				985	
26	Insurance Expense			(b) 200		200	
27	Depreciation Expense			(f) 50		50	
28	Miscellaneous Expense	455				455	
29		42,600	42,600	2,360	2,360	43,400	43,400
30							

NetSolutions
Balance Sheet
December 31, 2013

Assets

Current assets:			
Cash		$ 2,065	
Accounts receivable		2,720	
Supplies		760	
Prepaid insurance		2,200	
Total current assets			$ 7,745
Property, plant, and equipment:			
Land		$20,000	
Office equipment	$1,800		
Less accum. depreciation	50	1,750	
Total property, plant, and equipment			21,750
Total assets			$29,495

Liabilities

Current liabilities:		
Accounts payable	$900	
Wages payable	250	
Unearned rent	240	
Total liabilities		$ 1,390

Stockholders' Equity

Capital Stock	$25,000	
Retained Earnings	3,105	
Total stockholders' equity		28,105
Total liabilities and stockholders' equity		$29,495

NetSolutions
Retained Earnings Statement
For the Two Months Ended December 31, 2013

Retained earnings, November 1, 2013		$ 0
Net income for November and December	$7,105	
Less dividends	4,000	
Increase in retained earnings		3,105
Retained earnings, December 31, 2013		$3,105

NetSolutions
Income Statement
For the Two Months Ended December 31, 2013

Fees earned	$16,840	
Rent revenue	120	
Total revenues		$16,960
Expenses:		
Wages expense	$ 4,525	
Supplies expense	2,040	
Rent expense	1,600	
Utilities expense	985	
Insurance expense	200	
Depreciation expense	50	
Miscellaneous expense	455	
Total expenses		9,855
Net income		$ 7,105

Exhibit 1 illustrates the flow of accounts from the adjusted trial balance into the financial statements as follows:

1. The revenue and expense accounts (spreadsheet lines 20–28) flow into the income statement.
2. The dividends account (spreadsheet line 19) flows into the retained earnings statement. The net income of $7,105 also flows into the retained earnings statement from the income statement.
3. The asset, liability, and capital stock accounts (spreadsheet lines 8–18) flow into the balance sheet. The end-of-the-period retained earnings of $3,105 also flows into the balance sheet from the retained earnings statement.

To summarize, Exhibit 1 illustrates the process by which accounts are adjusted. In addition, Exhibit 1 illustrates how the adjusted accounts flow into the financial statements. The financial statements for NetSolutions can be prepared directly from Exhibit 1.

The spreadsheet in Exhibit 1 is not required. However, many accountants prepare such a spreadsheet, sometimes called a work sheet, as part of the normal end-of-period process. The primary advantage in doing so is that it allows managers and accountants to see the effect of adjustments on the financial statements. This is especially useful for adjustments that depend upon estimates. Such estimates and their effect on the financial statements are discussed in later chapters.[1]

Example Exercise 4-1 Flow of Accounts into Financial Statements (OBJ 1)

The balances for the accounts listed below appear in the Adjusted Trial Balance columns of the end-of-period spreadsheet. Indicate whether each account would flow into the income statement, retained earnings statement, or balance sheet.

1. Office Equipment
2. Utilities Expense
3. Accumulated Depreciation—Equipment
4. Unearned Rent
5. Fees Earned
6. Dividends
7. Rent Revenue
8. Supplies

Follow My Example 4-1

1. Balance sheet
2. Income statement
3. Balance sheet
4. Balance sheet
5. Income statement
6. Retained earnings statement
7. Income statement
8. Balance sheet

Practice Exercises: **PE 4-1A, PE 4-1B**

OBJ 2 Prepare financial statements from adjusted account balances.

Financial Statements

Using the adjusted trial balance shown in Exhibit 1, the financial statements for NetSolutions can be prepared. The income statement, the retained earnings statement, and the balance sheet are shown in Exhibit 2.

Income Statement

The income statement is prepared directly from the Adjusted Trial Balance columns of the Exhibit 1 spreadsheet, beginning with fees earned of $16,840. The expenses in the income statement in Exhibit 2 are listed in order of size, beginning with the larger items. Miscellaneous expense is the last item, regardless of its amount.

1 The appendix to this chapter describes and illustrates how to prepare an end-of-period spreadsheet (work sheet) that includes financial statement columns.

EXHIBIT 2 **Financial Statements—NetSolutions**

NetSolutions
Income Statement
For the Two Months Ended December 31, 2013

Fees earned	$16,840	
Rent revenue	120	
Total revenues		$16,960
Expenses:		
Wages expense	$ 4,525	
Supplies expense	2,040	
Rent expense	1,600	
Utilities expense	985	
Insurance expense	200	
Depreciation expense	50	
Miscellaneous expense	455	
Total expenses		9,855
Net income		$ 7,105

NetSolutions
Retained Earnings Statement
For the Two Months Ended December 31, 2013

Retained earnings, November 1, 2013		$ 0
Net income for November and December	$7,105	
Less dividends	4,000	
Increase in retained earnings		3,105
Retained earnings, December 31, 2013		$3,105

NetSolutions
Balance Sheet
December 31, 2013

Assets				**Liabilities**		
Current assets:				Current liabilities:		
Cash		$ 2,065		Accounts payable	$900	
Accounts receivable		2,720		Wages payable	250	
Supplies		760		Unearned rent	240	
Prepaid insurance		2,200		Total liabilities		$ 1,390
Total current assets			$ 7,745			
Property, plant, and equipment:						
Land		$20,000		**Stockholders' Equity**		
Office equipment	$1,800			Capital stock	$25,000	
Less accum. depreciation	50	1,750		Retained earnings	3,105	
Total property, plant, and equipment			21,750	Total stockholders' equity		28,105
Total assets			$29,495	Total liabilities and stockholders' equity		$29,495

Integrity, Objectivity, and Ethics in Business

CEO'S HEALTH?

How much and what information to disclose in financial statements and to investors presents a common ethical dilemma for managers and accountants. For example, Steve Jobs, co-founder and CEO of Apple Inc., had been diagnosed and treated for pancreatic cancer. Apple Inc. had insisted that the status of Steve Jobs's health was a "private" matter and did not have to be disclosed to investors. Apple maintained this position even though Jobs was a driving force behind Apple's innovation and financial success.

However, in response to increasing investor concerns and speculation, Jobs released a letter on January 5, 2009 to investors on his health. The letter indicated that his recent weight loss was due to a hormone imbalance and not due to the recurrence of cancer. On October 5, 2011, Steve Jobs died at the age of 56.

Retained Earnings Statement

The first item normally presented on the retained earnings statement is the balance of the retained earnings account at the beginning of the period. Since NetSolutions began operations on November 1, this balance is zero in Exhibit 2. Then, the retained earnings statement shows the net income for the two months ended December 31, 2013. The amount of dividends is deducted from the net income to arrive at the retained earnings as of December 31, 2013.

For the following period, the beginning balance of retained earnings for NetSolutions is the ending balance that was reported for the previous period. For example, assume that during 2014, NetSolutions earned net income of $149,695 and paid dividends of $24,000. The retained earnings statement for the year ending December 31, 2014, for NetSolutions is as follows:

NetSolutions
Retained Earnings Statement
For the Year Ended December 31, 2014

Retained earnings, January 1, 2014		$ 3,105
Net income for the year	$149,695	
Less dividends	24,000	
Increase in retained earnings		125,695
Retained earnings, December 31, 2014		$128,800

For NetSolutions, the amount of dividends was less than the net income. If the dividends had exceeded the net income, the order of the net income and the dividends would have been reversed. The difference between the two items would then be deducted from the beginning Retained Earnings balance. Other factors, such as a net loss, may also require some change in the form of the retained earnings statement, as shown in the following example:

Retained earnings, January 1, 20—		$45,000
Net loss for the year	$5,600	
Dividends	9,500	
Decrease in retained earnings		15,100
Retained earnings, December 31, 20—		$29,900

Example Exercise 4-2 Retained Earnings Statement

OBJ 2

Zack Gaddis owns and operates Gaddis Employment Services. On January 1, 2013, Retained Earnings had a balance of $186,000. During the year, Zack invested an additional $40,000 in the business in exchange for capital stock. In addition, dividends of $25,000 were paid during the year. For the year ended December 31, 2013, Gaddis Employment Services reported a net income of $18,750. Prepare a retained earnings statement for the year ended December 31, 2013.

(Continued)

Follow My Example 4-2

Gaddis Employment Services
Retained Earnings Statement
For the Year Ended December 31, 2013

Retained earnings, January 1, 2013		$186,000
Dividends	$25,000	
Less net income	18,750	
Decrease in retained earnings		6,250
Retained earnings, December 31, 2013		$179,750

Practice Exercises: **PE 4-2A, PE 4-2B**

Balance Sheet

The balance sheet is prepared directly from the Adjusted Trial Balance columns of the Exhibit 1 spreadsheet, beginning with Cash of $2,065. The asset and liability amounts are taken from the spreadsheet. The retained earnings amount, however, is taken from the retained earnings statement, as illustrated in Exhibit 2.

The balance sheet in Exhibit 2 shows subsections for assets and liabilities. Such a balance sheet is a *classified balance sheet*. These subsections are described next.

Assets Assets are commonly divided into two sections on the balance sheet: (1) current assets and (2) property, plant, and equipment.

Current Assets Cash and other assets that are expected to be converted to cash or sold or used up usually within one year or less, through the normal operations of the business, are called **current assets**. In addition to cash, the current assets may include notes receivable, accounts receivable, supplies, and other prepaid expenses.

Note:
Two common classes of assets are current assets and property, plant, and equipment.

Notes receivable are amounts that customers owe. They are written promises to pay the amount of the note and interest. Accounts receivable are also amounts customers owe, but they are less formal than notes. Accounts receivable normally result from providing services or selling merchandise on account. Notes receivable and accounts receivable are current assets because they are usually converted to cash within one year or less.

Property, Plant, and Equipment The property, plant, and equipment section may also be described as **fixed assets** or **plant assets**. These assets include equipment, machinery, buildings, and land. With the exception of land, as discussed in Chapter 3, fixed assets depreciate over a period of time. The original cost, accumulated depreciation, and book value of each major type of fixed asset are normally reported on the balance sheet or in the notes to the financial statements.

Liabilities Liabilities are the amounts the business owes to creditors. Liabilities are commonly divided into two sections on the balance sheet: (1) current liabilities and (2) long-term liabilities.

Current Liabilities Liabilities that will be due within a short time (usually one year or less) and that are to be paid out of current assets are called **current liabilities**. The most common liabilities in this group are notes payable and accounts payable. Other current liabilities may include Wages Payable, Interest Payable, Taxes Payable, and Unearned Fees.

Note:
Two common classes of liabilities are current liabilities and long-term liabilities.

Long-Term Liabilities Liabilities that will not be due for a long time (usually more than one year) are called **long-term liabilities**. If NetSolutions had long-term liabilities, they would be reported below the current liabilities. As long-term liabilities come due and are to be paid within one year, they are reported as current liabilities. If they are to be renewed rather than paid, they would continue to be reported as long term. When an asset is pledged as security for a liability, the obligation may be called a *mortgage note payable* or a *mortgage payable*.

Stockholders' Equity The stockholders' right to the assets of the business is presented on the balance sheet below the liabilities section. The stockholders' equity is added to the total liabilities, and this total must be equal to the total assets. The stockholders' equity consists of capital stock and retained earnings.

Example Exercise 4-3 Classified Balance Sheet

OBJ 2

The following accounts appear in an adjusted trial balance of Hindsight Consulting. Indicate whether each account would be reported in the (a) current asset; (b) property, plant, and equipment; (c) current liability; (d) long-term liability; or (e) stockholders' equity section of the December 31, 2013, balance sheet of Hindsight Consulting.

1. Capital Stock
2. Notes Receivable (due in 6 months)
3. Notes Payable (due in 2018)
4. Land
5. Cash
6. Unearned Rent (3 months)
7. Accumulated Depreciation—Equipment
8. Accounts Payable

Follow My Example 4-3

1. Stockholders' equity
2. Current asset
3. Long-term liability
4. Property, plant, and equipment
5. Current asset
6. Current liability
7. Property, plant, and equipment
8. Current liability

Practice Exercises: **PE 4-3A, PE 4-3B**

IFRS

International Connection

INTERNATIONAL DIFFERENCES

Financial statements prepared under accounting practices in other countries often differ from those prepared under generally accepted accounting principles in the United States. This is to be expected, since cultures and market structures differ from country to country.

To illustrate, BMW Group prepares its financial statements under International Financial Reporting Standards as adopted by the European Union. In doing so, BMW's balance sheet reports fixed assets first, followed by current assets. It also reports owner's equity before the liabilities. In contrast, balance sheets prepared under U.S. accounting principles report current assets followed by fixed assets and current liabilities followed by long-term liabilities and owner's equity. The U.S. form of balance sheet is organized to emphasize creditor interpretation and analysis. For example, current assets and current liabilities are presented first to facilitate their interpretation and analysis by creditors. Likewise, to emphasize their importance, liabilities are reported before owner's equity.*

Regardless of these differences, the basic principles underlying the accounting equation and the double-entry accounting system are the same in Germany and the United States. Even though differences in recording and reporting exist, the accounting equation holds true: The total assets still equal the total liabilities and owner's equity.

*Examples of U.S. and IFRS financial statement reporting differences are further discussed and illustrated in Appendix C.

OBJ 3 Prepare closing entries.

Closing Entries

As discussed in Chapter 3, the adjusting entries are recorded in the journal at the end of the accounting period. For NetSolutions, the adjusting entries are shown in Exhibit 9 of Chapter 3.

After the adjusting entries are posted to NetSolutions' ledger, shown in Exhibit 6 (on pages 160–161), the ledger agrees with the data reported on the financial statements.

The balances of the accounts reported on the balance sheet are carried forward from year to year. Because they are relatively permanent, these accounts are called **permanent accounts** or **real accounts**. For example, Cash, Accounts Receivable, Equipment, Accumulated Depreciation, Accounts Payable, Capital Stock, and Retained Earnings are permanent accounts.

The balances of the accounts reported on the income statement are not carried forward from year to year. Also, the balance of the dividends account, which is reported on the retained earnings statement, is not carried forward. Because these accounts report amounts for only one period, they are called **temporary accounts** or **nominal accounts**. Temporary accounts are not carried forward because they relate only to one period. For example, the Fees Earned of $16,840 and Wages Expense of $4,525 for NetSolutions shown in Exhibit 2 are for the two months ending December 31, 2013, and should not be carried forward to 2014.

At the beginning of the next period, temporary accounts should have zero balances. To achieve this, temporary account balances are transferred to permanent accounts at the end of the accounting period. The entries that transfer these balances are called **closing entries**. The transfer process is called the **closing process** and is sometimes referred to as **closing the books**.

Note:
Closing entries transfer the balances of temporary accounts to the retained earnings account.

The closing process involves the following four steps:

1. Revenue account balances are transferred to an account called Income Summary.
2. Expense account balances are transferred to an account called Income Summary.
3. The balance of Income Summary (net income or net loss) is transferred to the retained earnings account.
4. The balance of the dividends account is transferred to the retained earnings account.

Exhibit 3 diagrams the closing process.

EXHIBIT 3

The Closing Process

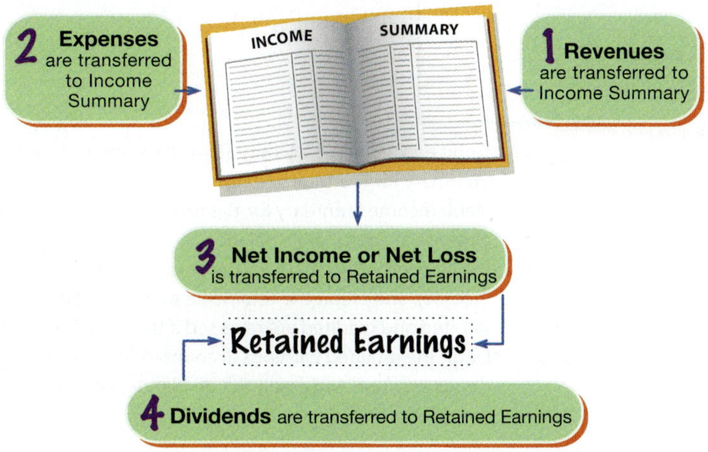

Income Summary is a temporary account that is only used during the closing process. At the beginning of the closing process, Income Summary has no balance. During the closing process, Income Summary will be debited and credited for various amounts. At the end of the closing process, Income Summary will again have no balance. Because Income Summary has the effect of clearing the revenue and expense accounts of their balances, it is sometimes called a **clearing account**. Other titles used for this account include Revenue and Expense Summary, Profit and Loss Summary, and Income and Expense Summary.

Note:
The income summary account does not appear on the financial statements.

The four closing entries required in the closing process are as follows:

1. Debit each revenue account for its balance and credit Income Summary for the total revenue.
2. Credit each expense account for its balance and debit Income Summary for the total expenses.
3. Debit Income Summary for its balance and credit the retained earnings account.
4. Debit the retained earnings account for the balance of the dividends account and credit the dividends account.

In the case of a net loss, Income Summary will have a debit balance after the first two closing entries. In this case, credit Income Summary for the amount of its balance and debit the retained earnings account for the amount of the net loss.

Closing entries are recorded in the journal and are dated as of the last day of the accounting period. In the journal, closing entries are recorded immediately following the adjusting entries. The caption, *Closing Entries*, is often inserted above the closing entries to separate them from the adjusting entries.

It is possible to close the temporary revenue and expense accounts without using a clearing account such as Income Summary. In this case, the balances of the revenue and expense accounts are closed directly to the retained earnings account.

Journalizing and Posting Closing Entries

A flowchart of the four closing entries for NetSolutions is shown in Exhibit 4. The balances in the accounts are those shown in the Adjusted Trial Balance columns of the end-of-period spreadsheet shown in Exhibit 1.

EXHIBIT 4 **Flowchart of Closing Entries for NetSolutions**

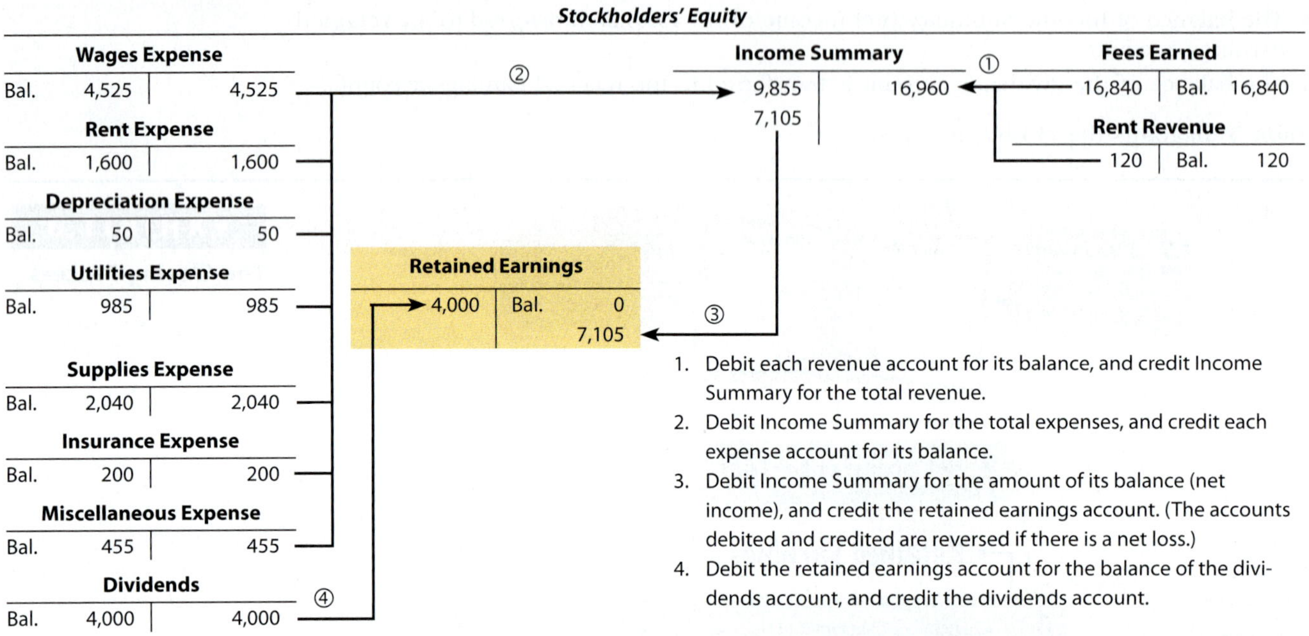

1. Debit each revenue account for its balance, and credit Income Summary for the total revenue.
2. Debit Income Summary for the total expenses, and credit each expense account for its balance.
3. Debit Income Summary for the amount of its balance (net income), and credit the retained earnings account. (The accounts debited and credited are reversed if there is a net loss.)
4. Debit the retained earnings account for the balance of the dividends account, and credit the dividends account.

The closing entries for NetSolutions are shown in Exhibit 5. The account titles and balances for these entries may be obtained from the end-of-period spreadsheet, the adjusted trial balance, the income statement, the retained earnings statement, or the ledger.

EXHIBIT 5

Closing Entries, NetSolutions

Journal *Page 6*

Date		Description	Post. Ref.	Debit	Credit
		Closing Entries			
2013 Dec.	31	Fees Earned	41	16,840	
		Rent Revenue	42	120	
		Income Summary	34		16,960
	31	Income Summary	34	9,855	
		Wages Expense	51		4,525
		Rent Expense	52		1,600
		Depreciation Expense	53		50
		Utilities Expense	54		985
		Supplies Expense	55		2,040
		Insurance Expense	56		200
		Miscellaneous Expense	59		455
	31	Income Summary	34	7,105	
		Retained Earnings	32		7,105
	31	Retained Earnings	32	4,000	
		Dividends	33		4,000

The closing entries are posted to NetSolutions' ledger as shown in Exhibit 6 (pages 160–161). Income Summary has been added to NetSolutions' ledger in Exhibit 6 as account number 34. After the closing entries are posted, NetSolutions' ledger has the following characteristics:

1. The balance of Retained Earnings of $3,105 agrees with the amount reported on the retained earnings statement and the balance sheet.
2. The revenue, expense, and dividends accounts will have zero balances.

As shown in Exhibit 6, the closing entries are normally identified in the ledger as "Closing." In addition, a line is often inserted in both balance columns after a closing entry is posted. This separates next period's revenue, expense, and dividend transactions from those of the current period. Next period's transactions will be posted directly below the closing entry.

Example Exercise 4-4 Closing Entries

OBJ 3

After the accounts have been adjusted at July 31, the end of the fiscal year, the following balances are taken from the ledger of Cabriolet Services Co.:

Retained Earnings	$615,850
Dividends	25,000
Fees Earned	380,450
Wages Expense	250,000
Rent Expense	65,000
Supplies Expense	18,250
Miscellaneous Expense	6,200

Journalize the four entries required to close the accounts.

Follow My Example 4-4

July	31	Fees Earned	380,450	
		Income Summary		380,450
	31	Income Summary	339,450	
		Wages Expense		250,000
		Rent Expense		65,000
		Supplies Expense		18,250
		Miscellaneous Expense		6,200
	31	Income Summary	41,000	
		Retained Earnings		41,000
	31	Retained Earnings	25,000	
		Dividends		25,000

Practice Exercises: **PE 4-4A, PE 4-4B**

Post-Closing Trial Balance

A post-closing trial balance is prepared after the closing entries have been posted. The purpose of the post-closing (after closing) trial balance is to verify that the ledger is in balance at the beginning of the next period. The accounts and amounts should agree exactly with the accounts and amounts listed on the balance sheet at the end of the period. The post-closing trial balance for NetSolutions is shown in Exhibit 7.

EXHIBIT 6 **Ledger, NetSolutions**

Account *Cash* — Account No. *11*

Date	Item	Post. Ref.	Debit	Credit	Balance Debit	Balance Credit
2013						
Nov. 1		1	25,000		25,000	
5		1		20,000	5,000	
18		1	7,500		12,500	
30		1		3,650	8,850	
30		1		950	7,900	
30		2		2,000	5,900	
Dec. 1		2		2,400	3,500	
1		2		800	2,700	
1		2	360		3,060	
6		2		180	2,880	
11		2		400	2,480	
13		3		950	1,530	
16		3	3,100		4,630	
20		3		900	3,730	
21		3	650		4,380	
23		3		1,450	2,930	
27		3		1,200	1,730	
31		3		310	1,420	
31		4		225	1,195	
31		4	2,870		4,065	
31		4		2,000	2,065	

Account *Accounts Receivable* — Account No. *12*

Date	Item	Post. Ref.	Debit	Credit	Balance Debit	Balance Credit
2013						
Dec. 16		3	1,750		1,750	
21		3		650	1,100	
31		4	1,120		2,220	
31	Adjusting	5	500		2,720	

Account *Supplies* — Account No. *14*

Date	Item	Post. Ref.	Debit	Credit	Balance Debit	Balance Credit
2013						
Nov. 10		1	1,350		1,350	
30		1		800	550	
Dec. 23		3	1,450		2,000	
31	Adjusting	5		1,240	760	

Account *Prepaid Insurance* — Account No. *15*

Date	Item	Post. Ref.	Debit	Credit	Balance Debit	Balance Credit
2013						
Dec. 1		2	2,400		2,400	
31	Adjusting	5		200	2,200	

Account *Land* — Account No. *17*

Date	Item	Post. Ref.	Debit	Credit	Balance Debit	Balance Credit
2013						
Nov. 5		1	20,000		20,000	

Account *Office Equipment* — Account No. *18*

Date	Item	Post. Ref.	Debit	Credit	Balance Debit	Balance Credit
2013						
Dec. 4		2	1,800		1,800	

Account *Accumulated Depreciation* — Account No. *19*

Date	Item	Post. Ref.	Debit	Credit	Balance Debit	Balance Credit
2013						
Dec. 31	Adjusting	5		50		50

Account *Accounts Payable* — Account No. *21*

Date	Item	Post. Ref.	Debit	Credit	Balance Debit	Balance Credit
2013						
Nov. 10		1		1,350		1,350
30		1	950			400
Dec. 4		2		1,800		2,200
11		2	400			1,800
20		3	900			900

Account *Wages Payable* — Account No. *22*

Date	Item	Post. Ref.	Debit	Credit	Balance Debit	Balance Credit
2013						
Dec. 31	Adjusting	5		250		250

Account *Unearned Rent* — Account No. *23*

Date	Item	Post. Ref.	Debit	Credit	Balance Debit	Balance Credit
2013						
Dec. 1		2		360		360
31	Adjusting	5	120			240

Account *Capital Stock* — Account No. *31*

Date	Item	Post. Ref.	Debit	Credit	Balance Debit	Balance Credit
2013						
Nov. 1				25,000		25,000

EXHIBIT 6 **Ledger, NetSolutions (*concluded*)**

Account *Retained Earnings* — Account No. 32

Date	Item	Post. Ref.	Debit	Credit	Balance Debit	Balance Credit
2013						
Dec. 31	Closing	6		7,105		7,105
31	Closing	6	4,000			3,105

Account *Dividends* — Account No. 33

Date	Item	Post. Ref.	Debit	Credit	Balance Debit	Balance Credit
2013						
Nov. 30		2	2,000		2,000	
Dec. 31		4	2,000		4,000	
31	Closing	6		4,000	—	—

Account *Income Summary* — Account No. 34

Date	Item	Post. Ref.	Debit	Credit	Balance Debit	Balance Credit
2013						
Dec. 31	Closing	6		16,960		16,960
31	Closing	6	9,855			7,105
31	Closing	6	7,105		—	—

Account *Fees Earned* — Account No. 41

Date	Item	Post. Ref.	Debit	Credit	Balance Debit	Balance Credit
2013						
Nov. 18		1		7,500		7,500
Dec. 16		3		3,100		10,600
16		3		1,750		12,350
31		4		2,870		15,220
31		4		1,120		16,340
31	Adjusting	5		500		16,840
31	Closing	6	16,840		—	—

Account *Rent Revenue* — Account No. 42

Date	Item	Post. Ref.	Debit	Credit	Balance Debit	Balance Credit
2013						
Dec. 31	Adjusting	5		120		120
31	Closing	6	120		—	—

Account *Wages Expense* — Account No. 51

Date	Item	Post. Ref.	Debit	Credit	Balance Debit	Balance Credit
2013						
Nov. 30		1	2,125		2,125	
Dec. 13		3	950		3,075	
27		3	1,200		4,275	
31	Adjusting	5	250		4,525	
31	Closing	6		4,525	—	—

Account *Rent Expense* — Account No. 52

Date	Item	Post. Ref.	Debit	Credit	Balance Debit	Balance Credit
2013						
Nov. 30		1	800		800	
Dec. 1		2	800		1,600	
31	Closing	6		1,600	—	—

Account *Depreciation Expense* — Account No. 53

Date	Item	Post. Ref.	Debit	Credit	Balance Debit	Balance Credit
2013						
Dec. 31	Adjusting	5	50		50	
31	Closing	6		50	—	—

Account *Utilities Expense* — Account No. 54

Date	Item	Post. Ref.	Debit	Credit	Balance Debit	Balance Credit
2013						
Nov. 30		1	450		450	
Dec. 31		3	310		760	
31		4	225		985	
31	Closing	6		985	—	—

Account *Supplies Expense* — Account No. 55

Date	Item	Post. Ref.	Debit	Credit	Balance Debit	Balance Credit
2013						
Nov. 30		1	800		800	
Dec. 31	Adjusting	5	1,240		2,040	
31	Closing	6		2,040	—	—

Account *Insurance Expense* — Account No. 56

Date	Item	Post. Ref.	Debit	Credit	Balance Debit	Balance Credit
2013						
Dec. 31	Adjusting	5	200		200	
31	Closing	6		200	—	—

Account *Miscellaneous Expense* — Account No. 59

Date	Item	Post. Ref.	Debit	Credit	Balance Debit	Balance Credit
2013						
Nov. 30		1	275		275	
Dec. 6		2	180		455	
31	Closing	6		455	—	—

EXHIBIT 7

Post-Closing Trial Balance, NetSolutions

NetSolutions Post-Closing Trial Balance December 31, 2013	Debit Balances	Credit Balances
Cash	2,065	
Accounts Receivable	2,720	
Supplies	760	
Prepaid Insurance	2,200	
Land	20,000	
Office Equipment	1,800	
Accumulated Depreciation		50
Accounts Payable		900
Wages Payable		250
Unearned Rent		240
Capital Stock		25,000
Retained Earnings		3,105
	29,545	29,545

OBJ 4 Describe the accounting cycle.

Accounting Cycle

The accounting process that begins with analyzing and journalizing transactions and ends with the post-closing trial balance is called the **accounting cycle**. The steps in the accounting cycle are as follows:

1. Transactions are analyzed and recorded in the journal.
2. Transactions are posted to the ledger.
3. An unadjusted trial balance is prepared.
4. Adjustment data are assembled and analyzed.
5. An optional end-of-period spreadsheet is prepared.
6. Adjusting entries are journalized and posted to the ledger.
7. An adjusted trial balance is prepared.
8. Financial statements are prepared.
9. Closing entries are journalized and posted to the ledger.
10. A post-closing trial balance is prepared.[2]

Example Exercise 4-5 Accounting Cycle

OBJ 4

From the following list of steps in the accounting cycle, identify what two steps are missing.

a. Transactions are analyzed and recorded in the journal.
b. Transactions are posted to the ledger.
c. Adjustment data are assembled and analyzed.
d. An optional end-of-period spreadsheet is prepared.
e. Adjusting entries are journalized and posted to the ledger.
f. Financial statements are prepared.
g. Closing entries are journalized and posted to the ledger.
h. A post-closing trial balance is prepared.

Follow My Example 4-5

The following two steps are missing: (1) the preparation of an unadjusted trial balance and (2) the preparation of the adjusted trial balance. The unadjusted trial balance should be prepared after step (b). The adjusted trial balance should be prepared after step (e).

Practice Exercises: **PE 4-5A, PE 4-5B**

2 Some accountants include the journalizing and posting of "reversing entries" as the last step in the accounting cycle. Because reversing entries are not required, they are described and illustrated in Appendix D, which is available on the product website at **www.cengagebrain.com.**

Exhibit 8 illustrates the accounting cycle in graphic form. It also illustrates how the accounting cycle begins with the source documents for a transaction and flows through the accounting system and into the financial statements.

EXHIBIT 8

Accounting Cycle

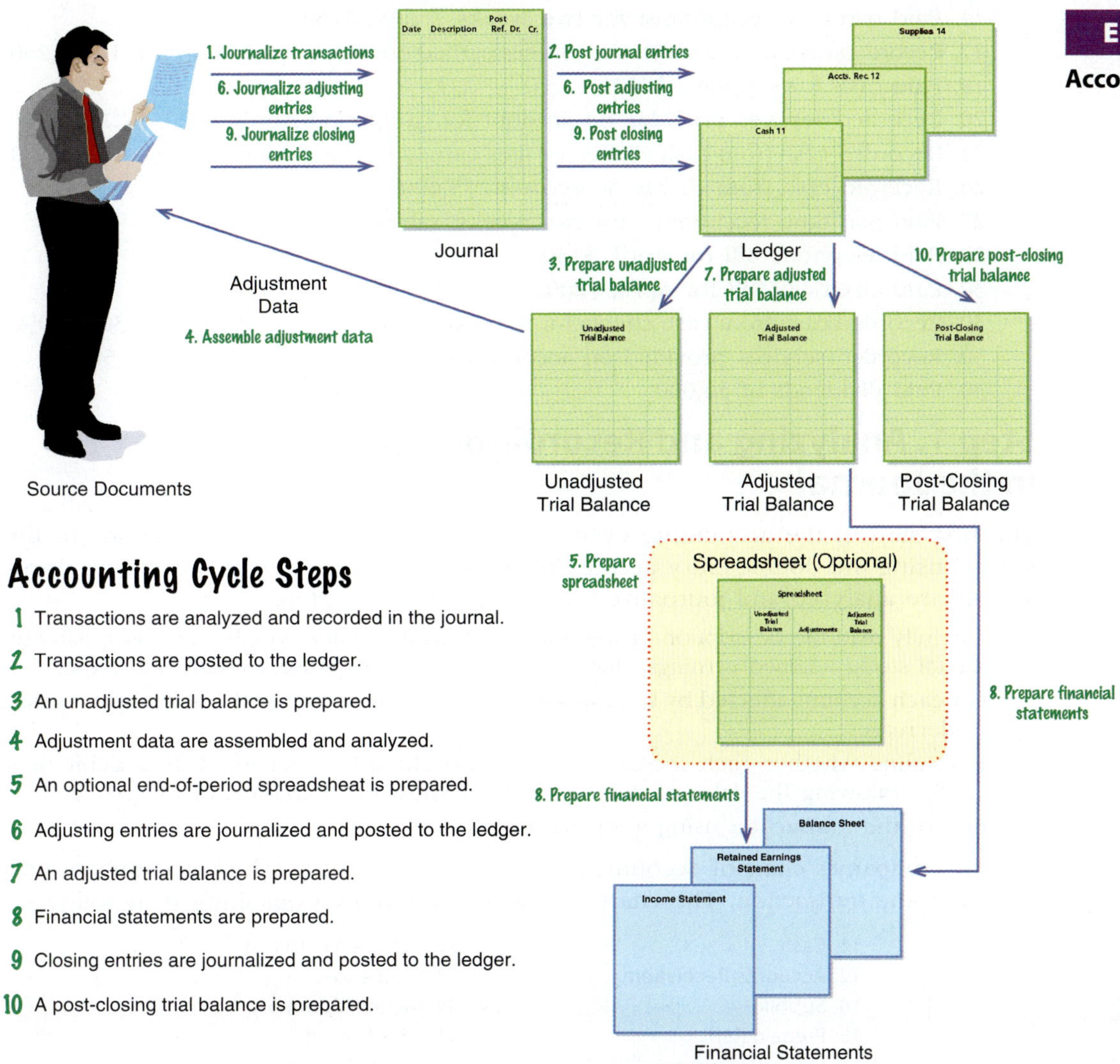

Accounting Cycle Steps

1 Transactions are analyzed and recorded in the journal.

2 Transactions are posted to the ledger.

3 An unadjusted trial balance is prepared.

4 Adjustment data are assembled and analyzed.

5 An optional end-of-period spreadsheet is prepared.

6 Adjusting entries are journalized and posted to the ledger.

7 An adjusted trial balance is prepared.

8 Financial statements are prepared.

9 Closing entries are journalized and posted to the ledger.

10 A post-closing trial balance is prepared.

Illustration of the Accounting Cycle

OBJ 5 Illustrate the accounting cycle for one period.

In this section, the complete accounting cycle for one period is illustrated. Assume that for several years Kelly Pitney has operated a part-time consulting business from her home. As of April 1, 2014, Kelly decided to move to rented quarters and to operate the business on a full-time basis as a professional corporation. The business will be known as Kelly Consulting, P.C. During April, Kelly Consulting entered into the following transactions:

Apr. 1. The following assets were received from Kelly Pitney in exchange for capital stock: cash, $13,100; accounts receivable, $3,000; supplies, $1,400; and office equipment, $12,500. There were no liabilities received.

1. Paid three months' rent on a lease rental contract, $4,800.

2. Paid the premiums on property and casualty insurance policies, $1,800.

4. Received cash from clients as an advance payment for services to be provided and recorded it as unearned fees, $5,000.

Apr. 5. Purchased additional office equipment on account from Office Station Co., $2,000.
6. Received cash from clients on account, $1,800.
10. Paid cash for a newspaper advertisement, $120.
12. Paid Office Station Co. for part of the debt incurred on April 5, $1,200.
12. Recorded services provided on account for the period April 1–12, $4,200.
14. Paid part-time receptionist for two weeks' salary, $750.
17. Recorded cash from cash clients for fees earned during the period April 1–16, $6,250.
18. Paid cash for supplies, $800.
20. Recorded services provided on account for the period April 13–20, $2,100.
24. Recorded cash from cash clients for fees earned for the period April 17–24, $3,850.
26. Received cash from clients on account, $5,600.
27. Paid part-time receptionist for two weeks' salary, $750.
29. Paid telephone bill for April, $130.
30. Paid electricity bill for April, $200.
30. Recorded cash from cash clients for fees earned for the period April 25–30, $3,050.
30. Recorded services provided on account for the remainder of April, $1,500.
30. Paid dividends of $6,000.

Step 1. Analyzing and Recording Transactions in the Journal

The first step in the accounting cycle is to analyze and record transactions in the journal using the double-entry accounting system. As illustrated in Chapter 2, transactions are analyzed and journalized using the following steps:

1. Carefully read the description of the transaction to determine whether an asset, liability, capital stock, retained earnings, dividends, revenue, or expense account is affected.
2. For each account affected by the transaction, determine whether the account increases or decreases.
3. Determine whether each increase or decrease should be recorded as a debit or a credit, following the rules of debit and credit shown in Exhibit 3 of Chapter 2.
4. Record the transaction using a journal entry.

The company's chart of accounts is useful in determining which accounts are affected by the transaction. The chart of accounts for Kelly Consulting is as follows:

11 Cash	32 Retained Earnings
12 Accounts Receivable	33 Dividends
14 Supplies	34 Income Summary
15 Prepaid Rent	41 Fees Earned
16 Prepaid Insurance	51 Salary Expense
18 Office Equipment	52 Rent Expense
19 Accumulated Depreciation	53 Supplies Expense
21 Accounts Payable	54 Depreciation Expense
22 Salaries Payable	55 Insurance Expense
23 Unearned Fees	59 Miscellaneous Expense
31 Capital Stock	

After analyzing each of Kelly Consulting's transactions for April, the journal entries are recorded as shown in Exhibit 9.

Step 2. Posting Transactions to the Ledger

Periodically, the transactions recorded in the journal are posted to the accounts in the ledger. The debits and credits for each journal entry are posted to the accounts in the order in which they occur in the journal. As illustrated in Chapters 2 and 3, journal entries are posted to the accounts using the following four steps:

1. The date is entered in the Date column of the account.
2. The amount is entered into the Debit or Credit column of the account.
3. The journal page number is entered in the Posting Reference column.
4. The account number is entered in the Posting Reference (Post. Ref.) column in the journal.

EXHIBIT 9

Journal Entries for April, Kelly Consulting, P.C.

Journal *Page 1*

Date		Description	Post. Ref.	Debit	Credit
2014 Apr.	1	Cash	11	13,100	
		Accounts Receivable	12	3,000	
		Supplies	14	1,400	
		Office Equipment	18	12,500	
		Capital Stock	31		30,000
	1	Prepaid Rent	15	4,800	
		Cash	11		4,800
	2	Prepaid Insurance	16	1,800	
		Cash	11		1,800
	4	Cash	11	5,000	
		Unearned Fees	23		5,000
	5	Office Equipment	18	2,000	
		Accounts Payable	21		2,000
	6	Cash	11	1,800	
		Accounts Receivable	12		1,800
	10	Miscellaneous Expense	59	120	
		Cash	11		120
	12	Accounts Payable	21	1,200	
		Cash	11		1,200
	12	Accounts Receivable	12	4,200	
		Fees Earned	41		4,200
	14	Salary Expense	51	750	
		Cash	11		750

Journal *Page 2*

Date		Description	Post. Ref.	Debit	Credit
2014 Apr.	17	Cash	11	6,250	
		Fees Earned	41		6,250
	18	Supplies	14	800	
		Cash	11		800
	20	Accounts Receivable	12	2,100	
		Fees Earned	41		2,100
	24	Cash	11	3,850	
		Fees Earned	41		3,850
	26	Cash	11	5,600	
		Accounts Receivable	12		5,600
	27	Salary Expense	51	750	
		Cash	11		750
	29	Miscellaneous Expense	59	130	
		Cash	11		130

(Continued)

EXHIBIT 9

Journal Entries for April, Kelly Consulting, P.C. (*concluded*)

Journal *Page 2*

Date		Description	Post. Ref.	Debit	Credit
2014 Apr.	30	Miscellaneous Expense	59	200	
		Cash	11		200
	30	Cash	11	3,050	
		Fees Earned	41		3,050
	30	Accounts Receivable	12	1,500	
		Fees Earned	41		1,500
	30	Dividends	33	6,000	
		Cash	11		6,000

The journal entries for Kelly Consulting have been posted to the ledger shown in Exhibit 17 on pages 172–173.

Step 3. Preparing an Unadjusted Trial Balance

An unadjusted trial balance is prepared to determine whether any errors have been made in posting the debits and credits to the ledger. The unadjusted trial balance shown in Exhibit 10 does not provide complete proof of the accuracy of the ledger. It indicates only that the debits and the credits are equal. This proof is of value, however, because errors often affect the equality of debits and credits. If the two totals of a trial balance are not equal, an error has occurred that must be discovered and corrected.

EXHIBIT 10

Unadjusted Trial Balance, Kelly Consulting, P.C.

Kelly Consulting, P.C.
Unadjusted Trial Balance
April 30, 2014

	Debit Balances	Credit Balances
Cash	22,100	
Accounts Receivable	3,400	
Supplies	2,200	
Prepaid Rent	4,800	
Prepaid Insurance	1,800	
Office Equipment	14,500	
Accumulated Depreciation		0
Accounts Payable		800
Salaries Payable		0
Unearned Fees		5,000
Capital Stock		30,000
Dividends	6,000	
Fees Earned		20,950
Salary Expense	1,500	
Rent Expense	0	
Supplies Expense	0	
Depreciation Expense	0	
Insurance Expense	0	
Miscellaneous Expense	450	
	56,750	56,750

The unadjusted account balances shown in Exhibit 10 were taken from Kelly Consulting's ledger shown in Exhibit 17, on pages 172–173, before any adjusting entries were recorded.

Step 4. Assembling and Analyzing Adjustment Data

Before the financial statements can be prepared, the accounts must be updated. The four types of accounts that normally require adjustment include prepaid expenses, unearned revenue, accrued revenue, and accrued expenses. In addition, depreciation expense must be recorded for fixed assets other than land. The following data have been assembled on April 30, 2014, for analysis of possible adjustments for Kelly Consulting:

a. Insurance expired during April is $300.
b. Supplies on hand on April 30 are $1,350.
c. Depreciation of office equipment for April is $330.
d. Accrued receptionist salary on April 30 is $120.
e. Rent expired during April is $1,600.
f. Unearned fees on April 30 are $2,500.

Step 5. Preparing an Optional End-of-Period Spreadsheet

Although an end-of-period spreadsheet is not required, it is useful in showing the flow of accounting information from the unadjusted trial balance to the adjusted trial balance. In addition, an end-of-period spreadsheet is useful in analyzing the impact of proposed adjustments on the financial statements. The end-of-period spreadsheet for Kelly Consulting is shown in Exhibit 11.

Step 6. Journalizing and Posting Adjusting Entries

Based on the adjustment data shown in Step 4, adjusting entries for Kelly Consulting are prepared as shown in Exhibit 12. Each adjusting entry affects at least one income statement account and one balance sheet account. Explanations for each adjustment including any computations are normally included with each adjusting entry.

EXHIBIT 11

End-of-Period Spreadsheet, Kelly Consulting, P.C.

	A	B	C	D	E	F	G
1				Kelly Consulting, P.C.			
2				End-of-Period Spreadsheet			
3				For the Month Ended April 30, 2014			
4		Unadjusted				Adjusted	
5		Trial Balance		Adjustments		Trial Balance	
6	Account Title	Dr.	Cr.	Dr.	Cr.	Dr.	Cr.
7							
8	Cash	22,100				22,100	
9	Accounts Receivable	3,400				3,400	
10	Supplies	2,200			(b) 850	1,350	
11	Prepaid Rent	4,800			(e) 1,600	3,200	
12	Prepaid Insurance	1,800			(a) 300	1,500	
13	Office Equipment	14,500				14,500	
14	Accum. Depreciation				(c) 330		330
15	Accounts Payable		800				800
16	Salaries Payable				(d) 120		120
17	Unearned Fees		5,000	(f) 2,500			2,500
18	Capital Stock		30,000				30,000
19	Dividends	6,000				6,000	
20	Fees Earned		20,950		(f) 2,500		23,450
21	Salary Expense	1,500		(d) 120		1,620	
22	Rent Expense			(e) 1,600		1,600	
23	Supplies Expense			(b) 850		850	
24	Depreciation Expense			(c) 330		330	
25	Insurance Expense			(a) 300		300	
26	Miscellaneous Expense	450				450	
27		56,750	56,750	5,700	5,700	57,200	57,200
28							

EXHIBIT 12

Adjusting Entries, Kelly Consulting, P.C.

Journal *Page 3*

Date		Description	Post. Ref.	Debit	Credit
		Adjusting Entries			
2014 Apr.	30	Insurance Expense	55	300	
		Prepaid Insurance	16		300
		Expired insurance.			
	30	Supplies Expense	53	850	
		Supplies	14		850
		Supplies used ($2,200 – $1,350).			
	30	Depreciation Expense	54	330	
		Accumulated Depreciation	19		330
		Depreciation of office equipment.			
	30	Salary Expense	51	120	
		Salaries Payable	22		120
		Accrued salary.			
	30	Rent Expense	52	1,600	
		Prepaid Rent	15		1,600
		Rent expired during April.			
	30	Unearned Fees	23	2,500	
		Fees Earned	41		2,500
		Fees earned ($5,000 – $2,500).			

Each of the adjusting entries shown in Exhibit 12 is posted to Kelly Consulting's ledger shown in Exhibit 17 on pages 172–173. The adjusting entries are identified in the ledger as "Adjusting."

Step 7. Preparing an Adjusted Trial Balance

After the adjustments have been journalized and posted, an adjusted trial balance is prepared to verify the equality of the total of the debit and credit balances. This is the last step before preparing the financial statements. If the adjusted trial balance does not balance, an error has occurred and must be found and corrected. The adjusted trial balance for Kelly Consulting as of April 30, 2014, is shown in Exhibit 13.

Step 8. Preparing the Financial Statements

The most important outcome of the accounting cycle is the financial statements. The income statement is prepared first, followed by the retained earnings statement and then the balance sheet. The statements can be prepared directly from the adjusted trial balance, the end-of-period spreadsheet, or the ledger. The net income or net loss shown on the income statement is reported on the retained earnings statement along with any dividends. The ending retained earnings is reported on the balance sheet and is added with total liabilities to equal total assets.

The financial statements for Kelly Consulting are shown in Exhibit 14. Kelly Consulting earned net income of $18,300 for April. As of April 30, 2014, Kelly Consulting has total assets of $45,720, total liabilities of $3,420, and total stockholders' equity of $42,300.

EXHIBIT 13

Adjusted Trial Balance, Kelly Consulting, P.C.

Kelly Consulting, P.C.
Adjusted Trial Balance
April 30, 2014

	Debit Balances	Credit Balances
Cash	22,100	
Accounts Receivable	3,400	
Supplies	1,350	
Prepaid Rent	3,200	
Prepaid Insurance	1,500	
Office Equipment	14,500	
Accumulated Depreciation		330
Accounts Payable		800
Salaries Payable		120
Unearned Fees		2,500
Capital Stock		30,000
Dividends	6,000	
Fees Earned		23,450
Salary Expense	1,620	
Rent Expense	1,600	
Supplies Expense	850	
Depreciation Expense	330	
Insurance Expense	300	
Miscellaneous Expense	450	
	57,200	57,200

EXHIBIT 14

Financial Statements, Kelly Consulting, P.C.

Kelly Consulting, P.C.
Income Statement
For the Month Ended April 30, 2014

Fees earned		$23,450
Expenses:		
Salary expense	$1,620	
Rent expense	1,600	
Supplies expense	850	
Depreciation expense	330	
Insurance expense	300	
Miscellaneous expense	450	
Total expenses		5,150
Net income		$18,300

Kelly Consulting, P.C.
Retained Earnings Statement
For the Month Ended April 30, 2014

Retained earnings, April 1, 2014		$ 0
Net income for April	$18,300	
Less dividends	6,000	
Increase in retained earnings		12,300
Retained earnings, April 30, 2014		$12,300

(Continued)

EXHIBIT 14 **Financial Statements, Kelly Consulting, P.C. (*concluded*)**

Kelly Consulting, P.C.
Balance Sheet
April 30, 2014

Assets			Liabilities		
Current assets:			Current liabilities:		
Cash	$22,100		Accounts payable	$ 800	
Accounts receivable	3,400		Salaries payable	120	
Supplies	1,350		Unearned fees	2,500	
Prepaid rent	3,200		Total liabilities		$ 3,420
Prepaid insurance	1,500				
Total current assets		$31,550	**Stockholders' Equity**		
Property, plant, and equipment:			Capital stock	$30,000	
Office equipment	$14,500		Retained earnings	12,300	
Less accumulated depreciation	330		Total stockholders' equity		42,300
Total property, plant, and equipment		14,170			
Total assets		$45,720	Total liabilities and stockholders' equity		$45,720

Step 9. Journalizing and Posting Closing Entries

As described earlier in this chapter, four closing entries are required at the end of an accounting period. These four closing entries are as follows:

1. Debit each revenue account for its balance and credit Income Summary for the total revenue.
2. Credit each expense account for its balance and debit Income Summary for the total expenses.
3. Debit Income Summary for its balance and credit the retained earnings account.
4. Debit the retained earnings account for the balance of the dividends account and credit the dividends account.

The four closing entries for Kelly Consulting are shown in Exhibit 15. The closing entries are posted to Kelly Consulting's ledger as shown in Exhibit 17 (pages 172–173). After the closing entries are posted, Kelly Consulting's ledger has the following characteristics:

1. The balance of Retained Earnings of $12,300 agrees with the amount reported on the retained earnings statement and the balance sheet.
2. The revenue, expense, and dividends accounts will have zero balances.

The closing entries are normally identified in the ledger as "Closing." In addition, a line is often inserted in both balance columns after a closing entry is posted. This separates next period's revenue, expense, and dividend transactions from those of the current period.

Step 10. Preparing a Post-Closing Trial Balance

A post-closing trial balance is prepared after the closing entries have been posted. The purpose of the post-closing trial balance is to verify that the ledger is in balance at the beginning of the next period. The accounts and amounts in the post-closing trial balance should agree exactly with the accounts and amounts listed on the balance sheet at the end of the period.

EXHIBIT 15

Closing Entries, Kelly Consulting, P.C.

Journal *Page 4*

Date		Description	Post. Ref.	Debit	Credit
		Closing Entries			
2014 Apr.	30	Fees Earned	41	23,450	
		Income Summary	34		23,450
	30	Income Summary	34	5,150	
		Salary Expense	51		1,620
		Rent Expense	52		1,600
		Supplies Expense	53		850
		Depreciation Expense	54		330
		Insurance Expense	55		300
		Miscellaneous Expense	59		450
	30	Income Summary	34	18,300	
		Retained Earnings	32		18,300
	30	Retained Earnings	32	6,000	
		Dividends	33		6,000

The post-closing trial balance for Kelly Consulting is shown in Exhibit 16. The balances shown in the post-closing trial balance are taken from the ending balances in the ledger shown in Exhibit 17. These balances agree with the amounts shown on Kelly Consulting's balance sheet in Exhibit 14.

EXHIBIT 16

Post-Closing Trial Balance, Kelly Consulting, P.C.

Kelly Consulting, P.C.
Post-Closing Trial Balance
April 30, 2014

	Debit Balances	Credit Balances
Cash	22,100	
Accounts Receivable	3,400	
Supplies	1,350	
Prepaid Rent	3,200	
Prepaid Insurance	1,500	
Office Equipment	14,500	
Accumulated Depreciation		330
Accounts Payable		800
Salaries Payable		120
Unearned Fees		2,500
Capital Stock		30,000
Retained Earnings		12,300
	46,050	46,050

EXHIBIT 17 **Ledger, Kelly Consulting, P.C.**

Ledger

Account *Cash* — Account No. *11*

					Balance	
Date	Item	Post. Ref.	Debit	Credit	Debit	Credit
2014						
Apr. 1		1	13,100		13,100	
1		1		4,800	8,300	
2		1		1,800	6,500	
4		1	5,000		11,500	
6		1	1,800		13,300	
10		1		120	13,180	
12		1		1,200	11,980	
14		1		750	11,230	
17		2	6,250		17,480	
18		2		800	16,680	
24		2	3,850		20,530	
26		2	5,600		26,130	
27		2		750	25,380	
29		2		130	25,250	
30		2		200	25,050	
30		2	3,050		28,100	
30		2		6,000	22,100	

Account *Accounts Receivable* — Account No. *12*

					Balance	
Date	Item	Post. Ref.	Debit	Credit	Debit	Credit
2014						
Apr. 1		1	3,000		3,000	
6		1		1,800	1,200	
12		1	4,200		5,400	
20		2	2,100		7,500	
26		2		5,600	1,900	
30		2	1,500		3,400	

Account *Supplies* — Account No. *14*

					Balance	
Date	Item	Post. Ref.	Debit	Credit	Debit	Credit
2014						
Apr. 1		1	1,400		1,400	
18		2	800		2,200	
30	Adjusting	3		850	1,350	

Account *Prepaid Rent* — Account No. *15*

					Balance	
Date	Item	Post. Ref.	Debit	Credit	Debit	Credit
2014						
Apr. 1		1	4,800		4,800	
30	Adjusting	3		1,600	3,200	

Account *Prepaid Insurance* — Account No. *16*

					Balance	
Date	Item	Post. Ref.	Debit	Credit	Debit	Credit
2014						
Apr. 2		1	1,800		1,800	
30	Adjusting	3		300	1,500	

Account *Office Equipment* — Account No. *18*

					Balance	
Date	Item	Post. Ref.	Debit	Credit	Debit	Credit
2014						
Apr. 1		1	12,500		12,500	
5		1	2,000		14,500	

Account *Accumulated Depreciation* — Account No. *19*

					Balance	
Date	Item	Post. Ref.	Debit	Credit	Debit	Credit
2014						
Apr. 30	Adjusting	3		330		330

Account *Accounts Payable* — Account No. *21*

					Balance	
Date	Item	Post. Ref.	Debit	Credit	Debit	Credit
2014						
Apr. 5		1		2,000		2,000
12		1	1,200			800

Account *Salaries Payable* — Account No. *22*

					Balance	
Date	Item	Post. Ref.	Debit	Credit	Debit	Credit
2014						
Apr. 30	Adjusting	3		120		120

Account *Unearned Fees* — Account No. *23*

					Balance	
Date	Item	Post. Ref.	Debit	Credit	Debit	Credit
2014						
Apr. 4		1		5,000		5,000
30	Adjusting	3	2,500			2,500

Account *Capital Stock* — Account No. *31*

					Balance	
Date	Item	Post. Ref.	Debit	Credit	Debit	Credit
2014						
Apr. 1				30,000		30,000

Account *Retained Earnings* — Account No. *32*

					Balance	
Date	Item	Post. Ref.	Debit	Credit	Debit	Credit
2014						
30	Closing	4		18,300		18,300
30	Closing	4	6,000			12,300

EXHIBIT 17 **Ledger, Kelly Consulting, P.C. (*concluded*)**

Account *Dividends* — Account No. *33*

Date	Item	Post. Ref.	Debit	Credit	Balance Debit	Balance Credit
2014 Apr. 30		2	6,000		6,000	
30	Closing	4		6,000	—	—

Account *Income Summary* — Account No. *34*

Date	Item	Post. Ref.	Debit	Credit	Balance Debit	Balance Credit
2014 Apr. 30	Closing	4		23,450		23,450
30	Closing	4	5,150			18,300
30	Closing	4	18,300		—	—

Account *Fees Earned* — Account No. *41*

Date	Item	Post. Ref.	Debit	Credit	Balance Debit	Balance Credit
2014 Apr. 12		1		4,200		4,200
17		2		6,250		10,450
20		2		2,100		12,550
24		2		3,850		16,400
30		2		3,050		19,450
30		2		1,500		20,950
30	Adjusting	3		2,500		23,450
30	Closing	4	23,450		—	—

Account *Salary Expense* — Account No. *51*

Date	Item	Post. Ref.	Debit	Credit	Balance Debit	Balance Credit
2014 Apr. 14		1	750		750	
27		2	750		1,500	
30	Adjusting	3	120		1,620	
30	Closing	4		1,620	—	—

Account *Rent Expense* — Account No. *52*

Date	Item	Post. Ref.	Debit	Credit	Balance Debit	Balance Credit
2014 Apr. 30	Adjusting	3	1,600		1,600	
30	Closing	4		1,600	—	—

Account *Supplies Expense* — Account No. *53*

Date	Item	Post. Ref.	Debit	Credit	Balance Debit	Balance Credit
2014 Apr. 30	Adjusting	3	850		850	
30	Closing	4		850	—	—

Account *Depreciation Expense* — Account No. *54*

Date	Item	Post. Ref.	Debit	Credit	Balance Debit	Balance Credit
2014 Apr. 30	Adjusting	3	330		330	
30	Closing	4		330	—	—

Account *Insurance Expense* — Account No. *55*

Date	Item	Post. Ref.	Debit	Credit	Balance Debit	Balance Credit
2014 Apr. 30	Adjusting	3	300		300	
30	Closing	4		300	—	—

Account *Miscellaneous Expense* — Account No. *59*

Date	Item	Post. Ref.	Debit	Credit	Balance Debit	Balance Credit
2014 Apr. 10		1	120		120	
29		2	130		250	
30		2	200		450	
30	Closing	4		450	—	—

Fiscal Year

OBJ 6 Explain what is meant by the fiscal year and the natural business year.

The annual accounting period adopted by a business is known as its **fiscal year**. Fiscal years begin with the first day of the month selected and end on the last day of the following twelfth month. The period most commonly used is the calendar year. Other periods are not unusual, especially for businesses organized as corporations. For example, a corporation may adopt a fiscal year that ends when business activities

Recent Fiscal Year-Ends of Some Well-Known Companies are shown below.

	Fiscal Year
Amazon	December 31
Apple Inc.	September 24
AT&T	December 31
Bank of America	December 31
Cardinal Health, Inc.	June 30
Cisco Systems	July 30
Costco Wholesale Corp.	August 28
Dell, Inc.	January 28
eBay	December 31
General Electric	December 31
Google Inc.	December 31
Microsoft Corporation	June 30
Nike, Inc.	May 31
Walgreen	August 31
Walmart	January 31
Walt Disney Company	October 1

have reached the lowest point in its annual operating cycle. Such a fiscal year is called the **natural business year**. At the low point in its operating cycle, a business has more time to analyze the results of operations and to prepare financial statements.

Because companies with fiscal years often have highly seasonal operations, investors and others should be careful in interpreting partial-year reports for such companies. That is, you should expect the results of operations for these companies to vary significantly throughout the fiscal year.

The financial history of a business may be shown by a series of balance sheets and income statements for several fiscal years. If the life of a business is expressed by a line moving from left to right, the series of balance sheets and income statements may be graphed as follows:

Financial History of a Business

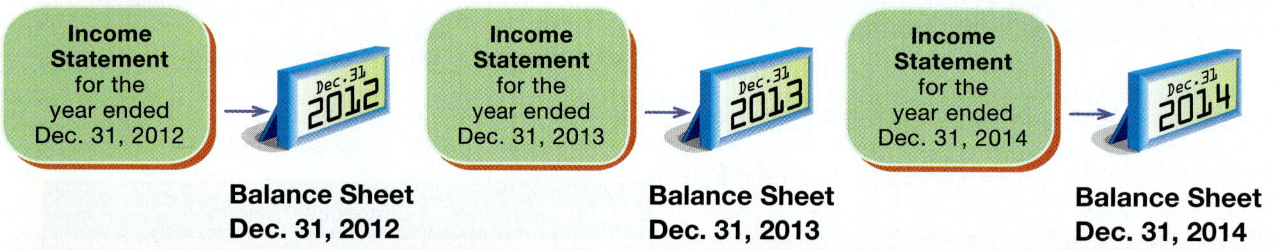

Business Connection

CHOOSING A FISCAL YEAR

CVS Caremark Corporation (CVS) operates over 7,000 pharmacies throughout the United States and fills more than one billion prescriptions annually. CVS recently chose December 31 as its fiscal year-end described as follows:

.... our Board of Directors approved a change in our fiscal year-end ... to December 31 of each year to better reflect our position in the health care ... industry.

In contrast, most large retailers such as Walmart and Target use fiscal years ending January 31, when their operations are the slowest following the December holidays.

F·A·I

Financial Analysis and Interpretation: Working Capital and Current Ratio

OBJ 7 Describe and illustrate the use of working capital and the current ratio in evaluating a company's financial condition.

The ability to convert assets into cash is called **liquidity**, while the ability of a business to pay its debts is called **solvency**. Two financial measures for evaluating a business's short-term liquidity and solvency are working capital and the current ratio.

Working capital is the excess of the current assets of a business over its current liabilities, as shown below.

$$\text{Working Capital} = \text{Current Assets} - \text{Current Liabilities}$$

Current assets are more liquid than long-term assets. Thus, an increase in a company's current assets increases or improves its liquidity. An increase in working capital increases or improves liquidity in the sense that current assets are available for uses other than paying current liabilities.

A positive working capital implies that the business is able to pay its current liabilities and is solvent. Thus, an increase in working capital increases or improves a company's short-term solvency.

To illustrate, NetSolutions' working capital at the end of 2013 is $6,355 as computed below. This amount of working capital implies that NetSolutions is able to pay its current liabilities.

$$\begin{aligned}\text{Working Capital} &= \text{Current Assets} - \text{Current Liabilities}\\ &= \$7{,}745 - \$1{,}390\\ &= \$6{,}355\end{aligned}$$

The **current ratio** is another means of expressing the relationship between current assets and current liabilities. The current ratio is computed by dividing current assets by current liabilities, as shown below.

$$\text{Current Ratio} = \frac{\text{Current Assets}}{\text{Current Liabilities}}$$

To illustrate, the current ratio for NetSolutions at the end of 2013 is 5.6, computed as follows:

$$\begin{aligned}\text{Current Ratio} &= \frac{\text{Current Assets}}{\text{Current Liabilities}}\\ &= \frac{\$7{,}745}{\$1{,}390}\\ &= 5.6 \text{ (Rounded)}\end{aligned}$$

The current ratio is more useful than working capital in making comparisons across companies or with industry averages. To illustrate, the following data (in millions) were taken from recent financial statements of Electronic Arts Inc. and Take-Two Interactive Software, Inc.

	Electronic Arts		Take-Two	
	Year 2	**Year 1**	**Year 2**	**Year 1**
Current assets	$3,032	$2,585	$566	$427
Current liabilities	2,001	1,574	231	210
Working capital	$1,031	$1,011	$335	$217
Current ratio*	1.52	1.64	2.45	2.03
	($3,032 ÷ $2,001)	($2,585 ÷ $1,574)	($566 ÷ $231)	($427 ÷ $210)

*Rounded to two decimal places.

Electronic Arts is larger than Take-Two and has Year 2 working capital of $1,031 as compared to Take-Two's Year 2 working capital of $335. Such size differences make comparisons across companies difficult. In contrast, the current ratio allows comparability across companies.

To illustrate, Electronic Arts has over three times more working capital ($1,031) than does Take-Two ($335). However, by using the current ratio the changes in liquidity of both companies can be directly compared. Specifically, Electronic Arts' current ratio declined from 1.64 to 1.52, or 0.12. In contrast, Take-Two's current ratio increased by 0.42 from 2.03 to 2.45. Thus, while Electronic Arts' liquidity declined in Year 2, Take-Two's short-term liquidity improved.

Example Exercise 4-6 Working Capital and Current Ratio

OBJ 7

Current assets and current liabilities for Fortson Company are shown below.

	2014	2013
Current assets	$310,500	$262,500
Current liabilities	172,500	150,000

a. Determine the working capital and current ratio for 2014 and 2013.

b. Does the change in the current ratio from 2013 to 2014 indicate a favorable or an unfavorable trend?

(Continued)

Follow My Example 4-6

a.

	2014	2013
Current assets	$310,500	$262,500
Current liabilities	172,500	150,000
Working capital	$138,000	$112,500
Current ratio	1.80	1.75
	($310,500 ÷ $172,500)	($262,500 ÷ $150,000)

b. The change from 1.75 to 1.80 indicates a favorable trend.

Practice Exercises: **PE 4-6A, PE 4-6B**

APPENDIX 1

End-of-Period Spreadsheet (Work Sheet)

Accountants often use working papers for analyzing and summarizing data. Such working papers are not a formal part of the accounting records. This is in contrast to the chart of accounts, the journal, and the ledger, which are essential parts of an accounting system. Working papers are usually prepared by using a computer spreadsheet program such as Microsoft's Excel™.

The end-of-period spreadsheet shown in Exhibit 1 is a working paper used to summarize adjusting entries and their effects on the accounts. As illustrated in the chapter, the financial statements for NetSolutions can be prepared directly from the spreadsheet's Adjusted Trial Balance columns.

Some accountants prefer to expand the end-of-period spreadsheet shown in Exhibit 1 to include financial statement columns. Exhibits 18 through 22 illustrate the step-by-step process of how to prepare this expanded spreadsheet. As a basis for illustration, NetSolutions is used.

Step 1. Enter the Title

The spreadsheet is started by entering the following data:

1. Name of the business: *NetSolutions*
2. Type of working paper: *End-of-Period Spreadsheet*
3. The period of time: *For the Two Months Ended December 31, 2013*

Exhibit 18 shows the preceding data entered for NetSolutions.

Step 2. Enter the Unadjusted Trial Balance

Enter the unadjusted trial balance on the spreadsheet. The spreadsheet in Exhibit 18 shows the unadjusted trial balance for NetSolutions at December 31, 2013.

Step 3. Enter the Adjustments

The adjustments for NetSolutions from Chapter 3 are entered in the Adjustments columns, as shown in Exhibit 19. Cross-referencing (by letters) the debit and credit of each adjustment is useful in reviewing the spreadsheet. It is also helpful for identifying the adjusting entries that need to be recorded in the journal. This cross-referencing process is sometimes referred to as *keying* the adjustments.

The adjustments are normally entered in the order in which the data are assembled. If the titles of the accounts to be adjusted do not appear in the unadjusted trial balance, the accounts are inserted in their proper order in the Account Title column.

EXHIBIT 18 **Spreadsheet (Work Sheet) with Unadjusted Trial Balance Entered**

	A	B	C	D	E	F	G	H	I	J	K
1			NetSolutions								
2			End-of-Period Spreadsheet (Work Sheet)								
3			For the Two Months Ended December 31, 2013								
4		Unadjusted				Adjusted					
5		Trial Balance		Adjustments		Trial Balance		Income Statement		Balance Sheet	
6	Account Title	Dr.	Cr.	Dr.	Cr.	Dr.	Cr.	Dr.	Cr.	Dr.	Cr.
7											
8	Cash	2,065									
9	Accounts Receivable	2,220									
10	Supplies	2,000									
11	Prepaid Insurance	2,400									
12	Land	20,000									
13	Office Equipment	1,800									
14	Accumulated Depreciation										
15	Accounts Payable		900								
16	Wages Payable										
17	Unearned Rent		360								
18	Capital Stock		25,000								
19	Dividends	4,000									
20	Fees Earned		16,340								
21	Rent Revenue										
22	Wages Expense	4,275									
23	Supplies Expense	800									
24	Rent Expense	1,600									
25	Utilities Expense	985									
26	Insurance Expense										
27	Depreciation Expense										
28	Miscellaneous Expense	455									
29		42,600	42,600								
30											
31											
32											

The spreadsheet (work sheet) is used for summarizing the effects of adjusting entries. It also aids in preparing financial statements.

The adjusting entries for NetSolutions that are entered in the Adjustments columns are as follows:

(a) **Supplies**. The supplies account has a debit balance of $2,000. The cost of the supplies on hand at the end of the period is $760. The supplies expense for December is the difference between the two amounts, or $1,240 ($2,000 – $760). The adjustment is entered as (1) $1,240 in the Adjustments Debit column on the same line as Supplies Expense and (2) $1,240 in the Adjustments Credit column on the same line as Supplies.

(b) **Prepaid Insurance**. The prepaid insurance account has a debit balance of $2,400. This balance represents the prepayment of insurance for 12 months beginning December 1. Thus, the insurance expense for December is $200 ($2,400 ÷ 12). The adjustment is entered as (1) $200 in the Adjustments Debit column on the same line as Insurance Expense and (2) $200 in the Adjustments Credit column on the same line as Prepaid Insurance.

(c) **Unearned Rent**. The unearned rent account has a credit balance of $360. This balance represents the receipt of three months' rent, beginning with December. Thus, the rent revenue for December is $120 ($360 ÷ 3). The adjustment is entered as (1) $120 in the Adjustments Debit column on the same line as Unearned Rent and (2) $120 in the Adjustments Credit column on the same line as Rent Revenue.

(d) **Accrued Fees**. Fees accrued at the end of December but not recorded total $500. This amount is an increase in an asset and an increase in revenue. The adjustment is entered as (1) $500 in the Adjustments Debit column on the same line as Accounts Receivable and (2) $500 in the Adjustments Credit column on the same line as Fees Earned.

EXHIBIT 19 **Spreadsheet (Work Sheet) with Unadjusted Trial Balance and Adjustments**

	A	B	C	D	E	F	G	H	I	J	K
1		NetSolutions									
2		End-of-Period Spreadsheet (Work Sheet)									
3		For the Two Months Ended December 31, 2013									
4		Unadjusted				Adjusted					
5		Trial Balance		Adjustments		Trial Balance		Income Statement		Balance Sheet	
6	**Account Title**	Dr.	Cr.	Dr.	Cr.	Dr.	Cr.	Dr.	Cr.	Dr.	Cr.
7											
8	Cash	2,065									
9	Accounts Receivable	2,220		(d) 500							
10	Supplies	2,000			(a) 1,240						
11	Prepaid Insurance	2,400			(b) 200						
12	Land	20,000									
13	Office Equipment	1,800									
14	Accumulated Depreciation				(f) 50						
15	Accounts Payable		900								
16	Wages Payable				(e) 250						
17	Unearned Rent		360	(c) 120							
18	Capital Stock		25,000								
19	Dividends	4,000									
20	Fees Earned		16,340		(d) 500						
21	Rent Revenue				(c) 120						
22	Wages Expense	4,275		(e) 250							
23	Supplies Expense	800		(a) 1,240							
24	Rent Expense	1,600									
25	Utilities Expense	985									
26	Insurance Expense			(b) 200							
27	Depreciation Expense			(f) 50							
28	Miscellaneous Expense	455									
29		42,600	42,600	2,360	2,360						
30											
31											
32											

The adjustments on the spreadsheet (work sheet) are used in preparing the adjusting journal entries.

(e) **Wages**. Wages accrued but not paid at the end of December total $250. This amount is an increase in expenses and an increase in liabilities. The adjustment is entered as (1) $250 in the Adjustments Debit column on the same line as Wages Expense and (2) $250 in the Adjustments Credit column on the same line as Wages Payable.

(f) **Depreciation**. Depreciation of the office equipment is $50 for December. The adjustment is entered as (1) $50 in the Adjustments Debit column on the same line as Depreciation Expense and (2) $50 in the Adjustments Credit column on the same line as Accumulated Depreciation.

After the adjustments have been entered, the Adjustments columns are totaled to verify the equality of the debits and credits. The total of the Debit column must equal the total of the Credit column.

Step 4. Enter the Adjusted Trial Balance

The adjusted trial balance is entered by combining the adjustments with the unadjusted balances for each account. The adjusted amounts are then extended to the Adjusted Trial Balance columns, as shown in Exhibit 20.

To illustrate, the cash amount of $2,065 is extended to the Adjusted Trial Balance Debit column since no adjustments affected Cash. Accounts Receivable has an initial balance of $2,220 and a debit adjustment of $500. Thus, $2,720 ($2,220 + $500) is entered in the Adjusted Trial Balance Debit column for Accounts Receivable. The same process continues until all account balances are extended to the Adjusted Trial Balance columns.

After the accounts and adjustments have been extended, the Adjusted Trial Balance columns are totaled to verify the equality of debits and credits. The total of the Debit column must equal the total of the Credit column.

EXHIBIT 20 **Spreadsheet (Work Sheet) with Unadjusted Trial Balance, Adjustments, and Adjusted Trial Balance Entered**

	A	B	C	D	E	F	G	H	I	J	K
1				NetSolutions							
2				End-of-Period Spreadsheet (Work Sheet)							
3				For the Two Months Ended December 31, 2013							
4		Unadjusted				Adjusted					
5		Trial Balance		Adjustments		Trial Balance		Income Statement		Balance Sheet	
6	**Account Title**	Dr.	Cr.	Dr.	Cr.	Dr.	Cr.	Dr.	Cr.	Dr.	Cr.
7											
8	Cash	2,065				2,065					
9	Accounts Receivable	2,220		(d) 500		2,720					
10	Supplies	2,000			(a) 1,240	760					
11	Prepaid Insurance	2,400			(b) 200	2,200					
12	Land	20,000				20,000					
13	Office Equipment	1,800				1,800					
14	Accumulated Depreciation				(f) 50		50				
15	Accounts Payable		900				900				
16	Wages Payable				(e) 250		250				
17	Unearned Rent		360	(c) 120			240				
18	Capital Stock		25,000				25,000				
19	Dividends	4,000				4,000					
20	Fees Earned		16,340		(d) 500		16,840				
21	Rent Revenue				(c) 120		120				
22	Wages Expense	4,275		(e) 250		4,525					
23	Supplies Expense	800		(a) 1,240		2,040					
24	Rent Expense	1,600				1,600					
25	Utilities Expense	985				985					
26	Insurance Expense			(b) 200		200					
27	Depreciation Expense			(f) 50		50					
28	Miscellaneous Expense	455				455					
29		42,600	42,600	2,360	2,360	43,400	43,400				
30											
31											
32											

The adjusted trial balance amounts are determined by adding the adjustments to or subtracting the adjustments from the trial balance amounts. For example, the Wages Expense debit of $4,525 is the trial balance amount of $4,275 plus the $250 adjustment debit.

Step 5. Extend the Accounts to the Income Statement and Balance Sheet Columns

The adjusted trial balance amounts are extended to the Income Statement and Balance Sheet columns. The amounts for revenues and expenses are extended to the Income Statement column. The amounts for assets, liabilities, capital stock, and dividends are extended to the Balance Sheet columns.[3]

The first account listed in the Adjusted Trial Balance columns is Cash with a debit balance of $2,065. Cash is an asset, is listed on the balance sheet, and has a debit balance. Therefore, $2,065 is extended to the Balance Sheet Debit column. The Fees Earned balance of $16,840 is extended to the Income Statement Credit column. The same process continues until all account balances have been extended to the proper columns, as shown in Exhibit 21.

3 The balance of the dividends account is extended to the Balance Sheet columns because the spreadsheet does not have separate Retained Earnings Statement columns.

EXHIBIT 21 **Spreadsheet (Work Sheet) with Amounts Extended to Income Statement and Balance Sheet Columns**

	A	B	C	D	E	F	G	H	I	J	K
1			NetSolutions								
2			End-of-Period Spreadsheet (Work Sheet)								
3			For the Two Months Ended December 31, 2013								
4		Unadjusted				Adjusted					
5		Trial Balance		Adjustments		Trial Balance		Income Statement		Balance Sheet	
6	Account Title	Dr.	Cr.	Dr.	Cr.	Dr.	Cr.	Dr.	Cr.	Dr.	Cr.
7											
8	Cash	2,065				2,065				2,065	
9	Accounts Receivable	2,220		(d) 500		2,720				2,720	
10	Supplies	2,000			(a) 1,240	760				760	
11	Prepaid Insurance	2,400			(b) 200	2,200				2,200	
12	Land	20,000				20,000				20,000	
13	Office Equipment	1,800				1,800				1,800	
14	Accumulated Depreciation				(f) 50		50				50
15	Accounts Payable		900				900				900
16	Wages Payable				(e) 250		250				250
17	Unearned Rent		360	(c) 120			240				240
18	Capital Stock		25,000				25,000				25,000
19	Dividends	4,000				4,000				4,000	
20	Fees Earned		16,340		(d) 500		16,840		16,840		
21	Rent Revenue				(c) 120		120		120		
22	Wages Expense	4,275		(e) 250		4,525		4,525			
23	Supplies Expense	800		(a) 1,240		2,040		2,040			
24	Rent Expense	1,600				1,600		1,600			
25	Utilities Expense	985				985		985			
26	Insurance Expense			(b) 200		200		200			
27	Depreciation Expense			(f) 50		50		50			
28	Miscellaneous Expense	455				455		455			
29		42,600	42,600	2,360	2,360	43,400	43,400				
30											
31											
32											

The revenue and expense amounts are extended to (entered in) the Income Statement columns.

The asset, liability, capital stock, and dividend amounts are extended to (entered in) the Balance Sheet columns.

Step 6. Total the Income Statement and Balance Sheet Columns, Compute the Net Income or Net Loss, and Complete the Spreadsheet

After the account balances are extended to the Income Statement and Balance Sheet columns, each of the columns is totaled. The difference between the two Income Statement column totals is the amount of the net income or the net loss for the period. This difference (net income or net loss) will also be the difference between the two Balance Sheet column totals.

If the Income Statement Credit column total (total revenue) is greater than the Income Statement Debit column total (total expenses), the difference is the net income. If the Income Statement Debit column total is greater than the Income Statement Credit column total, the difference is a net loss.

As shown in Exhibit 22, the total of the Income Statement Credit column is $16,960, and the total of the Income Statement Debit column is $9,855. Thus, the net income for NetSolutions is $7,105 as shown below.

Total of Income Statement Credit column (revenues)	$16,960
Total of Income Statement Debit column (expenses)	9,855
Net income (excess of revenues over expenses)	$ 7,105

The amount of the net income, $7,105, is entered in the Income Statement Debit column and the Balance Sheet Credit column. *Net income* is also entered in the Account Title column. Entering the net income of $7,105 in the Balance Sheet Credit column has the effect of transferring the net balance of the revenue and expense accounts to the retained earnings account.

If there was a net loss instead of net income, the amount of the net loss would be entered in the Income Statement Credit column and the Balance Sheet Debit column. *Net loss* would also be entered in the Account Title column.

EXHIBIT 22 **Completed Spreadsheet (Work Sheet) with Net Income Shown**

	A	B	C	D	E	F	G	H	I	J	K
1				NetSolutions							
2				End-of-Period Spreadsheet (Work Sheet)							
3				For the Two Months Ended December 31, 2013							
4		Unadjusted				Adjusted					
5		Trial Balance		Adjustments		Trial Balance		Income Statement		Balance Sheet	
6	**Account Title**	**Dr.**	**Cr.**	**Dr.**	**Cr.**	**Dr.**	**Cr.**	**Dr.**	**Cr.**	**Dr.**	**Cr.**
7											
8	Cash	2,065				2,065				2,065	
9	Accounts Receivable	2,220		(d) 500		2,720				2,720	
10	Supplies	2,000			(a) 1,240	760				760	
11	Prepaid Insurance	2,400			(b) 200	2,200				2,200	
12	Land	20,000				20,000				20,000	
13	Office Equipment	1,800				1,800				1,800	
14	Accumulated Depreciation				(f) 50		50				50
15	Accounts Payable		900				900				900
16	Wages Payable				(e) 250		250				250
17	Unearned Rent		360	(c) 120			240				240
18	Capital Stock		25,000				25,000				25,000
19	Dividends	4,000				4,000				4,000	
20	Fees Earned		16,340		(d) 500		16,840		16,840		
21	Rent Revenue				(c) 120		120		120		
22	Wages Expense	4,275		(e) 250		4,525		4,525			
23	Supplies Expense	800		(a) 1,240		2,040		2,040			
24	Rent Expense	1,600				1,600		1,600			
25	Utilities Expense	985				985		985			
26	Insurance Expense			(b) 200		200		200			
27	Depreciation Expense			(f) 50		50		50			
28	Miscellaneous Expense	455				455		455			
29		42,600	42,600	2,360	2,360	43,400	43,400	9,855	16,960	33,545	26,440
30	Net income							7,105			7,105
31								16,960	16,960	33,545	33,545
32											

The difference between the Income Statement column totals is the net income (or net loss) for the period. The difference between the Balance Sheet column totals is also the net income (or net loss) for the period.

After the net income or net loss is entered on the spreadsheet, the Income Statement and Balance Sheet columns are totaled. The totals of the two Income Statement columns must now be equal. The totals of the two Balance Sheet columns must also be equal.

Preparing the Financial Statements from the Spreadsheet

The spreadsheet can be used to prepare the income statement, the retained earnings statement, and the balance sheet shown in Exhibit 2. The income statement is normally prepared directly from the spreadsheet. The expenses are listed in the income statement in Exhibit 2 in order of size, beginning with the larger items. Miscellaneous expense is the last item, regardless of its amount.

The first item normally presented on the retained earnings statement is the balance of the retained earnings account at the beginning of the period. This amount along with the net income (or net loss) and the dividends amount shown in the spreadsheet, are used to determine the ending retained earnings account balance.

The balance sheet can be prepared directly from the spreadsheet columns except for the ending balance of retained earnings. The ending balance of retained earnings is taken from the retained earnings statement.

When a spreadsheet is used, the adjusting and closing entries are normally not journalized or posted until after the spreadsheet and financial statements have been prepared. The data for the adjusting entries are taken from the Adjustments columns of the spreadsheet. The data for the first two closing entries are taken from the Income Statement columns of the spreadsheet. The amount for the third closing entry is the net income or net loss appearing at the bottom of the spreadsheet. The amount for the fourth closing entry is the dividends account balance that appears in the Balance Sheet Debit column of the spreadsheet.

At a Glance 4

OBJ 1

Describe the flow of accounting information from the unadjusted trial balance into the adjusted trial balance and financial statements.

Key Points Exhibit 1 illustrates the end-of-period process by which accounts are adjusted and how the adjusted accounts flow into the financial statements.

Learning Outcome	Example Exercises	Practice Exercises
• Using an end-of-period spreadsheet, describe how the unadjusted trial balance accounts are affected by adjustments and how the adjusted trial balance accounts flow into the income statement, retained earnings statement, and balance sheet.	EE4-1	PE4-1A, 4-1B

OBJ 2 Prepare financial statements from adjusted account balances.

Key Points Using the end-of-period spreadsheet shown in Exhibit 1, the income statement, retained earnings statement, and balance sheet for NetSolutions can be prepared. A classified balance sheet has sections for current assets; property, plant, and equipment; current liabilities; long-term liabilities; and stockholders' equity.

Learning Outcomes	Example Exercises	Practice Exercises
• Describe how the net income or net loss from the period can be determined from an end-of-period spreadsheet.		
• Prepare an income statement, retained earnings statement, and a balance sheet.	EE4-2	PE4-2A, 4-2B
• Indicate how accounts would be reported on a classified balance sheet.	EE4-3	PE4-3A, 4-3B

OBJ 3 Prepare closing entries.

Key Points Four entries are required in closing the temporary accounts. The first entry closes the revenue accounts to Income Summary. The second entry closes the expense accounts to Income Summary. The third entry closes the balance of Income Summary (net income or net loss) to the retained earnings account. The fourth entry closes the dividends account to the retained earnings account.

After the closing entries have been posted to the ledger, the balance in the retained earnings account agrees with the amount reported on the retained earning statement and balance sheet. In addition, the revenue, expense, and dividends accounts will have zero balances.

Learning Outcomes	Example Exercises	Practice Exercises
• Prepare the closing entry for revenues.	EE4-4	PE4-4A, 4-4B
• Prepare the closing entry for expenses.	EE4-4	PE4-4A, 4-4B
• Prepare the closing entry for transferring the balance of Income Summary to the retained earnings account.	EE4-4	PE4-4A, 4-4B
• Prepare the closing entry for the dividends account.	EE4-4	PE4-4A, 4-4B

OBJ 4 Describe the accounting cycle.

Key Points The 10 basic steps of the accounting cycle are as follows:

1. Transactions are analyzed and recorded in the journal.
2. Transactions are posted to the ledger.
3. An unadjusted trial balance is prepared.
4. Adjustment data are assembled and analyzed.
5. An optional end-of-period spreadsheet is prepared.
6. Adjusting entries are journalized and posted to the ledger.
7. An adjusted trial balance is prepared.
8. Financial statements are prepared.
9. Closing entries are journalized and posted to the ledger.
10. A post-closing trial balance is prepared.

Learning Outcomes	Example Exercises	Practice Exercises
• List the 10 steps of the accounting cycle.	EE4-5	PE4-5A, 4-5B
• Determine whether any steps are out of order in a listing of accounting cycle steps.		
• Determine whether there are any missing steps in a listing of accounting cycle steps.		

OBJ 5 Illustrate the accounting cycle for one period.

Key Points The complete accounting cycle for Kelly Consulting for the month of April is described and illustrated on pages 163–173.

Learning Outcome	Example Exercises	Practice Exercises
• Complete the accounting cycle for a period from beginning to end.		

OBJ 6 Explain what is meant by the fiscal year and the natural business year.

Key Points The annual accounting period adopted by a business is its fiscal year. A company's fiscal year that ends when business activities have reached the lowest point in its annual operating cycle is called the natural business year.

Learning Outcome	Example Exercises	Practice Exercises
• Explain why companies use a fiscal year that is different from the calendar year.		

OBJ 7 Describe and illustrate the use of working capital and the current ratio in evaluating a company's financial condition.

Key Points The ability to convert assets into cash is called liquidity, while the ability of a business to pay its debts is called solvency. Two financial measures for evaluating a business's short-term liquidity and solvency are working capital and the current ratio. Working capital is computed by subtracting current liabilities from current assets. An excess of current assets over current liabilities implies that the business is able to pay its current liabilities. The current ratio is computed by dividing current assets by current liabilities. The current ratio is more useful than working capital in making comparisons across companies or with industry averages.

Learning Outcomes	Example Exercises	Practice Exercises
• Define liquidity and solvency.		
• Compute working capital.	EE4-6	PE4-6A, 4-6B
• Compute the current ratio.	EE4-6	PE4-6A, 4-6B

Key Terms

accounting cycle (162)
clearing account (157)
closing entries (157)
closing process (157)
closing the books (157)
current assets (155)
current liabilities (155)
current ratio (175)
fiscal year (173)
fixed (plant) assets (155)
Income Summary (157)
liquidity (174)
long-term liabilities (155)
natural business year (174)
notes receivable (155)
real (permanent) accounts (156)
solvency (174)
temporary (nominal) accounts (156)
working capital (174)

Illustrative Problem

Three years ago, T. Roderick organized Harbor Realty. At July 31, 2014, the end of the current fiscal year, the following end-of-period spreadsheet was prepared:

	A	B	C	D	E	F	G
1		Harbor Realty					
2		End-of-Period Spreadsheet					
3		For the Year Ended July 31, 2014					
4		Unadjusted				Adjusted	
5		Trial Balance		Adjustments		Trial Balance	
6	Account Title	Dr.	Cr.	Dr.	Cr.	Dr.	Cr.
7							
8	Cash	3,425				3,425	
9	Accounts Receivable	7,000		(e) 1,000		8,000	
10	Supplies	1,270			(a) 890	380	
11	Prepaid Insurance	620			(b) 315	305	
12	Office Equipment	51,650				51,650	
13	Accum. Depreciation		9,700		(c) 4,950		14,650
14	Accounts Payable		925				925
15	Unearned Fees		1,250	(f) 500			750
16	Wages Payable				(d) 440		440
17	Capital Stock		5,000				5,000
18	Retained Earnings		24,000				24,000
19	Dividends	5,200				5,200	
20	Fees Earned		59,125		(e) 1,000		60,625
21					(f) 500		
22	Wages Expense	22,415		(d) 440		22,855	
23	Depreciation Expense			(c) 4,950		4,950	
24	Rent Expense	4,200				4,200	
25	Utilities Expense	2,715				2,715	
26	Supplies Expense			(a) 890		890	
27	Insurance Expense			(b) 315		315	
28	Miscellaneous Expense	1,505				1,505	
29		100,000	100,000	8,095	8,095	106,390	106,390
30							

Instructions

1. Prepare an income statement, a retained earnings statement, and a balance sheet.
2. On the basis of the data in the end-of-period spreadsheet, journalize the closing entries.

Solution

1.

Harbor Realty
Income Statement
For the Year Ended July 31, 2014

Fees earned		$60,625
Expenses:		
Wages expense	$22,855	
Depreciation expense	4,950	
Rent expense	4,200	
Utilities expense	2,715	
Supplies expense	890	
Insurance expense	315	
Miscellaneous expense	1,505	
Total expenses		37,430
Net income		$23,195

Harbor Realty
Retained Earnings Statement
For the Year Ended July 31, 2014

Retained earnings, August 1, 2013		$24,000
Net income for the year	$23,195	
Less dividends	5,200	
Increase in retained earnings		17,995
Retained earnings, July 31, 2014		$41,995

Harbor Realty
Balance Sheet
July 31, 2014

Assets			Liabilities		
Current assets:			Current liabilities:		
Cash	$ 3,425		Accounts payable	$925	
Accounts receivable	8,000		Unearned fees	750	
Supplies	380		Wages payable	440	
Prepaid insurance	305		Total liabilities		$ 2,115
Total current assets		$12,110			
Property, plant, and equipment:			**Stockholders' Equity**		
Office equipment	$51,650		Capital stock	$ 5,000	
Less accum. depreciation	14,650		Retained earnings	41,995	
Total property, plant, and equipment		37,000	Total stockholders' equity		$46,995
Total assets		$49,110	Total liabilities and stockholders' equity		$49,110

2.

Journal *Page*

Date		Description	Post. Ref.	Debit	Credit
		Closing Entries			
2014 July	31	Fees Earned		60,625	
		Income Summary			60,625
	31	Income Summary		37,430	
		Wages Expense			22,855
		Depreciation Expense			4,950
		Rent Expense			4,200
		Utilities Expense			2,715
		Supplies Expense			890
		Insurance Expense			315
		Miscellaneous Expense			1,505
	31	Income Summary		23,195	
		Retained Earnings			23,195
	31	Retained Earnings		5,200	
		Dividends			5,200

Discussion Questions

1. Why do some accountants prepare an end-of-period spreadsheet?
2. Describe the nature of the assets that compose the following sections of a balance sheet: (a) current assets, (b) property, plant, and equipment.
3. What is the difference between a current liability and a long-term liability?
4. What types of accounts are referred to as temporary accounts?
5. Why are closing entries required at the end of an accounting period?
6. What is the difference between adjusting entries and closing entries?
7. What is the purpose of the post-closing trial balance?
8. (a) What is the most important output of the accounting cycle? (b) Do all companies have an accounting cycle? Explain.
9. What is the natural business year?
10. The fiscal years for several well-known companies are as follows:

Company	Fiscal Year Ending
Sears	January 30
JCPenney	January 30
Target Corp.	January 30
Home Depot	January 31
Tiffany & Co.	January 31
Limited Brands, Inc.	January 31

What general characteristic shared by these companies explains why they do not have fiscal years ending December 31?

Practice Exercises

Example Exercises

EE 4-1 *p. 152*

PE 4-1A Flow of accounts into financial statements — OBJ. 1

The balances for the accounts listed below appear in the Adjusted Trial Balance columns of the end-of-period spreadsheet. Indicate whether each account would flow into the income statement, retained earnings statement, or balance sheet.

1. Accounts Receivable
2. Depreciation Expense—Equipment
3. Capital Stock
4. Office Equipment
5. Rent Revenue
6. Supplies Expense
7. Unearned Revenue
8. Wages Payable

EE 4-1 *p. 152*

PE 4-1B Flow of accounts into financial statements — OBJ. 1

The balances for the accounts listed below appear in the Adjusted Trial Balance columns of the end-of-period spreadsheet. Indicate whether each account would flow into the income statement, retained earnings statement, or balance sheet.

1. Accumulated Depreciation—Building
2. Cash
3. Fees Earned
4. Insurance Expense
5. Prepaid Rent
6. Supplies
7. Dividends
8. Wages Expense

EE 4-2 *p. 154*

PE 4-2A Retained earnings statement — OBJ. 2

Francis Matthews owns and operates Daffodil Advertising Services. On January 1, 2013, Retained Earnings had a balance of $475,000. During the year, Francis invested an additional $50,000 in exchange for capital stock and $30,000 in dividends were paid. For the year ended December 31, 2013, Daffodil Advertising Services reported a net income of $139,500. Prepare a retained earnings statement for the year ended December 31, 2013.

EE 4-2 *p. 154*

PE 4-2B Retained earnings statement — OBJ. 2

Blake Knudson owns and operates Grab Bag Delivery Services. On January 1, 2013, Retained Earnings had a balance of $918,000. During the year, no additional capital stock was issued and $15,000 of dividends were paid. For the year ended December 31, 2013, Grab Bag Delivery Services reported a net loss of $43,500. Prepare a retained earnings statement for the year ended December 31, 2013.

EE 4-3 *p. 156*

PE 4-3A Classified balance sheet — OBJ. 2

The following accounts appear in an adjusted trial balance of Hampshire Consulting. Indicate whether each account would be reported in the (a) current asset; (b) property, plant, and equipment; (c) current liability; (d) long-term liability; or (e) stockholders' equity section of the December 31, 2013, balance sheet of Hampshire Consulting.

1. Building
2. Capital Stock
3. Notes Payable (due in 2020)
4. Prepaid Rent
5. Salaries Payable
6. Supplies
7. Taxes Payable
8. Unearned Service Fees

Example Exercises

EE 4-3 *p. 156*

PE 4-3B Classified balance sheet **OBJ. 2**

The following accounts appear in an adjusted trial balance of Kangaroo Consulting. Indicate whether each account would be reported in the (a) current asset; (b) property, plant, and equipment; (c) current liability; (d) long-term liability; or (e) stockholders' equity section of the December 31, 2013, balance sheet of Kangaroo Consulting.

1. Accounts Payable
2. Accounts Receivable
3. Accumulated Depreciation—Building
4. Cash
5. Capital Stock
6. Note Payable (due in 2021)
7. Supplies
8. Wages Payable

EE 4-4 *p. 159*

PE 4-4A Closing entries **OBJ. 3**

After the accounts have been adjusted at August 31, the end of the fiscal year, the following balances were taken from the ledger of Marcy Delivery Services Co.:

Retained Earnings	$1,400,000
Dividends	55,000
Fees Earned	880,000
Wages Expense	524,000
Rent Expense	80,000
Supplies Expense	16,000
Miscellaneous Expense	9,000

Journalize the four entries required to close the accounts.

EE 4-4 *p. 159*

PE 4-4B Closing entries **OBJ. 3**

After the accounts have been adjusted at April 30, the end of the fiscal year, the following balances were taken from the ledger of Nuclear Landscaping Co.:

Retained Earnings	$643,600
Dividends	10,500
Fees Earned	356,500
Wages Expense	283,100
Rent Expense	56,000
Supplies Expense	11,500
Miscellaneous Expense	13,000

Journalize the four entries required to close the accounts.

EE 4-5 *p. 162*

PE 4-5A Accounting cycle **OBJ. 4**

From the following list of steps in the accounting cycle, identify what two steps are missing.

a. Transactions are analyzed and recorded in the journal.
b. An unadjusted trial balance is prepared.
c. Adjustment data are assembled and analyzed.
d. An optional end-of-period spreadsheet is prepared.
e. Adjusting entries are journalized and posted to the ledger.
f. An adjusted trial balance is prepared.
g. Closing entries are journalized and posted to the ledger.
h. A post-closing trial balance is prepared.

EE 4-5 *p. 162*

PE 4-5B Accounting cycle **OBJ. 4**

From the following list of steps in the accounting cycle, identify what two steps are missing.

a. Transactions are analyzed and recorded in the journal.
b. Transactions are posted to the ledger.

(Continued)

Example Exercises

c. An unadjusted trial balance is prepared.
d. An optional end-of-period spreadsheet is prepared.
e. Adjusting entries are journalized and posted to the ledger.
f. An adjusted trial balance is prepared.
g. Financial statements are prepared.
h. A post-closing trial balance is prepared.

EE 4-6 *p. 175*

F·A·I

PE 4-6A Working capital and current ratio **OBJ. 7**

The following balance sheet data for Pecan Company are shown below.

	2014	2013
Current assets	$1,467,000	$1,269,000
Current liabilities	815,000	675,000

a. Determine the working capital and current ratio for 2014 and 2013.
b. Does the change in the current ratio from 2013 to 2014 indicate a favorable or an unfavorable trend?

EE 4-6 *p. 175*

F·A·I

PE 4-6B Working capital and current ratio **OBJ. 7**

The following balance sheet data for Brimstone Company are shown below.

	2014	2013
Current assets	$1,586,250	$1,210,000
Current liabilities	705,000	550,000

a. Determine the working capital and current ratio for 2014 and 2013.
b. Does the change in the current ratio from 2013 to 2014 indicate a favorable or an unfavorable trend?

Exercises

EX 4-1 Flow of accounts into financial statements **OBJ. 1, 2**

The balances for the accounts listed below appear in the Adjusted Trial Balance columns of the end-of-period spreadsheet. Indicate whether each account would flow into the income statement, retained earnings statement, or balance sheet.

1. Accounts Payable
2. Accounts Receivable
3. Cash
4. Dividends
5. Fees Earned
6. Supplies
7. Unearned Rent
8. Utilities Expense
9. Wages Expense
10. Wages Payable

EX 4-2 Classifying accounts **OBJ. 1, 2**

Balances for each of the following accounts appear in an adjusted trial balance. Identify each as (a) asset, (b) liability, (c) revenue, or (d) expense.

1. Accounts Receivable
2. Equipment
3. Fees Earned
4. Insurance Expense
5. Prepaid Advertising
6. Prepaid Rent
7. Rent Revenue
8. Salary Expense
9. Salary Payable
10. Supplies
11. Supplies Expense
12. Unearned Rent

EX 4-3 Financial statements from the end-of-period spreadsheet **OBJ. 1, 2**

Holism Consulting is a consulting firm owned and operated by Scott Cutler. The end-of-period spreadsheet shown below was prepared for the year ended May 31, 2014.

	A	B	C	D	E	F	G
1		Holism Consulting					
2		End-of-Period Spreadsheet					
3		For the Year Ended May 31, 2014					
4		Unadjusted				Adjusted	
5		Trial Balance		Adjustments		Trial Balance	
6	**Account Title**	**Dr.**	**Cr.**	**Dr.**	**Cr.**	**Dr.**	**Cr.**
7							
8	Cash	38,000				38,000	
9	Accounts Receivable	90,000				90,000	
10	Supplies	9,600			(a) 6,000	3,600	
11	Office Equipment	74,000				74,000	
12	Accumulated Depreciation		10,000		(b) 4,800		14,800
13	Accounts Payable		24,400				24,400
14	Salaries Payable				(c) 1,500		1,500
15	Capital Stock		10,000				10,000
16	Retained Earnings		80,400				80,400
17	Dividends	12,000				12,000	
18	Fees Earned		175,200				175,200
19	Salary Expense	69,000		(c) 1,500		70,500	
20	Supplies Expense			(a) 6,000		6,000	
21	Depreciation Expense			(b) 4,800		4,800	
22	Miscellaneous Expense	7,400				7,400	
23		300,000	300,000	12,300	12,300	306,300	306,300
24							

Based on the preceding spreadsheet, prepare an income statement, retained earnings statement, and balance sheet for Holism Consulting.

EX 4-4 Financial statements from the end-of-period spreadsheet **OBJ. 1, 2**

Olympia Consulting is a consulting firm owned and operated by Raul Hann. The following end-of-period spreadsheet was prepared for the year ended April 30, 2014.

	A	B	C	D	E	F	G
1		Olympia Consulting					
2		End-of-Period Spreadsheet					
3		For the Year Ended April 30, 2014					
4		Unadjusted				Adjusted	
5		Trial Balance		Adjustments		Trial Balance	
6	**Account Title**	**Dr.**	**Cr.**	**Dr.**	**Cr.**	**Dr.**	**Cr.**
7							
8	Cash	27,500				27,500	
9	Accounts Receivable	53,500				53,500	
10	Supplies	3,000			(a) 1,800	1,200	
11	Office Equipment	30,500				30,500	
12	Accumulated Depreciation		4,500		(b) 750		5,250
13	Accounts Payable		3,300				3,300
14	Salaries Payable				(c) 450		450
15	Capital Stock		30,000				30,000
16	Retained Earnings		52,200				52,200
17	Dividends	2,000				2,000	
18	Fees Earned		60,000				60,000
19	Salary Expense	32,000		(c) 450		32,450	
20	Supplies Expense			(a) 1,800		1,800	
21	Depreciation Expense			(b) 750		750	
22	Miscellaneous Expense	1,500				1,500	
23		150,000	150,000	3,000	3,000	151,200	151,200
24							

Based on the preceding spreadsheet, prepare an income statement, retained earnings statement, and balance sheet for Olympia Consulting.

EX 4-5 Income statement **OBJ. 2**

✔ Net income, $92,600

The following account balances were taken from the adjusted trial balance for Shanghai Messenger Service, a delivery service firm, for the current fiscal year ended September 30, 2014:

Depreciation Expense	$ 7,250	Rent Expense	$ 36,000
Fees Earned	440,000	Salaries Expense	265,150
Insurance Expense	1,200	Supplies Expense	2,200
Miscellaneous Expense	7,100	Utilities Expense	28,500

Prepare an income statement.

EX 4-6 Income statement; net loss **OBJ. 2**

✔ Net loss, $23,800

The following revenue and expense account balances were taken from the ledger of Veggie Health Services Co. after the accounts had been adjusted on February 28, 2014, the end of the current fiscal year:

Depreciation Expense	$ 9,000	Service Revenue	$270,900
Insurance Expense	4,000	Supplies Expense	3,000
Miscellaneous Expense	6,000	Utilities Expense	17,600
Rent Expense	42,000	Wages Expense	213,100

Prepare an income statement.

EX 4-7 Income statement **OBJ. 2**

Internet Project

✔ a. Net income: $1,452

FedEx Corporation had the following revenue and expense account balances (in millions) for a recent year ending May 31, 2011:

Depreciation	$1,973	Purchased Transportation	$ 5,674
Fuel	4,151	Rentals and Landing Fees	2,462
Maintenance and Repairs	1,979	Revenues	39,304
Other Expense (Income) Net	5,524	Salaries and Employee Benefits	15,276
Provision for Income Taxes	813		

a. Prepare an income statement.

b. Compare your income statement with the related income statement that is available at the FedEx Corporation Web site, which is linked to the text's Web site at **www.cengagebrain.com**. What similarities and differences do you see?

EX 4-8 Retained earnings statement **OBJ. 2**

✔ Retained Earnings, Oct. 31, 2014: $517,000

Well Systems Co. offers its services to residents in the Dallas area. Selected accounts from the ledger of Well Systems Co. for the current fiscal year ended October 31, 2014, are as follows:

Retained Earnings

Oct. 31	48,000	Nov. 1 (2013)	475,000
		Oct. 31	90,000

Dividends

Jan. 31	12,000	Oct. 31	48,000
Apr. 30	12,000		
July 31	12,000		
Oct. 31	12,000		

Income Summary

Oct. 31	270,000	Oct. 31	360,000
31	90,000		

Prepare a retained earnings statement for the year.

EX 4-9 Retained earnings statement; net loss **OBJ. 2**

✔ Retained Earnings, June 30, 2014: $70,900

Selected accounts from the ledger of Weird Sports for the current fiscal year ended June 30, 2014, are as follows:

Retained Earnings

June 30	20,900	July 1 (2013)	115,800
30	24,000		

Dividends

Sept. 30	6,000	June 30	24,000
Dec. 31	6,000		
March 31	6,000		
June 30	6,000		

	Income Summary		
June 30	201,400	June 30	180,500
		30	20,900

Prepare a retained earnings statement for the year.

EX 4-10 Classifying assets **OBJ. 2**

Identify each of the following as (a) a current asset or (b) property, plant, and equipment:

1. Accounts Receivable
2. Building
3. Cash
4. Equipment
5. Prepaid Insurance
6. Supplies

EX 4-11 Balance sheet classification **OBJ. 2**

At the balance sheet date, a business owes a mortgage note payable of $375,000, the terms of which provide for monthly payments of $1,250.

Explain how the liability should be classified on the balance sheet.

EX 4-12 Balance sheet **OBJ. 2**

✔ Total assets: $645,000

Labrador Weight Loss Co. offers personal weight reduction consulting services to individuals. After all the accounts have been closed on June 30, 2014, the end of the current fiscal year, the balances of selected accounts from the ledger of Labrador Weight Loss Co. are as follows:

Accounts Payable	$ 18,500	Prepaid Insurance	$ 19,200
Accounts Receivable	78,250	Prepaid Rent	18,000
Accumulated Depreciation—Equipment	103,300	Retained Earnings	509,000
Capital Stock	100,000	Salaries Payable	8,500
Cash	?	Supplies	5,350
Equipment	300,000	Unearned Fees	9,000
Land	290,000		

Prepare a classified balance sheet that includes the correct balance for Cash.

EX 4-13 Balance sheet **OBJ. 2**

✔ Corrected balance sheet, total assets: $625,000

List the errors you find in the following balance sheet. Prepare a corrected balance sheet.

Labyrinth Services Co.
Balance Sheet
For the Year Ended August 31, 2014

Assets			**Liabilities**		
Current assets:			Current liabilities:		
Cash	$ 18,500		Accounts receivable	$ 41,400	
Accounts payable	31,300		Accum. depr.—building	155,000	
Supplies	6,500		Accum. depr.—equipment	25,000	
Prepaid insurance	16,600		Net income	118,200	
Land	225,000		Total liabilities		$339,600
Total current assets		$297,900			
Property, plant, and equipment:			**Stockholders' Equity**		
Building	$400,000		Wages payable	$ 6,500	
Equipment	97,000		Capital stock	75,000	
Total property, plant, and equipment		635,400	Retained earnings	512,200	
			Total stockholders' equity		593,700
Total assets		$933,300	Total liabilities and stockholders' equity		$933,300

EX 4-14 Identifying accounts to be closed **OBJ. 3**

From the list at the top of the next page, identify the accounts that should be closed to Income Summary at the end of the fiscal year:

(Continued)

a. Accounts Payable
b. Accumulated Depreciation—Equipment
c. Capital Stock
d. Depreciation Expense—Equipment
e. Dividends
f. Equipment
g. Fees Earned
h. Land
i. Supplies
j. Supplies Expense
k. Wages Expense
l. Wages Payable

EX 4-15 Closing entries **OBJ. 3**

Prior to its closing, Income Summary had total debits of $1,190,500 and total credits of $1,476,300.

Briefly explain the purpose served by the income summary account and the nature of the entries that resulted in the $1,190,500 and the $1,476,300.

EX 4-16 Closing entries with net income **OBJ. 3**

After all revenue and expense accounts have been closed at the end of the fiscal year, Income Summary has a debit of $490,750 and a credit of $613,400. At the same date, Retained Earnings has a credit balance of $833,600, and Dividends has a balance of $55,000. (a) Journalize the entries required to complete the closing of the accounts. (b) Determine the amount of Retained Earnings at the end of the period.

EX 4-17 Closing entries with net loss **OBJ. 3**

Grande Services Co. offers its services to individuals desiring to improve their personal images. After the accounts have been adjusted at July 31, the end of the fiscal year, the following balances were taken from the ledger of Grande Services Co.

Retained Earnings	$842,500	Rent Expense	$54,000
Dividends	45,000	Supplies Expense	14,300
Fees Earned	337,900	Miscellaneous Expense	16,200
Wages Expense	277,500		

Journalize the four entries required to close the accounts.

EX 4-18 Identifying permanent accounts **OBJ. 3**

Which of the following accounts will usually appear in the post-closing trial balance?

a. Accounts Payable
b. Accumulated Depreciation
c. Capital Stock
d. Cash
e. Depreciation Expense
f. Dividends
g. Fees Earned
h. Office Equipment
i. Salaries Expense
j. Salaries Payable
k. Supplies

EX 4-19 Post-closing trial balance **OBJ. 3**

✔ Correct column totals, $160,000

An accountant prepared the following post-closing trial balance:

Igloo Treasures Co.
Post-Closing Trial Balance
January 31, 2014

	Debit Balances	Credit Balances
Cash	21,350	
Accounts Receivable	56,700	
Supplies		7,500
Equipment		74,450
Accumulated Depreciation—Equipment	12,400	
Accounts Payable	29,600	
Salaries Payable		3,200
Unearned Rent	11,000	
Capital Stock	25,000	
Retained Earnings	78,800	
	234,850	85,150

Prepare a corrected post-closing trial balance. Assume that all accounts have normal balances and that the amounts shown are correct.

EX 4-20 Steps in the accounting cycle **OBJ. 4**

Rearrange the following steps in the accounting cycle in proper sequence:

a. Financial statements are prepared.
b. An adjusted trial balance is prepared.
c. Adjustment data are asssembled and analyzed.
d. Adjusting entries are journalized and posted to the ledger.
e. Closing entries are journalized and posted to the ledger.
f. An unadjusted trial balance is prepared.
g. Transactions are posted to the ledger.
h. Transactions are analyzed and recorded in the journal.
i. An optional end-of-period spreadsheet (work sheet) is prepared.
j. A post-closing trial balance is prepared.

EX 4-21 Working capital and current ratio **OBJ. 7**

F·A·I

The following data (in thousands) were taken from recent financial statements of Under Armour, Inc.:

	December 31	
	Year 2	**Year 1**
Current assets	$555,850	$448,000
Current liabilities	149,147	120,162

a. Compute the working capital and the current ratio as of December 31, Year 2 and Year 1. Round to two decimal places.
b. What conclusions concerning the company's ability to meet its financial obligations can you draw from part (a)?

EX 4-22 Working capital and current ratio **OBJ. 7**

F·A·I

The following data (in thousands) were taken from recent financial statements of Starbucks Corporation:

	Year 2	**Year 1**
Current assets	$2,756,400	$2,035,800
Current liabilities	1,779,100	1,581,000

a. Compute the working capital and the current ratio for Year 2 and Year 1. Round to two decimal places.
b. What conclusions concerning the company's ability to meet its financial obligations can you draw from part (a)?

Appendix
EX 4-23 Completing an end-of-period spreadsheet (work sheet)

List (a) through (j) in the order they would be performed in preparing and completing an end-of-period spreadsheet (work sheet).

a. Add the Debit and Credit columns of the Unadjusted Trial Balance columns of the spreadsheet (work sheet) to verify that the totals are equal.
b. Add the Debit and Credit columns of the Balance Sheet and Income Statement columns of the spreadsheet (work sheet) to verify that the totals are equal.

(Continued)

c. Add or deduct adjusting entry data to trial balance amounts, and extend amounts to the Adjusted Trial Balance columns.

d. Add the Debit and Credit columns of the Adjustments columns of the spreadsheet (work sheet) to verify that the totals are equal.

e. Add the Debit and Credit columns of the Balance Sheet and Income Statement columns of the spreadsheet (work sheet) to determine the amount of net income or net loss for the period.

f. Add the Debit and Credit columns of the Adjusted Trial Balance columns of the spreadsheet (work sheet) to verify that the totals are equal.

g. Enter the adjusting entries into the spreadsheet (work sheet), based on the adjustment data.

h. Enter the amount of net income or net loss for the period in the proper Income Statement column and Balance Sheet column.

i. Enter the unadjusted account balances from the general ledger into the Unadjusted Trial Balance columns of the spreadsheet (work sheet).

j. Extend the adjusted trial balance amounts to the Income Statement columns and the Balance Sheet columns.

Appendix

EX 4-24 Adjustment data on an end-of-period spreadsheet (work sheet)

✔ Total debits of Adjustments column: $31

SPREADSHEET

Alert Security Services Co. offers security services to business clients. The trial balance for Alert Security Services Co. has been prepared on the end-of-period spreadsheet (work sheet) for the year ended October 31, 2014, shown below.

Alert Security Services Co.
End-of-Period Spreadsheet (Work Sheet)
For the Year Ended October 31, 2014

	Unadjusted Trial Balance		Adjustments		Adjusted Trial Balance	
Account Title	**Dr.**	**Cr.**	**Dr.**	**Cr.**	**Dr.**	**Cr.**
Cash	12					
Accounts Receivable	90					
Supplies	8					
Prepaid Insurance	12					
Land	190					
Equipment	50					
Accum. Depr.—Equipment		4				
Accounts Payable		36				
Wages Payable		0				
Capital Stock		50				
Retained Earnings		210				
Dividends	8					
Fees Earned		200				
Wages Expense	110					
Rent Expense	12					
Insurance Expense	0					
Utilities Expense	6					
Supplies Expense	0					
Depreciation Expense	0					
Miscellaneous Expense	2					
	500	500				

The data for year-end adjustments are as follows:

a. Fees earned, but not yet billed, $13.

b. Supplies on hand, $4.

c. Insurance premiums expired, $10.

d. Depreciation expense, $3.

e. Wages accrued, but not paid, $1.

Enter the adjustment data, and place the balances in the Adjusted Trial Balance columns.

Appendix

EX 4-25 Completing an end-of-period spreadsheet (work sheet)

✔ Net income: $65

SPREADSHEET

Alert Security Services Co. offers security services to business clients. Complete the following end-of-period spreadsheet (work sheet) for Alert Security Services Co.

Alert Security Services Co.
End-of-Period Spreadsheet (Work Sheet)
For the Year Ended October 31, 2014

	Adjusted Trial Balance		Income Statement		Balance Sheet	
Account Title	**Dr.**	**Cr.**	**Dr.**	**Cr.**	**Dr.**	**Cr.**
Cash	12					
Accounts Receivable	103					
Supplies	4					
Prepaid Insurance	2					
Land	190					
Equipment	50					
Accum. Depr.—Equipment		7				
Accounts Payable		36				
Wages Payable		1				
Capital Stock		50				
Retained Earnings		210				
Dividends	8					
Fees Earned		213				
Wages Expense	111					
Rent Expense	12					
Insurance Expense	10					
Utilities Expense	6					
Supplies Expense	4					
Depreciation Expense	3					
Miscellaneous Expense	2					
	517	517				
Net income (loss)						

Appendix

EX 4-26 Financial statements from an end-of-period spreadsheet (work sheet)

✔ Retained Earnings, October 31, 2014: $267

SPREADSHEET

Based on the data in Exercise 4-25, prepare an income statement, retained earnings statement, and balance sheet for Alert Security Services Co.

Appendix

EX 4-27 Adjusting entries from an end-of-period spreadsheet (work sheet)

Based on the data in Exercise 4-24, prepare the adjusting entries for Alert Security Services Co.

Appendix

EX 4-28 Closing entries from an end-of-period spreadsheet (work sheet)

Based on the data in Exercise 4-25, prepare the closing entries for Alert Security Services Co.

Problems Series A

PR 4-1A Financial statements and closing entries

OBJ. 1, 2, 3

✔ **3. Total assets: $359,500**

SPREADSHEET

GENERAL LEDGER

Watchdog Company maintains and repairs warning lights, such as those found on radio towers and lighthouses. Watchdog Company prepared the end-of-period spreadsheet shown below at July 31, 2014, the end of the current fiscal year:

	A	B	C	D	E	F	G
1				Watchdog Company			
2				End-of-Period Spreadsheet			
3				For the Year Ended July 31, 2014			
4		Unadjusted				Adjusted	
5		Trial Balance		Adjustments		Trial Balance	
6	Account Title	Dr.	Cr.	Dr.	Cr.	Dr.	Cr.
7							
8	Cash	10,800				10,800	
9	Accounts Receivable	38,900		(a) 4,400		43,300	
10	Prepaid Insurance	4,200			(b) 2,500	1,700	
11	Supplies	2,730			(c) 1,830	900	
12	Land	98,000				98,000	
13	Building	400,000				400,000	
14	Accum. Depr.—Building		205,300		(d) 1,600		206,900
15	Equipment	101,000				101,000	
16	Accum. Depr.—Equipment		85,100		(e) 4,200		89,300
17	Accounts Payable		15,700				15,700
18	Salaries & Wages Payable				(f) 1,800		1,800
19	Unearned Rent		2,100	(g) 1,000			1,100
20	Capital Stock		75,000				75,000
21	Retained Earnings		128,100				128,100
22	Dividends	10,000				10,000	
23	Fees Earned		363,700		(a) 4,400		368,100
24	Rent Revenue				(g) 1,000		1,000
25	Salaries & Wages Expense	163,100		(f) 1,800		164,900	
26	Advertising Expense	21,700				21,700	
27	Utilities Expense	11,400				11,400	
28	Repairs Expense	8,850				8,850	
29	Depr. Exp.—Equipment			(e) 4,200		4,200	
30	Insurance Expense			(b) 2,500		2,500	
31	Supplies Expense			(c) 1,830		1,830	
32	Depr. Exp.—Building			(d) 1,600		1,600	
33	Misc. Expense	4,320				4,320	
34		875,000	875,000	17,330	17,330	887,000	887,000
35							

Instructions

1. Prepare an income statement for the year ended July 31.
2. Prepare a retained earnings statement for the year ended July 31.
3. Prepare a balance sheet as of July 31.
4. Based upon the end-of-period spreadsheet, journalize the closing entries.
5. Prepare a post-closing trial balance.

PR 4-2A Financial statements and closing entries

OBJ. 2, 3

✔ **1. Retained Earnings, April 30 2014: $207,300**

Ironside Security Services is an investigative services firm that is owned and operated by Don Chadwell. On April 30, 2014, the end of the current fiscal year, the accountant for Ironside Security Services prepared an end-of-period spreadsheet, a part of which is shown on the next page.

	A	F	G
1	Ironside Security Services		
2	End-of-Period Spreadsheet		
3	For the Year Ended April 30, 2014		
4		Adjusted	
5		Trial Balance	
6	**Account Title**	Dr.	Cr.
7			
8	Cash	18,000	
9	Accounts Receivable	37,200	
10	Supplies	7,500	
11	Prepaid Insurance	4,800	
12	Building	240,500	
13	Accumulated Depreciation—Building		55,200
14	Accounts Payable		6,000
15	Salaries Payable		1,500
16	Unearned Rent		3,000
17	Capital Stock		35,000
18	Retained Earnings		144,300
19	Dividends	10,000	
20	Service Fees		480,000
21	Rent Revenue		25,000
22	Salaries Expense	336,000	
23	Rent Expense	62,500	
24	Supplies Expense	12,000	
25	Depreciation Expense—Building	6,000	
26	Utilities Expense	4,400	
27	Repairs Expense	3,200	
28	Insurance Expense	2,800	
29	Miscellaneous Expense	5,100	
30		750,000	750,000
31			

Instructions

1. Prepare an income statement, a retained earnings statement, and a balance sheet.
2. Journalize the entries that were required to close the accounts at April 30.
3. If Retained Earnings has instead decreased $47,500 after the closing entries were posted, and the dividends remained the same, what would have been the amount of net income or net loss?

✔ 5. Net income: $10,700

GENERAL LEDGER

PR 4-3A T accounts, adjusting entries, financial statements, and closing entries; optional end-of-period spreadsheet (work sheet) **OBJ. 2, 3**

The unadjusted trial balance of Epicenter Laundry at June 30, 2014, the end of the current fiscal year, is shown below.

Epicenter Laundry
Unadjusted Trial Balance
June 30, 2014

	Debit Balances	Credit Balances
Cash	11,000	
Laundry Supplies	21,500	
Prepaid Insurance	9,600	
Laundry Equipment	232,600	
Accumulated Depreciation		125,400
Accounts Payable		11,800
Capital Stock		40,000
Retained Earnings		65,600
Dividends	10,000	
Laundry Revenue		232,200
Wages Expense	125,200	
Rent Expense	40,000	
Utilities Expense	19,700	
Miscellaneous Expense	5,400	
	475,000	475,000

(Continued)

The data needed to determine year-end adjustments are as follows:

a. Laundry supplies on hand at June 30 are $3,600.
b. Insurance premiums expired during the year are $5,700.
c. Depreciation of laundry equipment during the year is $6,500.
d. Wages accrued but not paid at June 30 are $1,100.

Instructions

1. For each account listed in the unadjusted trial balance, enter the balance in a T account. Identify the balance as "June 30 Bal." In addition, add T accounts for Wages Payable, Depreciation Expense, Laundry Supplies Expense, Insurance Expense, and Income Summary.
2. (Optional.) Enter the unadjusted trial balance on an end-of-period spreadsheet (work sheet) and complete the spreadsheet. Add the accounts listed in part (1) as needed.
3. Journalize and post the adjusting entries. Identify the adjustments by "Adj." and the new balances as "Adj. Bal."
4. Prepare an adjusted trial balance.
5. Prepare an income statement, a retained earnings statement, and a balance sheet.
6. Journalize and post the closing entries. Identify the closing entries by "Clos."
7. Prepare a post-closing trial balance.

PR 4-4A Ledger accounts, adjusting entries, financial statements, and closing entries; optional spreadsheet (work sheet) OBJ. 2, 3

✔ 5. Net income: $51,150

SPREADSHEET

The unadjusted trial balance of Lakota Freight Co. at March 31, 2014, the end of the current year, is shown below.

Lakota Freight Co.
Unadjusted Trial Balance
March 31, 2014

		Debit Balances	Credit Balances
11	Cash	12,000	
13	Supplies	30,000	
14	Prepaid Insurance	3,600	
16	Equipment	110,000	
17	Accumulated Depreciation—Equipment		25,000
18	Trucks	60,000	
19	Accumulated Depreciation—Trucks		15,000
21	Accounts Payable		4,000
31	Capital Stock		26,000
32	Retained Earnings		70,000
33	Dividends	15,000	
41	Service Revenue		160,000
51	Wages Expense	45,000	
53	Rent Expense	10,600	
54	Truck Expense	9,000	
59	Miscellaneous Expense	4,800	
		300,000	300,000

The data needed to determine year-end adjustments are as follows:

a. Supplies on hand at March 31 are $7,500.
b. Insurance premiums expired during year are $1,800.
c. Depreciation of equipment during year is $8,350.
d. Depreciation of trucks during year is $6,200.
e. Wages accrued but not paid at March 31 are $600.

Instructions

1. For each account listed in the trial balance, enter the balance in the appropriate Balance column of a four-column account and place a check mark (✓) in the Posting Reference column.
2. (Optional.) Enter the unadjusted trial balance on an end-of-period spreadsheet (work sheet) and complete the spreadsheet. Add the accounts listed in part (3) as needed.
3. Journalize and post the adjusting entries, inserting balances in the accounts affected. Record the adjusting entries on Page 26 of the journal. The following additional accounts from Lakota Freight Co.'s chart of accounts should be used: Wages Payable, 22; Supplies Expense, 52; Depreciation Expense—Equipment, 55; Depreciation Expense—Trucks, 56; Insurance Expense, 57.
4. Prepare an adjusted trial balance.
5. Prepare an income statement, a retained earnings statement, and a balance sheet.
6. Journalize and post the closing entries. Record the closing entries on Page 27 of the journal. (Income Summary is account #34 in the chart of accounts.) Indicate closed accounts by inserting a line in both Balance columns opposite the closing entry.
7. Prepare a post-closing trial balance.

PR 4-5A Complete accounting cycle **OBJ. 4, 5**

✓ 8. Net income: $33,475

SPREADSHEET

For the past several years, Steffy Lopez has operated a part-time consulting business from his home. As of July 1, 2014, Steffy decided to move to rented quarters and to operate the business, which was to be known as Diamond Consulting, on a full-time basis. Diamond Consulting entered into the following transactions during July:

July 1. The following assets were received from Steffy Lopez in exchange for capital stock: cash, $13,500; accounts receivable, $20,800; supplies, $3,200; and office equipment, $7,500. There were no liabilities received.

1. Paid two months' rent on a lease rental contract, $4,800.

2. Paid the premiums on property and casualty insurance policies, $4,500.

4. Received cash from clients as an advance payment for services to be provided and recorded it as unearned fees, $5,500.

5. Purchased additional office equipment on account from Office Station Co., $6,500.

6. Received cash from clients on account, $15,300.

10. Paid cash for a newspaper advertisement, $400.

12. Paid Office Station Co. for part of the debt incurred on July 5, $5,200.

12. Recorded services provided on account for the period July 1–12, $13,300.

14. Paid receptionist for two weeks' salary, $1,750.

Record the following transactions on Page 2 of the journal.

17. Recorded cash from cash clients for fees earned during the period July 1–17, $9,450.

18. Paid cash for supplies, $600.

20. Recorded services provided on account for the period July 13–20, $6,650.

24. Recorded cash from cash clients for fees earned for the period July 17–24, $4,000.

26. Received cash from clients on account, $12,000.

27. Paid receptionist for two weeks' salary, $1,750.

29. Paid telephone bill for July, $325.

31. Paid electricity bill for July, $675.

31. Recorded cash from cash clients for fees earned for the period July 25–31, $5,200.

(Continued)

July 31. Recorded services provided on account for the remainder of July, $3,000.
31. Paid dividends of $12,500.

Instructions

1. Journalize each transaction in a two-column journal starting on Page 1, referring to the following chart of accounts in selecting the accounts to be debited and credited. (Do not insert the account numbers in the journal at this time.)

11	Cash	31	Capital Stock
12	Accounts Receivable	32	Retained Earnings
14	Supplies	33	Dividends
15	Prepaid Rent	41	Fees Earned
16	Prepaid Insurance	51	Salary Expense
18	Office Equipment	52	Rent Expense
19	Accumulated Depreciation	53	Supplies Expense
21	Accounts Payable	54	Depreciation Expense
22	Salaries Payable	55	Insurance Expense
23	Unearned Fees	59	Miscellaneous Expense

2. Post the journal to a ledger of four-column accounts.
3. Prepare an unadjusted trial balance.
4. At the end of July, the following adjustment data were assembled. Analyze and use these data to complete parts (5) and (6).
   a. Insurance expired during July is $375.
   b. Supplies on hand on July 31 are $1,525.
   c. Depreciation of office equipment for July is $750.
   d. Accrued receptionist salary on July 31 is $175.
   e. Rent expired during July is $2,400.
   f. Unearned fees on July 31 are $2,750.
5. (Optional.) Enter the unadjusted trial balance on an end-of-period spreadsheet (work sheet) and complete the spreadsheet.
6. Journalize and post the adjusting entries. Record the adjusting entries on Page 3 of the journal.
7. Prepare an adjusted trial balance.
8. Prepare an income statement, a retained earnings statement, and a balance sheet.
9. Prepare and post the closing entries. (Income Summary is account #34 in the chart of accounts.) Record the closing entries on Page 4 of the journal. Indicate closed accounts by inserting a line in both the Balance columns opposite the closing entry.
10. Prepare a post-closing trial balance.

Problems Series B

PR 4-1B Financial statements and closing entries

OBJ. 1, 2, 3

✔ 3. Total assets: $342,425

SPREADSHEET

GENERAL LEDGER

Last Chance Company offers legal consulting advice to prison inmates. Last Chance Company prepared the end-of-period spreadsheet at the top of the following page at June 30, 2014, the end of the current fiscal year.

Instructions

1. Prepare an income statement for the year ended June 30.
2. Prepare a retained earnings statement for the year ended June 30.
3. Prepare a balance sheet as of June 30.
4. On the basis of the end-of-period spreadsheet, journalize the closing entries.
5. Prepare a post-closing trial balance.

	A	B	C	D	E	F	G
1		**Last Chance Company**					
2		**End-of-Period Spreadsheet**					
3		**For the Year Ended June 30, 2014**					
4		**Unadjusted**				**Adjusted**	
5		**Trial Balance**		**Adjustments**		**Trial Balance**	
6	**Account Title**	**Dr.**	**Cr.**	**Dr.**	**Cr.**	**Dr.**	**Cr.**
7							
8	Cash	5,100				5,100	
9	Accounts Receivable	22,750		(a) 3,750		26,500	
10	Prepaid Insurance	3,600			(b) 1,300	2,300	
11	Supplies	2,025			(c) 1,500	525	
12	Land	80,000				80,000	
13	Building	340,000				340,000	
14	Accum. Depr.—Building		190,000		(d) 3,000		193,000
15	Equipment	140,000				140,000	
16	Accum. Depr.—Equipment		54,450		(e) 4,550		59,000
17	Accounts Payable		9,750				9,750
18	Salaries & Wages Payable				(f) 1,900		1,900
19	Unearned Rent		4,500	(g) 3,000			1,500
20	Capital Stock		90,000				90,000
21	Retained Earnings		271,300				271,300
22	Dividends	20,000				20,000	
23	Fees Earned		280,000		(a) 3,750		283,750
24	Rent Revenue				(g) 3,000		3,000
25	Salaries & Wages Expense	145,100		(f) 1,900		147,000	
26	Advertising Expense	86,800				86,800	
27	Utilities Expense	30,000				30,000	
28	Travel Expense	18,750				18,750	
29	Depr. Exp.—Equipment			(e) 4,550		4,550	
30	Depr. Exp.—Building			(d) 3,000		3,000	
31	Supplies Expense			(c) 1,500		1,500	
32	Insurance Expense			(b) 1,300		1,300	
33	Misc. Expense	5,875				5,875	
34		900,000	900,000	19,000	19,000	913,200	913,200
35							

PR 4-2B Financial statements and closing entries

OBJ. 2, 3

✔ **1. Retained Earnings, October 31: $288,000**

The Gorman Group is a financial planning services firm owned and operated by Nicole Gorman. As of October 31, 2014, the end of the current fiscal year, the accountant for The Gorman Group prepared an end-of-period spreadsheet (work sheet), part of which is shown below.

	A	F	G
1	**The Gorman Group**		
2	**End-of-Period Spreadsheet**		
3	**For the Year Ended October 31, 2014**		
4		**Adjusted**	
5		**Trial Balance**	
6	**Account Title**	**Dr.**	**Cr.**
7			
8	Cash	11,000	
9	Accounts Receivable	28,150	
10	Supplies	6,350	
11	Prepaid Insurance	9,500	
12	Land	75,000	
13	Buildings	250,000	
14	Accumulated Depreciation—Buildings		117,200
15	Equipment	240,000	
16	Accumulated Depreciation—Equipment		151,700
17	Accounts Payable		33,300
18	Salaries Payable		3,300
19	Unearned Rent		1,500
20	Capital Stock		25,000
21	Retained Earnings		195,000
22	Dividends	20,000	
23	Service Fees		468,000
24	Rent Revenue		5,000
25	Salaries Expense	291,000	
26	Depreciation Expense—Equipment	17,500	
27	Rent Expense	15,500	
28	Supplies Expense	9,000	
29	Utilities Expense	8,500	
30	Depreciation Expense—Buildings	6,600	
31	Repairs Expense	3,450	
32	Insurance Expense	3,000	
33	Miscellaneous Expense	5,450	
34		1,000,000	1,000,000
35			

(Continued)

Instructions

1. Prepare an income statement, a retained earnings statement, and a balance sheet.
2. Journalize the entries that were required to close the accounts at October 31.
3. If the balance of Retained Earnings had instead increased $115,000 after the closing entries were posted, and the dividends remained the same, what would have been the amount of net income or net loss?

PR 4-3B T accounts, adjusting entries, financial statements, and closing entries; optional end-of-period spreadsheet (work sheet) **OBJ. 2, 3**

✔ 5. Net income: $27,350

GENERAL LEDGER

The unadjusted trial balance of La Mesa Laundry at August 31, 2014, the end of the current fiscal year, is shown below.

La Mesa Laundry
Unadjusted Trial Balance
August 31, 2014

	Debit Balances	Credit Balances
Cash	3,800	
Laundry Supplies	9,000	
Prepaid Insurance	6,000	
Laundry Equipment	180,800	
Accumulated Depreciation		49,200
Accounts Payable		7,800
Capital Stock		15,000
Retained Earnings		80,000
Dividends	2,400	
Laundry Revenue		248,000
Wages Expense	135,800	
Rent Expense	43,200	
Utilities Expense	16,000	
Miscellaneous Expense	3,000	
	400,000	400,000

The data needed to determine year-end adjustments are as follows:

a. Wages accrued but not paid at August 31 are $2,200.
b. Depreciation of equipment during the year is $8,150.
c. Laundry supplies on hand at August 31 are $2,000.
d. Insurance premiums expired during the year are $5,300.

Instructions

1. For each account listed in the unadjusted trial balance, enter the balance in a T account. Identify the balance as "Aug. 31 Bal." In addition, add T accounts for Wages Payable, Depreciation Expense, Laundry Supplies Expense, Insurance Expense, and Income Summary.
2. (Optional.) Enter the unadjusted trial balance on an end-of-period spreadsheet (work sheet) and complete the spreadsheet. Add the accounts listed in part (1) as needed.
3. Journalize and post the adjusting entries. Identify the adjustments by "Adj." and the new balances as "Adj. Bal."
4. Prepare an adjusted trial balance.
5. Prepare an income statement, a retained earnings statement, and a balance sheet.
6. Journalize and post the closing entries. Identify the closing entries by "Clos."
7. Prepare a post-closing trial balance.

PR 4-4B Ledger accounts, adjusting entries, financial statements, and closing entries; optional end-of-period spreadsheet (work sheet) OBJ. 2, 3

✔ 5. Net income: $46,150

SPREADSHEET

The unadjusted trial balance of Recessive Interiors at January 31, 2014, the end of the current year, is shown below.

Recessive Interiors
Unadjusted Trial Balance
January 31, 2014

		Debit Balances	Credit Balances
11	Cash	13,100	
13	Supplies	8,000	
14	Prepaid Insurance	7,500	
16	Equipment	113,000	
17	Accumulated Depreciation—Equipment		12,000
18	Trucks	90,000	
19	Accumulated Depreciation—Trucks		27,100
21	Accounts Payable		4,500
31	Capital Stock		30,000
32	Retained Earnings		96,400
33	Dividends	3,000	
41	Service Revenue		155,000
51	Wages Expense	72,000	
52	Rent Expense	7,600	
53	Truck Expense	5,350	
59	Miscellaneous Expense	5,450	
		325,000	325,000

The data needed to determine year-end adjustments are as follows:

a. Supplies on hand at January 31 are $2,850.
b. Insurance premiums expired during the year are $3,150.
c. Depreciation of equipment during the year is $5,250.
d. Depreciation of trucks during the year is $4,000.
e. Wages accrued but not paid at January 31 are $900.

Instructions

1. For each account listed in the unadjusted trial balance, enter the balance in the appropriate Balance column of a four-column account and place a check mark (✓) in the Posting Reference column.
2. (Optional.) Enter the unadjusted trial balance on an end-of-period spreadsheet (work sheet) and complete the spreadsheet. Add the accounts listed in part (3) as needed.
3. Journalize and post the adjusting entries, inserting balances in the accounts affected. Record the adjusting entries on Page 26 of the journal. The following additional accounts from Recessive Interiors' chart of accounts should be used: Wages Payable, 22; Depreciation Expense—Equipment, 54; Supplies Expense, 55; Depreciation Expense—Trucks, 56; Insurance Expense, 57.
4. Prepare an adjusted trial balance.
5. Prepare an income statement, a retained earnings statement, and a balance sheet.
6. Journalize and post the closing entries. Record the closing entries on Page 27 of the journal. (Income Summary is account #34 in the chart of accounts.) Indicate closed accounts by inserting a line in both Balance columns opposite the closing entry.
7. Prepare a post-closing trial balance.

PR 4-5B Complete accounting cycle OBJ. 4, 5

✔ 8. Net income: $53,775

SPREADSHEET

For the past several years, Jeff Horton has operated a part-time consulting business from his home. As of April 1, 2014, Jeff decided to move to rented quarters and to operate the

(*Continued*)

business, which was to be known as Rosebud Consulting, on a full-time basis. Rosebud Consulting entered into the following transactions during April:

Apr. 1. The following assets were received from Jeff Horton in exchange for capital stock: cash, $20,000; accounts receivable, $14,700; supplies, $3,300; and office equipment, $12,000. There were no liabilities received.

1. Paid three months' rent on a lease rental contract, $6,000.

2. Paid the premiums on property and casualty insurance policies, $4,200.

4. Received cash from clients as an advance payment for services to be provided and recorded it as unearned fees, $9,400.

5. Purchased additional office equipment on account from Smith Office Supply Co., $8,000.

6. Received cash from clients on account, $11,700.

10. Paid cash for a newspaper advertisement, $350.

12. Paid Smith Office Supply Co. for part of the debt incurred on April 5, $6,400.

12. Recorded services provided on account for the period April 1–12, $21,900.

14. Paid receptionist for two weeks' salary, $1,650.

Record the following transactions on Page 2 of the journal.

17. Recorded cash from cash clients for fees earned during the period April 1–16, $6,600.

18. Paid cash for supplies, $725.

20. Recorded services provided on account for the period April 13–20, $16,800.

24. Recorded cash from cash clients for fees earned for the period April 17–24, $4,450.

26. Received cash from clients on account, $26,500.

27. Paid receptionist for two weeks' salary, $1,650.

29. Paid telephone bill for April, $540.

30. Paid electricity bill for April, $760.

30. Recorded cash from cash clients for fees earned for the period April 25–30, $5,160.

30. Recorded services provided on account for the remainder of April, $2,590.

30. Paid dividends of $18,000.

Instructions

1. Journalize each transaction in a two-column journal starting on Page 1, referring to the following chart of accounts in selecting the accounts to be debited and credited. (Do not insert the account numbers in the journal at this time.)

11	Cash	31	Capital Stock
12	Accounts Receivable	32	Retained Earnings
14	Supplies	33	Dividends
15	Prepaid Rent	41	Fees Earned
16	Prepaid Insurance	51	Salary Expense
18	Office Equipment	52	Supplies Expense
19	Accumulated Depreciation	53	Rent Expense
21	Accounts Payable	54	Depreciation Expense
22	Salaries Payable	55	Insurance Expense
23	Unearned Fees	59	Miscellaneous Expense

2. Post the journal to a ledger of four-column accounts.
3. Prepare an unadjusted trial balance.
4. At the end of April, the following adjustment data were assembled. Analyze and use these data to complete parts (5) and (6).
   a. Insurance expired during April is $350.
   b. Supplies on hand on April 30 are $1,225.

c. Depreciation of office equipment for April is $400.
d. Accrued receptionist salary on April 30 is $275.
e. Rent expired during April is $2,000.
f. Unearned fees on April 30 are $2,350.

5. (Optional.) Enter the unadjusted trial balance on an end-of-period spreadsheet (work sheet) and complete the spreadsheet.
6. Journalize and post the adjusting entries. Record the adjusting entries on Page 3 of the journal.
7. Prepare an adjusted trial balance.
8. Prepare an income statement, a retained earnings statement, and a balance sheet.
9. Prepare and post the closing entries. Record the closing entries on Page 4 of the journal. (Income Summary is account #34 in the chart of accounts.) Indicate closed accounts by inserting a line in both the Balance columns opposite the closing entry.
10. Prepare a post-closing trial balance.

Continuing Problem

✓ 2. Net income: $4,955

GENERAL LEDGER

The unadjusted trial balance of PS Music as of July 31, 2014, along with the adjustment data for the two months ended July 31, 2014, are shown in Chapter 3. Based upon the adjustment data, the adjusted trial balance shown below was prepared.

PS Music
Adjusted Trial Balance
July 31, 2014

	Debit Balances	Credit Balances
Cash	9,945	
Accounts Receivable	4,150	
Supplies	275	
Prepaid Insurance	2,475	
Office Equipment	7,500	
Accumulated Depreciation—Office Equipment		50
Accounts Payable		8,350
Wages Payable		140
Unearned Revenue		3,600
Capital Stock		9,000
Dividends	1,750	
Fees Earned		21,200
Music Expense	3,610	
Wages Expense	2,940	
Office Rent Expense	2,550	
Advertising Expense	1,500	
Equipment Rent Expense	1,375	
Utilities Expense	1,215	
Supplies Expense	925	
Insurance Expense	225	
Depreciation Expense	50	
Miscellaneous Expense	1,855	
	42,340	42,340

Instructions

1. (Optional.) Using the data from Chapter 3, prepare an end-of-period spreadsheet (work sheet).
2. Prepare an income statement, a retained earnings statement, and a balance sheet.

(Continued)

3. Journalize and post the closing entries. The income summary account is #34 in the ledger of PS Music. Indicate closed accounts by inserting a line in both Balance columns opposite the closing entry.
4. Prepare a post-closing trial balance.

Comprehensive Problem 1

✔ 8. Net income, $33,425

GENERAL LEDGER

Kelly Pitney began her consulting business, Kelly Consulting, P.C., on April 1, 2014. The accounting cycle for Kelly Consulting for April, including financial statements, was illustrated on pages 163–173. During May, Kelly Consulting entered into the following transactions:

May 3. Received cash from clients as an advance payment for services to be provided and recorded it as unearned fees, $4,500.
5. Received cash from clients on account, $2,450.
9. Paid cash for a newspaper advertisement, $225.
13. Paid Office Station Co. for part of the debt incurred on April 5, $640.
15. Recorded services provided on account for the period May 1–15, $9,180.
16. Paid part-time receptionist for two weeks' salary including the amount owed on April 30, $750.
17. Recorded cash from cash clients for fees earned during the period May 1–16, $8,360.

Record the following transactions on Page 6 of the journal.

20. Purchased supplies on account, $735.
21. Recorded services provided on account for the period May 16–20, $4,820.
25. Recorded cash from cash clients for fees earned for the period May 17–23, $7,900.
27. Received cash from clients on account, $9,520.
28. Paid part-time receptionist for two weeks' salary, $750.
30. Paid telephone bill for May, $260.
31. Paid electricity bill for May, $810.
31. Recorded cash from cash clients for fees earned for the period May 26–31, $3,300.
31. Recorded services provided on account for the remainder of May, $2,650.
31. Paid dividends, $10,500.

Instructions

1. The chart of accounts for Kelly Consulting is shown on page 164, and the post-closing trial balance as of April 30, 2014, is shown on page 171. For each account in the post-closing trial balance, enter the balance in the appropriate Balance column of a four-column account. Date the balances May 1, 2014, and place a check mark (✓) in the Posting Reference column. Journalize each of the May transactions in a two-column journal starting on Page 5 of the journal and using Kelly Consulting's chart of accounts. (Do not insert the account numbers in the journal at this time.)
2. Post the journal to a ledger of four-column accounts.
3. Prepare an unadjusted trial balance.
4. At the end of May, the following adjustment data were assembled. Analyze and use these data to complete parts (5) and (6).
   a. Insurance expired during May is $275.
   b. Supplies on hand on May 31 are $715.
   c. Depreciation of office equipment for May is $330.
   d. Accrued receptionist salary on May 31 is $325.
   e. Rent expired during May is $1,600.
   f. Unearned fees on May 31 are $3,210.

5. (Optional.) Enter the unadjusted trial balance on an end-of-period spreadsheet (work sheet) and complete the spreadsheet.
6. Journalize and post the adjusting entries. Record the adjusting entries on page 7 of the journal.
7. Prepare an adjusted trial balance.
8. Prepare an income statement, a retained earnings statement, and a balance sheet.
9. Prepare and post the closing entries. Record the closing entries on Page 8 of the journal. (Income Summary is account #34 in the chart of accounts.) Indicate closed accounts by inserting a line in both the Balance columns opposite the closing entry.
10. Prepare a post-closing trial balance.

Cases & Projects

CP 4-1 Ethics and professional conduct in business

Picasso Graphics is a graphics arts design consulting firm. Pablo Taylor, its treasurer and vice president of finance, has prepared a classified balance sheet as of July 31, 2014, the end of its fiscal year. This balance sheet will be submitted with Picasso Graphics' loan application to Paris Trust & Savings Bank.

In the Current Assets section of the balance sheet, Pablo reported a $56,000 receivable from Becky Holt, the president of Picasso Graphics, as a trade account receivable. Becky borrowed the money from Picasso Graphics in January 2012 for a down payment on a new home. She has orally assured Pablo that she will pay off the account receivable within the next year. Pablo reported the $56,000 in the same manner on the preceding year's balance sheet.

Evaluate whether it is acceptable for Pablo to prepare the July 31, 2014, balance sheet in the manner indicated above.

CP 4-2 Financial statements

The following is an excerpt from a telephone conversation between Ben Simpson, president of Main Street Co., and Tami Lundgren, owner of Reliable Employment Co.

Ben: Tami, you're going to have to do a better job of finding me a new computer programmer. That last guy was great at programming, but he didn't have any common sense.

Tami: What do you mean? The guy had a master's degree with straight A's.

Ben: Yes, well, last month he developed a new financial reporting system. He said we could do away with manually preparing an end-of-period spreadsheet (work sheet) and financial statements. The computer would automatically generate our financial statements with "a push of a button."

Tami: So what's the big deal? Sounds to me like it would save you time and effort.

Ben: Right! The balance sheet showed a minus for supplies!

Tami: Minus supplies? How can that be?

Ben: That's what I asked.

Tami: So, what did he say?

Ben: Well, after he checked the program, he said that it must be right. The minuses were greater than the pluses. . . .

Tami: Didn't he know that Supplies can't have a credit balance—it must have a debit balance?

Ben: He asked me what a debit and credit were.

Tami: I see your point.

1. Comment on (a) the desirability of computerizing Main Street Co.'s financial reporting system, (b) the elimination of the end-of-period spreadsheet (work sheet) in a computerized accounting system, and (c) the computer programmer's lack of accounting knowledge.
2. Explain to the programmer why Supplies could not have a credit balance.

CP 4-3 Financial statements

Assume that you recently accepted a position with Five Star National Bank & Trust as an assistant loan officer. As one of your first duties, you have been assigned the responsibility of evaluating a loan request for $300,000 from West Gate Auto Co., a small corporation. In support of the loan application, Joan Whalen, owner and sole stockholder, submitted a "Statement of Accounts" (trial balance) for the first year of operations ended October 31, 2014.

West Gate Auto Co.
Statement of Accounts
October 31, 2014

Cash	5,000	
Billings Due from Others	40,000	
Supplies (chemicals, etc.)	7,500	
Building	222,300	
Equipment	50,000	
Amounts Owed to Others		31,000
Investment in Business		179,000
Service Revenue		215,000
Wages Expense	75,000	
Utilities Expense	10,000	
Rent Expense	8,000	
Insurance Expense	6,000	
Other Expenses	1,200	
	425,000	425,000

1. Explain to Joan Whalen why a set of financial statements (income statement, retained earnings statement, and balance sheet) would be useful to you in evaluating the loan request.
2. In discussing the "Statement of Accounts" with Joan Whalen, you discovered that the accounts had not been adjusted at October 31. Analyze the "Statement of Accounts" and indicate possible adjusting entries that might be necessary before an accurate set of financial statements could be prepared.
3. Assuming that an accurate set of financial statements will be submitted by Joan Whalen in a few days, what other considerations or information would you require before making a decision on the loan request?

CP 4-4 Compare balance sheets

Internet Project

Group Project

In groups of three or four, compare the balance sheets of two different companies, and present to the class a summary of the similarities and differences of the two companies. You may obtain the balance sheets you need from one of the following sources:

1. Your school or local library.
2. The investor relations department of each company.
3. The company's Web site on the Internet.
4. EDGAR (Electronic Data Gathering, Analysis, and Retrieval), the electronic archives of financial statements filed with the Securities and Exchange Commission.

SEC documents can be retrieved using the EdgarScan™ service at **http://sec.gov**. To obtain annual report information, under Filings & Forms click on "Search for Company Filings," click on "Company or fund name, ticker symbol, ..." type in the company name, and then click on "Find Companies." Click on the CIK related to the company name, search for Form 10-K, and click on "Retrieve Selected Findings." Finally, click on the "html" for the latest period and the related document.

CHAPTER

5

SUSAN VAN ETTEN

Accounting for Merchandising Businesses

Dollar Tree Stores, Inc.

When you are low on cash but need to pick up party supplies, housewares, or other consumer items, where do you go? Many shoppers are turning to **Dollar Tree Stores, Inc.**, the nation's largest single price point dollar retailer with over 4,000 stores in 48 states. For the fixed price of $1 on merchandise in its stores, Dollar Tree has worked hard providing "new treasures" every week for the entire family.

Despite the fact that items cost only $1, the accounting for a merchandiser, like Dollar Tree, is more complex than for a service company. This is because a service company sells only services and has no inventory. With Dollar Tree's locations and merchandise, the company must design its accounting system to not only record the receipt of goods for resale, but also to keep track of what merchandise is available for sale as well as where the merchandise is located. In addition, Dollar Tree must record the sales and costs of the goods sold for each of its stores. Finally, Dollar Tree must record such data as delivery costs, merchandise discounts, and merchandise returns.

This chapter focuses on the accounting principles and concepts for a merchandising business. In doing so, the basic differences between merchandiser and service company activities are highlighted. The financial statements of a merchandising business and accounting for merchandise transactions are also described and illustrated.

Learning Objectives

After studying this chapter, you should be able to: *Example Exercises*

At a Glance 5 Page 241

OBJ 1 Distinguish between the activities and financial statements of service and merchandising businesses.

Nature of Merchandising Businesses

The activities of a service business differ from those of a merchandising business. These differences are illustrated in the following condensed income statements:

Service Business		Merchandising Business	
Fees earned	$XXX	Sales	$XXX
Operating expenses	–XXX	Cost of merchandise sold	–XXX
Net income	$XXX	Gross profit	$XXX
		Operating expenses	–XXX
		Net income	$XXX

The revenue activities of a service business involve providing services to customers. On the income statement for a service business, the revenues from services are reported as *fees earned*. The operating expenses incurred in providing the services are subtracted from the fees earned to arrive at *net income*.

In contrast, the revenue activities of a merchandising business involve the buying and selling of merchandise. A merchandising business first purchases merchandise to sell to its customers. When this merchandise is sold, the revenue is reported as **sales**, and its cost is recognized as an expense. This expense is called the **cost of merchandise sold**. The cost of merchandise sold is subtracted from sales to arrive at gross profit. This amount is called **gross profit** because it is the profit *before* deducting operating expenses.

Merchandise on hand (not sold) at the end of an accounting period is called **merchandise inventory**. Merchandise inventory is reported as a current asset on the balance sheet.

Business Connection

H&R BLOCK VERSUS THE HOME DEPOT

H&R Block is a service business that primarily offers tax planning and preparation to its customers. The Home Depot is a large home improvement retailer. The differences in the operations of a service and merchandise business are illustrated in their recent income statements, as shown below.

H&R Block
Condensed Income Statement
(in millions)

Revenue	$3,775
Operating expenses	3,109
Operating income	$ 666
Other expense (net)	2
Income before taxes	$ 664
Income taxes	258
Net income	$ 406

As discussed in a later chapter, corporations are subject to income taxes. Thus, the income statements of H&R Block and The Home Depot report "income taxes" as a deduction from "income before income taxes" in arriving at net income. This is in contrast to a proprietorship, such as NetSolutions, which is not subject to income taxes.

The Home Depot
Condensed Income Statement
(in millions)

Net sales	$67,997
Cost of merchandise sold	44,693
Gross profit	$23,304
Operating expenses	17,465
Operating income	$ 5,839
Other expense (net)	566
Income before taxes	$ 5,273
Income taxes	1,935
Net income	$ 3,338

Example Exercise 5-1 Gross Profit

OBJ 1

During the current year, merchandise is sold for $250,000 cash and for $975,000 on account. The cost of the merchandise sold is $735,000. What is the amount of the gross profit?

Follow My Example 5-1

The gross profit is $490,000 ($250,000 + $975,000 – $735,000).

Practice Exercises: **PE 5-1A, PE 5-1B**

THE OPERATING CYCLE

The operations of a merchandising business involve the purchase of merchandise for sale (purchasing), the sale of the products to customers (sales), and the receipt of cash from customers (collection). This overall process is referred to as the *operating cycle.* Thus, the operating cycle begins with spending cash, and it ends with receiving cash from customers. The operating cycle for a merchandising business is shown to the right.

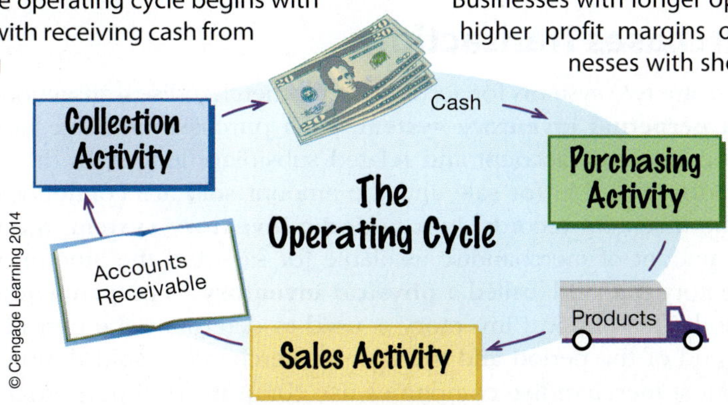

Operating cycles for retailers are usually shorter than for manufacturers because retailers purchase goods in a form ready for sale to the customer. Of course, some retailers will have shorter operating cycles than others because of the nature of their products. For example, a jewelry store or an automobile dealer normally has a longer operating cycle than a consumer electronics store or a grocery store.

Businesses with longer operating cycles normally have higher profit margins on their products than businesses with shorter operating cycles. For example, it is not unusual for jewelry stores to price their jewelry at 30%–50% above cost. In contrast, grocery stores operate on very small profit margins, often below 5%. Grocery stores make up the difference by selling their products more quickly.

OBJ 2 Describe and illustrate the accounting for merchandise transactions.

Merchandising Transactions

This section illustrates merchandise transactions for **NetSolutions** after it becomes a retailer of computer hardware and software. During 2013, Chris Clark implemented the second phase of NetSolutions' business plan. In doing so, Chris notified clients that beginning July 1, 2014, NetSolutions would no longer offer consulting services. Instead, it would become a retailer.

NetSolutions' business strategy is to offer personalized service to individuals and small businesses that are upgrading or purchasing new computer systems. NetSolutions' personal service includes a no-obligation, on-site assessment of the customer's computer needs. By providing personalized service and follow-up, Chris feels that NetSolutions can compete effectively against such retailers as Best Buy, Office Max, Office Depot, and Dell.

Merchandise transactions are recorded in the accounts, using the rules of debit and credit that are described and illustrated in Chapter 2. However, the accounting system for merchandise businesses is often modified to more efficiently record transactions. For example, an accounting system should be designed to provide information on the amounts due from various customers (accounts receivable) and amounts owed to various creditors (accounts payable). A separate account for each customer and creditor could be added to the ledger. However, as the number of customers and creditors increased, the ledger would become large and awkward to use.

A large number of individual accounts with a common characteristic can be grouped together in a separate ledger, called a **subsidiary ledger**. The primary ledger, which contains all of the balance sheet and income statement accounts, is then called the **general ledger**. Each subsidiary ledger is represented in the general ledger by a summarizing account, called a **controlling account**. The sum of the balances of the accounts in the subsidiary ledger must equal the balance of the related controlling account. Thus, a subsidiary ledger is a secondary ledger that supports a controlling account in the general ledger.

Common subsidiary ledgers are:

1. The **accounts receivable subsidiary ledger**, or *customers ledger*, lists the individual customer accounts in alphabetical order. The controlling account in the general ledger is Accounts Receivable.
2. The **accounts payable subsidiary ledger**, or *creditors ledger*, lists individual creditor accounts in alphabetical order. The controlling account in the general ledger is Accounts Payable.
3. The **inventory subsidiary ledger**, or *inventory ledger*, lists individual inventory by item (bar code) number. The controlling account in the general ledger is Inventory. An inventory subsidiary ledger is used in a perpetual inventory system.

Most merchandising companies also use computerized accounting systems that record similar transactions in separate journals, which generate purchase, sales, and inventory reports. These separate journals are called **special journals**. However, for simplicity, the journal entries in this chapter will be illustrated using a two-column general journal.[1]

Purchases Transactions

There are two systems for accounting for merchandise transactions: perpetual and periodic. In a **perpetual inventory system,** each purchase and sale of merchandise is recorded in the inventory account and related subsidiary ledger. In this way, the amount of merchandise available for sale and the amount sold are continuously (perpetually) updated in the inventory records. In a **periodic inventory system**, the inventory does not show the amount of merchandise available for sale and the amount sold. Instead, a listing of inventory on hand, called a **physical inventory**, is prepared at the end of the accounting period. This physical inventory is used to determine the cost of merchandise on hand at the end of the period and the cost of merchandise sold during the period.

Most merchandise companies use computerized perpetual inventory systems. Such systems use bar codes or radio frequency identification codes embedded in a product.

1 Subsidiary ledgers and special journals are further described and illustrated in online Appendix E, which appears on the product website at **www.cengagebrain.com.**

An optical scanner or radio frequency identification device is then used to read the product codes and track inventory on hand and sold.

Because computerized perpetual inventory systems are widely used, this chapter illustrates merchandise transactions using a perpetual inventory system. The periodic system is described and illustrated in an appendix at the end of this chapter.

Under the perpetual inventory system, cash purchases of merchandise are recorded as follows:

Journal *Page 24*

Date		Description	Post. Ref.	Debit	Credit
2015 Jan.	3	Merchandise Inventory		2,510	
		Cash			2,510
		Purchased inventory from Bowen Co.			

Purchases of merchandise on account are recorded as follows:

Jan.	4	Merchandise Inventory		9,250	
		Accounts Payable—Thomas Corporation			9,250
		Purchased inventory on account.			

The terms of purchases on account are normally indicated on the **invoice** or bill that the seller sends the buyer. An example of an invoice sent to NetSolutions by Alpha Technologies is shown in Exhibit 1.

Retailers, such as Best Buy, Sears Holding Corporation, and Walmart, and grocery store chains, such as Winn-Dixie Stores, Inc., and Kroger, use bar codes and optical scanners as part of their computerized inventory systems.

EXHIBIT 1

Invoice

Alpha Technologies
1000 Matrix Blvd.
San Jose, CA 95116-1000

Invoice
106-8

Made in U.S.A.

SOLD TO	**CUSTOMER ORDER NO.**	**ORDER DATE**
NetSolutions 5101 Washington Ave. Cincinnati, OH 45227-5101	412	Jan. 3, 2015

DATE SHIPPED	**HOW SHIPPED AND ROUTE**	**TERMS**	**INVOICE DATE**
Jan. 5, 2015	US Express Trucking Co.	2/10, n/30	Jan. 5, 2015
FROM	**F.O.B.**		
San Jose	Cincinnati		

QUANTITY	**DESCRIPTION**	**UNIT PRICE**	**AMOUNT**
20	3COM Wireless PC Card	150.00	3,000.00

The terms for when payments for merchandise are to be made are called the **credit terms**. If payment is required on delivery, the terms are cash or net cash. Otherwise, the buyer is allowed an amount of time, known as the **credit period**, in which to pay. The credit period usually begins with the date of the sale as shown on the invoice.

If payment is due within a stated number of days after the invoice date, such as 30 days, the terms are net 30 days. These terms may be written as *n/30*.[2] If payment is due by the end of the month in which the sale was made, the terms are written as *n/eom*.

2 The word *net* as used here does not have the usual meaning of a number after deductions have been subtracted, as in *net income*.

Purchases Discounts To encourage the buyer to pay before the end of the credit period, the seller may offer a discount. For example, a seller may offer a 2% discount if the buyer pays within 10 days of the invoice date. If the buyer does not take the discount, the total invoice amount is due within 30 days. These terms are expressed as 2/10, n/30 and are read as "2% discount if paid within 10 days, net amount due within 30 days." The credit terms of 2/10, n/30 are summarized in Exhibit 2, using the invoice in Exhibit 1.

EXHIBIT 2 **Credit Terms**

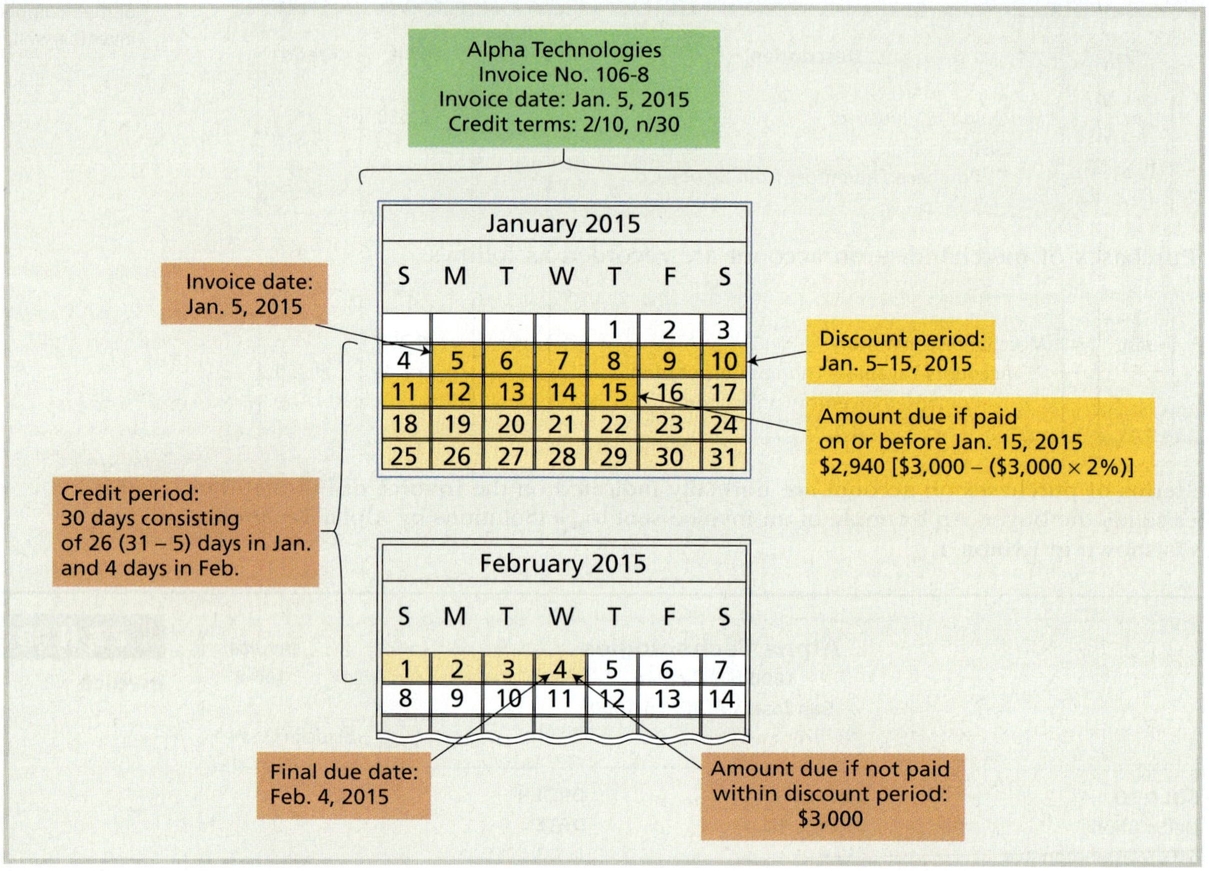

Discounts taken by the buyer for early payment of an invoice are called **purchases discounts**. Purchases discounts taken by a buyer reduce the cost of the merchandise purchased. Even if the buyer has to borrow to pay within a discount period, it is normally to the buyer's advantage to do so. For this reason, accounting systems are normally designed so that all available discounts are taken.

To illustrate, the invoice shown in Exhibit 1 is used. The last day of the discount period is January 15 (invoice date of January 5 plus 10 days). Assume that in order to pay the invoice on January 15, NetSolutions borrows $2,940, which is $3,000 less the discount of $60 ($3,000 × 2%). If an annual interest rate of 6% and a 360-day year is also assumed, the interest on the loan of $2,940 for the remaining 20 days of the credit period is $9.80 ($2,940 × 6% × 20/360).

The net savings to NetSolutions of taking the discount is $50.20, computed as follows:

Discount of 2% on $3,000	$60.00
Interest for 20 days at a rate of 6% on $2,940	9.80
Savings from taking the discount	$50.20

The savings can also be seen by comparing the interest rate on the money *saved* by taking the discount and the interest rate on the money *borrowed* to take the discount. The interest rate on the money saved in the prior example is estimated by converting 2% for 20 days to a yearly rate, as follows:

$$2\% \times \frac{360 \text{ days}}{20 \text{ days}} = 2\% \times 18 = 36\%$$

NetSolutions borrowed $2,940 at 6% to take the discount. If NetSolutions does not take the discount, it *pays* an estimated interest rate of 36% for using the $2,940 for the remaining 20 days of the credit period. Thus, buyers should normally take all available purchase discounts.

Under the perpetual inventory system, the buyer initially debits Merchandise Inventory for the amount of the invoice. When paying the invoice within the discount period, the buyer credits Merchandise Inventory for the amount of the discount. In this way, Merchandise Inventory shows the *net* cost to the buyer.

To illustrate, NetSolutions would record the Alpha Technologies invoice and its payment at the end of the discount period as follows:

Jan.	5	Merchandise Inventory		3,000	
		Accounts Payable—Alpha Technologies			3,000
	15	Accounts Payable—Alpha Technologies		3,000	
		Cash			2,940
		Merchandise Inventory			60

Assume that NetSolutions does not take the discount, but instead pays the invoice on February 4. In this case, NetSolutions would record the payment as follows:

Feb.	4	Accounts Payable—Alpha Technologies		3,000	
		Cash			3,000

Purchases Returns and Allowances A buyer may request an allowance for merchandise that is returned (purchases return) or a price allowance (purchases allowance) for damaged or defective merchandise. From a buyer's perspective, such returns and allowances are called **purchases returns and allowances**. In both cases, the buyer normally sends the seller a debit memorandum to notify the seller of reasons for the return (purchase return) or to request a price reduction (purchase allowance).

A **debit memorandum**, often called a **debit memo**, is shown in Exhibit 3. A debit memo informs the seller of the amount the buyer proposes to *debit* to the account payable due the seller. It also states the reasons for the return or the request for the price allowance.

EXHIBIT 3

Debit Memo

NetSolutions **No. 18**
5101 Washington Ave.
Cincinnati, OH 45227-5101

DEBIT MEMO

TO
Maxim Systems
7519 East Wilson Ave.
Seattle, WA 98101-7519

DATE
March 7, 2015

WE DEBITED YOUR ACCOUNT AS FOLLOWS

10	Server Network Interface Cards, your invoice No. 7291, are being returned via parcel post. Our order specified No. 825X.	@90.00	900.00

The buyer may use the debit memo as the basis for recording the return or allowance or wait for approval from the seller (creditor). In either case, the buyer debits Accounts Payable and credits Merchandise Inventory.

To illustrate, NetSolutions records the return of the merchandise indicated in the debit memo in Exhibit 3 as follows:

Mar.	7	Accounts Payable—Maxim Systems		900	
		Merchandise Inventory			900
		Debit Memo No. 18.			

A buyer may return merchandise or be granted a price allowance before paying an invoice. In this case, the amount of the debit memo is deducted from the invoice. The amount is deducted before the purchase discount is computed.

To illustrate, assume the following data concerning a purchase of merchandise by NetSolutions on May 2:

May 2. Purchased $5,000 of merchandise on account from Delta Data Link, terms 2/10, n/30.
4. Returned $3,000 of the merchandise purchased on May 2.
12. Paid for the purchase of May 2 less the return and discount.

NetSolutions would record these transactions as follows:

May	2	Merchandise Inventory		5,000	
		Accounts Payable—Delta Data Link			5,000
		Purchased merchandise.			
	4	Accounts Payable—Delta Data Link		3,000	
		Merchandise Inventory			3,000
		Returned portion of merch. purchased.			
	12	Accounts Payable—Delta Data Link		2,000	
		Cash			1,960
		Merchandise Inventory			40
		Paid invoice [($5,000 – $3,000) × 2% = $40; $2,000 – $40 = $1,960].			

Example Exercise 5-2 Purchases Transactions

OBJ 2

Rofles Company purchased merchandise on account from a supplier for $11,500, terms 2/10, n/30. Rofles Company returned $3,000 of the merchandise and received full credit.

a. If Rofles Company pays the invoice within the discount period, what is the amount of cash required for the payment?

b. Under a perpetual inventory system, what account is credited by Rofles Company to record the return?

Follow My Example 5-2

a. $8,330. Purchase of $11,500 less the return of $3,000 less the discount of $170 [($11,500 – $3,000) × 2%].

b. Merchandise Inventory

Practice Exercises: **PE 5-2A, PE 5-2B**

Sales Transactions

Revenue from merchandise sales is usually recorded as *Sales*. Sometimes a business may use the title *Sales of Merchandise*.

Cash Sales A business may sell merchandise for cash. Cash sales are normally entered on a cash register and recorded in the accounts. To illustrate, assume that on March 3, NetSolutions sells merchandise for $1,800. These cash sales are recorded as follows:

Journal					Page 25
Date		Description	Post. Ref.	Debit	Credit
2015 Mar.	3	Cash		1,800	
		Sales			1,800
		To record cash sales.			

Using the perpetual inventory system, the cost of merchandise sold and the decrease in merchandise inventory are also recorded. In this way, the merchandise inventory account indicates the amount of merchandise on hand (not sold).

To illustrate, assume that the cost of merchandise sold on March 3 is $1,200. The entry to record the cost of merchandise sold and the decrease in the merchandise inventory is as follows:

Mar.	3	Cost of Merchandise Sold		1,200	
		Merchandise Inventory			1,200
		To record the cost of merchandise sold.			

Sales may be made to customers using credit cards such as MasterCard or VISA. Such sales are recorded as cash sales. This is because these sales are normally processed by a clearinghouse that contacts the bank that issued the card. The issuing bank then electronically transfers cash directly to the retailer's bank account.[3] Thus, the retailer normally receives cash within a few days of making the credit card sale.

If customers use MasterCards to pay for their purchases, the sales would be recorded exactly as shown in the March 3 entry at the top of the page. Any processing fees charged by the clearinghouse or issuing bank are periodically recorded as an expense. This expense is normally reported on the income statement as an administrative expense. To illustrate, assume that NetSolutions paid credit card processing fees of $4,150 on March 31. These fees would be recorded as follows:

Mar.	31	Credit Card Expense		4,150	
		Cash			4,150
		To record service charges on credit card sales for the month.			

A retailer may accept MasterCard or VISA but not American Express. Why? American Express Co.'s service fees are normally higher than MasterCard's or VISA's. As a result, some retailers choose not to accept American Express cards. The disadvantage of this practice is that the retailer may lose customers to competitors who do accept American Express cards.

Instead of using MasterCard or VISA, a customer may use a credit card that is not issued by a bank. For example, a customer might use an American Express card. If the seller uses a clearinghouse, the clearinghouse will collect the receivable and transfer the cash to the retailer's bank account, similar to the way it would have if the customer had used MasterCard or VISA. Large businesses, however, may not

3 CyberSource is one of the major credit card clearinghouse. For a more detailed description of how credit card sales are processed, see the following CyberSource Web page: **http://www.cybersource.com,** click on Products & Services, click on Global Payment Services, and then click on Credit Card Processing.

use a clearinghouse. In such cases, nonbank credit card sales must first be reported to the card company before cash is received. Thus, a receivable is created with the nonbank credit card company. However, since most retailers use clearinghouses to process both bank and nonbank credit cards, all credit card sales will be recorded as cash sales.

Sales on Account A business may sell merchandise on account. The seller records such sales as a debit to Accounts Receivable and a credit to Sales. An example of an entry for a NetSolutions sale on account of $18,000 follows. The cost of merchandise sold was $10,800.

Mar.	10	Accounts Receivable—Digital Technologies		18,000	
		Sales			18,000
		Invoice No. 7172.			
	10	Cost of Merchandise Sold		10,800	
		Merchandise Inventory			10,800
		Cost of merch. sold on Invoice No. 7172.			

Sales Discounts As mentioned in the discussion of purchases transactions, a seller may offer the buyer credit terms that include a discount for early payment. The seller refers to such discounts as **sales discounts**.

Sales discounts reduce sales revenue. To reduce sales revenue, the sales account could be debited. However, managers usually want to know the amount of the sales discounts for a period. For this reason, sales discounts are recorded in a separate sales discounts account, which is a *contra* (or *offsetting*) account to Sales.

To illustrate, assume that NetSolutions sold $18,000 of merchandise to Digital Technologies on March 10 with credit terms 2/10, n/30. Under the credit terms, Digital Technologies has until March 20 (March 10 plus 10 days) to pay within the discount period. Assume that Digital Technologies pays the invoice on March 19. Since the invoice is paid within the discount period (10 days), Digital Technologies would deduct $360 ($18,000 × 2%) from the invoice amount of $18,000 and pay $17,640. NetSolutions would record the receipt of the cash as follows:

Mar.	19	Cash		17,640	
		Sales Discounts		360	
		Accounts Receivable—Digital Technologies			18,000
		Collection on Invoice No. 7172 of $18,000, less 2% discount.			

Sales Returns and Allowances Merchandise sold may be returned to the seller (sales return). In other cases, the seller may reduce the initial selling price (sales allowance). This might occur if the merchandise is defective, damaged during shipment, or does not meet the buyer's expectations. From a seller's perspective, such returns and allowances are called **sales returns and allowances**.

If the return or allowance is for a sale on account, the seller usually issues the buyer a **credit memorandum**, often called a **credit memo**. A credit memo authorizes a credit (decrease) to the buyer's account receivable. A credit memo indicates the amount and reason for the credit. An example of a credit memo issued by NetSolutions is shown in Exhibit 4.

EXHIBIT 4

Credit Memo

NetSolutions
5101 Washington Ave.
Cincinnati, OH 45227-5101

No. 321

CREDIT MEMO

TO	**DATE**
Krier Company 7608 Melton Avenue Los Angeles, CA 90025-3942	April 13, 2015

WE CREDIT YOUR ACCOUNT AS FOLLOWS

10	Graphic Video Card	2,250.00

Like sales discounts, sales returns and allowances reduce sales revenue. Also, returns often result in additional shipping and handling expenses. Thus, managers usually want to know the amount of returns and allowances for a period. For this reason, sales returns and allowances are recorded in a separate sales returns and allowances account, which is a *contra* (or *offsetting*) account to Sales.

The seller debits Sales Returns and Allowances for the amount of the return or allowance. If the sale was on account, the seller credits Accounts Receivable. Using a perpetual inventory system, the seller must also debit (increase) Merchandise Inventory and decrease (credit) Cost of Merchandise Sold for the cost of the returned merchandise.

To illustrate, the credit memo shown in Exhibit 4 is used. The selling price of the merchandise returned in Exhibit 4 is $2,250. Assuming that the cost of the merchandise returned is $1,600, the sales return and allowance would be recorded as follows:

Apr.	13	Sales Returns and Allowances		2,250	
		Accounts Receivable—Krier Company			2,250
		Credit Memo No. 321			
	13	Merchandise Inventory		1,600	
		Cost of Merchandise Sold			1,600
		Cost of merchandise returned, Credit Memo No. 321			

A buyer may pay for merchandise and then later return it. In this case, the seller may do one of the following:

1. Issue a credit that is applied against the buyer's other receivables.
2. Issue a cash refund.

If the credit is applied against the buyer's other receivables, the seller records the credit with entries similar to those shown above. If cash is refunded, the seller debits Sales Returns and Allowances and credits Cash.

Example Exercise 5-3 Sales Transactions

OBJ 2

Journalize the following merchandise transactions:

a. Sold merchandise on account, $7,500, with terms 2/10, n/30. The cost of the merchandise sold was $5,625.

b. Received payment less the discount.

Follow My Example 5-3

a.	Accounts Receivable	7,500	
	Sales		7,500
	Cost of Merchandise Sold	5,625	
	Merchandise Inventory		5,625
b.	Cash	7,350	
	Sales Discounts	150	
	Accounts Receivable		7,500

Practice Exercises: **PE 5-3A, PE 5-3B**

Integrity, Objectivity, and Ethics in Business

THE CASE OF THE FRAUDULENT PRICE TAGS

One of the challenges for a retailer is policing its sales return policy. There are many ways in which customers can unethically or illegally abuse such policies. In one case, a couple was accused of attaching Marshalls' store price tags to cheaper merchandise bought or obtained elsewhere. The couple then returned the cheaper goods and received the substantially higher refund amount. Company security officials discovered the fraud and had the couple arrested after they had allegedly bilked the company for over $1 million.

Freight

Purchases and sales of merchandise often involve freight. The terms of a sale indicate when ownership (title) of the merchandise passes from the seller to the buyer. This point determines whether the buyer or the seller pays the freight costs.[4]

Note:
The buyer bears the freight costs if the shipping terms are FOB shipping point.

The ownership of the merchandise may pass to the buyer when the seller delivers the merchandise to the freight carrier. In this case, the terms are said to be **FOB (free on board) shipping point**. This term means that the buyer pays the freight costs from the shipping point to the final destination. Such costs are part of the buyer's total cost of purchasing inventory and are added to the cost of the inventory by debiting Merchandise Inventory.

To illustrate, assume that on June 10, NetSolutions purchased merchandise as follows:

June 10. Purchased merchandise from Magna Data, $900, terms FOB shipping point.
10. Paid freight of $50 on June 10 purchase from Magna Data.

4 The passage of title also determines whether the buyer or seller must pay other costs, such as the cost of insurance, while the merchandise is in transit.

NetSolutions would record these two transactions as follows:

June	10	Merchandise Inventory		900	
		Accounts Payable—Magna Data			900
		Purchased merchandise, terms FOB shipping point.			
	10	Merchandise Inventory		50	
		Cash			50
		Paid shipping cost on merchandise purchased.			

The ownership of the merchandise may pass to the buyer when the buyer receives the merchandise. In this case, the terms are said to be **FOB (free on board) destination**. This term means that the seller pays the freight costs from the shipping point to the buyer's final destination. When the seller pays the delivery charges, the seller debits Delivery Expense or Freight Out. Delivery Expense is reported on the seller's income statement as a selling expense.

Sometimes FOB shipping point and FOB destination are expressed in terms of a specific location at which the title to the merchandise passes to the buyer. For example, if **Toyota Motor Corporation**'s assembly plant in Osaka, Japan, sells automobiles to a dealer in Chicago, FOB shipping point is expressed as FOB Osaka. Likewise, FOB destination is expressed as FOB Chicago.

To illustrate, assume that NetSolutions sells merchandise as follows:

June 15. Sold merchandise to Kranz Company on account, $700, terms FOB destination. The cost of the merchandise sold is $480.

15. NetSolutions pays freight of $40 on the sale of June 15.

NetSolutions records the sale, the cost of the sale, and the freight cost as follows:

June	15	Accounts Receivable—Kranz Company		700	
		Sales			700
		Sold merchandise, terms FOB destination.			
	15	Cost of Merchandise Sold		480	
		Merchandise Inventory			480
		Recorded cost of merchandise sold to Kranz Company.			
	15	Delivery Expense		40	
		Cash			40
		Paid shipping cost on merchandise sold.			

Note:
The seller bears the freight costs if the shipping terms are FOB destination.

The seller may prepay the freight, even though the terms are FOB shipping point. The seller will then add the freight to the invoice. The buyer debits Merchandise Inventory for the total amount of the invoice, including the freight. Any discount terms would not apply to the prepaid freight.

To illustrate, assume that NetSolutions sells merchandise as follows:

June 20. Sold merchandise to Planter Company on account, $800, terms FOB shipping point. NetSolutions paid freight of $45, which was added to the invoice. The cost of the merchandise sold is $360.

NetSolutions records the sale, the cost of the sale, and the freight as follows:

June	20	Accounts Receivable—Planter Company		800	
		Sales			800
		Sold merchandise, terms FOB shipping point.			
	20	Cost of Merchandise Sold		360	
		Merchandise Inventory			360
		Recorded cost of merchandise sold to Planter Company.			
	20	Accounts Receivable—Planter Company		45	
		Cash			45
		Prepaid shipping cost on merchandise sold.			

Shipping terms, the passage of title, and whether the buyer or seller is to pay the freight costs are summarized in Exhibit 5.

EXHIBIT 5 **Freight Terms**

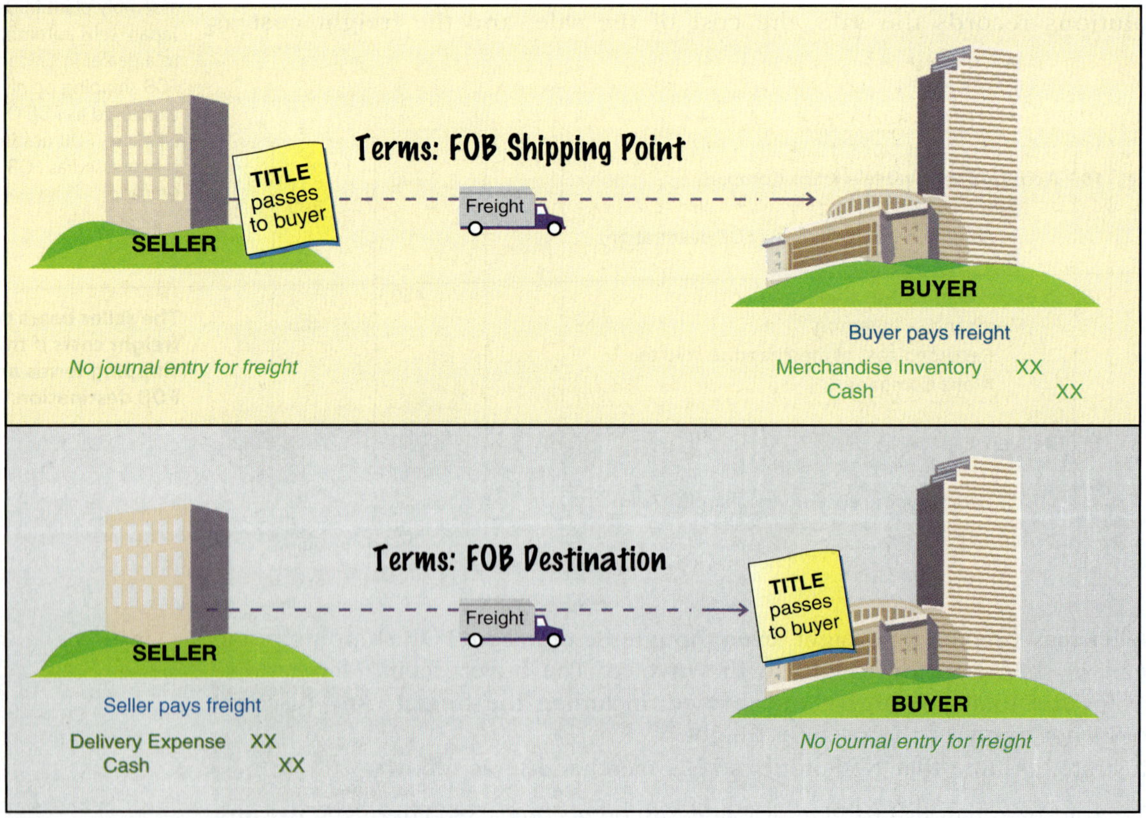

Example Exercise 5-4 Freight Terms

OBJ 2

Determine the amount to be paid in full settlement of each of the two invoices, (a) and (b), assuming that credit for returns and allowances was received prior to payment and that all invoices were paid within the discount period.

	Merchandise	Freight Paid by Seller	Freight Terms	Returns and Allowances
a.	$4,500	$200	FOB shipping point, 1/10, n/30	$ 800
b.	5,000	60	FOB destination, 2/10, n/30	2,500

Follow My Example 5-4

a. $3,863. Purchase of $4,500 less return of $800 less the discount of $37 [($4,500 – $800) × 1%] plus $200 of shipping.

b. $2,450. Purchase of $5,000 less return of $2,500 less the discount of $50 [($5,000 – $2,500) × 2%].

Practice Exercises: **PE 5-4A, PE 5-4B**

Summary: Recording Merchandise Inventory Transactions

Recording merchandise inventory transactions under the perpetual inventory system has been described and illustrated in the preceding sections. These transactions involved purchases, purchases discounts, purchases returns and allowances, freight, sales, and sales returns from customers. Exhibit 6 summarizes how these transactions are recorded in T account form.

EXHIBIT 6

Recording Merchandise Inventory Transactions

Merchandise Inventory

Debit		Credit	
Purchases of merchandise for sale	XXX	Purchases discounts	XXX
Freight for merchandise purchased FOB shipping point	XXX	Purchases returns and allowances	XXX
Merchandise returned from customer	XXX	Cost of merchandise sold	XXX

Cost of Merchandise Sold

Debit		Credit	
Cost of merchandise sold	XXX	Merchandise returned from customer	XXX

Dual Nature of Merchandise Transactions

Each merchandising transaction affects a buyer and a seller. In the following illustration, the same transactions for a seller and buyer are recorded. In this example, the seller is Scully Company and the buyer is Burton Co.

Transaction	Scully Company (Seller)			Burton Co. (Buyer)		
July 1. Scully Company sold merchandise on account to Burton Co., $7,500, terms FOB shipping point, n/45. The cost of the merchandise sold was $4,500.	Accounts Receivable—Burton Co.	7,500		Merchandise Inventory	7,500	
	Sales		7,500	Accounts Payable—Scully Co.		7,500
	Cost of Merchandise Sold	4,500				
	Merchandise Inventory		4,500			
July 2. Burton Co. paid freight of $150 on July 1 purchase from Scully Company.	No journal entry.			Merchandise Inventory	150	
				Cash		150
July 5. Scully Company sold merchandise on account to Burton Co., $5,000, terms FOB destination, n/30. The cost of the merchandise sold was $3,500.	Accounts Receivable—Burton Co.	5,000		Merchandise Inventory	5,000	
	Sales		5,000	Accounts Payable—Scully Co.		5,000
	Cost of Merchandise Sold	3,500				
	Merchandise Inventory		3,500			
July 7. Scully Company paid freight of $250 for delivery of merchandise sold to Burton Co. on July 5.	Delivery Expense	250		No journal entry.		
	Cash		250			
July 13. Scully Company issued Burton Co. a credit memo for merchandise returned, $1,000. The merchandise had been purchased by Burton Co. on account on July 5. The cost of the merchandise returned was $700.	Sales Returns and Allowances	1,000		Accounts Payable—Scully Co.	1,000	
	Accounts Receivable—Burton Co.		1,000	Merchandise Inventory		1,000
	Merchandise Inventory	700				
	Cost of Merchandise Sold		700			
July 15. Scully Company received payment from Burton Co. for purchase of July 5.	Cash	4,000		Accounts Payable—Scully Co.	4,000	
	Accounts Receivable—Burton Co.		4,000	Cash		4,000
July 18. Scully Company sold merchandise on account to Burton Co., $12,000, terms FOB shipping point, 2/10, n/eom. Scully Company prepaid freight of $500, which was added to the invoice. The cost of the merchandise sold was $7,200.	Accounts Receivable—Burton Co.	12,000		Merchandise Inventory	12,500	
	Sales		12,000	Accounts Payable—Scully Co.		12,500
	Accounts Receivable—Burton Co.	500				
	Cash		500			
	Cost of Merchandise Sold	7,200				
	Merchandise Inventory		7,200			
July 28. Scully Company received payment from Burton Co. for purchase of July 18, less discount (2% × $12,000).	Cash	12,260		Accounts Payable—Scully Co.	12,500	
	Sales Discounts	240		Merchandise Inventory		240
	Accounts Receivable—Burton Co.		12,500	Cash		12,260

Example Exercise 5-5 Transactions for Buyer and Seller

OBJ 2

Sievert Co. sold merchandise to Bray Co. on account, $11,500, terms 2/15, n/30. The cost of the merchandise sold is $6,900. Sievert Co. issued a credit memo for $900 for merchandise returned and later received the amount due within the discount period. The cost of the merchandise returned was $540. Journalize Sievert Co.'s and Bray Co.'s entries for the payment of the amount due.

Follow My Example 5-5

Sievert Co. journal entries:

Cash ($11,500 – $900 – $212)	10,388	
Sales Discounts [($11,500 – $900) × 2%]	212	
Accounts Receivable—Bray Co. ($11,500 – $900)		10,600

Bray Co. journal entries:

Accounts Payable—Sievert Co. ($11,500 – $900)	10,600	
Merchandise Inventory [($11,500 – $900) × 2%]		212
Cash ($11,500 – $900 – $212)		10,388

Practice Exercises: **PE 5-5A, PE 5-5B**

Chart of Accounts for a Merchandising Business

The chart of accounts for a merchandising business should reflect the types of merchandise transactions described and illustrated earlier in this chapter. The chart of accounts for NetSolutions is shown in Exhibit 7. The accounts related to merchandising transactions are shown in color.

EXHIBIT 7

Chart of Accounts for NetSolutions, a Merchandising Business

Balance Sheet Accounts	Income Statement Accounts
100 Assets	400 Revenues
110 Cash	410 Sales
112 Accounts Receivable	411 Sales Returns and Allowances
115 Merchandise Inventory	412 Sales Discounts
116 Office Supplies	500 Costs and Expenses
117 Prepaid Insurance	510 Cost of Merchandise Sold
120 Land	520 Sales Salaries Expense
123 Store Equipment	521 Advertising Expense
124 Accumulated Depreciation—Store Equipment	522 Depreciation Expense—Store Equipment
125 Office Equipment	523 Delivery Expense
126 Accumulated Depreciation—Office Equipment	529 Miscellaneous Selling Expense
200 Liabilities	530 Office Salaries Expense
210 Accounts Payable	531 Rent Expense
211 Salaries Payable	532 Depreciation Expense—Office Equipment
212 Unearned Rent	533 Insurance Expense
215 Notes Payable	534 Office Supplies Expense
300 Stockholders' Equity	539 Misc. Administrative Expense
310 Capital Stock	600 Other Income
311 Retained Earnings	610 Rent Revenue
312 Dividends	700 Other Expense
313 Income Summary	710 Interest Expense

As shown in Exhibit 7, NetSolutions' chart of accounts consists of three-digit account numbers. The first digit indicates the major financial statement classification (1 for assets, 2 for liabilities, and so on). The second digit indicates the subclassification (e.g., 11 for current assets, 12 for noncurrent assets, etc.). The third digit identifies the specific account (e.g., 110 for Cash, 123 for Store Equipment, etc.). Using a three-digit numbering system makes it easier to add new accounts as they are needed.

Sales Taxes and Trade Discounts

Sales of merchandise often involve sales taxes. Also, the seller may offer buyers trade discounts.

Sales Taxes Almost all states levy a tax on sales of merchandise.[5] The liability for the sales tax is incurred when the sale is made.

At the time of a cash sale, the seller collects the sales tax. When a sale is made on account, the seller charges the tax to the buyer by debiting Accounts Receivable. The seller credits the sales account for the amount of the sale and credits the tax to Sales Tax Payable. For example, the seller would record a sale of $100 on account, subject to a tax of 6%, as follows:

Aug.	12	Accounts Receivable—Lemon Co.		106	
		Sales			100
		Sales Tax Payable			6
		Invoice No. 339.			

On a regular basis, the seller pays to the taxing authority (state) the amount of the sales tax collected. The seller records such a payment as follows:

Sept.	15	Sales Tax Payable		2,900	
		Cash			2,900
		Payment for sales taxes collected during August.			

Business Connection

SALES TAXES

While there is no federal sales tax, most states have enacted statewide sales taxes. In addition, many states allow counties and cities to collect a "local option" sales tax. Delaware, Montana, New Hampshire, and Oregon have no state or local sales taxes. Tennessee (9.45%), Washington (8.8%), and Louisiana (8.75%) have the highest average combined rates (including state and local option taxes). Several towns in Tuscaloosa County, Alabama, have the highest combined rates in the United States of 11%, while Chicago, Illinois, has the highest combined city rate of 10.25%.

What about companies that sell merchandise through the Internet? The general rule is that if the company ships merchandise to a customer in a state where the company does not have a physical location, no sales tax is due. For example, a customer in Montana who purchases merchandise online from a New York retailer (and no physical location in Montana) does not have to pay sales tax to either Montana or New York.

Source: The Sales Tax Clearinghouse at **www.thestc.com/FAQ.stm** (accessed January 21, 2012).

Trade Discounts Wholesalers are companies that sell merchandise to other businesses rather than to the public. Many wholesalers publish sales catalogs. Rather than updating their catalogs, wholesalers may publish price updates. These updates may include large discounts from the catalog list prices. In addition, wholesalers often offer special discounts to government agencies or businesses that order large quantities. Such discounts are called **trade discounts**.

Sellers and buyers do not normally record the list prices of merchandise and trade discounts in their accounts. For example, assume that an item has a list price of $1,000 and a 40% trade discount. The seller records the sale of the item at $600 [$1,000 less the trade discount of $400 ($1,000 × 40%)]. Likewise, the buyer records the purchase at $600.

OBJ 3 Describe and illustrate the financial statements of a merchandising business.

Financial Statements for a Merchandising Business

Although merchandising transactions affect the balance sheet in reporting inventory, they primarily affect the income statement. An income statement for a merchandising business is normally prepared using either a multiple-step or single-step format.

5 Businesses that purchase merchandise for resale to others are normally exempt from paying sales taxes on their purchases. Only final buyers of merchandise normally pay sales taxes.

Multiple-Step Income Statement

The 2015 income statement for NetSolutions is shown in Exhibit 8.[6] This form of income statement, called a **multiple-step income statement**, contains several sections, subsections, and subtotals.

EXHIBIT 8

Multiple-Step Income Statement

NetSolutions
Income Statement
For the Year Ended December 31, 2015

Revenue from sales:			
Sales		$720,185	
Less: Sales returns and allowances	$ 6,140		
Sales discounts	5,790	11,930	
Net sales			$708,255
Cost of merchandise sold			525,305
Gross profit			$182,950
Operating expenses:			
Selling expenses:			
Sales salaries expense	$53,430		
Advertising expense	10,860		
Depreciation expense—store equipment	3,100		
Delivery expense	2,800		
Miscellaneous selling expense	630		
Total selling expenses		$ 70,820	
Administrative expenses:			
Office salaries expense	$21,020		
Rent expense	8,100		
Depreciation expense—office equipment	2,490		
Insurance expense	1,910		
Office supplies expense	610		
Miscellaneous administrative expense	760		
Total administrative expenses		34,890	
Total operating expenses			105,710
Income from operations			$ 77,240
Other income and expense:			
Rent revenue		$ 600	
Interest expense		(2,440)	(1,840)
Net income			$ 75,400

Revenue from Sales This section of the multiple-step income statement consists of sales, sales returns and allowances, sales discounts, and net sales. The total amount of sales to customers for cash and on account is reported in this section. From this total, sales returns and allowances and sales discounts are deducted to yield **net sales**. Some companies only report net sales in the income statement, and report sales, sales returns and allowances, and sales discounts in a note to the financial statements.

NetSolutions reported sales of $720,185, sales returns and allowances of $6,140, and sales discounts of $5,790 for the year ended December 31, 2015. As a result, net sales were $708,255.

Cost of Merchandise Sold As shown in Exhibit 8, NetSolutions reported cost of merchandise sold of $525,305 during 2015. This amount is the cost of merchandise sold to customers. Cost of merchandise sold may also be reported as *cost of goods sold* or *cost of sales*.

For many merchandising businesses, the cost of merchandise sold is usually the largest expense. For example, the approximate percentage of cost of merchandise sold to sales is 61% for JCPenney and 66% for The Home Depot.

Gross Profit The excess of net sales over cost of merchandise sold is gross profit. As shown in Exhibit 8, NetSolutions reported gross profit of $182,950 in 2015.

Income from Operations **Income from operations**, sometimes called operating income, is determined by subtracting operating expenses from gross profit. Operating expenses are normally classified as either selling expenses or administrative expenses.

6 The NetSolutions income statement for 2015 is used because it allows a better illustration of the computation of the cost of merchandise sold in the appendix to this chapter.

Selling expenses are incurred directly in the selling of merchandise. Examples of selling expenses include sales salaries, store supplies used, depreciation of store equipment, delivery expense, and advertising.

Administrative expenses, sometimes called **general expenses**, are incurred in the administration or general operations of the business. Examples of administrative expenses include office salaries, depreciation of office equipment, and office supplies used.

IFRS IFRS

See Appendix C for more information

Each selling and administrative expense may be reported separately as shown in Exhibit 8. However, many companies report selling, administrative, and operating expenses as single line items as shown below for NetSolutions.

Gross profit		$182,950
Operating expenses:		
Selling expenses	$70,820	
Administrative expenses	34,890	
Total operating expenses		105,710
Income from operations		$ 77,240

Other Income and Expense Other income and expense items are not related to the primary operations of the business. **Other income** is revenue from sources other than the primary operating activity of a business. Examples of other income include income from interest, rent, and gains resulting from the sale of fixed assets. **Other expense** is an expense that cannot be traced directly to the normal operations of the business. Examples of other expenses include interest expense and losses from disposing of fixed assets.

Other income and other expense are offset against each other on the income statement. If the total of other income exceeds the total of other expense, the difference is added to income from operations to determine net income. If the reverse is true, the difference is subtracted from income from operations. The other income and expense items of NetSolutions are reported as shown below and in Exhibit 8.

Income from operations		$77,240
Other income and expense:		
Rent revenue	$ 600	
Interest expense	(2,440)	(1,840)
Net income		$75,400

Single-Step Income Statement

An alternate form of income statement is the **single-step income statement.** As shown in Exhibit 9, the income statement for NetSolutions deducts the total of all expenses *in one step* from the total of all revenues.

The single-step form emphasizes total revenues and total expenses in determining net income. A criticism of the single-step form is that gross profit and income from operations are not reported.

EXHIBIT 9

Single-Step Income Statement

NetSolutions
Income Statement
For the Year Ended December 31, 2015

Revenues:		
Net sales		$708,255
Rent revenue		600
Total revenues		$708,855
Expenses:		
Cost of merchandise sold	$525,305	
Selling expenses	70,820	
Administrative expenses	34,890	
Interest expense	2,440	
Total expenses		633,455
Net income		$ 75,400

Retained Earnings Statement

The retained earnings statement for NetSolutions is shown in Exhibit 10. This statement is prepared in the same manner as for a service business.

EXHIBIT 10

Retained Earnings Statement for Merchandising Business

NetSolutions
Retained Earnings Statement
For the Year Ended December 31, 2015

Retained earnings, January 1, 2015		$128,800
Net income for the year	$75,400	
Less dividends	18,000	
Increase in retained earnings		57,400
Retained earnings, December 31, 2015		$186,200

Balance Sheet

The balance sheet may be presented with assets on the left-hand side and the liabilities and stockholders' equity on the right-hand side. This form of the balance sheet is called the **account form.** The balance sheet may also be presented in a downward sequence in three sections. This form of balance sheet is called the **report form.** The report form of balance sheet for NetSolutions is shown in Exhibit 11.

EXHIBIT 11

Report Form of Balance Sheet

NetSolutions
Balance Sheet
December 31, 2015

Assets			
Current assets:			
Cash		$52,950	
Accounts receivable		91,080	
Merchandise inventory		62,150	
Office supplies		480	
Prepaid insurance		2,650	
Total current assets			$209,310
Property, plant, and equipment:			
Land		$20,000	
Store equipment	$ 27,100		
Less accumulated depreciation	5,700	21,400	
Office equipment	$ 15,570		
Less accumulated depreciation	4,720	10,850	
Total property, plant, and equipment			52,250
Total assets			$261,560
Liabilities			
Current liabilities:			
Accounts payable		$22,420	
Note payable (current portion)		5,000	
Salaries payable		1,140	
Unearned rent		1,800	
Total current liabilities			$ 30,360
Long-term liabilities:			
Note payable (final payment due 2025)			20,000
Total liabilities			$ 50,360
Stockholders' Equity			
Capital stock	$ 25,000		
Retained earnings	186,200		
Total stockholders' equity			211,200
Total liabilities and stockholders' equity			$261,560

In Exhibit 11, merchandise inventory is reported as a current asset and the current portion of the note payable of $5,000 is reported as a current liability.

OBJ 4 Describe the adjusting and closing process for a merchandising business.

The Adjusting and Closing Process

Thus far, the recording of transactions, chart of accounts, and financial statements for a merchandising business (NetSolutions) have been described and illustrated. In the remainder of this chapter, the adjusting and closing process for a merchandising business will be described. In this discussion, the focus will be on the elements of the accounting cycle that differ from those of a service business.

Adjusting Entry for Inventory Shrinkage

Under the perpetual inventory system, the merchandise inventory account is continually updated for purchase and sales transactions. As a result, the balance of the merchandise inventory account is the amount of merchandise available for sale at that point in time. However, retailers normally experience some loss of inventory due to shoplifting, employee theft, or errors. Thus, the physical inventory on hand at the end of the accounting period is usually less than the balance of Merchandise Inventory. This difference is called **inventory shrinkage** or **inventory shortage**.

To illustrate, NetSolutions' inventory records indicate the following on December 31, 2015:

	Dec. 31, 2015
Account balance of Merchandise Inventory	$63,950
Physical merchandise inventory on hand	62,150
Inventory shrinkage	$ 1,800

At the end of the accounting period, inventory shrinkage is recorded by the following adjusting entry:

		Adjusting Entry			
Dec.	31	Cost of Merchandise Sold		1,800	
		Merchandise Inventory			1,800
		Inventory shrinkage ($63,950 – $62,150).			

After the preceding entry is recorded, the balance of Merchandise Inventory agrees with the physical inventory on hand at the end of the period. Since inventory shrinkage cannot be totally eliminated, it is considered a normal cost of operations. If, however, the amount of the shrinkage is unusually large, it may be disclosed separately on the income statement. In such cases, the shrinkage may be recorded in a separate account, such as Loss from Merchandise Inventory Shrinkage.[7]

7 The adjusting process for a merchandising business may be aided by preparing an end-of-period spreadsheet (work sheet). An end-of-period spreadsheet (work sheet) for a merchandising business is described and illustrated in an online appendix at **www.cengagebrain.com**.

Example Exercise 5-6 Inventory Shrinkage

OBJ 4

Pulmonary Company's perpetual inventory records indicate that $382,800 of merchandise should be on hand on March 31, 2014. The physical inventory indicates that $371,250 of merchandise is actually on hand. Journalize the adjusting entry for the inventory shrinkage for Pulmonary Company for the year ended March 31, 2014. Assume that the inventory shrinkage is a normal amount.

Follow My Example 5-6

Mar. 31	Cost of Merchandise Sold	11,550	
	Merchandise Inventory		11,550
	Inventory shrinkage ($382,800 – $371,250).		

Practice Exercises: **PE 5-6A, PE 5-6B**

Closing Entries

The closing entries for a merchandising business are similar to those for a service business. The four closing entries for a merchandising business are as follows:

1. Debit each temporary account with a credit balance, such as Sales, for its balance and credit Income Summary.
2. Credit each temporary account with a debit balance, such as the various expenses, and debit Income Summary. Since Sales Returns and Allowances, Sales Discounts, and Cost of Merchandise Sold are temporary accounts with debit balances, they are credited for their balances.
3. Debit Income Summary for the amount of its balance (net income) and credit the retained earnings account. The accounts debited and credited are reversed if there is a net loss.
4. Debit the retained earnings account for the balance of the dividends account and credit the dividends account.

The four closing entries for NetSolutions are shown at the top of the next page.

NetSolutions' income summary account after the closing entries have been posted is as follows:

Account *Income Summary* Account No. *313*

Date		Item	Post. Ref.	Debit	Credit	Balance Debit	Balance Credit
2015 Dec.	31	Revenues	29		720,785		720,785
	31	Expenses	29	645,385			75,400
	31	Net income	29	75,400		—	—

After the closing entries are posted to the accounts, a post-closing trial balance is prepared. The only accounts that should appear on the post-closing trial balance are the asset, contra asset, liability, and stockholders' equity accounts with balances. These are the same accounts that appear on the end-of-period balance sheet. If the two totals of the trial balance columns are not equal, an error has occurred that must be found and corrected.

Journal *Page 29*

Date		Item	Post. Ref.	Debit	Credit
		Closing Entries			
2015 Dec.	31	Sales	410	720,185	
		Rent Revenue	610	600	
		Income Summary	313		720,785
	31	Income Summary	313	645,385	
		Sales Returns and Allowances	411		6,140
		Sales Discounts	412		5,790
		Cost of Merchandise Sold	510		525,305
		Sales Salaries Expense	520		53,430
		Advertising Expense	521		10,860
		Depr. Expense—Store Equipment	522		3,100
		Delivery Expense	523		2,800
		Miscellaneous Selling Expense	529		630
		Office Salaries Expense	530		21,020
		Rent Expense	531		8,100
		Depr. Expense—Office Equipment	532		2,490
		Insurance Expense	533		1,910
		Office Supplies Expense	534		610
		Misc. Administrative Expense	539		760
		Interest Expense	710		2,440
	31	Income Summary	313	75,400	
		Retained Earnings	311		75,400
	31	Retained Earnings	311	18,000	
		Dividends	312		18,000

F·A·I

Financial Analysis and Interpretation: Ratio of Net Sales to Assets

OBJ 5 Describe and illustrate the use of the ratio of net sales to assets in evaluating a company's operating performance.

The **ratio of net sales to assets** measures how effectively a business is using its assets to generate sales. A high ratio indicates an effective use of assets. The assets used in computing the ratio may be the total assets at the end of the year, the average of the total assets at the beginning and end of the year, or the average of the monthly assets. For our purposes, the average of the total assets at the beginning and end of the year is used.

The ratio of net sales to assets is computed as follows:

$$\text{Ratio of Net Sales to Assets} = \frac{\text{Net Sales}}{\text{Average Total Assets}}$$

To illustrate the use of this ratio, the following data (in millions) were taken from recent annual reports of Dollar Tree, Inc.:

	Year 2	Year 1
Total revenues (net sales)	$5,882	$5,231
Total assets:		
Beginning of year	2,290	2,036
End of year	2,381	2,290

The ratios of net sales to assets for each year are as follows:

	Year 2	Year 1
Ratio of net sales to assets*	2.52	2.42
	$5,882/[($2,290 + $2,381)/2]	$5,231/[($2,036 + $2,290)/2]

*Rounded to two decimal places.

Based on the preceding ratios, Dollar Tree improved its ratio of net sales to assets from 2.42 in Year 1 to 2.52 in Year 2. Thus, Dollar Tree improved the utilization of its assets to generate sales in Year 2.

Using the ratio of net sales to assets for comparisons to competitors and with industry averages could also be beneficial in interpreting Dollar Tree's use of its assets. For example, the following data (in millions) were taken from recent annual reports of **Dollar General Corporation**:

	Year 2
Total revenues (net sales)	$13,035
Total assets:	
Beginning of year	8,864
End of year	9,546

Dollar General's ratio of net sales to assets for Year 2 is as follows:

	Year 2
Ratio of net sales to assets*	1.42
	$13,035/[($8,864 + $9,546)/2]

*Rounded to two decimal places.

Comparing Dollar General's Year 2 ratio of 1.42 to Dollar Tree's Year 2 ratio of 2.52 implies that Dollar Tree is using its assets more efficiently than is Dollar General.

Example Exercise 5-7 Ratio of Net Sales to Assets

OBJ 5

The following financial statement data for the years ending December 31, 2014 and 2013, for Gilbert Company are shown below.

	2014	2013
Net sales	$1,305,000	$962,500
Total assets:		
Beginning of year	840,000	700,000
End of year	900,000	840,000

a. Determine the ratio of net sales to assets for 2014 and 2013.

b. Does the change in the current ratio from 2013 to 2014 indicate a favorable or an unfavorable trend?

Follow My Example 5-7

a.

	2014	2013
Ratio of net sales to assets	1.50	1.25
	$1,305,000/[($840,000 + $900,000)/2]	$962,500/[($700,000 + $840,000)/2]

b. The change from 1.25 to 1.50 indicates a favorable trend in using assets to generate sales.

Practice Exercises: **PE 5-7A, PE 5-7B**

Freight In When merchandise is purchased FOB shipping point, the buyer pays for the freight. Under the periodic inventory system, freight paid when purchasing merchandise FOB shipping point is debited to Freight In, Transportation In, or a similar account.

The preceding periodic inventory accounts and their effect on the cost of merchandise purchased are summarized below.

Account	Entry to Increase	Normal Balance	Effect on Cost of Merchandise Purchased
Purchases	Debit	Debit	Increases
Purchases Discounts	Credit	Credit	Decreases
Purchases Returns and Allowances	Credit	Credit	Decreases
Freight In	Debit	Debit	Increases

Exhibit 14 illustrates the recording of merchandise transactions using the periodic system. As a review, Exhibit 14 also illustrates how each transaction would have been recorded using the perpetual system.

EXHIBIT 14 **Transactions Using the Periodic and Perpetual Inventory Systems**

Transaction	Periodic Inventory System			Perpetual Inventory System		
June 5. Purchased $30,000 of merchandise on account, terms 2/10, n/30.	Purchases	30,000		Merchandise Inventory	30,000	
	Accounts Payable		30,000	Accounts Payable		30,000
June 8. Returned merchandise purchased on account on June 5, $500.	Accounts Payable	500		Accounts Payable	500	
	Purchases Returns and Allowances		500	Merchandise Inventory		500
June 15. Paid for purchase of June 5, less return of $500 and discount of $590 [($30,000 – $500) × 2%].	Accounts Payable	29,500		Accounts Payable	29,500	
	Cash		28,910	Cash		28,910
	Purchases Discounts		590	Merchandise Inventory		590
June 18. Sold merchandise on account, $12,500, 1/10, n/30. The cost of the merchandise sold was $9,000.	Accounts Receivable	12,500		Accounts Receivable	12,500	
	Sales		12,500	Sales		12,500
				Cost of Merchandise Sold	9,000	
				Merchandise Inventory		9,000
June 21. Received merchandise returned on account, $4,000 from sale of June 18. The cost of the merchandise returned was $2,800.	Sales Returns and Allowances	4,000		Sales Returns and Allowances	4,000	
	Accounts Receivable		4,000	Accounts Receivable		4,000
				Merchandise Inventory	2,800	
				Cost of Merchandise Sold		2,800
June 22. Purchased merchandise, $15,000, terms FOB shipping point, 2/15, n/30, with prepaid freight of $750 added to the invoice.	Purchases	15,000		Merchandise Inventory	15,750	
	Freight In	750		Accounts Payable		15,750
	Accounts Payable		15,750			
June 28. Received $8,415 as payment on account from June 18 sale less return of June 21 and less discount of $85 [($12,500 – $4,000) × 1%].	Cash	8,415		Cash	8,415	
	Sales Discounts	85		Sales Discounts	85	
	Accounts Receivable		8,500	Accounts Receivable		8,500
June 29. Received $19,600 from cash sales. The cost of the merchandise sold was $13,800.	Cash	19,600		Cash	19,600	
	Sales		19,600	Sales		19,600
				Cost of Merchandise Sold	13,800	
				Merchandise Inventory		13,800

Adjusting Process Under the Periodic Inventory System

The adjusting process is the same under the periodic and perpetual inventory systems except for the inventory shrinkage adjustment. The ending merchandise inventory is determined by a physical count under both systems.

Under the perpetual inventory system, the ending inventory physical count is compared to the balance of Merchandise Inventory. The difference is the amount of inventory shrinkage. The inventory shrinkage is then recorded as a debit to Cost of Merchandise Sold and a credit to Merchandise Inventory.

Under the periodic inventory system, the merchandise inventory account is not kept up to date for purchases and sales. As a result, the inventory shrinkage cannot be directly determined. Instead, any inventory shrinkage is included indirectly in the computation of the cost of merchandise sold as shown in Exhibit 12. This is a major disadvantage of the periodic inventory system. That is, under the periodic inventory system, inventory shrinkage is not separately determined.

Financial Statements Under the Periodic Inventory System

The financial statements are similar under the perpetual and periodic inventory systems. When the multiple-step format of income statement is used, the cost of merchandise sold may be reported as shown in Exhibit 12.

Closing Entries Under the Periodic Inventory System

The closing entries differ in the periodic inventory system in that there is no cost of merchandise sold account to close to Income Summary. Instead, the purchases, purchases discounts, purchases returns and allowances, and freight in accounts are closed to Income Summary. In addition, the merchandise inventory account is adjusted to the end-of-period physical inventory count during the closing process.

The four closing entries under the periodic inventory system are as follows:

1. Debit each temporary account with a credit balance, such as Sales, for its balance and credit Income Summary. Since Purchases Discounts and Purchases Returns and Allowances are temporary accounts with credit balances, they are debited for their balances. In addition, Merchandise Inventory is debited for its end-of-period balance based on the end-of-period physical inventory.
2. Credit each temporary account with a debit balance, such as the various expenses, and debit Income Summary. Since Sales Returns and Allowances, Sales Discounts, Purchases, and Freight In are temporary accounts with debit balances, they are credited for their balances. In addition, Merchandise Inventory is credited for its balance as of the beginning of the period.
3. Debit Income Summary for the amount of its balance (net income) and credit the retained earnings account. The accounts debited and credited are reversed if there is a net loss.
4. Debit the retained earnings account for the balance of the dividends account and credit the dividends account.

The four closing entries for NetSolutions under the periodic inventory system are shown on the next page.

Journal					
Date		**Item**	**Post. Ref.**	**Debit**	**Credit**
2015		Closing Entries			
Dec.	31	Merchandise Inventory	115	62,150	
		Sales	410	720,185	
		Purchases Returns and Allowances	511	9,100	
		Purchases Discounts	512	2,525	
		Rent Revenue	610	600	
		Income Summary	313		794,560
	31	Income Summary	313	719,160	
		Merchandise Inventory	115		59,700
		Sales Returns and Allowances	411		6,140
		Sales Discounts	412		5,790
		Purchases	510		521,980
		Freight In	513		17,400
		Sales Salaries Expense	520		53,430
		Advertising Expense	521		10,860
		Depreciation Expense—Store Equipment	522		3,100
		Delivery Expense	523		2,800
		Miscellaneous Selling Expense	529		630
		Office Salaries Expense	530		21,020
		Rent Expense	531		8,100
		Depreciation Expense—Office Equipment	532		2,490
		Insurance Expense	533		1,910
		Office Supplies Expense	534		610
		Miscellaneous Administrative Expense	539		760
		Interest Expense	710		2,440
	31	Income Summary	313	75,400	
		Retained Earnings	311		75,400
	31	Retained Earnings	311	18,000	
		Dividends	312		18,000

In the first closing entry, Merchandise Inventory is debited for $62,150. This is the ending physical inventory count on December 31, 2015. In the second closing entry, Merchandise Inventory is credited for its January 1, 2015, balance of $59,700. In this way, the closing entries highlight the importance of the beginning and ending balances of Merchandise Inventory in determining the cost of merchandise sold, as shown in Exhibit 12. After the closing entries are posted, Merchandise Inventory will have a balance of $62,150. This is the amount reported on the December 31, 2015, balance sheet.

In the preceding closing entries, the periodic accounts are highlighted in color. Under the perpetual inventory system, the highlighted periodic inventory accounts are replaced by the cost of merchandise sold account.

At a Glance 5

OBJ 1 Distinguish between the activities and financial statements of service and merchandising businesses.

Key Points Merchandising businesses purchase merchandise for selling to customers. On a merchandising business's income statement, revenue from selling merchandise is reported as sales. The cost of the merchandise sold is subtracted from sales to arrive at gross profit. The operating expenses are subtracted from gross profit to arrive at net income. Merchandise inventory, which is merchandise not sold, is reported as a current asset on the balance sheet.

Learning Outcomes	Example Exercises	Practice Exercises
• Describe how the activities of a service and a merchandising business differ.		
• Describe the differences between the income statements of a service and a merchandising business.		
• Compute gross profit.	EE5-1	PE5-1A, 5-1B
• Describe how merchandise inventory is reported on the balance sheet.		

OBJ 2 Describe and illustrate the accounting for merchandise transactions.

Key Points Purchases of merchandise for cash or on account are recorded as merchandise inventory. Discounts for early payment of purchases on account are purchases discounts and are recorded by crediting Merchandise Inventory. Price adjustments or returned merchandise are purchases returns and allowances and are also recorded by crediting Merchandise Inventory.

Sales of merchandise for cash or on account are recorded as sales. The cost of merchandise sold and the reduction in merchandise inventory are also recorded at the time of sale. Discounts for early payment of sales on account are recorded as sales discounts. Price adjustments and returned merchandise are recorded as sales returns and allowances.

When merchandise is shipped FOB shipping point, the buyer pays the freight and debits Merchandise Inventory. When merchandise is shipped FOB destination, the seller pays the freight and debits Delivery Expense or Freight Out. Merchandise transactions can be summarized in T account form as shown in Exhibit 6. Each merchandising transaction affects a buyer and a seller. The chart of accounts for a merchandising business (NetSolutions) is shown in Exhibit 7. The liability for sales tax is incurred when the sale is made and is recorded by the seller as a credit to the sales tax payable account. Trade discounts are discounts off the list price of merchandise.

Learning Outcomes	Example Exercises	Practice Exercises
• Prepare journal entries to record the purchases of merchandise for cash.		
• Prepare journal entries to record the purchases of merchandise on account.	EE5-2	PE5-2A, 5-2B
• Prepare journal entries to record purchases discounts and purchases returns and allowances.	EE5-2	PE5-2A, 5-2B
• Prepare journal entries to record sales of merchandise for cash or using a credit card.		
• Prepare journal entries to record sales of merchandise on account.	EE5-3	PE5-3A, 5-3B
• Prepare journal entries to record sales discounts and sales returns and allowances.	EE5-3	PE5-3A, 5-3B
• Prepare journal entries for freight from the point of view of the buyer and seller.		
• Determine the total cost of the purchase of merchandise under differing freight terms.	EE5-4	PE5-4A, 5-4B
• Record the same merchandise transactions for the buyer and seller.	EE5-5	PE5-5A, 5-5B
• Prepare a chart of accounts for a merchandising business.		
• Determine the cost of merchandise purchased when a trade discount is offered by the seller.		
• Record sales transactions involving sales taxes and trade discounts.		

OBJ 3 Describe and illustrate the financial statements of a merchandising business.

Key Points The multiple-step income statement of a merchandiser reports sales, sales returns and allowances, sales discounts, and net sales. The cost of the merchandise sold is subtracted from net sales to determine the gross profit. Operating income is determined by subtracting selling and administrative expenses from gross profit. Net income is determined by adding or subtracting the net of other income and expense. The income statement may also be reported in a single-step form.

The retained earnings statement is similar to that for a service business.

The balance sheet reports merchandise inventory at the end of the period as a current asset.

Learning Outcomes	Example Exercises	Practice Exercises
• Prepare a multiple-step income statement for a merchandising business.		
• Prepare a single-step income statement.		
• Prepare a retained earnings statement for a merchandising business.		
• Prepare a report form of balance sheet for a merchandising business.		

OBJ 4

Describe the adjusting and closing process for a merchandising business.

Key Points The normal adjusting entry for inventory shrinkage is to debit Cost of Merchandise Sold and credit Merchandise Inventory.

The closing entries for a merchandising business are similar to those for a service business except that the cost of merchandise sold, sales discounts, and sales returns and allowances accounts are also closed to Income Summary.

Learning Outcomes	Example Exercises	Practice Exercises
• Prepare the adjusting journal entry for inventory shrinkage.	EE5-6	PE5-6A, 5-6B
• Prepare the closing entries for a merchandising business.		

OBJ 5

Describe and illustrate the use of the ratio of net sales to assets in evaluating a company's operating performance.

Key Points The ratio of net sales to assets measures how effectively a business is using its assets to generate sales. A high ratio indicates an effective use of assets. Using the average of the total assets at the beginning and end of the year, the ratio is computed as follows:

$$\text{Ratio of Net Sales to Assets} = \frac{\text{Net Sales}}{\text{Average Total Assets}}$$

Learning Outcomes	Example Exercises	Practice Exercises
• Interpret a high ratio of net sales to assets.		
• Compute the ratio of net sales to assets.	EE5-7	PE5-7A, 5-7B

Key Terms

account form (231)
accounts payable subsidiary ledger (214)
accounts receivable subsidiary ledger (214)
administrative expenses (general expenses) (230)
controlling account (214)
cost of merchandise sold (212)
credit memorandum (credit memo) (221)
credit period (215)
credit terms (215)
debit memorandum (debit memo) (217)
FOB (free on board) destination (223)
FOB (free on board) shipping point (222)
general ledger (214)
gross profit (212)
income from operations (operating income) (229)
inventory shrinkage (inventory shortage) (232)
inventory subsidiary ledger (214)
invoice (215)
merchandise inventory (212)
multiple-step income statement (229)
net sales (229)
other expense (230)
other income (230)
periodic inventory system (214)
perpetual inventory system (214)
physical inventory (214)
purchases discounts (216)
purchases returns and allowances (217)
ratio of net sales to assets (234)
report form (231)
sales (212)
sales discounts (220)
sales returns and allowances (220)
selling expenses (230)
single-step income statement (230)
special journals (214)
subsidiary ledger (214)
trade discounts (228)

Illustrative Problem

The following transactions were completed by Montrose Company during May of the current year. Montrose Company uses a perpetual inventory system.

May 3. Purchased merchandise on account from Floyd Co., $4,000, terms FOB shipping point, 2/10, n/30, with prepaid freight of $120 added to the invoice.

5. Purchased merchandise on account from Kramer Co., $8,500, terms FOB destination, 1/10, n/30.

6. Sold merchandise on account to C. F. Howell Co., list price $4,000, trade discount 30%, terms 2/10, n/30. The cost of the merchandise sold was $1,125.

8. Purchased office supplies for cash, $150.

10. Returned merchandise purchased on May 5 from Kramer Co., $1,300.

13. Paid Floyd Co. on account for purchase of May 3, less discount.

14. Purchased merchandise for cash, $10,500.

15. Paid Kramer Co. on account for purchase of May 5, less return of May 10 and discount.

16. Received cash on account from sale of May 6 to C. F. Howell Co., less discount.

19. Sold merchandise on MasterCard credit cards, $2,450. The cost of the merchandise sold was $980.

22. Sold merchandise on account to Comer Co., $3,480, terms 2/10, n/30. The cost of the merchandise sold was $1,400.

24. Sold merchandise for cash, $4,350. The cost of the merchandise sold was $1,750.

25. Received merchandise returned by Comer Co. from sale on May 22, $1,480. The cost of the returned merchandise was $600.

31. Paid a service processing fee of $140 for MasterCard sales.

Instructions

1. Journalize the preceding transactions.
2. Journalize the adjusting entry for merchandise inventory shrinkage, $3,750.

Solution

1.

May	3	Merchandise Inventory	4,120	
		Accounts Payable—Floyd Co.		4,120
	5	Merchandise Inventory	8,500	
		Accounts Payable—Kramer Co.		8,500
	6	Accounts Receivable—C. F. Howell Co.	2,800	
		Sales		2,800
		[$4,000 – (30% × $4,000)]		
	6	Cost of Merchandise Sold	1,125	
		Merchandise Inventory		1,125
	8	Office Supplies	150	
		Cash		150
	10	Accounts Payable—Kramer Co.	1,300	
		Merchandise Inventory		1,300
	13	Accounts Payable—Floyd Co.	4,120	
		Merchandise Inventory		80
		Cash		4,040
		[$4,000 – (2% × $4,000) + $120]		

	May 14	Merchandise Inventory	10,500	
		Cash		10,500
	15	Accounts Payable—Kramer Co.	7,200	
		Merchandise Inventory		72
		Cash		7,128
		[($8,500 – $1,300) × 1% = $72; $8,500 – $1,300 – $72 = $7,128]		
	16	Cash	2,744	
		Sales Discounts	56	
		Accounts Receivable—C. F. Howell Co.		2,800
	19	Cash	2,450	
		Sales		2,450
	19	Cost of Merchandise Sold	980	
		Merchandise Inventory		980
	22	Accounts Receivable—Comer Co.	3,480	
		Sales		3,480
	22	Cost of Merchandise Sold	1,400	
		Merchandise Inventory		1,400
	24	Cash	4,350	
		Sales		4,350
	24	Cost of Merchandise Sold	1,750	
		Merchandise Inventory		1,750
	25	Sales Returns and Allowances	1,480	
		Accounts Receivable—Comer Co.		1,480
	25	Merchandise Inventory	600	
		Cost of Merchandise Sold		600
	31	Credit Card Expense	140	
		Cash		140
2.	May 31	Cost of Merchandise Sold	3,750	
		Merchandise Inventory		3,750
		Inventory shrinkage.		

Discussion Questions

1. What distinguishes a merchandising business from a service business?
2. Can a business earn a gross profit but incur a net loss? Explain.
3. The credit period during which the buyer of merchandise is allowed to pay usually begins with what date?
4. What is the meaning of (a) 1/15, n/60; (b) n/30; (c) n/eom?
5. How are sales to customers using MasterCard and VISA recorded?
6. What is the nature of (a) a credit memo issued by the seller of merchandise, (b) a debit memo issued by the buyer of merchandise?
7. Who bears the freight when the terms of sale are (a) FOB shipping point, (b) FOB destination?
8. Name at least three accounts that would normally appear in the chart of accounts of a merchandising business but would not appear in the chart of accounts of a service business.
9. Audio Outfitter Inc., which uses a perpetual inventory system, experienced a normal inventory shrinkage of $13,675. What accounts would be debited and credited to record the adjustment for the inventory shrinkage at the end of the accounting period?
10. Assume that Audio Outfitter Inc. in Discussion Question 9 experienced an abnormal inventory shrinkage of $98,600. Audio Outfitter Inc. has decided to record the abnormal inventory shrinkage so that it would be separately disclosed on the income statement. What account would be debited for the abnormal inventory shrinkage?

Practice Exercises

Example Exercises

EE 5-1 *p. 213*

PE 5-1A Gross profit — OBJ. 1

During the current year, merchandise is sold for $450,000 cash and $1,350,000 on account. The cost of the merchandise sold is $1,100,000. What is the amount of the gross profit?

EE 5-1 *p. 213*

PE 5-1B Gross profit — OBJ. 1

During the current year, merchandise is sold for $18,300 cash and $295,700 on account. The cost of the merchandise sold is $188,000. What is the amount of the gross profit?

EE 5-2 *p. 218*

PE 5-2A Purchases transactions — OBJ. 2

Xanadu Company purchased merchandise on account from a supplier for $12,650, terms 2/10, n/30. Xanadu Company returned $3,950 of the merchandise and received full credit.

a. If Xanadu Company pays the invoice within the discount period, what is the amount of cash required for the payment?

b. What account is credited by Xanadu Company to record the return?

EE 5-2 *p. 218*

PE 5-2B Purchases transactions — OBJ. 2

Hoffman Company purchased merchandise on account from a supplier for $65,000, terms 1/10, n/30. Hoffman Company returned $7,500 of the merchandise and received full credit.

a. If Hoffman Company pays the invoice within the discount period, what is the amount of cash required for the payment?

b. What account is debited by Hoffman Company to record the return?

EE 5-3 *p. 222*

PE 5-3A Sales transactions — OBJ. 2

Journalize the following merchandise transactions:

a. Sold merchandise on account, $41,100 with terms 2/10, n/30. The cost of the merchandise sold was $26,750.

b. Received payment less the discount.

EE 5-3 *p. 222*

PE 5-3B Sales transactions — OBJ. 2

Journalize the following merchandise transactions:

a. Sold merchandise on account, $92,500 with terms 1/10, n/30. The cost of the merchandise sold was $55,500.

b. Received payment less the discount.

EE 5-4 *p. 225*

PE 5-4A Freight terms — OBJ. 2

Determine the amount to be paid in full settlement of each of two invoices, (a) and (b), assuming that credit for returns and allowances was received prior to payment and that all invoices were paid within the discount period.

	Merchandise	Freight Paid by Seller	Freight Terms	Returns and Allowances
a.	$180,000	$3,000	FOB shipping point, 1/10, n/30	$20,000
b.	88,000	1,250	FOB destination, 2/10, n/30	9,000

Example Exercises

EE 5-4 *p. 225*

PE 5-4B Freight terms

OBJ. 2

Determine the amount to be paid in full settlement of each of two invoices, (a) and (b), assuming that credit for returns and allowances was received prior to payment and that all invoices were paid within the discount period.

	Merchandise	Freight Paid by Seller	Freight Terms	Returns and Allowances
a.	$36,000	$800	FOB destination, 1/10, n/30	$4,000
b.	44,900	375	FOB shipping point, 2/10, n/30	2,400

EE 5-5 *p. 226*

PE 5-5A Transactions for buyer and seller

OBJ. 2

Sundance Co. sold merchandise to Butterfield Co. on account, $16,800, terms 2/15, n/30. The cost of the merchandise sold is $12,600. Sundance Co. issued a credit memo for $3,800 for merchandise returned and later received the amount due within the discount period. The cost of the merchandise returned was $2,850. Journalize Sundance Co.'s and Butterfield Co.'s entries for the payment of the amount due.

EE 5-5 *p. 226*

PE 5-5B Transactions for buyer and seller

OBJ. 2

Shore Co. sold merchandise to Blue Star Co. on account, $112,000, terms FOB shipping point, 2/10, n/30. The cost of the merchandise sold is $67,200. Shore Co. paid freight of $1,800 and later received the amount due within the discount period. Journalize Shore Co.'s and Blue Star Co.'s entries for the payment of the amount due.

EE 5-6 *p. 233*

PE 5-6A Inventory shrinkage

OBJ. 4

Modern Furnishings Company's perpetual inventory records indicate that $890,000 of merchandise should be on hand on April 30, 2014. The physical inventory indicates that $876,250 of merchandise is actually on hand. Journalize the adjusting entry for the inventory shrinkage for Modern Furnishings Company for the year ended April 30, 2014. Assume that the inventory shrinkage is a normal amount.

EE 5-6 *p. 233*

PE 5-6B Inventory shrinkage

OBJ. 4

Hahn Flooring Company's perpetual inventory records indicate that $1,333,150 of merchandise should be on hand on December 31, 2014. The physical inventory indicates that $1,309,900 of merchandise is actually on hand. Journalize the adjusting entry for the inventory shrinkage for Hahn Flooring Company for the year ended December 31, 2014. Assume that the inventory shrinkage is a normal amount.

EE 5-7 *p. 235*

F·A·I

PE 5-7A Ratio of net sales to assets

OBJ. 5

The following financial statement data for years ending December 31 for Latchkey Company are shown below.

	2014	2013
Net sales	$1,734,000	$1,645,000
Total assets:		
Beginning of year	480,000	460,000
End of year	540,000	480,000

a. Determine the ratio of net sales to assets for 2014 and 2013.

b. Does the change in the ratio of net sales to assets from 2013 to 2014 indicate a favorable or an unfavorable trend?

Example Exercises

EE 5-7 *p. 235*

F·A·I

PE 5-7B Ratio of net sales to assets **OBJ. 5**

The following financial statement data for years ending December 31 for Edison Company are shown below.

	2014	2013
Net sales	$1,884,000	$1,562,000
Total assets:		
Beginning of year	770,000	650,000
End of year	800,000	770,000

a. Determine the ratio of net sales to assets for 2014 and 2013.

b. Does the change in the ratio of net sales to assets from 2013 to 2014 indicate a favorable or an unfavorable trend?

Exercises

EX 5-1 Determining gross profit **OBJ. 1**

During the current year, merchandise is sold for $2,450,000. The cost of the merchandise sold is $1,519,000.

a. What is the amount of the gross profit?

b. Compute the gross profit percentage (gross profit divided by sales).

c. Will the income statement necessarily report a net income? Explain.

EX 5-2 Determining cost of merchandise sold **OBJ. 1**

For a recent year, Best Buy reported revenue of $50,272 million. Its gross profit was $12,637 million. What was the amount of Best Buy's cost of merchandise sold?

EX 5-3 Purchase-related transactions **OBJ. 2**

Locust Company purchased merchandise on account from a supplier for $34,900, terms 1/10, n/30. Locust Company returned $6,400 of the merchandise and received full credit.

a. If Locust Company pays the invoice within the discount period, what is the amount of cash required for the payment?

b. Under a perpetual inventory system, what account is credited by Locust Company to record the return?

EX 5-4 Purchase-related transactions **OBJ. 2**

A retailer is considering the purchase of 250 units of a specific item from either of two suppliers. Their offers are as follows:

Supplier One: $400 a unit, total of $100,000, 1/10, n/30, no charge for freight.

Supplier Two: $399 a unit, total of $99,750, 2/10, n/30, plus freight of $975.

Which of the two offers, Supplier One or Supplier Two, yields the lower price?

EX 5-5 Purchase-related transactions **OBJ. 2**

The debits and credits from four related transactions are presented in the following T accounts. Describe each transaction.

Cash

		(2)	300
		(4)	16,830

Merchandise Inventory

(1)	21,000	(3)	4,000
(2)	300	(4)	170

Accounts Payable

(3)	4,000	(1)	21,000
(4)	17,000		

✔ (c) Cash, cr. $47,040

EX 5-6 Purchase-related transactions **OBJ. 2**

Paramount Co., a women's clothing store, purchased $60,000 of merchandise from a supplier on account, terms FOB destination, 2/10, n/30. Paramount Co. returned $12,000 of the merchandise, receiving a credit memo, and then paid the amount due within the discount period. Journalize Paramount Co.'s entries to record (a) the purchase, (b) the merchandise return, and (c) the payment.

✔ (e) Cash, dr. $4,365

EX 5-7 Purchase-related transactions **OBJ. 2**

Journalize entries for the following related transactions of Platypus Company:

a. Purchased $71,500 of merchandise from Sitwell Co. on account, terms 1/10, n/30.

b. Paid the amount owed on the invoice within the discount period.

c. Discovered that $13,500 (before purchases discount of 1%) of the merchandise was defective and returned items, receiving credit.

d. Purchased $9,000 of merchandise from Sitwell Co. on account, terms n/30.

e. Received a check for the balance owed from the return in (c), after deducting for the purchase in (d).

EX 5-8 Sales-related transactions, including the use of credit cards **OBJ. 2**

Journalize the entries for the following transactions:

a. Sold merchandise for cash, $45,000. The cost of the merchandise sold was $27,000.

b. Sold merchandise on account, $115,000. The cost of the merchandise sold was $69,000.

c. Sold merchandise to customers who used MasterCard and VISA, $130,000. The cost of the merchandise sold was $78,000.

d. Sold merchandise to customers who used American Express, $100,000. The cost of the merchandise sold was $60,000.

e. Received an invoice from Foley Credit Co. for $9,200, representing a service fee paid for processing MasterCard, VISA, and American Express sales.

EX 5-9 Sales returns and allowances **OBJ. 2**

During the year, sales returns and allowances totaled $55,000. The cost of the merchandise returned was $33,000. The accountant recorded all the returns and allowances by debiting the sales account and crediting Cost of Merchandise Sold for $55,000.

Was the accountant's method of recording returns acceptable? Explain. In your explanation, include the advantages of using a sales returns and allowances account.

EX 5-10 Sales-related transactions **OBJ. 2**

After the amount due on a sale of $28,000, terms 2/10, n/eom, is received from a customer within the discount period, the seller consents to the return of the entire shipment. The cost of the merchandise returned was $16,800. (a) What is the amount of the refund owed to the customer? (b) Journalize the entries made by the seller to record the return and the refund.

EX 5-11 Sales-related transactions **OBJ. 2**

The debits and credits for three related transactions are presented in the following T accounts. Describe each transaction.

Cash

(5)	39,200		

Accounts Receivable

(1)	42,000	(3)	2,000
		(5)	40,000

Merchandise Inventory

(4)	1,200	(2)	25,200

Sales

		(1)	42,000

Sales Discounts

(5)	800		

Sales Returns and Allowances

(3)	2,000		

Cost of Merchandise Sold

(2)	25,200	(4)	1,200

EX 5-12 Sales-related transactions **OBJ. 2**

✔ d. $23,945

Merchandise is sold on account to a customer for $24,000, terms FOB shipping point, 2/10, n/30. The seller paid the freight of $425. Determine the following: (a) amount of the sale, (b) amount debited to Accounts Receivable, (c) amount of the discount for early payment, and (d) amount due within the discount period.

EX 5-13 Determining amounts to be paid on invoices **OBJ. 2**

✔ a. $49,600

Determine the amount to be paid in full settlement of each of the following invoices, assuming that credit for returns and allowances was received prior to payment and that all invoices were paid within the discount period.

	Merchandise	Freight Paid by Seller		Returns and Allowances
a.	$52,300	—	FOB destination, n/30	$2,700
b.	14,800	$200	FOB shipping point, 2/10, n/30	1,600
c.	19,100	—	FOB shipping point, 1/10, n/30	1,300
d.	6,700	80	FOB shipping point, 2/10, n/30	300
e.	22,600	—	FOB destination, 1/10, n/30	—

EX 5-14 Sales-related transactions **OBJ. 2**

Sombrero Co., a furniture wholesaler, sells merchandise to Belarus Co. on account, $64,300, terms 2/10, n/30. The cost of the merchandise sold is $38,000. Sombrero Co. issues a credit memo for $13,300 for merchandise returned and subsequently receives the amount due within the discount period. The cost of the merchandise returned is $8,000. Journalize Sombrero Co.'s entries for (a) the sale, including the cost of the merchandise sold, (b) the credit memo, including the cost of the returned merchandise, and (c) the receipt of the check for the amount due from Belarus Co.

EX 5-15 Purchase-related transactions **OBJ. 2**

Based on the data presented in Exercise 5-14, journalize Belarus Co.'s entries for (a) the purchase, (b) the return of the merchandise for credit, and (c) the payment of the invoice within the discount period.

EX 5-16 Chart of accounts **OBJ. 2**

Monet Paints Co. is a newly organized business with a list of accounts arranged in alphabetical order below.

Accounts Payable
Accounts Receivable
Accumulated Depreciation—Office Equipment
Accumulated Depreciation—Store Equipment
Advertising Expense
Capital Stock
Cash
Cost of Merchandise Sold
Delivery Expense
Depreciation Expense—Office Equipment
Depreciation Expense—Store Equipment
Dividends
Income Summary
Insurance Expense
Interest Expense
Land
Merchandise Inventory
Miscellaneous Administrative Expense
Miscellaneous Selling Expense
Notes Payable
Office Equipment
Office Salaries Expense
Office Supplies
Office Supplies Expense
Prepaid Insurance
Rent Expense
Retained Earnings
Salaries Payable
Sales
Sales Discounts
Sales Returns and Allowances
Sales Salaries Expense
Store Equipment
Store Supplies
Store Supplies Expense

Construct a chart of accounts, assigning account numbers and arranging the accounts in balance sheet and income statement order, as illustrated in Exhibit 7. Each account number is three digits: the first digit is to indicate the major classification (1 for assets, and so on); the second digit is to indicate the subclassification (11 for current assets, and so on); and the third digit is to identify the specific account (110 for Cash, 112 for Accounts Receivable, 114 for Merchandise Inventory, 115 for Store Supplies, and so on).

EX 5-17 Sales tax **OBJ. 2**

✔c. $38,880

A sale of merchandise on account for $36,000 is subject to an 8% sales tax. (a) Should the sales tax be recorded at the time of sale or when payment is received? (b) What is the amount of the sale? (c) What is the amount debited to Accounts Receivable? (d) What is the title of the account to which the $2,880 ($36,000 × 8%) is credited?

EX 5-18 Sales tax transactions **OBJ. 2**

Journalize the entries to record the following selected transactions:

a. Sold $22,600 of merchandise on account, subject to a sales tax of 5%. The cost of the merchandise sold was $13,600.

b. Paid $51,668 to the state sales tax department for taxes collected.

EX 5-19 Normal balances of merchandise accounts **OBJ. 2**

What is the normal balance of the following accounts: (a) Cost of Merchandise Sold, (b) Delivery Expense, (c) Merchandise Inventory, (d) Sales, (e) Sales Discounts, (f) Sales Returns and Allowances, (g) Sales Tax Payable?

EX 5-20 Income statement for merchandiser **OBJ. 3**

For the fiscal year, sales were $8,135,000, sales discounts were $795,000, sales returns and allowances were $475,000, and the cost of merchandise sold was $5,100,000.

a. What was the amount of net sales?

b. What was the amount of gross profit?

c. If total operating expenses were $1,350,000, could you determine net income?

EX 5-21 Income statement for merchandiser **OBJ. 3**

The following expenses were incurred by a merchandising business during the year. In which expense section of the income statement should each be reported: (a) selling, (b) administrative, or (c) other?

1. Advertising expense
2. Depreciation expense on store equipment
3. Insurance expense on office equipment
4. Interest expense on notes payable
5. Rent expense on office building
6. Salaries of office personnel
7. Salary of sales manager
8. Sales supplies used

EX 5-22 Determining amounts for items omitted from income statement **OBJ. 3**

✔ a. $20,250
✔ h. $1,500,000

Two items are omitted in each of the following four lists of income statement data. Determine the amounts of the missing items, identifying them by letter.

Sales	$525,000	$733,000	$1,440,000	$ (g)
Sales returns and allowances	(a)	28,000	(e)	85,000
Sales discounts	41,350	17,500	100,000	65,000
Net sales	463,400	(c)	1,295,000	(h)
Cost of merchandise sold	(b)	410,000	(f)	900,000
Gross profit	83,500	(d)	275,000	600,000

✔ **a. Net income: $475,000**

SPREADSHEET

EX 5-23 Multiple-step income statement **OBJ. 3**

On February 28, 2014, the balances of the accounts appearing in the ledger of Foldaway Furnishings Company, a furniture wholesaler, are as follows:

Accumulated Depreciation—Building	$ 150,000	Notes Payable	400,000
Administrative Expenses	290,000	Office Supplies	20,000
Building	1,130,000	Retained Earnings	416,000
Capital Stock	175,000	Salaries Payable	6,000
Cash	97,000	Sales	2,850,000
Cost of Merchandise Sold	1,641,000	Sales Discounts	25,000
Dividends	50,000	Sales Returns and Allowances	90,000
Interest Expense	29,000	Selling Expenses	300,000
Merchandise Inventory	$ 260,000	Store Supplies	65,000

a. Prepare a multiple-step income statement for the year ended February 28, 2014.

b. Compare the major advantages and disadvantages of the multiple-step and single-step forms of income statements.

EX 5-24 Multiple-step income statement **OBJ. 3**

Identify the errors in the following income statement:

Curbstone Company
Income Statement
For the Year Ended August 31, 2014

Revenue from sales:			
Sales		$9,132,000	
Add: Sales returns and allowances	$422,000		
Sales discounts	115,000	537,000	
Gross sales			$9,669,000
Cost of merchandise sold			6,110,000
Income from operations			$3,559,000
Expenses:			
Selling expenses		$ 800,000	
Administrative expenses		575,000	
Delivery expense		425,000	
Total expenses			1,800,000
			$1,759,000
Other expense:			
Interest revenue			45,000
Gross profit			$1,714,000

✔ **Net income: $475,000**

EX 5-25 Single-step income statement **OBJ. 3**

Summary operating data for Cummerbund Company during the current year ended June 30, 2014, are as follows: cost of merchandise sold, $2,400,000; administrative expenses, $420,000; interest expense, $30,000; rent revenue, $125,000; net sales, $3,750,000; and selling expenses, $550,000. Prepare a single-step income statement.

EX 5-26 Adjusting entry for merchandise inventory shrinkage **OBJ. 4**

Road Runner Tire Co.'s perpetual inventory records indicate that $1,498,200 of merchandise should be on hand on December 31, 2014. The physical inventory indicates that $1,483,750 of merchandise is actually on hand. Journalize the adjusting entry for the inventory shrinkage for Road Runner Tire Co. for the year ended December 31, 2014.

EX 5-27 Closing the accounts of a merchandiser — OBJ. 4

From the following list, identify the accounts that should be closed to Income Summary at the end of the fiscal year under a perpetual inventory system: (a) Accounts Payable, (b) Advertising Expense, (c) Cost of Merchandise Sold, (d) Dividends, (e) Merchandise Inventory, (f) Sales, (g) Sales Discounts, (h) Sales Returns and Allowances, (i) Supplies, (j) Supplies Expense, (k) Wages Payable.

EX 5-28 Closing entries; net income — OBJ. 4

Based on the data presented in Exercise 5-23, journalize the closing entries.

EX 5-29 Closing entries — OBJ. 4

On October 31, 2014, the balances of the accounts appearing in the ledger of Acorn Interiors Company, a furniture wholesaler, are as follows:

Accumulated Depr.—Building	$142,000	Notes Payable	$ 125,000
Administrative Expenses	300,000	Retained Earnings	105,000
Building	446,000	Sales	1,375,000
Capital Stock	75,000	Sales Discounts	20,000
Cash	60,000	Sales Returns and Allow.	13,000
Cost of Merchandise Sold	650,000	Sales Tax Payable	3,000
Dividends	25,000	Selling Expenses	140,000
Interest Expense	10,000	Store Supplies	23,000
Merchandise Inventory	126,000	Store Supplies Expense	12,000

Prepare the October 31, 2014, closing entries for Acorn Interiors Company.

EX 5-30 Ratio of net sales to assets — OBJ. 5

F·A·I

The Home Depot reported the following data (in millions) in its recent financial statements:

	Year 2	Year 1
Net sales	$67,997	$66,176
Total assets at the end of the year	40,125	40,877
Total assets at the beginning of the year	40,877	41,164

a. Determine the ratio of net sales to assets for The Home Depot for Year 2 and Year 1. Round to two decimal places.

b. What conclusions can be drawn from these ratios concerning the trend in the ability of The Home Depot to effectively use its assets to generate sales?

EX 5-31 Ratio of net sales to assets — OBJ. 5

F·A·I

Kroger, a national supermarket chain, reported the following data (in millions) in its financial statements for a recent year:

Total revenue	$82,189
Total assets at end of year	23,505
Total assets at beginning of year	23,126

a. Compute the ratio of net sales to assets. Round to two decimal places.

b. Tiffany & Co. is a large North American retailer of jewelry, with a ratio of net sales to assets of 0.85. Why would Tiffany's ratio of net sales to assets be lower than that of Kroger?

Appendix

EX 5-32 Identify items missing in determining cost of merchandise sold

For (a) through (d), identify the items designated by X and Y.

a. Purchases − (X + Y) = Net purchases.

b. Net purchases + X = Cost of merchandise purchased.

c. Merchandise inventory (beginning) + Cost of merchandise purchased = X.

d. Merchandise available for sale − X = Cost of merchandise sold.

Appendix

EX 5-33 Cost of merchandise sold and related items

✔ a. Cost of merchandise sold, $3,551,600

The following data were extracted from the accounting records of Harkins Company for the year ended April 30, 2014:

Merchandise inventory, May 1, 2013	$ 380,000
Merchandise inventory, April 30, 2014	415,000
Purchases	3,800,000
Purchases returns and allowances	150,000
Purchases discounts	80,000
Sales	5,850,000
Freight in	16,600

a. Prepare the cost of merchandise sold section of the income statement for the year ended April 30, 2014, using the periodic inventory system.

b. Determine the gross profit to be reported on the income statement for the year ended April 30, 2014.

c. Would gross profit be different if the perpetual inventory system was used instead of the periodic inventory system?

Appendix

EX 5-34 Cost of merchandise sold

Based on the following data, determine the cost of merchandise sold for November:

Merchandise inventory, November 1	$ 28,000
Merchandise inventory, November 30	31,500
Purchases	475,000
Purchases returns and allowances	15,000
Purchases discounts	9,000
Freight in	7,000

Appendix

EX 5-35 Cost of merchandise sold

Based on the following data, determine the cost of merchandise sold for July:

Merchandise inventory, July 1	$ 190,850
Merchandise inventory, July 31	160,450
Purchases	1,126,000
Purchases returns and allowances	46,000
Purchases discounts	23,000
Freight in	17,500

Appendix

EX 5-36 Cost of merchandise sold

✔ Correct cost of merchandise sold, $1,033,300

Identify the errors in the following schedule of the cost of merchandise sold for the current year ended May 31, 2014:

Cost of merchandise sold:			
Merchandise inventory, May 31, 2014			$ 105,000
Purchases		$1,110,000	
Plus: Purchases returns and allowances	$55,000		
Purchases discounts	30,000	85,000	
Gross purchases		$1,195,000	
Less freight in		22,000	
Cost of merchandise purchased			1,173,000
Merchandise available for sale			$1,278,000
Less merchandise inventory, June 1, 2013			91,300
Cost of merchandise sold			$1,186,700

Appendix
EX 5-37 Rules of debit and credit for periodic inventory accounts

Complete the following table by indicating for (a) through (g) whether the proper answer is debit or credit.

Account	Increase	Decrease	Normal Balance
Purchases	debit	(a)	(b)
Purchases Discounts	credit	(c)	credit
Purchases Returns and Allowances	(d)	(e)	(f)
Freight In	debit	(g)	debit

Appendix
EX 5-38 Journal entries using the periodic inventory system

The following selected transactions were completed by Air Systems Company during January of the current year. Air Systems Company uses the periodic inventory system.

Jan. 2. Purchased $18,200 of merchandise on account, FOB shipping point, terms 2/15, n/30.
5. Paid freight of $190 on the January 2 purchase.
6. Returned $2,750 of the merchandise purchased on January 2.
13. Sold merchandise on account, $37,300, FOB destination, 1/10, n/30. The cost of merchandise sold was $22,400.
15. Paid freight of $215 for the merchandise sold on January 13.
17. Paid for the purchase of January 2 less the return and discount.
23. Received payment on account for the sale of January 13 less the discount.

Journalize the entries to record the transactions of Air Systems Company.

Appendix
Ex 5-39 Journal entries using perpetual inventory system

Using the data shown in Exercise 5-38, journalize the entries for the transactions, assuming that Air Systems Company uses the perpetual inventory system.

Appendix
Ex 5-40 Closing entries using periodic inventory system

United Rug Company is a small rug retailer owned and operated by Pat Kirwan. After the accounts have been adjusted on December 31, the following selected account balances were taken from the ledger:

Advertising Expense	$ 36,000
Depreciation Expense	13,000
Dividends	65,000
Freight In	17,000
Merchandise Inventory, December 1	375,000
Merchandise Inventory, December 31	460,000
Miscellaneous Expense	9,000
Purchases	1,760,000
Purchases Discounts	35,000
Purchases Returns and Allowances	45,000
Salaries Expense	375,000
Sales	2,300,000
Sales Discounts	30,000
Sales Returns and Allowances	50,000

Journalize the closing entries on December 31.

Problems Series A

PR 5-1A Purchase-related transactions **OBJ. 2**

GENERAL LEDGER

The following selected transactions were completed by Capers Company during October of the current year:

Oct. 1. Purchased merchandise from UK Imports Co., $14,448, terms FOB destination, n/30.

3. Purchased merchandise from Hoagie Co., $9,950, terms FOB shipping point, 2/10, n/eom. Prepaid freight of $220 was added to the invoice.

4. Purchased merchandise from Taco Co., $13,650, terms FOB destination, 2/10, n/30.

6. Issued debit memo to Taco Co. for $4,550 of merchandise returned from purchase on October 4.

13. Paid Hoagie Co. for invoice of October 3, less discount.

14. Paid Taco Co. for invoice of October 4, less debit memo of October 6 and discount.

19. Purchased merchandise from Veggie Co., $27,300, terms FOB shipping point, n/eom.

19. Paid freight of $400 on October 19 purchase from Veggie Co.

20. Purchased merchandise from Caesar Salad Co., $22,000, terms FOB destination, 1/10, n/30.

30. Paid Caesar Salad Co. for invoice of October 20, less discount.

31. Paid UK Imports Co. for invoice of October 1.

31. Paid Veggie Co. for invoice of October 19.

Instructions

Journalize the entries to record the transactions of Capers Company for October.

PR 5-2A Sales-related transactions

OBJ. 2

SPREADSHEET

GENERAL LEDGER

The following selected transactions were completed by Amsterdam Supply Co., which sells office supplies primarily to wholesalers and occasionally to retail customers:

Mar. 2. Sold merchandise on account to Equinox Co., $18,900, terms FOB destination, 1/10, n/30. The cost of the merchandise sold was $13,300.

3. Sold merchandise for $11,350 plus 6% sales tax to retail cash customers. The cost of merchandise sold was $7,000.

4. Sold merchandise on account to Empire Co., $55,400, terms FOB shipping point, n/eom. The cost of merchandise sold was $33,200.

5. Sold merchandise for $30,000 plus 6% sales tax to retail customers who used MasterCard. The cost of merchandise sold was $19,400.

12. Received check for amount due from Equinox Co. for sale on March 2.

14. Sold merchandise to customers who used American Express cards, $13,700. The cost of merchandise sold was $8,350.

16. Sold merchandise on account to Targhee Co., $27,500, terms FOB shipping point, 1/10, n/30. The cost of merchandise sold was $16,000.

18. Issued credit memo for $4,800 to Targhee Co. for merchandise returned from sale on March 16. The cost of the merchandise returned was $2,900.

19. Sold merchandise on account to Vista Co., $8,250, terms FOB shipping point, 2/10, n/30. Added $75 to the invoice for prepaid freight. The cost of merchandise sold was $5,000.

26. Received check for amount due from Targhee Co. for sale on March 16 less credit memo of March 18 and discount.

28. Received check for amount due from Vista Co. for sale of March 19.

31. Received check for amount due from Empire Co. for sale of March 4.

31. Paid Fleetwood Delivery Service $5,600 for merchandise delivered during March to customers under shipping terms of FOB destination.

Apr. 3. Paid City Bank $940 for service fees for handling MasterCard and American Express sales during March.

15. Paid $6,544 to state sales tax division for taxes owed on sales.

Instructions

Journalize the entries to record the transactions of Amsterdam Supply Co.

PR 5-3A Sales-related and purchase-related transactions **OBJ. 2**

GENERAL LEDGER

The following were selected from among the transactions completed by Babcock Company during November of the current year:

Nov. 3. Purchased merchandise on account from Moonlight Co., list price $85,000, trade discount 25%, terms FOB destination, 2/10, n/30.

4. Sold merchandise for cash, $37,680. The cost of the merchandise sold was $22,600.

5. Purchased merchandise on account from Papoose Creek Co., $47,500, terms FOB shipping point, 2/10, n/30, with prepaid freight of $810 added to the invoice.

6. Returned $13,500 ($18,000 list price less trade discount of 25%) of merchandise purchased on November 3 from Moonlight Co.

11. Sold merchandise on account to Quinn Co., list price $24,000, trade discount 35%, terms 1/10, n/30. The cost of the merchandise sold was $9,400.

13. Paid Moonlight Co. on account for purchase of November 3, less return of November 6 and discount.

14. Sold merchandise on VISA, $236,000. The cost of the merchandise sold was $140,000.

15. Paid Papoose Creek Co. on account for purchase of November 5, less discount.

21. Received cash on account from sale of November 11 to Quinn Co., less discount.

24. Sold merchandise on account to Rabel Co., $56,900, terms 1/10, n/30. The cost of the merchandise sold was $34,000.

28. Paid VISA service fee of $3,540.

30. Received merchandise returned by Rabel Co. from sale on November 24, $8,400. The cost of the returned merchandise was $5,000.

Instructions

Journalize the transactions.

PR 5-4A Sales-related and purchase-related transactions for seller and buyer **OBJ. 2**

The following selected transactions were completed during August between Summit Company and Beartooth Co.:

Aug. 1. Summit Company sold merchandise on account to Beartooth Co., $48,000, terms FOB destination, 2/15, n/eom. The cost of the merchandise sold was $28,800.

2. Summit Company paid freight of $1,150 for delivery of merchandise sold to Beartooth Co. on August 1.

5. Summit Company sold merchandise on account to Beartooth Co., $66,000, terms FOB shipping point, n/eom. The cost of the merchandise sold was $40,000.

6. Beartooth Co. returned $10,500 of merchandise purchased on account on August 1 from Summit Company. The cost of the merchandise returned was $6,300.

9. Beartooth Co. paid freight of $2,300 on August 5 purchase from Summit Company.

15. Summit Company sold merchandise on account to Beartooth Co., $58,700, terms FOB shipping point, 1/10, n/30. Summit Company paid freight of $1,675, which was added to the invoice. The cost of the merchandise sold was $35,000.

16. Beartooth Co. paid Summit Company for purchase of August 1, less discount and less return of August 6.

25. Beartooth Co. paid Summit Company on account for purchase of August 15, less discount.

31. Beartooth Co. paid Summit Company on account for purchase of August 5.

Instructions

Journalize the August transactions for (1) Summit Company and (2) Beartooth Co.

✔ 1. Net income: $310,000

SPREADSHEET

GENERAL LEDGER

PR 5-5A Multiple-step income statement and report form of balance sheet OBJ. 3

The following selected accounts and their current balances appear in the ledger of Gloucester Co. for the fiscal year ended August 31, 2014:

Cash	$ 125,000	Sales	$4,576,000
Accounts Receivable	335,000	Sales Returns and Allowances	31,000
Merchandise Inventory	380,000	Sales Discounts	28,000
Office Supplies	12,000	Cost of Merchandise Sold	2,650,000
Prepaid Insurance	9,000	Sales Salaries Expense	745,000
Office Equipment	275,000	Advertising Expense	205,000
Accumulated Depreciation— Office Equipment	187,000	Depreciation Expense— Store Equipment	40,000
Store Equipment	859,000	Miscellaneous Selling Expense	18,000
Accumulated Depreciation— Store Equipment	293,000	Office Salaries Expense	410,000
		Rent Expense	60,000
Accounts Payable	193,000	Depreciation Expense— Office Equipment	30,000
Salaries Payable	12,000	Insurance Expense	18,000
Note Payable (final payment due 2037)	400,000	Office Supplies Expense	11,000
Capital Stock	125,000	Miscellaneous Administrative Exp.	8,000
Retained Earnings	550,000	Interest Expense	12,000
Dividends	75,000		

Instructions

1. Prepare a multiple-step income statement.
2. Prepare a retained earnings statement.
3. Prepare a report form of balance sheet, assuming that the current portion of the note payable is $16,000.
4. Briefly explain (a) how multiple-step and single-step income statements differ and (b) how report-form and account-form balance sheets differ.

✔ 3. Total assets: $1,515,000

SPREADSHEET

PR 5-6A Single-step income statement and account form of balance sheet OBJ. 3

Selected accounts and related amounts for Gloucester Co. for the fiscal year ended August 31, 2014, are presented in Problem 5-5A.

Instructions

1. Prepare a single-step income statement in the format shown in Exhibit 9.
2. Prepare a retained earnings statement.
3. Prepare an account form of balance sheet, assuming that the current portion of the note payable is $16,000.
4. Prepare closing entries as of August 31, 2014.

Appendix
PR 5-7A Purchase-related transactions using periodic inventory system

Selected transactions for Capers Company during October of the current year are listed in Problem 5-1A.

Instructions

Journalize the entries to record the transactions of Capers Company for October using the periodic inventory system.

Appendix
PR 5-8A Sales-related and purchase-related transactions using periodic inventory system

Selected transactions for Babcock Company during November of the current year are listed in Problem 5-3A.

Instructions

Journalize the entries to record the transactions of Babcock Company for November using the periodic inventory system.

Appendix

PR 5-9A Sales-related and purchase-related transactions for buyer and seller using periodic inventory system

Selected transactions during August between Summit Company and Beartooth Co. are listed in Problem 5-4A.

Instructions

Journalize the entries to record the transactions for (1) Summit Company and (2) Beartooth Co., assuming that both companies use the periodic inventory system.

Appendix

PR 5-10A Periodic inventory accounts, multiple-step income statement, closing entries

✔ 2. Net income, $180,000

SPREADSHEET

On December 31, 2014, the balances of the accounts appearing in the ledger of Wyman Company are as follows:

Cash	$ 13,500	Sales Returns and Allowances	$ 46,000
Accounts Receivable	72,000	Sales Discounts	29,000
Merchandise Inventory, January 1, 2014	257,000	Purchases	2,650,000
Office Supplies	3,000	Purchases Returns and Allowances	93,000
Prepaid Insurance	4,500	Purchases Discounts	37,000
Land	150,000	Freight In	48,000
Store Equipment	270,000	Sales Salaries Expense	300,000
Accumulated Depreciation—Store Equipment	55,900	Advertising Expense	45,000
Office Equipment	78,500	Delivery Expense	9,000
Accumulated Depreciation—Office Equipment	16,000	Depreciation Expense—Store Equipment	6,000
Accounts Payable	27,800	Miscellaneous Selling Expense	12,000
Salaries Payable	3,000	Office Salaries Expense	175,000
Unearned Rent	8,300	Rent Expense	28,000
Notes Payable	50,000	Insurance Expense	3,000
Capital Stock	150,000	Office Supplies Expense	2,000
Retained Earnings	430,500	Depreciation Expense—Office Equipment	1,500
Dividends	25,000	Miscellaneous Administrative Expense	3,500
Sales	3,355,000	Rent Revenue	7,000
		Interest Expense	2,000

Instructions

1. Does Wyman Company use a periodic or perpetual inventory system? Explain.
2. Prepare a multiple-step income statement for Wyman Company for the year ended December 31, 2014. The merchandise inventory as of December 31, 2014, was $305,000.
3. Prepare the closing entries for Wyman Company as of December 31, 2014.
4. What would be the net income if the perpetual inventory system had been used?

Problems Series B

PR 5-1B Purchase-related transactions

OBJ. 2

GENERAL LEDGER

The following selected transactions were completed by Niles Co. during March of the current year:

Mar. 1. Purchased merchandise from Haas Co., $43,250, terms FOB shipping point, 2/10, n/eom. Prepaid freight of $650 was added to the invoice.
5. Purchased merchandise from Whitman Co., $19,175, terms FOB destination, n/30.
10. Paid Haas Co. for invoice of March 1, less discount.
13. Purchased merchandise from Jost Co., $15,550, terms FOB destination, 2/10, n/30.
14. Issued debit memo to Jost Co. for $3,750 of merchandise returned from purchase on March 13.
18. Purchased merchandise from Fairhurst Company, $13,560, terms FOB shipping point, n/eom.
18. Paid freight of $140 on March 18 purchase from Fairhurst Company.
19. Purchased merchandise from Bickle Co., $6,500, terms FOB destination, 2/10, n/30.
23. Paid Jost Co. for invoice of March 13, less debit memo of March 14 and discount.
29. Paid Bickle Co. for invoice of March 19, less discount.
31. Paid Fairhurst Company for invoice of March 18.
31. Paid Whitman Co. for invoice of March 5.

Instructions

Journalize the entries to record the transactions of Niles Co. for March.

PR 5-2B Sales-related transactions

OBJ. 2

SPREADSHEET

GENERAL LEDGER

The following selected transactions were completed by Green Lawn Supplies Co., which sells irrigation supplies primarily to wholesalers and occasionally to retail customers:

July 1. Sold merchandise on account to Landscapes Co., $33,450, terms FOB shipping point, n/eom. The cost of merchandise sold was $20,000.
2. Sold merchandise for $86,000 plus 8% sales tax to retail cash customers. The cost of merchandise sold was $51,600.
5. Sold merchandise on account to Peacock Company, $17,500, terms FOB destination, 1/10, n/30. The cost of merchandise sold was $10,000.
8. Sold merchandise for $112,000 plus 8% sales tax to retail customers who used VISA cards. The cost of merchandise sold was $67,200.
13. Sold merchandise to customers who used MasterCard cards, $96,000. The cost of merchandise sold was $57,600.
14. Sold merchandise on account to Loeb Co., $16,000, terms FOB shipping point, 1/10, n/30. The cost of merchandise sold was $9,000.
15. Received check for amount due from Peacock Company for sale on July 5.
16. Issued credit memo for $3,000 to Loeb Co. for merchandise returned from sale on July 14. The cost of the merchandise returned was $1,800.
18. Sold merchandise on account to Jennings Company, $11,350, terms FOB shipping point, 2/10, n/30. Paid $475 for freight and added it to the invoice. The cost of merchandise sold was $6,800.
24. Received check for amount due from Loeb Co. for sale on July 14 less credit memo of July 16 and discount.
28. Received check for amount due from Jennings Company for sale of July 18.
31. Paid Black Lab Delivery Service $8,550 for merchandise delivered during July to customers under shipping terms of FOB destination.
31. Received check for amount due from Landscapes Co. for sale of July 1.

Aug. 3. Paid Hays Federal Bank $3,770 for service fees for handling MasterCard and VISA sales during July.
10. Paid $41,260 to state sales tax division for taxes owed on sales.

Instructions

Journalize the entries to record the transactions of Green Lawn Supplies Co.

PR 5-3B Sales-related and purchase-related transactions **OBJ. 2**

GENERAL LEDGER

The following were selected from among the transactions completed by Essex Company during July of the current year:

July 3. Purchased merchandise on account from Hamling Co., list price $72,000, trade discount 15%, terms FOB shipping point, 2/10, n/30, with prepaid freight of $1,450 added to the invoice.

5. Purchased merchandise on account from Kester Co., $33,450, terms FOB destination, 2/10, n/30.

6. Sold merchandise on account to Parsley Co., list price $45,000, trade discount 33%, terms 2/10, n/30. The cost of the merchandise sold was $25,000.

7. Returned $6,850 of merchandise purchased on July 5 from Kester Co.

13. Paid Hamling Co. on account for purchase of July 3, less discount.

15. Paid Kester Co. on account for purchase of July 5, less return of July 7 and discount.

16. Received cash on account from sale of July 6 to Parsley Co., less discount.

19. Sold merchandise on MasterCard, $108,000. The cost of the merchandise sold was $64,800.

22. Sold merchandise on account to Tabor Co., $16,650, terms 2/10, n/30. The cost of the merchandise sold was $10,000.

23. Sold merchandise for cash, $91,200. The cost of the merchandise sold was $55,000.

28. Received merchandise returned by Tabor Co. from sale on July 22, $3,600. The cost of the returned merchandise was $2,000.

31. Paid MasterCard service fee of $1,650.

Instructions

Journalize the transactions.

PR 5-4B Sales-related and purchase-related transactions for seller and buyer **OBJ. 2**

The following selected transactions were completed during April between Swan Company and Bird Company:

Apr. 2. Swan Company sold merchandise on account to Bird Company, $32,000, terms FOB shipping point, 2/10, n/30. Swan Company paid freight of $330, which was added to the invoice. The cost of the merchandise sold was $19,200.

8. Swan Company sold merchandise on account to Bird Company, $49,500, terms FOB destination, 1/15, n/eom. The cost of the merchandise sold was $29,700.

8. Swan Company paid freight of $710 for delivery of merchandise sold to Bird Company on April 8.

12. Bird Company returned $7,500 of merchandise purchased on account on April 8 from Swan Company. The cost of the merchandise returned was $4,800.

12. Bird Company paid Swan Company for purchase of April 2, less discount.

23. Bird Company paid Swan Company for purchase of April 8, less discount and less return of April 12.

24. Swan Company sold merchandise on account to Bird Company, $67,350, terms FOB shipping point, n/eom. The cost of the merchandise sold was $40,400.

26. Bird Company paid freight of $875 on April 24 purchase from Swan Company.

30. Bird Company paid Swan Company on account for purchase of April 24.

Instructions

Journalize the April transactions for (1) Swan Company and (2) Bird Company.

PR 5-5B Multiple-step income statement and report form of balance sheet

OBJ. 3

✔ 1. Net income: $1,340,000

SPREADSHEET

GENERAL LEDGER

The following selected accounts and their current balances appear in the ledger of Kanpur Co. for the fiscal year ended June 30, 2014:

Cash	$ 92,000	Sales	$9,175,000
Accounts Receivable	450,000	Sales Returns and Allowances	160,000
Merchandise Inventory	375,000	Sales Discounts	90,000
Office Supplies	10,000	Cost of Merchandise Sold	5,620,000
Prepaid Insurance	12,000	Sales Salaries Expense	850,000
Office Equipment	220,000	Advertising Expense	420,000
Accumulated Depreciation— Office Equipment	58,000	Depreciation Expense— Store Equipment	33,000
Store Equipment	650,000	Miscellaneous Selling Expense	18,000
Accumulated Depreciation— Store Equipment	87,500	Office Salaries Expense	540,000
		Rent Expense	48,000
Accounts Payable	48,500	Insurance Expense	24,000
Salaries Payable	4,000	Depreciation Expense— Office Equipment	10,000
Note Payable (final payment due 2032)	140,000	Office Supplies Expense	4,000
Capital Stock	50,000	Miscellaneous Administrative Exp.	6,000
Retained Earnings	381,000	Interest Expense	12,000
Dividends	300,000		

Instructions

1. Prepare a multiple-step income statement.
2. Prepare a retained earnings statement.
3. Prepare a report form of balance sheet, assuming that the current portion of the note payable is $7,000.
4. Briefly explain (a) how multiple-step and single-step income statements differ and (b) how report-form and account-form balance sheets differ.

PR 5-6B Single-step income statement and account form of balance sheet

OBJ. 3

✔ 3. Total assets: $1,663,500

SPREADSHEET

Selected accounts and related amounts for Kanpur Co. for the fiscal year ended June 30, 2014, are presented in Problem 5-5B.

Instructions

1. Prepare a single-step income statement in the format shown in Exhibit 9.
2. Prepare a retained earnings statement.
3. Prepare an account form of balance sheet, assuming that the current portion of the note payable is $7,000.
4. Prepare closing entries as of June 30, 2014.

Appendix

PR 5-7B Purchase-related transactions using periodic inventory system

Selected transactions for Niles Co. during March of the current year are listed in Problem 5-1B.

Instructions

Journalize the entries to record the transactions of Niles Co. for March using the periodic inventory system.

Appendix

PR 5-8B Sales-related and purchase-related transactions using periodic inventory system

Selected transactions for Essex Company during July of the current year are listed in Problem 5-3B.

Instructions

Journalize the entries to record the transactions of Essex Company for July using the periodic inventory system.

Appendix

PR 5-9B Sales-related and purchase-related transactions for buyer and seller using periodic inventory system

Selected transactions during April between Swan Company and Bird Company are listed in Problem 5-4B.

Instructions

Journalize the entries to record the transactions for (1) Swan Company and (2) Bird Company assuming that both companies use the periodic inventory system.

Appendix

PR 5-10B Periodic inventory accounts, multiple-step income statement, closing entries

✔ 2. Net income, $1,200,000

SPREADSHEET

On June 30, 2014, the balances of the accounts appearing in the ledger of Simkins Company are as follows:

Cash	$ 125,000	Sales Discounts	$ 66,000
Accounts Receivable	340,000	Purchases	4,100,000
Merchandise Inventory, July 1, 2013	415,000	Purchases Returns and Allowances	32,000
Office Supplies	9,000	Purchases Discounts	13,000
Prepaid Insurance	18,000	Freight In	45,000
Land	300,000	Sales Salaries Expense	580,000
Store Equipment	550,000	Advertising Expense	315,000
Accumulated Depreciation—		Delivery Expense	18,000
Store Equipment	190,000	Depreciation Expense—	
Office Equipment	250,000	Store Equipment	12,000
Accumulated Depreciation—		Miscellaneous Selling Expense	28,000
Office Equipment	110,000	Office Salaries Expense	375,000
Accounts Payable	85,000	Rent Expense	43,000
Salaries Payable	9,000	Insurance Expense	17,000
Unearned Rent	6,000	Office Supplies Expense	5,000
Notes Payable	50,000	Depreciation Expense—	
Capital Stock	300,000	Office Equipment	4,000
Retained Earnings	525,000	Miscellaneous Administrative Expense	16,000
Dividends	275,000	Rent Revenue	32,500
Sales	6,748,000	Interest Expense	2,500
Sales Returns and Allowances	92,000		

Instructions

1. Does Simkins Company use a periodic or perpetual inventory system? Explain.
2. Prepare a multiple-step income statement for Simkins Company for the year ended June 30, 2014. The merchandise inventory as of June 30, 2014, was $508,000.
3. Prepare the closing entries for Simkins Company as of June 30, 2014.
4. What would be the net income if the perpetual inventory system had been used?

Comprehensive Problem 2

✔ 8. Net income: $762,500

GENERAL LEDGER

Palisade Creek Co. is a merchandising business. The account balances for Palisade Creek Co. as of May 1, 2014 (unless otherwise indicated), are as follows:

110	Cash	$ 83,600
112	Accounts Receivable	233,900
115	Merchandise Inventory	602,400
116	Prepaid Insurance	16,800
117	Store Supplies	11,400
123	Store Equipment	569,500
124	Accumulated Depreciation—Store Equipment	56,700
210	Accounts Payable	96,600
211	Salaries Payable	—
310	Capital Stock	100,000
311	Retained Earnings	585,300
312	Dividends	135,000
313	Income Summary	—
410	Sales	5,221,100
411	Sales Returns and Allowances	92,700
412	Sales Discounts	59,400
510	Cost of Merchandise Sold	2,823,000
520	Sales Salaries Expense	664,800
521	Advertising Expense	281,000
522	Depreciation Expense	—
523	Store Supplies Expense	—
529	Miscellaneous Selling Expense	12,600
530	Office Salaries Expense	382,100
531	Rent Expense	83,700
532	Insurance Expense	—
539	Miscellaneous Administrative Expense	7,800

During May, the last month of the fiscal year, the following transactions were completed:

May 1. Paid rent for May, $5,000.

3. Purchased merchandise on account from Martin Co., terms 2/10, n/30, FOB shipping point, $36,000.

4. Paid freight on purchase of May 3, $600.

6. Sold merchandise on account to Korman Co., terms 2/10, n/30, FOB shipping point, $68,500. The cost of the merchandise sold was $41,000.

7. Received $22,300 cash from Halstad Co. on account, no discount.

10. Sold merchandise for cash, $54,000. The cost of the merchandise sold was $32,000.

13. Paid for merchandise purchased on May 3, less discount.

14. Received merchandise returned on sale of May 6, $13,500. The cost of the merchandise returned was $8,000.

15. Paid advertising expense for last half of May, $11,000.

16. Received cash from sale of May 6, less return of May 14 and discount.

19. Purchased merchandise for cash, $18,700.

19. Paid $33,450 to Buttons Co. on account, no discount.

Record the following transactions on Page 21 of the journal.

20. Sold merchandise on account to Crescent Co., terms 1/10, n/30, FOB shipping point, $110,000. The cost of the merchandise sold was $70,000.

21. For the convenience of Crescent Co., paid freight on sale of May 20, $2,300.

21. Received $42,900 cash from Gee Co. on account, no discount.

21. Purchased merchandise on account from Osterman Co., terms 1/10, n/30, FOB destination, $88,000.

24. Returned $5,000 of damaged merchandise purchased on May 21, receiving credit from the seller.

May 26. Refunded cash on sales made for cash, $7,500. The cost of the merchandise returned was $4,800.

28. Paid sales salaries of $56,000 and office salaries of $29,000.

29. Purchased store supplies for cash, $2,400.

30. Sold merchandise on account to Turner Co., terms 2/10, n/30, FOB shipping point, $78,750. The cost of the merchandise sold was $47,000.

30. Received cash from sale of May 20, less discount, plus freight paid on May 21.

31. Paid for purchase of May 21, less return of May 24 and discount.

Instructions

1. Enter the balances of each of the accounts in the appropriate balance column of a four-column account. Write *Balance* in the item section, and place a check mark (✓) in the Posting Reference column. Journalize the transactions for July, starting on Page 20 of the journal.
2. Post the journal to the general ledger, extending the month-end balances to the appropriate balance columns after all posting is completed. In this problem, you are not required to update or post to the accounts receivable and accounts payable subsidiary ledgers.
3. Prepare an unadjusted trial balance.
4. At the end of May, the following adjustment data were assembled. Analyze and use these data to complete (5) and (6).

a.	Merchandise inventory on May 31		$550,000
b.	Insurance expired during the year		12,000
c.	Store supplies on hand on May 31		4,000
d.	Depreciation for the current year		14,000
e.	Accrued salaries on May 31:		
	Sales salaries	$7,000	
	Office salaries	6,600	13,600

5. (**Optional.**) Enter the unadjusted trial balance on a 10-column end-of-period spreadsheet (work sheet), and complete the spreadsheet.
6. Journalize and post the adjusting entries. Record the adjusting entries on Page 22 of the journal.
7. Prepare an adjusted trial balance.
8. Prepare an income statement, a retained earnings statement, and a balance sheet.
9. Prepare and post the closing entries. Record the closing entries on Page 23 of the journal. Indicate closed accounts by inserting a line in both the Balance columns opposite the closing entry. Insert the new balance in the retained earnings account.
10. Prepare a post-closing trial balance.

Cases & Projects

CP 5-1 Ethics and professional conduct in business

On April 18, 2014, Bontanica Company, a garden retailer, purchased $9,800 of seed, terms 2/10, n/30, from Whitetail Seed Co. Even though the discount period had expired, Shelby Davey subtracted the discount of $196 when he processed the documents for payment on May 1, 2014.

Discuss whether Shelby Davey behaved in a professional manner by subtracting the discount, even though the discount period had expired.

Learning Objectives

After studying this chapter, you should be able to: *Example Exercises*

OBJ 1 Describe the importance of control over inventory.
- Control of Inventory
  - Safeguarding Inventory
  - Reporting Inventory

OBJ 2 Describe three inventory cost flow assumptions and how they impact the income statement and balance sheet.
- Inventory Cost Flow Assumptions — EE 6-1

OBJ 3 Determine the cost of inventory under the perpetual inventory system, using the FIFO, LIFO, and weighted average cost methods.
- Inventory Costing Methods Under a Perpetual Inventory System
  - First-In, First-Out Method — EE 6-2
  - Last-In, First-Out Method — EE 6-3
  - Weighted Average Cost Method — EE 6-4
  - Computerized Perpetual Inventory Systems

OBJ 4 Determine the cost of inventory under the periodic inventory system, using the FIFO, LIFO, and weighted average cost methods.
- Inventory Costing Methods Under a Periodic Inventory System
  - First-In, First-Out Method — EE 6-5
  - Last-In, First-Out Method — EE 6-5
  - Weighted Average Cost Method — EE 6-5

OBJ 5 Compare and contrast the use of the three inventory costing methods.
- Comparing Inventory Costing Methods

OBJ 6 Describe and illustrate the reporting of merchandise inventory in the financial statements.
- Reporting Merchandise Inventory in the Financial Statements
  - Valuation at Lower of Cost or Market — EE 6-6
  - Valuation at Net Realizable Value
  - Merchandise Inventory on the Balance Sheet
  - Effect of Inventory Errors on the Financial Statements — EE 6-7

OBJ 7 Describe and illustrate the inventory turnover and the number of days' sales in inventory in analyzing the efficiency and effectiveness of inventory management.
- Financial Analysis and Interpretation: Inventory Turnover and Number of Days' Sales in Inventory — EE 6-8

At a Glance 6 Page 292

OBJ 1 Describe the importance of control over inventory.

Control of Inventory

Two primary objectives of control over inventory are as follows:[1]

1. Safeguarding the inventory from damage or theft.
2. Reporting inventory in the financial statements.

Safeguarding Inventory

Controls for safeguarding inventory begin as soon as the inventory is ordered. The following documents are often used for inventory control:

Purchase order
Receiving report
Vendor's invoice

The **purchase order** authorizes the purchase of the inventory from an approved vendor. As soon as the inventory is received, a receiving report is completed.

1 Additional controls used by businesses are described and illustrated in Chapter 7, "Sarbanes-Oxley, Internal Control, and Cash."

The **receiving report** establishes an initial record of the receipt of the inventory. To make sure the inventory received is what was ordered, the receiving report is compared with the purchase order. The price, quantity, and description of the item on the purchase order and receiving report are then compared to the vendor's invoice. If the receiving report, purchase order, and vendor's invoice agree, the inventory is recorded in the accounting records. If any differences exist, they should be investigated and reconciled.

Recording inventory using a perpetual inventory system is also an effective means of control. The amount of inventory is always available in the **subsidiary inventory ledger**. This helps keep inventory quantities at proper levels. For example, comparing inventory quantities with maximum and minimum levels allows for the timely reordering of inventory and prevents ordering excess inventory.

Finally, controls for safeguarding inventory should include security measures to prevent damage and customer or employee theft. Some examples of security measures include the following:

1. Storing inventory in areas that are restricted to only authorized employees.
2. Locking high-priced inventory in cabinets.
3. Using two-way mirrors, cameras, security tags, and guards.

Best Buy uses scanners to screen customers as they leave the store for merchandise that has not been purchased. In addition, Best Buy stations greeters at the store's entrance to keep customers from bringing in bags that can be used to shoplift merchandise.

Reporting Inventory

A **physical inventory** or count of inventory should be taken near year-end to make sure that the quantity of inventory reported in the financial statements is accurate. After the quantity of inventory on hand is determined, the cost of the inventory is assigned for reporting in the financial statements. Most companies assign costs to inventory using one of three inventory cost flow assumptions. If a physical count is not possible or inventory records are not available, the inventory cost may be estimated as described in the appendix at the end of this chapter.

Inventory Cost Flow Assumptions

OBJ 2 Describe three inventory cost flow assumptions and how they impact the income statement and balance sheet.

An accounting issue arises when identical units of merchandise are acquired at different unit costs during a period. In such cases, when an item is sold, it is necessary to determine its cost using a cost flow assumption and related inventory costing method. Three common cost flow assumptions and related inventory costing methods are shown below.

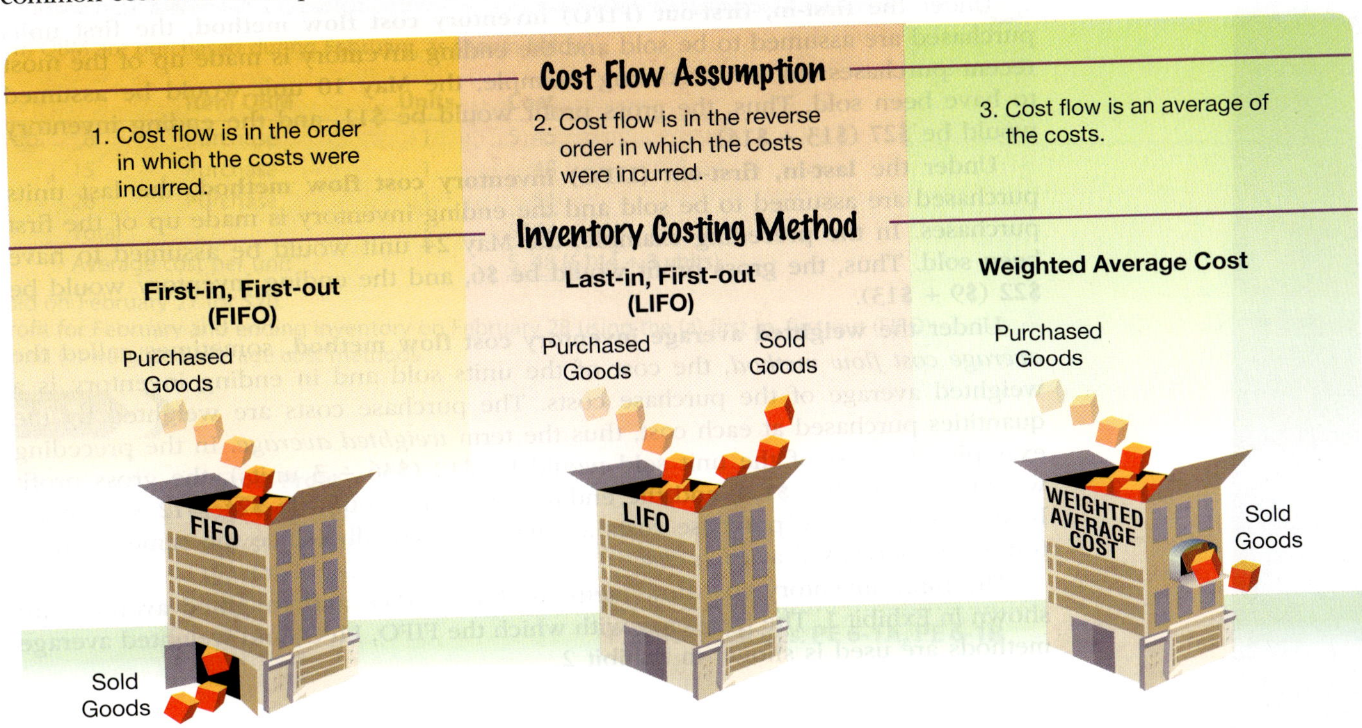

5. The January 28 sale and January 30 purchase are recorded in a similar manner.
6. The ending balance on January 31 is $18,280 (800 units × $22.85 per unit).

Example Exercise 6-4 Perpetual Inventory Using Weighted Average

OBJ 3

Beginning inventory, purchases, and sales for ER27 are as follows:

Nov.	1	Inventory	40 units at $5
	5	Sale	30 units
	11	Purchase	70 units at $7
	21	Sale	36 units

Assuming a perpetual inventory system using the weighted average method, determine (a) the weighted average unit cost after the November 11 purchase, (b) the cost of the merchandise sold on November 21, and (c) the inventory on November 30.

Follow My Example 6-4

a. Weighted average unit cost: $6.75
Inventory total cost after purchase on November 21:

	Cost
10 units at $5	$ 50
70 units at $7	490
80 units	$540

Weighted average unit cost = $6.75 ($540 ÷ 80 units)

b. Cost of merchandise sold (November 21):
$243 (36 units × $6.75)

c. Inventory, November 30:
$297 (44 units at $6.75)

Practice Exercises: **PE 6-4A, PE 6-4B**

The speci
method is
by autom
jewelry st
galleries.

Computerized Perpetual Inventory Systems

A perpetual inventory system may be used in a manual accounting system. However, if there are many inventory transactions, such a system is costly and time consuming. In almost all cases, perpetual inventory systems are computerized.

Computerized perpetual inventory systems are useful to managers in controlling and managing inventory. For example, fast-selling items can be reordered before the stock runs out. Sales patterns can also be analyzed to determine when to mark down merchandise or when to restock seasonal merchandise. Finally, inventory data can be used in evaluating advertising campaigns and sales promotions.

OBJ 4 Determine the cost of inventory under the periodic inventory system, using the FIFO, LIFO, and weighted average cost methods.

Inventory Costing Methods Under a Periodic Inventory System

When the periodic inventory system is used, only revenue is recorded each time a sale is made. No entry is made at the time of the sale to record the cost of the merchandise sold. At the end of the accounting period, a physical inventory is taken to determine the cost of the inventory and the cost of the merchandise sold.[2]

Like the perpetual inventory system, a cost flow assumption must be made when identical units are acquired at different unit costs during a period. In such cases, the FIFO, LIFO, or weighted average cost method is used.

First-In, First-Out Method

To illustrate the use of the FIFO method in a periodic inventory system, we use the same data for Item 127B as in the perpetual inventory example. The beginning inventory and purchases of Item 127B in January are as follows:

2 Determining the cost of merchandise sold using the periodic system was illustrated in the appendix to Chapter 5.

Jan. 1	Inventory	1,000 units at	$20.00	$20,000
10	Purchase	500 units at	22.40	11,200
30	Purchase	600 units at	23.30	13,980
Available for sale during month		2,100		$45,180

The physical count on January 31 shows that 800 units are on hand. Using the FIFO method, the cost of the merchandise on hand at the end of the period is made up of the most recent costs. The cost of the 800 units in the ending inventory on January 31 is determined as follows:

Most recent costs, January 30 purchase	600 units at	$23.30	$13,980
Next most recent costs, January 10 purchase	200 units at	$22.40	4,480
Inventory, January 31	800 units		$18,460

Deducting the cost of the January 31 inventory of $18,460 from the cost of merchandise available for sale of $45,180 yields the cost of merchandise sold of $26,720, as shown below.

Beginning inventory, January 1	$20,000
Purchases ($11,200 + $13,980)	25,180
Cost of merchandise available for sale in January	$45,180
Less ending inventory, January 31	18,460
Cost of merchandise sold	$26,720

The $18,460 cost of the ending merchandise inventory on January 31 is made up of the most recent costs. The $26,720 cost of merchandise sold is made up of the beginning inventory and the earliest costs. Exhibit 6 shows the relationship of the cost of merchandise sold for January and the ending inventory on January 31.

EXHIBIT 6

First-In, First-Out Flow of Costs

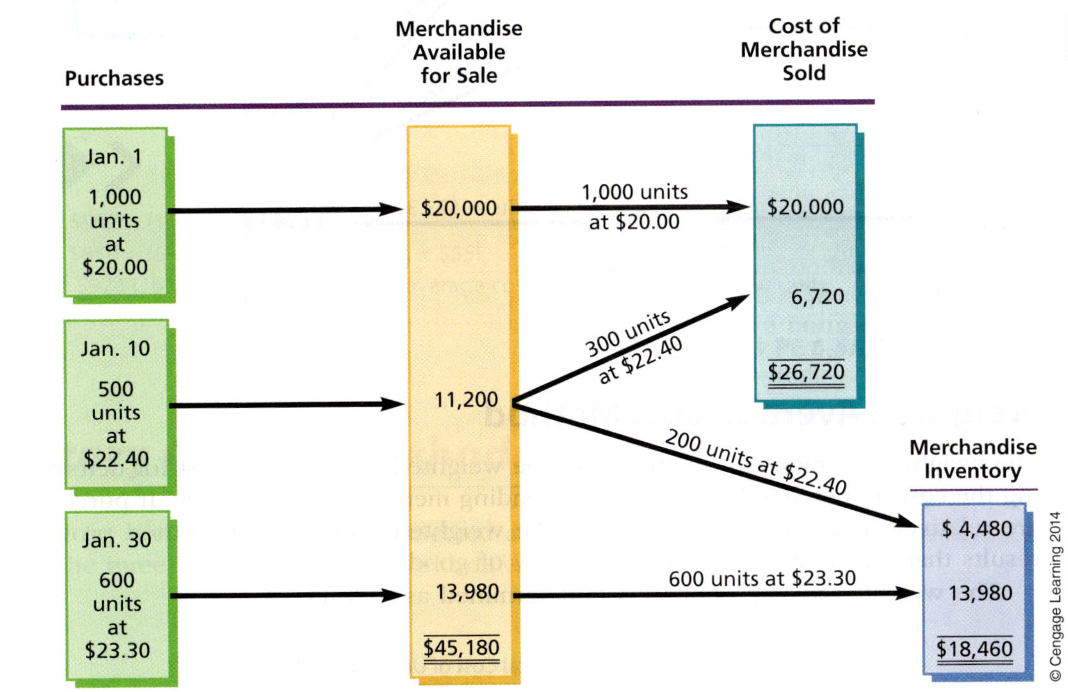

Last-In, First-Out Method

When the LIFO method is used, the cost of merchandise on hand at the end of the period is made up of the earliest costs. Based on the same data as in the FIFO example, the cost of the 800 units in ending inventory on January 31 is $16,000, which consists of 800 units from the beginning inventory at a cost of $20.00 per unit.

IFRS IFRS
See Appendix C for more information

IFRS IFRS

See Appendix C for more information

Using the perpetual inventory system illustration with sales of $39,000 (1,300 units × $30), these differences are illustrated below.[3]

Partial Income Statements

	First-In, First-Out	Weighted Average Cost	Last-In, First-Out
Net sales	$39,000	$39,000	$39,000
Cost of merchandise sold:	26,720	26,900	27,200
Gross profit	$12,280	$12,100	$11,800
Merchandise Inventory, Jan. 31	$18,460	$18,280	$17,980

The preceding differences show the effect of increasing costs (prices). If costs (prices) remain the same, all three methods would yield the same results. However, costs (prices) normally do change. The effects of changing costs (prices) on the FIFO and LIFO methods are summarized in Exhibit 8. The weighted average cost method will always yield results between those of FIFO and LIFO.

EXHIBIT 8

Effects of Changing Costs (Prices): FIFO and LIFO Cost Methods

	Increasing Costs (Prices)		Decreasing Costs (Prices)	
	Highest Amount	**Lowest Amount**	**Highest Amount**	**Lowest Amount**
Cost of merchandise sold	LIFO	FIFO	FIFO	LIFO
Gross profit	FIFO	LIFO	LIFO	FIFO
Net income	FIFO	LIFO	LIFO	FIFO
Ending merchandise inventory	FIFO	LIFO	LIFO	FIFO

FIFO reports higher gross profit and net income than the LIFO method when costs (prices) are increasing, as shown in Exhibit 8. However, in periods of rapidly rising costs, the inventory that is sold must be replaced at increasingly higher costs. In such cases, the larger FIFO gross profit and net income are sometimes called *inventory profits* or *illusory profits.*

During a period of increasing costs, LIFO matches more recent costs against sales on the income statement. Thus, it can be argued that the LIFO method more nearly matches current costs with current revenues. LIFO also offers an income tax savings during periods of increasing costs. This is because LIFO reports the lowest amount of gross profit and, thus, taxable net income.[4] However, under LIFO, the ending inventory on the balance sheet may be quite different from its current replacement cost. In such cases, the financial statements normally include a note that estimates what the inventory would have been if FIFO had been used.

The weighted average cost method is, in a sense, a compromise between FIFO and LIFO. The effect of cost (price) trends is averaged in determining the cost of merchandise sold and the ending inventory.

3 Similar results would also occur when comparing inventory costing methods under a periodic inventory system.
4 A proposal currently exists to not allow the use of LIFO for tax purposes.

Integrity, Objectivity, and Ethics in Business

WHERE'S THE BONUS?

Managers are often given bonuses based on reported earnings numbers. This can create a conflict. LIFO can improve the value of the company through lower taxes. However, in periods of rising costs (prices), LIFO also produces a lower earnings number and, therefore, lower management bonuses. Ethically, managers should select accounting procedures that will maximize the value of the firm, rather than their own compensation. Compensation specialists can help avoid this ethical dilemma by adjusting the bonus plan for the accounting procedure differences.

Reporting Merchandise Inventory in the Financial Statements

OBJ 6 Describe and illustrate the reporting of merchandise inventory in the financial statements.

Cost is the primary basis for valuing and reporting inventories in the financial statements. However, inventory may be valued at other than cost in the following cases:

1. The cost of replacing items in inventory is below the recorded cost.
2. The inventory cannot be sold at normal prices due to imperfections, style changes, or other causes.

Valuation at Lower of Cost or Market

IFRS IFRS See Appendix C for more information

If the cost of replacing inventory is lower than its recorded purchase cost, the **lower-of-cost-or-market (LCM) method** is used to value the inventory. *Market,* as used in *lower of cost or market,* is the cost to replace the inventory. The market value is based on normal quantities that would be purchased from suppliers.

The lower-of-cost-or-market method can be applied in one of three ways. The cost, market price, and any declines could be determined for the following:

1. Each item in the inventory.
2. Each major class or category of inventory.
3. Total inventory as a whole.

The amount of any price decline is included in the cost of merchandise sold. This, in turn, reduces gross profit and net income in the period in which the price declines occur. This matching of price declines to the period in which they occur is the primary advantage of using the lower-of-cost-or-market method.

To illustrate, assume the following data for 400 identical units of Item A in inventory on December 31, 2014:

Unit purchased cost	$10.25
Replacement cost on December 31, 2014	9.50

Since Item A could be replaced at $9.50 a unit, $9.50 is used under the lower-of-cost-or-market method.

Exhibit 9 illustrates applying the lower-of-cost-or-market method to each inventory item (Echo, Foxtrot, Sierra, Tango). As applied on an item-by-item basis, the total lower-of-cost-or-market is $15,070, which is a market decline of $450 ($15,520 – $15,070). This market decline of $450 is included in the cost of merchandise sold.

In Exhibit 9, Items Echo, Foxtrot, Sierra, and Tango could be viewed as a class of inventory items. If the lower-of-cost-or-market method is applied to the class, the inventory would be valued at $15,472, which is a market decline of $48 ($15,520 – $15,472). Likewise, if Items Echo, Foxtrot, Sierra, and Tango make up the total inventory, the lower-of-cost-or-market method as applied to the total inventory would be the same amount, $15,472.

EXHIBIT 9

Determining Inventory at Lower of Cost or Market

	A	B	C	D	E	F	G
1			Unit	Unit		Total	
2		Inventory	Cost	Market			Lower
3	Item	Quantity	Price	Price	Cost	Market	of C or M
4	Echo	400	$10.25	$ 9.50	$ 4,100	$ 3,800	$ 3,800
5	Foxtrot	120	22.50	24.10	2,700	2,892	2,700
6	Sierra	600	8.00	7.75	4,800	4,650	4,650
7	Tango	280	14.00	14.75	3,920	4,130	3,920
8	Total				$15,520	$15,472	$15,070
9							

Example Exercise 6-6 Lower-of-Cost-or-Market Method

OBJ 6

On the basis of the following data, determine the value of the inventory at the lower of cost or market. Apply lower of cost or market to each inventory item as shown in Exhibit 9.

Item	Inventory Quantity	Unit Cost Price	Unit Market Price
C17Y	10	$ 39	$40
B563	7	110	98

Follow My Example 6-6

	A	B	C	D	E	F	G
1			Unit	Unit		Total	
2		Inventory	Cost	Market			Lower
3	Item	Quantity	Price	Price	Cost	Market	of C or M
4	C17Y	10	$ 39	$40	$ 390	$ 400	$ 390
5	B563	7	110	98	770	686	686
6	Total				$1,160	$1,086	$1,076
7							

Practice Exercises: **PE 6-6A, PE 6-6B**

Valuation at Net Realizable Value

Merchandise that is out of date, spoiled, or damaged can often be sold only at a price below its original cost. Such merchandise should be valued at its **net realizable value**. Net realizable value is determined as follows:

Net Realizable Value = Estimated Selling Price – Direct Costs of Disposal

Direct costs of disposal include selling expenses such as special advertising or sales commissions. To illustrate, assume the following data about an item of damaged merchandise:

Original cost	$1,000
Estimated selling price	800
Selling expenses	150

The merchandise should be valued at its net realizable value of $650 as shown below.

Net Realizable Value = $800 – $150 = $650

Business Connection

INVENTORY WRITE-DOWNS

Worthington Industries, Inc., is a diversified metal processing company that manufactures metal products, such as metal framing and pressure cylinders. During a recent year, the company experienced rapidly changing business conditions. Due to the global financial crisis and recession, steel prices underwent a severe and rapid decline. As a result, the company recorded an inventory write-down of $105 million and an overall net loss of $108 million for the year.

Merchandise Inventory on the Balance Sheet

Merchandise inventory is usually reported in the Current Assets section of the balance sheet. In addition to this amount, the following are reported:

1. The method of determining the cost of the inventory (FIFO, LIFO, or weighted average)
2. The method of valuing the inventory (cost or the lower of cost or market)

IFRS IFRS

See Appendix C for more information

The financial statement reporting for the topics covered in Chapters 6–13 are illustrated using excerpts from the financial statements of Mornin' Joe. Mornin' Joe is a fictitious company that offers drip and espresso coffee in a coffeehouse setting. The complete financial statements of Mornin' Joe are illustrated at the end of Chapter 13 (pages 629–639).

The balance sheet presentation for merchandise inventory for Mornin' Joe is as follows:

Mornin' Joe
Balance Sheet
December 31, 2014

Current assets:		
Cash and cash equivalents		$235,000
Trading investments (at cost)	$420,000	
Plus valuation allowance on trading investments	45,000	465,000
Accounts receivable	$305,000	
Less allowance for doubtful accounts	12,300	292,700
Merchandise inventory—at lower of cost (first-in, first-out method) or market		120,000

It is not unusual for a large business to use different costing methods for segments of its inventories. Also, a business may change its inventory costing method. In such cases, the effect of the change and the reason for the change are disclosed in the financial statements.

Effect of Inventory Errors on the Financial Statements

Any errors in merchandise inventory will affect the balance sheet and income statement. Some reasons that inventory errors may occur include the following:

1. Physical inventory on hand was miscounted.
2. Costs were incorrectly assigned to inventory. For example, the FIFO, LIFO, or weighted average cost method was incorrectly applied.
3. Inventory in transit was incorrectly included or excluded from inventory.
4. Consigned inventory was incorrectly included or excluded from inventory.

Inventory errors often arise from merchandise that is in transit at year-end. As discussed in Chapter 5, shipping terms determine when the title to merchandise passes. When goods are purchased or sold *FOB shipping point*, title passes to the buyer when the goods are shipped. When the terms are *FOB destination*, title passes to the buyer when the goods are received.

To illustrate, assume that SysExpress ordered the following merchandise from American Products:

Date ordered:	December 27, 2013
Amount:	$10,000
Terms:	FOB shipping point, 2/10, n/30
Date shipped by seller:	December 30
Date delivered:	January 3, 2014

When SysExpress counts its physical inventory on December 31, 2013, the merchandise is still in transit. In such cases, it would be easy for SysExpress to not include the $10,000 of merchandise in its December 31 physical inventory. However, since the merchandise was purchased *FOB shipping point*, SysExpress owns the merchandise. Thus, it should be included in the December 31 inventory, even though it is not on hand. Likewise, any merchandise *sold* by SysExpress *FOB destination* is still SysExpress's inventory, even if it is in transit to the buyer on December 31.

Inventory errors often arise from **consigned inventory**. Manufacturers sometimes ship merchandise to retailers who act as the manufacturer's selling agent. The manufacturer, called the **consignor**, retains title until the goods are sold. Such merchandise is said to be shipped *on consignment* to the retailer, called the **consignee**. Any unsold merchandise at year-end is a part of the manufacturer's (consignor's) inventory, even though the merchandise is in the hands of the retailer (consignee). At year-end, it would be easy for the retailer (consignee) to incorrectly include the consigned merchandise in its physical inventory. Likewise, the manufacturer (consignor) should include consigned inventory in its physical inventory, even though the inventory is not on hand.

Income Statement Effects Inventory errors will misstate the income statement amounts for cost of merchandise sold, gross profit, and net income. The effects of inventory errors on the current period's income statement are summarized in Exhibit 10.

EXHIBIT 10

Effect of Inventory Errors on Current Period's Income Statement

	Income Statement Effect		
Inventory Error	**Cost of Merchandise Sold**	**Gross Profit**	**Net Income**
Beginning inventory is:			
Understated	*Understated*	*Overstated*	*Overstated*
Overstated	*Overstated*	*Understated*	*Understated*
Ending inventory is:			
Understated	*Overstated*	*Understated*	*Understated*
Overstated	*Understated*	*Overstated*	*Overstated*

To illustrate, the income statements of SysExpress shown in Exhibit 11 are used.[5] On December 31, 2013, assume that SysExpress incorrectly records its physical inventory as $50,000 instead of the correct amount of $60,000. Thus, the December 31, 2013, inventory is understated by $10,000 ($60,000 – $50,000). As a result, the cost of merchandise sold is overstated by $10,000. The gross profit and the net income for the year will also be understated by $10,000.

The December 31, 2013, merchandise inventory becomes the January 1, 2014, inventory. Thus, the beginning inventory for 2014 is understated by $10,000. As a result, the cost of merchandise sold is understated by $10,000 for 2014. The gross profit and net income for 2014 will be overstated by $10,000.

As shown in Exhibit 11, since the ending inventory of one period is the beginning inventory of the next period, the effects of inventory errors carry forward to the next period. Specifically, if uncorrected, the effects of inventory errors reverse themselves

5 The effect of inventory errors will be illustrated using the periodic system. This is because it is easier to see the impact of inventory errors on the income statement using the periodic system. The effect of inventory errors would be the same under the perpetual inventory system.

EXHIBIT 11 **Effects of Inventory Errors on Two Years' Income Statements**

SysExpress
Income Statement
For the Years Ended December 31, 2013 and 2014

	2013				**2014**			
	Correct		**Incorrect**		**Incorrect**		**Correct**	
Net sales		$980,000		$980,000		$1,100,000		$1,100,000
Merchandise inventory, January 1	$ 55,000		$ 55,000		**$ 50,000**		$ 60,000	
Purchases	650,000		650,000		700,000		700,000	
Merchandise available for sale	$705,000		$705,000		**$750,000**		$760,000	
Less merchandise inventory, December 31	60,000		**50,000**		70,000		70,000	
Cost of merchandise sold		645,000		**655,000**		**680,000**		690,000
Gross profit		$335,000		**$325,000**		**$ 420,000**		$ 410,000
Operating expenses		100,000		100,000		120,000		120,000
Net income		$235,000		**$225,000**		**$ 300,000**		$ 290,000

$10,000 Understatement of Net Income

$10,000 Overstatement of Net Income

Net Effect Is Zero for Two Years
The inventory errors reverse (or cancel) so that the combined net income for the two years of $525,000 ($225,000 + $300,000) is correct.

in the next period. In Exhibit 11, the combined net income for the two years of $525,000 is correct, even though the 2013 and 2014 income statements were incorrect.

Balance Sheet Effects Inventory errors misstate the merchandise inventory, current assets, total assets, and stockholders' equity on the balance sheet. The effects of inventory errors on the current period's balance sheet are summarized in Exhibit 12.

EXHIBIT 12 **Effect of Inventory Errors on Current Period's Balance Sheet**

	Balance Sheet Effect			
Ending Inventory Error	**Merchandise Inventory**	**Current Assets**	**Total Assets**	**Stockholders' Equity (Retained Earnings)**
Understated	*Understated*	*Understated*	*Understated*	*Understated*
Overstated	*Overstated*	*Overstated*	*Overstated*	*Overstated*

For the SysExpress illustration shown in Exhibit 11, the December 31, 2013, ending inventory was understated by $10,000. As a result, the merchandise inventory, current assets, and total assets would be understated by $10,000 on the December 31, 2013, balance sheet. Because the ending physical inventory is understated, the cost of merchandise sold for 2013 will be overstated by $10,000. Thus, the gross profit and the net income for 2013 are understated by $10,000. Since the net income is closed to stockholders' equity (Retained Earnings) at the end of the period, the stockholders' equity on the December 31, 2013, balance sheet is also understated by $10,000.

As discussed above, inventory errors reverse themselves within two years. As a result, the balance sheet will be correct as of December 31, 2014. Using the SysExpress illustration from Exhibit 11, these effects are summarized on the next page.

	Amount of Misstatement	
Balance Sheet:	December 31, 2013	December 31, 2014
Merchandise inventory overstated (understated)	$(10,000)	Correct
Current assets overstated (understated)	(10,000)	Correct
Total assets overstated (understated)	(10,000)	Correct
Stockholders' equity overstated (understated)	(10,000)	Correct
Income Statement:	2013	2014
Cost of merchandise sold overstated (understated)	$ 10,000	$(10,000)
Gross profit overstated (understated)	(10,000)	10,000
Net income overstated (understated)	(10,000)	10,000

Example Exercise 6-7 Effect of Inventory Errors

OBJ 6

Zula Repair Shop incorrectly counted its December 31, 2014, inventory as $250,000 instead of the correct amount of $220,000. Indicate the effect of the misstatement on Zula's December 31, 2014, balance sheet and income statement for the year ended December 31, 2014.

Follow My Example 6-7

	Amount of Misstatement Overstatement (Understatement)
Balance Sheet:	
Merchandise inventory overstated	$ 30,000
Current assets overstated	30,000
Total assets overstated	30,000
Stockholders' equity overstated	30,000
Income Statement:	
Cost of merchandise sold understated	$(30,000)
Gross profit overstated	30,000
Net income overstated	30,000

Practice Exercises: **PE 6-7A, PE 6-7B**

F·A·I

Financial Analysis and Interpretation: Inventory Turnover and Number of Days' Sales in Inventory

OBJ 7 Describe and illustrate the inventory turnover and the number of days' sales in inventory in analyzing the efficiency and effectiveness of inventory management.

A merchandising business should keep enough inventory on hand to meet its customers' needs. A failure to do so may result in lost sales. However, too much inventory ties up funds that could be used to improve operations. Also, excess inventory increases expenses such as storage and property taxes. Finally, excess inventory increases the risk of losses due to price declines, damage, or changes in customer tastes.

Two measures to analyze the efficiency and effectiveness of inventory management are:

1. inventory turnover and
2. number of days' sales in inventory.

Inventory turnover measures the relationship between the cost of merchandise sold and the amount of inventory carried during the period. It is computed as follows:

$$\text{Inventory Turnover} = \frac{\text{Cost of Merchandise Sold}}{\text{Average Inventory}}$$

Business Connection

RAPID INVENTORY AT COSTCO

Costco Wholesale Corporation operates over 500 membership warehouses that offer members low prices on a limited selection of nationally branded and selected private label products. Costco emphasizes high sales volumes and rapid inventory turnover. This enables Costco to operate profitably at lower gross margins than traditional wholesalers, discount retailers, and supermarkets. In addition, Costco's rapid inventory turnover allows it to conserve its working capital, as described below.

Because of our high sales volume and rapid inventory turnover, we generally have the opportunity to sell and be paid for inventory before we are required to pay . . . our merchandise vendors. . . . As sales increase and inventory turnover becomes more rapid, a greater percentage of inventory is financed through payment terms provided by suppliers rather than by our working capital.

© Don Ryan/AP Images

Source: Costco Wholesale Corporation, Annual Report on Form 10-K.

To illustrate, inventory turnover for Best Buy is computed from the following data (in millions) taken from two recent annual reports.

	For the Year Ended	
	Year 2	**Year 1**
Cost of merchandise sold	$37,635	$37,534
Inventories:		
Beginning of year	5,486	4,753
End of year	5,897	5,486
Average inventory:*		
($5,486 + $5,897) ÷ 2	5,691.5	
($4,753 + $5,486) ÷ 2		5,119.5
Inventory turnover:*		
$37,635 ÷ $5,691.5	6.6	
$37,534 ÷ $5,119.5		7.3

* Rounded to one decimal place.

Generally, the larger the inventory turnover the more efficient and effective the company is in managing inventory. As shown above, inventory turnover decreased from 7.3 to 6.6 during Year 2, and thus Best Buy's inventory efficiency decreased during Year 2.

The **number of days' sales in inventory** measures the length of time it takes to acquire, sell, and replace the inventory. It is computed as follows:

$$\text{Number of Days' Sales in Inventory} = \frac{\text{Average Inventory}}{\text{Average Daily Cost of Merchandise Sold}}$$

The average daily cost of merchandise sold is determined by dividing the cost of merchandise sold by 365. Based upon the preceding data, the number of days' sales in inventory for Best Buy is computed below.

	For the Year Ended	
	Year 2	**Year 1**
Cost of merchandise sold	$37,635	$37,534
Average daily cost of merchandise sold:*		
$37,635 ÷ 365 days	103.1	
$37,534 ÷ 365 days		102.8
Average inventory:*		
($5,486 + $5,897) ÷ 2	5,691.5	
($4,753 + $5,486) ÷ 2		5,119.5
Number of days' sales in inventory:*		
$5,691.5 ÷ $103.1	55.2 days	
$5,119.5 ÷ $102.8		49.8 days

* Rounded to one decimal place.

Generally, the lower the number of days' sales in inventory, the more efficient and effective the company is in managing inventory. As shown previously, the number of days' sales in inventory increased from 49.8 to 55.2 during Year 2, and thus Best Buy's inventory management did not improve. This is consistent with the decrease in inventory during the year.

As with most financial ratios, differences exist among industries. To illustrate, Zale Corporation is a large retailer of fine jewelry in the United States. Since jewelry doesn't sell as rapidly as Best Buy's consumer electronics, Zale's inventory turnover and number of days' sales in inventory should be significantly different than Best Buy's. For a recent year, this is confirmed as shown below.

	Best Buy	Zale
Inventory turnover	6.6	1.1
Number of days' sales in inventory	55.2 days	328.0 days

Example Exercise 6-8 Inventory Turnover and Number of Days' Sales in Inventory

OBJ 7

Financial statement data for years ending December 31 for Beadle Company are shown below.

	2014	2013
Cost of merchandise sold	$877,500	$615,000
Inventories:		
Beginning of year	225,000	185,000
End of year	315,000	225,000

a. Determine the inventory turnover for 2014 and 2013.
b. Determine the number of days' sales in inventory for 2014 and 2013.
c. Does the change in the inventory turnover and the number of days' sales in inventory from 2013 to 2014 indicate a favorable or an unfavorable trend?

Follow My Example 6-8

a. Inventory turnover:

	2014	2013
Average inventory:		
($225,000 + $315,000) ÷ 2	$270,000	
($185,000 + $225,000) ÷ 2		$205,000
Inventory turnover:		
$877,500 ÷ $270,000	3.25	
$615,000 ÷ $205,000		3.00

b. Number of days' sales in inventory:

Average daily cost of merchandise sold:		
$877,500 ÷ 365 days	$2,404	
$615,000 ÷ 365 days		$1,685
Average inventory:		
($225,000 + $315,000) ÷ 2	$270,000	
($185,000 + $225,000) ÷ 2		$205,000
Number of days' sales in inventory:		
$270,000 ÷ $2,404	112.3 days	
$205,000 ÷ $1,685		121.7 days

c. The increase in the inventory turnover from 3.00 to 3.25 and the decrease in the number of days' sales in inventory from 121.7 days to 112.3 days indicate favorable trends in managing inventory.

Practice Exercises: **PE 6-8A, PE 6-8B**

APPENDIX

Estimating Inventory Cost

A business may need to estimate the amount of inventory for the following reasons:

1. Perpetual inventory records are not maintained.
2. A disaster such as a fire or flood has destroyed the inventory records and the inventory.
3. Monthly or quarterly financial statements are needed, but a physical inventory is taken only once a year.

This appendix describes and illustrates two widely used methods of estimating inventory cost.

Retail Method of Inventory Costing

The **retail inventory method** of estimating inventory cost requires costs and retail prices to be maintained for the merchandise available for sale. A ratio of cost to retail price is then used to convert ending inventory at retail to estimate the ending inventory cost.

The retail inventory method is applied as follows:

Step 1. Determine the total merchandise available for sale at cost and retail.
Step 2. Determine the ratio of the cost to retail of the merchandise available for sale.
Step 3. Determine the ending inventory at retail by deducting the net sales from the merchandise available for sale at retail.
Step 4. Estimate the ending inventory cost by multiplying the ending inventory at retail by the cost to retail ratio.

Exhibit 13 illustrates the retail inventory method.

EXHIBIT 13

Determining Inventory by the Retail Method

		A	B	C
	1		Cost	Retail
	2	Merchandise inventory, January 1	$19,400	$ 36,000
	3	Purchases in January (net)	42,600	64,000
Step 1 →	4	Merchandise available for sale	$62,000	$100,000
Step 2 →	5	Ratio of cost to retail price: $\frac{\$62,000}{\$100,000} = 62\%$		
	6	Sales for January (net)		70,000
Step 3 →	7	Merchandise inventory, January 31, at retail		$ 30,000
Step 4 →	8	Merchandise inventory, January 31, at estimated cost		
	9	($30,000 × 62%)		$ 18,600
	10			

When estimating the cost to retail ratio, the mix of items in the ending inventory is assumed to be the same as the merchandise available for sale. If the ending inventory is made up of different classes of merchandise, cost to retail ratios may be developed for each class of inventory.

An advantage of the retail method is that it provides inventory figures for preparing monthly statements. Department stores and similar retailers often determine gross profit and operating income each month, but may take a physical inventory only once or twice a year. Thus, the retail method allows management to monitor operations more closely.

The retail method may also be used as an aid in taking a physical inventory. In this case, the items are counted and recorded at their retail (selling) prices instead of their costs. The physical inventory at retail is then converted to cost by using the cost to retail ratio.

Gross Profit Method of Inventory Costing

The **gross profit method** uses the estimated gross profit for the period to estimate the inventory at the end of the period. The gross profit is estimated from the preceding year, adjusted for any current-period changes in the cost and sales prices.

The gross profit method is applied as follows:

Step 1. Determine the merchandise available for sale at cost.

Step 2. Determine the estimated gross profit by multiplying the net sales by the gross profit percentage.

Step 3. Determine the estimated cost of merchandise sold by deducting the estimated gross profit from the net sales.

Step 4. Estimate the ending inventory cost by deducting the estimated cost of merchandise sold from the merchandise available for sale.

Exhibit 14 illustrates the gross profit method.

EXHIBIT 14

Estimating Inventory by Gross Profit Method

		A	B	C
	1			**Cost**
	2	Merchandise inventory, January 1		$ 57,000
	3	Purchases in January (net)		180,000
Step 1 →	4	Merchandise available for sale		$237,000
	5	Sales for January (net)	$250,000	
Step 2 →	6	Less estimated gross profit ($250,000 × 30%)	75,000	
Step 3 →	7	Estimated cost of merchandise sold		175,000
Step 4 →	8	Estimated merchandise inventory, January 31		$ 62,000
	9			

The gross profit method is useful for estimating inventories for monthly or quarterly financial statements. It is also useful in estimating the cost of merchandise destroyed by fire or other disasters.

At a Glance 6

OBJ 1 **Describe the importance of control over inventory.**

Key Points Two objectives of inventory control are safeguarding the inventory and properly reporting it in the financial statements. The perpetual inventory system and physical count enhance control over inventory.

Learning Outcomes	Example Exercises	Practice Exercises
• Describe controls for safeguarding inventory. • Describe how a perpetual inventory system enhances control over inventory. • Describe why taking a physical inventory enhances control over inventory.		

OBJ 2 Describe three inventory cost flow assumptions and how they impact the income statement and balance sheet.

Key Points The three common inventory cost flow assumptions used in business are the (1) first-in, first-out method (FIFO); (2) last-in, first-out method (LIFO); and (3) weighted average cost method. The cost flow assumption affects the income statement and balance sheet.

Learning Outcomes	Example Exercises	Practice Exercises
• Describe the FIFO, LIFO, and weighted average cost flow methods.		
• Describe how the choice of a cost flow method affects the income statement and balance sheet.	EE6-1	PE6-1A, 6-1B

OBJ 3 Determine the cost of inventory under the perpetual inventory system, using the FIFO, LIFO, and weighted average cost methods.

Key Points In a perpetual inventory system, the number of units and the cost of each type of merchandise are recorded in a subsidiary inventory ledger, with a separate account for each type of merchandise.

Learning Outcomes	Example Exercises	Practice Exercises
• Determine the cost of inventory and the cost of merchandise sold, using a perpetual inventory system under the FIFO method.	EE6-2	PE6-2A, 6-2B
• Determine the cost of inventory and the cost of merchandise sold, using a perpetual inventory system under the LIFO method.	EE6-3	PE6-3A, 6-3B
• Determine the cost of inventory and the cost of merchandise sold, using a perpetual inventory system under the weighted average cost method.	EE6-4	PE6-4A, 6-4B

OBJ 4 Determine the cost of inventory under the periodic inventory system, using the FIFO, LIFO, and weighted average cost methods.

Key Points In a periodic inventory system, a physical inventory is taken to determine the cost of the inventory and the cost of merchandise sold.

Learning Outcomes	Example Exercises	Practice Exercises
• Determine the cost of inventory and the cost of merchandise sold, using a periodic inventory system under the FIFO method.	EE6-5	PE6-5A, 6-5B
• Determine the cost of inventory and the cost of merchandise sold, using a periodic inventory system under the LIFO method.	EE6-5	PE6-5A, 6-5B
• Determine the cost of inventory and the cost of merchandise sold, using a periodic inventory system under the weighted average cost method.	EE6-5	PE6-5A, 6-5B

If the inventory of a particular model comprises one entire purchase plus a portion of another purchase acquired at a different unit cost, use a separate line for each purchase.

2. Determine the cost of the inventory on December 31, 2014, by the last-in, first-out method, following the procedures indicated in (1).
3. Determine the cost of the inventory on December 31, 2014, by the weighted average cost method, using the columnar headings indicated in (1).
4. Discuss which method (FIFO or LIFO) would be preferred for income tax purposes in periods of (a) rising prices and (b) declining prices.

PR 6-6B Lower-of-cost-or-market inventory

OBJ. 6

✔ Total LCM, $41,873

Data on the physical inventory of Katus Products Co. as of December 31, 2014, are presented below.

Description	Inventory Quantity	Unit Market Price
A54	37	$ 56
C77	24	178
F66	30	132
H83	21	545
K12	375	5
Q58	90	18
S36	8	235
V97	140	20
Y88	17	744

Quantity and cost data from the last purchases invoice of the year and the next-to-the-last purchases invoice are summarized as follows:

	Last Purchases Invoice		Next-to-the-Last Purchases Invoice	
Description	Quantity Purchased	Unit Cost	Quantity Purchased	Unit Cost
A54	30	$ 60	40	$ 58
C77	25	174	15	180
F66	20	130	15	128
H83	6	547	15	540
K12	500	6	500	7
Q58	75	25	80	26
S36	5	256	4	260
V97	100	17	115	16
Y88	10	750	8	740

Instructions

Determine the inventory at cost and also at the lower of cost or market, using the first-in, first-out method. Record the appropriate unit costs on the inventory sheet, and complete the pricing of the inventory. When there are two different unit costs applicable to an item:

1. Draw a line through the quantity, and insert the quantity and unit cost of the last purchase.
2. On the following line, insert the quantity and unit cost of the next-to-the-last purchase.
3. Total the cost and market columns and insert the lower of the two totals in the Lower of C or M column. The first item on the inventory sheet has been completed as an example.

Inventory Sheet
December 31, 2014

				Total		
Description	Unit Inventory Quantity	Unit Cost Price	Total Market Price	Cost	Market	Lower of C or M
A54	~~37~~ 30	60	$56	$1,800	$1,680	
	7	58	56	406	392	
				$2,206	$2,072	$2,072

Appendix
PR 6-7B Retail method; gross profit method

✔ 1. $630,000

Selected data on merchandise inventory, purchases, and sales for Jaffe Co. and Coronado Co. are as follows:

	Cost	Retail
Jaffe Co.		
Merchandise inventory, February 1	$ 400,000	$ 615,000
Transactions during February:		
Purchases (net)	4,055,000	5,325,000
Sales		5,220,000
Sales returns and allowances		120,000
Coronado Co.		
Merchandise inventory, May 1	$ 400,000	
Transactions during May thru October:		
Purchases (net)	3,150,000	
Sales	4,850,000	
Sales returns and allowances	100,000	
Estimated gross profit rate	35%	

Instructions

1. Determine the estimated cost of the merchandise inventory of Jaffe Co. on February 28 by the retail method, presenting details of the computations.
2. a. Estimate the cost of the merchandise inventory of Coronado Co. on October 31 by the gross profit method, presenting details of the computations.
   b. Assume that Coronado Co. took a physical inventory on October 31 and discovered that $366,500 of merchandise was on hand. What was the estimated loss of inventory due to theft or damage during May thru October?

Cases & Projects

CP 6-1 Ethics and professional conduct in business

Anstead Co. is experiencing a decrease in sales and operating income for the fiscal year ending October 31, 2014. Ryan Frazier, controller of Anstead Co., has suggested that all orders received before the end of the fiscal year be shipped by midnight, October 31, 2014, even if the shipping department must work overtime. Since Anstead Co. ships all merchandise FOB shipping point, it would record all such shipments as sales for the year ending October 31, 2014, thereby offsetting some of the decreases in sales and operating income.

Discuss whether Ryan Frazier is behaving in a professional manner.

CP 6-2 LIFO and inventory flow

The following is an excerpt from a conversation between Paula Marlo, the warehouse manager for Musick Foods Wholesale Co., and its accountant, Mike Hayes. Musick Foods operates a large regional warehouse that supplies produce and other grocery products to grocery stores in smaller communities.

Paula: Mike, can you explain what's going on here with these monthly statements?

Mike: Sure, Paula. How can I help you?

Paula: I don't understand this last-in, first-out inventory procedure. It just doesn't make sense.

Mike: Well, what it means is that we assume that the last goods we receive are the first ones sold. So the inventory consists of the items we purchased first.

Paula: Yes, but that's my problem. It doesn't work that way! We always distribute the oldest produce first. Some of that produce is perishable! We can't keep any of it very long or it'll spoil.

Mike: Paula, you don't understand. We only *assume* that the products we distribute are the last ones received. We don't actually have to distribute the goods in this way.

Paula: I always thought that accounting was supposed to show what really happened. It all sounds like "make believe" to me! Why not report what really happens?

Respond to Paula's concerns.

CP 6-3 Costing inventory

Golden Eagle Company began operations in 2014 by selling a single product. Data on purchases and sales for the year were as follows:

Purchases:

Date	Units Purchased	Unit Cost	Total Cost
April 6	31,000	$36.60	$1,134,600
May 18	33,000	39.00	1,287,000
June 6	40,000	39.60	1,584,000
July 10	40,000	42.00	1,680,000
August 10	27,200	42.75	1,162,800
October 25	12,800	43.50	556,800
November 4	8,000	44.85	358,800
December 10	8,000	48.00	384,000
	200,000		$8,148,000

Sales:

April	16,000 units
May	16,000
June	20,000
July	24,000
August	28,000
September	28,000
October	18,000
November	10,000
December	8,000
Total units	168,000
Total sales	$10,000,000

On January 4, 2015, the president of the company, Connie Kilmer, asked for your advice on costing the 32,000-unit physical inventory that was taken on December 31, 2014. Moreover, since the firm plans to expand its product line, she asked for your advice on the use of a perpetual inventory system in the future.

1. Determine the cost of the December 31, 2014, inventory under the periodic system, using the (a) first-in, first-out method, (b) last-in, first-out method, and (c) weighted average cost method.
2. Determine the gross profit for the year under each of the three methods in (1).
3. a. Explain varying viewpoints why each of the three inventory costing methods may best reflect the results of operations for 2014.

   b. Which of the three inventory costing methods may best reflect the replacement cost of the inventory on the balance sheet as of December 31, 2014?

   c. Which inventory costing method would you choose to use for income tax purposes? Why?

   d. Discuss the advantages and disadvantages of using a perpetual inventory system. From the data presented in this case, is there any indication of the adequacy of inventory levels during the year?

CP 6-4 Inventory ratios for Dell and HP

F·A·I

Dell, Inc. and Hewlett-Packard Development Company, L.P. (HP) are both manufacturers of computer equipment and peripherals. However, the two companies follow two different strategies. Dell follows primarily a build-to-order strategy, where the consumer orders the computer from a Web page. The order is then manufactured and shipped to the customer within days of the order. In contrast, HP follows a build-to-stock strategy, where the computer is first built for inventory, then sold from inventory to retailers, such as Best Buy. The two strategies can be seen in the difference between the inventory turnover and number of days' sales in inventory ratios for the two companies. The following financial statement information is provided for Dell and HP for a recent fiscal year (in millions):

	Dell	HP
Inventory, beginning of period	$ 1,051	$ 6,128
Inventory, end of period	1,301	6,466
Cost of goods sold	50,098	96,089

a. Determine the inventory turnover ratio and the number of days' sales in inventory ratio for each company. Round to one decimal place.

b. Interpret the difference between the ratios for the two companies.

CP 6-5 Comparing inventory ratios for two companies

F·A·I

Tiffany Co. is a high-end jewelry retailer, while Amazon.com uses its e-commerce services, features, and technologies to sell its products through the Internet. Recent balance sheet inventory disclosures for Tiffany and Amazon.com (in millons) are as follows:

	End-of-Period Inventory	Beginning-of-Period Inventory
Tiffany Co.	$1,625	$1,428
Amazon.com	3,202	2,171

The cost of merchandise sold reported by each company was as follows:

	Tiffany Co.	Amazon.com
Cost of merchandise sold	$1,263	$26,561

a. Determine the inventory turnover and number of days' sales in inventory for Tiffany and Amazon.com. Round to two decimal places.

b. Interpret your results.

CP 6-6 Comparing inventory ratios for three companies

F·A·I

The general merchandise retail industry has a number of segments represented by the following companies:

Company Name	Merchandise Concept
Costco Wholesale Corporation	Membership warehouse
Walmart	Discount general merchandise
JCPenney	Department store

For a recent year, the following cost of merchandise sold and beginning and ending inventories have been provided from corporate annual reports (in millions) for these three companies:

	Costco	Walmart	JCPenney
Cost of merchandise sold	$67,995	$315,287	$10,799
Merchandise inventory, beginning	5,405	32,713	3,024
Merchandise inventory, ending	5,638	36,318	3,213

a. Determine the inventory turnover ratio for all three companies. Round to one decimal place.

b. Determine the number of days' sales in inventory for all three companies. Round to one decimal place.

c. Interpret these results based on each company's merchandise concept.

CHAPTER 7

Sarbanes-Oxley, Internal Control, and Cash

eBay Inc.

Controls are a part of your everyday life. At one extreme, laws are used to limit your behavior. For example, speed limits are designed to control your driving for traffic safety. In addition, you may also use many nonlegal controls. For example, you can keep credit card receipts in order to compare your transactions to the monthly credit card statement. Comparing receipts to the monthly statement is a control designed to catch mistakes made by the credit card company. In addition, banks give you a personal identification number (PIN) as a control against unauthorized access to your cash if you lose your automated teller machine (ATM) card. Dairies use freshness dating on their milk containers as a control to prevent the purchase or sale of soured milk. As you can see, you use and encounter controls every day.

Just as there are many examples of controls throughout society, businesses must also implement controls to help guide the behavior of their managers, employees, and customers. For example, **eBay Inc.** maintains an Internet-based marketplace for the sale of goods and services. Using eBay's online platform, buyers and sellers can browse, buy, and sell a wide variety of items including antiques and used cars. However, in order to maintain the integrity and trust of its buyers and sellers, eBay must have controls to ensure that buyers pay for their items and sellers don't misrepresent their items or fail to deliver sales. One such control eBay uses is a feedback forum that establishes buyer and seller reputations. A prospective buyer or seller can view the member's reputation and feedback comments before completing a transaction. Dishonest or unfair trading can lead to a negative reputation and even suspension or cancellation of the member's ability to trade on eBay.

This chapter discusses controls that can be included in accounting systems to provide reasonable assurance that the financial statements are reliable. Controls to discover and prevent errors to a bank account are also discussed. This chapter begins by discussing the Sarbanes-Oxley Act of 2002 and its impact on controls and financial reporting.

Learning Objectives

After studying this chapter, you should be able to: | *Example Exercises*

At a Glance 7 Page 339

OBJ 1 Describe the Sarbanes-Oxley Act of 2002 and its impact on internal controls and financial reporting.

Sarbanes-Oxley Act of 2002

During the financial scandals of the early 2000s, stockholders, creditors, and other investors lost billions of dollars.[1] As a result, the U.S. Congress passed the **Sarbanes-Oxley Act of 2002**. This act, often referred to as *Sarbanes-Oxley*, is one of the most important laws affecting U.S. companies in recent history. The purpose of Sarbanes-Oxley is to maintain public confidence and trust in the financial reporting of companies.

Sarbanes-Oxley applies only to companies whose stock is traded on public exchanges, referred to as *publicly held companies*. However, Sarbanes-Oxley highlighted the importance of assessing the financial controls and reporting of all companies. As a result, companies of all sizes have been influenced by Sarbanes-Oxley.

Sarbanes-Oxley emphasizes the importance of effective internal control.[2] **Internal control** is defined as the procedures and processes used by a company to:

1. Safeguard its assets.
2. Process information accurately.
3. Ensure compliance with laws and regulations.

Sarbanes-Oxley requires companies to maintain effective internal controls over the recording of transactions and the preparing of financial statements. Such controls are important because they deter fraud and prevent misleading financial statements as shown on the next page.

1 Exhibit 2 in Chapter 1 briefly summarizes these scandals.

2 Sarbanes-Oxley also has important implications for corporate governance and the regulation of the public accounting profession. This chapter, however, focuses on the internal control implications of Sarbanes-Oxley.

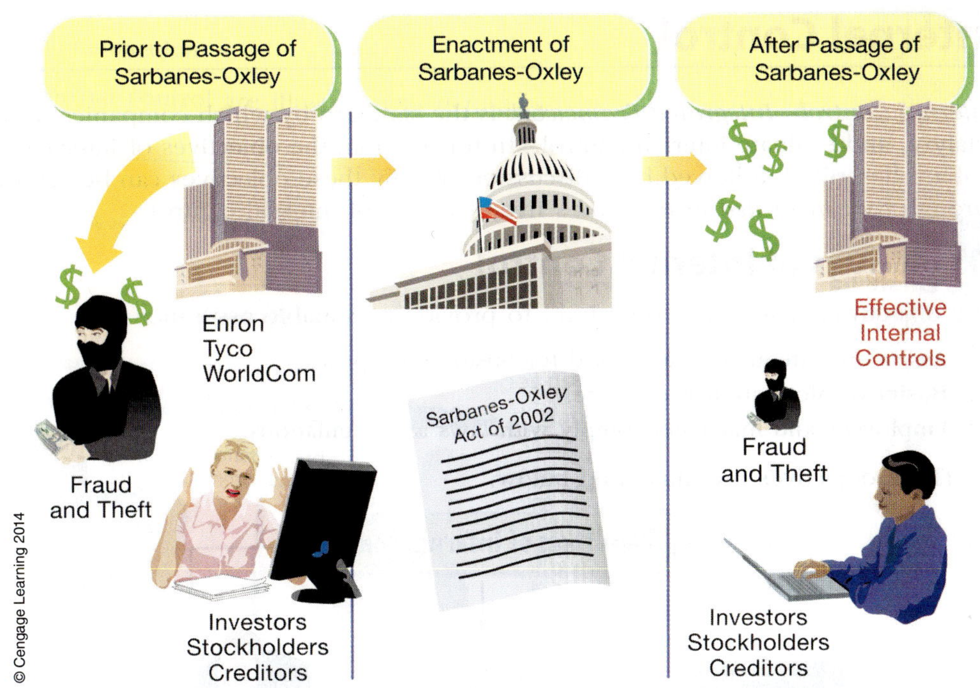

Sarbanes-Oxley also requires companies and their independent accountants to report on the effectiveness of the company's internal controls.[3] These reports are required to be filed with the company's annual 10-K report with the Securities and Exchange Commission. Companies are also encouraged to include these reports in their annual reports to stockholders. An example of such a report by the management of Nike is shown in Exhibit 1.

EXHIBIT 1

Sarbanes-Oxley Report of Nike

Management's Annual Report on Internal Control Over Financial Reporting

Management is responsible for establishing and maintaining adequate internal control over financial reporting....

Under the supervision and with the participation of our Chief Executive Officer and Chief Financial Officer, our management conducted an evaluation of the effectiveness of our internal control over financial reporting based upon the framework in *Internal Control—Integrated Framework* issued by the Committee of Sponsoring Organizations of the Treadway Commission. Based on that evaluation, our management concluded that our internal control over financial reporting is effective....

PricewaterhouseCoopers LLP, an independent registered public accounting firm, has audited . . . the effectiveness of our internal control over financial reporting . . . as stated in their report....

MARK G. PARKER
Chief Executive Officer and President

DONALD W. BLAIR
Chief Financial Officer

Exhibit 1 indicates that Nike based its evaluation of internal controls on *Internal Control—Integrated Framework*, which was issued by the Committee of Sponsoring Organizations (COSO) of the Treadway Commission. This framework is the standard by which companies design, analyze, and evaluate internal controls. For this reason, this framework is used as the basis for discussing internal controls.

Information on *Internal Control—Integrated Framework* can be found on COSO's Web site at **http://www.coso.org/**.

3 These reporting requirements are required under Section 404 of the act. As a result, these requirements and reports are often referred to as 404 requirements and 404 reports.

safeguarding prenumbered documents helps prevent fraudulent transactions from being recorded. For example, blank checks are prenumbered and safeguarded. Once a payment has been properly authorized and approved, the checks are filled out and issued.

Reconciliations are also an important control. Later in this chapter, the use of bank reconciliations as an aid in controlling cash is described and illustrated.

Security measures involve measures to safeguard assets. For example, cash on hand should be kept in a cash register or safe. Inventory not on display should be stored in a locked storeroom or warehouse. Accounting records such as the accounts receivable subsidiary ledger should also be safeguarded to prevent their loss. For example, electronically maintained accounting records should be safeguarded with access codes and backed up so that any lost or damaged files could be recovered if necessary.

Monitoring

Monitoring the internal control system is used to locate weaknesses and improve controls. Monitoring often includes observing employee behavior and the accounting system for indicators of control problems. Some such indicators are shown in Exhibit 4.[6]

EXHIBIT 4

Warning Signs of Internal Control Problems

Warning signs with regard to people

1. Abrupt change in lifestyle (without winning the lottery).
2. Close social relationships with suppliers.
3. Refusing to take a vacation.
4. Frequent borrowing from other employees.
5. Excessive use of alcohol or drugs.

Warning signs from the accounting system

1. Missing documents or gaps in transaction numbers (could mean documents are being used for fraudulent transactions).
2. An unusual increase in customer refunds (refunds may be phony).
3. Differences between daily cash receipts and bank deposits (could mean receipts are being pocketed before being deposited).
4. Sudden increase in slow payments (employee may be pocketing the payments).
5. Backlog in recording transactions (possibly an attempt to delay detection of fraud).

Evaluations of controls are often performed when there are major changes in strategy, senior management, business structure, or operations. Internal auditors, who are independent of operations, usually perform such evaluations. Internal auditors are also responsible for day-to-day monitoring of controls. External auditors also evaluate and report on internal control as part of their annual financial statement audit.

Information and Communication

Information and communication is an essential element of internal control. Information about the control environment, risk assessment, control procedures, and monitoring is used by management for guiding operations and ensuring compliance with reporting, legal, and regulatory requirements. Management also uses external

6 Edwin C. Bliss, "Employee Theft," *Boardroom Reports*, July 15, 1994, pp. 5–6.

information to assess events and conditions that impact decision making and external reporting. For example, management uses pronouncements of the Financial Accounting Standards Board (FASB) to assess the impact of changes in reporting standards on the financial statements.

Example Exercise 7-1 Internal Control Elements OBJ 2

Identify each of the following as relating to (a) the control environment, (b) risk assessment, or (c) control procedures.

1. Mandatory vacations
2. Personnel policies
3. Report of outside consultants on future market changes

Follow My Example 7-1

1. (c) control procedures
2. (a) the control environment
3. (b) risk assessment

Practice Exercises: **PE 7-1A, PE 7-1B**

Limitations of Internal Control

Internal control systems can provide only reasonable assurance for safeguarding assets, processing accurate information, and compliance with laws and regulations. In other words, internal controls are not a guarantee. This is due to the following factors:

1. The human element of controls
2. Cost-benefit considerations

The *human element* recognizes that controls are applied and used by humans. As a result, human errors can occur because of fatigue, carelessness, confusion, or misjudgment. For example, an employee may unintentionally shortchange a customer or miscount the amount of inventory received from a supplier. In addition, two or more employees may collude together to defeat or circumvent internal controls. This latter case often involves fraud and the theft of assets. For example, the cashier and the accounts receivable clerk might collude to steal customer payments on account.

Cost-benefit considerations recognize that the cost of internal controls should not exceed their benefits. For example, retail stores could eliminate shoplifting by searching all customers before they leave the store. However, such a control procedure would upset customers and result in lost sales. Instead, retailers use cameras or signs saying *"We prosecute all shoplifters."*

Cash Controls Over Receipts and Payments

OBJ 3 Describe and illustrate the application of internal controls to cash.

Cash includes coins, currency (paper money), checks, and money orders. Money on deposit with a bank or other financial institution that is available for withdrawal is also considered cash. Normally, you can think of cash as anything that a bank would accept for deposit in your account. For example, a check made payable to you could normally be deposited in a bank and, thus, is considered cash.

Businesses usually have several bank accounts. For example, a business might have one bank account for general cash payments and another for payroll. A separate ledger account is normally used for each bank account. For example, a bank account at City Bank could be identified in the ledger as *Cash in Bank—City Bank*. To simplify, this chapter assumes that a company has only *one* bank account, which is identified in the ledger as *Cash*.

Cash is the asset most likely to be stolen or used improperly in a business. For this reason, businesses must carefully control cash and cash transactions.

OBJ 2 Describe and illustrate the objectives and elements of internal control.

Key Points The objectives of internal control are to provide reasonable assurance that (1) assets are safeguarded and used for business purposes, (2) business information is accurate, and (3) laws and regulations are complied with. The elements of internal control are the control environment, risk assessment, control procedures, monitoring, and information and communication.

Learning Outcomes	Example Exercises	Practice Exercises
• List the objectives of internal control.		
• List the elements of internal control.		
• Describe each element of internal control and factors influencing each element.	EE7-1	PE7-1A, 7-1B

OBJ 3 Describe and illustrate the application of internal controls to cash.

Key Points A cash register is a control for protecting cash received in over-the-counter sales. A remittance advice is a control for cash received through the mail. Separating the duties of handling cash and recording cash is also a control. A voucher system is a control system for cash payments. Many companies use electronic funds transfers for cash receipts and cash payments.

Learning Outcomes	Example Exercises	Practice Exercises
• Describe and give examples of controls for cash received from cash sales, cash received in the mail, and cash received by EFT.		
• Describe and give examples of controls for cash payments made using a voucher system and cash payments made by EFT.		

OBJ 4 Describe the nature of a bank account and its use in controlling cash.

Key Points Bank accounts control cash by reducing the amount of cash on hand and facilitating the transfer of cash between businesses and locations. In addition, the bank statement allows a business to reconcile the cash transactions recorded in the accounting records to those recorded by the bank.

Learning Outcomes	Example Exercises	Practice Exercises
• Describe how the use of bank accounts helps control cash.	EE7-2	PE7-2A, 7-2B
• Describe a bank statement and provide examples of items that appear on a bank statement as debit and credit memos.		

OBJ 5 Describe and illustrate the use of a bank reconciliation in controlling cash.

Key Points A bank reconciliation is prepared using the nine steps as summarized on page 332. The items in the company section of a bank reconciliation must be journalized on the company's records.

Learning Outcomes	Example Exercises	Practice Exercises
• Describe a bank reconciliation.		
• Prepare a bank reconciliation.	EE7-3	PE7-3A, 7-3B
• Journalize any necessary entries on the company's records, based on the bank reconciliation.	EE7-3	PE7-3A, 7-3B

OBJ 6 Describe the accounting for special-purpose cash funds.

Key Points Special-purpose cash funds, such as a petty cash fund or travel funds, are used by businesses to meet specific needs. Each fund is established by cashing a check for the amount of cash needed. At periodic intervals, the fund is replenished and the disbursements recorded.

Learning Outcomes	Example Exercises	Practice Exercises
• Describe the use of special-purpose cash funds.		
• Journalize the entry to establish a petty cash fund.	EE7-4	PE7-4A, 7-4B
• Journalize the entry to replenish a petty cash fund.	EE7-4	PE7-4A, 7-4B

OBJ 7 Describe and illustrate the reporting of cash and cash equivalents in the financial statements.

Key Points Cash is listed as the first asset in the Current assets section of the balance sheet. Companies that have invested excess cash in highly liquid investments usually report *Cash and cash equivalents* on the balance sheet.

Learning Outcomes	Example Exercises	Practice Exercises
• Describe the reporting of cash and cash equivalents in the financial statements.		
• Illustrate the reporting of cash and cash equivalents in the financial statements.		

OBJ 8 Describe and illustrate the use of the ratio of cash to monthly cash expenses to assess the ability of a company to continue in business.

Key Points The ratio of cash to monthly cash expenses is useful for assessing how long a company can continue to operate without (1) additional financing or (2) generating positive cash flows from operations.

Learning Outcomes	Example Exercises	Practice Exercises
• Describe the use of the ratio of cash to monthly cash expenses.		
• Compute the ratio of cash to monthly cash expenses.	EE7-5	PE7-5A, 7-5B

Key Terms

bank reconciliation (331)
bank statement (328)
cash (325)
cash equivalents (336)
cash short and over account (326)
compensating balance (337)
control environment (321)
electronic funds transfer (EFT) (327)
elements of internal control (320)
employee fraud (320)
internal control (318)
petty cash fund (335)
ratio of cash to monthly cash expenses (337)
Sarbanes-Oxley Act of 2002 (318)
special-purpose funds (336)
voucher (328)
voucher system (328)

Illustrative Problem

The bank statement for Urethane Company for June 30, 2013, indicates a balance of $9,293.11. All cash receipts are deposited each evening in a night depository, after banking hours. The accounting records indicate the following summary data for cash receipts and payments for June:

Cash balance as of June 1	$ 3,943.50
Total cash receipts for June	28,971.60
Total amount of checks issued in June	28,388.85

Comparing the bank statement and the accompanying canceled checks and memos with the records reveals the following reconciling items:

a. The bank had collected for Urethane Company $1,030 on a note left for collection. The face amount of the note was $1,000.

b. A deposit of $1,852.21, representing receipts of June 30, had been made too late to appear on the bank statement.

c. Checks outstanding totaled $5,265.27.

d. A check drawn for $139 had been incorrectly charged by the bank as $157.

e. A check for $370 returned with the statement had been recorded in the company's records as $730. The check was for the payment of an obligation to Avery Equipment Company for the purchase of office supplies on account.

f. Bank service charges for June amounted to $18.20.

Instructions

1. Prepare a bank reconciliation for June.
2. Journalize the entries that should be made by Urethane Company.

Solution

1.

Urethane Company
Bank Reconciliation
June 30, 2013

Cash balance according to bank statement		$ 9,293.11
Add: Deposit of June 30 not recorded by bank	$1,852.21	
Bank error in charging check as $157 instead of $139	18.00	1,870.21
		$11,163.32
Deduct: Outstanding checks		5,265.27
Adjusted balance		$ 5,898.05
Cash balance according to company's records		$ 4,526.25*
Add: Proceeds of note collected by bank, including $30 interest	$1,030.00	
Error in recording check	360.00	1,390.00
		$ 5,916.25
Deduct: Bank service charges		18.20
Adjusted balance		$ 5,898.05

*$3,943.50 + $28,971.60 – $28,388.85

2.

June	30	Cash	1,390.00	
		Notes Receivable		1,000.00
		Interest Revenue		30.00
		Accounts Payable—Avery Equipment Company		360.00
	30	Miscellaneous Administrative Expense	18.20	
		Cash		18.20

Discussion Questions

1. (a) Name and describe the five elements of internal control. (b) Is any one element of internal control more important than another?
2. Why should the employee who handles cash receipts not have the responsibility for maintaining the accounts receivable records? Explain.
3. The ticket seller at a movie theater doubles as a ticket taker for a few minutes each day while the ticket taker is on a break. Which control procedure of a business's system of internal control is violated in this situation?
4. Why should the responsibility for maintaining the accounting records be separated from the responsibility for operations? Explain.
5. Assume that Brooke Miles, accounts payable clerk for West Coast Design Inc., stole $48,350 by paying fictitious invoices for goods that were never received. The clerk set up accounts in the names of the fictitious companies and cashed the checks at a local bank. Describe a control procedure that would have prevented or detected the fraud.
6. Before a voucher for the purchase of merchandise is approved for payment, supporting documents should be compared to verify the accuracy of the liability. Give an example of supporting documents for the purchase of merchandise.
7. The balance of Cash is likely to differ from the bank statement balance. What two factors are likely to be responsible for the difference?
8. What is the purpose of preparing a bank reconciliation?
9. Knott Inc. has a petty cash fund of $750. (a) Since the petty cash fund is only $750, should Knott Inc. implement controls over petty cash? (b) What controls, if any, could be used for the petty cash fund?
10. (a) How are cash equivalents reported in the financial statements? (b) What are some examples of cash equivalents?

Practice Exercises

Example Exercises

EE 7-1 *p. 325*

PE 7-1A Internal control elements **OBJ. 2**

Identify each of the following as relating to (a) the control environment, (b) control procedures, or (c) information and communication.

1. Management's philosophy and operating style
2. Report of company's conformity with environmental laws and regulations
3. Separating related operations

EE 7-1 *p. 325*

PE 7-1B Internal control elements **OBJ. 2**

Identify each of the following as relating to (a) the control environment, (b) control procedures, or (c) monitoring.

1. Hiring of external auditors to review the adequacy of controls
2. Personnel policies
3. Safeguarding inventory in a locked warehouse

EE 7-2 *p. 330*

PE 7-2A Items on company's bank statement **OBJ. 4**

The following items may appear on a bank statement:

1. Bank correction of an error from recording a $4,800 deposit as $8,400
2. EFT payment
3. Note collected for company
4. Service charge

Using the format shown below, indicate whether each item would appear as a debit or credit memo on the bank statement and whether the item would increase or decrease the balance of the company's account.

Item No.	Appears on the Bank Statement as a Debit or Credit Memo	Increases or Decreases the Balance of the Company's Bank Account

EE 7-2 *p. 330*

PE 7-2B Items on company's bank statement **OBJ. 4**

The following items may appear on a bank statement:

1. Bank correction of an error from posting another customer's check (disbursement) to the company's account
2. EFT deposit
3. Loan proceeds
4. NSF check

Using the format shown below, indicate whether each item would appear as a debit or credit memo on the bank statement and whether the item would increase or decrease the balance of the company's account.

Item No.	Appears on the Bank Statement as a Debit or Credit Memo	Increases or Decreases the Balance of the Company's Bank Account

Example Exercises

EE 7-3 *p. 334*

PE 7-3A Bank reconciliation — OBJ. 5

The following data were gathered to use in reconciling the bank account of Eves Company:

Balance per bank	$13,450
Balance per company records	11,655
Bank service charges	45
Deposit in transit	3,000
NSF check	1,800
Outstanding checks	6,640

a. What is the adjusted balance on the bank reconciliation?

b. Journalize any necessary entries for Eves Company based on the bank reconciliation.

EE 7-3 *p. 334*

PE 7-3B Bank reconciliation — OBJ. 5

The following data were gathered to use in reconciling the bank account of Conway Company:

Balance per bank	$23,900
Balance per company records	8,700
Bank service charges	50
Deposit in transit	5,500
Note collected by bank with $450 interest	9,450
Outstanding checks	11,300

a. What is the adjusted balance on the bank reconciliation?

b. Journalize any necessary entries for Conway Company based on the bank reconciliation.

EE 7-4 *p. 336*

PE 7-4A Petty cash fund — OBJ. 6

Prepare journal entries for each of the following:

a. Issued a check to establish a petty cash fund of $1,150.

b. The amount of cash in the petty cash fund is $250. Issued a check to replenish the fund, based on the following summary of petty cash receipts: repair expense, $725 and miscellaneous selling expense, $150. Record any missing funds in the cash short and over account.

EE 7-4 *p. 336*

PE 7-4B Petty cash fund — OBJ. 6

Prepare journal entries for each of the following:

a. Issued a check to establish a petty cash fund of $900.

b. The amount of cash in the petty cash fund is $115. Issued a check to replenish the fund, based on the following summary of petty cash receipts: store supplies, $550 and miscellaneous selling expense, $200. Record any missing funds in the cash short and over account.

EE 7-5 *p. 338*

F·A·I

PE 7-5A Ratio of cash to monthly cash expenses — OBJ. 8

Financial data for Otto Company are shown below.

	For Year Ended December 31, 2014
Cash on December 31, 2014	$ 69,350
Cash flow from operations	(114,000)

a. Compute the ratio of cash to monthly cash expenses.

b. Interpret the results computed in (a).

EE 7-5 *p. 338*

F·A·I

PE 7-5B Ratio of cash to monthly cash expenses — OBJ. 8

Financial data for Bonita Company are shown below.

	For Year Ended December 31, 2014
Cash on December 31, 2014	$ 187,180
Cash flow from operations	(458,400)

a. Compute the ratio of cash to monthly cash expenses.

b. Interpret the results computed in (a).

Exercises

EX 7-1 Sarbanes-Oxley internal control report **OBJ. 1**

Using Wikipedia (**www.wikipedia.com**), look up the entry for Sarbanes-Oxley Act. Look over the table of contents and find the section that describes Section 404.

What does Section 404 require of management's internal control report?

EX 7-2 Internal controls **OBJ. 2, 3**

Madonna Epstein has recently been hired as the manager of Beans Coffee Shop. Beans Coffee Shop is a national chain of franchised coffee shops. During her first month as store manager, Madonna encountered the following internal control situations:

a. Beans Coffee Shop has one cash register. Prior to Madonna's joining the coffee shop, each employee working on a shift would take a customer order, accept payment, and then prepare the order. Madonna made one employee on each shift responsible for taking orders and accepting the customer's payment. Other employees prepare the orders.

b. Since only one employee uses the cash register, that employee is responsible for counting the cash at the end of the shift and verifying that the cash in the drawer matches the amount of cash sales recorded by the cash register. Madonna expects each cashier to balance the drawer to the penny *every* time—no exceptions.

c. Madonna caught an employee putting a case of 500 single-serving tea bags in her car. Not wanting to create a scene, Madonna smiled and said, "I don't think you're putting those tea bags on the right shelf. Don't they belong inside the coffee shop?" The employee returned the tea bags to the stockroom.

State whether you agree or disagree with Madonna's method of handling each situation and explain your answer.

EX 7-3 Internal controls **OBJ. 2, 3**

Ramona's Clothing is a retail store specializing in women's clothing. The store has established a liberal return policy for the holiday season in order to encourage gift purchases. Any item purchased during November and December may be returned through January 31, with a receipt, for cash or exchange. If the customer does not have a receipt, cash will still be refunded for any item under $75. If the item is more than $75, a check is mailed to the customer.

Whenever an item is returned, a store clerk completes a return slip, which the customer signs. The return slip is placed in a special box. The store manager visits the return counter approximately once every two hours to authorize the return slips. Clerks are instructed to place the returned merchandise on the proper rack on the selling floor as soon as possible.

This year, returns at Ramona's Clothing have reached an all-time high. There are a large number of returns under $75 without receipts.

a. How can sales clerks employed at Ramona's Clothing use the store's return policy to steal money from the cash register?

b. What internal control weaknesses do you see in the return policy that make cash thefts easier?

c. Would issuing a store credit in place of a cash refund for all merchandise returned without a receipt reduce the possibility of theft? List some advantages and disadvantages of issuing a store credit in place of a cash refund.

d. Assume that Ramona's Clothing is committed to the current policy of issuing cash refunds without a receipt. What changes could be made in the store's procedures regarding customer refunds in order to improve internal control?

EX 7-4 Internal controls for bank lending **OBJ. 2, 3**

Pacific Bank provides loans to businesses in the community through its Commercial Lending Department. Small loans (less than $100,000) may be approved by an individual loan officer, while larger loans (greater than $100,000) must be approved by a board of loan officers. Once a loan is approved, the funds are made available to the loan applicant under agreed-upon terms. Pacific Bank has instituted a policy whereby its president has the individual authority to approve loans up to $5,000,000. The president believes that this policy will allow flexibility to approve loans to valued clients much quicker than under the previous policy.

As an internal auditor of Pacific Bank, how would you respond to this change in policy?

EX 7-5 Internal controls **OBJ. 2, 3**

One of the largest losses in history from unauthorized securities trading involved a securities trader for the French bank, Societe Generale. The trader was able to circumvent internal controls and create over $7 billion in trading losses in six months. The trader apparently escaped detection by using knowledge of the bank's internal control systems learned from a previous back-office monitoring job. Much of this monitoring involved the use of software to monitor trades. In addition, traders were usually kept to tight trading limits. Apparently, these controls failed in this case.

What general weaknesses in Societe Generale's internal controls contributed to the occurrence and size of the losses?

EX 7-6 Internal controls **OBJ. 2, 3**

An employee of JHT Holdings, Inc., a trucking company, was responsible for resolving roadway accident claims under $25,000. The employee created fake accident claims and wrote settlement checks of between $5,000 and $25,000 to friends or acquaintances acting as phony "victims." One friend recruited subordinates at his place of work to cash some of the checks. Beyond this, the JHT employee also recruited lawyers, who he paid to represent both the trucking company and the fake victims in the bogus accident settlements. When the lawyers cashed the checks, they allegedly split the money with the corrupt JHT employee. This fraud went undetected for two years.

Why would it take so long to discover such a fraud?

EX 7-7 Internal controls **OBJ. 2, 3**

All-Around Sound Co. discovered a fraud whereby one of its front office administrative employees used company funds to purchase goods, such as computers, digital cameras, and other electronic items for her own use. The fraud was discovered when employees noticed an increase in delivery frequency from vendors and the use of unusual vendors. After some investigation, it was discovered that the employee would alter the description or change the quantity on an invoice in order to explain the cost on the bill.

What general internal control weaknesses contributed to this fraud?

EX 7-8 Financial statement fraud **OBJ. 2, 3**

A former chairman, CFO, and controller of Donnkenny, Inc., an apparel company that makes sportswear for Pierre Cardin and Victoria Jones, pleaded guilty to financial statement fraud. These managers used false journal entries to record fictitious sales, hid inventory in public warehouses so that it could be recorded as "sold," and required sales orders to be backdated so that the sale could be moved back to an earlier period. The combined effect of these actions caused $25 million out of $40 million in quarterly sales to be phony.

a. Why might control procedures listed in this chapter be insufficient in stopping this type of fraud?

b. How could this type of fraud be stopped?

EX 7-9 Internal control of cash receipts **OBJ. 2, 3**

The procedures used for over-the-counter receipts are as follows. At the close of each day's business, the sales clerks count the cash in their respective cash drawers, after which they determine the amount recorded by the cash register and prepare the memo cash form, noting any discrepancies. An employee from the cashier's office counts the cash, compares the total with the memo, and takes the cash to the cashier's office.

a. Indicate the weak link in internal control.

b. How can the weakness be corrected?

EX 7-10 Internal control of cash receipts **OBJ. 2, 3**

Sergio Flores works at the drive-through window of Big & Bad Burgers. Occasionally, when a drive-through customer orders, Sergio fills the order and pockets the customer's money. He does not ring up the order on the cash register.

Identify the internal control weaknesses that exist at Big & Bad Burgers, and discuss what can be done to prevent this theft.

EX 7-11 Internal control of cash receipts **OBJ. 2, 3**

The mailroom employees send all remittances and remittance advices to the cashier. The cashier deposits the cash in the bank and forwards the remittance advices and duplicate deposit slips to the Accounting Department.

a. Indicate the weak link in internal control in the handling of cash receipts.

b. How can the weakness be corrected?

EX 7-12 Entry for cash sales; cash short **OBJ. 2, 3**

The actual cash received from cash sales was $114,850, and the amount indicated by the cash register total was $114,975. Journalize the entry to record the cash receipts and cash sales.

EX 7-13 Entry for cash sales; cash over **OBJ. 2, 3**

The actual cash received from cash sales was $32,730, and the amount indicated by the cash register total was $32,690. Journalize the entry to record the cash receipts and cash sales.

EX 7-14 Internal control of cash payments **OBJ. 2, 3**

Abbe Co. is a small merchandising company with a manual accounting system. An investigation revealed that in spite of a sufficient bank balance, a significant amount of available cash discounts had been lost because of failure to make timely payments. In addition, it was discovered that the invoices for several purchases had been paid twice.

Outline procedures for the payment of vendors' invoices, so that the possibilities of losing available cash discounts and of paying an invoice a second time will be minimized.

EX 7-15 Internal control of cash payments **OBJ. 2, 3**

Paragon Tech Company, a communications equipment manufacturer, recently fell victim to a fraud scheme developed by one of its employees. To understand the scheme, it is necessary to review Paragon Tech's procedures for the purchase of services.

The purchasing agent is responsible for ordering services (such as repairs to a photocopy machine or office cleaning) after receiving a service requisition from an authorized manager. However, since no tangible goods are delivered, a receiving report is not prepared. When the Accounting Department receives an invoice billing Paragon Tech for a service call, the accounts payable clerk calls the manager who requested the service in order to verify that it was performed.

The fraud scheme involves Mae Jansma, the manager of plant and facilities. Mae arranged for her uncle's company, Radiate Systems, to be placed on Paragon Tech's approved vendor list. Mae did not disclose the family relationship.

On several occasions, Mae would submit a requisition for services to be provided by Radiate Systems. However, the service requested was really not needed, and it was never performed. Radiate Systems would bill Paragon Tech for the service and then split the cash payment with Mae.

Explain what changes should be made to Paragon Tech's procedures for ordering and paying for services in order to prevent such occurrences in the future.

EX 7-16 Bank reconciliation **OBJ. 5**

Identify each of the following reconciling items as: (a) an addition to the cash balance according to the bank statement, (b) a deduction from the cash balance according to the bank statement, (c) an addition to the cash balance according to the company's records, or (d) a deduction from the cash balance according to the company's records. (None of the transactions reported by bank debit and credit memos have been recorded by the company.)

1. Bank service charges, $30.
2. Check of a customer returned by bank to company because of insufficient funds, $1,750.
3. Check for $390 incorrectly recorded by the company as $930.
4. Check for $50 incorrectly charged by bank as $500.
5. Deposit in transit, $9,700.
6. Outstanding checks, $33,110.
7. Note collected by bank, $24,600.

EX 7-17 Entries based on bank reconciliation **OBJ. 5**

Which of the reconciling items listed in Exercise 7-16 require an entry in the company's accounts?

EX 7-18 Bank reconciliation **OBJ. 5**

✔ **Adjusted balance: $31,670**

The following data were accumulated for use in reconciling the bank account of Allenby Co. for August:

1. Cash balance according to the company's records at August 31, $31,080.
2. Cash balance according to the bank statement at August 31, $38,280.
3. Checks outstanding, $12,460.
4. Deposit in transit, not recorded by bank, $5,850.
5. A check for $180 in payment of an account was erroneously recorded in the check register as $810.
6. Bank debit memo for service charges, $40.

a. Prepare a bank reconciliation, using the format shown in Exhibit 7.

b. If the balance sheet were prepared for Allenby Co. on August 31, what amount should be reported for cash?

c. Must a bank reconciliation always balance (reconcile)?

EX 7-19 Entries for bank reconciliation **OBJ. 5**

Using the data presented in Exercise 7-18, journalize the entry or entries that should be made by the company.

EX 7-20 Entries for note collected by bank **OBJ. 5**

Accompanying a bank statement for Borsa Company is a credit memo for $18,200, representing the principal ($17,500) and interest ($700) on a note that had been collected by the bank. The company had been notified by the bank at the time of the collection, but had made no entries. Journalize the entry that should be made by the company to bring the accounting records up to date.

EX 7-21 Bank reconciliation **OBJ. 5**

✔ **Adjusted balance: $23,915**

An accounting clerk for Chesner Co. prepared the following bank reconciliation:

(Continued)

Chesner Co.
Bank Reconciliation
July 31, 2014

Cash balance according to company's records		$11,100
Add: Outstanding checks	$ 3,585	
Error by Chesner Co. in recording Check No. 1056 as $950 instead of $590	360	
Note for $12,000 collected by bank, including interest	12,480	16,425
		$27,525
Deduct: Deposit in transit on July 31	$ 7,200	
Bank service charges	25	7,225
Cash balance according to bank statement		$20,300

a. From the data in the above bank reconciliation, prepare a new bank reconciliation for Chesner Co., using the format shown in the illustrative problem.

b. If a balance sheet were prepared for Chesner Co. on July 31, 2014, what amount should be reported for cash?

EX 7-22 Bank reconciliation

OBJ. 5

✔ **Corrected adjusted balance: $19,780**

Identify the errors in the following bank reconciliation:

Poway Co.
Bank Reconciliation
For the Month Ended June 30, 2014

Cash balance according to bank statement			$16,185
Add outstanding checks:			
No. 1067		$ 575	
1106		470	
1110		1,050	
1113		910	3,005
			$19,190
Deduct deposit of June 30, not recorded by bank			6,600
Adjusted balance			$12,590
Cash balance according to company's records			$ 8,985
Add: Proceeds of note collected by bank:			
Principal	$6,000		
Interest	300	$6,300	
Service charges		15	6,315
			$15,300
Deduct: Check returned because of insufficient funds		$ 890	
Error in recording June 17 deposit of $7,150 as $1,750		5,400	6,290
Adjusted balance			$ 9,010

EX 7-23 Using bank reconciliation to determine cash receipts stolen

OBJ. 2, 3, 5

Alaska Impressions Co. records all cash receipts on the basis of its cash register tapes. Alaska Impressions Co. discovered during October 2014 that one of its sales clerks had stolen an undetermined amount of cash receipts by taking the daily deposits to the bank. The following data have been gathered for October:

Cash in bank according to the general ledger	$11,680
Cash according to the October 31, 2014, bank statement	13,275
Outstanding checks as of October 31, 2014	3,670
Bank service charge for October	40
Note receivable, including interest collected by bank in October	2,100

No deposits were in transit on October 31.

a. Determine the amount of cash receipts stolen by the sales clerk.

b. What accounting controls would have prevented or detected this theft?

EX 7-24 Petty cash fund entries — OBJ. 6

Journalize the entries to record the following:

a. Check No. 33694 is issued to establish a petty cash fund of $900.

b. The amount of cash in the petty cash fund is now $70. Check No. 33749 is issued to replenish the fund, based on the following summary of petty cash receipts: office supplies, $525; miscellaneous selling expense, $190; miscellaneous administrative expense, $85. (Since the amount of the check to replenish the fund plus the balance in the fund do not equal $900, record the discrepancy in the cash short and over account.)

EX 7-25 Variation in cash flows — OBJ. 7

Mattel, Inc., designs, manufactures, and markets toy products worldwide. Mattel's toys include Barbie™ fashion dolls and accessories, Hot Wheels™, and Fisher-Price brands. For a recent year, Mattel reported the following net cash flows from operating activities (in thousands):

First quarter ending March 31	$ (41,844)
Second quarter ending June 30	(184,934)
Third quarter ending September 30	(55,548)
Fourth quarter ending December 31	955,600

Explain why Mattel reported negative net cash flows from operating activities during the first three quarters and a large positive cash flow for the fourth quarter, with overall net positive cash flow for the year.

EX 7-26 Cash to monthly cash expenses ratio — OBJ. 8

F·A·I

During 2014, El Dorado Inc. has monthly cash expenses of $168,500. On December 31, 2014, the cash balance is $1,415,400.

a. Compute the ratio of cash to monthly cash expenses.

b. Based on (a), what are the implications for El Dorado Inc.?

EX 7-27 Cash to monthly cash expenses ratio — OBJ. 8

F·A·I

Capstone Turbine Corporation produces and sells turbine generators for such applications as charging electric, hybrid vehicles. Capstone Turbine reported the following financial data for a recent year (in thousands):

Net cash flows from operating activities	$(21,899)
Cash and cash equivalents	33,456

a. Determine the monthly cash expenses. Round to one decimal place.

b. Determine the ratio of cash to monthly cash expenses. Round to one decimal place.

c. Based on your analysis, do you believe that Capstone Turbine will remain in business?

EX 7-28 Cash to monthly cash expenses ratio — OBJ. 8

F·A·I

Allos Therapeutics, Inc., is a biopharmaceutical company that develops drugs for the treatment of cancer. Allos Therapeutics reported the following financial data (in thousands) for three recent years:

	For Years Ended December 31		
	Year 3	Year 2	Year 1
Cash and cash equivalents	$ 48,402	$141,423	$ 30,696
Net cash flows from operations	(63,656)	(62,199)	(42,850)

(Continued)

a. Determine the monthly cash expenses for Year 3, Year 2, and Year 1. Round to one decimal place.

b. Determine the ratio of cash to monthly cash expenses for Year 3, Year 2, and Year 1 as of December 31. Round to one decimal place.

c. Based on (a) and (b), comment on Allos Therapeutics' ratio of cash to monthly operating expenses for Year 3, Year 2, and Year 1.

Problems Series A

PR 7-1A Evaluating internal control of cash — OBJ. 2, 3

The following procedures were recently installed by Raspberry Creek Company:

a. After necessary approvals have been obtained for the payment of a voucher, the treasurer signs and mails the check. The treasurer then stamps the voucher and supporting documentation as paid and returns the voucher and supporting documentation to the accounts payable clerk for filing.

b. The accounts payable clerk prepares a voucher for each disbursement. The voucher along with the supporting documentation is forwarded to the treasurer's office for approval.

c. Along with petty cash expense receipts for postage, office supplies, etc., several post-dated employee checks are in the petty cash fund.

d. At the end of the day, cash register clerks are required to use their own funds to make up any cash shortages in their registers.

e. At the end of each day, all cash receipts are placed in the bank's night depository.

f. At the end of each day, an accounting clerk compares the duplicate copy of the daily cash deposit slip with the deposit receipt obtained from the bank.

g. All mail is opened by the mail clerk, who forwards all cash remittances to the cashier. The cashier prepares a listing of the cash receipts and forwards a copy of the list to the accounts receivable clerk for recording in the accounts.

h. The bank reconciliation is prepared by the cashier, who works under the supervision of the treasurer.

Instructions

Indicate whether each of the procedures of internal control over cash represents (1) a strength or (2) a weakness. For each weakness, indicate why it exists.

PR 7-2A Transactions for petty cash, cash short and over — OBJ. 3, 6

SPREADSHEET

Picasso Restoration Company completed the following selected transactions during May 2014:

May 1. Established a petty cash fund of $800.

10. The cash sales for the day, according to the cash register records, totaled $3,345. The actual cash received from cash sales was $3,358.

31. Petty cash on hand was $275. Replenished the petty cash fund for the following disbursements, each evidenced by a petty cash receipt:

May 3. Store supplies, $290.

7. Express charges on merchandise sold, $70 (Delivery Expense).

9. Office supplies, $12.

13. Office supplies, $25.

19. Postage stamps, $18 (Office Supplies).

21. Repair to office file cabinet lock, $20 (Miscellaneous Administrative Expense).

May 22. Postage due on special delivery letter, $16 (Miscellaneous Administrative Expense).

24. Express charges on merchandise sold, $40 (Delivery Expense).

30. Office supplies, $10.

May 31. The cash sales for the day, according to the cash register records, totaled $6,155. The actual cash received from cash sales was $6,125.

31. Decreased the petty cash fund by $50.

Instructions

Journalize the transactions.

PR 7-3A Bank reconciliation and entries **OBJ. 5**

✔ 1. Adjusted balance: $22,485

SPREADSHEET

GENERAL LEDGER

The cash account for Remedy Medical Co. at April 30, 2014, indicated a balance of $18,885. The bank statement indicated a balance of $23,775 on April 30, 2014. Comparing the bank statement and the accompanying canceled checks and memos with the records revealed the following reconciling items:

a. Checks outstanding totaled $7,840.
b. A deposit of $3,580, representing receipts of April 30, had been made too late to appear on the bank statement.
c. The bank collected $3,780 on a note left for collection. The face of note was $3,600.
d. A check for $770 returned with the statement had been incorrectly recorded by Remedy Medical Co. as $700. The check was for the payment of an obligation to Copelin Co. for a purchase on account.
e. A check drawn for $330 had been erroneously charged by the bank as $3,300.
f. Bank service charges for April amounted to $110.

Instructions

1. Prepare a bank reconciliation.
2. Journalize the necessary entries. The accounts have not been closed.
3. If a balance sheet were prepared for Remedy Medical Co. on April 30, 2014, what amount should be reported as cash?

PR 7-4A Bank reconciliation and entries **OBJ. 5**

✔ 1. Adjusted balance: $8,260

SPREADSHEET

GENERAL LEDGER

The cash account for Fit Bike Co. at August 1, 2014, indicated a balance of $12,190. During August, the total cash deposited was $28,100 and checks written totaled $33,010. The bank statement indicated a balance of $12,550 on August 31. Comparing the bank statement, the canceled checks, and the accompanying memos with the records revealed the following reconciling items:

a. Checks outstanding totaled $7,440.
b. A deposit of $2,880, representing receipts of August 31, had been made too late to appear on the bank statement.
c. The bank had collected for Fit Bike Co. $2,080 on a note left for collection. The face of the note was $2,000.
d. A check for $580 returned with the statement had been incorrectly charged by the bank as $850.
e. A check for $640 returned with the statement had been recorded by Fit Bike Co. as $460. The check was for the payment of an obligation to Brown Co. on account.
f. Bank service charges for August amounted to $20.
g. A check for $900 from Murdock Co. was returned by the bank due to insufficient funds.

Instructions

1. Prepare a bank reconciliation as of August 31.
2. Journalize the necessary entries. The accounts have not been closed.
3. If a balance sheet were prepared for Fit Bike Co. on August 31, 2014, what amount should be reported as cash?

PR 7-5A Bank reconciliation and entries

OBJ. 5

✔ **1. Adjusted balance: $13,216**

SPREADSHEET

Beeler Furniture Company deposits all cash receipts each Wednesday and Friday in a night depository, after banking hours. The data required to reconcile the bank statement as of June 30 have been taken from various documents and records and are reproduced as follows. The sources of the data are printed in capital letters. All checks were written for payments on account.

CASH ACCOUNT:	
Balance as of June 1	$9,317.40
CASH RECEIPTS FOR MONTH OF JUNE	$9,223.76
DUPLICATE DEPOSIT TICKETS:	
Date and amount of each deposit in June:	

Date	Amount	Date	Amount	Date	Amount
June 1	$1,080.50	June 10	$ 996.61	June 22	$ 897.34
3	854.17	15	882.95	24	947.21
8	840.50	17	1,606.74	30	1,117.74

CHECKS WRITTEN:

Number and amount of each check issued in June:

Check No.	Amount	Check No.	Amount	Check No.	Amount
740	$237.50	747	Void	754	$ 449.75
741	495.15	748	$450.90	755	272.75
742	501.90	749	640.13	756	113.95
743	761.30	750	276.77	757	407.95
744	506.88	751	299.37	758	259.60
745	117.25	752	537.01	759	901.50
746	298.66	753	380.95	760	486.39
Total amount of checks issued in June					$8,395.66

BANK RECONCILIATION FOR PRECEDING MONTH:

Beeler Furniture Company
Bank Reconciliation
May 31, 20—

Cash balance according to bank statement		$ 9,447.20
Add deposit for May 31, not recorded by bank		690.25
		$10,137.45
Deduct outstanding checks:		
No. 731	$162.15	
736	345.95	
738	251.40	
739	60.55	820.05
Adjusted balance		$ 9,317.40
Cash balance according to company's records		$ 9,352.50
Deduct service charges		35.10
Adjusted balance		$ 9,317.40

Instructions

1. Prepare a bank reconciliation as of June 30. If errors in recording deposits or checks are discovered, assume that the errors were made by the company. Assume that all deposits are from cash sales. All checks are written to satisfy accounts payable.
2. Journalize the necessary entries. The accounts have not been closed.
3. What is the amount of Cash that should appear on the balance sheet as of June 30?
4. Assume that a canceled check for $390 has been incorrectly recorded by the bank as $930. Briefly explain how the error would be included in a bank reconciliation and how it should be corrected.

JUNE BANK STATEMENT:

PAGE 1

MEMBER FDIC

AMERICAN NATIONAL BANK
OF CHICAGO

CHICAGO, IL 60603 (312)441-1239

BEELER FURNITURE COMPANY

	ACCOUNT NUMBER	
	FROM 6/01/20–	TO 6/30/20–
	BALANCE	9,447.20
9	DEPOSITS	8,691.77
20	WITHDRAWALS	7,599.26
4	OTHER DEBITS AND CREDITS	3,085.00CR
	NEW BALANCE	13,624.71

CHECKS AND OTHER DEBITS				DEPOSITS	DATE	BALANCE
No.731	162.15	No.736	345.95	690.25	6/01	9,629.35
No.739	60.55	No.740	237.50	1,080.50	6/02	10,411.80
No.741	495.15	No.742	501.90	854.17	6/04	10,268.92
No.743	671.30	No.744	506.88	840.50	6/09	9,931.24
No.745	117.25	No.746	298.66	MS 3,500.00	6/09	13,015.33
No.748	450.90	No.749	640.13	MS 210.00	6/09	12,134.30
No.750	276.77	No.751	299.37	896.61	6/11	12,454.77
No.752	537.01	No.753	380.95	882.95	6/16	12,419.76
No.754	449.75	No.755	272.75	1,606.74	6/18	13,304.00
No.757	407.95	No.760	486.39	897.34	6/23	13,307.00
				942.71	6/25	14,249.71
		NSF	550.00		6/28	13,699.71
		SC	75.00		6/30	13,624.71

EC — ERROR CORRECTION
MS — MISCELLANEOUS
NSF — NOT SUFFICIENT FUNDS
OD — OVERDRAFT
PS — PAYMENT STOPPED
SC — SERVICE CHARGE

*** *** ***

THE RECONCILEMENT OF THIS STATEMENT WITH YOUR RECORDS IS ESSENTIAL.
ANY ERROR OR EXCEPTION SHOULD BE REPORTED IMMEDIATELY.

Problems Series B

PR 7-1B Evaluating internal control of cash

OBJ. 2, 3

The following procedures were recently installed by The China Shop:

a. All sales are rung up on the cash register, and a receipt is given to the customer. All sales are recorded on a record locked inside the cash register.

b. Each cashier is assigned a separate cash register drawer to which no other cashier has access.

c. At the end of a shift, each cashier counts the cash in his or her cash register, unlocks the cash register record, and compares the amount of cash with the amount on the record to determine cash shortages and overages.

d. Checks received through the mail are given daily to the accounts receivable clerk for recording collections on account and for depositing in the bank.

e. Vouchers and all supporting documents are perforated with a PAID designation after being paid by the treasurer.

f. Disbursements are made from the petty cash fund only after a petty cash receipt has been completed and signed by the payee.

g. The bank reconciliation is prepared by the cashier.

Instructions

Indicate whether each of the procedures of internal control over cash represents (1) a strength or (2) a weakness. For each weakness, indicate why it exists.

PR 7-2B Transactions for petty cash, cash short and over

OBJ. 3, 6

SPREADSHEET

Cedar Springs Company completed the following selected transactions during June 2014:

June 1. Established a petty cash fund of $1,000.

12. The cash sales for the day, according to the cash register records, totaled $9,440. The actual cash received from cash sales was $9,506.

30. Petty cash on hand was $46. Replenished the petty cash fund for the following disbursements, each evidenced by a petty cash receipt:

    June 2. Store supplies, $375.

    10. Express charges on merchandise purchased, $105 (Merchandise Inventory).

    14. Office supplies, $85.

    15. Office supplies, $90.

    18. Postage stamps, $33 (Office Supplies).

    20. Repair to fax, $100 (Miscellaneous Administrative Expense).

    21. Repair to office door lock, $25 (Miscellaneous Administrative Expense).

    22. Postage due on special delivery letter, $9 (Miscellaneous Administrative Expense).

    28. Express charges on merchandise purchased, $110 (Merchandise Inventory).

30. The cash sales for the day, according to the cash register records, totaled $13,390. The actual cash received from cash sales was $13,350.

30. Increased the petty cash fund by $200.

Instructions

Journalize the transactions.

PR 7-3B Bank reconciliation and entries

OBJ. 5

✔ 1. Adjusted balance: $24,305

SPREADSHEET

GENERAL LEDGER

The cash account for Stone Systems at July 31, 2014, indicated a balance of $17,750. The bank statement indicated a balance of $33,650 on July 31, 2014. Comparing the bank statement and the accompanying canceled checks and memos with the records reveals the following reconciling items:

a. Checks outstanding totaled $17,865.
b. A deposit of $9,150, representing receipts of July 31, had been made too late to appear on the bank statement.
c. The bank had collected $6,095 on a note left for collection. The face of the note was $5,750.
d. A check for $390 returned with the statement had been incorrectly recorded by Stone Systems as $930. The check was for the payment of an obligation to Holland Co. for the purchase of office supplies on account.
e. A check drawn for $1,810 had been incorrectly charged by the bank as $1,180.
f. Bank service charges for July amounted to $80.

Instructions

1. Prepare a bank reconciliation.
2. Journalize the necessary entries. The accounts have not been closed.
3. If a balance sheet were prepared for Stone Systems on July 31, 2014, what amount should be reported as cash?

PR 7-4B Bank reconciliation and entries

OBJ. 5

✔ 1. Adjusted balance: $78,535

SPREADSHEET

GENERAL LEDGER

The cash account for Collegiate Sports Co. on November 1, 2014, indicated a balance of $81,145. During November, the total cash deposited was $293,150, and checks written totaled $307,360. The bank statement indicated a balance of $112,675 on November 30, 2014. Comparing the bank statement, the canceled checks, and the accompanying memos with the records revealed the following reconciling items:

a. Checks outstanding totaled $41,840.
b. A deposit of $12,200, representing receipts of November 30, had been made too late to appear on the bank statement.
c. A check for $7,250 had been incorrectly charged by the bank as $2,750.

d. A check for $760 returned with the statement had been recorded by Collegiate Sports Co. as $7,600. The check was for the payment of an obligation to Ramirez Co. on account.

e. The bank had collected for Collegiate Sports Co. $7,385 on a note left for collection. The face of the note was $7,000.

f. Bank service charges for November amounted to $125.

g. A check for $2,500 from Hallen Academy was returned by the bank because of insufficient funds.

Instructions

1. Prepare a bank reconciliation as of November 30.
2. Journalize the necessary entries. The accounts have not been closed.
3. If a balance sheet were prepared for Collegiate Sports Co. on November 30, 2014, what amount should be reported as cash?

PR 7-5B Bank reconciliation and entries

OBJ. 5

✔ 1. Adjusted balance: $11,494

SPREADSHEET

Sunshine Interiors deposits all cash receipts each Wednesday and Friday in a night depository, after banking hours. The data required to reconcile the bank statement as of July 31 have been taken from various documents and records and are reproduced as follows. The sources of the data are printed in capital letters. All checks were written for payments on account.

BANK RECONCILIATION FOR PRECEDING MONTH (DATED JUNE 30):		
Cash balance according to bank statement		$ 9,422.80
Add deposit of June 30, not recorded by bank		780.80
		$10,203.60
Deduct outstanding checks:		
No. 580	$310.10	
No. 602	85.50	
No. 612	92.50	
No. 613	137.50	625.60
Adjusted balance		$ 9,578.00
Cash balance according to company's records		$ 9,605.70
Deduct service charges		27.70
Adjusted balance		$ 9,578.00
CASH ACCOUNT:		
Balance as of July 1		$ 9,578.00
CASH RECEIPTS FOR MONTH OF JULY		6,465.42

DUPLICATE DEPOSIT TICKETS:

Date and amount of each deposit in July:

Date	Amount	Date	Amount	Date	Amount
July 2	$569.50	July 12	$580.70	July 23	$ 713.45
5	701.80	16	600.10	26	601.50
9	819.24	19	701.26	31	1,177.87

CHECKS WRITTEN:

Number and amount of each check issued in July:

Check No.	Amount	Check No.	Amount	Check No.	Amount
614	$243.50	621	$309.50	628	$ 837.70
615	350.10	622	Void	629	329.90
616	279.90	623	Void	630	882.80
617	395.50	624	707.01	631	1,081.56
618	435.40	625	158.63	632	325.40
619	320.10	626	550.03	633	310.08
620	238.87	627	381.73	634	241.71
Total amount of checks issued in July					$8,379.42

(Continued)

JULY BANK STATEMENT:

MEMBER FDIC

AMERICAN NATIONAL BANK OF DETROIT

DETROIT, MI 48201-2500 (313)933-8547

SUNSHINE INTERIORS

	PAGE	1
	ACCOUNT NUMBER	
	FROM 7/01/20–	TO 7/31/20–
	BALANCE	9,422.80
9	DEPOSITS	6,086.35
20	WITHDRAWALS	7,656.74
4	OTHER DEBITS AND CREDITS	3,749.00CR
	NEW BALANCE	11,601.41

CHECKS AND OTHER DEBITS					DEPOSITS	DATE	BALANCE
No.580	310.10	No.612	92.50		780.80	07/01	9,801.00
No.602	85.50	No.614	243.50		569.50	07/03	10,041.50
No.615	350.10	No.616	279.90		701.80	07/06	10,113.30
No.617	395.50	No.618	435.40		819.24	07/11	10,101.64
No.619	320.10	No.620	238.87		580.70	07/13	10,123.37
No.621	309.50	No.624	707.01		MS 4,000.00	07/14	13,106.86
No.625	158.63	No.626	550.03		MS 160.00	07/14	12,558.20
No.627	318.73	No.629	329.90		600.10	07/17	12,509.67
No.630	882.80	No.631	1,081.56	NSF 375.00		07/20	10,170.31
No.632	325.40	No.634	241.71		701.26	07/21	10,304.46
					731.45	07/24	11,035.91
					601.50	07/28	11,637.41
		SC	36.00			07/31	11,601.41

EC — ERROR CORRECTION
MS — MISCELLANEOUS
NSF — NOT SUFFICIENT FUNDS
OD — OVERDRAFT
PS — PAYMENT STOPPED
SC — SERVICE CHARGE

* * *

THE RECONCILEMENT OF THIS STATEMENT WITH YOUR RECORDS IS ESSENTIAL.
ANY ERROR OR EXCEPTION SHOULD BE REPORTED IMMEDIATELY.

Instructions

1. Prepare a bank reconciliation as of July 31. If errors in recording deposits or checks are discovered, assume that the errors were made by the company. Assume that all deposits are from cash sales. All checks are written to satisfy accounts payable.
2. Journalize the necessary entries. The accounts have not been closed.
3. What is the amount of Cash that should appear on the balance sheet as of July 31?
4. Assume that a canceled check for $180 has been incorrectly recorded by the bank as $1,800. Briefly explain how the error would be included in a bank reconciliation and how it should be corrected.

Cases & Projects

CP 7-1 Ethics and professional conduct in business

During the preparation of the bank reconciliation for Building Concepts Co., Joel Kimmel, the assistant controller, discovered that Lone Peak National Bank incorrectly recorded a $3,290 check written by Building Concepts Co. as $329. Joel has decided not to notify the bank but wait for the bank to detect the error. Joel plans to record the $2,961 error as Other Income if the bank fails to detect the error within the next three months.

Discuss whether Joel is behaving in a professional manner.

CP 7-2 Internal controls

The following is an excerpt from a conversation between two sales clerks, Jean Moen and Sara Cheney. Jean and Sara are employed by Turpin Meadows Electronics, a locally owned and operated electronics retail store.

Jean: Did you hear the news?

Sara: What news?

Jean: Neal and Linda were both arrested this morning.

Sara: What? Arrested? You're putting me on!

Jean: No, really! The police arrested them first thing this morning. Put them in handcuffs, read them their rights—the whole works. It was unreal!

Sara: What did they do?

Jean: Well, apparently they were filling out merchandise refund forms for fictitious customers and then taking the cash.

Sara: I guess I never thought of that. How did they catch them?

Jean: The store manager noticed that returns were twice that of last year and seemed to be increasing. When he confronted Neal, he became flustered and admitted to taking the cash, apparently over $9,000 in just three months. They're going over the last six months' transactions to try to determine how much Linda stole. She apparently started stealing first.

Suggest appropriate control procedures that would have prevented or detected the theft of cash.

CP 7-3 Internal controls

The following is an excerpt from a conversation between the store manager of Wholesome Grocery Stores, Kara Dahl, and Lynn Shutes, president of Wholesome Grocery Stores.

Lynn: Kara, I'm concerned about this new scanning system.

Kara: What's the problem?

Lynn: Well, how do we know the clerks are ringing up all the merchandise?

Kara: That's one of the strong points about the system. The scanner automatically rings up each item, based on its bar code. We update the prices daily, so we're sure that the sale is rung up for the right price.

Lynn: That's not my concern. What keeps a clerk from pretending to scan items and then simply not charging his friends? If his friends were buying 10–15 items, it would be easy for the clerk to pass through several items with his finger over the bar code or just pass the merchandise through the scanner with the wrong side showing. It would look normal for anyone observing. In the old days, we at least could hear the cash register ringing up each sale.

Kara: I see your point.

Suggest ways that Wholesome Grocery Stores could prevent or detect the theft of merchandise as described.

CP 7-4 Ethics and professional conduct in business

Doris Tidwell and Jo Yost are both cash register clerks for Fuller's Organic Markets. Tom Ward is the store manager for Fuller's Organic Markets. The following is an excerpt of a conversation between Doris and Jo:

Doris: Jo, how long have you been working for Fuller's Organic Markets?

Jo: Almost five years this April. You just started two weeks ago . . . right?

Doris: Yes. Do you mind if I ask you a question?

Jo: No, go ahead.

Doris: What I want to know is, have they always had this rule that if your cash register is short at the end of the day, you have to make up the shortage out of your own pocket?

Jo: Yes, as long as I've been working here.

Doris: Well, it's the pits. Last week I had to pay in almost $40.

Jo: It's not that big a deal. I just make sure that I'm not short at the end of the day.

Doris: How do you do that?

Jo: I just shortchange a few customers early in the day. There are a few jerks that deserve it anyway. Most of the time, their attention is elsewhere and they don't think to check their change.

Doris: What happens if you're over at the end of the day?

Jo: Tom lets me keep it as long as it doesn't get to be too large. I've not been short in over a year. I usually clear about $20 to $30 extra per day.

Discuss this case from the viewpoint of proper controls and professional behavior.

CP 7-5 Bank reconciliation and internal control

The records of Parker Company indicate a July 31 cash balance of $10,400, which includes undeposited receipts for July 30 and 31. The cash balance on the bank statement as of July 31 is $10,575. This balance includes a note of $2,250 plus $150 interest collected by the bank but not recorded in the journal. Checks outstanding on July 31 were as follows: No. 2670, $1,050; No. 3679, $675; No. 3690, $1,650; No. 5148, $225; No. 5149, $750; and No. 5151, $800.

On July 25, the cashier resigned, effective at the end of the month. Before leaving on July 31, the cashier prepared the following bank reconciliation:

Cash balance per books, July 31		$10,400
Add outstanding checks:		
No. 5148	$225	
5149	750	
5151	800	1,675
		$12,075
Less undeposited receipts		1,500
Cash balance per bank, July 31		$10,575
Deduct unrecorded note with interest		2,400
True cash, July 31		$ 8,175

Calculator Tape of Outstanding Checks:
0*
225+
750+
800+
1,675*

Subsequently, the owner of Parker Company discovered that the cashier had stolen an unknown amount of undeposited receipts, leaving only $1,500 to be deposited on July 31. The owner, a close family friend, has asked your help in determining the amount that the former cashier has stolen.

1. Determine the amount the cashier stole from Parker Company. Show your computations in good form.
2. How did the cashier attempt to conceal the theft?
3. a. Identify two major weaknesses in internal controls, which allowed the cashier to steal the undeposited cash receipts.
   b. Recommend improvements in internal controls, so that similar types of thefts of undeposited cash receipts can be prevented.

CP 7-6 Observe internal controls over cash

Group Project

Select a business in your community and observe its internal controls over cash receipts and cash payments. The business could be a bank or a bookstore, restaurant, department store, or other retailer. In groups of three or four, identify and discuss the similarities and differences in each business's cash internal controls.

CP 7-7 Cash to monthly cash expenses ratio

F·A·I

TearLab Corp. is a health care company that specializes in developing diagnostic devices for eye disease. TearLab reported the following data (in thousands) for three recent years:

	For Years Ended December 31		
	Year 3	Year 2	Year 1
Cash and cash equivalents	$ 2,726	$ 106	$ 2,565
Net cash flows from operations	(4,540)	(4,098)	(9,435)

1. Determine the monthly cash expenses for Year 3, Year 2, and Year 1. Round to one decimal place.
2. Determine the ratio of cash to monthly cash expenses as of December 31, for Year 3, Year 2, and Year 1. Round to one decimal place.
3. Based on (1) and (2), comment on TearLab's ratio of cash to monthly operating expenses for Year 3, Year 2, and Year 1.

CHAPTER 8

Receivables

Oakley, Inc.

The sale and purchase of merchandise involves the exchange of goods for cash. However, the point at which cash actually changes hands varies with the transaction. Consider transactions by **Oakley, Inc.**, a worldwide leader in the design, development, manufacture, and distribution of premium sunglasses, goggles, prescription eyewear, apparel, footwear, and accessories. Not only does the company sell its products through three different company-owned retail chains, but it also has approximately 10,000 independent distributors.

If you were to buy a pair of sunglasses at an Oakley Vault, which is one of the company's retail outlet stores, you would have to pay cash or use a credit card to pay for the glasses before you left the store. However, Oakley allows its distributors to purchase sunglasses "on account." These sales on account are recorded as receivables due from the distributors.

As an individual, you also might build up a trusted financial history with a local company or department store that would allow you to purchase merchandise on account. Like Oakley's distributors, your purchase on account would be recorded as an account receivable. Such credit transactions facilitate sales and are a significant current asset for many businesses.

This chapter describes common classifications of receivables, illustrates how to account for uncollectible receivables, and demonstrates the reporting of receivables on the balance sheet.

Learning Objectives

After studying this chapter, you should be able to: *Example Exercises*

Obj.	Objective	Example Exercises
1	**Describe the common classes of receivables.**	
	Classification of Receivables	
	Accounts Receivable	
	Notes Receivable	
	Other Receivables	
2	**Describe the accounting for uncollectible receivables.**	
	Uncollectible Receivables	
3	**Describe the direct write-off method of accounting for uncollectible receivables.**	
	Direct Write-Off Method for Uncollectible Accounts	EE 8-1
4	**Describe the allowance method of accounting for uncollectible receivables.**	
	Allowance Method for Uncollectible Accounts	
	Write-Offs to the Allowance Account	EE 8-2
	Estimating Uncollectibles	EE 8-3
		EE 8-4
5	**Compare the direct write-off and allowance methods of accounting for uncollectible accounts.**	
	Comparing Direct Write-Off and Allowance Methods	
6	**Describe the accounting for notes receivable.**	
	Notes Receivable	
	Characteristics of Notes Receivable	
	Accounting for Notes Receivable	EE 8-5
7	**Describe the reporting of receivables on the balance sheet.**	
	Reporting Receivables on the Balance Sheet	
8	**Describe and illustrate the use of accounts receivable turnover and number of days' sales in receivables to evaluate a company's efficiency in collecting its receivables.**	
	Financial Analysis and Interpretation: Accounts Receivable Turnover and Number of Days' Sales in Receivables	EE 8-6

At a Glance 8 Page 379

OBJ 1 Describe the common classes of receivables.

Classification of Receivables

The receivables that result from sales on account are normally accounts receivable or notes receivable. The term **receivables** includes all money claims against other entities, including people, companies, and other organizations. Receivables are usually a significant portion of the total current assets.

A recent balance sheet of Caterpillar Inc. reported that receivables made up over 56% of its current assets.

Accounts Receivable

The most common transaction creating a receivable is selling merchandise or services on account (on credit). The receivable is recorded as a debit to Accounts Receivable. Such **accounts receivable** are normally collected within a short period, such as 30 or 60 days. They are classified on the balance sheet as a current asset.

Notes Receivable

Notes receivable are amounts that customers owe for which a formal, written instrument of credit has been issued. If notes receivable are expected to be collected within a year, they are classified on the balance sheet as a current asset.

Notes are often used for credit periods of more than 60 days. For example, an automobile dealer may require a down payment at the time of sale and accept a note or a series of notes for the remainder. Such notes usually provide for monthly payments.

Notes may also be used to settle a customer's account receivable. Notes and accounts receivable that result from sales transactions are sometimes called *trade receivables*. In this chapter, all notes and accounts receivable are from sales transactions.

Other Receivables

Other receivables include interest receivable, taxes receivable, and receivables from officers or employees. Other receivables are normally reported separately on the balance sheet. If they are expected to be collected within one year, they are classified as current assets. If collection is expected beyond one year, they are classified as noncurrent assets and reported under the caption *Investments.*

Uncollectible Receivables

OBJ 2 Describe the accounting for uncollectible receivables.

In prior chapters, the accounting for sales of merchandise or services on account (on credit) was described and illustrated. A major issue that has not yet been discussed is that some customers will not pay their accounts. That is, some accounts receivable will be uncollectible.

Companies may shift the risk of uncollectible receivables to other companies. For example, some retailers do not accept sales on account, but will only accept cash or credit cards. Such policies shift the risk to the credit card companies.

Companies may also sell their receivables. This is often the case when a company issues its own credit card. For example, Macy's and JCPenney issue their own credit cards. Selling receivables is called *factoring* the receivables. The buyer of the receivables is called a *factor.* An advantage of factoring is that the company selling its receivables immediately receives cash for operating and other needs. Also, depending on the factoring agreement, some of the risk of uncollectible accounts is shifted to the factor.

Regardless of how careful a company is in granting credit, some credit sales will be uncollectible. The operating expense recorded from uncollectible receivables is called **bad debt expense**, *uncollectible accounts expense*, or *doubtful accounts expense.*

There is no general rule for when an account becomes uncollectible. Some indications that an account may be uncollectible include the following:

1. The receivable is past due.
2. The customer does not respond to the company's attempts to collect.
3. The customer files for bankruptcy.
4. The customer closes its business.
5. The company cannot locate the customer.

Adams, Stevens & Bradley, Ltd. is a collection agency that operates on a contingency basis. That is, its fees are based on what it collects.

If a customer doesn't pay, a company may turn the account over to a collection agency. After the collection agency attempts to collect payment, any remaining balance in the account is considered worthless.

The two methods of accounting for uncollectible receivables are as follows:

1. The **direct write-off method** records bad debt expense only when an account is determined to be worthless.
2. The **allowance method** records bad debt expense by estimating uncollectible accounts at the end of the accounting period.

The direct write-off method is often used by small companies and companies with few receivables.[1] Generally accepted accounting principles (GAAP), however, require companies with a large amount of receivables to use the allowance method. As a result, most well-known companies such as General Electric, Pepsi, Intel, and FedEx use the allowance method.

Direct Write-Off Method for Uncollectible Accounts

OBJ 3 Describe the direct write-off method of accounting for uncollectible receivables.

Under the direct write-off method, Bad Debt Expense is not recorded until the customer's account is determined to be worthless. At that time, the customer's account receivable is written off.

1 The direct write-off method is also required for federal income tax purposes.

To illustrate, assume that on May 10 a $4,200 account receivable from D. L. Ross has been determined to be uncollectible. The entry to write off the account is as follows:

May	10	Bad Debt Expense	4,200	
		Accounts Receivable—D. L. Ross		4,200

An account receivable that has been written off may be collected later. In such cases, the account is reinstated by an entry that reverses the write-off entry. The cash received in payment is then recorded as a receipt on account.

To illustrate, assume that the D. L. Ross account of $4,200 written off on May 10 is later collected on November 21. The reinstatement and receipt of cash is recorded as follows:

Nov.	21	Accounts Receivable—D. L. Ross	4,200	
		Bad Debt Expense		4,200
	21	Cash	4,200	
		Accounts Receivable—D. L. Ross		4,200

The direct write-off method is used by businesses that sell most of their goods or services for cash or through the acceptance of MasterCard or VISA, which are recorded as cash sales. In such cases, receivables are a small part of the current assets and any bad debt expense is small. Examples of such businesses are a restaurant, a convenience store, and a small retail store.

Example Exercise 8-1 Direct Write-Off Method

OBJ 3

Journalize the following transactions, using the direct write-off method of accounting for uncollectible receivables:

July 9. Received $1,200 from Jay Burke and wrote off the remainder owed of $3,900 as uncollectible.
Oct. 11. Reinstated the account of Jay Burke and received $3,900 cash in full payment.

Follow My Example 8-1

July 9	Cash	1,200	
	Bad Debt Expense	3,900	
	Accounts Receivable—Jay Burke		5,100
Oct. 11	Accounts Receivable—Jay Burke	3,900	
	Bad Debt Expense		3,900
11	Cash	3,900	
	Accounts Receivable—Jay Burke		3,900

Practice Exercises: **PE 8-1A, PE 8-1B**

OBJ 4 Describe the allowance method of accounting for uncollectible receivables.

Allowance Method for Uncollectible Accounts

The allowance method estimates the uncollectible accounts receivable at the end of the accounting period. Based on this estimate, Bad Debt Expense is recorded by an adjusting entry.

To illustrate, assume that ExTone Company began operations August 1. As of the end of its accounting period on December 31, 2013, ExTone has an accounts receivable balance of $200,000. This balance includes some past due accounts. Based on industry averages, ExTone estimates that $30,000 of the December 31 accounts receivable will be uncollectible. However, on December 31, ExTone doesn't know which customer accounts will be uncollectible. Thus, specific customer accounts cannot be decreased or credited. Instead, a contra asset account, **Allowance for Doubtful Accounts**, is credited for the estimated bad debts.

Using the $30,000 estimate, the following adjusting entry is made on December 31:

2013 Dec.	31	Bad Debt Expense		30,000	
		Allowance for Doubtful Accounts			30,000
		Uncollectible accounts estimate.			

The preceding adjusting entry affects the income statement and balance sheet. On the income statement, the $30,000 of Bad Debt Expense will be matched against the related revenues of the period. On the balance sheet, the value of the receivables is reduced to the amount that is expected to be collected or realized. This amount, $170,000 ($200,000 – $30,000), is called the **net realizable value** of the receivables.

Note:
The adjusting entry reduces receivables to their net realizable value and matches the uncollectible expense with revenues.

After the preceding adjusting entry is recorded, Accounts Receivable still has a debit balance of $200,000. This balance is the total amount owed by customers on account on December 31 as supported by the accounts receivable subsidiary ledger. The accounts receivable contra account, Allowance for Doubtful Accounts, has a credit balance of $30,000.

Integrity, Objectivity, and Ethics in Business

SELLER BEWARE

A company in financial distress will still try to purchase goods and services on account. In these cases, rather than "buyer beware," it is more like "seller beware." Sellers must be careful in advancing credit to such companies, because trade creditors have low priority for cash payments in the event of bankruptcy. To help suppliers, third-party services specialize in evaluating court actions and payment decisions of financially distressed companies.

Write-Offs to the Allowance Account

When a customer's account is identified as uncollectible, it is written off against the allowance account. This requires the company to remove the specific accounts receivable and an equal amount from the allowance account.

To illustrate, on January 21, 2014, John Parker's account of $6,000 with ExTone Company is written off as follows:

2014 Jan.	21	Allowance for Doubtful Accounts		6,000	
		Accounts Receivable—John Parker			6,000

At the end of a period, Allowance for Doubtful Accounts will normally have a balance. This is because Allowance for Doubtful Accounts is based on an estimate. As a result, the total write-offs to the allowance account during the period will rarely equal the balance of the account at the beginning of the period. The allowance account will have a credit balance at the end of the period if the write-offs during the period are less than the beginning balance. It will have a debit balance if the write-offs exceed the beginning balance.

To illustrate, assume that during 2014 ExTone Company writes off $26,750 of uncollectible accounts, including the $6,000 account of John Parker recorded on January 21. Allowance for Doubtful Accounts will have a credit balance of $3,250 ($30,000 – $26,750), as shown below.

ALLOWANCE FOR DOUBTFUL ACCOUNTS

				Jan. 1	Balance	30,000
Total accounts written off $26,750	Jan.	21	6,000			
	Feb.	2	3,900			
	⋮		⋮			
				Dec. 31	Unadjusted balance	3,250

If ExTone Company had written off $32,100 in accounts receivable during 2014, Allowance for Doubtful Accounts would have a debit balance of $2,100, as shown below.

ALLOWANCE FOR DOUBTFUL ACCOUNTS

				Jan. 1	Balance	30,000
Total accounts written off $32,100	Jan.	21	6,000			
	Feb.	2	3,900			
	⋮		⋮			
Dec. 31	Unadjusted balance		2,100			

The allowance account balances (credit balance of $3,250 and debit balance of $2,100) in the preceding illustrations are *before* the end-of-period adjusting entry. After the end-of-period adjusting entry is recorded, Allowance for Doubtful Accounts should always have a credit balance.

An account receivable that has been written off against the allowance account may be collected later. Like the direct write-off method, the account is reinstated by an entry that reverses the write-off entry. The cash received in payment is then recorded as a receipt on account.

To illustrate, assume that Nancy Smith's account of $5,000 which was written off on April 2 is collected later on June 10. ExTone Company records the reinstatement and the collection as follows:

June	10	Accounts Receivable—Nancy Smith		5,000	
		Allowance for Doubtful Accounts			5,000
	10	Cash		5,000	
		Accounts Receivable—Nancy Smith			5,000

Example Exercise 8-2 Allowance Method

OBJ 4

Journalize the following transactions, using the allowance method of accounting for uncollectible receivables.

July 9. Received $1,200 from Jay Burke and wrote off the remainder owed of $3,900 as uncollectible.
Oct. 11. Reinstated the account of Jay Burke and received $3,900 cash in full payment.

Follow My Example 8-2

July 9	Cash	1,200	
	Allowance for Doubtful Accounts	3,900	
	Accounts Receivable—Jay Burke		5,100
Oct. 11	Accounts Receivable—Jay Burke	3,900	
	Allowance for Doubtful Accounts		3,900
11	Cash	3,900	
	Accounts Receivable—Jay Burke		3,900

Practice Exercises: **PE 8-2A, PE 8-2B**

Estimating Uncollectibles

The allowance method requires an estimate of uncollectible accounts at the end of the period. This estimate is normally based on past experience, industry averages, and forecasts of the future.

The two methods used to estimate uncollectible accounts are as follows:

1. Percent of sales method.
2. Analysis of receivables method.

Percent of Sales Method Since accounts receivable are created by credit sales, uncollectible accounts can be estimated as a percent of credit sales. If the portion of credit sales to sales is relatively constant, the percent may be applied to total sales or net sales.

Business Connection

ALLOWANCE PERCENTAGES ACROSS COMPANIES

The percent of the allowance for doubtful accounts to total accounts receivable will vary across companies and industries. For example, the following percentages were computed from recent annual reports:

Company	Industry	Percent of Allowance for Doubtful Accounts to Total Accounts Receivable
Apple Inc.	Computer/technology products	1.0%
Boeing	Aerospace & airplanes	1.0
Delta Air Lines	Transportation services	2.7
HCA Inc.	Health services	50.7
Sears	Retail	5.0

HCA's higher percent of allowance for doubtful accounts to total accounts receivable is due in part because Medicare reimbursements are often less than the amounts billed patients.

To illustrate, assume the following data for ExTone Company on December 31, 2014, before any adjustments:

Balance of Accounts Receivable	$ 240,000
Balance of Allowance for Doubtful Accounts	3,250 (Cr.)
Total credit sales	3,000,000
Bad debt as a percent of credit sales	¾%

Bad Debt Expense of $22,500 is estimated as follows:

Bad Debt Expense = Credit Sales × Bad Debt as a Percent of Credit Sales
Bad Debt Expense = $3,000,000 × ¾% = $22,500

The adjusting entry for uncollectible accounts on December 31, 2014, is as follows:

Dec.	31	Bad Debt Expense		22,500	
		Allowance for Doubtful Accounts			22,500
		Uncollectible accounts estimate ($3,000,000 × ¾% = $22,500).			

After the adjusting entry is posted to the ledger, Bad Debt Expense will have an adjusted balance of $22,500. Allowance for Doubtful Accounts will have an adjusted balance of $25,750 ($3,250 + $22,500). Both T accounts are shown below.

BAD DEBT EXPENSE

Dec. 31	Adjusting entry	22,500	
Dec. 31	Adjusted balance	22,500	

ALLOWANCE FOR DOUBTFUL ACCOUNTS

			Jan. 1	Balance	30,000
Total accounts written off $26,750	Jan. 21	6,000			
	Feb. 2	3,900			
	⋮	⋮			
			Dec. 31	Unadjusted balance	3,250
			Dec. 31	Adjusting entry	22,500
			Dec. 31	Adjusted balance	25,750

Under the percent of sales method, the amount of the adjusting entry is the amount estimated for Bad Debt Expense. This estimate is credited to whatever the unadjusted balance is for Allowance for Doubtful Accounts.

Note:
The estimate based on sales is added to any balance in Allowance for Doubtful Accounts.

To illustrate, assume that in the preceding example the unadjusted balance of Allowance for Doubtful Accounts on December 31, 2014, had been a $2,100 debit balance instead of a $3,250 credit balance. The adjustment would still have been $22,500. However, the December 31, 2014, ending adjusted balance of Allowance for Doubtful Accounts would have been $20,400 ($22,500 − $2,100).

Example Exercise 8-3 Percent of Sales Method

OBJ 4

At the end of the current year, Accounts Receivable has a balance of $800,000; Allowance for Doubtful Accounts has a credit balance of $7,500; and net sales for the year total $3,500,000. Bad debt expense is estimated at ½ of 1% of net sales.

Determine (a) the amount of the adjusting entry for uncollectible accounts; (b) the adjusted balances of Accounts Receivable, Allowance for Doubtful Accounts, and Bad Debt Expense; and (c) the net realizable value of accounts receivable.

Follow My Example 8-3

a. $17,500 ($3,500,000 × 0.005)

	Adjusted Balance
b. Accounts Receivable	$800,000
Allowance for Doubtful Accounts ($7,500 + $17,500)	25,000
Bad Debt Expense	17,500

c. $775,000 ($800,000 − $25,000)

Practice Exercises: **PE 8-3A, PE 8-3B**

Analysis of Receivables Method The analysis of receivables method is based on the assumption that the longer an account receivable is outstanding, the less likely that it will be collected. The analysis of receivables method is applied as follows:

Step 1. The due date of each account receivable is determined.

Step 2. The number of days each account is past due is determined. This is the number of days between the due date of the account and the date of the analysis.

Step 3. Each account is placed in an aged class according to its days past due. Typical aged classes include the following:

- Not past due
- 1–30 days past due
- 31–60 days past due
- 61–90 days past due
- 91–180 days past due
- 181–365 days past due
- Over 365 days past due

Step 4. The totals for each aged class are determined.

Step 5. The total for each aged class is multiplied by an estimated percentage of uncollectible accounts for that class.

Step 6. The estimated total of uncollectible accounts is determined as the sum of the uncollectible accounts for each aged class.

The preceding steps are summarized in an aging schedule, and this overall process is called **aging the receivables**.

To illustrate, assume that ExTone Company uses the analysis of receivables method instead of the percent of sales method. ExTone prepared an aging schedule for its accounts receivable of $240,000 as of December 31, 2014, as shown in Exhibit 1.

EXHIBIT 1 **Aging of Receivables Schedule, December 31, 2014**

		A	B	C	D	E	F	G	H	I
	1			Not	Days Past Due					
	2			Past						Over
	3	Customer	Balance	Due	1–30	31–60	61–90	91–180	181–365	365
Steps 1–3	4	Ashby & Co.	1,500			1,500				
	5	B. T. Barr	6,100					3,500	2,600	
	6	Brock Co.	4,700	4,700						
	21									
	22	Saxon Woods Co.	600					600		
Step 4 →	23	Total	240,000	125,000	64,000	13,100	8,900	5,000	10,000	14,000
Step 5 →	24	Percent uncollectible		2%	5%	10%	20%	30%	50%	80%
Step 6 →	25	Estimate of uncollectible accounts	26,490	2,500	3,200	1,310	1,780	1,500	5,000	11,200

Assume that ExTone Company sold merchandise to Saxon Woods Co. on August 29 with terms 2/10, n/30. Thus, the due date (Step 1) of Saxon Woods' account is September 28, as shown below.

Credit terms, net	30 days
Less: Aug. 29 to Aug. 31	2 days
Days in September	28 days

As of December 31, Saxon Woods' account is 94 days past due (Step 2), as shown below.

Number of days past due in September	2 days (30 – 28)
Number of days past due in October	31 days
Number of days past due in November	30 days
Number of days past due in December	31 days
Total number of days past due	94 days

Exhibit 1 shows that the $600 account receivable for Saxon Woods Co. was placed in the 91–180 days past due class (Step 3).

The total for each of the aged classes is determined (Step 4). Exhibit 1 shows that $125,000 of the accounts receivable are not past due, while $64,000 are 1–30 days past due. ExTone Company applies a different estimated percentage of uncollectible accounts to the totals of each of the aged classes (Step 5). As shown in Exhibit 1, the percent is 2% for accounts not past due, while the percent is 80% for accounts over 365 days past due.

The sum of the estimated uncollectible accounts for each aged class (Step 6) is the estimated uncollectible accounts on December 31, 2014. This is the desired adjusted balance for Allowance for Doubtful Accounts. For ExTone Company, this amount is $26,490, as shown in Exhibit 1.

Comparing the estimate of $26,490 with the unadjusted balance of the allowance account determines the amount of the adjustment for Bad Debt Expense. For ExTone, the unadjusted balance of the allowance account is a credit balance of $3,250. The amount to be added to this balance is therefore $23,240 ($26,490 – $3,250). The adjusting entry is as follows:

Note: **The estimate based on receivables is compared to the balance in the allowance account to determine the amount of the adjusting entry.**

Dec.	31	Bad Debt Expense		23,240	
		Allowance for Doubtful Accounts			23,240
		Uncollectible accounts estimate			
		($26,490 – $3,250).			

After the preceding adjusting entry is posted to the ledger, Bad Debt Expense will have an adjusted balance of $23,240. Allowance for Doubtful Accounts will have an adjusted balance of $26,490, and the net realizable value of the receivables is $213,510 ($240,000 – $26,490). Both T accounts are shown below.

BAD DEBT EXPENSE

Dec. 31	Adjusting entry	23,240			
Dec. 31	Adjusted balance	23,240			

ALLOWANCE FOR DOUBTFUL ACCOUNTS

			Dec. 31	Unadjusted balance	3,250
			Dec. 31	Adjusting entry	23,240
			Dec. 31	Adjusted balance	26,490

Under the analysis of receivables method, the amount of the adjusting entry is the amount that will yield an adjusted balance for Allowance for Doubtful Accounts equal to that estimated by the aging schedule.

To illustrate, if the unadjusted balance of the allowance account had been a debit balance of $2,100, the amount of the adjustment would have been $28,590 ($26,490 + $2,100). In this case, Bad Debt Expense would have an adjusted balance of $28,590. However, the adjusted balance of Allowance for Doubtful Accounts would still have been $26,490. After the adjusting entry is posted, both T accounts are shown below.

BAD DEBT EXPENSE

Dec. 31	Adjusting entry	28,590			
Dec. 31	Adjusted balance	28,590			

ALLOWANCE FOR DOUBTFUL ACCOUNTS

Dec. 31	Unadjusted balance	2,100			
			Dec. 31	Adjusting entry	28,590
			Dec. 31	Adjusted balance	26,490

Example Exercise 8-4 Analysis of Receivables Method

OBJ 4

At the end of the current year, Accounts Receivable has a balance of $800,000; Allowance for Doubtful Accounts has a credit balance of $7,500; and net sales for the year total $3,500,000. Using the aging method, the balance of Allowance for Doubtful Accounts is estimated as $30,000.

Determine (a) the amount of the adjusting entry for uncollectible accounts; (b) the adjusted balances of Accounts Receivable, Allowance for Doubtful Accounts, and Bad Debt Expense; and (c) the net realizable value of accounts receivable.

Follow My Example 8-4

a. $22,500 ($30,000 – $7,500)

		Adjusted Balance
b.	Accounts Receivable	$800,000
	Allowance for Doubtful Accounts	30,000
	Bad Debt Expense	22,500

c. $770,000 ($800,000 – $30,000)

Practice Exercises: **PE 8-4A, PE 8-4B**

Comparing Estimation Methods Both the percent of sales and analysis of receivables methods estimate uncollectible accounts. However, each method has a slightly different focus and financial statement emphasis.

Under the percent of sales method, Bad Debt Expense is the focus of the estimation process. The percent of sales method places more emphasis on matching revenues and expenses and, thus, emphasizes the income statement. That is, the amount of the adjusting entry is based on the estimate of Bad Debt Expense for the period. Allowance for Doubtful Accounts is then credited for this amount.

Under the analysis of receivables method, Allowance for Doubtful Accounts is the focus of the estimation process. The analysis of receivables method places more emphasis on the net realizable value of the receivables and, thus, emphasizes the balance sheet. That is, the amount of the adjusting entry is the amount that will yield an adjusted balance for Allowance for Doubtful Accounts equal to that estimated by the aging schedule. Bad Debt Expense is then debited for this amount.

Exhibit 2 summarizes these differences between the percent of sales and the analysis of receivables methods. Exhibit 2 also shows the results of the ExTone Company illustration for the percent of sales and analysis of receivables methods. The amounts shown in Exhibit 2 assume an unadjusted credit balance of $3,250 for Allowance for

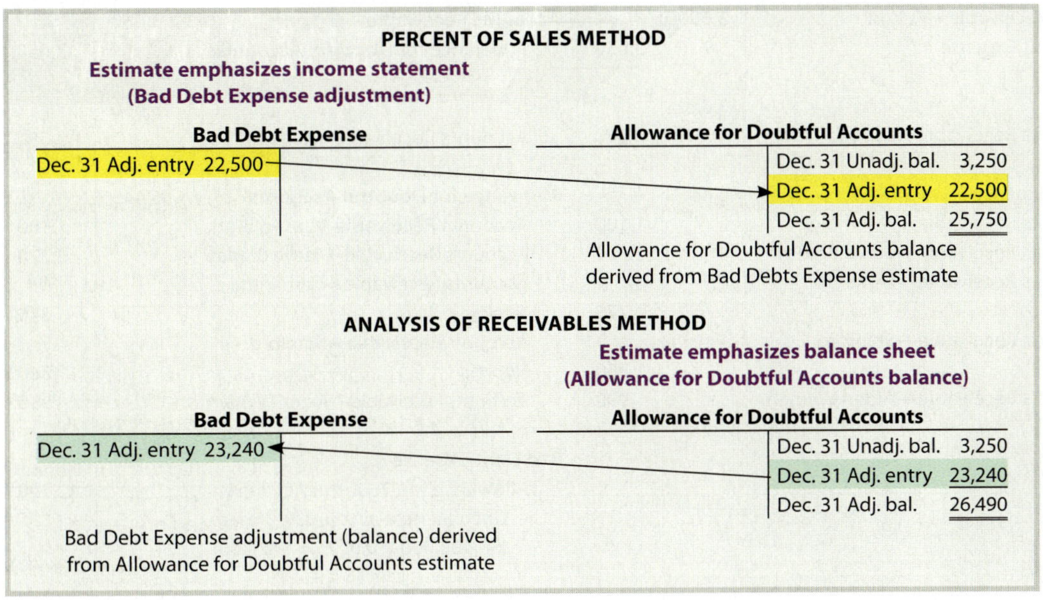

EXHIBIT 2

Difference Between Estimation Methods

Doubtful Accounts. While the methods normally yield different amounts for any one period, over several periods the amounts should be similar.

OBJ 5 Compare the direct write-off and allowance methods of accounting for uncollectible accounts.

Comparing Direct Write-Off and Allowance Methods

Journal entries for the direct write-off and allowance methods are illustrated and compared in this section. As a basis for illustration, the following transactions, taken from the records of Hobbs Co. for the year ending December 31, 2013, are used:

Mar. 1. Wrote off account of C. York, $3,650.

Apr. 12. Received $2,250 as partial payment on the $5,500 account of Cary Bradshaw. Wrote off the remaining balance as uncollectible.

June 22. Received the $3,650 from C. York, which had been written off on March 1. Reinstated the account and recorded the cash receipt.

Sept. 7. Wrote off the following accounts as uncollectible (record as one journal entry):

Jason Bigg	$1,100	Stanford Noonan	$1,360
Steve Bradey	2,220	Aiden Wyman	990
Samantha Neeley	775		

Dec. 31. Hobbs Company uses the percent of credit sales method of estimating uncollectible expenses. Based on past history and industry averages, 1.25% of credit sales are expected to be uncollectible. Hobbs recorded $3,400,000 of credit sales during 2013.

Exhibit 3 illustrates the journal entries for Hobbs Company using the direct write-off and allowance methods. Using the direct write-off method, there is no adjusting entry on December 31 for uncollectible accounts. In contrast, the allowance method records an adjusting entry for estimated uncollectible accounts of $42,500.

EXHIBIT 3 **Comparing Direct Write-Off and Allowance Methods**

		Direct Write-Off Method			Allowance Method		
2013 Mar.	1	Bad Debt Expense	3,650		Allowance for Doubtful Accounts	3,650	
		Accounts Receivable—C. York		3,650	Accounts Receivable—C. York		3,650
Apr.	12	Cash	2,250		Cash	2,250	
		Bad Debt Expense	3,250		Allowance for Doubtful Accounts	3,250	
		Accounts Receivable—Cary Bradshaw		5,500	Accounts Receivable—Cary Bradshaw		5,500
June	22	Accounts Receivable—C. York	3,650		Accounts Receivable—C. York	3,650	
		Bad Debt Expense		3,650	Allowance for Doubtful Accounts		3,650
	22	Cash	3,650		Cash	3,650	
		Accounts Receivable—C. York		3,650	Accounts Receivable—C. York		3,650
Sept.	7	Bad Debt Expense	6,445		Allowance for Doubtful Accounts	6,445	
		Accounts Receivable—Jason Bigg		1,100	Accounts Receivable—Jason Bigg		1,100
		Accounts Receivable—Steve Bradey		2,220	Accounts Receivable—Steve Bradey		2,220
		Accounts Receivable—Samantha Neeley		775	Accounts Receivable—Samantha Neeley		775
		Accounts Receivable—Stanford Noonan		1,360	Accounts Receivable—Stanford Noonan		1,360
		Accounts Receivable—Aiden Wyman		990	Accounts Receivable—Aiden Wyman		990
Dec.	31	No Entry			Bad Debt Expense	42,500	
					Allowance for Doubtful Accounts		42,500
					Uncollectible accounts estimate ($3,400,000 × 0.0125 = $42,500).		

The primary differences between the direct write-off and allowance methods are summarized below.

	Direct Write-Off Method	Allowance Method
Bad debt expense is recorded	When the specific customer accounts are determined to be uncollectible.	Using estimate based on (1) a percent of sales or (2) an analysis of receivables.
Allowance account	No allowance account is used.	The allowance account is used.
Primary users	Small companies and companies with few receivables.	Large companies and those with a large amount of receivables.

Notes Receivable

OBJ 6 Describe the accounting for notes receivable.

A note has some advantages over an account receivable. By signing a note, the debtor recognizes the debt and agrees to pay it according to its terms. Thus, a note is a stronger legal claim.

Characteristics of Notes Receivable

A promissory note is a written promise to pay the face amount, usually with interest, on demand or at a date in the future.[2] Characteristics of a promissory note are as follows:

1. The *maker* is the party making the promise to pay.
2. The *payee* is the party to whom the note is payable.
3. The *face amount* is the amount for which the note is written on its face.
4. The *issuance date* is the date a note is issued.
5. The *due date* or *maturity date* is the date the note is to be paid.
6. The *term* of a note is the amount of time between the issuance and due dates.
7. The *interest rate* is that rate of interest that must be paid on the face amount for the term of the note.

Exhibit 4 illustrates a promissory note. The maker of the note is Selig Company, and the payee is Pearland Company. The face value of the note is $2,000, the interest rate is 10%, and the issuance date is March 16, 2013. The term of the note is 90 days, which results in a due date of June 14, 2013, as shown below.

Days in March	31 days
Minus issuance date of note	16
Days remaining in March	15 days
Add days in April	30
Add days in May	31
Add days in June (due date of June 14)	14
Term of note	90 days

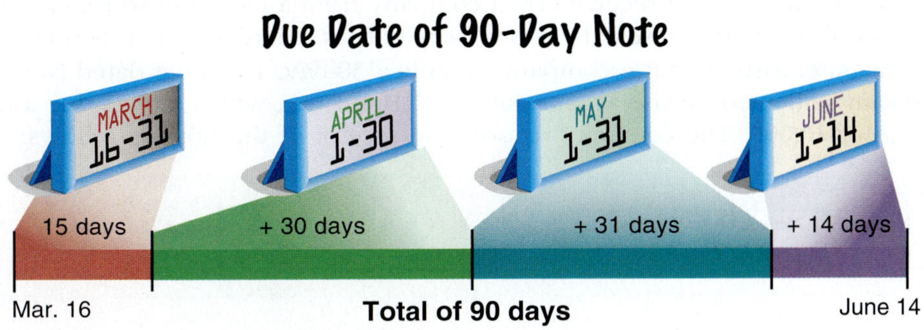

2 You may see references to non-interest-bearing notes. Such notes are not widely used and carry an assumed or implicit interest rate.

EXHIBIT 4 **Promissory Note**

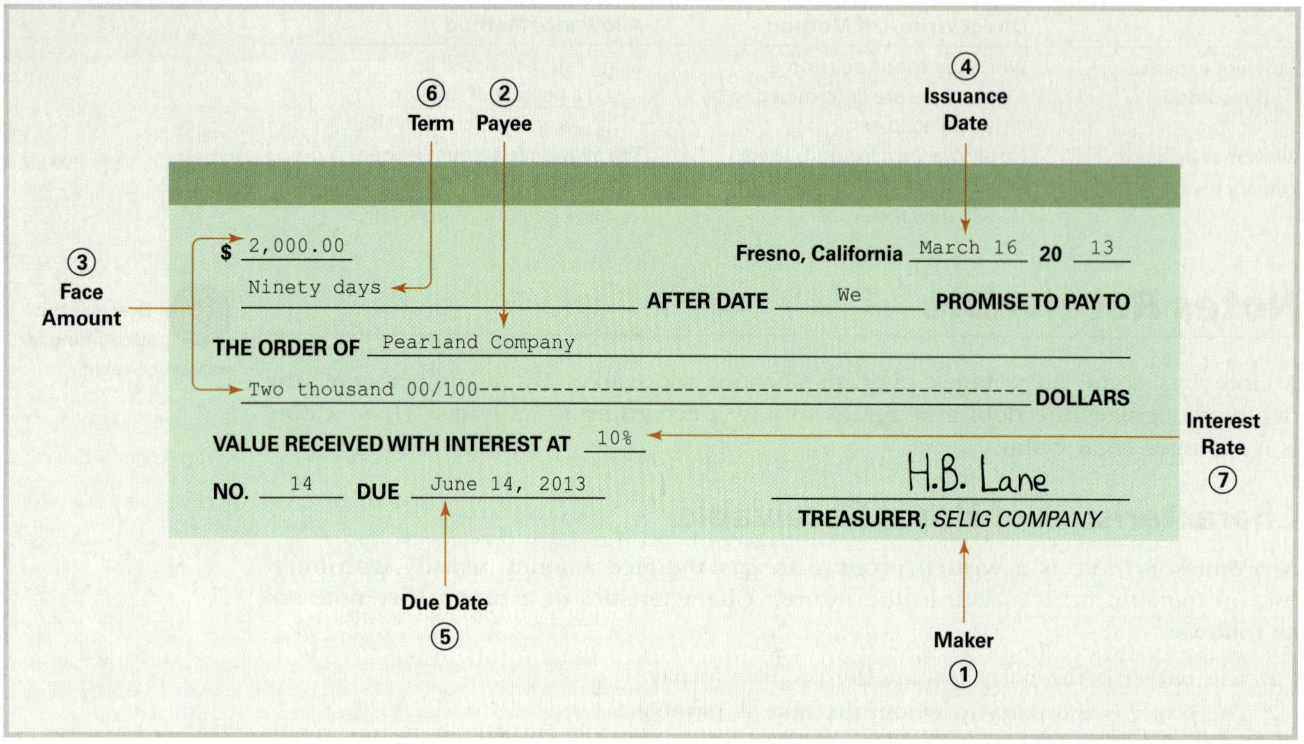

The interest on a note is computed as follows:

$$\text{Interest} = \text{Face Amount} \times \text{Interest Rate} \times (\text{Term}/360 \text{ days})$$

The interest rate is stated on an annual (yearly) basis, while the term is expressed as days. Thus, the interest on the note in Exhibit 4 is computed as follows:

$$\text{Interest} = \$2{,}000 \times 10\% \times (90/360) = \$50$$

To simplify, 360 days per year will be used. In practice, companies such as banks and mortgage companies use the exact number of days in a year, 365.

The **maturity value** is the amount that must be paid at the due date of the note, which is the sum of the face amount and the interest. The maturity value of the note in Exhibit 4 is $2,050 ($2,000 + $50).

Accounting for Notes Receivable

A promissory note may be received by a company from a customer to replace an account receivable. In such cases, the promissory note is recorded as a note receivable.[3]

To illustrate, assume that a company accepts a 30-day, 12% note dated November 21, 2014, in settlement of the account of W. A. Bunn Co., which is past due and has a balance of $6,000. The company records the receipt of the note as follows:

Nov.	21	Notes Receivable—W. A. Bunn Co.		6,000	
		Accounts Receivable—W. A. Bunn Co.			6,000

3 The accounting for notes payable is described and illustrated in Chapter 12.

At the due date, the company records the receipt of $6,060 ($6,000 face amount plus $60 interest) as follows:

Dec.	21	Cash	6,060	
		Notes Receivable—W. A. Bunn Co.		6,000
		Interest Revenue		60
		[$6,060 = $6,000 + ($6,000 × 12% × 30/360)].		

If the maker of a note fails to pay the note on the due date, the note is a **dishonored note receivable**. A company that holds a dishonored note transfers the face amount of the note plus any interest due back to an accounts receivable account. For example, assume that the $6,000, 30-day, 12% note received from W. A. Bunn Co. and recorded on November 21 is dishonored. The company holding the note transfers the note and interest back to the customer's account as follows:

Dec.	21	Accounts Receivable—W. A. Bunn Co.	6,060	
		Notes Receivable—W. A. Bunn Co.		6,000
		Interest Revenue		60

The company has earned the interest of $60, even though the note is dishonored. If the account receivable is uncollectible, the company will write off $6,060 against Allowance for Doubtful Accounts.

A company receiving a note should record an adjusting entry for any accrued interest at the end of the period. For example, assume that Crawford Company issues a $4,000, 90-day, 12% note dated December 1, 2014, to settle its account receivable. If the accounting period ends on December 31, the company receiving the note would record the following entries:

2014 Dec.	1	Notes Receivable—Crawford Company	4,000	
		Accounts Receivable—Crawford Company		4,000
	31	Interest Receivable	40	
		Interest Revenue		40
		Accrued interest		
		($4,000 × 12% × 30/360).		
2015 Mar.	1	Cash	4,120	
		Notes Receivable—Crawford Company		4,000
		Interest Receivable		40
		Interest Revenue		80
		Total interest of $120		
		($4,000 × 12% × 90/360).		

The interest revenue account is closed at the end of each accounting period. The amount of interest revenue is normally reported in the Other Income section of the income statement.

Example Exercise 8-5 Note Receivable

OBJ 6

Same Day Surgery Center received a 120-day, 6% note for $40,000, dated March 14, from a patient on account.

a. Determine the due date of the note.
b. Determine the maturity value of the note.
c. Journalize the entry to record the receipt of the payment of the note at maturity.

(Continued)

Follow My Example 8-5

a. The due date of the note is July 12, determined as follows:

March	17 days (31 – 14)
April	30 days
May	31 days
June	30 days
July	12 days
Total	120 days

b. $40,800 [$40,000 + ($40,000 × 6% × 120/360)]

c.

July 12	Cash	40,800	
	Notes Receivable		40,000
	Interest Revenue		800

Practice Exercises: **PE 8-5A, PE 8-5B**

OBJ 7 Describe the reporting of receivables on the balance sheet.

Reporting Receivables on the Balance Sheet

All receivables that are expected to be realized in cash within a year are reported in the Current assets section of the balance sheet. Current assets are normally reported in the order of their liquidity, beginning with cash and cash equivalents.

The balance sheet presentation for receivables for Mornin' Joe is shown below.

Mornin' Joe
Balance Sheet
December 31, 2014

Assets		
Current assets:		
Cash and cash equivalents		$235,000
Trading investments (at cost)	$420,000	
Plus valuation allowance for trading investments	45,000	465,000
Accounts receivable	$305,000	
Less allowance for doubtful accounts	12,300	292,700

In Mornin' Joe's financial statements, the allowance for doubtful accounts is subtracted from accounts receivable. Some companies report receivables at their net realizable value with a note showing the amount of the allowance.

Other disclosures related to receivables are reported either on the face of the financial statements or in the financial statement notes. Such disclosures include the market (fair) value of the receivables. In addition, if unusual credit risks exist within the receivables, the nature of the risks are disclosed. For example, if the majority of the receivables are due from one customer or are due from customers located in one area of the country or one industry, these facts are disclosed.[4]

F·A·I

OBJ 8 Describe and illustrate the use of accounts receivable turnover and number of days' sales in receivables to evaluate a company's efficiency in collecting its receivables.

Financial Analysis and Interpretation: Accounts Receivable Turnover and Number of Days' Sales in Receivables

Two financial measures that are especially useful in evaluating efficiency in collecting receivables are (1) the accounts receivable turnover and (2) the number of days' sales in receivables.

4 *FASB Accounting Standards Codification*, Section 210-10-50.

The **accounts receivable turnover** measures how frequently during the year the accounts receivable are being converted to cash. For example, with credit terms of n/30, the accounts receivable should turn over about 12 times per year.

The accounts receivable turnover is computed as follows:[5]

$$\text{Accounts Receivable Turnover} = \frac{\text{Net Sales}}{\text{Average Accounts Receivable}}$$

The average accounts receivable can be determined by using monthly data or by simply adding the beginning and ending accounts receivable balances and dividing by two. For example, using the following financial data (in millions) for FedEx, the Year 2 and Year 1 accounts receivable turnover is computed as 8.0 in Year 2 and 8.1 in Year 1, as shown below.

	Year 2	Year 1
Net sales	$39,304	$34,734
Accounts receivable:		
Beginning of year	4,692	3,902
End of year	5,191	4,692
Average accounts receivable:*		
($4,692 + $5,191)/2	4,941.5	
($3,902 + $4,692)/2		4,297.0
Accounts receivable turnover:*		
$39,304/$4,941.5	8.0	
$34,734/$4,297.0		8.1

* Rounded to one decimal place.

The **number of days' sales in receivables** is an estimate of the length of time the accounts receivable have been outstanding. With credit terms of n/30, the number of days' sales in receivables should be about 30 days. It is computed as follows:

$$\text{Number of Days' Sales in Receivables} = \frac{\text{Average Accounts Receivable}}{\text{Average Daily Sales}}$$

Average daily sales are determined by dividing net sales by 365 days. For example, using the preceding data for FedEx, the number of days' sales in receivables is 45.9 and 45.1 for Year 2 and Year 1, as shown below.

	Year 2	Year 1
Average daily sales:*		
$39,304/365	107.7	
$34,734/365		95.2
Number of days' sales in receivables:*		
$4,941.5/107.7	45.9	
$4,297.0/95.2		45.1

* Rounded to one decimal place.

The number of days' sales in receivables confirms that FedEx's efficiency in collecting accounts receivable decreased slightly from Year 1 to Year 2. Generally, the efficiency in collecting accounts receivable has improved when the accounts receivable turnover increases or the number of days' sales in receivables decreases.

Example Exercise 8-6 Accounts Receivable Turnover and Number of Days' Sales in Receivables

OBJ 8

Financial statement data for years ending December 31 for Osterman Company are as follows:

	2014	2013
Net sales	$4,284,000	$3,040,000
Accounts receivable:		
Beginning of year	550,000	400,000
End of year	640,000	550,000

(Continued)

5 If known, credit sales can be used in the numerator. However, because credit sales are not normally disclosed to external users, most analysts use net sales in the numerator.

Follow My Example 8-6

a. Determine the accounts receivable turnover for 2014 and 2013.

b. Determine the number of days' sales in receivables for 2014 and 2013. Round to one decimal place.

c. Does the change in accounts receivable turnover and the number of days' sales in receivable from 2013 to 2014 indicate a favorable or an unfavorable trend?

a. Accounts receivable turnover:

	2014	**2013**
Average accounts receivable:		
($550,000 + $640,000)/2	$595,000	
($400,000 + $550,000)/2		$475,000
Accounts receivable turnover:		
$4,284,000/$595,000	7.2	
$3,040,000/$475,000		6.4

b. Number of days' sales in receivables:

	2014	**2013**
Average daily sales:		
$4,284,000/365 days	$11,737.0	
$3,040,000/365 days		$8,328.8
Number of days' sales in receivables:		
$595,000/$11,737.0	50.7 days	
$475,000/$8,328.8		57.0 days

c. The increase in the accounts receivable turnover from 6.4 to 7.2 and the decrease in the number of days' sales in receivables from 57.0 days to 50.7 days indicate favorable trends in the efficiency of collecting accounts receivable.

Practice Exercises: **PE 8-6A, PE 8-6B**

Business Connection

DELTA AIR LINES

Delta Air Lines is a major air carrier that services cities throughout the United States and the world. In its operations, Delta generates accounts receivable as reported in the following note to its financial statements:

Our accounts receivable are generated largely from the sale of passenger airline tickets and cargo transportation services. The majority of these sales are processed through major credit card companies, resulting in accounts receivable. . . .

We also have receivables from the sale of mileage credits under our SkyMiles Program to participating airlines and nonairline businesses such as credit card companies, hotels, and car rental agencies. We believe the credit risk associated with these receivables is minimal and that the allowance for uncollectible accounts that we have provided is appropriate.

© AP Photo/Ric Feld

In a recent, balance sheet, Delta reported the following accounts receivable (in millions):

	Dec. 31, Year 2	**Dec. 31, Year 1**
Current Assets:		
⋮		
Accounts receivable, net of an allowance for uncollectible accounts of $40 at December 31 (Year 2) and $47 at December 31 (Year 1)	$1,456	$1,353

At a Glance 8

OBJ 1 Describe the common classes of receivables.

Key Points *Receivables* includes all money claims against other entities. Receivables are normally classified as accounts receivable, notes receivable, or other receivables.

Learning Outcomes	Example Exercises	Practice Exercises
• Define the term *receivables*.		
• List some common classifications of receivables.		

OBJ 2 Describe the accounting for uncollectible receivables.

Key Points The operating expense recorded from uncollectible receivables is called *bad debt expense*. The two methods of accounting for uncollectible receivables are the direct write-off method and the allowance method.

Learning Outcomes	Example Exercises	Practice Exercises
• Describe how a company may shift the risk of uncollectible receivables to other companies.		
• List factors that indicate an account receivable is uncollectible.		
• Describe two methods of accounting for uncollectible accounts receivable.		

OBJ 3 Describe the direct write-off method of accounting for uncollectible receivables.

Key Points Under the direct write-off method, the entry to write off an account debits Bad Debt Expense and credits Accounts Receivable. Neither an allowance account nor an adjusting entry is needed at the end of the period.

Learning Outcomes	Example Exercises	Practice Exercises
• Prepare journal entries to write off an account, using the direct write-off method.	**EE8-1**	**PE8-1A, 8-1B**
• Prepare journal entries for the reinstatement and collection of an account previously written off.	**EE8-1**	**PE8-1A, 8-1B**

OBJ 4 Describe the allowance method of accounting for uncollectible receivables.

Key Points Under the allowance method, an adjusting entry is made for uncollectible accounts. When an account is determined to be uncollectible, it is written off against the allowance account. The allowance account is a contra asset account that normally has a credit balance after the adjusting entry has been posted.

The estimate of uncollectibles may be based on a percent of sales or an analysis of receivables. Exhibit 2 compares and contrasts these two methods.

Learning Outcomes	Example Exercises	Practice Exercises
• Prepare journal entries to write off an account, using the allowance method.	EE8-2	PE8-2A, 8-2B
• Prepare journal entries for the reinstatement and collection of an account previously written off.	EE8-2	PE8-2A, 8-2B
• Determine the adjustment, bad debt expense, and net realizable value of accounts receivable, using the percent of sales method.	EE8-3	PE8-3A, 8-3B
• Determine the adjustment, bad debt expense, and net realizable value of accounts receivable, using the analysis of receivables method.	EE8-4	PE8-4A, 8-4B

OBJ 5 Compare the direct write-off and allowance methods of accounting for uncollectible accounts.

Key Points Exhibit 3 illustrates the differences between the direct write-off and allowance methods of accounting for uncollectible accounts.

Learning Outcomes	Example Exercises	Practice Exercises
• Describe the differences in accounting for uncollectible accounts under the direct write-off and allowance methods.		
• Record journal entries, using the direct write-off and allowance methods.		

OBJ 6 Describe the accounting for notes receivable.

Key Points A note received to settle an account receivable is recorded as a debit to Notes Receivable and a credit to Accounts Receivable. When a note is paid at maturity, Cash is debited, Notes Receivable is credited, and Interest Revenue is credited. If the maker of a note fails to pay, the dishonored note is recorded by debiting an account receivable for the amount due from the maker of the note.

Learning Outcomes	Example Exercises	Practice Exercises
• Describe the characteristics of a note receivable.		
• Determine the due date and maturity value of a note receivable.	EE8-5	PE8-5A, 8-5B
• Prepare journal entries for the receipt of the payment of a note receivable.	EE8-5	PE8-5A, 8-5B
• Prepare a journal entry for the dishonored note receivable.		

OBJ 7

Describe the reporting of receivables on the balance sheet.

Key Points All receivables that are expected to be realized in cash within a year are reported in the Current Assets section of the balance sheet. In addition to the allowance for doubtful accounts, additional receivable disclosures include the market (fair) value and unusual credit risks.

Learning Outcomes	Example Exercises	Practice Exercises
• Describe how receivables are reported in the Current Assets section of the balance sheet.		
• Describe the disclosures related to receivables that should be reported in the financial statements.		

OBJ 8

Describe and illustrate the use of accounts receivable turnover and number of days' sales in receivables to evaluate a company's efficiency in collecting its receivables.

Key Points Two financial measures that are especially useful in evaluating efficiency in collecting receivables are (1) the accounts receivable turnover and (2) the number of days' sales in receivables. Generally, the efficiency in collecting accounts receivable has improved when the accounts receivable turnover increases or there is a decrease in the number of days' sales in receivables.

Learning Outcomes	Example Exercises	Practice Exercises
• Describe two measures of the efficiency of managing receivables.		
• Compute and interpret the accounts receivable turnover and the number of days' sales in receivables.	EE8-6	PE8-6A, 8-6B

Key Terms

accounts receivable (362)
accounts receivable turnover (377)
aging the receivables (369)
Allowance for Doubtful Accounts (365)
allowance method (363)
bad debt expense (363)
direct write-off method (363)
dishonored note receivable (375)
maturity value (374)
net realizable value (365)
notes receivable (362)
number of days' sales in receivables (377)
receivables (362)

Illustrative Problem

Ditzler Company, a construction supply company, uses the allowance method of accounting for uncollectible accounts receivable. Selected transactions completed by Ditzler Company are as follows:

Feb. 1. Sold merchandise on account to Ames Co., $8,000. The cost of the merchandise sold was $4,500.

Mar. 15. Accepted a 60-day, 12% note for $8,000 from Ames Co. on account.

Apr. 9. Wrote off a $2,500 account from Dorset Co. as uncollectible.

21. Loaned $7,500 cash to Jill Klein, receiving a 90-day, 14% note.

May 14. Received the interest due from Ames Co. and a new 90-day, 14% note as a renewal of the loan. (Record both the debit and the credit to the notes receivable account.)

June 13. Reinstated the account of Dorset Co., written off on April 9, and received $2,500 in full payment.

July 20. Jill Klein dishonored her note.

Aug. 12. Received from Ames Co. the amount due on its note of May 14.

19. Received from Jill Klein the amount owed on the dishonored note, plus interest for 30 days at 15%, computed on the maturity value of the note.

Dec. 16. Accepted a 60-day, 12% note for $12,000 from Global Company on account.

31. It is estimated that 3% of the credit sales of $1,375,000 for the year ended December 31 will be uncollectible.

Instructions

1. Journalize the transactions.
2. Journalize the adjusting entry to record the accrued interest on December 31 on the Global Company note.

Solution

1.

Feb.	1	Accounts Receivable—Ames Co.		8,000.00	
		Sales			8,000.00
	1	Cost of Merchandise Sold		4,500.00	
		Merchandise Inventory			4,500.00
Mar.	15	Notes Receivable—Ames Co.		8,000.00	
		Accounts Receivable—Ames Co.			8,000.00
Apr.	9	Allowance for Doubtful Accounts		2,500.00	
		Accounts Receivable—Dorset Co.			2,500.00
	21	Notes Receivable—Jill Klein		7,500.00	
		Cash			7,500.00
May	14	Notes Receivable—Ames Co.		8,000.00	
		Cash		160.00	
		Notes Receivable—Ames Co.			8,000.00
		Interest Revenue			160.00
June	13	Accounts Receivable—Dorset Co.		2,500.00	
		Allowance for Doubtful Accounts			2,500.00
	13	Cash		2,500.00	
		Accounts Receivable—Dorset Co.			2,500.00
July	20	Accounts Receivable—Jill Klein		7,762.50	
		Notes Receivable—Jill Klein			7,500.00
		Interest Revenue			262.50
Aug.	12	Cash		8,280.00	
		Notes Receivable—Ames Co.			8,000.00
		Interest Revenue			280.00
	19	Cash		7,859.53	
		Accounts Receivable—Jill Klein			7,762.50
		Interest Revenue			97.03
		($7,762.50 × 15% × 30/360).			
Dec.	16	Notes Receivable—Global Company		12,000.00	
		Accounts Receivable—Global Company			12,000.00
	31	Bad Debt Expense		41,250.00	
		Allowance for Doubtful Accounts			41,250.00
		Uncollectible accounts estimate			
		($1,375,000 × 3%).			

2.

Dec.	31	Interest Receivable		60.00	
		Interest Revenue			60.00
		Accrued interest			
		($12,000 × 12% × 15/360).			

Discussion Questions

1. What are the three classifications of receivables?
2. Dan's Hardware is a small hardware store in the rural township of Twin Bridges. It rarely extends credit to its customers in the form of an account receivable. The few customers that are allowed to carry accounts receivable are long-time residents of Twin Bridges, with a history of doing business at Dan's Hardware. What method of accounting for uncollectible receivables should Dan's Hardware use? Why?
3. What kind of an account (asset, liability, etc.) is Allowance for Doubtful Accounts, and is its normal balance a debit or a credit?
4. After the accounts are adjusted and closed at the end of the fiscal year, Accounts Receivable has a balance of $673,400, and Allowance for Doubtful Accounts has a balance of $11,900. Describe how the accounts receivable and the allowance for doubtful accounts are reported on the balance sheet.
5. A firm has consistently adjusted its allowance account at the end of the fiscal year by adding a fixed percent of the period's net sales on account. After seven years, the balance in Allowance for Doubtful Accounts has become very large in relationship to the balance in Accounts Receivable. Give two possible explanations.
6. Which of the two methods of estimating uncollectibles provides for the most accurate estimate of the current net realizable value of the receivables?
7. Neptune Company issued a note receivable to Sailfish Company. (a) Who is the payee? (b) What is the title of the account used by Sailfish Company in recording the note?
8. If a note provides for payment of principal of $85,000 and interest at the rate of 6%, will the interest amount to $5,100? Explain.
9. The maker of a $240,000, 6%, 90-day note receivable failed to pay the note on the due date of November 30. What accounts should be debited and credited by the payee to record the dishonored note receivable?
10. The note receivable dishonored in Discussion Question 9 is paid on December 30 by the maker, plus interest for 30 days at 9%. What entry should be made to record the receipt of the payment?

Practice Exercises

Example Exercises

EE 8-1 *p. 364*

PE 8-1A Direct write-off method **OBJ. 3**

Journalize the following transactions, using the direct write-off method of accounting for uncollectible receivables:

Feb. 12. Received $800 from Leo Jorgenson and wrote off the remainder owed of $2,400 as uncollectible.

May 3. Reinstated the account of Leo Jorgenson and received $2,400 cash in full payment.

EE 8-1 *p. 364*

PE 8-1B Direct write-off method **OBJ. 3**

Journalize the following transactions, using the direct write-off method of accounting for uncollectible receivables:

Oct. 2. Received $600 from Rachel Elpel and wrote off the remainder owed of $1,350 as uncollectible.

Dec. 20. Reinstated the account of Rachel Elpel and received $1,350 cash in full payment.

Example Exercises

EE 8-2 *p. 367*

PE 8-2A Allowance method **OBJ. 4**

Journalize the following transactions, using the allowance method of accounting for uncollectible receivables:

Feb. 12. Received $800 from Leo Jorgenson and wrote off the remainder owed of $2,400 as uncollectible.

May 3. Reinstated the account of Leo Jorgenson and received $2,400 cash in full payment.

EE 8-2 *p. 367*

PE 8-2B Allowance method **OBJ. 4**

Journalize the following transactions, using the allowance method of accounting for uncollectible receivables:

Oct. 2. Received $600 from Rachel Elpel and wrote off the remainder owed of $1,350 as uncollectible.

Dec. 20. Reinstated the account of Rachel Elpel and received $1,350 cash in full payment.

EE 8-3 *p. 368*

PE 8-3A Percent of sales method **OBJ. 4**

At the end of the current year, Accounts Receivable has a balance of $685,000; Allowance for Doubtful Accounts has a credit balance of $9,000; and net sales for the year total $7,400,000. Bad debt expense is estimated at ¾ of 1% of net sales.

Determine (a) the amount of the adjusting entry for uncollectible accounts; (b) the adjusted balances of Accounts Receivable, Allowance for Doubtful Accounts, and Bad Debt Expense; and (c) the net realizable value of accounts receivable.

EE 8-3 *p. 368*

PE 8-3B Percent of sales method **OBJ. 4**

At the end of the current year, Accounts Receivable has a balance of $3,460,000; Allowance for Doubtful Accounts has a debit balance of $12,500; and net sales for the year total $46,300,000. Bad debt expense is estimated at ½ of 1% of net sales.

Determine (a) the amount of the adjusting entry for uncollectible accounts; (b) the adjusted balances of Accounts Receivable, Allowance for Doubtful Accounts, and Bad Debt Expense; and (c) the net realizable value of accounts receivable.

EE 8-4 *p. 371*

PE 8-4A Analysis of receivables method **OBJ. 4**

At the end of the current year, Accounts Receivable has a balance of $685,000; Allowance for Doubtful Accounts has a credit balance of $9,000; and net sales for the year total $7,400,000. Using the aging method, the balance of Allowance for Doubtful Accounts is estimated as $50,000.

Determine (a) the amount of the adjusting entry for uncollectible accounts; (b) the adjusted balances of Accounts Receivable, Allowance for Doubtful Accounts, and Bad Debt Expense; and (c) the net realizable value of accounts receivable.

EE 8-4 *p. 371*

PE 8-4B Analysis of receivables method **OBJ. 4**

At the end of the current year, Accounts Receivable has a balance of $3,460,000; Allowance for Doubtful Accounts has a debit balance of $12,500; and net sales for the year total $46,300,000. Using the aging method, the balance of Allowance for Doubtful Accounts is estimated as $245,000.

Determine (a) the amount of the adjusting entry for uncollectible accounts; (b) the adjusted balances of Accounts Receivable, Allowance for Doubtful Accounts, and Bad Debt Expense; and (c) the net realizable value of accounts receivable.

EE 8-5 *p. 375*

PE 8-5A Note receivable **OBJ. 6**

Lambert Supply Company received a 30-day, 5% note for $210,000, dated August 7 from a customer on account.

a. Determine the due date of the note.
b. Determine the maturity value of the note.
c. Journalize the entry to record the receipt of the payment of the note at maturity.

Example Exercises

EE 8-5 *p. 375*

PE 8-5B Note receivable **OBJ. 6**

Prefix Supply Company received a 120-day, 8% note for $450,000, dated April 9 from a customer on account.

a. Determine the due date of the note.

b. Determine the maturity value of the note.

c. Journalize the entry to record the receipt of the payment of the note at maturity.

EE 8-6 *p. 377*

F·A·I

PE 8-6A Accounts receivable turnover and number of days' sales in receivables **OBJ. 8**

Financial statement data for years ending December 31 for Chiro-Solutions Company are shown below.

	2014	2013
Net sales	$2,912,000	$2,958,000
Accounts receivable:		
Beginning of year	300,000	280,000
End of year	340,000	300,000

a. Determine the accounts receivable turnover for 2014 and 2013.

b. Determine the number of days' sales in receivables for 2014 and 2013. Round to one decimal place.

c. Does the change in accounts receivable turnover and the number of days' sales in receivables from 2013 to 2014 indicate a favorable or an unfavorable trend?

EE 8-6 *p. 377*

F·A·I

PE 8-6B Accounts receivable turnover and number of days' sales in receivables **OBJ. 8**

Financial statement data for years ending December 31 for Robinhood Company are shown below.

	2014	2013
Net sales	$7,906,000	$6,726,000
Accounts receivable:		
Beginning of year	600,000	540,000
End of year	580,000	600,000

a. Determine the accounts receivable turnover for 2014 and 2013.

b. Determine the number of days' sales in receivables for 2014 and 2013. Round to one decimal place.

c. Does the change in accounts receivable turnover and the number of days' sales in receivables from 2013 to 2014 indicate a favorable or an unfavorable trend?

Exercises

EX 8-1 Classifications of receivables **OBJ. 1**

Boeing is one of the world's major aerospace firms, with operations involving commercial aircraft, military aircraft, missiles, satellite systems, and information and battle management systems. As of a recent year, Boeing had $2,969 million of receivables involving U.S. government contracts and $1,241 million of receivables involving commercial aircraft customers, such as Delta Air Lines and United Airlines.

Should Boeing report these receivables separately in the financial statements, or combine them into one overall accounts receivable amount? Explain.

EX 8-2 Nature of uncollectible accounts — OBJ. 2

✔ a. 22.6%

MGM Resorts International owns and operates hotels and casinos including the MGM Grand and the Bellagio in Las Vegas, Nevada. As of a recent year, MGM reported accounts receivable of $415,654,000 and allowance for doubtful accounts of $93,760,000. Johnson & Johnson manufactures and sells a wide range of healthcare products including Band-Aids and Tylenol. As of a recent year, Johnson & Johnson reported accounts receivable of $10,114,000,000 and allowance for doubtful accounts of $340,000,000.

a. Compute the percentage of the allowance for doubtful accounts to the accounts receivable for MGM Resorts International. Round to one decimal place.

b. Compute the percentage of the allowance for doubtful accounts to the accounts receivable, for Johnson & Johnson. Round to one decimal place.

c. Discuss possible reasons for the difference in the two ratios computed in (a) and (b).

EX 8-3 Entries for uncollectible accounts, using direct write-off method — OBJ. 3

Journalize the following transactions in the accounts of Pro Medical Co., a medical equipment company that uses the direct write-off method of accounting for uncollectible receivables:

Jan. 30. Sold merchandise on account to Dr. Cindy Mott, $85,000. The cost of the merchandise sold was $50,000.

June 3. Received $48,000 from Dr. Cindy Mott and wrote off the remainder owed on the sale of January 30 as uncollectible.

Nov. 27. Reinstated the account of Dr. Cindy Mott that had been written off on June 3 and received $37,000 cash in full payment.

EX 8-4 Entries for uncollectible receivables, using allowance method — OBJ. 4

Journalize the following transactions in the accounts of Lamp Light Company, a restaurant supply company that uses the allowance method of accounting for uncollectible receivables:

Mar. 19. Sold merchandise on account to Midnight Delights Co., $37,500. The cost of the merchandise sold was $23,000.

Aug. 31. Received $22,000 from Midnight Delights Co. and wrote off the remainder owed on the sale of March 19 as uncollectible.

Dec. 22. Reinstated the account of Midnight Delights Co. that had been written off on August 31 and received $15,500 cash in full payment.

EX 8-5 Entries to write off accounts receivable — OBJ. 3, 4

Creative Solutions Company, a computer consulting firm, has decided to write off the $11,750 balance of an account owed by a customer, Wil Treadwell. Journalize the entry to record the write-off, assuming that (a) the direct write-off method is used and (b) the allowance method is used.

EX 8-6 Providing for doubtful accounts — OBJ. 4

✔ a. $501,000

✔ b. $493,000

At the end of the current year, the accounts receivable account has a debit balance of $6,125,000 and net sales for the year total $66,800,000. Determine the amount of the adjusting entry to provide for doubtful accounts under each of the following assumptions:

a. The allowance account before adjustment has a debit balance of $18,000. Bad debt expense is estimated at ¾ of 1% of net sales.

b. The allowance account before adjustment has a debit balance of $18,000. An aging of the accounts in the customer ledger indicates estimated doubtful accounts of $475,000.

c. The allowance account before adjustment has a credit balance of $10,000. Bad debt expense is estimated at ½ of 1% of net sales.

d. The allowance account before adjustment has a credit balance of $10,000. An aging of the accounts in the customer ledger indicates estimated doubtful accounts of $360,000.

✔ Avalanche Auto, 84 days

EX 8-7 Number of days past due

OBJ. 4

Toot Auto Supply distributes new and used automobile parts to local dealers throughout the Midwest. Toot's credit terms are n/30. As of the end of business on October 31, the following accounts receivable were past due:

Account	Due Date	Amount
Avalanche Auto	August 8	$12,000
Bales Auto	October 11	2,400
Derby Auto Repair	June 23	3,900
Lucky's Auto Repair	September 2	6,600
Pit Stop Auto	September 19	1,100
Reliable Auto Repair	July 15	9,750
Trident Auto	August 24	1,800
Valley Repair & Tow	May 17	4,000

Determine the number of days each account is past due as of October 31.

SPREADSHEET

EX 8-8 Aging of receivables schedule

OBJ. 4

The accounts receivable clerk for Thunderwood Industries prepared the following partially completed aging of receivables schedule as of the end of business on August 31:

	A	B	C	D	E	F	G
1			Not	Days Past Due			
2			Past				Over
3	Customer	Balance	Due	1–30	31–60	61–90	90
4	Allied Industries Inc.	3,000	3,000				
5	Archer Company	4,500		4,500			
21	Zussman Company	5,000			5,000		
22	Subtotals	750,000	480,000	160,000	75,000	28,000	7,000

The following accounts were unintentionally omitted from the aging schedule and not included in the subtotals above:

Customer	Balance	Due Date
Color World Industries	$33,000	March 13
Hawks Company	15,000	June 29
Osler Inc.	21,000	July 8
Sather Sales Company	8,000	September 6
Wisdom Company	6,500	August 25

a. Determine the number of days past due for each of the preceding accounts as of August 31.

b. Complete the aging of receivables schedule by adding the omitted accounts to the bottom of the schedule and updating the totals.

✔ Allowance for doubtful accounts, $74,170

SPREADSHEET

EX 8-9 Estimating allowance for doubtful accounts

OBJ. 4

Thunderwood Industries has a past history of uncollectible accounts, as shown below. Estimate the allowance for doubtful accounts, based on the aging of receivables schedule you completed in Exercise 8-8.

Age Class	Percent Uncollectible
Not past due	2%
1–30 days past due	6
31–60 days past due	12
61–90 days past due	30
Over 90 days past due	75

EX 8-10 Adjustment for uncollectible accounts **OBJ. 4**

Using data in Exercise 8-9, assume that the allowance for doubtful accounts for Thunderwood Industries has a credit balance of $6,350 before adjustment on August 31. Journalize the adjusting entry for uncollectible accounts as of August 31.

EX 8-11 Estimating doubtful accounts **OBJ. 4**

Traditional Bikes Co. is a wholesaler of motorcycle supplies. An aging of the company's accounts receivable on December 31, 2014, and a historical analysis of the percentage of uncollectible accounts in each age category are as follows:

Age Interval	Balance	Percent Uncollectible
Not past due	$ 740,000	½%
1–30 days past due	390,000	2
31–60 days past due	85,000	4
61–90 days past due	28,000	14
91–180 days past due	42,000	32
Over 180 days past due	15,000	80
	$1,300,000	

Estimate what the proper balance of the allowance for doubtful accounts should be as of December 31, 2014.

EX 8-12 Entry for uncollectible accounts **OBJ. 4**

Using the data in Exercise 8-11, assume that the allowance for doubtful accounts for Traditional Bikes Co. had a debit balance of $3,375 as of December 31, 2014.

Journalize the adjusting entry for uncollectible accounts as of December 31, 2014.

EX 8-13 Entries for bad debt expense under the direct write-off and allowance methods **OBJ. 5**

✔ c. $8,225 higher

The following selected transactions were taken from the records of Shipway Company for the first year of its operations ending December 31, 2014:

Apr. 13. Wrote off account of Dean Sheppard, $8,450.

May 15. Received $500 as partial payment on the $7,100 account of Dan Pyle. Wrote off the remaining balance as uncollectible.

July 27. Received $8,450 from Dean Sheppard, whose account had been written off on April 13. Reinstated the account and recorded the cash receipt.

Dec. 31. Wrote off the following accounts as uncollectible (record as one journal entry):

Paul Chapman	$2,225
Duane DeRosa	3,550
Teresa Galloway	4,770
Ernie Klatt	1,275
Marty Richey	1,690

31. If necessary, record the year-end adjusting entry for uncollectible accounts.

a. Journalize the transactions for 2014 under the direct write-off method.

b. Journalize the transactions for 2014 under the allowance method. Shipway Company uses the percent of credit sales method of estimating uncollectible accounts expense. Based on past history and industry averages, ¾% of credit sales are expected to be uncollectible. Shipway Company recorded $3,778,000 of credit sales during 2014.

c. How much higher (lower) would Shipway Company's net income have been under the direct write-off method than under the allowance method?

EX 8-14 Entries for bad debt expense under the direct write-off and allowance methods **OBJ. 5**

✔ c. $11,090 higher

The following selected transactions were taken from the records of Rustic Tables Company for the year ending December 31, 2014:

June 8. Wrote off account of Kathy Quantel, $8,440.

Aug. 14. Received $3,000 as partial payment on the $12,500 account of Rosalie Oakes. Wrote off the remaining balance as uncollectible.

Oct. 16. Received the $8,440 from Kathy Quantel, whose account had been written off on June 8. Reinstated the account and recorded the cash receipt.

Dec. 31. Wrote off the following accounts as uncollectible (record as one journal entry):

Wade Dolan	$4,600
Greg Gagne	3,600
Amber Kisko	7,150
Shannon Poole	2,975
Niki Spence	6,630

31. If necessary, record the year-end adjusting entry for uncollectible accounts.

a. Journalize the transactions for 2014 under the direct write-off method.

b. Journalize the transactions for 2014 under the allowance method, assuming that the allowance account had a beginning balance of $36,000 on January 1, 2014, and the company uses the analysis of receivables method. Rustic Tables Company prepared the following aging schedule for its accounts receivable:

Aging Class (Number of Days Past Due)	Receivables Balance on December 31	Estimated Percent of Uncollectible Accounts
0–30 days	$320,000	1%
31–60 days	110,000	3
61–90 days	24,000	10
91–120 days	18,000	33
More than 120 days	43,000	75
Total receivables	$515,000	

c. How much higher (lower) would Rustic Tables' 2014 net income have been under the direct write-off method than under the allowance method?

EX 8-15 Effect of doubtful accounts on net income **OBJ. 5**

During its first year of operations, Mack's Plumbing Supply Co. had net sales of $3,250,000, wrote off $27,800 of accounts as uncollectible using the direct write-off method, and reported net income of $487,500. Determine what the net income would have been if the allowance method had been used, and the company estimated that 1% of net sales would be uncollectible.

EX 8-16 Effect of doubtful accounts on net income **OBJ. 5**

✔ b. $11,700 credit balance

Using the data in Exercise 8-15, assume that during the second year of operations Mack's Plumbing Supply Co. had net sales of $4,100,000, wrote off $34,000 of accounts as uncollectible using the direct write-off method, and reported net income of $600,000.

a. Determine what net income would have been in the second year if the allowance method (using 1% of net sales) had been used in both the first and second years.

b. Determine what the balance of the allowance for doubtful accounts would have been at the end of the second year if the allowance method had been used in both the first and second years.

EX 8-17 Entries for bad debt expense under the direct write-off and allowance methods **OBJ. 5**

✔ c. $9,375 higher

Casebolt Company wrote off the following accounts receivable as uncollectible for the first year of its operations ending December 31, 2014:

Customer	Amount
Shawn Brooke	$ 4,650
Eve Denton	5,180
Art Malloy	11,050
Cassie Yost	9,120
Total	$30,000

a. Journalize the write-offs for 2014 under the direct write-off method.

b. Journalize the write-offs for 2014 under the allowance method. Also, journalize the adjusting entry for uncollectible accounts. The company recorded $5,250,000 of credit sales during 2014. Based on past history and industry averages, ¾% of credit sales are expected to be uncollectible.

c. How much higher (lower) would Casebolt Company's 2014 net income have been under the direct write-off method than under the allowance method?

EX 8-18 Entries for bad debt expense under the direct write-off and allowance methods **OBJ. 5**

Seaforth International wrote off the following accounts receivable as uncollectible for the year ending December 31, 2014:

Customer	Amount
Kim Abel	$ 21,550
Lee Drake	33,925
Jenny Green	27,565
Mike Lamb	19,460
Total	$102,500

The company prepared the following aging schedule for its accounts receivable on December 31, 2014:

Aging Class (Number of Days Past Due)	Receivables Balance on December 31	Estimated Percent of Uncollectible Accounts
0–30 days	$ 715,000	1%
31–60 days	310,000	2
61–90 days	102,000	15
91–120 days	76,000	30
More than 120 days	97,000	60
Total receivables	$1,300,000	

a. Journalize the write-offs for 2014 under the direct write-off method.

b. Journalize the write-offs and the year-end adjusting entry for 2014 under the allowance method, assuming that the allowance account had a beginning balance of $95,000 on January 1, 2014, and the company uses the analysis of receivables method.

c. How much higher (lower) would Seaforth International's 2014 net income have been under the allowance method than under the direct write-off method?

EX 8-19 Determine due date and interest on notes **OBJ. 6**

✔ a. Apr. 22, $1,100

SPREADSHEET

Determine the due date and the amount of interest due at maturity on the following notes dated in 2014:

	Date of Note	Face Amount	Interest Rate	Term of Note
a.	January 22	$55,000	8%	90 days
b.	March 9	36,000	5	60 days
c.	June 15	78,000	4	45 days
d.	September 4	13,800	7	60 days
e.	October 1	58,000	6	120 days

EX 8-20 Entries for notes receivable **OBJ. 6**

✔ b. $153,500

Doe Creek Interior Decorators issued a 120-day, 7% note for $150,000, dated February 18, 2014, to La Fleur Furniture Company on account.

a. Determine the due date of the note.

b. Determine the maturity value of the note.

c. Journalize the entries to record the following: (1) receipt of the note by La Fleur Furniture and (2) receipt of payment of the note at maturity.

EX 8-21 Entries for notes receivable **OBJ. 6**

The series of seven transactions recorded in the following T accounts were related to a sale to a customer on account and the receipt of the amount owed. Briefly describe each transaction.

CASH

(7)	61,509		

NOTES RECEIVABLE

(5)	60,000	(6)	60,000

ACCOUNTS RECEIVABLE

(1)	75,000	(3)	15,000
(6)	60,600	(5)	60,000
		(7)	60,600

SALES RETURNS AND ALLOWANCES

(3)	15,000		

MERCHANDISE INVENTORY

(4)	9,000	(2)	45,000

COST OF MERCHANDISE SOLD

(2)	45,000	(4)	9,000

SALES

		(1)	75,000

INTEREST REVENUE

		(6)	600
		(7)	909

EX 8-22 Entries for notes receivable, including year-end entries **OBJ. 6**

The following selected transactions were completed by Easy-Zip Co., a supplier of zippers for clothing:

2013

Dec. 16. Received from Lake Shore Clothing & Bags Co., on account, a $21,000, 90-day, 8% note dated December 16.

31. Recorded an adjusting entry for accrued interest on the note of December 16.

31. Recorded the closing entry for interest revenue.

2014

Mar. 16. Received payment of note and interest from Lake Shore Clothing & Bags Co.

Journalize the entries to record the transactions.

EX 8-23 Entries for receipt and dishonor of note receivable — OBJ. 6

Journalize the following transactions of Sanchez Productions:

July 12. Received a $240,000, 120-day, 7% note dated July 12 from Accolade Co. on account.

Nov. 9. The note is dishonored by Accolade Co.

Dec. 9. Received the amount due on the dishonored note plus interest for 30 days at 9% on the total amount charged to Accolade Co. on November 9.

EX 8-24 Entries for receipt and dishonor of notes receivable — OBJ. 4, 6

Journalize the following transactions in the accounts of Safari Games Co., which operates a riverboat casino:

Apr. 18. Received a $60,000, 30-day, 7% note dated April 18 from Glenn Cross on account.

30. Received a $42,000, 60-day, 8% note dated April 30 from Rhoni Melville on account.

May 18. The note dated April 18 from Glenn Cross is dishonored, and the customer's account is charged for the note, including interest.

June 29. The note dated April 30 from Rhoni Melville is dishonored, and the customer's account is charged for the note, including interest.

Aug. 16. Cash is received for the amount due on the dishonored note dated April 18 plus interest for 90 days at 8% on the total amount debited to Glenn Cross on May 18.

Oct. 22. Wrote off against the allowance account the amount charged to Rhoni Melville on June 29 for the dishonored note dated April 30.

EX 8-25 Receivables on the balance sheet — OBJ. 7

List any errors you can find in the following partial balance sheet:

Napa Vino Company
Balance Sheet
December 31, 2014

Assets		
Current assets:		
Cash		$ 78,500
Notes receivable	$ 300,000	
Less interest receivable	4,500	295,500
Accounts receivable	$1,200,000	
Plus allowance for doubtful accounts	11,500	1,211,500

EX 8-26 Accounts receivable turnover and days' sales in receivables — OBJ. 8

✔ a. Year 2: 10.5

F·A·I

Polo Ralph Lauren Corporation designs, markets, and distributes a variety of apparel, home decor, accessory, and fragrance products. The company's products include such brands as Polo by Ralph Lauren, Ralph Lauren Purple Label, Ralph Lauren, Polo Jeans Co., and Chaps. Polo Ralph Lauren reported the following (in thousands) for two recent years:

	For the Period Ending	
	Year 2	**Year 1**
Net sales	$5,660,300	$4,978,900
Accounts receivable	592,700	486,200

(Continued)

Assume that accounts receivable (in millions) were $576,700 at the beginning of Year 1.

a. Compute the accounts receivable turnover for Year 2 and Year 1. Round to one decimal place.

b. Compute the days' sales in receivables for Year 2 and Year 1. Round to one decimal place.

c. What conclusions can be drawn from these analyses regarding Ralph Lauren's efficiency in collecting receivables?

EX 8-27 Accounts receivable turnover and days' sales in receivables **OBJ. 8**

✔ a. Year 2: 9.3

F·A·I

H.J. Heinz Company was founded in 1869 at Sharpsburg, Pennsylvania, by Henry J. Heinz. The company manufactures and markets food products throughout the world, including ketchup, condiments and sauces, frozen food, pet food, soups, and tuna. For two recent years, H.J. Heinz reported the following (in thousands):

	Year 2	Year 1
Net sales	$10,706,588	$10,494,983
Accounts receivable	1,265,032	1,045,338

Assume that the accounts receivable (in thousands) were $1,171,797 at the beginning of Year 1.

a. Compute the accounts receivable turnover for Year 2 and Year 1. Round to one decimal place.

b. Compute the days' sales in receivables at the end of Year 2 and Year 1. Round to one decimal place.

c. What conclusions can be drawn from these analyses regarding Heinz's efficiency in collecting receivables?

EX 8-28 Accounts receivable turnover and days' sales in receivables **OBJ. 8**

F·A·I

The Limited Brands Inc. sells women's clothing and personal health care products through specialty retail stores including Victoria's Secret and Bath & Body Works stores. The Limited Brands reported the following (in millions) for two recent years:

	Year 2	Year 1
Net sales	$9,613	$8,632
Accounts receivable	267	249

Assume that accounts receivable (in millions) were $313 at the beginning of Year 1.

a. Compute the accounts receivable turnover for Year 2 and Year 1. Round to one decimal place.

b. Compute the day's sales in receivables for Year 2 and Year 1. Round to one decimal place.

c. What conclusions can be drawn from these analyses regarding The Limited Brands' efficiency in collecting receivables?

EX 8-29 Accounts receivable turnover **OBJ. 8**

F·A·I

Use the data in Exercises 8-27 and 8-28 to analyze the accounts receivable turnover ratios of H.J. Heinz Company and The Limited Brands Inc.

a. Compute the average accounts receivable turnover ratio for The Limited Brands Inc. and H.J. Heinz Company for the years shown in Exercises 8-27 and 8-28.

b. Does The Limited Brands or H.J. Heinz Company have the higher average accounts receivable turnover ratio?

c. Explain the logic underlying your answer in (b).

Problems Series A

PR 8-1A Entries related to uncollectible accounts

OBJ. 4

✔ 3. $1,749,300

GENERAL LEDGER

The following transactions were completed by The Irvine Company during the current fiscal year ended December 31:

Feb. 8. Received 40% of the $18,000 balance owed by DeCoy Co., a bankrupt business, and wrote off the remainder as uncollectible.

May 27. Reinstated the account of Seth Nelsen, which had been written off in the preceding year as uncollectible. Journalized the receipt of $7,350 cash in full payment of Seth's account.

Aug. 13. Wrote off the $6,400 balance owed by Kat Tracks Co., which has no assets.

Oct. 31. Reinstated the account of Crawford Co., which had been written off in the preceding year as uncollectible. Journalized the receipt of $3,880 cash in full payment of the account.

Dec. 31. Wrote off the following accounts as uncollectible (compound entry): Newbauer Co., $7,190; Bonneville Co., $5,500; Crow Distributors, $9,400; Fiber Optics, $1,110.

31. Based on an analysis of the $1,785,000 of accounts receivable, it was estimated that $35,700 will be uncollectible. Journalized the adjusting entry.

Instructions

1. Record the January 1 credit balance of $26,000 in a T account for Allowance for Doubtful Accounts.
2. Journalize the transactions. Post each entry that affects the following selected T accounts and determine the new balances:

   Allowance for Doubtful Accounts
   Bad Debt Expense

3. Determine the expected net realizable value of the accounts receivable as of December 31.
4. Assuming that instead of basing the provision for uncollectible accounts on an analysis of receivables, the adjusting entry on December 31 had been based on an estimated expense of ¼ of 1% of the net sales of $18,200,000 for the year, determine the following:
   a. Bad debt expense for the year.
   b. Balance in the allowance account after the adjustment of December 31.
   c. Expected net realizable value of the accounts receivable as of December 31.

PR 8-2A Aging of receivables; estimating allowance for doubtful accounts

OBJ. 4

✔ 3. $121,000

SPREADSHEET

Trophy Fish Company supplies flies and fishing gear to sporting goods stores and outfitters throughout the western United States. The accounts receivable clerk for Trophy Fish prepared the following partially completed aging of receivables schedule as of the end of business on December 31, 2013:

	A	B	C	D	E	F	G	H
1			Not	Days Past Due				
2			Past					
3	Customer	Balance	Due	1–30	31–60	61–90	91–120	Over 120
4	AAA Outfitters	20,000	20,000					
5	Brown Trout Fly Shop	7,500			7,500			
30	Zigs Fish Adventures	4,000		4,000				
31	Subtotals	1,300,000	750,000	290,000	120,000	40,000	20,000	80,000

(Continued)

The following accounts were unintentionally omitted from the aging schedule:

Customer	Due Date	Balance
Adams Sports & Flies	May 22, 2013	$5,000
Blue Dun Flies	Oct. 10, 2013	4,900
Cicada Fish Co.	Sept. 29, 2013	8,400
Deschutes Sports	Oct. 20, 2013	7,000
Green River Sports	Nov. 7, 2013	3,500
Smith River Co.	Nov. 28, 2013	2,400
Western Trout Company	Dec. 7, 2013	6,800
Wolfe Sports	Jan. 20, 2014	4,400

Trophy Fish has a past history of uncollectible accounts by age category, as follows:

Age Class	Percent Uncollectible
Not past due	1%
1–30 days past due	2
31–60 days past due	10
61–90 days past due	30
91–120 days past due	40
Over 120 days past due	80

Instructions

1. Determine the number of days past due for each of the preceding accounts.
2. Complete the aging of receivables schedule by adding the omitted accounts to the bottom of the schedule and updating the totals.
3. Estimate the allowance for doubtful accounts, based on the aging of receivables schedule.
4. Assume that the allowance for doubtful accounts for Trophy Fish Company has a debit balance of $3,600 before adjustment on December 31, 2013. Journalize the adjusting entry for uncollectible accounts.
5. Assume that the adjusting entry in (4) was inadvertently omitted, how would the omission affect the balance sheet and income statement?

PR 8-3A Compare two methods of accounting for uncollectible receivables OBJ. 3, 4, 5

✔ 1. Year 4: Balance of allowance account, end of year, $15,050

Call Systems Company, a telephone service and supply company, has just completed its fourth year of operations. The direct write-off method of recording bad debt expense has been used during the entire period. Because of substantial increases in sales volume and the amount of uncollectible accounts, the company is considering changing to the allowance method. Information is requested as to the effect that an annual provision of 1% of sales would have had on the amount of bad debt expense reported for each of the past four years. It is also considered desirable to know what the balance of Allowance for Doubtful Accounts would have been at the end of each year. The following data have been obtained from the accounts:

			Year of Origin of Accounts Receivable Written Off as Uncollectible			
Year	**Sales**	**Uncollectible Accounts Written Off**	**1st**	**2nd**	**3rd**	**4th**
1st	$ 900,000	$ 4,500	$4,500			
2nd	1,250,000	9,600	3,000	$6,600		
3rd	1,500,000	12,800	1,000	3,700	$8,100	
4th	2,200,000	16,550		1,500	4,300	$10,750

Instructions

1. Assemble the desired data, using the following column headings:

	Bad Debt Expense			
Year	Expense Actually Reported	Expense Based on Estimate	Increase (Decrease) in Amount of Expense	Balance of Allowance Account, End of Year

2. Experience during the first four years of operations indicated that the receivables were either collected within two years or had to be written off as uncollectible. Does the estimate of 1% of sales appear to be reasonably close to the actual experience with uncollectible accounts originating during the first two years? Explain.

PR 8-4A Details of notes receivable and related entries — OBJ. 6

✔ 1. Note 2: Due date, June 22; Interest due at maturity, $360

Flush Mate Co. wholesales bathroom fixtures. During the current fiscal year, Flush Mate Co. received the following notes:

	Date	Face Amount	Term	Interest Rate
1.	Mar. 6	$80,000	45 days	5%
2.	Apr. 23	24,000	60 days	9
3.	July 20	42,000	120 days	6
4.	Sept. 6	54,000	90 days	7
5.	Nov. 29	27,000	60 days	6
6.	Dec. 30	72,000	30 days	5

Instructions

1. Determine for each note (a) the due date and (b) the amount of interest due at maturity, identifying each note by number.
2. Journalize the entry to record the dishonor of Note (3) on its due date.
3. Journalize the adjusting entry to record the accrued interest on Notes (5) and (6) on December 31.
4. Journalize the entries to record the receipt of the amounts due on Notes (5) and (6) in January.

PR 8-5A Notes receivable entries — OBJ. 6

The following data relate to notes receivable and interest for CGH Cable Co., a cable manufacturer and supplier. (All notes are dated as of the day they are received.)

Apr. 10. Received a $144,000, 5%, 60-day note on account.

May 15. Received a $270,000, 7%, 120-day note on account.

June 9. Received $145,200 on note of April 10.

Aug. 22. Received a $150,000, 4%, 45-day note on account.

Sept. 12. Received $276,300 on note of May 15.

30. Received a $210,000, 8%, 60-day note on account.

Oct. 6. Received $150,750 on note of August 22.

18. Received a 120,000, 5%, 60-day note on account.

Nov. 29. Received $212,800 on note of September 30.

Dec. 17. Received $121,000 on note of October 18.

Instructions

Journalize the entries to record the transactions.

PR 8-6A Sales and notes receivable transactions

OBJ. 6

GENERAL LEDGER

The following were selected from among the transactions completed by Caldemeyer Co. during the current year. Caldemeyer Co. sells and installs home and business security systems.

Jan. 3. Loaned $18,000 cash to Trina Gelhaus, receiving a 90-day, 8% note.

Feb. 10. Sold merchandise on account to Bradford & Co., $24,000. The cost of the merchandise sold was $14,400.

13. Sold merchandise on account to Dry Creek Co., $60,000. The cost of merchandise sold was $54,000.

Mar. 12. Accepted a 60-day, 7% note for $24,000 from Bradford & Co. on account.

14. Accepted a 60-day, 9% note for $60,000 from Dry Creek Co. on account.

Apr. 3. Received the interest due from Trina Gelhaus and a new 120-day, 9% note as a renewal of the loan of January 3. (Record both the debit and the credit to the notes receivable account.)

May 11. Received from Bradford & Co. the amount due on the note of March 12.

13. Dry Creek Co. dishonored its note dated March 14.

July 12. Received from Dry Creek Co. the amount owed on the dishonored note, plus interest for 60 days at 12% computed on the maturity value of the note.

Aug. 1. Received from Trina Gelhaus the amount due on her note of April 3.

Oct. 5. Sold merchandise on account to Halloran Co., $13,500. The cost of the merchandise sold was $8,100.

15. Received from Halloran Co. the amount of the invoice of October 5, less 2% discount.

Instructions

Journalize the entries to record the transactions.

Problems Series B

PR 8-1B Entries related to uncollectible accounts

OBJ. 4

✔ 3. $2,290,000

GENERAL LEDGER

The following transactions were completed by The Wild Trout Gallery during the current fiscal year ended December 31:

Jan. 19. Reinstated the account of Arlene Gurley, which had been written off in the preceding year as uncollectible. Journalized the receipt of $2,660 cash in full payment of Arlene's account.

Apr. 3. Wrote off the $12,750 balance owed by Premier GS Co., which is bankrupt.

July 16. Received 25% of the $22,000 balance owed by Hayden Co., a bankrupt business, and wrote off the remainder as uncollectible.

Nov. 23. Reinstated the account of Harry Carr, which had been written off two years earlier as uncollectible. Recorded the receipt of $4,000 cash in full payment.

Dec. 31. Wrote off the following accounts as uncollectible (compound entry): Cavey Co., $3,300; Fogle Co., $8,100; Lake Furniture, $11,400; Melinda Shryer, $1,200.

31. Based on an analysis of the $2,350,000 of accounts receivable, it was estimated that $60,000 will be uncollectible. Journalized the adjusting entry.

Instructions

1. Record the January 1 credit balance of $50,000 in a T account for Allowance for Doubtful Accounts.

2. Journalize the transactions. Post each entry that affects the following T accounts and determine the new balances:

   Allowance for Doubtful Accounts
   Bad Debt Expense

3. Determine the expected net realizable value of the accounts receivable as of December 31.
4. Assuming that instead of basing the provision for uncollectible accounts on an analysis of receivables, the adjusting entry on December 31 had been based on an estimated expense of ½ of 1% of the net sales of $15,800,000 for the year, determine the following:
   a. Bad debt expense for the year.
   b. Balance in the allowance account after the adjustment of December 31.
   c. Expected net realizable value of the accounts receivable as of December 31.

✔ 3. $123,235

SPREADSHEET

PR 8-2B Aging of receivables; estimating allowance for doubtful accounts **OBJ. 4**

Wig Creations Company supplies wigs and hair care products to beauty salons throughout Texas and the Southwest. The accounts receivable clerk for Wig Creations prepared the following partially completed aging of receivables schedule as of the end of business on December 31, 2013:

	A	B	C	D	E	F	G	H
1			Not	Days Past Due				
2			Past					
3	Customer	Balance	Due	1–30	31–60	61–90	91–120	Over 120
4	ABC Beauty	15,000	15,000					
5	Angel Wigs	8,000			8,000			
30	Zodiac Beauty	3,000		3,000				
31	Subtotals	875,000	415,000	210,000	112,000	55,000	18,000	65,000

The following accounts were unintentionally omitted from the aging schedule:

Customer	Due Date	Balance
Arcade Beauty	Aug. 17, 2013	$10,000
Creative Images	Oct. 30, 2013	8,500
Excel Hair Products	July 3, 2013	7,500
First Class Hair Care	Sept. 8, 2013	6,600
Golden Images	Nov. 23, 2013	3,600
Oh That Hair	Nov. 29, 2013	1,400
One Stop Hair Designs	Dec. 7, 2013	4,000
Visions Hair & Nail	Jan. 11, 2014	9,000

Wig Creations has a past history of uncollectible accounts by age category, as follows:

Age Class	Percent Uncollectible
Not past due	1%
1–30 days past due	4
31–60 days past due	16
61–90 days past due	25
91–120 days past due	40
Over 120 days past due	80

Instructions

1. Determine the number of days past due for each of the preceding accounts.
2. Complete the aging of receivables schedule by adding the omitted accounts to the bottom of the schedule and updating the totals.

(Continued)

3. Estimate the allowance for doubtful accounts, based on the aging of receivables schedule.
4. Assume that the allowance for doubtful accounts for Wig Creations has a credit balance of $7,375 before adjustment on December 31, 2013. Journalize the adjustment for uncollectible accounts.
5. Assume that the adjusting entry in (4) was inadvertently omitted, how would the omission affect the balance sheet and income statement?

PR 8-3B Compare two methods of accounting for uncollectible receivables **OBJ. 3, 4, 5**

✔ 1. Year 4: Balance of allowance account, end of year, $32,550

Digital Depot Company, which operates a chain of 40 electronics supply stores, has just completed its fourth year of operations. The direct write-off method of recording bad debt expense has been used during the entire period. Because of substantial increases in sales volume and the amount of uncollectible accounts, the firm is considering changing to the allowance method. Information is requested as to the effect that an annual provision of ¼% of sales would have had on the amount of bad debt expense reported for each of the past four years. It is also considered desirable to know what the balance of Allowance for Doubtful Accounts would have been at the end of each year. The following data have been obtained from the accounts:

			Year of Origin of Accounts Receivable Written Off as Uncollectible			
Year	**Sales**	**Uncollectible Accounts Written Off**	**1st**	**2nd**	**3rd**	**4th**
1st	$12,500,000	$18,000	$18,000			
2nd	14,800,000	30,200	9,000	$21,200		
3rd	18,000,000	39,900	3,600	9,300	$27,000	
4th	24,000,000	52,600		5,100	12,500	$35,000

Instructions

1. Assemble the desired data, using the following column headings:

	Bad Debt Expense			
Year	**Expense Actually Reported**	**Expense Based on Estimate**	**Increase (Decrease) in Amount of Expense**	**Balance of Allowance Account, End of Year**

2. Experience during the first four years of operations indicated that the receivables were either collected within two years or had to be written off as uncollectible. Does the estimate of ¼% of sales appear to be reasonably close to the actual experience with uncollectible accounts originating during the first two years? Explain.

PR 8-4B Details of notes receivable and related entries **OBJ. 6**

✔ 1. Note 1: Due date, Feb. 13; Interest due at maturity, $110

Gen-X Ads Co. produces advertising videos. During the current fiscal year, Gen-X Ads Co. received the following notes:

	Date	Face Amount	Term	Interest Rate
1.	Jan. 14	$33,000	30 days	4%
2.	Mar. 9	60,000	45 days	7
3.	July 12	48,000	90 days	5
4.	Aug. 23	16,000	75 days	6
5.	Nov. 15	36,000	60 days	8
6.	Dec. 10	24,000	60 days	6

Instructions

1. Determine for each note (a) the due date and (b) the amount of interest due at maturity, identifying each note by number.

2. Journalize the entry to record the dishonor of Note (3) on its due date.
3. Journalize the adjusting entry to record the accrued interest on Notes (5) and (6) on December 31.
4. Journalize the entries to record the receipt of the amounts due on Notes (5) and (6) in January and February.

PR 8-5B Notes receivable entries **OBJ. 6**

The following data relate to notes receivable and interest for Owens Co., a financial services company. (All notes are dated as of the day they are received.)

Mar. 8. Received a $33,000, 5%, 60-day note on account.
31. Received an $80,000, 7%, 90-day note on account.
May 7. Received $33,275 on note of March 8.
16. Received a $72,000, 7%, 90-day note on account.
June 11. Received a $36,000, 6%, 45-day note on account.
29. Received $81,400 on note of March 31.
July 26. Received $36,270 on note of June 11.
Aug. 4. Received a $48,000, 9%, 120-day note on account.
14. Received $73,260 on note of May 16.
Dec. 2. Received $49,440 on note of August 4.

Instructions

Journalize the entries to record the transactions.

PR 8-6B Sales and notes receivable transactions **OBJ. 6**

GENERAL LEDGER

The following were selected from among the transactions completed during the current year by Danix Co., an appliance wholesale company:

Jan. 21. Sold merchandise on account to Black Tie Co., $28,000. The cost of merchandise sold was $16,800.
Mar. 18. Accepted a 60-day, 6% note for $28,000 from Black Tie Co. on account.
May 17. Received from Black Tie Co. the amount due on the note of March 18.
June 15. Sold merchandise on account to Pioneer Co. for $17,700. The cost of merchandise sold was $10,600.
21. Loaned $18,000 cash to JR Stutts, receiving a 30-day, 8% note.
25. Received from Pioneer Co. the amount due on the invoice of June 15, less 1% discount.
July 21. Received the interest due from JR Stutts and a new 60-day, 9% note as a renewal of the loan of June 21. (Record both the debit and the credit to the notes receivable account.)
Sept. 19. Received from JR Stutts the amount due on her note of July 21.
22. Sold merchandise on account to Wycoff Co., $20,000. The cost of merchandise sold was $12,000.
Oct. 14. Accepted a 30-day, 6% note for $20,000 from Wycoff Co. on account.
Nov. 13. Wycoff Co. dishonored the note dated October 14.
Dec. 28. Received from Wycoff Co. the amount owed on the dishonored note, plus interest for 45 days at 8% computed on the maturity value of the note.

Instructions

Journalize the entries to record the transactions.

Cases & Projects

CP 8-1 Ethics and professional conduct in business

Bev Wynn, vice president of operations for Dillon County Bank, has instructed the bank's computer programmer to use a 365-day year to compute interest on depository accounts (liabilities). Bev also instructed the programmer to use a 360-day year to compute interest on loans (assets).

Discuss whether Bev is behaving in a professional manner.

CP 8-2 Estimate uncollectible accounts

For several years, Xtreme Co.'s sales have been on a "cash only" basis. On January 1, 2011, however, Xtreme Co. began offering credit on terms of n/30. The amount of the adjusting entry to record the estimated uncollectible receivables at the end of each year has been ½ of 1% of credit sales, which is the rate reported as the average for the industry. Credit sales and the year-end credit balances in Allowance for Doubtful Accounts for the past four years are as follows:

Year	Credit Sales	Allowance for Doubtful Accounts
2011	$4,000,000	$ 5,000
2012	4,400,000	8,250
2013	4,800,000	10,200
2014	5,100,000	14,400

Laurie Jones, president of Xtreme Co., is concerned that the method used to account for and write off uncollectible receivables is unsatisfactory. She has asked for your advice in the analysis of past operations in this area and for recommendations for change.

1. Determine the amount of (a) the addition to Allowance for Doubtful Accounts and (b) the accounts written off for each of the four years.
2. a. Advise Laurie Jones as to whether the estimate of ½ of 1% of credit sales appears reasonable.

   b. Assume that after discussing (a) with Laurie Jones, she asked you what action might be taken to determine what the balance of Allowance for Doubtful Accounts should be at December 31, 2014, and what possible changes, if any, you might recommend in accounting for uncollectible receivables. How would you respond?

CP 8-3 Accounts receivable turnover and days' sales in receivables

F·A·I

Best Buy is a specialty retailer of consumer electronics, including personal computers, entertainment software, and appliances. Best Buy operates retail stores in addition to the Best Buy, Media Play, On Cue, and Magnolia Hi-Fi Web sites. For two recent years, Best Buy reported the following (in millions):

	Year 2	Year 1
Net sales	$50,272	$49,694
Accounts receivable at end of year	2,348	2,020

Assume that the accounts receivable (in millions) were $1,868 at the beginning of fiscal Year 1.

1. Compute the accounts receivable turnover for Year 2 and Year 1. Round to one decimal place.
2. Compute the days' sales in receivables at the end of Year 2 and Year 1. Round to one decimal place.

3. What conclusions can be drawn from (1) and (2) regarding Best Buy's efficiency in collecting receivables?
4. What assumption did we make about sales for the Best Buy ratio computations that might distort the ratios and therefore cause the ratios not to be comparable for Year 2 and Year 1?

CP 8-4 Accounts receivable turnover and days' sales in receivables

F·A·I

Apple Inc. designs, manufactures, and markets personal computers and related personal computing and communicating solutions for sale primarily to education, creative, consumer, and business customers. Substantially all of the company's net sales over the last five years are from sales of its Macs, iPods, iPads, and related software and peripherals. For two recent fiscal years, Apple reported the following (in millions):

	Year 2	Year 1
Net sales	$65,225	$42,905
Accounts receivable at end of year	5,510	3,361

Assume that the accounts receivable (in millions) were $2,422 at the beginning of fiscal Year 1.

1. Compute the accounts receivable turnover for Year 2 and Year 1. Round to one decimal place.
2. Compute the days' sales in receivables at the end of Year 2 and Year 1. Round to one decimal place.
3. What conclusions can be drawn from (1) and (2) regarding Apple's efficiency in collecting receivables?

CP 8-5 Accounts receivable turnover and days' sales in receivables

F·A·I

Costco Wholesale Corporation operates membership warehouses that sell a variety of branded and private label products. Headquartered in Issaquah, Washington, it also sells merchandise online in the United States (Costco.com) and in Canada (Costco.ca). For two recent years, Costco reported the following (in millions):

	Year 2	Year 1
Net sales	$77,946	$71,422
Accounts receivable at end of year	1,321	1,205

Assume that the accounts receivable (in thousands) were $1,009 at the beginning of Year 1.

1. Compute the accounts receivable turnover for Year 2 and Year 1. Round to one decimal place.
2. Compute the days' sales in receivables at the end of Year 2 and Year 1. Round to one decimal place.
3. What conclusions can be drawn from (1) and (2) regarding Costco's efficiency in collecting receivables?
4. Given the nature of Costco's operations, do you believe Costco's accounts receivable turnover ratio would be higher or lower than a typical manufacturing company, such as H.J. Heinz Company? Explain.

Learning Objectives

After studying this chapter, you should be able to: *Example Exercises*

Obj	Objective	Example Exercises
1	Define, classify, and account for the cost of fixed assets.	
	Nature of Fixed Assets	
	Classifying Costs	
	The Cost of Fixed Assets	
	Capital and Revenue Expenditures	EE 9-1
	Leasing Fixed Assets	
2	Compute depreciation, using the following methods: straight-line method, units-of-output method, and double-declining-balance method.	
	Accounting for Depreciation	
	Factors in Computing Depreciation Expense	
	Straight-Line Method	EE 9-2
	Units-of-Output Method	EE 9-3
	Double-Declining-Balance Method	EE 9-4
	Comparing Depreciation Methods	
	Depreciation for Federal Income Tax	
	Revising Depreciation Estimates	EE 9-5
3	Journalize entries for the disposal of fixed assets.	
	Disposal of Fixed Assets	
	Discarding Fixed Assets	
	Selling Fixed Assets	EE 9-6
4	Compute depletion and journalize the entry for depletion.	
	Natural Resources	EE 9-7
5	Describe the accounting for intangible assets, such as patents, copyrights, and goodwill.	
	Intangible Assets	
	Patents	EE 9-8
	Copyrights and Trademarks	
	Goodwill	EE 9-8
6	Describe how depreciation expense is reported in an income statement and prepare a balance sheet that includes fixed assets and intangible assets.	
	Financial Reporting for Fixed Assets and Intangible Assets	
7	Describe and illustrate the fixed asset turnover ratio to assess the efficiency of a company's use of its fixed assets.	
	Financial Analysis and Interpretation: Fixed Asset Turnover Ratio	EE 9-9

At a Glance 9 Page 430

OBJ 1 Define, classify, and account for the cost of fixed assets.

Nature of Fixed Assets

Fixed assets are long-term or relatively permanent assets such as equipment, machinery, buildings, and land. Other descriptive titles for fixed assets are *plant assets* or *property, plant, and equipment*. Fixed assets have the following characteristics:

1. They exist physically and, thus, are *tangible* assets.
2. They are owned and used by the company in its normal operations.
3. They are not offered for sale as part of normal operations.

Exhibit 1 shows the percent of fixed assets to total assets for some select companies. As shown in Exhibit 1, fixed assets are often a significant portion of the total assets of a company.

EXHIBIT 1

Fixed Assets as a Percent of Total Assets—Selected Companies

	Fixed Assets as a Percent of Total Assets
Alcoa Inc.	52%
Exxon Mobil Corporation	66
Ford Motor Company	21
Kroger	60
Office Depot Inc.	25
United Parcel Service, Inc.	52
Verizon Communications	40
Walgreen Co.	43
Walmart	60

Classifying Costs

A cost that has been incurred may be classified as a fixed asset, an investment, or an expense. Exhibit 2 shows how to determine the proper classification of a cost and how it should be recorded.

IFRS IFRS

See Appendix C for more information

EXHIBIT 2

Classifying Costs

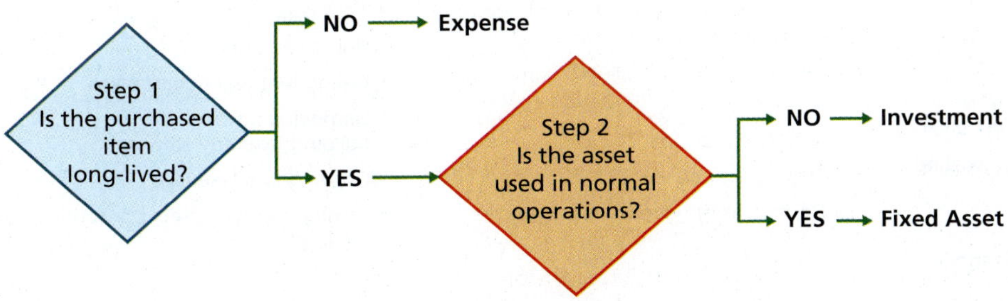

As shown in Exhibit 2, classifying a cost involves the following steps:

Step 1. Is the purchased item long-lived?

If *yes*, the item is recorded as an asset on the balance sheet, either as a fixed asset or an investment. Proceed to Step 2.

If *no*, the item is classified and recorded as an *expense*.

Step 2. Is the asset used in normal operations?

If *yes*, the asset is classified and recorded as a *fixed asset*.

If *no*, the asset is classified and recorded as an *investment*.

Items that are classified and recorded as fixed assets include land, buildings, or equipment. Such assets normally last more than a year and are used in the normal operations. However, standby equipment for use during peak periods or when other equipment breaks down is still classified as a fixed asset, even though it is not used very often. In contrast, fixed assets that have been abandoned or are no longer used in operations are not classified as fixed assets.

Although fixed assets may be sold, they should not be offered for sale as part of normal operations. For example, cars and trucks offered for sale by an automotive dealership are not fixed assets of the dealership. On the other hand, a tow truck used in the normal operations of the dealership is a fixed asset of the dealership.

Investments are long-lived assets that are not used in the normal operations and are held for future resale. Such assets are reported on the balance sheet in a section entitled *Investments*. For example, undeveloped land acquired for future resale would be classified and reported as an investment, not land.

The Cost of Fixed Assets

In addition to purchase price, the costs of acquiring fixed assets include all amounts spent getting the asset in place and ready for use. For example, freight costs and the costs of installing equipment are part of the asset's total cost.

Exhibit 3 summarizes some of the common costs of acquiring fixed assets. These costs are recorded by debiting the related fixed asset account, such as Land,[1] Building, Land Improvements, or Machinery and Equipment.

EXHIBIT 3 **Costs of Acquiring Fixed Assets**

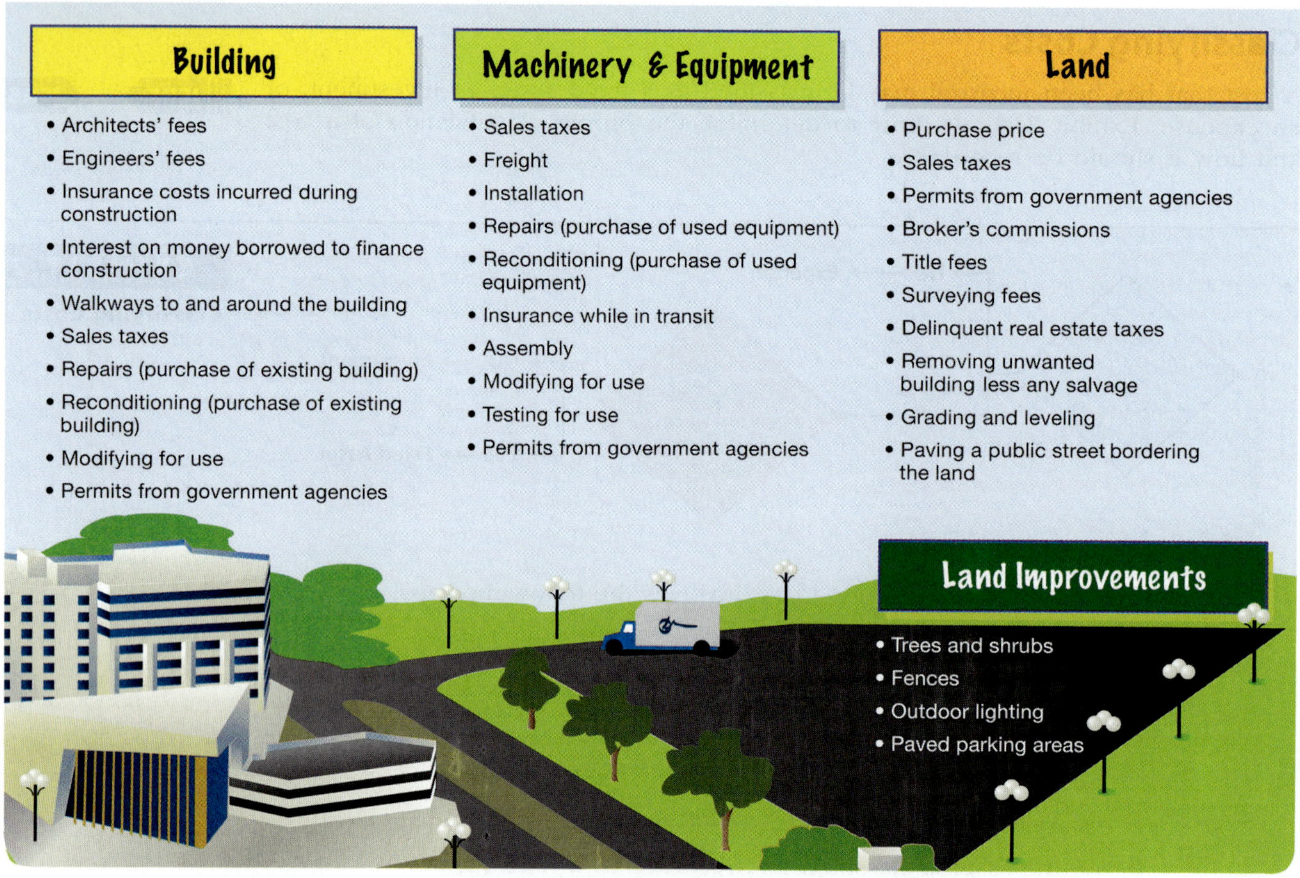

Only costs necessary for preparing the fixed asset for use are included as a cost of the asset. Unnecessary costs that do not increase the asset's usefulness are recorded as an expense. For example, the following costs are included as an expense:

1. Vandalism
2. Mistakes in installation
3. Uninsured theft
4. Damage during unpacking and installing
5. Fines for not obtaining proper permits from governmental agencies

A company may incur costs associated with constructing a fixed asset such as a new building. The direct costs incurred in the construction, such as labor and

1 As discussed here, land is assumed to be used only as a location or site and not for its mineral deposits or other natural resources.

materials, should be capitalized as a debit to an account entitled Construction in Progress. When the construction is complete, the costs are reclassified by crediting Construction in Progress and debiting the proper fixed asset account such as Building. For some companies, construction in progress can be significant.

Intel Corporation reported in a recent annual report construction in progress of $2.6 billion, which was 15% of its total fixed assets.

IFRS IFRS

See Appendix C for more information

Capital and Revenue Expenditures

Once a fixed asset has been acquired and placed into service, costs may be incurred for ordinary maintenance and repairs. In addition, costs may be incurred for improving an asset or for extraordinary repairs that extend the asset's useful life. Costs that benefit only the current period are called **revenue expenditures**. Costs that improve the asset or extend its useful life are **capital expenditures**.

Ordinary Maintenance and Repairs Costs related to the ordinary maintenance and repairs of a fixed asset are recorded as an expense of the current period. Such expenditures are *revenue expenditures* and are recorded as increases to Repairs and Maintenance Expense. For example, $300 paid for a tune-up of a delivery truck is recorded as follows:

		Repairs and Maintenance Expense		300	
		Cash			300

Asset Improvements After a fixed asset has been placed into service, costs may be incurred to improve the asset. For example, the service value of a delivery truck might be improved by adding a $5,500 hydraulic lift to allow for easier and quicker loading of cargo. Such costs are *capital expenditures* and are recorded as increases to the fixed asset account. In the case of the hydraulic lift, the expenditure is recorded as follows:

		Delivery Truck		5,500	
		Cash			5,500

Because the cost of the delivery truck has increased, depreciation for the truck will also change over its remaining useful life.

Extraordinary Repairs After a fixed asset has been placed into service, costs may be incurred to extend the asset's useful life. For example, the engine of a forklift that is near the end of its useful life may be overhauled at a cost of $4,500, extending its useful life by eight years. Such costs are *capital expenditures* and are recorded as a decrease in an accumulated depreciation account. In the case of the forklift, the expenditure is recorded as follows:

		Accumulated Depreciation—Forklift		4,500	
		Cash			4,500

Because the forklift's remaining useful life has changed, depreciation for the forklift will also change based on the new book value of the forklift.

Integrity, Objectivity, and Ethics in Business

CAPITAL CRIME

One of the largest alleged accounting frauds in history involved the improper accounting for capital expenditures. WorldCom, the second largest telecommunications company in the United States at the time, improperly treated maintenance expenditures on its telecommunications network as capital expenditures. As a result, the company had to restate its prior years' earnings downward by nearly $4 billion to correct this error. The company declared bankruptcy within months of disclosing the error, and the CEO was sentenced to 25 years in prison.

The accounting for revenue and capital expenditures is summarized below.

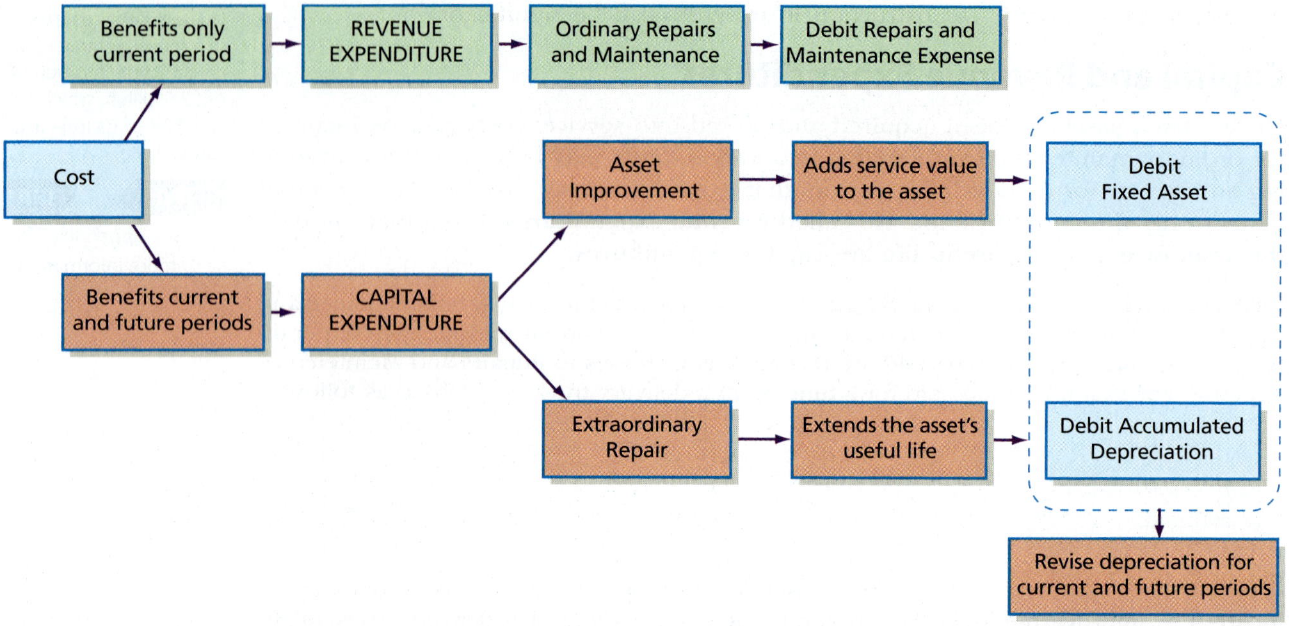

Example Exercise 9-1 **Capital and Revenue Expenditures**

OBJ 1

On June 18, GTS Co. paid $1,200 to upgrade a hydraulic lift and $45 for an oil change for one of its delivery trucks. Journalize the entries for the hydraulic lift upgrade and oil change expenditures.

Follow My Example 9-1

June 18	Delivery Truck	1,200	
	Cash		1,200
18	Repairs and Maintenance Expense	45	
	Cash		45

Practice Exercises: **PE 9-1A, PE 9-1B**

Leasing Fixed Assets

A *lease* is a contract for the use of an asset for a period of time. Leases are often used in business. For example, automobiles, computers, medical equipment, buildings, and airplanes are often leased.

The two parties to a lease contract are as follows:

1. The *lessor* is the party who owns the asset.
2. The *lessee* is the party to whom the rights to use the asset are granted by the lessor.

Delta Air Lines leases facilities, aircraft, and equipment, using both capital and operating leases.

Under a lease contract, the lessee pays rent on a periodic basis for the lease term. The lessee accounts for a lease contract in one of two ways depending on how the lease contract is classified. A lease contract can be classified as either:

1. A *capital lease* or
2. An *operating lease*

A **capital lease** is accounted for as if the lessee has purchased the asset. The lessee debits an asset account for the fair market value of the asset and credits a long-term lease liability account. The asset is then written off as an expense (amortized) over the life of the capital lease. The accounting for capital leases is discussed in more advanced accounting texts.

An **operating lease** is accounted for as if the lessee is renting the asset for the lease term. The lessee records operating lease payments by debiting *Rent Expense* and crediting *Cash*. The lessee's future lease obligations are not recorded in the accounts. However, such obligations are disclosed in notes to the financial statements.

The asset rentals described in earlier chapters of this text were accounted for as operating leases. To simplify, all leases are assumed to be operating leases throughout this text.

Accounting for Depreciation

OBJ 2 Compute depreciation, using the following methods: straight-line method, units-of-output method, and double-declining-balance method.

Over time, fixed assets, with the exception of land, lose their ability to provide services. Thus, the costs of fixed assets such as equipment and buildings should be recorded as an expense over their useful lives. This periodic recording of the cost of fixed assets as an expense is called **depreciation**. Because land has an unlimited life, it is not depreciated.

The adjusting entry to record depreciation debits *Depreciation Expense* and credits a *contra asset* account entitled *Accumulated Depreciation* or *Allowance for Depreciation*. The use of a contra asset account allows the original cost to remain unchanged in the fixed asset account.

Note:
The adjusting entry to record depreciation debits Depreciation Expense and credits Accumulated Depreciation.

Depreciation can be caused by physical or functional factors.

1. *Physical depreciation* factors include wear and tear during use or from exposure to weather.
2. *Functional depreciation* factors include obsolescence and changes in customer needs that cause the asset to no longer provide services for which it was intended. For example, equipment may become obsolete due to changing technology.

Two common misunderstandings that exist about *depreciation* as used in accounting include:

1. Depreciation does not measure a decline in the market value of a fixed asset. Instead, depreciation is an allocation of a fixed asset's cost to expense over the asset's useful life. Thus, the book value of a fixed asset (cost less accumulated depreciation) usually does not agree with the asset's market value. This is justified in accounting because a fixed asset is for use in a company's operations rather than for resale.
2. Depreciation does not provide cash to replace fixed assets as they wear out. This misunderstanding may occur because depreciation, unlike most expenses, does not require an outlay of cash when it is recorded.

Factors in Computing Depreciation Expense

Three factors determine the depreciation expense for a fixed asset. These three factors are as follows:

1. The asset's initial cost
2. The asset's expected useful life
3. The asset's estimated residual value

The initial *cost* of a fixed asset is determined using the concepts discussed and illustrated earlier in this chapter.

The *expected useful life* of a fixed asset is estimated at the time the asset is placed into service. Estimates of expected useful lives are available from industry trade associations. The Internal Revenue Service also publishes guidelines for useful lives, which may be helpful for financial reporting purposes. However, it is not uncommon for different companies to use a different useful life for similar assets.

The **residual value** of a fixed asset at the end of its useful life is estimated at the time the asset is placed into service. Residual value is sometimes referred to as *scrap* *value, salvage value*, or *trade-in value*. The difference between a fixed asset's initial cost and its residual value is called the asset's *depreciable cost*. The depreciable cost is the amount of the asset's cost that is allocated over its useful life as depreciation expense. If a fixed asset has no residual value, then its entire cost should be allocated to depreciation.

Exhibit 4 shows the relationship between depreciation expense and a fixed asset's initial cost, expected useful life, and estimated residual value.

EXHIBIT 4

Depreciation Expense Factors

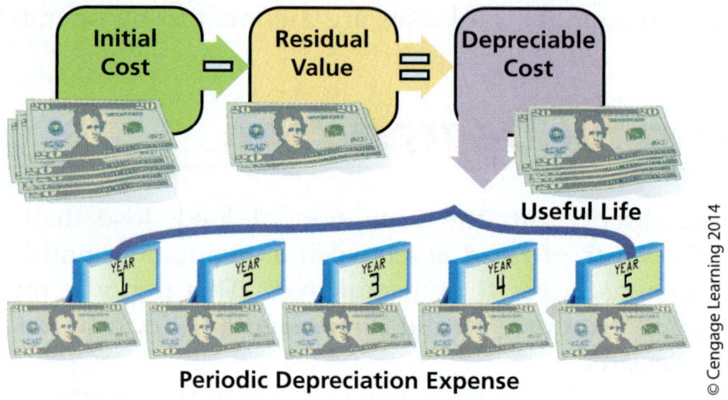

For an asset placed into or taken out of service during the first half of a month, many companies compute depreciation on the asset for the entire month. That is, the asset is treated as having been purchased or sold on the first day of *that* month. Likewise, purchases and sales during the second half of a month are treated as having occurred on the first day of the *next* month. To simplify, this practice is used in this chapter.

The three depreciation methods used most often are as follows:[2]

1. Straight-line depreciation
2. Units-of-output depreciation
3. Double-declining-balance depreciation

Exhibit 5 shows how often these methods are used in financial statements.

EXHIBIT 5

Use of Depreciation Methods

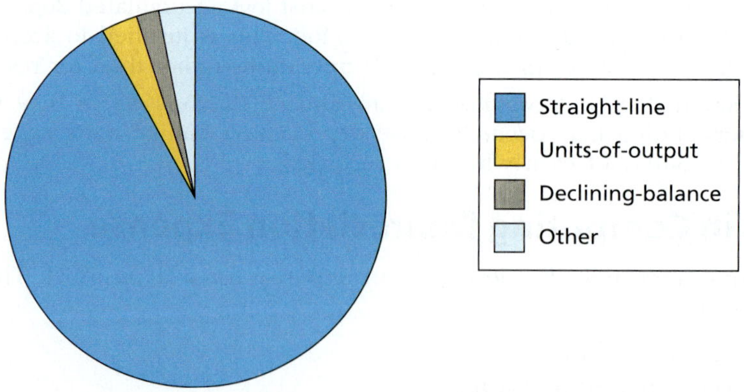

Source: *Accounting Trends & Techniques*, 65th ed., American Institute of Certified Public Accountants, New York, 2011.

It is not necessary for a company to use only one method of computing depreciation for all of its fixed assets. For example, a company may use one method for depreciating equipment and another method for depreciating buildings.

2 Another method not often used today, called the *sum-of-the-years-digits method*, is described and illustrated in an online appendix located at **www.cengagebrain.com**.

A company may also use different depreciation methods for determining income taxes and property taxes.

Straight-Line Method

The **straight-line method** provides for the same amount of depreciation expense for each year of the asset's useful life. As shown in Exhibit 5, the straight-line method is by far the most widely used depreciation method.

To illustrate, assume that equipment was purchased on January 1 as follows:

Initial cost	$24,000
Expected useful life	5 years
Estimated residual value	$2,000

The annual straight-line depreciation of $4,400 is computed below.

$$\text{Annual Depreciation} = \frac{\text{Cost} - \text{Residual Value}}{\text{Useful Life}} = \frac{\$24,000 - \$2,000}{5 \text{ Years}} = \$4,400$$

If an asset is used for only part of a year, the annual depreciation is prorated. For example, assume that the preceding equipment was purchased and placed into service on October 1. The depreciation for the year ending December 31 would be **$1,100**, computed as follows:

$$\text{First-Year Partial Depreciation} = \$4,400 \times 3/12 = \$1,100$$

The computation of straight-line depreciation may be simplified by converting the annual depreciation to a percentage of depreciable cost.[3] The straight-line percentage is determined by dividing 100% by the number of years of expected useful life, as shown below.

Expected Years of Useful Life	**Straight-Line Percentage**
5 years	20% (100%/5)
8 years	12.5% (100%/8)
10 years	10% (100%/10)
20 years	5% (100%/20)
25 years	4% (100%/25)

For the preceding equipment, the annual depreciation of $4,400 can be computed by multiplying the depreciable cost of $22,000 by 20% (100%/5).

Example Exercise 9-2 Straight-Line Depreciation

OBJ 2

Equipment acquired at the beginning of the year at a cost of $125,000 has an estimated residual value of $5,000 and an estimated useful life of 10 years. Determine (a) the depreciable cost, (b) the straight-line rate, and (c) the annual straight-line depreciation.

Follow My Example 9-2

a. $120,000 ($125,000 – $5,000)

b. 10% = 1/10

c. $12,000 ($120,000 × 10%), or ($120,000/10 years)

Practice Exercises: **PE 9-2A, PE 9-2B**

3 The depreciation rate may also be expressed as a fraction. For example, the annual straight-line rate for an asset with a three-year useful life is 1/3.

As shown on the previous page, the straight-line method is simple to use. When an asset's revenues are about the same from period to period, straight-line depreciation provides a good matching of depreciation expense with the asset's revenues.

Units-of-Output Method

Norfolk Southern Corporation depreciates its train engines based on hours of operation.

The **units-of-output method** provides the same amount of depreciation expense for each unit of output of the asset. Depending on the asset, the units of output can be expressed in terms of hours, miles driven, or quantity produced. For example, the unit of output for a truck is normally expressed in miles driven. For manufacturing assets, the units of output are often expressed as units of product. In this case, the units-of-output method may be called the *units-of-production method.*

The units-of-output method is applied in two steps.

Step 1. Determine the depreciation per unit as:

$$\text{Depreciation per Unit} = \frac{\text{Cost} - \text{Residual Value}}{\text{Total Units of Output}}$$

Step 2. Compute the depreciation expense as:

$$\text{Depreciation Expense} = \text{Depreciation per Unit} \times \text{Total Units of Output Used}$$

To illustrate, assume that the equipment in the preceding example is expected to have a useful life of 10,000 operating hours. During the year, the equipment was operated 2,100 hours. The units-of-output depreciation for the year is **$4,620**, as shown below.

Step 1. Determine the depreciation per hour as:

$$\text{Depreciation per Hour} = \frac{\text{Cost} - \text{Residual Value}}{\text{Total Units of Output}} = \frac{\$24{,}000 - \$2{,}000}{10{,}000 \text{ Hours}} = \$2.20 \text{ per Hour}$$

Step 2. Compute the depreciation expense as:

$$\text{Depreciation Expense} = \text{Depreciation per Unit} \times \text{Total Units of Output Used}$$

$$\text{Depreciation Expense} = \$2.20 \text{ per Hour} \times 2{,}100 \text{ Hours} = \$4{,}620$$

The units-of-output method is often used when a fixed asset's in-service time (or use) varies from year to year. In such cases, the units-of-output method matches depreciation expense with the asset's revenues.

Example Exercise 9-3 Units-of-Output Depreciation

OBJ 2

Equipment acquired at the beginning of the year at a cost of $180,000 has an estimated residual value of $10,000, has an estimated useful life of 40,000 hours, and was operated 3,600 hours during the year. Determine (a) the depreciable cost, (b) the depreciation rate, and (c) the unit-of-output depreciation for the year.

Follow My Example 9-3

a. $170,000 ($180,000 – $10,000)

b. $4.25 per hour ($170,000/40,000 hours)

c. $15,300 (3,600 hours × $4.25)

Practice Exercises: **PE 9-3A, PE 9-3B**

Double-Declining-Balance Method

The **double-declining-balance method** provides for a declining periodic expense over the expected useful life of the asset. The double-declining-balance method is applied in three steps.

Step 1. Determine the straight-line percentage, using the expected useful life.
Step 2. Determine the double-declining-balance rate by multiplying the straight-line rate from Step 1 by 2.
Step 3. Compute the depreciation expense by multiplying the double-declining-balance rate from Step 2 times the book value of the asset.

To illustrate, the equipment purchased in the preceding example is used to compute double-declining-balance depreciation. For the first year, the depreciation is **$9,600**, as shown below.

Step 1. Straight-line percentage = 20% (100%/5)
Step 2. Double-declining-balance rate = 40% (20% × 2)
Step 3. Depreciation expense = $9,600 ($24,000 × 40%)

For the first year, the book value of the equipment is its initial cost of $24,000. After the first year, the **book value** (cost minus accumulated depreciation) declines and, thus, the depreciation also declines. The double-declining-balance depreciation for the full five-year life of the equipment is shown below.

Year	Cost	Acc. Dep. at Beginning of Year	Book Value at Beginning of Year		Double-Declining-Balance Rate	Depreciation for Year	Book Value at End of Year
1	$24,000		$24,000.00	×	40%	$9,600.00	$14,400.00
2	24,000	$ 9,600.00	14,400.00	×	40%	5,760.00	8,640.00
3	24,000	15,360.00	8,640.00	×	40%	3,456.00	5,184.00
4	24,000	18,816.00	5,184.00	×	40%	2,073.60	3,110.40
5	24,000	20,889.60	3,110.40		—	1,110.40	2,000.00

When the double-declining-balance method is used, the estimated residual value is *not* considered. However, the asset should not be depreciated below its estimated residual value. In the above example, the estimated residual value was $2,000. Therefore, the depreciation for the fifth year is $1,110.40 ($3,110.40 − $2,000.00) instead of $1,244.16 (40% × $3,110.40).

Like straight-line depreciation, if an asset is used for only part of a year, the annual depreciation is prorated. For example, assume that the preceding equipment was purchased and placed into service on October 1. The depreciation for the year ending December 31 would be $2,400, computed as follows:

First-Year Partial Depreciation = $9,600 × 3/12 = $2,400

The depreciation for the second year would then be $8,640, computed as follows:

Second-Year Depreciation = $8,640 = [40% × ($24,000 – $2,400)]

The double-declining-balance method provides a higher depreciation in the first year of the asset's use, followed by declining depreciation amounts. For this reason, the double-declining-balance method is called an **accelerated depreciation method**.

An asset's revenues are often greater in the early years of its use than in later years. In such cases, the double-declining-balance method provides a good matching of depreciation expense with the asset's revenues.

Example Exercise 9-4 Double-Declining-Balance Depreciation OBJ 2

Equipment acquired at the beginning of the year at a cost of $125,000 has an estimated residual value of $5,000 and an estimated useful life of 10 years. Determine (a) the double-declining-balance rate and (b) the double-declining-balance depreciation for the first year.

Follow My Example 9-4

a. 20% [(1/10) × 2]
b. $25,000 ($125,000 × 20%)

Practice Exercises: **PE 9-4A, PE 9-4B**

Comparing Depreciation Methods

The three depreciation methods are summarized in Exhibit 6. All three methods allocate a portion of the total cost of an asset to an accounting period, while never depreciating an asset below its residual value.

EXHIBIT 6

Summary of Depreciation Methods

Method	Useful Life	Depreciable Cost	Depreciation Rate	Depreciation Expense
Straight-line	Years	Cost less residual value	Straight-line rate*	Constant
Units-of-output	Total units of output	Cost less residual value	Cost – Residual value / Total units of output	Variable
Double-declining-balance	Years	Declining book value, but not below residual value	Straight-line rate* × 2	Declining

*Straight-line rate = (100%/Useful life)

The straight-line method provides for the same periodic amounts of depreciation expense over the life of the asset. The units-of-output method provides for periodic amounts of depreciation expense that vary, depending on the amount the asset is used. The double-declining-balance method provides for a higher depreciation amount in the first year of the asset's use, followed by declining amounts.

The depreciation for the straight-line, units-of-output, and double-declining-balance methods is shown in Exhibit 7. The depreciation in Exhibit 7 is based on

EXHIBIT 7

Comparing Depreciation Methods

	Depreciation Expense		
Year	Straight-Line Method	Units-of-Output Method	Double-Declining-Balance Method
1	$ 4,400*	$ 4,620 ($2.20 × 2,100 hrs.)	$ 9,600.00 ($24,000 × 40%)
2	4,400	3,300 ($2.20 × 1,500 hrs.)	5,760.00 ($14,400 × 40%)
3	4,400	5,720 ($2.20 × 2,600 hrs.)	3,456.00 ($8,640 × 40%)
4	4,400	3,960 ($2.20 × 1,800 hrs.)	2,073.60 ($5,184 × 40%)
5	4,400	4,400 ($2.20 × 2,000 hrs.)	1,110.40**
Total	$22,000	$22,000	$22,000.00

*$4,400 = ($24,000 – $2,000)/5 years
**$3,110.40 – $2,000.00 because the equipment cannot be depreciated below its residual value of $2,000.

the equipment purchased in our prior illustrations. For the units-of-output method, we assume that the equipment was used as follows:

Year 1	2,100 hours
Year 2	1,500
Year 3	2,600
Year 4	1,800
Year 5	2,000
Total	10,000 hours

Depreciation for Federal Income Tax

The Internal Revenue Code uses the *Modified Accelerated Cost Recovery System (MACRS)* to compute depreciation for tax purposes. MACRS has eight classes of useful life and depreciation rates for each class. Two of the most common classes are the five-year class and the seven-year class.[4] The five-year class includes automobiles and light-duty trucks. The seven-year class includes most machinery and equipment. Depreciation for these two classes is similar to that computed using the double-declining-balance method.

In using the MACRS rates, residual value is ignored. Also, all fixed assets are assumed to be put in and taken out of service in the middle of the year. For the five-year-class assets, depreciation is spread over six years, as shown below.

Year	MACRS 5-Year-Class Depreciation Rates
1	20.0%
2	32.0
3	19.2
4	11.5
5	11.5
6	5.8
	100.0%

To simplify, a company will sometimes use MACRS for both financial statement and tax purposes. This is acceptable if MACRS does not result in significantly different amounts than would have been reported using one of the three depreciation methods discussed in this chapter.

Business Connection

DEPRECIATING ANIMALS?

Under MACRS, various farm animals may be depreciated. The period (years) over which some common classes of farm animals may be depreciated are shown in the table to the right.

Depreciation for farm animals begins when the animal reaches the age of maturity, which is normally when it can be worked, milked, or bred. For race horses, depreciation begins when a horse is put into training.

Class of Animal	Years
Dairy or breeding cattle	7–10
Goats and sheep	5
Hogs	3
Horses	3–12

4 Real estate is in either a 27½-year or a 31½-year class and is depreciated by the straight-line method.

Revising Depreciation Estimates

Estimates of residual values and useful lives of fixed assets may change due to abnormal wear and tear or obsolescence. When new estimates are determined, they are used to determine the depreciation expense in future periods. The depreciation expense recorded in earlier years is not affected.[5]

To illustrate, assume the following data for a machine that was purchased on January 1, 2013:

Initial machine cost	$140,000
Expected useful life	5 years
Estimated residual value	$10,000
Annual depreciation using the straight-line method [($140,000 – $10,000)/5 years]	$26,000

At the end of 2014, the machine's book value (undepreciated cost) is $88,000, as shown below.

Initial machine cost	$140,000
Less accumulated depreciation ($26,000 per year × 2 years)	52,000
Book value (undepreciated cost), end of second year	$ 88,000

At the beginning of 2015, the company estimates that the machine's remaining useful life is eight years (instead of three) and that its residual value is $8,000 (instead of $10,000). The depreciation expense for each of the remaining eight years is $10,000, computed as follows:

Book value (undepreciated cost), end of second year	$88,000
Less revised estimated residual value	8,000
Revised remaining depreciable cost	$80,000
Revised annual depreciation expense [($88,000 – $8,000)/8 years]	$10,000

Exhibit 8 shows the book value of the asset over its original and revised lives. After the depreciation is revised at the end of 2014, book value declines at a slower rate. At the end of year 2022, the book value reaches the revised residual value of $8,000.

EXHIBIT 8

Book Value of Asset with Change in Estimate

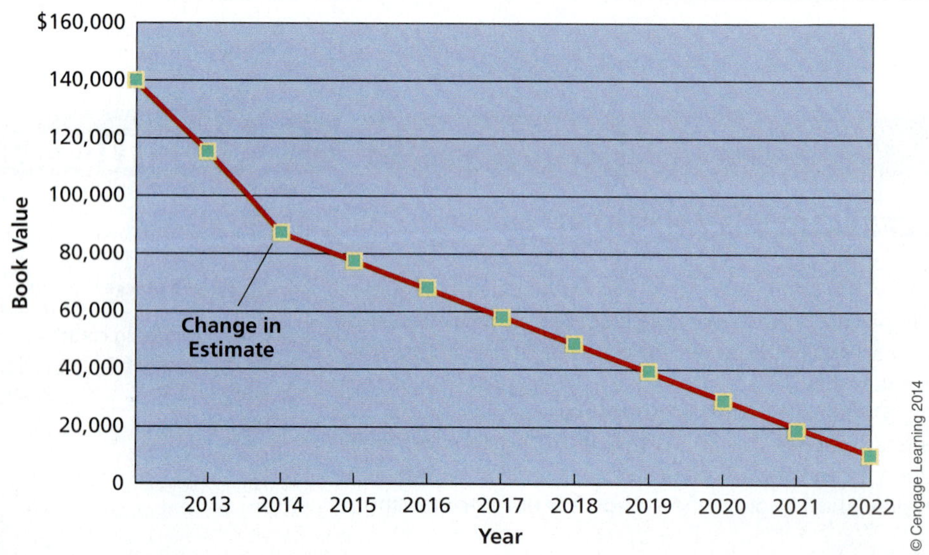

5 *FASB Accounting Standards Codification*, Section 250-10-05.

Example Exercise 9-5 Revision of Depreciation

OBJ 2

A warehouse with a cost of $500,000 has an estimated residual value of $120,000, has an estimated useful life of 40 years, and is depreciated by the straight-line method. (a) Determine the amount of the annual depreciation. (b) Determine the book value at the end of the twentieth year of use. (c) Assuming that at the start of the twenty-first year the remaining life is estimated to be 25 years and the residual value is estimated to be $150,000, determine the depreciation expense for each of the remaining 25 years.

Follow My Example 9-5

a. $9,500 [($500,000 – $120,000)/40]
b. $310,000 [$500,000 – ($9,500 × 20)]
c. $6,400 [($310,000 – $150,000)/25]

Practice Exercises: **PE 9-5A, PE 9-5B**

Disposal of Fixed Assets

OBJ 3 Journalize entries for the disposal of fixed assets.

Fixed assets that are no longer useful may be discarded or sold.[6] In such cases, the fixed asset is removed from the accounts. Just because a fixed asset is fully depreciated, however, does not mean that it should be removed from the accounts.

If a fixed asset is still being used, its cost and accumulated depreciation should remain in the ledger even if the asset is fully depreciated. This maintains accountability for the asset in the ledger. If the asset was removed from the ledger, the accounts would contain no evidence of the continued existence of the asset. In addition, cost and accumulated depreciation data on such assets are often needed for property tax and income tax reports.

Discarding Fixed Assets

If a fixed asset is no longer used and has no residual value, it is discarded. For example, assume that a fixed asset that is fully depreciated and has no residual value is discarded. The entry to record the discarding removes the asset and its related accumulated depreciation from the ledger.

To illustrate, assume that equipment acquired at a cost of $25,000 is fully depreciated at December 31, 2013. On February 14, 2014, the equipment is discarded. The entry to record the discard is as follows:

Feb.	14	Accumulated Depreciation—Equipment		25,000	
		Equipment			25,000
		To write off equipment discarded.			

Note:
The entry to record the disposal of a fixed asset removes the cost of the asset and its accumulated depreciation from the accounts.

If an asset has not been fully depreciated, depreciation should be recorded before removing the asset from the accounting records. To illustrate, assume that equipment costing $6,000 with no estimated residual value is depreciated at a straight-line rate of 10%. On December 31, 2013, the accumulated depreciation balance, after adjusting entries, is $4,650. On March 24, 2014, the asset is removed from service and discarded. The entry to record the depreciation for the three months of 2014 before the asset is discarded is as follows:

Mar.	24	Depreciation Expense—Equipment		150	
		Accumulated Depreciation—Equipment			150
		To record current depreciation on equipment discarded ($600 × 3/12).			

6 The accounting for the exchange of fixed assets is described and illustrated in the appendix at the end of this chapter.

The discarding of the equipment is then recorded as follows:

Mar.	24	Accumulated Depreciation—Equipment	4,800	
		Loss on Disposal of Equipment	1,200	
		Equipment		6,000
		To write off equipment discarded.		

The loss of $1,200 is recorded because the balance of the accumulated depreciation account ($4,800) is less than the balance in the equipment account ($6,000). Losses on the discarding of fixed assets are reported in the income statement.

Selling Fixed Assets

The entry to record the sale of a fixed asset is similar to the entry for discarding an asset. The only difference is that the receipt of cash is also recorded. If the selling price is more than the book value of the asset, a gain is recorded. If the selling price is less than the book value, a loss is recorded.

To illustrate, assume that equipment is purchased at a cost of $10,000 with no estimated residual value and is depreciated at a straight-line rate of 10%. The equipment is sold for cash on October 12 of the eighth year of its use. The balance of the accumulated depreciation account as of the preceding December 31 is $7,000. The entry to update the depreciation for the nine months of the current year is as follows:

Oct.	12	Depreciation Expense—Equipment	750	
		Accumulated Depreciation—Equipment		750
		To record current depreciation on equipment sold ($10,000 × 9/12 × 10%).		

After the current depreciation is recorded, the book value of the asset is $2,250 ($10,000 − $7,750). The entries to record the sale, assuming three different selling prices, are as follows:

Sold at book value, for $2,250. No gain or loss.

Oct.	12	Cash	2,250	
		Accumulated Depreciation—Equipment	7,750	
		Equipment		10,000

Sold below book value, for $1,000. Loss of $1,250.

Oct.	12	Cash	1,000	
		Accumulated Depreciation—Equipment	7,750	
		Loss on Sale of Equipment	1,250	
		Equipment		10,000

Sold above book value, for $2,800. Gain of $550.

Oct.	12	Cash	2,800	
		Accumulated Depreciation—Equipment	7,750	
		Equipment		10,000
		Gain on Sale of Equipment		550

Example Exercise 9-6 Sale of Equipment

OBJ 3

Equipment was acquired at the beginning of the year at a cost of $91,000. The equipment was depreciated using the straight-line method based on an estimated useful life of nine years and an estimated residual value of $10,000.

a. What was the depreciation for the first year?

b. Assuming the equipment was sold at the end of the second year for $78,000, determine the gain or loss on the sale of the equipment.

c. Journalize the entry to record the sale.

Follow My Example 9-6

a. $9,000 [($91,000 – $10,000)/9]

b. $5,000 gain {$78,000 – [$91,000 – ($9,000 × 2)]}

c.

Cash	78,000	
Accumulated Depreciation—Equipment	18,000	
Equipment		91,000
Gain on Sale of Equipment		5,000

Practice Exercises: **PE 9-6A, PE 9-6B**

Natural Resources

OBJ 4 Compute depletion and journalize the entry for depletion.

The fixed assets of some companies include timber, metal ores, minerals, or other natural resources. As these resources are harvested or mined and then sold, a portion of their cost is debited to an expense account. This process of transferring the cost of natural resources to an expense account is called **depletion**.

Depletion is determined as follows:[7]

Step 1. Determine the depletion rate as:

$$\text{Depletion Rate} = \frac{\text{Cost of Resource}}{\text{Estimated Total Units of Resource}}$$

Step 2. Multiply the depletion rate by the quantity extracted from the resource during the period.

$$\text{Depletion Expense} = \text{Depletion Rate} \times \text{Quantity Extracted}$$

To illustrate, assume that Karst Company purchased mining rights as follows:

Cost of mineral deposit	$400,000
Estimated total units of resource	1,000,000 tons
Tons mined during year	90,000 tons

The depletion expense of $36,000 for the year is computed as shown below.

Step 1.

$$\text{Depletion Rate} = \frac{\text{Cost of Resource}}{\text{Estimated Total Units of Resource}} = \frac{\$400{,}000}{1{,}000{,}000 \text{ Tons}} = \$0.40 \text{ per Ton}$$

Step 2.

$$\text{Depletion Expense} = \$0.40 \text{ per Ton} \times 90{,}000 \text{ Tons} = \$36{,}000$$

The adjusting entry to record the depletion is shown below.

Dec.	31	Depletion Expense		36,000	
		Accumulated Depletion			36,000
		Depletion of mineral deposit.			

7 We assume that there is no significant residual value after all the natural resource is extracted.

Like the accumulated depreciation account, Accumulated Depletion is a *contra asset* account. It is reported on the balance sheet as a deduction from the cost of the mineral deposit.

Example Exercise 9-7 Depletion

OBJ 4

Earth's Treasures Mining Co. acquired mineral rights for $45,000,000. The mineral deposit is estimated at 50,000,000 tons. During the current year, 12,600,000 tons were mined and sold.

a. Determine the depletion rate.

b. Determine the amount of depletion expense for the current year.

c. Journalize the adjusting entry on December 31 to recognize the depletion expense.

Follow My Example 9-7

a. $0.90 per ton ($45,000,000/50,000,000 tons)

b. $11,340,000 (12,600,000 tons × $0.90 per ton)

c.

Dec. 31	Depletion Expense	11,340,000	
	Accumulated Depreciation		11,340,000
	Depletion of mineral deposit.		

Practice Exercises: **PE 9-7A, PE 9-7B**

OBJ 5 Describe the accounting for intangible assets, such as patents, copyrights, and goodwill.

Intangible Assets

Patents, copyrights, trademarks, and goodwill are long-lived assets that are used in the operations of a business and are not held for sale. These assets are called **intangible assets** because they do not exist physically.

The accounting for intangible assets is similar to that for fixed assets. The major issues are:

IFRS IFRS

See Appendix C for more information

Determining the initial cost.

Determining the **amortization**, which is the amount of cost to transfer to expense.

Amortization results from the passage of time or a decline in the usefulness of the intangible asset.

Patents

Manufacturers may acquire exclusive rights to produce and sell goods with one or more unique features. Such rights are granted by **patents**, which the federal government issues to inventors. These rights continue in effect for 20 years. A business may purchase patent rights from others, or it may obtain patents developed by its own research and development.

The initial cost of a purchased patent, including any legal fees, is debited to an asset account. This cost is written off, or amortized, over the years of the patent's expected useful life. The expected useful life of a patent may be less than its legal life. For example, a patent may become worthless due to changing technology or consumer tastes.

Patent amortization is normally computed using the straight-line method. The amortization is recorded by debiting an amortization expense account and crediting the patents account. A separate contra asset account is usually *not* used for intangible assets.

To illustrate, assume that at the beginning of its fiscal year, a company acquires patent rights for $100,000. Although the patent will not expire for 14 years, its remaining useful life is estimated as five years. The adjusting entry to amortize the patent at the end of the year is as follows:

Dec.	31	Amortization Expense—Patents		20,000	
		Patents			20,000
		Patent amortization ($100,000/5).			

Some companies develop their own patents through research and development. In such cases, any *research and development costs* are usually recorded as current operating expenses in the period in which they are incurred. This accounting for research and development costs is justified on the basis that any future benefits from research and development are highly uncertain.

IFRS

International Connection

INTERNATIONAL FINANCIAL REPORTING STANDARDS (IFRS)

IFRS allow certain research and development (R&D) costs to be recorded as assets when incurred. Typically, R&D costs are classified as either research costs or development costs. If certain criteria are met, research costs can be recorded as an expense, while development costs can be recorded as an asset. This criterion includes such considerations as the company's intent to use or to sell the intangible asset. For example, Nokia Corporation (Finland) reported capitalized development costs of €40 million in a recent statement of financial position (balance sheet), where € represents the euro, the common currency of the European Economic Union.*

*Differences between U.S. GAAP and IFRS are further discussed and illustrated in Appendix C.

Copyrights and Trademarks

The exclusive right to publish and sell a literary, artistic, or musical composition is granted by a **copyright**. Copyrights are issued by the federal government and extend for 70 years beyond the author's death. The costs of a copyright include all costs of creating the work plus any other costs of obtaining the copyright. A copyright that is purchased is recorded at the price paid for it. Copyrights are amortized over their estimated useful lives.

A **trademark** is a name, term, or symbol used to identify a business and its products. Most businesses identify their trademarks with ® in their advertisements and on their products.

Under federal law, businesses can protect their trademarks by registering them for 10 years and renewing the registration for 10-year periods. Like a copyright, the legal costs of registering a trademark are recorded as an asset.

If a trademark is purchased from another business, its cost is recorded as an asset. In such cases, the cost of the trademark is considered to have an indefinite useful life. Thus, trademarks are not amortized. Instead, trademarks are reviewed periodically for impaired value. When a trademark is impaired, the trademark should be written down and a loss recognized.

Goodwill

Goodwill refers to an intangible asset of a business that is created from such favorable factors as location, product quality, reputation, and managerial skill. Goodwill allows a business to earn a greater rate of return than normal.

Generally accepted accounting principles (GAAP) allow goodwill to be recorded only if it is objectively determined by a transaction. An example of such a transaction is the purchase of an entity at a price in excess of the fair value of its net assets (assets − liabilities). The excess is recorded as goodwill and reported as an intangible asset.

Unlike patents and copyrights, goodwill is not amortized. However, a loss should be recorded if the future prospects of the purchased entity become impaired. This loss would normally be disclosed in the Other Expense section of the income statement.

To illustrate, assume that on December 31 FaceCard Company has determined that $250,000 of the goodwill created from the purchase of Electronic Systems is impaired. The entry to record the impairment is as follows:

Dec.	31	Loss from Impaired Goodwill		250,000	
		Goodwill			250,000
		Impaired goodwill.			

Exhibit 9 shows intangible asset disclosures for 500 large companies. Goodwill is the most often reported intangible asset. This is because goodwill arises from merger transactions, which are common.

EXHIBIT 9

Frequency of Intangible Asset Disclosures for 500 Companies

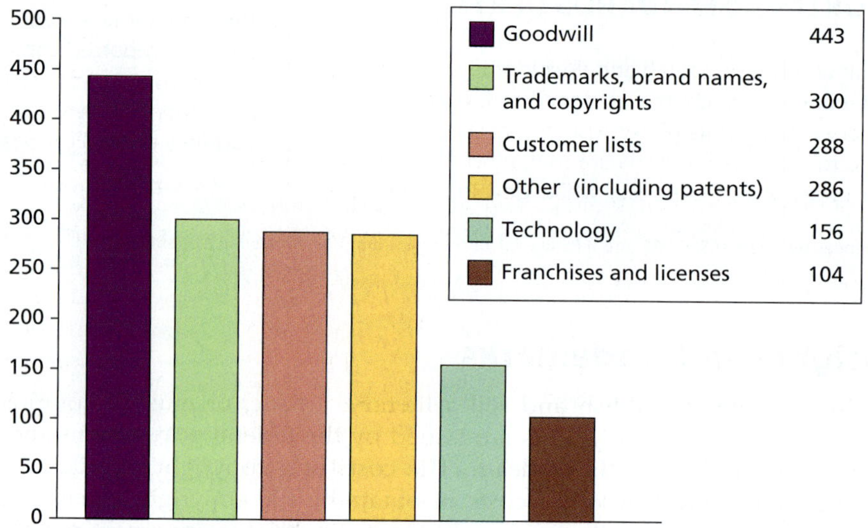

Source: *Accounting Trends & Techniques*, 65th ed., American Institute of Certified Public Accountants, New York, 2011.
Note: Some companies have multiple disclosures.

Exhibit 10 summarizes the characteristics of intangible assets.

EXHIBIT 10

Comparison of Intangible Assets

Intangible Asset	Description	Amortization Period	Periodic Expense
Patent	Exclusive right to benefit from an innovation.	Estimated useful life not to exceed legal life.	Amortization expense.
Copyright	Exclusive right to benefit from a literary, artistic, or musical composition.	Estimated useful life not to exceed legal life.	Amortization expense.
Trademark	Exclusive use of a name, term, or symbol.	None	Impairment loss if fair value less than carrying value (impaired).
Goodwill	Excess of purchase price of a business over the fair value of its net assets (assets − liabilities).	None	Impairment loss if fair value less than carrying value (impaired).

Example Exercise 9-8 Impaired Goodwill and Amortization of Patent

OBJ 5

On December 31, it was estimated that goodwill of $40,000 was impaired. In addition, a patent with an estimated useful economic life of 12 years was acquired for $84,000 on July 1.

a. Journalize the adjusting entry on December 31 for the impaired goodwill.

b. Journalize the adjusting entry on December 31 for the amortization of the patent rights.

Follow My Example 9-8

a.	Dec. 31	Loss from Impaired Goodwill	40,000	
		Goodwill		40,000
		Impaired goodwill.		
b.	Dec. 31	Amortization Expense—Patents	3,500	
		Patents		3,500
		Amortized patent rights [($84,000/12) × (6/12)].		

Practice Exercises: **PE 9-8A, PE 9-8B**

Financial Reporting for Fixed Assets and Intangible Assets

OBJ 6 Describe how depreciation expense is reported in an income statement and prepare a balance sheet that includes fixed assets and intangible assets.

In the income statement, depreciation and amortization expense should be reported separately or disclosed in a note. A description of the methods used in computing depreciation should also be reported.

In the balance sheet, each class of fixed assets should be disclosed on the face of the statement or in the notes. The related accumulated depreciation should also be disclosed, either by class or in total. The fixed assets may be shown at their *book value* (cost less accumulated depreciation), which can also be described as their *net* amount.

If there are many classes of fixed assets, a single amount may be presented in the balance sheet, supported by a note with a separate listing. Fixed assets may be reported under the more descriptive caption of property, plant, and equipment.

Intangible assets are usually reported in the balance sheet in a separate section following fixed assets. The balance of each class of intangible assets should be disclosed net of any amortization.

The balance sheet presentation for Mornin' Joe's fixed and intangible assets is shown below.

Mornin' Joe
Balance Sheet
December 31, 2014

Property, plant, and equipment:			
Land		$1,850,000	
Buildings	$2,650,000		
Less accumulated depreciation	420,000	2,230,000	
Office equipment	$ 350,000		
Less accumulated depreciation	102,000	248,000	
Total property, plant, and equipment			$4,328,000
Intangible assets:			
Patents			140,000

The cost and related accumulated depletion of mineral rights are normally shown as part of the Fixed Assets section of the balance sheet. The mineral rights may be shown net of depletion on the face of the balance sheet. In such cases, a supporting note discloses the accumulated depletion.

F·A·I

Financial Analysis and Interpretation: Fixed Asset Turnover Ratio

OBJ 7 Describe and illustrate the fixed asset turnover ratio to assess the efficiency of a company's use of its fixed assets.

A measure of a company's efficiency in using its fixed assets to generate revenue is the fixed asset turnover ratio. The **fixed asset turnover ratio** measures the number of dollars of sales earned per dollar of fixed assets. It is computed as follows:

$$\text{Fixed Asset Turnover Ratio} = \frac{\text{Net Sales}}{\text{Average Book Value of Fixed Assets}}$$

To illustrate, the following data (in millions) were taken from recent financial statements of Starbucks Corporation.

	Year 2	Year 1
Net sales	$10,707	$9,775
Fixed assets (net):		
Beginning of year	2,536	2,956
End of year	2,417	2,536

Starbucks' fixed asset turnover ratios for Year 2 and Year 1 are computed as follows:

	Year 2	Year 1
Net sales	$10,707	$9,775
Average fixed assets	$2,476.5	$2,746.0
	[($2,536 + $2,417) ÷ 2]	[($2,956 + $2,536) ÷ 2]
Fixed asset turnover ratio*	4.32	3.56
	($10,707 ÷ $2,476.5)	($9,775 ÷ $2,746.0)

* Rounded to two decimal places.

Business Connection

HUB-AND-SPOKE OR POINT-TO-POINT?

Southwest Airlines Co. uses a simple fare structure, featuring low, unrestricted, unlimited, everyday coach fares. These fares are made possible by Southwest's use of a point-to-point, rather than a hub-and-spoke, business approach.

United Airlines, Inc., Delta Air Lines, and American Airlines employ a hub-and-spoke approach in which an airline establishes major hubs that serve as connecting links to other cities. For example, Delta has major connecting hubs in Atlanta and Salt Lake City.

In contrast, Southwest focuses on nonstop, point-to-point service between selected cities. As a result, Southwest minimizes connections, delays, and total trip time. This operating approach permits Southwest to achieve high utilization of its fixed assets, such as its 737 aircraft.

© AP Photo/Matt Slocum

The higher the fixed asset turnover, the more efficiently a company is using its fixed assets in generating sales. For example, in Year 2 Starbucks earned $4.32 of sales for every dollar of fixed assets, which is more than $3.56 of sales for every dollar of fixed assets it earned in Year 1. Thus, Starbucks used its fixed assets more efficiently in Year 2.

As illustrated on the prior page, the fixed asset turnover ratio can be compared across time for a single company. In addition, the ratio can be compared across companies. For example, the fixed asset turnover ratio for a number of different companies and industries is shown below.

Company (industry)	Fixed Asset Turnover Ratio
Comcast Corporation (cable)	1.60
Google (Internet)	4.65
Manpower Inc. (temporary employment)	109.06
Norfolk Southern Corporation (railroad)	0.41
Ruby Tuesday, Inc. (restaurant)	1.28
Southwest Airlines Co. (airline)	1.14

The smaller ratios are associated with companies that require large fixed asset investments. The larger fixed asset turnover ratios are associated with companies that are more labor-intensive and require smaller fixed asset investments.

Example Exercise 9-9 Fixed Asset Turnover Ratio

OBJ 7

Financial statement data for years ending December 31 for Broadwater Company are shown below.

	2014	2013
Net sales	$2,862,000	$2,025,000
Fixed assets:		
Beginning of year	750,000	600,000
End of year	840,000	750,000

a. Determine the fixed asset turnover ratio for 2014 and 2013.

b. Does the change in the fixed asset turnover ratio from 2013 to 2014 indicate a favorable or an unfavorable trend?

Follow My Example 9-9

a. Fixed asset turnover:

	2014	2013
Net sales	$2,862,000	$2,025,000
Fixed assets:		
Beginning of year	$750,000	$600,000
End of year	$840,000	$750,000
Average fixed assets	$795,000	$675,000
	[($750,000 + $840,000) ÷ 2]	[($600,000 + $750,000) ÷ 2]
Fixed asset turnover	3.6	3.0
	($2,862,000 ÷ $795,000)	($2,025,000 ÷ $675,000)

b. The increase in the fixed asset turnover ratio from 3.0 to 3.6 indicates a favorable trend in the efficiency of using fixed assets to generate sales.

Practice Exercises: **PE 9-9A, PE 9-9B**

APPENDIX

Exchanging Similar Fixed Assets

Old equipment is often traded in for new equipment having a similar use. In such cases, the seller allows the buyer an amount for the old equipment traded in. This amount, called the **trade-in allowance**, may be either greater or less than the book value of the old equipment. The remaining balance—the amount owed—is either paid in cash or recorded as a liability. It is normally called **boot**, which is its tax name.

Accounting for the exchange of similar assets depends on whether the transaction has *commercial substance*.[8] An exchange has commercial substance if future cash flows change as a result of the exchange. If an exchange of similar assets has commercial substance, a gain or loss is recognized. In such cases, the exchange is accounted for similar to that of a sale of a fixed asset. The gain or loss is determined as the difference between the fair market value (trade-in allowance) of the asset given up (exchanged) and its book value. Alternatively, the gain or loss can be determined as the difference between the fair market value of the new asset received and the assets given up in the exchange (cash and book value of the old asset).

Gain on Exchange

To illustrate a gain on an exchange of similar assets, assume the following:

Similar equipment acquired (new):	
Price (fair market value) of new equipment	$5,000
Trade-in allowance on old equipment	1,100
Cash paid at June 19, date of exchange	$3,900

Equipment traded in (old):	
Cost of old equipment	$4,000
Accumulated depreciation at date of exchange	3,200
Book value at June 19, date of exchange	$ 800

The entry to record this exchange and payment of cash is as follows:

June 19	Accumulated Depreciation—Equipment	3,200	
	Equipment (new equipment)	5,000	
	Equipment (old equipment)		4,000
	Cash		3,900
	Gain on Exchange of Equipment		300

The gain on the exchange, $300, is the difference between the fair market value (trade-in allowance) of the asset given up (exchanged) of $1,100 and its book value of $800, as shown below.

Fair market value (trade-in allowance) of old equipment	$1,100
Less book value of old equipment	800
Gain on exchange of assets	$ 300

8 *FASB Accounting Standards Codification*, Section 360-10-30.

The gain on the exchange, $300, can also be determined as the difference between the fair market value of the new asset of $5,000 and the book value of the old asset traded in of $800 plus the cash paid of $3,900, as shown below.

Price (fair market value) of new equipment		$5,000
Less assets given up in exchange:		
Book value of old equipment ($4,000 – $3,200)	$ 800	
Cash paid on the exchange	3,900	4,700
Gain on exchange of assets		$ 300

Loss on Exchange

To illustrate a loss on an exchange of similar assets, assume that instead of a trade-in allowance of $1,100, a trade-in allowance of only $675 was allowed in the preceding example. In this case, the cash paid on the exchange is $4,325 as shown below.

Price (fair market value) of new equipment	$5,000
Trade-in allowance of old equipment	675
Cash paid at June 19, date of exchange	$4,325

The entry to record this exchange and payment of cash is as follows:

June 19	Accumulated Depreciation—Equipment	3,200	
	Equipment (new equipment)	5,000	
	Loss on Exchange of Equipment	125	
	Equipment (old equipment)		4,000
	Cash		4,325

The loss on the exchange, $125, is the difference between the fair market value (trade-in allowance) of the asset given up (exchanged) of $675 and its book value of $800, as shown below.

Fair market value (trade-in allowance) of old equipment	$ 675
Less book value of old equipment	800
Loss on exchange of assets	$(125)

The loss on the exchange, $125, can also be determined as the difference between the fair market value of the new asset of $5,000 and the book value of the old asset traded in of $800 plus the cash paid of $4,325, as shown below.

Price (fair market value) of new equipment		$5,000
Less assets given up in exchange:		
Book value of old equipment ($4,000 – $3,200)	$ 800	
Cash paid on the exchange	4,325	5,125
Loss on exchange of assets		$ (125)

In those cases where an asset exchange *lacks commercial substance*, no gain is recognized on the exchange. Instead, the cost of the new asset is adjusted for any gain. For example, in the first illustration, the gain of $300 would be subtracted from the purchase price of $5,000 and the new asset would be recorded at $4,700. Accounting for the exchange of assets that lack commercial substance is discussed in more advanced accounting texts.[9]

9 The exchange of similar assets also involves complex tax issues which are discussed in advanced accounting courses.

At a Glance 9

OBJ 1 Define, classify, and account for the cost of fixed assets.

Key Points Fixed assets are long-term tangible assets used in the normal operations of the business such as equipment, buildings, and land. The initial cost of a fixed asset includes all amounts spent to get the asset in place and ready for use. Revenue expenditures include ordinary repairs and maintenance. Capital expenditures include asset improvements and extraordinary repairs.

Learning Outcomes	Example Exercises	Practice Exercises
• Define *fixed assets*.		
• List the types of costs that should be included in the cost of a fixed asset.		
• Provide examples of ordinary repairs, asset improvements, and extraordinary repairs.		
• Prepare journal entries for ordinary repairs, asset improvements, and extraordinary repairs.	EE9-1	PE9-1A, 9-1B

OBJ 2 Compute depreciation, using the following methods: straight-line method, units-of-output method, and double-declining-balance method.

Key Points All fixed assets except land should be depreciated over time. Three factors are considered in determining depreciation: (1) the fixed asset's initial cost, (2) the useful life of the asset, and (3) the residual value of the asset.

Depreciation may be determined using the straight-line, units-of-output, and double-declining-balance methods.

Depreciation may be revised into the future for changes in an asset's useful life or residual value.

Learning Outcomes	Example Exercises	Practice Exercises
• Define and describe *depreciation*.		
• List the factors used in determining depreciation.		
• Compute straight-line depreciation.	EE9-2	PE9-2A, 9-2B
• Compute units-of-output depreciation.	EE9-3	PE9-3A, 9-3B
• Compute double-declining-balance depreciation.	EE9-4	PE9-4A, 9-4B
• Compute revised depreciation for a change in an asset's useful life and residual value.	EE9-5	PE9-5A, 9-5B

OBJ 3 Journalize entries for the disposal of fixed assets.

Key Points When discarding a fixed asset, any depreciation for the current period should be recorded, and the book value of the asset is then removed from the accounts.

When a fixed asset is sold, the book value is removed, and the cash or other asset received is recorded. If the selling price is more than the book value of the asset, the transaction results in a gain. If the selling price is less than the book value, there is a loss.

Learning Outcomes	Example Exercises	Practice Exercises
• Prepare the journal entry for discarding a fixed asset.		
• Prepare journal entries for the sale of a fixed asset.	EE9-6	PE9-6A, 9-6B

OBJ 4 Compute depletion and journalize the entry for depletion.

Key Points The amount of periodic depletion is computed by multiplying the quantity of minerals extracted during the period by a depletion rate. The depletion rate is computed by dividing the cost of the mineral deposit by its estimated total units of resource. The entry to record depletion debits a depletion expense account and credits an accumulated depletion account.

Learning Outcomes	Example Exercises	Practice Exercises
• Define and describe *depletion*.		
• Compute a depletion rate.	EE9-7	PE9-7A, 9-7B
• Prepare the journal entry to record depletion.	EE9-7	PE9-7A, 9-7B

OBJ 5 Describe the accounting for intangible assets, such as patents, copyrights, and goodwill.

Key Points Long-term assets such as patents, copyrights, trademarks, and goodwill are intangible assets. The cost of patents and copyrights should be amortized over the years of the asset's expected usefulness by debiting an expense account and crediting the intangible asset account. Trademarks and goodwill are not amortized, but are written down only upon impairment.

Learning Outcomes	Example Exercises	Practice Exercises
• Define, describe, and provide examples of intangible assets.		
• Prepare a journal entry for the purchase of an intangible asset.		
• Prepare a journal entry to amortize the costs of patents and copyrights.	EE9-8	PE9-8A, 9-8B
• Prepare the journal entry to record the impairment of goodwill.	EE9-8	PE9-8A, 9-8B

OBJ 6 Describe how depreciation expense is reported in an income statement and prepare a balance sheet that includes fixed assets and intangible assets.

Key Points The amount of depreciation expense and the depreciation methods used should be disclosed in the financial statements. Each major class of fixed assets should be disclosed, along with the related accumulated depreciation. Intangible assets are usually presented in a separate section following fixed assets. Each major class of intangible assets should be disclosed net of the amortization recorded to date.

Learning Outcomes	Example Exercises	Practice Exercises
• Describe and illustrate how fixed assets are reported on the income statement and balance sheet.		
• Describe and illustrate how intangible assets are reported on the income statement and balance sheet.		

Practice Exercises

Example Exercises

EE 9-1 *p. 410*

PE 9-1A Capital and revenue expenditures — OBJ. 1

On August 7, Green River Inflatables Co. paid $1,675 to install a hydraulic lift and $40 for an air filter for one of its delivery trucks. Journalize the entries for the new lift and air filter expenditures.

EE 9-1 *p. 410*

PE 9-1B Capital and revenue expenditures — OBJ. 1

On February 14, Garcia Associates Co. paid $2,300 to repair the transmission on one of its delivery vans. In addition, Garcia Associates paid $450 to install a GPS system in its van. Journalize the entries for the transmission and GPS system expenditures.

EE 9-2 *p. 413*

PE 9-2A Straight-line depreciation — OBJ. 2

Equipment acquired at the beginning of the year at a cost of $440,000 has an estimated residual value of $25,000 and an estimated useful life of 8 years. Determine (a) the depreciable cost, (b) the straight-line rate, and (c) the annual straight-line depreciation.

EE 9-2 *p. 413*

PE 9-2B Straight-line depreciation — OBJ. 2

A building acquired at the beginning of the year at a cost of $1,450,000 has an estimated residual value of $300,000 and an estimated useful life of 10 years. Determine (a) the depreciable cost, (b) the straight-line rate, and (c) the annual straight-line depreciation.

EE 9-3 *p. 414*

PE 9-3A Units-of-output depreciation — OBJ. 2

A tractor acquired at a cost of $275,000 has an estimated residual value of $39,000, has an estimated useful life of 40,000 hours, and was operated 2,660 hours during the year. Determine (a) the depreciable cost, (b) the depreciation rate, and (c) the units-of-output depreciation for the year.

EE 9-3 *p. 414*

PE 9-3B Units-of-output depreciation — OBJ. 2

A truck acquired at a cost of $69,000 has an estimated residual value of $12,000, has an estimated useful life of 300,000 miles, and was driven 77,000 miles during the year. Determine (a) the depreciable cost, (b) the depreciation rate, and (c) the units-of-output depreciation for the year.

EE 9-4 *p. 416*

PE 9-4A Double-declining-balance depreciation — OBJ. 2

Equipment acquired at the beginning of the year at a cost of $280,000 has an estimated residual value of $45,000 and an estimated useful life of 16 years. Determine (a) the double-declining-balance rate and (b) the double-declining-balance depreciation for the first year.

EE 9-4 *p. 416*

PE 9-4B Double-declining-balance depreciation — OBJ. 2

A building acquired at the beginning of the year at a cost of $1,375,000 has an estimated residual value of $250,000 and an estimated useful life of 40 years. Determine (a) the double-declining-balance rate and (b) the double-declining-balance depreciation for the first year.

Example Exercises

EE 9-5 *p. 419*

PE 9-5A Revision of depreciation **OBJ. 2**

A truck with a cost of $82,000 has an estimated residual value of $16,000, has an estimated useful life of 12 years, and is depreciated by the straight-line method. (a) Determine the amount of the annual depreciation. (b) Determine the book value at the end of the seventh year of use. (c) Assuming that at the start of the eighth year the remaining life is estimated to be six years and the residual value is estimated to be $12,000, determine the depreciation expense for each of the remaining six years.

EE 9-5 *p. 419*

PE 9-5B Revision of depreciation **OBJ. 2**

Equipment with a cost of $180,000 has an estimated residual value of $14,400, has an estimated useful life of 16 years, and is depreciated by the straight-line method. (a) Determine the amount of the annual depreciation. (b) Determine the book value at the end of the tenth year of use. (c) Assuming that at the start of the eleventh year the remaining life is estimated to be eight years and the residual value is estimated to be $10,500, determine the depreciation expense for each of the remaining eight years.

EE 9-6 *p. 421*

PE 9-6A Sale of equipment **OBJ. 3**

Equipment was acquired at the beginning of the year at a cost of $465,000. The equipment was depreciated using the straight-line method based on an estimated useful life of 15 years and an estimated residual value of $45,000.

a. What was the depreciation for the first year?

b. Assuming the equipment was sold at the end of the eighth year for $235,000, determine the gain or loss on the sale of the equipment.

c. Journalize the entry to record the sale.

EE 9-6 *p. 421*

PE 9-6B Sale of equipment **OBJ. 3**

Equipment was acquired at the beginning of the year at a cost of $600,000. The equipment was depreciated using the double-declining-balance method based on an estimated useful life of 16 years and an estimated residual value of $60,000.

a. What was the depreciation for the first year?

b. Assuming the equipment was sold at the end of the second year for $480,000, determine the gain or loss on the sale of the equipment.

c. Journalize the entry to record the sale.

EE 9-7 *p. 422*

PE 9-7A Depletion **OBJ. 4**

Caldwell Mining Co. acquired mineral rights for $127,500,000. The mineral deposit is estimated at 425,000,000 tons. During the current year, 42,000,000 tons were mined and sold.

a. Determine the depletion rate.

b. Determine the amount of depletion expense for the current year.

c. Journalize the adjusting entry on December 31 to recognize the depletion expense.

EE 9-7 *p. 422*

PE 9-7B Depletion **OBJ. 4**

Glacier Mining Co. acquired mineral rights for $494,000,000. The mineral deposit is estimated at 475,000,000 tons. During the current year, 31,500,000 tons were mined and sold.

a. Determine the depletion rate.

b. Determine the amount of depletion expense for the current year.

c. Journalize the adjusting entry on December 31 to recognize the depletion expense.

Example Exercises

EE 9-8 *p. 425*

PE 9-8A Impaired goodwill and amortization of patent **OBJ. 5**

On December 31, it was estimated that goodwill of $4,000,000 was impaired. In addition, a patent with an estimated useful economic life of 15 years was acquired for $900,000 on August 1.

a. Journalize the adjusting entry on December 31 for the impaired goodwill.

b. Journalize the adjusting entry on December 31 for the amortization of the patent rights.

EE 9-8 *p. 425*

PE 9-8B Impaired goodwill and amortization of patent **OBJ. 5**

On December 31, it was estimated that goodwill of $6,000,000 was impaired. In addition, a patent with an estimated useful economic life of 12 years was acquired for $1,500,000 on April 1.

a. Journalize the adjusting entry on December 31 for the impaired goodwill.

b. Journalize the adjusting entry on December 31 for the amortization of the patent rights.

EE 9-9 *p. 427*

F·A·I

PE 9-9A Fixed asset turnover ratio **OBJ. 7**

Financial statement data for years ending December 31 for DePuy Company are shown below.

	2014	2013
Net sales	$5,510,000	$4,880,000
Fixed assets:		
Beginning of year	1,600,000	1,450,000
End of year	2,200,000	1,600,000

a. Determine the fixed asset turnover ratio for 2014 and 2013.

b. Does the change in the fixed asset turnover ratio from 2013 to 2014 indicate a favorable or an unfavorable trend?

EE 9-9 *p. 427*

F·A·I

PE 9-9B Fixed asset turnover ratio **OBJ. 7**

Financial statement data for years ending December 31 for Davenport Company are shown below.

	2014	2013
Net sales	$1,668,000	$1,125,000
Fixed assets:		
Beginning of year	670,000	580,000
End of year	720,000	670,000

a. Determine the fixed asset turnover ratio for 2014 and 2013.

b. Does the change in the fixed asset turnover ratio from 2013 to 2014 indicate a favorable or an unfavorable trend?

Exercises

EX 9-1 Costs of acquiring fixed assets **OBJ. 1**

Dick Gaines owns and operates Gaines Print Co. During February, Gaines Print Co. incurred the following costs in acquiring two printing presses. One printing press was new, and the other was used by a business that recently filed for bankruptcy.

Costs related to new printing press:

1. Fee paid to factory representative for installation
2. Freight
3. Insurance while in transit
4. New parts to replace those damaged in unloading

5. Sales tax on purchase price
6. Special foundation

Costs related to used printing press:

7. Fees paid to attorney to review purchase agreement
8. Freight
9. Installation
10. Repair of damage incurred in reconditioning the press
11. Replacement of worn-out parts
12. Vandalism repairs during installation

a. Indicate which costs incurred in acquiring the new printing press should be debited to the asset account.

b. Indicate which costs incurred in acquiring the used printing press should be debited to the asset account.

EX 9-2 Determining cost of land **OBJ. 1**

Bridger Ski Co. has developed a tract of land into a ski resort. The company has cut the trees, cleared and graded the land and hills, and constructed ski lifts. (a) Should the tree cutting, land clearing, and grading costs of constructing the ski slopes be debited to the land account? (b) If such costs are debited to Land, should they be depreciated?

EX 9-3 Determining cost of land **OBJ. 1**

✔ $831,500

Intermountain Delivery Company acquired an adjacent lot to construct a new warehouse, paying $100,000 and giving a short-term note for $700,000. Legal fees paid were $5,000, delinquent taxes assumed were $18,500, and fees paid to remove an old building from the land were $12,000. Materials salvaged from the demolition of the building were sold for $4,000. A contractor was paid $950,000 to construct a new warehouse. Determine the cost of the land to be reported on the balance sheet.

EX 9-4 Capital and revenue expenditures **OBJ. 1**

Huffine Lines Co. incurred the following costs related to trucks and vans used in operating its delivery service:

1. Changed the oil and greased the joints of all the trucks and vans.
2. Changed the radiator fluid on a truck that had been in service for the past four years.
3. Installed a hydraulic lift to a van.
4. Installed security systems on four of the newer trucks.
5. Overhauled the engine on one of the trucks purchased three years ago.
6. Rebuilt the transmission on one of the vans that had been driven 40,000 miles. The van was no longer under warranty.
7. Removed a two-way radio from one of the trucks and installed a new radio with a greater range of communication.
8. Repaired a flat tire on one of the vans.
9. Replaced a truck's suspension system with a new suspension system that allows for the delivery of heavier loads.
10. Tinted the back and side windows of one of the vans to discourage theft of contents.

Classify each of the costs as a capital expenditure or a revenue expenditure.

EX 9-5 Capital and revenue expenditures
OBJ. 1

Jackie Fox owns and operates Platinum Transport Co. During the past year, Jackie incurred the following costs related to an 18-wheel truck:

1. Changed engine oil.
2. Installed a television in the sleeping compartment of the truck.
3. Installed a wind deflector on top of the cab to increase fuel mileage.
4. Modified the factory-installed turbo charger with a special-order kit designed to add 50 more horsepower to the engine performance.
5. Replaced a headlight that had burned out.
6. Replaced a shock absorber that had worn out.
7. Replaced fog and cab light bulbs.
8. Replaced the hydraulic brake system that had begun to fail during his latest trip through the Rocky Mountains.
9. Removed the old CB radio and replaced it with a newer model with a greater range.
10. Replaced the old radar detector with a newer model that is fastened to the truck with a locking device that prevents its removal.

Classify each of the costs as a capital expenditure or a revenue expenditure.

EX 9-6 Capital and revenue expenditures
OBJ. 1

Quality Move Company made the following expenditures on one of its delivery trucks:

Mar. 20. Replaced the transmission at a cost of $1,890.

June 11. Paid $1,350 for installation of a hydraulic lift.

Nov. 30. Paid $55 to change the oil and air filter.

Prepare journal entries for each expenditure.

EX 9-7 Nature of depreciation
OBJ. 2

Tri-City Ironworks Co. reported $44,500,000 for equipment and $29,800,000 for accumulated depreciation—equipment on its balance sheet.

Does this mean (a) that the replacement cost of the equipment is $44,500,000 and (b) that $29,800,000 is set aside in a special fund for the replacement of the equipment? Explain.

EX 9-8 Straight-line depreciation rates
OBJ. 2

✔ c. 10%

Convert each of the following estimates of useful life to a straight-line depreciation rate, stated as a percentage: (a) 4 years, (b) 8 years, (c) 10 years, (d) 16 years, (e) 25 years, (f) 40 years, (g) 50 years.

EX 9-9 Straight-line depreciation
OBJ. 2

✔ $3,950

A refrigerator used by a meat processor has a cost of $60,000, an estimated residual value of $12,600, and an estimated useful life of 12 years. What is the amount of the annual depreciation computed by the straight-line method?

EX 9-10 Depreciation by units-of-output method
OBJ. 2

✔ $644

A diesel-powered tractor with a cost of $214,000 and estimated residual value of $30,000 is expected to have a useful operating life of 50,000 hours. During January, the tractor was operated 175 hours. Determine the depreciation for the month.

✔ a. Truck #1, credit to Accumulated Depreciation, $5,460

EX 9-11 Depreciation by units-of-output method **OBJ. 2**

Prior to adjustment at the end of the year, the balance in Trucks is $296,900 and the balance in Accumulated Depreciation—Trucks is $99,740. Details of the subsidiary ledger are as follows:

Truck No.	Cost	Estimated Residual Value	Estimated Useful Life	Accumulated Depreciation at Beginning of Year	Miles Operated During Year
1	$80,000	$15,000	250,000 miles	—	21,000 miles
2	54,000	6,000	300,000	$14,400	33,500
3	72,900	10,900	200,000	60,140	8,000
4	90,000	22,800	240,000	25,200	22,500

a. Determine the depreciation rates per mile and the amount to be credited to the accumulated depreciation section of each of the subsidiary accounts for the miles operated during the current year.

b. Journalize the entry to record depreciation for the year.

✔ a. $4,500

EX 9-12 Depreciation by two methods **OBJ. 2**

A Kubota tractor acquired on January 6 at a cost of $90,000 has an estimated useful life of 20 years. Assuming that it will have no residual value, determine the depreciation for each of the first two years (a) by the straight-line method and (b) by the double-declining-balance method.

✔ a. $8,400

EX 9-13 Depreciation by two methods **OBJ. 2**

A storage tank acquired at the beginning of the fiscal year at a cost of $240,000 has an estimated residual value of $30,000 and an estimated useful life of 25 years. Determine the following: (a) the amount of annual depreciation by the straight-line method and (b) the amount of depreciation for the first and second years computed by the double-declining-balance method.

✔ a. First year, $2,250

EX 9-14 Partial-year depreciation **OBJ. 2**

Sandblasting equipment acquired at a cost of $36,000 has an estimated residual value of $6,000 and an estimated useful life of 10 years. It was placed into service on April 1 of the current fiscal year, which ends on December 31. Determine the depreciation for the current fiscal year and for the following fiscal year by (a) the straight-line method and (b) the double-declining-balance method.

✔ a. $17,250

EX 9-15 Revision of depreciation **OBJ. 2**

A building with a cost of $780,000 has an estimated residual value of $90,000, has an estimated useful life of 40 years, and is depreciated by the straight-line method. (a) What is the amount of the annual depreciation? (b) What is the book value at the end of the twenty-fourth year of use? (c) If at the start of the twenty-fifth year it is estimated that the remaining life is 10 years and that the residual value is $70,000, what is the depreciation expense for each of the remaining 10 years?

✔ b. Depreciation Expense, $800

EX 9-16 Capital expenditure and depreciation **OBJ. 1, 2**

Willow Creek Company purchased and installed carpet in its new general offices on April 30 for a total cost of $18,000. The carpet is estimated to have a 15-year useful life and no residual value.

a. Prepare the journal entry necessary for recording the purchase of the new carpet.

b. Record the December 31 adjusting entry for the partial-year depreciation expense for the carpet, assuming that Willow Creek Company uses the straight-line method.

EX 9-17 Entries for sale of fixed asset **OBJ. 3**

Equipment acquired on January 8, 2011, at a cost of $420,000, has an estimated useful life of 15 years, has an estimated residual value of $30,000, and is depreciated by the straight-line method.

a. What was the book value of the equipment at December 31, 2014, the end of the year?

b. Assuming that the equipment was sold on October 1, 2015, for $275,000, journalize the entries to record (1) depreciation for the nine months until the sale date, and (2) the sale of the equipment.

EX 9-18 Disposal of fixed asset **OBJ. 3**

✔ b. $546,600

Equipment acquired on January 6, 2011, at a cost of $714,000, has an estimated useful life of 12 years and an estimated residual value of $44,400.

a. What was the annual amount of depreciation for the years 2011, 2012, and 2013, using the straight-line method of depreciation?

b. What was the book value of the equipment on January 1, 2014?

c. Assuming that the equipment was sold on January 3, 2014, for $525,000, journalize the entry to record the sale.

d. Assuming that the equipment had been sold on January 3, 2014, for $560,000 instead of $525,000, journalize the entry to record the sale.

EX 9-19 Depletion entries **OBJ. 4**

✔ a. $5,220,000

Crazy Jim's Mining Co. acquired mineral rights for $21,750,000. The mineral deposit is estimated at 15,000,000 tons. During the current year, 3,600,000 tons were mined and sold.

a. Determine the amount of depletion expense for the current year.

b. Journalize the adjusting entry to recognize the depletion expense.

EX 9-20 Amortization entries **OBJ. 5**

✔ a. $76,000

Voss Company acquired patent rights on January 6, 2011, for $480,000. The patent has a useful life equal to its legal life of eight years. On January 3, 2014, Voss successfully defended the patent in a lawsuit at a cost of $80,000.

a. Determine the patent amortization expense for the current year ended December 31, 2014.

b. Journalize the adjusting entry to recognize the amortization.

EX 9-21 Book value of fixed assets **OBJ. 6**

Apple Inc. designs, manufactures, and markets personal computers and related software. Apple also manufactures and distributes music players (iPod) and mobile phones (iPhone) along with related accessories and services, including online distribution of third-party music, videos, and applications. The following information was taken from a recent annual report of Apple:

Property, Plant, and Equipment (in millions):

	Current Year	Preceding Year
Land and buildings	$1,471	$ 955
Machinery, equipment, and internal-use software	3,589	1,932
Office furniture and equipment	144	115
Other fixed assets related to leases	2,030	1,665
Accumulated depreciation and amortization	2,466	1,713

a. Compute the book value of the fixed assets for the current year and the preceding year and explain the differences, if any.

b. Would you normally expect Apple's book value of fixed assets to increase or decrease during the year?

EX 9-22 Balance sheet presentation **OBJ. 6**

List the errors you find in the following partial balance sheet:

Burnt Red Company
Balance Sheet
December 31, 2014

Assets

Total current assets			$350,000

	Replacement Cost	Accumulated Depreciation	Book Value
Property, plant, and equipment:			
Land	$ 250,000	$ 50,000	$200,000
Buildings	450,000	160,000	290,000
Factory equipment	375,000	140,000	235,000
Office equipment	125,000	60,000	65,000
Patents	90,000	—	90,000
Goodwill	60,000	10,000	50,000
Total property, plant, and equipment	$1,350,000	$420,000	$930,000

EX 9-23 Fixed asset turnover ratio **OBJ. 7**

F·A·I

Verizon Communications is a major telecommunications company in the United States. Two recent balance sheets for Verizon disclosed the following information regarding fixed assets:

	Year 2 (in millions)	Year 1 (in millions)
Plant, property, and equipment	$211,655	$229,743
Less accumulated depreciation	123,944	137,758
	$ 87,711	$ 91,985

Verizon's revenue for Year 2 was $106,565 million. Assume the fixed asset turnover for the telecommunications industry averages approximately 1.10.

a. Determine Verizon's fixed asset turnover ratio for Year 2. Round to two decimal places.

b. Interpret Verizon's fixed asset turnover ratio.

EX 9-24 Fixed asset turnover ratio **OBJ. 7**

F·A·I

The following table shows the revenue and average net fixed assets (in millions) for a recent fiscal year for Best Buy and RadioShack:

	Revenue	Average Net Fixed Assets
Best Buy	$50,272	$3,947
RadioShack	4,473	278

a. Compute the fixed asset turnover for each company. Round to two decimal places.

b. Which company uses its fixed assets more efficiently? Explain.

Appendix
EX 9-25 Asset traded for similar asset

✔ a. $185,000

A printing press priced at a fair market value of $275,000 is acquired in a transaction that has commercial substance by trading in a similar press and paying cash for the difference between the trade-in allowance and the price of the new press.

(Continued)

a. Assuming that the trade-in allowance is $90,000, what is the amount of cash given?

b. Assuming that the book value of the press traded in is $68,000, what is the gain or loss on the exchange?

Appendix
EX 9-26 Asset traded for similar asset

✔ b. $18,500 loss

Assume the same facts as in Exercise 9-25, except that the book value of the press traded in is $108,500. (a) What is the amount of cash given? (b) What is the gain or loss on the exchange?

Appendix
EX 9-27 Entries for trade of fixed asset

On July 1, Twin Pines Co., a water distiller, acquired new bottling equipment with a list price (fair market value) of $220,000. Twin Pines received a trade-in allowance (fair market value) of $45,000 on the old equipment of a similar type and paid cash of $175,000. The following information about the old equipment is obtained from the account in the equipment ledger: cost, $180,000; accumulated depreciation on December 31, the end of the preceding fiscal year, $120,000; annual depreciation, $12,000. Assuming the exchange has commercial substance, journalize the entries to record (a) the current depreciation of the old equipment to the date of trade-in and (b) the exchange transaction on July 1.

Appendix
EX 9-28 Entries for trade of fixed asset

On October 1, Bentley Delivery Services acquired a new truck with a list price (fair market value) of $75,000. Bentley Delivery received a trade-in allowance (fair market value) of $24,000 on an old truck of similar type and paid cash of $51,000. The following information about the old truck is obtained from the account in the equipment ledger: cost, $56,000; accumulated depreciation on December 31, the end of the preceding fiscal year, $35,000; annual depreciation, $7,000. Assuming the exchange has commercial substance, journalize the entries to record (a) the current depreciation of the old truck to the date of trade-in and (b) the transaction on October 1.

Problems Series A

PR 9-1A Allocating payments and receipts to fixed asset accounts **OBJ. 1**

✔ Land, $400,000

The following payments and receipts are related to land, land improvements, and buildings acquired for use in a wholesale ceramic business. The receipts are identified by an asterisk.

a.	Fee paid to attorney for title search	$ 2,500
b.	Cost of real estate acquired as a plant site: Land	285,000
	Building	55,000
c.	Delinquent real estate taxes on property, assumed by purchaser	15,500
d.	Cost of razing and removing building	5,000
e.	Proceeds from sale of salvage materials from old building	4,000*
f.	Special assessment paid to city for extension of water main to the property	29,000
g.	Architect's and engineer's fees for plans and supervision	60,000
h.	Premium on one-year insurance policy during construction	6,000
i.	Cost of filling and grading land	12,000
j.	Money borrowed to pay building contractor	900,000*
k.	Cost of repairing windstorm damage during construction	5,500
l.	Cost of paving parking lot to be used by customers	32,000
m.	Cost of trees and shrubbery planted	11,000
n.	Cost of floodlights installed on parking lot	2,000
o.	Cost of repairing vandalism damage during construction	2,500
p.	Proceeds from insurance company for windstorm and vandalism damage	7,500*
q.	Payment to building contractor for new building	800,000
r.	Interest incurred on building loan during construction	34,500
s.	Refund of premium on insurance policy (h) canceled after 11 months	500*

Instructions

1. Assign each payment and receipt to Land (unlimited life), Land Improvements (limited life), Building, or Other Accounts. Indicate receipts by an asterisk. Identify each item by letter and list the amounts in columnar form, as follows:

Item	Land	Land Improvements	Building	Other Accounts

2. Determine the amount debited to Land, Land Improvements, and Building.
3. The costs assigned to the land, which is used as a plant site, will not be depreciated, while the costs assigned to land improvements will be depreciated. Explain this seemingly contradictory application of the concept of depreciation.
4. What would be the effect on the income statement and balance sheet if the cost of filling and grading land of $12,000 [payment (i)] was incorrectly classified as Land Improvements rather than Land? Assume Land Improvements are depreciated over a 20-year life using the double-declining-balance method.

PR 9-2A Comparing three depreciation methods

OBJ. 2

✔ 1. a. 2012: straight-line depreciation, $40,500

SPREADSHEET

Waldum Company purchased packaging equipment on January 5, 2012, for $135,000. The equipment was expected to have a useful life of three years, or 18,000 operating hours, and a residual value of $13,500. The equipment was used for 8,600 hours during 2012, 5,300 hours in 2013, and 4,100 hours in 2014.

Instructions

1. Determine the amount of depreciation expense for the years ended December 31, 2012, 2013, and 2014, by (a) the straight-line method, (b) the units-of-output method, and (c) the double-declining-balance method. Also determine the total depreciation expense for the three years by each method. The following columnar headings are suggested for recording the depreciation expense amounts:

	Depreciation Expense		
Year	Straight-Line Method	Units-of-Output Method	Double-Declining-Balance Method

2. What method yields the highest depreciation expense for 2012?
3. What method yields the most depreciation over the three-year life of the equipment?

PR 9-3A Depreciation by three methods; partial years

OBJ. 2

✔ a. 2012: $65,250

SPREADSHEET

Perdue Company purchased equipment on April 1, 2012, for $270,000. The equipment was expected to have a useful life of three years, or 18,000 operating hours, and a residual value of $9,000. The equipment was used for 7,500 hours during 2012, 5,500 hours in 2013, 4,000 hours in 2014, and 1,000 hours in 2015.

Instructions

Determine the amount of depreciation expense for the years ended December 31, 2012, 2013, 2014, and 2015, by (a) the straight-line method, (b) the units-of-output method, and (c) the double-declining-balance method.

PR 9-4A Depreciation by two methods; sale of fixed asset

OBJ. 2, 3

✔ 1. b. Year 1: $320,000 depreciation expense

SPREADSHEET

GENERAL LEDGER

New lithographic equipment, acquired at a cost of $800,000 at the beginning of a fiscal year, has an estimated useful life of five years and an estimated residual value of $90,000. The manager requested information regarding the effect of alternative methods on the amount of depreciation expense each year. On the basis of the data presented to the manager, the double-declining-balance method was selected.

In the first week of the fifth year, the equipment was sold for $135,000.

Instructions

1. Determine the annual depreciation expense for each of the estimated five years of use, the accumulated depreciation at the end of each year, and the book value of the equipment at the end of each year by (a) the straight-line method and (b) the

(Continued)

2. What method yields the highest depreciation expense for 2013?
3. What method yields the most depreciation over the four-year life of the equipment?

PR 9-3B Depreciation by three methods; partial years

OBJ. 2

✔ a. 2012, $8,400

SPREADSHEET

Layton Company purchased tool sharpening equipment on October 1, 2012, for $108,000. The equipment was expected to have a useful life of three years, or 12,000 operating hours, and a residual value of $7,200. The equipment was used for 1,350 hours during 2012, 4,200 hours in 2013, 3,650 hours in 2014, and 2,800 hours in 2015.

Instructions

Determine the amount of depreciation expense for the years ended December 31, 2012, 2013, 2014, and 2015, by (a) the straight-line method, (b) the units-of-output method, and (c) the double-declining-balance method.

GENERAL LEDGER

PR 9-4B Depreciation by two methods; sale of fixed asset

OBJ. 2, 3

✔ 1. b. Year 1, $55,000 depreciation expense

SPREADSHEET

GENERAL LEDGER

New tire retreading equipment, acquired at a cost of $110,000 at the beginning of a fiscal year, has an estimated useful life of four years and an estimated residual value of $7,500. The manager requested information regarding the effect of alternative methods on the amount of depreciation expense each year. On the basis of the data presented to the manager, the double-declining-balance method was selected.

In the first week of the fourth year, the equipment was sold for $18,000.

Instructions

1. Determine the annual depreciation expense for each of the estimated four years of use, the accumulated depreciation at the end of each year, and the book value of the equipment at the end of each year by (a) the straight-line method and (b) the double-declining-balance method. The following columnar headings are suggested for each schedule:

Year	Depreciation Expense	Accumulated Depreciation, End of Year	Book Value, End of Year

2. Journalize the entry to record the sale.
3. Journalize the entry to record the sale, assuming that the equipment sold for $10,500 instead of $18,000.

PR 9-5B Transactions for fixed assets, including sale

OBJ. 1, 2, 3

GENERAL LEDGER

✔ 1. a. $

The following transactions, adjusting entries, and closing entries were completed by Robinson Furniture Co. during a three-year period. All are related to the use of delivery equipment. The double-declining-balance method of depreciation is used.

2012

Jan. 8. Purchased a used delivery truck for $24,000, paying cash.

Mar. 7. Paid garage $900 for changing the oil, replacing the oil filter, and tuning the engine on the delivery truck.

Dec. 31. Recorded depreciation on the truck for the fiscal year. The estimated useful life of the truck is four years, with a residual value of $4,000 for the truck.

2013

Jan. 9. Purchased a new truck for $50,000, paying cash.

Feb. 28. Paid garage $250 to tune the engine and make other minor repairs on the used truck.

Apr. 30. Sold the used truck for $9,500. (Record depreciation to date in 2013 for the truck.)

Dec. 31. Record depreciation for the new truck. It has an estimated residual value of $12,000 and an estimated life of eight years.

2014

Sept. 1. Purchased a new truck for $58,500, paying cash.

4. Sold the truck purchased January 9, 2013, for $36,000. (Record depreciation to date for 2014 for the truck.)

Dec. 31. Recorded depreciation on the remaining truck. It has an estimated residual value of $16,000 and an estimated useful life of 10 years.

Instructions

Journalize the transactions and the adjusting entries.

PR 9-6B Amortization and depletion entries

OBJ. 4, 5

✔ b. $150,000

Data related to the acquisition of timber rights and intangible assets during the current year ended December 31 are as follows:

a. On December 31, the company determined that $3,400,000 of goodwill was impaired.

b. Governmental and legal costs of $4,800,000 were incurred on September 30 in obtaining a patent with an estimated economic life of eight years. Amortization is to be for one-fourth year.

c. Timber rights on a tract of land were purchased for $2,975,000 on February 4. The stand of timber is estimated at 12,500,000 board feet. During the current year, 4,150,000 board feet of timber were cut and sold.

Instructions

1. Determine the amount of the amortization, depletion, or impairment for the current year for each of the foregoing items.
2. Journalize the adjusting entries to record the amortization, depletion, or impairment for each item.

Cases & Projects

CP 9-1 Ethics and professional conduct in business

Dave Elliott, CPA, is an assistant to the controller of Lyric Consulting Co. In his spare time, Dave also prepares tax returns and performs general accounting services for clients. Frequently, Dave performs these services after his normal working hours, using Lyric Consulting Co.'s computers and laser printers. Occasionally, Dave's clients will call him at the office during regular working hours.

Discuss whether Dave is performing in a professional manner.

CP 9-2 Financial vs. tax depreciation

The following is an excerpt from a conversation between two employees of WXT Technologies, Nolan Sears and Stacy Mays. Nolan is the accounts payable clerk, and Stacy is the cashier.

Nolan: Stacy, could I get your opinion on something?

Stacy: Sure, Nolan.

Nolan: Do you know Rita, the fixed assets clerk?

Stacy: I know who she is, but I don't know her real well. Why?

Nolan: Well, I was talking to her at lunch last Monday about how she liked her job, etc. You know, the usual . . . and she mentioned something about having to keep two sets of books . . . one for taxes and one for the financial statements. That can't be good accounting, can it? What do you think?

Stacy: Two sets of books? It doesn't sound right.

Nolan: It doesn't seem right to me either. I was always taught that you had to use generally accepted accounting principles. How can there be two sets of books? What can be the difference between the two?

How would you respond to Nolan and Stacy if you were Rita?

CP 9-3 Effect of depreciation on net income

Tuttle Construction Co. specializes in building replicas of historic houses. Tim Newman, president of Tuttle Construction, is considering the purchase of various items of equipment on July 1, 2012, for $400,000. The equipment would have a useful life of five years and no residual value. In the past, all equipment has been leased. For tax purposes, Tim is considering depreciating the equipment by the straight-line method. He discussed the matter with his CPA and learned that, although the straight-line method could be elected, it was to his advantage to use the Modified Accelerated Cost Recovery System (MACRS) for tax purposes. He asked for your advice as to which method to use for tax purposes.

1. Compute depreciation for each of the years (2012, 2013, 2014, 2015, 2016, and 2017) of useful life by (a) the straight-line method and (b) MACRS. In using the straight-line method, one-half year's depreciation should be computed for 2012 and 2017. Use the MACRS rates presented on page 417.
2. Assuming that income before depreciation and income tax is estimated to be $750,000 uniformly per year and that the income tax rate is 40%, compute the net income for each of the years 2012, 2013, 2014, 2015, 2016, and 2017 if (a) the straight-line method is used and (b) MACRS is used.
3. What factors would you present for Tim's consideration in the selection of a depreciation method?

CP 9-4 Applying for patents, copyrights, and trademarks

Group Project

Internet Project

Go to the Internet and review the procedures for applying for a patent, a copyright, and a trademark. You may find information available on Wikipedia (Wikipedia.org) useful for this purpose. Prepare a brief written summary of these procedures.

CP 9-5 Fixed asset turnover: three industries

F·A·I

The following table shows the revenues and average net fixed assets for a recent fiscal year for three different companies from three different industries: retailing, manufacturing, and communications.

	Revenues (in millions)	Average Net Fixed Assets (in millions)
Walmart	$421,849	$105,093
Occidental Petroleum Corporation	19,045	33,837
Comcast Corporation	37,937	23,685

a. For each company, determine the fixed asset turnover ratio. Round to two decimal places.

b. Explain Walmart's ratio relative to the other two companies.

CHAPTER 10

AP PHOTO/TOM GANNAM

Current Liabilities and Payroll

Panera Bread

Buying goods on credit is probably as old as business itself. In fact, the ancient Babylonians were lending money to support trade as early as 1300 B.C. The use of credit makes transactions more convenient and improves buying power. For *individuals*, the most common form of short-term credit is a credit card. Credit cards allow individuals to purchase items before they are paid for, while removing the need for individuals to carry large amounts of cash. They also provide documentation of purchases through a monthly credit card statement.

Short-term credit is also used by *businesses* to make purchasing items for manufacture or resale more convenient, and gives the business control over the payment for goods and services. For example, **Panera Bread**, a chain of bakery-cafés located throughout the United States, uses short-term trade credit, or accounts payable, to purchase ingredients for making bread products in its bakeries. Short-term trade credit gives Panera control over cash payments by separating the purchase function from the payment function. Thus, the employee responsible for purchasing the bakery ingredients is separated from the employee responsible for paying for the purchase. This separation of duties can help prevent unauthorized purchases or payments.

In addition to accounts payable, a business like Panera Bread can also have current liabilities related to payroll, payroll taxes, employee benefits, short-term notes, unearned revenue, and contingencies. This chapter discusses each of these types of current liabilities.

Learning Objectives

After studying this chapter, you should be able to: — Example Exercises

OBJ 1 Describe and illustrate current liabilities related to accounts payable, current portion of long-term debt, and notes payable.

- Current Liabilities
  - Accounts Payable
  - Current Portion of Long-Term Debt
  - Short-Term Notes Payable — EE 10-1

OBJ 2 Determine employer liabilities for payroll, including liabilities arising from employee earnings and deductions from earnings.

- Payroll and Payroll Taxes
  - Liability for Employee Earnings
  - Deductions from Employee Earnings — EE 10-2
  - Computing Employee Net Pay — EE 10-3
  - Liability for Employer's Payroll Taxes

OBJ 3 Describe payroll accounting systems that use a payroll register, employee earnings records, and a general journal.

- Accounting Systems for Payroll and Payroll Taxes
  - Payroll Register — EE 10-4, 10-5
  - Employee's Earnings Record
  - Payroll Checks
  - Computerized Payroll System
  - Internal Controls for Payroll Systems

OBJ 4 Journalize entries for employee fringe benefits, including vacation pay and pensions.

- Employees' Fringe Benefits
  - Vacation Pay
  - Pensions — EE 10-6
  - Postretirement Benefits Other than Pensions
  - Current Liabilities on the Balance Sheet

OBJ 5 Describe the accounting treatment for contingent liabilities and journalize entries for product warranties.

- Contingent Liabilities
  - Probable and Estimable — EE 10-7
  - Probable and Not Estimable
  - Reasonably Possible
  - Remote

OBJ 6 Describe and illustrate the use of the quick ratio in analyzing a company's ability to pay its current liabilities.

- Financial Analysis and Interpretation: Quick Ratio — EE 10-8

At a Glance 10 Page 472

OBJ 1 Describe and illustrate current liabilities related to accounts payable, current portion of long-term debt, and notes payable.

Current Liabilities

When a company or a bank advances *credit,* it is making a loan. The company or bank is called a *creditor* (or *lender*). The individuals or companies receiving the loan are called *debtors* (or *borrowers*).

Debt is recorded as a liability by the debtor. *Long-term liabilities* are debts due beyond one year. Thus, a 30-year mortgage used to purchase property is a long-term liability. *Current liabilities* are debts that will be paid out of current assets and are due within one year.

Three types of current liabilities are discussed in this section—accounts payable, the current portion of long-term debt, and short-term notes payable.

Accounts Payable

Accounts payable transactions have been described and illustrated in earlier chapters. These transactions involved a variety of purchases on account, including the purchase of merchandise and supplies. For most companies, accounts payable is the largest current liability. Exhibit 1 shows the accounts payable balance as a percent of total current liabilities for a number of companies.

Company	Accounts Payable as a Percent of Total Current Liabilities
Alcoa Inc.	45%
AT&T	65
Gap Inc.	50
IBM	20
Rite Aid Corp.	54
Chevron Corp.	66

EXHIBIT 1

Accounts Payable as a Percent of Total Current Liabilities

Current Portion of Long-Term Debt

Long-term liabilities are often paid back in periodic payments, called *installments*. Such installments that are due *within* the coming year are classified as a current liability. The installments due *after* the coming year are classified as a long-term liability.

To illustrate, The Coca-Cola Company reported the following debt payments schedule in its December 31, 2011, annual report to shareholders (in millions):

Fiscal year ending	
2012	$ 2,041
2013	1,515
2014	1,690
2015	1,462
2016	1,707
Thereafter	7,282
Total principal payments	$15,697

The debt of $2,041 due in 2012 would be reported as a current liability on the December 31 balance sheet for the preceding year. The remaining debt of $13,656 ($15,697 – $2,041) would be reported as a long-term liability on the balance sheet.

Short-Term Notes Payable

Notes may be issued to purchase merchandise or other assets. Notes may also be issued to creditors to satisfy an account payable created earlier.[1]

To illustrate, assume that Nature's Sunshine Company issued a 90-day, 12% note for $1,000, dated August 1, 2013, to Murray Co. for a $1,000 overdue account. The entry to record the issuance of the note is as follows:

Aug.	1	Accounts Payable—Murray Co.	1,000	
		Notes Payable		1,000
		Issued a 90-day, 12% note on account.		

When the note matures, the entry to record the payment of $1,000 plus $30 interest ($1,000 × 12% × 90/360) is as follows:

Oct.	30	Notes Payable	1,000	
		Interest Expense	30	
		Cash		1,030
		Paid principal and interest due on note.		

1 The accounting for notes received to satisfy an account receivable was described and illustrated in Chapter 8, *Receivables*.

The interest expense is reported in the Other Expense section of the income statement for the year ended December 31, 2013. The interest expense account is closed at December 31.

Each note transaction affects a debtor (borrower) and creditor (lender). The following illustration shows how the same transactions are recorded by the debtor and creditor. In this illustration, the debtor (borrower) is Bowden Co., and the creditor (lender) is Coker Co.

	Bowden Co. (Borrower)			Coker Co. (Creditor)		
May 1. Bowden Co. purchased merchandise on account from Coker Co., $10,000, 2/10, n/30. The merchandise cost Coker Co. $7,500.	Merchandise Inventory	10,000		Accounts Receivable	10,000	
	Accounts Payable		10,000	Sales		10,000
				Cost of Merchandise Sold	7,500	
				Merchandise Inventory		7,500
May 31. Bowden Co. issued a 60-day, 12% note for $10,000 to Coker Co. on account.	Accounts Payable	10,000		Notes Receivable	10,000	
	Notes Payable		10,000	Accounts Receivable		10,000
July 30. Bowden Co. paid Coker Co. the amount due on the note of May 31. Interest: $10,000 × 12% × 60/360.	Notes Payable	10,000		Cash	10,200	
	Interest Expense	200		Interest Revenue		200
	Cash		10,200	Notes Receivable		10,000

A company may also borrow from a bank by issuing a note. To illustrate, assume that on September 19 Iceburg Company borrowed cash from First National Bank by issuing a $4,000, 90-day, 15% note to the bank. The entry to record the issuance of the note and the cash proceeds is as follows:

Sept.	19	Cash		4,000	
		Notes Payable			4,000
		Issued a 90-day, 15% note to First National Bank.			

On the due date of the note (December 18), Iceburg Company owes First National Bank $4,000 plus interest of $150 ($4,000 × 15% × 90/360). The entry to record the payment of the note is as follows:

Dec.	18	Notes Payable		4,000	
		Interest Expense		150	
		Cash			4,150
		Paid principal and interest due on note.			

In some cases, a *discounted note* may be issued rather than an interest-bearing note. A discounted note has the following characteristics:

1. The interest rate on the note is called the *discount rate.*
2. The amount of interest on the note, called the *discount,* is computed by multiplying the discount rate times the face amount of the note.
3. The debtor (borrower) receives the face amount of the note less the discount, called the *proceeds.*
4. The debtor must repay the face amount of the note on the due date.

To illustrate, assume that on August 10, Cary Company issues a $20,000, 90-day discounted note to Western National Bank. The discount rate is 15%, and the amount of the discount is $750 ($20,000 × 15% × 90/360). Thus, the proceeds received by Cary Company are $19,250. The entry by Cary Company is as follows:

Aug.	10	Cash	19,250	
		Interest Expense	750	
		Notes Payable		20,000
		Issued a 90-day discounted note to Western National Bank at a 15% discount rate.		

The entry when Cary Company pays the discounted note on November 8 is as follows:[2]

Nov.	8	Notes Payable	20,000	
		Cash		20,000
		Paid note due.		

Other current liabilities that have been discussed in earlier chapters include accrued expenses, unearned revenue, and interest payable. The accounting for wages and salaries, termed *payroll accounting*, is discussed next.

Example Exercise 10-1 Proceeds from Notes Payable OBJ 1

On July 1, Bella Salon Company borrowed cash from Best Bank by issuing a 60-day note with a face amount of $60,000.

a. Determine the proceeds of the note, assuming the note carries an interest rate of 6%.

b. Determine the proceeds of the note, assuming the note is discounted at 6%.

Follow My Example 10-1

a. $60,000

b. $59,400 [$60,000 – ($60,000 × 6% × 60/360)]

Practice Exercises: **PE 10-1A, PE 10-1B**

Payroll and Payroll Taxes

OBJ 2 Determine employer liabilities for payroll, including liabilities arising from employee earnings and deductions from earnings.

In accounting, **payroll** refers to the amount paid to employees for services they provided during the period. A company's payroll is important for the following reasons:

1. Payroll and related payroll taxes significantly affect the net income of most companies.
2. Payroll is subject to federal and state regulations.
3. Good employee morale requires payroll to be paid timely and accurately.

Liability for Employee Earnings

Salary usually refers to payment for managerial and administrative services. Salary is normally expressed in terms of a month or a year. *Wages* usually refers to payment for employee manual labor. The rate of wages is normally stated on an hourly or a weekly basis. The salary or wage of an employee may be increased by bonuses, commissions, profit sharing, or cost-of-living adjustments.

Note: **Employee salaries and wages are expenses to an employer.**

2 If the accounting period ends before a discounted note is paid, an adjusting entry should record the prepaid (deferred) interest that is not yet an expense. This deferred interest would be deducted from Notes Payable in the Current Liabilities section of the balance sheet.

Companies engaged in interstate commerce must follow the Fair Labor Standards Act. This act, sometimes called the Federal Wage and Hour Law, requires employers to pay a minimum rate of 1½ times the regular rate for all hours worked in excess of 40 hours per week. Exemptions are provided for executive, administrative, and some supervisory positions. Increased rates for working overtime, nights, or holidays are common, even when not required by law. These rates may be as much as twice the regular rate.

To illustrate computing an employee's earnings, assume that John T. McGrath is a salesperson employed by McDermott Supply Co. McGrath's regular rate is $34 per hour, and any hours worked in excess of 40 hours per week are paid at 1½ times the regular rate. McGrath worked 42 hours for the week ended December 27. His earnings of **$1,462** for the week are computed as follows:

Earnings at regular rate (40 hrs. × $34)	$1,360
Earnings at overtime rate [2 hrs. × ($34 × 1½)]	102
Total earnings	$1,462

Deductions from Employee Earnings

The total earnings of an employee for a payroll period, including any overtime pay, are called **gross pay**. From this amount is subtracted one or more *deductions* to arrive at the **net pay**. Net pay is the amount paid the employee. The deductions normally include federal, state, and local income taxes, medical insurance, and pension contributions.

Income Taxes Employers normally withhold a portion of employee earnings for payment of the employees' federal income tax. Each employee authorizes the amount to be withheld by completing an "Employee's Withholding Allowance Certificate," called a W-4. Exhibit 2 is the W-4 form submitted by John T. McGrath.

On the W-4, an employee indicates marital status and the number of withholding allowances. A single employee may claim one withholding allowance. A married employee may claim an additional allowance for a spouse. An employee may also claim an allowance for each dependent other than a spouse. Each allowance reduces the federal income tax withheld from the employee's pay. Exhibit 2 indicates that John T. McGrath is single and, thus, claimed one withholding allowance.

The federal income tax withheld depends on each employee's gross pay and W-4 allowance. Withholding tables issued by the Internal Revenue Service (IRS) are used to determine amounts to withhold. Exhibit 3 is an example of an IRS wage withholding table for a single person who is paid weekly.[3]

EXHIBIT 2

Employee's Withholding Allowance Certificate (W-4 Form)

Separate here and give Form W-4 to your employer. Keep the top part for your records.

Form **W-4** — Department of the Treasury, Internal Revenue Service

Employee's Withholding Allowance Certificate

► Whether you are entitled to claim a certain number of allowances or exemption from withholding is subject to review by the IRS. Your employer may be required to send a copy of this form to the IRS.

OMB No. 1545-0074 — **2013**

1 Your first name and middle initial: John T. — Last name: McGrath — 2 Your social security number: 381 48 9120

Home address (number and street or rural route): 1830 4th Street — 3 ☒ Single ☐ Married ☐ Married, but withhold at higher Single rate.
Note. If married, but legally separated, or spouse is a nonresident alien, check the "Single" box.

City or town, state, and ZIP code: Clinton, Iowa 52732-6142 — 4 If your last name differs from that shown on your social security card, check here. You must call 1-800-772-1213 for a replacement card. ► ☐

5 Total number of allowances you are claiming (from line **H** above **or** from the applicable worksheet on page 2) — 5

6 Additional amount, if any, you want withheld from each paycheck . . . . — 6 $

7 I claim exemption from withholding for 2012, and I certify that I meet **both** of the following conditions for exemption.
• Last year I had a right to a refund of **all** federal income tax withheld because I had **no** tax liability, **and**
• This year I expect a refund of **all** federal income tax withheld because I expect to have **no** tax liability.
If you meet both conditions, write "Exempt" here . . . . ► 7

Under penalties of perjury, I declare that I have examined this certificate and, to the best of my knowledge and belief, it is true, correct, and complete.

Employee's signature (This form is not valid unless you sign it.) ► *John T. McGrath* — Date ► June 2, 2012

8 Employer's name and address (Employer: Complete lines 8 and 10 only if sending to the IRS.) — 9 Office code (optional) — 10 Employer identification number (EIN)

For Privacy Act and Paperwork Reduction Act Notice, see page 2. — Cat. No. 10220Q — Form **W-4** (2012)

3 IRS withholding tables are also available for married employees and for pay periods other than weekly.

In Exhibit 3, each row is the employee's wages after deducting the employee's withholding allowances. Each year, the amount of the standard withholding allowance is determined by the IRS. For ease of computation and because this amount changes each year, we assume that the standard withholding allowance to be deducted in Exhibit 3 for a single person paid weekly is $70.[4] Thus, if two withholding allowances are claimed, $140 ($70 × 2) is deducted.

To illustrate, John T. McGrath made $1,462 for the week ended December 27. McGrath's W-4 claims one withholding allowance of $70. Thus, the wages used in determining McGrath's withholding bracket in Exhibit 3 are $1,392 ($1,462 – $70).

After the person's withholding wage bracket has been computed, the federal income tax to be withheld is determined as follows:

Step 1. Locate the proper withholding wage bracket in Exhibit 3.

McGrath's wages after deducting one standard IRS withholding allowance are $1,392 ($1,462 – $70). Therefore, the wage bracket for McGrath is $704–$1,648.

Step 2. Compute the withholding for the proper wage bracket using the directions in the two right-hand columns in Exhibit 3.

For McGrath's wage bracket, the withholding is computed as "$91.40 plus 25% of the excess over $704." Hence, McGrath's withholding is $263.40, as shown below.

Initial withholding from wage bracket	*$ 91.40*
Plus [25% × ($1,392 – $704)]	*172.00*
Total withholding	*$263.40*

EXHIBIT 3

Wage Bracket Withholding Table

Table for Percentage Method of Withholding WEEKLY Payroll Period

(a) SINGLE person (including head of household)—

If the amount of wages (after subtracting withholding allowances) is:		The amount of income tax to withhold is:	
Not over $40		$0	
Over—	**But not over—**		**of excess over—**
$40	—$204	$0.00 plus 10%	—$40
$204	—$704	$16.40 plus 15%	—$204
$704	—$1,648	$91.40 plus 25%	—$704 ← McGrath wage bracket
$1,648	—$3,394	$327.40 plus 28%	—$1,648
$3,394	—$7,332	$816.28 plus 33%	—$3,394
$7,332		$2,115.82 plus 35%	—$7,332

Source: Publication 15, *Employer's Tax Guide*, Internal Revenue Service, 2011.

Residents of New York City must pay federal, state, and city income taxes.

Employers may also be required to withhold state or city income taxes. The amounts to be withheld are determined on state-by-state and city-by-city bases.

Example Exercise 10-2 Federal Income Tax Withholding

OBJ 2

Karen Dunn's weekly gross earnings for the present week were $2,250. Dunn has two exemptions. Using the wage bracket withholding table in Exhibit 3 with a $70 standard withholding allowance for each exemption, what is Dunn's federal income tax withholding?

(Continued)

4 The actual IRS standard withholding allowance changes every year and was $73.08 for 2012.

Follow My Example 10-2

Total wage payment		$ 2,250
One allowance (provided by IRS)	$70	
Multiplied by allowances claimed on Form W-4	× 2	140
Amount subject to withholding		$ 2,110
Initial withholding from wage bracket in Exhibit 3		$327.40
Plus additional withholding: 28% of excess over $1,648		129.36*
Federal income tax withholding		$456.76

*28% × ($2,110 – $1,648)

Practice Exercises: **PE 10-2A, PE 10-2B**

FICA Tax Employers are required by the Federal Insurance Contributions Act (FICA) to withhold a portion of the earnings of each employee. The **FICA tax** withheld contributes to the following two federal programs:

1. *Social security*, which provides payments for retirees, survivors, and disability insurance.
2. *Medicare*, which provides health insurance for senior citizens.

The amount withheld from each employee is based on the employee's earnings *paid* in the *calendar* year. The withholding tax rates and maximum earnings subject to tax are often revised by Congress.[5] To simplify, this chapter assumes the following rates and earnings subject to tax:

1. Social security: 6% on all earnings
2. Medicare: 1.5% on all earnings

To illustrate, assume that John T. McGrath's earnings for the week ending December 27 are $1,462 and the total FICA tax to be withheld is **$109.65**, as shown below.

Earnings subject to 6% social security tax	$1,462	
Social security tax rate	× 6%	
Social security tax		$ 87.72
Earnings subject to 1.5% Medicare tax	$1,462	
Medicare tax rate	× 1.5%	
Medicare tax		21.93
Total FICA tax		$109.65

Other Deductions Employees may choose to have additional amounts deducted from their gross pay. For example, an employee may authorize deductions for retirement savings, for charitable contributions, or life insurance. A union contract may also require the deduction of union dues.

Computing Employee Net Pay

Gross earnings less payroll deductions equals *net pay*, sometimes called *take-home pay*. Assuming that John T. McGrath authorized deductions for retirement savings and

5 For 2012, the social security tax rate was 6.2% and the Medicare tax rate was 1.45%. Earnings subject to the social security tax are limited to an annual threshold amount; but for text examples and problems, assume all accumulated annual earnings are below this threshold and subject to the tax.

for a United Fund contribution, McGrath's net pay for the week ended December 27 is $1,063.95, as shown below.

Gross earnings for the week		$1,462.00
Deductions:		
Social security tax	$ 87.72	
Medicare tax	21.93	
Federal income tax	263.40	
Retirement savings	20.00	
United Fund	5.00	
Total deductions		398.05
Net pay		$1,063.95

Example Exercise 10-3 Employee Net Pay OBJ 2

Karen Dunn's weekly gross earnings for the week ending December 3 were $2,250, and her federal income tax withholding was $456.76. Assuming the social security rate is 6% and Medicare is 1.5%, what is Dunn's net pay?

Follow My Example 10-3

Total wage payment		$2,250.00
Less: Federal income tax withholding	$456.76	
Social security tax ($2,250 × 6%)	135.00	
Medicare tax ($2,250 × 1.5%)	33.75	625.51
Net pay		$1,624.49

Practice Exercises: **PE 10-3A, PE 10-3B**

Liability for Employer's Payroll Taxes

Employers are subject to the following payroll taxes for amounts paid their employees:

1. *FICA Tax*: Employers must match the employee's FICA tax contribution.
2. *Federal Unemployment Compensation Tax (FUTA)*: This employer tax provides for temporary payments to those who become unemployed. The tax collected by the federal government is allocated among the states for use in state programs rather than paid directly to employees. Congress often revises the FUTA tax rate and maximum earnings subject to tax.
3. *State Unemployment Compensation Tax (SUTA)*: This employer tax also provides temporary payments to those who become unemployed. The FUTA and SUTA programs are closely coordinated, with the states distributing the unemployment checks.[6] SUTA tax rates and earnings subject to tax vary by state.[7]

The preceding employer taxes are an operating expense of the company. Exhibit 4 summarizes the responsibility for employee and employer payroll taxes.

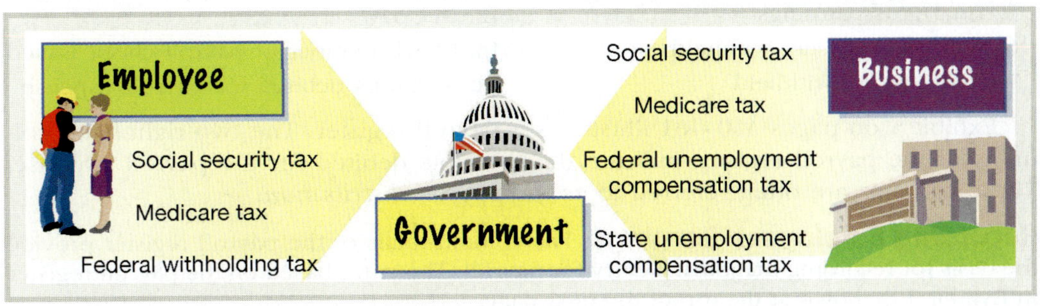

EXHIBIT 4

Responsibility for Tax Payments

6 This rate may be reduced to 0.8% for credits for state unemployment compensation tax.

7 For 2012, the maximum state rate credited against the federal unemployment rate was 5.4% of the first $7,000 of each employee's earnings during a calendar year.

Business Connection

THE MOST YOU WILL EVER PAY

In 1936, the Social Security Board described how the tax was expected to affect a worker's pay, as follows:

The taxes called for in this law will be paid both by your employer and by you. For the next 3 years you will pay maybe 15 cents a week, maybe 25 cents a week, maybe 30 cents or more, according to what you earn. That is to say, during the next 3 years, beginning January 1, 1937, you will pay 1 cent for every dollar you earn, and at the same time your employer will pay 1 cent for every dollar you earn, up to $3,000 a year. . . .

. . . Beginning in 1940 you will pay, and your employer will pay, 1½ cents for each dollar you earn, up to $3,000 a year . . . and then beginning in 1943, you will pay 2 cents, and so will your employer, for every dollar you earn for the next three years. After that, you and your employer will each pay half a cent more for 3 years, and finally, beginning in 1949, . . . you and your employer will each pay 3 cents on each dollar you earn, up to $3,000 a year. That is the most you will ever pay.

The rate on January 1, 2012, was 7.65 cents per dollar earned (7.65%). The social security portion was 6.20% on the first $110,100 of earnings. The Medicare portion was 1.45% on all earnings.*

*For the first two months of 2012, the social security tax rate was reduced by 2 percentage points for employees and for self-employed workers.

Source: Arthur Lodge, "That Is the Most You Will Ever Pay," *Journal of Accountancy*, October 1985, p. 44.

OBJ 3 Describe payroll accounting systems that use a payroll register, employee earnings records, and a general journal.

Accounting Systems for Payroll and Payroll Taxes

Payroll systems should be designed to:

1. Pay employees accurately and timely.
2. Meet regulatory requirements of federal, state, and local agencies.
3. Provide useful data for management decision-making needs.

Although payroll systems differ among companies, the major elements of most payroll systems are:

1. Payroll register
2. Employee's earnings record
3. Payroll checks

Payroll Register

The **payroll register** is a multicolumn report used for summarizing the data for each payroll period. Although payroll registers vary by company, a payroll register normally includes the following columns:

1. Employee name
2. Total hours worked
3. Regular earnings
4. Overtime earnings
5. Total gross earnings
6. Social security tax withheld
7. Medicare tax withheld
8. Federal income tax withheld
9. Retirement savings withheld
10. Miscellaneous items withheld
11. Total withholdings
12. Net pay
13. Check number of payroll check issued
14. Accounts debited for payroll expense

Exhibit 5 on pages 460–461 illustrates a payroll register. The two right-hand columns of the payroll register indicate the accounts debited for the payroll expense. These columns are often referred to as the *payroll distribution*.

Recording Employees' Earnings The column totals of the payroll register provide the basis for recording the journal entry for payroll. The entry based on the payroll register in Exhibit 5 is shown at the top of the next page.

Note: **Payroll taxes become a liability to the employer when the payroll is paid.**

Recording and Paying Payroll Taxes Payroll taxes are recorded as liabilities when the payroll is *paid* to employees. In addition, employers compute and report payroll taxes on a *calendar-year* basis, which may differ from the company's fiscal year.

Dec.	27	Sales Salaries Expense		11,122.00	
		Office Salaries Expense		2,780.00	
		Social Security Tax Payable			834.12
		Medicare Tax Payable			208.53
		Employees Federal Income Tax Payable			3,332.00
		Retirement Savings Deductions Payable			680.00
		United Fund Deductions Payable			520.00
		Salaries Payable			8,327.35
		Payroll for week ended December 27.			

Example Exercise 10-4 Journalize Period Payroll

OBJ 3

The payroll register of Chen Engineering Services indicates $900 of social security withheld and $225 of Medicare tax withheld on total salaries of $15,000 for the period. Federal withholding for the period totaled $2,925.

Provide the journal entry for the period's payroll.

Follow My Example 10-4

Salaries Expense	15,000	
Social Security Tax Payable		900
Medicare Tax Payable		225
Employees Federal Income Tax Payable		2,925
Salaries Payable		10,950

Practice Exercises: **PE 10-4A, PE 10-4B**

On December 27, McDermott Supply has the following payroll data:

Sales salaries	$11,122
Office salaries owed	2,780
Wages owed employees on December 27	$13,902
Wages subject to payroll taxes:	
Social security tax (6%)	$13,902
Medicare tax (1.5%)	13,902
State (5.4%) and federal (0.8%) unemployment compensation tax	2,710

Employers must match the employees' social security and Medicare tax contributions. In addition, the employer must pay state unemployment compensation tax (SUTA) of 5.4% and federal unemployment compensation tax (FUTA) of 0.8%. When payroll is paid on December 27, these payroll taxes are computed as follows:

Social security tax	$ 834.12 ($13,902 × 6%, and from Social Security Tax column of Exhibit 5)
Medicare tax	208.53 ($13,902 × 1.5%, and from Medicare Tax column of Exhibit 5)
SUTA	146.34 ($2,710 × 5.4%)
FUTA	21.68 ($2,710 × 0.8%)
Total payroll taxes	$1,210.67

The entry to journalize the payroll tax expense for Exhibit 5 is shown below.

Dec.	27	Payroll Tax Expense		1,210.67	
		Social Security Tax Payable			834.12
		Medicare Tax Payable			208.53
		State Unemployment Tax Payable			146.34
		Federal Unemployment Tax Payable			21.68
		Payroll taxes for week ended December 27.			

EXHIBIT 5 **Payroll Register**

			Earnings			
	Employee Name	**Total Hours**	**Regular**	**Overtime**	**Total**	
1	Abrams, Julie S.	40	500.00		500.00	1
2	Elrod, Fred G.	44	392.00	58.80	450.80	2
3	Gomez, Jose C.	40	840.00		840.00	3
4	**McGrath, John T.**	**42**	**1,360.00**	**102.00**	**1,462.00**	4
25	Wilkes, Glenn K.	40	480.00		480.00	25
26	Zumpano, Michael W.	40	600.00		600.00	26
27	Total		13,328.00	574.00	13,902.00	27
28						28

The preceding entry records a liability for each payroll tax. When the payroll taxes are paid, an entry is recorded debiting the payroll tax liability accounts and crediting Cash.

Example Exercise 10-5 Journalize Payroll Tax OBJ 3

The payroll register of Chen Engineering Services indicates $900 of social security withheld and $225 of Medicare tax withheld on total salaries of $15,000 for the period. Earnings of $5,250 are subject to state and federal unemployment compensation taxes at the federal rate of 0.8% and the state rate of 5.4%.

Provide the journal entry to record the payroll tax expense for the period.

Follow My Example 10-5

Payroll Tax Expense	1,450.50	
Social Security Tax Payable		900.00
Medicare Tax Payable		225.00
State Unemployment Tax Payable		283.50*
Federal Unemployment Tax Payable		42.00**

*$5,250 × 5.4%
**$5,250 × 0.8%

Practice Exercises: **PE 10-5A, PE 10-5B**

Employee's Earnings Record

Each employee's earnings to date must be determined at the end of each payroll period. This total is necessary for computing the employee's social security tax withholding and the employer's payroll taxes. Thus, detailed payroll records must be kept for each employee. This record is called an **employee's earnings record**.

Exhibit 6, on pages 462–463, shows a portion of John T. McGrath's employee's earnings record. An employee's earnings record and the payroll register are interrelated. For example, McGrath's earnings record for December 27 can be traced to the fourth line of the payroll register in Exhibit 5.

As shown in Exhibit 6, an employee's earnings record has quarterly and yearly totals. These totals are used for tax, insurance, and other reports. For example, one such report is the Wage and Tax Statement, commonly called a *W-2*. This form is

EXHIBIT 5 **(Concluded)**

	Deductions Withheld						Paid		Accounts Debited		
	Social Security Tax	Medicare Tax	Federal Income Tax	Retirement Savings	Misc.	Total	Net Pay	Check No.	Sales Salaries Expense	Office Salaries Expense	
1	30.00	7.50	50.30	20.00	UF 10.00	117.80	382.20	6857	500.00		1
2	27.05	6.76	42.92		UF 50.00	126.73	324.07	6858		450.80	2
3	50.40	12.60	107.90	25.00	UF 10.00	205.90	634.10	6859	840.00		3
4	87.72	21.93	263.40	20.00	UF 5.00	398.05	1,063.95	6860	1,462.00		4
25	28.80	7.20	47.30	10.00		93.30	386.70	6880	480.00		25
26	36.00	9.00	65.30	5.00	UF 2.00	117.30	482.70	6881		600.00	26
27	834.12	208.53	3,332.00	680.00	UF 520.00	5,574.65	8,327.35		11,122.00	2,780.00	27
28											28

Miscellaneous Deductions: UF—United Fund

provided annually to each employee as well as to the Social Security Administration. The W-2 shown below is based on John T. McGrath's employee's earnings record shown in Exhibit 6, on pages 462–463.

22222 Void ☐ | a Employee's social security number 381-48-9120 | For Official Use Only ▶ OMB No. 1545-0008

b Employer identification number (EIN): 61-8436524

c Employer's name, address, and ZIP code: McDermott Supply Co. 415 5th Ave. So. Dubuque, IA 52736-0142

d Control number

e Employee's first name and initial: John T. | Last name: McGrath | Suff.

1830 4th St.
Clinton, IA 52732-6142

f Employee's address and ZIP code

1 Wages, tips, other compensation: 100,500.00	2 Federal income tax withheld: 21,387.65
3 Social security wages: 100,500.00	4 Social security tax withheld: 6,030.00
5 Medicare wages and tips: 100,500.00	6 Medicare tax withheld: 1,507.50
7 Social security tips	8 Allocated tips
9	10 Dependent care benefits
11 Nonqualified plans	12a See instructions for box 12
13 Statutory employee ☐ Retirement plan ☐ Third-party sick pay ☐	12b
14 Other	12c
	12d

15 State / Employer's state ID number	16 State wages, tips, etc.	17 State income tax	18 Local wages, tips, etc.	19 Local income tax	20 Locality name
IA					Dubuque

Form **W-2** Wage and Tax Statement **2013**

Department of the Treasury—Internal Revenue Service

For Privacy Act and Paperwork Reduction Act Notice, see the separate instructions.

Cat. No. 10134D

Copy A For Social Security Administration — Send this entire page with Form W-3 to the Social Security Administration; photocopies are **not** acceptable.

Do Not Cut, Fold, or Staple Forms on This Page

Payroll Checks

Companies may pay employees, especially part-time employees, by issuing *payroll checks*. Each check includes a detachable statement showing how the net pay was computed. Exhibit 7, on page 464, illustrates a payroll check for John T. McGrath.

Most companies issuing payroll checks use a special payroll bank account. In such cases, payroll is processed as follows:

1. The total net pay for the period is determined from the payroll register.
2. The company authorizes an electronic funds transfer (EFT) from its regular bank account to the special payroll bank account for the total net pay.
3. Individual payroll checks are written from the payroll account.
4. The numbers of the payroll checks are inserted in the payroll register.

EXHIBIT 6

Employee's Earnings Record

John T. McGrath 1830 4th St. Clinton, IA 52732-6142						PHONE: 555-3148	
SINGLE		NUMBER OF WITHHOLDING ALLOWANCES: 1		PAY RATE:	$1,360.00 Per Week		
OCCUPATION:	Salesperson			EQUIVALENT HOURLY RATE: $34			

		Earnings					
	Period Ending	Total Hours	Regular Earnings	Overtime Earnings	Total Earnings	Total	
42	SEPT. 27	53	1,360.00	663.00	2,023.00	75,565.00	42
43	THIRD QUARTER		17,680.00	7,605.00	25,285.00		43
44	OCT. 4	51	1,360.00	561.00	1,921.00	77,486.00	44
50	NOV. 15	50	1,360.00	510.00	1,870.00	89,382.00	50
51	NOV. 22	53	1,360.00	663.00	2,023.00	91,405.00	51
52	NOV. 29	47	1,360.00	357.00	1,717.00	93,122.00	52
53	DEC. 6	53	1,360.00	663.00	2,023.00	95,145.00	53
54	DEC.13	52	1,360.00	612.00	1,972.00	97,117.00	54
55	DEC. 20	51	1,360.00	561.00	1,921.00	99,038.00	55
56	DEC. 27	42	1,360.00	102.00	1,462.00	100,500.00	56
57	FOURTH QUARTER		17,680.00	7,255.00	24,935.00		57
58	YEARLY TOTAL		70,720.00	29,780.00	100,500.00		58

An advantage of using a separate payroll bank account is that reconciling the bank statements is simplified. In addition, a payroll bank account establishes control over payroll checks and, thus, prevents their theft or misuse.

Many companies use electronic funds transfer to pay their employees. In such cases, each pay period an employee's net pay is deposited directly into the employee checking account. Later, employees receive a payroll statement summarizing how the net pay was computed.

Computerized Payroll System

The inputs into a payroll system may be classified as:

1. Constants, which are data that remain unchanged from payroll to payroll.

   Examples: Employee names, social security numbers, marital status, number of income tax withholding allowances, rates of pay, tax rates, and withholding tables.

2. Variables, which are data that change from payroll to payroll.

   Examples: Number of hours or days worked for each employee, accrued days of sick leave, vacation credits, total earnings to date, and total taxes withheld.

In a computerized accounting system, constants are stored within a payroll file. The variables are input each pay period by a payroll clerk. In some systems, employees swipe their identification (ID) cards when they report for and leave from work. In such cases, the hours worked by each employee are automatically updated.

A computerized payroll system also maintains electronic versions of the payroll register and employee earnings records. Payroll system outputs, such as payroll checks, EFTs, and tax records, are automatically produced each pay period.

EXHIBIT 6 **(Concluded)**

SOC. SEC. NO.: 381-48-9120 **EMPLOYEE NO.: 814**

DATE OF BIRTH: February 15, 1982

DATE EMPLOYMENT TERMINATED:

	Deductions							Paid		
	Social Security Tax	Medicare Tax	Federal Income Tax	Retirement Savings	Other		Total	Net Amount	Check No.	
42	121.38	30.35	412.80	20.00			584.53	1,438.47	6175	42
43	1,517.10	379.28	5,391.71	260.00	UF	40.00	7,588.09	17,696.91		43
44	115.26	28.82	384.24	20.00			548.32	1,372.68	6225	44
50	112.20	28.05	369.96	20.00			530.21	1,339.79	6530	50
51	121.38	30.35	412.80	20.00			589.53	1,433.47	6582	51
52	103.02	25.76	327.15	20.00			475.93	1,241.07	6640	52
53	121.38	30.35	412.80	20.00	UF	5.00	584.53	1,438.47	6688	53
54	118.32	29.58	398.52	20.00			566.42	1,405.58	6743	54
55	115.26	28.82	384.24	20.00			548.32	1,372.68	6801	55
56	87.72	21.93	263.40	20.00	UF	5.00	398.05	1,063.95	6860	56
57	1,496.10	374.03	5,293.71	260.00	UF	15.00	7,438.84	17,496.16		57
58	6,030.00	1,507.50	21,387.65	1,040.00	UF	100.00	30,065.15	70,434.85		58

Internal Controls for Payroll Systems

The cash payment controls described in Chapter 7, *Sarbanes-Oxley, Internal Control, and Cash*, also apply to payrolls. Some examples of payroll controls include the following:

1. If a check-signing machine is used, blank payroll checks and access to the machine should be restricted to prevent their theft or misuse.
2. The hiring and firing of employees should be properly authorized and approved in writing.
3. All changes in pay rates should be properly authorized and approved in writing.
4. Employees should be observed when arriving for work to verify that employees are "checking in" for work only once and only for themselves. Employees may "check in" for work by using a time card or by swiping their employee ID card.
5. Payroll checks should be distributed by someone other than employee supervisors.
6. A special payroll bank account should be used.

Integrity, Objectivity, and Ethics in Business

$8 MILLION FOR 18 MINUTES OF WORK

Computer system controls can be very important in issuing payroll checks. In one case, a Detroit schoolteacher was paid $4,015,625 after deducting $3,884,375 in payroll deductions for 18 minutes of overtime work. The error was caused by a computer glitch when the teacher's employee identification number was substituted incorrectly in the "hourly wage" field and wasn't caught by the payroll software. After six days, the error was discovered and the money was returned. "One of the things that came with (the software) is a fail-safe that prevents that. It doesn't work," a financial officer said. The district has since installed a program to flag any paycheck exceeding $10,000.

Source: Associated Press, September 27, 2002.

EXHIBIT 7

Payroll Check

McDermott Supply Co.
415 5th Ave. So.
Dubuque, IA 52736-0142

John T. McGrath
1830 4th St.
Clinton, IA 52732-6142

Check Number: 6860
Pay Period Ending: 12/27/13

HOURS & EARNINGS	
DESCRIPTION	AMOUNT
Rate of Pay Reg.	34
Rate of Pay O.T.	51
Hours Worked Reg.	40
Hours Worked O.T.	2
Net Pay	1,063.95
Total Gross Pay	1,462.00
Total Gross Y-T-D	100,500.00

TAXES & DEDUCTIONS		
DESCRIPTION	CURRENT AMOUNT	Y-T-D AMOUNT
Social Security Tax	87.72	6,030.00
Medicare Tax	21.93	1,507.50
Fed. Income Tax	263.40	21,387.65
U.S. Savings Bonds	20.00	1,040.00
United Fund	5.00	100.00
Total	398.05	30,365.15

STATEMENT OF EARNINGS. DETACH AND KEEP FOR YOUR RECORDS

McDermott Supply Co.
415 5th Ave. So.
Dubuque, IA 52736-0142

Pay Period Ending: 12/27/13

LaGesse Savings & Loan
33 Katie Avenue, Suite 33
Clinton, IA 52736-3581

24-2/531

6860

PAY ONE THOUSAND SIXTY-THREE AND 95/100 . . . . **DOLLARS**

To the Order of JOHN T. MCGRATH
1830 4TH ST.
CLINTON, IA 52732-6142

$1,063.95

Franklin D. McDermott

⑈6860⑈ ⑆153111123⑆ ⑈9385402⑈

OBJ 4 Journalize entries for employee fringe benefits, including vacation pay and pensions.

Employees' Fringe Benefits

Many companies provide their employees benefits in addition to salary and wages earned. Such **fringe benefits** may include vacation, medical, and retirement benefits.

The cost of employee fringe benefits is recorded as an expense by the employer. To match revenues and expenses, the estimated cost of fringe benefits is recorded as an expense during the period in which the employees earn the benefits.

Vacation Pay

Note:
Vacation pay becomes the employer's liability as the employee earns vacation rights.

Most employers provide employees vacations, sometimes called *compensated absences.* The liability to pay for employee vacations could be accrued as a liability at the end of each pay period. However, many companies wait and record an adjusting entry for accrued vacation at the end of the year.

To illustrate, assume that employees earn one day of vacation for each month worked. The estimated vacation pay for the year ending December 31 is $325,000. The adjusting entry for the accrued vacation is shown below.

Dec.	31	Vacation Pay Expense		325,000	
		Vacation Pay Payable			325,000
		Accrued vacation pay for the year.			

Employees may be required to take all their vacation time within one year. In such cases, any accrued vacation pay will be paid within one year. Thus, the vacation pay payable is reported as a current liability on the balance sheet. If employees are allowed to accumulate their vacation pay, the estimated vacation pay payable that will *not* be taken within a year is reported as a long-term liability.

When employees take vacations, the liability for vacation pay is decreased by debiting Vacation Pay Payable. Salaries or Wages Payable and the other related payroll accounts for taxes and withholdings are credited.

Pensions

A **pension** is a cash payment to retired employees. Pension rights are accrued by employees as they work, based on the employer's pension plan. Two basic types of pension plans are:

1. Defined contribution
2. Defined benefit

In a **defined contribution plan**, the company invests contributions on behalf of the employee during the employee's working years. Normally, the employee and employer contribute to the plan. The employee's pension depends on the total contributions and the investment returns earned on those contributions.

One of the more popular defined contribution plans is the 401k plan. Under this plan, employees contribute a portion of their gross pay to investments, such as mutual funds. A 401k plan offers employees two advantages.

1. The employee contribution is deducted before taxes.
2. The contributions and related earnings are not taxed until withdrawn at retirement.

In most cases, the employer matches some portion of the employee's contribution. The employer's cost is debited to *Pension Expense*. To illustrate, assume that Heaven Scent Perfumes Company contributes 10% of employee monthly salaries to an employee 401k plan. Assuming $500,000 of monthly salaries, the journal entry to record the monthly contribution is shown below.

Dec.	31	Pension Expense		50,000	
		Cash			50,000
		Contributed 10% of monthly salaries to pension plan.			

In a **defined benefit plan**, the company pays the employee a fixed annual pension based on a formula. The formula is normally based on such factors as the employee's years of service, age, and past salary.

In a defined benefit plan, the employer is obligated to pay for (fund) the employee's future pension benefits. As a result, many companies are replacing their defined benefit plans with defined contribution plans.

The pension cost of a defined benefit plan is debited to *Pension Expense*. Cash is credited for the amount contributed (funded) by the employer. Any unfunded amount is credited to *Unfunded Pension Liability*.

To illustrate, assume that the defined benefit plan of Hinkle Co. requires an annual pension cost of $80,000. This annual contribution is based on estimates of Hinkle's future pension liabilities. On December 31, Hinkle Co. pays $60,000 to the pension fund. The entry to record the payment and the unfunded liability is shown on the next page.

Dec.	31	Pension Expense	80,000	
		Cash		60,000
		Unfunded Pension Liability		20,000
		Annual pension cost and contribution.		

If the unfunded pension liability is to be paid within one year, it is reported as a current liability on the balance sheet. Any portion of the unfunded pension liability that will be paid beyond one year is a long-term liability.

The accounting for pensions is complex due to the uncertainties of estimating future pension liabilities. These estimates depend on such factors as employee life expectancies, employee turnover, expected employee compensation levels, and investment income on pension contributions. Additional accounting and disclosures related to pensions are covered in advanced accounting courses.

Example Exercise 10-6 Vacation Pay and Pension Benefits OBJ 4

Manfield Services Company provides its employees vacation benefits and a defined contribution pension plan. Employees earned vacation pay of $44,000 for the period. The pension plan requires a contribution to the plan administrator equal to 8% of employee salaries. Salaries were $450,000 during the period.

Provide the journal entry for the (a) vacation pay and (b) pension benefit.

Follow My Example 10-6

a.	Vacation Pay Expense	44,000	
	Vacation Pay Payable		44,000
	Vacation pay accrued for the period.		
b.	Pension Expense	36,000	
	Cash		36,000
	Pension contribution, 8% of $450,000 salary.		

Practice Exercises: **PE 10-6A, PE 10-6B**

Postretirement Benefits Other than Pensions

Employees may earn rights to other postretirement benefits from their employer. Such benefits may include dental care, eye care, medical care, life insurance, tuition assistance, tax services, and legal services.

The accounting for other postretirement benefits is similar to that of defined benefit pension plans. The estimate of the annual benefits expense is recorded by debiting *Postretirement Benefits Expense*. If the benefits are fully funded, Cash is credited for the same amount. If the benefits are not fully funded, a postretirement benefits plan liability account is also credited.

The financial statements should disclose the nature of the postretirement benefit liabilities. These disclosures are usually included as notes to the financial statements. Additional accounting and disclosures for postretirement benefits are covered in advanced accounting courses.

Current Liabilities on the Balance Sheet

Accounts payable, the current portion of long-term debt, notes payable, and any other debts that are due within one year are reported as current liabilities on the balance sheet. The balance sheet presentation of current liabilities for Mornin' Joe is as shown on the next page.

Mornin' Joe Balance Sheet December 31, 2014		
Liabilities		
Current liabilities:		
Accounts payable	$133,000	
Notes payable (current portion)	200,000	
Salaries and wages payable	42,000	
Payroll taxes payable	16,400	
Interest payable	40,000	
Total current liabilities		$431,400

Business Connection

GENERAL MOTORS' PENSION PROBLEMS

In June 2009, General Motors Company, the world's second-largest automaker, filed for bankruptcy. The company's troubles began decades earlier when the company agreed to provide employees with large pension benefits instead of giving them wage increases. While this strategy was initially successful, by the mid-1990s large numbers of employees began to retire, and the increasing pension costs began to put a financial strain on the company. In 2003, the company issued $18.5 billion in debt to fund its growing unfunded pension liability, but this only provided a temporary fix. From 1993 to 2007, General Motors spent $103 billion on pension and health care benefits for retirees, and the company had 4.61 retired union employees for every one active union employee. By June 2009, the combination of growing pension obligations and deteriorating sales forced the company into bankruptcy.

Source: R. Lowenstein, "Siphoning GM's Future," *The New York Times*, July 10, 2008.

Contingent Liabilities

OBJ 5 Describe the accounting treatment for contingent liabilities and journalize entries for product warranties.

Some liabilities may arise from past transactions only if certain events occur in the future. These *potential* liabilities are called **contingent liabilities**.

The accounting for contingent liabilities depends on the following two factors:

1. Likelihood of occurring: Probable, reasonably possible, or remote
2. Measurement: Estimable or not estimable

The likelihood that the event creating the liability occurring is classified as *probable*, *reasonably possible*, or *remote*. The ability to estimate the potential liability is classified as *estimable* or *not estimable*.

Probable and Estimable

If a contingent liability is *probable* and the amount of the liability can be *reasonably estimated*, it is recorded and disclosed. The liability is recorded by debiting an expense and crediting a liability.

To illustrate, assume that during June a company sold a product for $60,000 that includes a 36-month warranty for repairs. The average cost of repairs over the warranty period is 5% of the sales price. The entry to record the estimated product warranty expense for June is as shown below.

June	30	Product Warranty Expense		3,000	
		Product Warranty Payable			3,000
		Warranty expense for June, 5% × $60,000.			

The estimated costs of warranty work on new car sales are a contingent liability for Ford Motor Company.

The preceding entry records warranty expense in the same period in which the sale is recorded. In this way, warranty expense is matched with the related revenue (sales).

If the product is repaired under warranty, the repair costs are recorded by debiting *Product Warranty Payable* and crediting *Cash, Supplies, Wages Payable*, or other appropriate accounts. Thus, if a $200 part is replaced under warranty on August 16, the entry is as follows:

Aug.	16	Product Warranty Payable		200	
		Supplies			200
		Replaced defective part under warranty.			

Example Exercise 10-7 Estimated Warranty Liability

OBJ 5

Cook-Rite Co. sold $140,000 of kitchen appliances during August under a six-month warranty. The cost to repair defects under the warranty is estimated at 6% of the sales price. On September 11, a customer required a $200 part replacement plus $90 of labor under the warranty.

Provide the journal entry for (a) the estimated warranty expense on August 31 for August sales, and (b) the September 11 warranty work.

Follow My Example 10-7

a.	Product Warranty Expense	8,400	
	Product Warranty Payable		8,400
	To record warranty expense for August, 6% × $140,000.		
b.	Product Warranty Payable	290	
	Supplies		200
	Wages Payable		90
	Replaced defective part under warranty.		

Practice Exercises: **PE 10-7A, PE 10-7B**

Probable and Not Estimable

A contingent liability may be probable, but cannot be estimated. In this case, the contingent liability is disclosed in the notes to the financial statements. For example, a company may have accidentally polluted a local river by dumping waste products. At the end of the period, the cost of the cleanup and any fines may not be able to be estimated.

Reasonably Possible

A contingent liability may be only possible. For example, a company may have lost a lawsuit for infringing on another company's patent rights. However, the verdict is under appeal and the company's lawyers feel that the verdict will be reversed or significantly reduced. In this case, the contingent liability is disclosed in the notes to the financial statements.

Remote

A contingent liability may be remote. For example, a ski resort may be sued for injuries incurred by skiers. In most cases, the courts have found that a skier accepts the risk of injury when participating in the activity. Thus, unless the ski resort is grossly negligent, the resort will not incur a liability for ski injuries. In such cases, no disclosure needs to be made in the notes to the financial statements. The accounting treatment of contingent liabilities is summarized in Exhibit 8.

Common examples of contingent liabilities disclosed in notes to the financial statements are litigation, environmental matters, guarantees, and contingencies from the sale of receivables.

EXHIBIT 8 **Accounting Treatment of Contingent Liabilities**

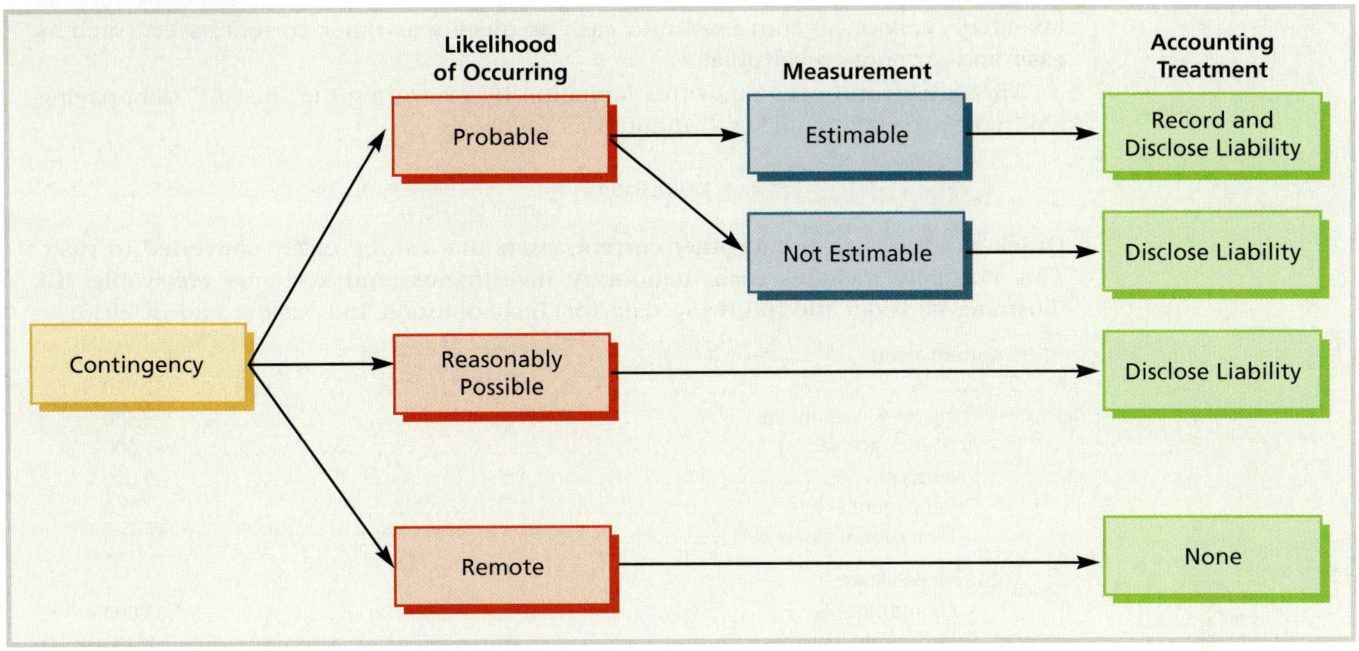

An example of a contingent liability disclosure from a recent annual report of Google Inc. is shown below.

> *We have also had copyright claims filed against us alleging that features of certain of our products and services, including Google Web Search, Google News, Google Video, Google Image Search, Google Book Search and YouTube, infringe their rights. Adverse results in these lawsuits may include awards of substantial monetary damages, costly royalty or licensing agreements or orders preventing us from offering certain functionalities, and may also result in a change in our business practices, which could result in a loss of revenue for us or otherwise harm our business. . . .*
>
> *Although the results of litigation and claims cannot be predicted with certainty, we believe that the final outcome of the matters discussed above will not have a material adverse effect on our business. . . .*

Professional judgment is necessary in distinguishing between classes of contingent liabilities. This is especially the case when distinguishing between probable and reasonably possible contingent liabilities.

Financial Analysis and Interpretation: Quick Ratio

F·A·I

OBJ 6 Describe and illustrate the use of the quick ratio in analyzing a company's ability to pay its current liabilities.

Current position analysis helps creditors evaluate a company's ability to pay its current liabilities. This analysis is based on the following three measures:

1. Working capital
2. Current ratio
3. Quick ratio

Working capital and the current ratio were discussed in Chapter 4 and are computed as follows:

$$\text{Working Capital} = \text{Current Assets} - \text{Current Liabilities}$$

$$\text{Current Ratio} = \frac{\text{Current Assets}}{\text{Current Liabilities}}$$

While these two measures can be used to evaluate a company's ability to pay its current liabilities, they do not provide insight into the company's ability to pay these liabilities within a short period of time. This is because some current assets, such as inventory, cannot be converted into cash as quickly as other current assets, such as cash and accounts receivable.

The **quick ratio** overcomes this limitation by measuring the "instant" debt-paying ability of a company and is computed as follows:

$$\text{Quick Ratio} = \frac{\text{Quick Assets}}{\text{Current Liabilities}}$$

Quick assets are cash and other current assets that can be easily converted to cash. This normally includes cash, temporary investments, and accounts receivable. To illustrate, consider the following data for TechSolutions, Inc., at the end of 2013:

Current assets:	
Cash	$2,020
Temporary investments	3,400
Accounts receivable	1,600
Inventory	2,000
Other current assets	160
Total current assets	$9,180
Current liabilities:	
Accounts payable	$3,000
Other current liabilities	2,400
Total current liabilities	$5,400
Working capital (current assets – current liabilities)	$3,780
Current ratio (current assets/current liabilities)	1.7

The quick ratio for TechSolutions, Inc., is computed as follows:

$$\text{Quick Ratio} = \frac{\$2,020 + \$3,400 + \$1,600}{\$5,400} = 1.3$$

The quick ratio of 1.3 indicates that the company has more than enough quick assets to pay its current liabilities in a short period of time. A quick ratio below 1.0 would indicate that the company does not have enough quick assets to cover its current liabilities.

Like the current ratio, the quick ratio is particularly useful in making comparisons across companies. To illustrate, the following selected balance sheet data (excluding ratios) were taken from recent financial statements of Panera Bread Company and Starbucks Corporation (in thousands):

	Panera Bread	Starbucks
Current assets:		
Cash and cash equivalents	$229,299	$1,164,000
Temporary investments	—	285,700
Accounts receivable	63,136	606,900
Inventory	14,345	543,300
Other current assets	23,905	156,500
Total current assets	$330,685	$2,756,400
Current liabilities:		
Accounts payable	$211,516	$1,365,000
Other current liabilities	—	414,000
Total current liabilities	$211,516	$1,779,000
Working capital (current assets – current liabilities)	$119,169	$ 977,400
Current ratio (current assets/current liabilities)	1.6	1.5
Quick ratio (quick assets/current liabilities)*	1.4	1.2

*The quick ratio for each company is computed as follows:
Panera Bread: ($229,299 + $0 + $63,136) ÷ $211,516 = 1.4
Starbucks: ($1,164,000 + $285,700 + $606,900) ÷ $1,779,000 = 1.2

Starbucks is larger than Panera Bread and has over eight times the amount of working capital. Such size differences make working capital comparisons between companies difficult. In contrast, the current and quick ratios provide better comparisons across companies. In this example, Panera Bread has a slightly higher current ratio than Starbucks. However, Starbucks' 1.2 quick ratio reveals that it has just enough quick assets to cover its current liabilities, while Panera Bread's quick ratio of 1.4 indicates that the company has more than enough quick assets to meet its current liabilities.

Example Exercise 10-8 Quick Ratio

OBJ 6

Sayer Company reported the following current assets and current liabilities for the years ended December 31, 2014 and 2013:

	2014	2013
Cash	$1,250	$1,000
Temporary investments	1,925	1,650
Accounts receivable	1,775	1,350
Inventory	1,900	1,700
Accounts payable	2,750	2,500

a. Compute the quick ratio for 2014 and 2013.

b. Interpret the company's quick ratio across the two time periods.

Follow My Example 10-8

a. December 31, 2014:
Quick Ratio = Quick Assets/Current Liabilities
Quick Ratio = ($1,250 + $1,925 + $1,775)/$2,750
Quick Ratio = 1.8

December 31, 2013:
Quick Ratio = Quick Assets/Current Liabilities
Quick Ratio = ($1,000 + $1,650 + $1,350)/$2,500
Quick Ratio = 1.6

b. The quick ratio of Sayer Company has improved from 1.6 in 2013 to 1.8 in 2014. This increase is the result of a large increase in the three types of quick assets (cash, temporary investments, and accounts receivable) compared to a relatively smaller increase in the current liability, accounts payable.

Practice Exercises: **PE 10-8A, PE 10-8B**

Illustrative Problem

Selected transactions of Taylor Company, completed during the fiscal year ended December 31, are as follows:

Mar. 1. Purchased merchandise on account from Kelvin Co., $20,000.

Apr. 10. Issued a 60-day, 12% note for $20,000 to Kelvin Co. on account.

June 9. Paid Kelvin Co. the amount owed on the note of April 10.

Aug. 1. Issued a $50,000, 90-day note to Harold Co. in exchange for a building. Harold Co. discounted the note at 15%.

Oct. 30. Paid Harold Co. the amount due on the note of August 1.

Dec. 27. Journalized the entry to record the biweekly payroll. A summary of the payroll record follows:

Salary distribution:		
Sales	$63,400	
Officers	36,600	
Office	10,000	$110,000
Deductions:		
Social security tax	$ 6,600	
Medicare tax	1,650	
Federal income tax withheld	17,600	
State income tax withheld	4,950	
Savings bond deductions	850	
Medical insurance deductions	1,120	32,770
Net amount		$ 77,230

27. Journalized the entry to record payroll taxes for social security and Medicare from the biweekly payroll.

30. Issued a check in payment of liabilities for employees' federal income tax of $17,600, social security tax of $13,200, and Medicare tax of $3,300.

31. Issued a check for $9,500 to the pension fund trustee to fully fund the pension cost for December.

31. Journalized an entry to record the employees' accrued vacation pay, $36,100.

31. Journalized an entry to record the estimated accrued product warranty liability, $37,240.

Instructions

Journalize the preceding transactions.

Solution

Mar.	1	Merchandise Inventory	20,000	
		Accounts Payable—Kelvin Co.		20,000
Apr.	10	Accounts Payable—Kelvin Co.	20,000	
		Notes Payable		20,000
June	9	Notes Payable	20,000	
		Interest Expense	400	
		Cash		20,400
Aug.	1	Building	48,125	
		Interest Expense	1,875	
		Notes Payable		50,000
Oct.	30	Notes Payable	50,000	
		Cash		50,000
Dec.	27	Sales Salaries Expense	63,400	
		Officers Salaries Expense	36,600	
		Office Salaries Expense	10,000	
		Social Security Tax Payable		6,600
		Medicare Tax Payable		1,650
		Employees Federal Income Tax Payable		17,600
		Employees State Income Tax Payable		4,950
		Bond Deductions Payable		850
		Medical Insurance Payable		1,120
		Salaries Payable		77,230
	27	Payroll Tax Expense	8,250	
		Social Security Tax Payable		6,600
		Medicare Tax Payable		1,650
	30	Employees Federal Income Tax Payable	17,600	
		Social Security Tax Payable	13,200	
		Medicare Tax Payable	3,300	
		Cash		34,100
	31	Pension Expense	9,500	
		Cash		9,500
		Fund pension cost.		
	31	Vacation Pay Expense	36,100	
		Vacation Pay Payable		36,100
		Accrue vacation pay.		
	31	Product Warranty Expense	37,240	
		Product Warranty Payable		37,240
		Accrue warranty expense.		

Discussion Questions

1. Does a discounted note payable provide credit without interest? Discuss.
2. Employees are subject to taxes withheld from their paychecks.
   a. List the federal taxes withheld from most employee paychecks.
   b. Give the title of the accounts credited by amounts withheld.
3. Why are deductions from employees' earnings classified as liabilities for the employer?
4. For each of the following payroll-related taxes, indicate whether they generally apply to (a) employees only, (b) employers only, or (c) both employees and employers:
   1. Federal income tax
   2. Medicare tax
   3. Social security tax
   4. Federal unemployment compensation tax
   5. State unemployment compensation tax
5. What are the principal reasons for using a special payroll bank account?
6. In a payroll system, what types of input data are referred to as (a) constants and (b) variables?
7. To match revenues and expenses properly, should the expense for employee vacation pay be recorded in the period during which the vacation privilege is earned or during the period in which the vacation is taken? Discuss.
8. Explain how a defined contribution pension plan works.
9. When should the liability associated with a product warranty be recorded? Discuss.
10. General Motors Corporation reported $2.6 billion of product warranties in the Current Liabilities section of a recent balance sheet. How would costs of repairing a defective product be recorded?

Practice Exercises

Example Exercises

EE 10-1 *p. 453*

PE 10-1A Proceeds from notes payable **OBJ. 1**

On October 12, Belleville Co. borrowed cash from Texas Bank by issuing a 30-day note with a face amount of $70,000.

a. Determine the proceeds of the note, assuming the note carries an interest rate of 6%.
b. Determine the proceeds of the note, assuming the note is discounted at 6%.

EE 10-1 *p. 453*

PE 10-1B Proceeds from notes payable **OBJ. 1**

On January 26, Nyree Co. borrowed cash from Conrad Bank by issuing a 45-day note with a face amount of $150,000.

a. Determine the proceeds of the note, assuming the note carries an interest rate of 10%.
b. Determine the proceeds of the note, assuming the note is discounted at 10%.

EE 10-2 *p. 455*

PE 10-2A Federal income tax withholding **OBJ. 2**

Bella Chen's weekly gross earnings for the present week were $2,600. Chen has two exemptions. Using the wage bracket withholding table in Exhibit 3 with a $70 standard withholding allowance for each exemption, what is Chen's federal income tax withholding?

Example Exercises

EE 10-2 *p. 455*

PE 10-2B Federal income tax withholding **OBJ. 2**

Todd Thompson's weekly gross earnings for the present week were $1,400. Thompson has one exemption. Using the wage bracket withholding table in Exhibit 3 with a $70 standard withholding allowance for each exemption, what is Thompson's federal income tax withholding?

EE 10-3 *p. 457*

PE 10-3A Employee net pay **OBJ. 2**

Bella Chen's weekly gross earnings for the week ended October 20 were $2,600, and her federal income tax withholding was $554.76. Assuming the social security rate is 6% and Medicare is 1.5% of all earnings, what is Chen's net pay?

EE 10-3 *p. 457*

PE 10-3B Employee net pay **OBJ. 2**

Todd Thompson's weekly gross earnings for the week ended May 23 were $1,400, and his federal income tax withholding was $247.90. Assuming the social security rate is 6% and Medicare is 1.5% of all earnings, what is Thompson's net pay?

EE 10-4 *p. 459*

PE 10-4A Journalize period payroll **OBJ. 3**

The payroll register of Konrath Co. indicates $13,200 of social security withheld and $3,300 of Medicare tax withheld on total salaries of $220,000 for the period. Federal withholding for the period totaled $43,560.

Provide the journal entry for the period's payroll.

EE 10-4 *p. 459*

PE 10-4B Journalize period payroll **OBJ. 3**

The payroll register of Longboat Co. indicates $5,400 of social security withheld and $1,350 of Medicare tax withheld on total salaries of $90,000 for the period. Retirement savings withheld from employee paychecks were $5,400 for the period. Federal withholding for the period totaled $17,820.

Provide the journal entry for the period's payroll.

EE 10-5 *p. 460*

PE 10-5A Journalize payroll tax **OBJ. 3**

The payroll register of Konrath Co. indicates $13,200 of social security withheld and $3,300 of Medicare tax withheld on total salaries of $220,000 for the period. Earnings of $35,000 are subject to state and federal unemployment compensation taxes at the federal rate of 0.8% and the state rate of 5.4%.

Provide the journal entry to record the payroll tax expense for the period.

EE 10-5 *p. 460*

PE 10-5B Journalize payroll tax **OBJ. 3**

The payroll register of Longboat Co. indicates $5,400 of social security withheld and $1,350 of Medicare tax withheld on total salaries of $90,000 for the period. Earnings of $10,000 are subject to state and federal unemployment compensation taxes at the federal rate of 0.8% and the state rate of 5.4%.

Provide the journal entry to record the payroll tax expense for the period.

EE 10-6 *p. 466*

PE 10-6A Vacation pay and pension benefits **OBJ. 4**

Fukushima Company provides its employees with vacation benefits and a defined contribution pension plan. Employees earned vacation pay of $19,500 for the period. The pension plan requires a contribution to the plan administrator equal to 6% of employee salaries. Salaries were $260,000 during the period.

Provide the journal entry for the (a) vacation pay and (b) pension benefit.

Example Exercises

EE 10-6 p. 466

PE 10-6B Vacation pay and pension benefits **OBJ. 4**

Regling Company provides its employees vacation benefits and a defined benefit pension plan. Employees earned vacation pay of $35,000 for the period. The pension formula calculated a pension cost of $201,250. Only $175,000 was contributed to the pension plan administrator.

Provide the journal entry for the (a) vacation pay and (b) pension benefit.

EE 10-7 p. 468

PE 10-7A Estimated warranty liability **OBJ. 5**

Kyrgyz Co. sold $200,000 of equipment during February under a one-year warranty. The cost to repair defects under the warranty is estimated at 6% of the sales price. On July 24, a customer required a $60 part replacement, plus $32 of labor under the warranty.

Provide the journal entry for (a) the estimated warranty expense on February 28 for February sales, and (b) the July 24 warranty work.

EE 10-7 p. 468

PE 10-7B Estimated warranty liability **OBJ. 5**

Quantas Industries sold $325,000 of consumer electronics during July under a nine-month warranty. The cost to repair defects under the warranty is estimated at 4.5% of the sales price. On November 11, a customer was given $220 cash under terms of the warranty.

Provide the journal entry for (a) the estimated warranty expense on July 31 for July sales, and (b) the November 11 cash payment.

EE 10-8 p. 471

PE 10-8A Quick ratio **OBJ. 6**

F·A·I

Nabors Company reported the following current assets and liabilities for December 31, 2014 and 2013:

	Dec. 31, 2014	Dec. 31, 2013
Cash	$ 650	$ 680
Temporary investments	1,500	1,550
Accounts receivable	700	770
Inventory	1,250	1,400
Accounts payable	2,375	2,000

a. Compute the quick ratio for December 31, 2014 and 2013.

b. Interpret the company's quick ratio. Is the quick ratio improving or declining?

EE 10-8 p. 471

PE 10-8B Quick ratio **OBJ. 6**

F·A·I

Adieu Company reported the following current assets and liabilities for December 31, 2014 and 2013:

	Dec. 31, 2014	Dec. 31, 2013
Cash	$1,000	$1,140
Temporary investments	1,200	1,400
Accounts receivable	800	910
Inventory	2,200	2,300
Accounts payable	1,875	2,300

a. Compute the quick ratio for December 31, 2014 and 2013.

b. Interpret the company's quick ratio. Is the quick ratio improving or declining?

Exercises

EX 10-1 Current liabilities **OBJ. 1**

✔ Total current liabilities, $1,929,750

Bon Nebo Co. sold 25,000 annual subscriptions of *Bjorn 20XX* for $85 during December 2014. These new subscribers will receive monthly issues, beginning in January 2015. In addition, the business had taxable income of $840,000 during the first calendar quarter of 2015. The federal tax rate is 40%. A quarterly tax payment will be made on April 12, 2015.

Prepare the Current Liabilities section of the balance sheet for Bon Nebo Co. on March 31, 2015.

EX 10-2 Entries for discounting notes payable **OBJ. 1**

Swain Enterprises issues a 60-day note for $800,000 to Hill Industries for merchandise inventory. Hill Industries discounts the note at 6%.

a. Journalize Swain Enterprises' entries to record:
   1. the issuance of the note.
   2. the payment of the note at maturity.

b. Journalize Hill Industries' entries to record:
   1. the receipt of the note.
   2. the receipt of the payment of the note at maturity.

EX 10-3 Evaluating alternative notes **OBJ. 1**

A borrower has two alternatives for a loan: (1) issue a $240,000, 60-day, 8% note or (2) issue a $240,000, 60-day note that the creditor discounts at 8%.

a. Calculate the amount of the interest expense for each option.

b. Determine the proceeds received by the borrower in each situation.

c. Which alternative is more favorable to the borrower? Explain.

EX 10-4 Entries for notes payable **OBJ. 1**

A business issued a 30-day, 7% note for $150,000 to a creditor on account. Journalize the entries to record (a) the issuance of the note and (b) the payment of the note at maturity, including interest.

EX 10-5 Entries for discounted note payable **OBJ. 1**

A business issued a 45-day note for $90,000 to a creditor on account. The note was discounted at 8%. Journalize the entries to record (a) the issuance of the note and (b) the payment of the note at maturity.

EX 10-6 Fixed asset purchases with note **OBJ. 1**

On June 30, Techcram Management Company purchased land for $350,000 and a building for $450,000, paying $400,000 cash and issuing a 6% note for the balance, secured by a mortgage on the property. The terms of the note provide for 20 semiannual payments of $20,000 on the principal plus the interest accrued from the date of the preceding payment. Journalize the entry to record (a) the transaction on June 30, (b) the payment of the first installment on December 31, and (c) the payment of the second installment the following June 30.

EX 10-7 Current portion of long-term debt **OBJ. 1**

The Coca-Cola Company reported the following information about its long-term debt in the notes to a recent financial statement (in millions):

Long-term debt is comprised of the following:

	December 31	
	Current Year	**Preceding Year**
Total long term-debt	$15,317	$5,110
Less current portion	(1,276)	(51)
Long-term debt	$14,041	$5,059

a. How much of the long-term debt was disclosed as a current liability on the current year's December 31 balance sheet?

b. How much did the total current liabilities change between the preceding year and the current year as a result of the current portion of long-term debt?

c. If Coca-Cola did not issue additional long-term debt next year, what would be the total long-term debt on December 31 of the upcoming year?

EX 10-8 Calculate payroll
OBJ. 2

✔ **b. Net pay, $2,089**

An employee earns $50 per hour and 2 times that rate for all hours in excess of 40 hours per week. Assume that the employee worked 50 hours during the week. Assume further that the social security tax rate was 6.0%, the Medicare tax rate was 1.5%, and federal income tax to be withheld was $686.

a. Determine the gross pay for the week.

b. Determine the net pay for the week.

EX 10-9 Calculate payroll
OBJ. 2

✔ **Administrator net pay, $1,856.44**

Snyder Company has three employees—a consultant, a computer programmer, and an administrator. The following payroll information is available for each employee:

	Consultant	Computer Programmer	Administrator
Regular earnings rate	$3,800 per week	$40 per hour	$44 per hour
Overtime earnings rate*	Not applicable	1.5 times hourly rate	2 times hourly rate
Number of withholding allowances	2	2	1

* For hourly employees, overtime is paid for hours worked in excess of 40 hours per week.

For the current pay period, the computer programmer worked 60 hours and the administrator worked 50 hours. The federal income tax withheld for all three employees, who are single, can be determined from the wage bracket withholding table in Exhibit 3 in the chapter. Assume further that the social security tax rate was 6.0%, the Medicare tax rate was 1.5%, and one withholding allowance is $70.

Determine the gross pay and the net pay for each of the three employees for the current pay period.

EX 10-10 Summary payroll data
OBJ. 2, 3

✔ **a. (3) Total earnings, $540,000**

In the following summary of data for a payroll period, some amounts have been intentionally omitted:

Earnings:	
1. At regular rate	?
2. At overtime rate	$80,000
3. Total earnings	?
Deductions:	
4. Social security tax	32,400
5. Medicare tax	8,100
6. Income tax withheld	135,000
7. Medical insurance	18,900
8. Union dues	?
9. Total deductions	201,150
10. Net amount paid	338,850
Accounts debited:	
11. Factory Wages	285,000
12. Sales Salaries	?
13. Office Salaries	120,000

a. Calculate the amounts omitted in lines (1), (3), (8), and (12).

b. Journalize the entry to record the payroll accrual.

c. Journalize the entry to record the payment of the payroll.

EX 10-11 Payroll tax entries
OBJ. 3

✔ **a. $68,480**

According to a summary of the payroll of Bailik Co., $880,000 was subject to the 6.0% social security tax and the 1.5% Medicare tax. Also, $40,000 was subject to state and federal unemployment taxes.

a. Calculate the employer's payroll taxes, using the following rates: state unemployment, 5.4%; federal unemployment, 0.8%.

b. Journalize the entry to record the accrual of payroll taxes.

EX 10-12 Payroll entries **OBJ. 3**

The payroll register for Jaffrey Company for the week ended May 16 indicated the following:

Salaries	$1,250,000
Social security tax withheld	58,750
Medicare tax withheld	18,750
Federal income tax withheld	250,000

In addition, state and federal unemployment taxes were calculated at the rate of 5.4% and 0.8%, respectively, on $225,000 of salaries.

a. Journalize the entry to record the payroll for the week of May 16.

b. Journalize the entry to record the payroll tax expense incurred for the week of May 16.

EX 10-13 Payroll entries **OBJ. 3**

Widmer Company had gross wages of $240,000 during the week ended June 17. The amount of wages subject to social security tax was $240,000, while the amount of wages subject to federal and state unemployment taxes was $35,000. Tax rates are as follows:

Social security	6.0%
Medicare	1.5%
State unemployment	5.4%
Federal unemployment	0.8%

The total amount withheld from employee wages for federal taxes was $48,000.

a. Journalize the entry to record the payroll for the week of June 17.

b. Journalize the entry to record the payroll tax expense incurred for the week of June 17.

EX 10-14 Payroll internal control procedures **OBJ. 3**

Big Howie's Hot Dog Stand is a fast-food restaurant specializing in hot dogs and hamburgers. The store employs 8 full-time and 12 part-time workers. The store's weekly payroll averages $5,600 for all 20 workers.

Big Howie's Hot Dog Stand uses a personal computer to assist in preparing paychecks. Each week, the store's accountant collects employee time cards and enters the hours worked into the payroll program. The payroll program calculates each employee's pay and prints a paycheck. The accountant uses a check-signing machine to sign the paychecks. Next, the restaurant's owner authorizes the transfer of funds from the restaurant's regular bank account to the payroll account.

For the week of May 12, the accountant accidentally recorded 100 hours worked instead of 40 hours for one of the full-time employees.

Does Big Howie's Hot Dog Stand have internal controls in place to catch this error? If so, how will this error be detected?

EX 10-15 Internal control procedures **OBJ. 3**

Dave's Scooters is a small manufacturer of specialty scooters. The company employs 14 production workers and four administrative persons. The following procedures are used to process the company's weekly payroll:

a. Whenever an employee receives a pay raise, the supervisor must fill out a wage adjustment form, which is signed by the company president. This form is used to change the employee's wage rate in the payroll system.

b. All employees are required to record their hours worked by clocking in and out on a time clock. Employees must clock out for lunch break. Due to congestion around the time clock area at lunch time, management has not objected to having one employee clock in and out for an entire department.

(Continued)

c. Whenever a salaried employee is terminated, Personnel authorizes Payroll to remove the employee from the payroll system. However, this procedure is not required when an hourly worker is terminated. Hourly employees only receive a paycheck if their time cards show hours worked. The computer automatically drops an employee from the payroll system when that employee has six consecutive weeks with no hours worked.

d. Paychecks are signed by using a check-signing machine. This machine is located in the main office so that it can be easily accessed by anyone needing a check signed.

e. Dave's Scooters maintains a separate checking account for payroll checks. Each week, the total net pay for all employees is transferred from the company's regular bank account to the payroll account.

State whether each of the procedures is appropriate or inappropriate, after considering the principles of internal control. If a procedure is inappropriate, describe the appropriate procedure.

EX 10-16 Accrued vacation pay **OBJ. 4**

A business provides its employees with varying amounts of vacation per year, depending on the length of employment. The estimated amount of the current year's vacation pay is $42,000.

a. Journalize the adjusting entry required on January 31, the end of the first month of the current year, to record the accrued vacation pay.

b. How is the vacation pay reported on the company's balance sheet? When is this amount removed from the company's balance sheet?

EX 10-17 Pension plan entries **OBJ. 4**

Yuri Co. operates a chain of gift shops. The company maintains a defined contribution pension plan for its employees. The plan requires quarterly installments to be paid to the funding agent, Whims Funds, by the fifteenth of the month following the end of each quarter. Assume that the pension cost is $365,000 for the quarter ended December 31.

a. Journalize the entries to record the accrued pension liability on December 31 and the payment to the funding agent on January 15.

b. How does a defined contribution plan differ from a defined benefit plan?

EX 10-18 Defined benefit pension plan terms **OBJ. 4**

In a recent year's financial statements, Procter & Gamble showed an unfunded pension liability of $4,267 million and a periodic pension cost of $538 million.

Explain the meaning of the $4,267 million unfunded pension liability and the $538 million periodic pension cost.

EX 10-19 Accrued product warranty **OBJ. 5**

Lowe Manufacturing Co. warrants its products for one year. The estimated product warranty is 4% of sales. Assume that sales were $560,000 for June. In July, a customer received warranty repairs requiring $140 of parts and $95 of labor.

a. Journalize the adjusting entry required at June 30, the end of the first month of the current fiscal year, to record the accrued product warranty.

b. Journalize the entry to record the warranty work provided in July.

EX 10-20 Accrued product warranty **OBJ. 5**

General Motors Corporation (GM) disclosed estimated product warranty payable for comparative years as follows:

	(in millions)	
	Year 2	**Year 1**
Current estimated product warranty payable	$2,587	$2,965
Noncurrent estimated product warranty payable	4,202	4,065
Total	$6,789	$7,030

GM's sales were $135,592 million in Year 2. Assume that the total paid on warranty claims during Year 2 was $3,000 million.

a. Why are short- and long-term estimated warranty liabilities separately disclosed?

b. Provide the journal entry for the Year 2 product warranty expense.

c. What two conditions must be met in order for a product warranty liability to be reported in the financial statements?

EX 10-21 Contingent liabilities — OBJ. 5

Several months ago, Ayers Industries Inc. experienced a hazardous materials spill at one of its plants. As a result, the Environmental Protection Agency (EPA) fined the company $240,000. The company is contesting the fine. In addition, an employee is seeking $220,000 in damages related to the spill. Lastly, a homeowner has sued the company for $310,000. The homeowner lives 35 miles from the plant, but believes that the incident has reduced the home's resale value by $310,000.

Ayers' legal counsel believes that it is probable that the EPA fine will stand. In addition, counsel indicates that an out-of-court settlement of $125,000 has recently been reached with the employee. The final papers will be signed next week. Counsel believes that the homeowner's case is much weaker and will be decided in favor of Ayers. Other litigation related to the spill is possible, but the damage amounts are uncertain.

a. Journalize the contingent liabilities associated with the hazardous materials spill. Use the account "Damage Awards and Fines" to recognize the expense for the period.

b. Prepare a note disclosure relating to this incident.

EX 10-22 Quick ratio — OBJ. 6

✔ a. 2014: 1.2

F·A·I

Gmeiner Co. had the following current assets and liabilities for two comparative years:

	Dec. 31, 2014	Dec. 31, 2013
Current assets:		
Cash	$ 486,000	$ 500,000
Accounts receivable	210,000	200,000
Inventory	375,000	350,000
Total current assets	$1,071,000	$1,050,000
Current liabilities:		
Current portion of long-term debt	$ 145,000	$ 110,000
Accounts payable	175,000	150,000
Accrued and other current liabilities	260,000	240,000
Total current liabilities	$ 580,000	$ 500,000

a. Determine the quick ratio for December 31, 2014 and 2013.

b. Interpret the change in the quick ratio between the two balance sheet dates.

EX 10-23 Quick ratio — OBJ. 6

✔ a. Apple, 1.8

F·A·I

The current assets and current liabilities for Apple Inc. and Dell, Inc., are shown as follows at the end of a recent fiscal period:

	Apple Inc. (in millions)	Dell, Inc. (in millions)
Current assets:		
Cash and cash equivalents	$11,261	$13,913
Short-term investments	14,359	452
Accounts receivable	11,560	10,136
Inventories	1,051	1,301
Other current assets*	3,447	3,219
Total current assets	$41,678	$29,021
Current liabilities:		
Accounts payable	$17,738	$15,474
Accrued and other current liabilities	2,984	4,009
Total current liabilities	$20,722	$19,483

*These represent prepaid expense and other nonquick current assets.

(Continued)

a. Determine the quick ratio for both companies.

b. Interpret the quick ratio difference between the two companies.

Problems Series A

PR 10-1A Liability transactions

OBJ. 1, 5

GENERAL LEDGER

The following items were selected from among the transactions completed by Warwick Co. during the current year:

Feb. 3. Purchased merchandise on account from Onifade Co., $410,000, terms n/30.

Mar. 3. Issued a 45-day, 6% note for $410,000 to Onifade Co., on account.

Apr. 17. Paid Onifade Co. the amount owed on the note of March 3.

June 1. Borrowed $250,000 from Aldhiezer Bank, issuing a 60-day, 7.5% note.

July 21. Purchased tools by issuing a $300,000, 60-day note to Nash Co., which discounted the note at the rate of 8%.

31. Paid Aldhiezer Bank the interest due on the note of June 1 and renewed the loan by issuing a new 30-day, 9% note for $250,000. (Journalize both the debit and credit to the notes payable account.)

Aug. 30. Paid Aldhiezer Bank the amount due on the note of July 31.

Sept. 19. Paid Nash Co. the amount due on the note of July 21.

Dec. 1. Purchased office equipment from Oso Co. for $340,000, paying $40,000 and issuing a series of ten 8% notes for $30,000 each, coming due at 30-day intervals.

12. Settled a product liability lawsuit with a customer for $165,000, payable in January. Warwick accrued the loss in a litigation claims payable account.

31. Paid the amount due Oso Co. on the first note in the series issued on December 1.

Instructions

1. Journalize the transactions.
2. Journalize the adjusting entry for each of the following accrued expenses at the end of the current year:
   a. Product warranty cost, $32,500.
   b. Interest on the nine remaining notes owed to Oso Co.

PR 10-2A Entries for payroll and payroll taxes

OBJ. 2, 3

✔ 1. (b) Dr. Payroll Tax Expense, $52,795

GENERAL LEDGER

The following information about the payroll for the week ended December 30 was obtained from the records of Qualitech Co.:

Salaries:		Deductions:	
Sales salaries	$350,000	Income tax withheld	$118,800
Warehouse salaries	180,000	Social security tax withheld	40,500
Office salaries	145,000	Medicare tax withheld	10,125
	$675,000	U.S. savings bonds	14,850
		Group insurance	12,150
			$196,425

Tax rates assumed:

Social security, 6%

Medicare, 1.5%

State unemployment (employer only), 5.4%

Federal unemployment (employer only), 0.8%

Instructions

1. Assuming that the payroll for the last week of the year is to be paid on December 31, journalize the following entries:
   a. December 30, to record the payroll.
   b. December 30, to record the employer's payroll taxes on the payroll to be paid on December 31. Of the total payroll for the last week of the year, $35,000 is subject to unemployment compensation taxes.
2. Assuming that the payroll for the last week of the year is to be paid on January 5 of the following fiscal year, journalize the following entries:
   a. December 30, to record the payroll.
   b. January 5, to record the employer's payroll taxes on the payroll to be paid on January 5. Since it is a new fiscal year, all $675,000 in salaries is subject to unemployment compensation taxes.

PR 10-3A Wage and tax statement data on employer FICA tax

OBJ. 2, 3

✔ 2. (e) $28,574.96

SPREADSHEET

Ehrlich Co. began business on January 2, 2013. Salaries were paid to employees on the last day of each month, and social security tax, Medicare tax, and federal income tax were withheld in the required amounts. An employee who is hired in the middle of the month receives half the monthly salary for that month. All required payroll tax reports were filed, and the correct amount of payroll taxes was remitted by the company for the calendar year. Early in 2014, before the Wage and Tax Statements (Form W-2) could be prepared for distribution to employees and for filing with the Social Security Administration, the employees' earnings records were inadvertently destroyed.

None of the employees resigned or were discharged during the year, and there were no changes in salary rates. The social security tax was withheld at the rate of 6.0% and Medicare tax at the rate of 1.5%. Data on dates of employment, salary rates, and employees' income taxes withheld, which are summarized as follows, were obtained from personnel records and payroll records:

Employee	Date First Employed	Monthly Salary	Monthly Income Tax Withheld
Arnett	Nov. 16	$ 5,500	$1,008
Cruz	Jan. 2	4,800	833
Edwards	Oct. 1	8,000	1,659
Harvin	Dec. 1	6,000	1,133
Nicks	Feb. 1	10,000	2,219
Shiancoe	Mar. 1	11,600	2,667
Ward	Nov. 16	5,220	938

Instructions

1. Calculate the amounts to be reported on each employee's Wage and Tax Statement (Form W-2) for 2013, arranging the data in the following form:

Employee	Gross Earnings	Federal Income Tax Withheld	Social Security Tax Withheld	Medicare Tax Withheld

2. Calculate the following employer payroll taxes for the year: (a) social security; (b) Medicare; (c) state unemployment compensation at 5.4% on the first $10,000 of each employee's earnings; (d) federal unemployment compensation at 0.8% on the first $10,000 of each employee's earnings; (e) total.

PR 10-4A Payroll register

OBJ. 2, 3

✔ 1. Total net pay $15,522.48

SPREADSHEET

The following data for Throwback Industries Inc. relate to the payroll for the week ended December 7, 2014:

Employee	Hours Worked	Hourly Rate	Weekly Salary	Federal Income Tax	U.S. Savings Bonds
Aaron	46	$68.00		$766.36	$100
Cobb	41	62.00		553.20	110
Clemente	48	70.00		691.60	120
DiMaggio	35	56.00		411.60	0
Griffey, Jr.	45	62.00		618.45	130
Mantle			$1,800	432.00	120
Robinson	36	54.00		291.60	130
Williams			2,000	440.00	125
Vaughn	42	62.00		533.20	50

Employees Mantle and Williams are office staff, and all of the other employees are sales personnel. All sales personnel are paid 1½ times the regular rate for all hours in excess of 40 hours per week. The social security tax rate is 6.0%, and Medicare tax is 1.5% of each employee's annual earnings. The next payroll check to be used is No. 901.

Instructions

1. Prepare a payroll register for Throwback Industries Inc. for the week ended December 7, 2014. Use the following columns for the payroll register: Employee, Total Hours, Regular Earnings, Overtime Earnings, Total Earnings, Social Security Tax, Medicare Tax, Federal Income Tax, U.S. Savings Bonds, Total Deductions, Net Pay, Ck. No., Sales Salaries Expense, and Office Salaries Expense.
2. Journalize the entry to record the payroll for the week.

PR 10-5A Payroll accounts and year-end entries

OBJ. 2, 3, 4

GENERAL LEDGER

The following accounts, with the balances indicated, appear in the ledger of Garcon Co. on December 1 of the current year:

211 Salaries Payable	—	218 Bond Deductions Payable	$ 3,400
212 Social Security Tax Payable	$ 9,273	219 Medical Insurance Payable	27,000
213 Medicare Tax Payable	2,318	411 Operations Salaries Expense	950,000
214 Employees Federal Income Tax Payable	15,455	511 Officers Salaries Expense	600,000
215 Employees State Income Tax Payable	13,909	512 Office Salaries Expense	150,000
216 State Unemployment Tax Payable	1,400	519 Payroll Tax Expense	137,951
217 Federal Unemployment Tax Payable	500		

The following transactions relating to payroll, payroll deductions, and payroll taxes occurred during December:

Dec. 2. Issued Check No. 410 for $3,400 to Jay Bank to purchase U.S. savings bonds for employees.

2. Issued Check No. 411 to Jay Bank for $27,046 in payment of $9,273 of social security tax, $2,318 of Medicare tax, and $15,455 of employees' federal income tax due.

13. Journalized the entry to record the biweekly payroll. A summary of the payroll record follows:

Salary distribution:		
Operations	$43,200	
Officers	27,200	
Office	6,800	$77,200
Deductions:		
Social security tax	$ 4,632	
Medicare tax	1,158	
Federal income tax withheld	15,440	
State income tax withheld	3,474	
Savings bond deductions	1,700	
Medical insurance deductions	4,500	30,904
Net amount		$46,296

Dec. 13. Issued Check No. 420 in payment of the net amount of the biweekly payroll.

13. Journalized the entry to record payroll taxes on employees' earnings of December 13: social security tax, $4,632; Medicare tax, $1,158; state unemployment tax, $350; federal unemployment tax, $125.

16. Issued Check No. 424 to Jay Bank for $27,020, in payment of $9,264 of social security tax, $2,316 of Medicare tax, and $15,440 of employees' federal income tax due.

19. Issued Check No. 429 to Sims-Walker Insurance Company for $31,500 in payment of the semiannual premium on the group medical insurance policy.

27. Journalized the entry to record the biweekly payroll. A summary of the payroll record follows:

Salary distribution:		
Operations	$42,800	
Officers	28,000	
Office	7,000	$77,800
Deductions:		
Social security tax	$ 4,668	
Medicare tax	1,167	
Federal income tax withheld	15,404	
State income tax withheld	3,501	
Savings bond deductions	1,700	26,440
Net amount		$51,360

27. Issued Check No. 541 in payment of the net amount of the biweekly payroll.

27. Journalized the entry to record payroll taxes on employees' earnings of December 27: social security tax, $4,668; Medicare tax, $1,167; state unemployment tax, $225; federal unemployment tax, $75.

27. Issued Check No. 543 for $20,884 to State Department of Revenue in payment of employees' state income tax due on December 31.

31. Issued Check No. 545 to Jay Bank for $3,400 to purchase U.S. savings bonds for employees.

31. Paid $45,000 to the employee pension plan. The annual pension cost is $60,000. (Record both the payment and unfunded pension liability.)

Instructions

1. Journalize the transactions.
2. Journalize the following adjusting entries on December 31:
   a. Salaries accrued: operations salaries, $8,560; officers salaries, $5,600; office salaries, $1,400. The payroll taxes are immaterial and are not accrued.
   b. Vacation pay, $15,000.

Problems Series B

PR 10-1B Liability transactions

OBJ. 1, 5

GENERAL LEDGER

The following items were selected from among the transactions completed by Aston Martin Inc. during the current year:

Apr. 15. Borrowed $225,000 from Audi Company, issuing a 30-day, 6% note for that amount.

May 1. Purchased equipment by issuing a $320,000, 180-day note to Spyder Manufacturing Co., which discounted the note at the rate of 6%.

15. Paid Audi Company the interest due on the note of April 15 and renewed the loan by issuing a new 60-day, 8% note for $225,000. (Record both the debit and credit to the notes payable account.)

July 14. Paid Audi Company the amount due on the note of May 15.

Aug. 16. Purchased merchandise on account from Exige Co., $90,000, terms, n/30.

Sept. 15. Issued a 45-day, 6% note for $90,000 to Exige Co., on account.

Oct. 28. Paid Spyder Manufacturing Co. the amount due on the note of May 1.

30. Paid Exige Co. the amount owed on the note of September 15.

Nov. 16. Purchased store equipment from Gallardo Co. for $450,000, paying $50,000 and issuing a series of twenty 9% notes for $20,000 each, coming due at 30-day intervals.

Dec. 16. Paid the amount due Gallardo Co. on the first note in the series issued on November 16.

28. Settled a personal injury lawsuit with a customer for $87,500, to be paid in January. Aston Martin Inc. accrued the loss in a litigation claims payable account.

Instructions

1. Journalize the transactions.
2. Journalize the adjusting entry for each of the following accrued expenses at the end of the current year:
   a. Product warranty cost, $26,800.
   b. Interest on the 19 remaining notes owed to Gallardo Co.

PR 10-2B Entries for payroll and payroll taxes — OBJ. 2, 3

✔ 1. (b) Dr. Payroll Tax Expense, $90,735

GENERAL LEDGER

The following information about the payroll for the week ended December 30 was obtained from the records of Saine Co.:

Salaries:		Deductions:	
Sales salaries	$ 625,000	Income tax withheld	$232,260
Warehouse salaries	240,000	Social security tax withheld	71,100
Office salaries	320,000	Medicare tax withheld	17,775
	$1,185,000	U.S. savings bonds	35,500
		Group insurance	53,325
			$409,960

Tax rates assumed:

Social security, 6%

Medicare, 1.5%

State unemployment (employer only), 5.4%

Federal unemployment (employer only), 0.8%

Instructions

1. Assuming that the payroll for the last week of the year is to be paid on December 31, journalize the following entries:
   a. December 30, to record the payroll.
   b. December 30, to record the employer's payroll taxes on the payroll to be paid on December 31. Of the total payroll for the last week of the year, $30,000 is subject to unemployment compensation taxes.
2. Assuming that the payroll for the last week of the year is to be paid on January 4 of the following fiscal year, journalize the following entries:
   a. December 30, to record the payroll.
   b. January 4, to record the employer's payroll taxes on the payroll to be paid on January 4. Since it is a new fiscal year, all $1,185,000 in salaries is subject to unemployment compensation taxes.

PR 10-3B Wage and tax statement data and employer FICA tax — OBJ. 2, 3

✔ 2. (e) $25,136.13

SPREADSHEET

Jocame Inc. began business on January 2, 2013. Salaries were paid to employees on the last day of each month, and social security tax, Medicare tax, and federal income tax were withheld in the required amounts. An employee who is hired in the middle of the month receives half the monthly salary for that month. All required payroll tax reports were filed, and the correct amount of payroll taxes was remitted by the company for the calendar year. Early in 2014, before the Wage and Tax Statements (Form W-2) could be prepared for distribution to employees and for filing with the Social Security Administration, the employees' earnings records were inadvertently destroyed.

None of the employees resigned or were discharged during the year, and there were no changes in salary rates. The social security tax was withheld at the rate of 6.0% and Medicare tax at the rate of 1.5% on salary. Data on dates of employment, salary rates, and employees' income taxes withheld, which are summarized as follows, were obtained from personnel records and payroll records:

Employee	Date First Employed	Monthly Salary	Monthly Income Tax Withheld
Addai	July 16	$ 8,160	$1,704
Kasay	June 1	3,600	533
McGahee	Feb. 16	6,420	1,238
Moss	Jan. 1	4,600	783
Stewart	Dec. 1	4,500	758
Tolbert	Nov. 16	3,250	446
Wells	May 1	10,500	2,359

Instructions

1. Calculate the amounts to be reported on each employee's Wage and Tax Statement (Form W-2) for 2013, arranging the data in the following form:

Employee	Gross Earnings	Federal Income Tax Withheld	Social Security Tax Withheld	Medicare Tax Withheld

2. Calculate the following employer payroll taxes for the year: (a) social security; (b) Medicare; (c) state unemployment compensation at 5.4% on the first $10,000 of each employee's earnings; (d) federal unemployment compensation at 0.8% on the first $10,000 of each employee's earnings; (e) total.

PR 10-4B Payroll register

OBJ. 2, 3

✔ **1. Total net pay, $16,592.58**

SPREADSHEET

The following data for Flexco Inc. relate to the payroll for the week ended December 7, 2014:

Employee	Hours Worked	Hourly Rate	Weekly Salary	Federal Income Tax	U.S. Savings Bonds
Carlton	52	$50.00		$667.00	$ 60
Grove			$4,000	860.00	100
Johnson	36	52.00		355.68	0
Koufax	45	58.00		578.55	44
Maddux	37	45.00		349.65	62
Seaver			3,200	768.00	120
Spahn	46	52.00		382.20	0
Winn	48	50.00		572.00	75
Young	43	54.00		480.60	80

Employees Grove and Seaver are office staff, and all of the other employees are sales personnel. All sales personnel are paid 1½ times the regular rate for all hours in excess of 40 hours per week. The social security tax rate is 6.0% of each employee's annual earnings, and Medicare tax is 1.5% of each employee's annual earnings. The next payroll check to be used is No. 328.

Instructions

1. Prepare a payroll register for Flexco Inc. for the week ended December 7, 2014. Use the following columns for the payroll register: Employee, Total Hours, Regular Earnings, Overtime Earnings, Total Earnings, Social Security Tax, Medicare Tax, Federal Income Tax, U.S. Savings Bonds, Total Deductions, Net Pay, Ck. No., Sales Salaries Expense, and Office Salaries Expense.
2. Journalize the entry to record the payroll for the week.

PR 10-5B Payroll accounts and year-end entries

OBJ. 2, 3, 4

GENERAL LEDGER

The following accounts, with the balances indicated, appear in the ledger of Codigo Co. on December 1 of the current year:

101 Salaries Payable	—	108 Bond Deductions Payable	$ 2,300
102 Social Security Tax Payable	$2,913	109 Medical Insurance Payable	2,520
103 Medicare Tax Payable	728	201 Sales Salaries Expense	700,000
104 Employees Federal Income Tax Payable	4,490	301 Officers Salaries Expense	340,000
105 Employees State Income Tax Payable	4,078	401 Office Salaries Expense	125,000
106 State Unemployment Tax Payable	1,260	408 Payroll Tax Expense	59,491
107 Federal Unemployment Tax Payable	360		

The following transactions relating to payroll, payroll deductions, and payroll taxes occurred during December:

Dec. 1. Issued Check No. 815 to Aberderas Insurance Company for $2,520, in payment of the semiannual premium on the group medical insurance policy.

1. Issued Check No. 816 to Alvarez Bank for $8,131, in payment for $2,913 of social security tax, $728 of Medicare tax, and $4,490 of employees' federal income tax due.

2. Issued Check No. 817 for $2,300 to Alvarez Bank to purchase U.S. savings bonds for employees.

12. Journalized the entry to record the biweekly payroll. A summary of the payroll record follows:

Salary distribution:		
Sales	$14,500	
Officers	7,100	
Office	2,600	$24,200
Deductions:		
Social security tax	$ 1,452	
Medicare tax	363	
Federal income tax withheld	4,308	
State income tax withheld	1,089	
Savings bond deductions	1,150	
Medical insurance deductions	420	8,782
Net amount		$15,418

12. Issued Check No. 822 in payment of the net amount of the biweekly payroll.

12. Journalized the entry to record payroll taxes on employees' earnings of December 12: social security tax, $1,452; Medicare tax, $363; state unemployment tax, $315; federal unemployment tax, $90.

15. Issued Check No. 830 to Alvarez Bank for $7,938, in payment of $2,904 of social security tax, $726 of Medicare tax, and $4,308 of employees' federal income tax due.

26. Journalized the entry to record the biweekly payroll. A summary of the payroll record follows:

Salary distribution:		
Sales	$14,250	
Officers	7,250	
Office	2,750	$24,250
Deductions:		
Social security tax	$ 1,455	
Medicare tax	364	
Federal income tax withheld	4,317	
State income tax withheld	1,091	
Savings bond deductions	1,150	8,377
Net amount		$15,873

26. Issued Check No. 840 for the net amount of the biweekly payroll.

Dec. 26. Journalized the entry to record payroll taxes on employees' earnings of December 26: social security tax, $1,455; Medicare tax, $364; state unemployment tax, $150; federal unemployment tax, $40.

30. Issued Check No. 851 for $6,258 to State Department of Revenue, in payment of employees' state income tax due on December 31.

30. Issued Check No. 852 to Alvarez Bank for $2,300 to purchase U.S. savings bonds for employees.

31. Paid $55,400 to the employee pension plan. The annual pension cost is $65,500. (Record both the payment and the unfunded pension liability.)

Instructions

1. Journalize the transactions.
2. Journalize the following adjusting entries on December 31:
   a. Salaries accrued: sales salaries, $4,275; officers salaries, $2,175; office salaries, $825. The payroll taxes are immaterial and are not accrued.
   b. Vacation pay, $13,350.

Comprehensive Problem 3

✔ **5. Total assets, $3,569,300**

GENERAL LEDGER

Selected transactions completed by Kornett Company during its first fiscal year ended December 31, 2014, were as follows:

Jan. 3. Issued a check to establish a petty cash fund of $4,500.

Feb. 26. Replenished the petty cash fund, based on the following summary of petty cash receipts: office supplies, $1,680; miscellaneous selling expense, $570; miscellaneous administrative expense, $880.

Apr. 14. Purchased $31,300 of merchandise on account, terms 1/10, n/30. The perpetual inventory system is used to account for inventory.

May 13. Paid the invoice of April 14 after the discount period had passed.

17. Received cash from daily cash sales for $21,200. The amount indicated by the cash register was $21,240.

June 2. Received a 60-day, 8% note for $180,000 on the Ryanair account.

Aug. 1. Received amount owed on June 2 note, plus interest at the maturity date.

24. Received $7,600 on the Finley account and wrote off the remainder owed on a $9,000 accounts receivable balance. (The allowance method is used in accounting for uncollectible receivables.)

Sept. 15. Reinstated the Finley account written off on August 24 and received $1,400 cash in full payment.

15. Purchased land by issuing a $670,000, 90-day note to Zahorik Co., which discounted it at 9%.

Oct. 17. Sold office equipment in exchange for $135,000 cash plus receipt of a $100,000, 90-day, 9% note. The equipment had a cost of $320,000 and accumulated depreciation of $64,000 as of October 17.

Nov. 30. Journalized the monthly payroll for November, based on the following data:

Salaries		Deductions	
Sales salaries	$135,000	Income tax withheld	$39,266
Office salaries	77,250	Social security tax withheld	12,735
	$212,250	Medicare tax withheld	3,184

Unemployment tax rates:	
State unemployment	5.4%
Federal unemployment	0.8%
Amount subject to unemployment taxes:	
State unemployment	$5,000
Federal unemployment	5,000

(Continued)

Nov. 30. Journalized the employer's payroll taxes on the payroll.

Dec. 14. Journalized the payment of the September 15 note at maturity.

31. The pension cost for the year was $190,400, of which $139,700 was paid to the pension plan trustee.

Instructions

1. Journalize the selected transactions.
2. Based on the following data, prepare a bank reconciliation for December of the current year:
   a. Balance according to the bank statement at December 31, $283,000.
   b. Balance according to the ledger at December 31, $245,410.
   c. Checks outstanding at December 31, $68,540.
   d. Deposit in transit, not recorded by bank, $29,500.
   e. Bank debit memo for service charges, $750.
   f. A check for $12,700 in payment of an invoice was incorrectly recorded in the accounts as $12,000.
3. Based on the bank reconciliation prepared in (2), journalize the entry or entries to be made by Kornett Company.
4. Based on the following selected data, journalize the adjusting entries as of December 31 of the current year:
   a. Estimated uncollectible accounts at December 31, $16,000, based on an aging of accounts receivable. The balance of Allowance for Doubtful Accounts at December 31 was $2,000 (debit).
   b. The physical inventory on December 31 indicated an inventory shrinkage of $3,300.
   c. Prepaid insurance expired during the year, $22,820.
   d. Office supplies used during the year, $3,920.
   e. Depreciation is computed as follows:

Asset	Cost	Residual Value	Acquisition Date	Useful Life in Years	Depreciation Method Used
Buildings	$900,000	$ 0	January 2	50	Double-declining-balance
Office Equip.	246,000	26,000	January 3	5	Straight-line
Store Equip.	112,000	12,000	July 1	10	Straight-line

   f. A patent costing $48,000 when acquired on January 2 has a remaining legal life of 10 years and is expected to have value for eight years.
   g. The cost of mineral rights was $546,000. Of the estimated deposit of 910,000 tons of ore, 50,000 tons were mined and sold during the year.
   h. Vacation pay expense for December, $10,500.
   i. A product warranty was granted beginning December 1 and covering a one-year period. The estimated cost is 4% of sales, which totaled $1,900,000 in December.
   j. Interest was accrued on the note receivable received on October 17.
5. Based on the following information and the post-closing trial balance shown below, prepare a balance sheet in report form at December 31 of the current year.

The merchandise inventory is stated at cost by the LIFO method.
The product warranty payable is a current liability.

Vacation pay payable:

Current liability	$7,140
Long-term liability	3,360

The unfunded pension liability is a long-term liability.

Notes payable:

Current liability	$ 70,000
Long-term liability	630,000

Kornett Company
Post-Closing Trial Balance
December 31, 2014

	Debit Balances	Credit Balances
Petty Cash	4,500	
Cash	243,960	
Notes Receivable	100,000	
Accounts Receivable	470,000	
Allowance for Doubtful Accounts		16,000
Merchandise Inventory	320,000	
Interest Receivable	1,875	
Prepaid Insurance	45,640	
Office Supplies	13,400	
Land	654,925	
Buildings	900,000	
Accumulated Depreciation—Buildings		36,000
Office Equipment	246,000	
Accumulated Depreciation—Office Equipment		44,000
Store Equipment	112,000	
Accumulated Depreciation—Store Equipment		5,000
Mineral Rights	546,000	
Accumulated Depletion		30,000
Patents	42,000	
Social Security Tax Payable		25,470
Medicare Tax Payable		4,710
Employees Federal Income Tax Payable		40,000
State Unemployment Tax Payable		270
Federal Unemployment Tax Payable		40
Salaries Payable		157,000
Accounts Payable		131,600
Interest Payable		28,000
Product Warranty Payable		76,000
Vacation Pay Payable		10,500
Unfunded Pension Liability		50,700
Notes Payable		700,000
Capital Stock		500,000
Retained Earnings		1,845,010
	3,700,300	3,700,300

Cases & Projects

CP 10-1 Ethics and professional conduct in business

Tonya Latirno is a certified public accountant (CPA) and staff accountant for Kennedy and Kennedy, a local CPA firm. It had been the policy of the firm to provide a holiday bonus equal to two weeks' salary to all employees. The firm's new management team announced on November 15 that a bonus equal to only one week's salary would be made available to employees this year. Tonya thought that this policy was unfair because she and her coworkers planned on the full two-week bonus. The two-week bonus had been given for 10 straight years, so it seemed as though the firm had breached an implied commitment. Thus, Tonya decided that she would make up the lost bonus week by working an extra six hours of overtime per week over the next five weeks until the end of the year. Kennedy and Kennedy's policy is to pay overtime at 150% of straight time.

Tonya's supervisor was surprised to see overtime being reported, since there is generally very little additional or unusual client service demands at the end of the calendar year. However, the overtime was not questioned, since firm employees are on the "honor system" in reporting their overtime.

Discuss whether the firm is acting in an ethical manner by changing the bonus. Is Tonya behaving in an ethical manner?

CP 10-2 Recognizing pension expense

The annual examination of Felton Company's financial statements by its external public accounting firm (auditors) is nearing completion. The following conversation took place between the controller of Felton Company (Francie) and the audit manager from the public accounting firm (Sumana).

Sumana: You know, Francie, we are about to wrap up our audit for this fiscal year. Yet, there is one item still to be resolved.

Francie: What's that?

Sumana: Well, as you know, at the beginning of the year, Felton began a defined benefit pension plan. This plan promises your employees an annual payment when they retire, using a formula based on their salaries at retirement and their years of service. I believe that a pension expense should be recognized this year, equal to the amount of pension earned by your employees.

Francie: Wait a minute. I think you have it all wrong. The company doesn't have a pension expense until it actually pays the pension in cash when the employee retires. After all, some of these employees may not reach retirement, and if they don't, the company doesn't owe them anything.

Sumana: You're not really seeing this the right way. The pension is earned by your employees during their working years. You actually make the payment much later—when they retire. It's like one long accrual—much like incurring wages in one period and paying them in the next. Thus, I think that you should recognize the expense in the period the pension is earned by the employees.

Francie: Let me see if I've got this straight. I should recognize an expense this period for something that may or may not be paid to the employees in 20 or 30 years, when they finally retire. How am I supposed to determine what the expense is for the current year? The amount of the final retirement depends on many uncertainties: salary levels, employee longevity, mortality rates, and interest earned on investments to fund the pension. I don't think that an amount can be determined, even if I accepted your arguments.

Evaluate Sumana's position. Is she right or is Francie correct?

CP 10-3 Ethics and professional conduct in business

Marvin Turner was discussing summer employment with Tina Song, president of Motown Construction Service:

Tina: I'm glad that you're thinking about joining us for the summer. We could certainly use the help.

Marvin: Sounds good. I enjoy outdoor work, and I could use the money to help with next year's school expenses.

Tina: I've got a plan that can help you out on that. As you know, I'll pay you $14 per hour, but in addition, I'd like to pay you with cash. Since you're only working for the summer, it really doesn't make sense for me to go to the trouble of formally putting you on our payroll system. In fact, I do some jobs for my clients on a strictly cash basis, so it would be easy to just pay you that way.

Marvin: Well, that's a bit unusual, but I guess money is money.

Tina: Yeah, not only that, it's tax-free!

Marvin: What do you mean?

Tina: Didn't you know? Any money that you receive in cash is not reported to the IRS on a W-2 form; therefore, the IRS doesn't know about the income—hence, it's the same as tax-free earnings.

a. Why does Tina Song want to conduct business transactions using cash (not check or credit card)?

b. How should Marvin respond to Tina's suggestion?

CP 10-4 Payroll forms

Group Project

Internet Project

Payroll accounting involves the use of government-supplied forms to account for payroll taxes. Three common forms are the W-2, Form 940, and Form 941. Form a team with three of your classmates and retrieve copies of each of these forms. They may be obtained from a local IRS office, a library, or downloaded from the Internet at **http://www.irs.gov** (go to forms and publications).

Briefly describe the purpose of each of the three forms.

CP 10-5 Contingent liabilities

Internet Project

Altria Group, Inc., has over 12 pages dedicated to describing contingent liabilities in the notes to recent financial statements. These pages include extensive descriptions of multiple contingent liabilities. Use the Internet to research Altria Group, Inc., at **http://www.altria.com**.

a. What are the major business units of Altria Group?

b. Based on your understanding of this company, why would Altria Group require 11 pages of contingency disclosure?

CHAPTER 11

Corporations: Organization, Stock Transactions, and Dividends

Google

If you purchase a share of stock from **Google**, you own a small interest in the company. You may request a Google stock certificate as an indication of your ownership.

Google is one of the most visible companies on the Internet. Many of us cannot visit the Web without using Google to power a search or to retrieve our e-mail using Google's gmail. Yet Google's Internet tools are free to online browsers. Google generates most of its revenue through online advertising.

Purchasing a share of stock from Google may be a great gift idea for the "hard-to-shop-for person." However, a stock certificate represents more than just a picture that you can frame. In fact, the stock certificate is a document that reflects legal ownership of the future financial prospects of Google. In addition, as a shareholder, it represents your claim against the assets and earnings of the corporation.

If you are purchasing Google stock as an investment, you should analyze Google financial statements and management's plans for the future. For example, Google first offered its stock to the public on August 19, 2004, for $100 per share. Google's stock recently sold for over $600 per share, even though it pays no dividends. In addition, Google recently expanded into developing and offering free software platforms for mobile devices such as cell phones. For example, your cell phone may use Google's Android™ operating system. So, should you purchase Google stock?

This chapter describes and illustrates the nature of corporations, including the accounting for stock and dividends. This discussion will aid you in making decisions such as whether or not to buy Google stock.

Learning Objectives

After studying this chapter, you should be able to:

	Example Exercises
OBJ 1 Describe the nature of the corporate form of organization.	
Nature of a Corporation	
Characteristics of a Corporation	
Forming a Corporation	
OBJ 2 Describe and illustrate the characteristics of stock, classes of stock, and entries for issuing stock.	
Paid-In Capital from Issuing Stock	
Characteristics of Stock	
Classes of Stock	EE 11-1
Issuing Stock	EE 11-2
Premium on Stock	EE 11-2
No-Par Stock	EE 11-2
OBJ 3 Describe and illustrate the accounting for cash dividends and stock dividends.	
Accounting for Dividends	
Cash Dividends	EE 11-3
Stock Dividends	EE 11-4
OBJ 4 Describe and illustrate the accounting for treasury stock transactions.	
Treasury Stock Transactions	EE 11-5
OBJ 5 Describe and illustrate the reporting of stockholders' equity.	
Reporting Stockholders' Equity	
Stockholders' Equity on the Balance Sheet	EE 11-6
Reporting Retained Earnings	EE 11-7
Statement of Stockholders' Equity	
Reporting Stockholders' Equity for Mornin' Joe	
OBJ 6 Describe the effect of stock splits on corporate financial statements.	
Stock Splits	
OBJ 7 Describe and illustrate the use of earnings per share in evaluating a company's profitability.	
Financial Analysis and Interpretation: Earnings per Share	EE 11-8

At a Glance 11 Page 517

OBJ 1 Describe the nature of the corporate form of organization.

Nature of a Corporation

Most large businesses are organized as corporations. As a result, corporations generate more than 90% of the total business dollars in the United States. In contrast, most small businesses are organized as proprietorships, partnerships, or limited liability companies.

Characteristics of a Corporation

A corporation was defined in the Dartmouth College case of 1819, in which Chief Justice Marshall of the U.S. Supreme Court stated: "A corporation is an artificial being, invisible, intangible, and existing only in contemplation of the law."

A *corporation* is a legal entity, distinct and separate from the individuals who create and operate it. As a legal entity, a corporation may acquire, own, and dispose of property in its own name. It may also incur liabilities and enter into contracts. Most importantly, it can sell shares of ownership, called **stock**. This characteristic gives corporations the ability to raise large amounts of capital.

The **stockholders** or *shareholders* who own the stock own the corporation. They can buy and sell stock without affecting the corporation's operations or continued existence. Corporations whose shares of stock are traded in public markets are called *public corporations*. Corporations whose shares of stock are not traded publicly are usually owned by a small group of investors and are called *nonpublic* or *private corporations*.

The stockholders of a corporation have *limited liability*. This means that creditors usually may not go beyond the assets of the corporation to satisfy their claims. Thus, the financial loss that a stockholder may suffer is limited to the amount invested.

The stockholders control a corporation by electing a *board of directors*. This board meets periodically to establish corporate policies. It also selects the chief executive officer (CEO) and other major officers to manage the corporation's day-to-day affairs. Exhibit 1 shows the organizational structure of a corporation.

EXHIBIT 1

Organizational Structure of a Corporation

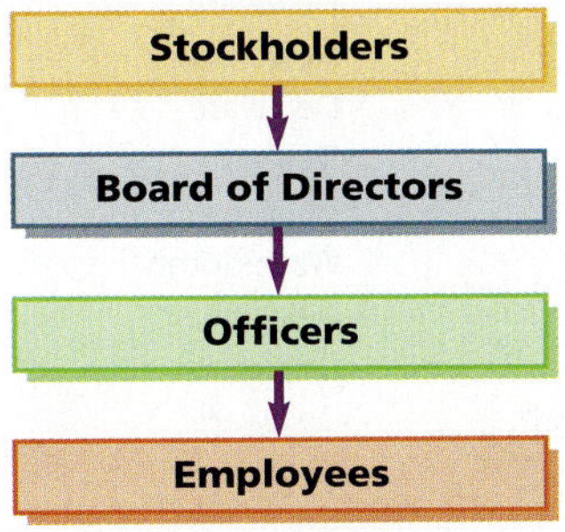

As a separate entity, a corporation is subject to taxes. For example, corporations must pay federal income taxes on their income.[1] Thus, corporate income that is distributed to stockholders in the form of *dividends* has already been taxed. In turn, stockholders must pay income taxes on the dividends they receive. This *double taxation* of corporate earnings is a major disadvantage of the corporate form. The advantages and disadvantages of the corporate form are listed in Exhibit 2.

Note:
Corporations have a separate legal existence, transferable units of ownership, and limited stockholder liability.

EXHIBIT 2 **Advantages and Disadvantages of the Corporate Form**

Advantages	**Explanation**
Separate legal existence	A corporation exists separately from its owners.
Continuous life	A corporation's life is separate from its owners; therefore, it exists indefinitely.
Raising large amounts of capital	The corporate form is suited for raising large amounts of money from shareholders.
Ownership rights are easily transferable	A corporation sells shares of ownership, called *stock*. The stockholders of a public company can transfer their shares of stock to other stockholders through stock markets, such as the New York Stock Exchange.
Limited liability	A corporation's creditors usually may not go beyond the assets of the corporation to satisfy their claims. Thus, the financial loss that a stockholder may suffer is limited to the amount invested.
Disadvantages	**Explanation**
Owner is separate from management	Stockholders control management through a board of directors. The board of directors should represent shareholder interests; however, the board is often more closely tied to management than to shareholders. As a result, the board of directors and management may not always behave in the best interests of stockholders.
Double taxation of dividends	As a separate legal entity, a corporation is subject to taxation. Thus, net income distributed as dividends will be taxed once at the corporation level, and then again at the individual level.
Regulatory costs	Corporations must satisfy many requirements, such as those required by the Sarbanes-Oxley Act of 2002.

Forming a Corporation

The first step in forming a corporation is to file an *application of incorporation* with the state. State incorporation laws differ, and corporations often organize in those states with the more favorable laws. For this reason, more than half of the largest companies are incorporated in Delaware. Exhibit 3 lists some corporations, their states of incorporation, and the location of their headquarters.

After the application of incorporation has been approved, the state grants a *charter* or *articles of incorporation*. The articles of incorporation formally create the corporation.[2]

1 A majority of states also require corporations to pay income taxes.

2 The articles of incorporation may also restrict a corporation's activities in certain areas, such as owning certain types of real estate, conducting certain types of business activities, or purchasing its own stock.

EXHIBIT 3

Examples of Corporations and their States of Incorporation

Corporation	State of Incorporation	Headquarters
Caterpillar	Delaware	Peoria, Ill.
Delta Air Lines	Delaware	Atlanta, Ga.
The Dow Chemical Company	Delaware	Midland, Mich.
Google	Delaware	Mountain View, Calif.
General Electric Company	New York	Fairfield, Conn.
The Home Depot	Delaware	Atlanta, Ga.
Kellogg Company	Delaware	Battle Creek, Mich.
R.J. Reynolds Tobacco Company	Delaware	Winston-Salem, N.C.
Starbucks Corporation	Washington	Seattle, Wash.
Sun Microsystems, Inc.	Delaware	Palo Alto, Calif.
3M	Delaware	St. Paul, Minn.
The Washington Post Company	Delaware	Washington, D.C.
Whirlpool Corporation	Delaware	Benton Harbor, Mich.

The corporate management and board of directors then prepare a set of *bylaws*, which are the rules and procedures for conducting the corporation's affairs.

Costs may be incurred in organizing a corporation. These costs include legal fees, taxes, state incorporation fees, license fees, and promotional costs. Such costs are debited to an expense account entitled *Organizational Expenses*.

To illustrate, a corporation's organizing costs of $8,500 on January 5 are recorded as shown below.

Jan.	5	Organizational Expenses		8,500	
		Cash			8,500
		Paid costs of organizing the corporation.			

OBJ 2 Describe and illustrate the characteristics of stock, classes of stock, and entries for issuing stock.

Paid-In Capital from Issuing Stock

The two main sources of stockholders' equity are paid-in capital (or contributed capital) and retained earnings. The main source of paid-in capital is from issuing stock.

Characteristics of Stock

Number of shares authorized, issued, and outstanding

The number of shares of stock that a corporation is *authorized* to issue is stated in its charter. The term *issued* refers to the shares issued to the stockholders. A corporation may reacquire some of the stock that it has issued. The stock remaining in the hands of stockholders is then called **outstanding stock**. The relationship between authorized, issued, and outstanding stock is shown in the graphic at the right.

Upon request, corporations may issue stock certificates to stockholders to document their ownership. Printed on a stock certificate is the name of the company, the name of the stockholder, and the number of shares owned. The stock certificate may also indicate a dollar amount assigned to each share of stock, called **par** value. Stock may be issued without par, in which case it is called *no-par stock*. In some states, the board of directors of a corporation is required to assign a *stated value* to no-par stock.

Corporations have limited liability and, thus, creditors have no claim against stockholders' personal assets. To protect creditors, however, some states require corporations to maintain a minimum amount of paid-in capital. This minimum amount, called *legal capital*, usually includes the par or stated value of the shares issued.

The major rights that accompany ownership of a share of stock are as follows:

1. The right to vote in matters concerning the corporation.
2. The right to share in distributions of earnings.
3. The right to share in assets upon liquidation.

These stock rights normally vary with the class of stock.

Classes of Stock

When only one class of stock is issued, it is called **common stock**. Each share of common stock has equal rights.

A corporation may also issue one or more classes of stock with various preference rights such as a preference to dividends. Such a stock is called a **preferred stock**. The dividend rights of preferred stock are stated either as dollars per share or as a percent of par. For example, a $50 par value preferred stock with a $4 per share dividend may be described as either:[3]

Note:
The two primary classes of paid-in capital are common stock and preferred stock.

preferred $4 stock, $50 par
or
preferred 8% stock, $50 par

Because they have first rights (preference) to any dividends, preferred stockholders have a greater chance of receiving dividends than common stockholders. However, since dividends are normally based on earnings, a corporation cannot guarantee dividends even to preferred stockholders.

The payment of dividends is authorized by the corporation's board of directors. When authorized, the directors are said to have *declared* a dividend.

Cumulative preferred stock has a right to receive regular dividends that were not declared (paid) in prior years. Noncumulative preferred stock does not have this right.

Cumulative preferred stock dividends that have not been paid in prior years are said to be **in arrears**. Any preferred dividends in arrears must be paid before any common stock dividends are paid. In addition, any dividends in arrears are normally disclosed in notes to the financial statements.

© Cengage Learning 2014

To illustrate, assume that a corporation has issued the following preferred and common stock:

1,000 shares of cumulative preferred $4 stock, $50 par
4,000 shares of common stock, $15 par

The corporation was organized on January 1, 2012, and paid no dividends in 2012 and 2013. In 2014, the corporation paid $22,000 in dividends, of which $12,000 was paid to preferred stockholders and $10,000 was paid to common stockholders as shown below.

Total dividends paid		$22,000
Preferred stockholders:		
2012 dividends in arrears (1,000 shares × $4)	$4,000	
2013 dividends in arrears (1,000 shares × $4)	4,000	
2014 dividend (1,000 shares × $4)	4,000	
Total preferred dividends paid		(12,000)
Dividends available to common stockholders		$10,000

As a result, preferred stockholders received $12.00 per share ($12,000 ÷ 1,000 shares) in dividends, while common stockholders received $2.50 per share ($10,000 ÷ 4,000 shares).

In addition to dividend preference, preferred stock may be given preferences to assets if the corporation goes out of business and is liquidated. However, claims of creditors must be satisfied first. Preferred stockholders are next in line to receive any remaining assets, followed by the common stockholders.

3 In some cases, preferred stock may receive additional dividends if certain conditions are met. Such stock, called *participating preferred stock*, is not often issued.

Example Exercise 11-1 Dividends per Share

OBJ 2

Sandpiper Company has 20,000 shares of cumulative preferred 1% stock of $100 par and 100,000 shares of $50 par common stock. The following amounts were distributed as dividends:

Year 1	$10,000
Year 2	45,000
Year 3	80,000

Determine the dividends per share for preferred and common stock for each year.

Follow My Example 11-1

	Year 1	Year 2	Year 3
Amount distributed	$10,000	$45,000	$80,000
Preferred dividend (20,000 shares)	10,000	30,000*	20,000
Common dividend (100,000 shares)	$ 0	$15,000	$60,000
*($10,000 + $20,000)			
Dividends per share:			
Preferred stock	$0.50	$1.50	$1.00
Common stock	None	$0.15	$0.60

Practice Exercises: **PE 11-1A, PE 11-1B**

Issuing Stock

A separate account is used for recording the amount of each class of stock issued to investors in a corporation. For example, assume that a corporation is authorized to issue 10,000 shares of $100 par preferred stock and 100,000 shares of $20 par common stock. The corporation issued 5,000 shares of preferred stock and 50,000 shares of common stock at par for cash. The corporation's entry to record the stock issue is as follows:[4]

		Cash	1,500,000	
		Preferred Stock		500,000
		Common Stock		1,000,000
		Issued preferred stock and common stock at par for cash.		

Stock is often issued by a corporation at a price other than its par. The price at which stock is sold depends on a variety of factors, such as the following:

1. The financial condition, earnings record, and dividend record of the corporation.
2. Investor expectations of the corporation's potential earning power.
3. General business and economic conditions and expectations.

If stock is issued (sold) for a price that is more than its par, the stock has been sold at a **premium**. For example, if common stock with a par of $50 is sold for $60 per share, the stock has sold at a premium of $10.

If stock is issued (sold) for a price that is less than its par, the stock has been sold at a **discount**. For example, if common stock with a par of $50 is sold for $45 per share, the stock has sold at a discount of $5. Many states do not permit stock to be sold at a discount. In other states, stock may be sold at a discount in only unusual cases. Since stock is rarely sold at a discount, it is not illustrated.

In order to distribute dividends, financial statements, and other reports, a corporation must keep track of its stockholders. Large public corporations normally use

4 The accounting for investments in stocks from the point of view of the investor is discussed in Chapter 13.

a financial institution, such as a bank, for this purpose.[5] In such cases, the financial institution is referred to as a *transfer agent* or *registrar*.

Premium on Stock

When stock is issued at a premium, Cash is debited for the amount received. Common Stock or Preferred Stock is credited for the par amount. The excess of the amount paid over par is part of the paid-in capital. An account entitled *Paid-In Capital in Excess of Par* is credited for this amount.

To illustrate, assume that Caldwell Company issues 2,000 shares of $50 par preferred stock for cash at $55. The entry to record this transaction is as follows:

		Cash		110,000	
		Preferred Stock			100,000
		Paid-In Capital in Excess of Par—Preferred Stock			10,000
		Issued $50 par preferred stock at $55.			

When stock is issued in exchange for assets other than cash, such as land, buildings, and equipment, the assets acquired are recorded at their fair market value. If this value cannot be determined, the fair market price of the stock issued is used.

To illustrate, assume that a corporation acquired land with a fair market value that cannot be determined. In exchange, the corporation issued 10,000 shares of its $10 par common stock. If the stock has a market price of $12 per share, the transaction is recorded as follows:

		Land		120,000	
		Common Stock			100,000
		Paid-In Capital in Excess of Par			20,000
		Issued $10 par common stock, valued at $12 per share, for land.			

No-Par Stock

In most states, no-par preferred and common stock may be issued. When no-par stock is issued, Cash is debited and Common Stock is credited for the proceeds. As no-par stock is issued over time, this entry is the same even if the issuing price varies.

To illustrate, assume that on January 9 a corporation issues 10,000 shares of no-par common stock at $40 a share. On June 27, the corporation issues an additional 1,000 shares at $36. The entries to record these issuances of the no-par stock are as follows:

Jan.	9	Cash		400,000	
		Common Stock			400,000
		Issued 10,000 shares of no-par common stock at $40.			
June	27	Cash		36,000	
		Common Stock			36,000
		Issued 1,000 shares of no-par common stock at $36.			

5 Small corporations may use a subsidiary ledger, called a *stockholders ledger.* in this case, the stock accounts (Preferred Stock and Common Stock) are controlling accounts for the subsidiary ledger.

In some states, no-par stock may be assigned a *stated value per share.* The stated value is recorded like a par value. Any excess of the proceeds over the stated value is credited to *Paid-In Capital in Excess of Stated Value.*

To illustrate, assume that in the preceding example the no-par common stock is assigned a stated value of $25. The issuance of the stock on January 9 and June 27 is recorded as follows:

Jan.	9	Cash	400,000	
		Common Stock		250,000
		Paid-In Capital in Excess of Stated Value		150,000
		Issued 10,000 shares of no-par common stock at $40; stated value, $25.		
June	27	Cash	36,000	
		Common Stock		25,000
		Paid-In Capital in Excess of Stated Value		11,000
		Issued 1,000 shares of no-par common stock at $36; stated value, $25.		

Business Connection

GOOGLE INC.

Some excepts from Google's bylaws are shown below.

ARTICLE I—CORPORATE OFFICES

1.1 REGISTERED OFFICE.

The registered office of Google Inc. shall be fixed in the corporation's certificate of incorporation. …

1.2 OTHER OFFICES.

The corporation's Board of Directors (the "Board") may at any time establish other offices at any place or places where the corporation is qualified to do business.

ARTICLE II—MEETINGS OF STOCKHOLDERS

2.2 ANNUAL MEETING.

The annual meeting of stockholders shall be held each year on a date and at a time designated by the Board. At the annual meeting, directors shall be elected and any other proper business may be transacted.

2.4 NOTICE OF STOCKHOLDERS' MEETINGS.

All notices of meetings of stockholders shall be sent … not less than ten (10) nor more than sixty (60) days before the date of the meeting to each stockholder entitled to vote at such meeting. … The notice shall specify the place, if any, date and hour of the meeting, the means of remote communication, if any, by which stockholders and proxy holders may be deemed to be present in person and vote at such meeting. …

2.8 ADMINISTRATION OF THE MEETING.

Meetings of stockholders shall be presided over by the chairman of the Board. …

ARTICLE V—OFFICERS

5.1 OFFICERS.

The officers of the corporation shall be a chief executive officer, one or more presidents (at the discretion of the Board), a chairman of the Board and a secretary. The corporation may also have, at the discretion of the Board, a vice chairman of the Board, a chief financial officer, a treasurer, one or more vice presidents, one or more assistant vice presidents, one or more assistant treasurers, one or more assistant secretaries, and any such other officers as may be appointed in accordance with the provisions of these bylaws.

5.6 CHAIRMAN OF THE BOARD.

The chairman of the Board shall be a member of the Board and, if present, preside at meetings of the Board. …

5.7 CHIEF EXECUTIVE OFFICER.

Subject to the control of the Board, … the chief executive officer shall, together with the president or presidents of the corporation, have general supervision, direction, and control of the business and affairs of the corporation. … The chief executive officer shall … preside at all meetings of the stockholders.

5.11 CHIEF FINANCIAL OFFICER.

The chief financial officer shall keep and maintain … adequate and correct books and records of accounts of the properties and business transactions of the corporation, including accounts of its assets, liabilities, receipts, disbursements, gains, losses, capital, retained earnings and shares. …

5.12 TREASURER.

The treasurer shall deposit all moneys and other valuables in the name and to the credit of the corporation. …

Source: Amended and Restated Bylaws of Google Inc., July 18, 2012. (Accessed at http://investor.google.com/corporate/bylaws.html.)

Example Exercise 11-2 Entries for Issuing Stock

OBJ 2

On March 6, Limerick Corporation issued for cash 15,000 shares of no-par common stock at $30. On April 13, Limerick issued at par 1,000 shares of preferred 4% stock, $40 par for cash. On May 19, Limerick issued for cash 15,000 shares of 4%, $40 par preferred stock at $42.

Journalize the entries to record the March 6, April 13, and May 19 transactions.

Follow My Example 11-2

Mar. 6	Cash	450,000	
	Common Stock		450,000
	(15,000 shares × $30).		
Apr. 13	Cash	40,000	
	Preferred Stock		40,000
	(1,000 shares × $40).		
May 19	Cash	630,000	
	Preferred Stock		600,000
	Paid-In Capital in Excess of Par		30,000
	(15,000 shares × $42).		

Practice Exercises: **PE 11-2A, PE 11-2B**

Accounting for Dividends

OBJ 3 Describe and illustrate the accounting for cash dividends and stock dividends.

When a board of directors declares a cash dividend, it authorizes the distribution of cash to stockholders. When a board of directors declares a stock dividend, it authorizes the distribution of its stock. In both cases, declaring a dividend reduces the retained earnings of the corporation.[6]

Cash Dividends

A cash distribution of earnings by a corporation to its shareholders is a **cash dividend**. Although dividends may be paid in other assets, cash dividends are the most common.

Three conditions for a cash dividend are as follows:

1. Sufficient retained earnings
2. Sufficient cash
3. Formal action by the board of directors

IFRS

International Connection

IFRS FOR SMES

In 2010, the International Accounting Standards Board (IASB) issued a set of accounting standards specifically designed for small- and medium-sized enterprises (SMEs) called International Financial Reporting Standards (IFRS) for SMEs. SMEs in the United States are private companies and such small corporations that they do not report to the Securities and Exchange Commission (SEC). IFRS for SMEs consist of only 230 pages, compared to 2,700 pages for full IFRS. These standards are designed to be cost effective for SMEs. Thus, IFRS for SMEs require fewer disclosures and contain no industry-specific standards or exceptions.

The American Institute of CPAs (AICPA) has accepted IFRS for SMEs as part of U.S. generally accepted accounting principles (GAAP) for private companies not reporting to the SEC. If users, such as bankers and investors, accept these financial statements, IFRS for SMEs may become popular in the United States.*

*Differences between U.S. GAAP and IFRS are further discussed and illustrated in Appendix C.

6 In rare cases, when a corporation is reducing its operations or going out of business, a dividend may be a distribution of paid-in capital. Such a dividend is called a *liquidating dividend*.

There must be a sufficient (large enough) balance in Retained Earnings to declare a cash dividend. That is, the balance of Retained Earnings must be large enough so that the dividend does not create a debit balance in the retained earnings account. However, a large Retained Earnings balance does not mean that there is cash available to pay dividends. This is because the balances of Cash and Retained Earnings are often unrelated.

Even if there are sufficient retained earnings and cash, a corporation's board of directors is not required to pay dividends. Nevertheless, many corporations pay quarterly cash dividends to make their stock more attractive to investors. *Special* or *extra* dividends may also be paid when a corporation experiences higher than normal profits.

Three dates included in a dividend announcement are as follows:

1. Date of declaration
2. Date of record
3. Date of payment

The *date of declaration* is the date the board of directors formally authorizes the payment of the dividend. On this date, the corporation incurs the liability to pay the amount of the dividend.

The *date of record* is the date the corporation uses to determine which stockholders will receive the dividend. During the period of time between the date of declaration and the date of record, the stock price is quoted as selling *with-dividends.* This means that any investors purchasing the stock before the date of record will receive the dividend.

Microsoft Corporation declared a dividend of $0.20 per share on March 13, 2012, to common stockholders of record as of May 17, 2012, payable on June 14, 2012.

The *date of payment* is the date the corporation will pay the dividend to the stockholders who owned the stock on the date of record. During the period of time between the record date and the payment date, the stock price is quoted as selling *ex-dividends.* This means that since the date of record has passed, any new investors will not receive the dividend.

To illustrate, assume that on October 1 Hiber Corporation declares the cash dividends shown below with a date of record of November 10 and a date of payment of December 2.

	Dividend per Share	Total Dividends
Preferred stock, $100 par, 5,000 shares outstanding....................	$2.50	$12,500
Common stock, $10 par, 100,000 shares outstanding	$0.30	30,000
Total		$42,500

On October 1, the declaration date, Hiber Corporation records the following entry:

Declaration Date

Oct.	1	Cash Dividends		42,500	
		Cash Dividends Payable			42,500
		Declared cash dividends.			

Date of Record

On November 10, the date of record, no entry is necessary. This date merely determines which stockholders will receive the dividends.

On December 2, the date of payment, Hiber Corporation records the payment of the dividends as follows:

Date of Payment

Dec.	2	Cash Dividends Payable		42,500	
		Cash			42,500
		Paid cash dividends.			

At the end of the accounting period, the balance in Cash Dividends will be transferred to Retained Earnings as part of the closing process. This closing entry debits Retained Earnings and credits Cash Dividends for the balance of the cash dividends account. If the cash dividends have not been paid by the end of the period, Cash Dividends Payable will be reported on the balance sheet as a current liability.

Example Exercise 11-3 Entries for Cash Dividends

OBJ 3

The important dates in connection with a cash dividend of $75,000 on a corporation's common stock are February 26, March 30, and April 2. Journalize the entries required on each date.

Follow My Example 11-3

Feb. 26	Cash Dividends	75,000	
	Cash Dividends Payable		75,000
Mar. 30	No entry required.		
Apr. 2	Cash Dividends Payable	75,000	
	Cash		75,000

Practice Exercises: **PE 11-3A, PE 11-3B**

Integrity, Objectivity, and Ethics in Business

THE PROFESSOR WHO KNEW TOO MUCH

A major Midwestern university released a quarterly "American Customer Satisfaction Index" based on its research of customers of popular U.S. products and services. Before the release of the index to the public, the professor in charge of the research bought and sold stocks of some of the companies in the report. The professor was quoted as saying that he thought it was important to test his theories of customer satisfaction with "real" [his own] money.

Is this proper or ethical? Apparently, the dean of the Business School didn't think so. In a statement to the press, the dean stated: "I have instructed anyone affiliated with the (index) not to make personal use of information gathered in the course of producing the quarterly index, prior to the index's release to the general public, and they [the researchers] have agreed."

Sources: Jon E. Hilsenrath and Dan Morse, "Researcher Uses Index to Buy, Short Stocks," *The Wall Street Journal*, February 18, 2003; and Jon E. Hilsenrath, "Satisfaction Theory: Mixed Results," *The Wall Street Journal*, February 19, 2003.

Stock Dividends

A **stock dividend** is a distribution of shares of stock to stockholders. Stock dividends are normally declared only on common stock and issued to common stockholders.

A stock dividend affects only stockholders' equity. Specifically, the amount of the stock dividend is transferred from Retained Earnings to Paid-In Capital. The amount transferred is normally the fair value (market price) of the shares issued in the stock dividend.[7]

To illustrate, assume that the stockholders' equity accounts of Hendrix Corporation as of December 15 are as follows:

Common Stock, $20 par (2,000,000 shares issued)	$40,000,000
Paid-In Capital in Excess of Par—Common Stock	9,000,000
Retained Earnings	26,600,000

On December 15, Hendrix Corporation declares a stock dividend of 5% or 100,000 shares (2,000,000 shares × 5%) to be issued on January 10 to stockholders of record on December 31. The market price of the stock on December 15 (the date of declaration) is $31 per share.

7 The use of fair market value is justified as long as the number of shares issued for the stock dividend is small (less than 25% of the shares outstanding).

The entry to record the stock dividend is as follows:

Dec.	15	Stock Dividends	3,100,000	
		Stock Dividends Distributable		2,000,000
		Paid-In Capital in Excess of Par—Common Stock		1,100,000
		Declared 5% (100,000 shares) stock dividend on $20 par common stock with a market price of $31 per share.		

After the preceding entry is recorded, Stock Dividends will have a debit balance of $3,100,000. Like cash dividends, the stock dividends account is closed to Retained Earnings at the end of the accounting period. This closing entry debits Retained Earnings and credits Stock Dividends.

At the end of the period, the *stock dividends distributable* and *paid-in capital in excess of par—common stock* accounts are reported in the Paid-In Capital section of the balance sheet. Thus, the effect of the preceding stock dividend is to transfer $3,100,000 of retained earnings to paid-in capital.

On January 10, the stock dividend is distributed to stockholders by issuing 100,000 shares of common stock. The issuance of the stock is recorded by the following entry:

Jan.	10	Stock Dividends Distributable	2,000,000	
		Common Stock		2,000,000
		Issued stock as stock dividend.		

A stock dividend does not change the assets, liabilities, or total stockholders' equity of a corporation. Likewise, a stock dividend does not change an individual stockholder's proportionate interest (equity) in the corporation.

To illustrate, assume a stockholder owns 1,000 of a corporation's 10,000 shares outstanding. If the corporation declares a 6% stock dividend, the stockholder's proportionate interest will not change, as shown below.

	***Before* Stock Dividend**	***After* Stock Dividend**
Total shares issued	10,000	10,600 [10,000 + (10,000 × 6%)]
Number of shares owned	1,000	1,060 [1,000 + (1,000 × 6%)]
Proportionate ownership	10% (1,000/10,000)	10% (1,060/10,600)

Example Exercise 11-4 Entries for Stock Dividends

OBJ 3

Vienna Highlights Corporation has 150,000 shares of $100 par common stock outstanding. On June 14, Vienna Highlights declared a 4% stock dividend to be issued August 15 to stockholders of record on July 1. The market price of the stock was $110 per share on June 14.

Journalize the entries required on June 14, July 1, and August 15.

Follow My Example 11-4

June 14	Stock Dividends (150,000 × 4% × $110)	660,000	
	Stock Dividends Distributable (6,000 × $100)		600,000
	Paid-In Capital in Excess of Par—Common Stock ($660,000 – $600,000)		60,000
July 1	No entry required.		
Aug. 15	Stock Dividends Distributable	600,000	
	Common Stock		600,000

Practice Exercises: **PE 11-4A, PE 11-4B**

Treasury Stock Transactions

OBJ 4 Describe and illustrate the accounting for treasury stock transactions.

Treasury stock is stock that a corporation has issued and then reacquired. A corporation may reacquire (purchase) its own stock for a variety of reasons, including the following:

1. To provide shares for resale to employees
2. To reissue as bonuses to employees, or
3. To support the market price of the stock

The 2011 edition of *Accounting Trends & Techniques* indicated that 64.6% of the companies surveyed reported treasury stock.

The *cost method* is normally used for recording the purchase and resale of treasury stock.[8] Using the cost method, *Treasury Stock* is debited for the cost (purchase price) of the stock. When the stock is resold, Treasury Stock is credited for its cost. Any difference between the cost and the selling price is debited or credited to *Paid-In Capital from Sale of Treasury Stock.*

To illustrate, assume that a corporation has the following paid-in capital on January 1:

Common stock, $25 par (20,000 shares authorized and issued)	$500,000
Excess of issue price over par	150,000
	$650,000

On February 13, the corporation purchases 1,000 shares of its common stock at $45 per share. The entry to record the purchase of the treasury stock is as follows:

Feb.	13	Treasury Stock	45,000	
		Cash		45,000
		Purchased 1,000 shares of treasury stock at $45.		

On April 29, the corporation sells 600 shares of the treasury stock for $60. The entry to record the sale is as follows:

Apr.	29	Cash	36,000	
		Treasury Stock		27,000
		Paid-In Capital from Sale of Treasury Stock		9,000
		Sold 600 shares of treasury stock at $60.		

A sale of treasury stock may result in a decrease in paid-in capital. To the extent that Paid-In Capital from Sale of Treasury Stock has a credit balance, it is debited for any such decrease. Any remaining decrease is then debited to the retained earnings account.

To illustrate, assume that on October 4, the corporation sells the remaining 400 shares of treasury stock for $40 per share. The entry to record the sale is as follows:

Oct.	4	Cash	16,000	
		Paid-In Capital from Sale of Treasury Stock	2,000	
		Treasury Stock		18,000
		Sold 400 shares of treasury stock at $40.		

The October 4 entry shown above decreases paid-in capital by $2,000. Since Paid-In Capital from Sale of Treasury Stock has a credit balance of $9,000, the entire $2,000 was debited to Paid-In Capital from Sale of Treasury Stock.

No dividends (cash or stock) are paid on the shares of treasury stock. To do so would result in the corporation earning dividend revenue from itself.

8 Another method that is infrequently used, called the *par value method*, is discussed in advanced accounting texts.

Example Exercise 11-5 Entries for Treasury Stock

OBJ 4

On May 3, Buzz Off Corporation reacquired 3,200 shares of its common stock at $42 per share. On July 22, Buzz Off sold 2,000 of the reacquired shares at $47 per share. On August 30, Buzz Off sold the remaining shares at $40 per share.

Journalize the transactions of May 3, July 22, and August 30.

Follow My Example 11-5

May 3	Treasury Stock (3,200 × $42)	134,400	
	Cash		134,400
July 22	Cash (2,000 × $47)	94,000	
	Treasury Stock (2,000 × $42)		84,000
	Paid-In Capital from Sale of Treasury Stock [2,000 × ($47 – $42)]		10,000
Aug. 30	Cash (1,200 × $40)	48,000	
	Paid-In Capital from Sale of Treasury Stock [1,200 × ($42 – $40)]	2,400	
	Treasury Stock (1,200 × $42)		50,400

Practice Exercises: **PE 11-5A, PE 11-5B**

OBJ 5 Describe and illustrate the reporting of stockholders' equity.

Reporting Stockholders' Equity

As with other sections of the balance sheet, alternative terms and formats may be used in reporting stockholders' equity. Also, changes in retained earnings and paid-in capital may be reported in separate statements or notes to the financial statements.

Stockholders' Equity on the Balance Sheet

Exhibit 4 shows two methods for reporting stockholders' equity for the December 31, 2014, balance sheet for Telex Inc.

Method 1. Each class of stock is reported, followed by its related paid-in capital accounts. Retained earnings is then reported followed by a deduction for treasury stock.

Method 2. The stock accounts are reported, followed by the paid-in capital reported as a single item, Additional paid-in capital. Retained earnings is then reported followed by a deduction for treasury stock.

EXHIBIT 4

Stockholders' Equity Section of a Balance Sheet

Telex Inc.
Balance Sheet
December 31, 2014

Stockholders' Equity

Paid-in capital:			
Preferred 10% stock, $50 par (2,000 shares authorized and issued)	$100,000		
Excess of issue price over par	10,000	$ 110,000	
Common stock, $20 par (50,000 shares authorized, 45,000 shares issued)	$900,000		
Excess of issue price over par	190,000	1,090,000	
From sale of treasury stock		2,000	
Total paid-in capital			$1,202,000
Retained earnings			350,000
Total			$1,552,000
Deduct treasury stock (600 shares at cost)			27,000
Total stockholders' equity			$1,525,000

Method 1

Telex Inc.
Balance Sheet
December 31, 2014

Stockholders' Equity

Contributed capital:		
Preferred 10% stock, $50 par (2,000 shares authorized and issued)	$100,000	
Common stock, $20 par (50,000 shares authorized, 45,000 shares issued)	900,000	
Additional paid-in capital	202,000	
Total contributed capital		$1,202,000
Retained earnings		350,000
Total		$1,552,000
Deduct treasury stock (600 shares at cost)		27,000
Total stockholders' equity		$1,525,000

EXHIBIT 4

Stockholders' Equity Section of a Balance Sheet (*Concluded*)

Method 2

Significant changes in stockholders' equity during a period may also be presented in a statement of stockholders' equity or in the notes to the financial statements. The statement of stockholders' equity is illustrated later in this section.

Relevant rights and privileges of the various classes of stock outstanding should also be reported.[9] Examples include dividend and liquidation preferences, conversion rights, and redemption rights. Such information may be disclosed on the face of the balance sheet or in the notes to the financial statements.

Example Exercise 11-6 Reporting Stockholders' Equity

OBJ 5

Using the following accounts and balances, prepare the Stockholders' Equity section of the balance sheet. Forty thousand shares of common stock are authorized, and 5,000 shares have been reacquired.

Common Stock, $50 par	$1,500,000
Paid-In Capital from Sale of Treasury Stock	44,000
Paid-In Capital in Excess of Par	160,000
Retained Earnings	4,395,000
Treasury Stock	120,000

Follow My Example 11-6

Stockholders' Equity

Paid-in capital:		
Common stock, $50 par (40,000 shares authorized, 30,000 shares issued)	$1,500,000	
Excess of issue price over par	160,000	$1,660,000
From sale of treasury stock		44,000
Total paid-in capital		$1,704,000
Retained earnings		4,395,000
Total		$6,099,000
Deduct treasury stock (5,000 shares at cost)		120,000
Total stockholders' equity		$5,979,000

Practice Exercises: **PE 11-6A, PE 11-6B**

9 *FASB Accounting Standards Codification*, Section 505-10-50.

Reporting Retained Earnings

Changes in retained earnings may be reported using one of the following:

1. Separate retained earnings statement
2. Combined income and retained earnings statement
3. Statement of stockholders' equity

Changes in retained earnings may be reported in a separate retained earnings statement. When a separate retained earnings statement is prepared, the beginning balance of retained earnings is reported. The net income is then added (or net loss is subtracted) and any dividends are subtracted to arrive at the ending retained earnings for the period.

To illustrate, a retained earnings statement for Telex Inc. is shown in Exhibit 5.

EXHIBIT 5

Retained Earnings Statement

Telex Inc.
Retained Earnings Statement
For the Year Ended December 31, 2014

Retained earnings, January 1, 2014			$245,000
Net income		$180,000	
Less dividends:			
Preferred stock	$10,000		
Common stock	65,000	75,000	
Increase in retained earnings			105,000
Retained earnings, December 31, 2014			$350,000

Changes in retained earnings may also be reported in combination with the income statement. This format emphasizes net income as the connecting link between the income statement and ending retained earnings. Since this format is not often used, we do not illustrate it.

Changes in retained earnings may also be reported in a statement of stockholders' equity. An example of reporting changes in retained earnings in a statement of stockholders' equity for Telex Inc. is shown in Exhibit 6.

Example Exercise 11-7 Retained Earnings Statement

OBJ 5

Dry Creek Cameras Inc. reported the following results for the year ending March 31, 2014:

Retained earnings, April 1, 2013	$3,338,500
Net income	461,500
Cash dividends declared	80,000
Stock dividends declared	120,000

Prepare a retained earnings statement for the fiscal year ended March 31, 2014.

Follow My Example 11-7

Dry Creek Cameras Inc.
Retained Earnings Statement
For the Year Ended March 31, 2014

Retained earnings, April 1, 2013		$3,338,500
Net income	$461,500	
Less dividends declared	200,000	
Increase in retained earnings		261,500
Retained earnings, March 31, 2014		$3,600,000

Practice Exercises: **PE 11-7A, PE 11-7B**

Restrictions The use of retained earnings for payment of dividends may be restricted by action of a corporation's board of directors. Such **restrictions**, sometimes called *appropriations,* remain part of the retained earnings.

Restrictions of retained earnings are classified as:

1. *Legal.* State laws may require a restriction of retained earnings.

   Example: States may restrict retained earnings by the amount of treasury stock purchased. In this way, legal capital cannot be used for dividends.

2. *Contractual.* A corporation may enter into contracts that require restrictions of retained earnings.

   Example: A bank loan may restrict retained earnings so that money for repaying the loan cannot be used for dividends.

3. *Discretionary.* A corporation's board of directors may restrict retained earnings voluntarily.

   Example: The board may restrict retained earnings and, thus, limit dividend distributions so that more money is available for expanding the business.

Restrictions of retained earnings must be disclosed in the financial statements. Such disclosures are usually included in the notes to the financial statements.

Prior Period Adjustments An error may arise from a mathematical mistake or from a mistake in applying accounting principles. Such errors may not be discovered within the same period in which they occur. In such cases, the effect of the error should not affect the current period's net income. Instead, the correction of the error, called a **prior period adjustment**, is reported in the retained earnings statement. Such corrections are reported as an adjustment to the beginning balance of retained earnings.[10]

Statement of Stockholders' Equity

When the only change in stockholders' equity is due to net income or net loss and dividends, a retained earnings statement is sufficient. However, when a corporation also has changes in stock and paid-in capital accounts, a **statement of stockholders' equity** is normally prepared.

A statement of stockholders' equity is normally prepared in a columnar format. Each column is a major stockholders' equity classification. Changes in each classification are then described in the left-hand column. Exhibit 6 illustrates a statement of stockholders' equity for Telex Inc.

EXHIBIT 6 **Statement of Stockholders' Equity**

Telex Inc.
Statement of Stockholders' Equity
For the Year Ended December 31, 2014

	Preferred Stock	Common Stock	Additional Paid-In Capital	Retained Earnings	Treasury Stock	Total
Balance, January 1, 2014	$100,000	$850,000	$177,000	$245,000	$(17,000)	$1,355,000
Net income				180,000		180,000
Dividends on preferred stock				(10,000)		(10,000)
Dividends on common stock				(65,000)		(65,000)
Issuance of additional common stock		50,000	25,000			75,000
Purchase of treasury stock					(10,000)	(10,000)
Balance, December 31, 2014	$100,000	$900,000	$202,000	$350,000	$(27,000)	$1,525,000

10 Prior period adjustments are illustrated in advanced texts.

Reporting Stockholders' Equity for Mornin' Joe

Mornin' Joe reports stockholders' equity in its balance sheet. Mornin' Joe also includes a retained earnings statement and statement of stockholders' equity in its financial statements.

The Stockholders' Equity section of Mornin' Joe's balance sheet as of December 31, 2014, is shown below.

Mornin' Joe
Balance Sheet
December 31, 2014

Stockholders' Equity

Paid-in capital:		
Preferred 10% stock, $50 par (6,000 shares authorized and issued)	$ 300,000	
Excess of issue price over par	50,000	$ 350,000
Common stock, $20 par (50,000 shares authorized, 45,000 shares issued)	$ 900,000	
Excess of issue price over par	1,450,000	2,350,000
Total paid-in capital		$2,700,000
Retained earnings		1,200,300
Total		$3,900,300
Deduct treasury stock (1,000 shares at cost)		46,000
Total stockholders' equity		$3,854,300
Total liabilities and stockholders' equity		$6,169,700

Mornin' Joe's retained earnings statement for the year ended December 31, 2014, is as follows:

Mornin' Joe
Retained Earnings Statment
For the Year Ended December 31, 2014

Retained earnings, January 1, 2014			$ 852,700
Net income		$421,600	
Less dividends:			
Preferred stock	$30,000		
Common stock	44,000	74,000	
Increase in retained earnings			347,600
Retained earnings, December 31, 2014			$1,200,300

The statement of stockholders' equity for Mornin' Joe is shown below.

Mornin' Joe
Statement of Stockholders' Equity
For the Year Ended December 31, 2014

	Preferred Stock	Common Stock	Additional Paid-In Capital	Retained Earnings	Treasury Stock	Total
Balance, January 1, 2014	$300,000	$800,000	$1,325,000	$ 852,700	$(36,000)	$3,241,700
Net income				421,600		421,600
Dividends on preferred stock				(30,000)		(30,000)
Dividends on common stock				(44,000)		(44,000)
Issuance of additional common stock		100,000	175,000			275,000
Purchase of treasury stock					(10,000)	(10,000)
Balance, December 31, 2014	$300,000	$900,000	$1,500,000	$1,200,300	$(46,000)	$3,854,300

Stock Splits

OBJ 6 Describe the effect of stock splits on corporate financial statements.

A **stock split** is a process by which a corporation reduces the par or stated value of its common stock and issues a proportionate number of additional shares. A stock split applies to all common shares including the unissued, issued, and treasury shares.

A major objective of a stock split is to reduce the market price per share of the stock. This attracts more investors and broadens the types and numbers of stockholders.

To illustrate, assume that Rojek Corporation has 10,000 shares of $100 par common stock outstanding with a current market price of $150 per share. The board of directors declares the following stock split:

1. Each common shareholder will receive 5 shares for each share held. This is called a 5-for-l stock split. As a result, 50,000 shares (10,000 shares × 5) will be outstanding.
2. The par of each share of common stock will be reduced to $20 ($100/5).

The par value of the common stock outstanding is $1,000,000 both before and after the stock split as shown below.

	Before Split	After Split
Number of shares	10,000	50,000
Par value per share	× $100	× $20
Total	$1,000,000	$1,000,000

In addition, each Rojek Corporation shareholder owns the same total par amount of stock before and after the stock split. For example, a stockholder who owned 4 shares of $100 par stock before the split (total par of $400) would own 20 shares of $20 par stock after the split (total par of $400). Only the number of shares and the par value per share have changed.

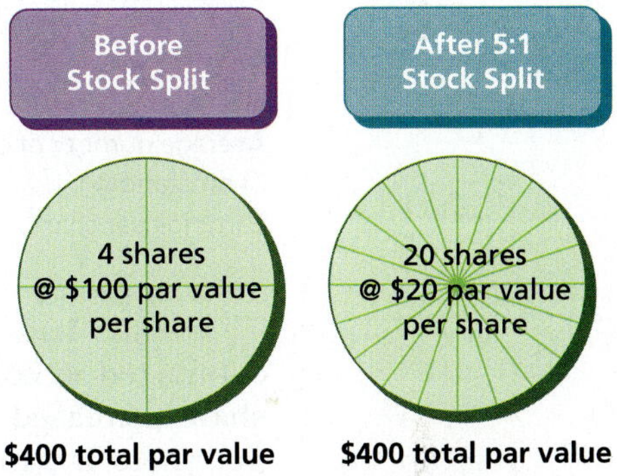

Since there are more shares outstanding after the stock split, the market price of the stock should decrease. For example, in the preceding example, there would be 5 times as many shares outstanding after the split. Thus, the market price of the stock would be expected to fall from $150 to about $30 ($150 ÷ 5).

Stock splits do not require a journal entry, since only the par (or stated) value and number of shares outstanding have changed. However, the details of stock splits are normally disclosed in the notes to the financial statements.

Note:
A stock split does not require a journal entry.

Business Connection

BUFFETT ON STOCK SPLITS

Warren E. Buffett, chairman and chief executive officer of Berkshire Hathaway Inc., opposes stock splits on the basis that they add no value to the company. Since its inception, Berkshire Hathaway has never declared a stock split on its primary (Class A) common stock. As a result, Berkshire Hathaway's Class A common stock sells well above $100,000 per share, which is the most expensive stock on the New York Stock Exchange. Such a high price doesn't bother Buffet, since he believes that high stock prices attract more sophisticated and long-term investors and discourage stock speculators and short-term investors.

In contrast, Microsoft Corporation has split its stock nine times since it went public in 1986. As a result, one share of Microsoft purchased in 1986 is equivalent to 288 shares today, which would be worth over $8,500.

F·A·I

Financial Analysis and Interpretation: Earnings per Share

OBJ 7 Describe and illustrate the use of earnings per share in evaluating a company's profitability.

Net income is often used by investors and creditors in evaluating a company's profitability. However, net income by itself is difficult to use in comparing companies of different sizes. Also, trends in net income may be difficult to evaluate if there have been significant changes in a company's stockholders' equity. Thus, the profitability of companies is often expressed as earnings per share.

Earnings per common share (EPS), sometimes called *basic earnings per share,* is the net income per share of common stock outstanding during a period.[11] Corporations whose stock is traded in a public market must report earnings per common share on their income statements.

Earnings per share is computed as follows:

$$\text{Earnings per Share} = \frac{\text{Net Income} - \text{Preferred Dividends}}{\text{Average Number of Common Shares Outstanding}}$$

If a company has preferred stock outstanding, any preferred dividends are subtracted from net income. This is because the numerator represents only those earnings available to the common shareholders.

To illustrate, the following data (in thousands) were taken from recent financial statements of Google:

	Year 2	Year 1
Net income	$8,505,000	$6,520,000
Average number of common shares outstanding	318,702 shares	316,221 shares
Earnings per share	$26.69 ($8,505,000 ÷ 318,702 shares)	$20.62 ($6,520,000 ÷ 316,221 shares)

Google had no preferred stock outstanding; thus, no preferred dividends were subtracted in computing earnings per share. As shown above, Google's earnings per share increased from $20.62 in Year 1 to $26.69 in Year 2. An increase in earnings per share is generally considered a favorable trend.

Earnings per share can be used to compare two companies with different net incomes. For example, the following data (in millions) were taken from a recent year's financial statements for Goldman Sachs Group, Inc., and Wells Fargo & Company.

	Goldman Sachs	Wells Fargo
Net income	$8,354	$12,362
Preferred dividends	$641	$730
Average number of common shares outstanding	545.0 shares	5,226.8 shares

Goldman Sachs:

$$\text{Earnings per Share} = \frac{\text{Net Income} - \text{Preferred Dividends}}{\text{Average Number of Common Shares Outstanding}} = \frac{\$8{,}354 - \$641}{545.0\text{ shares}} = \frac{\$7{,}713}{545.0\text{ shares}} = \$14.15$$

Wells Fargo:

$$\text{Earnings per Share} = \frac{\text{Net Income} - \text{Preferred Dividends}}{\text{Average Number of Common Shares Outstanding}} = \frac{\$12{,}362 - \$730}{5{,}226.8\text{ shares}} = \frac{\$11{,}632}{5{,}226.8\text{ shares}} = \$2.23$$

Based on earnings per share, Goldman Sachs is more profitable than Wells Fargo.

11 For complex capital structures, earnings per share assuming dilution may also be reported as described in Chapter 15.

Example Exercise 11-8 Earnings per Share

OBJ 7

Financial statement data for years ending December 31 for Finnegan Company are shown below.

	2014	2013
Net income	$350,000	$195,000
Preferred dividends	$20,000	$15,000
Average number of common shares outstanding	75,000 shares	50,000 shares

a. Determine earnings per share for 2014 and 2013.

b. Does the change in the earnings per share from 2013 to 2014 indicate a favorable or an unfavorable trend?

Follow My Example 11-8

a.

2014:

$$\text{Earnings per Share} = \frac{\text{Net Income} - \text{Preferred Dividends}}{\text{Average Number of Common Shares Outstanding}} = \frac{\$350{,}000 - \$20{,}000}{75{,}000 \text{ shares}} = \frac{\$330{,}000}{75{,}000 \text{ shares}} = \$4.40$$

2013:

$$\text{Earnings per Share} = \frac{\text{Net Income} - \text{Preferred Dividends}}{\text{Average Number of Common Shares Outstanding}} = \frac{\$195{,}000 - \$15{,}000}{50{,}000 \text{ shares}} = \frac{\$180{,}000}{50{,}000 \text{ shares}} = \$3.60$$

b. The increase in the earnings per share from $3.60 to $4.40 indicates a favorable trend in the company's profitability.

Practice Exercises: **PE 11-8A, PE 11-8B**

At a Glance 11

OBJ 1

Describe the nature of the corporate form of organization.

Key Points Corporations have a separate legal existence, transferable units of stock, unlimited life, and limited stockholders' liability. The advantages and disadvantages of the corporate form are summarized in Exhibit 2. Costs incurred in organizing a corporation are debited to Organizational Expenses.

Learning Outcomes	Example Exercises	Practice Exercises
• Describe the characteristics of corporations.		
• List the advantages and disadvantages of the corporate form.		
• Prepare a journal entry for the costs of organizing a corporation.		

OBJ 2 Describe and illustrate the characteristics of stock, classes of stock, and entries for issuing stock.

Key Points The main source of paid-in capital is from issuing common and preferred stock. Stock issued at par is recorded by debiting Cash and crediting the class of stock issued for its par amount. Stock issued for more than par is recorded by debiting Cash, crediting the class of stock for its par, and crediting Paid-In Capital in Excess of Par for the difference. When no-par stock is issued, the entire proceeds are credited to the stock account. No-par stock may be assigned a stated value per share, and the excess of the proceeds over the stated value may be credited to Paid-In Capital in Excess of Stated Value.

Learning Outcomes	Example Exercises	Practice Exercises
• Describe the characteristics of common and preferred stock including rights to dividends.	EE11-1	PE11-1A, 11-1B
• Journalize the entry for common and preferred stock issued at par.	EE11-2	PE11-2A, 11-2B
• Journalize the entry for common and preferred stock issued at more than par.	EE11-2	PE11-2A, 11-2B
• Journalize the entry for issuing no-par stock.	EE11-2	PE11-2A, 11-2B

OBJ 3 Describe and illustrate the accounting for cash dividends and stock dividends.

Key Points The entry to record a declaration of cash dividends debits Dividends and credits Dividends Payable. When a stock dividend is declared, Stock Dividends is debited for the fair value of the stock to be issued. Stock Dividends Distributable is credited for the par or stated value of the common stock to be issued. The difference between the fair value of the stock and its par or stated value is credited to Paid-In Capital in Excess of Par—Common Stock. When the stock is issued on the date of payment, Stock Dividends Distributable is debited and Common Stock is credited for the par or stated value of the stock issued.

Learning Outcomes	Example Exercises	Practice Exercises
• Journalize the entries for the declaration and payment of cash dividends.	EE11-3	PE11-3A, 11-3B
• Journalize the entries for the declaration and payment of stock dividends.	EE11-4	PE11-4A, 11-4B

OBJ 4 Describe and illustrate the accounting for treasury stock transactions.

Key Points When a corporation buys its own stock, the cost method of accounting is normally used. Treasury Stock is debited for its cost, and Cash is credited. If the stock is resold, Treasury Stock is credited for its cost and any difference between the cost and the selling price is normally debited or credited to Paid-In Capital from Sale of Treasury Stock.

Learning Outcomes	Example Exercises	Practice Exercises
• Define treasury stock.		
• Describe the accounting for treasury stock.		
• Journalize entries for the purchase and sale of treasury stock.	EE11-5	PE11-5A, 11-5B

OBJ 5 Describe and illustrate the reporting of stockholders' equity.

Key Points Two alternatives for reporting stockholders' equity are shown in Exhibit 4. Changes in retained earnings are reported in a retained earnings statement, as shown in Exhibit 5. Restrictions to retained earnings should be disclosed. Any prior period adjustments are reported in the retained earnings statement. Changes in stockholders' equity may be reported on a statement of stockholders' equity, as shown in Exhibit 6.

Learning Outcomes	Example Exercises	Practice Exercises
• Prepare the Stockholders' Equity section of the balance sheet.	EE11-6	PE11-6A, 11-6B
• Prepare a retained earnings statement.	EE11-7	PE11-7A, 11-7B
• Describe retained earnings restrictions and prior period adjustments.		
• Prepare a statement of stockholders' equity.		

OBJ 6 Describe the effect of stock splits on corporate financial statements.

Key Points When a corporation reduces the par or stated value of its common stock and issues a proportionate number of additional shares, a stock split has occurred. There are no changes in the balances of any accounts, and no entry is required for a stock split.

Learning Outcomes	Example Exercises	Practice Exercises
• Define and give an example of a stock split.		
• Describe the accounting for and effects of a stock split on the financial statements.		

OBJ 7 Describe and illustrate the use of earnings per share in evaluating a company's profitability.

Key Points The profitability of companies is often expressed as earnings per share. Earnings per share is computed by subtracting preferred dividends from net income and dividing by the average number of common shares outstanding.

Learning Outcomes	Example Exercises	Practice Exercises
• Describe the use of earnings per share in evaluating a company's profitability.		
• Compute and interpret earnings per share.	EE11-8	PE11-8A, 11-8B

Key Terms

cash dividend (505)
common stock (501)
cumulative preferred stock (501)
discount (502)
earnings per common share (EPS) (516)
in arrears (501)
outstanding stock (500)
par (500)
preferred stock (501)
premium (502)
prior period adjustments (513)
restrictions (513)
statement of stockholders' equity (513)
stock (498)
stock dividend (507)
stock split (515)
stockholders (498)
treasury stock (509)

Illustrative Problem

Altenburg Inc. is a lighting fixture wholesaler located in Arizona. During its current fiscal year, ended December 31, 2014, Altenburg Inc. completed the following selected transactions:

Feb. 3. Purchased 2,500 shares of its own common stock at $26, recording the stock at cost. (Prior to the purchase, there were 40,000 shares of $20 par common stock outstanding.)

May 1. Declared a semiannual dividend of $1 on the 10,000 shares of preferred stock and a $0.30 dividend on the common stock to stockholders of record on May 31, payable on June 15.

June 15. Paid the cash dividends.

Sept. 23. Sold 1,000 shares of treasury stock at $28, receiving cash.

Nov. 1. Declared semiannual dividends of $1 on the preferred stock and $0.30 on the common stock. In addition, a 5% common stock dividend was declared on the common stock outstanding, to be capitalized at the fair market value of the common stock, which is estimated at $30.

Dec. 1. Paid the cash dividends and issued the certificates for the common stock dividend.

Instructions

Journalize the entries to record the transactions for Altenburg Inc.

Solution

2014				
Feb.	3	Treasury Stock	65,000	
		Cash		65,000
May	1	Cash Dividends	21,250	
		Cash Dividends Payable		21,250
		(10,000 × $1) + [(40,000 – 2,500) × $0.30].		
June	15	Cash Dividends Payable	21,250	
		Cash		21,250
Sept.	23	Cash	28,000	
		Treasury Stock		26,000
		Paid-In Capital from Sale of Treasury Stock		2,000
Nov.	1	Cash Dividends	21,550	
		Cash Dividends Payable		21,550
		(10,000 × $1) + [(40,000 – 1,500) × $0.30].		
	1	Stock Dividends	57,750*	
		Stock Dividends Distributable		38,500
		Paid-In Capital in Excess of Par—Common Stock		19,250
		*(40,000 – 1,500) × 5% × $30.		
Dec.	1	Cash Dividends Payable	21,550	
		Stock Dividends Distributable	38,500	
		Cash		21,550
		Common Stock		38,500

Discussion Questions

1. Of two corporations organized at approximately the same time and engaged in competing businesses, one issued $80 par common stock, and the other issued $1 par common stock. Do the par designations provide any indication as to which stock is preferable as an investment? Explain.
2. A stockbroker advises a client to "buy preferred stock. . . . With that type of stock, . . . [you] will never have to worry about losing the dividends." Is the broker right?
3. A corporation with both preferred stock and common stock outstanding has a substantial credit balance in its retained earnings account at the beginning of the current fiscal year. Although net income for the current year is sufficient to pay the preferred dividend of $150,000 each quarter and a common dividend of $90,000 each quarter, the board of directors declares dividends only on the preferred stock. Suggest possible reasons for passing the dividends on the common stock.
4. An owner of 2,500 shares of Simmons Company common stock receives a stock dividend of 50 shares.
   a. What is the effect of the stock dividend on the stockholder's proportionate interest (equity) in the corporation?

b. How does the total equity of 2,550 shares compare with the total equity of 2,500 shares before the stock dividend?

5. a. Where should a declared but unpaid cash dividend be reported on the balance sheet?

   b. Where should a declared but unissued stock dividend be reported on the balance sheet?

6. A corporation reacquires 60,000 shares of its own $10 par common stock for $3,000,000, recording it at cost.

   a. What effect does this transaction have on revenue or expense of the period?

   b. What effect does it have on stockholders' equity?

7. The treasury stock in Discussion Question 6 is resold for $3,750,000.

   a. What is the effect on the corporation's revenue of the period?

   b. What is the effect on stockholders' equity?

8. What are the three classifications of restrictions of retained earnings, and how are such restrictions normally reported on the financial statements?

9. Indicate how prior period adjustments would be reported on the financial statements presented only for the current period.

10. What is the primary purpose of a stock split?

Practice Exercises

Example Exercises

EE 11-1 *p. 502*

PE 11-1A Dividends per share

OBJ. 2

Swan Creek Company has 40,000 shares of cumulative preferred 2% stock, $60 par and 50,000 shares of $50 par common stock. The following amounts were distributed as dividends:

Year 1	$ 30,000
Year 2	90,000
Year 3	125,000

Determine the dividends per share for preferred and common stock for each year.

EE 11-1 *p. 502*

PE 11-1B Dividends per share

OBJ. 2

Zero Calories Company has 16,000 shares of cumulative preferred 1% stock, $40 par and 80,000 shares of $150 par common stock. The following amounts were distributed as dividends:

Year 1	$ 21,600
Year 2	4,000
Year 3	100,800

Determine the dividends per share for preferred and common stock for each year.

EE 11-2 *p. 505*

PE 11-2A Entries for issuing stock

OBJ. 2

On May 10, Century Realty Inc. issued for cash 90,000 shares of no-par common stock (with a stated value of $30) at $42. On September 3, Century Realty Inc. issued at par value 36,000 shares of preferred 1% stock, $25 par for cash. On December 1, Century Realty Inc. issued for cash 14,000 shares of preferred 1% stock, $25 par at $33.

Journalize the entries to record the May 10, September 3, and December 1 transactions.

EE 11-2 *p. 505*

PE 11-2B Entries for issuing stock

OBJ. 2

On January 22, Zentric Corporation issued for cash 180,000 shares of no-par common stock at $4. On February 14, Zentric Corporation issued at par value 44,000 shares of

Example Exercises

preferred 2% stock, $55 par for cash. On August 30, Zentric Corporation issued for cash 9,000 shares of preferred 2% stock, $55 par at $60.

Journalize the entries to record the January 22, February 14, and August 30 transactions.

EE 11-3 *p. 507*

PE 11-3A Entries for cash dividends **OBJ. 3**

The declaration, record, and payment dates in connection with a cash dividend of $1,250,000 on a corporation's common stock are August 1, October 15, and November 14. Journalize the entries required on each date.

EE 11-3 *p. 507*

PE 11-3B Entries for cash dividends **OBJ. 3**

The declaration, record, and payment dates in connection with a cash dividend of $480,000 on a corporation's common stock are February 1, March 18, and May 1. Journalize the entries required on each date.

EE 11-4 *p. 508*

PE 11-4A Entries for stock dividends **OBJ. 3**

Olde Wine Corporation has 250,000 shares of $40 par common stock outstanding. On February 15, Olde Wine Corporation declared a 2% stock dividend to be issued May 2 to stockholders of record on March 27. The market price of the stock was $52 per share on February 15.

Journalize the entries required on February 15, March 27, and May 2.

EE 11-4 *p. 508*

PE 11-4B Entries for stock dividends **OBJ. 3**

Antique Buggy Corporation has 820,000 shares of $35 par common stock outstanding. On June 8, Antique Buggy Corporation declared a 5% stock dividend to be issued August 12 to stockholders of record on July 13. The market price of the stock was $63 per share on June 8.

Journalize the entries required on June 8, July 13, and August 12.

EE 11-5 *p. 510*

PE 11-5A Entries for treasury stock **OBJ. 4**

On January 31, Wilderness Resorts Inc. reacquired 22,500 shares of its common stock at $31 per share. On April 20, Wilderness Resorts sold 12,800 of the reacquired shares at $40 per share. On October 4, Wilderness Resorts sold the remaining shares at $28 per share.

Journalize the transactions of January 31, April 20, and October 4.

EE 11-5 *p. 510*

PE 11-5B Entries for treasury stock **OBJ. 4**

On May 27, Hydro Clothing Inc. reacquired 75,000 shares of its common stock at $8 per share. On August 3, Hydro Clothing sold 54,000 of the reacquired shares at $11 per share. On November 14, Hydro Clothing sold the remaining shares at $7 per share.

Journalize the transactions of May 27, August 3, and November 14.

EE 11-6 *p. 511*

PE 11-6A Reporting stockholders' equity **OBJ. 5**

Using the following accounts and balances, prepare the Stockholders' Equity section of the balance sheet. Two hundred fifty thousand shares of common stock are authorized, and 17,500 shares have been reacquired.

Common Stock, $60 par	$12,000,0000
Paid-In Capital from Sale of Treasury Stock	320,000
Paid-In Capital in Excess of Par—Common Stock	3,200,000
Retained Earnings	18,500,000
Treasury Stock	1,137,500

Example Exercises

EE 11-6 *p. 511*

PE 11-6B Reporting stockholders' equity

OBJ. 5

Using the following accounts and balances, prepare the Stockholders' Equity section of the balance sheet. Five-hundred thousand shares of common stock are authorized, and 40,000 shares have been reacquired.

Common Stock, $120 par	$48,000,000
Paid-In Capital from Sale of Treasury Stock	4,500,000
Paid-In Capital in Excess of Par—Common Stock	6,400,000
Retained Earnings	63,680,000
Treasury Stock	5,200,000

EE 11-7 *p. 512*

PE 11-7A Retained earnings statement

OBJ. 5

Rockwell Inc. reported the following results for the year ended June 30, 2014:

Retained earnings, July 1, 2013	$3,900,000
Net income	714,000
Cash dividends declared	100,000
Stock dividends declared	50,000

Prepare a retained earnings statement for the fiscal year ended June 30, 2014.

EE 11-7 *p. 512*

PE 11-7B Retained earnings statement

OBJ. 5

Noric Cruises Inc. reported the following results for the year ended October 31, 2014:

Retained earnings, November 1, 2013	$12,400,000
Net income	2,350,000
Cash dividends declared	175,000
Stock dividends declared	300,000

Prepare a retained earnings statement for the fiscal year ended October 31, 2014.

EE 11-8 *p. 518*

F·A·I

PE 11-8A Earnings per share

OBJ. 7

Financial statement data for the years ended December 31 for Dovetail Corporation are shown below.

	2014	2013
Net income	$448,750	$376,000
Preferred dividends	$40,000	$40,000
Average number of common shares outstanding	75,000 shares	60,000 shares

a. Determine the earnings per share for 2014 and 2013.

b. Does the change in the earnings per share from 2013 to 2014 indicate a favorable or an unfavorable trend?

EE 11-8 *p. 518*

F·A·I

PE 11-8B Earnings per share

OBJ. 7

Financial statement data for the years ended December 31 for Black Bull Inc. are shown below.

	2014	2013
Net income	$2,485,700	$1,538,000
Preferred dividends	$50,000	$50,000
Average number of common shares outstanding	115,000 shares	80,000 shares

a. Determine the earnings per share for 2014 and 2013.

b. Does the change in the earnings per share from 2013 to 2014 indicate a favorable or an unfavorable trend?

Exercises

EX 11-1 Dividends per share

OBJ. 2

✔ **Preferred stock, 1st year: $0.80**

Wallace Inc., a developer of radiology equipment, has stock outstanding as follows: 30,000 shares of cumulative preferred 2% stock, $90 par and 125,000 shares of $10 par common. During its first four years of operations, the following amounts were distributed as dividends:

first year, $24,000; second year, $81,000; third year, $92,000; fourth year, $139,000. Calculate the dividends per share on each class of stock for each of the four years.

EX 11-2 Dividends per share

OBJ. 2

✔ Preferred stock, 1st year: $0.90

Lightfoot Inc., a software development firm, has stock outstanding as follows: 40,000 shares of cumulative preferred 1% stock, $125 par, and 100,000 shares of $150 par common. During its first four years of operations, the following amounts were distributed as dividends: first year, $36,000; second year, $58,000; third year, $75,000; fourth year, $124,000. Calculate the dividends per share on each class of stock for each of the four years.

EX 11-3 Entries for issuing par stock

OBJ. 2

On February 25, Madison County Rocks Inc., a marble contractor, issued for cash 120,000 shares of $36 par common stock at $40, and on June 3, it issued for cash 50,000 shares of preferred stock, $8 par at $9.

a. Journalize the entries for February 25 and June 3.

b. What is the total amount invested (total paid-in capital) by all stockholders as of June 3?

EX 11-4 Entries for issuing no-par stock

OBJ. 2

On August 5, Synthetic Carpet Inc., a carpet wholesaler, issued for cash 500,000 shares of no-par common stock (with a stated value of $1) at $3, and on December 17, it issued for cash 5,000 shares of preferred stock, $180 par at $200.

a. Journalize the entries for August 5 and December 17, assuming that the common stock is to be credited with the stated value.

b. What is the total amount invested (total paid-in capital) by all stockholders as of December 17?

EX 11-5 Issuing stock for assets other than cash

OBJ. 2

On May 10, First Lift Corporation, a wholesaler of hydraulic lifts, acquired land in exchange for 3,600 shares of $4 par common stock with a current market price of $28. Journalize the entry to record the transaction.

EX 11-6 Selected stock transactions

OBJ. 2

Heavenly Sounds Corp., an electric guitar retailer, was organized by Mickey Blessing, John Frey, and Nancy Stein. The charter authorized 750,000 shares of common stock with a par of $20. The following transactions affecting stockholders' equity were completed during the first year of operations:

a. Issued 45,000 shares of stock at par to John Frey for cash.

b. Issued 400 shares of stock at par to Mickey Blessing for promotional services provided in connection with the organization of the corporation, and issued 60,000 shares of stock at par to Mickey Blessing for cash.

c. Purchased land and a building from Nancy Stein in exchange for stock issued at par. The building is mortgaged for $450,000 for 20 years at 4%, and there is accrued interest of $1,500 on the mortgage note at the time of the purchase. It is agreed that the land is to be priced at $150,000 and the building at $600,000, and that Nancy Stein's equity will be exchanged for stock at par. The corporation agreed to assume responsibility for paying the mortgage note and the accrued interest.

Journalize the entries to record the transactions.

EX 11-7 Issuing stock

OBJ. 2

Willow Creek Nursery, with an authorization of 75,000 shares of preferred stock and 200,000 shares of common stock, completed several transactions involving its stock on October 1, the first day of operations. The trial balance at the close of the day follows:

(Continued)

Cash	3,780,000	
Land	840,000	
Buildings	2,380,000	
Preferred 1% Stock, $80 par		2,800,000
Paid-In Capital in Excess of Par—Preferred Stock		420,000
Common Stock, $30 par		3,600,000
Paid-In Capital in Excess of Par—Common Stock		180,000
	7,000,000	7,000,000

All shares within each class of stock were sold at the same price. The preferred stock was issued in exchange for the land and buildings.

Journalize the two entries to record the transactions summarized in the trial balance.

EX 11-8 Issuing stock **OBJ. 2**

Workplace Products Inc., a wholesaler of office products, was organized on February 1 of the current year, with an authorization of 10,000 shares of preferred 2% stock, $120 par and 250,000 shares of $25 par common stock. The following selected transactions were completed during the first year of operations:

Feb. 1. Issued 180,000 shares of common stock at par for cash.

1. Issued 400 shares of common stock at par to an attorney in payment of legal fees for organizing the corporation.

Mar. 9. Issued 30,000 shares of common stock in exchange for land, buildings, and equipment with fair market prices of $200,000, $550,000, and $135,000, respectively.

Apr. 13. Issued 8,500 shares of preferred stock at $131 for cash.

Journalize the transactions.

EX 11-9 Entries for cash dividends **OBJ. 3**

The declaration, record, and payment dates in connection with a cash dividend of $187,500 on a corporation's common stock are July 10, August 9, and September 18. Journalize the entries required on each date.

EX 11-10 Entries for stock dividends **OBJ. 3**

✔ b. (1) $6,900,000
(3) $84,900,000

Healthy Living Co. is an HMO for businesses in the Seattle area. The following account balances appear on the balance sheet of Healthy Living Co.: Common stock (400,000 shares authorized; 300,000 shares issued), $18 par, $5,400,000; Paid-in capital in excess of par—common stock, $1,500,000; and Retained earnings, $78,000,000. The board of directors declared a 5% stock dividend when the market price of the stock was $40 a share. Healthy Living Co. reported no income or loss for the current year.

a. Journalize the entries to record (1) the declaration of the dividend, capitalizing an amount equal to market value, and (2) the issuance of the stock certificates.

b. Determine the following amounts before the stock dividend was declared: (1) total paid-in capital, (2) total retained earnings, and (3) total stockholders' equity.

c. Determine the following amounts after the stock dividend was declared and closing entries were recorded at the end of the year: (1) total paid-in capital, (2) total retained earnings, and (3) total stockholders' equity.

EX 11-11 Treasury stock transactions **OBJ. 4**

✔ b. $118,000 credit

Crystal Lake Inc. bottles and distributes spring water. On March 4 of the current year, Crystal Lake reacquired 33,000 shares of its common stock at $84 per share. On August 27, Crystal Lake Inc. sold 25,000 of the reacquired shares at $90 per share. The remaining 8,000 shares were sold at $80 per share on November 11.

a. Journalize the transactions of March 4, August 27, and November 11.

b. What is the balance in Paid-In Capital from Sale of Treasury Stock on December 31 of the current year?

c. For what reasons might Crystal Lake have purchased the treasury stock?

EX 11-12 Treasury stock transactions

OBJ. 4, 5

✔ b. $153,000 credit

Irrigate Smart Inc. develops and produces spraying equipment for lawn maintenance and industrial uses. On February 17 of the current year, Irrigate Smart Inc. reacquired 50,000 shares of its common stock at $12 per share. On April 29, 31,000 of the reacquired shares were sold at $15 per share, and on July 31, 12,000 of the reacquired shares were sold at $17.

a. Journalize the transactions of February 17, April 29, and July 31.

b. What is the balance in Paid-In Capital from Sale of Treasury Stock on December 31 of the current year?

c. What is the balance in Treasury Stock on December 31 of the current year?

d. How will the balance in Treasury Stock be reported on the balance sheet?

EX 11-13 Treasury stock transactions

OBJ. 4, 5

✔ b. $55,500 credit

Biscayne Bay Water Inc. bottles and distributes spring water. On May 14 of the current year, Biscayne Bay Water Inc. reacquired 23,500 shares of its common stock at $75 per share. On September 6, Biscayne Bay Water Inc. sold 14,000 of the reacquired shares at $81 per share. The remaining 9,500 shares were sold at $72 per share on November 30.

a. Journalize the transactions of May 14, September 6, and November 30.

b. What is the balance in Paid-In Capital from Sale of Treasury Stock on December 31 of the current year?

c. Where will the balance in Paid-In Capital from Sale of Treasury Stock be reported on the balance sheet?

d. For what reasons might Biscayne Bay Water Inc. have purchased the treasury stock?

EX 11-14 Reporting paid-in capital

OBJ. 5

✔ Total paid-in capital, $13,615,000

The following accounts and their balances were selected from the unadjusted trial balance of Point Loma Group Inc., a freight forwarder, at October 31, the end of the current fiscal year:

Common Stock, no par, $14 stated value	$ 4,480,000
Paid-In Capital from Sale of Treasury Stock	45,000
Paid-In Capital in Excess of Par—Preferred Stock	210,000
Paid-In Capital in Excess of Stated Value—Common Stock	480,000
Preferred 2% Stock, $120 par	8,400,000
Retained Earnings	39,500,000

Prepare the Paid-In Capital portion of the Stockholders' Equity section of the balance sheet using Method 1 of Exhibit 4. There are 375,000 shares of common stock authorized and 85,000 shares of preferred stock authorized.

EX 11-15 Stockholders' Equity section of balance sheet

OBJ. 5

✔ Total stockholders' equity, $23,676,000

The following accounts and their balances appear in the ledger of Goodale Properties Inc. on June 30 of the current year:

Common Stock, $45 par	$ 3,060,000
Paid-In Capital from Sale of Treasury Stock	115,000
Paid-In Capital in Excess of Par—Common Stock	272,000
Retained Earnings	20,553,000
Treasury Stock	324,000

Prepare the Stockholders' Equity section of the balance sheet as of June 30. Eighty thousand shares of common stock are authorized, and 9,000 shares have been reacquired.

EX 11-16 Stockholders' Equity section of balance sheet

OBJ. 5

✔ **Total stockholders' equity, $89,100,000**

Specialty Auto Racing Inc. retails racing products for BMWs, Porsches, and Ferraris. The following accounts and their balances appear in the ledger of Specialty Auto Racing Inc. on July 31, the end of the current year:

Common Stock, $36 par	$10,080,000
Paid-In Capital from Sale of Treasury Stock—Common	340,000
Paid-In Capital in Excess of Par—Common Stock	420,000
Paid-In Capital in Excess of Par—Preferred Stock	384,000
Preferred 1% Stock, $150 par	7,200,000
Retained Earnings	71,684,000
Treasury Stock—Common	1,008,000

Fifty thousand shares of preferred and 300,000 shares of common stock are authorized. There are 24,000 shares of common stock held as treasury stock.

Prepare the Stockholders' Equity section of the balance sheet as of July 31, the end of the current year using Method 1 of Exhibit 4.

EX 11-17 Retained earnings statement

OBJ. 5

✔ **Retained earnings, January 31, $55,040,000**

Atlas Pumps Corporation, a manufacturer of industrial pumps, reports the following results for the year ended January 31, 2014:

Retained earnings, February 1, 2013	$48,110,000
Net income	9,330,000
Cash dividends declared	2,000,000
Stock dividends declared	400,000

Prepare a retained earnings statement for the fiscal year ended January 31, 2014.

EX 11-18 Stockholders' Equity section of balance sheet

OBJ. 5

✔ **Corrected total stockholders' equity, $122,800,000**

List the errors in the following Stockholders' Equity section of the balance sheet prepared as of the end of the current year:

Stockholders' Equity

Paid-in capital:		
Preferred 2% stock, $80 par		
(125,000 shares authorized and issued)	$10,000,000	
Excess of issue price over par	500,000	$ 10,500,000
Retained earnings		96,700,000
Treasury stock (75,000 shares at cost)		1,755,000
Dividends payable		430,000
Total paid-in capital		$ 109,385,000
Common stock, $20 par (1,000,000 shares authorized, 825,000 shares issued)		17,655,000
Organizing costs		300,000
Total stockholders' equity		$127,340,000

EX 11-19 Statement of stockholders' equity

OBJ. 5

✔ **Total stockholders' equity, Dec. 31, $21,587,000**

SPREADSHEET

The stockholders' equity T accounts of I-Cards Inc. for the current fiscal year ended December 31, 2014, are as follows. Prepare a statement of stockholders' equity for the fiscal year ended December 31, 2014.

COMMON STOCK

	Jan. 1	Balance	4,800,000
	Apr. 14	Issued 30,000 shares	1,200,000
	Dec. 31	Balance	6,000,000

PAID-IN CAPITAL IN EXCESS OF PAR

			Jan. 1	Balance	960,000
			Apr. 14	Issued 30,000 shares	300,000
			Dec. 31	Balance	1,260,000

TREASURY STOCK

Aug. 7	Purchased 12,000 shares	552,000			

RETAINED EARNINGS

Mar. 31	Dividend	69,000	Jan. 1	Balance	11,375,000
June 30	Dividend	69,000	Dec. 31	Closing (net income)	3,780,000
Sept. 30	Dividend	69,000			
Dec. 31	Dividend	69,000	Dec. 31	Balance	14,879,000

EX 11-20 Effect of stock split **OBJ. 6**

Ironhaus Restaurant Corporation wholesales ovens and ranges to restaurants throughout the Southwest. Ironhaus Restaurant Corporation, which had 40,000 shares of common stock outstanding, declared a 4-for-1 stock split.

a. What will be the number of shares outstanding after the split?

b. If the common stock had a market price of $300 per share before the stock split, what would be an approximate market price per share after the split?

EX 11-21 Effect of cash dividend and stock split **OBJ. 3, 6**

Indicate whether the following actions would (+) increase, (–) decrease, or (0) not affect Indigo Inc.'s total assets, liabilities, and stockholders' equity:

	Assets	Liabilities	Stockholders' Equity
(1) Authorizing and issuing stock certificates in a stock split	_____	_____	_____
(2) Declaring a stock dividend	_____	_____	_____
(3) Issuing stock certificates for the stock dividend declared in (2)	_____	_____	_____
(4) Declaring a cash dividend	_____	_____	_____
(5) Paying the cash dividend declared in (4)	_____	_____	_____

EX 11-22 Selected dividend transactions, stock split **OBJ. 3, 6**

Selected transactions completed by Canyon Ferry Boating Corporation during the current fiscal year are as follows:

Jan. 8. Split the common stock 2 for 1 and reduced the par from $80 to $40 per share. After the split, there were 150,000 common shares outstanding.

Apr. 30. Declared semiannual dividends of $0.75 on 18,000 shares of preferred stock and $0.28 on the common stock payable on July 1.

July 1. Paid the cash dividends.

Oct. 31. Declared semiannual dividends of $0.75 on the preferred stock and $0.14 on the common stock (before the stock dividend). In addition, a 5% common stock dividend was declared on the common stock outstanding. The fair market value of the common stock is estimated at $52.

Dec. 31. Paid the cash dividends and issued the certificates for the common stock dividend.

Journalize the transactions.

EX 11-23 EPS **OBJ. 7**

F·A·I

Junkyard Arts, Inc., had earnings of $316,000 for 2014. The company had 40,000 shares of common stock outstanding during the year. In addition, the company issued 15,000 shares of $50 par value preferred stock on January 9, 2014. The preferred stock has a

(Continued)

dividend of $1.60 per share. There were no transactions in either common or preferred stock during 2014.

Determine the basic earnings per share for Junkyard Arts.

EX 11-24 EPS **OBJ. 7**

F·A·I

Pacific Gas and Electric Company is a large gas and electric utility operating in northern and central California. Three recent years of financial data for Pacific Gas and Electric Company are as follows:

	Fiscal Years Ended (in millions)		
	Year 3	**Year 2**	**Year 1**
Net income	$1,105	$1,208	$1,312
Preferred dividends	$14	$14	$14
Average number of common shares outstanding	382	368	357

a. Determine the earnings per share for fiscal Year 3, Year 2, and Year 1. Round to the nearest cent.

b. Evaluate the growth in earnings per share for the three years in comparison to the growth in net income for the three years.

EX 11-25 EPS **OBJ. 7**

F·A·I

For a recent year, OfficeMax and Staples are two companies competing in the retail office supply business. OfficeMax had a net income of $71,155,000, while Staples had a net income of $881,948,000. OfficeMax had preferred stock of $30,901,000 with preferred dividends of $2,527,000. Staples had no preferred stock. The average outstanding common shares for each company were as follows:

	Average Number of Common Shares Outstanding
OfficeMax	84,908,000
Staples	715,596,000

a. Determine the earnings per share for each company. Round to the nearest cent.

b. Evaluate the relative profitability of the two companies.

Problems Series A

PR 11-1A Dividends on preferred and common stock **OBJ. 2**

✔ 1. Common dividends in 2011: $48,000

SPREADSHEET

Partridge Theatre Inc. owns and operates movie theaters throughout Texas and Oklahoma. Partridge Theatre Inc. has declared the following annual dividends over a six-year period: 2009, $18,000; 2010, $40,000; 2011, $80,000; 2012, $120,000; 2013, $150,000; and 2014, $228,000. During the entire period ended December 31 of each year, the outstanding stock of the company was composed of 40,000 shares of cumulative, preferred 1% stock, $75 par, and 200,000 shares of common stock, $5 par.

Instructions

1. Calculate the total dividends and the per-share dividends declared on each class of stock for each of the six years. There were no dividends in arrears on January 1, 2009. Summarize the data in tabular form, using the following column headings:

		Preferred Dividends		Common Dividends	
Year	**Total Dividends**	**Total**	**Per Share**	**Total**	**Per Share**
2009	$ 18,000				
2010	40,000				
2011	80,000				
2012	120,000				
2013	150,000				
2014	228,000				

2. Calculate the average annual dividend per share for each class of stock for the six-year period.
3. Assuming a market price per share of $125 for the preferred stock and $7.60 for the common stock, calculate the average annual percentage return on initial shareholders' investment, based on the average annual dividend per share (a) for preferred stock and (b) for common stock.

PR 11-2A Stock transactions for corporate expansion

OBJ. 2

GENERAL LEDGER

On December 1 of the current year, the following accounts and their balances appear in the ledger of Latte Corp., a coffee processor:

Preferred 2% Stock, $50 par (250,000 shares authorized, 80,000 shares issued)	$ 4,000,000
Paid-In Capital in Excess of Par—Preferred Stock	560,000
Common Stock, $35 par (1,000,000 shares authorized, 400,000 shares issued)	14,000,000
Paid-In Capital in Excess of Par—Common Stock	1,200,000
Retained Earnings	180,000,000

At the annual stockholders' meeting on March 31, the board of directors presented a plan for modernizing and expanding plant operations at a cost of approximately $11,000,000. The plan provided (a) that a building, valued at $3,375,000, and the land on which it is located, valued at $1,500,000, be acquired in accordance with preliminary negotiations by the issuance of 125,000 shares of common stock, (b) that 40,000 shares of the unissued preferred stock be issued through an underwriter, and (c) that the corporation borrow $4,000,000. The plan was approved by the stockholders and accomplished by the following transactions:

May 11. Issued 125,000 shares of common stock in exchange for land and a building, according to the plan.

20. Issued 40,000 shares of preferred stock, receiving $52 per share in cash.

31. Borrowed $4,000,000 from Laurel National, giving a 5% mortgage note.

Instructions

Journalize the entries to record the May transactions.

PR 11-3A Selected stock transactions

OBJ. 2, 3, 4

✔ **f. Cash dividends, $71,750**

GENERAL LEDGER

The following selected accounts appear in the ledger of Orion Inc. on February 1, 2014, the beginning of the current fiscal year:

Preferred 1% Stock, $40 par (75,000 shares authorized, 45,000 shares issued)	$ 1,800,000
Paid-In Capital in Excess of Par—Preferred Stock	72,000
Common Stock, $12 par (2,000,000 shares authorized, 1,250,000 shares issued)	15,000,000
Paid-In Capital in Excess of Par—Common Stock	3,750,000
Retained Earnings	45,450,000

During the year, the corporation completed a number of transactions affecting the stockholders' equity. They are summarized as follows:

a. Issued 360,000 shares of common stock at $22, receiving cash.
b. Issued 14,000 shares of preferred 1% stock at $43.
c. Purchased 66,000 shares of treasury common for $18 per share.
d. Sold 51,000 shares of treasury common for $21 per share.
e. Sold 10,000 shares of treasury common for $16 per share.
f. Declared cash dividends of $0.40 per share on preferred stock and $0.03 per share on common stock.
g. Paid the cash dividends.

(Continued)

Instructions

Journalize the entries to record the transactions. Identify each entry by letter.

PR 11-4A Entries for selected corporate transactions

OBJ. 2, 3, 4, 5

✔ 4. Total stockholders' equity, $44,436,200

GENERAL LEDGER

SPREADSHEET

Morrow Enterprises Inc. manufactures bathroom fixtures. The stockholders' equity accounts of Morrow Enterprises Inc., with balances on January 1, 2014, are as follows:

Common Stock, $20 stated value (500,000 shares authorized, 375,000 shares issued)	$ 7,500,000
Paid-In Capital in Excess of Stated Value—Common Stock	825,000
Retained Earnings	33,600,000
Treasury Stock (25,000 shares, at cost)	450,000

The following selected transactions occurred during the year:

Jan. 22. Paid cash dividends of $0.08 per share on the common stock. The dividend had been properly recorded when declared on December 1 of the preceding fiscal year for $28,000.

Apr. 10. Issued 75,000 shares of common stock for $24 per share.

June 6. Sold all of the treasury stock for $26 per share.

July 5. Declared a 4% stock dividend on common stock, to be capitalized at the market price of the stock, which is $25 per share.

Aug. 15. Issued the certificates for the dividend declared on July 5.

Nov. 23. Purchased 30,000 shares of treasury stock for $19 per share.

Dec. 28. Declared a $0.10-per-share dividend on common stock.

31. Closed the credit balance of the income summary account, $1,125,000.

31. Closed the two dividends accounts to Retained Earnings.

Instructions

1. Enter the January 1 balances in T accounts for the stockholders' equity accounts listed. Also prepare T accounts for the following: Paid-In Capital from Sale of Treasury Stock; Stock Dividends Distributable; Stock Dividends; Cash Dividends.
2. Journalize the entries to record the transactions, and post to the eight selected accounts.
3. Prepare a retained earnings statement for the year ended December 31, 2014.
4. Prepare the Stockholders' Equity section of the December 31, 2014, balance sheet.

PR 11-5A Entries for selected corporate transactions

OBJ. 2, 3, 4, 6

✔ Oct. 1, cash dividends, $202,800

GENERAL LEDGER

Selected transactions completed by Primo Discount Corporation during the current fiscal year are as follows:

Jan. 9. Split the common stock 3 for 1 and reduced the par from $75 to $25 per share. After the split, there were 1,200,000 common shares outstanding.

Feb. 28. Purchased 40,000 shares of the corporation's own common stock at $28, recording the stock at cost.

May 1. Declared semiannual dividends of $0.80 on 75,000 shares of preferred stock and $0.12 on the common stock to stockholders of record on June 1, payable on July 10.

July 10. Paid the cash dividends.

Sept. 7. Sold 30,000 shares of treasury stock at $34, receiving cash.

Oct. 1. Declared semiannual dividends of $0.80 on the preferred stock and $0.12 on the common stock (before the stock dividend). In addition, a 2% common stock dividend was declared on the common stock outstanding. The fair market value of the common stock is estimated at $36.

Dec. 1. Paid the cash dividends and issued the certificates for the common stock dividend.

Instructions

Journalize the transactions.

Problems Series B

PR 11-1B Dividends on preferred and common stock **OBJ. 2**

✔ 1. Common dividends in 2011: $25,000

SPREADSHEET

Yosemite Bike Corp. manufactures mountain bikes and distributes them through retail outlets in California, Oregon, and Washington. Yosemite Bike Corp. has declared the following annual dividends over a six-year period ended December 31 of each year: 2009, $24,000; 2010, $10,000; 2011, $126,000; 2012, $100,000; 2013, $125,000; and 2014, $125,000. During the entire period, the outstanding stock of the company was composed of 25,000 shares of cumulative preferred 2% stock, $90 par, and 100,000 shares of common stock, $4 par.

Instructions

1. Determine the total dividends and the per-share dividends declared on each class of stock for each of the six years. There were no dividends in arrears on January 1, 2009. Summarize the data in tabular form, using the following column headings:

		Preferred Dividends		Common Dividends	
Year	**Total Dividends**	**Total**	**Per Share**	**Total**	**Per Share**
2009	$ 24,000				
2010	10,000				
2011	126,000				
2012	100,000				
2013	125,000				
2014	125,000				

2. Determine the average annual dividend per share for each class of stock for the six-year period.
3. Assuming a market price of $100 for the preferred stock and $5 for the common stock, calculate the average annual percentage return on initial shareholders' investment, based on the average annual dividend per share (a) for preferred stock and (b) for common stock.

PR 11-2B Stock transaction for corporate expansion **OBJ. 2**

GENERAL LEDGER

Pulsar Optics produces medical lasers for use in hospitals. The accounts and their balances appear in the ledger of Pulsar Optics on April 30 of the current year as follows:

Preferred 1% Stock, $120 par (300,000 shares authorized, 36,000 shares issued)	$ 4,320,000
Paid-In Capital in Excess of Par—Preferred Stock	180,000
Common Stock, $15 par (2,000,000 shares authorized, 1,400,000 shares issued)	21,000,000
Paid-In Capital in Excess of Par—Common Stock	3,500,000
Retained Earnings	78,000,000

At the annual stockholders' meeting on August 5, the board of directors presented a plan for modernizing and expanding plant operations at a cost of approximately $9,000,000. The plan provided (a) that the corporation borrow $1,500,000, (b) that 20,000 shares of the unissued preferred stock be issued through an underwriter, and (c) that a building, valued at $4,150,000, and the land on which it is located, valued at $800,000, be acquired in accordance with preliminary negotiations by the issuance of 300,000 shares of common stock. The plan was approved by the stockholders and accomplished by the following transactions:

Oct. 9. Borrowed $1,500,000 from St. Peter City Bank, giving a 4% mortgage note.

17. Issued 20,000 shares of preferred stock, receiving $126 per share in cash.

28. Issued 300,000 shares of common stock in exchange for land and a building, according to the plan.

Instructions

Journalize the entries to record the October transactions.

PR 11-3B Selected stock transactions

OBJ. 2, 3, 4

✔ f. Cash dividends, $234,775

GENERAL LEDGER

Diamondback Welding & Fabrication Corporation sells and services pipe welding equipment in Illinois. The following selected accounts appear in the ledger of Diamondback Welding & Fabrication Corporation on July 1, 2014, the beginning of the current fiscal year:

Preferred 2% Stock, $80 par (100,000 shares authorized, 60,000 shares issued)	$ 4,800,000
Paid-In Capital in Excess of Par—Preferred Stock	210,000
Common Stock, $9 par (3,000,000 shares authorized, 1,750,000 shares issued)	15,750,000
Paid-In Capital in Excess of Par—Common Stock	1,400,000
Retained Earnings	52,840,000

During the year, the corporation completed a number of transactions affecting the stockholders' equity. They are summarized as follows:

a. Purchased 87,500 shares of treasury common for $8 per share.
b. Sold 55,000 shares of treasury common for $11 per share.
c. Issued 20,000 shares of preferred 2% stock at $84.
d. Issued 400,000 shares of common stock at $13, receiving cash.
e. Sold 18,000 shares of treasury common for $7.50 per share.
f. Declared cash dividends of $1.60 per share on preferred stock and $0.05 per share on common stock.
g. Paid the cash dividends.

Instructions

Journalize the entries to record the transactions. Identify each entry by letter.

PR 11-4B Entries for selected corporate transactions

OBJ. 2, 3, 4, 5

✔ 4. Total stockholders' equity, $11,262,432

SPREADSHEET

GENERAL LEDGER

Nav-Go Enterprises Inc. produces aeronautical navigation equipment. The stockholders' equity accounts of Nav-Go Enterprises Inc., with balances on January 1, 2014, are as follows:

Common Stock, $5 stated value (900,000 shares authorized, 620,000 shares issued)	$3,100,000
Paid-In Capital in Excess of Stated Value—Common Stock	1,240,000
Retained Earnings	4,875,000
Treasury Stock (48,000 shares, at cost)	288,000

The following selected transactions occurred during the year:

Jan. 15. Paid cash dividends of $0.06 per share on the common stock. The dividend had been properly recorded when declared on December 1 of the preceding fiscal year for $34,320.

Mar. 15. Sold all of the treasury stock for $6.75 per share.

Apr. 13. Issued 200,000 shares of common stock for $8 per share.

June 14. Declared a 3% stock dividend on common stock, to be capitalized at the market price of the stock, which is $7.50 per share.

July 16. Issued the certificates for the dividend declared on June 14.

Oct. 30. Purchased 50,000 shares of treasury stock for $6 per share.

Dec. 30. Declared a $0.08-per-share dividend on common stock.

31. Closed the credit balance of the income summary account, $775,000.

31. Closed the two dividends accounts to Retained Earnings.

Instructions

1. Enter the January 1 balances in T accounts for the stockholders' equity accounts listed. Also prepare T accounts for the following: Paid-In Capital from Sale of Treasury Stock; Stock Dividends Distributable; Stock Dividends; Cash Dividends.
2. Journalize the entries to record the transactions, and post to the eight selected accounts.

3. Prepare a retained earnings statement for the year ended December 31, 2014.
4. Prepare the Stockholders' Equity section of the December 31, 2014, balance sheet.

PR 11-5B Entries for selected corporate transactions **OBJ. 2, 3, 4, 6**

✔ Sept. 1, Cash dividends, $95,200

GENERAL LEDGER

West Yellowstone Outfitters Corporation manufactures and distributes leisure clothing. Selected transactions completed by West Yellowstone Outfitters during the current fiscal year are as follows:

Jan. 15. Split the common stock 4 for 1 and reduced the par from $120 to $30 per share. After the split, there were 800,000 common shares outstanding.

Mar. 1. Declared semiannual dividends of $0.25 on 100,000 shares of preferred stock and $0.07 on the 800,000 shares of $30 par common stock to stockholders of record on March 31, payable on April 30.

Apr. 30. Paid the cash dividends.

May 31. Purchased 60,000 shares of the corporation's own common stock at $32, recording the stock at cost.

Aug. 17. Sold 40,000 shares of treasury stock at $38, receiving cash.

Sept. 1. Declared semiannual dividends of $0.25 on the preferred stock and $0.09 on the common stock (before the stock dividend). In addition, a 1% common stock dividend was declared on the common stock outstanding, to be capitalized at the fair market value of the common stock, which is estimated at $40.

Oct. 31. Paid the cash dividends and issued the certificates for the common stock dividend.

Instructions

Journalize the transactions.

Cases & Projects

CP 11-1 Board of directors' actions

Bernie Ebbers, the CEO of WorldCom, a major telecommunications company, was having personal financial troubles. Ebbers pledged a large stake of his WorldCom stock as security for some personal loans. As the price of WorldCom stock sank, Ebbers' bankers threatened to sell his stock in order to protect their loans. To avoid having his stock sold, Ebbers asked the board of directors of WorldCom to loan him nearly $400 million of corporate assets at 2.5% interest to pay off his bankers. The board agreed to lend him the money.

Comment on the decision of the board of directors in this situation.

CP 11-2 Ethics and professional conduct in business

Lou Hoskins and Shirley Crothers are organizing Red Lodge Metals Unlimited Inc. to undertake a high-risk gold-mining venture in Canada. Lou and Shirley tentatively plan to request authorization for 400,000,000 shares of common stock to be sold to the general public. Lou and Shirley have decided to establish par of $0.03 per share in order to appeal to a wide variety of potential investors. Lou and Shirley feel that investors would be more willing to invest in the company if they received a large quantity of shares for what might appear to be a "bargain" price.

Discuss whether Lou and Shirley are behaving in a professional manner.

CP 11-3 Issuing stock

Epstein Engineering Inc. began operations on January 5, 2014, with the issuance of 500,000 shares of $80 par common stock. The sole stockholders of Epstein Engineering Inc. are Barb Abrams and Dr. Amber Epstein, who organized Epstein Engineering Inc. with the objective of developing a new flu vaccine. Dr. Epstein claims that the flu vaccine, which is nearing the final development stage, will protect individuals against

(*Continued*)

90% of the flu types that have been medically identified. To complete the project, Epstein Engineering Inc. needs $25,000,000 of additional funds. The local banks have been unwilling to loan the funds because of the lack of sufficient collateral and the riskiness of the business.

The following is a conversation between Barb Abrams, the chief executive officer of Epstein Engineering Inc., and Amber Epstein, the leading researcher.

Barb: What are we going to do? The banks won't loan us any more money, and we've got to have $25 million to complete the project. We are so close! It would be a disaster to quit now. The only thing I can think of is to issue additional stock. Do you have any suggestions?

Amber: I guess you're right. But if the banks won't loan us any more money, how do you think we can find any investors to buy stock?

Barb: I've been thinking about that. What if we promise the investors that we will pay them 5% of net sales until they have received an amount equal to what they paid for the stock?

Amber: What happens when we pay back the $25 million? Do the investors get to keep the stock? If they do, it'll dilute our ownership.

Barb: How about, if after we pay back the $25 million, we make them turn in their stock for $120 per share? That's one and one-half times what they paid for it, plus they would have already gotten all their money back. That's a $120 profit per share for the investors.

Amber: It could work. We get our money, but don't have to pay any interest, dividends, or the $80 per share until we start generating net sales. At the same time, the investors could get their money back plus $120 per share profit.

Barb: We'll need current financial statements for the new investors. I'll get our accountant working on them and contact our attorney to draw up a legally binding contract for the new investors. Yes, this could work.

In late 2014, the attorney and the various regulatory authorities approved the new stock offering, and 312,500 shares of common stock were privately sold to new investors at the stock's par of $80.

In preparing financial statements for 2014, Barb Abrams and Dan Fisher, the controller for Epstein Engineering Inc., have the following conversation:

Dan: Barb, I've got a problem.

Barb: What's that, Dan?

Dan: Issuing common stock to raise that additional $25 million was a great idea. But . . .

Barb: But what?

Dan: I've got to prepare the 2014 annual financial statements, and I am not sure how to classify the common stock.

Barb: What do you mean? It's common stock.

Dan: I'm not so sure. I called the auditor and explained how we are contractually obligated to pay the new stockholders 5% of net sales until $80 per share is paid. Then, we may be obligated to pay them $120 per share.

Barb: So . . .

Dan: So the auditor thinks that we should classify the additional issuance of $25 million as debt, not stock! And, if we put the $25 million on the balance sheet as debt, we will violate our other loan agreements with the banks. And, if these agreements are violated, the banks may call in all our debt immediately. If they do that, we are in deep trouble. We'll probably have to file for bankruptcy. We just don't have the cash to pay off the banks.

1. Discuss the arguments for and against classifying the issuance of the $25 million of stock as debt.
2. What do you think might be a practical solution to this classification problem?

CP 11-4 Interpret stock exchange listing

F·A·I

The following stock exchange data for Microsoft Corporation were taken from the Yahoo! Finance Web site on February 29, 2012:

Microsoft Corporation (MSFT)

Last Trade:	31.74	Prev. Clos:	31.87
Trade Time:	4:00 PM EST	1y Target Est:	31.96
		Day's Range:	31.61–32.00
		52wk Range:	23.65–31.93
		Volume:	58,178,568
		Div & Yield:	0.80 (2.60%)

a. If you owned 500 shares of Mircosoft, what amount would you receive as a quarterly dividend?

b. Compute the percentage decrease in price from the Previous Close to the Last Trade. Round to two decimal places.

c. What is Microsoft's percentage change in market price from the 52-week low to the Previous Close on February 28, 2012? Round to one decimal place.

d. If you bought 500 shares of GE at the Last Trade price on February 29, 2012, how much would it cost, and who gets the money?

CP 11-5 Dividends

Motion Designs Inc. has paid quarterly cash dividends since 2003. These dividends have steadily increased from $0.05 per share to the latest dividend declaration of $0.50 per share. The board of directors would like to continue this trend and is hesitant to suspend or decrease the amount of quarterly dividends. Unfortunately, sales dropped sharply in the fourth quarter of 2014 because of worsening economic conditions and increased competition. As a result, the board is uncertain as to whether it should declare a dividend for the last quarter of 2014.

On October 1, 2014, Motion Designs Inc. borrowed $4,000,000 from Valley National Bank to use in modernizing its retail stores and to expand its product line in reaction to its competition. The terms of the 10-year, 6% loan require Motion Designs Inc. to:

a. Pay monthly interest on the last day of the month.

b. Pay $400,000 of the principal each October 1, beginning in 2015.

c. Maintain a current ratio (current assets/current liabilities) of 2.

d. Maintain a minimum balance (a compensating balance) of $100,000 in its Valley National Bank account.

On December 31, 2014, $1,000,000 of the $4,000,000 loan had been disbursed in modernization of the retail stores and in expansion of the product line. Motion Designs Inc.'s balance sheet as of December 31, 2014, is shown below.

Motion Designs Inc.
Balance Sheet
December 31, 2014

Assets			
Current assets:			
Cash		$ 250,000	
Marketable securities		3,000,000	
Accounts receivable	$ 800,000		
Less allowance for doubtful accounts	50,000	750,000	
Merchandise inventory		2,980,000	
Prepaid expenses		20,000	
Total current assets			$ 7,000,000
Property, plant, and equipment:			
Land		$1,500,000	
Buildings	$5,050,000		
Less accumulated depreciation	1,140,000	3,910,000	
Equipment	$3,320,000		
Less accumulated depreciation	730,000	2,590,000	
Total property, plant, and equipment			8,000,000
Total assets			$15,000,000

(Continued)

Liabilities			
Current liabilities:			
Accounts payable	$1,590,000		
Notes payable (Valley National Bank)	400,000		
Salaries payable	10,000		
Total current liabilities		$2,000,000	
Long-term liabilities:			
Notes payable (Valley National Bank)		3,600,000	
Total liabilities			$ 5,600,000
Stockholders' Equity			
Paid-in capital:			
Common stock, $25 par (200,000 shares authorized, 180,000 shares issued)	$4,500,000		
Excess of issue price over par	270,000		
Total paid-in capital		$4,770,000	
Retained earnings		4,630,000	
Total stockholders' equity			9,400,000
Total liabilities and stockholders' equity			$15,000,000

The board of directors is scheduled to meet January 10, 2015, to discuss the results of operations for 2014 and to consider the declaration of dividends for the fourth quarter of 2014. The chairman of the board has asked for your advice on the declaration of dividends.

1. What factors should the board consider in deciding whether to declare a cash dividend?
2. The board is considering the declaration of a stock dividend instead of a cash dividend. Discuss the issuance of a stock dividend from the point of view of (a) a stockholder and (b) the board of directors.

CP 11-6 Profiling a corporation

Group Project

Internet Project

Select a public corporation you are familiar with or which interests you. Using the Internet, develop a short (1 to 2 pages) profile of the corporation. Include in your profile the following information:

1. Name of the corporation.
2. State of incorporation.
3. Nature of its operations.
4. Total assets for the most recent balance sheet.
5. Total revenues for the most recent income statement.
6. Net income for the most recent income statement.
7. Classes of stock outstanding.
8. Market price of the stock outstanding.
9. High and low price of the stock for the past year.
10. Dividends paid for each share of stock during the past year.

In groups of three or four, discuss each corporate profile. Select one of the corporations, assuming that your group has $100,000 to invest in its stock. Summarize why your group selected the corporation it did and how financial accounting information may have affected your decision. Keep track of the performance of your corporation's stock for the remainder of the term.

Note: Most major corporations maintain "home pages" on the Internet. This home page provides a variety of information on the corporation and often includes the corporation's financial statements. In addition, the New York Stock Exchange Web site **(http://www.nyse.com)** includes links to the home pages of many listed companies that can be assessed by clicking on "Listings Directory." Financial statements can also be accessed using EDGAR, the electronic archives of financial statements filed with the Securities and Exchange Commission (SEC).

SEC documents can also be retrieved using the EdgarScan™ service at **http://www.sec.gov/edgar/searchedgar/companysearch.html.** To obtain annual report information, key in a company name in the appropriate space. Edgar will list the reports available to you for the company you've selected. Select the most recent annual report filing, identified as a 10-K or 10-K405.

CHAPTER 12

Long-Term Liabilities: Bonds and Notes

Dick's Sporting Goods

Most of us don't have enough money in our bank accounts to buy a house or a car by simply writing a check. Just imagine if you had to save the entire purchase price of a house before you could buy it! To help us make these types of purchases, banks will typically lend us the money, as long as we agree to repay the loan with interest in smaller future payments. Loans such as this, or long-term debt, allow us to purchase assets such as houses and cars today, which benefit us over the long term.

The use of debt can also help a business reach its objectives. Most businesses have to borrow money in order to acquire assets that they will use to generate income. For example, in 1948 Dick Stack borrowed $300 from his grandmother to start a sporting goods store in Binghamton, New York. Over the years the business grew, and in the early 1990s, **Dick's Sporting Goods** used long-term debt to transform itself from a small business to a Fortune 500 company with over 450 stores across the United States.

While debt can help companies like Dick's Sporting Goods grow to achieve financial success, too much debt can be a financial burden that may even lead to bankruptcy. Just like individuals, businesses must manage debt wisely. In this chapter, we will discuss the nature of, accounting for, analysis of, and investments in long-term debt.

Learning Objectives

After studying this chapter, you should be able to: *Example Exercises*

OBJ 1 Compute the potential impact of long-term borrowing on earnings per share.
Financing Corporations — EE 12-1

OBJ 2 Describe the characteristics and terminology of bonds payable.
Nature of Bonds Payable
- Bond Characteristics and Terminology
- Proceeds from Issuing Bonds

OBJ 3 Journalize entries for bonds payable.
Accounting for Bonds Payable
- Bonds Issued at Face Amount
- Bonds Issued at a Discount — EE 12-2
- Amortizing a Bond Discount — EE 12-3
- Bonds Issued at a Premium — EE 12-4
- Amortizing a Bond Premium — EE 12-5
- Bond Redemption — EE 12-6

OBJ 4 Describe and illustrate the accounting for installment notes.
Installment Notes
- Issuing an Installment Note
- Annual Payments — EE 12-7

OBJ 5 Describe and illustrate the reporting of long-term liabilities, including bonds and notes payable.
Reporting Long-Term Liabilities

OBJ 6 Describe and illustrate how the number of times interest charges are earned is used to evaluate a company's financial condition.
Financial Analysis and Interpretation: Number of Times Interest Charges Are Earned — EE 12-8

At a Glance 12 Page 563

OBJ 1 Compute the potential impact of long-term borrowing on earnings per share.

Financing Corporations

Corporations finance their operations using the following sources:

1. Short-term debt, such as purchasing goods or services on account.
2. Long-term debt, such as issuing bonds or notes payable.
3. Equity, such as issuing common or preferred stock.

Short-term debt, including the purchase of goods and services on account and the issuance of short-term notes payable, was discussed in Chapter 10. Issuing equity in the form of common or preferred stock was discussed in Chapter 11. This chapter focuses on the use of long-term debt such as bonds and notes payable to finance a company's operations.

A **bond** is a form of an interest-bearing note. Like a note, a bond requires periodic interest payments, with the face amount to be repaid at the maturity date. As creditors of the corporation, bondholder claims on the corporation's assets rank ahead of stockholders.

To illustrate the effects of long-term financing, assume Huckadee Corporation is considering the following plans to issue debt and equity:

	Plan 1		Plan 2		Plan 3	
	Amount	Percent	Amount	Percent	Amount	Percent
Issue 12% bonds	—	0%	—	0%	$2,000,000	50%
Issue preferred 9% stock, $50 par value	—	0	$2,000,000	50	1,000,000	25
Issue common stock, $10 par value	$4,000,000	100	2,000,000	50	1,000,000	25
Total amount of financing	$4,000,000	100%	$4,000,000	100%	$4,000,000	100%

Each of the preceding plans finances some of the corporation's operations by issuing common stock. However, the percentage financed by common stock varies from 100% (Plan 1) to 25% (Plan 3). In deciding among financing plans, the effect on earnings per share is often considered.

Earnings per share (EPS) measures the income earned by each share of common stock. It is computed as follows:[1]

$$\text{Earnings per Share} = \frac{\text{Net Income} - \text{Preferred Dividends}}{\text{Number of Common Shares Outstanding}}$$

To illustrate, assume the following data for Huckadee Corporation:

1. Earnings before interest and income taxes are $800,000.
2. The tax rate is 40%.
3. All bonds or stocks are issued at their par or face amount.

The effect of the preceding financing plans on Huckadee's net income and earnings per share is shown in Exhibit 1.

EXHIBIT 1

Effect of Alternative Financing Plans— $800,000 Earnings

	Plan 1	Plan 2	Plan 3
12% bonds	—	—	$2,000,000
Preferred 9% stock, $50 par	—	$2,000,000	1,000,000
Common stock, $10 par	$4,000,000	2,000,000	1,000,000
Total	$4,000,000	$4,000,000	$4,000,000
Earnings before interest and income tax	$ 800,000	$ 800,000	$ 800,000
Deduct interest on bonds	—	—	240,000
Income before income tax	$ 800,000	$ 800,000	$ 560,000
Deduct income tax	320,000	320,000	224,000
Net income	$ 480,000	$ 480,000	$ 336,000
Dividends on preferred stock	—	180,000	90,000
Available for dividends on common stock	$ 480,000	$ 300,000	$ 246,000
Shares of common stock outstanding	÷ 400,000	÷ 200,000	÷ 100,000
Earnings per share on common stock	$ 1.20	$ 1.50	$ 2.46

Exhibit 1 indicates that Plan 3 yields the highest earnings per share on common stock and, thus, is the most attractive for common stockholders. If the estimated earnings are more than $800,000, the difference between the earnings per share to common stockholders under Plans 1 and 3 is even greater.[2]

If smaller earnings occur, however, Plans 1 and 2 become more attractive to common stockholders. To illustrate, Exhibit 2 shows the effect on earnings per share if estimated earnings are $440,000 rather than $800,000 as estimated in Exhibit 1.

EXHIBIT 2

Effect of Alternative Financing Plans— $440,000 Earnings

	Plan 1	Plan 2	Plan 3
12% bonds	—	—	$2,000,000
Preferred 9% stock, $50 par	—	$2,000,000	1,000,000
Common stock, $10 par	$4,000,000	2,000,000	1,000,000
Total	$4,000,000	$4,000,000	$4,000,000
Earnings before interest and income tax	$ 440,000	$ 440,000	$ 440,000
Deduct interest on bonds	—	—	240,000
Income before income tax	$ 440,000	$ 440,000	$ 200,000
Deduct income tax	176,000	176,000	80,000
Net income	$ 264,000	$ 264,000	$ 120,000
Dividends on preferred stock	—	180,000	90,000
Available for dividends on common stock	$ 264,000	$ 84,000	$ 30,000
Shares of common stock outstanding	÷ 400,000	÷ 200,000	÷ 100,000
Earnings per share on common stock	$ 0.66	$ 0.42	$ 0.30

1 Earnings per share is also discussed in the *Financial Analysis and Interpretation* section of Chapter 11 and in Chapter 15.

2 The higher earnings per share under Plan 3 is due to a finance concept known as *leverage*. This concept is discussed further in Chapter 15.

OBJ 3 Journalize entries for bonds payable.

Accounting for Bonds Payable

Bonds may be issued at their face amount, a discount, or a premium. When bonds are issued at less or more than their face amount, the discount or premium must be amortized over the life of the bonds. At the maturity date, the face amount must be repaid. In some situations, a corporation may redeem bonds before their maturity date by repurchasing them from investors.

Bonds Issued at Face Amount

If the market rate of interest is equal to the contract rate of interest, the bonds will sell for their face amount or at a price of 100. To illustrate, assume that on January 1, 2013, Eastern Montana Communications Inc. issued the following bonds:

Face amount	$100,000
Contract rate of interest	12%
Interest paid semiannually on June 30 and December 31.	
Term of bonds	5 years
Market rate of interest	12%

Since the contract rate of interest and the market rate of interest are the same, the bonds will sell at their face amount. The entry to record the issuance of the bonds is as follows:

2013 Jan.	1	Cash		100,000	
		Bonds Payable			100,000
		Issued $100,000 bonds payable at face amount.			

Every six months (on June 30 and December 31) after the bonds are issued, interest of $6,000 ($100,000 × 12% × ½) is paid. The first interest payment on June 30, 2013, is recorded as follows:

2013 June	30	Interest Expense		6,000	
		Cash			6,000
		Paid six months' interest on bonds.			

At the maturity date, the payment of the principal of $100,000 is recorded as follows:

2017 Dec.	31	Bonds Payable		100,000	
		Cash			100,000
		Paid bond principal at maturity date.			

Bonds Issued at a Discount

If the market rate of interest is greater than the contract rate of interest, the bonds will sell for less than their face amount. This is because investors are not willing to pay the full face amount for bonds that pay a lower contract rate of interest than the rate they could earn on similar bonds (market rate). The difference between the face amount and the selling price of the bonds is the bond discount.[3]

To illustrate, assume that on January 1, 2013, Western Wyoming Distribution Inc. issued the following bonds:

3 The price that investors are willing to pay for the bonds depends on present value concepts. Present value concepts, including the computation of bond prices, are described and illustrated in Appendix 1 at the end of this chapter.

Face amount	$100,000
Contract rate of interest	12%
Interest paid semiannually on June 30 and December 31.	
Term of bonds	5 years
Market rate of interest	13%

Note:
Bonds will sell at a discount when the market rate of interest is higher than the contract rate.

Since the contract rate of interest is less than the market rate of interest, the bonds will sell at less than their face amount. Assuming the bonds sell for $96,406, the entry to record the issuance of the bonds is as follows:

2013 Jan.	1	Cash	96,406	
		Discount on Bonds Payable	3,594	
		Bonds Payable		100,000
		Issued $100,000 bonds at discount.		

The $96,406 is the amount investors are willing to pay for bonds that have a lower contract rate of interest (12%) than the market rate (13%). The discount is the market's way of adjusting the contract rate of interest to the higher market rate of interest.

The account, Discount on Bonds Payable, is a contra account to Bonds Payable and has a normal debit balance. It is subtracted from Bonds Payable to determine the carrying amount (or book value) of the bonds payable. Thus, after the preceding entry, the carrying amount of the bonds payable is $96,406 ($100,000 – $3,594).

Example Exercise 12-2 Issuing Bonds at a Discount

OBJ 3

On the first day of the fiscal year, a company issues a $1,000,000, 6%, five-year bond that pays semiannual interest of $30,000 ($1,000,000 × 6% × ½), receiving cash of $936,420. Journalize the entry to record the issuance of the bonds.

Follow My Example 12-2

Cash	936,420	
Discount on Bonds Payable	63,580	
Bonds Payable		1,000,000

Practice Exercises: **PE 12-2A, PE 12-2B**

Amortizing a Bond Discount

A bond discount must be amortized to interest expense over the life of the bond. The entry to amortize a bond discount is shown below.

		Interest Expense	XXX	
		Discount on Bonds Payable		XXX

The preceding entry may be made annually as an adjusting entry, or it may be combined with the semiannual interest payment. In the latter case, the entry would be as follows:

		Interest Expense	XXX	
		Discount on Bonds Payable		XXX
		Cash (amount of semiannual interest)		XXX

The two methods of computing the amortization of a bond discount are:

1. *Straight-line method*
2. *Effective interest rate method,* sometimes called the *interest method*

The **effective interest rate method** is required by generally accepted accounting principles. However, the straight-line method may be used if the results do not differ significantly from the interest method. The straight-line method is used in this chapter. The effective interest rate method is described and illustrated in Appendix 2 at the end of this chapter.

The straight-line method provides equal amounts of amortization each period. To illustrate, amortization of the Western Wyoming Distribution bond discount of $3,594 is computed below.

Discount on bonds payable	$3,594
Term of bonds	5 years
Semiannual amortization	$359.40 ($3,594/10 periods)

The combined entry to record the first interest payment and the amortization of the discount is as follows:

2013 June	30	Interest Expense		6,359.40	
		Discount on Bonds Payable			359.40
		Cash			6,000.00
		Paid semiannual interest and amortized 1/10 of bond discount.			

The preceding entry is made on each interest payment date. Thus, the amount of the semiannual interest expense on the bonds ($6,359.40) remains the same over the life of the bonds.

The effect of the discount amortization is to increase the interest expense from $6,000.00 to $6,359.40 on every semiannual interest payment date. In effect, this increases the contract rate of interest from 12% to a rate of interest that approximates the market rate of 13%. In addition, as the discount is amortized, the carrying amount of the bonds increases until it equals the face amount of the bonds on the maturity date.

Example Exercise 12-3 Discount Amortization

OBJ 3

Using the bond from Example Exercise 12-2, journalize the first interest payment and the amortization of the related bond discount.

Follow My Example 12-3

Interest Expense	36,358	
Discount on Bonds Payable		6,358
Cash		30,000
Paid interest and amortized the bond discount ($63,580/10).		

Practice Exercises: **PE 12-3A, PE 12-3B**

Note:
Bonds will sell at a premium when the market rate of interest is less than the contract rate.

Bonds Issued at a Premium

If the market rate of interest is less than the contract rate of interest, the bonds will sell for more than their face amount. This is because investors are willing to pay more for bonds that pay a higher contract rate of interest than the rate they could earn on similar bonds (market rate).

To illustrate, assume that on January 1, 2013, Northern Idaho Transportation Inc. issued the following bonds:

Face amount	$100,000
Contract rate of interest	12%
Interest paid semiannually on June 30 and December 31.	
Term of bonds	5 years
Market rate of interest	11%

Since the contract rate of interest is more than the market rate of interest, the bonds will sell for more than their face amount. Assuming the bonds sell for $103,769, the entry to record the issuance of the bonds is as follows:

2013 Jan.	1	Cash		103,769	
		Bonds Payable			100,000
		Premium on Bonds Payable			3,769
		Issued $100,000 bonds at a premium.			

The $3,769 premium is the extra amount investors are willing to pay for bonds that have a higher contract rate of interest (12%) than the market rate (11%). The premium is the market's way of adjusting the contract rate of interest to the lower market rate of interest.

The account, Premium on Bonds Payable, has a normal credit balance. It is added to Bonds Payable to determine the carrying amount (or book value) of the bonds payable. Thus, after the preceding entry, the carrying amount of the bonds payable is $103,769 ($100,000 + $3,769).

Example Exercise 12-4 Issuing Bonds at a Premium

OBJ 3

On the first day of the fiscal year, a company issues a $2,000,000, 12%, five-year bond that pays semiannual interest of $120,000 ($2,000,000 × 12% × ½), receiving cash of $2,154,440. Journalize the bond issuance.

Follow My Example 12-4

Cash	2,154,440	
Premium on Bonds Payable		154,440
Bonds Payable		2,000,000

Practice Exercises: **PE 12-4A, PE 12-4B**

Amortizing a Bond Premium

Like bond discounts, a bond premium must be amortized over the life of the bond. The amortization can be computed using either the straight-line or the effective interest rate method. The entry to amortize a bond premium is shown below.

		Premium on Bonds Payable		XXX	
		Interest Expense			XXX

The preceding entry may be made annually as an adjusting entry, or it may be combined with the semiannual interest payment. In the latter case, it would be:

		Interest Expense		XXX	
		Premium on Bonds Payable		XXX	
		Cash (amount of semiannual interest)			XXX

To illustrate, amortization of the preceding premium of $3,769 is computed using the straight-line method as shown below.

Premium on bonds payable	$3,769
Term of bonds	5 years
Semiannual amortization	$376.90 ($3,769/10 periods)

The combined entry to record the first interest payment and the amortization of the premium is as follows:

2013 June	30	Interest Expense		5,623.10	
		Premium on Bonds Payable		376.90	
		Cash			6,000.00
		Paid semiannual interest and amortized 1/10 of bond premium.			

The preceding entry is made on each interest payment date. Thus, the amount of the semiannual interest expense ($5,623.10) on the bonds remains the same over the life of the bonds.

The effect of the premium amortization is to decrease the interest expense from $6,000.00 to $5,623.10. In effect, this decreases the rate of interest from 12% to a rate of interest that approximates the market rate of 11%. In addition, as the premium is amortized, the carrying amount of the bonds decreases until it equals the face amount of bonds on the maturity date.

Example Exercise 12-5 Premium Amortization

OBJ 3

Using the bond from Example Exercise 12-4, journalize the first interest payment and the amortization of the related bond premium.

Follow My Example 12-5

Interest Expense	104,556	
Premium on Bonds Payable	15,444	
Cash		120,000
Paid interest and amortized the bond premium ($154,440/10).		

Practice Exercises: **PE 12-5A, PE 12-5B**

Business Connection

GENERAL MOTORS BONDS

In June 2009, after years of losses and a weakening financial condition, General Motors Corporation, maker of Chevrolet, Saturn, Pontiac, and Saab cars and trucks, was forced to file for bankruptcy. As part of the bankruptcy and restructuring plan, the U.S. government made a multibillion-dollar cash investment in the company in exchange for 60% of the restructured company's common stock. In addition, General Motors' bondholders were forced to exchange their bonds for the remaining common shares in the restructured company, which were worth only a fraction of the bonds' face value. Bondholders also lost the security of interest payments and repayment of the bonds' face value at maturity.

Source: C. Isidore, "GM Bankruptcy: End of an Era," *CNNMoney.com*, June 2, 2009.

Bond Redemption

A corporation may redeem or call bonds before they mature. This is often done when the market rate of interest declines below the contract rate of interest. In such cases, the corporation may issue new bonds at a lower interest rate and use the proceeds to redeem the original bond issue.

Callable bonds can be redeemed by the issuing corporation within the period of time and at the price stated in the bond indenture. Normally, the call price is above the face value. A corporation may also redeem its bonds by purchasing them on the open market.[4]

A corporation usually redeems its bonds at a price different from the carrying amount (or book value) of the bonds. The **carrying amount** of bonds payable is the face amount of the bonds less any unamortized discount or plus any unamortized premium. A gain or loss may be realized on a bond redemption as follows:

1. A *gain* is recorded if the price paid for redemption is below the bond carrying amount.
2. A *loss* is recorded if the price paid for the redemption is above the carrying amount.

Gains and losses on the redemption of bonds are reported in the *Other income (loss)* section of the income statement.

To illustrate, assume that on June 30, 2013, a corporation has the following bond issue:

Face amount of bonds	$100,000
Premium on bonds payable	4,000

On June 30, 2013, the corporation redeemed one-fourth ($25,000) of these bonds in the market for $24,000. The entry to record the redemption is as follows:

2013 June	30	Bonds Payable		25,000	
		Premium on Bonds Payable		1,000	
		Cash			24,000
		Gain on Redemption of Bonds			2,000
		Redeemed $25,000 bonds for $24,000.			

In the preceding entry, only the portion of the premium related to the redeemed bonds ($4,000 × 25% = $1,000) is written off. The difference between the carrying amount of the bonds redeemed, $26,000 ($25,000 + $1,000), and the redemption price, $24,000, is recorded as a gain.

Assume that the corporation calls the remaining $75,000 of outstanding bonds, which are held by a private investor, for $79,500 on July 1, 2013. The entry to record the redemption is as follows:

2013 July	1	Bonds Payable		75,000	
		Premium on Bonds Payable		3,000	
		Loss on Redemption of Bonds		1,500	
		Cash			79,500
		Redeemed $75,000 bonds for $79,500.			

Example Exercise 12-6 Redemption of Bonds Payable

OBJ 3

A $500,000 bond issue on which there is an unamortized discount of $40,000 is redeemed for $475,000. Journalize the redemption of the bonds.

(Continued)

4 Some bond indentures require the corporation issuing the bonds to transfer cash to a special cash fund, called a *sinking fund,* over the life of the bond. Such funds help assure investors that there will be adequate cash to pay the bonds at their maturity date.

Follow My Example 12-6

Bonds Payable	500,000	
Loss on Redemption of Bonds	15,000	
Discount on Bonds Payable		40,000
Cash		475,000

Practice Exercises: **PE 12-6A, PE 12-6B**

OBJ 4 Describe and illustrate the accounting for installment notes.

Installment Notes

Corporations often finance their operations by issuing bonds payable. As an alternative, corporations may issue installment notes. An **installment note** is a debt that requires the borrower to make equal periodic payments to the lender for the term of the note. Unlike bonds, each note payment includes the following:

1. Payment of a portion of the amount initially borrowed, called the *principal*
2. Payment of interest on the outstanding balance

Individuals typically use mortgage notes when buying a house or car.

At the end of the note's term, the principal will have been repaid in full.

Installment notes are often used to purchase specific assets such as equipment, and are often secured by the purchased asset. When a note is secured by an asset, it is called a **mortgage note**. If the borrower fails to pay a mortgage note, the lender has the right to take possession of the pledged asset and sell it to pay off the debt. Mortgage notes are typically issued by an individual bank.

Issuing an Installment Note

When an installment note is issued, an entry is recorded debiting Cash and crediting Notes Payable. To illustrate, assume that Lewis Company issues the following installment note to City National Bank on January 1, 2013.

Principal amount of note	$24,000
Interest rate	6%
Term of note	5 years
Annual payments	$5,698[5]

The entry to record the issuance of the note is as follows:

2013 Jan.	1	Cash		24,000	
		Notes Payable			24,000
		Issued installment note for cash.			

Annual Payments

The preceding note payable requires Lewis Company to repay the principal and interest in equal payments of $5,698 beginning December 31, 2013, for each of the next five years. Unlike bonds, however, each installment note payment includes an interest and principal component.

The interest portion of an installment note payment is computed by multiplying the interest rate by the carrying amount (book value) of the note at the beginning of the period. The principal portion of the payment is then computed as the difference between the total installment note payment (cash paid) and the interest component. These computations are illustrated in Exhibit 3 as shown on the following page.

5 The amount of the annual payment is calculated by using the present value concepts discussed in Appendix 1 at the end of this chapter. The annual payment of $5,698 is computed by dividing the $24,000 loan amount by the present value of an annuity of $1 for 5 periods at 6% (4.21236) from Exhibit 5 (rounded to the nearest dollar).

EXHIBIT 3 **Amortization of Installment Notes**

	A	B	C	D	E
For the Year Ending	**January 1 Carrying Amount**	**Note Payment (cash paid)**	**Interest Expense (6% of January 1 Note Carrying Amount)**	**Decrease in Notes Payable (B – C)**	**December 31 Carrying Amount (A – D)**
December 31, 2013	$24,000	$ 5,698	$ 1,440 (6% of $24,000)	$ 4,258	$19,742
December 31, 2014	19,742	5,698	1,185 (6% of $19,742)	4,513	15,229
December 31, 2015	15,229	5,698	914 (6% of $15,229)	4,784	10,445
December 31, 2016	10,445	5,698	627 (6% of $10,445)	5,071	5,374
December 31, 2017	5,374	5,698	324* (6% of $5,374)	5,374	0
		$28,490	**$4,490**	**$24,000**	

*Rounded ($5,374 – $5,698).

1. The January 1, 2013, carrying value (Column A) equals the amount borrowed from the bank. The January 1 balance in the following years equals the December 31 balance from the prior year.
2. The note payment (Column B) remains constant at $5,698, the annual cash payment required by the bank.
3. The interest expense (Column C) is computed at 6% of the installment note carrying amount at the beginning of each year. As a result, the interest expense decreases each year.
4. Notes payable decreases each year by the amount of the principal repayment (Column D). The principal repayment is computed by subtracting the interest expense (Column C) from the total payment (Column B). The principal repayment (Column D) increases each year as the interest expense decreases (Column C).
5. The carrying amount on December 31 (Column E) of the note decreases from $24,000, the initial amount borrowed, to $0 at the end of the five years.

The entry to record the first payment on December 31, 2013, is as follows:

2013 Dec.	31	Interest Expense	1,440	
		Notes Payable	4,258	
		Cash		5,698
		Paid principal and interest on installment note.		

The entry to record the second payment on December 31, 2014, is as follows:

2014 Dec.	31	Interest Expense	1,185	
		Notes Payable	4,513	
		Cash		5,698
		Paid principal and interest on installment note.		

As the prior entries show, the cash payment is the same in each year. The interest and principal repayment, however, change each year. This is because the carrying amount (book value) of the note decreases each year as principal is repaid, which decreases the interest component the next period.

The entry to record the final payment on December 31, 2017, is as follows:

2017 Dec.	31	Interest Expense	324	
		Notes Payable	5,374	
		Cash		5,698
		Paid principal and interest on installment note.		

After the final payment, the carrying amount on the note is zero, indicating that the note has been paid in full. Any assets that secure the note would then be released by the bank.

Example Exercise 12-7 Journalizing Installment Notes

OBJ 4

On the first day of the fiscal year, a company issues a $30,000, 10%, five-year installment note that has annual payments of $7,914. The first note payment consists of $3,000 of interest and $4,914 of principal repayment.

a. Journalize the entry to record the issuance of the installment note.

b. Journalize the first annual note payment.

Follow My Example 12-7

a.

		Cash	30,000	
		Notes Payable		30,000
		Issued $30,000 of installment note for cash.		

b.

		Interest Expense	3,000	
		Notes Payable	4,914	
		Cash		7,914
		Paid principal and interest on installment note.		

Practice Exercises: **PE 12-7A, PE 12-7B**

Integrity, Objectivity, and Ethics in Business

LIAR'S LOANS

One of the main causes of the 2008 financial crisis was a widespread inability of homeowners to repay their home mortgages. While the weak economy contributed to these problems, many mortgage defaults were the result of unethical lending practices in the form of "stated income," or "liar's" loans. In a conventional home mortgage, lenders base the amount of a loan on the borrower's income, expenses, and total assets. These amounts are verified by reviewing the borrower's tax returns, bank statements, and payroll records. Liar's loans, however, based the amount of the loan on the borrower's "stated income," without verifying it through sources such as tax returns, W-2 statements, or payroll records. Without independent verification, borrowers often falsified or lied about their "stated income" in order to obtain a larger loan than they were qualified for. Once in their homes, many of these borrowers were unable to make their loan payments, causing them to default on their home mortgages.

OBJ 5 Describe and illustrate the reporting of long-term liabilities, including bonds and notes payable.

Reporting Long-Term Liabilities

Bonds payable and notes payable are reported as liabilities on the balance sheet. Any portion of the bonds or notes that is due within one year is reported as a current liability. Any remaining bonds or notes are reported as a long-term liability.

Any unamortized premium is reported as an addition to the face amount of the bonds. Any unamortized discount is reported as a deduction from the face amount of the bonds. A description of the bonds and notes should also be reported either on the face of the financial statements or in the accompanying notes.

The reporting of bonds and notes payable for Mornin' Joe is shown below.

Mornin' Joe
Balance Sheet
December 31, 2014

Current liabilities:		
Accounts payable	$133,000	
Notes payable (current portion)	200,000	
Salaries and wages payable	42,000	
Payroll taxes payable	16,400	
Interest payable	40,000	
Total current liabilities		$ 431,400
Long-term liabilities:		
Bonds payable, 8%, due December 31, 2030	$500,000	
Less unamortized discount	16,000	$ 484,000
Notes payable		1,400,000
Total long-term liabilities		$1,884,000
Total liabilities		$2,315,400

Financial Analysis and Interpretation: Number of Times Interest Charges Are Earned

OBJ 6 Describe and illustrate how the number of times interest charges are earned is used to evaluate a company's financial condition.

As we have discussed, the assets of a company are subject to the (1) claims of creditors and (2) the rights of owners. As creditors, bondholders are primarily concerned with the company's ability to make its periodic interest payments and repay the face amount of the bonds at maturity.

Analysts assess the risk that bondholders will not receive their interest payments by computing the **number of times interest charges are earned** during the year as follows:

$$\text{Number of Times Interest Charges Are Earned} = \frac{\text{Income Before Income Tax} + \text{Interest Expense}}{\text{Interest Expense}}$$

This ratio computes the number of times interest payments could be paid out of current period earnings, measuring the company's ability to make its interest payments. Because interest payments reduce income tax expense, the ratio is computed using income before tax.

To illustrate, the following data were taken from a recent annual report of The Coca-Cola Company (in thousands):

Interest expense	$ 733,000
Income before income tax	14,243,000

The number of times interest charges are earned for The Coca-Cola Company is computed as follows:

$$\text{Number of Times Interest Charges Are Earned} = \frac{\$14{,}243{,}000 + \$733{,}000}{\$733{,}000} = 20.43$$

Compare this to the number of times interest charges are earned for United Continental Holdings (an airline), and Verizon Communications (a telecommunications company) shown on the next page (in thousands):

	Coca-Cola	United Continental	Verizon Communications
Interest expense	$733,000	$783,000	$2,523,000
Income before income tax expense	$14,243,000	$250,000	$12,684,000
Number of times interest charges are earned	20.43	1.32	6.03

Coca-Cola's number of times interest charges are earned is 20.43, indicating that the company generates enough income before taxes to pay (cover) its interest payments 20.43 times. As a result, debtholders have extremely good protection in the event of an earnings decline. Compare this to United Continental, which only generates enough income before taxes to pay (cover) its interest payments 1.32 times. A small decrease in United Continental's earnings could jeopardize the payment of interest. Verizon Communications falls in between, with a ratio of 6.03.

Example Exercise 12-8 Number of Times Interest Charges Are Earned

OBJ 6

Harris Industries reported the following on the company's income statement in 2014 and 2013:

	2014	2013
Interest expense	$ 200,000	$180,000
Income before income tax expense	1,000,000	720,000

a. Determine the number of times interest charges were earned for 2014 and 2013.
b. Is the number of times interest charges are earned improving or declining?

Follow My Example 12-8

a. 2014:

$$\text{Number of times interest charges are earned: } \frac{\$1{,}000{,}000 + \$200{,}000}{\$200{,}000} = 6.0$$

2013:

$$\text{Number of times interest charges are earned: } \frac{\$720{,}000 + \$180{,}000}{\$180{,}000} = 5.0$$

b. The number of times interest charges are earned has increased from 5.0 in 2013 to 6.0 in 2014. Thus, the debtholders have improved confidence in the company's ability to make its interest payments.

Practice Exercises: **PE 12-8A, PE 12-8B**

APPENDIX 1

Present Value Concepts and Pricing Bonds Payable

When a corporation issues bonds, the price that investors are willing to pay for the bonds depends on the following:

1. The face amount of the bonds, which is the amount due at the maturity date.
2. The periodic interest to be paid on the bonds.
3. The market rate of interest.

An investor determines how much to pay for the bonds by computing the present value of the bond's future cash receipts, using the market rate of interest. A bond's future cash receipts include its face value at maturity and the periodic interest payments.

Present Value Concepts

The concept of present value is based on the time value of money. The *time value of money concept* recognizes that cash received today is worth more than the same amount of cash to be received in the future.

To illustrate, what would you rather have: $1,000 today or $1,000 one year from now? You would rather have the $1,000 today because it could be invested to earn interest. For example, if the $1,000 could be invested to earn 10% per year, the $1,000 will accumulate to $1,100 ($1,000 plus $100 interest) in one year. In this sense, you can think of the $1,000 in hand today as the **present value** of $1,100 to be received a year from today. This present value is illustrated below.

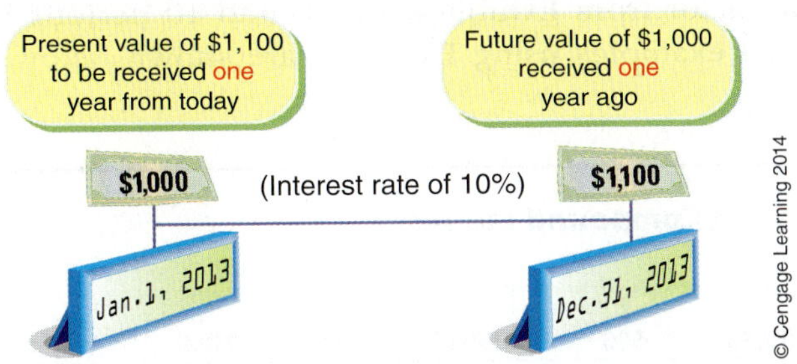

A related concept to present value is **future value**. To illustrate, using the preceding example, the $1,100 to be received on December 31, 2013, is the *future value* of $1,000 on January 1, 2013, assuming an interest rate of 10%.

Present Value of an Amount

To illustrate the present value of an amount, assume that $1,000 is to be received in one year. If the market rate of interest is 10%, the present value of the $1,000 is $909.09 ($1,000/1.10). This present value is illustrated below.

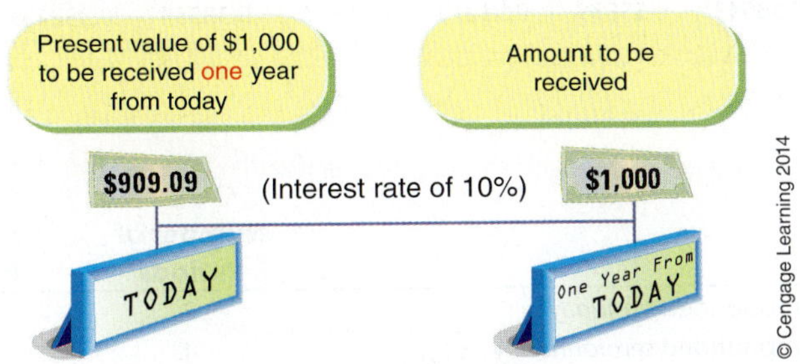

If the $1,000 is to be received in two years, with interest of 10% compounded at the end of the first year, the present value is $826.45 ($909.09/1.10).[6] This present value is illustrated below.

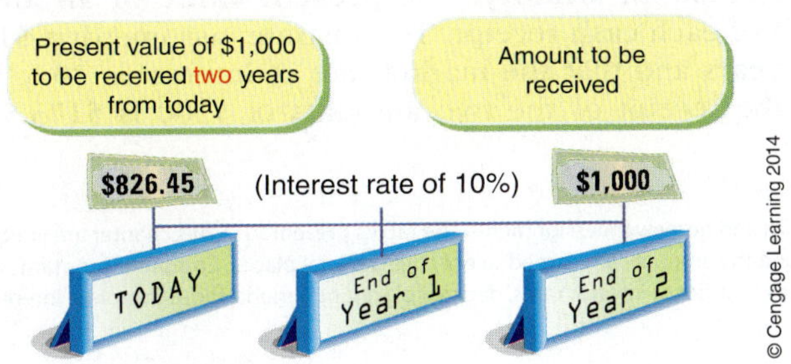

6 Note that the future value of $826.45 in two years, at an interest rate of 10% compounded annually, is $1,000.

Spreadsheet software with built-in present value functions can be used to calculate present values.

The present value of an amount to be received in the future can be determined by a series of divisions such as illustrated on the previous page. In practice, however, it is easier to use a table of present values.

The ***present value of $1*** table is used to find the present value factor for $1 to be received after a number of periods in the future. The amount to be received is then multiplied by this factor to determine its present value.

To illustrate, Exhibit 4 is a partial table of the present value of $1.[7] Exhibit 4 indicates that the present value of $1 to be received in two years with a market rate of interest of 10% a year is 0.82645. Multiplying $1,000 to be received in two years by 0.82645 yields $826.45 ($1,000 × 0.82645). This amount is the same amount computed earlier. In Exhibit 4, the Periods column represents the number of compounding periods, and the percentage columns represent the compound interest rate per period. Thus, the present value factor from Exhibit 4 for 12% for five years is 0.56743. If the interest is compounded semiannually, the interest rate is 6% (12% divided by 2), and the number of periods is 10 (5 years × 2 times per year). Thus, the present value factor from Exhibit 4 for 6% and 10 periods is 0.55839.

Some additional examples using Exhibit 4 are shown below.

EXHIBIT 4 **Present Value of $1 at Compound Interest**

Periods	4%	4½%	5%	5½%	6%	6½%	7%	10%	11%	12%	13%
1	0.96154	0.956940	0.95238	0.94787	0.94340	0.93897	0.93458	0.90909	0.90090	0.89286	0.88496
2	0.92456	0.915730	0.90703	0.89845	0.89000	0.88166	0.87344	0.82645	0.81162	0.79719	0.78315
3	0.88900	0.876300	0.86384	0.85161	0.83962	0.82785	0.81630	0.75131	0.73119	0.71178	0.69305
4	0.85480	0.838560	0.82270	0.80722	0.79209	0.77732	0.76290	0.68301	0.65873	0.63552	0.61332
5	0.82193	0.802450	0.78353	0.76513	0.74726	0.72988	0.71299	0.62092	0.59345	0.56743	0.54276
6	0.79031	0.767900	0.74622	0.72525	0.70496	0.68533	0.66634	0.56447	0.53464	0.50663	0.48032
7	0.75992	0.734830	0.71068	0.68744	0.66506	0.64351	0.62275	0.51316	0.48166	0.45235	0.42506
8	0.73069	0.703190	0.67684	0.65160	0.62741	0.60423	0.58201	0.46651	0.43393	0.40388	0.37616
9	0.70259	0.672900	0.64461	0.61763	0.59190	0.56735	0.54393	0.42410	0.39092	0.36061	0.33288
10	0.67556	0.643930	0.61391	0.58543	0.55839	0.53273	0.50835	0.38554	0.35218	0.32197	0.29459

	Number of Periods	Interest Rate	Present Value of $1 Factor from Exhibit 4
10% for *two* years compounded *annually*	2	10%	0.82645
10% for *two* years compounded *semiannually*	4	5%	0.82270
10% for *three* years compounded *semiannually*	6	5%	0.74622
12% for *five* years compounded *semiannually*	10	6%	0.55839

Present Value of the Periodic Receipts A series of equal cash receipts spaced equally in time is called an **annuity**. The **present value of an annuity** is the sum of the present values of each cash receipt. To illustrate, assume that $100 is to be received annually for two years and that the market rate of interest is 10%. Using Exhibit 4, the present value of the receipt of the two amounts of $100 is $173.55, as shown on the next page.

7 To simplify the illustrations and homework assignments, the tables presented in this chapter are limited to 10 periods for a small number of interest rates, and the amounts are carried to only five decimal places. Computer programs are available for determining present value factors for any number of interest rates, decimal places, or periods. More complete interest tables are presented in Appendix A of the text.

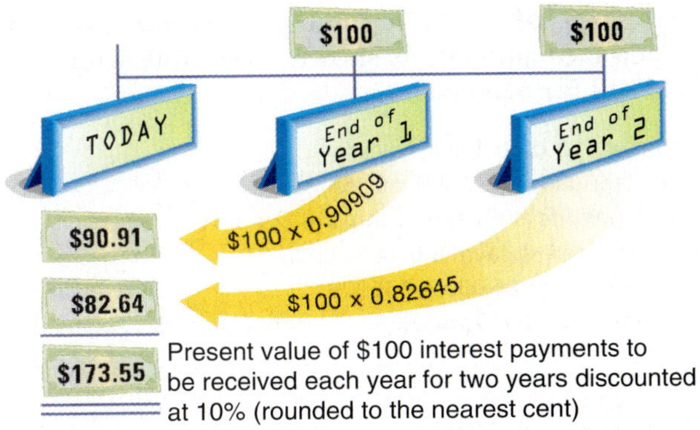

Instead of using present value of $1 tables to determine the present value of each cash flow separately, such as Exhibit 4, the present value of an annuity can be computed in a single step. Using a value from the *present value of an annuity of $1* table in Exhibit 5, the present value of the entire annuity can be calculated by multiplying the equal cash payment times the appropriate present value of an annuity of $1.

EXHIBIT 5 **Present Value of an Annuity of $1 at Compound Interest**

Periods	4%	4½%	5%	5½%	6%	6½%	7%	10%	11%	12%	13%
1	0.96154	0.95694	0.95238	0.94787	0.94340	0.93897	0.93458	0.90909	0.90090	0.89286	0.88496
2	1.88609	1.87267	1.85941	1.84632	1.83339	1.82063	1.80802	1.73554	1.71252	1.69005	1.66810
3	2.77509	2.74896	2.72325	2.69793	2.67301	2.64848	2.62432	2.48685	2.44371	2.40183	2.36115
4	3.62990	3.58753	3.54595	3.50515	3.46511	3.42580	3.38721	3.16987	3.10245	3.03735	2.97447
5	4.45182	4.38998	4.32948	4.27028	4.21236	4.15568	4.10020	3.79079	3.69590	3.60478	3.51723
6	5.24214	5.15787	5.07569	4.99553	4.91732	4.84101	4.76654	4.35526	4.23054	4.11141	3.99755
7	6.00205	5.89270	5.78637	5.68297	5.58238	5.48452	5.38929	4.86842	4.71220	4.56376	4.42261
8	6.73274	6.59589	6.46321	6.33457	6.20979	6.08875	5.97130	5.33493	5.14612	4.96764	4.79677
9	7.43533	7.26879	7.10782	6.95220	6.80169	6.65610	6.51523	5.75902	5.53705	5.32825	5.13166
10	8.11090	7.91272	7.72173	7.53763	7.36009	7.18883	7.02358	6.14457	5.88923	5.65022	5.42624

To illustrate, the present value of $100 to be received at the end of each of the next two years at 10% compound interest per period is $173.55 ($100 × 1.73554). This amount is the same amount computed above using the present value of $1.

Pricing Bonds

The selling price of a bond is the sum of the present values of:

1. The face amount of the bonds due at the maturity date
2. The periodic interest to be paid on the bonds

The market rate of interest is used to compute the present value of both the face amount and the periodic interest.

To illustrate the pricing of bonds, assume that Southern Utah Communications Inc. issued the following bond on January 1, 2013:

Face amount	$100,000
Contract rate of interest	12%
Interest paid semiannually on June 30 and December 31.	
Term of bonds..	5 years

Market Rate of Interest of 12% Assuming a market rate of interest of 12%, the bonds would sell for their face amount. As shown by the following present value computations, the bonds would sell for $100,000.

Present value of face amount of $100,000 due in 5 years, at 12% compounded semiannually: $100,000 × 0.55839 (present value of $1 for 10 periods at 6% from Exhibit 4)	$ 55,839
Present value of 10 semiannual interest payments of $6,000, at 12% compounded semiannually: $6,000 × 7.36009 (present value of an annuity of $1 for 10 periods at 6% from Exhibit 5)	44,161
Total present value of bonds	$100,000

Market Rate of Interest of 13% Assuming a market rate of interest of 13%, the bonds would sell at a discount. As shown by the following present value computations, the bonds would sell for $96,406.[8]

Present value of face amount of $100,000 due in 5 years, at 13% compounded semiannually: $100,000 × 0.53273 (present value of $1 for 10 periods at 6½% from Exhibit 4)	$53,273
Present value of 10 semiannual interest payments of $6,000, at 13% compounded semiannually: $6,000 × 7.18883 (present value of an annuity of $1 for 10 periods at 6½% from Exhibit 5)	43,133
Total present value of bonds	$96,406

Market Rate of Interest of 11% Assuming a market rate of interest of 11%, the bonds would sell at a premium. As shown by the following present value computations, the bonds would sell for $103,769.

Present value of face amount of $100,000 due in 5 years, at 11% compounded semiannually: $100,000 × 0.58543 (present value of $1 for 10 periods at 5½% from Exhibit 4)	$ 58,543
Present value of 10 semiannual interest payments of $6,000, at 11% compounded semiannually: $6,000 × 7.53763 (present value of an annuity of $1 for 10 periods at 5½% from Exhibit 5)	45,226
Total present value of bonds	$103,769

As shown above, the selling price of the bond varies with the present value of the bond's face amount at maturity, interest payments, and the market rate of interest.

APPENDIX 2

Effective Interest Rate Method of Amortization

The effective interest rate method of amortization provides for a constant *rate* of interest over the life of the bonds. As the discount or premium is amortized, the carrying amount of the bonds changes. As a result, interest expense also changes each period. This is in contrast to the straight-line method, which provides for a constant *amount* of interest expense each period.

The interest rate used in the effective interest rate method of amortization, sometimes called the *interest method*, is the market rate on the date the bonds are issued. The carrying amount of the bonds is multiplied by this interest rate to determine the interest expense for the period. The difference between the interest expense and the interest payment is the amount of discount or premium to be amortized for the period.

8 Some corporations issue bonds called **zero-coupon bonds** that provide for only the payment of the face amount at maturity. Such bonds sell for large discounts. In this example, such a bond would sell for $53,273, which is the present value of the face amount.

Amortization of Discount by the Interest Method

To illustrate, the following data taken from the chapter illustration of issuing bonds at a discount are used:

Face value of 12%, 5-year bonds, interest compounded semiannually	$100,000
Present value of bonds at effective (market) rate of interest of 13%	96,406
Discount on bonds payable	$ 3,594

Exhibit 6 illustrates the interest method for the preceding bonds. Exhibit 6 begins with six columns. The first column is not lettered. The remaining columns are lettered A through E. The exhibit was then prepared as follows:

Step 1. List the interest payments dates in the first column, which for the preceding bond are 10 interest payment dates (semiannual interest over five years). Also, list on the first line the initial amount of discount in Column D and the initial carrying amount (selling price) of the bonds in Column E.

Step 2. List in Column A the semiannual interest payments, which for the preceding bond are $6,000 ($100,000 × 6%).

Step 3. Compute the interest expense in Column B by multiplying the bond carrying amount at the beginning of each period times 6½%, which is the semiannual effective interest (market) rate (13% ÷ 2).

Step 4. In Column C, compute the discount to be amortized each period by subtracting the interest payment in Column A ($6,000) from the interest expense for the period shown in Column B.

Step 5. Compute the remaining unamortized discount by subtracting the amortized discount in Column C for the period from the unamortized discount at the beginning of the period in Column D.

Step 6. Compute the bond carrying amount at the end of the period by subtracting the unamortized discount at the end of the period in Column D from the face amount of the bonds ($100,000).

Steps 3–6 are repeated for each interest payment.

As shown in Exhibit 6, the interest expense increases each period as the carrying amount of the bond increases. Also, the unamortized discount decreases each period to zero at the maturity date. Finally, the carrying amount of the bonds increases from $96,406 to $100,000 (the face amount) at maturity.

EXHIBIT 6 **Amortization of Discount on Bonds Payable**

Interest Payment Date	A Interest Paid (6% of Face Amount)	B Interest Expense (6½% of Bond Carrying Amount)	C Discount Amortization (B – A)	D Unamortized Discount (D – C)	E Bond Carrying Amount ($100,000 – D)
				$3,594	$ 96,406
June 30, 2013	$6,000	$6,266 (6½% of $96,406)	$266	3,328	96,672
Dec. 31, 2013	6,000	6,284 (6½% of $96,672)	284	3,044	96,956
June 30, 2014	6,000	6,302 (6½% of $96,956)	302	2,742	97,258
Dec. 31, 2014	6,000	6,322 (6½% of $97,258)	322	2,420	97,580
June 30, 2015	6,000	6,343 (6½% of $97,580)	343	2,077	97,923
Dec. 31, 2015	6,000	6,365 (6½% of $97,923)	365	1,712	98,288
June 30, 2016	6,000	6,389 (6½% of $98,288)	389	1,323	98,677
Dec. 31, 2016	6,000	6,414 (6½% of $98,677)	414	909	99,091
June 30, 2017	6,000	6,441 (6½% of $99,091)	441	468	99,532
Dec. 31, 2017	6,000	6,470 (6½% of $99,532)	468*	—	100,000

*Cannot exceed unamortized discount.

The entry to record the first interest payment on June 30, 2013, and the related discount amortization is as follows:

2013 June	30	Interest Expense	6,266	
		Discount on Bonds Payable		266
		Cash		6,000
		Paid semiannual interest and amortized bond discount for 1/2 year.		

If the amortization is recorded only at the end of the year, the amount of the discount amortized on December 31, 2013, would be $550. This is the sum of the first two semiannual amortization amounts ($266 and $284) from Exhibit 6.

Amortization of Premium by the Interest Method

To illustrate, the following data taken from the chapter illustration of issuing bonds at a premium are used:

Present value of bonds at effective (market) rate of interest of 11%	$103,769
Face value of 12%, 5-year bonds, interest compounded semiannually	100,000
Premium on bonds payable	$ 3,769

Exhibit 7 illustrates the interest method for the preceding bonds. Exhibit 7 begins with six columns. The first column is not lettered. The remaining columns are lettered A through E. The exhibit was then prepared as follows:

Step 1. List the number of interest payments in the first column, which for the preceding bond are 10 interest payments (semiannual interest over 5 years). Also, list on the first line the initial amount of premium in Column D and the initial carrying amount of the bonds in Column E.

Step 2. List in Column A the semiannual interest payments, which for the preceding bond are $6,000 ($100,000 × 6%).

Step 3. Compute the interest expense in Column B by multiplying the bond carrying amount at the beginning of each period times 5½%, which is the semiannual effective interest (market) rate (11% ÷ 2).

Step 4. In Column C, compute the premium to be amortized each period by subtracting the interest expense for the period shown in Column B from the interest payment in Column A ($6,000).

EXHIBIT 7 **Amortization of Premium on Bonds Payable**

Interest Payment Date	A Interest Paid (6% of Face Amount)	B Interest Expense (5½% of Bond Carrying Amount)	C Premium Amortization (A – B)	D Unamortized Premium (D – C)	E Bond Carrying Amount ($100,000 + D)
				$3,769	$103,769
June 30, 2013	$6,000	$5,707 (5½% of $103,769)	$293	3,476	103,476
Dec. 31, 2013	6,000	5,691 (5½% of $103,476)	309	3,167	103,167
June 30, 2014	6,000	5,674 (5½% of $103,167)	326	2,841	102,841
Dec. 31, 2014	6,000	5,656 (5½% of $102,841)	344	2,497	102,497
June 30, 2015	6,000	5,637 (5½% of $102,497)	363	2,134	102,134
Dec. 31, 2015	6,000	5,617 (5½% of $102,134)	383	1,751	101,751
June 30, 2016	6,000	5,596 (5½% of $101,751)	404	1,347	101,347
Dec. 31, 2016	6,000	5,574 (5½% of $101,347)	426	921	100,921
June 30, 2017	6,000	5,551 (5½% of $100,921)	449	472	100,472
Dec. 31, 2017	6,000	5,526 (5½% of $100,472)	472*	—	100,000

*Cannot exceed unamortized premium.

Step 5. Compute the remaining unamortized premium by subtracting the amortized premium in Column C for the period from the unamortized premium at the beginning of the period in Column D.

Step 6. Compute the bond carrying amount at the end of the period by adding the unamortized premium at the end of the period in Column D to the face amount of the bonds ($100,000).

Steps 3–6 are repeated for each interest payment.

As shown in Exhibit 7, the interest expense decreases each period as the carrying amount of the bond decreases. Also, the unamortized premium decreases each period to zero at the maturity date. Finally, the carrying amount of the bonds decreases from $103,769 to $100,000 (the face amount) at maturity.

The entry to record the first interest payment on June 30, 2013, and the related premium amortization is as follows:

2013 June	30	Interest Expense		5,707	
		Premium on Bonds Payable		293	
		Cash			6,000
		Paid semiannual interest and amortized bond premium for 1/2 year.			

If the amortization is recorded only at the end of the year, the amount of the premium amortized on December 31, 2013, would be $602. This is the sum of the first two semiannual amortization amounts ($293 and $309) from Exhibit 7.

At a Glance 12

OBJ 1 Compute the potential impact of long-term borrowing on earnings per share.

Key Points Corporations can finance their operations by issuing short-term debt, long-term debt, or equity. One of the many factors that influence a corporation's decision on whether it should issue long-term debt or equity is the effect each alternative has on earnings per share.

Learning Outcomes	Example Exercises	Practice Exercises
• Define the concept of a bond.		
• Calculate and compare the effect of alternative long-term financing plans on earnings per share.	EE12-1	PE12-1A, 12-1B

OBJ 2 Describe the characteristics and terminology of bonds payable.

Key Points A corporation that issues bonds enters into a contract, or bond indenture.

When a corporation issues bonds, the price that buyers are willing to pay for the bonds depends on (1) the face amount of the bonds, (2) the periodic interest to be paid on the bonds, and (3) the market rate of interest.

Learning Outcomes	Example Exercises	Practice Exercises
• Define the characteristics of a bond.		
• Describe the various types of bonds.		
• Describe the factors that determine the price of a bond.		

OBJ 3 Journalize entries for bonds payable.

Key Points The journal entry for issuing bonds payable debits Cash and credits Bonds Payable. Any difference between the face amount of the bonds and the selling price is debited to Discount on Bonds Payable or credited to Premium on Bonds Payable when the bonds are issued. The discount or premium on bonds payable is amortized to interest expense over the life of the bonds.

At the maturity date, the entry to record the repayment of the face value of a bond is a debit to Bonds Payable and a credit to Cash.

When a corporation redeems bonds before they mature, Bonds Payable is debited for the face amount of the bonds, the premium (discount) on bonds payable account is debited (credited) for its unamoritized balance, Cash is credited, and any gain or loss on the redemption is recorded.

Learning Outcomes	Example Exercises	Practice Exercises
• Journalize the issuance of bonds at face value and the payment of periodic interest.		
• Journalize the issuance of bonds at a discount.	EE12-2	PE12-2A, 12-2B
• Journalize the amortization of a bond discount.	EE12-3	PE12-3A, 12-3B
• Journalize the issuance of bonds at a premium.	EE12-4	PE12-4A, 12-4B
• Journalize the amortization of a bond premium.	EE12-5	PE12-5A, 12-5B
• Describe bond redemptions.		
• Journalize the redemption of bonds payable	EE12-6	PE12-6A, 12-6B

OBJ 4 Describe and illustrate the accounting for installment notes.

Key Points An installment note requires the borrower to make equal periodic payments to the lender for the term of the note. Unlike bonds, the annual payment in an installment note consists of both principal and interest. The journal entry for the annual payment debits Interest Expense and Notes Payable and credits Cash for the amount of the payment. After the final payment, the carrying amount on the note is zero.

Learning Outcomes	Example Exercises	Practice Exercises
• Define the characteristics of an installment note.		
• Journalize the issuance of installment notes.	EE12-7	PE12-7A, 12-7B
• Journalize the annual payment for an installment note.		

OBJ 5

Describe and illustrate the reporting of long-term liabilities, including bonds and notes payable.

Key Points Bonds payable and notes payable are usually reported as long-term liabilities. If the balance sheet date is within one year, they are reported as current liabilities. A discount on bonds should be reported as a deduction from the related bonds payable. A premium on bonds should be reported as an addition to related bonds payable.

Learning Outcome	Example Exercises	Practice Exercises
• Illustrate the balance sheet presentation of bonds payable and notes payable.		

OBJ 6

Describe and illustrate how the number of times interest charges are earned is used to evaluate a company's financial condition.

Key Points The number of times interest charges are earned measures the risk to bondholders that a company will not be able to make its interest payments. It is computed by dividing income before income tax plus interest expense by interest expense. This ratio measures the number of times interest payments could be paid (covered) by current period earnings.

Learning Outcomes	Example Exercises	Practice Exercises
• Describe and compute the number of times interest charges are earned.	EE12-8	PE12-8A, 12-8B
• Interpret the number of times interest charges are earned.		

Key Terms

bond (542)
bond indenture (544)
carrying amount (551)
contract rate (545)
discount (545)
earnings per share (EPS) (543)
effective interest rate method (548)
effective rate of interest (545)
face amount (545)
installment note (552)
market rate of interest (545)
mortgage notes (552)
number of times interest charges are earned (555)
premium (545)

Illustrative Problem

The fiscal year of Russell Inc., a manufacturer of acoustical supplies, ends December 31. Selected transactions for the period 2013 through 2020, involving bonds payable issued by Russell Inc., are as follows:

2013

June 30. Issued $2,000,000 of 25-year, 7% callable bonds dated June 30, 2013, for cash of $1,920,000. Interest is payable semiannually on June 30 and December 31.

Dec. 31. Paid the semiannual interest on the bonds. The bond discount is amortized annually in a separate journal entry.

31. Recorded straight-line amortization of $1,600 of discount on the bonds.

31. Closed the interest expense account.

2014

June 30. Paid the semiannual interest on the bonds. The bond discount is amortized annually in a separate journal entry.

Dec. 31. Paid the semiannual interest on the bonds. The bond discount is amortized annually in a separate journal entry.

31. Recorded straight-line amortization of $3,200 of discount on the bonds.

31. Closed the interest expense account.

2020

June 30. Recorded the redemption of the bonds, which were called at 101.5. The balance in the bond discount account is $57,600 after the payment of interest and amortization of discount have been recorded. (Record the redemption only.)

Instructions

1. Journalize entries to record the preceding transactions.
2. Determine the amount of interest expense for 2013 and 2014.
3. Determine the carrying amount of the bonds as of December 31, 2014.

Solution

1.

2013 June	30	Cash		1,920,000	
		Discount on Bonds Payable		80,000	
		Bonds Payable			2,000,000
Dec.	31	Interest Expense		70,000	
		Cash			70,000
	31	Interest Expense		1,600	
		Discount on Bonds Payable			1,600
		Amortization of discount from July 1 to December 31.			
	31	Income Summary		71,600	
		Interest Expense			71,600
2014 June	30	Interest Expense		70,000	
		Cash			70,000
Dec.	31	Interest Expense		70,000	
		Cash			70,000
	31	Interest Expense		3,200	
		Discount on Bonds Payable			3,200
		Amortization of discount from January 1 to December 31.			
	31	Income Summary		143,200	
		Interest Expense			143,200
2020 June	30	Bonds Payable		2,000,000	
		Loss on Redemption of Bonds Payable		87,600	
		Discount on Bonds Payable			57,600
		Cash			2,030,000

2. a. 2013: $71,600 = $70,000 + $1,600

   b. 2014: $143,200 = $70,000 + $70,000 + $3,200

3.

Initial carrying amount of bonds	$1,920,000
Discount amortized on December 31, 2013	1,600
Discount amortized on December 31, 2014	3,200
Carrying amount of bonds, December 31, 2014	$1,924,800

Discussion Questions

1. Describe the two distinct obligations incurred by a corporation when issuing bonds.
2. Explain the meaning of each of the following terms as they relate to a bond issue: (a) convertible, (b) callable, and (c) debenture.
3. If you asked your broker to purchase for you a 12% bond when the market interest rate for such bonds was 11%, would you expect to pay more or less than the face amount for the bond? Explain.
4. A corporation issues $26,000,000 of 9% bonds to yield interest at the rate of 7%. (a) Was the amount of cash received from the sale of the bonds greater or less than $26,000,000? (b) Identify the following amounts as they relate to the bond issue: (1) face amount, (2) market or effective rate of interest, (3) contract rate of interest, and (4) maturity amount.
5. If bonds issued by a corporation are sold at a premium, is the market rate of interest greater or less than the contract rate?
6. The following data relate to a $15,000,000, 10% bond issued for a selected semiannual interest period:

Bond carrying amount at beginning of period	$15,593,454
Interest paid during period	750,000
Interest expense allocable to the period	809,345

   (a) Were the bonds issued at a discount or at a premium? (b) What is the unamortized amount of the discount or premium account at the beginning of the period? (c) What account was debited to amortize the discount or premium?
7. Bonds Payable has a balance of $5,000,000 and Discount on Bonds Payable has a balance of $150,000. If the issuing corporation redeems the bonds at 98, is there a gain or loss on the bond redemption?
8. What is a mortgage note?
9. Fleeson Company needs additional funds to purchase equipment for a new production facility and is considering either issuing bonds payable or borrowing the money from a local bank in the form of an installment note. How does an installment note differ from a bond payable?
10. In what section of the balance sheet would a bond payable be reported if: (a) it is payable within one year and (b) it is payable beyond one year?

Practice Exercises

Example Exercises

EE 12-1 *p. 544*

PE 12-1A Alternative financing plans

OBJ. 1

Texcar Co. is considering the following alternative financing plans:

	Plan 1	Plan 2
Issue 6% bonds (at face value)	$6,000,000	$5,000,000
Issue preferred $3 stock, $30 par	—	3,000,000
Issue common stock, $20 par	6,000,000	4,000,000

Income tax is estimated at 40% of income.

Determine the earnings per share of common stock, assuming income before bond interest and income tax is $1,200,000.

Example Exercises

EE 12-1 *p. 544*

PE 12-1B Alternative financing plans
OBJ. 1

Brower Co. is considering the following alternative financing plans:

	Plan 1	Plan 2
Issue 10% bonds (at face value)	$4,000,000	$2,500,000
Issue preferred $2.50 stock, $25 par	—	3,000,000
Issue common stock, $10 par	4,000,000	2,500,000

Income tax is estimated at 40% of income.

Determine the earnings per share of common stock, assuming income before bond interest and income tax is $2,000,000.

EE 12-2 *p. 547*

PE 12-2A Issuing bonds at a discount
OBJ. 3

On the first day of the fiscal year, a company issues a $2,000,000, 8%, five-year bond that pays semiannual interest of $80,000 ($2,000,000 × 8% × ½), receiving cash of $1,920,873. Journalize the bond issuance.

EE 12-2 *p. 547*

PE 12-2B Issuing bonds at a discount
OBJ. 3

On the first day of the fiscal year, a company issues a $3,000,000, 11%, five-year bond that pays semiannual interest of $165,000 ($3,000,000 × 11% × ½), receiving cash of $2,889,599. Journalize the bond issuance.

EE 12-3 *p. 548*

PE 12-3A Discount amortization
OBJ. 3

Using the bond from Practice Exercise 12-2A, journalize the first interest payment and the amortization of the related bond discount. Round to the nearest dollar.

EE 12-3 *p. 548*

PE 12-3B Discount amortization
OBJ. 3

Using the bond from Practice Exercise 12-2B, journalize the first interest payment and the amortization of the related bond discount. Round to the nearest dollar.

EE 12-4 *p. 549*

PE 12-4A Issuing bonds at a premium
OBJ. 3

On the first day of the fiscal year, a company issues a $4,000,000, 6%, five-year bond that pays semiannual interest of $120,000 ($4,000,000 × 6% × ½), receiving cash of $4,175,041. Journalize the bond issuance.

EE 12-4 *p. 549*

PE 12-4B Issuing bonds at a premium
OBJ. 3

On the first day of the fiscal year, a company issues an $8,000,000, 11%, five-year bond that pays semiannual interest of $440,000 ($8,000,000 × 11% × ½), receiving cash of $8,308,869. Journalize the bond issuance.

EE 12-5 *p. 550*

PE 12-5A Premium amortization
OBJ. 3

Using the bond from Practice Exercise 12-4A, journalize the first interest payment and the amortization of the related bond premium. Round to the nearest dollar.

EE 12-5 *p. 550*

PE 12-5B Premium amortization
OBJ. 3

Using the bond from Practice Exercise 12-4B, journalize the first interest payment and the amortization of the related bond premium. Round to the nearest dollar.

EE 12-6 *p. 551*

PE 12-6A Redemption of bonds payable
OBJ. 3

A $900,000 bond issue on which there is an unamortized discount of $87,000 is redeemed for $855,000. Journalize the redemption of the bonds.

Example Exercises

EE 12-6 *p. 551*

PE 12-6B Redemption of bonds payable **OBJ. 3**

A $500,000 bond issue on which there is an unamortized premium of $67,000 is redeemed for $490,000. Journalize the redemption of the bonds.

EE 12-7 *p. 554*

PE 12-7A Journalizing installment notes **OBJ. 4**

On the first day of the fiscal year, a company issues $80,000, 7%, seven-year installment notes that have annual payments of $14,844. The first note payment consists of $5,600 of interest and $9,244 of principal repayment.

a. Journalize the entry to record the issuance of the installment notes.

b. Journalize the first annual note payment.

EE 12-7 *p. 554*

PE 12-7B Journalizing installment notes **OBJ. 4**

On the first day of the fiscal year, a company issues $45,000, 8%, six-year installment notes that have annual payments of $9,734. The first note payment consists of $3,600 of interest and $6,134 of principal repayment.

a. Journalize the entry to record the issuance of the installment notes.

b. Journalize the first annual note payment.

EE 12-8 *p. 556*

F·A·I

PE 12-8A Number of times interest charges are earned **OBJ. 6**

Berry Company reported the following on the company's income statement in 2014 and 2013:

	2014	2013
Interest expense	$ 320,000	$ 300,000
Income before income tax expense	3,200,000	3,600,000

a. Determine the number of times interest charges are earned for 2014 and 2013. Round to one decimal place.

b. Is the number of times interest charges are earned improving or declining?

EE 12-8 *p. 556*

F·A·I

PE 12-8B Number of times interest charges are earned **OBJ. 6**

Averill Products Inc. reported the following on the company's income statement in 2014 and 2013:

	2014	2013
Interest expense	$ 440,000	$ 400,000
Income before income tax expense	5,544,000	4,400,000

a. Determine the number of times interest charges are earned for 2014 and 2013. Round to one decimal place.

b. Is the number of times interest charges are earned improving or declining?

Exercises

EX 12-1 Effect of financing on earnings per share **OBJ. 1**

✔ a. $2.10

SPREADSHEET

Rhett Co., which produces and sells biking equipment, is financed as follows:

Bonds payable, 7.5% (issued at face amount)	$30,000,000
Preferred $3 stock, $20 par	30,000,000
Common stock, $20 par	30,000,000

Income tax is estimated at 40% of income.

Determine the earnings per share of common stock, assuming that the income before bond interest and income tax is (a) $15,000,000, (b) $17,500,000, and (c) $20,000,000.

EX 12-2 Evaluate alternative financing plans **OBJ. 1**

Based on the data in Exercise 12-1, what factors other than earnings per share should be considered in evaluating these alternative financing plans?

EX 12-3 Corporate financing **OBJ. 1**

The financial statements for Nike, Inc., are presented in Appendix B at the end of the text. What is the major source of financing for Nike?

EX 12-4 Bond price **OBJ. 3**

Kohl's Corporation's 7.25% bonds due in 2029 were reported as selling for 115.948.

Were the bonds selling at a premium or at a discount? Why is Kohl's able to sell its bonds at this price?

EX 12-5 Entries for issuing bonds **OBJ. 3**

Amoruso Co. produces and distributes semiconductors for use by computer manufacturers. Amoruso Co. issued $7,500,000 of 15-year, 10% bonds on April 1 of the current year at face value, with interest payable on April 1 and October 1. The fiscal year of the company is the calendar year. Journalize the entries to record the following selected transactions for the current year:

Apr. 1. Issued the bonds for cash at their face amount.

Oct. 1. Paid the interest on the bonds.

Dec. 31. Recorded accrued interest for three months.

EX 12-6 Entries for issuing bonds and amortizing discount by straight-line method **OBJ. 2, 3**

✔ b. $1,109,546

On the first day of its fiscal year, Woodard Company issued $12,000,000 of 10-year, 8% bonds to finance its operations of producing and selling home improvement products. Interest is payable semiannually. The bonds were issued at a market (effective) interest rate of 10%, resulting in Woodard Company receiving cash of $10,504,541.

a. Journalize the entries to record the following:
   1. Issuance of the bonds.
   2. First semiannual interest payment. (Amortization of discount is to be recorded annually.)
   3. Second semiannual interest payment.
   4. Amortization of discount at the end of the first year, using the straight-line method. (Round to the nearest dollar.)

b. Determine the amount of the bond interest expense for the first year.

c. Explain why the company was able to issue the bonds for only $10,504,541 rather than for the face amount of $12,000,000.

EX 12-7 Entries for issuing bonds and amortizing premium by straight-line method **OBJ. 2, 3**

Yang Corporation wholesales repair products to equipment manufacturers. On May 1, 2014, Yang Corporation issued $20,000,000 of 10-year, 9% bonds at a market (effective) interest rate of 7%, receiving cash of $22,842,560. Interest is payable semiannually on May 1 and November 1. Journalize the entries to record the following:

a. Issuance of bonds on May 1, 2014.

b. First interest payment on November 1, 2014, and amortization of bond premium for six months, using the straight-line method. (Round to the nearest dollar.)

c. Explain why the company was able to issue the bonds for $22,842,560 rather than for the face amount of $20,000,000.

EX 12-8 Entries for issuing and calling bonds; loss OBJ. 3

Polders Corp., a wholesaler of office equipment, issued $40,000,000 of 10-year, 8% callable bonds on April 1, 2014, with interest payable on April 1 and October 1. The fiscal year of the company is the calendar year. Journalize the entries to record the following selected transactions:

2014

Apr. 1. Issued the bonds for cash at their face amount.

Oct. 1. Paid the interest on the bonds.

2018

Oct. 1. Called the bond issue at 104, the rate provided in the bond indenture. (Omit entry for payment of interest.)

EX 12-9 Entries for issuing and calling bonds; gain OBJ. 3

Robbins Corp. produces and sells wind-energy-driven engines. To finance its operations, Robbins Corp. issued $30,000,000 of 20-year, 10% callable bonds on March 1, 2014, with interest payable on March 1 and September 1. The fiscal year of the company is the calendar year. Journalize the entries to record the following selected transactions:

2014

Mar. 1. Issued the bonds for cash at their face amount.

Sept. 1. Paid the interest on the bonds.

2020

Sept. 1. Called the bond issue at 98, the rate provided in the bond indenture. (Omit entry for payment of interest.)

EX 12-10 Entries for installment note transactions OBJ. 4

On the first day of the fiscal year, Nash Company borrowed $50,000 by giving a six-year, 5% installment note to Buffet Bank. The note requires annual payments of $9,851, with the first payment occurring on the last day of the fiscal year. The first payment consists of interest of $2,500 and principal repayment of $7,351.

a. Journalize the entries to record the following:
   1. Issued the installment note for cash on the first day of the fiscal year.
   2. Paid the first annual payment on the note.
b. Explain how the notes payable would be reported on the balance sheet at the end of the first year.

EX 12-11 Entries for installment note transactions OBJ. 4

On January 1, 2014, O'Brien Company issued a $210,000, six-year, 9% installment note to Bulldog Bank. The note requires annual payments of $46,813, beginning on December 31, 2014. Journalize the entries to record the following:

2014

Jan. 1. Issued the notes for cash at their face amount.

Dec. 31. Paid the annual payment on the note, which consisted of interest of $18,900 and principal of $27,913.

2017

Dec. 31. Paid the annual payment on the note, included $10,665 of interest. The remainder of the payment reduced the principal balance on the note.

EX 12-12 Entries for installment note transactions **OBJ. 4**

On January 1, 2014, Parker Company obtained a $125,000, four-year, 6% installment note from Clark Bank. The note requires annual payments of $36,074, beginning on December 31, 2014.

a. Prepare an amortization table for this installment note, similar to the one presented in Exhibit 3.

b. Journalize the entries for the issuance of the note and the four annual note payments.

c. Describe how the annual note payment would be reported in the 2014 income statement.

EX 12-13 Reporting bonds **OBJ. 5**

At the beginning of the current year, two bond issues (Simmons Industries 7% 20-year bonds and Hunter Corporation 8% 10-year bonds) were outstanding. During the year, the Simmons Industries bonds were redeemed and a significant loss on the redemption of bonds was reported as an extraordinary item on the income statement. At the end of the year, the Hunter Corporation bonds were reported as a noncurrent liability. The maturity date on the Hunter Corporation bonds was early in the following year.

Identify the flaws in the reporting practices related to the two bond issues.

EX 12-14 Number of times interest charges are earned **OBJ. 6**

F·A·I

The following data were taken from recent annual reports of Southwest Airlines, which operates a low-fare airline service to over 50 cities in the United States:

	Current Year	Preceding Year
Interest expense	$167,000,000	$186,000,000
Income before income tax	745,000,000	164,000,000

a. Determine the number of times interest charges are earned for the current and preceding years. Round to one decimal place.

b. What conclusions can you draw?

EX 12-15 Number of times interest charges are earned **OBJ. 6**

F·A·I

Loomis, Inc. reported the following on the company's income statement in 2014 and 2013:

	2014	2013
Interest expense	$ 13,500,000	$ 16,000,000
Income before income tax expense	310,500,000	432,000,000

a. Determine the number of times interest charges were earned for 2014 and 2013. Round to one decimal place.

b. Is the number of times interest charges are earned improving or declining?

EX 12-16 Number of times interest charges are earned **OBJ. 6**

F·A·I

Iacouva Company reported the following on the company's income statement for 2014 and 2013:

	2014	2013
Interest expense	$5,000,000	$5,000,000
Income before income tax	3,500,000	6,000,000

a. Determine the number of times interest charges are earned for 2014 and 2013. Round to one decimal place.

b. What conclusions can you draw?

Appendix 1
EX 12-17 Present value of amounts due

Tommy John is going to receive $1,000,000 in three years. The current market rate of interest is 10%.

a. Using the present value of $1 table in Exhibit 4, determine the present value of this amount compounded annually.

b. Why is the present value less than the $1,000,000 to be received in the future?

Appendix 1
EX 12-18 Present value of an annuity

Determine the present value of $200,000 to be received at the end of each of four years, using an interest rate of 7%, compounded annually, as follows:

a. By successive computations, using the present value table in Exhibit 4.

b. By using the present value table in Exhibit 5.

c. Why is the present value of the four $200,000 cash receipts less than the $800,000 to be received in the future?

Appendix 1
EX 12-19 Present value of an annuity

✔ $52,676,850

On January 1, 2014, you win $75,000,000 in the state lottery. The $75,000,000 prize will be paid in equal installments of $7,500,000 over 10 years. The payments will be made on December 31 of each year, beginning on December 31, 2014. If the current interest rate is 7%, determine the present value of your winnings. Use the present value tables in Appendix A.

Appendix 1
EX 12-20 Present value of an annuity

Assume the same data as in Appendix 1 Exercise 12-19, except that the current interest rate is 12%.

Will the present value of your winnings using an interest rate of 12% be more than the present value of your winnings using an interest rate of 7%? Why or why not?

Appendix 1
EX 12-21 Present value of bonds payable; discount

Pinder Co. produces and sells high-quality video equipment. To finance its operations, Pinder Co. issued $25,000,000 of five-year, 7% bonds, with interest payable semiannually, at a market (effective) interest rate of 9%. Determine the present value of the bonds payable, using the present value tables in Exhibits 4 and 5. Round to the nearest dollar.

Appendix 1
EX 12-22 Present value of bonds payable; premium

✔ $32,019,810

Roehm Co. issued $30,000,000 of four-year, 10% bonds, with interest payable semiannually, at a market (effective) interest rate of 8%. Determine the present value of the bonds payable, using the present value tables in Exhibits 4 and 5. Round to the nearest dollar.

Appendix 2
EX 12-23 Amortize discount by interest method

✔ b. $3,923,959

On the first day of its fiscal year, Ebert Company issued $50,000,000 of 10-year, 7% bonds to finance its operations. Interest is payable semiannually. The bonds were issued at a market (effective) interest rate of 9%, resulting in Ebert Company receiving cash of $43,495,895. The company uses the interest method.

a. Journalize the entries to record the following:
   1. Sale of the bonds.
   2. First semiannual interest payment, including amortization of discount. Round to the nearest dollar.
   3. Second semiannual interest payment, including amortization of discount. Round to the nearest dollar.

b. Compute the amount of the bond interest expense for the first year.

c. Explain why the company was able to issue the bonds for only $43,495,895 rather than for the face amount of $50,000,000.

Appendix 2
EX 12-24 Amortize premium by interest method

✔ b. $1,662,619

Shunda Corporation wholesales parts to appliance manufacturers. On January 1, 2014, Shunda Corporation issued $22,000,000 of five-year, 9% bonds at a market (effective) interest rate of 7%, receiving cash of $23,829,684. Interest is payable semiannually. Shunda Corporation's fiscal year begins on January 1. The company uses the interest method.

a. Journalize the entries to record the following:
   1. Sale of the bonds.
   2. First semiannual interest payment, including amortization of premium. Round to the nearest dollar.
   3. Second semiannual interest payment, including amortization of premium. Round to the nearest dollar.

b. Determine the bond interest expense for the first year.

c. Explain why the company was able to issue the bonds for $23,829,684 rather than for the face amount of $22,000,000.

Appendix 1 and Appendix 2
EX 12-25 Compute bond proceeds, amortizing premium by interest method, and interest expense

✔ a. $37,702,483
✔ c. $225,620

Ware Co. produces and sells motorcycle parts. On the first day of its fiscal year, Ware Co. issued $35,000,000 of five-year, 12% bonds at a market (effective) interest rate of 10%, with interest payable semiannually. Compute the following, presenting figures used in your computations.

a. The amount of cash proceeds from the sale of the bonds. Use the tables of present values in Exhibits 4 and 5. Round to the nearest dollar.

b. The amount of premium to be amortized for the first semiannual interest payment period, using the interest method. Round to the nearest dollar.

c. The amount of premium to be amortized for the second semiannual interest payment period, using the interest method. Round to the nearest dollar.

d. The amount of the bond interest expense for the first year.

Appendix 1 and Appendix 2
EX 12-26 Compute bond proceeds, amortizing discount by interest method, and interest expense

✔ a. $71,167,524
✔ b. $670,051

Boyd Co. produces and sells aviation equipment. On the first day of its fiscal year, Boyd Co. issued $80,000,000 of five-year, 9% bonds at a market (effective) interest rate of 12%, with interest payable semiannually. Compute the following, presenting figures used in your computations.

a. The amount of cash proceeds from the sale of the bonds. Use the tables of present values in Exhibits 4 and 5. Round to the nearest dollar.

b. The amount of discount to be amortized for the first semiannual interest payment period, using the interest method. Round to the nearest dollar.

c. The amount of discount to be amortized for the second semiannual interest payment period, using the interest method. Round to the nearest dollar.

d. The amount of the bond interest expense for the first year.

Problems Series A

PR 12-1A Effect of financing on earnings per share **OBJ. 1**

✔ 1. Plan 3: $1.44

SPREADSHEET

Three different plans for financing an $18,000,000 corporation are under consideration by its organizers. Under each of the following plans, the securities will be issued at their par or face amount, and the income tax rate is estimated at 40% of income.

	Plan 1	Plan 2	Plan 3
8% Bonds	—	—	$ 9,000,000
Preferred 4% stock, $20 par	—	$ 9,000,000	4,500,000
Common stock, $10 par	$18,000,000	9,000,000	4,500,000
Total	$18,000,000	$18,000,000	$18,000,000

Instructions

1. Determine the earnings per share of common stock for each plan, assuming that the income before bond interest and income tax is $2,100,000.
2. Determine the earnings per share of common stock for each plan, assuming that the income before bond interest and income tax is $1,050,000.
3. Discuss the advantages and disadvantages of each plan.

PR 12-2A Bond discount, entries for bonds payable transactions **OBJ. 2, 3**

✔ 3. $4,714,477

GENERAL LEDGER

On July 1, 2014, Bryant Industries Inc. issued $100,000,000 of 20-year, 9% bonds at a market (effective) interest rate of 10%, receiving cash of $91,420,905. Interest on the bonds is payable semiannually on December 31 and June 30. The fiscal year of the company is the calendar year.

Instructions

1. Journalize the entry to record the amount of cash proceeds from the issuance of the bonds on July 1, 2014.
2. Journalize the entries to record the following:
   a. The first semiannual interest payment on December 31, 2014, and the amortization of the bond discount, using the straight-line method. (Round to the nearest dollar.)
   b. The interest payment on June 30, 2015, and the amortization of the bond discount, using the straight-line method. (Round to the nearest dollar.)
3. Determine the total interest expense for 2014.
4. Will the bond proceeds always be less than the face amount of the bonds when the contract rate is less than the market rate of interest?
5. (Appendix 1) Compute the price of $91,420,905 received for the bonds by using the present value tables in Appendix A at the end of the text. (Round to the nearest dollar.)

PR 12-3A Bond premium, entries for bonds payable transactions **OBJ. 2, 3**

✔ 3. $7,964,907

GENERAL LEDGER

Wishaw, Inc. produces and sells outdoor equipment. On July 1, 2014, Wishaw, Inc. issued $150,000,000 of 20-year, 12% bonds at a market (effective) interest rate of 9%, receiving cash of $191,403,720. Interest on the bonds is payable semiannually on December 31 and June 30. The fiscal year of the company is the calendar year.

Instructions

1. Journalize the entry to record the amount of cash proceeds from the issuance of the bonds on July 1, 2014.
2. Journalize the entries to record the following:
   a. The first semiannual interest payment on December 31, 2014, and the amortization of the bond premium, using the straight-line method. (Round to the nearest dollar.)
   b. The interest payment on June 30, 2015, and the amortization of the bond premium, using the straight-line method. (Round to the nearest dollar.)
3. Determine the total interest expense for 2014.
4. Will the bond proceeds always be greater than the face amount of the bonds when the contract rate is greater than the market rate of interest?
5. (Appendix 1) Compute the price of 191,403,720 received for the bonds by using the present value tables in Appendix A at the end of the text. (Round to the nearest dollar.)

PR 12-4A Entries for bonds payable and installment note transactions OBJ. 3, 4

✔ 3. $79,420,141

SPREADSHEET

GENERAL LEDGER

The following transactions were completed by Navarez Inc., whose fiscal year is the calendar year:

2014

July 1. Issued $88,000,000 of 10-year, 10% callable bonds dated July 1, 2014, at a market (effective) rate of 12%, receiving cash of $77,906,048. Interest is payable semiannually on December 31 and June 30.

Oct. 1. Borrowed $240,000 by issuing a five-year, 5% installment note to Setzer Bank. The note requires annual payments of $55,434, with the first payment occurring on September 30, 2015.

Dec. 31. Accrued $3,000 of interest on the installment note. The interest is payable on the date of the next installment note payment.

31. Paid the semiannual interest on the bonds. The bond discount is amortized annually in a separate journal entry.

31. Recorded bond discount amortization of $504,698, which was determined using the straight-line method.

31. Closed the interest expense account.

2015

June 30. Paid the semiannual interest on the bonds. The bond discount is amortized annually in a separate journal entry.

Sept. 30. Paid the annual payment on the note, which consisted of interest of $12,000 and principal of $43,434.

Dec. 31. Accrued $2,457 of interest on the installment note. The interest is payable on the date of the next installment note payment.

31. Paid the semiannual interest on the bonds. The bond discount is amortized annually in a separate journal entry.

31. Recorded bond discount amortization of $1,009,396, which was determined using the straight-line method.

31. Closed the interest expense account.

2016

June 30. Recorded the redemption of the bonds, which were called at 97. The balance in the bond discount account is $8,075,160 after payment of interest and amortization of discount have been recorded. (Record the redemption only.)

Sept. 30. Paid the second annual payment on the note, which consisted of interest of $9,828 and principal of $45,606.

Instructions

1. Journalize the entries to record the foregoing transactions.
2. Indicate the amount of the interest expense in (a) 2014 and (b) 2015.
3. Determine the carrying amount of the bonds as of December 31, 2015.

Appendix 1 and Appendix 2

PR 12-5A Bond discount, entries for bonds payable transactions, interest method of amortizing bond discount

✔ 3. $4,571,045

On July 1, 2014, Bryant Industries Inc. issued $100,000,000 of 20-year, 9% bonds at a market (effective) interest rate of 10%, receiving cash of $91,420,905. Interest on the bonds is payable semiannually on December 31 and June 30. The fiscal year of the company is the calendar year.

Instructions

1. Journalize the entry to record the amount of cash proceeds from the issuance of the bonds.
2. Journalize the entries to record the following:
   a. The first semiannual interest payment on December 31, 2014, and the amortization of the bond discount, using the interest method. (Round to the nearest dollar.)
   b. The interest payment on June 30, 2015, and the amortization of the bond discount, using the interest method. (Round to the nearest dollar.)
3. Determine the total interest expense for 2014.

Appendix 1 and Appendix 2

PR 12-6A Bond premium, entries for bonds payable transactions, interest method of amortizing bond premium

✔ 3. $8,613,167

Wishaw, Inc. produces and sells outdoor equipment. On July 1, 2014, Wishaw, Inc. issued $150,000,000 of 20-year, 12% bonds at a market (effective) interest rate of 9%, receiving cash of $191,403,720. Interest on the bonds is payable semiannually on December 31 and June 30. The fiscal year of the company is the calendar year.

Instructions

1. Journalize the entry to record the amount of cash proceeds from the issuance of the bonds.
2. Journalize the entries to record the following:
   a. The first semiannual interest payment on December 31, 2014, and the amortization of the bond premium, using the interest method. (Round to the nearest dollar.)
   b. The interest payment on June 30, 2015, and the amortization of the bond premium, using the interest method. (Round to the nearest dollar.)
3. Determine the total interest expense for 2014.

Problems Series B

PR 12-1B Effect of financing on earnings per share

OBJ. 1

✔ 1. Plan 3: $2.84

SPREADSHEET

Three different plans for financing an $80,000,000 corporation are under consideration by its organizers. Under each of the following plans, the securities will be issued at their par or face amount, and the income tax rate is estimated at 40% of income.

	Plan 1	Plan 2	Plan 3
9% Bonds	—	—	$40,000,000
Preferred 5% stock, $25 par	—	$40,000,000	20,000,000
Common stock, $20 par	$80,000,000	40,000,000	20,000,000
Total	$80,000,000	$80,000,000	$80,000,000

Instructions

1. Determine for each plan the earnings per share of common stock, assuming that the income before bond interest and income tax is $10,000,000.
2. Determine for each plan the earnings per share of common stock, assuming that the income before bond interest and income tax is $6,000,000.
3. Discuss the advantages and disadvantages of each plan.

PR 12-2B Bond discount, entries for bonds payable transactions

OBJ. 2, 3

✔ 3. $2,392,269

GENERAL LEDGER

On July 1, 2014, Livingston Corporation, a wholesaler of manufacturing equipment, issued $46,000,000 of 20-year, 10% bonds at a market (effective) interest rate of 11%, receiving cash of $42,309,236. Interest on the bonds is payable semiannually on December 31 and June 30. The fiscal year of the company is the calendar year.

(Continued)

Instructions

1. Journalize the entry to record the amount of cash proceeds from the issuance of the bonds on July 1, 2014.
2. Journalize the entries to record the following:
   a. The first semiannual interest payment on December 31, 2014, and the amortization of the bond discount, using the straight-line method. (Round to the nearest dollar.)
   b. The interest payment on June 30, 2015, and the amortization of the bond discount, using the straight-line method. (Round to the nearest dollar.)
3. Determine the total interest expense for 2014.
4. Will the bond proceeds always be less than the face amount of the bonds when the contract rate is less than the market rate of interest?
5. (Appendix 1) Compute the price of $42,309,236 received for the bonds by using the present value tables in Appendix A at the end of the text. (Round to the nearest dollar.)

✔ 3. $3,494,977

GENERAL LEDGER

PR 12-3B Bond premium, entries for bonds payable transactions — OBJ. 2, 3

Rodgers Corporation produces and sells football equipment. On July 1, 2014, Rodgers Corporation issued $65,000,000 of 10-year, 12% bonds at a market (effective) interest rate of 10%, receiving cash of $73,100,469. Interest on the bonds is payable semiannually on December 31 and June 30. The fiscal year of the company is the calendar year.

Instructions

1. Journalize the entry to record the amount of cash proceeds from the issuance of the bonds on July 1, 2014.
2. Journalize the entries to record the following:
   a. The first semiannual interest payment on December 31, 2014, and the amortization of the bond premium, using the straight-line method. (Round to the nearest dollar.)
   b. The interest payment on June 30, 2015, and the amortization of the bond premium, using the straight-line method. (Round to the nearest dollar.)
3. Determine the total interest expense for 2014.
4. Will the bond proceeds always be greater than the face amount of the bonds when the contract rate is greater than the market rate of interest?
5. (Appendix 1) Compute the price of $73,100,469 received for the bonds by using the present value tables in Appendix A at the end of the text. (Round to the nearest dollar.)

✔ 3. $61,644,484

SPREADSHEET

GENERAL LEDGER

PR 12-4B Entries for bonds payable and installment note transactions — OBJ. 3, 4

The following transactions were completed by Montague Inc., whose fiscal year is the calendar year:

2014

July 1. Issued $55,000,000 of 10-year, 9% callable bonds dated July 1, 2014, at a market (effective) rate of 7%, receiving cash of $62,817,040. Interest is payable semiannually on December 31 and June 30.

Oct. 1. Borrowed $450,000 by issuing a six-year, 8% installment note to Intexicon Bank. The note requires annual payments of $97,342, with the first payment occurring on September 30, 2015.

Dec. 31. Accrued $9,000 of interest on the installment note. The interest is payable on the date of the next installment note payment.

31. Paid the semiannual interest on the bonds. The bond premium is amortized annually in a separate journal entry.

31. Recorded bond premium amortization of $390,852 which was determined using the straight-line method.

31. Closed the interest expense account.

2015

June 30. Paid the semiannual interest on the bonds. The bond premium is amortized annually in a separate journal entry.

Sept. 30. Paid the annual payment on the note, which consisted of interest of $36,000 and principal of $61,342.

Dec. 31. Accrued $7,773 of interest on the installment note. The interest is payable on the date of the next installment note payment.

31. Paid the semiannual interest on the bonds. The bond premium is amortized annually in a separate journal entry.

31. Recorded bond premium amortization of $781,704, which was determined using the straight-line method.

31. Closed the interest expense account.

2016

June 30. Recorded the redemption of the bonds, which were called at 103. The balance in the bond premium account is $6,253,632 after payment of interest and amortization of premium have been recorded. (Record the redemption only.)

Sept. 30. Paid the second annual payment on the note, which consisted of interest of $31,093 and principal of $66,249.

Instructions

1. Journalize the entries to record the foregoing transactions.
2. Indicate the amount of the interest expense in (a) 2014 and (b) 2015.
3. Determine the carrying amount of the bonds as of December 31, 2015.

Appendix 1 and Appendix 2

PR 12-5B Bond discount, entries for bonds payable transactions, interest method of amortizing bond discount

✔ 3. $2,327,008

On July 1, 2014, Livingston Corporation, a wholesaler of manufacturing equipment, issued $46,000,000 of 20-year, 10% bonds at a market (effective) interest rate of 11%, receiving cash of $42,309,236. Interest on the bonds is payable semiannually on December 31 and June 30. The fiscal year of the company is the calendar year.

Instructions

1. Journalize the entry to record the amount of cash proceeds from the issuance of the bonds.
2. Journalize the entries to record the following:
   a. The first semiannual interest payment on December 31, 2014, and the amortization of the bond discount, using the interest method. (Round to the nearest dollar.)
   b. The interest payment on June 30, 2015, and the amortization of the bond discount, using the interest method. (Round to the nearest dollar.)
3. Determine the total interest expense for 2014.

Appendix 1 and Appendix 2

PR 12-6B Bond premium, entries for bonds payable transactions, interest method of amortizing bond premium

✔ 3. $3,655,023

Rodgers Corporation produces and sells football equipment. On July 1, 2014, Rodgers Corporation issued $65,000,000 of 10-year, 12% bonds at a market (effective) interest rate of 10%, receiving cash of $73,100,469. Interest on the bonds is payable semiannually on December 31 and June 30. The fiscal year of the company is the calendar year.

(Continued)

Instructions

1. Journalize the entry to record the amount of cash proceeds from the issuance of the bonds.
2. Journalize the entries to record the following:
   a. The first semiannual interest payment on December 31, 2014, and the amortization of the bond premium, using the interest method. (Round to the nearest dollar.)
   b. The interest payment on June 30, 2015, and the amortization of the bond premium, using the interest method. (Round to the nearest dollar.)
3. Determine the total interest expense for 2014.

Cases & Projects

CP 12-1 General Electric bond issuance

General Electric Capital, a division of General Electric, uses long-term debt extensively. In a recent year, GE Capital issued $11 billion in long-term debt to investors, then within days filed legal documents to prepare for another $50 billion long-term debt issue. As a result of the $50 billion filing, the price of the initial $11 billion offering declined (due to higher risk of more debt).

> *Bill Gross, a manager of a bond investment fund, "denounced a 'lack in candor' related to GE's recent debt deal. 'It was the most recent and most egregious example of how bondholders are mistreated.' Gross argued that GE was not forthright when GE Capital recently issued $11 billion in bonds, one of the largest issues ever from a U.S. corporation. What bothered Gross is that three days after the issue the company announced its intention to sell as much as $50 billion in additional debt, warrants, preferred stock, guarantees, letters of credit and promissory notes at some future date."*

In your opinion, did GE Capital act unethically by selling $11 billion of long-term debt without telling those investors that a few days later it would be filing documents to prepare for another $50 billion debt offering?

Source: Jennifer Ablan, "Gross Shakes the Bond Market; GE Calms It, a Bit," *Barron's,* March 25, 2002.

CP 12-2 Ethics and professional conduct in business

Solar Industries develops and produces high-efficiency solar panels. The company has an outstanding $10,000,000, 30-year, 10% bond issue dated July 1, 2009. The bond issue is due June 30, 2038. Some bond indentures require the corporation issuing the bonds to transfer cash to a special cash fund, called a sinking fund, over the life of the bond. Such funds help assure investors that there will be adequate cash to pay the bonds at their maturity date.

The bond indenture requires a bond sinking fund, which has a balance of $1,200,000 as of July 1, 2014. The company is currently experiencing a shortage of funds due to a recent acquisition. Bob Lachgar, the company's treasurer, is considering using the funds from the bond sinking fund to cover payroll and other bills that are coming due at the end of the month. Bob's brother-in-law, a trustee of Solar's sinking fund, has indicated willingness to allow Bob to use the funds from the sinking fund to temporarily meet the company's cash needs.

Discuss whether Bob's proposal is appropriate.

CP 12-3 Present values

Alex Kelton recently won the jackpot in the Colorado lottery while he was visiting his parents. When he arrived at the lottery office to collect his winnings, he was offered the following three payout options:

a. Receive $100,000,000 in cash today.

b. Receive $25,000,000 today and $9,000,000 per year for 8 years, with the first payment being received one year from today.

c. Receive $15,000,000 per year for 10 years, with the first payment being received one year from today.

Assuming that the effective rate of interest is 7%, which payout option should Alex select? Use the present value tables in Appendix A. Explain your answer and provide any necessary supporting calculations.

CP 12-4 Preferred stock vs. bonds

Xentec Inc. has decided to expand its operations to owning and operating golf courses. The following is an excerpt from a conversation between the chief executive officer, Peter Kilgallon, and the vice president of finance, Dan Baron.

Peter: Dan, have you given any thought to how we're going to the acquisition of Sweeping Bluff Golf Course?

Dan: Well, the two basic options, as I see it, are to issue either preferred stock or bonds. The equity market is a little depressed right now. The rumor is that the Federal Reserve Bank's going to increase the interest rates either this month or next.

Peter: Yes, I've heard the rumor. The problem is that we can't wait around to see what's going to happen. We'll have to move on this next week if we want any chance to complete the acquisition of Sweeping Bluff Golf Course.

Dan: Well, the bond market is strong right now. Maybe we should issue debt this time around.

Peter: That's what I would have guessed as well. Sweeping Bluff Golf Course's financial statements look pretty good, except for the volatility of its income and cash flows. But that's characteristic of the industry.

Discuss the advantages and disadvantages of issuing preferred stock versus bonds.

CP 12-5 Financing business expansion

You hold a 25% common stock interest in YouOwnIt, a family-owned construction equipment company. Your sister, who is the manager, has proposed an expansion of plant facilities at an expected cost of $26,000,000. Two alternative plans have been suggested as methods of financing the expansion. Each plan is briefly described as follows:

Plan 1. Issue $26,000,000 of 20-year, 8% notes at face amount.

Plan 2. Issue an additional 550,000 shares of $10 par common stock at $20 per share, and $15,000,000 of 20-year, 8% notes at face amount.

The balance sheet as of the end of the previous fiscal year is as follows:

YouOwnIt, Inc.
Balance Sheet
December 31, 2014

Assets	
Current assets	$15,000,000
Property, plant, and equipment	22,500,000
Total assets	$37,500,000
Liabilities and Stockholders' Equity	
Liabilities	$11,250,000
Common stock, $10	4,000,000
Paid-in capital in excess of par	500,000
Retained earnings	21,750,000
Total liabilities and stockholders' equity	$37,500,000

Net income has remained relatively constant over the past several years. The expansion program is expected to increase yearly income before bond interest and income tax from $2,667,000 in the previous year to $5,000,000 for this year. Your sister has asked you, as the company treasurer, to prepare an analysis of each financing plan.

1. Prepare a table indicating the expected earnings per share on the common stock under each plan. Assume an income tax rate of 40%. Round to the nearest cent.
2. a. Discuss the factors that should be considered in evaluating the two plans.
   b. Which plan offers the greater benefit to the present stockholders? Give reasons for your opinion.

CP 12-6 Number of times interest charges are earned

F·A·I

The following financial data (in thousands) were taken from recent financial statements of Staples, Inc.

	Year 3	Year 2	Year 1
Interest expense	$ 214,824	$ 237,025	$ 149,774
Earnings before taxes	1,356,595	1,155,894	1,243,084

1. What is the number of times interest charges are earned for Staples in Year 3, Year 2, and Year 1? (Round your answers to one decimal place.)
2. Evaluate this ratio for Staples.

FRED PROUSER/REUTERS/LANDOV

CHAPTER 13

Investments and Fair Value Accounting

News Corporation

You invest cash to earn more cash. For example, you could deposit cash in a bank account to earn interest. You could also invest cash in preferred or common stocks and in corporate or U.S. government notes and bonds.

Preferred and common stock can be purchased through a stock exchange, such as the **New York Stock Exchange (NYSE)**. Preferred stock is purchased primarily with the expectation of earning dividends. Common stock is purchased with the expectation of earning dividends or realizing gains from a price increase in the stock.

Corporate and U.S. government bonds can also be purchased through a bond exchange. Bonds are purchased with the primary expectation of earning interest revenue.

Companies make investments for many of the same reasons that you would as an individual. For example, **News Corporation**, a diversified media company, which produces such popular television shows as *The Simpsons* and *American Idol*, has invested approximately $652 million of available cash in stocks and bonds. These investments are held by News Corporation for interest, dividends, and expected price increases.

Unlike most individuals, however, companies also purchase significant amounts of the outstanding common stock of other companies for strategic reasons. For example, News Corporation invested in 32% of Hulu, an online video joint venture with other major media companies.

Investments in debt and equity securities give rise to a number of accounting issues. These issues are described and illustrated in this chapter.

Learning Objectives

After studying this chapter, you should be able to: *Example Exercises*

At a Glance 13 Page 604

OBJ 1 Describe why companies invest in debt and equity securities.

Why Companies Invest

Most companies generate cash from their operations. This cash can be used for the following purposes:

1. Investing in current operations
2. Investing in temporary investments to earn additional revenue
3. Investing in long-term investments in stock of other companies for strategic reasons

Investing Cash in Current Operations

Cash is often used to support the current operating activities of a company. For example, cash may be used to replace worn-out equipment or to purchase new, more efficient and productive equipment. In addition, cash may be reinvested in the company to expand its current operations. For example, a retailer based in the northwest United States might decide to expand by opening stores in the Midwest.

To support its current level of operations, a company also uses cash to pay:

1. expenses.
2. suppliers of merchandise and other assets.
3. interest to creditors.
4. dividends to stockholders.

The accounting for the use of cash in current operations has been described and illustrated in earlier chapters. For example, Chapter 9, "Fixed Assets and Intangible

Assets," illustrated the use of cash for purchasing property, plant, and equipment. In this chapter, we describe and illustrate the use of cash for investing in temporary investments and the stock of other companies.

Investing Cash in Temporary Investments

A company may temporarily have excess cash that is not needed for use in its current operations. This is often the case when a company has a seasonal operating cycle. For example, a significant portion of the annual merchandise sales of a retailer occurs during the fall holiday season. As a result, retailers often experience a large increase in cash during this period, which is not needed until the spring buying season.

Instead of letting excess cash remain idle in a checking account, most companies invest their excess cash in temporary investments. In doing so, companies invest in securities such as:

1. **Debt securities**, which are notes and bonds that pay interest and have a fixed maturity date.
2. **Equity securities**, which are preferred and common stock that represent ownership in a company and do not have a fixed maturity date.

Investments in debt and equity securities, termed **Investments** or *Temporary Investments*, are reported in the Current Assets section of the balance sheet.

The primary objective of investing in temporary investments is to:

1. earn interest revenue.
2. receive dividends.
3. realize gains from increases in the market price of the securities.

Investments in certificates of deposit and other securities that do not normally change in value are disclosed on the balance sheet as *cash and cash equivalents*. Such investments are held primarily for their interest revenue.

Investing Cash in Long-Term Investments

A company may invest cash in the debt or equity of another company as a long-term investment. Long-term investments may be held for the same investment objectives as temporary investments. However, long-term investments often involve the purchase of a significant portion of the stock of another company. Such investments usually have a strategic purpose, such as:

1. *Reduction of costs*: When one company buys another company, the combined company may be able to reduce administrative expenses. For example, a combined company does not need two chief executive officers (CEOs) or chief financial officers (CFOs).
2. *Replacement of management*: If the purchased company has been mismanaged, the acquiring company may replace the company's management and, thus, improve operations and profits.
3. *Expansion*: The acquiring company may purchase a company because it has a complementary product line, territory, or customer base. The new combined company may be able to serve customers better than the two companies could separately.
4. *Integration*: A company may integrate operations by acquiring a supplier or customer. Acquiring a supplier may provide a more stable or uninterrupted supply of resources. Acquiring a customer may also provide a market for the company's products or services.

The Walt Disney Company purchased Marvel Entertainment in order to expand into action/adventure characters, movies, and products.

Accounting for Debt Investments

OBJ 2 Describe and illustrate the accounting for debt investments.

Debt securities include notes and bonds, issued by corporations and governmental organizations. Most companies invest excess cash in bonds as investments to earn interest revenue.

The accounting for bond investments[1] includes recording the following:

1. Purchase of bonds
2. Interest revenue
3. Sale of bonds

Purchase of Bonds

The purchase of bonds is recorded by debiting an investments account for the purchase price of the bonds, including any brokerage commissions. If the bonds are purchased between interest dates, the purchase price includes accrued interest since the last interest payment. This is because the seller has earned the accrued interest, but the buyer will receive the accrued interest when it is paid.

To illustrate, assume that Homer Company purchases $18,000 of U.S. Treasury bonds at their face amount on March 17, 2014, plus accrued interest for 45 days. The bonds have an interest rate of 6%, payable on July 31 and January 31.

The entry to record the purchase of the Treasury bonds is as follows:

2014 Mar.	17	Investments—U.S. Treasury Bonds		18,000	
		Interest Receivable		135	
		Cash			18,135
		Purchased $18,000, 6% Treasury bonds.			

Since Homer Company purchased the bonds on March 17, it is also purchasing the accrued interest for 45 days (January 31 to March 17), as shown in Exhibit 1. The accrued interest of $135 is computed as follows:[2]

$$\text{Accrued Interest} = \$18,000 \times 6\% \times (45/360) = \$135$$

The accrued interest is recorded by debiting Interest Receivable for $135. Investments is debited for the purchase price of the bonds of $18,000.

Interest Revenue

On July 31, Homer Company receives a semiannual interest payment of $540 ($18,000 × 6% × ½). The $540 interest includes the $135 accrued interest that Homer Company purchased with the bonds on March 17. Thus, Homer Company has earned $405 ($540 − $135) of interest revenue since purchasing the bonds, as shown in Exhibit 1.

The receipt of the interest on July 31 is recorded as follows:

2014 July	31	Cash		540	
		Interest Receivable			135
		Interest Revenue			405
		Received semiannual interest.			

Homer Company's accounting period ends on December 31. Thus, an adjusting entry must be made to accrue interest for five months (August 1 to December 31) of $450 ($18,000 × 6% × 5/12), as shown in Exhibit 1. The adjusting entry to record the accrued interest is as follows:

2014 Dec.	31	Interest Receivable		450	
		Interest Revenue			450
		Accrued interest.			

1 Debt investments may also include installment notes and short-term notes. The basic accounting for notes is similar to bonds and, thus, is not illustrated.

2 To simplify, a 360-day year is used to compute interest.

EXHIBIT 1 **Interest Timeline**

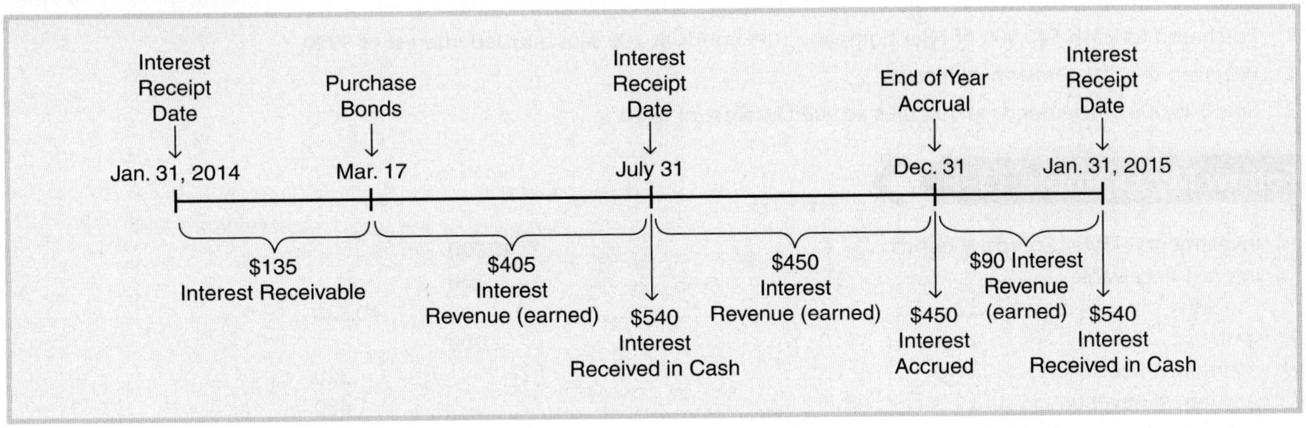

For the year ended December 31, 2014, Homer Company would report *Interest revenue* of $855 ($405 + $450) as part of *Other income* on its income statement.

The receipt of the semiannual interest of $540 on January 31, 2015, is recorded as follows:

2015 Jan.	31	Cash		540	
		Interest Revenue			90
		Interest Receivable			450
		Received interest on Treasury bonds.			

Sale of Bonds

The sale of a bond investment normally results in a gain or loss. If the proceeds from the sale exceed the book value (cost) of the bonds, then a gain is recorded. If the proceeds are less than the book value (cost) of the bonds, a loss is recorded.

To illustrate, on January 31, 2015, Homer Company sells the Treasury bonds at 98, which is a price equal to 98% of their face amount. The sale results in a loss of $360, as shown below.

Proceeds from sale	$17,640*
Less book value (cost) of the bonds	18,000
Loss on sale of bonds	$ (360)

*$18,000 × 98%

The entry to record the sale is as follows:

2015 Jan.	31	Cash		17,640	
		Loss on Sale of Investment		360	
		Investments—U.S. Treasury Bonds			18,000
		Sold U.S. Treasury bonds.			

There is no accrued interest upon the sale, since the interest payment date is also January 31. If the sale were between interest dates, interest accrued since the last interest payment date would be added to the sale proceeds and credited to Interest Revenue. The loss on the sale of bond investments is reported as part of *Other income (loss)* on Homer Company's income statement.

Example Exercise 13-1 Bond Investment Transactions OBJ 2

Journalize the entries to record the following selected bond investment transactions for Fly Company:

1. Purchased for cash $40,000 of Tyler Company 10% bonds at 100 plus accrued interest of $320.
2. Received the first semiannual interest.
3. Sold $30,000 of the bonds at 102 plus accrued interest of $110.

Follow My Example 13-1

1.	Investments—Tyler Company Bonds	40,000	
	Interest Receivable	320	
	Cash		40,320
2.	Cash	2,000*	
	Interest Receivable		320
	Interest Revenue		1,680
	*$40,000 × 10% × ½		
3.	Cash	30,710*	
	Interest Revenue		110
	Gain on Sale of Investments		600
	Investments—Tyler Company Bonds		30,000

*Sale proceeds ($30,000 × 102%)	$30,600
Accrued interest	110
Total proceeds from sale	$30,710

Practice Exercises: **PE 13-1A, PE 13-1B**

OBJ 3 Describe and illustrate the accounting for equity investments.

Accounting for Equity Investments

A company may invest in the preferred or common stock of another company. The company investing in another company's stock is the **investor**. The company whose stock is purchased is the **investee**.

The percent of the investee's outstanding stock purchased by the investor determines the degree of control that the investor has over the investee. This, in turn, determines the accounting method used to record the stock investment, as shown in Exhibit 2.

EXHIBIT 2

Stock Investments

Percent of Outstanding Stock Owned by Investor	Degree of Control of Investor over Investee	Accounting Method
Less than 20%	No control	Cost method
Between 20% and 50%	Significant influence	Equity method
Greater than 50%	Control	Consolidation

Less Than 20% Ownership

If the investor purchases less than 20% of the outstanding stock of the investee, the investor is considered to have no control over the investee. In this case, it is assumed that the investor purchased the stock primarily to earn dividends or to realize gains on price increases of the stock.

Investments of less than 20% of the investee's outstanding stock are accounted for using the **cost method**. Under the cost method, entries are recorded for the following transactions:

1. Purchase of stock
2. Receipt of dividends
3. Sale of stock

Purchase of Stock The purchase of stock is recorded at its cost. Any brokerage commissions are included as part of the cost.

To illustrate, assume that on May 1, Bart Company purchases 2,000 shares of Lisa Company common stock at $49.90 per share plus a brokerage fee of $200. The entry to record the purchase of the stock is as follows:

May	1	Investments—Lisa Company Stock		100,000	
		Cash			100,000
		Purchased 2,000 shares of Lisa Company common stock [($49.90 × 2,000 shares) + $200].			

Receipt of Dividends On July 31, Bart Company receives a dividend of $0.40 per share from Lisa Company. The entry to record the receipt of the dividend is as follows:

July	31	Cash		800	
		Dividend Revenue			800
		Received dividend on Lisa Company common stock (2,000 shares × $0.40).			

Dividend revenue is reported as part of *Other income* on Bart Company's income statement.

Sale of Stock The sale of a stock investment normally results in a gain or loss. A gain is recorded if the proceeds from the sale exceed the book value (cost) of the stock. A loss is recorded if the proceeds from the sale are less than the book value (cost).

To illustrate, on September 1, Bart Company sells 1,500 shares of Lisa Company stock for $54.50 per share, less a $160 commission. The sale results in a gain of $6,590, as shown below.

Proceeds from sale	$81,590*
Book value (cost) of the stock	75,000**
Gain on sale	$ 6,590

*($54.50 × 1,500 shares) – $160
**($100,000/2,000 shares) × 1,500 shares

The entry to record the sale is as follows:

Sept.	1	Cash		81,590	
		Gain on Sale of Investments			6,590
		Investments—Lisa Company Stock			75,000
		Sold 1,500 shares of Lisa Company common stock.			

The gain on the sale of investments is reported as part of *Other income* on Bart Company's income statement.

Example Exercise 13-2 Stock Investment Transactions OBJ 3

On September 1, 1,500 shares of Monroe Company are acquired at a price of $24 per share plus a $40 brokerage fee. On October 14, a $0.60-per-share dividend was received on the Monroe Company stock. On November 11, 750 shares (half) of Monroe Company stock were sold for $20 per share, less a $45 brokerage fee. Prepare the journal entries for the original purchase, dividend, and sale.

Follow My Example 13-2

Sept. 1	Investments—Monroe Company Stock	36,040*	
	Cash		36,040
	*(1,500 shares × $24 per share) + $40		
Oct. 14	Cash	900*	
	Dividend Revenue		900
	*$0.60 per share × 1,500 shares		
Nov. 11	Cash	14,955*	
	Loss on Sale of Investments	3,065	
	Investments—Monroe Company Stock		18,020**
	*(750 shares × $20) – $45		
	**$36,040 × ½		

Practice Exercises: **PE 13-2A, PE 13-2B**

Between 20%–50% Ownership

If the investor purchases between 20% and 50% of the outstanding stock of the investee, the investor is considered to have a significant influence over the investee. In this case, it is assumed that the investor purchased the stock primarily for strategic reasons, such as developing a supplier relationship.

Investments of between 20% and 50% of the investee's outstanding stock are accounted for using the **equity method**. Under the equity method, the stock is recorded initially at its cost, including any brokerage commissions. This is the same as under the cost method.

Under the equity method, the investment account is adjusted for the investor's share of the *net income* and *dividends* of the investee. These adjustments are as follows:

1. *Net Income:* The investor records its share of the net income of the investee as an increase in the investment account. Its share of any net loss is recorded as a decrease in the investment account.
2. *Dividends:* The investor's share of cash dividends received from the investee decreases the investment account.

Purchase of Stock To illustrate, assume that Simpson Inc. purchased its 40% interest in Flanders Corporation's common stock on January 2, 2014, for $350,000. The entry to record the purchase is as follows:

2014 Jan.	2	Investment in Flanders Corporation Stock		350,000	
		Cash			350,000
		Purchased 40% of Flanders Corporation stock.			

Recording Investee Net Income For the year ended December 31, 2014, Flanders Corporation reported net income of $105,000. Under the equity method, Simpson Inc. (the investor) records its share of Flanders net income, as shown on the next page.

2014 Dec.	31	Investment in Flanders Corporation Stock	42,000	
		Income of Flanders Corporation		42,000
		Recorded 40% share of Flanders Corporation net income, $105,000 × 40%.		

Income of Flanders Corporation is reported on Simpson Inc.'s income statement. Depending on its significance, it may be reported separately or as part of *Other income*. If Flanders Corporation had a loss during the period, then the journal entry would be a debit to Loss of Flanders Corporation and a credit to the investment account.

Recording Investee Dividends During the year, Flanders declared and paid cash dividends of $45,000. Under the equity method, Simpson Inc. (the investor) records its share of Flanders dividends as follows:

2014 Dec.	31	Cash	18,000	
		Investment in Flanders Corporation Stock		18,000
		Recorded 40% share of Flanders Corporation dividends, $45,000 × 40%.		

The effect of recording 40% of Flanders Corporation's net income and dividends is to increase the investment account by $24,000 ($42,000 − $18,000). Thus, Investment in Flanders Corporation Stock increases from $350,000 to $374,000, as shown below.

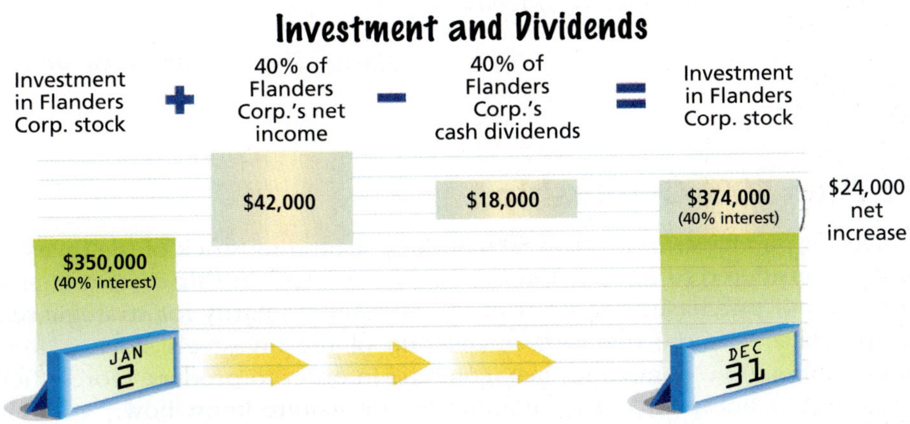

Under the equity method, the investment account reflects the investor's proportional changes in the net book value of the investee. For example, Flanders Corporation's net book value increased by $60,000 (net income of $105,000 less dividends of $45,000) during the year. As a result, Simpson's share of Flanders' net book value increased by $24,000 ($60,000 × 40%). Investments accounted for under the equity method are classified on the balance sheet as noncurrent assets.

Sale of Stock Under the equity method, a gain or loss is normally recorded from the sale of an investment. A gain is recorded if the proceeds exceed the *book value* of the investment. A loss is recorded if the proceeds are less than the *book value* of the investment.

To illustrate, if Simpson Inc. sold Flanders Corporation's stock on January 1, 2015, for $400,000, a gain of $26,000 would be reported, as shown below.

Proceeds from sale	$400,000
Book value of stock investment	374,000
Gain on sale	$ 26,000

The entry to record the sale is as follows:

2015 Jan.	1	Cash	400,000	
		Investment in Flanders Corporation Stock		374,000
		Gain on Sale of Flanders Corporation Stock		26,000
		Sold Flanders Corporation stock.		

Example Exercise 13-3 Equity Method

OBJ 3

On January 2, Olson Company acquired 35% of the outstanding stock of Bryant Company for $140,000. For the year ended December 31, Bryant Company earned income of $44,000 and paid dividends of $20,000. Prepare the entries for Olson Company for the purchase of the stock, the share of Bryant income, and the dividends received from Bryant Company.

Follow My Example 13-3

Jan. 2	Investment in Bryant Company Stock	140,000	
	Cash		140,000
Dec. 31	Investment in Bryant Company Stock	15,400*	
	Income of Bryant Company		15,400
	*Recorded 35% of Bryant income, 35% × $44,000		
Dec. 31	Cash	7,000*	
	Investment in Bryant Company Stock		7,000
	*Recorded 35% of Bryant's $20,000 dividend, 35% × $20,000		

Practice Exercises: **PE 13-3A, PE 13-3B**

More Than 50% Ownership

If the investor purchases more than 50% of the outstanding stock of the investee, the investor is considered to have control over the investee. In this case, it is assumed that the investor purchased the stock of the investee primarily for strategic reasons.

The purchase of more than 50% ownership of the investee's stock is termed a **business combination**. Companies may combine in order to produce more efficiently, diversify product lines, expand geographically, or acquire know-how.

A corporation owning all or a majority of the voting stock of another corporation is called a **parent company**. The corporation that is controlled is called the **subsidiary company**.

Parent and subsidiary corporations often continue to maintain separate accounting records and prepare their own financial statements. In such cases, at the end of the year, the financial statements of the parent and subsidiary are combined and reported as a single company. These combined financial statements are called **consolidated financial statements**. Such statements are normally identified by adding *and Subsidiary(ies)* to the name of the parent corporation or by adding *Consolidated* to the statement title.

To the external stakeholders of the parent company, consolidated financial statements are more meaningful than separate statements for each corporation. This is because the parent company, in substance, controls the subsidiaries. The accounting for business combinations, including preparing consolidated financial statements, is described and illustrated in advanced accounting courses and textbooks.

Business Connection

APPLE'S ENTRANCE TO STREAMING MUSIC

Apple's iTunes is the dominant provider of music downloads. However, companies such as Pandora and Grooveshark are challenging iTunes by providing permanent access to web songs that can be streamed live from a web browser, but cannot be downloaded onto a device. These companies can stream customized radio stations for free, or individual songs for as little as 10 cents. This compares to downloading a song from iTunes for $0.99 or more.

In late 2009, Apple acquired online music provider Lala in order to establish a presence in streaming music. Apparently, Apple believed that it was easier to acquire this technology by purchasing Lala, rather than build it in-house. Apple closed the Lala service in May of 2010 and incorporated Lala's assets and technology into its iTunes platform.

Source: Ethan Smith and Yakari Iwatani Kane, "Apple Acquires Lala Media," *The Wall Street Journal*, December 6, 2009.

Valuing and Reporting Investments

OBJ 4 Describe and illustrate valuing and reporting investments in the financial statements.

Debt and equity securities are *financial assets* that are often traded on public exchanges such as the New York Stock Exchange. As a result, their market value can be observed and, thus, objectively determined. For this reason, generally accepted accounting principles (GAAP) allows some debt securities, and requires equity securities where there is less than a 20% ownership interest to be valued in the accounting records and financial statements at their fair market values.

These securities are classified as follows:

1. Trading securities
2. Available-for-sale securities
3. Held-to-maturity securities

Trading Securities

Trading securities are debt and equity securities that are purchased to earn short-term profits from changes in their market prices. Trading securities are often held by banks, mutual funds, insurance companies, and other financial institutions.

Since trading securities are held as a short-term investment, they are reported as a current asset on the balance sheet. Trading securities are valued as a portfolio (group) of securities using the securities' fair values. **Fair value** is the market price that the company would receive for a security if it were sold. A change in the fair value of the portfolio (group) of trading securities is recognized as an **unrealized gain or loss** for the period.

SunTrust Banks Inc. holds $6 billion in trading securities as current assets.

To illustrate, assume Maggie Company purchased a portfolio of trading securities during 2014. On December 31, 2014, the cost and fair values of the securities were as follows:

Name	Number of Shares	Total Cost	Total Fair Value
Armour Company	400	$ 5,000	$ 7,200
Maven, Inc.	500	11,000	7,500
Polaris Co.	200	8,000	10,600
Total		$24,000	$25,300

The portfolio of trading securities is reported at its fair value of $25,300. An adjusting entry is made to record the increase in the fair value of $1,300 ($25,300 – $24,000). In order to maintain a record of the original cost of the securities, a valuation account, called *Valuation Allowance for Trading Investments*, is debited for $1,300, and *Unrealized Gain on Trading Investments* is credited for $1,300.[3] The adjusting entry on December 31, 2014, to record the fair value of the portfolio of trading securities is shown below.

2014 Dec.	31	Valuation Allowance for Trading Investments	1,300	
		Unrealized Gain on Trading Investments		1,300
		To record increase in fair value of trading securities.		

Unrealized Gain on Trading Investments is reported on the income statement. Depending on its significance, it may be reported separately or as *Other income* on the income statement. The valuation allowance is reported on the December 31, 2014, balance sheet as follows:

Maggie Company
Balance Sheet (selected items)
December 31, 2014

Current assets:		
Cash		$120,000
Trading investments (at cost)	$24,000	
Plus valuation allowance for trading investments	1,300	
Trading investments (at fair value)		25,300

If the fair value of the portfolio of trading securities was less than the cost, then the adjustment would debit *Unrealized Loss on Trading Investments* and credit *Valuation Allowance for Trading Investments* for the difference. Unrealized Loss on Trading Investments would be reported on the income statement as Other expenses. Valuation Allowance for Trading Investments would be shown on the balance sheet as a *deduction* from Trading Investments (at cost).

Over time, the valuation allowance account is adjusted to reflect the difference between the cost and the fair value of the portfolio. Thus, increases in the valuation allowance account from the beginning of the period will result in an adjustment to record an unrealized gain, similar to the journal entry illustrated above. Likewise, decreases in the valuation allowance account from the beginning of the period will result in an adjustment to record an unrealized loss.

Example Exercise 13-4 Valuing Trading Securities at Fair Value

OBJ 4

On January 1, 2014, Valuation Allowance for Trading Investments had a zero balance. On December 31, 2014, the cost of the trading securities portfolio was $79,200, and the fair value was $76,800. Prepare the December 31, 2014, adjusting journal entry to record the unrealized gain or loss on trading investments.

3 We assume that the valuation allowance account has a beginning balance of zero to simplify our illustrations.

Follow My Example 13-4

2014			
Dec. 31	Unrealized Loss on Trading Investments	2,400	
	Valuation Allowance for Trading Investments		2,400*
	To record decrease in fair value of trading investments.		

*Trading investments at fair value, December 31, 2014	$ 76,800
Less trading investments at cost, December 31, 2014	79,200
Unrealized loss on trading investments	$ (2,400)

Practice Exercises: **PE 13-4A, PE 13-4B**

Integrity, Objectivity, and Ethics in Business

LOAN LOSS WOES

During the economic crisis of 2008, many of the largest U.S. banks were accused of having provided mortgages to marginally qualified borrowers. Such loans, called "subprime" and "Alt-A" loans, were made to earn mortgage fees. When the borrowers were unable to pay their mortgages, the banks incurred large losses on defaulted loans. These losses were so large that the U.S. government had to provide money (TARP funds) to many banks to bail them out of their financial distress.

During the middle of the crisis, the FASB voted to provide banks more flexibility in applying fair value accounting for bank assets, such as defaulted loans. These FASB rule changes allowed banks to minimize the impact of their defaulted loan write-downs and improve their earnings. Some criticized the FASB as succumbing to political pressure and reducing overall financial statement fairness.

Source: Ian Katz, "FASB Eases Fair-Value Rules Amid Lawmaker Pressure," *Bloomberg*, April 2, 2009.

Available-for-Sale Securities

Available-for-sale securities are debt and equity securities that are neither held for trading, held to maturity, nor held for strategic reasons. The accounting for available-for-sale securities is similar to the accounting for trading securities, except for the reporting of changes in fair values. Specifically, changes in the fair values of *trading securities* are reported as an unrealized gain or loss on the income statement. In contrast, changes in the fair values of *available-for-sale securities* are reported as part of stockholders' equity and, thus, excluded from the income statement.

To illustrate, assume that Maggie Company purchased the three securities during 2014 as available-for-sale securities instead of trading securities. On December 31, 2014, the cost and fair values of the securities were as follows:

Name	Number of Shares	Total Cost	Total Fair Value
Armour Company	400	$ 5,000	$ 7,200
Maven, Inc.	500	11,000	7,500
Polaris Co.	200	8,000	10,600
Total		$24,000	$25,300

Microsoft Corporation holds over $30 billion in available-for-sale securities as current assets.

The portfolio of available-for-sale securities is reported at its fair value of $25,300. An adjusting entry is made to record the increase in fair value of $1,300 ($25,300 – $24,000). In order to maintain a record of the original cost of the securities, a valuation account, called *Valuation Allowance for Available-for-Sale Investments*, is debited for $1,300. This account is similar to the valuation account used for trading securities.

Unlike trading securities, the December 31, 2014, adjusting entry credits a stockholders' equity account instead of an income statement account.[4] The $1,300 increase in fair value is credited to *Unrealized Gain (Loss) on Available-for-Sale Investments.*

The adjusting entry on December 31, 2014, to record the fair value of the portfolio of available-for-sale securities is as follows:

2014 Dec.	31	Valuation Allowance for Available-for-Sale Investments		1,300	
		Unrealized Gain (Loss) on Available-for-Sale Investments			1,300
		To record increase in fair value of available-for-sale investments.			

A credit balance in Unrealized Gain (Loss) on Available-for-Sale Investments is added to stockholders' equity, while a debit balance is subtracted from stockholders' equity.

The valuation allowance and the unrealized gain are reported on the December 31, 2014, balance sheet as follows:

Maggie Company
Balance Sheet
December 31, 2014

Current assets:		
Cash		$120,000
Available-for-sale investments (at cost)	$24,000	
Plus valuation allowance for available-for-sale investments	1,300	
Available-for-sale investments (at fair value)		25,300
Stockholders' equity:		
Common stock		$ 10,000
Paid-in capital in excess of par		150,000
Retained earnings		250,000
Unrealized gain (loss) on available-for-sale investments		1,300
Total stockholders' equity		$411,300

Equal

As shown above, Unrealized Gain (Loss) on Available-for-Sale Investments is reported as an addition to stockholders' equity. In future years, the cumulative effects of unrealized gains and losses are reported in this account. Since 2014 was the first year that Maggie Company purchased available-for-sale securities, the unrealized gain is reported as the balance of *Unrealized Gain (Loss) on Available-for-Sale Investments.* This treatment is supported under the theory that available-for-sale securities will be held longer than trading securities, so changes in fair value over time have a greater opportunity to cancel out. Thus, these changes are not reported on the income statement, as is the case with trading securities.

If the fair value was less than the cost, then the adjustment would debit Unrealized Gain (Loss) on Available-for-Sale Investments and credit Valuation Allowance for Available-for-Sale Investments for the difference. Unrealized Gain (Loss) on Trading Investments would be reported in the Stockholders' Equity section as a negative

4 This is a rare exception to the rule that every adjusting entry must affect an income statement and a balance sheet account.

item. Valuation Allowance for Available-for-Sale Investments would be shown on the balance sheet as a deduction from Available-for-Sale Investments (at cost).

Over time, the valuation allowance account is adjusted to reflect the difference between the cost and the fair value of the portfolio. Thus, increases in the valuation allowance from the beginning of the period will result in an adjustment to record an increase in the valuation and unrealized gain (loss) accounts, similar to the journal entry illustrated earlier. Likewise, decreases in the valuation allowance from the beginning of the period will result in an adjustment to record decreases in the valuation and unrealized gain (loss) accounts.

Example Exercise 13-5 Valuing Available-for-Sale Securities at Fair Value OBJ 4

On January 1, 2014, Valuation Allowance for Available-for-Sale Investments had a zero balance. On December 31, 2014, the cost of the available-for-sale securities was $45,700, and the fair value was $50,000.

Prepare the adjusting entry to record the unrealized gain or loss for available-for-sale investments on December 31, 2014.

Follow My Example 13-5

2014			
Dec. 31	Valuation Allowance for Available-for-Sale Investments	4,300*	
	Unrealized Gain (Loss) on Available-for-Sale Investments		4,300
	To record increase in fair value of available-for-sale securities.		

*Available-for-sale investments at fair value, December 31, 2014	$50,000
Less available-for-sale investments at cost, December 31, 2014	45,700
Unrealized gain (loss) on available-for-sale investments	$ 4,300

Practice Exercises: **PE 13-5A, PE 13-5B**

Held-to-Maturity Securities

Held-to-maturity securities are debt investments, such as notes or bonds, that a company intends to hold until their maturity date. Held-to-maturity securities are primarily purchased to earn interest revenue.

If a held-to-maturity security will mature within a year, it is reported as a current asset on the balance sheet. Held-to-maturity securities maturing beyond a year are reported as noncurrent assets.

Only securities with maturity dates, such as corporate notes and bonds, are classified as held-to-maturity securities. Equity securities are not held-to-maturity securities because they have no maturity date.

Held-to-maturity bond investments are recorded at their cost, including any brokerage commissions, as illustrated earlier in this chapter. If the interest rate on the bonds differs from the market rate of interest, the bonds may be purchased at a premium or discount. In such cases, the premium or discount is amortized over the life of the bonds.

Held-to-maturity bond investments are reported on the balance sheet at their amortized cost. The accounting for held-to-maturity investments, including premium and discount amortization, is described in advanced accounting texts.

Summary

Exhibit 3 summarizes the valuation and balance sheet reporting of trading, available-for-sale, and held-to-maturity securities.

EXHIBIT 3

Summary of Valuing and Reporting of Investments

	Trading Securities	**Available-for-Sale Securities**	**Held-to-Maturity Securities**
Valued at:	**Fair Value**	**Fair Value**	**Amortized Cost**
Changes in valuation are reported as:	Unrealized gain or loss in the income statement as Other income (loss).	Accumulated unrealized gain or loss is reported in stockholders' equity on the balance sheet.	Premium or discount amortization is reported as part of interest revenue on the income statement.
Reported on the balance sheet as:	Cost of investments plus or minus valuation allowance.	Cost of investments plus or minus valuation allowance.	Amortized cost of investment.
Classified on balance sheet as:	A current asset.	Either as a current or noncurrent asset, depending on management's intent.	Either as a current or noncurrent asset, depending on remaining term to maturity.

Common stock investments in trading and available-for-sale securities are normally less than 20% of the outstanding common stock of the investee. The portfolios are reported at fair value using the valuation allowance account, while the individual securities are accounted for using the cost method. Investments between 20% and 50% of the outstanding common stock of the investee are accounted for using the equity method illustrated earlier in this chapter. Equity method investments are classified as noncurrent assets on the balance sheet. Moreover, such investments are permitted to be valued using fair values. To simplify, it is assumed that the investor does not elect this option.

The balance sheet reporting for the investments of Mornin' Joe is shown below.

Mornin' Joe
Balance Sheet
December 31, 2014

Assets			
Current assets:			
Cash and cash equivalents		$235,000	
Trading investments (at cost)	$420,000		
Plus valuation allowance for trading investments	45,000	465,000	
Accounts receivable	$305,000		
Less allowance for doubtful accounts	12,300	292,700	
Merchandise inventory—at lower of cost (first-in, first-out method) or market		120,000	
Prepaid insurance		24,000	
Total current assets			$1,136,700
Investments:			
Investment in AM Coffee (equity method)			565,000
Property, plant, and equipment:			

Mornin' Joe invests in trading securities and does not have investments in held-to-maturity or available-for-sale securities. Mornin' Joe also owns 40% of AM Coffee Corporation, which is accounted for using the equity method. Mornin' Joe intends to keep its investment in AM Coffee indefinitely for strategic reasons; thus, its investment in AM Coffee is classified as a noncurrent asset. Such investments are normally reported before property, plant, and equipment.

Mornin' Joe reported an Unrealized Gain on Trading Investments of $5,000 and Equity Income in AM Coffee of $57,000 in the Other Income and Expense section of its income statement, as shown below.

Mornin' Joe
Income Statement
For the Year Ended December 31, 2014

Revenue from sales:			
Sales		$5,450,000	
Less: Sales returns and allowances	$26,500		
Sales discounts	21,400	47,900	
Net sales			$5,402,100
Cost of merchandise sold			2,160,000
Gross profit			$3,242,100
Total operating expenses			2,608,700
Income from operations			$ 633,400
Other income and expense:			
Interest revenue		$ 18,000	
Interest expense		(136,000)	
Loss on disposal of fixed asset		(23,000)	
Unrealized gain on trading investments		5,000	
Equity income in AM Coffee		57,000	(79,000)
Income before income taxes			$ 554,400
Income tax expense			132,800
Net income			$ 421,600

Business Connection

WARREN BUFFETT: THE SAGE OF OMAHA

Beginning in 1962, Warren Buffett, one of the world's wealthiest and most successful investors, began buying shares of Berkshire Hathaway. He eventually took control of the company and transformed it from a textile manufacturing company into an investment holding company. Today, Berkshire Hathaway holds over $125 billion in cash and cash equivalents, equity securities, and debt securities. Berkshire's largest holdings include The Coca-Cola Company, American Express, Wells Fargo, and Procter & Gamble. Berkshire Class A common stock trades near $121,900 per share, the highest priced share on the New York Stock Exchange. These shares would have given an investor over a 1,400% return since 1990.

Buffett compares his investment style to hitting a baseball: "Ted Williams, one of the greatest hitters in the game, stated, 'my argument is, to be a good hitter, you've got to get a good ball to hit. It's the first rule of the book. If I have to bite at stuff that is out of my happy zone, I'm not a .344 hitter. I might only be a .250 hitter.'" Buffett states, "Charlie (Buffett's partner) and I agree and will try to wait for (investment) opportunities that are well within our 'happy zone.'" One of Buffet's recent "happy zone" investments was the acquisition of Burlington Northern Santa Fe Railroad for $34 billion.

Warren Buffett as the CEO of Berkshire Hathaway earns a salary of only $100,000 per year, which is the lowest CEO salary for a company of its size in the United States. However, he personally owns approximately 38% of the company, making him worth over $40 billion. What will Buffett do with this wealth? He has decided to give nearly all of it to philanthropic causes through the Bill and Melinda Gates Foundation.

Source: Warren E. Buffett, *The Essays of Warren Buffett: Lessons for Corporate America*, edited by Lawrence A. Cunningham, p. 234.

OBJ 5 Describe fair value accounting and its implications for the future.

Fair Value Accounting

Fair value is the price that would be received to sell an asset or pay off a liability. Fair value assumes that this transaction occurs under *normal* business conditions.

As illustrated earlier, generally accepted accounting principles require trading and available-for-sale investments to be recorded at fair value.

In contrast, many assets and liabilities are recorded and reported at amounts that differ significantly from their fair values. For example, when property, plant, and equipment is purchased, it is initially recorded at its purchase price, or cost. This purchase price, called *historical cost*, is allocated to income over its useful life through depreciation. As a result, the book value of property, plant, and equipment reflects the portion of the historical cost of the asset that has not been depreciated, and normally differs significantly from fair value.

Trend to Fair Value Accounting

The current trend is for the Financial Accounting Standards Board (FASB) and other accounting regulators to adopt accounting principles using fair values for valuing and reporting assets and liabilities. Factors contributing to this trend include:

1. Current generally accepted accounting principles are a hybrid of varying measurement methods that often conflict with one another. For example, property, plant, and equipment are normally reported at their depreciated book values. However, GAAP require that if a fixed asset value is *impaired*, that it be written down to its fair value. Such conflicting accounting principles could confuse users of financial statements.
2. A greater percentage of the total assets of many companies consists of financial assets such as receivables and securities that have readily available fair values. Fair values for such assets can often be readily obtained from stock market quotations or computed using current interest rates and present values. Likewise, many liabilities can be valued using readily available market quotations or current interest rates and present values.
3. The world economy has compelled accounting regulators to adopt a worldwide set of accounting principles and standards. International Financial Reporting Standards (IFRSs) are issued by the International Accounting Standards Board (IASB) and are used by the European Economic Union (EU). As a result, the FASB is under increasing pressure to conform U.S. accounting standards to international standards. One area where differences exist is in the use of fair values, which are more often used by International Financial Reporting Standards.

IFRS IFRS See Appendix C for more information

While there is an increasing trend to fair value accounting, fair value measures also have several potential disadvantages. These disadvantages include:

1. Fair values may not be readily obtainable for some assets or liabilities. As a result, accounting reports may become more subjective and less reliable. For example, fair values (market quotations) are normally available for trading and available-for-sale securities. However, fair values may not be as available for assets such as property, plant, and equipment or intangible assets such as goodwill.
2. Fair values make it more difficult to compare companies that use different methods of determining (measuring) fair values. This would be especially true for assets and liabilities for which fair values are not readily available.
3. Using fair values could result in more fluctuations in accounting reports because fair values normally change from year to year. Such volatility may confuse users of the financial statements. It may also make it more difficult for users to determine current operating trends and to predict future trends.

Effect of Fair Value Accounting on the Financial Statements

The use of fair values for valuing assets and liabilities affects the financial statements. Specifically, the balance sheet and income statement could be affected.

Balance Sheet When an asset or a liability is reported at its fair value, any difference between the asset's original cost or prior period's fair value must be recorded. As we illustrated for trading and available-for-sale securities, one method for doing this is to use a valuation allowance. The account, *Valuation Allowance for Trading Investments*, was used earlier in this chapter to adjust trading securities to their fair values.

Available-for-sale securities are recorded at fair value. Changes in their fair values are not recognized on the income statement, but are included as part of stockholders' equity.

Income Statement Instead of recording the unrealized gain or loss on changes in fair values as part of stockholders' equity, the unrealized gains or losses may be reported on the income statement. This method was illustrated earlier in this chapter for *trading* securities.

As shown above, differences exist as to how to best report changes in fair values—that is, whether to report gains or losses on fair values on the income statement or the balance sheet.

In an attempt to bridge these differences, the FASB introduced the concepts of *comprehensive income* and *accumulated other comprehensive income*. These concepts are described in the appendix to this chapter.

Financial Analysis and Interpretation: Dividend Yield

F·A·I

OBJ 6 Describe and illustrate the computation of dividend yield.

The **dividend yield** measures the rate of return to stockholders, based on cash dividends. Dividend yield is most often computed for common stock because preferred stock has a stated dividend rate. In contrast, the cash dividends paid on common stock normally vary with the profitability of the corporation.

The dividend yield is computed as follows:

$$\text{Dividend Yield} = \frac{\text{Dividends per Share of Common Stock}}{\text{Market Price per Share of Common Stock}}$$

To illustrate, the market price of News Corporation was \$16.98 on November 8, 2011. During the preceding year, News Corporation had paid dividends of \$0.19 per share. Thus, the dividend yield of News Corporation's common stock is computed as follows:

$$\text{Dividend Yield} = \frac{\text{Dividends per Share of Common Stock}}{\text{Market Price per Share of Common Stock}} = \frac{\$0.19}{\$16.98} = 1.1\%$$

News Corporation pays a dividend yield of slightly more than 1%. The dividend yield is first a function of a company's profitability, or ability to pay a dividend. For example, many banks nearly eliminated their dividends during the banking crisis of 2008 because they had significant losses. News Corporation has sufficient profitability to pay a dividend. Secondly, a company's dividend yield is a function of management's alternative use of funds. If a company has sufficient growth opportunities, funds may be directed toward internal investment, rather than toward paying dividends. This would explain News Corporation's small dividend yield.

The dividend yield will vary from day to day, because the market price of a corporation's stock varies day to day. Current dividend yields are provided with news service quotations of market prices, such as The Wall Street Journal or Yahoo! Finance.

Recent dividend yields for some selected companies are as follows:

Company	Dividend Yield (%)
Apple	None
Best Buy	2.30
Coca-Cola Company	2.80
Duke Energy	4.80
Google	None
Hewlett-Packard	1.80
Microsoft	3.00
Verizon Communications	5.40

As can be seen, the dividend yield varies widely across firms. Growth firms tend to retain their earnings to fund future growth. Thus, Apple and Google pay no dividends, and Hewlett-Packard has a relatively small dividend. Common stockholders of these companies expect to earn most of their return from stock price appreciation. In contrast, Duke Energy and Verizon Communications are regulated utilities that provide a return to common stockholders mostly through dividends. Best Buy, Coca-Cola, and Microsoft provide a mix of dividends and expected stock price appreciation to their common stockholders.

Example Exercise 13-6 Dividend Yield

OBJ 6

On March 11, 2014, Sheldon Corporation had a market price of $58 per share of common stock. For the previous year, Sheldon paid an annual dividend of $2.90 per share. Compute the dividend yield for Sheldon Corporation.

Follow My Example 13-6

$$\text{Dividend Yield} = \frac{\text{Dividends per Share of Common Stock}}{\text{Market Price per Share of Common Stock}}$$

$$\text{Dividend Yield} = \frac{\$2.90}{\$58} = 0.05\text{, or }5\%$$

Practice Exercises: **PE 13-6A, PE 13-6B**

APPENDIX

Comprehensive Income

Comprehensive income is defined as all changes in stockholders' equity during a period, except those resulting from dividends and stockholders' investments. Comprehensive income is computed by adding or subtracting *other comprehensive income* from net income, as follows:

Net income	$XXX
Other comprehensive income	XXX
Comprehensive income	$XXX

Other comprehensive income items include unrealized gains and losses on available-for-sale securities as well as other items such as foreign currency and pension liability adjustments. The *cumulative* effect of other comprehensive income is reported on the balance sheet, as **accumulated other comprehensive income**.

Companies are required to report comprehensive income in the financial statements in one of the following two ways:

1. On the income statement, or
2. In a separate statement of comprehensive income that immediately follows the income statement.

In the earlier illustration, Maggie Company had reported an unrealized gain of $1,300 on available-for-sale investments. This unrealized gain would be reported in the Stockholders' Equity section of Maggie's 2014 balance sheet, as follows:

Maggie Company
Balance Sheet
December 31, 2014

Stockholders' equity:	
Common stock	$ 10,000
Paid-in capital in excess of par	150,000
Retained earnings	250,000
Unrealized gain (loss) on available-for-sale investments	1,300
Total stockholders' equity	$411,300

Alternatively, Maggie Company could have reported the unrealized gain as part of accumulated other comprehensive income as follows:

Maggie Company
Balance Sheet
December 31, 2014

Stockholders' equity:	
Common stock	$ 10,000
Paid-in capital in excess of par	150,000
Retained earnings	250,000
Accumulated other comprehensive income:	
Unrealized gain on available-for-sale investments	1,300
Total stockholders' equity	$411,300

At a Glance 13

OBJ 1 Describe why companies invest in debt and equity securities.

Key Points Cash can be used to (1) invest in current operations, (2) invest to earn additional revenue in marketable securities, or (3) invest in marketable securities for strategic reasons.

Learning Outcomes	Example Exercises	Practice Exercises
• Describe the ways excess cash is used by a business.		
• Describe the purpose of temporary investments.		
• Describe the strategic purpose of long-term investments.		

OBJ 2 Describe and illustrate the accounting for debt investments.

Key Points The accounting for debt investments includes recording the purchase, interest revenue, and sale of the debt. Both the purchase and sale date may include accrued interest.

Learning Outcomes	Example Exercises	Practice Exercises
• Prepare journal entries to record the purchase of a debt investment, including accrued interest.	**EE13-1**	**PE13-1A, 13-1B**
• Prepare journal entries for interest revenue from debt investments.	**EE13-1**	**PE13-1A, 13-1B**
• Prepare journal entries to record the sale of a debt investment at a gain or loss.	**EE13-1**	**PE13-1A, 13-1B**

OBJ 3 Describe and illustrate the accounting for equity investments.

Key Points The accounting for equity investments differs, depending on the degree of control. Accounting for investments of less than 20% of the outstanding stock (no control) of the investee includes recording the purchase of stock, the receipt of dividends, and the sale of stock at a gain or loss. Investments of 20%–50% of the outstanding stock of an investee are considered to have significant influence and accounted for under the *equity method*. An investment for more than 50% of the outstanding stock of an investee is treated as a *business combination* and accounted for using *consolidated financial statements*.

Learning Outcomes	Example Exercises	Practice Exercises
• Describe the accounting for less than 20%, 20%–50%, and greater than 50% investments.		
• Prepare journal entries to record the purchase of a stock investment.	**EE13-2**	**PE13-2A, 13-2B**
• Prepare journal entries for the receipt of dividends.	**EE13-2**	**PE13-2A, 13-2B**
• Prepare journal entries for the sale of a stock investment at a gain or loss.	**EE13-2**	**PE13-2A, 13-2B**
• Prepare journal entries for the equity earnings of an equity method investee.	**EE13-3**	**PE13-3A, 13-3B**
• Prepare journal entries for the dividends received from an equity method investee.	**EE13-3**	**PE13-3A, 13-3B**
• Describe a business combination, parent company, and subsidiary company.		
• Describe consolidated financial statements.		

OBJ 4 Describe and illustrate valuing and reporting investments in the financial statements.

Key Points Debt and equity securities are classified as (1) trading securities, (2) available-for-sale securities, and (3) held-to-maturity securities for reporting and valuation purposes. *Trading securities* are debt and equity securities valued at *fair value*, with unrealized gains and losses reported on the income statement. *Available-for-sale securities* are debt and equity securities that are not classified as trading or held to maturity. Available-for-sale securities are reported at fair value with unrealized gains or losses reported in the Stockholders' Equity section of the balance sheet. *Held-to-maturity* investments are debt securities only that are intended to be held until their maturity date. Held-to-maturity debt investments are valued at amortized cost.

Learning Outcomes	Example Exercises	Practice Exercises
• Describe trading securities, held-to-maturity securities, and available-for-sale securities.		
• Prepare journal entries to record the change in the fair value of a trading security portfolio.	EE13-4	PE13-4A, 13-4B
• Describe and illustrate the reporting of trading securities on the balance sheet.		
• Prepare journal entries to record the change in fair value of an available-for-sale security portfolio.	EE13-5	PE13-5A, 13-5B
• Describe and illustrate the reporting of available-for-sale securities on the balance sheet.		
• Describe the accounting for held-to-maturity debt securities.		

OBJ 5 Describe fair value accounting and its implications for the future.

Key Points There is a trend toward fair value accounting in generally accepted accounting principles. Fair value is the price that would be received to sell an asset or pay off a liability.

Learning Outcomes	Example Exercises	Practice Exercises
• Describe the reasons why there is a trend toward fair value accounting.		
• Describe the advantages and disadvantages of fair value accounting.		
• Describe how fair value accounting impacts the balance sheet and income statement.		
• Describe the future of fair value accounting.		

OBJ 6 Describe and illustrate the computation of dividend yield.

Key Points The dividend yield measures the cash return from common dividends as a percent of the market price of the common stock. The ratio is computed as dividends per share of common stock divided by the market price per share of common stock.

Learning Outcomes	Example Exercises	Practice Exercises
• Compute dividend yield.	EE13-6	13-6A, 13-6B
• Describe how dividend yield measures the return to stockholders from dividends.		

Key Terms

accumulated other comprehensive income (603)
available-for-sale securities (595)
business combination (592)
comprehensive income (602)
consolidated financial statements (592)
cost method (589)
debt securities (585)
dividend yield (601)
equity method (590)
equity securities (585)
fair value (593)
held-to-maturity securities (597)
investee (588)
investments (585)
investor (588)
other comprehensive income (602)
parent company (592)
subsidiary company (592)
trading securities (593)
unrealized gain or loss (593)

Illustrative Problem

The following selected investment transactions were completed by Rosewell Company during 2014, its first year of operations:

2014

Jan. 11. Purchased 800 shares of Bryan Company stock as an available-for-sale security at $23 per share plus an $80 brokerage commission.

Feb. 6. Purchased $40,000 of 8% U.S. Treasury bonds at their face amount plus accrued interest for 36 days. The bonds pay interest on January 1 and July 1. The bonds were classified as held-to-maturity securities.

Mar. 3. Purchased 1,900 shares of Cohen Company stock as a trading security at $48 per share plus a $152 brokerage commission.

Apr. 5. Purchased 2,400 shares of Lyons Inc. stock as an available-for-sale security at $68 per share plus a $120 brokerage commission.

May 12. Purchased 200,000 shares of Myers Company at $37 per share plus an $8,000 brokerage commission. Myers Company has 800,000 common shares issued and outstanding. The equity method was used for this investment.

July 1. Received semiannual interest on bonds purchased on February 6.

Aug. 29. Sold 1,200 shares of Cohen Company stock at $61 per share less a $90 brokerage commission.

Oct. 5. Received an $0.80-per-share dividend on Bryan Company stock.

Nov. 11. Received a $1.10-per-share dividend on Myers Company stock.

16. Purchased 3,000 shares of Morningside Company stock as a trading security for $52 per share plus a $150 brokerage commission.

Dec. 31. Accrued interest on U.S. Treasury bonds.

31. Myers Company earned $1,200,000 during the year. Rosewell recorded its share of Myers Company earnings, using the equity method.

31. Prepared adjusting entries for the portfolios of trading and available-for-sale securities, based upon the following fair values (stock prices):

Bryan Company	$21
Cohen Company	43
Lyons Inc.	88
Myers Company	40
Morningside Company	45

Instructions

1. Journalize the preceding transactions.
2. Prepare the balance sheet disclosure for Rosewell Company's investments on December 31, 2014. Assume held-to-maturity investments are classified as noncurrent assets.

Solution

1.

2014 Jan.	11	Investments—Bryan Company	18,480*	
		Cash		18,480
		*(800 shares × $23 per share) + $80		

Feb.	6	Investments—U.S. Treasury Bonds	40,000	
		Interest Receivable	320*	
		Cash		40,320
		*$40,000 × 8% × (36 days/360 days)		

Mar.	3	Investments—Cohen Company	91,352*	
		Cash		91,352
		*(1,900 shares × $48 per share) + $152		

Apr.	5	Investments—Lyons Inc.	163,320*	
		Cash		163,320
		*(2,400 shares × $68 per share) + $120		

May	12	Investment in Myers Company	7,408,000*	
		Cash		7,408,000
		*(200,000 shares × $37 per share) + $8,000		

July	1	Cash	1,600*	
		Interest Receivable		320
		Interest Revenue		1,280
		*$40,000 × 8% × ½		

Aug.	29	Cash	73,110*	
		Investments—Cohen Company		57,696**
		Gain on Sale of Investments		15,414
		*(1,200 shares × $61 per share) – $90		
		**1,200 shares × ($91,352/1,900 shares)		

Practice Exercises

Example Exercises

EE 13-1 p. 588

PE 13-1A Bond investment transactions — OBJ. 2

Journalize the entries to record the following selected bond investment transactions for Supper Club Trust:

a. Purchased for cash $400,000 of Tyler City 6% bonds at 100 plus accrued interest of $2,000.

b. Received first semiannual interest payment.

c. Sold $200,000 of the bonds at 98 plus accrued interest of $1,000.

EE 13-1 p. 588

PE 13-1B Bond investment transactions — OBJ. 2

Journalize the entries to record the following selected bond investment transactions for Starks Products:

a. Purchased for cash $120,000 of Iceline, Inc. 5% bonds at 100 plus accrued interest of $1,000.

b. Received first semiannual interest payment.

c. Sold $60,000 of the bonds at 101 plus accrued interest of $500.

EE 13-2 p. 590

PE 13-2A Stock investment transactions — OBJ. 3

On March 20, 10,000 shares of Thorlite Company are acquired at a price of $30 per share plus a $250 brokerage fee. On May 30, a $0.25-per-share dividend was received on the Thorlite Company stock. On June 15, 5,000 shares of the Thorlite Company stock were sold for $36 per share less a $200 brokerage fee. Prepare the journal entries for the original purchase, the dividend, and the sale under the cost method.

EE 13-2 p. 590

PE 13-2B Stock investment transactions — OBJ. 3

On September 12, 2,000 shares of Aspen Company are acquired at a price of $50 per share plus a $200 brokerage fee. On October 15, a $0.50-per-share dividend was received on the Aspen Company stock. On November 10, 1,200 shares of the Aspen Company stock were sold for $42 per share less a $150 brokerage fee. Prepare the journal entries for the original purchase, the dividend, and the sale under the cost method.

EE 13-3 p. 592

PE 13-3A Equity method — OBJ. 3

On January 2, Leonberger Company acquired 30% of the outstanding stock of ARO Company for $300,000. For the year ended December 31, ARO Company earned income of $60,000 and paid dividends of $15,000. Prepare the entries for Leonberger Company for the purchase of the stock, the share of ARO income, and the dividends received from ARO Company.

EE 13-3 p. 592

PE 13-3B Equity method — OBJ. 3

On January 2, Yorkshire Company acquired 40% of the outstanding stock of Fain Company for $500,000. For the year ended December 31, Fain Company earned income of $140,000 and paid dividends of $50,000. Prepare the entries for Yorkshire Company for the purchase of the stock, the share of Fain income, and the dividends received from Fain Company.

Example Exercises

EE 13-4 *p. 594*

PE 13-4A Valuing trading securities at fair value
OBJ. 4

On January 1, 2014, Valuation Allowance for Trading Investments had a zero balance. On December 31, 2014, the cost of the trading securities portfolio was $212,500, and the fair value was $203,600. Prepare the December 31, 2014, adjusting journal entry to record the unrealized gain or loss on trading investments.

EE 13-4 *p. 594*

PE 13-4B Valuing trading securities at fair value
OBJ. 4

On January 1, 2014, Valuation Allowance for Trading Investments had a zero balance. On December 31, 2014, the cost of the trading securities portfolio was $41,500, and the fair value was $46,300. Prepare the December 31, 2014, adjusting journal entry to record the unrealized gain or loss on trading investments.

EE 13-5 *p. 597*

PE 13-5A Valuing available-for-sale securities at fair value
OBJ. 4

On January 1, 2014, Valuation Allowance for Available-for-Sale Investments had a zero balance. On December 31, 2014, the cost of the available-for-sale securities was $78,400, and the fair value was $72,600. Prepare the adjusting entry to record the unrealized gain or loss on available-for-sale investments on December 31, 2014.

EE 13-5 *p. 597*

PE 13-5B Valuing available-for-sale securities at fair value
OBJ. 4

On January 1, 2014, Valuation Allowance for Available-for-Sale Investments had a zero balance. On December 31, 2014, the cost of the available-for-sale securities was $24,260, and the fair value was $26,350. Prepare the adjusting entry to record the unrealized gain or loss on available-for-sale investments on December 31, 2014.

EE 13-6 *p. 602*

F·A·I

PE 13-6A Dividend yield
OBJ. 6

On June 30, 2014, Setzer Corporation had a market price of $100 per share of common stock. For the previous year, Setzer paid an annual dividend of $4.00. Compute the dividend yield for Setzer Corporation.

EE 13-6 *p. 602*

F·A·I

PE 13-6B Dividend yield
OBJ. 6

On October 23, 2014, Wilkerson Company had a market price of $40 per share of common stock. For the previous year, Wilkerson paid an annual dividend of $1.20. Compute the dividend yield for Wilkerson Company.

Exercises

EX 13-1 Entries for investment in bonds, interest, and sale of bonds
OBJ. 2

Sorrey Company acquired $75,000 of Clayton Co., 6% bonds on April 1, 2014, at their face amount. Interest is paid semiannually on April 1 and October 1. On October 1, 2014, Sorrey Company sold $25,000 of the bonds for 98.

Journalize entries to record the following:

a. The initial acquisition of the bonds on April 1.

b. The semiannual interest received on October 1.

c. The sale of the bonds on October 1.

d. The accrual of $750 interest on December 31, 2014.

EX 13-7 Entries for inves

✔ May 26, Loss on sale of investments, $10,110

The following equity in
in 2014:

Feb. 8. Purchased 2,400
brokerage comm

Apr. 22. Received a quar
investment.

May 26. Sold 1,000 share
$60.

Journalize the entries for

EX 13-8 Entries for stock

✔ Oct. 12, Dividend revenue, $408

Murray Corp. manufactur
following selected equity

Jan. 16. Purchased for ca
a $140 brokerag

Mar. 23. Received divider

May 25. Purchased 1,000
brokerage comm

July 10. Sold 3,200 share
age commission.
first investments

Oct. 12. Received dividen

EX 13-9 Entries for stock

Seamus Industries Inc. buy
The following investment

Feb. 24. Acquired 1,000 s
commission.

May 16. Acquired 2,500 s
commission.

July 14. Sold 400 shares c
commission.

Aug. 12. Sold 750 shares c
brokerage commi

Oct. 31. Received divideno

Journalize the entries for t

EX 13-10 Equity method f

At a total cost of $2,000,00
common stock as a long-
of accounting for this inv
outstanding, including the

a. Journalize the entries b

1. Larson Corp. reports

2. A cash dividend of $
current period.

b. Why is the equ

EX 13-2 Entries for i

Mars Investments acq
September 1, 2014. T
2015, Mars sold $75,(
Journalize the ent

a. The initial acquisi
b. The adjusting ent
bonds on Decemb
c. The receipt of sen
d. The sale of $75,0C

✔ Dec. 1, Loss on sale of investments, $600

EX 13-3 Entries for i

Crabtree Co. purchase
rectly from the county,
interest on May 1 and
Thomas County bonds
Provide journal en

a. The purchase of th
b. Semiannual interes
c. Sale of the bonds
d. Adjusting entry for

✔ Aug. 29, Loss on sale of investments, $700

EX 13-4 Entries for in

The following bond
Company:

Jan. 31. Purchased 75
The bonds pa
July 1. Received sen
Aug. 29. Sold 35, $1,0

a. Journalize the entri
b. Provide the Decemb
on the bonds.

EX 13-5 Interest on bo

On April 1, 2014, Rizzo
bonds at their face amo
March 1 and Septembe
Energizer Company bo
December 31, 2014, for
Determine the inter
2014.

✔ c. Gain on sale of investments, $14,104

EX 13-6 Entries for inv

On March 10, Fly Corp
of Dickson Co. commo
a cash dividend of $1.4
sold at $38, less commi
Using the cost meth
receipt of dividends, an

EX 13-11 Equity method for stock investment OBJ. 3

✔ b. $5,567,600

SPREADSHEET

On January 4, 2014, Penman Company purchased 124,000 shares of Hi Energy Company directly from one of the founders for a price of $44 per share. Hi Energy has 400,000 shares outstanding, including the Penman shares. On July 2, 2014, Hi Energy paid $440,000 in total dividends to its shareholders. On December 31, 2014, Hi Energy reported a net income of $800,000 for the year. Penman uses the equity method in accounting for its investment in Hi Energy.

a. Provide the Penman Inc. journal entries for the transactions involving its investment in Hi Energy Inc. during 2014.
b. Determine the December 31, 2014, balance of the Investment in Hi Energy Company. Stock account.

EX 13-12 Equity method for stock investment with loss OBJ. 3

On January 6, 2014, Bulldog Co. purchased 34% of the outstanding stock of Gator Co. for $212,000. Gator Co. paid total dividends of $24,000 to all shareholders on June 30. Gator had a net loss of $56,000 for 2014.

a. Journalize Bulldog's purchase of the stock, receipt of the dividends, and the adjusting entry for the equity loss in Gator Co. stock.
b. Compute the balance of Investment in Gator Co. Stock on December 31, 2014.
c. How does valuing an investment under the equity method differ from valuing an investment at fair value?

EX 13-13 Equity method for stock investment OBJ. 3

Hawkeye Company's balance sheet reported, under the equity method, its long-term investment in Raven Company for comparative years as follows:

	Dec. 31, 2015	Dec. 31, 2014
Investment in Raven Company stock (in millions)	$281	$264

In addition, the 2015 Hawkeye Company income statement disclosed equity earnings in the Raven Company investment as $25 million. Hawkeye Company neither purchased nor sold Raven Company stock during 2015. The fair value of the Raven Company stock investment on December 31, 2015, was $310 million.

Explain the change in Investment in Raven Company Stock from December 31, 2014, to December 31, 2015.

EX 13-14 Missing statement items, trading investments OBJ. 4

✔ g. $6,000

JED Capital Inc. makes investments in trading securities. Selected income statement items for the years ended December 31, 2014 and 2015, plus selected items from comparative balance sheets, are as follows:

JED Capital Inc.
Selected Income Statement Items
For the Years Ended December 31, 2014 and 2015

	2014	2015
Operating income	a.	e.
Unrealized gain (loss)	b.	$(11,000)
Net income	c.	28,000

JED Capital Inc.
Selected Balance Sheet Items
December 31, 2013, 2014, and 2015

	Dec. 31, 2013	Dec. 31, 2014	Dec. 31, 2015
Trading investments, at cost	$144,000	$168,000	$205,000
Valuation allowance for trading investments	(12,000)	17,000	g.
Trading investments, at fair value	d.	f.	h.
Retained earnings	$210,000	$245,000	i.

There were no dividends.

Determine the missing lettered items.

EX 13-15 Fair value journal entries, trading investments **OBJ. 3, 4**

The investments of Charger Inc. include a single investment: 14,500 shares of Raiders Inc. common stock purchased on February 24, 2014, for $38 per share including brokerage commission. These shares were classified as trading securities. As of the December 31, 2014, balance sheet date, the share price had increased to $42 per share.

a. Journalize the entries to acquire the investment on February 24, and record the adjustment to fair value on December 31, 2014.

b. How is the unrealized gain or loss for trading investments reported on the financial statements?

EX 13-16 Fair value journal entries, trading investments **OBJ. 3, 4**

Jets Bancorp Inc. purchased a portfolio of trading securities during 2014. The cost and fair value of this portfolio on December 31, 2014, was as follows:

Name	Number of Shares	Total Cost	Total Fair Value
Dolphins Inc.	1,400	$28,000	$30,800
Marino Company	1,200	30,000	27,600
Namath Company	800	28,000	26,400
Total		$86,000	$84,800

On May 10, 2015, Jets Bancorp Inc. purchased 1,000 shares of Giants Inc. at $24 per share plus a $150 brokerage fee.

Provide the journal entries to record the following:

a. The adjustment of the trading security portfolio to fair value on December 31, 2014.

b. The May 10, 2015, purchase of Giants Inc. stock.

EX 13-17 Fair value journal entries, trading investments **OBJ. 3, 4**

✔ **a. Dec. 31, 2014, Unrealized gain on trading investments, $17,500**

SPREADSHEET

Last Unguaranteed Financial Inc. purchased the following trading securities during 2014, its first year of operations:

Name	Number of Shares	Cost
Arden Enterprises Inc.	5,000	$150,000
French Broad Industries Inc.	2,750	66,000
Pisgah Construction Inc.	1,600	104,000
Total		$320,000

The market price per share for the trading security portfolio on December 31, 2014, was as follows:

	Market Price per Share, Dec. 31, 2014
Arden Enterprises Inc.	$34
French Broad Industries Inc.	26
Pisgah Construction Inc.	60

(Continued)

a. Provide the journal entry to adjust the trading security portfolio to fair value on December 31, 2014.

b. Assume the market prices of the portfolio were the same on December 31, 2015, as they were on December 31, 2014. What would be the journal entry to adjust the portfolio to fair value?

EX 13-18 Balance sheet presentation, trading investments **OBJ. 4**

The income statement for Delta-tec Inc. for the year ended December 31, 2014, was as follows:

Delta-tec Inc.
Income Statement (selected items)
For the Year Ended December 31, 2014

Income from operations	$299,700
Gain on sale of investments	17,800
Less unrealized loss on trading investments	72,500
Net income	$245,000

The balance sheet dated December 31, 2013, showed a Retained Earnings balance of $825,000. During 2014, the company purchased trading investments for the first time at a cost of $346,000. In addition, trading investments with a cost of $66,000 were sold at a gain during 2014. The company paid $65,000 in dividends during 2014.

a. Determine the December 31, 2014, Retained Earnings balance.

b. Provide the December 31, 2014, balance sheet presentation for Trading Investments.

EX 13-19 Missing statement items, available-for-sale securities **OBJ. 4**

✔ f. ($11,000)

Highland Industries Inc. makes investments in available-for-sale securities. Selected income statement items for the years ended December 31, 2014 and 2015, plus selected items from comparative balance sheets, are as follows:

Highland Industries Inc.
Selected Income Statement Items
For the Years Ended December 31, 2014 and 2015

	2014	2015
Operating income	a.	g.
Gain (loss) from sale of investments	$7,500	$(12,000)
Net income (loss)	b.	(21,000)

Highland Industries Inc.
Selected Balance Sheet Items
December 31, 2013, 2014, and 2015

	Dec. 31, 2013	Dec. 31, 2014	Dec. 31, 2015
Assets			
Available-for-sale investments, at cost	$ 90,000	$ 86,000	$102,000
Valuation allowance for available-for-sale investments	12,000	(11,000)	h.
Available-for-sale investments, at fair value	c.	e.	i.
Stockholders' Equity			
Unrealized gain (loss) on available-for-sale investments	d.	f.	(16,400)
Retained earnings	$175,400	$220,000	j.

There were no dividends.

Determine the missing lettered items.

EX 13-20 Fair value journal entries, available-for-sale investments **OBJ. 3, 4**

The investments of Steelers Inc. include a single investment: 33,100 shares of Bengals Inc. common stock purchased on September 12, 2014, for $13 per share including brokerage commission. These shares were classified as available-for-sale securities. As of the December 31, 2014, balance sheet date, the share price declined to $11 per share.

a. Journalize the entries to acquire the investment on September 12 and record the adjustment to fair value on December 31, 2014.

b. How is the unrealized gain or loss for available-for-sale investments disclosed on the financial statements?

EX 13-21 Fair value journal entries, available-for-sale investments — OBJ. 3, 4

Hurricane Inc. purchased a portfolio of available-for-sale securities in 2014, its first year of operations. The cost and fair value of this portfolio on December 31, 2014, was as follows:

Name	Number of Shares	Total Cost	Total Fair Value
Tornado Inc.	800	$14,000	$15,600
Tsunami Corp.	1,250	31,250	35,000
Typhoon Corp.	2,140	43,870	42,800
Total		$89,120	$93,400

On June 12, 2015, Hurricane purchased 1,450 shares of Rogue Wave Inc. at $45 per share plus a $100 brokerage fee.

a. Provide the journal entries to record the following:

1. The adjustment of the available-for-sale security portfolio to fair value on December 31, 2014.
2. The June 12, 2015, purchase of Rogue Wave Inc. stock.

b. How are unrealized gains and losses treated differently for available-for-sale securities than for trading securities?

EX 13-22 Fair value journal entries, available-for-sale investments — OBJ. 3, 4

SPREADSHEET

Storm, Inc. purchased the following available-for-sale securities during 2014, its first year of operations:

Name	Number of Shares	Cost
Dust Devil, Inc.	1,900	$ 81,700
Gale Co.	850	68,000
Whirlwind Co.	2,850	114,000
Total		$263,700

The market price per share for the available-for-sale security portfolio on December 31, 2014, was as follows:

	Market Price per Share, Dec. 31, 2014
Dust Devil, Inc.	$40
Gale Co.	75
Whirlwind Co.	42

a. Provide the journal entry to adjust the available-for-sale security portfolio to fair value on December 31, 2014.

b. Describe the income statement impact from the December 31, 2014, journal entry.

EX 13-23 Balance sheet presentation of available-for-sale investments — OBJ. 4

During 2014, its first year of operations, Galileo Company purchased two available-for-sale investments as follows:

Security	Shares Purchased	Cost
Hawking Inc.	900	$44,000
Pavlov Co.	1,780	38,000

(Continued)

Assume that as of December 31, 2014, the Hawking Inc. stock had a market value of $50 per share, and the Pavlov Co. stock had a market value of $24 per share. Galileo Company had net income of $300,000, and paid no dividends for the year ended December 31, 2014. All of the available-for-sale investments are classified as current assets.

a. Prepare the Current Assets section of the balance sheet presentation for the available-for-sale investments.

b. Prepare the Stockholders' Equity section of the balance sheet to reflect the earnings and unrealized gain (loss) for the available-for-sale investments.

EX 13-24 Balance sheet presentation of available-for-sale investments **OBJ. 4**

During 2014, Copernicus Corporation held a portfolio of available-for-sale securities having a cost of $185,000. There were no purchases or sales of investments during the year. The market values at the beginning and end of the year were $225,000 and $160,000, respectively. The net income for 2014 was $180,000, and no dividends were paid during the year. The Stockholders' Equity section of the balance sheet was as follows on December 31, 2013:

Copernicus Corporation
Stockholders' Equity
December 31, 2013

Common stock	$ 50,000
Paid-in capital in excess of par	250,000
Retained earnings	340,000
Unrealized gain (loss) on available-for-sale investments	40,000
Total	$680,000

Prepare the Stockholders' Equity section of the balance sheet for December 31, 2014.

EX 13-25 Dividend yield **OBJ. 6**

F·A·I

At the market close on October 27 of a recent year, McDonald's Corporation had a closing stock price of $93.49. In addition, McDonald's Corporation had a dividend per share of $2.44 during the previous year.

Determine McDonald's Corporation's dividend yield. (Round to one decimal place.)

EX 13-26 Dividend yield **OBJ. 6**

✔ a. Dec. 31, Year 1, 1.71%

F·A·I

The market price for Microsoft Corporation closed at $30.48 and $27.91 on December 31, Year 1, and Year 2, respectively. The dividends per share were $0.52 for Year 1 and $0.52 for Year 2.

a. Determine the dividend yield for Microsoft on December 31, Year 1, and Year 2. (Round percentages to two decimal places.)

b. Interpret these measures.

EX 13-27 Dividend yield **OBJ. 6**

F·A·I

eBay Inc. developed a Web-based marketplace at **http://www.ebay.com**, in which individuals can buy and sell a variety of items. eBay also acquired PayPal, an online payments system that allows businesses and individuals to send and receive online payments securely. In a recent annual report, eBay published the following dividend policy:

We have never paid cash dividends on our stock and currently anticipate that we will continue to retain any future earnings for the foreseeable future.

Given eBay's dividend policy, why would an investor be attracted to its stock?

Appendix
EX 13-28 Comprehensive income

On May 12, 2014, Chewco Co. purchased 2,000 shares of Jedi Inc. for $112 per share, including the brokerage commission. The Jedi investment was classified as an available-for-sale security.

On December 31, 2014, the fair value of Jedi Inc. was $124 per share. The net income of Chewco Co. was $50,000 for 2014.

Compute the comprehensive income for Chewco Co. for the year ended December 31, 2014.

Appendix
EX 13-29 Comprehensive income

On December 31, 2013, Valur Co. had the following available-for-sale investment disclosure within the Current Assets section of the balance sheet:

Available-for-sale investments (at cost)	$145,000
Plus valuation allowance for available-for-sale investments	40,000
Available-for-sale investments (at fair value)	$185,000

There were no purchases or sales of available-for-sale investments during 2014. On December 31, 2014, the fair value of the available-for-sale investment portfolio was $200,000. The net income of Valur Co. was $210,000 for 2014.

Compute the comprehensive income for Valur Co. for the year ended December 31, 2014.

Problems Series A

PR 13-1A Debt investment transactions, available-for-sale valuation — OBJ. 2, 4

GENERAL LEDGER

Baldwin Inc. is an athletic footware company that began operations on January 1, 2014. The following transactions relate to debt investments acquired by Baldwin Inc., which has a fiscal year ending on December 31:

2014

Mar. 1. Purchased $50,000 of Buncombe Co. 6%, 10-year bonds at their face amount plus accrued interest of $250. The bonds pay interest semiannually on February 1 and August 1.

16. Purchased $84,000 of French Broad 5%, 15-year bonds at their face amount plus accrued interest of $175. The bonds pay interest semiannually on March 1 and September 1.

Aug. 1. Received semiannual interest on the Buncombe Co. bonds.

31. Sold $20,000 of Buncombe Co. bonds at 99 plus accrued interest of $100.

Sept. 1. Received semiannual interest on the French Broad bonds.

Dec. 31. Accrued $750 interest on the Buncombe Co. bonds.

31. Accrued $1,400 interest on the French Broad bonds.

2015

Feb. 1. Received semiannual interest on the Buncombe Co. bonds.

Mar. 1. Received semiannual interest on the French Broad bonds.

Instructions

1. Journalize the entries to record these transactions.
2. If the bond portfolio is classified as available for sale, what impact would this have on financial statement disclosure?

PR 13-2A Stock investment transactions, trading securities — OBJ. 3, 4

SPREADSHEET

Scofield Financial Co. is a regional insurance company that began operations on January 1, 2014. The following transactions relate to trading securities acquired by Scofield Financial Co., which has a fiscal year ending on December 31:

2014

Mar. 14. Purchased 5,000 shares of Wilkomm Inc. as a trading security at $40 per share plus a brokerage commission of $500.

(Continued)

Apr. 24. Purchased 1,800 shares of McMarsh Inc. as a trading security at $50 plus a brokerage commission of $198.

June 1. Sold 2,600 shares of Wilkomm Inc. for $38 per share less a $100 brokerage commission.

30. Received an annual dividend of $0.35 per share on Wilkomm Inc. stock.

Dec. 31. The portfolio of trading securities was adjusted to fair values of $38 and $49 per share for Wilkomm Inc. and McMarsh Inc., respectively.

2015

Apr. 4. Purchased 3,500 shares of Daley Inc. as a trading security at $30 per share plus a $175 brokerage commission.

June 28. Received an annual dividend of $0.40 per share on Wilkomm Inc. stock.

Sept. 9. Sold 700 shares of Daley Inc. for $32 per share less a $50 brokerage commission.

Dec. 31. The portfolio of trading securities had a cost of $270,578 and a fair value of $350,000, requiring a debit balance in Valuation Allowance for Trading Investments of $79,422 ($350,000 − $270,578). Thus, the credit balance from December 31, 2014, is to be adjusted to the new balance.

Instructions

1. Journalize the entries to record these transactions.
2. Prepare the investment-related current asset balance sheet presentation for Scofield Financial Co. on December 31, 2015.
3. How are unrealized gains or losses on trading investments presented in the financial statements of Scofield Financial Co.?

PR 13-3A Stock investment transactions, equity method and available-for-sale securities OBJ. 3, 4

SPREADSHEET

Daffitar Inc. produces and sells theater set designs and costumes. The company began operations on January 1, 2014. The following transactions relate to securities acquired by Daffitar Inc., which has a fiscal year ending on December 31:

2014

Feb. 1. Purchased 12,000 shares of Acuity Inc. as an available-for-sale security at $27 per share, including the brokerage commission.

Mar. 18. Received a cash dividend of $0.18 per share on Acuity Inc. stock.

Sept. 12. A cash dividend of $0.24 per share was received on the Acuity stock.

28. Sold 1,000 shares of Acuity Inc. stock at $21 per share, less a brokerage commission of $50.

Dec. 31. Acuity Inc. is classified as an available-for-sale investment and is adjusted to a fair value of $33 per share. Use the valuation allowance for available-for-sale investments account in making the adjustment.

2015

Jan. 23. Purchased an influential interest in Shouse Inc. for $376,000 by purchasing 70,000 shares directly from the estate of the founder of Shouse Inc. There are 250,000 shares of Shouse Inc. stock outstanding.

Mar. 16. Received a cash dividend of $0.24 per share on Acuity Inc. stock.

Sept. 16. Received a cash dividend of $0.24 per share plus an extra dividend of $0.06 per share on Acuity Inc. stock.

Dec. 31. Received $30,100 of cash dividends on Shouse Inc. stock. Shouse Inc. reported net income of $190,000 in 2015. Daffitar Inc. uses the equity method of accounting for its investment in Shouse Inc.

31. Acuity Inc. is classified as an available-for-sale investment and is adjusted to a fair value of $30 per share. Use the valuation allowance for available-for-sale investments account in making the adjustment for the decrease in fair value from $33 to $30 per share.

Instructions

1. Journalize the entries to record these transactions.
2. Prepare the investment-related asset and stockholders' equity balance sheet presentation for Daffitar Inc. on December 31, 2015, assuming the Retained Earnings balance on December 31, 2015, is $465,000.

✔ h. ($5,800)

SPREADSHEET

PR 13-4A Investment reporting

OBJ. 2, 3, 4

O'Brien Industries Inc. is a book publisher. The comparative unclassified balance sheets for December 31, 2015 and 2014 are provided below. Selected missing balances are shown by letters.

O'Brien Industries Inc.
Balance Sheet
December 31, 2015 and 2014

	Dec. 31, 2015	Dec. 31, 2014
Cash	$233,000	$220,000
Accounts receivable (net)	136,530	138,000
Available-for-sale investments (at cost)—Note 1	a.	103,770
Less valuation allowance for available-for-sale investments	b.	2,500
Available-for-sale investments (fair value)	$ c.	$101,270
Interest receivable	$ d.	—
Investment in Jolly Roger Co. stock—Note 2	e.	$ 77,000
Office equipment (net)	115,000	130,000
Total assets	$ f.	$666,270
Accounts payable	$ 69,400	$ 60,000
Common stock	70,000	70,000
Excess of issue price over par	225,000	225,000
Retained earnings	g.	308,770
Unrealized gain (loss) on available-for-sale investments	h.	2,500
Total liabilities and stockholders' equity	$ i.	$666,270

Note 1. Investments are classified as available for sale. The investments at cost and fair value on December 31, 2014, are as follows:

	No. of Shares	Cost per Share	Total Cost	Total Fair Value
Bernard Co. stock	2,250	$17	$ 38,250	$ 37,500
Chadwick Co. stock	1,260	52	65,520	63,770
			$103,770	$101,270

Note 2. The investment in Jolly Roger Co. stock is an equity method investment representing 30% of the outstanding shares of Jolly Roger Co.

The following selected investment transactions occurred during 2015:

May 5. Purchased 3,080 shares of Gozar Inc. at $30 per share including brokerage commission. Gozar Inc. is classified as an available-for-sale security.

Oct. 1. Purchased $40,000 of Nightline Co. 6%, 10-year bonds at 100. The bonds are classified as available for sale. The bonds pay interest on October 1 and April 1.

9. Dividends of $12,500 are received on the Jolly Roger Co. investment.

(Continued)

Dec. 31. Jolly Roger Co. reported a total net income of $112,000 for 2015. O'Brien Industries Inc. recorded equity earnings for its share of Jolly Roger Co. net income.

31. Accrued three months of interest on the Nightline bonds.

31. Adjusted the available-for-sale investment portfolio to fair value, using the following fair value per-share amounts:

Available-for-Sale Investments	Fair Value
Bernard Co. stock	$15.40 per share
Chadwick Co. stock	$46.00 per share
Gozar Inc. stock	$32.00 per share
Nightline Co. bonds	$98 per $100 of face amount

31. Closed the O'Brien Industries Inc. net income of $146,230 for 2015. O'Brien Industries Inc. paid no dividends during 2015.

Instructions

Determine the missing letters in the unclassified balance sheet. Provide appropriate supporting calculations.

Problems Series B

PR 13-1B Debt investment transactions, available-for-sale valuation OBJ. 2, 4

GENERAL LEDGER

Rekya Mart Inc. is a general merchandise retail company that began operations on January 1, 2014. The following transactions relate to debt investments acquired by Rekya Mart Inc., which has a fiscal year ending on December 31:

2014

Apr. 1. Purchased $90,000 of Smoke Bay 6%, 10-year bonds at their face amount plus accrued interest of $900. The bonds pay interest semiannually on February 1 and August 1.

May 16. Purchased $42,000 of Geotherma Co. 4%, 12-year bonds at their face amount plus accrued interest of $70. The bonds pay interest semiannually on May 1 and November 1.

Aug. 1. Received semiannual interest on the Smoke Bay bonds.

Sept. 1. Sold $12,000 of Smoke Bay bonds at 101 plus accrued interest of $60.

Nov. 1. Received semiannual interest on the Geotherma Co. bonds.

Dec. 31. Accrued $1,950 interest on the Smoke Bay bonds.

31. Accrued $280 interest on the Geotherma Co. bonds.

2015

Feb. 1. Received semiannual interest on the Smoke Bay bonds.

May 1. Received semiannual interest on the Geotherma Co. bonds.

Instructions

1. Journalize the entries to record these transactions.
2. If the bond portfolio is classified as available for sale, what impact would this have on financial statement disclosure?

PR 13-2B Stock investment transactions, trading securities OBJ. 3, 4

SPREADSHEET

Zeus Investments Inc. is a regional investment company that began operations on January 1, 2014. The following transactions relate to trading securities acquired by Zeus Investments Inc., which has a fiscal year ending on December 31:

2014

Feb. 14. Purchased 4,800 shares of Apollo Inc. as a trading security at $26 per share plus a brokerage commission of $192.

Apr. 1. Purchased 2,300 shares of Ares Inc. as a trading security at $19 per share plus a brokerage commission of $92.

June 1. Sold 600 shares of Apollo Inc. for $32 per share less a $100 brokerage commission.

27. Received an annual dividend of $0.20 per share on Apollo Inc. stock.

Dec. 31. The portfolio of trading securities was adjusted to fair values of $33 and $18.50 per share for Apollo Inc. and Ares Inc., respectively.

2015

Mar. 14. Purchased 1,200 shares of Athena Inc. as a trading security at $65 per share plus a $120 brokerage commission.

June 26. Received an annual dividend of $0.21 per share on Apollo Inc. stock.

July 30. Sold 480 shares of Athena Inc. for $60 per share less a $50 brokerage commission.

Dec. 31. The portfolio of trading securities had a cost of $200,032 and a fair value of $188,000, requiring a credit balance in Valuation Allowance for Trading Investments of $12,032 ($200,032 − $188,000). Thus, the debit balance from December 31, 2014, is to be adjusted to the new balance.

Instructions

1. Journalize the entries to record these transactions.
2. Prepare the investment-related current asset balance sheet presentation for Zeus Investments Inc. on December 31, 2015.
3. How are unrealized gains or losses on trading investments presented in the financial statements of Zeus Investments Inc.?

PR 13-3B Stock investment transactions, equity method and available-for-sale securities — OBJ. 3, 4

SPREADSHEET

Glacier Products Inc. is a wholesaler of rock climbing gear. The company began operations on January 1, 2014. The following transactions relate to securities acquired by Glacier Products Inc., which has a fiscal year ending on December 31:

2014

Jan. 18. Purchased 9,000 shares of Malmo Inc. as an available-for-sale investment at $40 per share, including the brokerage commission.

July 22. A cash dividend of $3.00 per share was received on the Malmo stock.

Oct. 5. Sold 500 shares of Malmo Inc. stock at $58.00 per share, less a brokerage commission of $100.

Dec. 18. Received a regular cash dividend of $3.00 per share on Malmo Inc. stock.

31. Malmo Inc. is classified as an available-for-sale investment and is adjusted to a fair value of $36.00 per share. Use the valuation allowance for available-for-sale investments account in making the adjustment.

2015

Jan. 25. Purchased an influential interest in Helsi Co. for $800,000 by purchasing 75,000 shares directly from the estate of the founder of Helsi. There are 250,000 shares of Helsi Co. stock outstanding.

July 16. Received a cash dividend of $3.00 per share on Malmo Inc. stock.

Dec. 16. Received a cash dividend of $3.00 per share plus an extra dividend of $0.20 per share on Malmo Inc. stock.

(Continued)

Dec. 31. Received $38,000 of cash dividends on Helsi Co. stock. Helsi Co. reported net income of $170,000 in 2015. Glacier Products Inc. uses the equity method of accounting for its investment in Helsi Co.

31. Malmo Inc. is classified as an available-for-sale investment and is adjusted to a fair value of $44 per share. Use the valuation allowance for available-for-sale investments account in making the adjustment for the increase in fair value from $36 to $44 per share.

Instructions

1. Journalize the entries to record the preceding transactions.
2. Prepare the investment-related asset and stockholders' equity balance sheet presentation for Glacier Products Inc. on December 31, 2015, assuming the Retained Earnings balance on December 31, 2015, is $700,000.

✔ b. $4,680

SPREADSHEET

PR 13-4B Investment reporting

OBJ. 2, 3, 4

Teasdale Inc. manufactures and sells commercial and residential security equipment. The comparative unclassified balance sheets for December 31, 2015 and 2014 are provided below. Selected missing balances are shown by letters.

Teasdale Inc.
Balance Sheet
December 31, 2015 and 2014

	Dec. 31, 2015	Dec. 31, 2014
Cash	$160,000	$156,000
Accounts receivable (net)	115,000	108,000
Available-for-sale investments (at cost)—Note 1	a.	91,200
Plus valuation allowance for available-for-sale investments	b.	8,776
Available-for-sale investments (fair value)	$ c.	$ 99,976
Interest receivable	$ d.	—
Investment in Wright Co. stock—Note 2	e.	$ 69,200
Office equipment (net)	96,000	105,000
Total assets	$ f.	$538,176
Accounts payable	$ 91,000	$ 72,000
Common stock	80,000	80,000
Excess of issue price over par	250,000	250,000
Retained earnings	g.	127,400
Unrealized gain (loss) on available-for-sale investments	h.	8,776
Total liabilities and stockholders' equity	$ i.	$538,176

Note 1. Investments are classified as available for sale. The investments at cost and fair value on December 31, 2014, are as follows:

	No. of Shares	Cost per Share	Total Cost	Total Fair Value
Alvarez Inc. stock	960	$38.00	$36,480	$39,936
Hirsch Inc. stock	1,900	28.80	54,720	60,040
			$91,200	$99,976

Note 2. The Investment in Wright Co. stock is an equity method investment representing 30% of the outstanding shares of Wright Co.

The following selected investment transactions occurred during 2015:

Mar. 18. Purchased 800 shares of Richter Inc. at $40 including brokerage commission. Richter is classified as an available-for-sale security.

July 12. Dividends of $12,000 are received on the Wright Co. investment.

Oct. 1. Purchased $24,000 of Toon Co. 4%, 10-year bonds at 100. The bonds are classified as available for sale. The bonds pay interest on October 1 and April 1.

Dec. 31. Wright Co. reported a total net income of $80,000 for 2015. Teasdale recorded equity earnings for its share of Wright Co. net income.

Dec. 31. Accrued interest for three months on the Toon Co. bonds purchased on October 1.

31. Adjusted the available-for-sale investment portfolio to fair value, using the following fair value per-share amounts:

Available-for-Sale Investments	Fair Value
Alvarez Inc. stock	$41.50 per share
Hirsch Inc. stock	$26.00 per share
Richter Inc. stock	$48.00 per share
Toon Co. bonds	101 per $100 of face amount

31. Closed the Teasdale Inc. net income of $51,240 for 2015. Teasdale Inc. paid no dividends during 2015.

Instructions

Determine the missing letters in the unclassified balance sheet. Provide appropriate supporting calculations.

Comprehensive Problem 4

GENERAL LEDGER

Selected transactions completed by Equinox Products Inc. during the fiscal year ended December 31, 2014, were as follows:

a. Issued 15,000 shares of $20 par common stock at $30, receiving cash.

b. Issued 4,000 shares of $80 par preferred 5% stock at $100, receiving cash.

c. Issued $500,000 of 10-year, 5% bonds at 104, with interest payable semiannually.

d. Declared a quarterly dividend of $0.50 per share on common stock and $1.00 per share on preferred stock. On the date of record, 100,000 shares of common stock were outstanding, no treasury shares were held, and 20,000 shares of preferred stock were outstanding.

e. Paid the cash dividends declared in (d).

f. Purchased 7,500 shares of Solstice Corp. at $40 per share, plus a $150 brokerage commission. The investment is classified as an available-for-sale investment.

g. Purchased 8,000 shares of treasury common stock at $33 per share.

h. Purchased 40,000 shares of Pinkberry Co. stock directly from the founders for $24 per share. Pinkberry has 125,000 shares issued and outstanding. Equinox Products Inc. treated the investment as an equity method investment.

i. Declared a $1.00 quarterly cash dividend per share on preferred stock. On the date of record, 20,000 shares of preferred stock had been issued.

j. Paid the cash dividends to the preferred stockholders.

k. Received $27,500 dividend from Pinkberry Co. investment in (h).

l. Purchased $90,000 of Dream Inc. 10-year, 5% bonds, directly from the issuing company, at their face amount plus accrued interest of $375. The bonds are classified as a held-to-maturity long-term investment.

m. Sold, at $38 per share, 2,600 shares of treasury common stock purchased in (g).

n. Received a dividend of $0.60 per share from the Solstice Corp. investment in (f).

o. Sold 1,000 shares of Solstice Corp. at $45, including commission.

p. Recorded the payment of semiannual interest on the bonds issued in (c) and the amortization of the premium for six months. The amortization is determined using the straight-line method.

q. Accrued interest for three months on the Dream Inc. bonds purchased in (l).

r. Pinkberry Co. recorded total earnings of $240,000. Equinox Products recorded equity earnings for its share of Pinkberry Co. net income.

(Continued)

s. The fair value for Solstice Corp. stock was $39.02 per share on December 31, 2014. The investment is adjusted to fair value, using a valuation allowance account. Assume Valuation Allowance for Available-for-Sale Investments had a beginning balance of zero.

Instructions

1. Journalize the selected transactions.
2. After all of the transactions for the year ended December 31, 2014, had been posted [including the transactions recorded in part (1) and all adjusting entries], the data below and on the following page were taken from the records of Equinox Products Inc.
   a. Prepare a multiple-step income statement for the year ended December 31, 2014, concluding with earnings per share. In computing earnings per share, assume that the average number of common shares outstanding was 100,000 and preferred dividends were $100,000. (Round earnings per share to the nearest cent.)
   b. Prepare a retained earnings statement for the year ended December 31, 2014.
   c. Prepare a balance sheet in report form as of December 31, 2014.

Income statement data:	
Advertising expense	$ 150,000
Cost of merchandise sold	3,700,000
Delivery expense	30,000
Depreciation expense—office buildings and equipment	30,000
Depreciation expense—store buildings and equipment	100,000
Dividend revenue	4,500
Gain on sale of investment	4,980
Income from Pinkberry Co. investment	76,800
Income tax expense	140,500
Interest expense	21,000
Interest revenue	2,720
Miscellaneous administrative expense	7,500
Miscellaneous selling expense	14,000
Office rent expense	50,000
Office salaries expense	170,000
Office supplies expense	10,000
Sales	5,254,000
Sales commissions	185,000
Sales salaries expense	385,000
Store supplies expense	21,000

Retained earnings and balance sheet data:	
Accounts payable	$ 194,300
Accounts receivable	545,000
Accumulated depreciation—office buildings and equipment	1,580,000
Accumulated depreciation—store buildings and equipment	4,126,000
Allowance for doubtful accounts	8,450
Available-for-sale investments (at cost)	260,130
Bonds payable, 5%, due 2022	500,000
Cash	246,000
Common stock, $20 par (400,000 shares authorized; 100,000 shares issued, 94,600 outstanding)	2,000,000
Dividends:	
Cash dividends for common stock	155,120
Cash dividends for preferred stock	100,000
Stock dividends for common stock	66,240
Goodwill	500,000
Income tax payable	44,000
Interest receivable	1,125
Investment in Pinkberry Co. stock (equity method)	1,009,300
Investment in Dream Inc. bonds (long term)	90,000

Merchandise inventory (December 31, 2014), at lower of cost (FIFO) or market	$ 778,000
Office buildings and equipment	4,320,000
Paid-in capital from sale of treasury stock	13,000
Excess of issue price over par—common stock	886,800
Excess of issue price over par—preferred stock	150,000
Preferred 5% stock, $80 par (30,000 shares authorized; 20,000 shares issued)	1,600,000
Premium on bonds payable	19,000
Prepaid expenses	27,400
Retained earnings, January 1, 2014	9,319,725
Store buildings and equipment	12,560,000
Treasury stock (5,400 shares of common stock at cost of $33 per share)	178,200
Unrealized gain (loss) on available-for-sale investments	(6,500)
Valuation allowance for available-for-sale investments	(6,500)

Cases & Projects

CP 13-1 Benefits of fair value

On July 16, 1996, Wyatt Corp. purchased 40 acres of land for $350,000. The land has been held for a future plant site until the current date, December 31, 2014. On December 18, 2014, TexoPete Inc. purchased 40 acres of land for $2,000,000 to be used for a distribution center. The TexoPete land is located next to the Wyatt Corp. land. Thus, both Wyatt Corp. and TexoPete Inc. own nearly identical pieces of land.

1. What are the valuations of land on the balance sheets of Wyatt Corp. and TexoPete, Inc., using generally accepted accounting principles?
2. How might fair value accounting aid comparability when evaluating these two companies?

CP 13-2 International fair value accounting

International Financial Reporting Standard No. 16 provides companies the option of valuing property, plant, and equipment at either historical cost or fair value. If fair value is selected, then the property, plant, and equipment must be revalued periodically to fair value. Under fair value, if there is an increase in the value of the property, plant, and equipment over the reporting period, then the increase is credited to stockholders' equity. However, if there is a decrease in fair value, then the decrease is reported as an expense for the period.

1. Why do International Financial Reporting Standards influence U.S. GAAP?
2. What would be some of the disadvantages of using fair value accounting for property, plant, and equipment?
3. How is the international accounting treatment for changes in fair value for property, plant, and equipment similar to investments?

CP 13-3 Ethics and fair value measurement

Financial assets include stocks and bonds. These are fairly simple securities that can often be valued using quoted market prices. However, there are more complex financial instruments that do not have quoted market prices. These complex securities must still be valued on the balance sheet at fair value. Generally accepted accounting principles require that the reporting entity use assumptions in valuing investments when market prices or critical valuation inputs are unobservable.

What are the ethical considerations in making subjective valuations of these complex financial instruments?

IFRS Activity 2

IFRS

The following is a recent consolidated statement of financial position on December 31 of a recent year for **LVMH**, a French company that markets the Louis Vuitton® and Moët Hennessy® brands.

LVMH Statement of Financial Position December 31 (in millions of euros)	
Assets	
Brands and other intangible assets—net	€ 9,104
Goodwill—net	5,027
Property, plant, and equipment—net	6,733
Investment in associates	223
Non-current available for sale financial assets	3,891
Other non-current assets	319
Deferred tax	668
Non-current assets	€25,965
Inventories	€ 5,991
Trade accounts receivable	1,565
Income taxes receivable	96
Other current assets	1,255
Cash and cash equivalents	2,292
Current assets	€11,199
TOTAL ASSETS	€37,164
Liabilities and Equity	
Share capital	€ 147
Share premium	1,782
Treasury shares	(607)
Revaluation reserves	1,244
Other reserves	11,370
Cumulative translation adjustment	230
Net profit, group share	3,032
Equity, group share	€17,198
Minority interests	1,006
Total equity	€18,204
Long-term borrowings	€ 3,432
Provisions	1,167
Deferred tax	3,354
Other non-current liabilities	3,947
Total non-current liabilities	€11,900
Short-term borrowings	€ 1,834
Trade accounts payable	2,298
Income taxes payable	446
Provisions	339
Other current liabilities	2,143
Total current liabilities	€ 7,060
TOTAL LIABILITIES AND EQUITY	€37,164

Source: LVNH., Form 10-K. Annual Report pursuant to Section 13 or 15(d) of the Securities Exchange Act of 1934. For the fiscal year ended December 31, 2010. Securities and Exchange Commission, Washington D.C. 20549.

a. Identify presentation differences between the balance sheet of LVMH and a balance sheet prepared under U.S. GAAP. Use the Mornin' Joe balance sheet on page 626 as an example of a U.S. GAAP balance sheet. (Ignore minority interests and cumulative translation adjustment.)

b. Compare the terms used in this balance sheet with the terms used by Mornin' Joe (page 626), using the table below.

LVMH Term	Mornin' Joe U.S. GAAP Term
Statement of financial position	
Share capital	
Share premium	
Other reserves	
Provisions	

c. What does the "Revaluation reserves" in the Equity section of the balance sheet represent?

IFRS Activity 3

IFRS

Under U.S. GAAP, LIFO is an acceptable inventory method. Listed below is financial statement information for three companies that use LIFO. All table numbers are in millions of dollars.

	LIFO Inventory	FIFO Inventory (from notes)	Impact on Net Income from Using LIFO Rather than FIFO (from notes)	Total Current Assets	Net Income as Reported
ExxonMobil	$9,852	$31,200	$317	$58,984	$30,460
Kroger	4,966	5,793	(57)	7,621	1,116
Ford Motor*	5,917	6,782	4	34,368	4,690

*Autos and trucks only

Assume these companies adopted IFRS, and thus were required to use FIFO, rather than LIFO.

a. Prepare a table with the following columns:

(1)	(2)	(3)	(4)
FIFO less LIFO	IFRS Net Income	(FIFO less LIFO) / Total Current Assets	IFRS Net Income (Col. 2) / Reported Net Income

(1) Difference between FIFO and LIFO inventory valuation.

(2) Revised IFRS net income using FIFO.

(3) Difference between FIFO and LIFO inventory valuation as a percent of total current assets.

(4) Revised IFRS net income as a percent of the reported net income.

b. Complete the table for the three companies.

c. For which company would a change to IFRS for inventory valuation have the largest percentage impact on total current assets (Col. 3)?

d. For which company would a change to IFRS for inventory valuation have the largest percentage impact on net income (Col. 4)?

e. Why might Kroger have a negative impact on net income from using LIFO, while the other two companies have a positive impact on net income from using LIFO?

AP PHOTO/ELAINE THOMPSON

CHAPTER 14

Statement of Cash Flows

Jones Soda Co.

Suppose you were to receive $100 from an event. Would it make a difference what the event was? Yes, it would! If you received $100 for your birthday, then it's a gift. If you received $100 as a result of working part time for a week, then it's the result of your effort. If you received $100 as a loan, then it's money that you will have to pay back in the future. If you received $100 as a result of selling your iPod, then it's the result of selling an asset. Thus, $100 received can be associated with different types of events, and these events have different meanings to you, and different implications for your future. You would much rather receive a $100 gift than take out a $100 loan. Likewise, company stakeholders view inflows and outflows of cash differently, depending on their source.

Companies are required to report information about the events causing a change in cash over a period of time. This information is reported in the statement of cash flows. One such company is **Jones Soda Co.** Jones began in the late 1980s as an alternative beverage company, known for its customer-provided labels, unique flavors, and support for extreme sports. You have probably seen Jones Soda at **Barnes & Noble**, **Panera Bread**, or **Starbucks**, or maybe sampled some of its unique flavors, such as Fufu Berry®, Blue Bubblegum®, or Lemon Drop®. As with any company, cash is important to Jones Soda. Without cash, Jones would be unable to expand its brands, distribute its product, support extreme sports, or provide a return for its owners. Thus, its managers are concerned about the sources and uses of cash.

In previous chapters, we have used the income statement, balance sheet, statement of retained earnings, and other information to analyze the effects of management decisions on a business's financial position and operating performance. In this chapter, we focus on the events causing a change in cash by presenting the preparation and use of the statement of cash flows.

Learning Objectives

After studying this chapter, you should be able to: *Example Exercises*

OBJ 1 Describe the cash flow activities reported in the statement of cash flows.
Reporting Cash Flows
- Cash Flows from Operating Activities
- Cash Flows from Investing Activities
- Cash Flows from Financing Activities — EE 14-1
- Noncash Investing and Financing Activities
- No Cash Flow per Share

OBJ 2 Prepare a statement of cash flows, using the indirect method.
Statement of Cash Flows—The Indirect Method
- Retained Earnings
- Adjustments to Net Income — EE 14-2, 3, 4
- Dividends
- Common Stock
- Bonds Payable
- Building
- Land — EE 14-5
- Preparing the Statement of Cash Flows

OBJ 3 Prepare a statement of cash flows, using the direct method.
Statement of Cash Flows—The Direct Method
- Cash Received from Customers — EE 14-6
- Cash Payments for Merchandise — EE 14-7
- Cash Payments for Operating Expenses
- Gain on Sale of Land
- Interest Expense
- Cash Payments for Income Taxes
- Reporting Cash Flows from Operating Activities—Direct Method

OBJ 4 Describe and illustrate the use of free cash flow in evaluating a company's cash flow.
Financial Analysis and Interpretation: Free Cash Flow — EE 14-8

At a Glance 14 Page 665

OBJ 1 Describe the cash flow activities reported in the statement of cash flows.

Reporting Cash Flows

The **statement of cash flows** reports a company's cash inflows and outflows for a period.[1] The statement of cash flows provides useful information about a company's ability to do the following:

1. Generate cash from operations
2. Maintain and expand its operating capacity
3. Meet its financial obligations
4. Pay dividends

The statement of cash flows is used by managers in evaluating past operations and in planning future investing and financing activities. It is also used by external users such as investors and creditors to assess a company's profit potential and ability to pay its debt and pay dividends.

The statement of cash flows reports three types of cash flow activities, as follows:

Cash flows from operating activities are the cash flows from transactions that affect the net income of the company.

Example: Purchase and sale of merchandise by a retailer.

Cash flows from investing activities are the cash flows from transactions that affect investments in the noncurrent assets of the company.

Example: Purchase and sale of fixed assets, such as equipment and buildings.

1 As used in this chapter, *cash* refers to cash and cash equivalents. Examples of cash equivalents include short-term, highly liquid investments, such as money market accounts, bank certificates of deposit, and U.S. Treasury bills.

Cash flows from financing activities are the cash flows from transactions that affect the debt and equity of the company.

Example: Issuing or retiring equity and debt securities.

The cash flows are reported in the statement of cash flows as follows:

Cash flows from operating activities	$XXX
Cash flows from investing activities	XXX
Cash flows from financing activities	XXX
Net increase or decrease in cash for the period	$XXX
Cash at the beginning of the period	XXX
Cash at the end of the period	$XXX

The ending cash on the statement of cash flows equals the cash reported on the company's balance sheet at the end of the year.

Exhibit 1 illustrates the sources (increases) and uses (decreases) of cash by each of the three cash flow activities. A *source* of cash causes the cash flow to increase and is called a *cash inflow*. A *use* of cash causes cash flow to decrease and is called *cash outflow*.

Note:
The statement of cash flows reports cash flows from operating, investing, and financing activities.

EXHIBIT 1

Sources and Uses of Cash

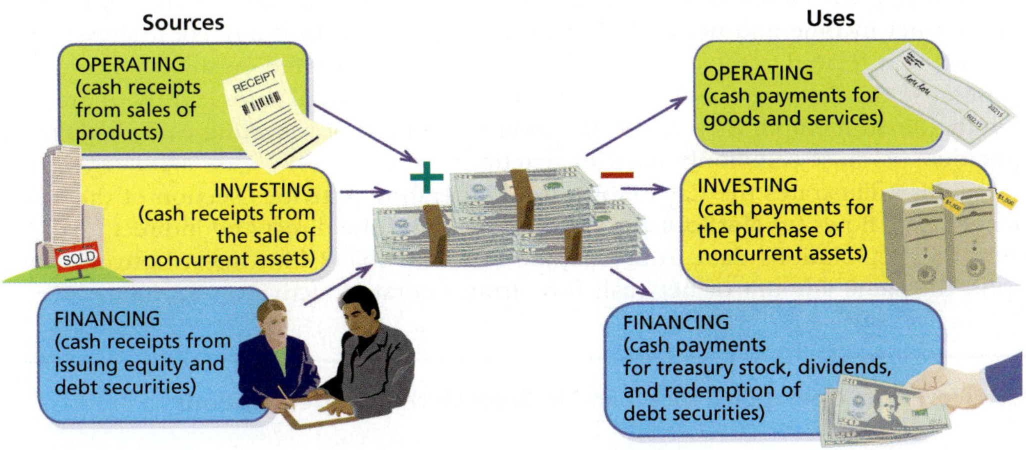

Cash Flows from Operating Activities

Cash flows from operating activities reports the cash inflows and outflows from a company's day-to-day operations. Companies may select one of two alternative methods for reporting cash flows from operating activities in the statement of cash flows:

1. The direct method
2. The indirect method

Both methods result in the same amount of cash flows from operating activities. They differ in the way they report cash flows from operating activities.

The **direct method** reports operating cash inflows (receipts) and cash outflows (payments) as follows:

Cash flows from operating activities:		
Cash received from customers		$XXX
Less: Cash payments for merchandise	$XXX	
Cash payments for operating expenses	XXX	
Cash payments for interest	XXX	
Cash payments for income taxes	XXX	XXX
Net cash flow from operating activities		$XXX

The primary operating cash inflow is cash received from customers. The primary operating cash outflows are cash payments for merchandise, operating expenses, interest, and income tax payments. The cash received from operating activities less the cash payments for operating activities is the net cash flow from operating activities.

The primary advantage of the direct method is that it *directly* reports cash receipts and cash payments in the statement of cash flows. Its primary disadvantage is that these data may not be readily available in the accounting records. Thus, the direct method is normally more costly to prepare and, as a result, is used infrequently in practice.

The **indirect method** reports cash flows from operating activities by beginning with net income and adjusting it for revenues and expenses that do not involve the receipt or payment of cash, as follows:

Cash flows from operating activities:		
Net income	$XXX	
Adjustments to reconcile net income to net cash flow from operating activities	XXX	
Net cash flow from operating activities		$XXX

The adjustments to reconcile net income to net cash flow from operating activities include such items as depreciation and gains or losses on fixed assets. Changes in current operating assets and liabilities such as accounts receivable or accounts payable are also added or deducted, depending on their effect on cash flows. In effect, these additions and deductions adjust net income, which is reported on an accrual accounting basis, to cash flows from operating activities, which is a cash basis.

A primary advantage of the indirect method is that it reconciles the differences between net income and net cash flows from operations. In doing so, it shows how net income is related to the ending cash balance that is reported on the balance sheet.

Because the data are readily available, the indirect method is less costly to prepare than the direct method. As a result, the indirect method of reporting cash flows from operations is most commonly used in practice.

Exhibit 2 illustrates the Cash Flows from Operating Activities section of the statement of cash flows for **NetSolutions**. Exhibit 2 shows the direct and indirect methods using the NetSolutions data from Chapter 1. As Exhibit 2 illustrates, both methods report the same amount of net cash flow from operating activities, $2,900.

EXHIBIT 2 **Cash Flow from Operations: Direct and Indirect Methods—NetSolutions**

Direct Method	
Cash flows from operating activities:	
Cash received from customers	$7,500
Deduct cash payments for expenses and payments to creditors	4,600
Net cash flow from operating activities	$2,900

Indirect Method	
Cash flows from operating activities:	
Net income	$3,050
Add increase in accounts payable	400
	$3,450
Deduct increase in supplies	550
Net cash flow from operating activities	$2,900

the same

Cash Flows from Investing Activities

In October 2008, the U.S. government invested $250 billion of cash into U.S. banks to help stabilize the financial system.

Cash flows from investing activities show the cash inflows and outflows related to changes in a company's long-term assets. Cash flows from investing activities are reported on the statement of cash flows as follows:

Cash flows from investing activities:		
Cash inflows from investing activities	$XXX	
Less cash used for investing activities	XXX	
Net cash flows from investing activities		$XXX

Cash inflows from investing activities normally arise from selling fixed assets, investments, and intangible assets. Cash outflows normally include payments to purchase fixed assets, investments, and intangible assets.

In fiscal 2011, Apple Inc. generated $37.5 billion in net cash flow from operating activities.

Cash Flows from Financing Activities

Cash flows from financing activities show the cash inflows and outflows related to changes in a company's long-term liabilities and stockholders' equity. Cash flows from financing activities are reported on the statement of cash flows as follows:

Cash flows from financing activities:		
Cash inflows from financing activities	$XXX	
Less cash used for financing activities	XXX	
Net cash flow from financing activities		$XXX

Cash inflows from financing activities normally arise from issuing long-term debt or equity securities. For example, issuing bonds, notes payable, preferred stock, and common stock creates cash inflows from financing activities. Cash outflows from financing activities include paying cash dividends, repaying long-term debt, and acquiring treasury stock.

Noncash Investing and Financing Activities

A company may enter into transactions involving investing and financing activities that do not *directly* affect cash. For example, a company may issue common stock to retire long-term debt. Although this transaction does not directly affect cash, it does eliminate future cash payments for interest and for paying the bonds when they mature. Because such transactions *indirectly* affect cash flows, they are reported in a separate section of the statement of cash flows. This section usually appears at the bottom of the statement of cash flows.

Example Exercise 14-1 Classifying Cash Flows (OBJ 1)

Identify whether each of the following would be reported as an operating, investing, or financing activity in the statement of cash flows.

a. Purchase of patent
b. Payment of cash dividend
c. Disposal of equipment
d. Cash sales
e. Purchase of treasury stock
f. Payment of wages expense

Follow My Example 14-1

a. Investing
b. Financing
c. Investing
d. Operating
e. Financing
f. Operating

Practice Exercises: **PE 14-1A, PE 14-1B**

No Cash Flow per Share

Cash flow per share is sometimes reported in the financial press. As reported, cash flow per share is normally computed as *cash flow from operations per share*. However, such reporting may be misleading because of the following:

1. Users may misinterpret cash flow per share as the per-share amount available for dividends. This would not be the case if the cash generated by operations is required for repaying loans or for reinvesting in the business.
2. Users may misinterpret cash flow per share as equivalent to (or better than) earnings per share.

For these reasons, the financial statements, including the statement of cash flows, should not report cash flow per share.

OBJ 2 Prepare a statement of cash flows, using the indirect method.

Statement of Cash Flows—The Indirect Method

The indirect method of reporting cash flows from operating activities uses the logic that a change in any balance sheet account (including cash) can be analyzed in terms of changes in the other balance sheet accounts. Thus, by analyzing changes in noncash balance sheet accounts, any change in the cash account can be *indirectly* determined.

To illustrate, the accounting equation can be solved for cash as shown below.

$$\text{Assets} = \text{Liabilities} + \text{Stockholders' Equity}$$
$$\text{Cash} + \text{Noncash Assets} = \text{Liabilities} + \text{Stockholders' Equity}$$
$$\text{Cash} = \text{Liabilities} + \text{Stockholders' Equity} - \text{Noncash Assets}$$

Therefore, any change in the cash account can be determined by analyzing changes in the liability, stockholders' equity, and noncash asset accounts as shown below.

$$\textit{Change}\text{ in Cash} = \textit{Change}\text{ in Liabilities} + \textit{Change}\text{ in Stockholders' Equity} - \textit{Change}\text{ in Noncash Assets}$$

Under the indirect method, there is no order in which the balance sheet accounts must be analyzed. However, net income (or net loss) is the first amount reported on the statement of cash flows. Since net income (or net loss) is a component of any change in Retained Earnings, the first account normally analyzed is Retained Earnings.

To illustrate the indirect method, the income statement and comparative balance sheets for Rundell Inc., shown in Exhibit 3, are used. Ledger accounts and other data supporting the income statement and balance sheet are presented as needed.[2]

EXHIBIT 3 **Income Statement and Comparative Balance Sheet**

Rundell Inc.
Income Statement
For the Year Ended December 31, 2014

Sales		$1,180,000
Cost of merchandise sold		790,000
Gross profit		$ 390,000
Operating expenses:		
Depreciation expense	$ 7,000	
Other operating expenses	196,000	
Total operating expenses		203,000
Income from operations		$ 187,000
Other income:		
Gain on sale of land	$ 12,000	
Other expense:		
Interest expense	8,000	4,000
Income before income tax		$ 191,000
Income tax expense		83,000
Net income		$ 108,000

(Continued)

2 An appendix that discusses using a spreadsheet (work sheet) as an aid in assembling data for the statement of cash flows is presented at the end of this chapter. This appendix illustrates the use of this spreadsheet in reporting cash flows from operating activities using the indirect method.

EXHIBIT 3 **Income Statement and Comparative Balance Sheet *(concluded)***

Rundell Inc.
Comparative Balance Sheet
December 31, 2014 and 2013

	2014	2013	Increase (Decrease)
Assets			
Cash	$ 97,500	$ 26,000	$ 71,500
Accounts receivable (net)	74,000	65,000	9,000
Inventories	172,000	180,000	(8,000)
Land	80,000	125,000	(45,000)
Building	260,000	200,000	60,000
Accumulated depreciation—building	(65,300)	(58,300)	7,000**
Total assets	$618,200	$537,700	$ 80,500
Liabilities			
Accounts payable (merchandise creditors)	$ 43,500	$ 46,700	$ (3,200)
Accrued expenses payable (operating expenses)	26,500	24,300	2,200
Income taxes payable	7,900	8,400	(500)
Dividends payable	14,000	10,000	4,000
Bonds payable	100,000	150,000	(50,000)
Total liabilities	$191,900	$239,400	$ 47,500*
Stockholders' Equity			
Common stock ($2 par)	$ 24,000	$ 16,000	$ 8,000
Paid-in capital in excess of par	120,000	80,000	40,000
Retained earnings	282,300	202,300	80,000
Total stockholders' equity	$426,300	$298,300	$128,000
Total liabilities and stockholders' equity	$618,200	$537,700	$ 80,500

**There is a $7,000 increase to Accumulated Depreciation—Building, which is a contra asset account. As a result, the $7,000 increase in this account must be subtracted in summing to the increase in Total assets of $80,500.

Retained Earnings

The comparative balance sheet for Rundell Inc. shows that retained earnings increased $80,000 during the year. The retained earnings account shown below indicates how this change occurred.

Account *Retained Earnings* Account No.

Date		Item	Debit	Credit	Balance Debit	Balance Credit
2014 Jan.	1	Balance				202,300
Dec.	31	Net income		108,000		310,300
	31	Cash dividends	28,000			282,300

The retained earnings account indicates that the $80,000 ($108,000 – $28,000) change resulted from net income of $108,000 and cash dividends of $28,000. The net income of $108,000 is the first amount reported in the Cash Flows from Operating Activities section.

Adjustments to Net Income

The net income of $108,000 reported by Rundell Inc. does not equal the cash flows from operating activities for the period. This is because net income is determined using the accrual method of accounting.

Under the accrual method of accounting, revenues and expenses are recorded at different times from when cash is received or paid. For example, merchandise may be sold on account and the cash received at a later date. Likewise, insurance premiums may be paid in the current period, but expensed in a following period.

Thus, under the indirect method, adjustments to net income must be made to determine cash flows from operating activities. The typical adjustments to net income are shown in Exhibit 4.[3]

EXHIBIT 4

Adjustments to Net Income (Loss) Using the Indirect Method

		Increase (Decrease)
	Net income (loss)	$ XXX
	Adjustments to reconcile net income to net cash flow from operating activities:	
Step 1	Depreciation of fixed assets	XXX
	Amortization of intangible assets	XXX
Step 2	Losses on disposal of assets	XXX
	Gains on disposal of assets	(XXX)
Step 3	Changes in current operating assets and liabilities:	
	Increases in noncash current operating assets	(XXX)
	Decreases in noncash current operating assets	XXX
	Increases in current operating liabilities	XXX
	Decreases in current operating liabilities	(XXX)
	Net cash flow from operating activities	$ XXX or $(XXX)

Subtract	Add
Increases in accounts receivable	Decreases in accounts receivable
Increases in inventory	Decreases in inventory
Increases in prepaid expenses	Decreases in prepaid expenses
Decreases in accounts payable	Increases in accounts payable
Decreases in accrued expenses payable	Increases in accrued expenses payable
Decreases in income taxes payable	Increases in income taxes payable

Net income is normally adjusted to cash flows from operating activities, using the following steps:

Step 1. Expenses that do not affect cash are added. Such expenses decrease net income but do not involve cash payments and, thus, are added to net income.

Examples: *Depreciation* of fixed assets and *amortization* of intangible assets are added to net income.

Step 2. Losses on the disposal of assets are added and gains on the disposal of assets are deducted. The disposal (sale) of assets is an investing activity rather than an operating activity. However, such losses and gains are reported as part of net income. As a result, any *losses* on disposal of assets are *added* back to net income. Likewise, any *gains* on disposal of assets are *deducted* from net income.

Example: Land costing $100,000 is sold for $90,000. The loss of $10,000 is added back to net income.

3 Other items that also require adjustments to net income to obtain cash flows from operating activities include amortization of bonds payable discounts (add), losses on debt retirement (add), amortization of bonds payable premiums (deduct), and gains on retirement of debt (deduct).

Step 3. Changes in current operating assets and liabilities are added or deducted as follows:

Increases in noncash current operating assets are deducted.
Decreases in noncash current operating assets are added.
Increases in current operating liabilities are added.
Decreases in current operating liabilities are deducted.

Example: A sale of $10,000 on account increases sales, accounts receivable, and net income by $10,000. However, cash is not affected. Thus, the $10,000 increase in accounts receivable is deducted. Similar adjustments are required for the changes in the other current asset and liability accounts, such as inventory, prepaid expenses, accounts payable, accrued expenses payable, and income taxes payable, as shown in Exhibit 4.

Example Exercise 14-2 Adjustments to Net Income—Indirect Method

OBJ 2

Omni Corporation's accumulated depreciation increased by $12,000, while $3,400 of patent amortization was recognized between balance sheet dates. There were no purchases or sales of depreciable or intangible assets during the year. In addition, the income statement showed a gain of $4,100 from the sale of land. Reconcile Omni's net income of $50,000 to net cash flow from operating activities.

Follow My Example 14-2

Net income	$50,000
Adjustments to reconcile net income to net cash flow from operating activities:	
Depreciation	12,000
Amortization of patents	3,400
Gain from sale of land	(4,100)
Net cash flow from operating activities	$61,300

Practice Exercises: **PE 14-2A, PE 14-2B**

The Cash Flows from Operating Activities section of Rundell's statement of cash flows is shown in Exhibit 5. Rundell's net income of $108,000 is converted to cash flows from operating activities of $100,500 as follows:

EXHIBIT 5

Cash Flows from Operating Activities—Indirect Method

	Cash flows from operating activities:		
	Net income	$108,000	
	Adjustments to reconcile net income to net cash flow from operating activities:		
Step 1 →	Depreciation	7,000	
Step 2 →	Gain on sale of land	(12,000)	
	Changes in current operating assets and liabilities:		
Step 3 →	Increase in accounts receivable	(9,000)	
	Decrease in inventories	8,000	
	Decrease in accounts payable	(3,200)	
	Increase in accrued expenses payable	2,200	
	Decrease in income taxes payable	(500)	
	Net cash flow from operating activities		$100,500

Step 1. Add depreciation of $7,000.
Analysis: The comparative balance sheet in Exhibit 3 indicates that Accumulated Depreciation—Building increased by $7,000. The account, shown on the following page, indicates that depreciation for the year was $7,000 for the building.

Account *Accumulated Depreciation—Building* Account No.

Date		Item	Debit	Credit	Balance	
					Debit	Credit
2014 Jan.	1	Balance				58,300
Dec.	31	Depreciation for year		7,000		65,300

Step 2. Deduct the gain on the sale of land of $12,000.
Analysis: The income statement in Exhibit 3 reports a gain of $12,000 from the sale of land. The proceeds, which include the gain, are reported in the Investing section of the statement of cash flows.[4] Thus, the gain of $12,000 is deducted from net income in determining cash flows from operating activities.

Step 3. Add and deduct changes in current operating assets and liabilities.
Analysis: The increases and decreases in the current operating asset and current liability accounts are shown below.

Accounts	December 31 2014	December 31 2013	Increase Decrease*
Accounts Receivable (net)	$ 74,000	$ 65,000	$9,000
Inventories	172,000	180,000	8,000*
Accounts Payable (merchandise creditors)	43,500	46,700	3,200*
Accrued Expenses Payable (operating expenses)	26,500	24,300	2,200
Income Taxes Payable	7,900	8,400	500*

Accounts receivable (net): The $9,000 increase is deducted from net income. This is because the $9,000 increase in accounts receivable indicates that sales on account were $9,000 more than the cash received from customers. Thus, sales (and net income) includes $9,000 that was not received in cash during the year.

Business Connection

CASH CRUNCH!

Automobile manufacturers such as Chrysler Group LLC sell their cars and trucks through a network of independently owned and operated dealerships. The vehicles are sold to the dealerships on credit by issuing a trade receivable, which is repaid to Chrysler Group LLC after the vehicles are sold by the dealership. The economic crisis of 2008 created a slump in car sales that lasted well into 2009. By spring 2009, Chrysler dealers around the world found themselves with large inventories of unsold cars and trucks, resulting in their inability to repay their trade receivables from Chrysler Group LLC. This led to a significant decline in Chrysler's cash flow from operating activities that forced the company into a financial restructuring. Ultimately, the company was rescued by a significant investment (cash inflow from financing activities) from Fiat and loans and investments (cash inflow from financing activities) from the U.S. and Canadian governments. Chrysler's cash position improved in the years that followed. In May 2011, the company repaid the majority of the loans outstanding from the U.S. and Canadian governments (cash used for financing activities).

Source: "Chrysler Restructuring Plan for Long-Term Viability," Chrysler Group LLC, February 17, 2009.

Inventories: The $8,000 decrease is added to net income. This is because the $8,000 decrease in inventories indicates that the cost of merchandise *sold* exceeds the cost of the merchandise *purchased* during the year by $8,000. In other words, the cost of merchandise sold includes $8,000 of goods from inventory that were not purchased (used cash) during the year.

Accounts payable (merchandise creditors): The $3,200 decrease is deducted from net income. This is because a decrease in accounts payable indicates that the cash *payments* to merchandise creditors exceed the merchandise *purchased on account* by $3,200. Therefore, the cost of merchandise sold is $3,200 less than the cash paid to merchandise creditors during the year.

4 The reporting of the proceeds (cash flows) from the sale of land as part of investing activities is discussed later in this chapter.

Accrued expenses payable (operating expenses): The $2,200 increase is added to net income. This is because an increase in accrued expenses payable indicates that operating expenses exceed the cash payments for operating expenses by $2,200. In other words, operating expenses reported on the income statement include $2,200 that did not require a cash outflow during the year.

Income taxes payable: The $500 decrease is deducted from net income. This is because a decrease in income taxes payable indicates that taxes paid exceed the amount of taxes incurred during the year by $500. In other words, the amount reported on the income statement for income tax expense is less than the amount paid by $500.

Example Exercise 14-3 Changes in Current Operating Assets and Liabilities—Indirect Method

OBJ 2

Victor Corporation's current operating assets and liabilities from the company's comparative balance sheet were as follows:

	Dec. 31, 2015	Dec. 31, 2014
Accounts receivable	$ 6,500	$ 4,900
Inventory	12,300	15,000
Accounts payable	4,800	5,200
Dividends payable	5,000	4,000

Adjust Victor's net income of $70,000 for changes in operating assets and liabilities to arrive at cash flows from operating activities.

Follow My Example 14-3

Net income	$70,000
Adjustments to reconcile net income to net cash flow from operating activities:	
Changes in current operating assets and liabilities:	
Increase in accounts receivable	(1,600)
Decrease in inventory	2,700
Decrease in accounts payable	(400)
Net cash flow from operating activities	$70,700

Note: The change in dividends payable impacts the cash paid for dividends, which is disclosed under financing activities.

Practice Exercises: **PE 14-3A, PE 14-3B**

Using the preceding analyses, Rundell's net income of $108,000 is converted to cash flows from operating activities of $100,500 as shown in Exhibit 5, on page 649.

Integrity, Objectivity, and Ethics in Business

CREDIT POLICY AND CASH FLOW

One would expect customers to pay for products and services sold on account. Unfortunately, that is not always the case. Collecting accounts receivable efficiently is the key to turning a current asset into positive cash flow. Most entrepreneurs would rather think about the exciting aspects of their business—such as product development, marketing, sales, and advertising—than credit collection. This can be a mistake. Hugh McHugh of Overhill Flowers, Inc., decided that he would have no more trade accounts after dealing with Christmas orders that weren't paid for until late February, or sometimes not paid at all. As stated by one collection service, "One thing business owners always tell me is that they never thought about [collections] when they started their own business." To the small business owner, the collection of accounts receivable may mean the difference between succeeding and failing.

Source: Paulette Thomas, "Making Them Pay: The Last Thing Most Entrepreneurs Want to Think About Is Bill Collection; It Should Be One of the First Things," *The Wall Street Journal*, September 19, 2005, p. R6.

Example Exercise 14-4 Cash Flows from Operating Activities—Indirect Method

OBJ 2

Omicron Inc. reported the following data:

Net income	$120,000
Depreciation expense	12,000
Loss on disposal of equipment	15,000
Increase in accounts receivable	5,000
Decrease in accounts payable	2,000

Prepare the Cash Flows from Operating Activities section of the statement of cash flows, using the indirect method.

Follow My Example 14-4

Cash flows from operating activities:		
Net income	$120,000	
Adjustments to reconcile net income to net cash flow from operating activities:		
Depreciation expense........................	12,000	
Loss on disposal of equipment..............	15,000	
Changes in current operating assets and liabilities:		
Increase in accounts receivable	(5,000)	
Decrease in accounts payable................	(2,000)	
Net cash flow from operating activities..........		$140,000

Practice Exercises: **PE 14-4A, PE 14-4B**

Dividends

The retained earnings account of Rundell Inc., shown on page 647, indicates cash dividends of $28,000 were declared during the year. However, the dividends payable account, shown below, indicates that only $24,000 of dividends were paid during the year.

Account *Dividends Payable* — Account No.

Date		Item	Debit	Credit	Balance Debit	Balance Credit
2014 Jan.	1	Balance				10,000
	10	Cash paid	10,000		—	—
June	20	Dividends declared		14,000		14,000
July	10	Cash paid	14,000		—	—
Dec.	20	Dividends declared		14,000		14,000

Since dividend payments are a financing activity, the dividend payment of $24,000 is reported in the Financing Activities section of the statement of cash flows, as shown below.

Cash flows from financing activities:	
Cash paid for dividends....................................	$24,000

Common Stock

The common stock account increased by $8,000, and the paid-in capital in excess of par—common stock account increased by $40,000, as shown below. These increases were from issuing 4,000 shares of common stock for $12 per share.

Account *Common Stock*						Account No.
					Balance	
Date		Item	Debit	Credit	Debit	Credit
2014 Jan.	1	Balance				16,000
Nov.	1	4,000 shares issued for cash		8,000		24,000

Account *Paid-In Capital in Excess of Par—Common Stock*						Account No.
					Balance	
Date		Item	Debit	Credit	Debit	Credit
2014 Jan.	1	Balance				80,000
Nov.	1	4,000 shares issued for cash		40,000		120,000

This cash inflow is reported in the Financing Activities section as follows:

Cash flows from financing activities:	
Cash received from sale of common stock	$48,000

Bonds Payable

The bonds payable account decreased by $50,000, as shown below. This decrease is from retiring the bonds by a cash payment for their face amount.

Account *Bonds Payable*						Account No.
					Balance	
Date		Item	Debit	Credit	Debit	Credit
2014 Jan.	1	Balance				150,000
June	1	Retired by payment of cash at face amount	50,000			100,000

This cash outflow is reported in the Financing Activities section as follows:

Cash flows from financing activities:	
Cash paid to retire bonds payable	$50,000

Building

The building account increased by $60,000, and the accumulated depreciation—building account increased by $7,000, as shown below.

Account *Building* — Account No.

Date		Item	Debit	Credit	Balance Debit	Balance Credit
2014 Jan.	1	Balance			200,000	
Dec.	27	Purchased for cash	60,000		260,000	

Account *Accumulated Depreciation—Building* — Account No.

Date		Item	Debit	Credit	Balance Debit	Balance Credit
2014 Jan.	1	Balance				58,300
Dec.	31	Depreciation for the year		7,000		65,300

The purchase of a building for cash of $60,000 is reported as an outflow of cash in the Investing Activities section as follows:

Cash flows from investing activities:	
Cash paid for purchase of building	$60,000

The credit in the accumulated depreciation—building account represents depreciation expense for the year. This depreciation expense of $7,000 on the building was added to net income in determining cash flows from operating activities, as reported in Exhibit 5, on page 649.

Land

The $45,000 decline in the land account was from two transactions, as shown below.

Account *Land* — Account No.

Date		Item	Debit	Credit	Balance Debit	Balance Credit
2014 Jan.	1	Balance			125,000	
June	8	Sold for $72,000 cash		60,000	65,000	
Oct.	12	Purchased for $15,000 cash	15,000		80,000	

The June 8 transaction is the sale of land with a cost of $60,000 for $72,000 in cash. The $72,000 proceeds from the sale are reported in the Investing Activities section, as follows:

Cash flows from investing activities:	
Cash received from sale of land	$72,000

The proceeds of $72,000 include the $12,000 gain on the sale of land and the $60,000 cost (book value) of the land. As shown in Exhibit 5, on page 649, the $12,000 gain is deducted from net income in the Cash Flows from Operating Activities section. This is so that the $12,000 cash inflow related to the gain is not included twice as a cash inflow.

The October 12 transaction is the purchase of land for cash of $15,000. This transaction is reported as an outflow of cash in the Investing Activities section, as follows:

Cash flows from investing activities:	
Cash paid for purchase of land	$15,000

Example Exercise 14-5 Land Transactions on the Statement of Cash Flows

OBJ 2

Alpha Corporation purchased land for $125,000. Later in the year, the company sold a different piece of land with a book value of $165,000 for $200,000. How are the effects of these transactions reported on the statement of cash flows?

Follow My Example 14-5

The gain on the sale of the land is deducted from net income, as shown below.

Gain on sale of land	$ (35,000)

The purchase and sale of land is reported as part of cash flows from investing activities, as shown below.

Cash received from sale of land	200,000
Cash paid for purchase of land	(125,000)

Practice Exercises: **PE 14-5A, PE 14-5B**

Preparing the Statement of Cash Flows

The statement of cash flows for Rundell Inc., using the indirect method, is shown in Exhibit 6. The statement of cash flows indicates that cash increased by $71,500 during the year. The most significant increase in net cash flows ($100,500) was from operating activities. The most significant use of cash ($26,000) was for financing activities. The ending balance of cash on December 31, 2014, is $97,500. This ending cash balance is also reported on the December 31, 2014, balance sheet shown in Exhibit 3 on pages 646–647.

EXHIBIT 6

Statement of Cash Flows—Indirect Method

Rundell Inc.
Statement of Cash Flows
For the Year Ended December 31, 2014

Cash flows from operating activities:			
Net income		$108,000	
Adjustments to reconcile net income to net cash flow from operating activities:			
Depreciation		7,000	
Gain on sale of land		(12,000)	
Changes in current operating assets and liabilities:			
Increase in accounts receivable		(9,000)	
Decrease in inventories		8,000	
Decrease in accounts payable		(3,200)	
Increase in accrued expenses payable		2,200	
Decrease in income taxes payable		(500)	
Net cash flow from operating activities			$100,500
Cash flows from investing activities:			
Cash received from sale of land		$ 72,000	
Less: Cash paid for purchase of land	$15,000		
Cash paid for purchase of building	60,000	75,000	
Net cash flow used for investing activities			(3,000)
Cash flows from financing activities:			
Cash received from sale of common stock		$ 48,000	
Less: Cash paid to retire bonds payable	$50,000		
Cash paid for dividends	24,000	74,000	
Net cash flow used for financing activities			(26,000)
Increase in cash			$ 71,500
Cash at the beginning of the year			26,000
Cash at the end of the year			$ 97,500

OBJ 3 Prepare a statement of cash flows, using the direct method.

Statement of Cash Flows—The Direct Method

The direct method reports cash flows from operating activities as follows:

Cash flows from operating activities:		
Cash received from customers		$ XXX
Less: Cash payments for merchandise	$ XXX	
Cash payments for operating expenses	XXX	
Cash payments for interest	XXX	
Cash payments for income taxes	XXX	XXX
Net cash flow from operating activities		$ XXX

The Cash Flows from Investing and Financing Activities sections of the statement of cash flows are exactly the same under both the direct and indirect methods. The amount of net cash flow from operating activities is also the same, but the manner in which it is reported is different.

Under the direct method, the income statement is adjusted to cash flows from operating activities as follows:

Income Statement	Adjusted to	Cash Flows from Operating Activities
Sales	→	Cash received from customers
Cost of merchandise sold	→	Cash payments for merchandise
Operating expenses:		
Depreciation expense	N/A	N/A
Other operating expenses	→	Cash payments for operating expenses
Gain on sale of land	N/A	N/A
Interest expense	→	Cash payments for interest
Income tax expense	→	Cash payments for income taxes
Net income	→	Net cash flow from operating activities

N/A—Not applicable

As shown above, depreciation expense is not adjusted or reported as part of cash flows from operating activities. This is because deprecation expense does not involve a cash outflow. The gain on the sale of the land is also not adjusted and is not reported as part of cash flows from operating activities. This is because the cash flow from operating activities is determined directly, rather than by reconciling net income. The cash proceeds from the sale of the land are reported as an investing activity.

To illustrate the direct method, the income statement and comparative balance sheet for Rundell Inc., shown in Exhibit 3 on pages 646–647, are used.

Cash Received from Customers

The income statement (shown in Exhibit 3) of Rundell Inc. reports sales of $1,180,000. To determine the *cash received from customers*, the $1,180,000 is adjusted for any increase or decrease in accounts receivable. The adjustment is summarized below.

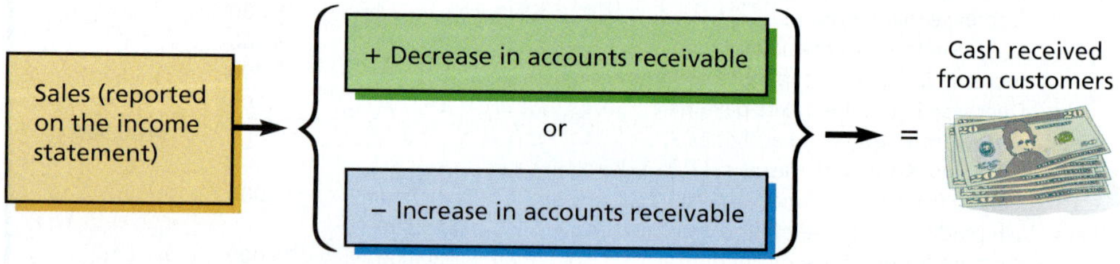

The cash received from customers is $1,171,000, computed as follows:

Sales	$1,180,000
Less increase in accounts receivable	9,000
Cash received from customers	$1,171,000

The increase of $9,000 in accounts receivable (shown in Exhibit 3) during 2014 indicates that sales on account exceeded cash received from customers by $9,000. In other words, sales include $9,000 that did not result in a cash inflow during the year. Thus, $9,000 is deducted from sales to determine the *cash received from customers*.

Example Exercise 14-6 Cash Received from Customers—Direct Method

OBJ 3

Sales reported on the income statement were $350,000. The accounts receivable balance declined $8,000 over the year. Determine the amount of cash received from customers.

Follow My Example 14-6

Sales	$350,000
Add decrease in accounts receivable	8,000
Cash received from customers	$358,000

Practice Exercises: **PE 14-6A, PE 14-6B**

Cash Payments for Merchandise

The income statement (shown in Exhibit 3) for Rundell Inc. reports cost of merchandise sold of $790,000. To determine the *cash payments for merchandise*, the $790,000 is adjusted for any increases or decreases in inventories and accounts payable. Assuming the accounts payable are owed to merchandise suppliers, the adjustment is summarized below.

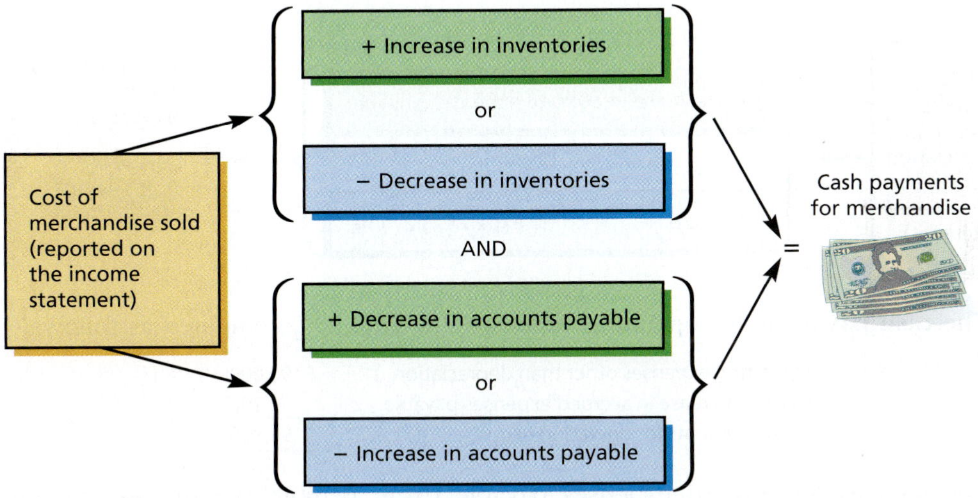

The cash payments for merchandise are $785,200, computed as follows:

Cost of merchandise sold	$790,000
Deduct decrease in inventories	(8,000)
Add decrease in accounts payable	3,200
Cash payments for merchandise	$785,200

The $8,000 decrease in inventories (from Exhibit 3) indicates that the merchandise sold exceeded the cost of the merchandise purchased by $8,000. In other words, the cost of merchandise sold includes $8,000 of goods sold from inventory that did not require a cash outflow during the year. Thus, $8,000 is deducted from the cost of merchandise sold in determining the *cash payments for merchandise.*

The $3,200 decrease in accounts payable (from Exhibit 3) indicates that cash payments for merchandise were $3,200 more than the purchases on account during 2014. Therefore, $3,200 is added to the cost of merchandise sold in determining the *cash payments for merchandise.*

Example Exercise 14-7 Cash Payments for Merchandise—Direct Method

OBJ 3

The cost of merchandise sold reported on the income statement was $145,000. The accounts payable balance increased by $4,000, and the inventory balance increased by $9,000 over the year. Determine the amount of cash paid for merchandise.

Follow My Example 14-7

Cost of merchandise sold	$145,000
Add increase in inventories	9,000
Deduct increase in accounts payable	(4,000)
Cash paid for merchandise	$150,000

Practice Exercises: **PE 14-7A, PE 14-7B**

Cash Payments for Operating Expenses

The income statement (from Exhibit 3) for Rundell Inc. reports total operating expenses of $203,000, which includes depreciation expense of $7,000. Since depreciation expense does not require a cash outflow, it is omitted from *cash payments for operating expenses.*

To determine the *cash payments for operating expenses*, the other operating expenses (excluding depreciation) of $196,000 ($203,000 – $7,000) are adjusted for any increase or decrease in accrued expenses payable. Assuming that the accrued expenses payable are all operating expenses, this adjustment is summarized below.

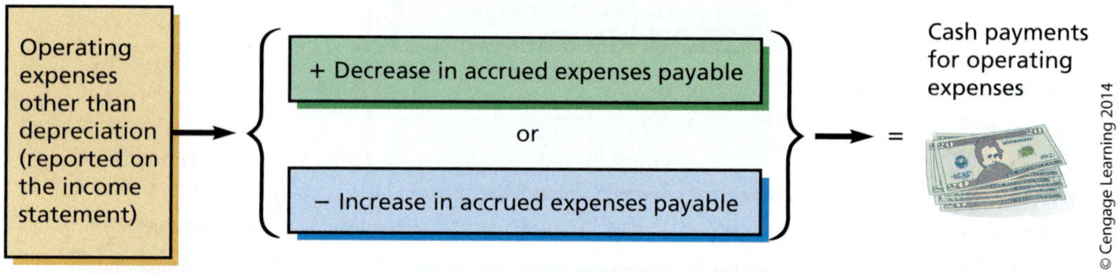

The cash payments for operating expenses are $193,800, computed as follows:

Operating expenses other than depreciation	$196,000
Deduct increase in accrued expenses payable	(2,200)
Cash payments for operating expenses	$193,800

The increase in accrued expenses payable (from Exhibit 3) indicates that the cash payments for operating expenses were $2,200 less than the amount reported for operating expenses during the year. Thus, $2,200 is deducted from the operating expenses in determining the *cash payments for operating expenses.*

Gain on Sale of Land

The income statement for Rundell Inc. (from Exhibit 3) reports a gain of $12,000 on the sale of land. The sale of land is an investing activity. Thus, the proceeds from the sale, which include the gain, are reported as part of the cash flows from investing activities.

Interest Expense

The income statement (from Exhibit 3) for Rundell Inc. reports interest expense of $8,000. To determine the *cash payments for interest*, the $8,000 is adjusted for any increases or decreases in interest payable. The adjustment is summarized as follows:

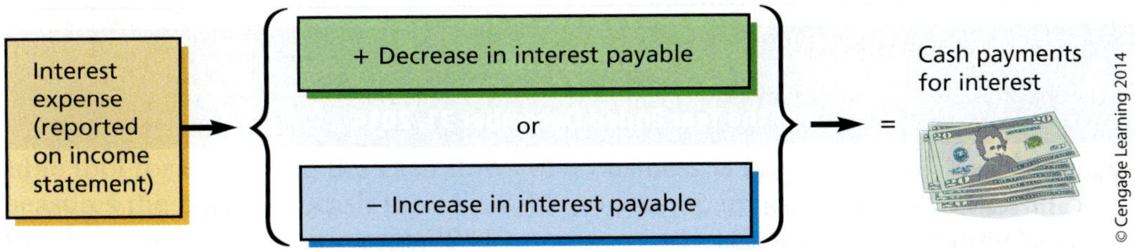

The comparative balance sheet of Rundell Inc. in Exhibit 3 indicates no interest payable. This is because the interest expense on the bonds payable is paid on June 1 and December 31. Since there is no interest payable, no adjustment of the interest expense of $8,000 is necessary.

Cash Payments for Income Taxes

The income statement (from Exhibit 3) for Rundell Inc. reports income tax expense of $83,000. To determine the *cash payments for income taxes*, the $83,000 is adjusted for any increases or decreases in income taxes payable. The adjustment is summarized below.

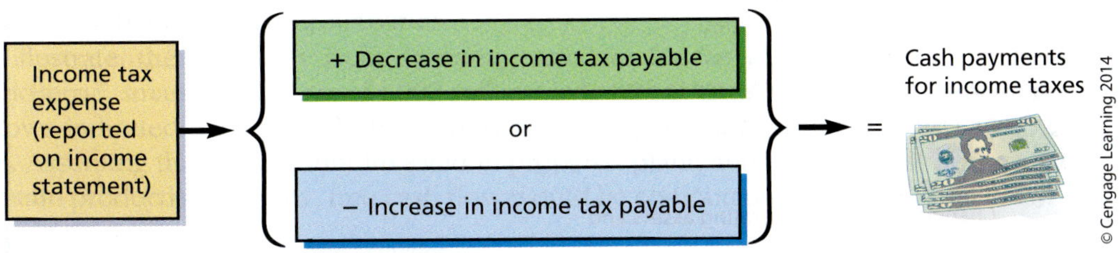

The cash payments for income taxes are $83,500, computed as follows:

Income tax expense	$83,000
Add decrease in income taxes payable	500
Cash payments for income taxes	$83,500

The $500 decrease in income taxes payable (from Exhibit 3) indicates that the cash payments for income taxes were $500 more than the amount reported for income tax expense during 2014. Thus, $500 is added to the income tax expense in determining the *cash payments for income taxes*.

Reporting Cash Flows from Operating Activities—Direct Method

The statement of cash flows for Rundell Inc., using the direct method for reporting cash flows from operating activities, is shown in Exhibit 7. The portions of the statement that differ from those prepared under the indirect method are highlighted in color.

EXHIBIT 7

Statement of Cash Flows—Direct Method

Rundell Inc.
Statement of Cash Flows
For the Year Ended December 31, 2014

Cash flows from operating activities:			
Cash received from customers		$1,171,000	
Deduct: Cash payments for merchandise	$785,200		
Cash payments for operating expenses	193,800		
Cash payments for interest	8,000		
Cash payments for income taxes	83,500	1,070,500	
Net cash flow from operating activities			$100,500

(Continued)

Example Exercise 14-8 Free Cash Flow OBJ 4

Omnicron Inc. reported the following on the company's cash flow statement in 2014 and 2013:

	2014	2013
Net cash flow from operating activities	$140,000	$120,000
Net cash flow used for investing activities	(120,000)	(80,000)
Net cash flow used for financing activities	(20,000)	(32,000)

Seventy-five percent of the net cash flow used for investing activities was used to replace existing capacity.

a. Determine Omnicron's free cash flow.

b. Has Omnicron's free cash flow improved or declined from 2013 to 2014?

Follow My Example 14-8

a.

	2014	2013
Net cash flow from operating activities	$140,000	$120,000
Less: Investments in fixed assets to maintain current production	90,000[1]	60,000[2]
Free cash flow	$ 50,000	$ 60,000

[1] $120,000 × 75%
[2] $80,000 × 75%

b. The change from $60,000 to $50,000 indicates an unfavorable trend.

Practice Exercises: **PE 14-8A, PE 14-8B**

APPENDIX

Spreadsheet (Work Sheet) for Statement of Cash Flows—The Indirect Method

A spreadsheet (work sheet) may be used in preparing the statement of cash flows. However, whether or not a spreadsheet (work sheet) is used, the concepts presented in this chapter are not affected.

The data for Rundell Inc., presented in Exhibit 3 on pages 646–647, are used as a basis for illustrating the spreadsheet (work sheet) for the indirect method. The steps in preparing this spreadsheet (work sheet), shown in Exhibit 8, are as follows:

Step 1. List the title of each balance sheet account in the Accounts column.

Step 2. For each balance sheet account, enter its balance as of December 31, 2013, in the first column and its balance as of December 31, 2014, in the last column. Place the credit balances in parentheses.

Step 3. Add the December 31, 2013 and 2014 column totals, which should total to zero.

Step 4. Analyze the change during the year in each noncash account to determine its net increase (decrease) and classify the change as affecting cash flows from operating activities, investing activities, financing activities, or noncash investing and financing activities.

Step 5. Indicate the effect of the change on cash flows by making entries in the Transactions columns.

EXHIBIT 8 **End-of-Period Spreadsheet (Work Sheet) for Statement of Cash Flows—Indirect Method**

Step 2

	A	B	C	D	E	F	G
1	**Rundell Inc.**						
2	**End-of-Period Spreadsheet (Work Sheet) for Statement of Cash Flows**						
3	**For the Year Ended December 31, 2014**						
4	Accounts	**Balance,**		**Transactions**			**Balance,**
5		**Dec. 31, 2013**		**Debit**		**Credit**	**Dec. 31, 2014**
6	Cash	26,000	(o)	71,500			97,500
7	Accounts receivable (net)	65,000	(n)	9,000			74,000
8	Inventories	180,000			(m)	8,000	172,000
9	Land	125,000	(k)	15,000	(l)	60,000	80,000
10	Building	200,000	(j)	60,000			260,000
11	Accumulated depreciation—building	(58,300)			(i)	7,000	(65,300)
12	Accounts payable (merchandise creditors)	(46,700)	(h)	3,200			(43,500)
13	Accrued expenses payable (operating expenses)	(24,300)			(g)	2,200	(26,500)
14	Income taxes payable	(8,400)	(f)	500			(7,900)
15	Dividends payable	(10,000)			(e)	4,000	(14,000)
16	Bonds payable	(150,000)	(d)	50,000			(100,000)
17	Common stock	(16,000)			(c)	8,000	(24,000)
18	Paid-in capital in excess of par	(80,000)			(c)	40,000	(120,000)
19	Retained earnings	(202,300)	(b)	28,000	(a)	108,000	(282,300)
20	Totals **Step 3 →**	0		237,200		237,200	0 **← Step 3**
21	Operating activities:						
22	Net income		(a)	108,000			
23	Depreciation of building		(i)	7,000			
24	Gain on sale of land				(l)	12,000	
25	Increase in accounts receivable				(n)	9,000	
26	Decrease in inventories		(m)	8,000			
27	Decrease in accounts payable				(h)	3,200	
28	Increase in accrued expenses payable		(g)	2,200			
29	Decrease in income taxes payable				(f)	500	
30	Investing activities:						
31	Sale of land		(l)	72,000			
32	Purchase of land				(k)	15,000	
33	Purchase of building				(j)	60,000	
34	Financing activities:						
35	Issued common stock		(c)	48,000			
36	Retired bonds payable				(d)	50,000	
37	Declared cash dividends				(b)	28,000	
38	Increase in dividends payable		(e)	4,000			
39	Net increase in cash				(o)	71,500	
40	Totals			249,200		249,200	

Step 1 (rows 6–20)

Steps 4–7

Step 6. After all noncash accounts have been analyzed, enter the net increase (decrease) in cash during the period.

Step 7. Add the Debit and Credit Transactions columns. The totals should be equal.

Analyzing Accounts

In analyzing the noncash accounts (Step 4), try to determine the type of cash flow activity (operating, investing, or financing) that led to the change in the account. As each noncash account is analyzed, an entry (Step 5) is made on the spreadsheet (work sheet) for the type of cash flow activity that caused the change. After all noncash accounts have been analyzed, an entry (Step 6) is made for the increase (decrease) in cash during the period.

The entries made on the spreadsheet are not posted to the ledger. They are only used in preparing and summarizing the data on the spreadsheet.

The order in which the accounts are analyzed is not important. However, it is more efficient to begin with Retained Earnings and proceed upward in the account listing.

Retained Earnings

The spreadsheet (work sheet) shows a Retained Earnings balance of $202,300 at December 31, 2013, and $282,300 at December 31, 2014. Thus, Retained Earnings increased $80,000 during the year. This increase is from the following:

1. Net income of $108,000
2. Declaring cash dividends of $28,000

To identify the cash flows from these activities, two entries are made on the spreadsheet.

The $108,000 is reported on the statement of cash flows as part of "cash flows from operating activities." Thus, an entry is made in the Transactions columns on the spreadsheet, as follows:

(a)	Operating Activities—Net Income	108,000	
	Retained Earnings		108,000

The preceding entry accounts for the net income portion of the change to Retained Earnings. It also identifies the cash flow in the bottom portion of the spreadsheet as related to operating activities.

The $28,000 of dividends is reported as a financing activity on the statement of cash flows. Thus, an entry is made in the Transactions columns on the spreadsheet, as follows:

(b)	Retained Earnings	28,000	
	Financing Activities—Declared Cash Dividends		28,000

The preceding entry accounts for the dividends portion of the change to Retained Earnings. It also identifies the cash flow in the bottom portion of the spreadsheet as related to financing activities. The $28,000 of declared dividends will be adjusted later for the actual amount of cash dividends paid during the year.

Other Accounts

The entries for the other noncash accounts are made in the spreadsheet in a manner similar to entries (a) and (b). A summary of these entries is as follows:

(c)	Financing Activities—Issued Common Stock	48,000	
	Common Stock		8,000
	Paid-In Capital in Excess of Par—Common Stock		40,000
(d)	Bonds Payable	50,000	
	Financing Activities—Retired Bonds Payable		50,000
(e)	Financing Activities—Increase in Dividends Payable	4,000	
	Dividends Payable		4,000
(f)	Income Taxes Payable	500	
	Operating Activities—Decrease in Income Taxes Payable		500
(g)	Operating Activities—Increase in Accrued Expenses Payable	2,200	
	Accrued Expenses Payable		2,200

(h)	Accounts Payable	3,200	
	Operating Activities—Decrease in Accounts Payable		3,200
(i)	Operating Activities—Depreciation of Building	7,000	
	Accumulated Depreciation—Building		7,000
(j)	Building	60,000	
	Investing Activities—Purchase of Building		60,000
(k)	Land	15,000	
	Investing Activities—Purchase of Land		15,000
(l)	Investing Activities—Sale of Land	72,000	
	Operating Activities—Gain on Sale of Land		12,000
	Land		60,000
(m)	Operating Activities—Decrease in Inventories	8,000	
	Inventories		8,000
(n)	Accounts Receivable	9,000	
	Operating Activities—Increase in Accounts Receivable		9,000
(o)	Cash	71,500	
	Net Increase in Cash		71,500

After all the balance sheet accounts are analyzed and the entries made on the spreadsheet (work sheet), all the operating, investing, and financing activities are identified in the bottom portion of the spreadsheet. The accuracy of the entries is verified by totaling the Debit and Credit Transactions columns. The totals of the columns should be equal.

Preparing the Statement of Cash Flows

The statement of cash flows prepared from the spreadsheet is identical to the statement in Exhibit 6 on page 655. The data for the three sections of the statement are obtained from the bottom portion of the spreadsheet.

At a Glance 14

OBJ 1 Describe the cash flow activities reported in the statement of cash flows.

Key Points The statement of cash flows reports cash receipts and cash payments by three types of activities: operating activities, investing activities, and financing activities. Cash flows from operating activities reports the cash inflows and outflows from a company's day-to-day operations. Cash flows from investing activities reports the cash inflows and outflows related to changes in a company's long-term assets. Cash flows from financing activities reports the cash inflows and outflows related to changes in a company's long-term liabilities and stockholders' equity. Investing and financing for a business may be affected by transactions that do not involve cash. The effect of such transactions should be reported in a separate schedule accompanying the statement of cash flows.

Learning Outcome	Example Exercises	Practice Exercises
• Classify transactions that either provide or use cash into either operating, investing, or financing activities.	EE14-1	PE14-1A, 14-1B

OBJ 2 Prepare a statement of cash flows, using the indirect method.

Key Points The indirect method reports cash flows from operating activities by adjusting net income for revenues and expenses that do not involve the receipt or payment of cash. Noncash expenses such as depreciation are added back to net income. Gains and losses on the disposal of assets are added to or deducted from net income. Changes in current operating assets and liabilities are added to or subtracted from net income, depending on their effect on cash. Cash flows from investing activities and cash flows from financing activities are reported below cash flows from operating activities in the statement of cash flows.

Learning Outcomes	Example Exercises	Practice Exercises
• Determine cash flows from operating activities under the indirect method by adjusting net income for noncash expenses and gains and losses from asset disposals.	EE14-2	PE14-2A, 14-2B
• Determine cash flows from operating activities under the indirect method by adjusting net income for changes in current operating assets and liabilities.	EE14-3	PE14-3A, 14-3B
• Prepare the Cash Flows from Operating Activities section of the statement of cash flows, using the indirect method.	EE14-4	PE14-4A, 14-4B
• Prepare the Cash Flows from Investing Activities and Cash Flows from Financing Activities sections of the statement of cash flows.	EE14-5	PE14-5A, 14-5B

OBJ 3 Prepare a statement of cash flows, using the direct method.

Key Points The amount of cash flows from operating activities is the same under both the direct and indirect methods, but the manner in which cash flows operating activities is reported is different. The direct method reports cash flows from operating activities by major classes of operating cash receipts and cash payments. The difference between the major classes of total operating cash receipts and total operating cash payments is the net cash flow from operating activities. The Cash Flows from Investing and Financing Activities sections of the statement are the same under both the direct and indirect methods.

Learning Outcome	Example Exercises	Practice Exercises
• Prepare the cash flows from operating activities section of the statement of cash flows under the direct method.	EE14-6 EE14-7	PE14-6A, 14-6B PE14-7A, 14-7B

OBJ 4 Describe and illustrate the use of free cash flow in evaluating a company's cash flow.

Key Points Free cash flow measures the operating cash flow available for company use after purchasing the fixed assets that are necessary to maintain current productive capacity. It is calculated by subtracting these fixed asset purchases from net cash flow from operating activities. A company with strong free cash flow is able to fund internal growth, retire debt, pay dividends, and enjoy financial flexibility. A company with weak free cash flow has much less financial flexibility.

Learning Outcomes	Example Exercises	Practice Exercises
• Describe free cash flow.		
• Calculate and evaluate free cash flow.	EE14-8	PE14-8A, 14-8B

Key Terms

cash flow per share (645)
cash flows from financing activities (643)
cash flows from investing activities (642)
cash flows from operating activities (642)
direct method (643)
free cash flow (661)
indirect method (644)
statement of cash flows (642)

Illustrative Problem

The comparative balance sheet of Dowling Company for December 31, 2014 and 2013, is as follows:

Dowling Company
Comparative Balance Sheet
December 31, 2014 and 2013

	2014	2013
Assets		
Cash	$ 140,350	$ 95,900
Accounts receivable (net)	95,300	102,300
Inventories	165,200	157,900
Prepaid expenses	6,240	5,860
Investments (long-term)	35,700	84,700
Land	75,000	90,000
Buildings	375,000	260,000
Accumulated depreciation—buildings	(71,300)	(58,300)
Machinery and equipment	428,300	428,300
Accumulated depreciation—machinery and equipment	(148,500)	(138,000)
Patents	58,000	65,000
Total assets	$1,159,290	$1,093,660
Liabilities and Stockholders' Equity		
Accounts payable (merchandise creditors)	$ 43,500	$ 46,700
Accrued expenses payable (operating expenses)	14,000	12,500
Income taxes payable	7,900	8,400
Dividends payable	14,000	10,000
Mortgage note payable, due 2023	40,000	0
Bonds payable	150,000	250,000
Common stock, $30 par	450,000	375,000
Excess of issue price over par—common stock	66,250	41,250
Retained earnings	373,640	349,810
Total liabilities and stockholders' equity	$1,159,290	$1,093,660

The income statement for Dowling Company is shown here.

Dowling Company Income Statement For the Year Ended December 31, 2014		
Sales		$1,100,000
Cost of merchandise sold		710,000
Gross profit		$ 390,000
Operating expenses:		
Depreciation expense	$ 23,500	
Patent amortization	7,000	
Other operating expenses	196,000	
Total operating expenses		226,500
Income from operations		$ 163,500
Other income:		
Gain on sale of investments	$ 11,000	
Other expense:		
Interest expense	26,000	(15,000)
Income before income tax		$ 148,500
Income tax expense		50,000
Net income		$ 98,500

An examination of the accounting records revealed the following additional information applicable to 2014:

a. Land costing $15,000 was sold for $15,000.

b. A mortgage note was issued for $40,000.

c. A building costing $115,000 was constructed.

d. 2,500 shares of common stock were issued at $40 in exchange for the bonds payable.

e. Cash dividends declared were $74,670.

Instructions

1. Prepare a statement of cash flows, using the indirect method of reporting cash flows from operating activities.

2. Prepare a statement of cash flows, using the direct method of reporting cash flows from operating activities.

Solution

1.

Dowling Company
Statement of Cash Flows—Indirect Method
For the Year Ended December 31, 2014

Cash flows from operating activities:			
Net income		$ 98,500	
Adjustments to reconcile net income to net cash flow from operating activities:			
Depreciation		23,500	
Amortization of patents		7,000	
Gain on sale of investments		(11,000)	
Changes in current operating assets and liabilities:			
Decrease in accounts receivable		7,000	
Increase in inventories		(7,300)	
Increase in prepaid expenses		(380)	
Decrease in accounts payable		(3,200)	
Increase in accrued expenses payable		1,500	
Decrease in income taxes payable		(500)	
Net cash flow from operating activities			$115,120
Cash flows from investing activities:			
Cash received from sale of:			
Investments	$60,000[1]		
Land	15,000	$ 75,000	
Less: Cash paid for construction of building		115,000	
Net cash flow used for investing activities			(40,000)
Cash flows from financing activities:			
Cash received from issuing mortgage note payable		$ 40,000	
Less: Cash paid for dividends		70,670[2]	
Net cash flow used for financing activities			(30,670)
Increase in cash			$ 44,450
Cash at the beginning of the year			95,900
Cash at the end of the year			$140,350
Schedule of Noncash Investing and Financing Activities:			
Issued common stock to retire bonds payable			$100,000

[1] $60,000 = $11,000 gain + $49,000 (decrease in investments)

[2] $70,670 = $74,670 – $4,000 (increase in dividends)

2.

Dowling Company
Statement of Cash Flows—Direct Method
For the Year Ended December 31, 2014

Cash flows from operating activities:			
Cash received from customers[1]		$1,107,000	
Deduct: Cash paid for merchandise[2]	$720,500		
Cash paid for operating expenses[3]	194,880		
Cash paid for interest expense	26,000		
Cash paid for income tax[4]	50,500	991,880	
Net cash flow from operating activities			$115,120
Cash flows from investing activities:			
Cash received from sale of:			
Investments	$ 60,000[5]		
Land	15,000	$ 75,000	
Less: Cash paid for construction of building		115,000	
Net cash flow used for investing activities			(40,000)
Cash flows from financing activities:			
Cash received from issuing mortgage note payable		$ 40,000	
Less: Cash paid for dividends[6]		70,670	
Net cash flow used for financing activities			(30,670)
Increase in cash			$ 44,450
Cash at the beginning of the year			95,900
Cash at the end of the year			$140,350
Schedule of Noncash Investing and Financing Activities:			
Issued common stock to retire bonds payable			$100,000
Schedule Reconciling Net Income with Cash Flows from Operating Activities[7]			

Computations:

[1]$1,100,000 + $7,000 = $1,107,000
[2]$710,000 + $3,200 + $7,300 = $720,500
[3]$196,000 + $380 − $1,500 = $194,880
[4]$50,000 + $500 = $50,500
[5]$60,000 = $11,000 gain + $49,000 (decrease in investments)
[6]$74,670 + $10,000 − $14,000 = $70,670
[7]The content of this schedule is the same as the Operating Activities section of part (1) of this solution and is not reproduced here for the sake of brevity.

Discussion Questions

1. What is the principal disadvantage of the direct method of reporting cash flows from operating activities?
2. What are the major advantages of the indirect method of reporting cash flows from operating activities?
3. A corporation issued $2,000,000 of common stock in exchange for $2,000,000 of fixed assets. Where would this transaction be reported on the statement of cash flows?
4. A retail business, using the accrual method of accounting, owed merchandise creditors (accounts payable) $320,000 at the beginning of the year and $350,000 at the end of the year. How would the $30,000 increase be used to adjust net income in determining the amount of cash flows from operating activities by the indirect method? Explain.
5. If salaries payable was $100,000 at the beginning of the year and $75,000 at the end of the year, should $25,000 be added to or deducted from income to determine the amount of cash flows from operating activities by the indirect method? Explain.

6. A long-term investment in bonds with a cost of $500,000 was sold for $600,000 cash. (a) What was the gain or loss on the sale? (b) What was the effect of the transaction on cash flows? (c) How should the transaction be reported on the statement of cash flows if cash flows from operating activities are reported by the indirect method?

7. A corporation issued $2,000,000 of 20-year bonds for cash at 98. How would the transaction be reported on the statement of cash flows?

8. Fully depreciated equipment costing $50,000 was discarded. What was the effect of the transaction on cash flows if (a) $15,000 cash is received, (b) no cash is received?

9. For the current year, Packers Company decided to switch from the indirect method to the direct method for reporting cash flows from operating activities on the statement of cash flows. Will the change cause the amount of net cash flow from operating activities to be larger, smaller, or the same as if the indirect method had been used? Explain.

10. Name five common major classes of operating cash receipts or operating cash payments presented on the statement of cash flows when the cash flows from operating activities are reported by the direct method.

Practice Exercises

Example Exercises

EE 14-1 *p. 645*

PE 14-1A Classifying cash flows **OBJ. 1**

Identify whether each of the following would be reported as an operating, investing, or financing activity on the statement of cash flows.

a. Payment of accounts payable
b. Payment for administrative expenses
c. Purchase of land
d. Issuance of common stock
e. Retirement of bonds payable
f. Cash received from customers

EE 14-1 *p. 645*

PE 14-1B Classifying cash flows **OBJ. 1**

Identify whether each of the following would be reported as an operating, investing, or financing activity on the statement of cash flows.

a. Purchase of investments
b. Disposal of equipment
c. Payment for selling expenses
d. Collection of accounts receivable
e. Cash sales
f. Issuance of bonds payable

EE 14-2 *p. 649*

PE 14-2A Adjustments to net income—indirect method **OBJ. 2**

Carlyn Corporation's accumulated depreciation—furniture account increased by $7,500, while $2,750 of patent amortization was recognized between balance sheet dates. There were no purchases or sales of depreciable or intangible assets during the year. In addition, the income statement showed a loss of $4,000 from the sale of land. Reconcile a net income of $107,500 to net cash flow from operating activities.

EE 14-2 *p. 649*

PE 14-2B Adjustments to net income—indirect method **OBJ. 2**

Ya Wen Corporation's accumulated depreciation—equipment account increased by $8,750, while $3,250 of patent amortization was recognized between balance sheet dates. There were no purchases or sales of depreciable or intangible assets during the year. In addition, the income statement showed a gain of $18,750 from the sale of investments. Reconcile a net income of $175,000 to net cash flow from operating activities.

Example Exercises

EE 14-3 *p. 651*

PE 14-3A Changes in current operating assets and liabilities—indirect method **OBJ. 2**

Macavoy Corporation's comparative balance sheet for current assets and liabilities was as follows:

	Dec. 31, 2014	Dec. 31, 2013
Accounts receivable	$33,000	$39,600
Inventory	22,000	18,920
Accounts payable	19,800	17,380
Dividends payable	60,500	64,900

Adjust net income of $253,000 for changes in operating assets and liabilities to arrive at net cash flow from operating activities.

EE 14-3 *p. 651*

PE 14-3B Changes in current operating assets and liabilities—indirect method **OBJ. 2**

Huluduey Corporation's comparative balance sheet for current assets and liabilities was as follows:

	Dec. 31, 2014	Dec. 31, 2013
Accounts receivable	$18,000	$14,400
Inventory	34,800	29,700
Accounts payable	27,600	20,700
Dividends payable	8,400	10,800

Adjust net income of $160,000 for changes in operating assets and liabilities to arrive at net cash flow from operating activities.

EE 14-4 *p. 652*

PE 14-4A Cash flows from operating activities—indirect method **OBJ. 2**

Avenger Inc. reported the following data:

Net income	$270,000
Depreciation expense	30,000
Gain on disposal of equipment	24,600
Decrease in accounts receivable	16,800
Decrease in accounts payable	4,320

Prepare the Cash Flows from Operating Activities section of the statement of cash flows, using the indirect method.

EE 14-4 *p. 652*

PE 14-4B Cash flows from operating activities—indirect method **OBJ. 2**

Staley Inc. reported the following data:

Net income	$280,000
Depreciation expense	48,000
Loss on disposal of equipment	19,520
Increase in accounts receivable	17,280
Increase in accounts payable	8,960

Prepare the Cash Flows from Operating Activities section of the statement of cash flows, using the indirect method.

EE 14-5 *p. 655*

PE 14-5A Land transactions on the statement of cash flows **OBJ. 2**

Rainbow Corporation purchased land for $360,000. Later in the year, the company sold a different piece of land with a book value of $180,000 for $120,000. How are the effects of these transactions reported on the statement of cash flows?

Example Exercises

EE 14-5 *p. 655*

PE 14-5B Land transactions on the statement of cash flows **OBJ. 2**

IZ Corporation purchased land for $400,000. Later in the year, the company sold a different piece of land with a book value of $200,000 for $240,000. How are the effects of these transactions reported on the statement of cash flows?

EE 14-6 *p. 657*

PE 14-6A Cash received from customers—direct method **OBJ. 3**

Sales reported on the income statement were $480,000. The accounts receivable balance increased $54,000 over the year. Determine the amount of cash received from customers.

EE 14-6 *p. 657*

PE 14-6B Cash received from customers—direct method **OBJ. 3**

Sales reported on the income statement were $112,000. The accounts receivable balance decreased $10,500 over the year. Determine the amount of cash received from customers.

EE 14-7 *p. 658*

PE 14-7A Cash payments for merchandise—direct method **OBJ. 3**

The cost of merchandise sold reported on the income statement was $770,000. The accounts payable balance decreased $44,000, and the inventory balance decreased by $66,000 over the year. Determine the amount of cash paid for merchandise.

EE 14-7 *p. 658*

PE 14-7B Cash payments for merchandise—direct method **OBJ. 3**

The cost of merchandise sold reported on the income statement was $240,000. The accounts payable balance increased $12,000, and the inventory balance increased by $19,200 over the year. Determine the amount of cash paid for merchandise.

EE 14-8 *p. 662*

F·A·I

PE 14-8A Free cash flow **OBJ. 4**

McMahon Inc. reported the following on the company's statement of cash flows in 2014 and 2013:

	2014	2013
Net cash flow from operating activities	$ 294,000	$ 280,000
Net cash flow used for investing activities	(224,000)	(252,000)
Net cash flow used for financing activities	(63,000)	(42,000)

Seventy percent of the net cash flow used for investing activities was used to replace existing capacity.

a. Determine McMahon's free cash flow for both years.

b. Has McMahon's free cash flow improved or declined from 2013 to 2014?

EE 14-8 *p. 662*

F·A·I

PE 14-8B Free cash flow **OBJ. 4**

Dillin Inc. reported the following on the company's statement of cash flows in 2014 and 2013:

	2014	2013
Net cash flow from operating activities	$ 476,000	$ 455,000
Net cash flow used for investing activities	(427,000)	(378,000)
Net cash flow used for financing activities	(42,000)	(58,800)

Eighty percent of the net cash flow used for investing activities was used to replace existing capacity.

a. Determine Dillin's free cash flow for both years.

b. Has Dillin's free cash flow improved or declined from 2013 to 2014?

Exercises

EX 14-1 Cash flows from operating activities—net loss **OBJ. 1**

On its income statement for a recent year, Continental Airlines, Inc., reported a net *loss* of $471 million from operations. On its statement of cash flows, it reported $1,241 million of cash flows from operating activities.

Explain this apparent contradiction between the loss and the positive cash flows.

EX 14-2 Effect of transactions on cash flows **OBJ. 1**

✔ c. Cash payment, $475,000

State the effect (cash receipt or payment and amount) of each of the following transactions, considered individually, on cash flows:

a. Sold equipment with a book value of $78,000 for $94,000.

b. Sold a new issue of $250,000 of bonds at 102.

c. Retired $400,000 of bonds, on which there was $4,000 of unamortized discount, for $475,000.

d. Purchased 3,000 shares of $30 par common stock as treasury stock at $40 per share.

e. Sold 4,000 shares of $25 par common stock for $50 per share.

f. Paid dividends of $1.50 per share. There were 40,000 shares issued and 5,000 shares of treasury stock.

g. Purchased land for $287,000 cash.

h. Purchased a building by paying $60,000 cash and issuing a $50,000 mortgage note payable.

EX 14-3 Classifying cash flows **OBJ. 1**

Identify the type of cash flow activity for each of the following events (operating, investing, or financing):

a. Redeemed bonds

b. Purchased patents

c. Purchased buildings

d. Purchased treasury stock

e. Sold long-term investments

f. Paid cash dividends

g. Issued common stock

h. Issued preferred stock

i. Net income

j. Issued bonds

k. Sold equipment

EX 14-4 Cash flows from operating activities—indirect method **OBJ. 2**

Indicate whether each of the following would be added to or deducted from net income in determining net cash flow from operating activities by the indirect method:

a. Increase in notes payable due in 90 days to vendors

b. Decrease in prepaid expenses

c. Increase in merchandise inventory

d. Loss on disposal of fixed assets

e. Decrease in accounts receivable

f. Decrease in salaries payable

g. Gain on retirement of long-term debt

h. Increase in notes receivable due in 90 days from customers

i. Depreciation of fixed assets

j. Amortization of patent

k. Decrease in accounts payable

✔ Net cash flow from operating activities, $626,400

EX 14-5 Cash flows from operating activities—indirect method **OBJ. 2**

The net income reported on the income statement for the current year was $600,000. Depreciation recorded on store equipment for the year amounted to $24,000. Balances of the current asset and current liability accounts at the beginning and end of the year are as follows:

	End of Year	Beginning of Year
Cash	$62,400	$57,600
Accounts receivable (net)	45,600	42,000
Merchandise inventory	60,000	66,000
Prepaid expenses	7,200	5,400
Accounts payable (merchandise creditors)	60,000	54,000
Wages payable	31,800	36,000

a. Prepare the Cash Flows from Operating Activities section of the statement of cash flows, using the indirect method.

b. Briefly explain why net cash flow from operating activities is different than net income.

✔ Net cash flow from operating activities, $295,800

EX 14-6 Cash flows from operating activities—indirect method **OBJ. 1, 2**

The net income reported on the income statement for the current year was $240,000. Depreciation recorded on equipment and a building amounted to $72,000 for the year. Balances of the current asset and current liability accounts at the beginning and end of the year are as follows:

	End of Year	Beginning of Year
Cash	$ 67,200	$ 72,000
Accounts receivable (net)	84,000	88,800
Inventories	168,000	150,000
Prepaid expenses	9,600	10,800
Accounts payable (merchandise creditors)	72,000	78,000
Salaries payable	12,000	10,200

a. Prepare the Cash Flows from Operating Activities section of the statement of cash flows, using the indirect method.

b. If the direct method had been used, would the net cash flow from operating activities have been the same? Explain.

✔ Net cash flow from operating activities, $657,400

EX 14-7 Cash flows from operating activities—indirect method **OBJ. 1, 2**

The income statement disclosed the following items for 2014:

Depreciation expense	$ 72,000
Gain on disposal of equipment	42,000
Net income	635,000

Balances of the current assets and current liability accounts changed between December 31, 2013, and December 31, 2014, as follows:

Accounts receivable	$11,200
Inventory	6,400*
Prepaid insurance	2,400*
Accounts payable	7,600*
Income taxes payable	2,400
Dividends payable	1,700

*Decrease

a. Prepare the Cash Flows from Operating Activities section of the statement of cash flows, using the indirect method.

b. Briefly explain why net cash flows from operating activities is different than net income.

In a vertical analysis of the income statement, each item is stated as a percent of net sales. Exhibit 6 illustrates the vertical analysis of the 2014 and 2013 income statements of Lincoln Company.

Exhibit 6 indicates a decrease in the gross profit rate from 31.7% in 2013 to 30.4% in 2014. Although this is only a 1.3 percentage point (31.7% – 30.4%) decrease, in dollars of potential gross profit, it represents a decrease of $19,500 (1.3% × $1,498,000) based on 2014 net sales. Thus, a small percentage decrease can have a large dollar effect.

EXHIBIT 6

Comparative Income Statement—Vertical Analysis

Lincoln Company
Comparative Income Statement
For the Years Ended December 31, 2014 and 2013

	2014 Amount	2014 Percent	2013 Amount	2013 Percent
Sales	$1,530,500	102.2%	$1,234,000	102.8%
Sales returns and allowances	32,500	2.2	34,000	2.8
Net sales	$1,498,000	100.0%	$1,200,000	100.0%
Cost of goods sold	1,043,000	69.6	820,000	68.3
Gross profit	$ 455,000	30.4%	$ 380,000	31.7%
Selling expenses	$ 191,000	12.8%	$ 147,000	12.3%
Administrative expenses	104,000	6.9	97,400	8.1
Total operating expenses	$ 295,000	19.7%	$ 244,400	20.4%
Income from operations	$ 160,000	10.7%	$ 135,600	11.3%
Other income	8,500	0.6	11,000	0.9
	$ 168,500	11.3%	$ 146,600	12.2%
Other expense (interest)	6,000	0.4	12,000	1.0
Income before income tax	$ 162,500	10.9%	$ 134,600	11.2%
Income tax expense	71,500	4.8	58,100	4.8
Net income	$ 91,000	6.1%	$ 76,500	6.4%

Example Exercise 15-2 Vertical Analysis OBJ 1

Income statement information for Lee Corporation is provided below.

Sales	$100,000
Cost of goods sold	65,000
Gross profit	$ 35,000

Prepare a vertical analysis of the income statement for Lee Corporation.

Follow My Example 15-2

	Amount	Percentage	
Sales	$100,000	100%	($100,000 ÷ $100,000)
Cost of goods sold	65,000	65	($65,000 ÷ $100,000)
Gross profit	$ 35,000	35%	($35,000 ÷ $100,000)

Practice Exercises: **PE 15-2A, PE 15-2B**

Common-Sized Statements

In a **common-sized statement**, all items are expressed as percentages, with no dollar amounts shown. Common-sized statements are often useful for comparing one company with another or for comparing a company with industry averages.

Exhibit 7 illustrates common-sized income statements for Lincoln Company and Madison Corporation. Exhibit 7 indicates that Lincoln Company has a slightly higher

	Lincoln Company	Madison Corporation
Sales	102.2%	102.3%
Sales returns and allowances	2.2	2.3
Net sales	100.0%	100.0%
Cost of goods sold	69.6	70.0
Gross profit	30.4%	30.0%
Selling expenses	12.8%	11.5%
Administrative expenses	6.9	4.1
Total operating expenses	19.7%	15.6%
Income from operations	10.7%	14.4%
Other income	0.6	0.6
	11.3%	15.0%
Other expense (interest)	0.4	0.5
Income before income tax	10.9%	14.5%
Income tax expense	4.8	5.5
Net income	6.1%	9.0%

EXHIBIT 7

Common-Sized Income Statements

rate of gross profit (30.4%) than Madison Corporation (30.0%). However, Lincoln has a higher percentage of selling expenses (12.8%) and administrative expenses (6.9%) than does Madison (11.5% and 4.1%). As a result, the income from operations of Lincoln (10.7%) is less than that of Madison (14.4%).

The unfavorable difference of 3.7 (14.4% – 10.7%) percentage points in income from operations would concern the managers and other stakeholders of Lincoln. The underlying causes of the difference should be investigated and possibly corrected. For example, Lincoln Company may decide to outsource some of its administrative duties so that its administrative expenses are more comparative to that of Madison Corporation.

Other Analytical Measures

Other relationships may be expressed in ratios and percentages. Often, these relationships are compared within the same statement and, thus, are a type of vertical analysis. Comparing these items with items from earlier periods is a type of horizontal analysis.

Analytical measures are not a definitive conclusion. They are only guides in evaluating financial and operating data. Many other factors, such as trends in the industry and general economic conditions, should also be considered when analyzing a company.

Liquidity and Solvency Analysis

OBJ 2 Use financial statement analysis to assess the solvency of a business.

All users of financial statements are interested in the ability of a company to do the following:

1. Maintain **liquidity** and **solvency**
2. Earn income, called **profitability**

The ability of a company to convert assets into cash is called liquidity, while the ability of a company to pay its debts is called solvency. Liquidity, solvency, and profitability are interrelated. For example, a company that cannot convert assets into cash may have difficulty taking advantage of profitable courses of action requiring immediate cash outlays. Likewise, a company that cannot pay its debts will have difficulty obtaining credit. A lack of credit will, in turn, limit the company's ability to purchase merchandise or expand operations, which decreases its profitability.

Liquidity and solvency are normally assessed using the following:

1. Current position analysis
    - Working capital
    - Current ratio
    - Quick ratio

One popular printed source for industry ratios is *Annual Statement Studies* from Risk Management Association. Online analysis is available from Zacks Investment Research site, which is linked to the text's Web site at **www.cengagebrain.com.**

2. Accounts receivable analysis
    - Accounts receivable turnover
    - Number of days' sales in receivables
3. Inventory analysis
    - Inventory turnover
    - Number of days' sales in inventory
4. The ratio of fixed assets to long-term liabilities
5. The ratio of liabilities to stockholders' equity
6. The number of times interest charges are earned

The Lincoln Company financial statements presented earlier are used to illustrate the preceding analyses.

Current Position Analysis

A company's ability to pay its current liabilities is called **current position analysis.** It is a solvency measure of special interest to short-term creditors and includes the computation and analysis of the following:

1. Working capital
2. Current ratio
3. Quick ratio

Working Capital

A company's **working capital** is computed as follows:

$$\text{Working Capital} = \text{Current Assets} - \text{Current Liabilities}$$

To illustrate, the working capital for Lincoln Company for 2014 and 2013 is computed below.

	2014	2013
Current assets	$550,000	$533,000
Less current liabilities	210,000	243,000
Working capital	$340,000	$290,000

The working capital is used to evaluate a company's ability to pay current liabilities. A company's working capital is often monitored monthly, quarterly, or yearly by creditors and other debtors. However, it is difficult to use working capital to compare companies of different sizes. For example, working capital of $250,000 may be adequate for a local hardware store, but it would be inadequate for The Home Depot.

Current Ratio

The **current ratio**, sometimes called the *working capital ratio*, is computed as follows:

$$\text{Current Ratio} = \frac{\text{Current Assets}}{\text{Current Liabilities}}$$

To illustrate, the current ratio for Lincoln Company is computed below.

	2014	2013
Current assets	$550,000	$533,000
Current liabilities	$210,000	$243,000
Current ratio	2.6 ($550,000/$210,000)	2.2 ($533,000/$243,000)

The current ratio is a more reliable indicator of a company's ability to pay its current liabilities than is working capital, and it is much easier to compare across companies. To illustrate, assume that as of December 31, 2014, the working capital of a competitor is much greater than $340,000, but its current ratio is only 1.3. Considering these facts alone, Lincoln Company, with its current ratio of 2.6, is in a more favorable position to obtain short-term credit than the competitor, which has the greater amount of working capital.

Quick Ratio One limitation of working capital and the current ratio is that they do not consider the types of current assets a company has and how easily they can be turned in to cash. Because of this, two companies may have the same working capital and current ratios, but differ significantly in their ability to pay their current liabilities.

To illustrate, the current assets and liabilities for Lincoln Company and Jefferson Corporation as of December 31, 2014, are as follows:

	Lincoln Company	Jefferson Corporation
Current assets:		
Cash	$ 90,500	$ 45,500
Temporary investments	75,000	25,000
Accounts receivable (net)	115,000	90,000
Inventories	264,000	380,000
Prepaid expenses	5,500	9,500
Total current assets	$550,000	$550,000
Total current assets	$550,000	$550,000
Less current liabilities	210,000	210,000
Working capital	$340,000	$340,000
Current ratio ($550,000/$210,000)	2.6	2.6

Lincoln and Jefferson both have a working capital of $340,000 and current ratios of 2.6. Jefferson, however, has more of its current assets in inventories. These inventories must be sold and the receivables collected before all the current liabilities can be paid. This takes time. In addition, if the market for its product declines, Jefferson may have difficulty selling its inventory. This, in turn, could impair its ability to pay its current liabilities.

In contrast, Lincoln's current assets contain more cash, temporary investments, and accounts receivable, which can easily be converted to cash. Thus, Lincoln is in a stronger current position than Jefferson to pay its current liabilities.

A ratio that measures the "instant" debt-paying ability of a company is the **quick ratio**, sometimes called the *acid-test ratio*. The quick ratio is computed as follows:

$$\text{Quick Ratio} = \frac{\text{Quick Assets}}{\text{Current Liabilities}}$$

Quick assets are cash and other current assets that can be easily converted to cash. Quick assets normally include cash, temporary investments, and receivables, but exclude inventories and prepaid assets.

To illustrate, the quick ratio for Lincoln Company is computed below.

	2014	2013
Quick assets:		
Cash	$ 90,500	$ 64,700
Temporary investments	75,000	60,000
Accounts receivable (net)	115,000	120,000
Total quick assets	$280,500	$244,700
Current liabilities	$210,000	$243,000
Quick ratio	1.3 ($280,500 ÷ $210,000)	1.0 ($244,700 ÷ $243,000)

Example Exercise 15-3 Current Position Analysis

OBJ 2

The following items are reported on a company's balance sheet:

Cash	$300,000
Temporary investments	100,000
Accounts receivable (net)	200,000
Inventory	200,000
Accounts payable	400,000

Determine (a) the current ratio and (b) the quick ratio.

Follow My Example 15-3

a. Current Ratio = Current Assets ÷ Current Liabilities

Current Ratio = ($300,000 + $100,000 + $200,000 + $200,000) ÷ $400,000

Current Ratio = 2.0

b. Quick Ratio = Quick Assets ÷ Current Liabilities

Quick Ratio = ($300,000 + $100,000 + $200,000) ÷ $400,000

Quick Ratio = 1.5

Practice Exercises: **PE 15-3A, PE 15-3B**

Accounts Receivable Analysis

A company's ability to collect its accounts receivable is called **accounts receivable analysis**. It includes the computation and analysis of the following:

1. Accounts receivable turnover
2. Number of days' sales in receivables

Collecting accounts receivable as quickly as possible improves a company's liquidity. In addition, the cash collected from receivables may be used to improve or expand operations. Quick collection of receivables also reduces the risk of uncollectible accounts.

Accounts Receivable Turnover The **accounts receivable turnover** is computed as follows:

$$\text{Accounts Receivable Turnover} = \frac{\text{Net Sales}^2}{\text{Average Accounts Receivable}}$$

To illustrate, the accounts receivable turnover for Lincoln Company for 2014 and 2013 is computed below. Lincoln's accounts receivable balance at the beginning of 2013 is $140,000.

	2014	2013
Net sales	$1,498,000	$1,200,000
Accounts receivable (net):		
Beginning of year	$ 120,000	$ 140,000
End of year	115,000	120,000
Total	$ 235,000	$ 260,000
Average accounts receivable	$117,500 ($235,000 ÷ 2)	$130,000 ($260,000 ÷ 2)
Accounts receivable turnover	12.7 ($1,498,000 ÷ $117,500)	9.2 ($1,200,000 ÷ $130,000)

The increase in Lincoln's accounts receivable turnover from 9.2 to 12.7 indicates that the collection of receivables has improved during 2014. This may be due to a change in how credit is granted, collection practices, or both.

For Lincoln Company, the average accounts receivable was computed using the accounts receivable balance at the beginning and the end of the year. When sales

2 If known, *credit* sales should be used in the numerator. Because credit sales are not normally known by external users, we use net sales in the numerator.

are seasonal and, thus, vary throughout the year, monthly balances of receivables are often used. Also, if sales on account include notes receivable as well as accounts receivable, notes and accounts receivable are normally combined for analysis.

Number of Days' Sales in Receivables The **number of days' sales in receivables** is computed as follows:

$$\text{Number of Days' Sales in Receivables} = \frac{\text{Average Accounts Receivable}}{\text{Average Daily Sales}}$$

where

$$\text{Average Daily Sales} = \frac{\text{Net Sales}}{\text{365 days}}$$

To illustrate, the number of days' sales in receivables for Lincoln Company is computed below.

	2014	2013
Average accounts receivable	$117,500 ($235,000 ÷ 2)	$130,000 ($260,000 ÷ 2)
Average daily sales	$4,104 ($1,498,000 ÷ 365)	$3,288 ($1,200,000 ÷ 365)
Number of days' sales in receivables	28.6 ($117,500 ÷ $4,104)	39.5 ($130,000 ÷ $3,288)

The number of days' sales in receivables is an estimate of the time (in days) that the accounts receivable have been outstanding. The number of days' sales in receivables is often compared with a company's credit terms to evaluate the efficiency of the collection of receivables.

To illustrate, if Lincoln's credit terms are 2/10, n/30, then Lincoln was very *inefficient* in collecting receivables in 2013. In other words, receivables should have been collected in 30 days or less, but were being collected in 39.5 days. Although collections improved during 2014 to 28.6 days, there is probably still room for improvement. On the other hand, if Lincoln's credit terms are n/45, then there is probably little room for improving collections.

Example Exercise 15-4 Accounts Receivable Analysis

OBJ 2

A company reports the following:

Net sales	$960,000
Average accounts receivable (net)	48,000

Determine (a) the accounts receivable turnover and (b) the number of days' sales in receivables. Round to one decimal place.

Follow My Example 15-4

a. Accounts Receivable Turnover = Net Sales ÷ Average Accounts Receivable
Accounts Receivable Turnover = $960,000 ÷ $48,000
Accounts Receivable Turnover = 20.0

b. Number of Days' Sales in Receivables = Average Accounts Receivable ÷ Average Daily Sales
Number of Days' Sales in Receivables = $48,000 ÷ ($960,000 ÷ 365) = $48,000 ÷ $2,630
Number of Days' Sales in Receivables = 18.3 days

Practice Exercises: **PE 15-4A, PE 15-4B**

Inventory Analysis

A company's ability to manage its inventory effectively is evaluated using **inventory analysis**. It includes the computation and analysis of the following:

1. Inventory turnover
2. Number of days' sales in inventory

Excess inventory decreases liquidity by tying up funds (cash) in inventory. In addition, excess inventory increases insurance expense, property taxes, storage costs, and other related expenses. These expenses further reduce funds that could be used elsewhere to improve or expand operations.

Excess inventory also increases the risk of losses because of price declines or obsolescence of the inventory. On the other hand, a company should keep enough inventory in stock so that it doesn't lose sales because of lack of inventory.

Inventory Turnover The **inventory turnover** is computed as follows:

$$\text{Inventory Turnover} = \frac{\text{Cost of Goods Sold}}{\text{Average Inventory}}$$

To illustrate, the inventory turnover for Lincoln Company for 2014 and 2013 is computed below. Lincoln's inventory balance at the beginning of 2013 is $311,000.

	2014	2013
Cost of goods sold	$1,043,000	$820,000
Inventories:		
Beginning of year	$ 283,000	$311,000
End of year	264,000	283,000
Total	$ 547,000	$594,000
Average inventory	$273,500 ($547,000 ÷ 2)	$297,000 ($594,000 ÷ 2)
Inventory turnover	3.8 ($1,043,000 ÷ $273,500)	2.8 ($820,000 ÷ $297,000)

The increase in Lincoln's inventory turnover from 2.8 to 3.8 indicates that the management of inventory has improved in 2014. The inventory turnover improved because of an increase in the cost of goods sold, which indicates more sales, and a decrease in the average inventories.

What is considered a good inventory turnover varies by type of inventory, companies, and industries. For example, grocery stores have a higher inventory turnover than jewelers or furniture stores. Likewise, within a grocery store, perishable foods have a higher turnover than the soaps and cleansers.

Number of Days' Sales in Inventory The **number of days' sales in inventory** is computed as follows:

$$\text{Number of Days' Sales in Inventory} = \frac{\text{Average Inventory}}{\text{Average Daily Cost of Goods Sold}}$$

where

$$\text{Average Daily Cost of Goods Sold} = \frac{\text{Cost of Goods Sold}}{\text{365 days}}$$

To illustrate, the number of days' sales in inventory for Lincoln Company is computed below.

	2014	2013
Average inventory	$273,500 ($547,000 ÷ 2)	$297,000 ($594,000 ÷ 2)
Average daily cost of goods sold	$2,858 ($1,043,000 ÷ 365)	$2,247 ($820,000 ÷ 365)
Number of days' sales in inventory	95.7 ($273,500 ÷ $2,858)	132.2 ($297,000 ÷ $2,247)

The number of days' sales in inventory is a rough measure of the length of time it takes to purchase, sell, and replace the inventory. Lincoln's number of days' sales in inventory improved from 132.2 days to 95.7 days during 2014. This is a major improvement in managing inventory.

Example Exercise 15-5 Inventory Analysis OBJ 2

A company reports the following:

Cost of goods sold	$560,000
Average inventory	112,000

Determine (a) the inventory turnover and (b) the number of days' sales in inventory. Round to one decimal place.

Follow My Example 15-5

a. Inventory Turnover = Cost of Goods Sold ÷ Average Inventory
   Inventory Turnover = $560,000 ÷ $112,000
   Inventory Turnover = 5.0

b. Number of Days' Sales in Inventory = Average Inventory ÷ Average Daily Cost of Goods Sold
   Number of Days' Sales in Inventory = $112,000 ÷ ($560,000 ÷ 365) = $112,000 ÷ $1,534
   Number of Days' Sales in Inventory = 73.0 days

Practice Exercises: **PE 15-5A, PE 15-5B**

Ratio of Fixed Assets to Long-Term Liabilities

The **ratio of fixed assets to long-term liabilities** provides a measure of whether noteholders or bondholders will be paid. Since fixed assets are often pledged as security for long-term notes and bonds, it is computed as follows:

$$\text{Ratio of Fixed Assets to Long-Term Liabilities} = \frac{\text{Fixed Assets (net)}}{\text{Long-Term Liabilities}}$$

To illustrate, the ratio of fixed assets to long-term liabilities for Lincoln Company is computed below.

	2014	2013
Fixed assets (net)	$444,500	$470,000
Long-term liabilities	$100,000	$200,000
Ratio of fixed assets to long-term liabilities	4.4 ($444,500 ÷ $100,000)	2.4 ($470,000 ÷ $200,000)

During 2014, Lincoln's ratio of fixed assets to long-term liabilities increased from 2.4 to 4.4. This increase was due primarily to Lincoln paying off one-half of its long-term liabilities in 2014.

Ratio of Liabilities to Stockholders' Equity

The **ratio of liabilities to stockholders' equity** measures how much of the company is financed by debt and equity. It is computed as follows:

$$\text{Ratio of Liabilities to Stockholders' Equity} = \frac{\text{Total Liabilities}}{\text{Total Stockholders' Equity}}$$

To illustrate, the ratio of liabilities to stockholders' equity for Lincoln Company is computed below.

	2014	2013
Total liabilities	$310,000	$443,000
Total stockholders' equity	$829,500	$787,500
Ratio of liabilities to stockholders' equity	0.4 ($310,000 ÷ $829,500)	0.6 ($443,000 ÷ $787,500)

Lincoln's ratio of liabilities to stockholders' equity decreased from 0.6 to 0.4 during 2014. This is an improvement and indicates that Lincoln's creditors have an adequate margin of safety.

Example Exercise 15-6 Long-Term Solvency Analysis

OBJ 2

The following information was taken from Acme Company's balance sheet:

Fixed assets (net)	$1,400,000
Long-term liabilities	400,000
Total liabilities	560,000
Total stockholders' equity	1,400,000

Determine the company's (a) ratio of fixed assets to long-term liabilities and (b) ratio of liabilities to total stockholders' equity.

Follow My Example 15-6

a. Ratio of Fixed Assets to Long-Term Liabilities = Fixed Assets ÷ Long-Term Liabilities
   Ratio of Fixed Assets to Long-Term Liabilities = $1,400,000 ÷ $400,000
   Ratio of Fixed Assets to Long-Term Liabilities = 3.5

b. Ratio of Liabilities to Total Stockholders' Equity = Total Liabilities ÷ Total Stockholders' Equity
   Ratio of Liabilities to Total Stockholders' Equity = $560,000 ÷ $1,400,000
   Ratio of Liabilities to Total Stockholders' Equity = 0.4

Practice Exercises: **PE 15-6A, PE 15-6B**

Number of Times Interest Charges Are Earned

The **number of times interest charges are earned**, sometimes called the *fixed charge coverage ratio*, measures the risk that interest payments will not be made if earnings decrease. It is computed as follows:

$$\text{Number of Times Interest Charges Are Earned} = \frac{\text{Income Before Income Tax} + \text{Interest Expense}}{\text{Interest Expense}}$$

Interest expense is paid before income taxes. In other words, interest expense is deducted in determining taxable income and, thus, income tax. For this reason, income *before taxes* is used in computing the number of times interest charges are earned.

The *higher* the ratio the more likely interest payments will be paid if earnings decrease. To illustrate, the number of times interest charges are earned for Lincoln Company is computed below.

	2014	2013
Income before income tax	$162,500	$134,600
Add interest expense	6,000	12,000
Amount available to pay interest	$168,500	$146,600
Number of times interest charges are earned	28.1 ($168,500 ÷ $6,000)	12.2 ($146,600 ÷ $12,000)

The number of times interest charges are earned improved from 12.2 to 28.1 during 2014. This indicates that Lincoln Company has sufficient earnings to pay interest expense.

The number of times interest charges are earned can be adapted for use with dividends on preferred stock. In this case, the *number of times preferred dividends are earned* is computed as follows:

$$\text{Number of Times Preferred Dividends Are Earned} = \frac{\text{Net Income}}{\text{Preferred Dividends}}$$

Since dividends are paid after taxes, net income is used in computing the number of times preferred dividends are earned. The *higher* the ratio, the more likely preferred dividend payments will be paid if earnings decrease.

Example Exercise 15-7 Times Interest Charges Are Earned

OBJ 2

A company reports the following:

Income before income tax	$250,000
Interest expense	100,000

Determine the number of times interest charges are earned.

Follow My Example 15-7

Number of Times Interest Charges Are Earned = (Income Before Income Tax + Interest Expense) ÷ Interest Expense
Number of Times Interest Charges Are Earned = ($250,000 + $100,000) ÷ $100,000
Number of Times Interest Charges Are Earned = 3.5

Practice Exercises: **PE 15-7A, PE 15-7B**

Profitability Analysis

OBJ 3 Use financial statement analysis to assess the profitability of a business.

Profitability analysis focuses on the ability of a company to earn profits. This ability is reflected in the company's operating results, as reported in its income statement. The ability to earn profits also depends on the assets the company has available for use in its operations, as reported in its balance sheet. Thus, income statement and balance sheet relationships are often used in evaluating profitability.

Common profitability analyses include the following:

1. Ratio of net sales to assets
2. Rate earned on total assets
3. Rate earned on stockholders' equity
4. Rate earned on common stockholders' equity
5. Earnings per share on common stock
6. Price-earnings ratio
7. Dividends per share
8. Dividend yield

Note:
Profitability analysis focuses on the relationship between operating results and the resources available to a business.

Ratio of Net Sales to Assets

The **ratio of net sales to assets** measures how effectively a company uses its assets. It is computed as follows:

$$\text{Ratio of Net Sales to Assets} = \frac{\text{Net Sales}}{\text{Average Total Assets (excluding long-term investments)}}$$

As shown above, any long-term investments are excluded in computing the ratio of net sales to assets. This is because long-term investments are unrelated to normal operations and net sales.

To illustrate, the ratio of net sales to assets for Lincoln Company is computed below. Total assets (excluding long-term investments) are $1,010,000 at the beginning of 2013.

	2014	2013
Net sales	$1,498,000	$1,200,000
Total assets (excluding long-term investments):		
Beginning of year	$1,053,000*	$1,010,000
End of year	1,044,500**	1,053,000***
Total	$2,097,500	$2,063,000
Average total assets	$1,048,750 ($2,097,500 ÷ 2)	$1,031,500 ($2,063,000 ÷ 2)
Ratio of net sales to assets	1.4 ($1,498,000 ÷ $1,048,750)	1.2 ($1,200,000 ÷ $1,031,500)

*($1,230,500 – $177,500)
**($1,139,500 – $95,000)
***($1,230,500 – $177,500)

For Lincoln Company, the average total assets was computed using total assets (excluding long-term investments) at the beginning and end of the year. The average total assets could also be based on monthly or quarterly averages.

The ratio of net sales to assets indicates that Lincoln's use of its operating assets has improved in 2014. This was primarily due to the increase in net sales in 2014.

Example Exercise 15-8 Net Sales to Assets

OBJ 3

A company reports the following:

Net sales	$2,250,000
Average total assets	1,500,000

Determine the ratio of net sales to assets.

Follow My Example 15-8

Ratio of Net Sales to Assets = Net Sales ÷ Average Total Assets
Ratio of Net Sales to Assets = $2,250,000 ÷ $1,500,000
Ratio of Net Sales to Assets = 1.5

Practice Exercises: **PE 15-8A, PE 15-8B**

Rate Earned on Total Assets

The **rate earned on total assets** measures the profitability of total assets, without considering how the assets are financed. In other words, this rate is not affected by the portion of assets financed by creditors or stockholders. It is computed as follows:

$$\text{Rate Earned on Total Assets} = \frac{\text{Net Income} + \text{Interest Expense}}{\text{Average Total Assets}}$$

The rate earned on total assets is computed by adding interest expense to net income. By adding interest expense to net income, the effect of whether the assets are financed by creditors (debt) or stockholders (equity) is eliminated. Because net income includes any income earned from long-term investments, the average total assets includes long-term investments as well as the net operating assets.

To illustrate, the rate earned on total assets by Lincoln Company is computed below. Total assets are $1,187,500 at the beginning of 2013.

	2014	2013
Net income	$ 91,000	$ 76,500
Plus interest expense	6,000	12,000
Total	$ 97,000	$ 88,500
Total assets:		
Beginning of year	$1,230,500	$1,187,500
End of year	1,139,500	1,230,500
Total	$2,370,000	$2,418,000
Average total assets	$1,185,000 ($2,370,000 ÷ 2)	$1,209,000 ($2,418,000 ÷ 2)
Rate earned on total assets	8.2% ($97,000 ÷ $1,185,000)	7.3% ($88,500 ÷ $1,209,000)

The rate earned on total assets improved from 7.3% to 8.2% during 2014.

The *rate earned on operating assets* is sometimes computed when there are large amounts of nonoperating income and expense. It is computed as follows:

$$\text{Rate Earned on Operating Assets} = \frac{\text{Income from Operations}}{\text{Average Operating Assets}}$$

Since Lincoln Company does not have a significant amount of nonoperating income and expense, the rate earned on operating assets is not illustrated.

Example Exercise 15-9 Rate Earned on Total Assets OBJ 3

A company reports the following income statement and balance sheet information for the current year:

Net income	$ 125,000
Interest expense	25,000
Average total assets	2,000,000

Determine the rate earned on total assets.

Follow My Example 15-9

Rate Earned on Total Assets = (Net Income + Interest Expense) ÷ Average Total Assets
Rate Earned on Total Assets = ($125,000 + $25,000) ÷ $2,000,000
Rate Earned on Total Assets = $150,000 ÷ $2,000,000
Rate Earned on Total Assets = 7.5%

Practice Exercises: **PE 15-9A, PE 15-9B**

Rate Earned on Stockholders' Equity

The **rate earned on stockholders' equity** measures the rate of income earned on the amount invested by the stockholders. It is computed as follows:

$$\text{Rate Earned on Stockholders' Equity} = \frac{\text{Net Income}}{\text{Average Total Stockholders' Equity}}$$

To illustrate, the rate earned on stockholders' equity for Lincoln Company is computed below. Total stockholders' equity is $750,000 at the beginning of 2013.

	2014	2013
Net income	$ 91,000	$ 76,500
Stockholders' equity:		
Beginning of year	$ 787,500	$ 750,000
End of year	829,500	787,500
Total	$1,617,000	$1,537,500
Average stockholders' equity	$808,500 ($1,617,000 ÷ 2)	$768,750 ($1,537,500 ÷ 2)
Rate earned on stockholders' equity	11.3% ($91,000 ÷ $808,500)	10.0% ($76,500 ÷ $768,750)

The rate earned on stockholders' equity improved from 10.0% to 11.3% during 2014.

Leverage involves using debt to increase the return on an investment. The rate earned on stockholders' equity is normally higher than the rate earned on total assets. This is because of the effect of leverage.

For Lincoln Company, the effect of leverage for 2014 is 3.1% and for 2013 is 2.7% computed as follows:

	2014	2013
Rate earned on stockholders' equity	11.3%	10.0%
Less rate earned on total assets	8.2	7.3
Effect of leverage	3.1%	2.7%

Exhibit 8 shows the 2014 and 2013 effects of leverage for Lincoln Company.

Rate Earned on Common Stockholders' Equity

The **rate earned on common stockholders' equity** measures the rate of profits earned on the amount invested by the common stockholders. It is computed as follows:

$$\text{Rate Earned on Common Stockholders' Equity} = \frac{\text{Net Income} - \text{Preferred Dividends}}{\text{Average Common Stockholders' Equity}}$$

EXHIBIT 8

Effect of Leverage

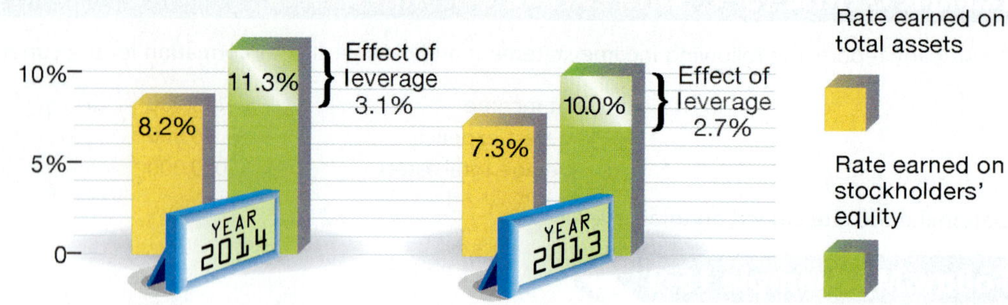

Because preferred stockholders rank ahead of the common stockholders in their claim on earnings, any preferred dividends are subtracted from net income in computing the rate earned on common stockholders' equity.

Lincoln Company had $150,000 of 6% preferred stock outstanding on December 31, 2014 and 2013. Thus, preferred dividends of $9,000 ($150,000 × 6%) are deducted from net income. Lincoln's common stockholders' equity is determined as follows:

	December 31		
	2014	**2013**	**2012**
Common stock, $10 par	$500,000	$500,000	$500,000
Retained earnings	179,500	137,500	100,000
Common stockholders' equity	$679,500	$637,500	$600,000

The retained earnings on December 31, 2012, of $100,000 is the same as the retained earnings on January 1, 2013, as shown in Lincoln's retained earnings statement in Exhibit 4.

Using this information, the rate earned on common stockholders' equity for Lincoln Company is computed below.

	2014	2013
Net income	$ 91,000	$ 76,500
Less preferred dividends	9,000	9,000
Total	$ 82,000	$ 67,500
Common stockholders' equity:		
Beginning of year	$ 637,500	$ 600,000
End of year	679,500*	637,500**
Total	$1,317,000	$1,237,500
Average common stockholders' equity	$658,500 ($1,317,000 ÷ 2)	$618,750 ($1,237,500 ÷ 2)
Rate earned on common stockholders' equity	12.5% ($82,000 ÷ $658,500)	10.9% ($67,500 ÷ $618,750)

*($829,500 – $150,000)
**($787,500 – $150,000)

Lincoln Company's rate earned on common stockholders' equity improved from 10.9% to 12.5% in 2014. This rate differs from the rates earned by Lincoln Company on total assets and stockholders' equity as shown below.

	2014	2013
Rate earned on total assets	8.2%	7.3%
Rate earned on stockholders' equity	11.3%	10.0%
Rate earned on common stockholders' equity	12.5%	10.9%

These rates differ because of leverage, as discussed in the preceding section.

Example Exercise 15-10 Common Stockholders' Profitability Analysis

OBJ 3

A company reports the following:

Net income	$ 125,000
Preferred dividends	5,000
Average stockholders' equity	1,000,000
Average common stockholders' equity	800,000

Determine (a) the rate earned on stockholders' equity and (b) the rate earned on common stockholders' equity.

Follow My Example 15-10

a. Rate Earned on Stockholders' Equity = Net Income ÷ Average Stockholders' Equity

Rate Earned on Stockholders' Equity = $125,000 ÷ $1,000,000

Rate Earned on Stockholders' Equity = 12.5%

b. Rate Earned on Common Stockholders' Equity = (Net Income – Preferred Dividends) ÷ Average Common Stockholders' Equity

Rate Earned on Common Stockholders' Equity = ($125,000 – $5,000) ÷ $800,000

Rate Earned on Common Stockholders' Equity = 15%

Practice Exercises: **PE 15-10A, PE 15-10B**

Earnings per Share on Common Stock

Earnings per share (EPS) on common stock measures the share of profits that are earned by a share of common stock. Earnings per share must be reported in the income statement. As a result, earnings per share (EPS) is often reported in the financial press. It is computed as follows:

$$\text{Earnings per Share (EPS) on Common Stock} = \frac{\text{Net Income} - \text{Preferred Dividends}}{\text{Shares of Common Stock Outstanding}}$$

When preferred and common stock are outstanding, preferred dividends are subtracted from net income to determine the income related to the common shares.

To illustrate, the earnings per share (EPS) of common stock for Lincoln Company is computed below.

	2014	2013
Net income	$91,000	$76,500
Preferred dividends	9,000	9,000
Total	$82,000	$67,500
Shares of common stock outstanding	50,000	50,000
Earnings per share on common stock	$1.64 ($82,000 ÷ 50,000)	$1.35 ($67,500 ÷ 50,000)

Lincoln Company had $150,000 of 6% preferred stock outstanding on December 31, 2014 and 2013. Thus, preferred dividends of $9,000 ($150,000 × 6%) are deducted from net income in computing earnings per share on common stock.

Lincoln did not issue any additional shares of common stock in 2014. If Lincoln had issued additional shares in 2014, a weighted average of common shares outstanding during the year would have been used.

Lincoln's earnings per share (EPS) on common stock improved from $1.35 to $1.64 during 2014.

Lincoln Company has a simple capital structure with only common stock and preferred stock outstanding. Many corporations, however, have complex capital structures with various types of equity securities outstanding, such as convertible preferred stock,

stock options, and stock warrants. In such cases, the possible effects of such securities on the shares of common stock outstanding are considered in reporting earnings per share. These possible effects are reported separately as *earnings per common share assuming dilution* or *diluted earnings per share*. This topic is described and illustrated in advanced accounting courses and textbooks.

Price-Earnings Ratio

The **price-earnings (P/E) ratio** on common stock measures a company's future earnings prospects. It is often quoted in the financial press and is computed as follows:

$$\text{Price-Earnings (P/E) Ratio} = \frac{\text{Market Price per Share of Common Stock}}{\text{Earnings per Share on Common Stock}}$$

To illustrate, the price-earnings (P/E) ratio for Lincoln Company is computed below.

	2014	**2013**
Market price per share of common stock	$41.00	$27.00
Earnings per share on common stock	$1.64	$1.35
Price-earnings ratio on common stock	25 ($41 ÷ $1.64)	20 ($27 ÷ $1.35)

The price-earnings ratio improved from 20 to 25 during 2014. In other words, a share of common stock of Lincoln Company was selling for 20 times earnings per share at the end of 2013. At the end of 2014, the common stock was selling for 25 times earnings per share. This indicates that the market expects Lincoln to experience favorable earnings in the future.

Example Exercise 15-11 Earnings per Share and Price-Earnings Ratio OBJ 3

A company reports the following:

Net income	$250,000
Preferred dividends	$15,000
Shares of common stock outstanding	20,000
Market price per share of common stock	$35.25

a. Determine the company's earnings per share on common stock.

b. Determine the company's price-earnings ratio. Round to one decimal place.

Follow My Example 15-11

a. Earnings per Share on Common Stock = (Net Income – Preferred Dividends) ÷ Shares of Common Stock Outstanding

Earnings per Share = ($250,000 – $15,000) ÷ 20,000

Earnings per Share = $11.75

b. Price-Earnings Ratio = Market Price per Share of Common Stock ÷ Earnings per Share on Common Stock

Price-Earnings Ratio = $35.25 ÷ $11.75

Price-Earnings Ratio = 3.0

Practice Exercises: **PE 15-11A, PE 15-11B**

Dividends per Share

Dividends per share measures the extent to which earnings are being distributed to common shareholders. It is computed as follows:

$$\text{Dividends per Share} = \frac{\text{Dividends on Common Stock}}{\text{Shares of Common Stock Outstanding}}$$

To illustrate, the dividends per share for Lincoln Company are computed below.

	2014	2013
Dividends on common stock	$40,000	$30,000
Shares of common stock outstanding	50,000	50,000
Dividends per share of common stock	$0.80 ($40,000 ÷ 50,000)	$0.60 ($30,000 ÷ 50,000)

The dividends per share of common stock increased from $0.60 to $0.80 during 2014.

Dividends per share are often reported with earnings per share. Comparing the two per-share amounts indicates the extent to which earnings are being retained for use in operations. To illustrate, the dividends and earnings per share for Lincoln Company are shown in Exhibit 9.

EXHIBIT 9

Dividends and Earnings per Share of Common Stock

Dividend Yield

The **dividend yield** on common stock measures the rate of return to common stockholders from cash dividends. It is of special interest to investors whose objective is to earn revenue (dividends) from their investment. It is computed as follows:

$$\text{Dividend Yield} = \frac{\text{Dividends per Share of Common Stock}}{\text{Market Price per Share of Common Stock}}$$

To illustrate, the dividend yield for Lincoln Company is computed below.

	2014	2013
Dividends per share of common stock	$0.80	$0.60
Market price per share of common stock	$41.00	$27.00
Dividend yield on common stock	2.0% ($0.80 ÷ $41)	2.2% ($0.60 ÷ $27)

The dividend yield declined slightly from 2.2% to 2.0% in 2014. This decline was primarily due to the increase in the market price of Lincoln's common stock.

The dividends per share, dividend yield, and P/E ratio of a common stock are normally quoted on the daily listing of stock prices in *The Wall Street Journal* and on Yahoo!'s finance Web site.

Summary of Analytical Measures

Exhibit 10 shows a summary of the solvency and profitability measures discussed in this chapter. The type of industry and the company's operations usually affect which measures are used. In many cases, additional measures are used for a specific industry. For example, airlines use *revenue per passenger mile* and *cost per available seat* as profitability measures. Likewise, hotels use *occupancy rates* as a profitability measure.

The analytical measures shown in Exhibit 10 are a useful starting point for analyzing a company's solvency and profitability. However, they are not a substitute for sound judgment. For example, the general economic and business environment should always be considered in analyzing a company's future prospects. In addition, any trends and interrelationships among the measures should be carefully studied.

EXHIBIT 10 **Summary of Analytical Measures**

Liquidity and solvency measures:	Method of Computation	Use
Working Capital	Current Assets – Current Liabilities	To indicate the ability to meet currently maturing obligations (measures solvency)
Current Ratio	$\frac{\text{Current Assets}}{\text{Current Liabilities}}$	To indicate the ability to meet currently maturing obligations (measures solvency)
Quick Ratio	$\frac{\text{Quick Assets}}{\text{Current Liabilities}}$	To indicate instant debt-paying ability (measures solvency)
Accounts Receivable Turnover	$\frac{\text{Net Sales}}{\text{Average Accounts Receivable}}$	To assess the efficiency in collecting receivables and in the management of credit (measures liquidity)
Numbers of Days' Sales in Receivables	$\frac{\text{Average Accounts Receivable}}{\text{Average Daily Sales}}$	To assess the efficiency in collecting receivables and in the management of credit (measures liquidity)
Inventory Turnover	$\frac{\text{Cost of Goods Sold}}{\text{Average Inventory}}$	To assess the efficiency in the management of inventory (measures liquidity)
Number of Days' Sales in Inventory	$\frac{\text{Average Inventory}}{\text{Average Daily Cost of Goods Sold}}$	To assess the efficiency in the management of inventory (measures liquidity)
Ratio of Fixed Assets to Long-Term Liabilities	$\frac{\text{Fixed Assets (net)}}{\text{Long-Term Liabilities}}$	To indicate the margin of safety to long-term creditors (measures solvency)
Ratio of Liabilities to Stockholders' Equity	$\frac{\text{Total Liabilities}}{\text{Total Stockholders' Equity}}$	To indicate the margin of safety to creditors (measures solvency)
Number of Times Interest Charges Are Earned	$\frac{\text{Income Before Income Tax + Interest Expense}}{\text{Interest Expense}}$	To assess the risk to debtholders in terms of number of times interest charges were earned (measures solvency)
Number of Times Preferred Dividends Are Earned	$\frac{\text{Net Income}}{\text{Preferred Dividends}}$	To assess the risk to preferred stockholders in terms of the number of times preferred dividends were earned (measures solvency)
Profitability measures:		
Ratio of Net Sales to Assets	$\frac{\text{Net Sales}}{\text{Average Total Assets (excluding long-term investments)}}$	To assess the effectiveness in the use of assets
Rate Earned on Total Assets	$\frac{\text{Net Income + Interest Expense}}{\text{Average Total Assets}}$	To assess the profitability of the assets
Rate Earned on Stockholders' Equity	$\frac{\text{Net Income}}{\text{Average Total Stockholders' Equity}}$	To assess the profitability of the investment by stockholders
Rate Earned on Common Stockholders' Equity	$\frac{\text{Net Income – Preferred Dividends}}{\text{Average Common Stockholders' Equity}}$	To assess the profitability of the investment by common stockholders
Earnings per Share (EPS) on Common Stock	$\frac{\text{Net Income – Preferred Dividends}}{\text{Shares of Common Stock Outstanding}}$	To assess the profitability of the investment by common stockholders
Price-Earnings (P/E) Ratio	$\frac{\text{Market Price per Share of Common Stock}}{\text{Earnings per Share on Common Stock}}$	To indicate future earnings prospects, based on the relationship between market value of common stock and earnings
Dividends per Share	$\frac{\text{Dividends on Common Stock}}{\text{Shares of Common Stock Outstanding}}$	To indicate the extent to which earnings are being distributed to common stockholders
Dividend Yield	$\frac{\text{Dividends per Share of Common Stock}}{\text{Market Price per Share of Common Stock}}$	To indicate the rate of return to common stockholders in terms of dividends

Integrity, Objectivity, and Ethics in Business

CHIEF FINANCIAL OFFICER BONUSES

A recent study by compensation experts at Temple University found that chief financial officer salaries are correlated with the complexity of a company's operations, but chief financial officer bonuses are correlated with the company's ability to meet analysts' earnings forecasts. These results suggest that financial bonuses may provide chief financial officers with an incentive to use questionable accounting practices to improve earnings. While the study doesn't conclude that bonuses lead to accounting fraud, it does suggest that bonuses give chief financial officers a reason to find ways to use accounting to increase apparent earnings.

Source: E. Jelesiewicz, "Today's CFO: More Challenge but Higher Compensation," *News Communications* (Temple University, August 2009).

Corporate Annual Reports

OBJ 4 Describe the contents of corporate annual reports.

Public corporations issue annual reports summarizing their operating activities for the past year and plans for the future. Such annual reports include the financial statements and the accompanying notes. In addition, annual reports normally include the following sections:

- Management discussion and analysis
- Report on internal control
- Report on fairness of the financial statements

IFRS IFRS

See Appendix C for more information

Management Discussion and Analysis

Management's Discussion and Analysis (MD&A) is required in annual reports filed with the Securities and Exchange Commission. It includes management's analysis of current operations and its plans for the future. Typical items included in the MD&A are as follows:

- Management's analysis and explanations of any significant changes between the current and prior years' financial statements.
- Important accounting principles or policies that could affect interpretation of the financial statements, including the effect of changes in accounting principles or the adoption of new accounting principles.
- Management's assessment of the company's liquidity and the availability of capital to the company.
- Significant risk exposures that might affect the company.
- Any "off-balance-sheet" arrangements such as leases not included directly in the financial statements. Such arrangements are discussed in advanced accounting courses and textbooks.

Report on Internal Control

The Sarbanes-Oxley Act of 2002 requires a report on internal control by management. The report states management's responsibility for establishing and maintaining internal control. In addition, management's assessment of the effectiveness of internal controls over financial reporting is included in the report.

Sarbanes-Oxley also requires a public accounting firm to verify management's conclusions on internal control. Thus, two reports on internal control, one by management and one by a public accounting firm, are included in the annual report. In some situations, these may be combined into a single report on internal control.

Report on Fairness of the Financial Statements

All publicly held corporations are required to have an independent audit (examination) of their financial statements. The Certified Public Accounting (CPA) firm that conducts the audit renders an opinion, called the *Report of Independent Registered Public Accounting Firm*, on the fairness of the statements.

An opinion stating that the financial statements present fairly the financial position, results of operations, and cash flows of the company is said to be an *unqualified opinion*, sometimes called a *clean opinion*. Any report other than an unqualified opinion raises a "red flag" for financial statement users and requires further investigation as to its cause.

The annual report of Nike, Inc. is shown in Appendix B. The Nike report includes the financial statements as well as the MD&A Report on Internal Control, and the Report on Fairness of the Financial Statements.

Integrity, Objectivity, and Ethics in Business

BUY LOW, SELL HIGH

Research analysts work for banks, brokerages, or other financial institutions. Their job is to estimate the value of a company's common stock by reviewing and evaluating the company's business model, strategic plan, and financial performance. Based on this analysis, the analyst develops an estimate of a stock's value, which is called its *fundamental value*. Analysts then advise their clients to "buy" or "sell" a company's stock based on the following guidelines:

Current market price is greater than fundamental value	Sell
Current market price is lower than fundamental value	Buy

If analysts are doing their job well, their clients will enjoy large returns by buying stocks at low prices and selling them at high prices.

APPENDIX

Unusual Items on the Income Statement

Generally accepted accounting principles require that unusual items be reported separately on the income statement. This is because such items do not occur frequently and are typically unrelated to current operations. Without separate reporting of these items, users of the financial statements might be misled about current and future operations.

Unusual items on the income statement are classified as one of the following:

1. Affecting the *current period* income statement
2. Affecting a *prior period* income statement

Unusual Items Affecting the Current Period's Income Statement

Unusual items affecting the current period's income statement include the following:

1. Discontinued operations
2. Extraordinary items

These items are reported separately on the income statement for any period in which they occur.

Discontinued Operations A company may discontinue a segment of its operations by selling or abandoning the segment's operations. For example, a retailer might decide to sell its product only online and, thus, discontinue selling its merchandise at its retail outlets (stores).

Any gain or loss on discontinued operations is reported on the income statement as a *Gain (or loss) from discontinued operations*. It is reported immediately following *Income from continuing operations*.

To illustrate, assume that Jones Corporation produces and sells electrical products, hardware supplies, and lawn equipment. Because of a lack of profits, Jones discontinues its electrical products operation and sells the remaining inventory and other assets at a loss of $100,000. Exhibit 11 illustrates the reporting of the loss on discontinued operations.[3]

EXHIBIT 11

Unusual Items in the Income Statement

Jones Corporation
Income Statement
For the Year Ended December 31, 2014

Net sales	$12,350,000
Cost of merchandise sold	5,800,000
Gross profit	$ 6,550,000
Selling and administrative expenses	5,240,000
Income from continuing operations before income tax	$ 1,310,000
Income tax expense	620,000
Income from continuing operations	$ 690,000
Loss on discontinued operations	100,000
Income before extraordinary items	$ 590,000
Extraordinary items:	
Gain on condemnation of land	150,000
Net income	$ 740,000

In addition, a note accompanying the income statement should describe the operations sold, including such details as the date operations were discontinued, the assets sold, and the effect (if any) on current and future operations.

Extraordinary Items An **extraordinary item** is defined as an event or a transaction that has both of the following characteristics:

1. Unusual in nature
2. Infrequent in occurrence

Gains and losses from natural disasters such as floods, earthquakes, and fires are normally reported as extraordinary items, provided that they occur infrequently. Gains or losses from land or buildings taken (condemned) for public use are also reported as extraordinary items.

Any gain or loss from extraordinary items is reported on the income statement as *Gain (or loss) from extraordinary item*. It is reported immediately following *Income from continuing operations* and any *Gain (or loss) on discontinued operations*.

To illustrate, assume that land owned by Jones Corporation was taken for public use (condemned) by the local government. The condemnation of the land resulted in a gain of $150,000. Exhibit 11 illustrates the reporting of the extraordinary gain.[4]

Reporting Earnings per Share Earnings per common share should be reported separately for discontinued operations and extraordinary items. To illustrate, a partial income statement for Jones Corporation is shown in Exhibit 12. The company has 200,000 shares of common stock outstanding.

Exhibit 12 reports earnings per common share for income from continuing operations, discontinued operations, and extraordinary items. However, only earnings per share for income from continuing operations and net income are required by generally accepted accounting principles. The other per-share amounts may be presented in the notes to the financial statements.

3 The gain or loss on discontinued operations is reported net of any tax effects. To simplify, the tax effects are not specifically identified in Exhibit 11.

4 The gain or loss on extraordinary operations is reported net of any tax effects.

EXHIBIT 12

Income Statement with Earnings per Share

Jones Corporation
Income Statement
For the Year Ended December 31, 2014

Earnings per common share:	
Income from continuing operations	$3.45
Loss on discontinued operations	0.50
Income before extraordinary items	$2.95
Extraordinary items:	
Gain on condemnation of land	0.75
Net income	$3.70

Unusual Items Affecting the Prior Period's Income Statement

An unusual item may occur that affects a prior period's income statement. Two such items are as follows:

1. Errors in applying generally accepted accounting principles
2. Changes from one generally accepted accounting principle to another

If an error is discovered in a prior period's financial statement, the prior-period statement and all following statements are restated and thus corrected.

A company may change from one generally accepted accounting principle to another. In this case, the prior-period financial statements are restated as if the new accounting principle had always been used.[5]

For both of the preceding items, the current-period earnings are not affected. That is, only the earnings reported in prior periods are restated. However, because the prior earnings are restated, the beginning balance of Retained Earnings may also have to be restated. This, in turn, may cause the restatement of other balance sheet accounts. Illustrations of these types of adjustments and restatements are provided in advanced accounting courses.

5 Changes from one acceptable depreciation method to another acceptable depreciation method are an exception to this general rule and are to be treated prospectively as a change in estimate, as discussed in Chapter 9.

At a Glance 15

OBJ 1 **Describe basic financial statement analytical methods.**

Key Points The basic financial statements provide much of the information users need to make economic decisions. Analytical procedures are used to compare items on a current financial statement with related items on earlier statements, or to examine relationships within a financial statement.

Learning Outcomes	Example Exercises	Practice Exercises
• Prepare a vertical analysis from a company's financial statements.	EE15-1	PE15-1A, 15-1B
• Prepare a horizontal analysis from a company's financial statements.	EE15-2	PE15-2A, 15-2B
• Prepare common-sized financial statements.		

OBJ 2 Use financial statement analysis to assess the solvency of a business.

Key Points All users of financial statements are interested in the ability of a business to convert assets into cash (liquidity), pay its debts (solvency), and earn income (profitability). Liquidity, solvency, and profitability are interrelated. Liquidity and solvency are normally assessed by examining the following: current position analysis, accounts receivable analysis, inventory analysis, the ratio of fixed assets to long-term liabilities, the ratio of liabilities to stockholders' equity, and the number of times interest charges are earned.

Learning Outcomes	Example Exercises	Practice Exercises
• Determine working capital.		
• Compute and interpret the current ratio.	EE15-3	PE15-3A, 15-3B
• Compute and interpret the quick ratio.	EE15-3	PE15-3A, 15-3B
• Compute and interpret accounts receivable turnover.	EE15-4	PE15-4A, 15-4B
• Compute and interpret the number of days' sales in receivables.	EE15-4	PE15-4A, 15-4B
• Compute and interpret inventory turnover.	EE15-5	PE15-5A, 15-5B
• Compute and interpret the number of days' sales in inventory.	EE15-5	PE15-5A, 15-5B
• Compute and interpret the ratio of fixed assets to long-term liabilities.	EE15-6	PE15-6A, 15-6B
• Compute and interpret the ratio of liabilities to stockholders' equity.	EE15-6	PE15-6A, 15-6B
• Compute and interpret the number of times interest charges are earned.	EE15-7	PE15-7A, 15-7B

OBJ 3 Use financial statement analysis to assess the profitability of a business.

Key Points Profitability analysis focuses on the ability of a company to earn profits. This ability is reflected in the company's operating results as reported on the income statement and resources available as reported on the balance sheet. Major analyses include the ratio of net sales to assets, the rate earned on total assets, the rate earned on stockholders' equity, the rate earned on common stockholders' equity, earnings per share on common stock, the price-earnings ratio, dividends per share, and dividend yield.

Learning Outcomes	Example Exercises	Practice Exercises
• Compute and interpret the ratio of net sales to assets.	EE15-8	PE15-8A, 15-8B
• Compute and interpret the rate earned on total assets.	EE15-9	PE15-9A, 15-9B
• Compute and interpret the rate earned on stockholders' equity.	EE15-10	PE15-10A, 15-10B
• Compute and interpret the rate earned on common stockholders' equity.	EE15-10	PE15-10A, 15-10B
• Compute and interpret the earnings per share on common stock.	EE15-11	PE15-11A, 15-11B
• Compute and interpret the price-earnings ratio.	EE15-11	PE15-11A, 15-11B
• Compute and interpret the dividends per share and dividend yield.		
• Describe the uses and limitations of analytical measures.		

OBJ 4 Describe the contents of corporate annual reports.

Key Points Corporations normally issue annual reports to their stockholders and other interested parties. Such reports summarize the corporation's operating activities for the past year and plans for the future.

Learning Outcome	Example Exercises	Practice Exercises
• Describe the elements of a corporate annual report.		

Key Terms

accounts receivable analysis (706)
accounts receivable turnover (706)
common-sized statement (702)
current position analysis (704)
current ratio (704)
dividend yield (717)
dividends per share (716)
earnings per share (EPS) on common stock (715)
extraordinary item (721)
horizontal analysis (698)
inventory analysis (707)
inventory turnover (708)
leverage (713)
liquidity (703)
Management's Discussion and Analysis (MD&A) (719)
number of days' sales in inventory (708)
number of days' sales in receivables (707)
number of times interest charges are earned (710)
price-earnings (P/E) ratio (716)
profitability (703)
quick assets (705)
quick ratio (705)
rate earned on common stockholders' equity (713)
rate earned on stockholders' equity (713)
rate earned on total assets (712)
ratio of fixed assets to long-term liabilities (709)
ratio of liabilities to stockholders' equity (709)
ratio of net sales to assets (711)
solvency (703)
vertical analysis (701)
working capital (704)

Illustrative Problem

Rainbow Paint Co.'s comparative financial statements for the years ending December 31, 2014 and 2013, are as follows. The market price of Rainbow Paint Co.'s common stock was $25 on December 31, 2014, and $30 on December 31, 2013.

Rainbow Paint Co.
Comparative Income Statement
For the Years Ended December 31, 2014 and 2013

	2014	2013
Sales	$5,125,000	$3,257,600
Sales returns and allowances	125,000	57,600
Net sales	$5,000,000	$3,200,000
Cost of goods sold	3,400,000	2,080,000
Gross profit	$1,600,000	$1,120,000
Selling expenses	$ 650,000	$ 464,000
Administrative expenses	325,000	224,000
Total operating expenses	$ 975,000	$ 688,000
Income from operations	$ 625,000	$ 432,000
Other income	25,000	19,200
	$ 650,000	$ 451,200
Other expense (interest)	105,000	64,000
Income before income tax	$ 545,000	$ 387,200
Income tax expense	300,000	176,000
Net income	$ 245,000	$ 211,200

Rainbow Paint Co.
Comparative Retained Earnings Statement
For the Years Ended December 31, 2014 and 2013

	2014	2013
Retained earnings, January 1	$723,000	$581,800
Add net income for year	245,000	211,200
Total	$968,000	$793,000
Deduct dividends:		
On preferred stock	$ 40,000	$ 40,000
On common stock	45,000	30,000
Total	$ 85,000	$ 70,000
Retained earnings, December 31	$883,000	$723,000

Rainbow Paint Co.
Comparative Balance Sheet
December 31, 2014 and 2013

	Dec. 31, 2014	Dec. 31, 2013
Assets		
Current assets:		
Cash	$ 175,000	$ 125,000
Temporary investments	150,000	50,000
Accounts receivable (net)	425,000	325,000
Inventories	720,000	480,000
Prepaid expenses	30,000	20,000
Total current assets	$1,500,000	$1,000,000
Long-term investments	250,000	225,000
Property, plant, and equipment (net)	2,093,000	1,948,000
Total assets	$3,843,000	$3,173,000
Liabilities		
Current liabilities	$ 750,000	$ 650,000
Long-term liabilities:		
Mortgage note payable, 10%, due 2017	$ 410,000	—
Bonds payable, 8%, due 2020	800,000	$ 800,000
Total long-term liabilities	$1,210,000	$ 800,000
Total liabilities	$1,960,000	$1,450,000
Stockholders' Equity		
Preferred 8% stock, $100 par	$ 500,000	$ 500,000
Common stock, $10 par	500,000	500,000
Retained earnings	883,000	723,000
Total stockholders' equity	$1,883,000	$1,723,000
Total liabilities and stockholders' equity	$3,843,000	$3,173,000

Instructions

Determine the following measures for 2014:

1. Working capital
2. Current ratio
3. Quick ratio
4. Accounts receivable turnover
5. Number of days' sales in receivables
6. Inventory turnover
7. Number of days' sales in inventory

8. Ratio of fixed assets to long-term liabilities
9. Ratio of liabilities to stockholders' equity
10. Number of times interest charges are earned
11. Number of times preferred dividends are earned
12. Ratio of net sales to assets
13. Rate earned on total assets
14. Rate earned on stockholders' equity
15. Rate earned on common stockholders' equity
16. Earnings per share on common stock
17. Price-earnings ratio
18. Dividends per share
19. Dividend yield

Solution

(Ratios are rounded to the nearest single digit after the decimal point.)

1. Working capital: $750,000
   $1,500,000 – $750,000
2. Current ratio: 2.0
   $1,500,000 ÷ $750,000
3. Quick ratio: 1.0
   $750,000 ÷ $750,000
4. Accounts receivable turnover: 13.3
   $5,000,000 ÷ [($425,000 + $325,000) ÷ 2]
5. Number of days' sales in receivables: 27.4 days
   $5,000,000 ÷ 365 days = $13,699
   $375,000 ÷ $13,699
6. Inventory turnover: 5.7
   $3,400,000 ÷ [($720,000 + $480,000) ÷ 2]
7. Number of days' sales in inventory: 64.4 days
   $3,400,000 ÷ 365 days = $9,315
   $600,000 ÷ $9,315
8. Ratio of fixed assets to long-term liabilities: 1.7
   $2,093,000 ÷ $1,210,000
9. Ratio of liabilities to stockholders' equity: 1.0
   $1,960,000 ÷ $1,883,000
10. Number of times interest charges are earned: 6.2
    ($545,000 + $105,000) ÷ $105,000
11. Number of times preferred dividends are earned: 6.1
    $245,000 ÷ $40,000
12. Ratio of net sales to assets: 1.5
    $5,000,000 ÷ [($3,593,000 + $2,948,000) ÷ 2]
13. Rate earned on total assets: 10.0%
    ($245,000 + $105,000) ÷ [($3,843,000 + $3,173,000) ÷ 2]
14. Rate earned on stockholders' equity: 13.6%
    $245,000 ÷ [($1,883,000 + $1,723,000) ÷ 2]
15. Rate earned on common stockholders' equity: 15.7%
    ($245,000 – $40,000) ÷ [($1,383,000 + $1,223,000) ÷ 2]

16. Earnings per share on common stock: $4.10
    ($245,000 – $40,000) ÷ 50,000 shares
17. Price-earnings ratio: 6.1
    $25 ÷ $4.10
18. Dividends per share: $0.90
    $45,000 ÷ 50,000 shares
19. Dividend yield: 3.6%
    $0.90 ÷ $25

Discussion Questions

1. What is the difference between horizontal and vertical analysis of financial statements?
2. What is the advantage of using comparative statements for financial analysis rather than statements for a single date or period?
3. The current year's amount of net income (after income tax) is 25% larger than that of the preceding year. Does this indicate an improved operating performance? Discuss.
4. How would the current and quick ratios of a service business compare?
5. a. Why is it advantageous to have a high inventory turnover?
   b. Is it possible to have a high inventory turnover and a high number of days' sales in inventory? Discuss.
6. What do the following data taken from a comparative balance sheet indicate about the company's ability to borrow additional funds on a long-term basis in the current year as compared to the preceding year?

	Current Year	Preceding Year
Fixed assets (net)	$1,260,000	$1,360,000
Total long-term liabilities	300,000	400,000

7. a. How does the rate earned on total assets differ from the rate earned on stockholders' equity?
   b. Which ratio is normally higher? Explain.
8. a. Why is the rate earned on stockholders' equity by a thriving business ordinarily higher than the rate earned on total assets?
   b. Should the rate earned on common stockholders' equity normally be higher or lower than the rate earned on total stockholders' equity? Explain.
9. The net income (after income tax) of McCants Inc. was $2 per common share in the latest year and $6 per common share for the preceding year. At the beginning of the latest year, the number of shares outstanding was doubled by a stock split. There were no other changes in the amount of stock outstanding. What were the earnings per share in the preceding year, adjusted for comparison with the latest year?
10. Describe two reports provided by independent auditors in the annual report to shareholders.

Practice Exercises

Example Exercises

EE 15-1 *p. 701*

PE 15-1A Horizontal analysis

OBJ. 1

The comparative temporary investments and inventory balances of a company are provided below.

	2014	2013
Temporary investments	$46,400	$40,000
Inventory	73,600	80,000

Based on this information, what is the amount and percentage of increase or decrease that would be shown in a balance sheet with horizontal analysis?

EE 15-1 *p. 701*

PE 15-1B Horizontal analysis

OBJ. 1

The comparative accounts payable and long-term debt balances for a company are provided below.

	2014	2013
Accounts payable	$111,000	$100,000
Long-term debt	132,680	124,000

Based on this information, what is the amount and percentage of increase or decrease that would be shown in a balance sheet with horizontal analysis?

EE 15-2 *p. 702*

PE 15-2A Vertical analysis

OBJ. 1

Income statement information for Thain Corporation is provided below.

Sales	$850,000
Cost of goods sold	493,000
Gross profit	357,000

Prepare a vertical analysis of the income statement for Thain Corporation.

EE 15-2 *p. 702*

PE 15-2B Vertical analysis

OBJ. 1

Income statement information for Einsworth Corporation is provided below.

Sales	$1,200,000
Cost of goods sold	780,000
Gross profit	420,000

Prepare a vertical analysis of the income statement for Einsworth Corporation.

EE 15-3 *p. 706*

PE 15-3A Current position analysis

OBJ. 2

The following items are reported on a company's balance sheet:

Cash	$130,000
Marketable securities	50,000
Accounts receivable (net)	60,000
Inventory	120,000
Accounts payable	150,000

Determine (a) the current ratio and (b) the quick ratio. Round to one decimal place.

Example Exercises

EE 15-3 *p. 706*

PE 15-3B Current position analysis **OBJ. 2**

The following items are reported on a company's balance sheet:

Cash	$210,000
Marketable securities	120,000
Accounts receivable (net)	110,000
Inventory	160,000
Accounts payable	200,000

Determine (a) the current ratio and (b) the quick ratio. Round to one decimal place.

EE 15-4 *p. 707*

PE 15-4A Accounts receivable analysis **OBJ. 2**

A company reports the following:

Net sales	$1,200,000
Average accounts receivable (net)	100,000

Determine (a) the accounts receivable turnover and (b) the number of days' sales in receivables. Round to one decimal place.

EE 15-4 *p. 707*

PE 15-4B Accounts receivable analysis **OBJ. 2**

A company reports the following:

Net sales	$3,150,000
Average accounts receivable (net)	210,000

Determine (a) the accounts receivable turnover and (b) the number of days' sales in receivables. Round to one decimal place.

EE 15-5 *p. 709*

PE 15-5A Inventory analysis **OBJ. 2**

A company reports the following:

Cost of goods sold	$630,000
Average inventory	90,000

Determine (a) the inventory turnover and (b) the number of days' sales in inventory. Round to one decimal place.

EE 15-5 *p. 709*

PE 15-5B Inventory analysis **OBJ. 2**

A company reports the following:

Cost of goods sold	$435,000
Average inventory	72,500

Determine (a) the inventory turnover and (b) the number of days' sales in inventory. Round to one decimal place.

EE 15-6 *p. 710*

PE 15-6A Long-term solvency analysis **OBJ. 2**

The following information was taken from Einar Company's balance sheet:

Fixed assets (net)	$1,800,000
Long-term liabilities	600,000
Total liabilities	900,000
Total stockholders' equity	750,000

Determine the company's (a) ratio of fixed assets to long-term liabilities and (b) ratio of liabilities to stockholders' equity.

Example Exercises

EE 15-6 *p. 710*

PE 15-6B Long-term solvency analysis **OBJ. 2**

The following information was taken from Charu Company's balance sheet:

Fixed assets (net)	$2,000,000
Long-term liabilities	800,000
Total liabilities	1,000,000
Total stockholders' equity	625,000

Determine the company's (a) ratio of fixed assets to long-term liabilities and (b) ratio of liabilities to stockholders' equity.

EE 15-7 *p. 711*

PE 15-7A Times interest charges are earned **OBJ. 2**

A company reports the following:

Income before income tax	$4,000,000
Interest expense	400,000

Determine the number of times interest charges are earned.

EE 15-7 *p. 711*

PE 15-7B Times interest charges are earned **OBJ. 2**

A company reports the following:

Income before income tax	$8,000,000
Interest expense	500,000

Determine the number of times interest charges are earned.

EE 15-8 *p. 712*

PE 15-8A Net sales to assets **OBJ. 3**

A company reports the following:

Net sales	$1,800,000
Average total assets	1,125,000

Determine the ratio of net sales to assets.

EE 15-8 *p. 712*

PE 15-8B Net sales to assets **OBJ. 3**

A company reports the following:

Net sales	$4,400,000
Average total assets	2,000,000

Determine the ratio of net sales to assets.

EE 15-9 *p. 713*

PE 15-9A Rate earned on total assets **OBJ. 3**

A company reports the following income statement and balance sheet information for the current year:

Net income	$ 250,000
Interest expense	100,000
Average total assets	2,500,000

Determine the rate earned on total assets.

EE 15-9 *p. 713*

PE 15-9B Rate earned on total assets **OBJ. 3**

A company reports the following income statement and balance sheet information for the current year:

Net income	$ 410,000
Interest expense	90,000
Average total assets	5,000,000

Determine the rate earned on total assets.

Example Exercises

EE 15-10 p. 715

PE 15-10A Common stockholders' profitability analysis **OBJ. 3**

A company reports the following:

Net income	$ 375,000
Preferred dividends	75,000
Average stockholders' equity	2,500,000
Average common stockholders' equity	1,875,000

Determine (a) the rate earned on stockholders' equity and (b) the rate earned on common stockholders' equity. Round to one decimal place.

EE 15-10 p. 715

PE 15-10B Common stockholders' profitability analysis **OBJ. 3**

A company reports the following:

Net income	$1,000,000
Preferred dividends	50,000
Average stockholders' equity	6,250,000
Average common stockholders' equity	3,800,000

Determine (a) the rate earned on stockholders' equity and (b) the rate earned on common stockholders' equity. Round to one decimal place.

EE 15-11 p. 716

PE 15-11A Earnings per share and price-earnings ratio **OBJ. 3**

A company reports the following:

Net income	$185,000
Preferred dividends	$25,000
Shares of common stock outstanding	100,000
Market price per share of common stock	$20

a. Determine the company's earnings per share on common stock.

b. Determine the company's price-earnings ratio.

EE 15-11 p. 716

PE 15-11B Earnings per share and price-earnings ratio **OBJ. 3**

A company reports the following:

Net income	$410,000
Preferred dividends	$60,000
Shares of common stock outstanding	50,000
Market price per share of common stock	$84

a. Determine the company's earnings per share on common stock.

b. Determine the company's price-earnings ratio.

Exercises

EX 15-1 Vertical analysis of income statement **OBJ. 1**

✔ a. 2014 net income: $30,000; 2.0% of sales

Revenue and expense data for Soldner Inc. are as follows:

	2014	2013
Sales	$1,500,000	$1,450,000
Cost of goods sold	930,000	812,000
Selling expenses	210,000	261,000
Administrative expenses	255,000	232,000
Income tax expense	52,500	72,500

(Continued)

EX 15-19 Six measures of solvency or profitability **OBJ. 2, 3**

✔ c. Ratio of net sales to assets, 4.2

The following data were taken from the financial statements of Gates Inc. for the current fiscal year. Assuming that long-term investments totaled $3,000,000 throughout the year and that total assets were $7,000,000 at the beginning of the current fiscal year, determine the following: (a) ratio of fixed assets to long-term liabilities, (b) ratio of liabilities to stockholders' equity, (c) ratio of net sales to assets, (d) rate earned on total assets, (e) rate earned on stockholders' equity, and (f) rate earned on common stockholders' equity. Round to one decimal place.

Property, plant, and equipment (net)			$ 3,200,000
Liabilities:			
Current liabilities		$ 1,000,000	
Mortgage note payable, 6%, issued 2003, due 2019		2,000,000	
Total liabilities			$ 3,000,000
Stockholders' equity:			
Preferred $10 stock, $100 par (no change during year)			$ 1,000,000
Common stock, $10 par (no change during year)			2,000,000
Retained earnings:			
Balance, beginning of year	$1,570,000		
Net income	930,000	$2,500,000	
Preferred dividends	$ 100,000		
Common dividends	400,000	500,000	
Balance, end of year			2,000,000
Total stockholders' equity			$ 5,000,000
Net sales			$18,900,000
Interest expense			$ 120,000

EX 15-20 Six measures of solvency or profitability **OBJ. 2, 3**

✔ d. Price-earnings ratio, 10.0

The balance sheet for Garcon Inc. at the end of the current fiscal year indicated the following:

Bonds payable, 8% (issued in 2004, due in 2024)	$5,000,000
Preferred $4 stock, $50 par	2,500,000
Common stock, $10 par	5,000,000

Income before income tax was $3,000,000, and income taxes were $1,200,000 for the current year. Cash dividends paid on common stock during the current year totaled $1,200,000. The common stock was selling for $32 per share at the end of the year. Determine each of the following: (a) number of times bond interest charges are earned, (b) number of times preferred dividends are earned, (c) earnings per share on common stock, (d) price-earnings ratio, (e) dividends per share of common stock, and (f) dividend yield. Round to one decimal place, except earnings per share, which should be rounded to two decimal places.

EX 15-21 Earnings per share, price-earnings ratio, dividend yield **OBJ. 3**

✔ b. Price-earnings ratio, 15.0

The following information was taken from the financial statements of Tolbert Inc. for December 31 of the current fiscal year:

Common stock, $20 par (no change during the year)	$10,000,000
Preferred $4 stock, $40 par (no change during the year)	2,500,000

The net income was $1,750,000 and the declared dividends on the common stock were $1,125,000 for the current year. The market price of the common stock is $45 per share.

For the common stock, determine (a) the earnings per share, (b) the price-earnings ratio, (c) the dividends per share, and (d) the dividend yield. Round to one decimal place, except earnings per share, which should be rounded to two decimal places.

OBJ. 3

EX 15-22 Price-earnings ratio; dividend yield

The table below shows the stock price, earnings per share, and dividends per share for three companies for a recent year:

	Price	Earnings per Share	Dividends per Share
Deere & Co.	$ 65.70	$ 4.40	$1.16
Google	528.33	27.72	0.00
The Coca-Cola Company	69.05	5.37	1.88

a. Determine the price-earnings ratio and dividend yield for the three companies. Round to one decimal place.

b. Explain the differences in these ratios across the three companies.

Appendix

EX 15-23 Earnings per share, extraordinary item

✔ b. Earnings per share on common stock, $7.60

The net income reported on the income statement of Cutler Co. was $4,000,000. There were 500,000 shares of $10 par common stock and 100,000 shares of $2 preferred stock outstanding throughout the current year. The income statement included two extraordinary items: an $800,000 gain from condemnation of land and a $400,000 loss arising from flood damage, both after applicable income tax. Determine the per-share figures for common stock for (a) income before extraordinary items and (b) net income.

✔ 2. c.
ratio, 2.
SPREAD

Appendix

EX 15-24 Extraordinary item

Assume that the amount of each of the following items is material to the financial statements. Classify each item as either normally recurring (NR) or extraordinary (E).

a. Loss on the disposal of equipment considered to be obsolete because of the development of new technology.

b. Uninsured loss on building due to hurricane damage. The building was purchased by the company in 1910 and had not previously incurred hurricane damage.

c. Gain on sale of land condemned by the local government for a public works project.

d. Uninsured flood loss. (Flood insurance is unavailable because of periodic flooding in the area.)

e. Interest revenue on notes receivable.

f. Uncollectible accounts expense.

g. Loss on sale of investments in stocks and bonds.

Appendix

EX 15-25 Income statement and earnings per share for extraordinary items and discontinued operations

Cruz Inc. reports the following for 2014:

Income from continuing operations before income tax	$1,000,000
Extraordinary property loss from hurricane	$140,000*
Loss from discontinued operations	$240,000*
Weighted average number of shares outstanding	20,000
Applicable tax rate	40%

*Net of any tax effect.

a. Prepare a partial income statement for Cruz Inc., beginning with income from continuing operations before income tax.

b. Calculate the earnings per common share for Cruz Inc., including per-share amounts for unusual items.

PR 15-4A Nineteen measures of solvency and profitability

OBJ. 2, 3

✔ 5. Number of days' sales in receivables, 36.5

SPREADSHEET

The comparative financial statements of Bettancort Inc. are as follows. The market price of Bettancort Inc. common stock was $71.25 on December 31, 2014.

Bettancort Inc.
Comparative Retained Earnings Statement
For the Years Ended December 31, 2014 and 2013

	2014	2013
Retained earnings, January 1	$2,655,000	$2,400,000
Add net income for year	300,000	280,000
Total	$2,955,000	$2,680,000
Deduct dividends:		
On preferred stock	$ 15,000	$ 15,000
On common stock	10,000	10,000
Total	$ 25,000	$ 25,000
Retained earnings, December 31	$2,930,000	$2,655,000

Bettancort Inc.
Comparative Income Statement
For the Years Ended December 31, 2014 and 2013

	2014	2013
Sales (all on account)	$1,212,000	$1,010,000
Sales returns and allowances	12,000	10,000
Net sales	$1,200,000	$1,000,000
Cost of goods sold	500,000	475,000
Gross profit	$ 700,000	$ 525,000
Selling expenses	$ 240,000	$ 200,000
Administrative expenses	180,000	150,000
Total operating expenses	$ 420,000	$ 350,000
Income from operations	$ 280,000	$ 175,000
Other income	166,000	225,000
	$ 446,000	$ 400,000
Other expense (interest)	66,000	60,000
Income before income tax	$ 380,000	$ 340,000
Income tax expense	80,000	60,000
Net income	$ 300,000	$ 280,000

Bettancort Inc.
Comparative Balance Sheet
December 31, 2014 and 2013

	Dec. 31, 2014	Dec. 31, 2013
Assets		
Current assets:		
Cash	$ 450,000	$ 400,000
Marketable securities	300,000	260,000
Accounts receivable (net)	130,000	110,000
Inventories	67,000	58,000
Prepaid expenses	153,000	139,000
Total current assets	$1,100,000	$ 967,000
Long-term investments	2,350,000	2,200,000
Property, plant, and equipment (net)	1,320,000	1,188,000
Total assets	$4,770,000	$4,355,000
Liabilities		
Current liabilities	$ 440,000	$ 400,000
Long-term liabilities:		
Mortgage note payable, 8%, due 2019	$ 100,000	$ 0
Bonds payable, 10%, due 2015	1,000,000	1,000,000
Total long-term liabilities	$1,100,000	$1,000,000
Total liabilities	$1,540,000	$1,400,000
Stockholders' Equity		
Preferred $0.75 stock, $10 par	$ 200,000	$ 200,000
Common stock, $10 par	100,000	100,000
Retained earnings	2,930,000	2,655,000
Total stockholders' equity	$3,230,000	$2,955,000
Total liabilities and stockholders' equity	$4,770,000	$4,355,000

Instructions

Determine the following measures for 2014, rounding to one decimal place:

1. Working capital
2. Current ratio
3. Quick ratio
4. Accounts receivable turnover
5. Number of days' sales in receivables
6. Inventory turnover
7. Number of days' sales in inventory
8. Ratio of fixed assets to long-term liabilities
9. Ratio of liabilities to stockholders' equity
10. Number of times interest charges are earned
11. Number of times preferred dividends are earned
12. Ratio of net sales to assets
13. Rate earned on total assets
14. Rate earned on stockholders' equity
15. Rate earned on common stockholders' equity
16. Earnings per share on common stock
17. Price-earnings ratio
18. Dividends per share of common stock
19. Dividend yield

PR 15-5A Solvency and profitability trend analysis

OBJ. 2, 3

Addai Company has provided the following comparative information:

	2014	2013	2012	2011	2010
Net income	$ 273,406	$ 367,976	$ 631,176	$ 884,000	$ 800,000
Interest expense	616,047	572,003	528,165	495,000	440,000
Income tax expense	31,749	53,560	106,720	160,000	200,000
Total assets (ending balance)	4,417,178	4,124,350	3,732,443	3,338,500	2,750,000
Total stockholders' equity (ending balance)	3,706,557	3,433,152	3,065,176	2,434,000	1,550,000
Average total assets	4,270,764	3,928,396	3,535,472	3,044,250	2,475,000
Average total stockholders' equity	3,569,855	3,249,164	2,749,588	1,992,000	1,150,000

You have been asked to evaluate the historical performance of the company over the last five years.

Selected industry ratios have remained relatively steady at the following levels for the last five years:

	2010–2014
Rate earned on total assets	28%
Rate earned on stockholders' equity	18%
Number of times interest charges are earned	2.7
Ratio of liabilities to stockholders' equity	0.4

Instructions

1. Prepare four line graphs with the ratio on the vertical axis and the years on the horizontal axis for the following four ratios (rounded to one decimal place):
   a. Rate earned on total assets
   b. Rate earned on stockholders' equity
   c. Number of times interest charges are earned
   d. Ratio of liabilities to stockholders' equity

   Display both the company ratio and the industry benchmark on each graph. That is, each graph should have two lines.
2. Prepare an analysis of the graphs in (1).

Problems Series B

✔ 1. Net sales, 30.0% increase

SPREADSHEET

GENERAL LEDGER

PR 15-1B Horizontal analysis of income statement

OBJ. 1

For 2014, Macklin Inc. reported its most significant increase in net income in years. At the end of the year, John Mayer, the president, is presented with the following condensed comparative income statement:

Macklin Inc.
Comparative Income Statement
For the Years Ended December 31, 2014 and 2013

	2014	2013
Sales	$936,000	$720,000
Sales returns and allowances	26,000	20,000
Net sales	$910,000	$700,000
Cost of goods sold	441,000	350,000
Gross profit	$469,000	$350,000
Selling expenses	$ 139,150	$115,000
Administrative expenses	99,450	85,000
Total operating expenses	$238,600	$200,000
Income from operations	$230,400	$150,000
Other income	65,000	50,000
Income before income tax	$295,400	$200,000
Income tax expense	65,000	50,000
Net income	$230,400	$150,000

Instructions

1. Prepare a comparative income statement with horizontal analysis for the two-year period, using 2013 as the base year. Round to one decimal place.
2. To the extent the data permit, comment on the significant relationships revealed by the horizontal analysis prepared in (1).

✔ 1. Net income, 2013, 14.0%

SPREADSHEET

GENERAL LEDGER

PR 15-2B Vertical analysis of income statement

OBJ. 1

For 2014, Fielder Industries Inc. initiated a sales promotion campaign that included the expenditure of an additional $40,000 for advertising. At the end of the year, Leif Grando, the president, is presented with the following condensed comparative income statement:

Fielder Industries Inc.
Comparative Income Statement
For the Years Ended December 31, 2014 and 2013

	2014	2013
Sales	$1,325,000	$1,200,000
Sales returns and allowances	25,000	20,000
Net sales	$1,300,000	$1,180,000
Cost of goods sold	682,500	613,600
Gross profit	$ 617,500	$ 566,400
Selling expenses	$ 260,000	$ 188,800
Adminstrative expenses	169,000	177,000
Total operating expenses	$ 429,000	$ 365,800
Income from operations	$ 188,500	$ 200,600
Other income	78,000	70,800
Income before income tax	$ 266,500	$ 271,400
Income tax expense	117,000	106,200
Net income	$ 149,500	$ 165,200

Instructions

1. Prepare a comparative income statement for the two-year period, presenting an analysis of each item in relationship to net sales for each of the years. Round to one decimal place.
2. To the extent the data permit, comment on the significant relationships revealed by the vertical analysis prepared in (1).

✔ 2. g. Quick ratio, 1.6

SPREADSHEET

PR 15-3B Effect of transactions on current position analysis

OBJ. 2

Data pertaining to the current position of Lucroy Industries Inc. are as follows:

Cash	$ 800,000
Marketable securities	550,000
Accounts and notes receivable (net)	850,000
Inventories	700,000
Prepaid expenses	300,000
Accounts payable	1,200,000
Notes payable (short-term)	700,000
Accrued expenses	100,000

Instructions

1. Compute (a) the working capital, (b) the current ratio, and (c) the quick ratio. Round to one decimal place.
2. List the following captions on a sheet of paper:

Transaction	Working Capital	Current Ratio	Quick Ratio

Compute the working capital, the current ratio, and the quick ratio after each of the following transactions, and record the results in the appropriate columns. *Consider each transaction separately* and assume that only that transaction affects the data given above. Round to one decimal place.

a. Sold marketable securities at no gain or loss, $500,000.
b. Paid accounts payable, $287,500.
c. Purchased goods on account, $400,000.
d. Paid notes payable, $125,000.
e. Declared a cash dividend, $325,000.
f. Declared a common stock dividend on common stock, $150,000.
g. Borrowed cash from bank on a long-term note, $1,000,000.
h. Received cash on account, $75,000.
i. Issued additional shares of stock for cash, $2,000,000.
j. Paid cash for prepaid expenses, $200,000.

✔ 9. Ratio of liabilities to stockholders' equity, 0.4

SPREADSHEET

PR 15-4B Nineteen measures of solvency and profitability

OBJ. 2, 3

The comparative financial statements of Stargel Inc. are as follows. The market price of Stargel Inc. common stock was $119.70 on December 31, 2014.

Stargel Inc.
Comparative Retained Earnings Statement
For the Years Ended December 31, 2014 and 2013

	2014	2013
Retained earnings, January 1	$5,375,000	$4,545,000
Add net income for year	900,000	925,000
Total	$6,275,000	$5,470,000
Deduct dividends:		
On preferred stock	$ 45,000	$ 45,000
On common stock	50,000	50,000
Total	$ 95,000	$ 95,000
Retained earnings, December 31	$6,180,000	$5,375,000

(Continued)

Stargel Inc.
Comparative Income Statement
For the Years Ended December 31, 2014 and 2013

	2014	2013
Sales (all on account)	$10,050,000	$9,450,000
Sales returns and allowances	50,000	50,000
Net sales	$10,000,000	$9,400,000
Cost of goods sold	5,350,000	4,950,000
Gross profit	$ 4,650,000	$4,450,000
Selling expenses	$ 2,000,000	$1,880,000
Administrative expenses	1,500,000	1,410,000
Total operating expenses	$ 3,500,000	$3,290,000
Income from operations	$ 1,150,000	$1,160,000
Other income	150,000	140,000
	$ 1,300,000	$1,300,000
Other expense (interest)	170,000	150,000
Income before income tax	$ 1,130,000	$1,150,000
Income tax expense	230,000	225,000
Net income	$ 900,000	$ 925,000

Stargel Inc.
Comparative Balance Sheet
December 31, 2014 and 2013

	Dec. 31, 2014	Dec. 31, 2013
Assets		
Current assets:		
Cash	$ 500,000	$ 400,000
Marketable securities	1,010,000	1,000,000
Accounts receivable (net)	740,000	510,000
Inventories	1,190,000	950,000
Prepaid expenses	250,000	229,000
Total current assets	$3,690,000	$3,089,000
Long-term investments	2,350,000	2,300,000
Property, plant, and equipment (net)	3,740,000	3,366,000
Total assets	$9,780,000	$8,755,000
Liabilities		
Current liabilities	$ 900,000	$ 880,000
Long-term liabilities:		
Mortgage note payable, 8%, due 2019	$ 200,000	$ 0
Bonds payable, 10%, due 2015	1,500,000	1,500,000
Total long-term liabilities	$1,700,000	$1,500,000
Total liabilities	$2,600,000	$2,380,000
Stockholders' Equity		
Preferred $0.90 stock, $10 par	$ 500,000	$ 500,000
Common stock, $5 par	500,000	500,000
Retained earnings	6,180,000	5,375,000
Total stockholders' equity	$7,180,000	$6,375,000
Total liabilities and stockholders' equity	$9,780,000	$8,755,000

Instructions

Determine the following measures for 2014, rounding to one decimal place, except per share amounts which should be rounded to the nearest penny:

1. Working capital
2. Current ratio
3. Quick ratio
4. Accounts receivable turnover
5. Number of days' sales in receivables
6. Inventory turnover
7. Number of days' sales in inventory
8. Ratio of fixed assets to long-term liabilities

9. Ratio of liabilities to stockholders' equity
10. Number of times interest charges are earned
11. Number of times preferred dividends are earned
12. Ratio of net sales to assets
13. Rate earned on total assets
14. Rate earned on stockholders' equity
15. Rate earned on common stockholders' equity
16. Earnings per share on common stock
17. Price-earnings ratio
18. Dividends per share of common stock
19. Dividend yield

PR 15-5B Solvency and profitability trend analysis

OBJ. 2, 3

Crosby Company has provided the following comparative information:

	2014	2013	2012	2011	2010
Net income	$ 5,571,720	$ 3,714,480	$ 2,772,000	$ 1,848,000	$ 1,400,000
Interest expense	1,052,060	891,576	768,600	610,000	500,000
Income tax expense	1,225,572	845,222	640,320	441,600	320,000
Total assets (ending balance)	29,378,491	22,598,839	17,120,333	12,588,480	10,152,000
Total stockholders' equity (ending balance)	18,706,200	13,134,480	9,420,000	6,648,000	4,800,000
Average total assets	25,988,665	19,859,586	14,854,406	11,370,240	8,676,000
Average total stockholders' equity	15,920,340	11,277,240	8,034,000	5,724,000	4,100,000

You have been asked to evaluate the historical performance of the company over the last five years.

Selected industry ratios have remained relatively steady at the following levels for the last five years:

	2010–2014
Rate earned on total assets	19%
Rate earned on stockholders' equity	26%
Number of times interest charges are earned	3.4
Ratio of liabilities to stockholders' equity	1.4

Instructions

1. Prepare four line graphs with the ratio on the vertical axis and the years on the horizontal axis for the following four ratios (rounded to one decimal place):
   a. Rate earned on total assets
   b. Rate earned on stockholders' equity
   c. Number of times interest charges are earned
   d. Ratio of liabilities to stockholders' equity

   Display both the company ratio and the industry benchmark on each graph. That is, each graph should have two lines.
2. Prepare an analysis of the graphs in (1).

Nike, Inc., Problem

Financial Statement Analysis

The financial statements for Nike, Inc., are presented in Appendix B at the end of the text. The following additional information (in thousands) is available:

Accounts receivable at May 31, 2008	$ 2,884
Inventories at May 31, 2008	2,357
Total assets at May 31, 2008	13,249
Stockholders' equity at May 31, 2008	8,693

Instructions

1. Determine the following measures for the fiscal years ended May 31, 2011 (fiscal 2010), and May 31, 2010 (fiscal 2009), rounding to one decimal place.
   a. Working capital
   b. Current ratio
   c. Quick ratio
   d. Accounts receivable turnover
   e. Number of days' sales in receivables
   f. Inventory turnover
   g. Number of days' sales in inventory
   h. Ratio of liabilities to stockholders' equity
   i. Ratio of net sales to assets
   j. Rate earned on total assets, assuming interest expense is $4 million for the year ending May 31, 2011, and $6 million for the year ending May 31, 2010
   k. Rate earned on common stockholders' equity
   l. Price-earnings ratio, assuming that the market price was $75.70 per share on May 31, 2011, and $73.50 per share on May 31, 2010
   m. Percentage relationship of net income to net sales
2. What conclusions can be drawn from these analyses?

Cases & Projects

CP 15-1 Analysis of financing corporate growth

Assume that the president of Freeman Industries Inc. made the following statement in the Annual Report to Shareholders:

"The founding family and majority shareholders of the company do not believe in using debt to finance future growth. The founding family learned from hard experience during Prohibition and the Great Depression that debt can cause loss of flexibility and eventual loss of corporate control. The company will not place itself at such risk. As such, all future growth will be financed either by stock sales to the public or by internally generated resources."

As a public shareholder of this company, how would you respond to this policy?

CP 15-2 Receivables and inventory turnover

Rodgers Industries Inc. has completed its fiscal year on December 31, 2014. The auditor, Josh McCoy, has approached the CFO, Aaron Mathews, regarding the year-end receivables and inventory levels of Rodgers Industries. The following conversation takes place:

Josh: We are beginning our audit of Rodgers Industries and have prepared ratio analyses to determine if there have been significant changes in operations or financial position. This helps us guide the audit process. This analysis indicates that the inventory turnover has decreased from 5.1 to 2.7, while the accounts receivable turnover has decreased from 11 to 7. I was wondering if you could explain this change in operations.

Aaron: There is little need for concern. The inventory represents computers that we were unable to sell during the holiday buying season. We are confident, however, that we will be able to sell these computers as we move into the next fiscal year.

Josh: What gives you this confidence?

Aaron: We will increase our advertising and provide some very attractive price concessions to move these machines. We have no choice. Newer technology is already out there, and we have to unload this inventory.

Josh: ... and the receivables?

Aaron: As you may be aware, the company is under tremendous pressure to expand sales and profits. As a result, we lowered our credit standards to our commercial customers so that we would be able to sell products to a broader customer base. As a result of this policy change, we have been able to expand sales by 35%.

Josh: Your responses have not been reassuring to me.

Aaron: I'm a little confused. Assets are good, right? Why don't you look at our current ratio? It has improved, hasn't it? I would think that you would view that very favorably.

Why is Josh concerned about the inventory and accounts receivable turnover ratios and Aaron's responses to them? What action may Josh need to take? How would you respond to Aaron's last comment?

CP 15-3 Vertical analysis

The condensed income statements through income from operations for Dell Inc. and Apple Inc. are reproduced below for recent fiscal years (numbers in millions of dollars).

	Dell Inc.	Apple Inc.
Sales (net)	$61,494	$65,225
Cost of sales	50,098	39,541
Gross profit	$11,396	$25,684
Selling, general, and administrative expenses	$ 7,302	$ 5,517
Research and development	661	1,782
Operating expenses	$ 7,963	$ 7,299
Income from operations	$ 3,433	$18,385

Prepare comparative common-sized statements, rounding percents to one decimal place. Interpret the analyses.

CP 15-4 Profitability and stockholder ratios

Deere & Co. manufactures and distributes farm and construction machinery that it sells around the world. In addition to its manufacturing operations, Deere & Co.'s credit division loans money to customers to finance the purchase of their farm and construction equipment.

The following information is available for three recent years (in millions except per-share amounts):

	Year 3	Year 2	Year 1
Net income (loss)	$1,865	$874	$2,053
Preferred dividends	$0.00	$0.00	$0.00
Interest expense	$811	$1,042	$1,137
Shares outstanding for computing earnings per share	424	423	431
Cash dividend per share	$1.16	$1.12	$1.06
Average total assets	$42,200	$39,934	$38,655
Average stockholders' equity	$5,555	$5,676	$6,844
Average stock price per share	$60.95	$47.06	$58.01

1. Calculate the following ratios for each year:
   a. Rate earned on total assets
   b. Rate earned on stockholders' equity
   c. Earnings per share
   d. Dividend yield
   e. Price-earnings ratio
2. What is the ratio of average liabilities to average stockholders' equity for Year 3?
3. Based on these data, evaluate Deere & Co.'s performance.

CP 15-5 Comprehensive profitability and solvency analysis

Marriott International, Inc., and Hyatt Hotels Corporation are two major owners and managers of lodging and resort properties in the United States. Abstracted income statement information for the two companies is as follows for a recent year:

	Marriott (in millions)	Hyatt (in millions)
Operating profit before other expenses and interest	$ 677	$ 39
Other income (expenses)	54	118
Interest expense	(180)	(54)
Income before income taxes	$ 551	$103
Income tax expense	93	37
Net income	$ 458	$ 66

Balance sheet information is as follows:

	Marriott (in millions)	Hyatt (in millions)
Total liabilities	$7,398	$2,125
Total stockholders' equity	1,585	5,118
Total liabilities and stockholders' equity	$8,983	$7,243

The average liabilities, average stockholders' equity, and average total assets were as follows:

	Marriott (in millions)	Hyatt (in millions)
Average total liabilities	$7,095	$2,132
Average total stockholders' equity	1,364	5,067
Average total assets	8,458	7,199

1. Determine the following ratios for both companies (round to one decimal place after the whole percent):
   a. Rate earned on total assets
   b. Rate earned on stockholders' equity
   c. Number of times interest charges are earned
   d. Ratio of liabilities to stockholders' equity
2. Analyze and compare the two companies, using the information in (1).

Example Exercises

EE 16-2 p. 761

PE 16-2A Direct materials, direct labor, and factory overhead **OBJ. 2**

Identify the following costs as direct materials (DM), direct labor (DL), or factory overhead (FO) for an automobile manufacturer.

a. Wages of employees that operate painting equipment

b. Wages of the plant supervisor

c. Steel

d. Oil used for assembly line machinery

EE 16-2 p. 761

PE 16-2B Direct materials, direct labor, and factory overhead **OBJ. 2**

Identify the following costs as direct materials (DM), direct labor (DL), or factory overhead (FO) for a magazine publisher.

a. Staples used to bind magazines

b. Wages of printing machine employees

c. Maintenance on printing machines

d. Paper used in the magazine

EE 16-3 p. 762

PE 16-3A Prime and conversion costs **OBJ. 2**

Identify the following costs as a prime cost (P), conversion cost (C), or both (B) for an automobile manufacturer.

a. Wages of employees that operate painting equipment

b. Wages of the plant manager

c. Steel

d. Oil used for assembly line machinery

EE 16-3 p. 762

PE 16-3B Prime and conversion costs **OBJ. 2**

Identify the following costs as a prime cost (P), conversion cost (C), or both (B) for a magazine publisher.

a. Paper used for the magazine

b. Wages of printing machine employees

c. Glue used to bind magazine

d. Maintenance on printing machines

EE 16-4 p. 764

PE 16-4A Product and period costs **OBJ. 2**

Identify the following costs as a product cost or a period cost for an automobile manufacturer.

a. Steel

b. Wages of employees that operate painting equipment

c. Rent on office building

d. Sales staff salaries

EE 16-4 p. 764

PE 16-4B Product and period costs **OBJ. 2**

Identify the following costs as a product cost or a period cost for a magazine publisher.

a. Sales salaries

b. Paper used for the magazine

c. Maintenance on printing machines

d. Depreciation expense—corporate headquarters

f. Payments of cash or the cc generating revenues are (co

g. A product, sales territory, de (direct cost, cost object).

EX 16-6 Concepts and termino

From the choices presented in each of the following sentences

a. The wages of an assembly w

b. Short-term plans are called (

c. The phase of the manageme source of problems in a pro the correct quantities is calle

d. Direct materials costs combine

e. Materials for use in productio

f. The plant manager's salary w

g. An example of factory overh

EX 16-7 Classifying costs in a se

A partial list of the costs for Wis is provided below. Classify each sifying each cost, use the train a

a. Cost to lease (rent) train loco

b. Salaries of dispatching and cc

c. Costs of accident cleanup

d. Wages of switch and classifica

e. Cost of track and bed (ballast

f. Wages of train engineers

g. Payroll clerk salaries

h. Safety training costs

i. Fuel costs

j. Maintenance costs of right of

k. Cost to lease (rent) railroad ca

l. Depreciation of terminal facilit

EX 16-8 Classifying costs

The following report was prepare of Farrar Inc. Evaluate and correct

For th	
Materials used in producti	
$62,500 of indirect mate	
Direct labor (including $93	
Factory overhead:	
Supervisor salaries	
Heat, light, and power..	
Sales salaries	
Promotional expenses..	
Insurance and property t	
Insurance and property t	
Depreciation—plant and	
Depreciation—corporate	
Total	

Example Exercises

OBJ. 3

EE 16-5 *p. 768* **PE 16-5A Cost of goods sold, cost of goods manufactured**

Hill Company has the following information for January:

Cost of direct materials used in production	$16,800
Direct labor	43,400
Factory overhead	28,000
Work in process inventory, January 1	70,000
Work in process inventory, January 31	74,200
Finished goods inventory, January 1	29,400
Finished goods inventory, January 31	33,600

For January, determine (a) the cost of goods manufactured and (b) the cost of goods sold.

OBJ. 3

EE 16-5 *p. 768* **PE 16-5B Cost of goods sold, cost of goods manufactured**

Ebony Company has the following information for July:

Cost of direct materials used in production	$67,200
Direct labor	88,000
Factory overhead	44,800
Work in process inventory, July 1	32,800
Work in process inventory, July 31	29,600
Finished goods inventory, July 1	37,600
Finished goods inventory, July 31	27,200

For July, determine (a) the cost of goods manufactured and (b) the cost of goods sold.

Exercises

OBJ. 2

EX 16-1 Classifying costs as materials, labor, or factory overhead

Indicate whether each of the following costs of an automobile manufacturer would be classified as direct materials cost, direct labor cost, or factory overhead cost:

a. Steering wheel

b. Salary of test driver

c. Depreciation of welding equipment

d. V8 automobile engine

e. Wages of assembly line worker

f. Steel used in body

g. Tires

h. Assembly machinery lubricants

OBJ. 2

EX 16-2 Classifying costs as materials, labor, or factory overhead

Indicate whether the following costs of Colgate-Palmolive Company, a maker of consumer products, would be classified as direct materials cost, direct labor cost, or factory overhead cost:

a. Maintenance supplies

b. Wages of production line employees

c. Depreciation on production machinery

d. Resins for soap and shampoo products

e. Plant manager salary for the Clarksville, Indiana, soap plant

f. Packaging materials

(Continued)

g. Depreciation on the Mori
h. Wages paid to Packaging
i. Scents and fragrances
j. Salary of process enginee

EX 16-3 Classifying costs as

Which of the following iten Caterpillar, a maker of heavy
a. Factory supplies used in t
b. Interest expense on debt
c. Amortization of patents oi
d. Steel plate
e. Plant manager's salary at
f. Vice president of finance's
g. Property taxes on the Aur
h. Consultant fees for a study
i. Sales incentive fees to dea
j. Depreciation on Peoria, Ill

EX 16-4 Classifying costs as p

For apparel manufacturer Ann product cost or a period cost:
a. Depreciation on office equi
b. Property taxes on factory b
c. Advertising expenses
d. Sales commissions
e. Salaries of distribution cent
f. Factory supervisors' salaries
g. Factory janitorial supplies
h. Repairs and maintenance cc
i. Research and development
j. Travel costs of media relatic
k. Chief financial officer's salar
l. Oil used to lubricate sewing
m. Depreciation on sewing mac
n. Utility costs for office buildi
o. Salary of production quality
p. Fabric used during productic
q. Wages of sewing machine oj

EX 16-5 Concepts and terminol

From the choices presented in p each of the following sentences:
a. Feedback is often used to (ir
b. The implementation of auto decreases) the direct labor cc
c. Advertising costs are usually
d. The balance sheet of a manufa work in process inventory).
e. Factory overhead costs comb sion) costs.

Discussion Questions

1. a. Name two principal types of cost accounting systems.
   b. Which system provides for a separate record of each particular quantity of product that passes through the factory?
   c. Which system accumulates the costs for each department or process within the factory?
2. What kind of firm would use a job order cost system?
3. Which account is used in the job order cost system to accumulate direct materials, direct labor, and factory overhead applied to production costs for individual jobs?
4. What document is the source for (a) debiting the accounts in the materials ledger and (b) crediting the accounts in the materials ledger?
5. What is a job cost sheet?
6. What is the difference between a clock card and time ticket?
7. Discuss how the predetermined factory overhead rate can be used in job order cost accounting to assist management in pricing jobs.
8. a. How is a predetermined factory overhead rate calculated?
   b. Name three common bases used in calculating the rate.
9. a. What is (1) overapplied factory overhead and (2) underapplied factory overhead?
   b. If the factory overhead account has a debit balance, was factory overhead underapplied or overapplied?
   c. If the factory overhead account has a credit balance at the end of the first month of the fiscal year, where will the amount of this balance be reported on the interim balance sheet?
10. Describe how a job order cost system can be used for professional service businesses.

Practice Exercises

Example Exercises

EE 17-1 p. 795

PE 17-1A Issuance of materials **OBJ. 2**

On February 8, Gross Company purchased on account 72,000 units of raw materials at $8 per unit. On February 19, raw materials were requisitioned for production as follows: 32,000 units for Job 60 at $7 per unit and 37,000 units for Job 61 at $8 per unit. Journalize the entry on February 8 to record the purchase and on February 19 to record the requisition from the materials storeroom.

EE 17-1 p. 795

PE 17-1B Issuance of materials **OBJ. 2**

On August 4, Rothchild Company purchased on account 12,000 units of raw materials at $14 per unit. On August 24, raw materials were requisitioned for production as follows: 5,000 units for Job 40 at $8 per unit and 6,200 units for Job 42 at $14 per unit. Journalize the entry on August 4 to record the purchase and on August 24 to record the requisition from the materials storeroom.

Example Exercises

EE 17-2 *p. 797*

PE 17-2A Direct labor costs **OBJ. 2**

During February, Gross Company accumulated 15,000 hours of direct labor costs on Job 60 and 18,000 hours on Job 61. The total direct labor was incurred at a rate of $24.00 per direct labor hour for Job 60 and $26.50 per direct labor hour for Job 61. Journalize the entry to record the flow of labor costs into production during February.

EE 17-2 *p. 797*

PE 17-2B Direct labor costs **OBJ. 2**

During August, Rothchild Company accumulated 3,500 hours of direct labor costs on Job 40 and 4,200 hours on Job 42. The total direct labor was incurred at a rate of $25.00 per direct labor hour for Job 40 and $23.50 per direct labor hour for Job 42. Journalize the entry to record the flow of labor costs into production during August.

EE 17-3 *p. 798*

PE 17-3A Factory overhead costs **OBJ. 2**

During February, Gross Company incurred factory overhead costs as follows: indirect materials, $34,000; indirect labor, $81,000; utilities cost, $10,000; and factory depreciation, $61,000. Journalize the entry to record the factory overhead incurred during February.

EE 17-3 *p. 798*

PE 17-3B Factory overhead costs **OBJ. 2**

During August, Rothchild Company incurred factory overhead costs as follows: indirect materials, $17,500; indirect labor, $22,000; utilities cost, $9,600; and factory depreciation, $17,500. Journalize the entry to record the factory overhead incurred during August.

EE 17-4 *p. 801*

PE 17-4A Applying factory overhead **OBJ. 2**

Gross Company estimates that total factory overhead costs will be $2,200,000 for the year. Direct labor hours are estimated to be 400,000. For Gross Company, (a) determine the predetermined factory overhead rate using direct labor hours as the activity base, (b) determine the amount of factory overhead applied to Jobs 60 and 61 in February using the data on direct labor hours from Practice Exercise 17-2A, and (c) prepare the journal entry to apply factory overhead to both jobs in February according to the predetermined overhead rate.

EE 17-4 *p. 801*

PE 17-4B Applying factory overhead **OBJ. 2**

Rothchild Company estimates that total factory overhead costs will be $810,000 for the year. Direct labor hours are estimated to be 90,000. For Rothchild Company, (a) determine the predetermined factory overhead rate using direct labor hours as the activity base, (b) determine the amount of factory overhead applied to Jobs 40 and 42 in August using the data on direct labor hours from Practice Exercise 17-2B, and (c) prepare the journal entry to apply factory overhead to both jobs in August according to the predetermined overhead rate.

EE 17-5 *p. 803*

PE 17-5A Job costs **OBJ. 2**

At the end of February, Gross Company had completed Jobs 60 and 61. Job 60 is for 25,000 units, and Job 61 is for 32,000 units. Using the data from Practice Exercises 17-1A, 17-2A, and 17-4A, determine (a) the balance on the job cost sheets for Jobs 60 and 61 at the end of February and (b) the cost per unit for Jobs 60 and 61 at the end of February.

EE 17-5 *p. 803*

PE 17-5B Job costs **OBJ. 2**

At the end of August, Rothchild Company had completed Jobs 40 and 42. Job 40 is for 10,000 units, and Job 42 is for 11,000 units. Using the data from Practice Exercises 17-1B, 17-2B, and 17-4B, determine (a) the balance on the job cost sheets for Jobs 40 and 42 at the end of August and (b) the cost per unit for Jobs 40 and 42 at the end of August.

Example Exercises

EE 17-6 p. 804

PE 17-6A Cost of goods sold **OBJ. 2**

Curl Company completed 500,000 units during the year at a cost of $24,000,000. The beginning finished goods inventory was 50,000 units at $1,600,000. Determine the cost of goods sold for 525,000 units, assuming a FIFO cost flow.

EE 17-6 p. 804

PE 17-6B Cost of goods sold **OBJ. 2**

Skeleton Company completed 200,000 units during the year at a cost of $3,000,000. The beginning finished goods inventory was 25,000 units at $310,000. Determine the cost of goods sold for 210,000 units, assuming a FIFO cost flow.

Exercises

EX 17-1 Transactions in a job order cost system **OBJ. 2**

Five selected transactions for the current month are indicated by letters in the following T accounts in a job order cost accounting system:

Materials	
	(a)

Work in Process	
(a)	(d)
(b)	
(c)	

Wages Payable	
	(b)

Finished Goods	
(d)	(e)

Factory Overhead	
(a)	(c)
(b)	

Cost of Goods Sold	
(e)	

Describe each of the five transactions.

EX 17-2 Cost flow relationships **OBJ. 2**

✔ c. $1,589,400

The following information is available for the first month of operations of Icahn Inc., a manufacturer of art and craft items:

Sales	$4,500,000
Gross profit	810,000
Indirect labor	270,000
Indirect materials	117,000
Other factory overhead	54,000
Materials purchased	1,530,000
Total manufacturing costs for the period	3,330,000
Materials inventory, end of period	113,400

Factory overhead was applied during the year. Using the above information, determine the following missing amounts:

a. Cost of goods sold

b. Direct materials cost

c. Direct labor cost

✔ b. $3,840

SPREADSHEET

EX 17-3 Cost of materials issuances under the FIFO method **OBJ. 2**

An incomplete subsidiary ledger of wire cable for July is as follows:

RECEIVED			ISSUED			BALANCE			
Receiving Report Number	**Quantity**	**Unit Price**	**Materials Requisition Number**	**Quantity**	**Amount**	**Date**	**Quantity**	**Unit Price**	**Amount**
						July 1	300	$18.00	$5,400
31	200	$20.00				July 2	____	____	____
			106	320		July 6	____	____	____
37	140	32.00				July 12	____	____	____
			115	200		July 21	____	____	____

a. Complete the materials issuances and balances for the wire cable subsidiary ledger under FIFO.

b. Determine the balance of wire cable at the end of July.

c. Journalize the summary entry to transfer materials to work in process.

d. Explain how the materials ledger might be used as an aid in maintaining inventory quantities on hand.

EX 17-4 Entry for issuing materials **OBJ. 2**

Materials issued for the current month are as follows:

Requisition No.	Material	Job No.	Amount
410	Steel	800	$42,700
411	Plastic	802	32,900
412	Glue	Indirect	2,800
413	Rubber	812	2,450
414	Aluminum	820	77,000

Journalize the entry to record the issuance of materials.

✔ c. fabric, $74,490

EX 17-5 Entries for materials **OBJ. 2**

European Designs Company manufactures furniture. European Designs uses a job order cost system. Balances on May 1 from the materials ledger are as follows:

Fabric	$ 56,000
Polyester filling	16,800
Lumber	125,300
Glue	5,460

The materials purchased during May are summarized from the receiving reports as follows:

Fabric	$282,240
Polyester filling	392,000
Lumber	770,000
Glue	27,300

Materials were requisitioned to individual jobs as follows:

	Fabric	Polyester Filling	Lumber	Glue	Total
Job 91	$106,400	$134,400	$358,400		$ 599,200
Job 92	81,750	121,000	312,500		515,250
Job 93	75,600	98,700	175,000		349,300
Factory overhead—indirect materials				$29,000	29,000
Total	$263,750	$354,100	$845,900	$29,000	$1,492,750

(Continued)

The glue is not a significant cost, so it is treated as indirect materials (factory overhead).

a. Journalize the entry to record the purchase of materials in May.

b. Journalize the entry to record the requisition of materials in May.

c. Determine the May 31 balances that would be shown in the materials ledger accounts.

EX 17-6 Entry for factory labor costs **OBJ. 2**

A summary of the time tickets for the current month follows:

Job No.	Amount	Job No.	Amount
201	$ 5,120	Indirect	$ 7,200
202	3,920	212	5,520
204	6,200	214	6,000
206	23,200	215	20,000

Journalize the entry to record the factory labor costs.

EX 17-7 Entry for factory labor costs **OBJ. 2**

The weekly time tickets indicate the following distribution of labor hours for three direct labor employees:

	Hours			
	Job 501	Job 502	Job 503	Process Improvement
Frank Davis	12	14	11	3
Miles Coultrain	14	10	12	4
John Morgan	10	12	14	4

The direct labor rate earned per hour by the three employees is as follows:

Frank Davis	$35
Miles Coultrain	40
John Morgan	30

The process improvement category includes training, quality improvement, and other indirect tasks.

a. Journalize the entry to record the factory labor costs for the week.

b. Assume that Jobs 501 and 502 were completed but not sold during the week and that Job 503 remained incomplete at the end of the week. How would the direct labor costs for all three jobs be reflected on the financial statements at the end of the week?

EX 17-8 Entries for direct labor and factory overhead **OBJ. 2**

VOC Industries Inc. manufactures recreational vehicles. VOC uses a job order cost system. The time tickets from May jobs are summarized below.

Job 301	$6,700
Job 302	5,100
Job 303	5,000
Job 304	5,800
Factory supervision	3,900

Factory overhead is applied to jobs on the basis of a predetermined overhead rate of $20 per direct labor hour. The direct labor rate is $40 per hour.

a. Journalize the entry to record the factory labor costs.

b. Journalize the entry to apply factory overhead to production for May.

EX 17-9 Factory overhead rates, entries, and account balance **OBJ. 2**

✔ b. $41 per direct labor hour

Almer Company operates two factories. The company applies factory overhead to jobs on the basis of machine hours in Factory 1 and on the basis of direct labor hours in Factory 2. Estimated factory overhead costs, direct labor hours, and machine hours are as follows:

	Factory 1	Factory 2
Estimated factory overhead cost for fiscal year beginning July 1	$1,008,000	$861,000
Estimated direct labor hours for year		21,000
Estimated machine hours for year	42,000	
Actual factory overhead costs for July	$74,480	$77,500
Actual direct labor hours for July		2,000
Actual machine hours for July	3,050	

a. Determine the factory overhead rate for Factory 1.

b. Determine the factory overhead rate for Factory 2.

c. Journalize the entries to apply factory overhead to production in each factory for July.

d. Determine the balances of the factory overhead accounts for each factory as of July 31, and indicate whether the amounts represent overapplied or underapplied factory overhead.

EX 17-10 Predetermined factory overhead rate **OBJ. 2**

Amoruso Engine Shop uses a job order cost system to determine the cost of performing engine repair work. Estimated costs and expenses for the coming period are as follows:

Engine parts	$ 980,000
Shop direct labor	750,000
Shop and repair equipment depreciation	53,500
Shop supervisor salaries	140,000
Shop property taxes	26,300
Shop supplies	20,200
Advertising expense	19,900
Administrative office salaries	84,000
Administrative office depreciation expense	11,200
Total costs and expenses	$2,085,100

The average shop direct labor rate is $25 per hour.

Determine the predetermined shop overhead rate per direct labor hour.

EX 17-11 Predetermined factory overhead rate **OBJ. 2**

✔ a. $325 per hour

Reithofer Medical Center has a single operating room that is used by local physicians to perform surgical procedures. The cost of using the operating room is accumulated by each patient procedure and includes the direct materials costs (drugs and medical devices), physician surgical time, and operating room overhead. On January 1 of the current year, the annual operating room overhead is estimated to be:

Disposable supplies	$340,000
Depreciation expense	64,000
Utilities	26,000
Nurse salaries	312,400
Technician wages	131,200
Total operating room overhead	$873,600

(Continued)

The overhead costs will be assigned to procedures, based on the number of surgical room hours. Reithofer Medical Center expects to use the operating room an average of eight hours per day, seven days per week. In addition, the operating room will be shut down four weeks per year for general repairs.

a. Determine the predetermined operating room overhead rate for the year.

b. Wayne Lawrence had a four-hour procedure on January 15. How much operating room overhead would be charged to his procedure, using the rate determined in part (a)?

c. During January, the operating room was used 232 hours. The actual overhead costs incurred for January were $65,500. Determine the overhead under- or overapplied for the period.

✔ b. $53,000

EX 17-12 Entry for jobs completed; cost of unfinished jobs **OBJ. 2**

The following account appears in the ledger prior to recognizing the jobs completed in June:

Work in Process	
Balance, June 1	$ 40,000
Direct materials	270,000
Direct labor	320,000
Factory overhead	176,000

Jobs finished during June are summarized as follows:

Job 320	$160,000	Job 327	$ 100,000
Job 326	175,000	Job 350	318,000

a. Journalize the entry to record the jobs completed.

b. Determine the cost of the unfinished jobs at June 30.

✔ d. $22,580

EX 17-13 Entries for factory costs and jobs completed **OBJ. 2**

Law Publishing Inc. began printing operations on January 1. Jobs 401 and 402 were completed during the month, and all costs applicable to them were recorded on the related cost sheets. Jobs 403 and 404 are still in process at the end of the month, and all applicable costs except factory overhead have been recorded on the related cost sheets. In addition to the materials and labor charged directly to the jobs, $2,000 of indirect materials and $9,000 of indirect labor were used during the month. The cost sheets for the four jobs entering production during the month are as follows, in summary form:

Job 401		Job 402	
Direct materials	$ 8,240	Direct materials	$3,800
Direct labor	3,200	Direct labor	3,000
Factory overhead	2,240	Factory overhead	2,100
Total	$13,680	Total	$8,900

Job 403		Job 404	
Direct materials	$11,600	Direct materials	$2,350
Direct labor	3,500	Direct labor	500
Factory overhead	—	Factory overhead	—

Journalize the summary entry to record each of the following operations for January (one entry for each operation):

a. Direct and indirect materials used.

b. Direct and indirect labor used.

c. Factory overhead applied to all four jobs (a single overhead rate is used based on direct labor cost).

d. Completion of Jobs 401 and 402.

EX 17-14 Financial statements of a manufacturing firm — OBJ. 2

✔ a. Income from operations, $115,000

SPREADSHEET

The following events took place for Kirchhoff Inc. during April 2014, the first month of operations as a producer of road bikes:

- Purchased $320,000 of materials.
- Used $275,000 of direct materials in production.
- Incurred $236,250 of direct labor wages.
- Applied factory overhead at a rate of 80% of direct labor cost.
- Transferred $670,000 of work in process to finished goods.
- Sold goods with a cost of $635,000.
- Sold goods for $1,125,000.
- Incurred $275,000 of selling expenses.
- Incurred $100,000 of administrative expenses.

a. Prepare the April income statement for Kirchhoff. Assume that Kirchhoff uses the perpetual inventory method.

b. Determine the inventory balances at the end of the first month of operations.

EX 17-15 Decision making with job order costs — OBJ. 3

Alvarez Manufacturing Inc. is a job shop. The management of Alvarez Manufacturing Inc. uses the cost information from the job sheets to assess cost performance. Information on the total cost, product type, and quantity of items produced is as follows:

Date	Job No.	Product	Quantity	Amount
Jan. 2	1	TT	520	$16,120
Jan. 15	22	SS	1,610	20,125
Feb. 3	30	SS	1,420	25,560
Mar. 7	41	TT	670	15,075
Mar. 24	49	SLK	2,210	22,100
May 19	58	SLK	2,550	31,875
June 12	65	TT	620	10,540
Aug. 18	78	SLK	3,110	48,205
Sept. 2	82	SS	1,210	16,940
Nov. 14	92	TT	750	8,250
Dec. 12	98	SLK	2,700	52,650

a. Develop a graph for *each* product (three graphs), with Job Number (in date order) on the horizontal axis and Unit Cost on the vertical axis. Use this information to determine Alvarez Manufacturing Inc.'s cost performance over time for the three products.

b. What additional information would you require in order to investigate Alvarez Manufacturing Inc.'s cost performance more precisely?

EX 17-16 Decision making with job order costs — OBJ. 3

Raneri Trophies Inc. uses a job order cost system for determining the cost to manufacture award products (plaques and trophies). Among the company's products is an engraved plaque that is awarded to participants who complete a training program at a local business. The company sells the plaques to the local business for $80 each.

Each plaque has a brass plate engraved with the name of the participant. Engraving requires approximately 30 minutes per name. Improperly engraved names must be redone. The plate is screwed to a walnut backboard. This assembly takes approximately 15 minutes per unit. Improper assembly must be redone using a new walnut backboard.

(Continued)

During the first half of the year, Raneri had two separate plaque orders. The job cost sheets for the two separate jobs indicated the following information:

Job 101	May 4		
	Cost per Unit	Units	Job Cost
Direct materials:			
Wood	$20/unit	40 units	$ 800
Brass	15/unit	40 units	600
Engraving labor	20/hr.	20 hrs.	400
Assembly labor	30/hr.	10 hrs.	300
Factory overhead	10/hr.	30 hrs.	300
			$2,400
Plaques shipped			÷ 40
Cost per plaque			$ 60

Job 105	June 10		
	Cost per Unit	Units	Job Cost
Direct materials:			
Wood	$20/unit	34 units	$ 680
Brass	15/unit	34 units	510
Engraving labor	20/hr.	17 hrs.	340
Assembly labor	30/hr.	8.5 hrs.	255
Factory overhead	10/hr.	25.5 hrs.	255
			$2,040
Plaques shipped			÷ 30
Cost per plaque			$ 68

a. Why did the cost per plaque increase from $60 to $68?

b. What improvements would you recommend for Raneri Trophies Inc.?

✔ b. Underapplied, $7,000

EX 17-17 Job order cost accounting entries for a service business OBJ. 4

The law firm of Clark and Lankau accumulates costs associated with individual cases, using a job order cost system. The following transactions occurred during May:

May 2. Charged 200 hours of professional (lawyer) time to the Peterson Co. breech of contract suit to prepare for the trial, at a rate of $140 per hour.

7. Reimbursed travel costs to employees for depositions related to the Peterson case, $14,600.

11. Charged 300 hours of professional time for the Peterson trial at a rate of $175 per hour.

16. Received invoice from consultants Davis and Harris for $40,000 for expert testimony related to the Peterson trial.

21. Applied office overhead at a rate of $50 per professional hour charged to the Peterson case.

31. Paid secretarial and administrative salaries of $26,000 for the month.

31. Used office supplies for the month, $6,000.

31. Paid professional salaries of $38,640 for the month.

31. Billed Peterson $185,000 for successful defense of the case.

a. Provide the journal entries for each of the above transactions.

b. How much office overhead is over- or underapplied?

c. Determine the gross profit on the Peterson case, assuming that over- or underapplied office overhead is closed monthly to cost of services.

✔ d. Dr. Cost of Services, $1,927,550

EX 17-18 Job order cost accounting entries for a service business **OBJ. 4**

The Crosby Company provides advertising services for clients across the nation. The Crosby Company is presently working on four projects, each for a different client. The Crosby Company accumulates costs for each account (client) on the basis of both direct costs and allocated indirect costs. The direct costs include the charged time of professional personnel and media purchases (air time and ad space). Overhead is allocated to each project as a percentage of media purchases. The predetermined overhead rate is 70% of media purchases.

On June 1, the four advertising projects had the following accumulated costs:

	June 1 Balances
Starks Bank	$180,000
Finley Airlines	54,000
Branch Hotels	140,000
Sanders Beverages	76,500
Total	$450,500

During June, The Crosby Company incurred the following direct labor and media purchase costs related to preparing advertising for each of the four accounts:

	Direct Labor	Media Purchases
Starks Bank	$126,000	$ 472,500
Finley Airlines	56,250	416,500
Branch Hotels	247,500	303,750
Sanders Beverages	281,250	227,250
Total	$711,000	$1,420,000

At the end of June, both the Starks Bank and Finley Airlines campaigns were completed. The costs of completed campaigns are debited to the cost of services account.

Journalize the summary entry to record each of the following for the month:

a. Direct labor costs
b. Media purchases
c. Overhead applied
d. Completion of Starks Bank and Finley Airlines campaigns

Problems Series A

PR 17-1A Entries for costs in a job order cost system **OBJ. 2**

GENERAL LEDGER

Churchill Co. uses a job order cost system. The following data summarize the operations related to production for November:

a. Materials purchased on account, $528,000.
b. Materials requisitioned, $462,000, of which $58,800 was for general factory use.
c. Factory labor used, $545,200, of which $76,400 was indirect.
d. Other costs incurred on account for factory overhead, $123,400; selling expenses, $195,500; and administrative expenses, $121,800.
e. Prepaid expenses expired for factory overhead were $24,360; for selling expenses, $20,600; and for administrative expenses, $14,900.
f. Depreciation of office building was $70,500; of office equipment, $36,120; and of factory equipment, $24,360.
g. Factory overhead costs applied to jobs, $300,400.
h. Jobs completed, $840,000.
i. Cost of goods sold, $740,000.

Instructions

Journalize the entries to record the summarized operations.

PR 17-2A Entries and schedules for unfinished jobs and completed jobs

OBJ. 2

✔ 3. Work in Process balance, $37,020

SPREADSHEET

GENERAL LEDGER

Sinatra Industries Inc. uses a job order cost system. The following data summarize the operations related to production for January 2014, the first month of operations:

a. Materials purchased on account, $39,300.

b. Materials requisitioned and factory labor used:

Job	Materials	Factory Labor
201	$ 3,950	$3,700
202	4,830	5,000
203	3,200	2,500
204	10,800	9,150
205	6,800	7,000
206	5,000	4,450
For general factory use	1,440	5,500

c. Factory overhead costs incurred on account, $7,500.

d. Depreciation of machinery and equipment, $2,640.

e. The factory overhead rate is $60 per machine hour. Machine hours used:

Job	Machine Hours
201	31
202	46
203	36
204	96
205	48
206	31
Total	288

f. Jobs completed: 201, 202, 203 and 205.

g. Jobs were shipped and customers were billed as follows: Job 201, $11,000; Job 202, $14,820; Job 203, $19,920.

Instructions

1. Journalize the entries to record the summarized operations.
2. Post the appropriate entries to T accounts for Work in Process and Finished Goods, using the identifying letters as transaction codes. Insert memo account balances as of the end of the month.
3. Prepare a schedule of unfinished jobs to support the balance in the work in process account.
4. Prepare a schedule of completed jobs on hand to support the balance in the finished goods account.

PR 17-3A Job order cost sheet

OBJ. 2, 3

SPREADSHEET

Cheng Furniture Company refinishes and reupholsters furniture. Cheng Furniture uses a job order cost system. When a prospective customer asks for a price quote on a job, the estimated cost data are inserted on an unnumbered job cost sheet. If the offer is accepted, a number is assigned to the job, and the costs incurred are recorded in the usual manner on the job cost sheet. After the job is completed, reasons for the variances between the estimated and actual costs are noted on the sheet. The data are then available to management in evaluating the efficiency of operations and in preparing quotes on future jobs. On September 3, 2014, an estimate of $3,050 for reupholstering a sofa and loveseat was given to John Jobs. The estimate was based on the following data:

Estimated direct materials:	
40 meters at $25 per meter	$1,000.00
Estimated direct labor:	
30 hours at $30 per hour	900.00
Estimated factory overhead (60% of direct labor cost)	540.00
Total estimated costs	$2,440.00
Markup (25% of production costs)	610.00
Total estimate	$3,050.00

On September 6, the sofa and loveseat were picked up from the residence of John Jobs, 220 Apple Lane, Cupertino, CA, with a commitment to return it on October 31. The job was completed on October 28.

The related materials requisitions and time tickets are summarized as follows:

Materials Requisition No.	Description	Amount
508	18 meters at $25	$450
510	25 meters at $25	625

Time Ticket No.	Description	Amount
H40	14 hours at $30	$420
H43	20 hours at $30	600

Instructions

1. Complete that portion of the job order cost sheet that would be prepared when the estimate is given to the customer.
2. Record the costs incurred, and prepare a job order cost sheet. Comment on the reasons for the variances between actual costs and estimated costs. For this purpose, assume that three meters of materials were spoiled, the factory overhead rate has proven to be satisfactory, and an inexperienced employee performed the work.

✔ G. $751,870

SPREADSHEET

PR 17-4A Analyzing manufacturing cost accounts

OBJ. 2

Fire Rock Company manufactures designer paddle boards in a wide variety of sizes and styles. The following incomplete ledger accounts refer to transactions that are summarized for June:

Materials

June	1	Balance	82,500	June 30	Requisitions	(A)
	30	Purchases	330,000			

Work in Process

June	1	Balance	(B)	June 30	Completed jobs	(F)
	30	Materials	(C)			
	30	Direct labor	(D)			
	30	Factory overhead applied	(E)			

Finished Goods

June	1	Balance	0	June 30	Cost of goods sold	(G)
	30	Completed jobs	(F)			

Wages Payable

				June 30	Wages incurred	330,000

Factory Overhead

June	1	Balance	33,000	June 30	Factory overhead applied	(E)
	30	Indirect labor	(H)			
	30	Indirect materials	44,000			
	30	Other overhead	237,500			

(Continued)

In addition, the following information is available:

a. Materials and direct labor were applied to six jobs in June:

Job No.	Style	Quantity	Direct Materials	Direct Labor
201	T100	550	$ 55,000	$ 41,250
202	T200	1,100	93,500	71,500
203	T400	550	38,500	22,000
204	S200	660	82,500	69,300
205	T300	480	60,000	48,000
206	S100	380	22,000	12,400
	Total	3,720	$351,500	$264,450

b. Factory overhead is applied to each job at a rate of 140% of direct labor cost.

c. The June 1 Work in Process balance consisted of two jobs, as follows:

Job No.	Style	Work in Process, June 1
Job 201	T100	$16,500
Job 202	T200	44,000
Total		$60,500

d. Customer jobs completed and units sold in June were as follows:

Job No.	Style	Completed in June	Units Sold in June
201	T100	X	440
202	T200	X	880
203	T400		0
204	S200	X	570
205	T300	X	420
206	S100		0

Instructions

1. Determine the missing amounts associated with each letter. Provide supporting calculations by completing a table with the following headings:

Job No.	Quantity	June 1 Work in Process	Direct Materials	Direct Labor	Factory Overhead	Total Cost	Unit Cost	Units Sold	Cost of Goods Sold

2. Determine the June 30 balances for each of the inventory accounts and factory overhead.

PR 17-5A Flow of costs and income statement **OBJ. 2**

✔ 1. Income from operations, $432,000

SPREADSHEET

Ginocera Inc. is a designer, manufacturer, and distributor of low-cost, high-quality stainless steel kitchen knives. A new kitchen knife series called the Kitchen Ninja was released for production in early 2014. In January, the company spent $600,000 to develop a late night advertising infomercial for the new product. During 2014, the company spent $1,400,000 promoting the product through these infomercials, and $800,000 in legal costs. The knives were ready for manufacture on January 1, 2014.

Ginocera uses a job order cost system to accumulate costs associated with the kitchen knife. The unit direct materials cost for the knife is:

Hardened steel blanks (used for knife shaft and blade)	$4.00
Wood (for handle)	1.50
Packaging	0.50

The production process is straightforward. First, the hardened steel blanks, which are purchased directly from a raw material supplier, are stamped into a single piece of metal that includes both the blade and the shaft. The stamping machine requires one hour per 250 knives.

After the knife shafts are stamped, they are brought to an assembly area where an employee attaches the handle to the shaft and packs the knife into a decorative box. The direct labor cost is $0.50 per unit.

The knives are sold to stores. Each store is given promotional materials, such as posters and aisle displays. Promotional materials cost $60 per store. In addition, shipping costs average $0.20 per knife.

Total completed production was 1,200,000 units during the year. Other information is as follows:

Number of customers (stores)	60,000
Number of knives sold	1,120,000
Wholesale price (to store) per knife	$16

Factory overhead cost is applied to jobs at the rate of $800 per stamping machine hour after the knife blanks are stamped. There were an additional 25,000 stamped knives, handles, and cases waiting to be assembled on December 31, 2014.

Instructions

1. Prepare an annual income statement for the Kitchen Ninja knife series, including supporting calculations, from the information above.
2. Determine the balances in the work in process and finished goods inventories for the Kitchen Ninja knife series on December 31, 2014.

Problems Series B

PR 17-1B Entries for costs in a job order cost system — OBJ. 2

GENERAL LEDGER

Royal Technology Company uses a job order cost system. The following data summarize the operations related to production for March:

a. Materials purchased on account, $770,000.

b. Materials requisitioned, $680,000, of which $75,800 was for general factory use.

c. Factory labor used, $756,000, of which $182,000 was indirect.

d. Other costs incurred on account for factory overhead, $245,000; selling expenses, $171,500; and administrative expenses, $110,600.

e. Prepaid expenses expired for factory overhead were $24,500; for selling expenses, $28,420; and for administrative expenses, $16,660.

f. Depreciation of factory equipment was $49,500; of office equipment, $61,800; and of office building, $14,900.

g. Factory overhead costs applied to jobs, $568,500.

h. Jobs completed, $1,500,000.

i. Cost of goods sold, $1,375,000.

Instruction

Journalize the entries to record the summarized operations.

PR 17-2B Entries and schedules for unfinished jobs and completed jobs — OBJ. 2

✔ 3. Work in Process balance, $127,880

SPREADSHEET

GENERAL LEDGER

Hildreth Company uses a job order cost system. The following data summarize the operations related to production for April 2014, the first month of operations:

a. Materials purchased on account, $147,000.

b. Materials requisitioned and factory labor used:

Job No.	Materials	Factory Labor
101	$19,320	$19,500
102	23,100	28,140
103	13,440	14,000
104	38,200	36,500
105	18,050	15,540
106	18,000	18,700
For general factory use	9,000	20,160

(Continued)

c. Factory overhead costs incurred on account, $6,000.
d. Depreciation of machinery and equipment, $4,100.
e. The factory overhead rate is $40 per machine hour. Machine hours used:

Job	Machine Hours
101	154
102	160
103	126
104	238
105	160
106	174
Total	1,012

f. Jobs completed: 101, 102, 103, and 105.
g. Jobs were shipped and customers were billed as follows: Job 101, $62,900; Job 102, $80,700; Job 105, $45,500.

Instructions

1. Journalize the entries to record the summarized operations.
2. Post the appropriate entries to T accounts for Work in Process and Finished Goods, using the identifying letters as transaction codes. Insert memo account balances as of the end of the month.
3. Prepare a schedule of unfinished jobs to support the balance in the work in process account.
4. Prepare a schedule of completed jobs on hand to support the balance in the finished goods account.

PR 17-3B Job order cost sheet

OBJ. 2, 3

SPREADSHEET

Refco Furniture Company refinishes and reupholsters furniture. Refco Furniture uses a job order cost system. When a prospective customer asks for a price quote on a job, the estimated cost data are inserted on an unnumbered job cost sheet. If the offer is accepted, a number is assigned to the job, and the costs incurred are recorded in the usual manner on the job cost sheet. After the job is completed, reasons for the variances between the estimated and actual costs are noted on the sheet. The data are then available to management in evaluating the efficiency of operations and in preparing quotes on future jobs. On January 21, 2014, an estimate of $1,391 for reupholstering a sofa and a loveseat was given to Steve Scully. The estimate was based on the following data:

Estimated direct materials:	
22 meters at $20 per meter	$ 440.00
Estimated direct labor:	
14 hours at $25 per hour	350.00
Estimated factory overhead (80% of direct labor cost)	280.00
Total estimated costs	$1,070.00
Markup (30% of production costs)	321.00
Total estimate	$1,391.00

On January 26, the sofa and loveseat were picked up from the residence of Steve Scully, 160 Soda Alley, Purchase, NY, with a commitment to return them on March 3. The job was completed on March 1.

The related materials requisitions and time tickets are summarized as follows:

Materials Requisition No.	Description	Amount
400	10 meters at $20	$200
403	14 meters at $20	280

Time Ticket No.	Description	Amount
H9	10 hours at $24	$240
H12	10 hours at $24	240

Instructions

1. Complete that portion of the job order cost sheet that would be prepared when the estimate is given to the customer.
2. Record the costs incurred, and prepare a job order cost sheet. Comment on the reasons for the variances between actual costs and estimated costs. For this purpose, assume that two meters of materials were spoiled, the factory overhead rate has proven to be satisfactory, and an inexperienced employee performed the work.

✔ G. $700,284

SPREADSHEET

PR 17-4B Analyzing manufacturing cost accounts

OBJ. 2

Clapton Company manufactures custom guitars in a wide variety of styles. The following incomplete ledger accounts refer to transactions that are summarized for May:

Materials

May	1	Balance	105,600	May	31	Requisitions	(A)
	31	Purchases	500,000				

Work in Process

May	1	Balance	(B)	May	31	Completed jobs	(F)
	31	Materials	(C)				
	31	Direct labor	(D)				
	31	Factory overhead applied	(E)				

Finished Goods

May	1	Balance	0	May	31	Cost of goods sold	(G)
	31	Completed jobs	(F)				

Wages Payable

				May	31	Wages incurred	396,000

Factory Overhead

May	1	Balance	26,400	May	31	Factory overhead applied	(E)
	31	Indirect labor	(H)				
	31	Indirect materials	15,400				
	31	Other overhead	122,500				

In addition, the following information is available:

a. Materials and direct labor were applied to six jobs in May:

Job No.	Style	Quantity	Direct Materials	Direct Labor
101	AF1	330	$ 82,500	$ 59,400
102	AF3	380	105,400	72,600
103	AF2	500	132,000	110,000
104	VY1	400	66,000	39,600
105	VY2	660	118,800	66,000
106	AF4	330	66,000	30,800
	Total	2,600	$570,700	$378,400

b. Factory overhead is applied to each job at a rate of 50% of direct labor cost.

c. The May 1 Work in Process balance consisted of two jobs, as follows:

Job No.	Style	Work in Process, May 1
Job 101	AF1	$26,400
Job 102	AF3	46,000
Total		$72,400

(Continued)

d. Customer jobs completed and units sold in May were as follows:

Job No.	Style	Completed in May	Units Sold in May
101	AF1	X	264
102	AF3	X	360
103	AF2		0
104	VY1	X	384
105	VY2	X	530
106	AF4		0

Instructions

1. Determine the missing amounts associated with each letter. Provide supporting calculations by completing a table with the following headings:

Job No.	Quantity	May 1 Work in Process	Direct Materials	Direct Labor	Factory Overhead	Total Cost	Unit Cost	Units Sold	Cost of Goods Sold

2. Determine the May 31 balances for each of the inventory accounts and factory overhead.

PR 17-5B Flow of costs and income statement

OBJ. 2

✔ 1. Income from operations, $656,000

SPREADSHEET

Technology Accessories Inc. is a designer, manufacturer, and distributor of accessories for consumer electronic products. Early in 2014, the company began production of a leather cover for tablet computers, called the iLeather. The cover is made of stitched leather with a velvet interior and fits snuggly around most tablet computers. In January, $750,000 was spent on developing marketing and advertising materials. For the first six months of 2014, the company spent $1,400,000 promoting the iLeather. The product was ready for manufacture on January 21, 2014.

Technology Accessories Inc. uses a job order cost system to accumulate costs for the iLeather. Direct materials unit costs for the iLeather are as follows:

Leather	$10.00
Velvet	5.00
Packaging	0.40
Total	$15.40

The actual production process for the iLeather is fairly straightforward. First, leather is brought to a cutting and stitching machine. The machine cuts the leather and stitches an exterior edge into the product. The machine requires one hour per 125 iLeatherss.

After the iLeather is cut and stitched, it is brought to assembly, where assembly personnel affix the velvet interior and pack the iLeather for shipping. The direct labor cost for this work is $0.50 per unit.

The completed packages are then sold to retail outlets through a sales force. The sales force is compensated by a 20% commission on the wholesale price for all sales.

Total completed production was 500,000 units during the year. Other information is as follows:

Number of iLeather units sold in 2014	460,000
Wholesale price per unit	$40

Factory overhead cost is applied to jobs at the rate of $1,250 per machine hour. There were an additional 22,000 cut and stitched iLeathers waiting to be assembled on December 31, 2014.

Instructions

1. Prepare an annual income statement for the iLeather product, including supporting calculations, from the information above.
2. Determine the balances in the finished goods and work in process inventories for the iLeather product on December 31, 2014.

Cases & Projects

CP 17-1 Managerial analysis

The controller of the plant of Minsky Company prepared a graph of the unit costs from the job cost reports for Product One. The graph appeared as follows:

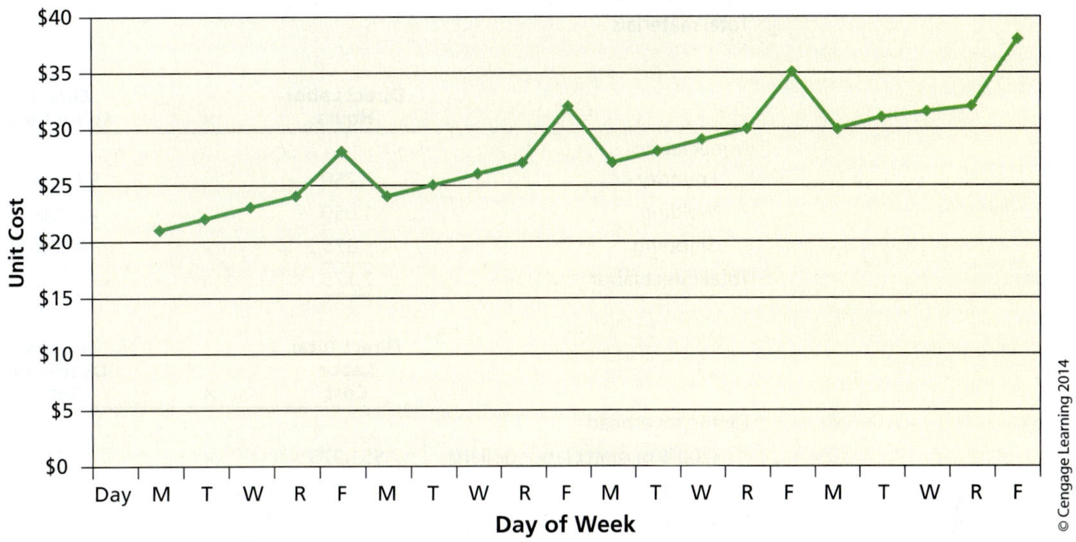

How would you interpret this information? What further information would you request?

CP 17-2 Job order decision making and rate deficiencies

RIRA Company makes attachments, such as backhoes and grader and bulldozer blades, for construction equipment. The company uses a job order cost system. Management is concerned about cost performance and evaluates the job cost sheets to learn more about the cost effectiveness of the operations. To facilitate a comparison, the cost sheet for Job 206 (50 backhoe buckets completed in October) was compared with Job 228, which was for 75 backhoe buckets completed in December. The two job cost sheets follow.

Job 206

Item: 50 backhoe buckets

Materials:	**Direct Materials Quantity**	×	**Direct Materials Price**	=	**Amount**
Steel (tons)	105		$1,200		$126,000
Steel components (pieces)	630		7		4,410
Total materials					$130,410
Direct labor:	**Direct Labor Hours**	×	**Direct Labor Rate**	=	**Amount**
Foundry	400		$22.50		$ 9,000
Welding	550		27.00		14,850
Shipping	180		18.00		3,240
Total direct labor	1,130				$ 27,090
	Direct Total Labor Cost	×	**Factory Overhead Rate**	=	**Amount**
Factory overhead (200% of direct labor dollars)	$27,090	×	200%		$ 54,180
Total cost					$ 211,680
Total units					÷ 50
Unit cost (rounded)					$4,233.60

(Continued)

Job 228

Item: 75 backhoe buckets

	Direct Materials Quantity	×	Direct Materials Price	=	Amount
Materials:					
Steel (tons)	195		$1,100		$214,500
Steel components (pieces)	945		7		6,615
Total materials					$221,115

	Direct Labor Hours	×	Direct Labor Rate	=	Amount
Direct labor:					
Foundry	750		$22.50		$ 16,875
Welding	1,050		27.00		28,350
Shipping	375		18.00		6,750
Total direct labor	2,175				$ 51,975

	Direct Total Labor Cost	×	Factory Overhead Rate	=	Amount
Factory overhead					
(200% of direct labor dollars)	$51,975	×	200%		$ 103,950
Total cost					$ 377,040
Total units					÷ 75
Unit cost					$5,027.20

Management is concerned with the increase in unit costs over the months from October to December. To understand what has occurred, management interviewed the purchasing manager and quality manager.

Purchasing Manager: Prices have been holding steady for our raw materials during the first half of the year. I found a new supplier for our bulk steel that was willing to offer a better price than we received in the past. I saw these lower steel prices and jumped at them, knowing that a reduction in steel prices would have a very favorable impact on our costs.

Quality Manager: Something happened around mid-year. All of a sudden, we were experiencing problems with respect to the quality of our steel. As a result, we've been having all sorts of problems on the shop floor in our foundry and welding operation.

1. Analyze the two job cost sheets, and identify why the unit costs have changed for the backhoe buckets. Complete the following schedule to help you in your analysis:

Item	Input Quantity per Unit—Job 206	Input Quantity per Unit—Job 228
Steel		
Foundry labor		
Welding labor		

2. How would you interpret what has happened in light of your analysis and the interviews?

CP 17-3 Factory overhead rate

Salvo Inc., a specialized equipment manufacturer, uses a job order costing system. The overhead is allocated to jobs on the basis of direct labor hours. The overhead rate is now $1,500 per direct labor hour. The design engineer thinks that this is illogical. The design engineer has stated the following:

Our accounting system doesn't make any sense to me. It tells me that every labor hour carries an additional burden of $1,500. This means that direct labor makes up only 6%

of our total product cost, yet it drives all our costs. In addition, these rates give my design engineers incentives to "design out" direct labor by using machine technology. Yet, over the past years as we have had less and less direct labor, the overhead rate keeps going up and up. I won't be surprised if next year the rate is $2,000 per direct labor hour. I'm also concerned because small errors in our estimates of the direct labor content can have a large impact on our estimated costs. Just a 30-minute error in our estimate of assembly time is worth $750. Small mistakes in our direct labor time estimates really swing our bids around. I think this puts us at a disadvantage when we are going after business.

1. What is the engineer's concern about the overhead rate going "up and up"?
2. What did the engineer mean about the large overhead rate being a disadvantage when placing bids and seeking new business?
3. What do you think is a possible solution?

CP 17-4 Recording manufacturing costs

Todd Lay just began working as a cost accountant for Enteron Industries Inc., which manufactures gift items. Todd is preparing to record summary journal entries for the month. Todd begins by recording the factory wages as follows:

Wages Expense	60,000	
Wages Payable		60,000

Then the factory depreciation:

Depreciation Expense—Factory Machinery	20,000	
Accumulated Depreciation—Factory Machinery		20,000

Todd's supervisor, Jeff Fastow, walks by and notices the entries. The following conversation takes place:

Jeff: That's a very unusual way to record our factory wages and depreciation for the month.

Todd: What do you mean? This is exactly the way we were taught to record wages and depreciation in school. You know, debit an expense and credit Cash or payables, or in the case of depreciation, credit Accumulated Depreciation.

Jeff: Well, it's not the credits I'm concerned about. It's the debits—I don't think you've recorded the debits correctly. I wouldn't mind if you were recording the administrative wages or office equipment depreciation this way, but I've got real questions about recording factory wages and factory machinery depreciation this way.

Todd: Now I'm really confused. You mean this is correct for administrative costs, but not for factory costs? Well, what am I supposed to do—and why?

1. Play the role of Jeff and answer Todd's questions.
2. Why would Jeff accept the journal entries if they were for administrative costs?

CP 17-5 Predetermined overhead rates

As an assistant cost accountant for Mississippi Industries, you have been assigned to review the activity base for the predetermined factory overhead rate. The president, Tony Favre, has expressed concern that the over- or underapplied overhead has fluctuated excessively over the years.

An analysis of the company's operations and use of the current overhead rate (direct labor cost) has narrowed the possible alternative overhead bases to direct labor cost and machine hours. For the past five years, the following data have been gathered:

	2014	2013	2012	2011	2010
Actual overhead	$ 790,000	$ 870,000	$ 935,000	$ 845,000	$ 760,000
Applied overhead	777,000	882,000	924,000	840,000	777,000
(Over-) underapplied overhead	$ 13,000	$ (12,000)	$ 11,000	$ 5,000	$ (17,000)
Direct labor cost	$3,885,000	$4,410,000	$4,620,000	$4,200,000	$3,885,000
Machine hours	93,000	104,000	111,000	100,400	91,600

(Continued)

Learning Objectives

After studying this chapter, you should be able to: *Example Exercises*

Objective	Example Exercises
OBJ 1 Describe process cost systems.	
Process Cost Systems	
Comparing Job Order and Process Cost Systems	EE 18-1
Cost Flows for a Process Manufacturer	
OBJ 2 Prepare a cost of production report.	
Cost of Production Report	
Step 1: Determine the Units to Be Assigned Costs	EE 18-2
Step 2: Compute Equivalent Units of Production	EE 18-3, 18-4
Step 3: Determine the Cost per Equivalent Unit	EE 18-5
Step 4: Allocate Costs to Units Transferred Out and Partially Completed Units	EE 18-6
Preparing the Cost of Production Report	
OBJ 3 Journalize entries for transactions using a process cost system.	
Journal Entries for a Process Cost System	EE 18-7
OBJ 4 Describe and illustrate the use of cost of production reports for decision making.	
Using the Cost of Production Report for Decision Making	
Frozen Delight	
Holland Beverage Company	EE 18-8
Yield	
OBJ 5 Compare just-in-time processing with traditional manufacturing processing.	
Just-in-Time Processing	

At a Glance 18 Page 859

OBJ 1 Describe process cost systems.

Process Cost Systems

A **process manufacturer** produces products that are indistinguishable from each other using a continuous production process. For example, an oil refinery processes crude oil through a series of steps to produce a barrel of gasoline. One barrel of gasoline, the product, cannot be distinguished from another barrel. Other examples of process manufacturers include paper producers, chemical processors, aluminum smelters, and food processors.

The cost accounting system used by process manufacturers is called the **process cost system**. A process cost system records product costs for each manufacturing department or process.

In contrast, a job order manufacturer produces custom products for customers or batches of similar products. For example, a custom printer produces wedding invitations, graduation announcements, or other special print items that are tailored to the specifications of each customer. Each item manufactured is unique to itself. Other examples of job order manufacturers include furniture manufacturers, shipbuilders, and home builders.

As described and illustrated in Chapter 17, the cost accounting system used by job order manufacturers is called the *job order cost system*. A job order cost system records product cost for each job, using job cost sheets.

Some examples of process and job order companies and their products are shown on the next page.

Process Manufacturing Companies		Job Order Companies	
Company	**Product**	**Company**	**Product**
Pepsi	soft drinks	Walt Disney	movies
Alcoa	aluminum	Nike, Inc.	athletic shoes
Intel	computer chip	Nicklaus Design	golf courses
Apple	iPhone	Heritage Log Homes	log homes
Hershey Foods	chocolate bars	DDB Advertising Agency	advertising

Comparing Job Order and Process Cost Systems

Process and job order cost systems are similar in that each system:

1. Records and summarizes product costs.
2. Classifies product costs as direct materials, direct labor, and factory overhead.
3. Allocates factory overhead costs to products.
4. Uses perpetual inventory system for materials, work in process, and finished goods.
5. Provides useful product cost information for decision making.

Process and job costing systems are different in several ways. As a basis for illustrating these differences, the cost systems for Frozen Delight and Legend Guitars are used.

Integrity, Objectivity, and Ethics in Business

ON BEING GREEN

Process manufacturing often involves significant energy and material resources, which can be harmful to the environment. Thus, many process manufacturing companies, such as chemical, electronic, and metal processors, must address environmental issues. Companies, such as DuPont, Intel, Apple, and Alcoa, are at the forefront of providing environmental solutions for their products and processes.

For example, Apple provides free recycling programs for Macs®, iPhones®, and iPads®. Apple recovers over 90% by weight of the original product in reusable components, glass, and plastic. You can even receive a free gift card for voluntarily recycling an older Apple product.

Source: Apple Web site.

Exhibit 1 illustrates the process cost system for Frozen Delight, an ice cream manufacturer. As a basis for comparison, Exhibit 1 also illustrates the job order cost system for Legend Guitars, a custom guitar manufacturer. Legend Guitars was described and illustrated in Chapters 16 and 17.

Exhibit 1 indicates that Frozen Delight manufactures ice cream, using two departments:

1. The Mixing Department mixes the ingredients, using large vats.
2. The Packaging Department puts the ice cream into cartons for shipping to customers.

Since each gallon of ice cream is similar, product costs are recorded in each department's work in process account. As shown in Exhibit 1, Frozen Delight accumulates (records) the cost of making ice cream in *work in process accounts* for the Mixing and Packaging departments. The product costs of making a gallon of ice cream include:

1. *Direct materials costs,* which include milk, cream, sugar, and packing cartons. All materials costs are added at the beginning of the process for both the Mixing Department and the Packaging Department.

c. The cost of direct labor used by the Mixing and Packaging departments is recorded in work in process accounts for each department.
d. The cost of factory overhead incurred for indirect materials and other factory overhead such as depreciation is recorded in the factory overhead accounts for each department.
e. The factory overhead incurred in the Mixing and Packaging departments is applied to the work in process accounts for each department.
f. The cost of units completed in the Mixing Department is transferred to the Packaging Department.
g. The cost of units completed in the Packaging Department is transferred to Finished Goods.
h. The cost of units sold is transferred to Cost of Goods Sold.

As shown in Exhibit 3, the Mixing and Packaging departments have separate factory overhead accounts. The factory overhead costs incurred for indirect materials, depreciation, and other overhead are debited to each department's factory overhead account. The overhead is applied to work in process by debiting each department's work in process account and crediting the department's factory overhead account.

Exhibit 3 illustrates how the Mixing and Packaging departments have separate work in process accounts. Each work in process account is debited for direct materials, direct labor, and applied factory overhead. In addition, the work in process account for the Packaging Department is debited for the cost of the units transferred in from the Mixing Department. Each work in process account is credited for the cost of the units transferred to the next department.

Lastly, Exhibit 3 shows that the finished goods account is debited for the cost of the units transferred from the Packaging Department. The finished goods account is credited for the cost of the units sold, which is debited to the cost of goods sold account.

Business Connection

FRIDGE PACK

Go to any food store and you will see beverage cans sold in popular 12-can fridge packs. The fridge pack was introduced to the soft drink industry in 1998 by Alcoa Inc.

The fridge pack story began when Alcoa was looking for ways to sell more aluminum can sheet, one of its major products. After extensive market research, Alcoa thought of a fiberboard package design that would make it easier for consumers to store canned beverages in a refrigerator by taking up the "dead space." Alcoa believed if more cans could be stored in the refrigerator it would result in more cans being consumed, and hence more overall sales.

The fridge pack was first adopted by Coca-Cola Australia, where it saw an instant increase in sales as Alcoa predicted. As a result, the remaining soft beverage industry quickly adopted the package design. Miller Brewing introduced the fridge pack for beer in 2004. The fridge pack is an excellent example of a process manufacturer, like Alcoa, creating innovations to benefit its customers (and itself).

Source: Alcoa Recycling Company, "Fridge Vendor: A Cool Idea that Is Paying Off," Web site, 2010.

OBJ 2 Prepare a cost of production report.

Cost of Production Report

In a process cost system, the cost of units transferred out of each processing department must be determined along with the cost of any partially completed units remaining in the department. The report that summarizes these costs is a cost of production report.

The **cost of production report** summarizes the production and cost data for a department as follows:

1. The units the department is accountable for and the disposition of those units.
2. The product costs incurred by the department and the allocation of those costs between completed (transferred out) and partially completed units.

EXHIBIT 3 Cost Flows for a Process Manufacturer—Frozen Delight

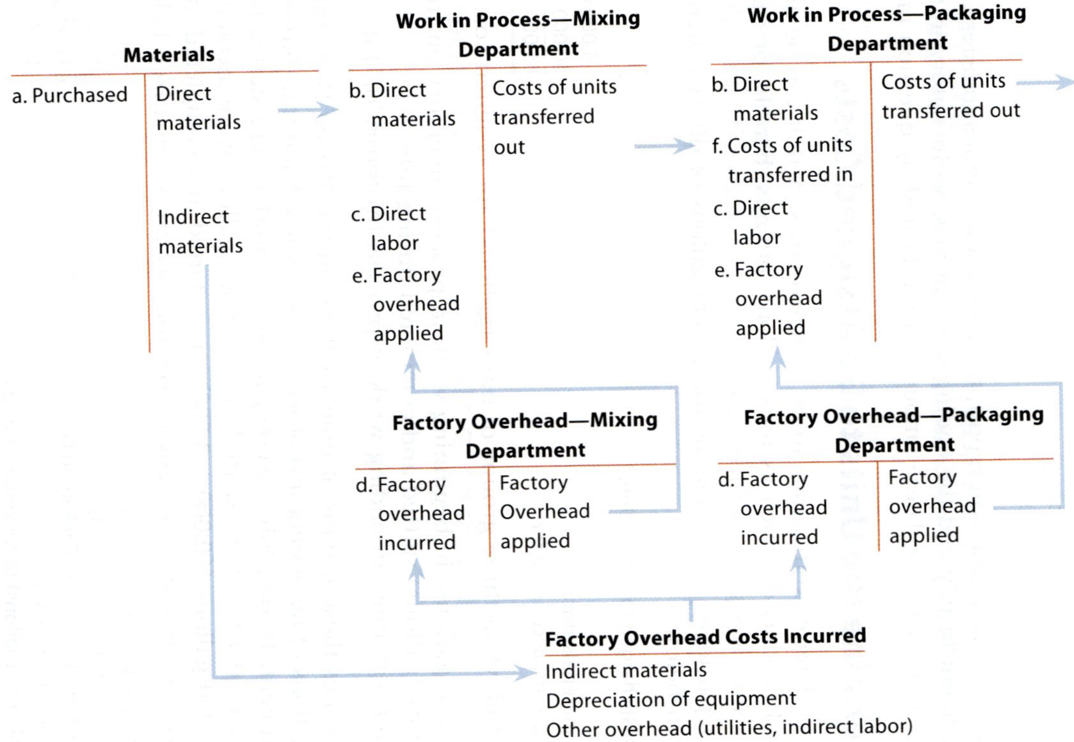

Cost Flows for Frozen Delight

a. The cost of materials purchased is recorded in the materials account.
b. The cost of direct materials used by the Mixing and Packaging departments is recorded in the work in process accounts for each department.
c. The cost of direct labor used by the Mixing and Packaging departments is recorded in work in process accounts for each department.
d. The cost of factory overhead incurred for indirect materials and other factory overhead such as depreciation is recorded in the factory overhead accounts for each department.
e. The factory overhead incurred in the Mixing and Packaging departments is applied to the work in process accounts for each department.
f. The cost of units completed in the Mixing Department is transferred to the Packaging Department.
g. The cost of units completed in the Packaging Department is transferred to Finished Goods.
h. The cost of units sold is transferred to Cost of Goods Sold.

$$\text{Direct Materials Cost per Equivalent Unit} = \frac{\$66{,}000}{60{,}000 \text{ gallons}} = \$1.10 \text{ per gallon}$$

$$\text{Conversion Cost per Equivalent Unit} = \frac{\text{Total Conversion Costs for the Period}}{\text{Total Equivalent Units of Conversion Costs}}$$

$$\text{Conversion Cost per Equivalent Unit} = \frac{\$17{,}775}{59{,}250 \text{ gallons}} = \$0.30 \text{ per gallon}$$

The preceding costs per equivalent unit are used in Step 4 to allocate the direct materials and conversion costs to the completed and partially completed units.

Example Exercise 18-5 Cost per Equivalent Unit OBJ 2

The cost of direct materials transferred into the Bottling Department of Rocky Springs Beverage Company is $22,800. The conversion cost for the period in the Bottling Department is $8,790. The total equivalent units for direct materials and conversion are 57,000 liters and 58,600 liters, respectively. Determine the direct materials and conversion costs per equivalent unit.

Follow My Example 18-5

$$\text{Direct Materials Cost per Equivalent Unit} = \frac{\$22{,}800}{57{,}000 \text{ liters}} = \$0.40 \text{ per liter}$$

$$\text{Conversion Cost per Equivalent Unit} = \frac{\$8{,}790}{58{,}600 \text{ liters}} = \$0.15 \text{ per liter}$$

Practice Exercises: **PE 18-5A, PE 18-5B**

Step 4: Allocate Costs to Units Transferred Out and Partially Completed Units

Product costs must be allocated to the units transferred out and the partially completed units on hand at the end of the period. The product costs are allocated using the costs per equivalent unit for materials and conversion costs that were computed in Step 3.

The total production costs to be assigned for Frozen Delight in July are $90,000 as shown below and on page 840.

Inventory in process, July 1, 5,000 gallons:	
Direct materials cost, for 5,000 gallons	$ 5,000
Conversion costs, for 5,000 gallons, 70% completed	1,225
Total inventory in process, July 1	$ 6,225
Direct materials cost for July, 60,000 gallons	66,000
Direct labor cost for July	10,500
Factory overhead applied for July	7,275
Total production costs to account for	$90,000

The units to be assigned these costs are shown below. The costs to be assigned these units are indicated by question marks (?).

		Units	Total Cost
Group 1	Inventory in process, July 1, completed in July	5,000 gallons	?
Group 2	Started and completed in July	57,000	?
	Transferred out to the Packaging Department in July	62,000 gallons	?
Group 3	Inventory in process, July 31	3,000	?
	Total	65,000 gallons	$90,000

Group 1: Inventory in Process on July 1 The 5,000 gallons of inventory in process on July 1 (Group 1) were completed and transferred out to the Packaging Department in July. The cost of these units of $6,675 is determined as follows:

	Direct Materials Costs	Conversion Costs	Total Costs
Inventory in process, July 1 balance			$6,225
Equivalent units for completing the July 1 in-process inventory	0	1,500	
Cost per equivalent unit	× $1.10	× $0.30	
Cost of completed July 1 in-process inventory	0	$450	450
Cost of July 1 in-process inventory transferred to Packaging Department			$6,675

As shown above, $6,225 of the cost of the July 1 in-process inventory of 5,000 gallons was carried over from June. This cost plus the cost of completing the 5,000 gallons in July was transferred to the Packaging Department during July. The cost of completing the 5,000 gallons during July is $450. The $450 represents the conversion costs necessary to complete the remaining 30% of the processing. There were no direct materials costs added in July because all the materials costs had been added in June. Thus, the cost of the 5,000 gallons in process on July 1 (Group 1) transferred to the Packaging Department is $6,675.

Group 2: Started and Completed The 57,000 units started and completed in July (Group 2) incurred all (100%) of their direct materials and conversion costs in July. Thus, the cost of the 57,000 gallons started and completed is $79,800, computed by multiplying 57,000 gallons by the costs per equivalent unit for materials and conversion costs as shown below.

	Direct Materials Costs	Conversion Costs	Total Costs
Units started and completed in July	57,000 gallons	57,000 gallons	
Cost per equivalent unit	× $1.10	× $0.30	
Cost of the units started and completed in July	$62,700	$17,100	$79,800

The total cost of $86,475 transferred to the Packaging Department in July is the sum of the beginning inventory cost and the costs of the units started and completed in July as shown below.

Group 1	Cost of July 1 in-process inventory	$ 6,675
Group 2	Cost of the units started and completed in July	79,800
	Total costs transferred to Packaging Department in July	$86,475

Group 3: Inventory in Process on July 31 The 3,000 gallons in process on July 31 (Group 3) incurred all their direct materials costs and 25% of their conversion costs in July. The cost of these partially completed units of $3,525 is computed below.

	Direct Materials Costs	Conversion Costs	Total Costs
Equivalent units in ending inventory	3,000 gallons	750 gallons	
Cost per equivalent unit	× $1.10	× $0.30	
Cost of July 31 in-process inventory	$3,300	$225	$3,525

The 3,000 gallons in process on July 31 received all (100%) of their materials in July. Therefore, the direct materials cost incurred in July is $3,300 (3,000 × $1.10). The conversion costs of $225 represent the cost of the 750 (3,000 × 25%) equivalent gallons multiplied by the cost of $0.30 per equivalent unit for conversion costs.

The sum of the direct materials cost ($3,300) and the conversion costs ($225) equals the total cost of the July 31 work in process inventory of $3,525 ($3,300 + $225).

To summarize, the total manufacturing costs for Frozen Delight in July were assigned as shown below. In doing so, the question marks(?) on page 846 have been answered.

		Units	Total Cost
Group 1	Inventory in process, July 1, completed in July	5,000 gallons	$ 6,675
Group 2	Started and completed in July	57,000	79,800
	Transferred out to the Packaging Department in July	62,000 gallons	$86,475
Group 3	Inventory in process, July 31	3,000	3,525
	Total	65,000 gallons	$90,000

Example Exercise 18-6 Cost of Units Transferred Out and Ending Work in Process

OBJ 2

The costs per equivalent unit of direct materials and conversion in the Bottling Department of Rocky Springs Beverage Company are $0.40 and $0.15, respectively. The equivalent units to be assigned costs are as follows:

	Equivalent Units	
	Direct Materials	**Conversion**
Inventory in process, beginning of period	0	2,800
Started and completed during the period	54,000	54,000
Transferred out of Bottling (completed)	54,000	56,800
Inventory in process, end of period	3,000	1,800
Total units to be assigned costs	57,000	58,600

The beginning work in process inventory had a cost of $1,860. Determine the cost of units transferred out and the ending work in process inventory.

Follow My Example 18-6

	Direct Materials Costs		Conversion Costs	Total Costs
Inventory in process, beginning of period				$ 1,860
Inventory in process, beginning of period	0	+	2,800 × $0.15	420
Started and completed during the period	54,000 × $0.40	+	54,000 × $0.15	29,700
Transferred out of Bottling (completed)				$31,980
Inventory in process, end of period	3,000 × $0.40	+	1,800 × $0.15	1,470
Total costs assigned by the Bottling Department				$33,450
Completed and transferred out of production	$31,980			
Inventory in process, ending	$ 1,470			

Practice Exercises: **PE 18-6A, PE 18-6B**

Preparing the Cost of Production Report

A cost of production report is prepared for each processing department at periodic intervals. The report summarizes the following production quantity and cost data:

1. The units for which the department is accountable and the disposition of those units.
2. The production costs incurred by the department and the allocation of those costs between completed (transferred out) and partially completed units.

Using Steps 1–4, the July cost of production report for Frozen Delight's Mixing Department is shown in Exhibit 7. During July, the Mixing Department was accountable for 65,000 units (gallons). Of these units, 62,000 units were completed and transferred to the Packaging Department. The remaining 3,000 units are partially completed and are part of the in-process inventory as of July 31.

The Mixing Department was responsible for $90,000 of production costs during July. The cost of goods transferred to the Packaging Department in July was $86,475. The remaining cost of $3,525 is part of the in-process inventory as of July 31.

EXHIBIT 7 **Cost of Production Report for Frozen Delight's Mixing Department—FIFO**

	A	B	C	D	E	
1		**Frozen Delight**				
2		**Cost of Production Report—Mixing Department**				
3		**For the Month Ended July 31, 2014**				
4						Step 1 Step 2
5		Whole Units	Equivalent Units			
6	**UNITS**		Direct Materials	Conversion		
7	Units charged to production:					
8	Inventory in process, July 1	5,000				
9	Received from materials storeroom	60,000				
10	Total units accounted for by the Mixing Department	65,000				
11						
12	Units to be assigned costs:					
13	Inventory in process, July 1 (70% completed)	5,000	0	1,500		
14	Started and completed in July	57,000	57,000	57,000		
15	Transferred to Packaging Department in July	62,000	57,000	58,500		
16	Inventory in process, July 31 (25% completed)	3,000	3,000	750		
17	Total units to be assigned costs	65,000	60,000	59,250		
18						
19				**Costs**		
20	**COSTS**		Direct Materials	Conversion	Total	
21						
22	Costs per equivalent unit:					
23	Total costs for July in Mixing Department		$ 66,000	$ 17,775		
24	Total equivalent units (from Step 2 above)		÷60,000	÷59,250		
25	Cost per equivalent unit		$ 1.10	$ 0.30		
26						Step 3
27	Costs assigned to production:					
28	Inventory in process, July 1				$ 6,225	
29	Costs incurred in July				83,775[a]	
30	Total costs accounted for by the Mixing Department				$90,000	
31						
32						
33	Cost allocated to completed and partially					
34	completed units:					
35	Inventory in process, July 1—balance				$ 6,225	
36	To complete inventory in process, July 1		$ 0 +	$ 450[b] =	450	
37	Cost of completed July 1 work in process				$ 6,675	Step 4
38	Started and completed in July		62,700[c] +	17,100[d] =	79,800	
39	Transferred to Packaging Department in July				$86,475	
40	Inventory in process, July 31		$ 3,300[e] +	$ 225[f] =	3,525	
41	Total costs assigned by the Mixing Department				$90,000	
42						

[a]$66,000 + $10,500 + $7,275 = $83,775 [b]1,500 units × $0.30 = $450 [c]57,000 units × $1.10 = $62,700 [d]57,000 units × $0.30 = $17,100
[e]3,000 units × $1.10 = $3,300 [f]750 units × $0.30 = $225

OBJ 3 Journalize entries for transactions using a process cost system.

Journal Entries for a Process Cost System

The journal entries to record the cost flows and transactions for a process cost system are illustrated in this section. As a basis for illustration, the July transactions for Frozen Delight are used. To simplify, the entries are shown in summary form, even though many of the transactions would be recorded daily.

a. Purchased materials, including milk, cream, sugar, packaging, and indirect materials on account, $88,000.

Materials		88,000		
Accounts Payable			88,000	

b. The Mixing Department requisitioned milk, cream, and sugar, $66,000. This is the amount indicated on page 840. Packaging materials of $8,000 were requisitioned by the Packaging Department. Indirect materials for the Mixing and Packaging departments were $4,125 and $3,000, respectively.

Work in Process—Mixing		66,000	
Work in Process—Packaging		8,000	
Factory Overhead—Mixing		4,125	
Factory Overhead—Packaging		3,000	
Materials			81,125

c. Incurred direct labor in the Mixing and Packaging departments of $10,500 and $12,000, respectively.

Work in Process—Mixing		10,500	
Work in Process—Packaging		12,000	
Wages Payable			22,500

d. Recognized equipment depreciation for the Mixing and Packaging departments of $3,350 and $1,000, respectively.

Factory Overhead—Mixing		3,350	
Factory Overhead—Packaging		1,000	
Accumulated Depreciation—Equipment			4,350

e. Applied factory overhead to Mixing and Packaging departments of $7,275 and $3,500, respectively.

Work in Process—Mixing		7,275	
Work in Process—Packaging		3,500	
Factory Overhead—Mixing			7,275
Factory Overhead—Packaging			3,500

f. Transferred costs of $86,475 from the Mixing Department to the Packaging Department per the cost of production report in Exhibit 7.

Work in Process—Packaging		86,475	
Work in Process—Mixing			86,475

g. Transferred goods of $106,000 out of the Packaging Department to Finished Goods according to the Packaging Department cost of production report (not illustrated).

		Finished Goods—Ice Cream	106,000	
		Work in Process—Packaging		106,000

h. Recorded the cost of goods sold out of the finished goods inventory of $107,000.

		Cost of Goods Sold	107,000	
		Finished Goods—Ice Cream		107,000

Exhibit 8 shows the flow of costs for each transaction. The highlighted amounts in Exhibit 8 were determined from assigning the costs in the Mixing Department. These amounts were computed and are shown at the bottom of the cost of production report for the Mixing Department in Exhibit 7 on page 849. Likewise, the amount transferred out of the Packaging Department to Finished Goods would have also been determined from a cost of production report for the Packaging Department.

EXHIBIT 8 **Frozen Delight's Cost Flows**

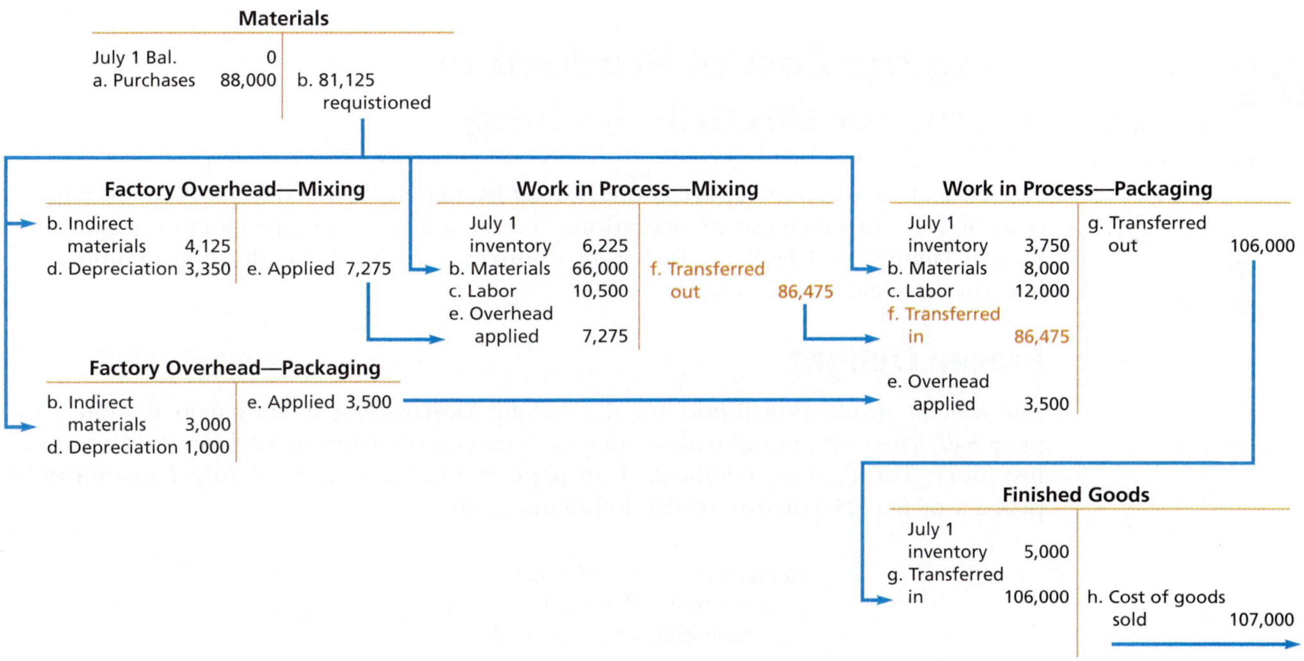

The ending inventories for Frozen Delight are reported on the July 31 balance sheet as follows:

Materials	$ 6,875
Work in Process—Mixing Department	3,525
Work in Process—Packaging Department	7,725
Finished Goods	4,000
Total inventories	$22,125

The $3,525 balance of Work in Process—Mixing Department is the amount determined from the bottom of the cost of production report in Exhibit 7.

Example Exercise 18-7 **Process Cost Journal Entries** OBJ 3

The cost of materials transferred into the Bottling Department of Rocky Springs Beverage Company is $22,800, including $20,000 from the Blending Department and $2,800 from the materials storeroom. The conversion cost for the period in the Bottling Department is $8,790 ($3,790 factory overhead applied and $5,000 direct labor). The total cost transferred to Finished Goods for the period was $31,980. The Bottling Department had a beginning inventory of $1,860.

a. Journalize (1) the cost of transferred-in materials, (2) conversion costs, and (3) the costs transferred out to Finished Goods.
b. Determine the balance of Work in Process—Bottling at the end of the period.

Follow My Example 18-7

a.	1. Work in Process—Bottling	22,800	
	Work in Process—Blending		20,000
	Materials		2,800
	2. Work in Process—Bottling	8,790	
	Factory Overhead—Bottling		3,790
	Wages Payable		5,000
	3. Finished Goods	31,980	
	Work in Process—Bottling		31,980

b. $1,470 ($1,860 + $22,800 + $8,790 − $31,980)

Practice Exercises: **PE 18-7A, PE 18-7B**

OBJ 4 Describe and illustrate the use of cost of production reports for decision making.

Using the Cost of Production Report for Decision Making

The cost of production report is often used by managers for decisions involving the control and improvement of operations. To illustrate, cost of production reports for Frozen Delight and Holland Beverage Company are used. Finally, the computation and use of yield are discussed.

Frozen Delight

The cost of production report for the Mixing Department is shown in Exhibit 7 on page 849. The cost per equivalent unit for June can be determined from the beginning inventory. The Frozen Delight data on page 840 indicate that the July 1 inventory in process of $6,225 consists of the following costs:

Direct materials cost, 5,000 gallons	$5,000
Conversion costs, 5,000 gallons, 70% completed	1,225
Total inventory in process, July 1	$6,225

Using the preceding data, the June costs per equivalent unit of materials and conversion costs can be determined as follows:

$$\text{Direct Materials Cost per Equivalent Unit} = \frac{\text{Total Direct Materials Cost for the Period}}{\text{Total Equivalent Units of Direct Materials}}$$

$$\text{Direct Materials Cost per Equivalent Unit} = \frac{\$5{,}000}{5{,}000 \text{ gallons}} = \$1.00 \text{ per gallon}$$

$$\text{Conversion Cost per Equivalent Unit} = \frac{\text{Total Conversion Costs for the Period}}{\text{Total Equivalent Units of Conversion Costs}}$$

$$\text{Conversion Cost per Equivalent Unit} = \frac{\$1,225}{(5,000 \times 70\%) \text{ gallons}} = \$0.35 \text{ per gallon}$$

In July, the cost per equivalent unit of materials increased by $0.10 per gallon, while the cost per equivalent unit for conversion costs decreased by $0.05 per gallon, as shown below.

	July*	June	Increase (Decrease)
Cost per equivalent unit for direct materials	$1.10	$1.00	$0.10
Cost per equivalent unit for conversion costs	0.30	0.35	(0.05)

*From Exhibit 7, p. 849

Frozen Delight's management could use the preceding analysis as a basis for investigating the increase in the direct materials cost per equivalent unit and the decrease in the conversion cost per equivalent unit.

Holland Beverage Company

A cost of production report may be prepared showing more cost categories beyond just direct materials and conversion costs. This greater detail can help managers isolate problems and seek opportunities for improvement.

To illustrate, the Blending Department of Holland Beverage Company prepared cost of production reports for April and May. To simplify, assume that the Blending Department had no beginning or ending work in process inventory in either month. That is, all units started were completed in each month. The cost of production reports showing multiple cost categories for April and May in the Blending Department are as follows:

	A	B	C
1	**Cost of Production Reports**		
2	**Holland Beverage Company—Blending Department**		
3	**For the Months Ended April 30 and May 31, 2014**		
4		**April**	**May**
5	Direct materials	$ 20,000	$ 40,600
6	Direct labor	15,000	29,400
7	Energy	8,000	20,000
8	Repairs	4,000	8,000
9	Tank cleaning	3,000	8,000
10	Total	$ 50,000	$106,000
11	Units completed	÷100,000	÷200,000
12	Cost per unit	$ 0.50	$ 0.53
13			

The May results indicate that total unit costs have increased from $0.50 to $0.53, or 6% in May. To determine the possible causes for this increase, the cost of production report is restated in per-unit terms by dividing the costs by the number of units completed, as shown below.

	A	B	C	D
1	**Blending Department**			
2	**Per-Unit Expense Comparisons**			
3		**April**	**May**	**% Change**
4	Direct materials	$0.200	$0.203	1.50%
5	Direct labor	0.150	0.147	−2.00%
6	Energy	0.080	0.100	25.00%
7	Repairs	0.040	0.040	0.00%
8	Tank cleaning	0.030	0.040	33.33%
9	Total	$0.500	$0.530	6.00%
10				

Both energy and tank cleaning per-unit costs have increased significantly in May. These increases should be further investigated. For example, the increase in energy may be due to the machines losing fuel efficiency. This could lead management to repair the machines. The tank cleaning costs could be investigated in a similar fashion.

Yield

In addition to unit costs, managers of process manufacturers are also concerned about yield. The **yield** is computed as follows:

$$\text{Yield} = \frac{\text{Quantity of Material Output}}{\text{Quantity of Material Input}}$$

To illustrate, assume that 1,000 pounds of sugar enter the Packaging Department, and 980 pounds of sugar were packed. The yield is 98% as computed below.

$$\text{Yield} = \frac{\text{Quantity of Material Output}}{\text{Quantity of Material Input}} = \frac{\text{980 pounds}}{\text{1,000 pounds}} = 98\%$$

Thus, two percent (100% – 98%) or 20 pounds of sugar were lost or spilled during the packing process. Managers can investigate significant changes in yield over time or significant differences in yield from industry standards.

Example Exercise 18-8 Using Process Costs for Decision Making

OBJ 4

The cost of energy consumed in producing good units in the Bottling Department of Rocky Springs Beverage Company was $4,200 and $3,700 for March and April, respectively. The number of equivalent units produced in March and April was 70,000 liters and 74,000 liters, respectively. Evaluate the change in the cost of energy between the two months.

Follow My Example 18-8

$$\text{Energy cost per liter, March} = \frac{\$4,200}{\text{70,000 liters}} = \$0.06$$

$$\text{Energy cost per liter, April} = \frac{\$3,700}{\text{74,000 liters}} = \$0.05$$

The cost of energy has improved by 1 cent per liter between March and April.

Practice Exercises: **PE 18-8A, PE 18-8B**

OBJ 5 Compare just-in-time processing with traditional manufacturing processing.

Just-in-Time Processing

The objective of most manufacturers is to produce products with high quality, low cost, and instant availability. In attempting to achieve this objective, many manufacturers have implemented just-in-time processing. **Just-in-time (JIT) processing** is a management approach that focuses on reducing time and cost and eliminating poor quality. A JIT system obtains efficiencies and flexibility by reorganizing the traditional production process.

A traditional manufacturing process for a furniture manufacturer is shown in Exhibit 9. The product (chair) moves through seven processes. In each process, workers are assigned a specific job, which is performed repeatedly as unfinished products are received from the preceding department. The product moves from process to process as each function or step is completed.

EXHIBIT 9 **Traditional Production Line**

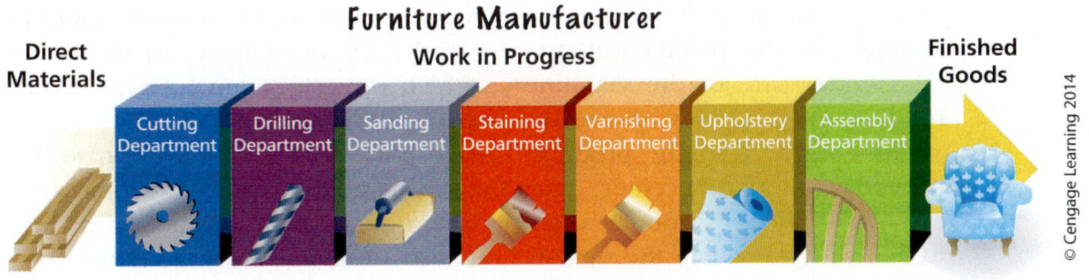

For the furniture maker in Exhibit 9, the product (chair) moves through the following processes:

1. In the Cutting Department, the wood is cut to design specifications.
2. In the Drilling Department, the wood is drilled to design specifications.
3. In the Sanding Department, the wood is sanded.
4. In the Staining Department, the wood is stained.
5. In the Varnishing Department, varnish and other protective coatings are applied.
6. In the Upholstery Department, fabric and other materials are added.
7. In the Assembly Department, the product (chair) is assembed.

In the traditional production process, supervisors enter materials into manufacturing so as to keep all the manufacturing departments (processes) operating. Some departments, however, may process materials more rapidly than others. In addition, if one department stops because of machine breakdowns, for example, the preceding departments usually continue production in order to avoid idle time. In such cases, a buildup of work in process inventories results in some departments.

In a just-in-time system, processing functions are combined into work centers, sometimes called **manufacturing cells**. For example, the seven departments illustrated in Exhibit 9 might be reorganized into the following three work centers:

1. Work Center 1 performs the cutting, drilling, and sanding functions.
2. Work Center 2 performs the staining and varnishing functions.
3. Work Center 3 performs the upholstery and assembly functions.

The preceding JIT manufacturing process is illustrated in Exhibit 10.

EXHIBIT 10 **Just-in-Time Production Line**

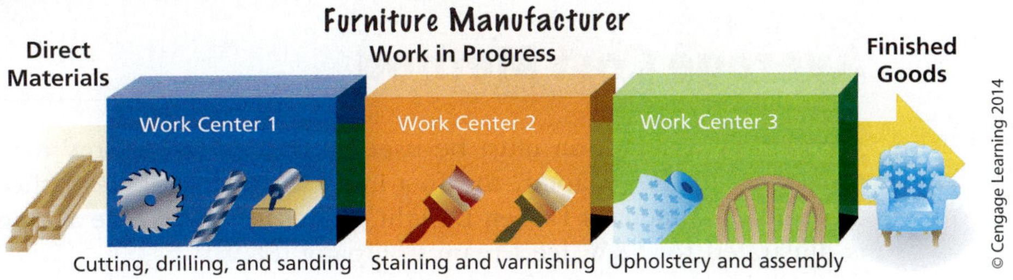

In traditional manufacturing, a worker typically performs only one function. However, in JIT manufacturing, work centers complete several functions. Thus, workers are often cross-trained to perform more than one function. Research has indicated that workers who perform several functions identify better with the end product. This creates pride in the product and improves quality and productivity.

The activities supporting the manufacturing process are called *service activities*. For example, repair and maintenance of manufacturing equipment are service activities.

Before Caterpillar implemented JIT, a transmission traveled 10 miles through the factory and required 1,000 pieces of paper to support the manufacturing process. After implementing JIT, a transmission travels only 200 feet and requires only 10 pieces of paper.

In a JIT manufacturing process, service activities may be assigned to individual work centers, rather than to centralized service departments. For example, each work center may be assigned responsibility for the repair and maintenance of its machinery and equipment. This creates an environment in which workers gain a better understanding of the production process and their machinery. In turn, workers tend to take better care of the machinery, which decreases repairs and maintenance costs, reduces machine downtime, and improves product quality.

In a JIT system, the product is often placed on a movable carrier that is centrally located in the work center. After the workers in a work center have completed their activities with the product, the entire carrier and any additional materials are moved just in time to satisfy the demand or need of the next work center. In this sense, the product is said to be "pulled through." Each work center is connected to other work centers through information contained on a Kanban, which is a Japanese term for cards.

In summary, the primary objective of JIT systems is to increase the efficiency of operations. This is achieved by eliminating waste and simplifying the production process. At the same time, JIT systems emphasize continually improving the manufacturing process and product quality. JIT systems, including cost management in JIT systems, are further described and illustrated in Chapter 27.

Business Connection

RADICAL IMPROVEMENT: JUST IN TIME FOR PULASKI'S CUSTOMERS

Pulaski Furniture Corporation embraced just-in-time manufacturing principles and revolutionized its business. The company wanted to "be easier to do business with" by offering its customers smaller shipments more frequently. It was able to accomplish this by taking the following steps:

- Mapping processes to properly align labor, machines, and materials.
- Eliminating 100 feet of conveyor line.
- Moving machines into manufacturing cells.
- Reducing manufacturing run sizes by simplifying the product design.
- Making every product more frequently in order to reduce the customer's waiting time for a product.

As a result of these just-in-time changes, the company significantly improved its inventory position while simultaneously improving its shipping times to the customer. Its lumber inventory was reduced by 25%, finished goods inventory was reduced by 40%, and work in process inventory was reduced by 50%. At the same time, customers' shipment waiting times were shortened from months to weeks.

Source: Jeff Linville, "Pulaski's Passion for Lean Plumps up Dealer Service," *Furniture Today,* June 2006.

APPENDIX

Average Cost Method

A cost flow assumption must be used as product costs flow through manufacturing processes. In this chapter, the first-in, first-out cost flow method was used for the Mixing Department of Frozen Delight. In this appendix, the average cost flow method is illustrated for S&W Ice Cream Company (S&W).

Determining Costs Using the Average Cost Method

S&W's operations are similar to those of Frozen Delight. Like Frozen Delight, S&W mixes direct materials (milk, cream, sugar) in refrigerated vats and has two manufacturing departments, Mixing and Packaging.

The manufacturing data for the Mixing Department for July 2014 are as follows:

Inventory in process, July 1, 5,000 gallons (70% completed)	$ 6,200
Direct materials cost incurred in July, 60,000 gallons	66,000
Direct labor cost incurred in July	10,500
Factory overhead applied in July	6,405
Total production costs to account for	$89,105
Cost of goods transferred to Packaging in July (includes units in process on July 1), 62,000 gallons	?
Cost of work in process inventory, July 31, 3,000 gallons, 25% completed as to conversion costs	?

Using the average cost method, the objective is to allocate the total costs of production of $89,105 to the following:

1. The 62,000 gallons completed and transferred to the Packaging Department
2. The 3,000 gallons in the July 31 (ending) work in process inventory

The preceding costs show two question marks. These amounts are determined by preparing a cost of production report, using the following four steps:

Step 1. Determine the units to be assigned costs.
Step 2. Compute equivalent units of production.
Step 3. Determine the cost per equivalent unit.
Step 4. Allocate costs to transferred out and partially completed units.

Under the average cost method, all production costs (materials and conversion costs) are combined together for determining equivalent units and cost per equivalent unit.

Step 1: Determine the Units to Be Assigned Costs The first step is to determine the units to be assigned costs. A unit can be any measure of completed production, such as tons, gallons, pounds, barrels, or cases. For S&W, a unit is a gallon of ice cream.

S&W's Mixing Department had 65,000 gallons of direct materials to account for during July, as shown here.

Total gallons to account for:	
Inventory in process, July 1	5,000 gallons
Received from materials storeroom	60,000
Total units to account for by the Packaging Department	65,000 gallons

There are two groups of units to be assigned costs for the period.

Group 1	Units completed and transferred out
Group 2	Units in the July 31 (ending) work in process inventory

During July, the Mixing Department completed and transferred 62,000 gallons to the Packaging Department. Of the 60,000 gallons started in July, 57,000 (60,000 − 3,000) gallons were completed and transferred to the Packaging Department. Thus, the ending work in process inventory consists of 3,000 gallons.

The total units (gallons) to be assigned costs for S&W can be summarized as follows:

Group 1	Units transferred out to the Packaging Department in July	62,000 gallons
Group 2	Inventory in process, July 31	3,000
	Total gallons to be assigned costs	65,000 gallons

The total units (gallons) to be assigned costs (65,000 gallons) equal the total units to account for (65,000 gallons).

Step 2: Compute Equivalent Units of Production S&W has 3,000 gallons of whole units in the work in process inventory for the Mixing Department on July 31. Since these units are 25% complete, the number of equivalent units in process in the Mixing Department on July 31 is 750 gallons (3,000 gallons × 25%). Since the units transferred to the Packaging Department have been completed, the whole units (62,000 gallons) transferred are the same as the equivalent units transferred.

The total equivalent units of production for the Mixing Department are determined by adding the equivalent units in the ending work in process inventory to the units transferred and completed during the period as shown below.

Equivalent units completed and transferred to the Packaging Department during July	62,000 gallons
Equivalent units in ending work in process, July 31	750
Total equivalent units	62,750 gallons

Step 3: Determine the Cost per Equivalent Unit Since materials and conversion costs are combined under the average cost method, the cost per equivalent unit is determined by dividing the total production costs by the total equivalent units of production as follows:

$$\text{Cost per Equivalent Unit} = \frac{\text{Total Production Costs}}{\text{Total Equivalent Units}}$$

$$\text{Cost per Equivalent Unit} = \frac{\text{Total Production Costs}}{\text{Total Equivalent Units}} = \frac{\$89{,}105}{62{,}750 \text{ gallons}} = \$1.42$$

The cost per equivalent unit shown above is used in Step 4 to allocate the production costs to the completed and partially completed units.

Step 4: Allocate Costs to Transferred Out and Partially Completed Units The cost of transferred and partially completed units is determined by multiplying the cost per equivalent unit times the equivalent units of production. For the Mixing Department, these costs are determined as follows:

Group 1	Transferred out to the Packaging Department (62,000 gallons × $1.42)	$88,040
Group 2	Inventory in process, July 31 (3,000 gallons × 25% × $1.42)	1,065
	Total production costs assigned	$89,105

The Cost of Production Report

The July cost of production report for S&W's Mixing Department is shown in Exhibit 11. This cost of production report summarizes the following:

1. The units for which the department is accountable and the disposition of those units
2. The production costs incurred by the department and the allocation of those costs between completed and partially completed units

EXHIBIT 11 **Cost of Production Report for S&W's Mixing Department—Average Cost**

	A	B	C
1	**S&W Ice Cream Company**		
2	**Cost of Production Report—Mixing Department**		
3	**For the Month Ended July 31, 2014**		
4	**UNITS**	Step 1	Step 2
5		Whole Units	Equivalent Units
6			of Production
7	Units to account for during production:		
8	Inventory in process, July 1	5,000	
9	Received from materials storeroom	60,000	
10	Total units accounted for by the Mixing Department	65,000	
11			
12	Units to be assigned costs:		
13	Transferred to Packaging Department in July	62,000	62,000
14	Inventory in process, July 31 (25% completed)	3,000	750
15	Total units to be assigned costs	65,000	62,750
16			
17	**COSTS**		**Costs**
18			
19	Cost per equivalent unit: (Step 3)		
20	Total production costs for July in Mixing Department		$89,105
21	Total equivalent units (from Step 2 above)		÷62,750
22	Cost per equivalent unit		$ 1.42
23			
24	Costs assigned to production:		
25	Inventory in process, July 1		$ 6,200
26	Direct materials, direct labor, and factory overhead incurred in July		82,905
27	Total costs accounted for by the Mixing Department		$89,105
28			
29			
30	Costs allocated to completed and partially completed units: (Step 4)		
31	Transferred to Packaging Department in July (62,000 gallons × $1.42)		$88,040
32	Inventory in process, July 31 (3,000 gallons × 25% × $1.42)		1,065
33	Total costs assigned by the Mixing Department		$89,105
34			

At a Glance 18

OBJ 1 Describe process cost systems.

Key Points The process cost system is best suited for industries that mass produce identical units of a product. Costs are charged to processing departments, rather than to jobs as with the job order cost system. These costs are transferred from one department to the next until production is completed.

Learning Outcomes	*Example Exercises*	*Practice Exercises*
• Identify the characteristics of a process manufacturer.		
• Compare and contrast the job order cost system with the process cost system.	EE18-1	PE18-1A, 18-1B
• Describe the physical and cost flows of a process manufacturer.		

Determine the following for the Pressing Department:

a. Total conversion cost

b. Conversion cost per equivalent unit

c. Direct materials cost per equivalent unit

EX 18-11 Equivalent units of production and related costs **OBJ. 2**

✔ a. 640 units

SPREADSHEET

The charges to Work in Process—Assembly Department for a period, together with information concerning production, are as follows. All direct materials are placed in process at the beginning of production.

Work in Process—Assembly Department

Bal., 900 units, 35% completed	22,450	To Finished Goods, 16,260 units	?
Direct materials, 16,000 units @ $21	336,000		
Direct labor	101,380		
Factory overhead	93,416		
Bal. ? units, 45% completed	?		

Determine the following:

a. The number of units in work in process inventory at the end of the period.

b. Equivalent units of production for direct materials and conversion.

c. Costs per equivalent unit for direct materials and conversion.

d. Cost of the units started and completed during the period.

EX 18-12 Cost of units completed and in process **OBJ. 2, 4**

✔ a. 1. $29,470

a. Based on the data in Exercise 18-11, determine the following:

1. Cost of beginning work in process inventory completed this period.
2. Cost of units transferred to finished goods during the period.
3. Cost of ending work in process inventory.
4. Cost per unit of the completed beginning work in process inventory, rounded to the nearest cent.

b. Did the production costs change from the preceding period? Explain.

c. Assuming that the direct materials cost per unit did not change from the preceding period, did the conversion costs per equivalent unit increase, decrease, or remain the same for the current period?

EX 18-13 Errors in equivalent unit computation **OBJ. 2**

Napco Refining Company processes gasoline. On June 1 of the current year, 6,400 units were ⅗ completed in the Blending Department. During June, 55,000 units entered the Blending Department from the Refining Department. During June, the units in process at the beginning of the month were completed. Of the 55,000 units entering the department, all were completed except 5,200 units that were ⅕ completed. The equivalent units for conversion costs for June for the Blending Department were computed as follows:

Equivalent units of production in June:	
To process units in inventory on June 1: 6,400 × ⅗	3,840
To process units started and completed in June: 55,000 – 6,400	48,600
To process units in inventory on June 30: 5,200 × ⅕	1,040
Equivalent units of production	53,480

List the errors in the computation of equivalent units for conversion costs for the Blending Department for June.

EX 18-14 Cost per equivalent unit **OBJ. 2**

✔ a. 8,600 units

The following information concerns production in the Forging Department for November. All direct materials are placed into the process at the beginning of production, and conversion costs are incurred evenly throughout the process. The beginning inventory consists of $17,400 of direct materials.

ACCOUNT ***Work in Process—Forging Department*** **ACCOUNT NO.**

Date		Item	Debit	Credit	Balance Debit	Balance Credit
Nov.	1	Bal., 1,200 units, 60% completed			20,856	
	30	Direct materials, 8,300 units	124,500		145,356	
	30	Direct labor	18,950		164,306	
	30	Factory overhead	20,196	?	184,502	
	30	Goods transferred, ? units			?	
	30	Bal., 900 units, 70% completed			?	

a. Determine the number of units transferred to the next department.

b. Determine the costs per equivalent unit of direct materials and conversion.

c. Determine the cost of units started and completed in November.

EX 18-15 Costs per equivalent unit and production costs **OBJ. 2, 4**

✔ a. $23,064

Based on the data in Exercise 18-14, determine the following:

a. Cost of beginning work in process inventory completed in November.

b. Cost of units transferred to the next department during November.

c. Cost of ending work in process inventory on November 30.

d. Costs per equivalent unit of direct materials and conversion included in the November 1 beginning work in process.

e. The November increase or decrease in costs per equivalent unit for direct materials and conversion from the previous month.

EX 18-16 Cost of production report **OBJ. 2, 4**

✔ d. $2,092

SPREADSHEET

The debits to Work in Process—Roasting Department for Morning Brew Coffee Company for August 2014, together with information concerning production, are as follows:

Work in process, August 1, 700 pounds, 20% completed		$ 3,479*
*Direct materials (700 × $4.70)	$3,290	
Conversion (700 × 20% × $1.35)	189	
	$3,479	
Coffee beans added during August, 14,300 pounds		65,780
Conversion costs during August		21,942
Work in process, August 31, 400 pounds, 42% completed		?
Goods finished during August, 14,600 pounds		?

All direct materials are placed in process at the beginning of production.

a. Prepare a cost of production report, presenting the following computations:

1. Direct materials and conversion equivalent units of production for August.
2. Direct materials and conversion costs per equivalent unit for August.
3. Cost of goods finished during August.
4. Cost of work in process at August 31, 2014.

b. Compute and evaluate the change in cost per equivalent unit for direct materials and conversion from the previous month (July).

EX 18-17 Cost of production report **OBJ. 2, 4**

✔ Conversion cost per equivalent unit, $5.10

The Cutting Department of Karachi Carpet Company provides the following data for January 2014. Assume that all materials are added at the beginning of the process.

(Continued)

EX 18-22 Just-in-time manufacturing **OBJ. 5**

The following are some quotes provided by a number of managers at Hawkeye Machining Company regarding the company's planned move toward a just-in-time manufacturing system:

Director of Sales: I'm afraid we'll miss some sales if we don't keep a large stock of items on hand just in case demand increases. It only makes sense to me to keep large inventories in order to assure product availability for our customers.

Director of Purchasing: I'm very concerned about moving to a just-in-time system for materials. What would happen if one of our suppliers were unable to make a shipment? A supplier could fall behind in production or have a quality problem. Without some safety stock in our materials, our whole plant would shut down.

Director of Manufacturing: If we go to just-in-time, I think our factory output will drop. We need in-process inventory in order to "smooth out" the inevitable problems that occur during manufacturing. For example, if a machine that is used to process a product breaks down, it would starve the next machine if I don't have in-process inventory between the two machines. If I have in-process inventory, then I can keep the next operation busy while I fix the broken machine. Thus, the in-process inventories give me a safety valve that I can use to keep things running when things go wrong.

How would you respond to these managers?

Appendix
EX 18-23 Equivalent units of production: average cost method

✔ a. 17,000

The Converting Department of Tender Soft Tissue Company uses the average cost method and had 1,900 units in work in process that were 60% complete at the beginning of the period. During the period, 15,800 units were completed and transferred to the Packing Department. There were 1,200 units in process that were 30% complete at the end of the period.

a. Determine the number of whole units to be accounted for and to be assigned costs for the period.

b. Determine the number of equivalent units of production for the period.

Appendix
EX 18-24 Equivalent units of production: average cost method

✔ a. 12,100 units to be accounted for

Units of production data for the two departments of Atlantic Cable and Wire Company for July of the current fiscal year are as follows:

	Drawing Department	Winding Department
Work in process, July 1	500 units, 50% completed	350 units, 30% completed
Completed and transferred to next processing department during July	11,400 units	10,950 units
Work in process, July 31	700 units, 55% completed	800 units, 25% completed

Each department uses the average cost method.

a. Determine the number of whole units to be accounted for and to be assigned costs and the equivalent units of production for the Drawing Department.

b. Determine the number of whole units to be accounted for and to be assigned costs and the equivalent units of production for the Winding Department.

Appendix
EX 18-25 Equivalent units of production: average cost method

✔ a. 3,100

The following information concerns production in the Finishing Department for May. The Finishing Department uses the average cost method.

ACCOUNT *Work in Process—Finishing Department* ACCOUNT NO.

Date		Item	Debit	Credit	Balance Debit	Balance Credit
May	1	Bal., 4,200 units, 70% completed			36,500	
	31	Direct materials, 23,600 units	125,800		162,300	
	31	Direct labor	75,400		237,700	
	31	Factory overhead	82,675		320,375	
	31	Goods transferred, 24,700 units		308,750	11,625	
	31	Bal., ? units, 30% completed			11,625	

a. Determine the number of units in work in process inventory at the end of the month.
b. Determine the number of whole units to be accounted for and to be assigned costs and the equivalent units of production for May.

✔ b. 8,820 units

SPREADSHEET

Appendix
EX 18-26 Equivalent units of production and related costs

The charges to Work in Process—Baking Department for a period as well as information concerning production are as follows. The Baking Department uses the average cost method, and all direct materials are placed in process during production.

Work in Process—Baking Department

Bal., 900 units, 40% completed	2,466	To Finished Goods, 8,100 units	?
Direct materials, 8,400 units	34,500		
Direct labor	16,200		
Factory overhead	8,574		
Bal., 1,200 units, 60% completed	?		

Determine the following:
a. The number of whole units to be accounted for and to be assigned costs.
b. The number of equivalent units of production.
c. The cost per equivalent unit.
d. The cost of units transferred to Finished Goods.
e. The cost of units in ending Work in Process.

✔ a. $26.00

Appendix
EX 18-27 Cost per equivalent unit: average cost method

The following information concerns production in the Forging Department for June. The Forging Department uses the average cost method.

ACCOUNT *Work in Process—Forging Department* ACCOUNT NO.

Date		Item	Debit	Credit	Balance Debit	Balance Credit
June	1	Bal., 500 units, 40% completed			5,000	
	30	Direct materials, 3,700 units	49,200		54,200	
	30	Direct labor	25,200		79,400	
	30	Factory overhead	25,120		104,520	
	30	Goods transferred, 3,600 units		?	?	
	30	Bal., 600 units, 70% completed			?	

a. Determine the cost per equivalent unit.
b. Determine cost of units transferred to Finished Goods.
c. Determine the cost of units in ending Work in Process.

✔ Cost per equivalent unit, $3.60

Appendix
EX 18-28 Cost of production report: average cost method

The increases to Work in Process—Roasting Department for Highlands Coffee Company for May 2014 as well as information concerning production are as follows:

Work in process, May 1, 1,150 pounds, 40% completed	$ 1,700
Coffee beans added during May, 10,900 pounds	28,600
Conversion costs during May	12,504
Work in process, May 31, 800 pounds, 80% completed	—
Goods finished during May, 11,250 pounds	—

Prepare a cost of production report, using the average cost method.

Appendix

EX 18-29 Cost of production report: average cost method

✔ Cost per equivalent unit, $9.00

SPREADSHEET

Prepare a cost of production report for the Cutting Department of Dalton Carpet Company for January 2014. Use the average cost method with the following data:

Work in process, January 1, 3,400 units, 75% completed	$ 23,000
Materials added during January from Weaving Department, 64,000 units	366,200
Direct labor for January	105,100
Factory overhead for January	80,710
Goods finished during January (includes goods in process, January 1), 63,500 units	—
Work in process, January 31, 3,900 units, 10% completed	—

Problems Series A

PR 18-1A Entries for process cost system — OBJ. 1, 3

✔ 2. Materials August 31 balance, $3,000

GENERAL LEDGER

Homepride Carpet Company manufactures carpets. Fiber is placed in process in the Spinning Department, where it is spun into yarn. The output of the Spinning Department is transferred to the Tufting Department, where carpet backing is added at the beginning of the process and the process is completed. On August 1, Homepride Carpet Company had the following inventories:

Finished Goods	$4,800
Work in Process—Spinning Department	1,200
Work in Process—Tufting Department	1,900
Materials	3,700

Departmental accounts are maintained for factory overhead, and both have zero balances on August 1.

Manufacturing operations for August are summarized as follows:

a. Materials purchased on account	$ 74,200
b. Materials requisitioned for use:	
Fiber—Spinning Department	$ 38,300
Carpet backing—Tufting Department	31,200
Indirect materials—Spinning Department	3,000
Indirect materials—Tufting Department	2,400
c. Labor used:	
Direct labor—Spinning Department	$ 22,300
Direct labor—Tufting Department	16,900
Indirect labor—Spinning Department	11,900
Indirect labor—Tufting Department	10,200
d. Depreciation charged on fixed assets:	
Spinning Department	$ 4,900
Tufting Department	3,000
e. Expired prepaid factory insurance:	
Spinning Department	$ 1,000
Tufting Department	800
f. Applied factory overhead:	
Spinning Department	$ 21,400
Tufting Department	15,600
g. Production costs transferred from Spinning Department to Tufting Department	$ 83,000
h. Production costs transferred from Tufting Department to Finished Goods	$143,700
i. Cost of goods sold during the period	$146,900

Instructions

1. Journalize the entries to record the operations, identifying each entry by letter.
2. Compute the August 31 balances of the inventory accounts.
3. Compute the August 31 balances of the factory overhead accounts.

✔ 1. Conversion cost per equivalent unit, $1.10

SPREADSHEET

PR 18-2A Cost of production report — OBJ. 2, 4

Abica Coffee Company roasts and packs coffee beans. The process begins by placing coffee beans into the Roasting Department. From the Roasting Department, coffee beans are then transferred to the Packing Department. The following is a partial work in process account of the Roasting Department at May 31, 2014:

ACCOUNT *Work in Process—Roasting Department* ACCOUNT NO.

Date		Item	Debit	Credit	Balance Debit	Balance Credit
May	1	Bal., 1,200 units, 30% completed			5,610	
	31	Direct materials, 18,900 units	81,270		86,880	
	31	Direct labor	12,400		99,280	
	31	Factory overhead	8,060		107,340	
	31	Goods transferred, 18,200 units		?		
	31	Bal., ? units, 40% completed			?	

Instructions

1. Prepare a cost of production report, and identify the missing amounts for Work in Process—Roasting Department.
2. Assuming that the May 1 work in process inventory includes $5,232 of direct materials, determine the increase or decrease in the cost per equivalent unit for direct materials and conversion between April and May.

✔ 2. Transferred to Packaging Dept., $38,365

SPREADSHEET

PR 18-3A Equivalent units and related costs; cost of production report; entries — OBJ. 2, 3, 4

Lily Flour Company manufactures flour by a series of three processes, beginning with wheat grain being introduced in the Milling Department. From the Milling Department, the materials pass through the Sifting and Packaging departments, emerging as packaged refined flour.

The balance in the account Work in Process—Sifting Department was as follows on July 1, 2014:

Work in Process—Sifting Department (700 units, $^3/_5$ completed):	
Direct materials (700 × $2.58)	$1,806
Conversion (700 × $^3/_5$ × $0.55)	231
	$2,037

The following costs were charged to Work in Process—Sifting Department during July:

Direct materials transferred from Milling Department:	
12,300 units at $2.60 a unit	$31,980
Direct labor	4,670
Factory overhead	2,758

During July, 12,000 units of flour were completed. Work in Process—Sifting Department on July 31 was 1,000 units, $^4/_5$ completed.

Instructions

1. Prepare a cost of production report for the Sifting Department for July.
2. Journalize the entries for costs transferred from Milling to Sifting and the costs transferred from Sifting to Packaging.
3. Determine the increase or decrease in the cost per equivalent unit from June to July for direct materials and conversion costs.
4. Discuss the uses of the cost of production report and the results of part (3).

PR 18-4A Work in process account data for two months; cost of production reports OBJ. 1, 2, 3, 4

✔ 1. c. Transferred to finished goods in April, $49,818

SPREADSHEET

Hearty Soup Co. uses a process cost system to record the costs of processing soup, which requires the cooking and filling processes. Materials are entered from the cooking process at the beginning of the filling process. The inventory of Work in Process—Filling on Apirl 1 and debits to the account during April 2014 were as follows:

Bal., 800 units, 30% completed:	
Direct materials (800 × $4.30)	$ 3,440
Conversion (800 × 30% × $1.75)	420
	$ 3,860
From Cooking Department, 7,800 units	$34,320
Direct labor	8,562
Factory overhead	6,387

During April, 800 units in process on April 1 were completed, and of the 7,800 units entering the department, all were completed except 550 units that were 90% completed.

Charges to Work in Process—Filling for May were as follows:

From Cooking Department, 9,600 units	$44,160
Direct labor	12,042
Factory overhead	6,878

During May, the units in process at the beginning of the month were completed, and of the 9,600 units entering the department, all were completed except 300 units that were 35% completed.

Instructions

1. Enter the balance as of April 1, 2014, in a four-column account for Work in Process—Filling. Record the debits and the credits in the account for April. Construct a cost of production report, and present computations for determining (a) equivalent units of production for materials and conversion, (b) costs per equivalent unit, (c) cost of goods finished, differentiating between units started in the prior period and units started and finished in April, and (d) work in process inventory.
2. Provide the same information for May by recording the May transactions in the four-column work in process account. Construct a cost of production report, and present the May computations (a through d) listed in part (1).
3. Comment on the change in costs per equivalent unit for March through May for direct materials and conversion costs.

Appendix

PR 18-5A Cost of production report: average cost method

✔ Cost per equivalent unit, $2.70

SPREADSHEET

Sunrise Coffee Company roasts and packs coffee beans. The process begins in the Roasting Department. From the Roasting Department, the coffee beans are transferred to the Packing Department. The following is a partial work in process account of the Roasting Department at December 31, 2014:

ACCOUNT *Work in Process—Roasting Department* ACCOUNT NO.

Date		Item	Debit	Credit	Balance Debit	Balance Credit
Dec.	1	Bal., 10,500 units, 75% completed			21,000	
	31	Direct materials, 210,400 units	246,800		267,800	
	31	Direct labor	135,700		403,500	
	31	Factory overhead	168,630		572,130	
	31	Goods transferred, 208,900 units		?	?	
	31	Bal., ? units, 25% completed			?	

Instructions

Prepare a cost of production report, using the average cost method, and identify the missing amounts for Work in Process—Roasting Department.

Problems Series B

PR 18-1B Entries for process cost system

OBJ. 1, 3

✔ **2. Materials July 31 balance, $11,390**

GENERAL LEDGER

Preston & Grover Soap Company manufactures powdered detergent. Phosphate is placed in process in the Making Department, where it is turned into granulars. The output of Making is transferred to the Packing Department, where packaging is added at the beginning of the process. On July 1, Preston & Grover Soap Company had the following inventories:

Finished Goods	$13,500
Work in Process—Making	6,790
Work in Process—Packing	7,350
Materials	5,100

Departmental accounts are maintained for factory overhead, which both have zero balances on July 1.

Manufacturing operations for July are summarized as follows:

a. Materials purchased on account	$149,800
b. Materials requisitioned for use:	
Phosphate—Making Department	$105,700
Packaging—Packing Department	31,300
Indirect materials—Making Department	4,980
Indirect materials—Packing Department	1,530
c. Labor used:	
Direct labor—Making Department	$ 32,400
Direct labor—Packing Department	40,900
Indirect labor—Making Department	15,400
Indirect labor—Packing Department	18,300
d. Depreciation charged on fixed assets:	
Making Department	$ 10,700
Packing Department	7,900
e. Expired prepaid factory insurance:	
Making Department	$ 2,000
Packing Department	1,500
f. Applied factory overhead:	
Making Department	$ 32,570
Packing Department	30,050
g. Production costs transferred from Making Department to Packing Department	$166,790
h. Production costs transferred from Packing Department to Finished Goods	$263,400
i. Cost of goods sold during the period	$265,200

Instructions

1. Journalize the entries to record the operations, identifying each entry by letter.
2. Compute the July 31 balances of the inventory accounts.
3. Compute the July 31 balances of the factory overhead accounts.

PR 18-2B Cost of production report

OBJ. 2, 4

✔ **1. Conversion cost per equivalent unit, $6.00**

SPREADSHEET

Bavarian Chocolate Company processes chocolate into candy bars. The process begins by placing direct materials (raw chocolate, milk, and sugar) into the Blending Department. All materials are placed into production at the beginning of the blending process. After blending, the milk chocolate is then transferred to the Molding Department, where the milk chocolate is formed into candy bars. The following is a partial work in process account of the Blending Department at October 31, 2014:

(Continued)

ACCOUNT *Work in Process—Blending Department*					ACCOUNT NO.	
					Balance	
Date		Item	Debit	Credit	Debit	Credit
Oct.	1	Bal., 2,300 units, 3/5 completed			46,368	
	31	Direct materials, 26,000 units	429,000		475,368	
	31	Direct labor	100,560		575,928	
	31	Factory overhead	48,480		624,408	
	31	Goods transferred, 25,700 units		?		
	31	Bal., ? units, 1/5 completed			?	

Instructions

1. Prepare a cost of production report, and identify the missing amounts for Work in Process—Blending Department.
2. Assuming that the October 1 work in process inventory includes direct materials of $38,295, determine the increase or decrease in the cost per equivalent unit for direct materials and conversion between September and October.

PR 18-3B Equivalent units and related costs; cost of production report; entries **OBJ. 2, 3, 4**

✔ 2. Transferred to finished goods, $705,376

SPREADSHEET

Dover Chemical Company manufactures specialty chemicals by a series of three processes, all materials being introduced in the Distilling Department. From the Distilling Department, the materials pass through the Reaction and Filling departments, emerging as finished chemicals.

The balance in the account Work in Process—Filling was as follows on January 1, 2014:

Work in Process—Filling Department	
(3,400 units, 60% completed):	
Direct materials (3,400 × $9.58)	$32,572
Conversion (3,400 × 60% × $3.90)	7,956
	$40,528

The following costs were charged to Work in Process—Filling during January.

Direct materials transferred from Reaction	
Department: 52,300 units at $9.50 a unit	$496,850
Direct labor	101,560
Factory overhead	95,166

During January, 53,000 units of specialty chemicals were completed. Work in Process—Filling Department on January 31 was 2,700 units, 30% completed.

Instructions

1. Prepare a cost of production report for the Filling Department for January.
2. Journalize the entries for costs transferred from Reaction to Filling and the costs transferred from Filling to Finished Goods.
3. Determine the increase or decrease in the cost per equivalent unit from December to January for direct materials and conversion costs.
4. Discuss the uses of the cost of production report and the results of part (3).

PR 18-4B Work in process account data for two months; cost of production reports **OBJ. 1, 2, 3, 4**

✔ 1. d. Transferred to finished goods in September, $702,195

Pittsburgh Aluminum Company uses a process cost system to record the costs of manufacturing rolled aluminum, which consists of the smelting and rolling processes. Materials

SPREADSHEET

are entered from smelting at the beginning of the rolling process. The inventory of Work in Process—Rolling on September 1, 2014, and debits to the account during September were as follows:

Bal., 2,600 units, ¼ completed:	
Direct materials (2,600 × $15.50)	$40,300
Conversion (2,600 × ¼ × $8.50)	5,525
	$45,825
From Smelting Department, 28,900 units	462,400
Direct labor	158,920
Factory overhead	101,402

During September, 2,600 units in process on September 1 were completed, and of the 28,900 units entering the department, all were completed except 2,900 units that were ⅘ completed.

Charges to Work in Process—Rolling for October were as follows:

From Smelting Department, 31,000 units	$511,500
Direct labor	162,850
Factory overhead	104,494

During October, the units in process at the beginning of the month were completed, and of the 31,000 units entering the department, all were completed except 2,000 units that were ⅖ completed.

Instructions

1. Enter the balance as of September 1, 2014, in a four-column account for Work in Process—Rolling. Record the debits and the credits in the account for September. Construct a cost of production report and present computations for determining (a) equivalent units of production for materials and conversion, (b) costs per equivalent unit, (c) cost of goods finished, differentiating between units started in the prior period and units started and finished in September, and (d) work in process inventory.
2. Provide the same information for October by recording the October transactions in the four-column work in process account. Construct a cost of production report, and present the October computations (a through d) listed in part (1).
3. Comment on the change in costs per equivalent unit for August through October for direct materials and conversion cost.

Appendix

PR 18-5B Cost of production report: average cost method

✔ Transferred to Packaging Dept., $54,000

SPREADSHEET

Blue Ribbon Flour Company manufactures flour by a series of three processes, beginning in the Milling Department. From the Milling Department, the materials pass through the Sifting and Packaging departments, emerging as packaged refined flour.

The balance in the account Work in Process—Sifting Department was as follows on May 1, 2014:

Work in Process—Sifting Department (1,500 units, 75% completed)	$3,400

The following costs were charged to Work in Process—Sifting Department during May:

Direct materials transferred from Milling Department: 18,300 units	$32,600
Direct labor	14,560
Factory overhead	7,490

During May, 18,000 units of flour were completed and transferred to finished goods. Work in Process—Sifting Department on May 31 was 1,800 units, 75% completed.

Instructions

Prepare a cost of production report for the Sifting Department for May, using the average cost method.

Cases & Projects

CP 18-1 Ethics and professional conduct in business

Assume you are the division controller for Auntie M's Cookie Company. Auntie M has introduced a new chocolate chip cookie called Full of Chips, and it is a success. As a result, the product manager responsible for the launch of this new cookie was promoted to division vice president and became your boss. A new product manager, Bishop, has been brought in to replace the promoted manager. Bishop notices that the Full of Chips cookie uses a lot of chips, which increases the cost of the cookie. As a result, Bishop has ordered that the amount of chips used in the cookies be reduced by 10%. The manager believes that a 10% reduction in chips will not adversely affect sales, but will reduce costs, and hence improve margins. The increased margins would help Bishop meet profit targets for the period.

You are looking over some cost of production reports segmented by cookie line. You notice that there is a drop in the materials costs for Full of Chips. On further investigation, you discover why the chip costs have declined (fewer chips). Both you and Bishop report to the division vice president, who was the original product manager for Full of Chips. You are trying to decide what to do, if anything.

Discuss the options you might consider.

CP 18-2 Accounting for materials costs

In papermaking operations for companies such as International Paper Company, wet pulp is fed into paper machines, which press and dry pulp into a continuous sheet of paper. The paper is formed at very high speeds (60 mph). Once the paper is formed, the paper is rolled onto a reel at the back end of the paper machine. One of the characteristics of papermaking is the creation of "broke" paper. Broke is paper that fails to satisfy quality standards and is therefore rejected for final shipment to customers. Broke is recycled back to the beginning of the process by combining the recycled paper with virgin (new) pulp material. The combination of virgin pulp and recycled broke is sent to the paper machine for papermaking. Broke is fed into this recycle process continuously from all over the facility.

In this industry, it is typical to charge the papermaking operation with the cost of direct materials, which is a mixture of virgin materials and broke. Broke has a much lower cost than does virgin pulp. Therefore, the more broke in the mixture, the lower the average cost of direct materials to the department. Papermaking managers will frequently comment on the importance of broke for keeping their direct materials costs down.

a. How do you react to this accounting procedure?

b. What "hidden costs" are not considered when accounting for broke as described above?

CP 18-3 Analyzing unit costs

Midstate Containers Inc. manufactures cans for the canned food industry. The operations manager of a can manufacturing operation wants to conduct a cost study investigating the relationship of tin content in the material (can stock) to the energy cost for enameling the cans. The enameling was necessary to prepare the cans for labeling. A higher percentage of tin content in the can stock increases the cost of material. The operations manager believed that a higher tin content in the can stock would reduce the amount of energy used in enameling. During the analysis period, the amount of tin content in the steel can stock was increased for every month, from April to September. The following operating reports were available from the controller:

	A	B	C	D	E	F	G
1		April	May	June	July	August	September
2	Energy	$ 14,000	$ 34,800	$ 33,000	$ 21,700	$ 28,800	$ 33,000
3	Materials	13,000	28,800	24,200	14,000	17,100	16,000
4	Total cost	$ 27,000	$ 63,600	$ 57,200	$ 35,700	$ 45,900	$ 49,000
5	Units produced	÷50,000	÷120,000	÷110,000	÷ 70,000	÷ 90,000	÷100,000
6	Cost per unit	$ 0.54	$ 0.53	$ 0.52	$ 0.51	$ 0.51	$ 0.49
7							

Differences in materials unit costs were entirely related to the amount of tin content.

Interpret this information and report to the operations manager your recommendations with respect to tin content.

CP 18-4 Decision making

Jamarcus Bradshaw, plant manager of Georgia Paper Company's papermaking mill, was looking over the cost of production reports for July and August for the Papermaking Department. The reports revealed the following:

	July	August
Pulp and chemicals	$295,600	$304,100
Conversion cost	146,000	149,600
Total cost	$441,600	$453,700
Number of tons	÷ 1,200	÷ 1,130
Cost per ton	$ 368	$ 401.50

Jamarcus was concerned about the increased cost per ton from the output of the department. As a result, he asked the plant controller to perform a study to help explain these results. The controller, Leann Brunswick, began the analysis by performing some interviews of key plant personnel in order to understand what the problem might be. Excerpts from an interview with Len Tyson, a paper machine operator, follow:

Len: We have two papermaking machines in the department. I have no data, but I think paper machine No. 1 is applying too much pulp, and thus is wasting both conversion and materials resources. We haven't had repairs on paper machine No. 1 in a while. Maybe this is the problem.

Leann: How does too much pulp result in wasted resources?

Len: Well, you see, if too much pulp is applied, then we will waste pulp material. The customer will not pay for the extra weight. Thus, we just lose that amount of material. Also, when there is too much pulp, the machine must be slowed down in order to complete the drying process. This results in a waste of conversion costs.

Leann: Do you have any other suspicions?

Len: Well, as you know, we have two products—green paper and yellow paper. They are identical except for the color. The color is added to the papermaking process in the paper machine. I think that during August these two color papers have been behaving very differently. I don't have any data, but it just seems as though the amount of waste associated with the green paper has increased.

Leann: Why is this?

Len: I understand that there has been a change in specifications for the green paper, starting near the beginning of August. This change could be causing the machines to run poorly when making green paper. If this is the case, the cost per ton would increase for green paper.

Leann also asked for a database printout providing greater detail on August's operating results.

September 9 Requested by: Leann Brunswick

Papermaking Department—August detail

	A	B	C	D	E	F
1	Production					
2	Run	Paper		Material	Conversion	
3	Number	Machine	Color	Costs	Costs	Tons
4	1	1	Green	40,300	18,300	150
5	2	1	Yellow	41,700	21,200	140
6	3	1	Green	44,600	22,500	150
7	4	1	Yellow	36,100	18,100	120
8	5	2	Green	38,300	18,900	160
9	6	2	Yellow	33,900	15,200	140
10	7	2	Green	35,600	18,400	130
11	8	2	Yellow	33,600	17,000	140
12		Total		304,100	149,600	1,130
13						

Assuming that you're Leann Brunswick, write a memo to Jamarcus Bradshaw with a recommendation to management. You should analyze the August data to determine whether the paper machine or the paper color explains the increase in the unit cost from July. Include any supporting schedules that are appropriate.

Learning Objectives

After studying this chapter, you should be able to: *Example Exercises*

At a Glance 19 Page 909

OBJ 1 Classify costs as variable costs, fixed costs, or mixed costs.

Cost Behavior

Cost behavior is the manner in which a cost changes as a related activity changes. The behavior of costs is useful to managers for a variety of reasons. For example, knowing how costs behave allows managers to predict profits as sales and production volumes change. Knowing how costs behave is also useful for estimating costs, which affects a variety of decisions such as whether to replace a machine.

Understanding the behavior of a cost depends on:

1. Identifying the activities that cause the cost to change. These activities are called **activity bases** (or *activity drivers*).
2. Specifying the range of activity over which the changes in the cost are of interest. This range of activity is called the **relevant range**.

To illustrate, assume that a hospital is concerned about planning and controlling patient food costs. A good activity base is the number of patients who *stay* overnight in the hospital. The number of patients who are *treated* is not as good an activity base since some patients are outpatients and, thus, do not consume food. Once an activity base is identified, food costs can then be analyzed over the range of the number of patients who normally stay in the hospital (the relevant range).

Costs are normally classified as variable costs, fixed costs, or mixed costs.

Variable Costs

Variable costs are costs that vary in proportion to changes in the activity base. When the activity base is units produced, direct materials and direct labor costs are normally classified as variable costs.

To illustrate, assume that Jason Sound Inc. produces stereo systems. The parts for the stereo systems are purchased from suppliers for $10 per unit and are assembled by Jason Sound Inc. For Model JS-12, the direct materials costs for the relevant range of 5,000 to 30,000 units of production are shown below.

Number of Units of Model JS-12 Produced	Direct Materials Cost per Unit	Total Direct Materials Cost
5,000 units	$10	$ 50,000
10,000	10	100,000
15,000	10	150,000
20,000	10	200,000
25,000	10	250,000
30,000	10	300,000

As shown above, variable costs have the following characteristics:

1. *Cost per unit* remains the same regardless of changes in the activity base. For Jason Sound Inc., units produced is the activity base. For Model JS-12, the cost per unit is $10.
2. *Total cost* changes in proportion to changes in the activity base. For Model JS-12, the direct materials cost for 10,000 units ($100,000) is twice the direct materials cost for 5,000 units ($50,000).

Exhibit 1 illustrates how the variable costs for direct materials for Model JS-12 behave in total and on a per-unit basis as production changes.

EXHIBIT 1 **Variable Cost Graphs**

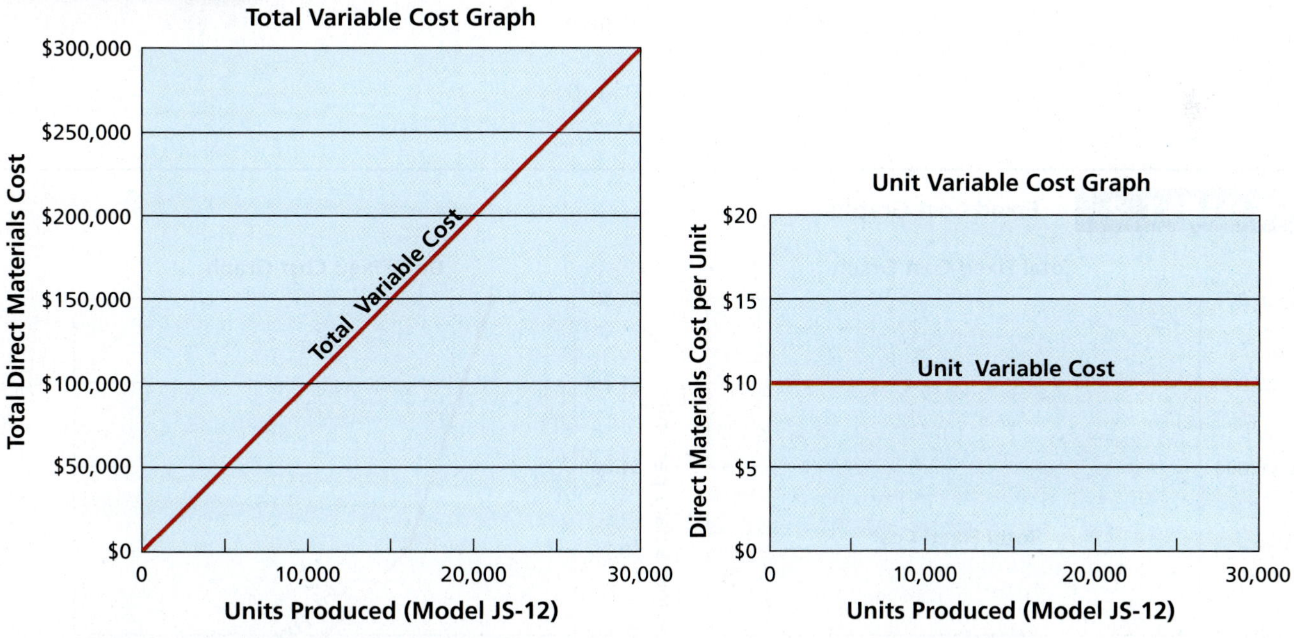

Some examples of variable costs and their related activity bases for various types of businesses are shown below.

Type of Business	Cost	Activity Base
University	Instructor salaries	Number of classes
Passenger airline	Fuel	Number of miles flown
Manufacturing	Direct materials	Number of units produced
Hospital	Nurse wages	Number of patients
Hotel	Maid wages	Number of guests
Bank	Teller wages	Number of banking transactions

Fixed Costs

Fixed costs are costs that remain the same in total dollar amount as the activity base changes. When the activity base is units produced, many factory overhead costs such as straight-line depreciation are classified as fixed costs.

To illustrate, assume that Minton Inc. manufactures, bottles, and distributes perfume. The production supervisor is Jane Sovissi, who is paid a salary of $75,000 per year. For the relevant range of 50,000 to 300,000 bottles of perfume, the total fixed cost of $75,000 does not vary as production increases. As a result, the fixed cost per bottle decreases as the units produced increase. This is because the fixed cost is spread over a larger number of bottles, as shown below.

Number of Bottles of Perfume Produced	Total Salary for Jane Sovissi	Salary per Bottle of Perfume Produced
50,000 bottles	$75,000	$1.500
100,000	75,000	0.750
150,000	75,000	0.500
200,000	75,000	0.375
250,000	75,000	0.300
300,000	75,000	0.250

As shown above, fixed costs have the following characteristics:

1. *Cost per unit* decreases as the activity level increases, and increases as the activity level decreases. For Jane Sovissi's salary, the cost per unit decreased from $1.50 for 50,000 bottles produced to $0.25 for 300,000 bottles produced.
2. *Total cost* remains the same regardless of changes in the activity base. Jane Sovissi's salary of $75,000 remained the same regardless of whether 50,000 bottles or 300,000 bottles were produced.

Exhibit 2 illustrates how Jane Sovissi's salary (fixed cost) behaves in total and on a per-unit basis as production changes.

EXHIBIT 2 **Fixed Cost Graphs**

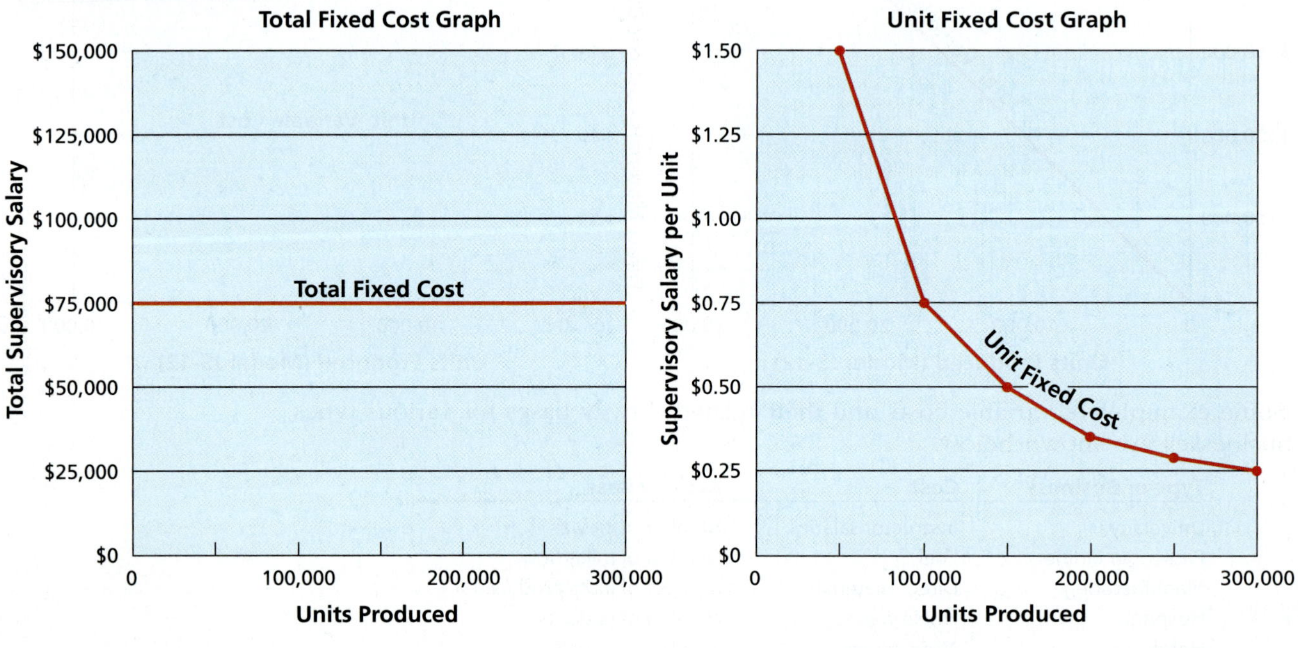

Some examples of fixed costs and their related activity bases for various types of businesses are shown below.

Type of Business	Fixed Cost	Activity Base
University	Building (straight-line) depreciation	Number of students
Passenger airline	Airplane (straight-line) depreciation	Number of miles flown
Manufacturing	Plant manager salary	Number of units produced
Hospital	Property insurance	Number of patients
Hotel	Property taxes	Number of guests
Bank	Branch manager salary	Number of customer accounts

Mixed Costs

A salesperson's compensation can be a mixed cost comprised of a salary (fixed portion) plus a commission as a percent of sales (variable portion).

Mixed costs are costs that have characteristics of both a variable and a fixed cost. Mixed costs are sometimes called *semivariable* or *semifixed* costs.

To illustrate, assume that Simpson Inc. manufactures sails, using rented machinery. The rental charges are as follows:

Rental Charge = $15,000 per year + $1 for each hour used in excess of 10,000 hours

The rental charges for various hours used within the relevant range of 8,000 hours to 40,000 hours are as follows:

Hours Used	Rental Charge
8,000 hours	$15,000
12,000	$17,000 {$15,000 + [(12,000 hrs. – 10,000 hrs.) × $1]}
20,000	$25,000 {$15,000 + [(20,000 hrs. – 10,000 hrs.) × $1]}
40,000	$45,000 {$15,000 + [(40,000 hrs. – 10,000 hrs.) × $1]}

Exhibit 3 illustrates the preceding mixed cost behavior.

EXHIBIT 3

Mixed Costs

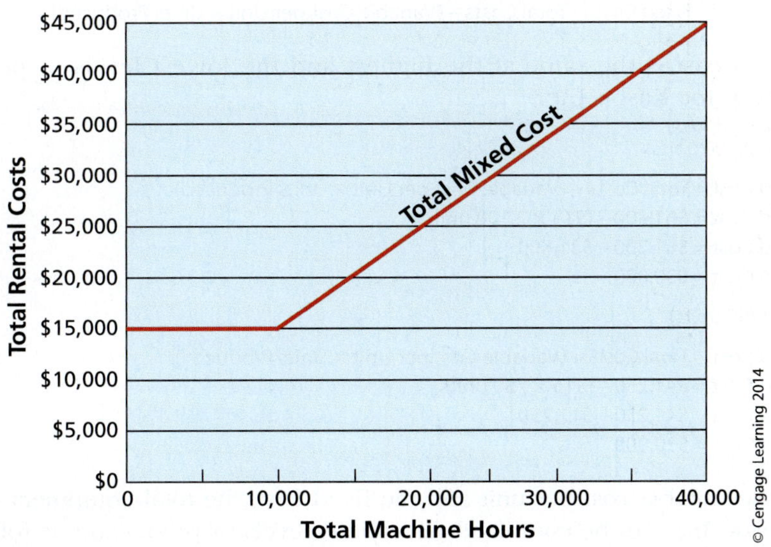

For purposes of analysis, mixed costs are usually separated into their fixed and variable components. The **high-low method** is a cost estimation method that may be used for this purpose.[1] The high-low method uses the highest and lowest activity levels and their related costs to estimate the variable cost per unit and the fixed cost.

1 Other methods of estimating costs, such as the scattergraph method and the least squares method, are discussed in cost accounting textbooks.

To illustrate, assume that the Equipment Maintenance Department of Kason Inc. incurred the following costs during the past five months:

	Units Produced	Total Cost
June	1,000 units	$45,550
July	1,500	52,000
August	2,100	61,500
September	1,800	57,500
October	750	41,250

The number of units produced is the activity base, and the relevant range is the units produced between June and October. For Kason Inc., the difference between the units produced and the total costs at the highest and lowest levels of production are as follows:

	Units Produced	Total Cost
Highest level	2,100 units	$61,500
Lowest level	750	41,250
Difference	1,350 units	$20,250

The total fixed cost does not change with changes in production. Thus, the $20,250 difference in the total cost is the change in the total variable cost. Dividing this difference of $20,250 by the difference in production is an estimate of the variable cost per unit. For Kason Inc., this estimate is $15, as computed below.

$$\text{Variable Cost per Unit} = \frac{\text{Difference in Total Cost}}{\text{Difference in Units Produced}}$$

$$\text{Variable Cost per Unit} = \frac{\$20{,}250}{1{,}350 \text{ units}} = \$15 \text{ per unit}$$

The fixed cost is estimated by subtracting the total variable costs from the total costs for the units produced, as shown below.

Fixed Cost = Total Costs – (Variable Cost per Unit × Units Produced)

The fixed cost is the same at the highest and the lowest levels of production, as shown below for Kason Inc.

Highest level (2,100 units)

Fixed Cost = Total Costs – (Variable Cost per Unit × Units Produced)
Fixed Cost = $61,500 – ($15 × 2,100 units)
Fixed Cost = $61,500 – $31,500
Fixed Cost = $30,000

Lowest level (750 units)

Fixed Cost = Total Costs – (Variable Cost per Unit × Units Produced)
Fixed Cost = $41,250 – ($15 × 750 units)
Fixed Cost = $41,250 – $11,250
Fixed Cost = $30,000

Using the variable cost per unit and the fixed cost, the total equipment maintenance cost for Kason Inc. can be computed for various levels of production as follows:

Total Cost = (Variable Cost per Unit × Units Produced) + Fixed Costs
Total Cost = ($15 × Units Produced) + $30,000

To illustrate, the estimated total cost of 2,000 units of production is $60,000, as computed below.

Total Cost = ($15 × Units Produced) + $30,000
Total Cost = ($15 × 2,000 units) + $30,000 = $30,000 + $30,000
Total Cost = $60,000

Example Exercise 19-1 High-Low Method

OBJ 1

The manufacturing costs of Alex Industries for the first three months of the year are provided below.

	Total Cost	Production
January	$ 80,000	1,000 units
February	125,000	2,500
March	100,000	1,800

Using the high-low method, determine (a) the variable cost per unit and (b) the total fixed cost.

Follow My Example 19-1

a. $30 per unit = ($125,000 – $80,000)/(2,500 – 1,000)
b. $50,000 = $125,000 – ($30 × 2,500), or $80,000 – ($30 × 1,000)

Practice Exercises: **PE 19-1A, PE 19-1B**

Summary of Cost Behavior Concepts

The cost behavior of variable costs and fixed costs is summarized below.

	Effect of Changing Activity Level	
Cost	**Total Amount**	**Per-Unit Amount**
Variable	Increases and decreases proportionately with activity level.	Remains the same regardless of activity level.
Fixed	Remains the same regardless of activity level.	Increases and decreases inversely with activity level.

Mixed costs contain a fixed cost component that is incurred even if nothing is produced. For analysis, the fixed and variable cost components of mixed costs are separated using the high-low method.

Some examples of variable, fixed, and mixed costs for the activity base of *units produced* are as follows:

Variable Costs	Fixed Costs	Mixed Costs
Direct materials	Straight-line depreciation	Quality Control Department salaries
Direct labor	Property taxes	Purchasing Department salaries
Electricity expense	Production supervisor salaries	Maintenance expenses
Supplies	Insurance expense	Warehouse expenses

One method of reporting variable and fixed costs is called **variable costing** or *direct costing*. Under variable costing, only the variable manufacturing costs (direct materials, direct labor, and variable factory overhead) are included in the product cost. The fixed factory overhead is treated as an expense of the period in which it is incurred. Variable costing is described and illustrated in the appendix to this chapter.

Business Connection

FRANCHISING

Many restaurant chains such as McDonald's, Wendy's, Dunkin' Donuts, and Fatburger operate as franchises. In a franchise, the restaurant chain (called the franchisor) sells the right to sell products using its trademark or brand name to a franchisee. The franchisee typically pays an initial franchise fee, which is a fixed cost. In addition, the franchisee must normally make royalty payments to the franchisor based on a percentage of sales revenues, which is a variable cost. Prior to signing a franchise agreement, most franchisees conduct a break-even analysis to determine how much sales volume their franchise must generate to earn a profit. For example, McDonald's franchises require an initial investment of over $500,000 and typically take several years to break even.

Source: B. Beshel, *An Introduction to Franchising*, IFA Educational Foundation, 2000.

OBJ 2 Compute the contribution margin, the contribution margin ratio, and the unit contribution margin.

Cost-Volume-Profit Relationships

Cost-volume-profit analysis is the examination of the relationships among selling prices, sales and production volume, costs, expenses, and profits. Cost-volume-profit analysis is useful for managerial decision making. Some of the ways cost-volume-profit analysis may be used include:

1. Analyzing the effects of changes in selling prices on profits
2. Analyzing the effects of changes in costs on profits
3. Analyzing the effects of changes in volume on profits
4. Setting selling prices
5. Selecting the mix of products to sell
6. Choosing among marketing strategies

Contribution Margin

Contribution margin is especially useful because it provides insight into the profit potential of a company. **Contribution margin** is the excess of sales over variable costs, as shown below.

$$\text{Contribution Margin} = \text{Sales} - \text{Variable Costs}$$

To illustrate, assume the following data for Lambert Inc.:

Sales	50,000 units
Sales price per unit	$20 per unit
Variable cost per unit	$12 per unit
Fixed costs	$300,000

Exhibit 4 illustrates an income statement for Lambert Inc. prepared in a contribution margin format.

EXHIBIT 4

Contribution Margin Income Statement

Sales (50,000 units × $20)	$1,000,000
Variable costs (50,000 units × $12)	600,000
Contribution margin (50,000 units × $8)	$ 400,000
Fixed costs	300,000
Income from operations	$ 100,000

Lambert's contribution margin of $400,000 is available to cover the fixed costs of $300,000. Once the fixed costs are covered, any additional contribution margin increases income from operations.

Contribution Margin Ratio

Contribution margin can also be expressed as a percentage. The **contribution margin ratio**, sometimes called the *profit-volume ratio*, indicates the percentage of each sales dollar available to cover fixed costs and to provide income from operations. The contribution margin ratio is computed as follows:

$$\text{Contribution Margin Ratio} = \frac{\text{Contribution Margin}}{\text{Sales}}$$

The contribution margin ratio is 40% for Lambert Inc., computed as follows:

$$\text{Contribution Margin Ratio} = \frac{\$400,000}{\$1,000,000} = 40\%$$

The contribution margin ratio is most useful when the increase or decrease in sales volume is measured in sales *dollars*. In this case, the change in sales dollars multiplied by the contribution margin ratio equals the change in income from operations, as shown below.

Change in Income from Operations = Change in Sales Dollars × Contribution Margin Ratio

To illustrate, if Lambert Inc. adds $80,000 in sales from the sale of an additional 4,000 units, its income from operations will increase by $32,000, as computed below.

Change in Income from Operations = Change in Sales Dollars × Contribution Margin Ratio
Change in Income from Operations = $80,000 × 40% = $32,000

The preceding analysis is confirmed by the following contribution margin income statement of Lambert Inc.:

Sales (54,000 units × $20)	$1,080,000
Variable costs (54,000 units × $12)	648,000*
Contribution margin (54,000 units × $8)	$ 432,000**
Fixed costs	300,000
Income from operations	$ 132,000

*$1,080,000 × 60%
**$1,080,000 × 40%

Income from operations increased from $100,000 to $132,000 when sales increased from $1,000,000 to $1,080,000. Variable costs as a percentage of sales are equal to 100% minus the contribution margin ratio. Thus, in the above income statement, the variable costs are 60% (100% – 40%) of sales, or $648,000 ($1,080,000 × 60%). The total contribution margin, $432,000, can also be computed directly by multiplying the total sales by the contribution margin ratio ($1,080,000 × 40%).

In the preceding analysis, factors other than sales volume, such as variable cost per unit and sales price, are assumed to remain constant. If such factors change, their effect must also be considered.

The contribution margin ratio is also useful in developing business strategies. For example, assume that a company has a high contribution margin ratio and is producing below 100% of capacity. In this case, a large increase in income from operations can be expected from an increase in sales volume. Therefore, the company might consider implementing a special sales campaign to increase sales. In contrast, a company with a small contribution margin ratio will probably want to give more attention to reducing costs before attempting to promote sales.

Unit Contribution Margin

The unit contribution margin is also useful for analyzing the profit potential of proposed decisions. The **unit contribution margin** is computed as follows:

Unit Contribution Margin = Sales Price per Unit – Variable Cost per Unit

To illustrate, if Lambert Inc.'s unit selling price is $20 and its variable cost per unit is $12, the unit contribution margin is $8, as shown below.

Unit Contribution Margin = Sales Price per Unit – Variable Cost per Unit
Unit Contribution Margin = $20 – $12 = $8

The unit contribution margin is most useful when the increase or decrease in sales volume is measured in sales *units* (quantities). In this case, the change in sales volume (units) multiplied by the unit contribution margin equals the change in income from operations, as shown below.

Change in Income from Operations = Change in Sales Units × Unit Contribution Margin

To illustrate, assume that Lambert Inc.'s sales could be increased by 15,000 units, from 50,000 units to 65,000 units. Lambert's income from operations would increase by $120,000 (15,000 units × $8), as shown below.

Change in Income from Operations = Change in Sales Units × Unit Contribution Margin
Change in Income from Operations = 15,000 units × $8 = $120,000

The preceding analysis is confirmed by the following contribution margin income statement of Lambert Inc., which shows that income increased to $220,000 when 65,000 units are sold. The prior income statement on page 890 indicates income of $100,000 when 50,000 units are sold. Thus, selling an additional 15,000 units increases income by $120,000 ($220,000 – $100,000).

A room night at Hilton Hotels has a high contribution margin. The high contribution margin per room night is necessary to cover the high fixed costs of the hotel.

Sales (65,000 units × $20)	$1,300,000
Variable costs (65,000 units × $12)	780,000
Contribution margin (65,000 units × $8)	$ 520,000
Fixed costs	300,000
Income from operations	$ 220,000

Unit contribution margin analysis is useful information for managers. For example, in the preceding illustration, Lambert Inc. could spend up to $120,000 for special advertising or other product promotions to increase sales by 15,000 units and still increase income by $100,000, the $220,000 increase in sales minus the $120,000 cost of special advertising.

Example Exercise 19-2 Contribution Margin

OBJ 2

Molly Company sells 20,000 units at $12 per unit. Variable costs are $9 per unit, and fixed costs are $25,000. Determine the (a) contribution margin ratio, (b) unit contribution margin, and (c) income from operations.

Follow My Example 19-2

a. 25% = ($12 – $9)/$12, or ($240,000 – $180,000)/$240,000
b. $3 per unit = $12 – $9
c.

Sales	$240,000	(20,000 units × $12 per unit)
Variable costs	180,000	(20,000 units × $9 per unit)
Contribution margin	$ 60,000	[20,000 units × ($12 – $9)]
Fixed costs	25,000	
Income from operations	$ 35,000	

Practice Exercises: **PE 19-2A, PE 19-2B**

OBJ 3 Determine the break-even point and sales necessary to achieve a target profit.

Mathematical Approach to Cost-Volume-Profit Analysis

The mathematical approach to cost-volume-profit analysis uses equations to determine the following:

1. Sales necessary to break even
2. Sales necessary to make a target or desired profit

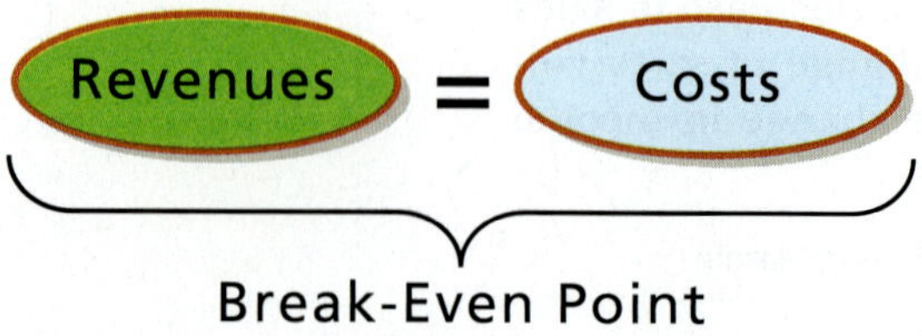

Break-Even Point

The **break-even point** is the level of operations at which a company's revenues and expenses are equal. At break-even, a company reports neither an income nor a loss from operations. The break-even point in *sales units* is computed as follows:

$$\text{Break-Even Sales (units)} = \frac{\text{Fixed Costs}}{\text{Unit Contribution Margin}}$$

To illustrate, assume the following data for Baker Corporation:

Fixed costs	$90,000
Unit selling price	$25
Unit variable cost	15
Unit contribution margin	$10

The break-even point is 9,000 units, as shown below.

$$\text{Break-Even Sales (units)} = \frac{\text{Fixed Costs}}{\text{Unit Contribution Margin}} = \frac{\$90{,}000}{\$10} = 9{,}000 \text{ units}$$

The following income statement verifies the break-even point of 9,000 units:

Sales (9,000 units × $25)	$225,000
Variable costs (9,000 units × $15)	135,000
Contribution margin	$ 90,000
Fixed costs	90,000
Income from operations	$ 0

As shown in the preceding income statement, the break-even point is $225,000 (9,000 units × $25) of sales. The break-even point in *sales dollars* can be determined directly as follows:

$$\text{Break-Even Sales (dollars)} = \frac{\text{Fixed Costs}}{\text{Contribution Margin Ratio}}$$

The contribution margin ratio can be computed using the unit contribution margin and unit selling price as follows:

$$\text{Contribution Margin Ratio} = \frac{\text{Unit Contribution Margin}}{\text{Unit Selling Price}}$$

The contribution margin ratio for Baker Corporation is 40%, as shown below.

$$\text{Contribution Margin Ratio} = \frac{\text{Unit Contribution Margin}}{\text{Unit Selling Price}} = \frac{\$10}{\$25} = 40\%$$

Thus, the break-even sales dollars for Baker Corporation of $225,000 can be computed directly as follows:

$$\text{Break-Even Sales (dollars)} = \frac{\text{Fixed Costs}}{\text{Contribution Margin Ratio}} = \frac{\$90{,}000}{40\%} = \$225{,}000$$

The break-even point is affected by changes in the fixed costs, unit variable costs, and the unit selling price.

Effect of Changes in Fixed Costs Fixed costs do not change in total with changes in the level of activity. However, fixed costs may change because of other factors such as advertising campaigns, changes in property tax rates, or changes in factory supervisors' salaries.

Changes in fixed costs affect the break-even point as follows:

1. Increases in fixed costs increase the break-even point.
2. Decreases in fixed costs decrease the break-even point.

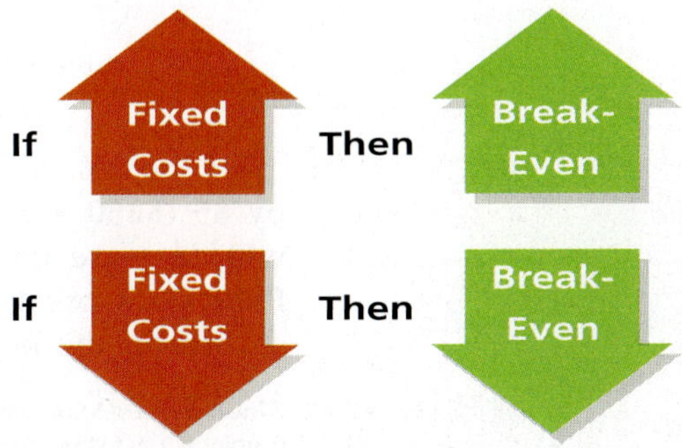

To illustrate, assume that Bishop Co. is evaluating a proposal to budget an additional $100,000 for advertising. The data for Bishop Co. are as follows:

	Current	Proposed
Unit selling price	$90	$90
Unit variable cost	70	70
Unit contribution margin	$20	$20
Fixed costs	$600,000	$700,000

Bishop Co.'s break-even point *before* the additional advertising expense of $100,000 is 30,000 units, as shown below.

$$\text{Break-Even Sales (units)} = \frac{\text{Fixed Costs}}{\text{Unit Contribution Margin}} = \frac{\$600{,}000}{\$20} = 30{,}000 \text{ units}$$

Bishop Co.'s break-even point *after* the additional advertising expense of $100,000 is 35,000 units, as shown below.

$$\text{Break-Even Sales (units)} = \frac{\text{Fixed Costs}}{\text{Unit Contribution Margin}} = \frac{\$700{,}000}{\$20} = 35{,}000 \text{ units}$$

As shown above, the $100,000 increase in advertising (fixed costs) requires an additional 5,000 units (35,000 – 30,000) of sales to break even.[2] In other words, an increase in sales of 5,000 units is required in order to generate an additional $100,000 of total contribution margin (5,000 units × $20) to cover the increased fixed costs.

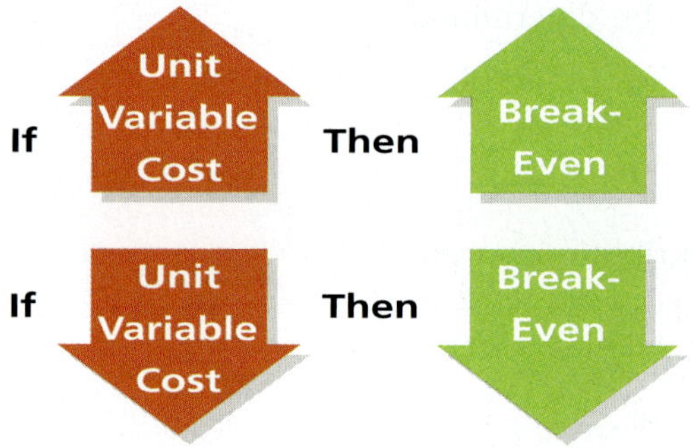

© Cengage Learning 2014

Effect of Changes in Unit Variable Costs Unit variable costs do not change with changes in the level of activity. However, unit variable costs may be affected by other factors such as changes in the cost per unit of direct materials, changes in the wage rate for direct labor, or changes in the sales commission paid to salespeople.

Changes in unit variable costs affect the break-even point as follows:

1. Increases in unit variable costs increase the break-even point.
2. Decreases in unit variable costs decrease the break-even point.

To illustrate, assume that Park Co. is evaluating a proposal to pay an additional 2% commission on sales to its salespeople as an incentive to increase sales. The data for Park Co. are as follows:

	Current	Proposed
Unit selling price	$250	$250
Unit variable cost	145	150*
Unit contribution margin	$105	$100
Fixed costs	$840,000	$840,000

*$150 = $145 + (2% × $250 unit selling price).

Park Co.'s break-even point *before* the additional 2% commission is 8,000 units, as shown below.

$$\text{Break-Even Sales (units)} = \frac{\text{Fixed Costs}}{\text{Unit Contribution Margin}} = \frac{\$840{,}000}{\$105} = 8{,}000 \text{ units}$$

If the 2% sales commission proposal is adopted, unit variable costs will increase by $5 ($250 × 2%), from $145 to $150 per unit. This increase in unit variable costs will decrease the unit contribution margin from $105 to $100 ($250 – $150). Thus, Park Co.'s break-even point *after* the additional 2% commission is 8,400 units, as shown on the next page.

2 The increase of 5,000 units can also be computed by dividing the increase in fixed costs of $100,000 by the unit contribution margin, $20, as follows: 5,000 units = $100,000/$20.

$$\text{Break-Even Sales (units)} = \frac{\text{Fixed Costs}}{\text{Unit Contribution Margin}} = \frac{\$840{,}000}{\$100} = 8{,}400 \text{ units}$$

As shown above, an additional 400 units of sales will be required in order to break even. This is because if 8,000 units are sold, the new unit contribution margin of $100 provides only $800,000 (8,000 units × $100) of contribution margin. Thus, $40,000 more contribution margin is necessary to cover the total fixed costs of $840,000. This additional $40,000 of contribution margin is provided by selling 400 more units (400 units × $100).

Effect of Changes in Unit Selling Price Changes in the unit selling price affect the unit contribution margin and, thus, the break-even point. Specifically, changes in the unit selling price affect the break-even point as follows:

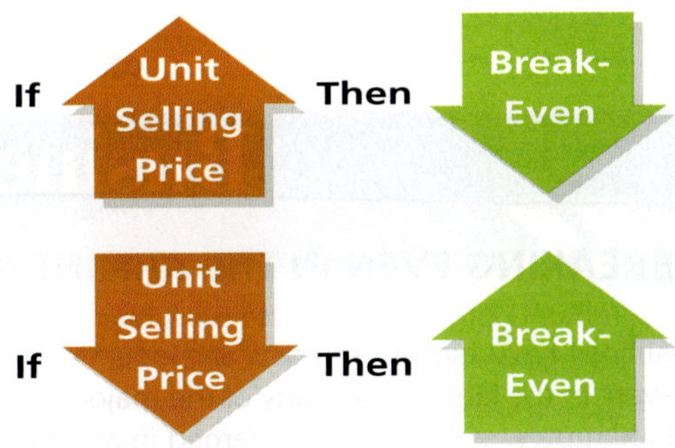

1. Increases in the unit selling price decrease the break-even point.
2. Decreases in the unit selling price increase the break-even point.

To illustrate, assume that Graham Co. is evaluating a proposal to increase the unit selling price of its product from $50 to $60. The data for Graham Co. are as follows:

	Current	Proposed
Unit selling price	$50	$60
Unit variable cost	30	30
Unit contribution margin	$20	$30
Fixed costs	$600,000	$600,000

Graham Co.'s break-even point *before* the price increase is 30,000 units, as shown below.

$$\text{Break-Even Sales (units)} = \frac{\text{Fixed Costs}}{\text{Unit Contribution Margin}} = \frac{\$600{,}000}{\$20} = 30{,}000 \text{ units}$$

The increase of $10 per unit in the selling price increases the unit contribution margin by $10. Thus, Graham Co.'s break-even point *after* the price increase is 20,000 units, as shown below.

$$\text{Break-Even Sales (units)} = \frac{\text{Fixed Costs}}{\text{Unit Contribution Margin}} = \frac{\$600{,}000}{\$30} = 20{,}000 \text{ units}$$

As shown above, the price increase of $10 increased the unit contribution margin by $10, which decreased the break-even point by 10,000 units (30,000 units – 20,000 units).

Summary of Effects of Changes on Break-Even Point The break-even point in sales changes in the same direction as changes in the variable cost per unit and fixed costs. In contrast, the break-even point in sales changes in the opposite direction as changes in the unit selling price. These changes on the break-even point in sales are summarized below.

Type of Change	Direction of Change	Effect of Change on Break-Even Sales
Fixed cost	Increase	Increase
	Decrease	Decrease
Unit variable cost	Increase	Increase
	Decrease	Decrease
Unit selling price	Increase	Decrease
	Decrease	Increase

Therefore, the current sales may decline $50,000, 2,000 units, or 20% before an operating loss occurs.

Example Exercise 19-7 Margin of Safety OBJ 5

Rachel Company has sales of $400,000, and the break-even point in sales dollars is $300,000. Determine the company's margin of safety as a percent of current sales.

Follow My Example 19-7

$$\text{Margin of Safety} = \frac{\text{Sales} - \text{Sales at Break-Even Point}}{\text{Sales}} = \frac{\$400{,}000 - \$300{,}000}{\$400{,}000} = \frac{\$100{,}000}{\$400{,}000} = 25\%$$

Practice Exercises: **PE 19-7A, PE 19-7B**

APPENDIX

Variable Costing

The cost of manufactured products consists of direct materials, direct labor, and factory overhead. The reporting of all these costs in financial statements is called **absorption costing**. Absorption costing is required under generally accepted accounting principles for financial statements distributed to external users. However, alternative reports may be prepared for decision-making purposes by managers and other internal users. One such alternative reporting is *variable costing* or *direct costing*.

In *variable costing*, the cost of goods manufactured is composed only of variable costs. Thus, the cost of goods manufactured consists of direct materials, direct labor, and *variable* factory overhead.

In a variable costing income statement, *fixed* factory overhead costs do not become a part of the cost of goods manufactured. Instead, fixed factory overhead costs are treated as a period expense.

Cost of Goods Manufactured

Absorption Costing	Variable Costing
Direct materials	Direct materials
Direct labor	Direct labor
Variable factory overhead	Variable factory overhead
Fixed factory overhead	

The form of a variable costing income statement is as follows:

Sales		$XXX
Variable cost of goods sold		XXX
Manufacturing margin		$XXX
Variable selling and administrative expenses		XXX
Contribution margin		$XXX
Fixed costs:		
Fixed manufacturing costs	$XXX	
Fixed selling and administrative expenses	XXX	XXX
Income from operations		$XXX

Manufacturing margin is sales less variable cost of goods sold. *Variable cost of goods sold* consists of direct materials, direct labor, and variable factory overhead for the units sold. *Contribution margin* is manufacturing margin less variable selling and administrative expenses. Subtracting fixed costs from contribution margin yields *income from operations*.

The variable costing income statement facilitates managerial decision making, since manufacturing margin and contribution margin are reported directly. As illustrated in this chapter, contribution margin is used in break-even analysis and other analyses.

To illustrate the variable costing income statement, assume that 15,000 units are manufactured and sold at a price of $50. The related costs and expenses are as follows:

	Total Cost	Number of Units	Unit Cost
Manufacturing costs:			
Variable	$375,000	15,000	$25
Fixed	150,000	15,000	10
Total	$525,000		$35
Selling and administrative expenses:			
Variable ($5 per unit sold)	$ 75,000		
Fixed	50,000		
Total	$125,000		

Exhibit 9 shows the variable costing income statement prepared from the above data. The computations are shown in parentheses.

EXHIBIT 9

Variable Costing Income Statement

Sales (15,000 × $50)		$750,000
Variable cost of goods sold (15,000 × $25)		375,000
Manufacturing margin		$375,000
Variable selling and administrative expenses (15,000 × $5)		75,000
Contribution margin		$300,000
Fixed costs:		
Fixed manufacturing costs	$150,000	
Fixed selling and administrative expenses	50,000	200,000
Income from operations		$100,000

Exhibit 10 illustrates the absorption costing income statement prepared from the same data. The absorption costing income statement does not distinguish between variable and fixed costs. All manufacturing costs are included in the cost of goods sold. Deducting the cost of goods sold from sales yields the *gross profit*. Deducting the selling and administrative expenses from gross profit yields the *income from operations*.

EXHIBIT 10

Absorption Costing Income Statement

Sales (15,000 × $50)	$750,000
Cost of goods sold (15,000 × $35)	525,000
Gross profit	$225,000
Selling and administrative expenses ($75,000 + $50,000)	125,000
Income from operations	$100,000

The relationship between variable and absorption costing *income from operations* is summarized on the next page.

In Exhibits 9 and 10, 15,000 units were manufactured and sold. Thus, the variable and absorption costing income statements reported the same income from operations of $100,000. However, assume that in the preceding example only 12,000 units of the 15,000 units manufactured were sold. Exhibit 11 shows the related variable and absorption costing income statements.

EXHIBIT 11

Units Manufactured Exceed Units Sold

Variable Costing Income Statement		
Sales (12,000 × $50)		$600,000
Variable cost of goods sold:		
Variable cost of goods manufactured (15,000 × $25)	$375,000	
Less ending inventory (3,000 × $25)	75,000	
Variable cost of goods sold		300,000
Manufacturing margin		$300,000
Variable selling and administrative expenses (12,000 × $5)		60,000
Contribution margin		$240,000
Fixed costs:		
Fixed manufacturing costs	$150,000	
Fixed selling and administrative expenses	50,000	200,000
Income from operations		$ 40,000
Absorption Costing Income Statement		
Sales (12,000 × $50)		$600,000
Cost of goods sold:		
Cost of goods manufactured (15,000 × $35)	$525,000	
Less ending inventory (3,000 × $35)	105,000	
Cost of goods sold		420,000
Gross profit		$180,000
Selling and administrative expenses [(12,000 × $5) + $50,000]		110,000
Income from operations		$ 70,000

Exhibit 11 shows a $30,000 ($70,000 – $40,000) difference in income from operations. This difference is due to the fixed manufacturing costs. All of the $150,000 of fixed manufacturing costs is included as a period expense in the variable costing statement. However, the 3,000 units of ending inventory in the absorption costing statement include $30,000 (3,000 units × $10) of fixed manufacturing costs. By being included in inventory, this $30,000 is thus excluded from the current cost of goods sold. Thus, the absorption costing income from operations is $30,000 higher than the income from operations for variable costing.

A similar analysis could be used to illustrate that income from operations under variable costing is greater than income from operations under absorption costing when the units manufactured are less than the units sold.

Under absorption costing, increases or decreases in income from operations can result from changes in inventory levels. For example, in the preceding illustration, a 3,000 increase in ending inventory created a $30,000 increase in income from operations under absorption costing. Such increases (decreases) could be misinterpreted by managers using absorption costing as operating efficiencies (inefficiencies). This is one of the reasons that variable costing is often used by managers for cost control, product pricing, and production planning. Such uses of variable costing are discussed in advanced accounting texts.

At a Glance 19

OBJ 1 Classify costs as variable costs, fixed costs, or mixed costs.

Key Points Variable costs vary in proportion to changes in the level of activity. Fixed costs remain the same in total dollar amount as the level of activity changes. Mixed costs are comprised of both fixed and variable costs.

Learning Outcomes	Example Exercises	Practice Exercises
• Describe variable costs.		
• Describe fixed costs.		
• Describe mixed costs.		
• Separate mixed costs, using the high-low method.	EE19-1	PE19-1A, 19-1B

OBJ 2 Compute the contribution margin, the contribution margin ratio, and the unit contribution margin.

Key Points Contribution margin is the excess of sales revenue over variable costs and can be expressed as a ratio (contribution margin ratio) or a dollar amount (unit contribution margin).

Learning Outcomes	Example Exercises	Practice Exercises
• Describe the contribution margin.		
• Compute the contribution margin ratio.	EE19-2	PE19-2A, 19-2B
• Compute the unit contribution margin.	EE19-2	PE19-2A, 19-2B

OBJ 3 Determine the break-even point and sales necessary to achieve a target profit.

Key Points The break-even point is the point at which a business's revenues exactly equal costs. The mathematical approach to cost-volume-profit analysis uses the unit contribution margin concept and mathematical equations to determine the break-even point and the volume necessary to achieve a target profit.

Learning Outcomes	Example Exercises	Practice Exercises
• Compute the break-even point in units.	EE19-3	PE19-3A, 19-3B
• Describe how changes in fixed costs affect the break-even point.		
• Describe how changes in unit variable costs affect the break-even point.		
• Describe how a change in the unit selling price affects the break-even point.	EE19-3	PE19-3A, 19-3B
• Modify the break-even equation to compute the unit sales required to earn a target profit.	EE19-4	PE19-4A, 19-4B

CHAPTER 20

© PAUL SAKURA/ASSOCIATED PRESS

Variable Costing for Management Analysis

Adobe Systems, Inc.

Assume that you have three different options for a summer job. How would you evaluate these options? Naturally there are many things to consider, including how much you could earn from each job.

Determining how much you could earn from each job may not be as simple as comparing the wage rate per hour. For example, a job as an office clerk at a local company pays $8 per hour. A job delivering pizza pays $10 per hour (including estimated tips), although you must use your own transportation. Another job working in a beach resort over 500 miles away from your home pays $8 per hour. All three jobs offer 40 hours per week for the whole summer. If these options were ranked according to their pay per hour, the pizza delivery job would be the most attractive. However, the costs associated with each job must also be evaluated. For example, the office job may require that you pay for downtown parking and purchase office clothes. The pizza delivery job will require you to pay for gas and maintenance for your car. The resort job will require you to move to the resort city and incur additional living costs. Only by considering the costs for each job will you be able to determine which job will provide you with the most income.

Just as you should evaluate the relative income of various choices, a business also evaluates the income earned from its choices. Important choices include the products offered and the geographical regions to be served.

A company will often evaluate the profitability of products and regions. For example, **Adobe Systems Inc.**, one of the largest software companies in the world, determines the income earned from its various product lines, such as Acrobat®, Photoshop®, Premier®, and Dreamweaver® software. Adobe uses this information to establish product line pricing, as well as sales, support, and development effort. Likewise, Adobe evaluates the income earned in the geographic regions it serves, such as the United States, Europe, and Asia. Again, such information aids management in managing revenue and expenses within the regions.

In this chapter, how businesses measure profitability using absorption costing and variable costing is discussed. After illustrating and comparing these concepts, how businesses use them for controlling costs, pricing products, planning production, analyzing market segments, and analyzing contribution margins is described and illustrated.

Learning Objectives

After studying this chapter, you should be able to: — *Example Exercises*

At a Glance 20 Page 955

OBJ 1 Describe and illustrate reporting income from operations under absorption and variable costing.

Income from Operations Under Absorption Costing and Variable Costing

Income from operations is one of the most important items reported by a company. Depending on the decision-making needs of management, income from operations can be determined using absorption or variable costing.

Absorption Costing

Absorption costing is required under generally accepted accounting principles for financial statements distributed to external users. Under absorption costing, the cost of goods manufactured includes direct materials, direct labor, and factory overhead costs. Both fixed and variable factory costs are included as part of factory overhead. In the financial statements, these costs are included in the cost of goods sold (income statement) and inventory (balance sheet).

The reporting of income from operations under absorption costing is as follows:

Sales	$XXX
Cost of goods sold	XXX
Gross profit	$XXX
Selling and administrative expenses	XXX
Income from operations	$XXX

The income statements illustrated in the preceding chapters of this text have used absorption costing.

Variable Costing

For internal use in decision making, managers often use variable costing. Under **variable costing**, sometimes called *direct costing*, the cost of goods manufactured includes only variable manufacturing costs. Thus, the cost of goods manufactured consists of the following:

1. Direct materials
2. Direct labor
3. *Variable* factory overhead

Under variable costing, *fixed* factory overhead costs are not a part of the cost of goods manufactured. Instead, fixed factory overhead costs are treated as a period expense.

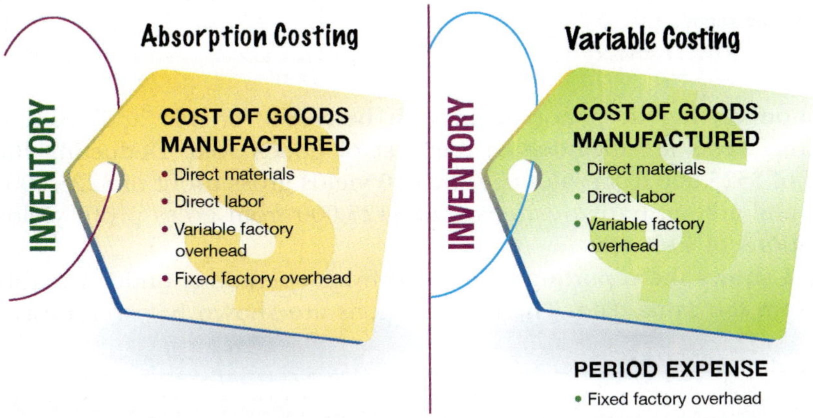

The reporting of income from operations under variable costing is as follows:

Sales		$XXX
Variable cost of goods sold		XXX
Manufacturing margin		$XXX
Variable selling and administrative expenses		XXX
Contribution margin		$XXX
Fixed costs:		
Fixed manufacturing costs	$XXX	
Fixed selling and administrative expenses	XXX	XXX
Income from operations		$XXX

Manufacturing margin is sales less variable cost of goods sold. **Variable cost of goods sold** consists of direct materials, direct labor, and variable factory overhead for the units sold. **Contribution margin** is manufacturing margin less variable selling and administrative expenses. Subtracting fixed costs from contribution margin yields income from operations.

To illustrate variable costing and absorption costing, assume that 15,000 units are manufactured and sold at a price of $50. The related costs and expenses are as follows:

	Number of Units	Unit Cost	Total Cost
Manufacturing costs:			
Variable	15,000	$25	$375,000
Fixed	15,000	10	150,000
Total		$35	$525,000
Selling and administrative expenses:			
Variable	15,000	$ 5	$ 75,000
Fixed	15,000	—	50,000
Total			$125,000

Exhibit 1 illustrates the reporting of income from operations under absorption costing prepared from the data on the previous page. The computations are shown in parentheses.

EXHIBIT 1

Absorption Costing Income Statement

Sales (15,000 × $50)	$750,000
Cost of goods sold (15,000 × $35)	525,000
Gross profit	$225,000
Selling and administrative expenses ($75,000 + $50,000)	125,000
Income from operations	$100,000

Absorption costing does not distinguish between variable and fixed costs. All manufacturing costs are included in the cost of goods sold. Deducting the cost of goods sold of $525,000 from sales of $750,000 yields gross profit of $225,000. Deducting selling and administrative expenses of $125,000 from gross profit yields income from operations of $100,000.

Exhibit 2 shows the reporting of income from operations under variable costing prepared from the same data. The computations are shown in parentheses.

EXHIBIT 2

Variable Costing Income Statement

Sales (15,000 × $50)		$750,000
Variable cost of goods sold (15,000 × $25)		375,000
Manufacturing margin		$375,000
Variable selling and administrative expenses (15,000 × $5)		75,000
Contribution margin		$300,000
Fixed costs:		
Fixed manufacturing costs	$150,000	
Fixed selling and administrative expenses	50,000	200,000
Income from operations		$100,000

Note:
The variable costing income statement includes only variable manufacturing costs in the cost of goods sold.

Variable costing income reports variable costs separately from fixed costs. Deducting the variable cost of goods sold of $375,000 from sales of $750,000 yields the manufacturing margin of $375,000. Deducting variable selling and administrative expenses of $75,000 from the manufacturing margin yields the contribution margin of $300,000. Deducting fixed costs of $200,000 from the contribution margin yields income from operations of $100,000.

The contribution margin reported in Exhibit 2 is the same as that used in Chapter 19. That is, the contribution margin is sales less variable costs and expenses. The only difference is that Exhibit 2 reports manufacturing margin before deducting variable selling and administrative expenses.

Example Exercise 20-1 Variable Costing

OBJ 1

Leone Company has the following information for March:

Sales	$450,000
Variable cost of goods sold	220,000
Fixed manufacturing costs	80,000
Variable selling and administrative expenses	50,000
Fixed selling and administrative expenses	35,000

Determine (a) the manufacturing margin, (b) the contribution margin, and (c) income from operations for Leone Company for the month of March.

Follow My Example 20-1

a. $230,000 ($450,000 – $220,000)
b. $180,000 ($230,000 – $50,000)
c. $65,000 ($180,000 – $80,000 – $35,000)

Practice Exercises: **PE 20-1A, PE 20-1B**

Units Manufactured Equal Units Sold

In Exhibits 1 and 2, 15,000 units were manufactured and sold. Both variable and absorption costing reported the same income from operations of $100,000. Thus, when the number of units manufactured equals the number of units sold, income from operations will be the same under both methods.

Units Manufactured Exceed Units Sold

When units manufactured exceed the units sold, the variable costing income from operations will be *less* than it is for absorption costing. To illustrate, assume that in the preceding example only 12,000 units of the 15,000 units manufactured were sold.

Exhibit 3 shows the reporting of income from operations under absorption and variable costing.

Different regions of the world emphasize different approaches to reporting income. For example, Scandinavian companies have a strong variable costing tradition, while German cost accountants have developed some of the most advanced absorption costing practices in the world.

EXHIBIT 3

Units Manufactured Exceed Units Sold

Absorption Costing Income Statement

Sales (12,000 × $50)		$600,000
Cost of goods sold:		
Cost of goods manufactured (15,000 × $35)	$525,000	
Less ending inventory (3,000 × $35)	105,000	
Cost of goods sold		420,000
Gross profit		$180,000
Selling and administrative expenses [(12,000 × $5) + $50,000]		110,000
Income from operations		$ 70,000

Variable Costing Income Statement

Sales (12,000 × $50)		$600,000
Variable cost of goods sold:		
Variable cost of goods manufactured (15,000 × $25)	$375,000	
Less ending inventory (3,000 × $25)	75,000	
Variable cost of goods sold		300,000
Manufacturing margin		$300,000
Variable selling and administrative expenses (12,000 × $5)		60,000
Contribution margin		$240,000
Fixed costs:		
Fixed manufacturing costs	$150,000	
Fixed selling and administrative expenses	50,000	200,000
Income from operations		$ 40,000

Exhibit 3 shows a $30,000 difference in income from operations ($70,000 – $40,000). This difference is due to the fixed manufacturing costs. All of the $150,000 of fixed manufacturing costs is included as a period expense in the variable costing statement. However, the 3,000 units of ending inventory in the absorption costing statement includes $30,000 (3,000 units × $10) of fixed manufacturing costs. By including the $30,000 in inventory, it is excluded from the cost of goods sold. Thus, the absorption costing income from operations is $30,000 higher than the income from operations for variable costing.

Example Exercise 20-2 Variable Costing—Production Exceeds Sales OBJ 1

Fixed manufacturing costs are $40 per unit, and variable manufacturing costs are $120 per unit. Production was 125,000 units, while sales were 120,000 units. Determine (a) whether variable costing income from operations is less than or greater than absorption costing income from operations, and (b) the difference in variable costing and absorption costing income from operations.

Follow My Example 20-2

a. Variable costing income from operations is less than absorption costing income from operations.
b. $200,000 ($40 per unit × 5,000 units)

Practice Exercises: **PE 20-2A, PE 20-2B**

Units Manufactured Less Than Units Sold

When the units manufactured are less than the number of units sold, the variable costing income from operations will be *greater* than that of absorption costing. To illustrate, assume that beginning inventory, units manufactured, and units sold were as follows:

Beginning inventory	5,000 units
Units manufactured during current period	10,000 units
Units sold during the current period at $50 per unit	15,000 units

The manufacturing costs and selling and administrative expenses are as follows:

	Number of Units	Unit Cost	Total Cost
Beginning inventory (5,000 units):			
Manufacturing costs:			
Variable	5,000	$25	$125,000
Fixed	5,000	10	50,000
Total		$35	$175,000
Current period (10,000 units):			
Manufacturing costs:			
Variable	10,000	$25	$250,000
Fixed	10,000	15	150,000
Total		$40	$400,000
Selling and administrative expenses:			
Variable	15,000	$5	$ 75,000
Fixed	15,000	—	50,000
Total			$125,000

Exhibit 4 shows the reporting of income from operations under absorption and variable costing based on the preceding data.

EXHIBIT 4

Units Manufactured Are Less Than Units Sold

Absorption Costing Income Statement

Sales (15,000 × $50)		$750,000
Cost of goods sold:		
Beginning inventory (5,000 × $35)	$175,000	
Cost of goods manufactured (10,000 × $40)	400,000	
Cost of goods sold		575,000
Gross profit		$175,000
Selling and administrative expenses ($75,000 + $50,000)		125,000
Income from operations		$ 50,000

Variable Costing Income Statement

Sales (15,000 × $50)		$750,000
Variable cost of goods sold:		
Beginning inventory (5,000 × $25)	$125,000	
Variable cost of goods manufactured (10,000 × $25)	250,000	
Variable cost of goods sold		375,000
Manufacturing margin		$375,000
Variable selling and administrative expenses (15,000 × $5)		75,000
Contribution margin		$300,000
Fixed costs:		
Fixed manufacturing costs	$150,000	
Fixed selling and administrative expenses	50,000	200,000
Income from operations		$100,000

Exhibit 4 shows a $50,000 difference in income from operations ($100,000 – $50,000). This difference is due to the fixed manufacturing costs. The beginning inventory under absorption costing includes $50,000 (5,000 units × $10) of fixed manufacturing costs incurred in the preceding period. By being included in the beginning inventory, this $50,000 is included in the cost of goods sold for the current period. Under variable costing, this $50,000 was included as an expense in an income statement of a prior period. Thus, the variable costing income from operations is $50,000 higher than the income from operations for absorption costing.

***Example Exercise* 20-3 Variable Costing—Sales Exceed Production** OBJ 1

The beginning inventory is 6,000 units. All of the units that were manufactured during the period and the 6,000 units of beginning inventory were sold. The beginning inventory fixed manufacturing costs are $60 per unit, and variable manufacturing costs are $300 per unit. Determine (a) whether variable costing income from operations is less than or greater than absorption costing income from operations, and (b) the difference in variable costing and absorption costing income from operations.

Follow My Example 20-3

a. Variable costing income from operations is greater than absorption costing income from operations.
b. $360,000 ($60 per unit × 6,000 units)

Practice Exercises: **PE 20-3A, PE 20-3B**

Effects on Income from Operations

The preceding examples illustrate the effects on income from operations of using absorption and variable costing. These effects are summarized below.

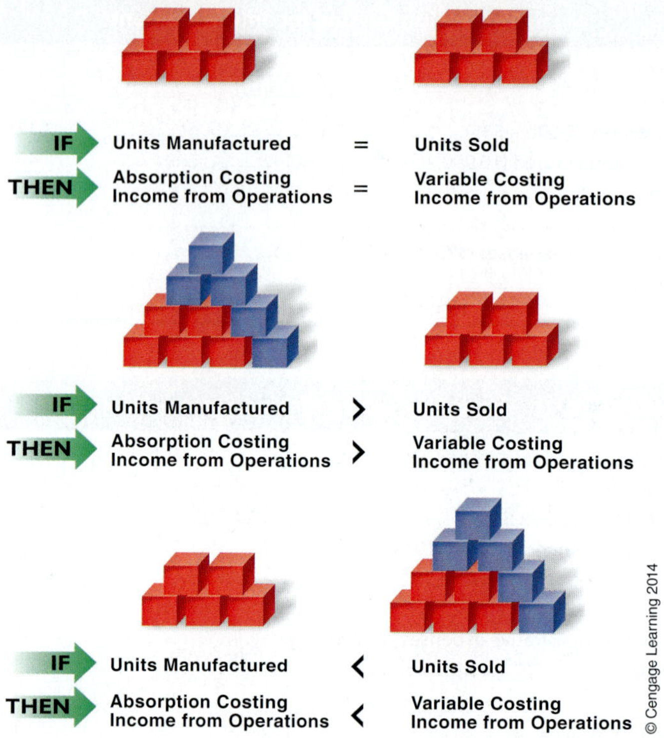

OBJ 2 Describe and illustrate the effects of absorption and variable costing on analyzing income from operations.

Income Analysis Under Absorption and Variable Costing

Whenever the units manufactured differ from the units sold, finished goods inventory is affected. When the units manufactured are greater than the units sold, finished goods inventory increases. Under absorption costing, a portion of this increase is related to the allocation of fixed manufacturing overhead to ending inventory. As a result, increases or decreases in income from operations can be due to changes in inventory levels. In analyzing income from operations, such increases and decreases could be misinterpreted as operating efficiencies or inefficiencies.

To illustrate, assume that Frand Manufacturing Company has no beginning inventory and sales are estimated to be 20,000 units at $75 per unit. Also, assume that sales will not change if more than 20,000 units are manufactured.

The management of Frand Manufacturing Company is evaluating whether to manufacture 20,000 units (Proposal 1) or 25,000 units (Proposal 2). The costs and expenses related to each proposal are shown below.

Proposal 1: 20,000 Units to Be Manufactured and Sold

	Number of Units	Unit Cost	Total Cost
Manufacturing costs:			
Variable	20,000	$35	$ 700,000
Fixed	20,000	20*	400,000
Total		$55	$1,100,000
Selling and administrative expenses:			
Variable	20,000	$ 5	$ 100,000
Fixed	20,000	—	100,000
Total			$ 200,000

*$400,000/20,000 units

Proposal 2: 25,000 Units to Be Manufactured and 20,000 Units to Be Sold

	Number of Units	Unit Cost	Total Cost
Manufacturing costs:			
Variable	25,000	$35	$ 875,000
Fixed	25,000	16*	400,000
Total		$51	$1,275,000
Selling and administrative expenses:			
Variable	20,000	$ 5	$ 100,000
Fixed	20,000	—	100,000
Total			$ 200,000

*$400,000/25,000 units

The absorption costing income statements for each proposal are shown in Exhibit 5.

EXHIBIT 5

Absorption Costing Income Statements for Two Production Levels

Frand Manufacturing Company
Absorption Costing Income Statements

	Proposal 1 20,000 Units Manufactured	Proposal 2 25,000 Units Manufactured
Sales (20,000 units × $75)	$1,500,000	$1,500,000
Cost of goods sold:		
Cost of goods manufactured:		
(20,000 units × $55)	$1,100,000	
(25,000 units × $51)		$1,275,000
Less ending inventory:		
(5,000 units × $51)		255,000
Cost of goods sold	$1,100,000	$1,020,000
Gross profit	$ 400,000	$ 480,000
Selling and administrative expenses:		
($100,000 + $100,000)	200,000	200,000
Income from operations	$ 200,000	$ 280,000

Exhibit 5 shows that if Frand manufactures 25,000 units, sells 20,000 units, and adds the 5,000 units to finished goods inventory (Proposal 2), income from operations will be $280,000. In contrast, if Frand manufactures and sells 20,000 units (Proposal 1), income from operations will be $200,000. In other words, Frand can increase income from operations by $80,000 ($280,000 – $200,000) by simply increasing finished goods inventory by 5,000 units.

The $80,000 increase in income from operations under Proposal 2 is caused by the allocation of the fixed manufacturing costs of $400,000 over a greater number of units manufactured. Specifically, an increase in production from 20,000 units to 25,000 units means that the fixed manufacturing cost per unit decreases from $20 ($400,000/20,000 units) to $16 ($400,000/25,000 units). Thus, the cost of goods sold when 25,000 units are manufactured is $4 per unit less, or $80,000 less in total (20,000 units sold × $4). Since the cost of goods sold is less, income from operations is $80,000 more when 25,000 units rather than 20,000 units are manufactured.

Managers should be careful in analyzing income from operations under absorption costing when finished goods inventory changes. As shown above, increases in income from operations may be created by simply increasing finished goods inventory. Thus, managers could misinterpret such increases (or decreases) in income from operations as due to changes in sales volume, prices, or costs.

Under variable costing, income from operations is $200,000, regardless of whether 20,000 units or 25,000 units are manufactured. This is because no fixed manufacturing costs are allocated to the units manufactured. Instead, all fixed manufacturing costs are treated as a period expense.

To illustrate, Exhibit 6 shows the variable costing income statements for Frand Manufacturing Company for the production of 20,000 units, 25,000 units, and 30,000 units. In each case, the income from operations is $200,000.

EXHIBIT 6

Variable Costing Income Statements for Three Production Levels

Frand Manufacturing Company
Variable Costing Income Statements

	20,000 Units Manufactured	25,000 Units Manufactured	30,000 Units Manufactured
Sales (20,000 units × $75)	$1,500,000	$1,500,000	$1,500,000
Variable cost of goods sold:			
Variable cost of goods manufactured:			
(20,000 units × $35)	$ 700,000		
(25,000 units × $35)		$ 875,000	
(30,000 units × $35)			$1,050,000
Less ending inventory:			
(0 units × $35)	0		
(5,000 units × $35)		175,000	
(10,000 units × $35)			350,000
Variable cost of goods sold	$ 700,000	$ 700,000	$ 700,000
Manufacturing margin	$ 800,000	$ 800,000	$ 800,000
Variable selling and administrative expenses	100,000	100,000	100,000
Contribution margin	$ 700,000	$ 700,000	$ 700,000
Fixed costs:			
Fixed manufacturing costs	$ 400,000	$ 400,000	$ 400,000
Fixed selling and administrative expenses	100,000	100,000	100,000
Total fixed costs	$ 500,000	$ 500,000	$ 500,000
Income from operations	$ 200,000	$ 200,000	$ 200,000

Integrity, Objectivity, and Ethics in Business

TAKING AN "ABSORPTION HIT"

Aligning production to demand is a critical decision in business. Managers must not allow the temporary benefits of excess production through higher absorption of fixed costs to guide their decisions. Likewise, if demand falls, production should be dropped and inventory liquidated to match the new demand level, even though earnings will be penalized. The following interchange provides an example of an appropriate response to lowered demand for H.J. Heinz Company:

Analyst's question: *It seems.... that you're guiding to a little bit of a drop in performance between 3Q (third Quarter) and 4Q (fourth Quarter.... if so, maybe you could walk us through some of the drivers of that relative softness.*

Heinz executive's response: *No, I think, frankly, we're real pleased with the performance in the business.... We're also aggressively taking out inventory in the fourth quarter. And as you know, as you reduce inventory, you take an absorption hit. You're pulling basically fixed costs off the balance sheet into the P&L and there's a hit associated with that, but we think that's the right thing to do, to pull inventory out and to drive cash flow. So now, we feel very good about the business and feel very good about the fact that we're taking it to the middle of the range and taking up the bottom end of our guidance.*

Management operating with integrity will seek the tangible benefits of reducing inventory, even though there may be an adverse impact on published financial statements caused by absorption costing.

Source of question and response from http://seekingalpha.com/article/375151-h-j-heinz-management-discusses-q3-2012-results-earnings-call-transcript?page=6&p=qanda. Accessed February 2012.

As shown previously, absorption costing may encourage managers to produce inventory. This is because producing inventory absorbs fixed manufacturing costs, which increases income from operations. However, producing inventory leads to higher handling, storage, financing, and obsolescence costs. For this reason, many accountants believe that variable costing should be used by management for evaluating operating performance.

Example Exercise 20-4 Analyzing Income Under Absorption and Variable Costing

OBJ 5

Variable manufacturing costs are $100 per unit, and fixed manufacturing costs are $50,000. Sales are estimated to be 4,000 units.

a. How much would absorption costing income from operations differ between a plan to produce 4,000 units and a plan to produce 5,000 units?
b. How much would variable costing income from operations differ between the two production plans?

Follow My Example 20-4

a. $10,000 greater in producing 5,000 units. 4,000 units × ($12.50[1] – $10.00[2]), or [1,000 units × ($50,000/5,000 units)].
b. There would be no difference in variable costing income from operations between the two plans.

[1]$50,000/4,000 units
[2]$50,000/5,000 units

Practice Exercises: **PE 20-4A, PE 20-4B**

Using Absorption and Variable Costing

OBJ 3 Describe management's use of absorption and variable costing.

Each decision-making situation should be carefully analyzed in deciding whether absorption or variable costing reporting would be more useful. As a basis for discussion, the use of absorption and variable costing in the following decision-making situations is described:

1. Controlling costs
2. Pricing products
3. Planning production
4. Analyzing contribution margins
5. Analyzing market segments

The role of accounting reports in these decision-making situations is shown in Exhibit 7.

EXHIBIT 7

Accounting Reports and Management Decisions

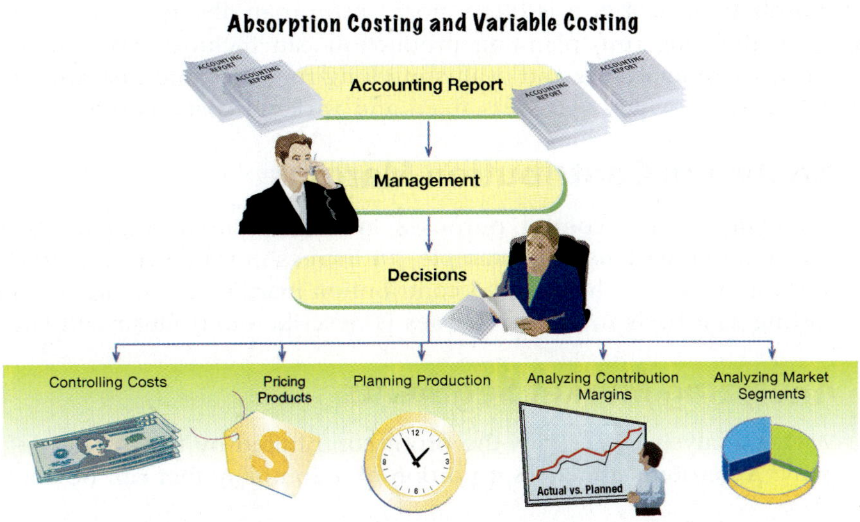

Controlling Costs

All costs are controllable in the long run by someone within a business. However, not all costs are controllable at the same level of management. For example, plant supervisors control the use of direct materials in their departments. They have no control, though, over insurance costs related to the property, plant, and equipment.

For a level of management, **controllable costs** are costs that can be influenced (increased or decreased) by management at that level. **Noncontrollable costs** are costs that another level of management controls. This distinction is useful for reporting costs to those responsible for their control.

Variable manufacturing costs are controlled by operating management. In contrast, fixed manufacturing overhead costs such as the salaries of production supervisors are normally controlled at a higher level of management. Likewise, control of the variable and fixed operating expenses usually involves different levels of management. Since fixed costs and expenses are reported separately under variable costing, variable costing reports are normally more useful than absorption costing reports for controlling costs.

Pricing Products

Major hotel chains, such as Marriott, Hilton, and Hyatt, often provide "weekend getaway" packages, which provide discounts for weekend stays in their city hotels. As long as the weekend rates exceed the variable costs, the "weekend getaway" pricing will contribute to the hotel's short-run profitability.

Many factors enter into determining the selling price of a product. However, the cost of making the product is significant in all pricing decisions.

In the short run, fixed costs cannot be avoided. Thus, the selling price of a product should at least be equal to the variable costs of making and selling it. Any price above this minimum selling price contributes to covering fixed costs and generating income. Since variable costing reports variable and fixed costs and expenses separately, it is often more useful than absorption costing for setting short-run prices.

In the long run, a company must set its selling price high enough to cover all costs and expenses (variable and fixed) and generate income. Since absorption costing includes fixed and variable costs in the cost of manufacturing a product, absorption costing is often more useful than variable costing for setting long-term prices.

Planning Production

In the short run, planning production is limited to existing capacity. In many cases, operating decisions must be made quickly before opportunities are lost.

To illustrate, a company with seasonal demand for its products may have an opportunity to obtain an off-season order that will not interfere with its current production schedule. The relevant factors for such a short-run decision are the additional revenues and the additional variable costs associated with the order. If the revenues from the order exceed the related variable costs, the order will increase contribution margin and, thus, increase the company's income from operations. Since variable costing reports contribution margin, it is often more useful than absorption costing in such cases.

In the long run, planning production can include expanding existing capacity. Thus, when analyzing and evaluating long-run sales and operating decisions, absorption costing, which considers fixed and variable costs, is often more useful.

Analyzing Contribution Margins

For planning and control purposes, managers often compare planned and actual contribution margins. For example, an increase in the price of fuel could have a significant impact on the planned contribution margins of an airline. The use of variable costing as a basis for such analyses is described and illustrated later in this chapter.

Analyzing Market Segments

Market analysis determines the profit contributed by the market segments of a company. A **market segment** is a portion of a company that can be analyzed using sales,

Business Connection

INVENTORY WRITE-DOWNS

Apple has become one of the most financially successful companies of the past decade by using variable cost information to carefully price its iPod family of products. The cost of an iPod consists almost entirely of direct materials and other variable costs. For example, Apple's sixth generation iPod nano is estimated to have a total cost of $45.10, of which $43.73 is direct materials. Thus, when designing a new iPod, Apple has to carefully balance product features with the variable cost of direct materials. For the sixth generation iPod nano, Apple added touch screen technology and a more powerful battery, while removing the camera feature. This careful balancing of cost and functionality allowed Apple to offer a new generation of iPod nano at an enticing price, highlighting how Apple's awareness and understanding of variable cost information has been a key element of the company's financial success.

Source: A. Rassweiler, "ISuppli Estimates New iPod Nano Bill of Materials at $43.73," iSuppli, Applied Market Intelligence.

costs, and expenses to determine its profitability. Examples of market segments include sales territories, products, salespersons, and customers. Variable costing as an aid in decision making regarding market segments is discussed next.

Analyzing Market Segments

OBJ 4 Use variable costing for analyzing market segments, including product, territories, and salespersons segments.

Companies can report income for internal decision making using either absorption or variable costing. Absorption costing is often used for long-term analysis of market segments. This type of analysis is illustrated in Chapter 26, "Cost Allocation and Activity-Based Costing." Variable costing is often used for short-term analysis of market segments. In this section, segment profitability reporting using variable costing is described and illustrated.

Most companies prepare variable costing reports for each product. These reports are often used for product pricing and deciding whether to discontinue a product. In addition, variable costing reports may be prepared for geographic areas, customers, distribution channels, or salespersons. A distribution channel is the method for selling a product to a customer.

To illustrate analysis of market segments using variable costing, the following data for the month ending March 31, 2014, for Camelot Fragrance Company are used:

Camelot Fragrance Company
Sales and Production Data
For the Month Ended March 31, 2014

	Northern Territory	Southern Territory	Total
Sales:			
Gwenevere	$60,000	$30,000	$ 90,000
Lancelot	20,000	50,000	70,000
Total territory sales	$80,000	$80,000	$160,000
Variable production costs:			
Gwenevere (12% of sales)	$ 7,200	$ 3,600	$ 10,800
Lancelot (12% of sales)	2,400	6,000	8,400
Total variable production cost by territory	$ 9,600	$ 9,600	$ 19,200
Promotion costs:			
Gwenevere (variable at 30% of sales)	$18,000	$ 9,000	$ 27,000
Lancelot (variable at 20% of sales)	4,000	10,000	14,000
Total promotion cost by territory	$22,000	$19,000	$ 41,000
Sales commissions:			
Gwenevere (variable at 20% of sales)	$12,000	$ 6,000	$ 18,000
Lancelot (variable at 10% of sales)	2,000	5,000	7,000
Total sales commissions by territory	$14,000	$11,000	$ 25,000

Camelot Fragrance Company manufactures and sells the Gwenevere perfume for women and the Lancelot cologne for men. To simplify, no inventories are assumed to exist at the beginning or end of March.

Sales Territory Profitability Analysis

An income statement presenting the contribution margin by sales territories is often used in evaluating past performance and in directing future sales efforts. Sales territory profitability analysis may lead management to do the following:

1. Reduce costs in lower-profit sales territories
2. Increase sales efforts in higher-profit territories

To illustrate sales territory profitability analysis, Exhibit 8 shows the contribution margin for the Northern and Southern territories of Camelot Fragrance Company. As Exhibit 8 indicates, the Northern Territory is generating $34,400 of contribution margin, while the Southern Territory is generating $40,400 of contribution margin.

In addition to the contribution margin, the contribution margin ratio for each territory is shown in Exhibit 8. The contribution margin ratio is computed as follows:

$$\text{Contribution Margin Ratio} = \frac{\text{Contribution Margin}}{\text{Sales}}$$

Exhibit 8 indicates that the Northern Territory has a contribution margin ratio of 43% ($34,400/$80,000). In contrast, the Southern Territory has a contribution margin ratio of 50.5% ($40,400/$80,000).

EXHIBIT 8

Contribution Margin by Sales Territory Report

Camelot Fragrance Company
Contribution Margin by Sales Territory
For the Month Ended March 31, 2014

	Northern Territory		Southern Territory	
Sales		$80,000		$80,000
Variable cost of goods sold		9,600		9,600
Manufacturing margin		$70,400		$70,400
Variable selling expenses:				
Promotion costs	$22,000		$19,000	
Sales commissions	14,000	36,000	11,000	30,000
Contribution margin		$34,400		$40,400
Contribution margin ratio		43%		50.5%

The Coca-Cola Company earns over 75% of its total corporate profits outside of the United States. As a result, Coca-Cola management continues to expand operations and sales efforts around the world.

The difference in profit of the Northern and Southern territories is due to the difference in sales mix between the territories. **Sales mix**, sometimes referred to as *product mix*, is the relative amount of sales among the various products. The sales mix is computed by dividing the sales of each product by the total sales of each territory. Sales mix of the Northern and Southern territories is as follows:

	Northern Territory		Southern Territory	
Product	**Sales**	**Sales Mix**	**Sales**	**Sales Mix**
Gwenevere	$60,000	75%	$30,000	37.5%
Lancelot	20,000	25	50,000	62.5
Total	$80,000	100%	$80,000	100.0%

As shown on the previous page, 62.5% of the Southern Territory's sales are sales of Lancelot. Since the Southern Territory's contribution margin ($40,400) is higher (as shown in Exhibit 8) than that of the Northern Territory ($34,400), Lancelot must be more profitable than Gwenevere. To verify this, product profitability analysis is performed.

Product Profitability Analysis

A company should focus its sales efforts on products that will provide the maximum total contribution margin. In doing so, product profitability analysis is often used by management in making decisions regarding product sales and promotional efforts.

To illustrate product profitability analysis, Exhibit 9 shows the contribution margin by product for Camelot Fragrance Company.

EXHIBIT 9

Contribution Margin by Product Line Report

Camelot Fragrance Company
Contribution Margin by Product Line
For the Month Ended March 31, 2014

	Gwenevere		Lancelot	
Sales		$90,000		$70,000
Variable cost of goods sold		10,800		8,400
Manufacturing margin		$79,200		$61,600
Variable selling expenses:				
Promotion costs	$27,000		$14,000	
Sales commissions	18,000	45,000	7,000	21,000
Contribution margin		$34,200		$40,600
Contribution margin ratio		38%		58%

Exhibit 9 indicates that Lancelot's contribution margin ratio (58%) is greater than Gwenevere's (38%). Lancelot's higher contribution margin ratio is a result of its lower promotion and sales commissions costs. Thus, management should consider the following:

1. Emphasizing Lancelot in its marketing plans
2. Reducing Gwenevere's promotion and sales commissions costs
3. Increasing the price of Gwenevere

Salesperson Profitability Analysis

A salesperson profitability report is useful in evaluating sales performance. Such a report normally includes total sales, variable cost of goods sold, variable selling expenses, contribution margin, and contribution margin ratio for each salesperson.

Exhibit 10 illustrates such a salesperson profitability report for three salespersons in the Northern Territory of Camelot Fragrance Company. The exhibit indicates that Beth Williams produced the greatest contribution margin ($15,200), but had the lowest contribution margin ratio (38%). Beth sold $40,000 of product, which is twice as much product as the other two salespersons. However, Beth sold only Gwenevere, which has the lowest contribution margin ratio (from Exhibit 9). The other two salespersons sold equal amounts of Gwenevere and Lancelot. As a result, Inez Rodriguez and Tom Ginger had higher contribution margin ratios because they sold more Lancelot. The Northern Territory manager could use this report to encourage Inez and Tom to sell more total product, while encouraging Beth to sell more Lancelot.

2. **Unit price factor** or unit cost factor: The effect of a difference in unit sales price or unit cost on the number of units sold. The *unit price factor* and *unit cost factor* are computed as follows:

Unit Price Factor = (Actual Selling Price per Unit – Planned Selling Price per Unit) × Actual Units Sold

Unit Cost Factor = (Planned Cost per Unit – Actual Cost per Unit) × Actual Units Sold

The preceding factors are computed so that a positive amount increases contribution margin and a negative amount decreases contribution margin.

The effects of the preceding factors on contribution margin are summarized in Exhibit 11.

EXHIBIT 11

Contribution Margin Analysis

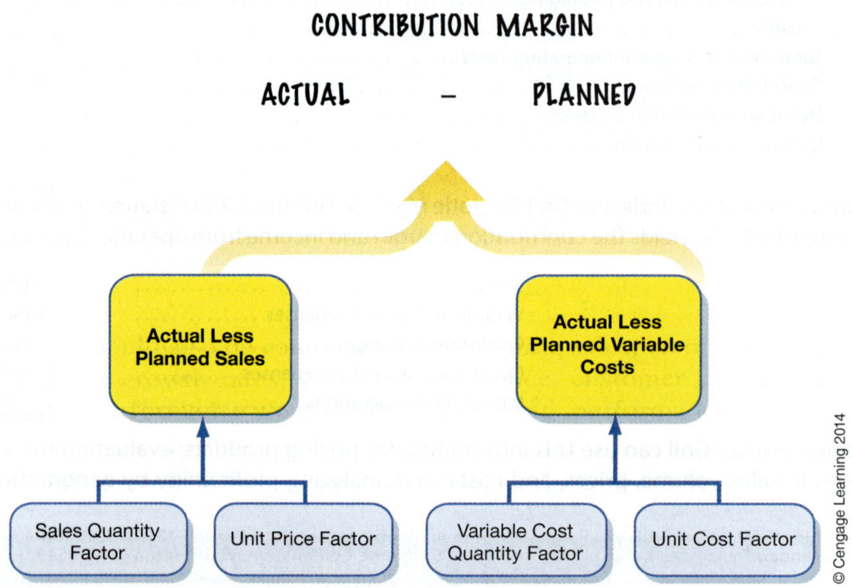

To illustrate, the following data for the year ended December 31, 2014, for Noble Inc., which sells a single product, are used.[1]

	Actual	Planned
Sales	$937,500	$800,000
Less: Variable cost of goods sold	$425,000	$350,000
Variable selling and administrative expenses	162,500	125,000
Total	$587,500	$475,000
Contribution margin	$350,000	$325,000
Number of units sold	125,000	100,000
Per unit:		
Sales price	$7.50	$8.00
Variable cost of goods sold	3.40	3.50
Variable selling and administrative expenses	1.30	1.25

Exhibit 12 shows the contribution margin analysis report for Noble Inc. for the year ended December 31, 2014. The exhibit indicates that the favorable difference of $25,000 ($350,000 – $325,000) between the actual and planned contribution margins was due in large part to an increase in the quantity sold (sales quantity factor) of $200,000. This $200,000 increase was partially offset by a decrease in the unit sales price (unit price factor) of $62,500 and an increase in the amount of variable costs of $112,500 ($75,000 + $37,500).

[1] To simplify, it is assumed that Noble Inc. sells a single product. The analysis would be more complex, but the principles would be the same, if more than one product were sold.

EXHIBIT 12

Contribution Margin Analysis Report

Noble Inc. Contribution Margin Analysis For the Year Ended December 31, 2014		
Planned contribution margin		$325,000
Effect of changes in sales:		
Sales quantity factor (125,000 units – 100,000 units) × $8.00	$200,000	
Unit price factor ($7.50 – $8.00) × 125,000 units	–62,500	
Total effect of changes in sales		137,500
Effect of changes in variable cost of goods sold:		
Variable cost quantity factor (100,000 units – 125,000 units) × $3.50	–$ 87,500	
Unit cost factor ($3.50 – $3.40) × 125,000 units	12,500	
Total effect of changes in variable cost of goods sold		–75,000
Effect of changes in selling and administrative expenses:		
Variable cost quantity factor (100,000 units – 125,000 units) × $1.25	–$ 31,250	
Unit cost factor ($1.25 – $1.30) × 125,000 units	–6,250	
Total effect of changes in selling and administrative expenses		–37,500
Actual contribution margin		$350,000

The contribution margin analysis reports are useful to management in evaluating past performance and in planning future operations. For example, the impact of the $0.50 reduction in the unit sales price by Noble Inc. on the number of units sold and on the total sales for the year is useful information in determining whether further price reductions might be desirable.

The contribution margin analysis report also highlights the impact of changes in unit variable costs and expenses. For example, the $0.05 increase in the unit variable selling and administrative expenses might be a result of increased advertising expenditures. If so, the increase in the number of units sold in 2014 could be attributed to both the $0.50 price reduction and the increased advertising.

Example Exercise 20-6 Contribution Margin Analysis

OBJ 5

The actual price for a product was $48 per unit, while the planned price was $40 per unit. The volume increased by 5,000 units to 60,000 actual total units. Determine (a) the quantity factor and (b) the price factor for sales.

Follow My Example 20-6

a. $200,000 increase in sales (5,000 units × $40 per unit)
b. $480,000 increase in sales [($48 – $40) × 60,000 units]

Practice Exercises: **PE 20-6A, PE 20-6B**

Variable Costing for Service Firms

OBJ 6 Describe and illustrate the use of variable costing for service firms.

Variable costing and the use of variable costing for manufacturing firms have been discussed earlier in this chapter. Service companies also use variable costing, contribution margin analysis, and segment analysis.

Reporting Income from Operations Using Variable Costing for a Service Company

Unlike a manufacturing company, a service company does not make or sell a product. Thus, service companies do not have inventory. Since service companies have no inventory, they do not use absorption costing to allocate fixed costs. In addition, variable costing reports of service companies do not report a manufacturing margin.

To illustrate variable costing for a service company, Blue Skies Airlines Inc., which operates as a small commercial airline, is used. The variable and fixed costs of Blue Skies are shown in Exhibit 13.

EXHIBIT 13

Costs of Blue Skies Airlines Inc.

Cost	Amount	Cost Behavior	Activity Base
Depreciation expense	$3,600,000	Fixed	
Food and beverage service expense.......	444,000	Variable	Number of passengers
Fuel expense	4,080,000	Variable	Number of miles flown
Rental expense..........................	800,000	Fixed	
Selling expense	3,256,000	Variable	Number of passengers
Wages expense..........................	6,120,000	Variable	Number of miles flown

As discussed in the prior chapter, a cost is classified as a fixed or variable cost according to how it changes relative to an activity base. A common activity for a manufacturing firm is the number of units produced. In contrast, most service companies use several activity bases.

To illustrate, Blue Skies Airlines uses the activity base *number of passengers* for food and beverage service and selling expenses. Blue Skies uses *number of miles flown* for fuel and wage expenses.

The variable costing income statement for Blue Skies, assuming revenue of $19,238,000, is shown in Exhibit 14.

EXHIBIT 14

Variable Costing Income Statement

Blue Skies Airlines Inc.
Variable Costing Income Statement
For the Month Ended April 30, 2014

Revenue		$19,238,000
Variable costs:		
Fuel expense	$4,080,000	
Wages expense	6,120,000	
Food and beverage service expense.........................	444,000	
Selling expense...	3,256,000	
Total variable costs		13,900,000
Contribution margin..		$ 5,338,000
Fixed costs:		
Depreciation expense.....................................	$3,600,000	
Rental expense	800,000	
Total fixed costs		4,400,000
Income from operations		$ 938,000

Unlike a manufacturing company, Exhibit 14 does not report cost of goods sold, inventory, or manufacturing margin. However, as shown in Exhibit 14, contribution margin is reported separately from income from operations.

Market Segment Analysis for Service Company

A contribution margin report for service companies can be used to analyze and evaluate market segments. Typical segments for various service companies are shown below.

Service Industry	Market Segments
Electric power	Regions, customer types (industrial, consumer)
Banking	Customer types (commercial, retail), products (loans, savings accounts)
Airlines	Products (passengers, cargo), routes
Railroads	Products (commodity type), routes
Hotels	Hotel properties
Telecommunications	Customer type (commercial, retail), service type (voice, data)
Health care	Procedure, payment type (Medicare, insured)

To illustrate, a contribution margin report segmented by route is used for Blue Skies Airlines. In preparing the report, the following data for April 2014 are used:

	Chicago/Atlanta	Atlanta/LA	LA/Chicago
Average ticket price per passenger	$400	$1,075	$805
Total passengers served	16,000	7,000	6,600
Total miles flown	56,000	88,000	60,000

The variable costs per unit are as follows:

Fuel	$ 20 per mile
Wages	30 per mile
Food and beverage service	15 per passenger
Selling	110 per passenger

A contribution margin report for Blue Skies Airlines is shown in Exhibit 15. The report is segmented by the routes (city pairs) flown.

EXHIBIT 15

Contribution Margin by Segment Report—Service Firm

Blue Skies Airlines Inc.
Contribution Margin by Route
For the Month Ended April 30, 2014

	Chicago/ Atlanta	Atlanta/ Los Angeles	Los Angeles/ Chicago	Total
Revenue				
(Ticket price × No. of passengers)	$ 6,400,000	$ 7,525,000	$ 5,313,000	$19,238,000
Aircraft fuel				
($20 × No. of miles flown)	(1,120,000)	(1,760,000)	(1,200,000)	(4,080,000)
Wages and benefits				
($30 × No. of miles flown)	(1,680,000)	(2,640,000)	(1,800,000)	(6,120,000)
Food and beverage service				
($15 × No. of passengers)	(240,000)	(105,000)	(99,000)	(444,000)
Selling expenses				
($110 × No. of passengers)	(1,760,000)	(770,000)	(726,000)	(3,256,000)
Contribution margin......................	$ 1,600,000	$ 2,250,000	$ 1,488,000	$ 5,338,000
Contribution margin ratio* (rounded)	25%	30%	28%	28%

*Contribution margin/revenue

Exhibit 15 indicates that the Chicago/Atlanta route has the lowest contribution margin ratio of 25%. In contrast, the Atlanta/Los Angeles route has the highest contribution margin ratio of 30%.

Contribution Margin Analysis

Blue Skies Airlines Inc. is also used to illustrate contribution margin analysis. Specifically, assume that Blue Skies decides to try to improve the contribution margin of its Chicago/Atlanta route during May by decreasing ticket prices. Thus, Blue Skies decreases the ticket price from $400 to $380 beginning May 1. As a result, the number of tickets sold (passengers) increased from 16,000 to 20,000. However, the cost per mile also increased during May from $20 to $22 due to increasing fuel prices.

The actual and planned results for the Chicago/Atlanta route during May are shown below. The planned amounts are based on the April results without considering the price change or cost per mile increase. The highlighted numbers indicate changes during May.

	Chicago/Atlanta Route	
	Actual, May	**Planned, May**
Revenue	$7,600,000	$6,400,000
Less variable expenses:		
Aircraft fuel	$1,232,000	$1,120,000
Wages and benefits	1,680,000	1,680,000
Food and beverage service	300,000	240,000
Selling expenses and commissions	2,200,000	1,760,000
Total	$5,412,000	$4,800,000
Contribution margin	$2,188,000	$1,600,000
Contribution margin ratio	29%	25%
Number of miles flown	56,000	56,000
Number of passengers flown	20,000	16,000
Per unit:		
Ticket price	$380	$400
Fuel expense	22	20
Wages expense	30	30
Food and beverage service expense	15	15
Selling expense	110	110

Using the preceding data, a contribution margin analysis report can be prepared for the Chicago/Atlanta route for May as shown in Exhibit 16. Since the planned and actual wages and benefits expense are the same ($1,680,000), its quantity and unit cost factors are not included in Exhibit 16.

Exhibit 16 indicates that the price decrease generated an additional $1,200,000 in revenue. This consists of $1,600,000 from an increased number of passengers (revenue quantity factor) and a $400,000 revenue reduction from the decrease in ticket price (unit price factor).

EXHIBIT 16

Contribution Margin Analysis Report—Service Company

Blue Skies Airlines Inc.
Contribution Margin Analysis
Chicago/Atlanta Route
For the Month Ended May 31, 2014

Planned contribution margin		$1,600,000
Effect of changes in revenue:		
Revenue quantity factor (20,000 pass. – 16,000 pass.) × $400	$1,600,000	
Unit price factor ($380 – $400) × 20,000 passengers	–400,000	
Total effect of changes in revenue		1,200,000
Effect of changes in fuel cost:		
Variable cost quantity factor (56,000 miles – 56,000 miles) × $20	$ 0	
Unit cost factor ($20 – $22) × 56,000 miles	–112,000	
Total effect of changes in fuel costs		–112,000
Effect of changes in food and beverage expenses:		
Variable cost quantity factor (16,000 pass. – 20,000 pass.) × $15	–$ 60,000	
Unit cost factor ($15 – $15) × 20,000 passengers	0	
Total effect of changes in food and beverage expenses		–60,000
Effect of changes in selling and commission expenses:		
Variable cost quantity factor (16,000 pass. – 20,000 pass.) × $110	–$ 440,000	
Unit cost factor ($110 – $110) × 20,000 passengers	0	
Total effect of changes in selling and administrative expenses		–440,000
Actual contribution margin		$2,188,000

The increased fuel costs (by $2 per mile) reduced the contribution margin by $112,000 (unit cost factor). The increased number of passengers also increased the food and beverage service costs by $60,000 and the selling costs by $440,000 (variable cost quantity factors). The net increase in contribution margin is $588,000 ($2,188,000 − $1,600,000).

At a Glance 20

OBJ 1 Describe and illustrate reporting income from operations under absorption and variable costing.

Key Points Under absorption costing, the cost of goods manufactured is comprised of all direct materials, direct labor, and factory overhead costs (both fixed and variable). Under variable costing, the cost of goods manufactured is composed of only variable costs: direct materials, direct labor, and variable factory overhead costs. Fixed factory overhead costs are considered a period expense.

The variable costing income statement is structured differently than a traditional absorption costing income statement. Sales less variable cost of goods sold is presented as manufacturing margin. Manufacturing margin less variable selling and administrative expenses is presented as contribution margin. Contribution margin less fixed costs is presented as income from operations.

Learning Outcomes	Example Exercises	Practice Exercises
• Describe the difference between absorption and variable costing.		
• Prepare a variable costing income statement for a manufacturer.	EE20-1	PE20-1A, 20-1B
• Evaluate the difference between the variable and absorption costing income statements when production exceeds sales.	EE20-2	PE20-2A, 20-2B
• Evaluate the difference between the variable and absorption costing income statements when sales exceed production.	EE20-3	PE20-3A, 20-3B

OBJ 2 Describe and illustrate the effects of absorption and variable costing on analyzing income from operations.

Key Points Management should be aware of the effects of changes in inventory levels on income from operations reported under variable costing and absorption costing. If absorption costing is used, managers could misinterpret increases or decreases in income from operations due to changes in inventory levels to be the result of operating efficiencies or inefficiencies.

Learning Outcome	Example Exercises	Practice Exercises
• Determine absorption costing and variable costing income under different planned levels of production for a given sales level.	EE20-4	PE20-4A, 20-4B

2.

Variable Costing Income Statement		
Sales (60,000 × $30)		$1,800,000
Variable cost of goods sold:		
Beginning inventory (10,000 × $24)	$ 240,000	
Variable cost of goods manufactured (50,000 × $25)	1,250,000	
Variable cost of goods sold		1,490,000
Manufacturing margin		$ 310,000
Variable selling and administrative expenses		65,000
Contribution margin		$ 245,000
Fixed costs:		
Fixed manufacturing costs	$ 100,000	
Fixed selling and administrative expenses	45,000	145,000
Income from operations		$ 100,000

3. The difference of $20,000 ($100,000 – $80,000) in the amount of income from operations is attributable to the different treatment of the fixed manufacturing costs. The beginning inventory in the absorption costing income statement includes $20,000 (10,000 units × $2) of fixed manufacturing costs incurred in the preceding period. This $20,000 was included as an expense in a variable costing income statement of a prior period. Therefore, none of it is included as an expense in the current period variable costing income statement.

Discussion Questions

1. What types of costs are customarily included in the cost of manufactured products under (a) the absorption costing concept and (b) the variable costing concept?
2. Which type of manufacturing cost (direct materials, direct labor, variable factory overhead, fixed factory overhead) is included in the cost of goods manufactured under the absorption costing concept but is excluded from the cost of goods manufactured under the variable costing concept?
3. Which of the following costs would be included in the cost of a manufactured product according to the variable costing concept: (a) rent on factory building, (b) direct materials, (c) property taxes on factory building, (d) electricity purchased to operate factory equipment, (e) salary of factory supervisor, (f) depreciation on factory building, (g) direct labor?
4. In the variable costing income statement, how are the fixed manufacturing costs reported, and how are the fixed selling and administrative expenses reported?
5. Since all costs of operating a business are controllable, what is the significance of the term *noncontrollable cost*?
6. Discuss how financial data prepared on the basis of variable costing can assist management in the development of short-run pricing policies.
7. Why might management analyze product profitability?
8. Explain why rewarding sales personnel on the basis of total sales might not be in the best interests of a business whose goal is to maximize profits.
9. Discuss the two factors affecting both sales and variable costs to which a change in contribution margin can be attributed.
10. How is the quantity factor for an increase or a decrease in the amount of sales computed in using contribution margin analysis?
11. How is the unit cost factor for an increase or a decrease in the amount of variable cost of goods sold computed in using contribution margin analysis?

Practice Exercises

Example Exercises

EE 20-1 *p. 937*

PE 20-1A Variable costing **OBJ. 1**

Kohler Company has the following information for June:

Sales	$540,000
Variable cost of goods sold	194,400
Fixed manufacturing costs	129,600
Variable selling and administrative expenses	43,200
Fixed selling and administrative expenses	32,400

Determine (a) the manufacturing margin, (b) the contribution margin, and (c) income from operations for Kohler Company for the month of June.

EE 20-1 *p. 937*

PE 20-1B Variable costing **OBJ. 1**

Cassy Company has the following information for October:

Sales	$760,000
Variable cost of goods sold	395,200
Fixed manufacturing costs	68,400
Variable selling and administrative expenses	197,600
Fixed selling and administrative expenses	45,600

Determine (a) the manufacturing margin, (b) the contribution margin, and (c) income from operations for Cassy Company for the month of October.

EE 20-2 *p. 938*

PE 20-2A Variable costing—production exceeds sales **OBJ. 1**

Fixed manufacturing costs are $70 per unit, and variable manufacturing costs are $132 per unit. Production was 384,000 units, while sales were 345,600 units. Determine (a) whether variable costing income from operations is less than or greater than absorption costing income from operations, and (b) the difference in variable costing and absorption costing income from operations.

EE 20-2 *p. 938*

PE 20-2B Variable costing—production exceeds sales **OBJ. 1**

Fixed manufacturing costs are $44 per unit, and variable manufacturing costs are $100 per unit. Production was 67,200 units, while sales were 50,400 units. Determine (a) whether variable costing income from operations is less than or greater than absorption costing income from operations, and (b) the difference in variable costing and absorption costing income from operations.

EE 20-3 *p. 939*

PE 20-3A Variable costing—sales exceed production **OBJ. 1**

The beginning inventory is 9,600 units. All of the units that were manufactured during the period and 9,600 units of the beginning inventory were sold. The beginning inventory fixed manufacturing costs are $21 per unit, and variable manufacturing costs are $60 per unit. Determine (a) whether variable costing income from operations is less than or greater than absorption costing income from operations, and (b) the difference in variable costing and absorption costing income from operations.

EE 20-3 *p. 939*

PE 20-3B Variable costing—sales exceed production **OBJ. 1**

The beginning inventory is 52,800 units. All of the units that were manufactured during the period and 52,800 units of the beginning inventory were sold. The beginning inventory

Example Exercises

fixed manufacturing costs are $14.70 per unit, and variable manufacturing costs are $30 per unit. Determine (a) whether variable costing income from operations is less than or greater than absorption costing income from operations, and (b) the difference in variable costing and absorption costing income from operations.

EE 20-4 p. 943

PE 20-4A Analyzing income under absorption and variable costing **OBJ. 2**

Variable manufacturing costs are $13 per unit, and fixed manufacturing costs are $75,000. Sales are estimated to be 12,000 units.

a. How much would absorption costing income from operations differ between a plan to produce 12,000 units and a plan to produce 15,000 units?

b. How much would variable costing income from operations differ between the two production plans?

EE 20-4 p. 943

PE 20-4B Analyzing income under absorption and variable costing **OBJ. 2**

Variable manufacturing costs are $126 per unit, and fixed manufacturing costs are $157,500. Sales are estimated to be 10,000 units.

a. How much would absorption costing income from operations differ between a plan to produce 10,000 units and a plan to produce 15,000 units?

b. How much would variable costing income from operations differ between the two production plans?

EE 20-5 p. 948

PE 20-5A Contribution margin by segment **OBJ. 4**

The following information is for Olivio Coaster Bikes Inc.:

	North	South
Sales volume (units):		
Red Dream	50,000	66,000
Blue Marauder	112,000	140,000
Sales price:		
Red Dream	$480	$500
Blue Marauder	$560	$600
Variable cost per unit:		
Red Dream	$248	$248
Blue Marauder	$260	$260

Determine the contribution margin for (a) Red Dream and (b) North Region.

EE 20-5 p. 948

PE 20-5B Contribution margin by segment **OBJ. 4**

The following information is for LaPlanche Industries Inc.:

	East	West
Sales volume (units):		
Product XX	45,000	38,000
Product YY	60,000	50,000
Sales price:		
Product XX	$700	$660
Product YY	$728	$720
Variable cost per unit:		
Product XX	$336	$336
Product YY	$360	$360

Determine the contribution margin for (a) Product YY and (b) West Region.

Example Exercises

EE 20-6 *p. 951*

PE 20-6A Contribution margin analysis **OBJ. 5**

The actual price for a product was $28 per unit, while the planned price was $25 per unit. The volume decreased by 20,000 units to 410,000 actual total units. Determine (a) the sales quantity factor and (b) the unit price factor for sales.

EE 20-6 *p. 951*

PE 20-6B Contribution margin analysis **OBJ. 5**

The actual variable cost of goods sold for a product was $140 per unit, while the planned variable cost of goods sold was $136 per unit. The volume increased by 2,400 units to 14,000 actual total units. Determine (a) the variable cost quantity factor and (b) the unit cost factor for variable cost of goods sold.

Exercises

EX 20-1 Inventory valuation under absorption costing and variable costing **OBJ. 1**

✔ b. Inventory, $1,428,750

At the end of the first year of operations, 11,250 units remained in the finished goods inventory. The unit manufacturing costs during the year were as follows:

Direct materials	$78
Direct labor	38
Fixed factory overhead	12
Variable factory overhead	11

Determine the cost of the finished goods inventory reported on the balance sheet under (a) the absorption costing concept and (b) the variable costing concept.

EX 20-2 Income statements under absorption costing and variable costing **OBJ. 1**

✔ a. Income from operations, $1,215,000

Beach Motors Inc. assembles and sells Dune Buggy engines. The company began operations on July 1, 2014, and operated at 100% of capacity during the first month. The following data summarize the results for July:

Sales (30,000 units)		$9,000,000
Production costs (40,500 units):		
Direct materials	$4,495,500	
Direct labor	2,187,000	
Variable factory overhead	1,093,500	
Fixed factory overhead	729,000	8,505,000
Selling and administrative expenses:		
Variable selling and administrative expenses	$1,260,000	
Fixed selling and administrative expenses	225,000	1,485,000

a. Prepare an income statement according to the absorption costing concept.

b. Prepare an income statement according to the variable costing concept.

c. What is the reason for the difference in the amount of income from operations reported in (a) and (b)?

EX 20-3 Income statements under absorption costing and variable costing **OBJ. 1**

✔ b. Income from operations, $7,330,500

Ekin Inc. manufactures and sells high-quality sporting goods equipment under its highly recognizable inverse swoosh logo. The company began operations on January 1, 2014, and operated at 100% of capacity (99,000 units) during the first month, creating an ending inventory of 9,000 units. During February, the company produced 90,000 garments during the month but sold 99,000 units at $250 per unit. The February manufacturing costs and selling and administrative expenses were as follows:

	Number of Units	Unit Cost	Total Cost
Manufacturing costs in February beginning inventory:			
Variable	9,000	$100	$ 900,000
Fixed	9,000	20	180,000
Total		$120	$ 1,080,000
February manufacturing costs:			
Variable	90,000	$100	$ 9,000,000
Fixed	90,000	22	1,980,000
Total		$122	$10,980,000
Selling and administrative expenses:			
Variable			$ 4,752,000
Fixed			787,500
Total			$ 5,539,500

a. Prepare an income statement according to the absorption costing concept for February.
b. Prepare an income statement according to the variable costing concept for February.
c. What is the reason for the difference in the amount of income from operations reported in (a) and (b)?

EX 20-4 Cost of goods manufactured, using variable costing and absorption costing

OBJ. 1

✔ b. Unit cost of goods manufactured, $2,800

On June 30, the end of the first year of operations, Monfelli Inc. manufactured 10,800 units and sold 10,000 units. The following income statement was prepared, based on the variable costing concept:

Monfelli Inc.
Variable Costing Income Statement
For the Year Ended June 30, 2015

Sales		$40,000,000
Variable cost of goods sold:		
Variable cost of goods manufactured	$20,736,000	
Less inventory, June 30	1,536,000	
Variable cost of goods sold		19,200,000
Manufacturing margin		$20,800,000
Variable selling and administrative expenses		4,800,000
Contribution margin		$16,000,000
Fixed costs:		
Fixed manufacturing costs	$ 9,504,000	
Fixed selling and administrative expenses	4,000,000	13,504,000
Income from operations		$ 2,496,000

Determine the unit cost of goods manufactured, based on (a) the variable costing concept and (b) the absorption costing concept.

EX 20-5 Variable costing income statement

OBJ. 1

✔ Income from operations, $211,680

On June 30, the end of the first month of operations, Haman Company prepared the following income statement, based on the absorption costing concept:

Haman Company
Absorption Costing Income Statement
For the Month Ended June 30, 2015

Sales (14,400 units)		$1,209,600
Cost of goods sold:		
Cost of goods manufactured (16,800 units)	$1,008,000	
Less inventory, June 30 (2,400 units)	144,000	
Cost of goods sold		864,000
Gross profit		$ 345,600
Selling and administrative expenses		123,120
Income from operations		$ 222,480

If the fixed manufacturing costs were $75,600 and the variable selling and administrative expenses were $68,400 prepare an income statement according to the variable costing concept.

✔ Income from operations, $1,237,500

EX 20-6 Absorption costing income statement **OBJ. 1**

On July 31, the end of the first month of operations, Covelli Equipment Company prepared the following income statement, based on the variable costing concept:

Covelli Equipment Company
Variable Costing Income Statement
For the Month Ended July 31, 2014

Sales (45,000 units)		$6,750,000
Variable cost of goods sold:		
Variable cost of goods manufactured	$3,240,000	
Less inventory, July 31 (9,000 units)	540,000	
Variable cost of goods sold		2,700,000
Manufacturing margin		$4,050,000
Variable selling and administrative expenses		1,710,000
Contribution margin		$2,340,000
Fixed costs:		
Fixed manufacturing costs	$ 675,000	
Fixed selling and administrative expenses	540,000	1,215,000
Income from operations		$1,125,000

Prepare an income statement under absorption costing.

✔ a. Income from operations, $15,818

EX 20-7 Variable costing income statement **OBJ. 1**

The following data were adapted from a recent income statement of Procter & Gamble Company:

	(in millions)
Net sales	$82,559
Operating costs:	
Cost of products sold	$40,768
Marketing, administrative, and other expenses	25,973
Total operating costs	$66,741
Income from operations	$15,818

Assume that the variable amount of each category of operating costs is as follows:

	(in millions)
Cost of products sold	$22,830
Marketing, administrative, and other expenses	10,400

a. Based on the above data, prepare a variable costing income statement for Procter & Gamble Company, assuming that the company maintained constant inventory levels during the period.

b. If Procter & Gamble reduced its inventories during the period, what impact would that have on the income from operations determined under absorption costing?

EX 20-8 Estimated income statements, using absorption and variable costing **OBJ. 1, 2**

✔ a. 1. Income from operations, $136,700 (36,000 units)

Prior to the first month of operations ending July 31, 2014, Muzenski Industries Inc. estimated the following operating results:

Sales (28,800 × $75)	$2,160,000
Manufacturing costs (28,800 units):	
Direct materials	1,324,800
Direct labor	316,800
Variable factory overhead	144,000
Fixed factory overhead	216,000
Fixed selling and administrative expenses	29,400
Variable selling and administrative expenses	35,500

The company is evaluating a proposal to manufacture 36,000 units instead of 28,800 units, thus creating an ending inventory of 7,200 units. Manufacturing the additional units will not change sales, unit variable factory overhead costs, total fixed factory overhead cost, or total selling and administrative expenses.

a. Prepare an estimated income statement, comparing operating results if 28,800 and 36,000 units are manufactured in (1) the absorption costing format and (2) the variable costing format.

b. What is the reason for the difference in income from operations reported for the two levels of production by the absorption costing income statement?

EX 20-9 Variable and absorption costing **OBJ. 1**

✔ a. Contribution margin, $6,042

Whirlpool Corporation had the following abbreviated income statement for a recent year:

	(in millions)
Net sales	$18,666
Cost of goods sold	$16,089
Selling, administrative, and other expenses	1,621
Total expenses	$17,710
Income from operations	$ 956

Assume that there were $4,024 million fixed manufacturing costs and $930 million fixed selling, administrative, and other costs for the year.

The finished goods inventories at the beginning and end of the year from the balance sheet were as follows:

January 1	$2,792 million
December 31	$2,354 million

Assume that 30% of the beginning and ending inventory consists of fixed costs. Assume work in process and materials inventory were unchanged during the period.

a. Prepare an income statement according to the variable costing concept for Whirlpool Corporation for the recent year.

b. Explain the difference between the amount of income from operations reported under the absorption costing and variable costing concepts.

EX 20-10 Variable and absorption costing—three products **OBJ. 2, 3**

Kobeer Inc. manufactures and sells three types of shoes. The income statements prepared under the absorption costing method for the three shoes are as follows:

Kobeer Inc.
Product Income Statements—Absorption Costing
For the Year Ended December 31, 2014

	Basketball Shoes	Cross Training Shoes	Running Shoes
Revenues	$696,000	$588,000	$ 504,000
Cost of goods sold	360,000	288,000	336,000
Gross profit	$336,000	$300,000	$ 168,000
Selling and administrative expenses	288,000	216,000	282,000
Income from operations	$ 48,000	$ 84,000	$(114,000)

In addition, you have determined the following information with respect to allocated fixed costs:

	Basketball Shoes	Cross Training Shoes	Running Shoes
Fixed costs:			
Cost of goods sold	$108,000	$78,000	$96,000
Selling and administrative expenses	84,000	72,000	96,000

These fixed costs are used to support all three product lines. In addition, you have determined that the inventory is negligible.

The management of the company has deemed the profit performance of the running shoe line as unacceptable. As a result, it has decided to eliminate the running shoe line. Management does not expect to be able to increase sales in the other two lines. However, as a result of eliminating the running shoe line, management expects the profits of the company to increase by $114,000.

a. Do you agree with management's decision and conclusions?

b. Prepare a variable costing income statement for the three products.

c. Use the report in (b) to determine the profit impact of eliminating the running shoe line, assuming no other changes.

EX 20-11 Change in sales mix and contribution margin OBJ. 4

Noise Candy Inc. manufactures two models of noise-canceling headphones: No Noise and Silent Candy models. The company is operating at less than full capacity. Market research indicates that 35,700 additional No Noise and 39,600 additional Silent Candy headphones could be sold. The income from operations by unit of product is as follows:

	No Noise Headphone	Silent Candy Headphone
Sales price	$60.00	$84.00
Variable cost of goods sold	33.60	47.00
Manufacturing margin	$26.40	$37.00
Variable selling and administrative expenses	12.00	16.80
Contribution margin	$14.40	$20.20
Fixed manufacturing costs	6.00	8.50
Income from operations	$ 8.40	$11.70

Prepare an analysis indicating the increase or decrease in total profitability if 35,700 additional No Noise and 39,600 additional Silent Candy headphones are produced and sold, assuming that there is sufficient capacity for the additional production.

EX 20-12 Product profitability analysis OBJ. 4

✔ a. Cat contribution margin, $1,258,400

Snow Motor Sports Inc. manufactures and sells two styles of snowmobiles, Arctic and Cat from a single manufacturing facility. The manufacturing facility operates at 100% of capacity. The following per unit information is available for the two products:

(Continued)

	Arctic	Cat
Sales price	$4,200	$2,600
Variable cost of goods sold	2,480	1,680
Manufacturing margin	$1,720	$ 920
Variable selling expenses	628	348
Contribution margin	$1,092	$ 572
Fixed expenses	370	160
Income from operations	$ 722	$ 412

In addition, the following unit volume information for the period is as follows:

	Arctic	Cat
Sales unit volume	3,000	2,200

a. Prepare a contribution margin by product report. Calculate the contribution margin ratio for each product as a whole percent, rounded to two decimal places.

b. What advice would you give to the management of Snow Motor Sports Inc. regarding the relative profitability of the two products?

EX 20-13 Territory and product profitability analysis **OBJ. 4**

✔ a. East contribution margin, $640,000

Coast to Coast Surfboards Inc. manufactures and sells two styles of surfboards, Atlantic Wave and Pacific Pounder. These surfboards are sold in two regions, East and West. Information about the two surfboards is as follows:

	Atlantic Waves	Pacific Pounder
Sales price	$200	$120
Variable cost of goods sold per unit	150	90
Manufacturing margin per unit	$ 50	$ 30
Variable selling expense per unit	34	16
Contribution margin per unit	$ 16	$ 14

The sales unit volume for the sales territories and products for the period is as follows:

	East	West
Atlantic Wave	40,000	25,000
Pacific Pounder	0	25,000

a. Prepare a contribution margin by sales territory report. Calculate the contribution margin ratio for each territory as a whole percent, rounded to two decimal places.

b. What advice would you give to the management of Coast to Coast Surfboards regarding the relative profitability of the two territories?

EX 20-14 Sales territory and salesperson profitability analysis **OBJ. 4**

✔ a. Todd contribution margin, $887,040

Reyes Industries Inc. manufactures and sells a variety of commercial vehicles in the North east and South west regions. There are two salespersons assigned to each territory. Higher commission rates go to the most experienced salespersons. The following sales statistics are available for each salesperson:

	Northeast		Southwest	
	Cassy G.	Todd	Tim	Jeff
Average per unit:				
Sales price	$96,000	$84,000	$108,000	$78,000
Variable cost of goods sold	57,600	33,600	64,800	31,200
Commission rate	12%	16%	16%	12%
Units sold	28	24	24	38
Manufacturing margin ratio	40%	60%	40%	60%

a. 1. Prepare a contribution margin by salesperson report. Calculate the contribution margin ratio for each salesperson.
   2. Interpret the report.

b. 1. Prepare a contribution margin by territory report. Calculate the contribution margin for each territory as a whole percent, rounded to one decimal place.
   2. Interpret the report.

EX 20-15 Segment profitability analysis **OBJ. 4**

✔ a. Electric Power, $824.92

Provided below are the marketing segment sales for Caterpillar, Inc., for a recent year.

Caterpillar, Inc.
Machinery and Engines Marketing Segment Sales
(in millions)

	Building Construction Products	Cat Japan	Core Components	Earth-moving	Electric Power	Excavation	Large Power Systems	Logistics	Marine & Petroleum Power	Mining	Turbines
Sales	$2,217	$1,225	$1,234	$5,045	$2,847	$4,562	$2,885	$659	$2,132	$3,975	$3,321

In addition, assume the following information:

	Building Construction Products	Cat Japan	Core Components	Earth-moving	Electric Power	Excavation	Large Power Systems	Logistics	Marine & Petroleum Power	Mining	Turbines
Variable cost of goods sold as a percent of sales	45%	55%	49%	51%	54%	52%	53%	50%	50%	52%	48%
Dealer commissions as a percent of sales	9%	11%	8%	8%	10%	6%	5%	10%	9%	7%	9%
Variable promotion expenses (in millions)	310	120	150	600	200	600	300	75	270	480	400

a. Use the sales information and the additional assumed information to prepare a contribution margin by segment report. Round to two decimal places. In addition, calculate the contribution margin ratio for each segment as a whole percent, rounded to one decimal place.

b. Prepare a table showing the manufacturing margin, dealer commissions, and variable promotion expenses as a percent of sales for each segment. Round whole percents to one decimal place.

c. Use the information in (a) and (b) to interpret the segment performance.

OBJ. 4, 6

✔ a. Filmed entertainment, $7,777.44, 66%

EX 20-16 Segment contribution margin analysis

The operating revenues of the three largest business segments for Time Warner, Inc., for a recent year are shown below. Each segment includes a number of businesses, examples of which are indicated in parentheses.

Time Warner, Inc.
Segment Revenues
(in millions)

Filmed Entertainment (Warner Bros.)	$11,784
Networks (CNN, HBO, WB)	13,562
Publishing (*Time, People, Sports Illustrated*)	6,328

Assume that the variable costs as a percent of sales for each segment are as follows:

Filmed Entertainment	34%
Networks	32%
Publishing	70%

a. Determine the contribution margin (round to whole millions) and contribution margin ratio (round to whole percents) for each segment from the above information.

(Continued)

b. Why is the contribution margin ratio for the Publishing segment smaller than for the other segments?

c. Does your answer to (b) mean that the other segments are more profitable businesses than the Publishing segment?

EX 20-17 Contribution margin analysis—sales **OBJ. 5**

SPREADSHEET

Buy Best Inc. sells electronic equipment. Management decided early in the year to reduce the price of the speakers in order to increase sales volume. As a result, for the year ended December 31, 2015 the sales increased by $31,875 from the planned level of $1,048,125. The following information is available from the accounting records for the year ended December 31, 2015:

	Actual	Planned	Increase or (Decrease)
Sales	$1,080,000	$1,048,125	$31,875
Number of units sold	36,000	32,250	3,750
Sales price	$30.00	$32.50	$(2.50)
Variable cost per unit	$10.00	$10.00	0

a. Prepare an analysis of the sales quantity and unit price factors.

b. Did the price decrease generate sufficient volume to result in a net increase in contribution margin if the actual variable cost per unit was $10, as planned?

EX 20-18 Contribution margin analysis—sales **OBJ. 5**

✔ Sales quantity factor, –$(600,000)

SPREADSHEET

The following data for Romero Products Inc. are available:

For the Year Ended December 31, 2014	Actual	Planned	Difference—Increase or (Decrease)
Sales	$8,360,000	$8,200,000	$160,000
Less:			
Variable cost of goods sold	$3,496,000	$3,280,000	$216,000
Variable selling and administrative expenses	760,000	902,000	(142,000)
Total variable costs	$4,256,000	$4,182,000	$ 74,000
Contribution margin	$4,104,000	$4,018,000	$ 86,000
Number of units sold	38,000	41,000	
Per unit:			
Sales price	$220	$200	
Variable cost of goods sold	92	80	
Variable selling and administrative expenses	20	22	

Prepare an analysis of the sales quantity and unit price factors.

EX 20-19 Contribution margin analysis—variable costs **OBJ. 5**

✔ Variable cost of goods sold quantity factor, $240,000

SPREADSHEET

Based on the data in Exercise 20-18, prepare a contribution analysis of the variable costs for Romero Products Inc. for the year ended December 31, 2014.

EX 20-20 Variable costing income statement—service company **OBJ. 4, 6**

East Coast Railroad Company transports commodities among three routes (city-pairs): Atlanta/Baltimore, Baltimore/Pittsburgh, and Pittsburgh/Atlanta. Significant costs, their cost behavior, and activity rates for April 2014, are as follows:

Cost	Amount	Cost Behavior	Activity Rate
Labor costs for loading and unloading railcars	$ 175,582	Variable	$46.00 per railcar
Fuel costs	460,226	Variable	12.40 per train-mile
Train crew labor costs	267,228	Variable	7.20 per train-mile
Switchyard labor costs	118,327	Variable	31.00 per railcar
Track and equipment depreciation	194,400	Fixed	
Maintenance	129,600	Fixed	
	$1,345,363		

Operating statistics from the management information system reveal the following for April:

	Atlanta/ Baltimore	Baltimore/ Pittsburgh	Pittsburgh/ Atlanta	Total
Number of train-miles	12,835	10,200	14,080	37,115
Number of railcars	425	2,160	1,232	3,817
Revenue per railcar	$600	$275	$440	

a. Prepare a contribution margin by route report for East Coast Railroad Company for the month of April. Calculate the contribution margin ratio in whole percents, rounded to one decimal place.

b. Evaluate the route performance of the railroad using the report in (a).

EX 20-21 Contribution margin reporting and analysis—service company **OBJ. 5, 6**

SPREADSHEET

The management of East Coast Railroad Company introduced in Exercise 20-20 improved the profitability of the Atlanta/Baltimore route in May by reducing the price of a railcar from $600 to $500. This price reduction increased the demand for rail services. Thus, the number of railcars increased by 275 railcars to a total of 700 railcars. This was accomplished by increasing the size of each train but not the number of trains. Thus, the number of train-miles was unchanged. All the activity rates remained unchanged.

a. Prepare a contribution margin report for the Atlanta/Baltimore route for May. Calculate the contribution margin ratio in percentage terms to one decimal place.

b. Prepare a contribution margin analysis to evaluate management's actions in May. Assume that the May planned quantity, price, and unit cost was the same as April.

EX 20-22 Variable costing income statement and contribution margin analysis—service company **OBJ. 5, 6**

SPREADSHEET

The actual and planned data for Underwater University for the Fall term 2014 were as follows:

	Actual	Planned
Enrollment	4,500	4,125
Tuition per credit hour	$120	$135
Credit hours	60,450	43,200
Registration, records, and marketing cost per enrolled student	$275	$275
Instructional costs per credit hour	$64	$60
Depreciation on classrooms and equipment	$825,600	$825,600

Registration, records, and marketing costs vary by the number of enrolled students, while instructional costs vary by the number of credit hours. Depreciation is a fixed cost.

a. Prepare a variable costing income statement showing the contribution margin and income from operations for the Fall 2014 term.

b. Prepare a contribution margin analysis report comparing planned with actual performance for the Fall 2014 term.

(Continued)

Problems Series A

PR 20-1A Absorption and variable costing income statements — OBJ. 1, 2

✔ 2. Income from operations, $359,940

During the first month of operations ended May 31, 2014, Ice Cold Fridge Company manufactured 17,500 dormitory refrigerators, of which 16,380 were sold. Operating data for the month are summarized as follows:

Sales		$4,095,000
Manufacturing costs:		
Direct materials	$2,065,000	
Direct labor	612,500	
Variable manufacturing cost	525,000	
Fixed manufacturing cost	262,500	3,465,000
Selling and administrative expenses:		
Variable	$ 327,600	
Fixed	147,420	475,020

Instructions

1. Prepare an income statement based on the absorption costing concept.
2. Prepare an income statement based on the variable costing concept.
3. Explain the reason for the difference in the amount of income from operations reported in (1) and (2).

PR 20-2A Income statements under absorption costing and variable costing — OBJ. 1, 2

✔ 2. Contribution margin, $67,275

The demand for solvent, one of numerous products manufactured by Heyward Industries Inc., has dropped sharply because of recent competition from a similar product. The company's chemists are currently completing tests of various new formulas, and it is anticipated that the manufacture of a superior product can be started on June 1, one month in the future. No changes will be needed in the present production facilities to manufacture the new product because only the mixture of the various materials will be changed.

The controller has been asked by the president of the company for advice on whether to continue production during May or to suspend the manufacture of solvent until June 1. The controller has assembled the following pertinent data:

Heyward Industries Inc.
Income Statement—Solvent
For the Month Ended April 31, 2015

Sales (3,900 units)	$421,200
Cost of goods sold	354,700
Gross profit	$ 66,500
Selling and administrative expenses	83,300
Loss from operations	$ (16,800)

The production costs and selling and administrative expenses, based on production of 3,900 units in April, are as follows:

Direct materials	$40 per unit
Direct labor	18 per unit
Variable manufacturing cost	15 per unit
Variable selling and administrative expenses	12 per unit
Fixed manufacturing cost	$70,000 for April
Fixed selling and administrative expenses	36,500 for April

Sales for May are expected to drop about 25% below those of the preceding month. No significant changes are anticipated in the fixed costs or variable costs per unit. No extra costs will be incurred in discontinuing operations in the portion of the plant associated with solvent. The inventory of solvent at the beginning and end of May is expected to be inconsequential.

Instructions

1. Prepare an estimated income statement in absorption costing form for May for solvent, assuming that production continues during the month. Round amounts to two decimals.
2. Prepare an estimated income statement in variable costing form for May for solvent, assuming that production continues during the month. Round amounts to two decimals.
3. What would be the estimated loss in income from operations if the solvent production were temporarily suspended for May?
4. What advice should the controller give to management?

PR 20-3A Absorption and variable costing income statements for two months and analysis

OBJ. 1, 2

✔ 1. b. Income from operations, $38,205

During the first month of operations ended January 31, 2015, Hip and Conscious Clothing Company produced 55,500 designer cowboy hats, of which 51,450 were sold. Operating data for the month are summarized as follows:

Sales		$771,750
Manufacturing costs:		
Direct materials	$471,750	
Direct labor	127,650	
Variable manufacturing cost	61,050	
Fixed manufacturing cost	55,500	715,950
Selling and administrative expenses:		
Variable	$ 36,015	
Fixed	25,725	61,740

During February, Hip and Conscious Clothing produced 47,400 designer cowboy hats and sold 51,450 cowboy hats. Operating data for February are summarized as follows:

Sales		$771,750
Manufacturing costs:		
Direct materials	$402,900	
Direct labor	109,020	
Variable manufacturing cost	52,140	
Fixed manufacturing cost	55,500	619,560
Selling and administrative expenses:		
Variable	$ 36,015	
Fixed	25,725	61,740

Instructions

1. Using the absorption costing concept, prepare income statements for (a) January and (b) February.
2. Using the variable costing concept, prepare income statements for (a) January and (b) February.
3. a. Explain the reason for the differences in the amount of income from operations in (1) and (2) for January.

   b. Explain the reason for the differences in the amount of income from operations in (1) and (2) for February.
4. Based on your answers to (1) and (2), did Hip and Conscious Clothing Company operate more profitably in January or in February Explain.

Instructions

1. Prepare a table indicating contribution margin, variable cost of goods sold as a percent of sales, variable selling expenses as a percent of sales, and contribution margin ratio by salesperson. (Round whole percent to one digit after decimal point.)
2. Which salesperson generated the highest contribution margin ratio for the year and why?
3. Briefly list factors other than contribution margin that should be considered in evaluating the performance of salespersons.

PR 20-5B Variable costing income statement and effect on income of change in operations

OBJ. 4

✔ 3. Income from operations, $106,280

SPREADSHEET

Kimbrell Inc. manufactures three sizes of utility tables—small (S), medium (M), and large (L). The income statement has consistently indicated a net loss for the M size, and management is considering three proposals: (1) continue Size M, (2) discontinue Size M and reduce total output accordingly, or (3) discontinue Size M and conduct an advertising campaign to expand the sales of Size S so that the entire plant capacity can continue to be used.

If Proposal 2 is selected and Size M is discontinued and production curtailed, the annual fixed production costs and fixed operating expenses could be reduced by $142,500 and $28,350, respectively. If Proposal 3 is selected, it is anticipated that an additional annual expenditure of $85,050 for the salary of an assistant brand manager (classified as a fixed operating expense) would yield an additional 130% in Size S sales volume. It is also assumed that the increased production of Size S would utilize the plant facilities released by the discontinuance of Size M.

The sales and costs have been relatively stable over the past few years, and they are expected to remain so for the foreseeable future. The income statement for the past year ended January 31, 2015, is as follows:

	Size			
	S	**M**	**L**	**Total**
Sales	$990,000	$1,087,500	$945,000	$3,022,500
Cost of goods sold:				
Variable costs	$538,500	$ 718,500	$567,000	$1,824,000
Fixed costs	241,000	288,000	250,000	779,000
Total cost of goods sold	$779,500	$1,006,500	$817,000	$2,603,000
Gross profit	$210,500	$ 81,000	$128,000	$ 419,500
Less operating expenses:				
Variable expenses	$118,100	$ 108,750	$ 85,050	$ 311,900
Fixed expenses	32,125	42,525	14,250	88,900
Total operating expenses	$150,225	$ 151,275	$ 99,300	$ 400,800
Income from operations	$ 60,275	$ (70,275)	$ 28,700	$ 18,700

Instructions

1. Prepare an income statement for the past year in the variable costing format. Use the following headings:

Size			
S	M	L	Total

   Data for each style should be reported through contribution margin. The fixed costs should be deducted from the total contribution margin, as reported in the "Total" column, to determine income from operations.
2. Based on the income statement prepared in (1) and the other data presented above, determine the amount by which total annual income from operations would be reduced below its present level if Proposal 2 is accepted.
3. Prepare an income statement in the variable costing format, indicating the projected annual income from operations if Proposal 3 is accepted. Use the following headings:

Size		
S	L	Total

Data for each style should be reported through contribution margin. The fixed costs should be deducted from the total contribution margin as reported in the "Total" column. For purposes of this problem, the additional expenditure of $85,050 for the assistant brand manager's salary can be added to the fixed operating expenses.

4. By how much would total annual income increase above its present level if Proposal 3 is accepted? Explain.

PR 20-6B Contribution margin analysis

OBJ. 5

✔ **1. Sales quantity factor, $310,500**

SPREADSHEET

Mathews Company manufactures only one product. For the year ended December 31, 2014, the contribution margin decreased by $126,000 from the planned level of $540,000. The president of Mathews Company has expressed some concern about this decrease and has requested a follow-up report.

The following data have been gathered from the accounting records for the year ended December 31, 2014.

	Actual	Planned	Difference—Increase or (Decrease)
Sales	$2,277,000	$2,070,000	$207,000
Less:			
Variable cost of goods sold	$1,035,000	$ 990,000	$ 45,000
Variable selling and administrative expenses	828,000	540,000	288,000
Total	$1,863,000	$1,530,000	$333,000
Contribution margin	$ 414,000	$ 540,000	$(126,000)
Number of units sold	34,500	30,000	
Per unit:			
Sales price	$66	$69	
Variable cost of goods sold	30	33	
Variable selling and administrative expenses	24	18	

Instructions

1. Prepare a contribution margin analysis report for the year ended December 31, 2014.
2. At a meeting of the board of directors on January 30, 2015, the president, after reviewing the contribution margin analysis report, made the following comment:

"It looks as if the price decrease of $3.00 had the effect of increasing sales. However, we lost control over the variable cost of goods sold and variable selling and administrative expenses. Let's look into these expenses and get them under control! Also, let's consider decreasing the sales price to $60 to increase sales further."

Do you agree with the president's comment? Explain.

Cases & Projects

CP 20-1 Ethics and professional conduct in business

The Southwest Division of Texcaliber Inc. uses absorption costing for profit reporting. The general manager of the Southwest Division is concerned about meeting the income objectives of the division. At the beginning of the reporting period, the division had an adequate supply of inventory. The general manager has decided to increase production of goods in the plant in order to allocate fixed manufacturing cost over a greater number of units. Unfortunately, the increased production cannot be sold and will increase the inventory. However, the impact on earnings will be positive because the lower cost per unit will be matched against sales. The general manager has come to Aston Melon, the controller, to determine exactly how much additional production is required in order to increase net income enough to meet the division's profit objectives. Aston analyzes the data and determines that the inventory will need to be increased by 30% in order to absorb enough fixed costs and meet the income objective. Aston reports this information to the division manager.

Discuss whether Aston is acting in an ethical manner.

CP 20-2 Inventories under absorption costing

BendOR, Inc. manufactures control panels for the electronics industry and has just completed its first year of operations. The following discussion took place between the controller, Gordon Merrick, and the company president, Matt McCray:

Matt: I've been looking over our first year's performance by quarters. Our earnings have been increasing each quarter, even though our sales have been flat and our prices and costs have not changed. Why is this?

Gordon: Our actual sales have stayed even throughout the year, but we've been increasing the utilization of our factory every quarter. By keeping our factory utilization high, we will keep our costs down by allocating the fixed plant costs over a greater number of units. Naturally, this causes our cost per unit to be lower than it would be otherwise.

Matt: Yes, but what good is this if we have been unable to sell everything that we make? Our inventory is also increasing.

Gordon: This is true. However, our unit costs are lower because of the additional production. When these lower costs are matched against sales, it has a positive impact on our earnings.

Matt: Are you saying that we are able to create additional earnings merely by building inventory? Can this be true?

Gordon: Well, I've never thought about it quite that way . . . but I guess so.

Matt: And another thing. What will happen if we begin to reduce our production in order to liquidate the inventory? Don't tell me our earnings will go down even though our production effort drops!

Gordon: Well . . .

Matt: There must be a better way. I'd like our quarterly income statements to reflect what's really going on. I don't want our income reports to reward building inventory and penalize reducing inventory.

Gordon: I'm not sure what I can do—we have to follow generally accepted accounting principles.

1. Why does reporting income under generally accepted accounting principles "reward" building inventory and "penalize" reducing inventory?
2. What advice would you give to Gordon in responding to Matt's concern about the present method of profit reporting?

CP 20-3 Segmented contribution margin analysis

Bon Jager Inc. manufactures and sells devices used in cardiovascular surgery. The company has two salespersons, Dean and Martin.

A contribution margin by salesperson report was prepared as follows:

Bon Jager Inc.
Contribution Margin by Salesperson

	Dean	Martin
Sales	$400,000	$480,000
Variable cost of goods sold	184,000	264,000
Manufacturing margin	216,000	216,000
Variable promotion expenses	72,000	43,200
Variable sales commission expenses	56,000	67,200
	128,000	110,400
Contribution margin	88,000	105,600
Manufacturing margin as a percent of sales (manufacturing margin ratio)	54%	45%
Contribution margin ratio	22%	22%

Interpret the report, and provide recommendations to the two salespersons for improving profitability.

CP 20-4 Margin analysis

Jellnick Equipment Inc. manufactures and sells kitchen cooking products throughout the state. The company employs four salespersons. The following contribution margin by salesperson analysis was prepared:

Jellnick Equipment Inc.
Contribution Margin Analysis by Salesperson

	Danica	Kyle	Richard	Tom
Sales	$165,000	$187,000	$176,000	$132,000
Variable cost of goods sold	57,750	93,500	88,000	66,000
Manufacturing margin	$107,250	$ 93,500	$ 88,000	$ 66,000
Variable selling expenses:				
Commissions	$ 6,600	$ 7,480	$ 7,040	$ 5,280
Promotion expenses	47,850	44,880	42,240	31,680
Total variable selling expenses	$ 54,450	$ 52,360	$ 49,280	$ 36,960
Contribution margin	$ 52,800	$ 41,140	$ 38,720	$ 29,040

1. Calculate the manufacturing margin as a percent of sales and the contribution margin ratio for each salesperson.
2. Explain the results of the analysis.

CP 20-5 Contribution margin analysis

Trans Sport Company sells sporting goods to retailers in three different states—Florida, Georgia, and Tennessee. The following profit analysis by state was prepared by the company:

	Florida	Georgia	Tennessee
Revenue	$1,125,000	$1,000,000	$1,181,250
Cost of goods sold	562,500	535,000	562,500
Gross profit	$ 562,500	$ 465,000	$ 618,750
Selling expenses	365,600	337,500	420,000
Income from operations	$ 196,900	$ 127,500	$ 198,750

The following fixed costs have also been provided:

	Florida	Georgia	Tennessee
Fixed manufacturing costs	$112,500	$225,000	$126,500
Fixed selling expenses	84,375	135,000	113,625

In addition, assume that inventories have been negligible.

Management believes it could increase state sales by 20%, without increasing any of the fixed costs, by spending an additional $42,200 per state on advertising.

1. Prepare a contribution margin by state report for Trans Sport Company.
2. Determine how much state operating profit will be generated for an additional $42,200 per state on advertising.
3. Which state will provide the greatest profit return for a $42,200 increase in advertising? Why?

CP 20-6 Absorption costing

Group Project

Craig Company is a family-owned business in which you own 20% of the common stock and your brothers and sisters own the remaining shares. The employment contract of Craig's new president, Ajay Pinder, stipulates a base salary of $140,000 per year plus 10% of income from operations in excess of $670,000. Craig uses the absorption costing method of reporting income from operations, which has averaged approximately $670,000 for the past several years.

Sales for 2014, Pinder's first year as president of Craig Company, are estimated at 44,000 units at a selling price of $106 per unit. To maximize the use of Craig's productive capacity, Pinder has decided to manufacture 55,000 units, rather than the 44,000 units of estimated sales. The beginning inventory at January 1, 2014, is insignificant in amount, and the manufacturing costs and selling and administrative expenses for the production of 44,000 and 55,000 units are as follows:

44,000 Units to Be Manufactured

	Number of Units	Unit Cost	Total Cost
Manufacturing costs:			
Variable	44,000	$50.00	$2,200,000
Fixed	44,000	11.00	484,000
Total		$61.00	$2,684,000
Selling and administrative expenses:			
Variable	$ 1,050,000		
Fixed	330,000		
Total	$1,380,000		

55,000 Units to Be Manufactured

	Number of Units	Unit Cost	Total Cost
Manufacturing costs:			
Variable	55,000	$50.00	$2,750,000
Fixed	55,000	8.80	484,000
Total		$58.80	$3,234,000
Selling and administrative expenses:			
Variable	$1,050,000		
Fixed	330,000		
Total	$1,380,000		

1. In one group, prepare an absorption costing income statement for the year ending December 31, 2014, based on sales of 44,000 units and the manufacture of 44,000 units. In the other group, conduct the same analysis, assuming production of 55,000 units.
2. Explain the difference in the income from operations reported in (1).
3. Compute Pinder's total salary for the year 2014, based on sales of 44,000 units and the manufacture of 44,000 units (Group 1) and 55,000 units (Group 2). Compare your answers.
4. In addition to maximizing the use of Craig Company's productive capacity, why might Pinder wish to manufacture 55,000 units rather than 44,000 units?
5. Can you suggest an alternative way in which Pinder's salary could be determined, using a base salary of $140,000 and 10% of income from operations in excess of $670,000, so that the salary could not be increased by simply manufacturing more units?

CHAPTER 21

Budgeting

The North Face

You may have financial goals for your life. To achieve these goals, it is necessary to plan for future expenses. For example, you may consider taking a part-time job to save money for school expenses for the coming school year. How much money would you need to earn and save in order to pay these expenses? One way to find an answer to this question would be to prepare a budget. A budget would show an estimate of your expenses associated with school, such as tuition, fees, and books. In addition, you would have expenses for day-to-day living, such as rent, food, and clothing. You might also have expenses for travel and entertainment. Once the school year begins, you can use the budget as a tool for guiding your spending priorities during the year.

The budget is used in businesses in much the same way as it can be used in personal life. For example, **The North Face** sponsors mountain climbing expeditions throughout the year for professional and amateur climbers. These events require budgeting to plan trip expenses, much like you might use a budget to plan a vacation.

Budgeting is also used by The North Face to plan the manufacturing costs associated with its outdoor clothing and equipment production. For example, budgets would be used to determine the number of coats to be produced, number of people to be employed, and amount of material to be purchased. The budget provides the company with a "game plan" for the year. In this chapter, you will see how budgets can be used for financial planning and control.

Learning Objectives

After studying this chapter, you should be able to: *Example Exercises*

OBJ 1 Describe budgeting, its objectives, and its impact on human behavior.
- Nature and Objectives of Budgeting
  - Objectives of Budgeting
  - Human Behavior and Budgeting

OBJ 2 Describe the basic elements of the budget process, the two major types of budgeting, and the use of computers in budgeting.
- Budgeting Systems
  - Static Budget
  - Flexible Budget — EE 21-1
  - Computerized Budgeting Systems

OBJ 3 Describe the master budget for a manufacturing company.
- Master Budget

OBJ 4 Prepare the basic income statement budgets for a manufacturing company.
- Income Statement Budgets
  - Sales Budget
  - Production Budget — EE 21-2
  - Direct Materials Purchases Budget — EE 21-3
  - Direct Labor Cost Budget — EE 21-4
  - Factory Overhead Cost Budget
  - Cost of Goods Sold Budget — EE 21-5
  - Selling and Administrative Expenses Budget
  - Budgeted Income Statement

OBJ 5 Prepare balance sheet budgets for a manufacturing company.
- Balance Sheet Budgets
  - Cash Budget — EE 21-6
  - Capital Expenditures Budget
  - Budgeted Balance Sheet

At a Glance 21 Page 1002

Nature and Objectives of Budgeting

OBJ 1 Describe budgeting, its objectives, and its impact on human behavior.

Budgets play an important role for organizations of all sizes and forms. For example, budgets are used in managing the operations of government agencies, churches, hospitals, and other nonprofit organizations. Individuals and families also use budgeting in managing their financial affairs. This chapter describes and illustrates budgeting for a manufacturing company.

The chart below shows the estimated portion of your total monthly income that should be budgeted for various living expenses, according to the Consumer Credit Counseling Service.

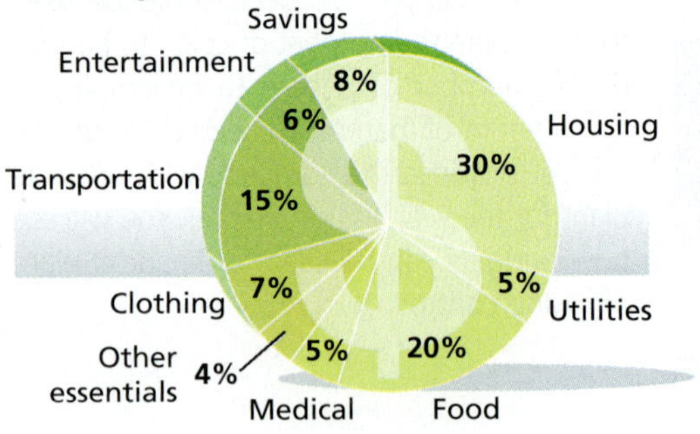

Objectives of Budgeting

Budgeting involves (1) establishing specific goals, (2) executing plans to achieve the goals, and (3) periodically comparing actual results with the goals. In doing so, budgeting affects the following managerial functions:

1. Planning
2. Directing
3. Controlling

The relationships of these activities are illustrated in Exhibit 1.

Planning involves setting goals to guide decisions and help motivate employees. The planning process often identifies where operations can be improved.

EXHIBIT 1 **Planning, Directing, and Controlling**

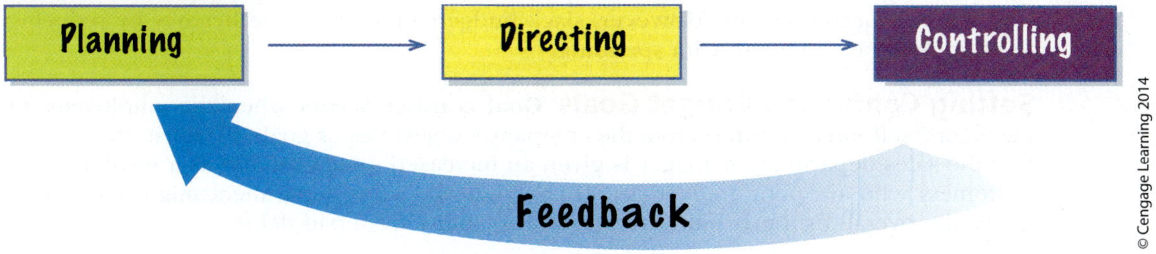

Directing involves decisions and actions to achieve budgeted goals. A budgetary unit of a company is called a **responsibility center**. Each responsibility center is led by a manager who has the authority and responsibility for achieving the center's budgeted goals.

Controlling involves comparing actual performance against the budgeted goals. Such comparisons provide feedback to managers and employees about their performance. If necessary, responsibility centers can use such feedback to adjust their activities in the future.

Human Behavior and Budgeting

Human behavior problems can arise in the budgeting process in the following situations:

1. Budgeted goals are set too tight, which are very hard or impossible to achieve
2. Budgeted goals are set too loose, which are very easy to achieve
3. Budgeted goals conflict with the objectives of the company and employees

These behavior problems are illustrated in Exhibit 2.

EXHIBIT 2 **Human Behavior Problems in Budgeting**

Setting Budget Goals Too Tightly

Employees and managers may become discouraged if budgeted goals are set too high. That is, if budgeted goals are viewed as unrealistic or unachievable, the budget may have a negative effect on the ability of the company to achieve its goals.

Reasonable, attainable goals are more likely to motivate employees and managers. For this reason, it is important for employees and managers to be involved in the budgeting process. Involving employees in the budgeting process provides them with a sense of control and, thus, more of a commitment in meeting budgeted goals.

Setting Budget Goals Too Loosely Although it is desirable to establish attainable goals, it is undesirable to plan budget goals that are too easy. Such budget "padding" is termed **budgetary slack**. Managers may plan slack in their budgets to provide a "cushion" for unexpected events. However, slack budgets may create inefficiency by reducing the budgetary incentive to trim spending.

Setting Conflicting Budget Goals **Goal conflict** occurs when the employees' or managers' self-interest differs from the company's objectives or goals. To illustrate, assume that the sales department manager is given an increased sales goal and as a result accepts customers who are poor credit risks. Thus, while the sales department might meet sales goals, the overall firm may suffer reduced profitability from bad debts.

Integrity, Objectivity, and Ethics in Business

BUDGET GAMES

The budgeting system is designed to plan and control a business. However, it is common for the budget to be "gamed" by its participants. For example, managers may pad their budgets with excess resources. In this way, the managers have additional resources for unexpected events during the period. If the budget is being used to establish the incentive plan, then sales managers have incentives to understate the sales potential of a territory to ensure hitting their quotas. Other times, managers engage in "land grabbing," which occurs when they overstate the sales potential of a territory to guarantee access to resources. If managers believe that unspent resources will not roll over to future periods, then they may be encouraged to "spend it or lose it," causing wasteful expenditures. These types of problems can be partially overcome by separating the budget into planning and incentive components. This is why many organizations have two budget processes, one for resource planning and another, more challenging budget, for motivating managers.

OBJ 2 Describe the basic elements of the budget process, the two major types of budgeting, and the use of computers in budgeting.

Budgeting Systems

Budgeting systems vary among companies and industries. For example, the budget system used by Ford Motor Company differs from that used by Delta Air Lines. However, the basic budgeting concepts discussed in this section apply to all types of businesses and organizations.

The budgetary period for operating activities normally includes the fiscal year of a company. A year is short enough that future operations can be estimated fairly accurately, yet long enough that the future can be viewed in a broad context. However, for control purposes, annual budgets are usually subdivided into shorter time periods, such as quarters of the year, months, or weeks.

A variation of fiscal-year budgeting, called **continuous budgeting**, maintains a 12-month projection into the future. The 12-month budget is continually revised by replacing the data for the month just ended with the budget data for the same month in the next year. A continuous budget is illustrated in Exhibit 3.

Developing an annual budget usually begins several months prior to the end of the current year. This responsibility is normally assigned to a budget committee. Such a committee often consists of the budget director, the controller, the treasurer, the production manager, and the sales manager. The budget process is monitored and summarized by the Accounting Department, which reports to the committee.

EXHIBIT 3 **Continuous Budgeting**

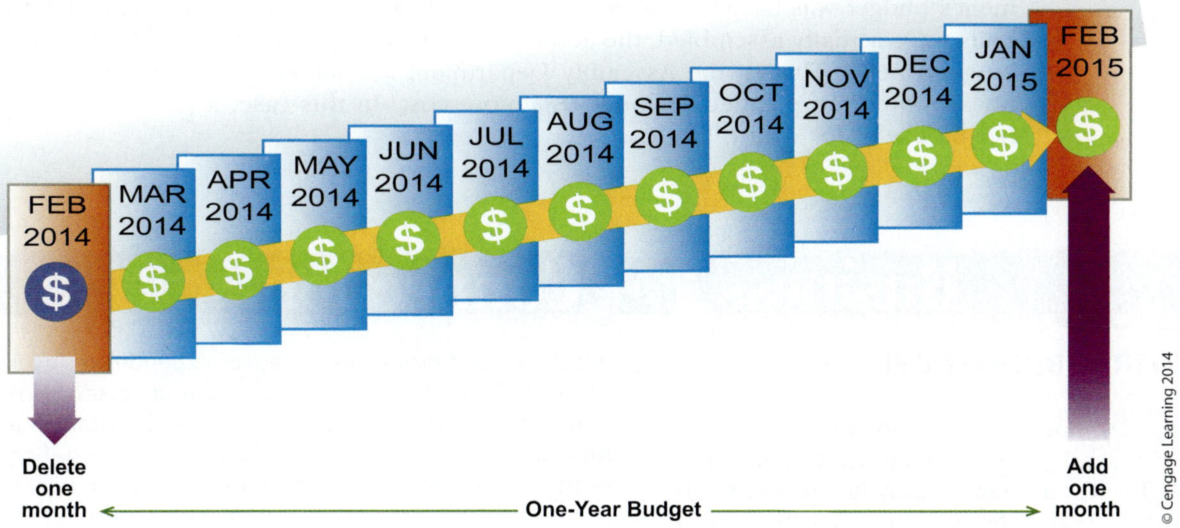

There are several methods of developing budget estimates. One method, termed **zero-based budgeting**, requires managers to estimate sales, production, and other operating data as though operations are being started for the first time. This approach has the benefit of taking a fresh view of operations each year. A more common approach is to start with last year's budget and revise it for actual results and expected changes for the coming year. Two major budgets using this approach are the static budget and the flexible budget.

Static Budget

A **static budget** shows the expected results of a responsibility center for only one activity level. Once the budget has been determined, it is not changed, even if the activity changes. Static budgeting is used by many service companies, governmental entities, and for some functions of manufacturing companies, such as purchasing, engineering, and accounting.

To illustrate, the static budget for the Assembly Department of Colter Manufacturing Company is shown in Exhibit 4.

EXHIBIT 4 **Static Budget**

	A	B
1	**Colter Manufacturing Company**	
2	**Assembly Department Budget**	
3	**For the Year Ending July 31, 2014**	
4	Direct labor	$40,000
5	Electric power	5,000
6	Supervisor salaries	15,000
7	Total department costs	$60,000
8		

A disadvantage of static budgets is that they do not adjust for changes in activity levels. For example, assume that the Assembly Department of Colter Manufacturing spent $70,800 for the year ended July 31, 2014. Thus, the Assembly Department spent

$10,800 ($70,800 – $60,000), or 18% ($10,800/$60,000) more than budgeted. Is this good news or bad news?

The first reaction is that this is bad news and the Assembly Department was inefficient in spending more than budgeted. However, assume that the Assembly Department's budget was based on plans to assemble 8,000 units during the year. If 10,000 units were actually assembled, the additional $10,800 spent in excess of budget might be good news. That is, the Assembly Department assembled 25% (2,000 units/8,000 units) more than planned for only 18% more cost. In this case, a static budget may not be useful for controlling costs.

Business Connection

U.S. FEDERAL BUDGET DEFICIT

Budgeting is an important tool used by municipalities, states, and federal governments to control expenditures. Many states are required by law to have balanced budgets. That is, the amount of money received from taxes and other revenues must be greater than or equal to the planned expenditures for state services. The U.S. federal government, however, may run a budget deficit. A *deficit* is the excess of expenditures over revenues. The deficit is paid for by issuing government debt. The amount of deficit a nation can sustain is a function of the size of its economy. Thus, the deficit is often measured as a percentage of gross domestic product (GDP), a measure of the nation's output of goods and services. The deficit as a percent of GDP for the United States over the last several decades is as follows:

U.S. Federal Deficit as Percent of GDP
Government Spending in U.S. from FY 1980 to FY 2011

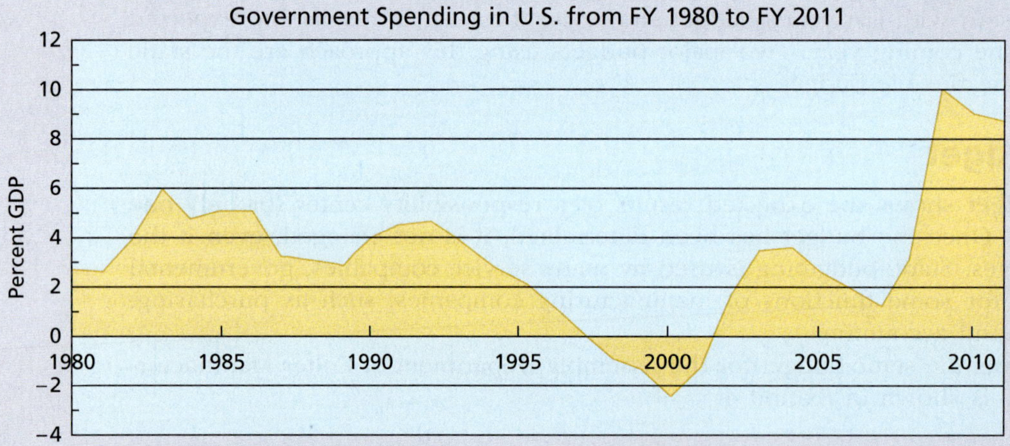

As can be seen, the budget deficit has jumped higher in response to the recession that began in 2008. While a nation may increase a deficit to near 10% of GDP temporarily, keeping a budget deficit above 10% for a long period of time typically slows a nation's economic growth.

Source: Carmen Reinhart and Kenneth Rogoff, *This Time Its Different: Eight Centuries of Financial Folly* (Princeton University Press, 2009). Congressional Budget Office, 2012.

Flexible Budget

Note:
Flexible budgets show expected results for several activity levels.

Unlike static budgets, **flexible budgets** show the expected results of a responsibility center for several activity levels. A flexible budget is, in effect, a series of static budgets for different levels of activity.

To illustrate, a flexible budget for the Assembly Department of Colter Manufacturing Company is shown in Exhibit 5.

EXHIBIT 5

Flexible Budget

	A	B	C	D
1	**Colter Manufacturing Company**			
2	**Assembly Department Budget**			
3	**For the Year Ending July 31, 2014**			
4		**Level 1**	**Level 2**	**Level 3**
5	Units of production	8,000	9,000	10,000
6	Variable cost:			
7	Direct labor ($5 per unit)	$40,000	$45,000	$50,000
8	Electric power ($0.50 per unit)	4,000	4,500	5,000
9	Total variable cost	$44,000	$49,500	$55,000
10	Fixed cost:			
11	Electric power	$ 1,000	$ 1,000	$ 1,000
12	Supervisor salaries	15,000	15,000	15,000
13	Total fixed cost	$16,000	$16,000	$16,000
14	Total department costs	$60,000	$65,500	$71,000

Step 1 (row 5, units of production); Step 2 (rows 6–12, cost components); Step 3 (columns B–D, budget for each level)

A flexible budget is constructed as follows:

Step 1. Identify the relevant activity levels. The relevant levels of activity could be expressed in units, machine hours, direct labor hours, or some other activity base. In Exhibit 5, the levels of activity are 8,000, 9,000, and 10,000 units of production.

Step 2. Identify the fixed and variable cost components of the costs being budgeted. In Exhibit 5, the electric power cost is separated into its fixed cost ($1,000 per year) and variable cost ($0.50 per unit). The direct labor is a variable cost, and the supervisor salaries are all fixed costs.

Step 3. Prepare the budget for each activity level by multiplying the variable cost per unit by the activity level and then adding the monthly fixed cost.

With a flexible budget, actual costs can be compared to the budgeted costs for actual activity. To illustrate, assume that the Assembly Department spent $70,800 to produce 10,000 units. Exhibit 5 indicates that the Assembly Department was *under* budget by $200 ($71,000 – $70,800).

Under the static budget in Exhibit 4, the Assembly Department was $10,800 *over* budget. This comparison is illustrated in Exhibit 6.

The flexible budget for the Assembly Department is much more accurate and useful than the static budget. This is because the flexible budget adjusts for changes in the level of activity.

EXHIBIT 6 **Static and Flexible Budgets**

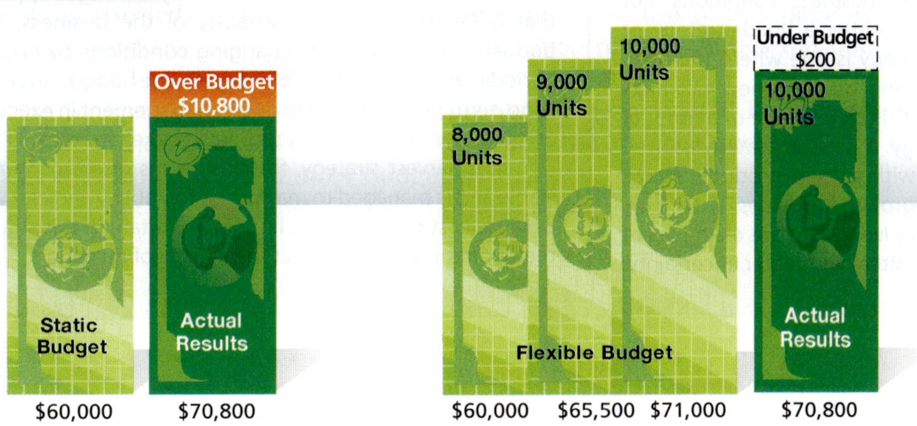

The estimated direct labor hourly rates for the Cutting and Sewing departments during 2014 are shown below.

	Hourly Rate
Cutting Department	$12
Sewing Department	15

Exhibit 11 illustrates the direct labor cost budget for Elite Accessories Inc.

EXHIBIT 11

Direct Labor Cost Budget

	A	B	C	D	E
1		**Elite Accessories Inc.**			
2		**Direct Labor Cost Budget**			
3		**For the Year Ending December 31, 2014**			
4			**Cutting**	**Sewing**	**Total**
5	Hours required for production:				
6	Wallet (Note A)		52,000	130,000	
7	Handbag (Note B)		43,800	116,800	
8	Total		95,800	246,800	
9	Hourly rate		× $12.00	× $15.00	
10	Total direct labor cost		$1,149,600	$3,702,000	$4,851,600
11					
12	Note A:	Cutting Department: 520,000 units × 0.10 hr. per unit = 52,000 hrs.			
13		Sewing Department: 520,000 units × 0.25 hr. per unit = 130,000 hrs.			
14					
15	Note B:	Cutting Department: 292,000 units × 0.15 hr. per unit = 43,800 hrs.			
16		Sewing Department: 292,000 units × 0.40 hr. per unit = 116,800 hrs.			

As shown in Exhibit 11, for Elite Accessories Inc. to produce 520,000 wallets, 52,000 hours (520,000 units × 0.10 hr. per unit) of labor are required in the Cutting Department. Likewise, to produce 292,000 handbags, 43,800 hours (292,000 units × 0.15 hour per unit) of labor are required in the Cutting Department. Thus, the estimated total direct labor cost for the Cutting Department is $1,149,600 [(52,000 hrs. + 43,800 hrs.) × $12 per hr.). In a similar manner, the direct labor hours and cost for the Sewing Department are determined.

The direct labor needs should be coordinated between the production and personnel departments so that there will be enough labor available for production.

Example Exercise 21-4 Direct Labor Cost Budget

OBJ 4

Landon Awards Co. budgeted production of 47,000 brass plaques in 2014. Each plaque requires engraving. Assume that 12 minutes are required to engrave each plaque. If engraving labor costs $11.00 per hour, determine the direct labor cost budget for 2014.

Follow My Example 21-4

Hours required for engraving:	
Brass plaque (47,000 × 12 min.)	564,000 min.
Convert minutes to hours	÷ 60 min.
Engraving hours	9,400 hrs.
Hourly rate	× $11.00
Total direct labor cost	$103,400

Practice Exercises: **PE 21-4A, PE 21-4B**

Selling and Administrative Expenses Budget

The sales budget is often used as the starting point for the selling and adm tive expenses budget. For example, a budgeted increase in sales may requir advertising expenses.

Exhibit 14 illustrates the selling and administrative expenses budget fc Accessories Inc.

	A	B	C
1	Elite Accessories Inc.		
2	Selling and Administrative Expenses Budget		
3	For the Year Ending December 31, 2014		
4	Selling expenses:		
5	Sales salaries expense	$715,000	
6	Advertising expense	360,000	
7	Travel expense	115,000	
8	Total selling expenses		$1,190,000
9	Administrative expenses:		
10	Officers' salaries expense	$360,000	
11	Office salaries expense	258,000	
12	Office rent expense	34,500	
13	Office supplies expense	17,500	
14	Miscellaneous administrative expenses	25,000	
15	Total administrative expenses		695,000
16	Total selling and administrative expenses		$1,885,000

The selling and administrative expenses budget shown in Exhibit 14 is no supported by departmental schedules. For example, an advertising expense scl for the Marketing Department could include the advertising media to be used (paper, direct mail, television), quantities (column inches, number of pieces, mi and related costs per unit.

Budgeted Income Statement

The budgeted income statement is prepared by integrating the following bud

1. Sales budget (Exhibit 8)
2. Cost of goods sold budget (Exhibit 13)
3. Selling and administrative expenses budget (Exhibit 14)

In addition, estimates of other income, other expense, and income tax ar integrated into the budgeted income statement.

Exhibit 15 illustrates the budgeted income statement for Elite Accessories Inc budget summarizes the budgeted operating activities of the company. In doi the budgeted income statement allows management to assess the effects of esti sales, costs, and expenses on profits for the year.

Balance Sheet Budgets

While the income statement budgets reflect the operating activities of the com the balance sheet budgets reflect the financing and investing activities. In this se the following balance sheet budgets are described and illustrated:

1. Cash budget (financing activity)
2. Capital expenditures budget (investing activity)

Factory Overhead Cost Budget

The **factory overhead cost budget** estimates the cost for each item of factory overhead needed to support budgeted production.

Exhibit 12 illustrates the factory overhead cost budget for Elite Accessories Inc.

EXHIBIT 12

Factory Overhead Cost Budget

	A	B
1	Elite Accessories Inc.	
2	Factory Overhead Cost Budget	
3	For the Year Ending December 31, 2014	
4	Indirect factory wages	$ 732,800
5	Supervisor salaries	360,000
6	Power and light	306,000
7	Depreciation of plant and equipment	288,000
8	Indirect materials	182,800
9	Maintenance	140,280
10	Insurance and property taxes	79,200
11	Total factory overhead cost	$2,089,080

The factory overhead cost budget shown in Exhibit 12 may be supported by departmental schedules. Such schedules normally separate factory overhead costs into fixed and variable costs to better enable department managers to monitor and evaluate costs during the year.

The factory overhead cost budget should be integrated with the production budget to ensure that production is not interrupted during the year.

Cost of Goods Sold Budget

The **cost of goods sold budget** is prepared by integrating the following budgets:

1. Direct materials purchases budget (Exhibit 10)
2. Direct labor cost budget (Exhibit 11)
3. Factory overhead cost budget (Exhibit 12)

In addition, the estimated and desired inventories for direct materials, work in process, and finished goods must be integrated into the cost of goods sold budget.

Elite Accessories Inc. expects the following direct materials, work in process, and finished goods inventories:

	Estimated Inventory, January 1, 2014	Desired Inventory, December 31, 2014
Direct materials:		
Leather	$ 81,000 (18,000 sq. yds. × $4.50)	$ 90,000 (20,000 sq. yds. × $4.50)
Lining	18,000 (15,000 sq. yds. × $1.20)	14,400 (12,000 sq. yds. × $1.20)
Total direct materials	$ 99,000	$ 104,400
Work in process	$ 214,400	$ 220,000
Finished goods	$1,095,600	$1,565,000

Exhibit 13 illustrates the cost of goods sold budget for Elite Accessories Inc. It indicates that total manufacturing costs of $9,522,780 are budgeted to be incurred in 2014. Of this total, $2,582,100 is budgeted for direct materials, $4,851,600 is budgeted for direct labor, and $2,089,080 is budgeted for factory overhead. After considering work in process inventories, the total budgeted cost of goods manufactured and transferred to finished goods during 2014 is $9,517,180. Based on expected sales, the budgeted cost of goods sold is $9,047,780.

EXHIBIT 13

Cost of Goods Sold Budget

	A	B	C	D
1		**Elite Accessories Inc.**		
2		**Cost of Goods Sold Budget**		
3		**For the Year Ending December 31, 2014**		
4	Finished goods inventory, January 1, 2014			
5	Work in process inventory, January 1, 2014			
6	Direct materials:			
7	Direct materials inventory,			
8	January 1, 2014		$ 99,000	
9	Direct materials purchases (from Exhibit 10)		2,587,500	
10	Cost of direct materials available for use		$2,686,500	
11	Less direct materials inventory,			
12	December 31, 2014		104,400	
13	Cost of direct materials placed in production		$2,582,100	
14	Direct labor (from Exhibit 11)		4,851,600	
15	Factory overhead (from Exhibit 12)		2,089,080	
16	Total manufacturing costs			
17	Total work in process during period			
18	Less work in process inventory,			
19	December 31, 2014			
20	Cost of goods manufactured			
21	Cost of finished goods available for sale			
22	Less finished goods inventory,			
23	December 31, 2014			
24	Cost of goods sold			
25				

Example Exercise 21-5 Cost of Goods Sold Budget

Prepare a cost of goods sold budget for Landon Awards Co. using the information in E
Assume the estimated inventories on January 1, 2014, for finished goods and work in p
respectively. Also assume the desired inventories on December 31, 2014, for finished g
$50,000 and $49,000, respectively. Factory overhead was budgeted for $126,000.

Follow My Example 21-5

Finished goods inventory, January 1, 2014	
Work in process inventory, January 1, 2014	
Direct materials:	
Direct materials inventory, January 1, 2014	
(240,000 × $0.12, from EE 21-3)	$ 28,800
Direct materials purchases (from EE 21-3)	536,640
Cost of direct materials available for use	$565,440
Less direct materials inventory, December 31, 2014	
(200,000 × $0.12, from EE 21-3)	24,000
Cost of direct materials placed in production	$541,440
Direct labor (from EE 21-4)	103,400
Factory overhead	126,000
Total manufacturing costs	
Total work in process during period	
Less work in process inventory, December 31, 2014	
Cost of goods manufactured	
Cost of finished goods available for sale	
Less finished goods inventory, December 31, 2014	
Cost of goods sold	

Practi

Budgeted Balance Sheet

The budgeted balance sheet is prepared based on the operating, financing, and investing budgets of the master budget. The budgeted balance sheet is dated as of the end of the budget period and is similar to a normal balance sheet except that estimated amounts are used. For this reason, a budgeted balance sheet for Elite Accessories Inc. is not illustrated.

At a Glance 21

OBJ 1 Describe budgeting, its objectives, and its impact on human behavior.

Key Points Budgeting involves (1) establishing plans (planning), (2) directing operations (directing), and (3) evaluating performance (controlling). In addition, budgets should be established to avoid human behavior problems.

Learning Outcomes	Example Exercises	Practice Exercises
• Describe the planning, directing, controlling, and feedback elements of the budget process.		
• Describe the behavioral issues associated with tight goals, loose goals, and goal conflict.		

OBJ 2 Describe the basic elements of the budget process, the two major types of budgeting, and the use of computers in budgeting.

Key Points The budget estimates received by the budget committee should be carefully studied, analyzed, revised, and integrated. The static and flexible budgets are two major budgeting approaches. Computers can be used to make the budget process more efficient and organizationally integrated.

Learning Outcomes	Example Exercises	Practice Exercises
• Describe a static budget and explain when it might be used.		
• Describe and prepare a flexible budget and explain when it might be used.	EE21-1	PE21-1A, 21-1B
• Describe the role of computers in the budget process.		

OBJ 3 Describe the master budget for a manufacturing company.

Key Points The master budget consists of the budgeted income statement and budgeted balance sheet.

Learning Outcome	Example Exercises	Practice Exercises
• Illustrate the connection between the major income statement and balance sheet budgets.		

OBJ 4

Prepare the basic income statement budgets for a manufacturing company.

Key Points The basic income statement budgets are the sales budget, production budget, direct materials purchases budget, direct labor cost budget, factory overhead cost budget, cost of goods sold budget, and selling and administrative expenses budget.

Learning Outcomes	Example Exercises	Practice Exercises
• Prepare a sales budget.		
• Prepare a production budget.	EE21-2	PE21-2A, 21-2B
• Prepare a direct materials purchases budget.	EE21-3	PE21-3A, 21-3B
• Prepare a direct labor cost budget.	EE21-4	PE21-4A, 21-4B
• Prepare a factory overhead cost budget.		
• Prepare a cost of goods sold budget.	EE21-5	PE21-5A, 21-5B
• Prepare a selling and administrative expenses budget.		

OBJ 5

Prepare balance sheet budgets for a manufacturing company.

Key Points The cash budget and capital expenditures budget can be used in preparing the budgeted balance sheet.

Learning Outcomes	Example Exercises	Practice Exercises
• Prepare cash receipts and cash payments budgets.	EE21-6	PE21-6A, 21-6B
• Prepare a capital expenditures budget.		

Key Terms

budget (982)
budgetary slack (984)
capital expenditures budget (1001)
cash budget (998)
continuous budgeting (984)
cost of goods sold budget (995)
direct labor cost budget (993)
direct materials purchases budget (992)
factory overhead cost budget (995)
flexible budget (986)
goal conflict (984)
master budget (989)
production budget (991)
responsibility center (983)
sales budget (990)
static budget (985)
zero-based budgeting (985)

Illustrative Problem

Selected information concerning sales and production for Cabot Co. for July 2014 are summarized as follows:

a. Estimated sales:

Product K:	40,000 units at $30 per unit
Product L:	20,000 units at $65 per unit

b. Estimated inventories, July 1, 2014:

Material A:	4,000 lbs.	Product K:	3,000 units at $17 per unit	$ 51,000
Material B:	3,500 lbs.	Product L:	2,700 units at $35 per unit	94,500
		Total		$145,500

There were no work in process inventories estimated for July 1, 2014.

c. Desired inventories at July 31, 2014:

Material A:	3,000 lbs.	Product K:	2,500 units at $17 per unit	$ 42,500
Material B:	2,500 lbs.	Product L:	2,000 units at $35 per unit	70,000
		Total		$112,500

There were no work in process inventories desired for July 31, 2014.

d. Direct materials used in production:

	Product K	Product L
Material A:	0.7 lb. per unit	3.5 lbs. per unit
Material B:	1.2 lbs. per unit	1.8 lbs. per unit

e. Unit costs for direct materials:

Material A: $4.00 per lb.
Material B: $2.00 per lb.

f. Direct labor requirements:

	Department 1	Department 2
Product K	0.4 hr. per unit	0.15 hr. per unit
Product L	0.6 hr. per unit	0.25 hr. per unit

g.

	Department 1	Department 2
Direct labor rate	$12.00 per hr.	$16.00 per hr.

h. Estimated factory overhead costs for July:

Indirect factory wages	$200,000
Depreciation of plant and equipment	40,000
Power and light	25,000
Indirect materials	34,000
Total	$299,000

Instructions

1. Prepare a sales budget for July.
2. Prepare a production budget for July.
3. Prepare a direct materials purchases budget for July.
4. Prepare a direct labor cost budget for July.
5. Prepare a cost of goods sold budget for July.

Solution

1.

	A	B	C	D
1	Cabot Co.			
2	Sales Budget			
3	For the Month Ending July 31, 2014			
4	Product	Unit Sales Volume	Unit Selling Price	Total Sales
5	Product K	40,000	$30.00	$1,200,000
6	Product L	20,000	65.00	1,300,000
7	Total revenue from sales			$2,500,000

2.

Cabot Co.		
Production Budget		
For the Month Ending July 31, 2014		
	Units	
	Product K	**Product L**
Sales	40,000	20,000
Plus desired inventories at July 31, 2014	2,500	2,000
Total	42,500	22,000
Less estimated inventories, July 1, 2014	3,000	2,700
Total production	39,500	19,300

3.

Cabot Co.			
Direct Materials Purchases Budget			
For the Month Ending July 31, 2014			
	Direct Materials		
	Material A	**Material B**	**Total**
Units required for production:			
Product K (39,500 × lbs. per unit)	27,650 lbs.*	47,400 lbs.*	
Product L (19,300 × lbs. per unit)	67,550 **	34,740 **	
Plus desired units of inventory, July 31, 2014	3,000	2,500	
Total	98,200 lbs.	84,640 lbs.	
Less estimated units of inventory, July 1, 2014	4,000	3,500	
Total units to be purchased	94,200 lbs.	81,140 lbs.	
Unit price	× $4.00	× $2.00	
Total direct materials purchases	$376,800	$162,280	$539,080

*27,650 = 39,500 × 0.7 — 47,400 = 39,500 × 1.2

**67,550 = 19,300 × 3.5 — 34,740 = 19,300 × 1.8

4.

Cabot Co.			
Direct Labor Cost Budget			
For the Month Ending July 31, 2014			
	Department 1	**Department 2**	**Total**
Hours required for production:			
Product K (39,500 × hrs. per unit)	15,800 *	5,925 *	
Product L (19,300 × hrs. per unit)	11,580 **	4,825 **	
Total	27,380	10,750	
Hourly rate	×$12.00	×$16.00	
Total direct labor cost	$328,560	$172,000	$500,560

*15,800 = 39,500 × 0.4 — 5,925 = 39,500 × 0.15

**11,580 = 19,300 × 0.6 — 4,825 = 19,300 × 0.25

5.

	A	B	C	D
1	**Cabot Co.**			
2	**Cost of Goods Sold Budget**			
3	**For the Month Ending July 31, 2014**			
4	Finished goods inventory, July 1, 2014			$ 145,500
5	Direct materials:			
6	Direct materials inventory, July 1, 2014 (Note A)		$ 23,000	
7	Direct materials purchases		539,080	
8	Cost of direct materials available for use		$562,080	
9	Less direct materials inventory, July 31, 2014 (Note B)		17,000	
10	Cost of direct materials placed in production		$545,080	
11	Direct labor		500,560	
12	Factory overhead		299,000	
13	Cost of goods manufactured			1,344,640
14	Cost of finished goods available for sale			$1,490,140
15	Less finished goods inventory, July 31, 2014			112,500
16	Cost of goods sold			$1,377,640
17				
18	Note A:			
19	Material A 4,000 lbs. at $4.00 per lb.	$16,000		
20	Material B 3,500 lbs. at $2.00 per lb.	7,000		
21	Direct materials inventory, July 1, 2014	$23,000		
22				
23	Note B:			
24	Material A 3,000 lbs. at $4.00 per lb.	$12,000		
25	Material B 2,500 lbs. at $2.00 per lb.	5,000		
26	Direct materials inventory, July 31, 2014	$17,000		

Discussion Questions

1. What are the three major objectives of budgeting?
2. Briefly describe the type of human behavior problems that might arise if budget goals are set too tightly.
3. What behavioral problems are associated with setting a budget too loosely?
4. What behavioral problems are associated with establishing conflicting goals within the budget?
5. Under what circumstances would a static budget be appropriate?
6. How do computerized budgeting systems aid firms in the budgeting process?
7. Why should the production requirements set forth in the production budget be carefully coordinated with the sales budget?
8. Why should the timing of direct materials purchases be closely coordinated with the production budget?
9. a. Discuss the purpose of the cash budget.
   b. If the cash for the first quarter of the fiscal year indicates excess cash at the end of each of the first two months, how might the excess cash be used?
10. Give an example of how the capital expenditures budget affects other operating budgets.

Practice Exercises

Example Exercises

EE 21-1 *p. 988*

PE 21-1A Flexible budgeting **OBJ. 2**

At the beginning of the period, the Assembly Department budgeted direct labor of $123,500 and property tax of $10,000 for 6,500 hours of production. The department actually completed 7,300 hours of production. Determine the budget for the department, assuming that it uses flexible budgeting.

EE 21-1 *p. 988*

PE 21-1B Flexible budgeting **OBJ. 2**

At the beginning of the period, the Fabricating Department budgeted direct labor of $9,280 and equipment depreciation of $2,300 for 640 hours of production. The department actually completed 600 hours of production. Determine the budget for the department, assuming that it uses flexible budgeting.

EE 21-2 *p. 992*

PE 21-2A Production budget **OBJ. 4**

LifeTyme Publishers Inc. projected sales of 190,000 diaries for 2014. The estimated January 1, 2014, inventory is 18,400 units, and the desired December 31, 2014, inventory is 20,300 units. What is the budgeted production (in units) for 2014?

EE 21-2 *p. 992*

PE 21-2B Production budget **OBJ. 4**

Magnolia Candle Co. projected sales of 75,000 candles for 2014. The estimated January 1, 2014, inventory is 3,500 units, and the desired December 31, 2014, inventory is 2,700 units. What is the budgeted production (in units) for 2014?

EE 21-3 *p. 993*

PE 21-3A Direct materials purchases budget **OBJ. 4**

LifeTyme Publishers Inc. budgeted production of 191,900 diaries in 2014. Paper is required to produce a diary. Assume seven square yards of paper are required for each diary. The estimated January 1, 2014, paper inventory is 29,100 square yards. The desired December 31, 2014, paper inventory is 32,900 square yards. If paper costs $0.80 per square yard, determine the direct materials purchases budget for 2014.

EE 21-3 *p. 993*

PE 21-3B Direct materials purchases budget **OBJ. 4**

Magnolia Candle Co. budgeted production of 74,200 candles in 2014. Wax is required to produce a candle. Assume eight ounces (one-half of a pound) of wax is required for each candle. The estimated January 1, 2014, wax inventory is 2,500 pounds. The desired December 31, 2014, wax inventory is 2,100 pounds. If candle wax costs $4.10 per pound, determine the direct materials purchases budget for 2014.

EE 21-4 *p. 994*

PE 21-4A Direct labor cost budget **OBJ. 4**

LifeTyme Publishers Inc. budgeted production of 191,900 diaries in 2014. Each diary requires assembly. Assume that nine minutes are required to assemble each diary. If assembly labor costs $16.00 per hour, determine the direct labor cost budget for 2014.

Example Exercises

EE 21-4 *p. 994* **PE 21-4B Direct labor cost budget** **OBJ. 4**

Magnolia Candle Co. budgeted production of 74,200 candles in 2014. Each candle requires molding. Assume that 12 minutes are required to mold each candle. If molding labor costs $14.00 per hour, determine the direct labor cost budget for 2014.

EE 21-5 *p. 996* **PE 21-5A Cost of goods sold budget** **OBJ. 4**

Prepare a cost of goods sold budget for LifeTyme Publishers Inc., using the information in Practice Exercises 21-3A and 21-4A. Assume the estimated inventories on January 1, 2014, for finished goods and work in process were $28,000 and $17,000, respectively. Also assume the desired inventories on December 31, 2014, for finished goods and work in process were $23,700 and $19,500, respectively. Factory overhead was budgeted at $205,800.

EE 21-5 *p. 996* **PE 21-5B Cost of goods sold budget** **OBJ. 4**

Prepare a cost of goods sold budget for Magnolia Candle Co., using the information in Practice Exercises 21-3B and 21-4B. Assume the estimated inventories on January 1, 2014, for finished goods and work in process were $9,800 and $3,600, respectively. Also assume the desired inventories on December 31, 2014, for finished goods and work in process were $12,900 and $3,500, respectively. Factory overhead was budgeted at $109,600.

EE 21-6 *p. 996* **PE 21-6A Cash budget** **OBJ. 5**

LifeTyme Publishers Inc. collects 30% of its sales on account in the month of the sale and 70% in the month following the sale. If sales on account are budgeted to be $320,000 for June and $350,000 for July, what are the budgeted cash receipts from sales on account for July?

EE 21-6 *p. 996* **PE 21-6B Cash budget** **OBJ. 5**

Magnolia Candle Co. pays 10% of its purchases on account in the month of the purchase and 90% in the month following the purchase. If purchases are budgeted to be $11,900 for March and $12,700 for April, what are the budgeted cash payments for purchases on account for April?

Exercises

EX 21-1 Personal budget **OBJ. 2, 5**

✔ a. December 31 cash balance, $4,000

SPREADSHEET

At the beginning of the 2014 school year, Jen Lassiter decided to prepare a cash budget for the months of September, October, November, and December. The budget must plan for enough cash on December 31 to pay the spring semester tuition, which is the same as the fall tuition. The following information relates to the budget:

Cash balance, September 1 (from a summer job)	$5,970
Purchase season football tickets in September	150
Additional entertainment for each month	300
Pay fall semester tuition in September	4,500
Pay rent at the beginning of each month	300
Pay for food each month	180
Pay apartment deposit on September 2 (to be returned December 15)	500
Part-time job earnings each month (net of taxes)	1,450

a. Prepare a cash budget for September, October, November, and December.

b. Are the four monthly budgets that are presented prepared as static budgets or flexible budgets?

c. What are the budget implications for Jen Lassiter?

EX 21-2 Flexible budget for selling and administrative expenses **OBJ. 2, 4**

✔ Total selling and administrative expenses at $120,000 sales, $88,700

SPREADSHEET

Cyberware uses flexible budgets that are based on the following data:

Sales commissions	12% of sales
Advertising expense	22% of sales
Miscellaneous selling expense	$4,200 per month plus 15% of sales
Office salaries expense	$16,000 per month
Office supplies expense	4% of sales
Miscellaneous administrative expense	$2,500 per month plus 2% of sales

Prepare a flexible selling and administrative expenses budget for March 2014 for sales volumes of $80,000, $100,000, and $120,000. (Use Exhibit 5 as a model.)

EX 21-3 Static budget vs. flexible budget **OBJ. 2, 4**

✔ b. Excess of actual over budget for March, $18,000

SPREADSHEET

The production supervisor of the Machining Department for Gilman Company agreed to the following monthly static budget for the upcoming year:

Gilman Company
Machining Department
Monthly Production Budget

Wages	$450,000
Utilities	54,000
Depreciation	60,000
Total	$564,000

The actual amount spent and the actual units produced in the first three months of 2014 in the Machining Department were as follows:

	Amount Spent	Units Produced
January	$450,000	90,000
February	492,000	100,000
March	540,000	110,000

The Machining Department supervisor has been very pleased with this performance, since actual expenditures have been less than the monthly budget. However, the plant manager believes that the budget should not remain fixed for every month but should "flex" or adjust to the volume of work that is produced in the Machining Department. Additional budget information for the Machining Department is as follows:

Wages per hour	$15.00
Utility cost per direct labor hour	$1.80
Direct labor hours per unit	0.25
Planned monthly unit production	120,000

a. Prepare a flexible budget for the actual units produced for January, February, and March in the Machining Department. Assume depreciation is a fixed cost.

b. Compare the flexible budget with the actual expenditures for the first three months. What does this comparison suggest?

EX 21-4 Flexible budget for Fabrication Department **OBJ. 2**

✔ Total department cost at 12,000 units, $566,000

SPREADSHEET

Steelcase Inc. is one of the largest manufacturers of office furniture in the United States. In Grand Rapids, Michigan, it produces filing cabinets in two departments: Fabrication and Trim Assembly. Assume the following information for the Fabrication Department:

Steel per filing cabinet	55 pounds
Direct labor per filing cabinet	20 minutes
Supervisor salaries	$180,000 per month
Depreciation	$28,000 per month
Direct labor rate	$21 per hour
Steel cost	$0.40 per pound

b. Estimated inventories at December 1:

Direct materials:		Finished products:	
Wood	200 ft.	Bird house	320 units at $27 per unit
Plastic	240 lbs.	Bird feeder	270 units at $40 per unit

c. Desired inventories at December 31:

Direct materials:		Finished products:	
Wood	220 ft.	Bird house	290 units at $27 per unit
Plastic	200 lbs.	Bird feeder	250 units at $41 per unit

d. Direct materials used in production:

In manufacture of Bird House:		In manufacture of Bird Feeder:	
Wood	0.80 ft. per unit of product	Wood	1.20 ft. per unit of product
Plastic	0.50 lb. per unit of product	Plastic	0.75 lb. per unit of product

e. Anticipated cost of purchases and beginning and ending inventory of direct materials:

Wood	$7.00 per ft.	Plastic	$1.00 per lb.

f. Direct labor requirements:

Bird House:	
Fabrication Department	0.20 hr. at $16 per hr.
Assembly Department	0.30 hr. at $12 per hr.
Bird Feeder:	
Fabrication Department	0.40 hr. at $16 per hr.
Assembly Department	0.35 hr. at $12 per hr.

g. Estimated factory overhead costs for December:

Indirect factory wages	$75,000	Power and light	$6,000
Depreciation of plant and equipment	23,000	Insurance and property tax	5,000

h. Estimated operating expenses for December:

Sales salaries expense	$70,000
Advertising expense	18,000
Office salaries expense	21,000
Depreciation expense—office equipment	600
Telephone expense—selling	550
Telephone expense—administrative	250
Travel expense—selling	4,000
Office supplies expense	200
Miscellaneous administrative expense	400

i. Estimated other income and expense for December:

Interest revenue	$200
Interest expense	122

j. Estimated tax rate: 30%

Instructions

1. Prepare a sales budget for December.
2. Prepare a production budget for December.
3. Prepare a direct materials purchases budget for December.
4. Prepare a direct labor cost budget for December.
5. Prepare a factory overhead cost budget for December.
6. Prepare a cost of goods sold budget for December. Work in process at the beginning of December is estimated to be $29,000, and work in process at the end of December is estimated to be $35,400.
7. Prepare a selling and administrative expenses budget for December.
8. Prepare a budgeted income statement for December.

✔ 1. July deficiency, $2,200

SPREADSHEET

PR 21-4A Cash budget **OBJ. 5**

The controller of Sonoma Housewares Inc. instructs you to prepare a monthly cash budget for the next three months. You are presented with the following budget information:

	May	June	July
Sales	$86,000	$90,000	$95,000
Manufacturing costs	34,000	39,000	44,000
Selling and administrative expenses	15,000	16,000	22,000
Capital expenditures			80,000

The company expects to sell about 10% of its merchandise for cash. Of sales on account, 70% are expected to be collected in the month following the sale and the remainder the following month (second month following sale). Depreciation, insurance, and property tax expense represent $3,500 of the estimated monthly manufacturing costs. The annual insurance premium is paid in September, and the annual property taxes are paid in November. Of the remainder of the manufacturing costs, 80% are expected to be paid in the month in which they are incurred and the balance in the following month.

Current assets as of May 1 include cash of $33,000, marketable securities of $40,000, and accounts receivable of $90,000 ($72,000 from April sales and $18,000 from March sales). Sales on account for March and April were $60,000 and $72,000, respectively. Current liabilities as of May 1 include $6,000 of accounts payable incurred in April for manufacturing costs. All selling and administrative expenses are paid in cash in the period they are incurred. An estimated income tax payment of $14,000 will be made in June. Sonoma's regular quarterly dividend of $5,000 is expected to be declared in June and paid in July. Management desires to maintain a minimum cash balance of $30,000.

Instructions

1. Prepare a monthly cash budget and supporting schedules for May, June, and July 2014.
2. On the basis of the cash budget prepared in part (1), what recommendation should be made to the controller?

✔ 1. Budgeted net income, $96,600

SPREADSHEET

PR 21-5A Budgeted income statement and balance sheet **OBJ. 4, 5**

As a preliminary to requesting budget estimates of sales, costs, and expenses for the fiscal year beginning January 1, 2015, the following tentative trial balance as of December 31, 2014, is prepared by the Accounting Department of Regina Soap Co.:

Cash	$ 85,000	
Accounts Receivable	125,600	
Finished Goods	69,300	
Work in Process	32,500	
Materials	48,900	
Prepaid Expenses	2,600	
Plant and Equipment	325,000	
Accumulated Depreciation—Plant and Equipment		$156,200
Accounts Payable		62,000
Common Stock, $10 par		180,000
Retained Earnings		290,700
	$688,900	$688,900

Factory output and sales for 2015 are expected to total 200,000 units of product, which are to be sold at $5.00 per unit. The quantities and costs of the inventories at December 31, 2015, are expected to remain unchanged from the balances at the beginning of the year.

Budget estimates of manufacturing costs and operating expenses for the year are summarized as follows:

	Estimated Costs and Expenses	
	Fixed (Total for Year)	**Variable (Per Unit Sold)**
Cost of goods manufactured and sold:		
Direct materials	—	$1.10
Direct labor	—	0.65
Factory overhead:		
Depreciation of plant and equipment	$40,000	—
Other factory overhead	12,000	0.40
Selling expenses:		
Sales salaries and commissions	46,000	0.45
Advertising	64,000	—
Miscellaneous selling expense	6,000	0.25
Administrative expenses:		
Office and officers salaries	72,400	0.12
Supplies	5,000	0.10
Miscellaneous administrative expense	4,000	0.05

Balances of accounts receivable, prepaid expenses, and accounts payable at the end of the year are not expected to differ significantly from the beginning balances. Federal income tax of $30,000 on 2015 taxable income will be paid during 2015. Regular quarterly cash dividends of $0.15 per share are expected to be declared and paid in March, June, September, and December on 18,000 shares of common stock outstanding. It is anticipated that fixed assets will be purchased for $75,000 cash in May.

Instructions

1. Prepare a budgeted income statement for 2015.
2. Prepare a budgeted balance sheet as of December 31, 2015, with supporting calculations.

Problems Series B

PR 21-1B Forecast sales volume and sales budget

OBJ. 4

✔ 3. Total revenue from sales, $2,148,950

SPREADSHEET

Sentinel Systems Inc. prepared the following sales budget for the current year:

Sentinel Systems Inc.
Sales Budget
For the Year Ending December 31, 2014

Product and Area	Unit Sales Volume	Unit Selling Price	Total Sales
Home Alert System:			
United States	1,700	$200	$ 340,000
Europe	580	200	116,000
Asia	450	200	90,000
Total	2,730		$ 546,000
Business Alert System:			
United States	980	$750	$ 735,000
Europe	350	750	262,500
Asia	240	750	180,000
Total	1,570		$1,177,500
Total revenue from sales			$1,723,500

At the end of December 2014, the following unit sales data were reported for the year:

	Unit Sales	
	Home Alert System	**Business Alert System**
United States	1,734	1,078
Europe	609	329
Asia	432	252

For the year ending December 31, 2015, unit sales are expected to follow the patterns established during the year ending December 31, 2014. The unit selling price for the Home Alert System is expected to increase to $250, and the unit selling price for the Business Alert System is expected to be decreased to $820, effective January 1, 2015.

Instructions

1. Compute the increase or decrease of actual unit sales for the year ended December 31, 2014, over budget. Place your answers in a columnar table with the following format:

	Unit Sales, Year Ended 2014		Increase (Decrease) Actual Over Budget	
	Budget	**Actual Sales**	**Amount**	**Percent**
Home Alert System:				
United States				
Europe				
Asia				
Business Alert System:				
United States				
Europe				
Asia				

2. Assuming that the increase or decrease in actual sales to budget indicated in part (1) is to continue in 2015, compute the unit sales volume to be used for preparing the sales budget for the year ending December 31, 2015. Place your answers in a columnar table similar to that in part (1) above but with the following column heads. Round budgeted units to the nearest unit.

2014 Actual Units	Percentage Increase (Decrease)	2015 Budgeted Units (rounded)

3. Prepare a sales budget for the year ending December 31, 2015.

✔ 3. Total direct materials purchases, $987,478

SPREADSHEET

PR 21-2B Sales, production, direct materials purchases, and direct labor cost budgets OBJ. 4

The budget director of Royal Furniture Company requests estimates of sales, production, and other operating data from the various administrative units every month. Selected information concerning sales and production for February 2014 is summarized as follows:

a. Estimated sales of King and Prince chairs for February by sales territory:

Northern Domestic:	
King	610 units at $780 per unit
Prince	750 units at $550 per unit
Southern Domestic:	
King	340 units at $780 per unit
Prince	440 units at $550 per unit
International:	
King	360 units at $850 per unit
Prince	290 units at $600 per unit

b. Estimated inventories at February 1:

Direct materials:		Finished products:	
Fabric	420 sq. yds.	King..................	90 units
Wood	580 linear ft.	Prince	25 units
Filler	250 cu. ft.		
Springs.................	660 units		

c. Desired inventories at February 28:

Direct materials:		Finished products:	
Fabric	390 sq. yds.	King	80 units
Wood	650 linear ft.	Prince	35 units
Filler	300 cu. ft.		
Springs	540 units		

d. Direct materials used in production:

In manufacture of King:	
Fabric	6.0 sq. yds. per unit of product
Wood	38 linear ft. per unit of product
Filler	4.2 cu. ft. per unit of product
Springs	16 units per unit of product
In manufacture of Prince:	
Fabric	4.0 sq. yds. per unit of product
Wood	26 linear ft. per unit of product
Filler	3.4 cu. ft. per unit of product
Springs	12 units per unit of product

e. Anticipated purchase price for direct materials:

Fabric	$12.00 per sq. yd.	Filler	$3.00 per cu. ft.
Wood	7.00 per linear ft.	Springs	4.50 per unit

f. Direct labor requirements:

King:	
Framing Department	1.2 hrs. at $12 per hr.
Cutting Department	0.5 hr. at $14 per hr.
Upholstery Department	0.8 hr. at $15 per hr.
Prince:	
Framing Department	1.0 hr. at $12 per hr.
Cutting Department	0.4 hr. at $14 per hr.
Upholstery Department	0.6 hr. at $15 per hr.

Instructions

1. Prepare a sales budget for February.
2. Prepare a production budget for February.
3. Prepare a direct materials purchases budget for February.
4. Prepare a direct labor cost budget for February.

PR 21-3B Budgeted income statement and supporting budgets — OBJ. 4

✔ 4. Total direct labor cost in Assembly Dept., $171,766

SPREADSHEET

The budget director of Gold Medal Athletic Co., with the assistance of the controller, treasurer, production manager, and sales manager, has gathered the following data for use in developing the budgeted income statement for March 2014:

a. Estimated sales for March:

Batting helmet	1,200 units at $40 per unit
Football helmet	6,500 units at $160 per unit

b. Estimated inventories at March 1:

Direct materials:		Finished products:	
Plastic	90 lbs.	Batting helmet	40 units at $25 per unit
Foam lining	80 lbs.	Football helmet	240 units at $77 per unit

c. Desired inventories at March 31:

Direct materials:		Finished products:	
Plastic	50 lbs.	Batting helmet	50 units at $25 per unit
Foam lining	65 lbs.	Football helmet	220 units at $78 per unit

d. Direct materials used in production:

In manufacture of batting helmet:	
Plastic	1.20 lbs. per unit of product
Foam lining	0.50 lb. per unit of product
In manufacture of football helmet:	
Plastic	3.50 lbs. per unit of product
Foam lining	1.50 lbs. per unit of product

e. Anticipated cost of purchases and beginning and ending inventory of direct materials:

Plastic	$6.00 per lb.
Foam lining	$4.00 per lb.

f. Direct labor requirements:

Batting helmet:	
Molding Department	0.20 hr. at $20 per hr.
Assembly Department	0.50 hr. at $14 per hr.
Football helmet:	
Molding Department	0.50 hr. at $20 per hr.
Assembly Department	1.80 hrs. at $14 per hr.

g. Estimated factory overhead costs for March:

Indirect factory wages	$86,000	Power and light	$4,000
Depreciation of plant and equipment	12,000	Insurance and property tax	2,300

h. Estimated operating expenses for March:

Sales salaries expense	$184,300
Advertising expense	87,200
Office salaries expense	32,400
Depreciation expense—office equipment	3,800
Telephone expense—selling	5,800
Telephone expense—administrative	1,200
Travel expense—selling	9,000
Office supplies expense	1,100
Miscellaneous administrative expense	1,000

i. Estimated other income and expense for March:

Interest revenue	$940
Interest expense	872

j. Estimated tax rate: 30%

Instructions

1. Prepare a sales budget for March.
2. Prepare a production budget for March.
3. Prepare a direct materials purchases budget for March.
4. Prepare a direct labor cost budget for March.
5. Prepare a factory overhead cost budget for March.
6. Prepare a cost of goods sold budget for March. Work in process at the beginning of March is estimated to be $15,300, and work in process at the end of March is desired to be $14,800.
7. Prepare a selling and administrative expenses budget for March.
8. Prepare a budgeted income statement for March.

✔ 1. August deficiency, $9,000

SPREADSHEET

PR 21-4B Cash budget **OBJ. 5**

The controller of Mercury Shoes Inc. instructs you to prepare a monthly cash budget for the next three months. You are presented with the following budget information:

	June	July	August
Sales	$160,000	$185,000	$200,000
Manufacturing costs	66,000	82,000	105,000
Selling and administrative expenses	40,000	46,000	51,000
Capital expenditures	—	—	120,000

The company expects to sell about 10% of its merchandise for cash. Of sales on account, 60% are expected to be collected in the month following the sale and the remainder the following month (second month after sale). Depreciation, insurance, and property tax expense represent $12,000 of the estimated monthly manufacturing costs. The annual insurance premium is paid in February, and the annual property taxes are paid in November. Of the remainder of the manufacturing costs, 80% are expected to be paid in the month in which they are incurred and the balance in the following month.

Current assets as of June 1 include cash of $42,000, marketable securities of $25,000, and accounts receivable of $198,000 ($150,000 from May sales and $48,000 from April sales). Sales on account in April and May were $120,000 and $150,000, respectively. Current liabilities as of June 1 include $13,000 of accounts payable incurred in May for manufacturing costs. All selling and administrative expenses are paid in cash in the period they are incurred. An estimated income tax payment of $24,000 will be made in July. Mercury Shoes' regular quarterly dividend of $15,000 is expected to be declared in July and paid in August. Management desires to maintain a minimum cash balance of $40,000.

Instructions

1. Prepare a monthly cash budget and supporting schedules for June, July, and August 2014.
2. On the basis of the cash budget prepared in part (1), what recommendation should be made to the controller?

✔ 1. Budgeted net income, $114,660

SPREADSHEET

PR 21-5B Budgeted income statement and balance sheet **OBJ. 4, 5**

As a preliminary to requesting budget estimates of sales, costs, and expenses for the fiscal year beginning January 1, 2015, the following tentative trial balance as of December 31, 2014, is prepared by the Accounting Department of Mesa Publishing Co.:

Cash	$ 26,000	
Accounts Receivable	23,800	
Finished Goods	16,900	
Work in Process	4,200	
Materials	6,400	
Prepaid Expenses	600	
Plant and Equipment	82,000	
Accumulated Depreciation—Plant and Equipment		$ 32,000
Accounts Payable		14,800
Common Stock, $1.50 par		30,000
Retained Earnings		83,100
	$159,900	$159,900

Factory output and sales for 2015 are expected to total 3,800 units of product, which are to be sold at $120 per unit. The quantities and costs of the inventories at December 31, 2015, are expected to remain unchanged from the balances at the beginning of the year.

Budget estimates of manufacturing costs and operating expenses for the year are summarized as follows:

	Estimated Costs and Expenses	
	Fixed (Total for Year)	**Variable (Per Unit Sold)**
Cost of goods manufactured and sold:		
Direct materials	—	$30.00
Direct labor	—	8.40
Factory overhead:		
Depreciation of plant and equipment	$ 4,000	—
Other factory overhead	1,400	4.80
Selling expenses:		
Sales salaries and commissions	12,800	13.50
Advertising	13,200	—
Miscellaneous selling expense	1,000	2.50
Administrative expenses:		
Office and officers salaries	7,800	7.00
Supplies	500	1.20
Miscellaneous administrative expense	400	2.40

Balances of accounts receivable, prepaid expenses, and accounts payable at the end of the year are not expected to differ significantly from the beginning balances. Federal income tax of $35,000 on 2015 taxable income will be paid during 2015. Regular quarterly cash dividends of $0.20 per share are expected to be declared and paid in March, June, September, and December on 20,000 shares of common stock outstanding. It is anticipated that fixed assets will be purchased for $22,000 cash in May.

Instructions

1. Prepare a budgeted income statement for 2015.
2. Prepare a budgeted balance sheet as of December 31, 2015, with supporting calculations.

Cases & Projects

CP 21-1 Ethics and professional conduct in business

The director of marketing for Starr Computer Co., Megan Hewitt, had the following discussion with the company controller, Cam Morley, on July 26 of the current year:

Megan: Cam, it looks like I'm going to spend much less than indicated on my July budget.

Cam: I'm glad to hear it.

Megan: Well, I'm not so sure it's good news. I'm concerned that the president will see that I'm under budget and reduce my budget in the future. The only reason that I look good is that we've delayed an advertising campaign. Once the campaign hits in September, I'm sure my actual expenditures will go up. You see, we are also having our sales convention in September. Having the advertising campaign and the convention at the same time is going to kill my September numbers.

Cam: I don't think that's anything to worry about. We all expect some variation in actual spending month to month. What's really important is staying within the budgeted targets for the year. Does that look as if it's going to be a problem?

Megan: I don't think so, but just the same, I'd like to be on the safe side.

Cam: What do you mean?

Megan: Well, this is what I'd like to do. I want to pay the convention-related costs in advance this month. I'll pay the hotel for room and convention space and purchase the airline tickets in advance. In this way, I can charge all these expenditures to July's budget. This would cause my actual expenses to come close to budget for July. Moreover, when the big advertising campaign hits in September, I won't have to worry about expenditures for the convention on my September budget as well. The convention costs will already be paid. Thus, my September expenses should be pretty close to budget.

Cam: I can't tell you when to make your convention purchases, but I'm not too sure that it should be expensed on July's budget.

Megan: What's the problem? It looks like "no harm, no foul" to me. I can't see that there's anything wrong with this—it's just smart management.

How should Cam Morley respond to Megan Hewitt's request to expense the advanced payments for convention-related costs against July's budget?

CP 21-2 Evaluating budgeting systems

Children's Hospital of the King's Daughters Health System in Norfolk, Virginia, introduced a new budgeting method that allowed the hospital's annual plan to be updated for changes in operating plans. For example, if the budget was based on 400 patient-days (number of patients × number of days in the hospital) and the actual count rose to 450 patient-days, the variable costs of staffing, lab work, and medication costs could be adjusted to reflect this change. The budget manager stated, "I work with hospital directors to turn data into meaningful information and effect change before the month ends."

a. What budgeting methods are being used under the new approach?

b. Why are these methods superior to the former approaches?

CP 21-3 Service company static decision making

A bank manager of City Savings Bank Inc. uses the managerial accounting system to track the costs of operating the various departments within the bank. The departments include Cash Management, Trust, Commercial Loans, Mortgage Loans, Operations, Credit Card, and Branch Services. The static budget and actual results for the Operations Department are as follows:

Resources	Budget	Actual
Salaries	$200,000	$200,000
Benefits	30,000	30,000
Supplies	45,000	42,000
Travel	20,000	30,000
Training	25,000	35,000
Overtime	25,000	20,000
Total	$345,000	$357,000
Excess of actual over budget		$ 12,000

a. What information is provided by the budget? Specifically, what questions can the bank manager ask of the Operations Department manager?

b. What information does the static budget fail to provide? Specifically, could the budget information be presented differently to provide even more insight for the bank manager?

CP 21-4 Objectives of the master budget

Domino's Pizza L.L.C. operates pizza delivery and carry-out restaurants. The annual report describes its business as follows:

We offer a focused menu of high-quality, value-priced pizza with three types of crust (Hand-Tossed, Thin Crust, and Deep Dish), along with buffalo wings, bread sticks, cheesy bread, CinnaStix®, and Coca-Cola® products. Our hand-tossed pizza is made from fresh dough produced in our regional distribution centers. We prepare every pizza using real cheese, pizza sauce made from fresh tomatoes, and a choice of high-quality meat and vegetable toppings in generous portions. Our focused menu and use of premium ingredients enable us to consistently and efficiently produce the highest-quality pizza.

Over the 41 years since our founding, we have developed a simple, cost-efficient model. We offer a limited menu, our stores are designed for delivery and carry-out, and we do not generally offer dine-in service. As a result, our stores require relatively small, lower-rent locations and limited capital expenditures.

How would a master budget support planning, directing, and control for Domino's?

CP 21-5 Integrity and evaluating budgeting systems

The city of Milton has an annual budget cycle that begins on July 1 and ends on June 30. At the beginning of each budget year, an annual budget is established for each department. The annual budget is divided by 12 months to provide a constant monthly static budget. On June 30, all unspent budgeted monies for the budget year from the various city departments must be "returned" to the General Fund. Thus, if department heads fail to use their budget by year-end, they will lose it. A budget analyst prepared a chart of the difference between the monthly actual and budgeted amounts for the recent fiscal year. The chart was as follows:

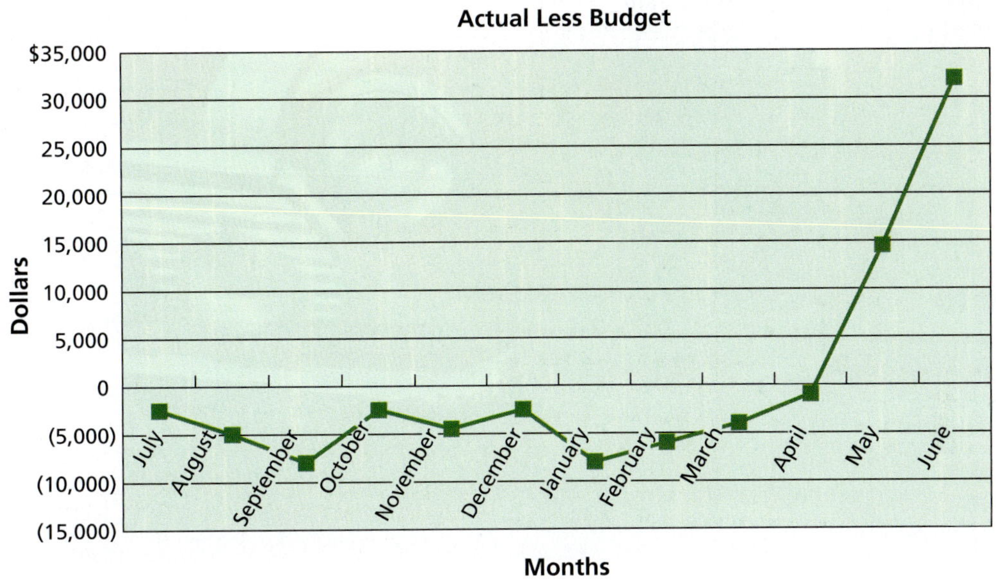

a. Interpret the chart.

b. Suggest an improvement in the budget system.

CP 21-6 Budget for a state government

Internet Project

Group Project

In a group, find the home page of the state in which you presently live. The home page will be of the form *www.statename.gov*. For example, the state of Tennessee would be found at **www.tennessee.gov**. At the home page site, search for annual budget information.

1. What are the budgeted sources of revenue and their percentage breakdown?
2. What are the major categories of budgeted expenditures (or appropriations) and their percentage breakdown?
3. Is the projected budget in balance?

Learning Objectives

After studying this chapter, you should be able to: *Example Exercises*

OBJ	Objective	Example Exercises
1	**Describe the types of standards and how they are established.**	
	Standards	
	Setting Standards	
	Types of Standards	
	Reviewing and Revising Standards	
	Criticisms of Standard Costs	
2	**Describe and illustrate how standards are used in budgeting.**	
	Budgetary Performance Evaluation	
	Budget Performance Report	
	Manufacturing Cost Variances	
3	**Compute and interpret direct materials and direct labor variances.**	
	Direct Materials and Direct Labor Variances	
	Direct Materials Variances	EE 22-1
	Direct Labor Variances	EE 22-2
4	**Compute and interpret factory overhead controllable and volume variances.**	
	Factory Overhead Variances	
	The Factory Overhead Flexible Budget	
	Variable Factory Overhead Controllable Variance	EE 22-3
	Fixed Factory Overhead Volume Variance	EE 22-4
	Reporting Factory Overhead Variances	
	Factory Overhead Account	
5	**Journalize the entries for recording standards in the accounts and prepare an income statement that includes variances from standard.**	
	Recording and Reporting Variances from Standards	EE 22-5, 22-6
6	**Describe and provide examples of nonfinancial performance measures.**	
	Nonfinancial Performance Measures	EE 22-7

At a Glance 22 Page 1052

OBJ 1 Describe the types of standards and how they are established.

Drivers for United Parcel Service (UPS) are expected to drive a standard distance per day. Salespersons for The Limited are expected to meet sales standards.

Standards

Standards are performance goals. Manufacturing companies normally use **standard cost** for each of the three following product costs:

1. Direct materials
2. Direct labor
3. Factory overhead

Accounting systems that use standards for product costs are called **standard cost systems**. Standard cost systems enable management to determine the following:

1. How much a product *should* cost (standard cost)
2. How much it does cost (actual cost)

When actual costs are compared with standard costs, the exceptions or cost variances are reported. This reporting by the *principle of exceptions* allows management to focus on correcting the cost variances.

Setting Standards

The standard-setting process normally requires the joint efforts of accountants, engineers, and other management personnel. The accountant converts the results of judgments and process studies into dollars and cents. Engineers with the aid of operation managers identify the materials, labor, and machine requirements needed to produce the product. For example, engineers estimate direct materials by studying the product specifications and estimating normal spoilage. Time and motion studies may be used to determine the direct labor required for each manufacturing operation. Engineering studies may also be used to determine standards for factory overhead, such as the amount of power needed to operate machinery.

Types of Standards

Standards imply an acceptable level of production efficiency. One of the major objectives in setting standards is to motivate employees to achieve efficient operations.

Ideal standards, or *theoretical standards*, are standards that can be achieved only under perfect operating conditions, such as no idle time, no machine breakdowns, and no materials spoilage. Such standards may have a negative impact on performance, because they may be viewed by employees as unrealistic.

Currently attainable standards, sometimes called *normal standards*, are standards that can be attained with reasonable effort. Such standards, which are used by most companies, allow for normal production difficulties and mistakes. When reasonable standards are used, employees focus more on cost and are more likely to put forth their best efforts.

An example from the game of golf illustrates the distinction between ideal and normal standards. In golf, "par" is an ideal standard for most players. Each player's USGA (United States Golf Association) handicap is the player's normal standard. The motivation of average players is to beat their handicaps because beating par is unrealistic for most players.

Reviewing and Revising Standards

Standard costs should be periodically reviewed to ensure that they reflect current operating conditions. Standards should not be revised, however, just because they differ from actual costs. For example, the direct labor standard would not be revised just because employees are unable to meet properly set standards. On the other hand, standards should be revised when prices, product designs, labor rates, or manufacturing methods change.

Criticisms of Standard Costs

Some criticisms of using standard costs for performance evaluation include the following:

1. Standards limit operating improvements by discouraging improvement beyond the standard.
2. Standards are too difficult to maintain in a dynamic manufacturing environment, resulting in "stale standards."

Integrity, Objectivity, and Ethics in Business

COMPANY REPUTATION: THE BEST OF THE BEST

Harris Interactive annually ranks American corporations in terms of reputation. The ranking is based on how respondents rate corporations on 20 attributes in six major areas. The six areas are emotional appeal, products and services, financial performance, workplace environment, social responsibility, and vision and leadership. What are the five highest ranked companies in its 2011 survey? The five highest (best) ranked companies were Apple Inc., Google, Amazon.com, The Coca-Cola Company, and Kraft Foods.

Source: Harris Interactive, February 2012.

Business Connection

MAKING THE GRADE IN THE REAL WORLD—THE 360-DEGREE REVIEW

When you leave school and take your first job, you will likely be subject to an employee evaluation. These reviews provide feedback on performance that is often very detailed, providing insights to strengths and weaknesses that often go beyond mere grades.

One feedback trend is the 360-degree review. As stated by the human resources consulting firm Towers Perrin, the 360-degree review "is a huge wave that's just hitting—not only here, but all over the world." In a 360-degree review, six to twelve evaluators who encircle an employee's sphere of influence, such as superiors, peers, and subordinates, are selected to fill out anonymous questionnaires. These questionnaires rate the employee on various criteria including the ability to work in groups, form a consensus, make timely decisions, motivate employees, and achieve objectives. The results are summarized and used to identify and strengthen weaknesses.

For example, one individual at Intel Corporation was very vocal during team meetings. In the 360-degree review, the manager thought this behavior was "refreshing." However, the employee's peers thought the vocal behavior monopolized conversations. Thus, what the manager viewed as a positive, the peer group viewed as a negative. The 360-degree review provided valuable information to both the manager and the employee to adjust behavior.

Sources: Llana DeBare, "360-Degrees of Evaluation: More Companies Turning to Full-Circle Job Reviews," *San Francisco Chronicle*, May 5, 1997; Francie Dalton, "Using 360 Degree Feedback Mechanisms," *Occupational Health and Safety*, Vol. 74, Issue 7, 2005.

3. Standards can cause employees to lose sight of the larger objectives of the organization by focusing only on efficiency improvement.
4. Standards can cause employees to unduly focus on their own operations to the possible harm of other operations that rely on them.

Regardless of these criticisms, standards are widely used. In addition, standard costs are only one part of the performance evaluation system used by most companies. As discussed in this chapter, other nonfinancial performance measures are often used to supplement standard costs, with the result that many of the preceding criticisms are overcome.

OBJ 2 Describe and illustrate how standards are used in budgeting.

Budgetary Performance Evaluation

As discussed in Chapter 21, the master budget assists a company in planning, directing, and controlling performance. The control function, or budgetary performance evaluation, compares the actual performance against the budget.

To illustrate, Western Rider Inc., a manufacturer of blue jeans, uses standard costs in its budgets. The standards for direct materials, direct labor, and factory overhead are separated into the following two components.

1. Standard price
2. Standard quantity

The standard cost per unit for direct materials, direct labor, and factory overhead is computed as follows:

Standard Cost per Unit = Standard Price × Standard Quantity

Western Rider's standard costs per unit for its XL jeans are shown in Exhibit 1.

EXHIBIT 1

Standard Cost for XL Jeans

Manufacturing Costs	Standard Price	×	Standard Quantity per Pair	=	Standard Cost per Pair of XL Jeans
Direct materials	$5.00 per sq. yd.		1.5 sq. yds.		$ 7.50
Direct labor	$9.00 per hr.		0.80 hr. per pair		7.20
Factory overhead	$6.00 per hr.		0.80 hr. per pair		4.80
Total standard cost per pair					$19.50

As shown in Exhibit 1, the standard cost per pair of XL jeans is $19.50, which consists of $7.50 for direct materials, $7.20 for direct labor, and $4.80 for factory overhead.

The standard price and standard quantity are separated for each product cost. For example, Exhibit 1 indicates that for each pair of XL jeans, the standard price for direct materials is $5.00 per square yard and the standard quantity is 1.5 square yards. The standard price and quantity are separated because the department responsible for their control is normally different. For example, the direct materials price per square yard is controlled by the Purchasing Department, and the direct materials quantity per pair is controlled by the Production Department.

As illustrated in Chapter 21, the master budget is prepared based on planned sales and production. The budgeted costs for materials purchases, direct labor, and factory overhead are determined by multiplying their standard costs per unit by the planned level of production. Budgeted (standard) costs are then compared to actual costs during the year for control purposes.

Budget Performance Report

The report that summarizes actual costs, standard costs, and the differences for the units produced is called a **budget performance report**. To illustrate, assume that Western Rider produced the following pairs of jeans during June:

XL jeans produced and sold	5,000 pairs
Actual costs incurred in June:	
Direct materials	$ 40,150
Direct labor	38,500
Factory overhead	22,400
Total costs incurred	$101,050

Exhibit 2 illustrates the budget performance report for June for Western Rider Inc. The report summarizes the actual costs, standard costs, and the differences for each product cost. The differences between actual and standard costs are called **cost variances**. A **favorable cost variance** occurs when the actual cost is less than the standard cost. An **unfavorable cost variance** occurs when the actual cost exceeds the standard cost.

Note:

Favorable cost variance: Actual cost < Standard cost at actual volumes

Unfavorable cost variance: Actual cost > Standard cost at actual volumes

EXHIBIT 2 Budget Performance Report

Western Rider Inc.
Budget Performance Report
For the Month Ended June 30, 2014

Manufacturing Costs	Actual Costs	Standard Cost at Actual Volume (5,000 pairs of XL Jeans)*	Cost Variance— (Favorable) Unfavorable
Direct materials	$ 40,150	$37,500	$ 2,650
Direct labor	38,500	36,000	2,500
Factory overhead	22,400	24,000	(1,600)
Total manufacturing costs	$101,050	$97,500	$ 3,550

*5,000 pairs × $7.50 per pair = $37,500
5,000 pairs × $7.20 per pair = $36,000
5,000 pairs × $4.80 per pair = $24,000

The budget performance report shown in Exhibit 2 is based on the actual units produced in June of 5,000 XL jeans. Even though 6,000 XL jeans might have been *planned* for production, the budget performance report is based on *actual* production.

Manufacturing Cost Variances

The **total manufacturing cost variance** is the difference between total standard costs and total actual cost for the units produced. As shown in Exhibit 2, the total manufacturing cost unfavorable variance and the variance for each product cost is as follows:

	Cost Variance (Favorable) Unfavorable
Direct materials	$ 2,650
Direct labor	2,500
Factory overhead	(1,600)
Total manufacturing variance	$ 3,550

For control purposes, each product cost variance is separated into two additional variances as shown in Exhibit 3.

EXHIBIT 3 Manufacturing Cost Variances

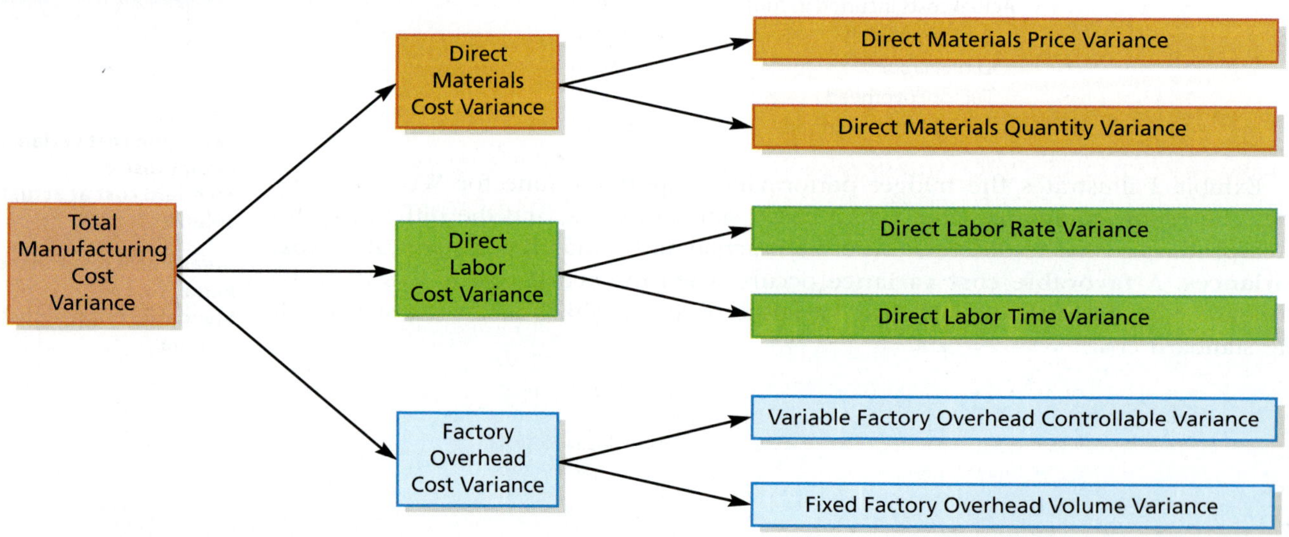

The total direct materials variance is separated into a *price* variance and a *quantity* variance. This is because standard and actual direct materials costs are computed as follows:

Actual Direct Materials Cost	=	Actual Price	×	Actual Quantity
Standard Direct Materials Cost	=	–Standard Price	×	Standard Quantity
Direct Materials Cost Variance	=	Price Difference	+	Quantity Difference

Thus, the actual and standard direct materials costs may differ because of a price difference (variance), a quantity difference (variance), or both.

Likewise, the total direct labor variance is separated into a *rate* variance and a *time* variance. This is because standard and actual direct labor costs are computed as follows:

Actual Direct Labor Cost	=	Actual Rate	×	Actual Time
Standard Direct Labor Cost	=	–Standard Rate	×	Standard Time
Direct Labor Cost Variance	=	Rate Difference	+	Time Difference

Therefore, the actual and standard direct labor costs may differ because of a rate difference (variance), a time difference (variance), or both.

The total factory overhead variance is separated into a *controllable* variance and a *volume* variance. Because factory overhead has fixed and variable cost elements, it uses different variances than direct materials and direct labor, which are variable costs.

In the next sections, the price and quantity variances for direct materials, the rate and time variances for direct labor, and the controllable and volume variances for factory overhead are further described and illustrated.

Direct Materials and Direct Labor Variances

OBJ 3 Compute and interpret direct materials and direct labor variances.

As indicated in the prior section, the total direct materials and direct labor variances are separated into the following variances for analysis and control purposes:

Total Direct Materials Cost Variance ⟶ { Direct Materials Price Variance; Direct Materials Quantity Variance }

Total Direct Labor Cost Variance ⟶ { Direct Labor Rate Variance; Direct Labor Time Variance }

As a basis for illustration, the variances for Western Rider Inc.'s June operations shown in Exhibit 2 are used.

Direct Materials Variances

During June, Western Rider reported an unfavorable total direct materials cost variance of $2,650 for the production of 5,000 XL style jeans, as shown in Exhibit 2. This variance was based on the following actual and standard costs:

Actual costs	$40,150
Standard costs	37,500
Total direct materials cost variance	$ 2,650

The actual costs incurred of $40,150 consist of the following:

Actual Direct Materials Cost = Actual Price × Actual Quantity
Actual Direct Materials Cost = ($5.50 per sq. yd.) × (7,300 sq. yds.)
Actual Direct Materials Cost = $40,150

The standard costs of $37,500 consist of the following:

Standard Direct Materials Cost = Standard Price × Standard Quantity
Standard Direct Materials Cost = ($5.00 per sq. yd.) × (7,500 sq. yds.)
Standard Direct Materials Cost = $37,500

The standard price of $5.00 per square yard is taken from Exhibit 1. In addition, Exhibit 1 indicates that 1.5 square yards is the standard for producing one pair of XL jeans. Thus, 7,500 (5,000 × 1.5) square yards is the standard for producing 5,000 pairs of XL jeans.

Comparing the actual and standard cost computations shown above indicates that the total direct materials unfavorable cost variance of $2,650 is caused by the following:

1. A price per square yard of $0.50 ($5.50 – $5.00) more than standard
2. A quantity usage of 200 square yards (7,300 sq. yds. – 7,500 sq. yds.) less than standard

The impact of these differences from standard is reported and analyzed as a direct materials *price* variance and direct materials *quantity* variance.

Direct Materials Price Variance The **direct materials price variance** is computed as follows:

Direct Materials Price Variance = (Actual Price – Standard Price) × Actual Quantity

If the actual price per unit exceeds the standard price per unit, the variance is unfavorable. This positive amount (unfavorable variance) can be thought of as increasing costs (a debit). If the actual price per unit is less than the standard price per unit, the variance is favorable. This negative amount (favorable variance) can be thought of as decreasing costs (a credit).

To illustrate, the direct materials price variance for Western Rider Inc. is computed as follows:[1]

Direct Materials Price Variance = (Actual Price – Standard Price) × Actual Quantity
Direct Materials Price Variance = ($5.50 – $5.00) × 7,300 sq. yds.
Direct Materials Price Variance = $3,650 Unfavorable Variance

As shown above, Western Rider has an unfavorable direct materials price variance of $3,650 for June.

Direct Materials Quantity Variance The **direct materials quantity variance** is computed as follows:

Direct Materials Quantity Variance = (Actual Quantity – Standard Quantity) × Standard Price

If the actual quantity for the units produced exceeds the standard quantity, the variance is unfavorable. This positive amount (unfavorable variance) can be thought of as increasing costs (a debit). If the actual quantity for the units produced is less than the standard quantity, the variance is favorable. This negative amount (favorable variance) can be thought of as decreasing costs (a credit).

To illustrate, the direct materials quantity variance for Western Rider Inc. is computed as follows:

Direct Materials Quantity Variance = (Actual Quantity – Standard Quantity) × Standard Price
Direct Materials Quantity Variance = (7,300 sq. yds. – 7,500 sq. yds.) × $5.00
Direct Materials Quantity Variance = –$1,000 Favorable Variance

As shown above, Western Rider has a favorable direct materials quantity variance of $1,000 for June.

Direct Materials Variance Relationships The relationship among the *total* direct materials cost variance, the direct materials *price* variance, and the direct materials *quantity* variance is shown in Exhibit 4.

1 To simplify, it is assumed that there is no change in the beginning and ending materials inventories. Thus, the amount of materials budgeted for production equals the amount purchased.

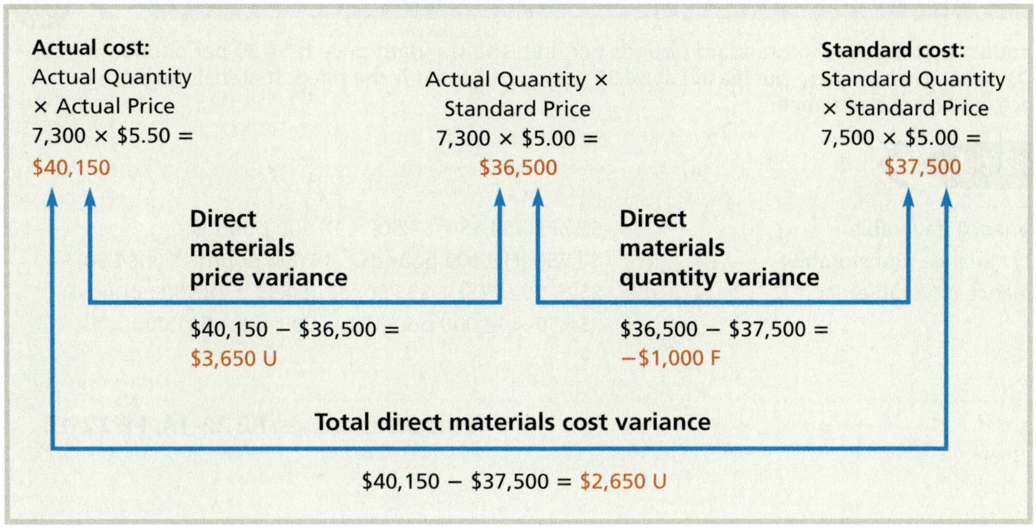

EXHIBIT 4

Direct Materials Variance Relationships

Reporting Direct Materials Variances The direct materials quantity variances should be reported to the manager responsible for the variance. For example, an unfavorable quantity variance might be caused by either of the following:

1. Equipment that has not been properly maintained
2. Low-quality (inferior) direct materials

In the first case, the operating department responsible for maintaining the equipment should be held responsible for the variance. In the second case, the Purchasing Department should be held responsible.

Not all variances are controllable. For example, an unfavorable materials price variance might be due to market-wide price increases. In this case, there is nothing the Purchasing Department might have done to avoid the unfavorable variance. On the other hand, if materials of the same quality could have been purchased from another supplier at the standard price, the variance was controllable.

Business Connection

WOULD YOU LIKE DESSERT?

Many restaurants use standards to manage the business. Food quantity standards are used to control the amount of food that is served to a customer. For example, Darden Restaurants, Inc., the operator of the Red Lobster chain, establishes food quantity standards for the number of shrimp, scallops, or clams on a seafood plate.

A food price variance can be used to control the price paid for food products. For example, Uno Restaurant Holdings Corp. controls food prices by using "forward contracts" for about 80% of its cheese and 50% of its wheat. Such a contract locks in the price for a period of time, thus eliminating materials price variances (favorable or unfavorable) for these items over the contract term.

Standards can also be used in innovative ways to monitor revenues. Brinker International, the operator of popular chains such as Chili's and On the Border, uses "theoretical food system" software that enables it to compare customer traffic and menu item volumes over a period of time. Thus, actual order revenue can be compared to expected (standard) revenues, based on actual traffic volumes. In this way, the restaurant can monitor trends and check composition and size.

Source: Edward Teach, "Table Stakes," *CFO* (December 2008), pp. 44–49.

Example Exercise 22-1 Direct Materials Variances

OBJ 3

Tip Top Corp. produces a product that requires six standard pounds per unit. The standard price is $4.50 per pound. If 3,000 units required 18,500 pounds, which were purchased at $4.35 per pound, what is the direct materials (a) price variance, (b) quantity variance, and (c) cost variance?

Follow My Example 22-1

a.	Direct materials price variance (favorable)	–$2,775 [($4.35 – $4.50) × 18,500 pounds]
b.	Direct materials quantity variance (unfavorable)	$2,250 [(18,500 pounds – 18,000 pounds*) × $4.50]
c.	Direct materials cost variance (favorable)	–$525 [(\$2,775) + $2,250] or [($4.35 × 18,500 pounds) – ($4.50 × 18,000 pounds)] = $80,475 – $81,000

*3,000 units × 6 pounds

Practice Exercises: **PE 22-1A, PE 22-1B**

The Internal Revenue Service publishes a time standard for completing a tax return. The average 1040EZ return is expected to require eight hours to prepare.

Direct Labor Variances

During June, Western Rider reported an unfavorable total direct labor cost variance of $2,500 for the production of 5,000 XL style jeans, as shown in Exhibit 2. This variance was based on the following actual and standard costs:

Actual costs	$38,500
Standard costs	36,000
Total direct labor cost variance	$ 2,500

The actual costs incurred of $38,500 consist of the following:

Actual Direct Labor Cost = Actual Rate per Hour × Actual Time
Actual Direct Labor Cost = $10.00 per hr. × 3,850 hrs.
Actual Direct Labor Cost = $38,500

The standard costs of $36,000 consist of the following:

Standard Direct Labor Cost = Standard Rate per Hour × Standard Time
Standard Direct Labor Cost = $9.00 per hr. × 4,000 hrs.
Standard Direct Labor Cost = $36,000

The standard rate of $9.00 per direct labor hour is taken from Exhibit 1. In addition, Exhibit 1 indicates that 0.80 hour is the standard time required for producing one pair of XL jeans. Thus, 4,000 (5,000 units × 0.80 hr.) direct labor hours is the standard for producing 5,000 pairs of XL jeans.

Comparing the actual and standard cost computations shown above indicates that the total direct labor unfavorable cost variance of $2,500 is caused by the following:

1. A rate of $1.00 per hour ($10.00 – $9.00) more than standard
2. A quantity of 150 hours (4,000 hrs. – 3,850 hrs.) less than standard

The impact of these differences from standard is reported and analyzed as a direct labor *rate* variance and a direct labor *time* variance.

Direct Labor Rate Variance The **direct labor rate variance** is computed as follows:

Direct Labor Rate Variance = (Actual Rate per Hour – Standard Rate per Hour) × Actual Hours

If the actual rate per hour exceeds the standard rate per hour, the variance is unfavorable. This positive amount (unfavorable variance) can be thought of as increasing costs (a debit). If the actual rate per hour is less than the standard rate per hour, the variance is favorable. This negative amount (favorable variance) can be thought of as decreasing costs (a credit).

To illustrate, the direct labor rate variance for Western Rider Inc. is computed as follows:

Direct Labor Rate Variance = (Actual Rate per Hour – Standard Rate per Hour) × Actual Hours
Direct Labor Rate Variance = ($10.00 – $9.00) × 3,850 hours
Direct Labor Rate Variance = $3,850 Unfavorable Variance

As shown above, Western Rider has an unfavorable direct labor rate variance of $3,850 for June.

Direct Labor Time Variance The **direct labor time variance** is computed as follows:

Direct Labor Time Variance = (Actual Direct Labor Hours – Standard Direct Labor Hours) × Standard Rate per Hour

If the actual direct labor hours for the units produced exceeds the standard direct labor hours, the variance is unfavorable. This positive amount (unfavorable variance) can be thought of as increasing costs (a debit). If the actual direct labor hours for the units produced is less than the standard direct labor hours, the variance is favorable. This negative amount (favorable variance) can be thought of as decreasing costs (a credit).

To illustrate, the direct labor time variance for Western Rider Inc. is computed as follows:

Direct Labor Time Variance = (Actual Direct Labor Hours – Standard Direct Labor Hours) × Standard Rate per Hour
Direct Labor Time Variance = (3,850 hours – 4,000 direct labor hours) × $9.00
Direct Labor Time Variance = – $1,350 Favorable Variance

As shown above, Western Rider has a favorable direct labor time variance of $1,350 for June.

Direct Labor Variance Relationships The relationships among the *total* direct labor cost variance, the direct labor *rate* variance, and the direct labor *time* variance is shown in Exhibit 5.

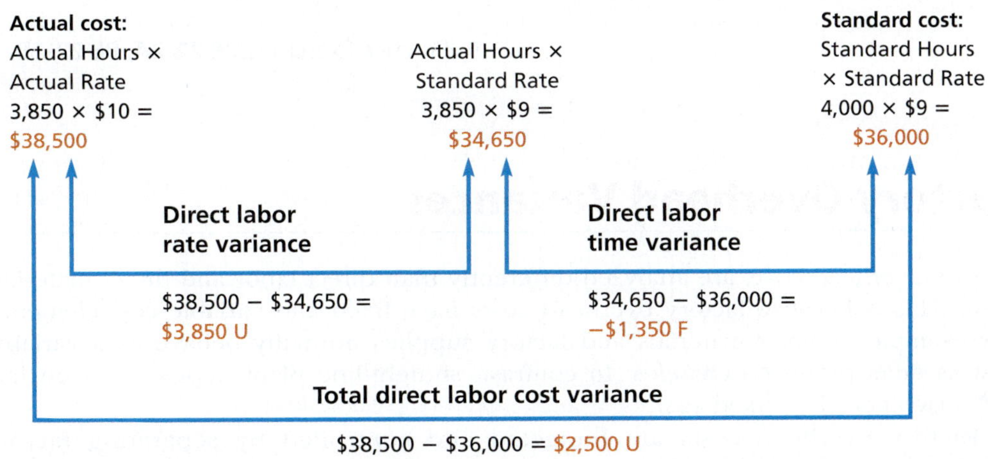

EXHIBIT 5

Direct Labor Variance Relationships

Reporting Direct Labor Variances Production supervisors are normally responsible for controlling direct labor cost. For example, an investigation could reveal the following causes for unfavorable rate and time variances:

1. An unfavorable rate variance may be caused by the improper scheduling and use of employees. In such cases, skilled, highly paid employees may be used in jobs that are normally performed by unskilled, lower-paid employees. In this case, the unfavorable rate variance should be reported to the managers who schedule work assignments.

2. An unfavorable time variance may be caused by a shortage of skilled employees. In such cases, there may be an abnormally high turnover rate among skilled employees. In this case, production supervisors with high turnover rates should be questioned as to why their employees are quitting.

Direct Labor Standards for Nonmanufacturing Activities Direct labor time standards can also be developed for use in administrative, selling, and service activities. This is most appropriate when the activity involves a repetitive task that produces a common output. In these cases, the use of standards is similar to that for a manufactured product.

To illustrate, standards could be developed for customer service personnel who process sales orders. A standard time for processing a sales order (the output) could be developed and used to control sales order processing costs. Similar standards could be developed for computer help desk operators, nurses, and insurance application processors.

When labor-related activities are not repetitive, direct labor time standards are less commonly used. For example, the time spent by a senior executive or the work of a research and development scientist would not normally be controlled using time standards.

Example Exercise 22-2 Direct Labor Variances OBJ 3

Tip Top Corp. produces a product that requires 2.5 standard hours per unit at a standard hourly rate of $12 per hour. If 3,000 units required 7,420 hours at an hourly rate of $12.30 per hour, what is the (a) direct labor rate variance, (b) direct labor time variance, and (c) total direct labor cost variance?

Follow My Example 22-2

a. Direct labor rate variance (unfavorable)	$2,226 [($12.30 – $12.00) × 7,420 hours]
b. Direct labor time variance (favorable)	–$960 [(7,420 hours – 7,500 hours*) × $12.00]
c. Total direct labor cost variance (unfavorable)	$1,266 [$2,226 + ($960)] or [($12.30 × 7,420 hours) – ($12.00 × 7,500 hours)] = $91,266 – $90,000

*3,000 units × 2.5 hours

Practice Exercises: **PE 22-2A, PE 22-2B**

OBJ 4 Compute and interpret factory overhead controllable and volume variances.

Factory Overhead Variances

Factory overhead costs are analyzed differently than direct labor and direct materials costs. This is because factory overhead costs have fixed and variable cost elements. For example, indirect materials and factory supplies normally behave as a variable cost as units produced changes. In contrast, straight-line plant depreciation on factory machinery is a fixed cost.

Factory overhead costs are budgeted and controlled by separating factory overhead into fixed and variable components. Doing so allows the preparation of flexible budgets and the analysis of factory overhead controllable and volume variances.

The Factory Overhead Flexible Budget

The preparation of a flexible budget was described and illustrated in Chapter 21. Exhibit 6 illustrates a flexible factory overhead budget for Western Rider Inc. for June 2014.

EXHIBIT 6

Factory Overhead Cost Budget Indicating Standard Factory Overhead Rate

	A	B	C	D	E
1	Western Rider Inc.				
2	Factory Overhead Cost Budget				
3	For the Month Ending June 30, 2014				
4	Percent of normal capacity	80%	90%	100%	110%
5	Units produced	5,000	5,625	6,250	6,875
6	Direct labor hours (0.80 hr. per unit)	4,000	4,500	5,000	5,500
7	Budgeted factory overhead:				
8	Variable costs:				
9	Indirect factory wages	$ 8,000	$ 9,000	$10,000	$11,000
10	Power and light	4,000	4,500	5,000	5,500
11	Indirect materials	2,400	2,700	3,000	3,300
12	Total variable cost	$14,400	$16,200	$18,000	$19,800
13	Fixed costs:				
14	Supervisory salaries	$ 5,500	$ 5,500	$ 5,500	$ 5,500
15	Depreciation of plant				
16	and equipment	4,500	4,500	4,500	4,500
17	Insurance and property taxes	2,000	2,000	2,000	2,000
18	Total fixed cost	$12,000	$12,000	$12,000	$12,000
19	Total factory overhead cost	$26,400	$28,200	$30,000	$31,800
20					
21	Factory overhead rate per direct labor hour, $30,000/5,000 hours = $6.00				
22					

Exhibit 6 indicates that the budgeted factory overhead rate for Western Rider is $6.00, as computed below.

$$\text{Factory Overhead Rate} = \frac{\text{Budgeted Factory Overhead at Normal Capacity}}{\text{Normal Productive Capacity}}$$

$$\text{Factory Overhead Rate} = \frac{\$30{,}000}{5{,}000 \text{ direct labor hrs.}} = \$6.00 \text{ per direct labor hr.}$$

The normal productive capacity is expressed in terms of an activity base such as direct labor hours, direct labor cost, or machine hours. For Western Rider, 100% of normal capacity is 5,000 direct labor hours. The budgeted factory overhead cost at 100% of normal capacity is $30,000, which consists of variable overhead of $18,000 and fixed overhead of $12,000.

For analysis purposes, the budgeted factory overhead rate is subdivided into a variable factory overhead rate and a fixed factory overhead rate. For Western Rider, the variable overhead rate is $3.60 per direct labor hour, and the fixed overhead rate is $2.40 per direct labor hour, as computed below.

$$\text{Variable Factory Overhead Rate} = \frac{\text{Budgeted Variable Overhead at Normal Capacity}}{\text{Normal Productive Capacity}}$$

$$\text{Variable Factory Overhead Rate} = \frac{\$18{,}000}{5{,}000 \text{ direct labor hrs.}} = \$3.60 \text{ per direct labor hr.}$$

$$\text{Fixed Factory Overhead Rate} = \frac{\text{Budgeted Fixed Overhead at Normal Capacity}}{\text{Normal Productive Capacity}}$$

$$\text{Fixed Factory Overhead Rate} = \frac{\$12{,}000}{5{,}000 \text{ direct labor hrs.}} = \$2.40 \text{ per direct labor hr.}$$

To summarize, the budgeted factory overhead rates for Western Rider Inc. are as follows:

Variable factory overhead rate	$3.60
Fixed factory overhead rate	2.40
Total factory overhead rate	$6.00

As mentioned earlier, factory overhead variances can be separated into a controllable variance and a volume variance as discussed in the next sections.

Variable Factory Overhead Controllable Variance

The variable factory overhead **controllable variance** is the difference between the actual variable overhead costs and the budgeted variable overhead for actual production. It is computed as shown below.

$$\text{Variable Factory Overhead Controllable Variance} = \text{Actual Variable Factory Overhead} - \text{Budgeted Variable Factory Overhead}$$

If the actual variable overhead is less than the budgeted variable overhead, the variance is favorable. If the actual variable overhead exceeds the budgeted variable overhead, the variance is unfavorable.

The **budgeted variable factory overhead** is the standard variable overhead for the *actual* units produced. It is computed as follows:

$$\text{Budgeted Variable Factory Overhead} = \text{Standard Hours for Actual Units Produced} \times \text{Variable Factory Overhead Rate}$$

To illustrate, the budgeted variable overhead for Western Rider for June, when 5,000 units of XL jeans were produced, is $14,400, as computed below.

$$\text{Budgeted Variable Factory Overhead} = \text{Standard Hours for Actual Units Produced} \times \text{Variable Factory Overhead Rate}$$
$$\text{Budgeted Variable Factory Overhead} = 4{,}000 \text{ direct labor hrs.} \times \$3.60$$
$$\text{Budgeted Variable Factory Overhead} = \$14{,}400$$

The preceding computation is based on the fact that Western Rider produced 5,000 XL jeans, which requires a standard of 4,000 (5,000 units × 0.8 hr.) direct labor hours. The variable factory overhead rate of $3.60 was computed earlier. Thus, the budgeted variable factory overhead is $14,400 (4,000 direct labor hrs. × $3.60).

During June, assume that Western Rider incurred the following actual factory overhead costs:

	Actual Costs in June
Variable factory overhead	$10,400
Fixed factory overhead	12,000
Total actual factory overhead	$22,400

Based on the actual variable factory overhead incurred in June, the variable factory overhead controllable variance is a $4,000 favorable variance, as computed below.

$$\text{Variable Factory Overhead Controllable Variance} = \text{Actual Variable Factory Overhead} - \text{Budgeted Variable Factory Overhead}$$
$$\text{Variable Factory Overhead Controllable Variance} = \$10{,}400 - \$14{,}400$$
$$\text{Variable Factory Overhead Controllable Variance} = -\$4{,}000 \text{ Favorable Variance}$$

The variable factory overhead controllable variance indicates the ability to keep the factory overhead costs within the budget limits. Since variable factory overhead costs are normally controllable at the department level, responsibility for controlling this variance usually rests with department supervisors.

Example Exercise 22-3 Factory Overhead Controllable Variance OBJ 4

Tip Top Corp. produced 3,000 units of product that required 2.5 standard hours per unit. The standard variable overhead cost per unit is $2.20 per hour. The actual variable factory overhead was $16,850. Determine the variable factory overhead controllable variance.

Follow My Example 22-3

Variable Factory Overhead Controllable Variance = Actual Variable Factory Overhead – Budgeted Variable Factory Overhead
Variable Factory Overhead Controllable Variance = $16,850 – [(3,000 units × 2.5 hrs.) × $2.20]
Variable Factory Overhead Controllable Variance = $16,850 – $16,500
Variable Factory Overhead Controllable Variance = $350 Unfavorable Variance

Practice Exercises: **PE 22-3A, PE 22-3B**

Fixed Factory Overhead Volume Variance

Western Rider's budgeted factory overhead is based on a 100% normal capacity of 5,000 direct labor hours, as shown in Exhibit 6. This is the expected capacity that management believes will be used under normal business conditions. Exhibit 6 indicates that the 5,000 direct labor hours is less than the total available capacity of 110%, which is 5,500 direct labor hours.

The fixed factory overhead **volume variance** is the difference between the budgeted fixed overhead at 100% of normal capacity and the standard fixed overhead for the actual units produced. It is computed as follows:

$$\text{Fixed Factory Overhead Volume Variance} = \left(\text{Standard Hours for 100\% of Normal Capacity} - \text{Standard Hours for Actual Units Produced}\right) \times \text{Fixed Factory Overhead Rate}$$

The volume variance measures the use of fixed overhead resources (plant and equipment). The interpretation of an unfavorable and a favorable fixed factory overhead volume variance is as follows:

1. *Unfavorable* fixed factory overhead volume variance. The actual units produced is *less than* 100% of normal capacity; thus, the company used its fixed overhead resources (plant and equipment) less than would be expected under normal operating conditions.
2. *Favorable* fixed factory overhead volume variance. The actual units produced is *more than* 100% of normal capacity; thus, the company used its fixed overhead resources (plant and equipment) more than would be expected under normal operating conditions.

To illustrate, the fixed factory overhead volume variance for Western Rider is a $2,400 unfavorable variance, as computed below.

$$\text{Fixed Factory Overhead Volume Variance} = \left(\text{Standard Hours for 100\% of Normal Capacity} - \text{Standard Hours for Actual Units Produced}\right) \times \text{Fixed Factory Overhead Rate}$$

$$\text{Fixed Factory Overhead Volume Variance} = \left(\text{5,000 direct labor hrs.} - \text{4,000 direct labor hrs.}\right) \times \$2.40$$

$$\text{Fixed Factory Overhead Volume Variance} = \text{\$2,400 Unfavorable Variance}$$

Since Western Rider produced 5,000 XL jeans during June, the standard for the actual units produced is 4,000 (5,000 units × 0.80) direct labor hours. This is 1,000 hours less than the 5,000 standard hours of normal capacity. The fixed overhead rate of $2.40 was computed earlier. Thus, the unfavorable fixed factory overhead volume variance is $2,400 (1,000 direct labor hrs. × $2.40).

Exhibit 7 illustrates graphically the fixed factory overhead volume variance for Western Rider Inc. The budgeted fixed overhead does not change and is $12,000 at all levels of production. At 100% of normal capacity (5,000 direct labor hours), the standard fixed overhead line intersects the budgeted fixed costs line. For production levels *more than* 100% of normal capacity (5,000 direct labor hours), the volume variance is *favorable*. For production levels *less than* 100% of normal capacity (5,000 direct labor hours), the volume variance is *unfavorable*.

EXHIBIT 7

Graph of Fixed Overhead Volume Variance

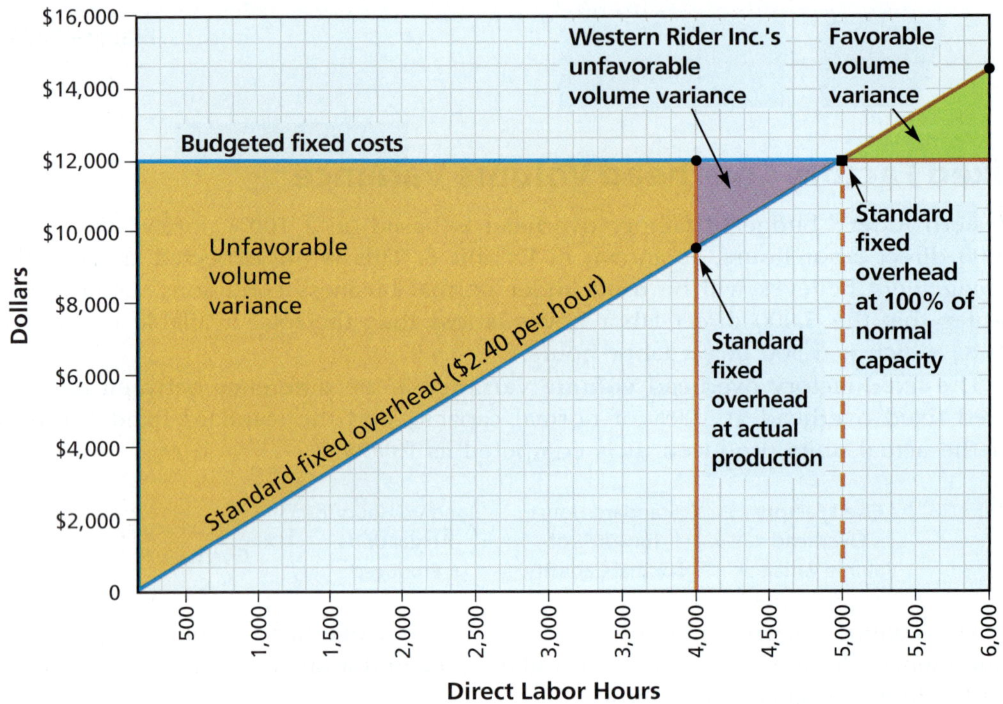

Exhibit 7 indicates that Western Rider's fixed factory overhead volume variance is unfavorable in June because the actual production is 4,000 direct labor hours, or 80% of normal volume. The unfavorable volume variance of $2,400 can be viewed as the cost of the unused capacity (1,000 direct labor hours).

An unfavorable volume variance may be due to factors such as the following:

1. Failure to maintain an even flow of work
2. Machine breakdowns
3. Work stoppages caused by lack of materials or skilled labor
4. Lack of enough sales orders to keep the factory operating at normal capacity

Management should determine the causes of the unfavorable variance and consider taking corrective action. For example, a volume variance caused by an uneven flow of work could be remedied by changing operating procedures. Lack of sales orders may be corrected through increased advertising.

Favorable volume variances may not always be desirable. For example, in an attempt to create a favorable volume variance, manufacturing managers might run the factory above the normal capacity. However, if the additional production cannot be sold, it must be stored as inventory, which would incur storage costs.

Example Exercise 22-4 Factory Overhead Volume Variance

OBJ 4

Tip Top Corp. produced 3,000 units of product that required 2.5 standard hours per unit. The standard fixed overhead cost per unit is $0.90 per hour at 8,000 hours, which is 100% of normal capacity. Determine the fixed factory overhead volume variance.

Follow My Example 22-4

Fixed Factory Overhead Volume Variance = (Standard Hours for 100% of Normal Capacity – Standard Hours for Actual Units Produced) × Fixed Factory Overhead Rate
Fixed Factory Overhead Volume Variance = [8,000 hrs. – (3,000 units × 2.5 hrs.)] × $0.90
Fixed Factory Overhead Volume Variance = (8,000 hrs. – 7,500 hrs.) × $0.90
Fixed Factory Overhead Volume Variance = $450 Unfavorable Variance

Practice Exercises: **PE 22-4A, PE 22-4B**

Reporting Factory Overhead Variances

The total factory overhead cost variance can also be determined as the sum of the variable factory overhead controllable and fixed factory overhead volume variances, as shown below for Western Rider Inc.

Variable factory overhead controllable variance	–$4,000 Favorable Variance
Fixed factory overhead volume variance	2,400 Unfavorable Variance
Total factory overhead cost variance	–$1,600 Favorable Variance

A **factory overhead cost variance report** is useful to management in controlling factory overhead costs. Budgeted and actual costs for variable and fixed factory overhead along with the related controllable and volume variances are reported by each cost element.

Exhibit 8 illustrates a factory overhead cost variance report for Western Rider Inc. for June.

Factory Overhead Account

To illustrate, the applied factory overhead for Western Rider for the 5,000 XL jeans produced in June is $24,000, as computed below.

$$\text{Applied Factory Overhead} = \text{Standard Hours for Actual Units Produced} \times \text{Total Factory Overhead Rate}$$

Applied Factory Overhead = (5,000 jeans × 0.80 direct labor hr. per pair of jeans) × $6.00
Applied Factory Overhead = 4,000 direct labor hrs. × $6.00 = $24,000

The total actual factory overhead for Western Rider, as shown in Exhibit 8, was $22,400. Thus, the total factory overhead cost variance for Western Rider for June is a $1,600 favorable variance, as computed below.

Total Factory Overhead Cost Variance = Actual Factory Overhead – Applied Factory Overhead

Total Factory Overhead Cost Variance = $22,400 – $24,000 = –$1,600 Favorable Variance

At the end of the period, the factory overhead account normally has a balance. A debit balance in Factory Overhead represents underapplied overhead. Underapplied overhead occurs when actual factory overhead costs exceed the applied factory overhead. A credit balance in Factory Overhead represents overapplied overhead. Overapplied overhead occurs when actual factory overhead costs are less than the applied factory overhead.

EXHIBIT 8

Factory Overhead Cost Variance Report

	A	B	C	D	E
1	**Western Rider Inc.**				
2	**Factory Overhead Cost Variance Report**				
3	**For the Month Ending June 30, 2014**				
4	Productive capacity for the month (100% of normal)		5,000 hours		
5	Actual production for the month		4,000 hours		
6					
7		**Budget**			
8		**(at Actual**		**Variances**	
9		**Production)**	**Actual**	**Favorable**	**Unfavorable**
10	Variable factory overhead costs:				
11	Indirect factory wages	$ 8,000	$ 5,100	$2,900	
12	Power and light	4,000	4,200		$ 200
13	Indirect materials	2,400	1,100	1,300	
14	Total variable factory				
15	overhead cost	$14,400	$10,400		
16	Fixed factory overhead costs:				
17	Supervisory salaries	$ 5,500	$ 5,500		
18	Depreciation of plant and				
19	equipment	4,500	4,500		
20	Insurance and property taxes	2,000	2,000		
21	Total fixed factory				
22	overhead cost	$12,000	$12,000		
23	Total factory overhead cost	$26,400	$22,400		
24	Total controllable variances			$4,200	$ 200
25					
26					
27	Net controllable variance—favorable				$4,000
28	Volume variance—unfavorable:				
29	Capacity not used at the standard rate for fixed				
30	factory overhead—1,000 × $2.40				2,400
31	Total factory overhead cost variance—favorable				$1,600
32					

The difference between the actual factory overhead and the applied factory overhead is the total factory overhead cost variance. Thus, underapplied and overapplied factory overhead account balances represent the following total factory overhead cost variances:

1. *Underapplied* Factory Overhead = *Unfavorable* Total Factory Overhead Cost Variance
2. *Overapplied* Factory Overhead = *Favorable* Total Factory Overhead Cost Variance

The factory overhead account for Western Rider Inc. for the month ending June 30, 2014, is shown below.

Factory Overhead

Actual factory overhead ($10,400 + $12,000)	22,400		24,000 Applied factory overhead (4,000 hrs. × $6.00 per hr.)
		Bal., June 30	1,600 Overapplied factory overhead

The $1,600 overapplied factory overhead account balance shown above and the favorable total factory overhead cost variance shown in Exhibit 8 are the same.

The variable factory overhead controllable variance and the volume variance can be computed by comparing the factory overhead account with the budgeted total overhead for the actual level produced, as shown on the next page.

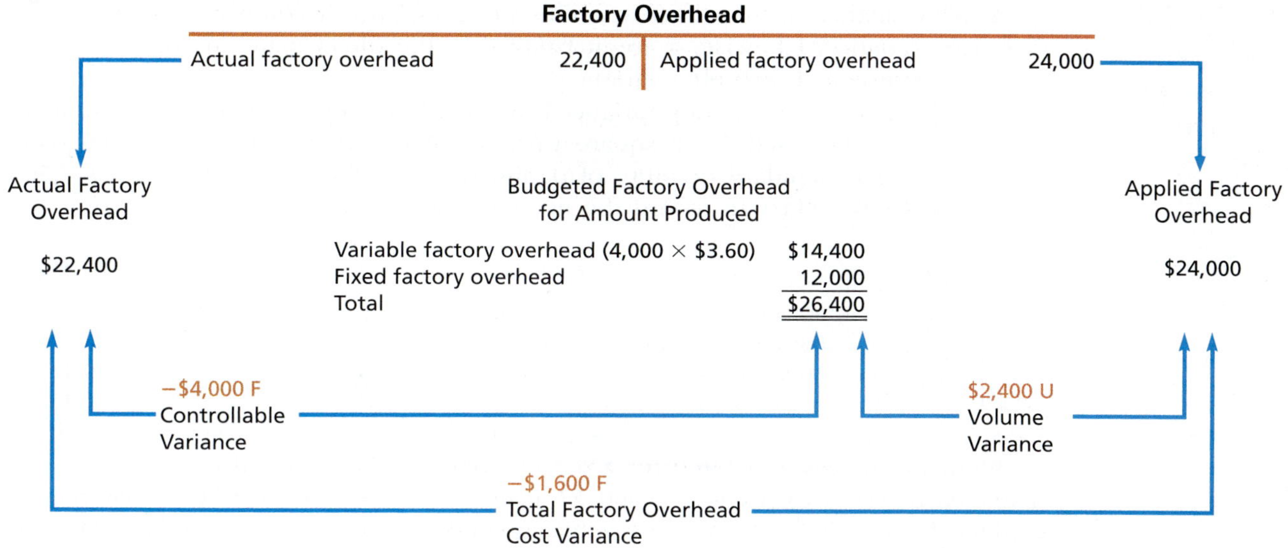

The controllable and volume variances are determined as follows:

1. The difference between the actual overhead incurred and the budgeted overhead is the *controllable* variance.
2. The difference between the applied overhead and the budgeted overhead is the *volume* variance.

If the actual factory overhead exceeds (is less than) the budgeted factory overhead, the controllable variance is unfavorable (favorable). In contrast, if the applied factory overhead is less than (exceeds) the budgeted factory overhead, the volume variance is unfavorable (favorable).

Recording and Reporting Variances from Standards

OBJ 5 Journalize the entries for recording standards in the accounts and prepare an income statement that includes variances from standard.

Standard costs may be used as a management tool to control costs separately from the accounts in the general ledger. However, many companies include standard costs in their accounts. One method for doing so records standard costs and variances at the same time the actual product costs are recorded.

To illustrate, assume that Western Rider Inc. purchased, on account, the 7,300 square yards of blue denim used at $5.50 per square yard. The standard price for direct materials is $5.00 per square yard. The entry to record the purchase and the unfavorable direct materials price variance is as follows:

		Materials (7,300 sq. yds. × $5.00)		36,500	
		Direct Materials Price Variance		3,650	
		Accounts Payable (7,300 sq. yds. × $5.50)			40,150

The materials account is debited for the *actual quantity* purchased at the *standard price*, $36,500 (7,300 square yards × $5.00). Accounts Payable is credited for the $40,150 actual cost and the amount due the supplier. The difference of $3,650 is the unfavorable direct materials price variance [($5.50 – $5.00) × 7,300 sq. yds.]. It is recorded by debiting *Direct Materials Price Variance*. If the variance had been favorable, Direct Materials Price Variance would have been credited for the variance.

A debit balance in the direct materials price variance account represents an unfavorable variance. Likewise, a credit balance in the direct materials price variance account represents a favorable variance.

The direct materials quantity variance is recorded in a similar manner. For example, Western Rider Inc. used 7,300 square yards of blue denim to produce 5,000 pairs of XL jeans. The standard quantity of denim for the 5,000 jeans produced is 7,500 square yards. The entry to record the materials used is as follows:

		Work in Process (7,500 sq. yds. × $5.00)		37,500	
		Direct Materials Quantity Variance			1,000
		Materials (7,300 sq. yds. × $5.00)			36,500

Work in Process is debited for $37,500, which is the standard cost of the direct materials required to produce 5,000 XL jeans (7,500 sq. yds. × $5.00). Materials is credited for $36,500, which is the actual quantity of materials used at the standard price (7,300 sq. yds. × $5.00). The difference of $1,000 is the favorable direct materials quantity variance [(7,300 sq. yds. – 7,500 sq. yds.) × $5.00]. It is recorded by crediting *Direct Materials Quantity Variance*. If the variance had been unfavorable, Direct Materials Quantity Variance would have been debited for the variance.

A debit balance in the direct materials quantity variance account represents an unfavorable variance. Likewise, a credit balance in the direct materials quantity variance account represents a favorable variance.

Example Exercise 22-5 Standard Cost Journal Entries

OBJ 5

Tip Top Corp. produced 3,000 units that require six standard pounds per unit at the $4.50 standard price per pound. The company actually used 18,500 pounds in production. Journalize the entry to record the standard direct materials used in production.

Follow My Example 22-5

Work in Process (18,000* pounds × $4.50)	81,000	
Direct Materials Quantity Variance [(18,500 pounds – 18,000 pounds) × $4.50]	2,250	
Materials (18,500 pounds × $4.50)		83,250

*3,000 units × 6 pounds per unit = 18,000 standard pounds for units produced

Practice Exercises: **PE 22-5A, PE 22-5B**

The journal entries to record the standard costs and variances for *direct labor* are similar to those for direct materials. These entries are summarized below.

1. Work in Process is debited for the standard cost of direct labor.
2. Wages Payable is credited for the actual direct labor cost incurred.
3. Direct Labor Rate Variance is debited for an unfavorable variance and credited for a favorable variance.
4. Direct Labor Time Variance is debited for an unfavorable variance and credited for a favorable variance.

As illustrated in the prior section, the factory overhead account already incorporates standard costs and variances into its journal entries. That is, Factory Overhead is debited for actual factory overhead and credited for applied (standard) factory overhead. The ending balance of factory overhead (overapplied or underapplied) is the total factory overhead cost variance. By comparing the actual factory overhead with the budgeted factory overhead, the controllable variance can be determined. By comparing the budgeted factory overhead with the applied factory overhead, the volume variance can be determined.

When goods are completed, Finished Goods is debited and Work in Process is credited for the standard cost of the product transferred.

At the end of the period, the balances of each of the variance accounts indicate the net favorable or unfavorable variance for the period. These variances may be reported in an income statement prepared for management's use.

Exhibit 9 is an example of an income statement for Western Rider Inc. that includes variances. In Exhibit 9, a sales price of $28 per pair of jeans, selling expenses of $14,500, and administrative expenses of $11,225 are assumed.

EXHIBIT 9

Variance from Standards in Income Statement

Western Rider Inc.
Income Statement
For the Month Ended June 30, 2014

	Favorable	Unfavorable	
Sales			$140,000[1]
Cost of goods sold—at standard			97,500[2]
Gross profit—at standard			$ 42,500
Less variances from standard cost:			
Direct materials price		$ 3,650	
Direct materials quantity	$1,000		
Direct labor rate		3,850	
Direct labor time	1,350		
Factory overhead controllable	4,000		
Factory overhead volume		2,400	3,550
Gross profit			$ 38,950
Operating expenses:			
Selling expenses		$14,500	
Administrative expenses		11,225	25,725
Income before income tax			$ 13,225

[1]5,000 × $28
[2]$37,500 + $36,000 + $24,000 (from Exhibit 2), or 5,000 × $19.50 (from Exhibit 1)

The income statement shown in Exhibit 9 is for internal use by management. That is, variances are not reported to external users. Thus, the variances shown in Exhibit 9 must be transferred to other accounts in preparing an income statement for external users.

In preparing an income statement for external users, the balances of the variance accounts are normally transferred to Cost of Goods Sold. However, if the variances are significant or if many of the products manufactured are still in inventory, the variances should be allocated to Work in Process, Finished Goods, and Cost of Goods Sold. Such an allocation, in effect, converts these account balances from standard cost to actual cost.

Example Exercise 22-6 Income Statement with Variances

OBJ 5

Prepare an income statement for the year ended December 31, 2014, through gross profit for Tip Top Corp. using the variance data in Example Exercises 22-1 through 22-4. Assume Tip Top sold 3,000 units at $100 per unit.

(Continued)

Follow My Example 22-6

Tip Top Corp.
Income Statement through Gross Profit
For the Year Ended December 31, 2014

	Favorable	Unfavorable	
Sales (3,000 units × $100)			$300,000
Cost of goods sold—at standard			194,250*
Gross profit—at standard			$105,750
Less variances from standard cost:			
Direct materials price (EE 22-1)	$2,775		
Direct materials quantity (EE 22-1)		$2,250	
Direct labor rate (EE 22-2)		2,226	
Direct labor time (EE 22-2)	960		
Factory overhead controllable (EE 22-3)		350	
Factory overhead volume (EE 22-4)		450	1,541
Gross profit—actual			$104,209

*Direct materials (3,000 units × 6 lbs. × $4.50)	$ 81,000
Direct labor (3,000 units × 2.5 hrs. × $12.00)	90,000
Factory overhead [3,000 units × 2.5 hrs. × ($2.20 + $0.90)]	23,250
Cost of goods sold at standard	$194,250

Practice Exercises: **PE 22-6A, PE 22-6B**

OBJ 6 Describe and provide examples of nonfinancial performance measures.

Nonfinancial Performance Measures

Many companies supplement standard costs and variances from standards with nonfinancial performance measures. A **nonfinancial performance measure** expresses performance in a measure other than dollars. For example, airlines use on-time performance, percent of bags lost, and number of customer complaints as nonfinancial performance measures. Such measures are often used to evaluate the time, quality, or quantity of a business activity.

Using financial and nonfinancial performance measures aids managers and employees in considering multiple performance objectives. Such measures often bring additional perspectives, such as quality of work, to evaluating performance. Some examples of nonfinancial performance measures include the following:

Nonfinancial Performance Measures
Inventory turnover
Percent on-time delivery
Elapsed time between a customer order and product delivery
Customer preference rankings compared to competitors
Response time to a service call
Time to develop new products
Employee satisfaction
Number of customer complaints

Nonfinancial measures are often linked to either the inputs or outputs of an activity or process. A **process** is a sequence of activities for performing a task. The relationship between an activity or a process and its inputs and outputs is shown below.

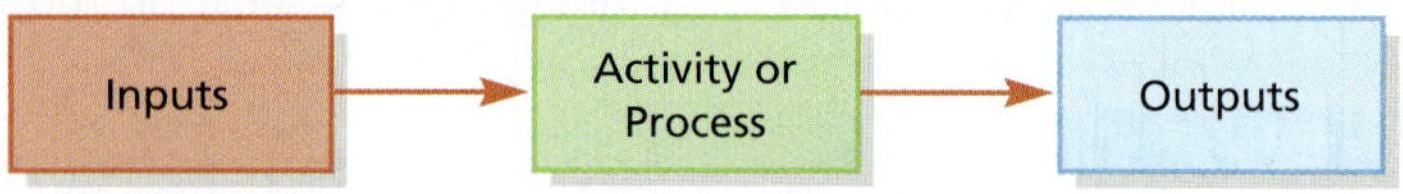

To illustrate, the counter service activity of a fast-food restaurant is used. The following inputs/outputs could be identified for providing customer service:

The customer service outputs of the counter service activity include the following:

1. Line wait for the customer
2. Percent order accuracy in serving the customer
3. Friendly service experience for the customer

Some of the inputs that impact the customer service outputs include the following:

1. Number of employees
2. Employee experience
3. Employee training
4. Fryer (and other cooking equipment) reliability
5. Number of new menu items
6. Fountain drink availability

A fast-food restaurant can develop a set of linked nonfinancial performance measures across inputs and outputs. The output measures tell management how the activity is performing, such as keeping the line wait to a minimum. The input measures are used to improve the output measures. For example, if the customer line wait is too long, then improving employee training or hiring more employees could improve the output (decrease customer line wait).

Example Exercise 22-7 Activity Inputs and Outputs

OBJ 6

The following are inputs and outputs to the baggage claim process of an airline:

Baggage handler training
Time customers wait for returned baggage
Maintenance of baggage handling equipment
Number of baggage handlers
Number of damaged bags
On-time flight performance

Identify whether each is an input or output to the baggage claim process.

Follow My Example 22-7

Baggage handler training	Input
Time customers wait for returned baggage	Output
Maintenance of baggage handling equipment	Input
Number of baggage handlers	Input
Number of damaged bags	Output
On-time flight performance	Input

Practice Exercises: **PE 22-7A, PE 22-7B**

Key Terms

budget performance report (1033)
budgeted variable factory overhead (1042)
controllable variance (1042)
cost variance (1033)
currently attainable standards (1031)
direct labor rate variance (1038)
direct labor time variance (1039)
direct materials price variance (1036)
direct materials quantity variance (1036)
factory overhead cost variance report (1045)
favorable cost variance (1033)
ideal standards (1031)
nonfinancial performance measure (1050)
process (1050)
standard cost (1030)
standard cost systems (1030)
standards (1030)
total manufacturing cost variance (1034)
unfavorable cost variance (1033)
volume variance (1043)

Illustrative Problem

Hawley Inc. manufactures woven baskets for national distribution. The standard costs for the manufacture of Folk Art style baskets were as follows:

	Standard Costs	Actual Costs
Direct materials	1,500 lbs. at $35	1,600 lbs. at $32
Direct labor	4,800 hrs. at $11	4,500 hrs. at $11.80
Factory overhead	Rates per labor hour, based on 100% of normal capacity of 5,500 labor hrs.:	
	Variable cost, $2.40	$12,300 variable cost
	Fixed cost, $3.50	$19,250 fixed cost

Instructions

1. Determine the direct materials price variance, direct materials quantity variance, and total direct materials cost variance for the Folk Art style baskets.
2. Determine the direct labor rate variance, direct labor time variance, and total direct labor cost variance for the Folk Art style baskets.
3. Determine the variable factory overhead controllable variance, fixed factory overhead volume variance, and total factory overhead cost variance for the Folk Art style baskets.

Solution

1. **Direct Materials Cost Variance**

Price variance:

Direct Materials Price Variance = (Actual Price – Standard Price) × Actual Quantity
Direct Materials Price Variance = ($32 per lb. – $35 per lb.) × 1,600 lbs.
Direct Materials Price Variance = –$4,800 Favorable Variance

Quantity variance:

Direct Materials Quantity Variance = (Actual Quantity – Standard Quantity) × Standard Price
Direct Materials Quantity Variance = (1,600 lbs. – 1,500 lbs.) × $35 per lb.
Direct Materials Quantity Variance = $3,500 Unfavorable Variance

Total direct materials cost variance:

Direct Materials Cost Variance = Direct Materials Quantity Variance + Direct Materials Price Variance
Direct Materials Cost Variance = $3,500 + ($4,800)
Direct Materials Cost Variance = –$1,300 Favorable Variance

2. **Direct Labor Cost Variance**

Rate variance:

Direct Labor Rate Variance = (Actual Rate per Hour – Standard Rate per Hour) × Actual Hours
Direct Labor Rate Variance = ($11.80 – $11.00) × 4,500 hrs.
Direct Labor Rate Variance = $3,600 Unfavorable Variance

Time variance:

Direct Labor Time Variance = (Actual Direct Labor Hours – Standard Direct Labor Hours) × Standard Rate per Hour
Direct Labor Time Variance = (4,500 hrs. – 4,800 hrs.) × $11.00 per hour
Direct Labor Time Variance = –$3,300 Favorable Variance

Total direct labor cost variance:

Direct Labor Cost Variance = Direct Labor Time Variance + Direct Labor Rate Variance
Direct Labor Cost Variance = ($3,300) + $3,600
Direct Labor Cost Variance = $300 Unfavorable Variance

3. **Factory Overhead Cost Variance**

Variable factory overhead controllable variance:

Variable Factory Overhead Controllable Variance = Actual Variable Factory Overhead – Budgeted Variable Factory Overhead
Variable Factory Overhead Controllable Variance = $12,300 – $11,520*
Variable Factory Overhead Controllable Variance = $780 Unfavorable Variance
*4,800 hrs. × $2.40 per hour

Fixed factory overhead volume variance:

Fixed Factory Overhead Volume Variance = (Standard Hours for 100% of Normal Capacity – Standard Hours for Actual Units Produced) × Fixed Factory Overhead Rate
Fixed Factory Overhead Volume Variance = (5,500 hrs. – 4,800 hrs.) × $3.50 per hr.
Fixed Factory Overhead Volume Variance = $2,450 Unfavorable Variance

Total factory overhead cost variance:

Factory Overhead Cost Variance = Variable Factory Overhead Controllable Variance + Fixed Factory Overhead Volume Variance
Factory Overhead Cost Variance = $780 + $2,450
Factory Overhead Cost Variance = $3,230 Unfavorable Variance

Discussion Questions

1. What are the basic objectives in the use of standard costs?
2. What is meant by reporting by the "principle of exceptions," as the term is used in reference to cost control?
3. What are the two variances between the actual cost and the standard cost for direct materials?
4. The materials cost variance report for Nickols Inc. indicates a large favorable materials price variance and a significant unfavorable materials quantity variance. What might have caused these offsetting variances?
5. a. What are the two variances between the actual cost and the standard cost for direct labor?

   b. Who generally has control over the direct labor cost variances?
6. A new assistant controller recently was heard to remark: "All the assembly workers in this plant are covered by union contracts, so there should be no labor variances." Was the controller's remark correct? Discuss.
7. Would the use of standards be appropriate in a nonmanufacturing setting, such as a fast-food restaurant?
8. a. Describe the two variances between the actual costs and the standard costs for factory overhead.

   b. What is a factory overhead cost variance report?
9. If variances are recorded in the accounts at the time the manufacturing costs are incurred, what does a debit balance in Direct Materials Price Variance represent?
10. Briefly explain why firms might use nonfinancial performance measures.

Practice Exercises

Example Exercises

EE 22-1 *p. 1038*

PE 22-1A Direct materials variances

OBJ. 3

Giovanni Company produces a product that requires four standard gallons per unit. The standard price is $34.00 per gallon. If 3,500 units required 14,400 gallons, which were purchased at $33.25 per gallon, what is the direct materials (a) price variance, (b) quantity variance, and (c) cost variance?

EE 22-1 *p. 1038*

PE 22-1B Direct materials variances

OBJ. 3

Dvorak Company produces a product that requires five standard pounds per unit. The standard price is $2.50 per pound. If 1,000 units required 4,500 pounds, which were purchased at $3.00 per pound, what is the direct materials (a) price variance, (b) quantity variance, and (c) cost variance?

EE 22-2 *p. 1040*

PE 22-2A Direct labor variances

OBJ. 3

Giovanni Company produces a product that requires five standard hours per unit at a standard hourly rate of $30 per hour. If 3,500 units required 17,700 hours at an hourly rate of $30.50 per hour, what is the direct labor (a) rate variance, (b) time variance, and (c) cost variance?

Example Exercises

EE 22-2 *p. 1040*

PE 22-2B Direct labor variances — OBJ. 3

Dvorak Company produces a product that requires three standard hours per unit at a standard hourly rate of $17 per hour. If 1,000 units required 2,800 hours at an hourly rate of $16.50 per hour, what is the direct labor (a) rate variance, (b) time variance, and (c) cost variance?

EE 22-3 *p. 1043*

PE 22-3A Factory overhead controllable variance — OBJ. 4

Giovanni Company produced 3,500 units of product that required five standard hours per unit. The standard variable overhead cost per unit is $3.50 per hour. The actual variable factory overhead was $63,400. Determine the variable factory overhead controllable variance.

EE 22-3 *p. 1043*

PE 22-3B Factory overhead controllable variance — OBJ. 4

Dvorak Company produced 1,000 units of product that required three standard hours per unit. The standard variable overhead cost per unit is $1.40 per hour. The actual variable factory overhead was $4,000. Determine the variable factory overhead controllable variance.

EE 22-4 *p. 1045*

PE 22-4A Factory overhead volume variance — OBJ. 4

Giovanni Company produced 3,500 units of product that required five standard hours per unit. The standard fixed overhead cost per unit is $1.80 per hour at 17,000 hours, which is 100% of normal capacity. Determine the fixed factory overhead volume variance.

EE 22-4 *p. 1045*

PE 22-4B Factory overhead volume variance — OBJ. 4

Dvorak Company produced 1,000 units of product that required three standard hours per unit. The standard fixed overhead cost per unit is $0.60 per hour at 3,500 hours, which is 100% of normal capacity. Determine the fixed factory overhead volume variance.

EE 22-5 *p. 1048*

PE 22-5A Standard cost journal entries — OBJ. 5

Giovanni Company produced 3,500 units that require four standard gallons per unit at $34.00 standard price per gallon. The company actually used 14,400 gallons in production. Journalize the entry to record the standard direct materials used in production.

EE 22-5 *p. 1048*

PE 22-5B Standard cost journal entries — OBJ. 5

Dvorak Company produced 1,000 units that require five standard pounds per unit at $2.50 standard price per pound. The company actually used 4,500 pounds in production. Journalize the entry to record the standard direct materials used in production.

EE 22-6 *p. 1049*

PE 22-6A Income statement with variances — OBJ. 5

Prepare a 2014 income statement through gross profit for Giovanni Company, using the variance data in Practice Exercises 22-1A, 22-2A, 22-3A, and 22-4A. Assume Giovanni sold 3,500 units at $400 per unit.

EE 22-6 *p. 1049*

PE 22-6B Income statement with variances — OBJ. 5

Prepare a 2014 income statement through gross profit for Dvorak Company, using the variance data in Practice Exercises 22-1B, 22-2B, 22-3B, and 22-4B. Assume Dvorak sold 1,000 units at $90 per unit.

Example Exercises

EE 22-7 *p. 1051*

PE 22-7A Activity inputs and outputs — OBJ. 6

The following are inputs and outputs to the copying process of a copy shop:

Number of employee errors
Number of times paper supply runs out
Copy machine downtime (broken)
Number of pages copied per hour
Number of customer complaints
Percent jobs done on time

Identify whether each is an input or output to the copying process.

EE 22-7 *p. 1051*

PE 22-7B Activity inputs and outputs — OBJ. 6

The following are inputs and outputs to the cooking process of a restaurant:

Number of times ingredients are missing
Number of customer complaints
Number of hours kitchen equipment is down for repairs
Number of server order mistakes
Percent of meals prepared on time
Number of unexpected cook absences

Identify whether each is an input or output to the cooking process.

Exercises

EX 22-1 Standard direct materials cost per unit — OBJ. 2

De la Renta Chocolate Company produces chocolate bars. The primary materials used in producing chocolate bars are cocoa, sugar, and milk. The standard costs for a batch of chocolate (4,800 bars) are as follows:

Ingredient	Quantity	Price
Cocoa	650 lbs.	$0.90 per lb.
Sugar	200 lbs.	$1.50 per lb.
Milk	150 gal.	$2.10 per gal.

Determine the standard direct materials cost per bar of chocolate.

EX 22-2 Standard product cost — OBJ. 2

Wood Designs Company manufactures unfinished oak furniture. Wood Designs uses a standard cost system. The direct labor, direct materials, and factory overhead standards for an unfinished dining room table are as follows:

Direct labor:	standard rate	$18.00 per hr.
	standard time per unit	2.0 hrs.
Direct materials (oak):	standard price	$15.00 per bd. ft.
	standard quantity	20.0 bd. ft.
Variable factory overhead:	standard rate	$2.75 per direct labor hr.
Fixed factory overhead:	standard rate	$1.25 per direct labor hr.

a. Determine the standard cost per dining room table.

b. Why would Wood Designs Company use a standard cost system?

EX 22-3 Budget performance report — OBJ. 2

✔ b. Direct labor cost variance, $1,090 F

Time in a Bottle Company (TBC) manufactures plastic two-liter bottles for the beverage industry. The cost standards per 100 two-liter bottles are as follows:

SPREADSHEET

Cost Category	Standard Cost per 100 Two-Liter Bottles
Direct labor	$ 1.80
Direct materials	8.25
Factory overhead	0.50
Total	$10.55

At the beginning of May, TBC management planned to produce 600,000 bottles. The actual number of bottles produced for May was 610,000 bottles. The actual costs for May of the current year were as follows:

Cost Category	Actual Cost for the Month Ended May 31, 2014
Direct labor	$ 9,890
Direct materials	48,450
Factory overhead	3,460
Total	$61,800

a. Prepare the May manufacturing standard cost budget (direct labor, direct materials, and factory overhead) for TBC, assuming planned production.

b. Prepare a budget performance report for manufacturing costs, showing the total cost variances for direct materials, direct labor, and factory overhead for May.

c. Interpret the budget performance report.

EX 22-4 Direct materials variances **OBJ. 3**

✔ a. Price variance, $5,350 U

The following data relate to the direct materials cost for the production of 2,400 automobile tires:

Actual:	53,500 lbs. at $2.60	$139,100
Standard:	55,120 lbs. at $2.50	$137,800

a. Determine the direct materials price variance, direct materials quantity variance, and total direct materials cost variance.

b. To whom should the variances be reported for analysis and control?

EX 22-5 Direct materials variances **OBJ. 3**

✔ Quantity variance, $138 U

Techno Tyme Inc. produces electronic timepieces. The company uses mini-LCD displays for its products. Each timepiece uses one display. The company produced 430 timepieces during October. However, due to LCD defects, the company actually used 450 LCD displays during October. Each display has a standard cost of $6.90. Four hundred fifty LCD displays were purchased for October production at a cost of $2,925.

Determine the price variance, quantity variance, and total direct materials cost variance for October.

EX 22-6 Standard direct materials cost per unit from variance data **OBJ. 2, 3**

The following data relating to direct materials cost for October of the current year are taken from the records of Good Clean Fun Inc., a manufacturer of organic toys:

Quantity of direct materials used	3,000 lbs.
Actual unit price of direct materials	$5.50 per lb.
Units of finished product manufactured	1,400 units
Standard direct materials per unit of finished product	2 lbs.
Direct materials quantity variance—unfavorable	$1,000
Direct materials price variance—unfavorable	$1,500

Determine the standard direct materials cost per unit of finished product, assuming that there was no inventory of work in process at either the beginning or the end of the month.

EX 22-7 Standard product cost, direct materials variance **OBJ. 2, 3**

H.J. Heinz Company uses standards to control its materials costs. Assume that a batch of ketchup (1,880 pounds) has the following standards:

	Standard Quantity	Standard Price
Whole tomatoes	3,360 lbs.	$ 0.50 per lb.
Vinegar	220 gal.	3.00 per gal.
Corn syrup	20 gal.	12.00 per gal.
Salt	80 lbs.	3.00 per lb.

The actual materials in a batch may vary from the standard due to tomato characteristics. Assume that the actual quantities of materials for batch K-54 were as follows:

3,556 lbs. of tomatoes
230 gal. of vinegar
18 gal. of corn syrup
75 lbs. of salt

a. Determine the standard unit materials cost per pound for a standard batch.

b. Determine the direct materials quantity variance for batch K-54.

EX 22-8 Direct labor variances **OBJ. 3**

✔ a. Rate variance, $1,620 F

The following data relate to labor cost for production of 8,000 cellular telephones:

Actual:	4,050 hrs. at $20.00	$81,000
Standard:	4,000 hrs. at $20.40	$81,600

a. Determine the direct labor rate variance, direct labor time variance, and total direct labor cost variance.

b. Discuss what might have caused these variances.

EX 22-9 Direct labor variances **OBJ. 3, 5**

✔ a. Time variance, $800 U

Hoschild Bicycle Company manufactures bicycles. The following data for September of the current year are available:

Quantity of direct labor used	850 hrs.
Actual rate for direct labor	$15.60 per hr.
Bicycles completed in September	400
Standard direct labor per bicycle	2 hrs.
Standard rate for direct labor	$16.00 per hr.

a. Determine the direct labor rate and time variances.

b. How much direct labor should be debited to Work in Process?

EX 22-10 Direct labor variances **OBJ. 3**

✔ a. Cutting Department rate variance, $638 favorable

The Greeson Clothes Company produced 25,000 units during June of the current year. The Cutting Department used 6,380 direct labor hours at an actual rate of $10.90 per hour. The Sewing Department used 9,875 direct labor hours at an actual rate of $11.12 per hour. Assume there were no work in process inventories in either department at the beginning or end of the month. The standard labor rate is $11.00. The standard labor time for the Cutting and Sewing departments is 0.25 hour and 0.4 hour per unit, respectively.

a. Determine the direct labor rate, direct labor time, and total direct labor cost variance for the (1) Cutting Department and (2) Sewing Department.

b. Interpret your results.

EX 22-11 Direct labor standards for nonmanufacturing expenses **OBJ. 3**

✔ a. $2,400

Englert Hospital began using standards to evaluate its Admissions Department. The standard was broken into two types of admissions as follows:

Type of Admission	Standard Time to Complete Admission Record
Unscheduled admission	30 min.
Scheduled admission	15 min.

The unscheduled admission took longer, since name, address, and insurance information needed to be determined and verified at the time of admission. Information was collected on scheduled admissions prior to the admissions, which was less time consuming.

The Admissions Department employs four full-time people (40 productive hours per week, with no overtime) at $15 per hour. For the most recent week, the department handled 140 unscheduled and 350 scheduled admissions.

a. How much was actually spent on labor for the week?

b. What are the standard hours for the actual volume for the week?

c. Calculate a time variance, and report how well the department performed for the week.

EX 22-12 Direct labor standards for nonmanufacturing operations **OBJ. 2, 3**

One of the operations in the United States Postal Service is a mechanical mail sorting operation. In this operation, letter mail is sorted at a rate of two letters per second. The letter is mechanically sorted from a three-digit code input by an operator sitting at a keyboard. The manager of the mechanical sorting operation wishes to determine the number of temporary employees to hire for December. The manager estimates that there will be an additional 41,472,000 pieces of mail in December, due to the upcoming holiday season.

Assume that the sorting operators are temporary employees. The union contract requires that temporary employees be hired for one month at a time. Each temporary employee is hired to work 160 hours in the month.

a. How many temporary employees should the manager hire for December?

b. If each employee earns a standard $15 per hour, what would be the labor time variance if the actual number of letters sorted in December was 41,220,000?

EX 22-13 Direct materials and direct labor variances **OBJ. 3**

✔ Direct materials quantity variance, $750 U

At the beginning of June, Veneskey Printing Company budgeted 19,200 books to be printed in June at standard direct materials and direct labor costs as follows:

Direct materials	$36,000
Direct labor	26,880
Total	$62,880

The standard materials price is $1.25 per pound. The standard direct labor rate is $14.00 per hour. At the end of June, the actual direct materials and direct labor costs were as follows:

Actual direct materials	$34,500
Actual direct labor	24,500
Total	$59,000

There were no direct materials price or direct labor rate variances for June. In addition, assume no changes in the direct materials inventory balances in June. Veneskey Printing Company actually produced 18,000 units during June.

Determine the direct materials quantity and direct labor time variances.

EX 22-14 Flexible overhead budget

OBJ. 4

✔ Total factory overhead, 22,000 hrs., $443,600

Leno Manufacturing Company prepared the following factory overhead cost budget for the Press Department for October 2014, during which it expected to require 20,000 hours of productive capacity in the department:

Variable overhead cost:		
Indirect factory labor	$180,000	
Power and light	12,000	
Indirect materials	64,000	
Total variable overhead cost		$256,000
Fixed overhead cost:		
Supervisory salaries	$ 80,000	
Depreciation of plant and equipment	50,000	
Insurance and property taxes	32,000	
Total fixed overhead cost		162,000
Total factory overhead cost		$418,000

Assuming that the estimated costs for November are the same as for October, prepare a flexible factory overhead cost budget for the Press Department for November for 18,000, 20,000, and 22,000 hours of production.

EX 22-15 Flexible overhead budget

OBJ. 4

Wiki Wiki Company has determined that the variable overhead rate is $4.50 per direct labor hour in the Fabrication Department. The normal production capacity for the Fabrication Department is 10,000 hours for the month. Fixed costs are budgeted at $60,000 for the month.

a. Prepare a monthly factory overhead flexible budget for 9,000, 10,000, and 11,000 hours of production.

b. How much overhead would be applied to production if 9,000 hours were used in the department during the month?

EX 22-16 Factory overhead cost variances

OBJ. 4

✔ Volume variance, $6,000 U

The following data relate to factory overhead cost for the production of 10,000 computers:

Actual:	Variable factory overhead	$262,000
	Fixed factory overhead	90,000
Standard:	14,000 hrs. at $25	350,000

If productive capacity of 100% was 15,000 hours and the total factory overhead cost budgeted at the level of 14,000 standard hours was $356,000, determine the variable factory overhead controllable variance, fixed factory overhead volume variance, and total factory overhead cost variance. The fixed factory overhead rate was $6.00 per hour.

EX 22-17 Factory overhead cost variances

OBJ. 4

✔ a. $13,000 F

SPREADSHEET

Blumen Textiles Corporation began January with a budget for 90,000 hours of production in the Weaving Department. The department has a full capacity of 100,000 hours under normal business conditions. The budgeted overhead at the planned volumes at the beginning of April was as follows:

Variable overhead	$540,000
Fixed overhead	240,000
Total	$780,000

The actual factory overhead was $782,000 for April. The actual fixed factory overhead was as budgeted. During April, the Weaving Department had standard hours at actual production volume of 92,500 hours.

a. Determine the variable factory overhead controllable variance.

b. Determine the fixed factory overhead volume variance.

EX 22-18 Factory overhead variance corrections **OBJ. 4**

The data related to Shunda Enterprises Inc.'s factory overhead cost for the production of 100,000 units of product are as follows:

Actual:	Variable factory overhead	$458,000
	Fixed factory overhead	494,000
Standard:	132,000 hrs. at $7.30 ($3.50 for variable factory overhead)	963,600

Productive capacity at 100% of normal was 130,000 hours, and the factory overhead cost budgeted at the level of 132,000 standard hours was $956,000. Based on these data, the chief cost accountant prepared the following variance analysis:

Variable factory overhead controllable variance:		
Actual variable factory overhead cost incurred	$458,000	
Budgeted variable factory overhead for 132,000 hours	462,000	
Variance—favorable		–$ 4,000
Fixed factory overhead volume variance:		
Normal productive capacity at 100%	130,000 hrs.	
Standard for amount produced	132,000	
Productive capacity not used	2,000 hrs.	
Standard variable factory overhead rate	× $7.30	
Variance—unfavorable		14,600
Total factory overhead cost variance—unfavorable		$10,600

Identify the errors in the factory overhead cost variance analysis.

EX 22-19 Factory overhead cost variance report **OBJ. 4**

✔ Net controllable variance, $900 U

SPREADSHEET

Tannin Products Inc. prepared the following factory overhead cost budget for the Trim Department for July 2014, during which it expected to use 20,000 hours for production:

Variable overhead cost:		
Indirect factory labor	$46,000	
Power and light	12,000	
Indirect materials	20,000	
Total variable overhead cost		$ 78,000
Fixed overhead cost:		
Supervisory salaries	$54,500	
Depreciation of plant and equipment	40,000	
Insurance and property taxes	35,500	
Total fixed overhead cost		130,000
Total factory overhead cost		$208,000

Tannin has available 25,000 hours of monthly productive capacity in the Trim Department under normal business conditions. During July, the Trim Department actually used 22,000 hours for production. The actual fixed costs were as budgeted. The actual variable overhead for July was as follows:

Actual variable factory overhead cost:	
Indirect factory labor	$49,700
Power and light	13,000
Indirect materials	24,000
Total variable cost	$86,700

Construct a factory overhead cost variance report for the Trim Department for July.

EX 22-20 Recording standards in accounts **OBJ. 5**

Cioffi Manufacturing Company incorporates standards in its accounts and identifies variances at the time the manufacturing costs are incurred. Journalize the entries to record the following transactions:

a. Purchased 2,450 units of copper tubing on account at $52.00 per unit. The standard price is $48.50 per unit.

b. Used 1,900 units of copper tubing in the process of manufacturing 200 air conditioners. Ten units of copper tubing are required, at standard, to produce one air conditioner.

EX 22-21 Recording standards in accounts **OBJ. 5**

The Assembly Department produced 5,000 units of product during March. Each unit required 2.20 standard direct labor hours. There were 11,500 actual hours used in the Assembly Department during March at an actual rate of $17.60 per hour. The standard direct labor rate is $18.00 per hour. Assuming direct labor for a month is paid on the fifth day of the following month, journalize the direct labor in the Assembly Department on March 31.

EX 22-22 Income statement indicating standard cost variances **OBJ. 5**

✔ Income before income tax, $85,900

The following data were taken from the records of Griggs Company for December 2014:

Administrative expenses	$100,800
Cost of goods sold (at standard)	550,000
Direct materials price variance—unfavorable	1,680
Direct materials quantity variance—favorable	560
Direct labor rate variance—favorable	1,120
Direct labor time variance—unfavorable	490
Variable factory overhead controllable variance—favorable	210
Fixed factory overhead volume variance—unfavorable	3,080
Interest expense	2,940
Sales	868,000
Selling expenses	125,000

Prepare an income statement for presentation to management.

EX 22-23 Nonfinancial performance measures **OBJ. 6**

Diamond Inc. is an Internet retailer of woodworking equipment. Customers order woodworking equipment from the company, using an online catalog. The company processes these orders and delivers the requested product from its warehouse. The company wants to provide customers with an excellent purchase experience in order to expand the business through favorable word-of-mouth advertising and to drive repeat business. To help monitor performance, the company developed a set of performance measures for its order placement and delivery process:

Average computer response time to customer "clicks"
Dollar amount of returned goods
Elapsed time between customer order and product delivery
Maintenance dollars divided by hardware investment
Number of customer complaints divided by the number of orders
Number of misfilled orders divided by the number of orders
Number of orders per warehouse employee
Number of page faults or errors due to software programming errors
Number of software fixes per week
Server (computer) downtime
Training dollars per programmer

a. For each performance measure, identify it as either an input or output measure related to the "order placement and delivery" process.

b. Provide an explanation for each performance measure.

EX 22-24 Nonfinancial performance measures **OBJ. 6**

Alpha University wishes to monitor the efficiency and quality of its course registration process.

a. Identify three input and three output measures for this process.

b. Why would Alpha University use nonfinancial measures for monitoring this process?

Problems Series A

PR 22-1A Direct materials and direct labor variance analysis **OBJ. 2, 3**

✔ c. Direct labor time variance, $3,360 U

Oasis Faucet Company manufactures faucets in a small manufacturing facility. The faucets are made from zinc. Manufacturing has 80 employees. Each employee presently provides 40 hours of labor per week. Information about a production week is as follows:

Standard wage per hr.	$16.80
Standard labor time per faucet	15 min.
Standard number of lbs. of zinc	2.6 lbs.
Standard price per lb. of zinc	$22.00
Actual price per lb. of zinc	$21.85
Actual lbs. of zinc used during the week	31,750 lbs.
Number of faucets produced during the week	12,000
Actual wage per hr.	$17.00
Actual hrs. for the week	3,200 hrs.

Instructions

Determine (a) the standard cost per unit for direct materials and direct labor; (b) the direct materials price variance, direct materials quantity variance, and total direct materials cost variance; and (c) the direct labor rate variance, direct labor time variance, and total direct labor cost variance.

PR 22-2A Flexible budgeting and variance analysis **OBJ. 1, 2, 3**

✔ 1. a. Direct materials quantity variance, $625 F

SPREADSHEET

I Love My Chocolate Company makes dark chocolate and light chocolate. Both products require cocoa and sugar. The following planning information has been made available:

	Standard Amount per Case		
	Dark Chocolate	**Light Chocolate**	**Standard Price per Pound**
Cocoa	12 lbs.	8 lbs.	$7.25
Sugar	10 lbs.	14 lbs.	1.40
Standard labor time	0.50 hr.	0.60 hr.	

	Dark Chocolate	**Light Chocolate**
Planned production	4,700 cases	11,000 cases
Standard labor rate	$15.50 per hr.	$15.50 per hr.

I Love My Chocolate Company does not expect there to be any beginning or ending inventories of cocoa or sugar. At the end of the budget year, I Love My Chocolate Company had the following actual results:

	Dark Chocolate	**Light Chocolate**
Actual production (cases)	5,000	10,000
	Actual Price per Pound	**Actual Pounds Purchased and Used**
Cocoa	$7.33	140,300
Sugar	1.35	188,000
	Actual Labor Rate	**Actual Labor Hours Used**
Dark chocolate	$15.25 per hr.	2,360
Light chocolate	15.80 per hr.	6,120

(Continued)

Instructions

1. Prepare the following variance analyses for both chocolates and the total, based on the actual results and production levels at the end of the budget year:
   a. Direct materials price, quantity, and total variance.
   b. Direct labor rate, time, and total variance.
2. Why are the standard amounts in part (1) based on the actual production for the year instead of the planned production for the year?

PR 22-3A Direct materials, direct labor, and factory overhead cost variance analysis OBJ. 3, 4

✔ c. Controllable variance, $400 F

SPREADSHEET

Sticky Polymers Inc. processes a base chemical into plastic. Standard costs and actual costs for direct materials, direct labor, and factory overhead incurred for the manufacture of 10,750 units of product were as follows:

	Standard Costs	Actual Costs
Direct materials	3,700 lbs. at $12.00	3,500 lbs. at $12.50
Direct labor	4,300 hrs. at $20.00	4,200 hrs. at $20.40
Factory overhead	Rates per direct labor hr., based on 100% of normal capacity of 4,500 direct labor hrs.:	
	Variable cost, $4.00	$16,800 variable cost
	Fixed cost, $3.00	$13,500 fixed cost

Each unit requires 0.4 hour of direct labor.

Instructions

Determine (a) the direct materials price variance, direct materials quantity variance, and total direct materials cost variance; (b) the direct labor rate variance, direct labor time variance, and total direct labor cost variance; and (c) the variable factory overhead controllable variance, fixed factory overhead volume variance, and total factory overhead cost variance.

PR 22-4A Factory overhead cost variance report OBJ. 4

✔ Controllable variance, $770 U

SPREADSHEET

GENERAL LEDGER

Tiger Equipment Inc., a manufacturer of construction equipment, prepared the following factory overhead cost budget for the Welding Department for May 2014. The company expected to operate the department at 100% of normal capacity of 8,400 hours.

Variable costs:		
Indirect factory wages	$30,240	
Power and light	20,160	
Indirect materials	16,800	
Total variable cost		$ 67,200
Fixed costs:		
Supervisory salaries	$20,000	
Depreciation of plant and equipment	36,200	
Insurance and property taxes	15,200	
Total fixed cost		71,400
Total factory overhead cost		$138,600

During May, the department operated at 8,860 standard hours, and the factory overhead costs incurred were indirect factory wages, $32,400; power and light, $21,000; indirect materials, $18,250; supervisory salaries, $20,000; depreciation of plant and equipment, $36,200; and insurance and property taxes, $15,200.

Instructions

Prepare a factory overhead cost variance report for May. To be useful for cost control, the budgeted amounts should be based on 8,860 hours.

✔ 3. $1,600 U

PR 22-5A Standards for nonmanufacturing expenses OBJ. 3, 6

CodeHead Software Inc. does software development. One important activity in software development is writing software code. The manager of the WordPro Development Team determined that the average software programmer could write 25 lines of code in an hour. The plan for the first week in May called for 4,650 lines of code to be written on the WordPro product. The WordPro Team has five programmers. Each programmer is hired from an employment firm that requires temporary employees to be hired for a minimum of a 40-hour week. Programmers are paid $32.00 per hour. The manager offered a bonus if the team could generate more lines for the week, without overtime. Due to a project emergency, the programmers wrote more code in the first week of May than planned. The actual amount of code written in the first week of May was 5,650 lines, without overtime. As a result, the bonus caused the average programmer's hourly rate to increase to $40.00 per hour during the first week in May.

Instructions

1. If the team generated 4,650 lines of code according to the original plan, what would have been the labor time variance?
2. What was the actual labor time variance as a result of generating 5,650 lines of code?
3. What was the labor rate variance as a result of the bonus?
4. Are there any performance-related issues that the labor time and rate variances fail to consider? Explain.
5. The manager is trying to determine if a better decision would have been to hire a temporary programmer to meet the higher programming demand in the first week of May, rather than paying out the bonus. If another employee was hired from the employment firm, what would have been the labor time variance in the first week?
6. Which decision is better, paying the bonus or hiring another programmer?

Problems Series B

✔ c. Rate variance, $200 F

PR 22-1B Direct materials and direct labor variance analysis OBJ. 2, 3

Lenni Clothing Co. manufactures clothing in a small manufacturing facility. Manufacturing has 25 employees. Each employee presently provides 40 hours of productive labor per week. Information about a production week is as follows:

Standard wage per hr.	$12.00
Standard labor time per unit	12 min.
Standard number of yds. of fabric per unit	5.0 yds.
Standard price per yd. of fabric	$5.00
Actual price per yd. of fabric	$5.10
Actual yds. of fabric used during the week	26,200 yds.
Number of units produced during the week	5,220
Actual wage per hr.	$11.80
Actual hrs. for the week	1,000 hrs.

Instructions

Determine (a) the standard cost per unit for direct materials and direct labor; (b) the price variance, quantity variance, and total direct materials cost variance; and (c) the rate variance, time variance, and total direct labor cost variance.

✔ 1. a. Direct materials price variance, $12,220 U

SPREADSHEET

PR 22-2B Flexible budgeting and variance analysis OBJ. 1, 2, 3

I'm Really Cold Coat Company makes women's and men's coats. Both products require filler and lining material. The following planning information has been made available:

	Standard Amount per Unit		
	Women's Coats	**Men's Coats**	**Standard Price per Unit**
Filler	4.0 lbs.	5.20 lbs.	$2.00 per lb.
Liner	7.00 yds.	9.40 yds.	8.00 per yd.
Standard labor time	0.40 hr.	0.50 hr.	

	Women's Coats	**Men's Coats**
Planned production	5,000 units	6,200 units
Standard labor rate	$14.00 per hr.	$13.00 per hr.

I'm Really Cold Coat Company does not expect there to be any beginning or ending inventories of filler and lining material. At the end of the budget year, I'm Really Cold Coat Company experienced the following actual results:

	Women's Coats	**Men's Coats**
Actual production	4,400	5,800
	Actual Price per Unit	**Actual Quantity Purchased and Used**
Filler	$1.90 per lb.	48,000
Liner	8.20 per yd.	85,100
	Actual Labor Rate	**Actual Labor Hours Used**
Women's coats	$14.10 per hr.	1,825
Men's coats	13.30 per hr.	2,800

The expected beginning inventory and desired ending inventory were realized.

Instructions

1. Prepare the following variance analyses for both coats and the total, based on the actual results and production levels at the end of the budget year:
   a. Direct materials price, quantity, and total variance.
   b. Direct labor rate, time, and total variance.
2. Why are the standard amounts in part (1) based on the actual production at the end of the year instead of the planned production at the beginning of the year?

PR 22-3B Direct materials, direct labor, and factory overhead cost variance analysis OBJ. 3, 4

✔ a. Direct materials price variance, $10,100 U

SPREADSHEET

Road Gripper Tire Co. manufactures automobile tires. Standard costs and actual costs for direct materials, direct labor, and factory overhead incurred for the manufacture of 4,160 tires were as follows:

	Standard Costs	**Actual Costs**
Direct materials	100,000 lbs. at $6.40	101,000 lbs. at $6.50
Direct labor	2,080 hrs. at $15.75	2,000 hrs. at $15.40
Factory overhead	Rates per direct labor hr., based on 100% of normal capacity of 2,000 direct labor hrs.:	
	Variable cost, $4.00	$8,200 variable cost
	Fixed cost, $6.00	$12,000 fixed cost

Each tire requires 0.5 hour of direct labor.

Instructions

Determine (a) the direct materials price variance, direct materials quantity variance, and total direct materials cost variance; (b) the direct labor rate variance, direct labor time variance, and total direct labor cost variance; and (c) the variable factory overhead controllable variance, fixed factory overhead volume variance, and total factory overhead cost variance.

✔ Controllable variance, $1,450 F

SPREADSHEET

GENERAL LEDGER

PR 22-4B Factory overhead cost variance report **OBJ. 4**

Feeling Better Medical Inc., a manufacturer of disposable medical supplies, prepared the following factory overhead cost budget for the Assembly Department for October 2014. The company expected to operate the department at 100% of normal capacity of 30,000 hours.

Variable costs:		
Indirect factory wages	$247,500	
Power and light	189,000	
Indirect materials	52,500	
Total variable cost		$489,000
Fixed costs:		
Supervisory salaries	$126,000	
Depreciation of plant and equipment	70,000	
Insurance and property taxes	44,000	
Total fixed cost		240,000
Total factory overhead cost		$729,000

During October, the department operated at 28,500 hours, and the factory overhead costs incurred were indirect factory wages, $234,000 power and light, $178,500 indirect materials, $50,600 supervisory salaries, $126,000 depreciation of plant and equipment, $70,000 and insurance and property taxes, $44,000.

Instructions

Prepare a factory overhead cost variance report for October. To be useful for cost control, the budgeted amounts should be based on 28,500 hours.

PR 22-5B Standards for nonmanufacturing expenses **OBJ. 3, 6**

✔ 2. $161 F

The Radiology Department provides imaging services for Emergency Medical Center. One important activity in the Radiology Department is transcribing digitally recorded analyses of images into a written report. The manager of the Radiology Department determined that the average transcriptionist could type 700 lines of a report in an hour. The plan for the first week in May called for 81,900 typed lines to be written. The Radiology Department has three transcriptionists. Each transcriptionist is hired from an employment firm that requires temporary employees to be hired for a minimum of a 40-hour week. Transcriptionists are paid $23.00 per hour. The manager offered a bonus if the department could type more lines for the week, without overtime. Due to high service demands, the transcriptionists typed more lines in the first week of May than planned. The actual amount of lines typed in the first week of May was 88,900 lines, without overtime. As a result, the bonus caused the average transcriptionist hourly rate to increase to $30.00 per hour during the first week in May.

Instructions

1. If the department typed 81,900 lines according to the original plan, what would have been the labor time variance?
2. What was the labor time variance as a result of typing 88,900 lines?
3. What was the labor rate variance as a result of the bonus?
4. The manager is trying to determine if a better decision would have been to hire a temporary transcriptionist to meet the higher typing demands in the first week of May, rather than paying out the bonus. If another employee was hired from the employment firm, what would have been the labor time variance in the first week?
5. Which decision is better, paying the bonus or hiring another transcriptionist?
6. Are there any performance-related issues that the labor time and rate variances fail to consider? Explain.

Comprehensive Problem 5

✔ 2. $55.60

✔ 6. Bottles purchased, $8,070

✔ 11. Mixing time variance, $216 F

✔ 12. $5 U

Genuine Spice Inc. began operations on January 1, 2014. The company produces a hand and body lotion in an eight-ounce bottle called *Eternal Beauty*. The lotion is sold wholesale in 12-bottle cases for $100 per case. There is a selling commission of $20 per case. The January direct materials, direct labor, and factory overhead costs are as follows:

DIRECT MATERIALS

	Cost Behavior	Units per Case	Cost per Unit	Direct Materials Cost per Case
Cream base	Variable	100 ozs.	$0.02	$ 2.00
Natural oils	Variable	30 ozs.	0.30	9.00
Bottle (8-oz.)	Variable	12 bottles	0.50	6.00
				$17.00

DIRECT LABOR

Department	Cost Behavior	Time per Case	Labor Rate per Hour	Direct Labor Cost per Case
Mixing	Variable	20 min.	$18.00	$6.00
Filling	Variable	5	14.40	1.20
		25 min.		$7.20

FACTORY OVERHEAD

	Cost Behavior	Total Cost
Utilities	Mixed	$ 600
Facility lease	Fixed	14,000
Equipment depreciation	Fixed	4,300
Supplies	Fixed	660
		$19,560

Part A—Break-Even Analysis

The management of Genuine Spice Inc. wishes to determine the number of cases required to break even per month. The utilities cost, which is part of factory overhead, is a mixed cost. The following information was gathered from the first six months of operation regarding this cost:

2014	Case Production	Utility Total Cost
January	500	$600
February	800	660
March	1,200	740
April	1,100	720
May	950	690
June	1,025	705

Instructions

1. Determine the fixed and variable portion of the utility cost, using the high-low method.
2. Determine the contribution margin per case.
3. Determine the fixed costs per month, including the utility fixed cost from part (1).
4. Determine the break-even number of cases per month.

Part B—August Budgets

During July of the current year, the management of Genuine Spice Inc. asked the controller to prepare August manufacturing and income statement budgets. Demand was expected to be 1,500 cases at $100 per case for August. Inventory planning information is provided as follows:

Finished Goods Inventory:

	Cases	Cost
Estimated finished goods inventory, August 1, 2014	300	$12,000
Desired finished goods inventory, August 31, 2014	175	7,000

Materials Inventory:

	Cream Base (ozs.)	Oils (ozs.)	Bottles (bottles)
Estimated materials inventory, August 1, 2014	250	290	600
Desired materials inventory, August 31, 2014	1,000	360	240

There was negligible work in process inventory assumed for either the beginning or end of the month; thus, none was assumed. In addition, there was no change in the cost per unit or estimated units per case operating data from January.

Instructions

5. Prepare the August production budget.
6. Prepare the August direct materials purchases budget.
7. Prepare the August direct labor budget. Round the hours required for production to the nearest hour.
8. Prepare the August factory overhead budget.
9. Prepare the August budgeted income statement, including selling expenses.

Part C—August Variance Analysis

During September of the current year, the controller was asked to perform variance analyses for August. The January operating data provided the standard prices, rates, times, and quantities per case. There were 1,500 actual cases produced during August, which was 250 more cases than planned at the beginning of the month. Actual data for August were as follows:

	Actual Direct Materials Price per Unit	Actual Direct Materials Quantity per Case
Cream base	$0.016 per oz.	102 ozs.
Natural oils	$0.32 per oz.	31 ozs.
Bottle (8-oz.)	$0.42 per bottle	12.5 bottles

	Actual Direct Labor Rate	Actual Direct Labor Time per Case
Mixing	$18.20	19.50 min.
Filling	14.00	5.60 min.

Actual variable overhead	$305.00
Normal volume	1,600 cases

The prices of the materials were different than standard due to fluctuations in market prices. The standard quantity of materials used per case was an ideal standard. The Mixing Department used a higher grade labor classification during the month, thus causing the actual labor rate to exceed standard. The Filling Department used a lower grade labor classification during the month, thus causing the actual labor rate to be less than standard.

Instructions

10. Determine and interpret the direct materials price and quantity variances for the three materials.
11. Determine and interpret the direct labor rate and time variances for the two departments. Round hours to the nearest hour.
12. Determine and interpret the factory overhead controllable variance.
13. Determine and interpret the factory overhead volume variance.
14. Why are the standard direct labor and direct materials costs in the calculations for parts (10) and (11) based on the actual 1,500-case production volume rather than the planned 1,250 cases of production used in the budgets for parts (6) and (7)?

Cases & Projects

CP 22-1 Ethics and professional conduct in business using nonmanufacturing standards

Dash Riprock is a cost analyst with Safe Insurance Company. Safe is applying standards to its claims payment operation. Claims payment is a repetitive operation that could be evaluated with standards. Dash used time and motion studies to identify an ideal standard of 36 claims processed per hour. The Claims Processing Department manager, Henry Tudor, has rejected this standard and has argued that the standard should be 30 claims processed per hour. Henry and Dash were unable to agree, so they decided to discuss this matter openly at a joint meeting with the vice president of operations, who would arbitrate a final decision. Prior to the meeting, Dash wrote the following memo to Anne Boleyn, Vice President of Operations.

To: Anne Boleyn, Vice President of Operations
From: Dash Riprock
Re: Standards in the Claims Processing Department

As you know, Henry and I are scheduled to meet with you to discuss our disagreement with respect to the appropriate standards for the Claims Processing Department. I have conducted time and motion studies and have determined that the ideal standard is 36 claims processed per hour. Henry argues that 30 claims processed per hour would be more appropriate. I believe he is trying to "pad" the budget with some slack. I'm not sure what he is trying to get away with, but I believe a tight standard will drive efficiency up in his area. I hope you will agree when we meet with you next week.

Discuss the ethical and professional issues in this situation.

CP 22-2 Nonfinancial performance measures

The senior management of Tungston Company has proposed the following three performance measures for the company:

1. Net income as a percent of stockholders' equity
2. Revenue growth
3. Employee satisfaction

Management believes these three measures combine both financial and nonfinancial measures and are thus superior to using just financial measures.

What advice would you give Tungston Company for improving its performance measurement system?

CP 22-3 Variance interpretation

You have been asked to investigate some cost problems in the Assembly Department of Ruthenium Electronics Co., a consumer electronics company. To begin your investigation, you have obtained the following budget performance report for the department for the last quarter:

Ruthenium Electronics Co.
Assembly Department Quarterly Budget Performance Report

	Standard Quantity at Standard Rates	Actual Quantity at Standard Rates	Quantity Variances
Direct labor	$157,500	$227,500	$ 70,000 U
Direct materials	297,500	385,000	87,500 U
Total	$455,000	$612,500	$157,500 U

The following reports were also obtained:

Ruthenium Electronics Co.
Purchasing Department Quarterly Budget Performance Report

	Actual Quantity at Standard Rates	Actual Quantity at Actual Rates	Price Variance
Direct materials	$437,500	$385,000	–$52,500 F

Ruthenium Electronics Co.
Fabrication Department Quarterly Budget Performance Report

	Standard Quantity at Standard Rates	Actual Quantity at Standard Rates	Quantity Variances
Direct labor	$245,000	$203,000	–$42,000 F
Direct materials	140,000	140,000	0
Total	$385,000	$343,000	–$42,000 F

You also interviewed the Assembly Department supervisor. Excerpts from the interview follow.

Q: *What explains the poor performance in your department?*

A: *Listen, you've got to understand what it's been like in this department recently. Lately, it seems no matter how hard we try, we can't seem to make the standards. I'm not sure what is going on, but we've been having a lot of problems lately.*

Q: *What kind of problems?*

A: *Well, for instance, all this quarter we've been requisitioning purchased parts from the material storeroom, and the parts just didn't fit together very well. During most of this quarter we've had to scrap and sort purchased parts—just to get our assemblies put together. Naturally, all this takes time and material. And that's not all.*

Q: *Go on.*

A: *All this quarter, the work that we've been receiving from the Fabrication Department has been shoddy. I mean, maybe around 20% of the material that comes in from Fabrication just can't be assembled. The fabrication is all wrong. As a result, we've had to scrap and rework a lot of the stuff. Naturally, this has just shot our quantity variances.*

Interpret the variance reports in light of the comments by the Assembly Department supervisor.

CP 22-4 Variance interpretation

Vanadium Audio Inc. is a small manufacturer of electronic musical instruments. The plant manager received the following variable factory overhead report for the period:

	Actual	Budgeted Variable Factory Overhead at Actual Production	Controllable Variance
Supplies	$ 42,000	$ 39,780	$ 2,220 U
Power and light	52,500	50,900	1,600 U
Indirect factory wages	39,100	30,600	8,500 U
Total	$133,600	$121,280	$12,320 U

Actual units produced: 15,000 (90% of practical capacity)

The plant manager is not pleased with the $12,320 unfavorable variable factory overhead controllable variance and has come to discuss the matter with the controller. The following discussion occurred:

Plant Manager: I just received this factory report for the latest month of operation. I'm not very pleased with these figures. Before these numbers go to headquarters, you and I will need to reach an understanding.

Controller: Go ahead, what's the problem?

Plant Manager: What's the problem? Well, everything. Look at the variance. It's too large. If I understand the accounting approach being used here, you are assuming that my costs are variable to the units produced. Thus, as the production volume declines, so should these costs. Well, I don't believe that these costs are variable at all. I think they are fixed costs. As a result, when we operate below capacity, the costs really don't go down at all. I'm being penalized for costs I have no control over at all. I need this report to be redone to reflect this fact. If anything, the difference between actual and budget is essentially a volume variance. Listen, I know that you're a team player. You really need to reconsider your assumptions on this one.

If you were in the controller's position, how would you respond to the plant manager?

CP 22-5 Nonmanufacturing performance measures—government

Internet Project

Group Project

Municipal governments are discovering that you can control only what you measure. As a result, many municipal governments are introducing nonfinancial performance measures to help improve municipal services. In a group, use the Google search engine to perform a search for "municipal government performance measurement." Google will provide a list of Internet sites that outline various city efforts in using nonfinancial performance measures. As a group, report on the types of measures used by one of the cities from the search.

CHAPTER 23

CLAUDIAVEJA/ISTOCKPHOTO.COM

Performance Evaluation for Decentralized Operations

E.W. Scripps

Have you ever wondered why large retail stores like **Macy's**, **JC Penney**, and **Sears** are divided into departments? Organizing into departments allows retailers to provide products and expertise in specialized areas, while offering a wide range of products. Departments also allow companies to assign responsibility for financial performance. This information can be used to make product decisions, evaluate operations, and guide company strategy. Strong departmental performance might be attributable to a good department manager, while weak departmental performance may be the result of a product mix that has low customer appeal. By tracking departmental performance, companies can identify and reward excellent performance and take corrective action in departments that are performing poorly.

Like retailers, most businesses organize into operational units, such as divisions and departments. For example, **E.W. Scripps Company** operates a variety of media companies and is organized into three business segments: Newspapers, TV Stations, and United Media. The Newspapers segment includes the Scripps Media Center and a variety of local newspapers such as the *Ventura County Star* and the *Knoxville News Sentinel*. The TV Stations segment operates network-affiliated television stations. United Media licenses media brands and creative content, such as the comic strips *Peanuts* and *Dilbert*, and distributes many of these brands internationally.

Managers at E.W. Scripps are responsible for running their business segment. Each segment is evaluated on segment profit, which excludes certain expense items from the calculation of profit that are not within the control of the business segment. The company uses segment profit to determine how to allocate resources between business segments and to plan and control the company's operations.

In this chapter, the role of accounting in assisting managers in planning and controlling organizational units, such as departments, divisions, and stores, is described and illustrated.

Learning Objectives

After studying this chapter, you should be able to: | *Example Exercises*

Objective	Example Exercises
OBJ 1 Describe the advantages and disadvantages of decentralized operations.	
Centralized and Decentralized Operations	
Advantages of Decentralization	
Disadvantages of Decentralization	
Responsibility Accounting	
OBJ 2 Prepare a responsibility accounting report for a cost center.	
Responsibility Accounting for Cost Centers	EE 23-1
OBJ 3 Prepare responsibility accounting reports for a profit center.	
Responsibility Accounting for Profit Centers	
Service Department Charges	EE 23-2
Profit Center Reporting	EE 23-3
OBJ 4 Compute and interpret the rate of return on investment, the residual income, and the balanced scorecard for an investment center.	
Responsibility Accounting for Investment Centers	
Rate of Return on Investment	EE 23-4
Residual Income	EE 23-5
The Balanced Scorecard	
OBJ 5 Describe and illustrate how the market price, negotiated price, and cost price approaches to transfer pricing may be used by decentralized segments of a business.	
Transfer Pricing	
Market Price Approach	
Negotiated Price Approach	EE 23-6
Cost Price Approach	

At a Glance 23 Page 1094

OBJ 1 Describe the advantages and disadvantages of decentralized operations.

Centralized and Decentralized Operations

In a *centralized* company, all major planning and operating decisions are made by top management. For example, a one-person, owner-manager-operated company is centralized because all plans and decisions are made by one person. In a small owner-manager-operated business, centralization may be desirable. This is because the owner-manager's close supervision ensures that the business will be operated in the way the owner-manager wishes.

In a *decentralized* company, managers of separate divisions or units are delegated operating responsibility. The division (unit) managers are responsible for planning and controlling the operations of their divisions. Divisions are often structured around products, customers, or regions.

The proper amount of decentralization for a company depends on the company's unique circumstances. For example, in some companies, division managers have authority over all operations, including fixed asset purchases. In other companies, division managers have authority over profits but not fixed asset purchases.

Advantages of Decentralization

For large companies, it is difficult for top management to:

1. Maintain daily contact with all operations, and
2. Maintain operating expertise in all product lines and services

In such cases, delegating authority to managers closest to the operations usually results in better decisions. These managers often anticipate and react to operating data more quickly than could top management. These managers can also focus their attention on becoming "experts" in their area of operation.

Decentralized operations provide excellent training for managers. Delegating responsibility allows managers to develop managerial experience early in their careers. This helps a company retain managers, some of whom may be later promoted to top management positions.

Managers of decentralized operations often work closely with customers. As a result, they tend to identify with customers and thus are often more creative in suggesting operating and product improvements. This helps create good customer relations.

Disadvantages of Decentralization

A primary disadvantage of decentralized operations is that decisions made by one manager may negatively affect the profits of the company. For example, managers of divisions whose products compete with one another might start a price war that decreases the profits of both divisions and thus the overall company.

Another disadvantage of decentralized operations is that assets and expenses may be duplicated across divisions. For example, each manager of a product line might have a separate sales force and office support staff.

The advantages and disadvantages of decentralization are summarized in Exhibit 1.

EXHIBIT 1

Advantages and Disadvantages of Decentralized Operations

Advantages of Decentralization
Allows managers closest to the operations to make decisions
Provides excellent training for managers
Allows managers to become experts in their area of operation
Helps retain managers
Improves creativity and customer relations

Disadvantages of Decentralization
Decisions made by managers may negatively affect the profits of the company
Duplicates assets and expenses

Business Connection

STEVE JOBS: CENTRALIZED OPERATIONS AT APPLE

Apple Inc.'s meteoric rise from a second-tier computer maker in the early 2000s to the standard for all things technology by the end of the decade was no accident. The company's success was the result of a centralized operation, where Apple CEO Steve Jobs had ultimate control over the company's strategic and operational decisions. As Andrew Keen noted in his interview of Job's biographer Walter Isaacson, it was Jobs' "obsessive end-to-end control of products—from chip manufacture to retail experience—that most defined Steve's remarkable tenure as Apple CEO." This centralized business model also drove Apple's success. Unfortunately, Steve Jobs died in October 2011, creating a void at the top of the company's centralized operation. Apple must now struggle with how to adapt its highly successful centralized business model to the loss of the person that controlled the company's decisions.

Source: A. Keen, "Keen On ... Walter Isaacson: Sometimes It's Nice to Be In The Hands of a Control Freak," *AOLTech.com*, December 19, 2011.

Responsibility Accounting

In a decentralized business, accounting assists managers in evaluating and controlling their areas of responsibility, called *responsibility centers*. **Responsibility accounting** is the process of measuring and reporting operating data by responsibility center.

Three types of responsibility centers are:

1. Cost centers, which have responsibility over costs
2. Profit centers, which have responsibility over revenues and costs
3. Investment centers, which have responsibility over revenues, costs, and investment in assets

OBJ 2 Prepare a responsibility accounting report for a cost center.

Responsibility Accounting for Cost Centers

A **cost center** manager has responsibility for controlling costs. For example, the supervisor of the Power Department has responsibility for the costs of providing power. A cost center manager does not make decisions concerning sales or the amount of fixed assets invested in the center.

Cost centers may vary in size from a small department to an entire manufacturing plant. In addition, cost centers may exist within other cost centers. For example, an entire university or college could be viewed as a cost center, and each college and department within the university could also be a cost center, as shown in Exhibit 2.

EXHIBIT 2 **Cost Centers in a University**

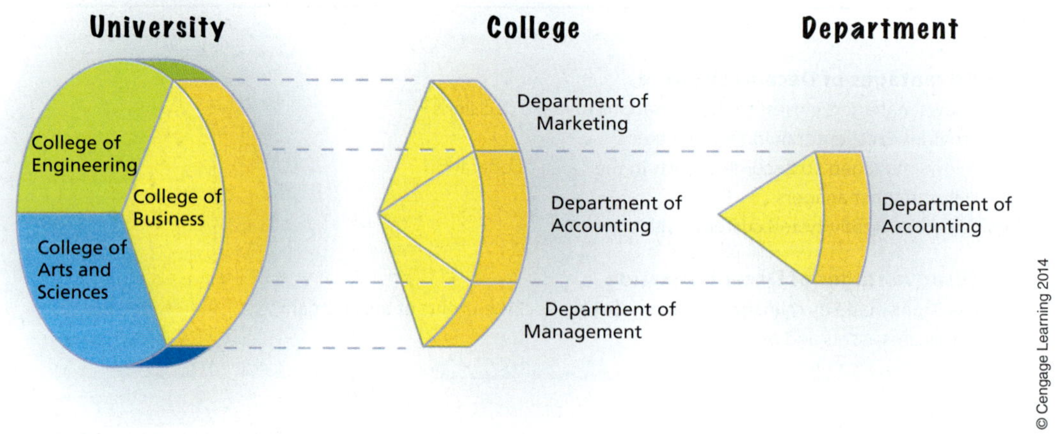

Responsibility accounting for cost centers focuses on the controlling and reporting of costs. Budget performance reports that report budgeted and actual costs are normally prepared for each cost center.

Exhibit 3 illustrates budget performance reports for the following cost centers:

1. Vice President, Production
2. Manager, Plant A
3. Supervisor, Department 1—Plant A

Exhibit 3 shows how cost centers are often linked together within a company. For example, the budget performance report for Department 1—Plant A supports the report for Plant A, which supports the report for the vice president of production.

The reports in Exhibit 3 show the budgeted costs and actual costs along with the differences. Each difference is classified as either *over* budget or *under* budget. Such reports allow cost center managers to focus on areas of significant differences.

For example, the supervisor for Department 1 of Plant A can focus on why the materials cost was over budget. The supervisor might discover that excess materials were scrapped. This could be due to such factors as machine malfunctions, improperly trained employees, or low-quality materials.

As shown in Exhibit 3, responsibility accounting reports are usually more summarized for higher levels of management. For example, the budget performance report for the manager of Plant A shows only administration and departmental data. This report enables the plant manager to identify the departments responsible for major differences. Likewise, the report for the vice president of production summarizes the cost data for each plant.

EXHIBIT 3

Responsibility Accounting Reports for Cost Centers

Budget Performance Report
Vice President, Production
For the Month Ended October 31, 2014

	Budget	Actual	Over Budget	Under Budget
Administration	$ 19,500	$ 19,700	$ 200	
Plant A	467,475	470,330	2,855	
Plant B	395,225	394,300		$925
	$882,200	$884,330	$3,055	$925

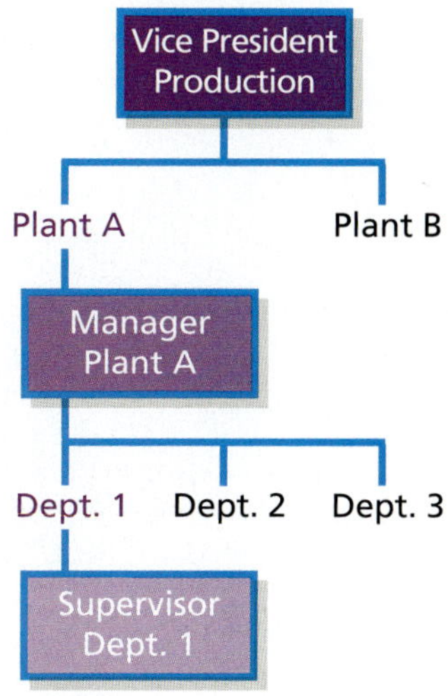

Budget Performance Report
Manager, Plant A
For the Month Ended October 31, 2014

	Budget	Actual	Over Budget	Under Budget
Administration	$ 17,500	$ 17,350		$150
Department 1	109,725	111,280	$1,555	
Department 2	190,500	192,600	2,100	
Department 3	149,750	149,100		650
	$467,475	$470,330	$3,655	$800

Budget Performance Report
Supervisor, Department 1 — Plant A
For the Month Ended October 31, 2014

	Budget	Actual	Over Budget	Under Budget
Factory wages	$ 58,100	$ 58,000		$100
Materials	32,500	34,225	$1,725	
Supervisory salaries	6,400	6,400		
Power and light	5,750	5,690		60
Depreciation of plant and equipment	4,000	4,000		
Maintenance	2,000	1,990		10
Insurance and property taxes	975	975		
	$109,725	$111,280	$1,725	$170

Example Exercise 23-1 Budgetary Performance for Cost Center

OBJ 2

Nuclear Power Company's costs were over budget by $24,000. The company is divided into North and South regions. The North Region's costs were under budget by $2,000. Determine the amount that the South Region's costs were over or under budget.

Follow My Example 23-1

$26,000 over budget ($24,000 + $2,000)

Practice Exercises: **PE 23-1A, PE 23-1B**

OBJ 3 Prepare responsibility accounting reports for a profit center.

Responsibility Accounting for Profit Centers

A **profit center** manager has the responsibility and authority for making decisions that affect revenues and costs and thus profits. Profit centers may be divisions, departments, or products.

The manager of a profit center does not make decisions concerning the fixed assets invested in the center. However, profit centers are an excellent training assignment for new managers.

Responsibility accounting for profit centers focuses on reporting revenues, expenses, and income from operations. Thus, responsibility accounting reports for profit centers take the form of income statements.

The profit center income statement should include only revenues and expenses that are controlled by the manager. **Controllable revenues** are revenues earned by the profit center. **Controllable expenses** are costs that can be influenced (controlled) by the decisions of profit center managers.

Service Department Charges

The controllable expenses of profit centers include *direct operating expenses* such as sales salaries and utility expenses. In addition, a profit center may incur expenses provided by internal centralized *service departments*. Examples of such service departments include the following:

1. Research and Development
2. Legal
3. Telecommunications
4. Information and Computer Systems
5. Facilities Management
6. Purchasing
7. Publications and Graphics
8. Payroll Accounting
9. Transportation
10. Personnel Administration

Service department charges are *indirect* expenses to a profit center. They are similar to the expenses that would be incurred if the profit center purchased the services from outside the company. A profit center manager has control over service department expenses if the manager is free to choose how much service is used. In such cases, **service department charges** are allocated to profit centers based on the usage of the service by each profit center.

To illustrate, Nova Entertainment Group (NEG), a diversified entertainment company, is used. NEG has the following two operating divisions organized as profit centers:

1. Theme Park Division
2. Movie Production Division

Employees of IBM speak of "green money" and "blue money." Green money comes from customers. Blue money comes from providing services to other IBM departments via service department charges. IBM employees note that blue money is easier to earn than green money; yet from the stockholders' perspective, green money is the only money that counts.

The revenues and direct operating expenses for the two divisions are shown below. The operating expenses consist of direct expenses, such as the wages and salaries of a division's employees.

	Theme Park Division	Movie Production Division
Revenues	$6,000,000	$2,500,000
Operating expenses	2,495,000	405,000

NEG's service departments and the expenses they incurred for the year ended December 31, 2014, are as follows:

Purchasing	$400,000
Payroll Accounting	255,000
Legal	250,000
Total	$905,000

An activity base for each service department is used to charge service department expenses to the Theme Park and Movie Production divisions. The activity base for each service department is a measure of the services performed. For NEG, the service department activity bases are as follows:

Department	Activity Base
Purchasing	Number of purchase requisitions
Payroll Accounting	Number of payroll checks
Legal	Number of billed hours

The use of services by the Theme Park and Movie Production divisions is as follows:

	Service Usage		
Division	**Purchasing**	**Payroll Accounting**	**Legal**
Theme Park	25,000 purchase requisitions	12,000 payroll checks	100 billed hrs.
Movie Production	15,000	3,000	900
Total	40,000 purchase requisitions	15,000 payroll checks	1,000 billed hrs.

The rates at which services are charged to each division are called *service department charge rates*. These rates are computed as follows:

$$\text{Service Department Charge Rate} = \frac{\text{Service Department Expense}}{\text{Total Service Department Usage}}$$

NEG's service department charge rates are computed as follows:

$$\text{Purchasing Charge Rate} = \frac{\$400{,}000}{40{,}000 \text{ purchase requisitions}} = \$10 \text{ per purchase requisition}$$

$$\text{Payroll Charge Rate} = \frac{\$255{,}000}{15{,}000 \text{ payroll checks}} = \$17 \text{ per payroll check}$$

$$\text{Legal Charge Rate} = \frac{\$250{,}000}{1{,}000 \text{ billed hrs.}} = \$250 \text{ per hr.}$$

The services used by each division are multiplied by the service department charge rates to determine the service charges for each division, as shown below.

$$\text{Service Department Charge} = \text{Service Usage} \times \text{Service Department Charge Rate}$$

Exhibit 4 illustrates the service department charges and related computations for NEG's Theme Park and Movie Production divisions.

EXHIBIT 4

Service Department Charges to NEG Divisions

Nova Entertainment Group
Service Department Charges to NEG Divisions
For the Year Ended December 31, 2014

Service Department	Theme Park Division	Movie Production Division
Purchasing (Note A)	$250,000	$150,000
Payroll Accounting (Note B)	204,000	51,000
Legal (Note C)	25,000	225,000
Total service department charges	$479,000	$426,000

Note A:
25,000 purchase requisitions × $10 per purchase requisition = $250,000
15,000 purchase requisitions × $10 per purchase requisition = $150,000
Note B:
12,000 payroll checks × $17 per check = $204,000
3,000 payroll checks × $17 per check = $51,000
Note C:
100 hours × $250 per hour = $25,000
900 hours × $250 per hour = $225,000

The differences in the service department charges between the two divisions can be explained by the nature of their operations and thus usage of services. For example, the Theme Park Division employs many part-time employees who are paid weekly. As a result, the Theme Park Division requires 12,000 payroll checks and incurs a $204,000 payroll service department charge (12,000 × $17). In contrast, the Movie Production Division has more permanent employees who are paid monthly. Thus, the Movie Production Division requires only 3,000 payroll checks and incurs a payroll service department charge of $51,000 (3,000 × $17).

Example Exercise 23-2 Service Department Charges

OBJ 3

The centralized legal department of Johnson Company has expenses of $600,000. The department has provided a total of 2,000 hours of service for the period. The East Division has used 500 hours of legal service during the period, and the West Division has used 1,500 hours. How much should each division be charged for legal services?

Follow My Example 23-2

East Division Service Charge for Legal Department:
$150,000 = 500 billed hours × ($600,000/2,000 hours)

West Division Service Charge for Legal Department:
$450,000 = 1,500 billed hours × ($600,000/2,000 hours)

Practice Exercises: **PE 23-2A, PE 23-2B**

Profit Center Reporting

The divisional income statements for NEG are shown in Exhibit 5.

EXHIBIT 5

Divisional Income Statements—NEG

Nova Entertainment Group
Divisional Income Statements
For the Year Ended December 31, 2014

	Theme Park Division	Movie Production Division
Revenues*	$6,000,000	$2,500,000
Operating expenses	2,495,000	405,000
Income from operations before service department charges	$3,505,000	$2,095,000
Less service department charges:		
Purchasing	$ 250,000	$ 150,000
Payroll Accounting	204,000	51,000
Legal	25,000	225,000
Total service department charges	$ 479,000	$ 426,000
Income from operations	$3,026,000	$1,669,000

*For a profit center that sells products, the income statement would show: Net sales – Cost of goods sold = Gross profit. The operating expenses would be deducted from the gross profit to get the income from operations before service department charges.

In evaluating the profit center manager, the income from operations should be compared over time to a budget. However, it should not be compared across profit centers, since the profit centers are usually different in terms of size, products, and customers.

Example Exercise 23-3 Income from Operations for Profit Center

OBJ 3

Using the data for Johnson Company from Example Exercise 23-2 along with the data given below, determine the divisional income from operations for the East and West divisions.

	East Division	West Division
Sales	$3,000,000	$8,000,000
Cost of goods sold	1,650,000	4,200,000
Selling expenses	850,000	1,850,000

Follow My Example 23-3

	East Division	West Division
Net sales	$3,000,000	$8,000,000
Cost of goods sold	1,650,000	4,200,000
Gross profit	$1,350,000	$3,800,000
Selling expenses	850,000	1,850,000
Income from operations before service department charges	$ 500,000	$1,950,000
Service department charges	150,000	450,000
Income from operations	$ 350,000	$1,500,000

Practice Exercises: **PE 23-3A, PE 23-3B**

Responsibility Accounting for Investment Centers

OBJ 4 Compute and interpret the rate of return on investment, the residual income, and the balanced scorecard for an investment center.

An **investment center** manager has the responsibility and the authority to make decisions that affect not only costs and revenues but also the assets invested in the center. Investment centers are often used in diversified companies organized by divisions. In such cases, the divisional manager has authority similar to that of a chief operating officer or president of a company.

Since investment center managers have responsibility for revenues and expenses, *income from operations* is part of investment center reporting. In addition, because the manager has responsibility for the assets invested in the center, the following two additional measures of performance are used:

1. Rate of return on investment
2. Residual income

To illustrate, DataLink Inc., a cellular phone company with three regional divisions, is used. Condensed divisional income statements for the Northern, Central, and Southern divisions of DataLink are shown in Exhibit 6.

EXHIBIT 6

Divisional Income Statements—DataLink Inc.

DataLink Inc.
Divisional Income Statements
For the Year Ended December 31, 2014

	Northern Division	Central Division	Southern Division
Revenues	$560,000	$672,000	$750,000
Operating expenses	336,000	470,400	562,500
Income from operations before service department charges	$224,000	$201,600	$187,500
Service department charges	154,000	117,600	112,500
Income from operations	$ 70,000	$ 84,000	$ 75,000

Using only income from operations, the Central Division is the most profitable division. However, income from operations does not reflect the amount of assets invested in each center. For example, the Central Division could have twice as many assets as the Northern Division. For this reason, performance measures that consider the amount of invested assets, such as the rate of return on investment and residual income, are used.

Rate of Return on Investment

Since investment center managers control the amount of assets invested in their centers, they should be evaluated based on the use of these assets. One measure that considers the amount of assets invested is the **rate of return on investment (ROI)** or *rate of return on assets*. It is computed as follows:

$$\text{Rate of Return on Investment (ROI)} = \frac{\text{Income from Operations}}{\text{Invested Assets}}$$

The rate of return on investment is useful because the three factors subject to control by divisional managers (revenues, expenses, and invested assets) are considered. The higher the rate of return on investment, the better the division is using its assets to generate income. In effect, the rate of return on investment measures the income (return) on each dollar invested. As a result, the rate of return on investment can be used as a common basis for comparing divisions with each other.

To illustrate, the invested assets of DataLink's three divisions are as follows:

	Invested Assets
Northern Division	$350,000
Central Division	700,000
Southern Division	500,000

Using the income from operations for each division shown in Exhibit 6, the rate of return on investment for each division is computed below.

Northern Division:

$$\text{Rate of Return on Investment} = \frac{\text{Income from Operations}}{\text{Invested Assets}} = \frac{\$70{,}000}{\$350{,}000} = 20\%$$

Central Division:

$$\text{Rate of Return on Investment} = \frac{\text{Income from Operations}}{\text{Invested Assets}} = \frac{\$84{,}000}{\$700{,}000} = 12\%$$

Southern Division:

$$\text{Rate of Return on Investment} = \frac{\text{Income from Operations}}{\text{Invested Assets}} = \frac{\$75{,}000}{\$500{,}000} = 15\%$$

Although the Central Division generated the largest income from operations, its rate of return on investment (12%) is the lowest. Hence, relative to the assets invested, the Central Division is the least profitable division. In comparison, the rate of return on investment of the Northern Division is 20%, and the Southern Division is 15%.

To analyze differences in the rate of return on investment across divisions, the **DuPont formula** for the rate of return on investment is often used.[1] The DuPont formula views the rate of return on investment as the product of the following two factors:

1. **Profit margin**, which is the ratio of income from operations to sales.
2. **Investment turnover**, which is the ratio of sales to invested assets.

1 The DuPont formula was created by a financial executive of E. I. du Pont de Nemours and Company in 1919.

Using the DuPont formula, the rate of return on investment is expressed as follows:

$$\text{Rate of Return on Investment} = \text{Profit Margin} \times \text{Investment Turnover}$$

$$\text{Rate of Return on Investment} = \frac{\text{Income from Operations}}{\text{Sales}} \times \frac{\text{Sales}}{\text{Invested Assets}}$$

The DuPont formula is useful in evaluating divisions. This is because the profit margin and the investment turnover reflect the following underlying operating relationships of each division:

1. Profit margin indicates *operating profitability* by computing the rate of profit earned on each sales dollar.
2. Investment turnover indicates *operating efficiency* by computing the number of sales dollars generated by each dollar of invested assets.

If a division's profit margin increases, and all other factors remain the same, the division's rate of return on investment will increase. For example, a division might add more profitable products to its sales mix and thus increase its operating profit, profit margin, and rate of return on investment.

If a division's investment turnover increases, and all other factors remain the same, the division's rate of return on investment will increase. For example, a division might attempt to increase sales through special sales promotions and thus increase operating efficiency, investment turnover, and rate of return on investment.

The rate of return on investment, profit margin, and investment turnover operate in relationship to one another. Specifically, more income can be earned by either increasing the investment turnover, increasing the profit margin, or both.

Using the DuPont formula yields the same rate of return on investment for each of DataLink's divisions, as shown below.

$$\text{Rate of Return on Investment} = \frac{\text{Income from Operations}}{\text{Sales}} \times \frac{\text{Sales}}{\text{Invested Assets}}$$

Northern Division:

$$\text{Rate of Return on Investment} = \frac{\$70{,}000}{\$560{,}000} \times \frac{\$560{,}000}{\$350{,}000} = 12.5\% \times 1.6 = 20\%$$

Central Division:

$$\text{Rate of Return on Investment} = \frac{\$84{,}000}{\$672{,}000} \times \frac{\$672{,}000}{\$700{,}000} = 12.5\% \times 0.96 = 12\%$$

Southern Division:

$$\text{Rate of Return on Investment} = \frac{\$75{,}000}{\$750{,}000} \times \frac{\$750{,}000}{\$500{,}000} = 10\% \times 1.5 = 15\%$$

The Northern and Central divisions have the same profit margins of 12.5%. However, the Northern Division's investment turnover of 1.6 is larger than that of the Central Division's turnover of 0.96. By using its invested assets more efficiently, the Northern Division's rate of return on investment of 20% is 8 percentage points higher than the Central Division's rate of return of 12%.

The Southern Division's profit margin of 10% and investment turnover of 1.5 are lower than those of the Northern Division. The product of these factors results in a return on investment of 15% for the Southern Division, compared to 20% for the Northern Division.

Even though the Southern Division's profit margin is lower than the Central Division's, its higher turnover of 1.5 results in a rate of return of 15%, which is greater than the Central Division's rate of return of 12%.

To increase the rate of return on investment, the profit margin and investment turnover for a division may be analyzed. For example, assume that the Northern Division is in a highly competitive industry in which the profit margin cannot be easily increased. As a result, the division manager might focus on increasing the investment turnover.

To illustrate, assume that the revenues of the Northern Division could be increased by \$56,000 through increasing operating expenses, such as advertising, to \$385,000. The Northern Division's income from operations will increase from \$70,000 to \$77,000, as shown below.

Revenues (\$560,000 + \$56,000)	\$616,000
Operating expenses	385,000
Income from operations before service department charges	\$231,000
Service department charges	154,000
Income from operations	\$ 77,000

The rate of return on investment for the Northern Division, using the DuPont formula, is recomputed as follows:

$$\text{Rate of Return on Investment} = \frac{\text{Income from Operations}}{\text{Sales}} \times \frac{\text{Sales}}{\text{Invested Assets}}$$

$$\text{Rate of Return on Investment} = \frac{\$77{,}000}{\$616{,}000} \times \frac{\$616{,}000}{\$350{,}000} = 12.5\% \times 1.76 = 22\%$$

Although the Northern Division's profit margin remains the same (12.5%), the investment turnover has increased from 1.6 to 1.76, an increase of 10% (0.16 ÷ 1.6). The 10% increase in investment turnover increases the rate of return on investment by 10% (from 20% to 22%).

The rate of return on investment is also useful in deciding where to invest additional assets or expand operations. For example, DataLink should give priority to expanding operatons in the Northern Division because it earns the highest rate of return on investment. In other words, an investment in the Northern Division will return 20 cents (20%) on each dollar invested. In contrast, investments in the Central and Southern divisions will earn only 12 cents and 15 cents, respectively, per dollar invested.

A disadvantage of the rate of return on investment as a performance measure is that it may lead divisional managers to reject new investments that could be profitable for the company as a whole. To illustrate, assume the following rates of return for the Northern Division of DataLink:

Current rate of return on investment	20%
Minimum acceptable rate of return on investment set by top management	10%
Expected rate of return on investment for new project	14%

If the manager of the Northern Division invests in the new project, the Northern Division's overall rate of return will decrease from 20% due to averaging. Thus, the division manager might decide to reject the project, even though the new project's expected rate of return of 14% exceeds DataLink's minimum acceptable rate of return of 10%.

Example Exercise 23-4 Profit Margin, Investment Turnover, and ROI

OBJ 4

Campbell Company has income from operations of \$35,000, invested assets of \$140,000, and sales of \$437,500. Use the DuPont formula to compute the rate of return on investment and show (a) the profit margin, (b) the investment turnover, and (c) the rate of return on investment.

Follow My Example 23-4

a. Profit Margin = \$35,000 ÷ \$437,500 = 8%

b. Investment Turnover = \$437,500 ÷ \$140,000 = 3.125

c. Rate of Return on Investment = 8% × 3.125 = 25%

Practice Exercises: **PE 23-4A, PE 23-4B**

Business Connection

BOOSTING ROI

Investment centers can use the rate of return on investment (ROI) to identify operational and strategic decisions that improve their financial performance. For example, a group of consultants worked with a golf ball manufacturer to find ways to improve their rate of return on investment. After examining the company's operations, the consultants found that if the golf ball manufacturer outsourced a portion of the production process, changed the company's product mix, and slightly altered its brand strategy, they could increase the company's rate of return on investment by more than 70%.

Source: M. Cvar and J. Quelch, "Which Levers Boost ROI?" *Harvard Business Review*, June 1, 2007.

Residual Income

Residual income is useful in overcoming some of the disadvantages of the rate of return on investment. **Residual income** is the excess of income from operations over a minimum acceptable income from operations, as shown below.

Income from operations	$XXX
Less minimum acceptable income from operations as a percent of invested assets	XXX
Residual income	$XXX

The minimum acceptable income from operations is computed by multiplying the company minimum rate of return by the invested assets. The minimum rate is set by top management, based on such factors as the cost of financing.

To illustrate, assume that DataLink Inc. has established 10% as the minimum acceptable rate of return on divisional assets. The residual incomes for the three divisions are as follows:

	Northern Division	Central Division	Southern Division
Income from operations	$70,000	$84,000	$75,000
Less minimum acceptable income from operations as a percent of invested assets:			
$350,000 × 10%	35,000		
$700,000 × 10%		70,000	
$500,000 × 10%			50,000
Residual income	$35,000	$14,000	$25,000

The Northern Division has more residual income ($35,000) than the other divisions, even though it has the least amount of income from operations ($70,000). This is because the invested assets are less for the Northern Division than for the other divisions.

The major advantage of residual income as a performance measure is that it considers both the minimum acceptable rate of return, invested assets, and the income from operations for each division. In doing so, residual income encourages division managers to maximize income from operations in excess of the minimum. This provides an incentive to accept any project that is expected to have a rate of return in excess of the minimum.

To illustrate, assume the following rates of return for the Northern Division of DataLink:

Current rate of return on investment	20%
Minimum acceptable rate of return on investment set by top management	10%
Expected rate of return on investment for new project	14%

If the manager of the Northern Division is evaluated on new projects using only return on investment, the division manager might decide to reject the new project. This is because investing in the new project will decrease Northern's current rate of return of 20%. While this helps the division maintain its high ROI, it hurts the company as a whole because the expected rate of return of 14% exceeds DataLink's minimum acceptable rate of return of 10%.

In contrast, if the manager of the Northern Division is evaluated using residual income, the new project would probably be accepted because it will increase the Northern Division's residual income. In this way, residual income supports both divisional and overall company objectives.

Example Exercise 23-5 Residual Income

OBJ 4

The Wholesale Division of PeanutCo has income from operations of $87,000 and assets of $240,000. The minimum acceptable rate of return on assets is 12%. What is the residual income for the division?

Follow My Example 23-5

Income from operations	$87,000
Minimum acceptable income from operations as a percent of assets ($240,000 × 12%)	28,800
Residual income	$58,200

Practice Exercises: **PE 23-5A, PE 23-5B**

The Balanced Scorecard[2]

The **balanced scorecard** is a set of multiple performance measures for a company. In addition to financial performance, a balanced scorecard normally includes performance measures for customer service, innovation and learning, and internal processes, as shown in Exhibit 7.

Performance measures for learning and innovation often revolve around a company's research and development efforts. For example, the number of new products

EXHIBIT 7

The Balanced Scorecard

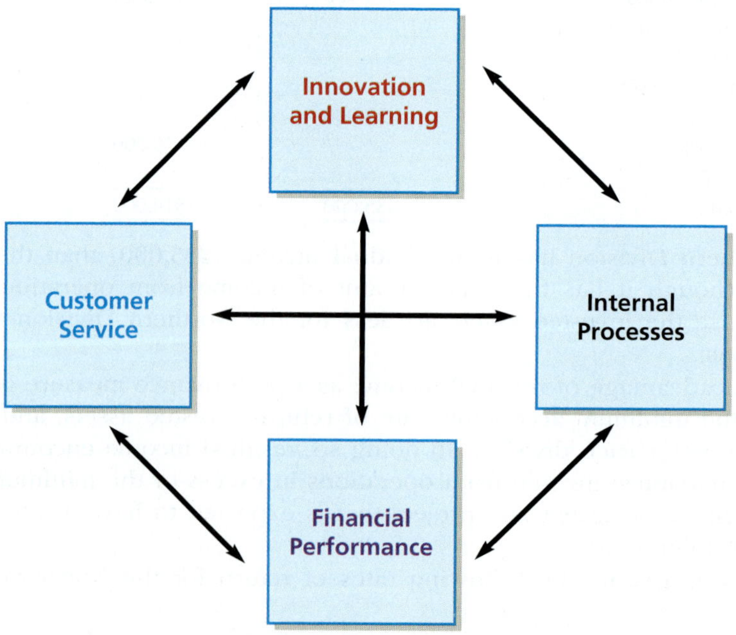

2 The balanced scorecard was developed by R. S. Kaplan and D. P. Norton and explained in *The Balanced Scorecard: Translating Strategy into Action* (Cambridge: Harvard Business School Press, 1996).

developed during a year and the time it takes to bring new products to the market are performance measures for innovation. Performance measures for learning could include the number of employee training sessions and the number of employees who are cross-trained in several skills.

Performance measures for customer service include the number of customer complaints and the number of repeat customers. Customer surveys can also be used to gather measures of customer satisfaction with the company as compared to competitors.

Performance measures for internal processes include the length of time it takes to manufacture a product. The amount of scrap and waste is a measure of the efficiency of a company's manufacturing processes. The number of customer returns is a performance measure of both the manufacturing and sales ordering processes.

All companies will use financial performance measures. Some financial performance measures have been discussed earlier in this chapter and include income from operations, rate of return on investment, and residual income.

The balanced scorecard attempts to identify the underlying nonfinancial drivers, or causes, of financial performance related to innovation and learning, customer service, and internal processes. In this way, the financial performance may be improved. For example, customer satisfaction is often measured by the number of repeat customers. By increasing the number of repeat customers, sales and income from operations can be increased.

Some common performance measures used in the balanced scorecard approach are shown below.

Hilton Hotels Corporation uses a balanced scorecard to measure employee satisfaction, customer loyalty, and financial performance.

Innovation and Learning

Number of new products
Number of new patents
Number of cross-trained employees
Number of training hours
Number of ethics violations
Employee turnover

Customer Service

Number of repeat customers
Customer brand recognition
Delivery time to customer
Customer satisfaction
Number of sales returns
Customer complaints

Internal Processes

Waste and scrap
Time to manufacture products
Number of defects
Number of rejected sales orders
Number of stockouts
Labor utilization

Financial

Sales
Income from operations
Return on investment
Profit margin and investment turnover
Residual income
Actual versus budgeted (standard) costs

Transfer Pricing

OBJ 5 Describe and illustrate how the market price, negotiated price, and cost price approaches to transfer pricing may be used by decentralized segments of a business.

When divisions transfer products or render services to each other, a **transfer price** is used to charge for the products or services.[3] Since transfer prices will affect a division's financial performance, setting a transfer price is a sensitive matter for the managers of both the selling and buying divisions.

Three common approaches to setting transfer prices are as follows:

1. Market price approach
2. Negotiated price approach
3. Cost approach

Transfer prices may be used for cost, profit, or investment centers. The objective of setting a transfer price is to motivate managers to behave in a manner that will

3 The discussion in this chapter highlights the essential concepts of transfer pricing. In-depth discussion of transfer pricing can be found in advanced texts.

increase the overall company income. As will be illustrated, however, transfer prices may be misused in such a way that overall company income suffers.

Transfer prices can be set as low as the variable cost per unit or as high as the market price. Often, transfer prices are negotiated at some point between variable cost per unit and market price. Exhibit 8 shows the possible range of transfer prices.

EXHIBIT 8

Commonly Used Transfer Prices

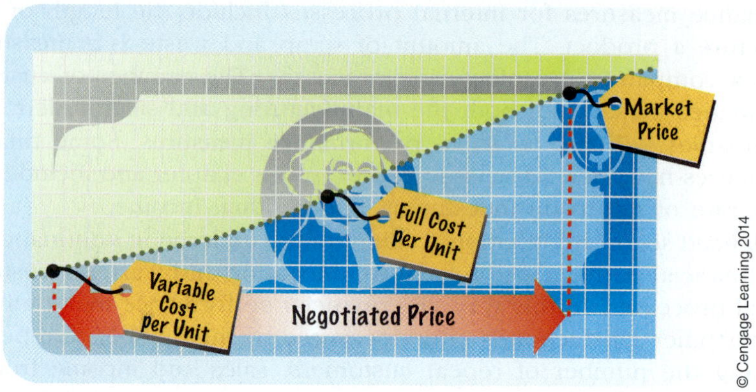

To illustrate, Wilson Company, a packaged snack food company with no service departments, is used. Wilson Company has two operating divisions (Eastern and Western) that are organized as investment centers. Condensed income statements for Wilson Company, assuming no transfers between divisions, are shown in Exhibit 9.

EXHIBIT 9

Income Statements—No Transfers Between Divisions

Wilson Company
Income Statements
For the Year Ended December 31, 2014

	Eastern Division	Western Division	Total Company
Sales:			
50,000 units × $20 per unit	$1,000,000		$1,000,000
20,000 units × $40 per unit		$800,000	800,000
			$1,800,000
Expenses:			
Variable:			
50,000 units × $10 per unit	$ 500,000		$ 500,000
20,000 units × $30* per unit		$600,000	600,000
Fixed	300,000	100,000	400,000
Total expenses	$ 800,000	$700,000	$1,500,000
Income from operations	$ 200,000	$100,000	$ 300,000

*$20 of the $30 per unit represents materials costs, and the remaining $10 per unit represents other variable conversion expenses incurred within the Western Division.

Market Price Approach

Using the **market price approach**, the transfer price is the price at which the product or service transferred could be sold to outside buyers. If an outside market exists for the product or service transferred, the current market price may be a proper transfer price.

Transfer Price = Market Price

To illustrate, assume that materials used by Wilson Company in producing snack food in the Western Division are currently purchased from an outside supplier at $20 per unit. The same materials are produced by the Eastern Division. The Eastern Division is operating at full capacity of 50,000 units and can sell all it produces to either the Western Division or to outside buyers.

A transfer price of $20 per unit (the market price) has no effect on the Eastern Division's income or total company income. The Eastern Division will earn revenues of $20 per unit on all its production and sales, regardless of who buys its product.

Likewise, the Western Division will pay $20 per unit for materials (the market price). Thus, the use of the market price as the transfer price has no effect on the Eastern Division's income or total company income.

In this situation, the use of the market price as the transfer price is proper. The condensed divisional income statements for Wilson Company would be the same as shown in Exhibit 9.

Negotiated Price Approach

If unused or excess capacity exists in the supplying division (the Eastern Division), and the transfer price is equal to the market price, total company profit may not be maximized. This is because the manager of the Western Division will be indifferent toward purchasing materials from the Eastern Division or from outside suppliers. That is, in both cases the Western Division manager pays $20 per unit (the market price). As a result, the Western Division may purchase the materials from outside suppliers.

If, however, the Western Division purchases the materials from the Eastern Division, the difference between the market price of $20 and the variable costs of the Eastern Division of $10 per unit (from Exhibit 9) can cover fixed costs and contribute to overall company profits. Thus, the Western Division manager should be encouraged to purchase the materials from the Eastern Division.

The **negotiated price approach** allows the managers to agree (negotiate) among themselves on a transfer price. The only constraint is that the transfer price be less than the market price, but greater than the supplying division's variable costs per unit, as shown below.

Variable Costs per Unit < Transfer Price < Market Price

To illustrate, assume that instead of a capacity of 50,000 units, the Eastern Division's capacity is 70,000 units. In addition, assume that the Eastern Division can continue to sell only 50,000 units to outside buyers.

A transfer price less than $20 would encourage the manager of the Western Division to purchase from the Eastern Division. This is because the Western Division is currently purchasing its materials from outside suppliers at a cost of $20 per unit. Thus, its materials cost would decrease, and its income from operations would increase.

At the same time, a transfer price above the Eastern Division's variable costs per unit of $10 (from Exhibit 10) would encourage the manager of the Eastern Division to supply materials to the Western Division. In doing so, the Eastern Division's income from operations would also increase.

Exhibit 10 illustrates the divisional and company income statements, assuming that the Eastern and Western division managers agree to a transfer price of $15.

The Eastern Division increases its sales by $300,000 (20,000 units × $15 per unit) to $1,300,000. As a result, the Eastern Division's income from operations increases by $100,000 ($300,000 sales − $200,000 variable costs) to $300,000, as shown in Exhibit 10.

EXHIBIT 10

Income Statements—Negotiated Transfer Price

Wilson Company Income Statements For the Year Ended December 31, 2014	Eastern Division	Western Division	Total Company
Sales:			
50,000 units × $20 per unit	$1,000,000		$1,000,000
20,000 units × $15 per unit	300,000		300,000
20,000 units × $40 per unit		$800,000	800,000
	$1,300,000	$800,000	$2,100,000
Expenses:			
Variable:			
70,000 units × $10 per unit	$ 700,000		$ 700,000
20,000 units × $25* per unit		$500,000	500,000
Fixed	300,000	100,000	400,000
Total expenses	$1,000,000	$600,000	$1,600,000
Income from operations	$ 300,000	$200,000	$ 500,000

*$10 of the $25 represents variable conversion expenses incurred solely within the Western Division, and $15 per unit represents the transfer price per unit from the Eastern Division.

The increase of $100,000 in the Eastern Division's income can also be computed as follows:

Increase in Eastern (Supplying) Division's Income from Operations = (Transfer Price – Variable Cost per Unit) × Units Transferred

Increase in Eastern (Supplying) Division's Income from Operations = ($15 – $10) × 20,000 units = $100,000

The Western Division's materials cost decreases by $5 per unit ($20 – $15) for a total of $100,000 (20,000 units × $5 per unit). Thus, the Western Division's income from operations increases by $100,000 to $200,000, as shown in Exhibit 10.

The increase of $100,000 in the Western Division's income can also be computed as follows:

Increase in Western (Purchasing) Division's Income from Operations = (Market Price – Transfer Price) × Units Transferred

Increase in Western (Purchasing) Division's Income from Operations = ($20 – $15) × 20,000 units = $100,000

Comparing Exhibits 9 and 10 shows that Wilson Company's income from operations increased by $200,000, as shown below.

	Income from Operations		
	No Units Transferred (Exhibit 9)	20,000 Units Transferred at $15 per Unit (Exhibit 10)	Increase (Decrease)
Eastern Division	$200,000	$300,000	$100,000
Western Division	100,000	200,000	100,000
Wilson Company	$300,000	$500,000	$200,000

In the preceding illustration, any negotiated transfer price between $10 and $20 is acceptable, as shown below.

Variable Costs per Unit < Transfer Price < Market Price

$10 < Transfer Price < $20

Any transfer price within this range will increase the overall income from operations for Wilson Company by $200,000. However, the increases in the Eastern and Western divisions' income from operations will vary depending on the transfer price.

To illustrate, a transfer price of $16 would increase the Eastern Division's income from operations by $120,000, as shown below.

Increase in Eastern (Supplying) Division's Income from Operations = (Transfer Price – Variable Cost per Unit) × Units Transferred

Increase in Eastern (Supplying) Division's Income from Operations = ($16 – $10) × 20,000 units = $120,000

A transfer price of $16 would increase the Western Division's income from operations by $80,000, as shown below.

Increase in Western (Purchasing) Division's Income from Operations = (Market Price – Transfer Price) × Units Transferred

Increase in Western (Purchasing) Division's Income from Operations = ($20 – $16) × 20,000 units = $80,000

With a transfer price of $16, Wilson Company's income from operations still increases by $200,000, which consists of the Eastern Division's increase of $120,000 plus the Western Division's increase of $80,000.

As shown above, a negotiated price provides each division manager with an incentive to negotiate the transfer of materials. At the same time, the overall company's income from operations will also increase. However, the negotiated approach only applies when the supplying division has excess capacity. In other words, the supplying division cannot sell all its production to outside buyers at the market price.

Example Exercise 23-6 Transfer Pricing OBJ 5

The materials used by the Winston-Salem Division of Fox Company are currently purchased from outside suppliers at $30 per unit. These same materials are produced by Fox's Flagstaff Division. The Flagstaff Division can produce the materials needed by the Winston-Salem Division at a variable cost of $15 per unit. The division is currently producing 70,000 units and has capacity of 100,000 units. The two divisions have recently negotiated a transfer price of $22 per unit for 30,000 units. By how much will each division's income increase as a result of this transfer?

Follow My Example 23-6

Increase in Flagstaff (Supplying) Division's Income from Operations = (Transfer Price – Variable Cost per Unit) × Units Transferred

Increase in Flagstaff (Supplying) Division's Income from Operations = ($22 – $15) × 30,000 units = $210,000

Increase in Winston-Salem (Purchasing) Division's Income from Operations = (Market Price – Transfer Price) × Units Transferred

Increase in Winston-Salem (Purchasing) Division's Income from Operations = ($30 – $22) × 30,000 units = $240,000

Practice Exercises: **PE 23-6A, PE 23-6B**

Cost Price Approach

Under the **cost price approach**, cost is used to set transfer prices. A variety of costs may be used in this approach, including the following:

1. Total product cost per unit
2. Variable product cost per unit

If total product cost per unit is used, direct materials, direct labor, and factory overhead are included in the transfer price. If variable product cost per unit is used, the fixed factory overhead cost is excluded from the transfer price.

Actual costs or standard (budgeted) costs may be used in applying the cost price approach. If actual costs are used, inefficiencies of the producing (supplying) division are transferred to the purchasing division. Thus, there is little incentive for the producing (supplying) division to control costs. For this reason, most companies use standard costs in the cost price approach. In this way, differences between actual and standard costs remain with the producing (supplying) division for cost control purposes.

The cost price approach is most often used when the responsibility centers are organized as cost centers. When the responsibility centers are organized as profit or investment centers, the cost price approach is normally not used.

For example, using the cost price approach when the supplying division is organized as a profit center ignores the supplying division manager's responsibility for earning profits. In this case, using the cost price approach prevents the supplying division from reporting any profit (revenues – costs) on the units transferred. As a result, the division manager has little incentive to transfer units to another division, even though it may be in the best interests of the company.

Integrity, Objectivity, and Ethics in Business

SHIFTING INCOME THROUGH TRANSFER PRICES

Transfer prices allow companies to minimize taxes by shifting taxable income from countries with high tax rates to countries with low taxes. For example, GlaxoSmithKline, a British company and the second biggest drug maker in the world, had been in a dispute with the U.S. Internal Revenue Service (IRS) over international transfer prices since the early 1990s. The company pays U.S. taxes on income from its U.S. Division and British taxes on income from the British Division. The IRS, however, claimed that the transfer prices on sales from the British Division to the U.S. Division were too high, which reduced profits and taxes in the U.S. Division. The company received a new tax bill from the IRS in 2005 for almost $1.9 billion related to the transfer pricing issue, raising the total bill to almost $5 billion. In January 2006, the company agreed to settle this dispute with the IRS for $3.4 billion, the largest tax settlement in history.

Source: J. Whalen, "Glaxo Gets New IRS Bill Seeking Another $1.9 Billion in BackTax," *The Wall Street Journal*, January 27, 2005.

At a Glance 23

OBJ 1 **Describe the advantages and disadvantages of decentralized operations.**

Key Points In a centralized business, all major planning and operating decisions are made by top management. In a decentralized business, these responsibilities are delegated to unit managers. Decentralization may be more effective because operational decisions are made by the managers closest to the operations.

Learning Outcomes	Example Exercises	Practice Exercises
• Describe the advantages of decentralization.		
• Describe the disadvantages of decentralization.		
• Describe the common types of responsibility centers and the role of responsibility accounting.		

OBJ 2 Prepare a responsibility accounting report for a cost center.

Key Points Cost centers limit the responsibility and authority of managers to decisions related to the costs of their unit. The primary tools for planning and controlling are budgets and budget performance reports.

Learning Outcomes	Example Exercises	Practice Exercises
• Describe cost centers.		
• Describe the responsibility reporting for a cost center.		
• Compute the costs over (under) budget for a cost center.	EE23-1	PE23-1A, 23-1B

OBJ 3 Prepare responsibility accounting reports for a profit center.

Key Points In a profit center, managers have the responsibility and authority to make decisions that affect both revenues and costs. Responsibility reports for a profit center usually show income from operations for the unit.

Learning Outcomes	Example Exercises	Practice Exercises
• Describe profit centers.		
• Determine how service department charges are allocated to profit centers.	EE23-2	PE23-2A, 23-2B
• Describe the responsibility reporting for a profit center.		
• Compute income from operations for a profit center.	EE23-3	PE23-3A, 23-3B

OBJ 4 Compute and interpret the rate of return on investment, the residual income, and the balanced scorecard for an investment center.

Key Points In an investment center, the unit manager has the responsibility and authority to make decisions that affect the unit's revenues, expenses, and assets invested in the center. Three measures are commonly used to assess investment center performance: return on investment (ROI), residual income, and the balanced scorecard. These measures are often used to compare investment center performance.

Learning Outcomes	Example Exercises	Practice Exercises
• Describe investment centers.		
• Describe the responsibility reporting for an investment center.		
• Compute the profit margin, investment turnover, and rate of return on investment (ROI).	EE23-4	PE23-4A, 23-4B
• Compute residual income.	EE23-5	PE23-5A, 23-5B
• Describe the balanced scorecard approach.		

OBJ 5

Describe and illustrate how the market price, negotiated price, and cost price approaches to transfer pricing may be used by decentralized segments of a business.

Key Points When divisions within a company transfer products or provide services to each other, a transfer price is used to charge for the products or services. Transfer prices should be set so that the overall company income is increased when goods are transferred between divisions. One of three approaches is typically used to establish transfer prices: market price, negotiated price, or cost price.

Learning Outcomes	Example Exercises	Practice Exercises
• Describe how companies determine the price used to transfer products or services between divisions.		
• Determine transfer prices using the market price approach.		
• Determine transfer prices using the negotiated price approach.	EE23-4	PE23-4A, 23-4B
• Describe the cost price approach to determining transfer price.		

Key Terms

balanced scorecard (1088)
controllable expenses (1080)
controllable revenues (1080)
cost center (1078)
cost price approach (1093)
DuPont formula (1084)
investment center (1083)
investment turnover (1084)
market price approach (1090)
negotiated price approach (1091)
profit center (1080)
profit margin (1084)
rate of return on investment (ROI) (1084)
residual income (1087)
responsibility accounting (1077)
service department charges (1080)
transfer price (1089)

Illustrative Problem

Quinn Company has two divisions, Domestic and International. Invested assets and condensed income statement data for each division for the year ended December 31, 2014, are as follows:

	Domestic Division	International Division
Revenues	$675,000	$480,000
Operating expenses	450,000	372,400
Service department charges	90,000	50,000
Invested assets	600,000	384,000

Instructions

1. Prepare condensed income statements for the past year for each division.
2. Using the DuPont formula, determine the profit margin, investment turnover, and rate of return on investment for each division.
3. If management's minimum acceptable rate of return is 10%, determine the residual income for each division.

Solution

1.

Quinn Company
Divisional Income Statements
For the Year Ended December 31, 2014

	Domestic Division	International Division
Revenues	$675,000	$480,000
Operating expenses	450,000	372,400
Income from operations before service department charges	$225,000	$107,600
Service department charges	90,000	50,000
Income from operations	$135,000	$ 57,600

2. Rate of Return on Investment = Profit Margin × Investment Turnover

$$\text{Rate of Return on Investment} = \frac{\text{Income from Operations}}{\text{Sales}} \times \frac{\text{Sales}}{\text{Invested Assets}}$$

$$\text{Domestic Division: ROI} = \frac{\$135{,}000}{\$675{,}000} \times \frac{\$675{,}000}{\$600{,}000}$$

$$\text{ROI} = 20\% \times 1.125$$

$$\text{ROI} = 22.5\%$$

$$\text{International Division: ROI} = \frac{\$57{,}600}{\$480{,}000} \times \frac{\$480{,}000}{\$384{,}000}$$

$$\text{ROI} = 12\% \times 1.25$$

$$\text{ROI} = 15\%$$

3. Domestic Division: $75,000 [$135,000 – (10% × $600,000)]
International Division: $19,200 [$57,600 – (10% × $384,000)]

Discussion Questions

1. Differentiate between centralized and decentralized operations.
2. Differentiate between a profit center and an investment center.
3. Weyerhaeuser developed a system that assigns service department expenses to user divisions on the basis of actual services consumed by the division. Here are a number of Weyerhaeuser's activities in its central Financial Services Department:
   - Payroll
   - Accounts payable
   - Accounts receivable
   - Database administration—report preparation

   For each activity, identify an activity base that could be used to charge user divisions for service.
4. What is the major shortcoming of using income from operations as a performance measure for investment centers?
5. In a decentralized company in which the divisions are organized as investment centers, how could a division be considered the least profitable even though it earned the largest amount of income from operations?
6. How does using the rate of return on investment facilitate comparability between divisions of decentralized companies?
7. Why would a firm use a balanced scorecard in evaluating divisional performance?
8. What is the objective of transfer pricing?
9. When is the negotiated price approach preferred over the market price approach in setting transfer prices?
10. When using the negotiated price approach to transfer pricing, within what range should the transfer price be established?

Practice Exercises

Example Exercises

EE 23-1 p. 1079

PE 23-1A Budgetary performance for cost center **OBJ. 2**

Mandel Company's costs were over budget by $252,000. The company is divided into West and East regions. The East Region's costs were under budget by $74,000. Determine the amount that the West Region's costs were over or under budget.

EE 23-1 p. 1079

PE 23-1B Budgetary performance for cost center **OBJ. 2**

Conley Company's costs were under budget by $198,000. The company is divided into North and South regions. The North Region's costs were over budget by $52,000. Determine the amount that the South Region's costs were over or under budget.

EE 23-2 p. 1082

PE 23-2A Service department charges **OBJ. 3**

The centralized employee travel department of Kensy Company has expenses of $435,000. The department has serviced a total of 4,000 travel reservations for the period. The Northeast Division has made 1,800 reservations during the period, and the Pacific Division has made 2,200 reservations. How much should each division be charged for travel services?

EE 23-2 p. 1082

PE 23-2B Service department charges **OBJ. 3**

The centralized computer technology department of Lee Company has expenses of $264,000. The department has provided a total of 2,500 hours of service for the period. The Retail Division has used 1,125 hours of computer technology service during the period, and the Commercial Division has used 1,375 hours of computer technology service. How much should each division be charged for computer technology department services?

EE 23-3 p. 1083

PE 23-3A Income from operations for profit center **OBJ. 3**

Using the data for Kensy Company from Practice Exercise 23-2A along with the data provided below, determine the divisional income from operations for the Northeast and Pacific divisions.

	Northeast Division	Pacific Division
Sales	$1,155,000	$1,204,000
Cost of goods sold	590,800	658,000
Selling expenses	231,000	252,000

EE 23-3 p. 1083

PE 23-3B Income from operations for profit center **OBJ. 3**

Using the data for Lee Company from Practice Exercise 23-2B along with the data provided below, determine the divisional income from operations for the Retail Division and the Commercial Division.

	Retail Division	Commercial Division
Sales	$945,000	$966,000
Cost of goods sold	504,000	559,300
Selling expenses	156,800	175,000

Example Exercises

EE 23-4 *p. 1086*

PE 23-4A Profit margin, investment turnover, and ROI **OBJ. 4**

McBreen Company has income from operations of $96,000, invested assets of $400,000, and sales of $1,200,000. Use the DuPont formula to compute the rate of return on investment and show (a) the profit margin, (b) the investment turnover, and (c) the rate of return on investment.

EE 23-4 *p. 1086*

PE 23-4B Profit margin, investment turnover, and ROI **OBJ. 4**

Briggs Company has income from operations of $36,000, invested assets of $180,000, and sales of $720,000. Use the DuPont formula to compute the rate of return on investment and show (a) the profit margin, (b) the investment turnover, and (c) the rate of return on investment.

EE 23-5 *p. 1088*

PE 23-5A Residual income **OBJ. 4**

The Consumer Division of Hernandez Company has income from operations of $90,000 and assets of $450,000. The minimum acceptable rate of return on assets is 10%. What is the residual income for the division?

EE 23-5 *p. 1088*

PE 23-5B Residual income **OBJ. 4**

The Commercial Division of Herring Company has income from operations of $420,000 and assets of $910,000. The minimum acceptable rate of return on assets is 8%. What is the residual income for the division?

EE 23-6 *p. 1093*

PE 23-6A Transfer pricing **OBJ. 5**

The materials used by the North Division of Horton Company are currently purchased from outside suppliers at $60 per unit. These same materials are produced by Horton's South Division. The South Division can produce the materials needed by the North Division at a variable cost of $42 per unit. The division is currently producing 200,000 units and has capacity of 250,000 units. The two divisions have recently negotiated a transfer price of $52 per unit for 30,000 units. By how much will each division's income increase as a result of this transfer?

EE 23-6 *p. 1093*

PE 23-6B Transfer pricing **OBJ. 5**

The materials used by the Multinomah Division of Isbister Company are currently purchased from outside suppliers at $90 per unit. These same materials are produced by the Pembroke Division. The Pembroke Division can produce the materials needed by the Multinomah Division at a variable cost of $75 per unit. The division is currently producing 120,000 units and has capacity of 150,000 units. The two divisions have recently negotiated a transfer price of $82 per unit for 15,000 units. By how much will each division's income increase as a result of this transfer?

Exercises

EX 23-1 Budget performance reports for cost centers **OBJ. 2**

✔ a. (c) $2,832

Partially completed budget performance reports for Maguire Company, a manufacturer of air conditioners, are provided on the following page.

Maguire Company
Budget Performance Report—Vice President, Production
For the Month Ended May 31, 2014

Plant	Budget	Actual	Over Budget	Under Budget
Mid-Atlantic Region	$748,800	$747,000		$1,800
West Region	535,680	532,800		2,880
South Region	(g)	(h)	(i)	
	(j)	(k)	$ (l)	$4,680

Maguire Company
Budget Performance Report—Manager, South Region Plant
For the Month Ended May 31, 2014

Department	Budget	Actual	Over Budget	Under Budget
Chip Fabrication	(a)	(b)	(c)	
Electronic Assembly	$153,216	$155,232	$ 2,016	
Final Assembly	246,600	245,952		$648
	(d)	(e)	$ (f)	$648

Maguire Company
Budget Performance Report—Supervisor, Chip Fabrication
For the Month Ended May 31, 2014

Cost	Budget	Actual	Over Budget	Under Budget
Factory wages	$ 47,952	$ 49,200	$1,248	
Materials	125,280	124,416		$864
Power and light	6,912	8,208	1,296	
Maintenance	12,096	13,248	1,152	
	$192,240	$195,072	$3,696	$864

a. Complete the budget performance reports by determining the correct amounts for the lettered spaces.

b. Compose a memo to Holly Keller, vice president of production for Maguire Company, explaining the performance of the production division for May.

✔ Commercial Division income from operations, $141,512

EX 23-2 Divisional income statements **OBJ. 3**

The following data were summarized from the accounting records for Endless River Construction Company for the year ended June 30, 2014:

Cost of goods sold:		Service department charges:	
Commercial Division	$732,200	Commercial Division	$ 90,048
Residential Division	338,940	Residential Division	54,264
Administrative expenses:		Net sales:	
Commercial Division	$119,840	Commercial Division	$1,083,600
Residential Division	102,900	Residential Division	595,000

Prepare divisional income statements for Endless River Construction Company.

EX 23-3 Service department charges and activity bases **OBJ. 3**

For each of the following service departments, identify an activity base that could be used for charging the expense to the profit center.

a. Legal
b. Duplication services
c. Electronic data processing
d. Central purchasing
e. Telecommunications
f. Accounts receivable

✔ c. 6

EX 23-4 Activity bases for service department charges

OBJ. 3

For each of the following service departments, select the activity base listed that is most appropriate for charging service expenses to responsible units.

Service Department	Activity Base
a. Conferences	1. Number of conference attendees
b. Telecommunications	2. Number of computers
c. Accounts Receivable	3. Number of employees trained
d. Payroll Accounting	4. Number of telephone lines
e. Employee Travel	5. Number of purchase requisitions
f. Central Purchasing	6. Number of sales invoices
g. Training	7. Number of payroll checks
h. Computer Support	8. Number of travel claims

✔ b. Commercial payroll, $30,800

EX 23-5 Service department charges

OBJ. 3

In divisional income statements prepared for Wilborne Construction Company, the Payroll Department costs are charged back to user divisions on the basis of the number of payroll checks, and the Purchasing Department costs are charged back on the basis of the number of purchase requisitions. The Payroll Department had expenses of $119,280, and the Purchasing Department had expenses of $57,750 for the year. The following annual data for Residential, Commercial, and Government Contract divisions were obtained from corporate records:

	Residential	Commercial	Government Contract
Sales	$900,000	$1,218,750	$2,800,000
Number of employees:			
Weekly payroll (52 weeks per year)	250	125	150
Monthly payroll	50	100	60
Number of purchase requisitions per year	3,750	3,125	2,750

a. Determine the total amount of payroll checks and purchase requisitions processed per year by the company and each division.

b. Using the activity base information in (a), determine the annual amount of payroll and purchasing costs charged back to the Residential, Commercial, and Government Contract divisions from payroll and purchasing services.

c. Why does the Residential Division have a larger service department charge than the other two divisions, even though its sales are lower?

✔ b. Help desk, $93,600

EX 23-6 Service department charges and activity bases

OBJ. 3

Middler Corporation, a manufacturer of electronics and communications systems, uses a service department charge system to charge profit centers with Computing and Communications Services (CCS) service department costs. The following table identifies an abbreviated list of service categories and activity bases used by the CCS department. The table also includes some assumed cost and activity base quantity information for each service for October.

CCS Service Category	Activity Base	Budgeted Cost	Budgeted Activity Base Quantity
Help desk	Number of calls	$160,000	3,200
Network center	Number of devices monitored	735,000	9,800
Electronic mail	Number of user accounts	100,000	10,000
Local voice support	Number of phone extensions	124,600	8,900

One of the profit centers for Middler Corporation is the Communication Systems (COMM) sector. Assume the following information for the COMM sector:

- The sector has 5,200 employees, of whom 25% are office employees.
- All the office employees have a phone, and 96% of them have a computer on the network.

- One hundred percent of the employees with a computer also have an e-mail account.
- The average number of help desk calls for October was 1.5 calls per individual with a computer.
- There are 600 additional printers, servers, and peripherals on the network beyond the personal computers.

a. Determine the service charge rate for the four CCS service categories for October.

b. Determine the charges to the COMM sector for the four CCS service categories for October.

EX 23-7 Divisional income statements with service department charges **OBJ. 3**

✔ Commercial income from operations, $787,940

SPREADSHEET

Van Emburgh Technology has two divisions, Consumer and Commercial, and two corporate service departments, Tech Support and Accounts Payable. The corporate expenses for the year ended December 31, 2014, are as follows:

Tech Support Department	$ 676,000
Accounts Payable Department	256,000
Other corporate administrative expenses	402,000
Total corporate expense	$1,334,000

The other corporate administrative expenses include officers' salaries and other expenses required by the corporation. The Tech Support Department charges the divisions for services rendered, based on the number of computers in the department, and the Accounts Payable Department charges divisions for services, based on the number of checks issued for each department. The usage of service by the two divisions is as follows:

	Tech Support	Accounts Payable
Consumer Division	250 computers	3,400 checks
Commercial Division	150	6,600
Total	400 computers	10,000 checks

The service department charges of the Tech Support Department and the Accounts Payable Department are considered controllable by the divisions. Corporate administrative expenses are not considered controllable by the divisions. The revenues, cost of goods sold, and operating expenses for the two divisions are as follows:

	Consumer	Commercial
Revenues	$5,944,000	$4,947,200
Cost of goods sold	3,298,400	2,500,000
Operating expenses	1,172,000	1,236,800

Prepare the divisional income statements for the two divisions.

EX 23-8 Corrections to service department charges **OBJ. 3**

✔ b. Income from operations, Cargo Division, $84,400

Wild Sun Airlines Inc. has two divisions organized as profit centers, the Passenger Division and the Cargo Division. The following divisional income statements were prepared:

Wild Sun Airlines Inc.
Divisional Income Statements
For the Year Ended December 31, 2014

	Passenger Division		Cargo Division	
Revenues		$3,025,000		$3,025,000
Operating expenses		2,450,000		2,736,000
Income from operations before service department charges		$ 575,000		$ 289,000
Less service department charges:				
Training	$125,000		$125,000	
Flight scheduling	108,000		108,000	
Reservations	151,200	384,200	151,200	384,200
Income from operations		$ 190,800		$ (95,200)

The service department charge rate for the service department costs was based on revenues. Since the revenues of the two divisions were the same, the service department charges to each division were also the same.

The following additional information is available:

	Passenger Division	Cargo Division	Total
Number of personnel trained	350	150	500
Number of flights	800	1,200	2,000
Number of reservations requested	20,000	0	20,000

a. Does the income from operations for the two divisions accurately measure performance? Explain.

b. Correct the divisional income statements, using the activity bases provided above in revising the service department charges.

EX 23-9 Profit center responsibility reporting — OBJ. 3

✔ Income from operations, Summer Sports Division, $4,350,000

SPREADSHEET

Full Throttle Sporting Goods Co. operates two divisions—the Winter Sports Division and the Summer Sports Division. The following income and expense accounts were provided from the trial balance as of December 31, 2014, the end of the current fiscal year, after all adjustments, including those for inventories, were recorded and posted:

Sales—Winter Sports Division	$31,500,000
Sales—Summer Sports Division	36,400,000
Cost of Goods Sold—Winter Sports Division	18,900,000
Cost of Goods Sold—Summer Sports Division	21,112,000
Sales Expense—Winter Sports Division	5,040,000
Sales Expense—Summer Sports Division	5,096,000
Administrative Expense—Winter Sports Division	3,150,000
Administrative Expense—Summer Sports Division	3,239,600
Advertising Expense	1,357,900
Transportation Expense	595,000
Accounts Receivable Collection Expense	240,000
Warehouse Expense	2,650,000

The bases to be used in allocating expenses, together with other essential information, are as follows:

a. Advertising expense—incurred at headquarters, charged back to divisions on the basis of usage: Winter Sports Division, $611,000; Summer Sports Division, $746,900.

b. Transportation expense—charged back to divisions at a charge rate of $14.00 per bill of lading: Winter Sports Division, 20,400 bills of lading; Summer Sports Division, 22,100 bills of lading.

c. Accounts receivable collection expense—incurred at headquarters, charged back to divisions at a charge rate of $7.50 per invoice: Winter Sports Division, 13,120 sales invoices; Summer Sports Division, 18,880 sales invoices.

d. Warehouse expense—charged back to divisions on the basis of floor space used in storing division products: Winter Sports Division, 124,550 square feet; Summer Sports Division, 140,450 square feet.

Prepare a divisional income statement with two column headings: Winter Sports Division and Summer Sports Division. Provide supporting calculations for service department charges.

EX 23-10 Rate of return on investment — OBJ. 4

✔ a. Retail, 20%

The income from operations and the amount of invested assets in each division of Steele Industries are as follows:

	Income from Operations	Invested Assets
Retail Division	$130,000	$650,000
Commercial Division	72,000	400,000
Internet Division	137,500	550,000

a. Compute the rate of return on investment for each division.

b. Which division is the most profitable per dollar invested?

EX 23-11 Residual income **OBJ. 4**

✔ a. Internet Division, $93,500

Based on the data in Exercise 23-10, assume that management has established an 8% minimum acceptable rate of return for invested assets.

a. Determine the residual income for each division.

b. Which division has the most residual income?

EX 23-12 Determining missing items in rate of return computation **OBJ. 4**

✔ d. 2.25

One item is omitted from each of the following computations of the rate of return on investment:

Rate of Return on Investment	=	Profit Margin	×	Investment Turnover
12%	=	5%	×	(a)
(b)	=	8%	×	2.00
14%	=	(c)	×	1.40
13.5%	=	6%	×	(d)
(e)	=	15%	×	1.20

Determine the missing items, identifying each by the appropriate letter.

EX 23-13 Profit margin, investment turnover, and rate of return on investment **OBJ. 4**

✔ a. ROI, 35%

The condensed income statement for the Consumer Products Division of Milner Industries Inc. is as follows (assuming no service department charges):

Sales	$7,000,000
Cost of goods sold	4,500,000
Gross profit	$2,500,000
Administrative expenses	750,000
Income from operations	$1,750,000

The manager of the Consumer Products Division is considering ways to increase the rate of return on investment.

a. Using the DuPont formula for rate of return on investment, determine the profit margin, investment turnover, and rate of return on investment of the Consumer Products Division, assuming that $5,000,000 of assets have been invested in the Consumer Products Division.

b. If expenses could be reduced by $350,000 without decreasing sales, what would be the impact on the profit margin, investment turnover, and rate of return on investment for the Consumer Products Division?

EX 23-14 Rate of return on investment **OBJ. 4**

✔ a. Media Networks ROI, 22.6%

The Walt Disney Company has four profitable business segments, described as follows:

- **Media Networks:** The ABC television and radio network, Disney channel, ESPN, A&E, E!, and Disney.com.
- **Parks and Resorts:** Walt Disney World Resort, Disneyland, Disney Cruise Line, and other resort properties.
- **Studio Entertainment:** Walt Disney Pictures, Touchstone Pictures, Hollywood Pictures, Miramax Films, and Buena Vista Theatrical Productions.
- **Consumer Products:** Character merchandising, Disney stores, books, and magazines.

Disney recently reported sector income from operations, revenue, and invested assets (in millions) as follows:

	Income from Operations	Revenue	Invested Assets
Media Networks	$6,146	$18,714	$27,244
Parks and Resorts	1,553	11,797	19,530
Studio Entertainment	618	6,351	12,221
Consumer Products	816	3,049	4,992

a. Use the DuPont formula to determine the rate of return on investment for the four Disney sectors. Round whole percents to one decimal place and investment turnover to two decimal places.

b. How do the four sectors differ in their profit margin, investment turnover, and return on investment?

EX 23-15 Determining missing items in rate of return and residual income computations **OBJ. 4**

✔ c. $68,800

Data for Magnum Company are presented in the following table of rates of return on investment and residual incomes:

Invested Assets	Income from Operations	Rate of Return on Investment	Minimum Rate of Return	Minimum Acceptable Income from Operations	Residual Income
$860,000	$215,000	(a)	17%	(b)	(c)
$540,000	(d)	(e)	(f)	$70,200	$27,000
$320,000	(g)	20%	(h)	$48,000	(i)
$460,000	$92,000	(j)	16%	(k)	(l)

Determine the missing items, identifying each item by the appropriate letter.

EX 23-16 Determining missing items from computations **OBJ. 4**

✔ a. (e) $350,000

Data for the North, South, East, and West divisions of Free Bird Company are as follows:

	Sales	Income from Operations	Invested Assets	Rate of Return on Investment	Profit Margin	Investment Turnover
North	$750,000	(a)	(b)	20%	8%	(c)
South	(d)	$75,600	(e)	(f)	12%	1.8
East	$840,000	(g)	$280,000	18%	(h)	(i)
West	$1,100,000	$99,000	$550,000	(j)	(k)	(l)

a. Determine the missing items, identifying each by the letters (a) through (l). Round percents and investment turnover to one decimal place.

b. Determine the residual income for each division, assuming that the minimum acceptable rate of return established by management is 10%.

c. Which division is the most profitable in terms of (1) return on investment and (2) residual income?

EX 23-17 Rate of return on investment, residual income **OBJ. 4**

Starwood Hotels & Resorts Worldwide provides lodging services around the world. The company is separated into two major divisions.

- **Hotel Ownership:** Hotels owned and operated by Starwood.
- **Vacation Ownership:** Resort properties developed, owned, and operated for timeshare vacation owners.

Financial information for each division, from a recent annual report, is as follows (in millions):

	Hotel Ownership	Vacation Ownership
Revenues	$4,383	$ 688
Income from operations	571	105
Total assets	6,440	2,139

a. Use the DuPont formula to determine the return on investment for each of the Starwood business divisions. Round whole percents to one decimal place and investment turnover to two decimal places.

b. Determine the residual income for each division, assuming a minimum acceptable income of 5% of total assets. Round minimal acceptable return to the nearest million dollars.

c. Interpret your results.

EX 23-18 Balanced scorecard **OBJ. 4**

American Express Company is a major financial services company, noted for its American Express® card. Below are some of the performance measures used by the company in its balanced scorecard.

- Average card member spending
- Cards in force
- Earnings growth
- Hours of credit consultant training
- Investment in information technology
- Number of card choices
- Number of Internet features
- Number of merchant signings
- Number of new card launches
- Return on equity
- Revenue growth

For each measure, identify whether the measure best fits the innovation, customer, internal process, or financial dimension of the balanced scorecard.

EX 23-19 Balanced scorecard **OBJ. 4**

Several years ago, United Parcel Service (UPS) believed that the Internet was going to change the parcel delivery market and would require UPS to become a more nimble and customer-focused organization. As a result, UPS replaced its old measurement system, which was 90% oriented toward financial performance, with a balanced scorecard. The scorecard emphasized four "point of arrival" measures, which were:

1. Customer satisfaction index—a measure of customer satisfaction.
2. Employee relations index—a measure of employee sentiment and morale.
3. Competitive position—delivery performance relative to competition.
4. Time in transit—the time from order entry to delivery.

a. Why did UPS introduce a balanced scorecard and nonfinancial measures in its new performance measurement system?

b. Why do you think UPS included a factor measuring employee sentiment?

EX 23-20 Decision on transfer pricing **OBJ. 5**

✔ a. $2,200,000

Materials used by the Instrument Division of Dart Industries are currently purchased from outside suppliers at a cost of $180 per unit. However, the same materials are available from the Components Division. The Components Division has unused capacity and can produce the materials needed by the Instrument Division at a variable cost of $125 per unit.

a. If a transfer price of $145 per unit is established and 40,000 units of materials are transferred, with no reduction in the Components Division's current sales, how much would Dart Industries' total income from operations increase?

b. How much would the Instrument Division's income from operations increase?

c. How much would the Components Division's income from operations increase?

✔ b. $880,000

EX 23-21 Decision on transfer pricing — OBJ. 5

Based on Dart Industries' data in Exercise 23-20, assume that a transfer price of $158 has been established and that 40,000 units of materials are transferred, with no reduction in the Components Division's current sales.

a. How much would Dart Industries' total income from operations increase?

b. How much would the Instrument Division's income from operations increase?

c. How much would the Components Division's income from operations increase?

d. If the negotiated price approach is used, what would be the range of acceptable transfer prices and why?

Problems Series A

SPREADSHEET

PR 23-1A Budget performance report for a cost center — OBJ. 2

E-Net Company sells electronics over the Internet. The Consumer Products Division is organized as a cost center. The budget for the Consumer Products Division for the month ended January 31, 2014, is as follows (in thousands):

Customer service salaries	$ 390,600
Insurance and property taxes	81,900
Distribution salaries	623,100
Marketing salaries	734,550
Engineer salaries	597,750
Warehouse wages	418,650
Equipment depreciation	131,280
Total	$2,977,830

During January, the costs incurred in the Consumer Products Division were as follows:

Customer service salaries	$ 500,040
Insurance and property taxes	79,440
Distribution salaries	616,800
Marketing salaries	822,600
Engineer salaries	585,720
Warehouse wages	401,880
Equipment depreciation	131,250
Total	$3,137,730

Instructions

1. Prepare a budget performance report for the director of the Consumer Products Division for the month of January.
2. For which costs might the director be expected to request supplemental reports?

✔ 1. Income from operations, Central Division, $430,560

SPREADSHEET

PR 23-2A Profit center responsibility reporting — OBJ. 3

Traxonia Railroad Inc. has three regional divisions organized as profit centers. The chief executive officer (CEO) evaluates divisional performance, using income from operations as a percent of revenues. The following quarterly income and expense accounts were provided from the trial balance as of December 31, 2014:

Revenues—East	$ 870,000
Revenues—West	1,032,000
Revenues—Central	1,872,000
Operating Expenses—East	563,300
Operating Expenses—West	618,240
Operating Expenses—Central	1,166,940
Corporate Expenses—Shareholder Relations	154,000
Corporate Expenses—Customer Support	400,000
Corporate Expenses—Legal	270,000
General Corporate Officers' Salaries	275,000

The company operates three service departments: Shareholder Relations, Customer Support, and Legal. The Shareholder Relations Department conducts a variety of services for shareholders of the company. The Customer Support Department is the company's point of contact for new service, complaints, and requests for repair. The department believes that the number of customer contacts is an activity base for this work. The Legal Department provides legal services for division management. The department believes that the number of hours billed is an activity base for this work. The following additional information has been gathered:

	East	West	Central
Number of customer contacts	5,000	6,000	9,000
Number of hours billed	1,350	2,160	1,890

Instructions

1. Prepare quarterly income statements showing income from operations for the three divisions. Use three column headings: East, West, and Central.
2. Identify the most successful division according to the profit margin.
3. Provide a recommendation to the CEO for a better method for evaluating the performance of the divisions. In your recommendation, identify the major weakness of the present method.

PR 23-3A Divisional income statements and rate of return on investment analysis OBJ. 4

✔ 2. Mutual Fund Division, ROI, 22.4%

SPREADSHEET

E.F. Lynch Company is a diversified investment company with three operating divisions organized as investment centers. Condensed data taken from the records of the three divisions for the year ended June 30, 2014, are as follows:

	Mutual Fund Division	Electronic Brokerage Division	Investment Banking Division
Fee revenue	$4,140,000	$3,360,000	$4,560,000
Operating expenses	2,980,800	3,091,200	3,739,200
Invested assets	5,175,000	1,120,000	3,800,000

The management of E.F. Lynch Company is evaluating each division as a basis for planning a future expansion of operations.

Instructions

1. Prepare condensed divisional income statements for the three divisions, assuming that there were no service department charges.
2. Using the DuPont formula for rate of return on investment, compute the profit margin, investment turnover, and rate of return on investment for each division.
3. If available funds permit the expansion of operations of only one division, which of the divisions would you recommend for expansion, based on parts (1) and (2)? Explain.

PR 23-4A Effect of proposals on divisional performance OBJ. 4

✔ 1. ROI, 16.8%

SPREADSHEET

A condensed income statement for the Commercial Division of Maxell Manufacturing Inc. for the year ended December 31, 2014, is as follows:

Sales	$3,500,000
Cost of goods sold	2,480,000
Gross profit	$1,020,000
Operating expenses	600,000
Income from operations	$ 420,000
Invested assets	$2,500,000

Assume that the Commercial Division received no charges from service departments. The president of Maxell Manufacturing has indicated that the division's rate of return on a

$2,500,000 investment must be increased to at least 21% by the end of the next year if operations are to continue. The division manager is considering the following three proposals:

Proposal 1: Transfer equipment with a book value of $312,500 to other divisions at no gain or loss and lease similar equipment. The annual lease payments would exceed the amount of depreciation expense on the old equipment by $105,000. This increase in expense would be included as part of the cost of goods sold. Sales would remain unchanged.

Proposal 2: Purchase new and more efficient machining equipment and thereby reduce the cost of goods sold by $560,000. Sales would remain unchanged, and the old equipment, which has no remaining book value, would be scrapped at no gain or loss. The new equipment would increase invested assets by an additional $1,875,000 for the year.

Proposal 3: Reduce invested assets by discontinuing a product line. This action would eliminate sales of $595,000, reduce cost of goods sold by $406,700, and reduce operating expenses by $175,000. Assets of $1,338,000 would be transferred to other divisions at no gain or loss.

Instructions

1. Using the DuPont formula for rate of return on investment, determine the profit margin, investment turnover, and rate of return on investment for the Commercial Division for the past year.
2. Prepare condensed estimated income statements and compute the invested assets for each proposal.
3. Using the DuPont formula for rate of return on investment, determine the profit margin, investment turnover, and rate of return on investment for each proposal.
4. Which of the three proposals would meet the required 21% rate of return on investment?
5. If the Commercial Division were in an industry where the profit margin could not be increased, how much would the investment turnover have to increase to meet the president's required 21% rate of return on investment? Round to one decimal place.

✔ 2. Business Division ROI, 20.0%

SPREADSHEET

PR 23-5A Divisional performance analysis and evaluation

OBJ. 4

The vice president of operations of Pavone Company is evaluating the performance of two divisions organized as investment centers. Invested assets and condensed income statement data for the past year for each division are as follows:

	Business Division	Consumer Division
Sales	$2,500,000	$2,550,000
Cost of goods sold	1,320,000	1,350,000
Operating expenses	930,000	843,000
Invested assets	1,250,000	2,125,000

Instructions

1. Prepare condensed divisional income statements for the year ended December 31, 2014, assuming that there were no service department charges.
2. Using the DuPont formula for rate of return on investment, determine the profit margin, investment turnover, and rate of return on investment for each division.
3. If management desires a minimum acceptable rate of return of 17%, determine the residual income for each division.
4. Discuss the evaluation of the two divisions, using the performance measures determined in parts (1), (2), and (3).

✔ 3. Total income from operations, $1,759,680

SPREADSHEET

PR 23-6A Transfer pricing

OBJ. 5

Garcon Inc. manufactures electronic products, with two operating divisions, the Consumer and Commercial divisions. Condensed divisional income statements, which involve no intracompany transfers and which include a breakdown of expenses into variable and fixed components, are as follows:

Garcon Inc.
Divisional Income Statements
For the Year Ended December 31, 2014

	Consumer Division	Commercial Division	Total
Sales:			
14,400 units @ $144 per unit	$2,073,600		$2,073,600
21,600 units @ $275 per unit		$5,940,000	5,940,000
	$2,073,600	$5,940,000	$8,013,600
Expenses:			
Variable:			
14,400 units @ $104 per unit	$1,497,600		$1,497,600
21,600 units @ $193* per unit		$4,168,800	4,168,800
Fixed	200,000	520,000	720,000
Total expenses	$1,697,600	$4,688,800	$6,386,400
Income from operations	$ 376,000	$1,251,200	$1,627,200

*$150 of the $193 per unit represents materials costs, and the remaining $43 per unit represents other variable conversion expenses incurred within the Commercial Division.

The Consumer Division is presently producing 14,400 units out of a total capacity of 17,280 units. Materials used in producing the Commercial Division's product are currently purchased from outside suppliers at a price of $150 per unit. The Consumer Division is able to produce the materials used by the Commercial Division. Except for the possible transfer of materials between divisions, no changes are expected in sales and expenses.

Instructions

1. Would the market price of $150 per unit be an appropriate transfer price for Garcon Inc.? Explain.
2. If the Commercial Division purchases 2,880 units from the Consumer Division, rather than externally, at a negotiated transfer price of $115 per unit, how much would the income from operations of each division and the total company income from operations increase?
3. Prepare condensed divisional income statements for Garcon Inc. based on the data in part (2).
4. If a transfer price of $126 per unit is negotiated, how much would the income from operations of each division and the total company income from operations increase?
5. a. What is the range of possible negotiated transfer prices that would be acceptable for Garcon Inc.?

   b. Assuming that the managers of the two divisions cannot agree on a transfer price, what price would you suggest as the transfer price?

Problems Series B

PR 23-1B Budget performance report for a cost center **OBJ. 2**

SPREADSHEET

The Eastern District of Adelson Inc. is organized as a cost center. The budget for the Eastern District of Adelson Inc. for the month ended December 31, 2014, is as follows:

Sales salaries	$ 819,840
System administration salaries	448,152
Customer service salaries	152,600
Billing salaries	98,760
Maintenance	271,104
Depreciation of plant and equipment	92,232
Insurance and property taxes	41,280
Total	$1,923,968

During December, the costs incurred in the Eastern District were as follows:

Sales salaries	$ 818,880
System administration salaries	447,720
Customer service salaries	183,120
Billing salaries	98,100
Maintenance	273,000
Depreciation of plant and equipment	92,232
Insurance and property taxes	41,400
Total	$1,954,452

Instructions

1. Prepare a budget performance report for the manager of the Eastern District of Adelson for the month of December.
2. For which costs might the supervisor be expected to request supplemental reports?

PR 23-2B Profit center responsibility reporting

OBJ. 3

✔ 1. Income from operations, West Region, $820,800

SPREADSHEET

Thomas Railroad Company organizes its three divisions, the North (N), South (S), and West (W) regions, as profit centers. The chief executive officer (CEO) evaluates divisional performance, using income from operations as a percent of revenues. The following quarterly income and expense accounts were provided from the trial balance as of December 31, 2014:

Revenues—N Region	$3,780,000
Revenues—S Region	5,673,000
Revenues—W Region	5,130,000
Operating Expenses—N Region	2,678,500
Operating Expenses—S Region	4,494,890
Operating Expenses—W Region	3,770,050
Corporate Expenses—Dispatching	182,000
Corporate Expenses—Equipment Management	1,200,000
Corporate Expenses—Treasurer's	734,000
General Corporate Officers' Salaries	1,380,000

The company operates three service departments: the Dispatching Department, the Equipment Management Department, and the Treasurer's Department. The Dispatching Department manages the scheduling and releasing of completed trains. The Equipment Management Department manages the railroad cars inventories. It makes sure the right freight cars are at the right place at the right time. The Treasurer's Department conducts a variety of services for the company as a whole. The following additional information has been gathered:

	North	South	West
Number of scheduled trains	650	1,105	845
Number of railroad cars in inventory	6,000	8,400	9,600

Instructions

1. Prepare quarterly income statements showing income from operations for the three regions. Use three column headings: North, South, and West.
2. Identify the most successful region according to the profit margin.
3. Provide a recommendation to the CEO for a better method for evaluating the performance of the regions. In your recommendation, identify the major weakness of the present method.

✔ 2. Cereal Division ROI, 12.0%

SPREADSHEET

PR 23-3B Divisional income statements and rate of return on investment analysis OBJ. 4

The Whole Earth Food Company is a diversified food company with three operating divisions organized as investment centers. Condensed data taken from the records of the three divisions for the year ended June 30, 2014, are as follows:

	Cereal Division	Snack Cake Division	Retail Bakeries Division
Sales	$12,000,000	$6,600,000	$5,740,000
Cost of goods sold	8,000,000	4,600,000	4,000,000
Operating expenses	3,280,000	1,340,000	1,051,200
Invested assets	6,000,000	4,400,000	4,100,000

The management of The Whole Earth Food Company is evaluating each division as a basis for planning a future expansion of operations.

Instructions

1. Prepare condensed divisional income statements for the three divisions, assuming that there were no service department charges.
2. Using the DuPont formula for rate of return on investment, compute the profit margin, investment turnover, and rate of return on investment for each division.
3. If available funds permit the expansion of operations of only one division, which of the divisions would you recommend for expansion, based on parts (1) and (2)? Explain.

✔ 3. Proposal 3 ROI, 16.0%

SPREADSHEET

PR 23-4B Effect of proposals on divisional performance OBJ. 4

A condensed income statement for the Electronics Division of Gihbli Industries Inc. for the year ended December 31, 2014, is as follows:

Sales	$1,575,000
Cost of goods sold	891,000
Gross profit	$ 684,000
Operating expenses	558,000
Income from operations	$ 126,000
Invested assets	$1,050,000

Assume that the Electronics Division received no charges from service departments.

The president of Gihbli Industries Inc. has indicated that the division's rate of return on a $1,050,000 investment must be increased to at least 20% by the end of the next year if operations are to continue. The division manager is considering the following three proposals:

Proposal 1: Transfer equipment with a book value of $300,000 to other divisions at no gain or loss and lease similar equipment. The annual lease payments would be less than the amount of depreciation expense on the old equipment by $31,400. This decrease in expense would be included as part of the cost of goods sold. Sales would remain unchanged.

Proposal 2: Reduce invested assets by discontinuing a product line. This action would eliminate sales of $180,000, reduce cost of goods sold by $119,550, and reduce operating expenses by $60,000. Assets of $112,500 would be transferred to other divisions at no gain or loss.

Proposal 3: Purchase new and more efficient machinery and thereby reduce the cost of goods sold by $189,000. Sales would remain unchanged, and the old machinery, which has no remaining book value, would be scrapped at no gain or loss. The new machinery would increase invested assets by $918,750 for the year.

Instructions

1. Using the DuPont formula for rate of return on investment, determine the profit margin, investment turnover, and rate of return on investment for the Electronics Division for the past year. Round investment turnover and the rate of return to one decimal place.
2. Prepare condensed estimated income statements and compute the invested assets for each proposal.

3. Using the DuPont formula for rate of return on investment, determine the profit margin, investment turnover, and rate of return on investment for each proposal.
4. Which of the three proposals would meet the required 20% rate of return on investment?
5. If the Electronics Division were in an industry where the profit margin could not be increased, how much would the investment turnover have to increase to meet the president's required 20% rate of return on investment? Round to one decimal place.

✔ 2. Road Bike Division ROI, 12.0%

SPREADSHEET

PR 23-5B Divisional performance analysis and evaluation **OBJ. 4**

The vice president of operations of Free Ride Bike Company is evaluating the performance of two divisions organized as investment centers. Invested assets and condensed income statement data for the past year for each division are as follows:

	Road Bike Division	Mountain Bike Division
Sales	$1,728,000	$1,760,000
Cost of goods sold	1,380,000	1,400,000
Operating expenses	175,200	236,800
Invested assets	1,440,000	800,000

Instructions

1. Prepare condensed divisional income statements for the year ended December 31, 2014, assuming that there were no service department charges.
2. Using the DuPont formula for rate of return on investment, determine the profit margin, investment turnover, and rate of return on investment for each division.
3. If management's minimum acceptable rate of return is 10%, determine the residual income for each division.
4. Discuss the evaluation of the two divisions, using the performance measures determined in parts (1), (2), and (3).

✔ 3. Navigational Systems Division, $179,410

SPREADSHEET

PR 23-6B Transfer pricing **OBJ. 5**

Exoplex Industries Inc. is a diversified aerospace company, including two operating divisions, Semiconductors and Navigational Systems divisions. Condensed divisional income statements, which involve no intracompany transfers and which include a breakdown of expenses into variable and fixed components, are as follows:

Exoplex Industries Inc.
Divisional Income Statements
For the Year Ended December 31, 2014

	Semiconductors Division	Navigational Systems Division	Total
Sales:			
2,240 units @ $396 per unit	$887,040		$ 887,040
3,675 units @ $590 per unit		$2,168,250	2,168,250
	$887,040	$2,168,250	$3,055,290
Expenses:			
Variable:			
2,240 units @ $232 per unit	$519,680		$ 519,680
3,675 units @ $472* per unit		$1,734,600	1,734,600
Fixed	220,000	325,000	545,000
Total expenses	$739,680	$2,059,600	$2,799,280
Income from operations	$147,360	$ 108,650	$ 256,010

*$432 of the $472 per unit represents materials costs, and the remaining $40 per unit represents other variable conversion expenses incurred within the Navigational Systems Division.

The Semiconductors Division is presently producing 2,240 units out of a total capacity of 2,820 units. Materials used in producing the Navigational Systems Division's product are currently purchased from outside suppliers at a price of $432 per unit. The

Learning Objectives

After studying this chapter, you should be able to: *Example Exercises*

OBJ 1 Prepare differential analysis reports for a variety of managerial decisions.
Differential Analysis
- Lease or Sell — EE 24-1
- Discontinue a Segment or Product — EE 24-2
- Make or Buy — EE 24-3
- Replace Equipment — EE 24-4
- Process or Sell — EE 24-5
- Accept Business at a Special Price — EE 24-6

OBJ 2 Determine the selling price of a product, using the product cost concept.
Setting Normal Product Selling Prices
- Product Cost Concept — EE 24-7
- Target Costing

OBJ 3 Compute the relative profitability of products in bottleneck production processes.
Production Bottlenecks — EE 24-8

At a Glance 24 Page 1139

OBJ 1 Prepare differential analysis reports for a variety of managerial decisions.

Differential Analysis

Managerial decision making involves choosing between alternative courses of action. Although the managerial decision-making process varies by the type of decision, it normally involves the following steps:

Step 1. Identify the objective of the decision, which is normally maximizing income.
Step 2. Identify alternative courses of action.
Step 3. Gather information and perform a differential analysis.
Step 4. Make a decision.
Step 5. Review, analyze, and assess the results of the decision.

To illustrate, assume Bryant Restaurants Inc. is deciding whether to replace some of its customer seating (tables) with a salad bar. The differential analysis decision-making process is as follows:

Step 1. Bryant Restaurants' objective is to increase its income.
Step 2. The alternative courses of action are:
1. Use floor space for existing tables.
2. Replace the tables with a salad bar.

Step 3. The following relevant data have been gathered:

	Tables (Alternative 1)	Salad Bar (Alternative 2)
Revenues	$100,000	$120,000
Costs	60,000	65,000
Income (loss)	$ 40,000	$ 55,000

The preceding information is used to perform differential analysis. **Differential analysis**, sometimes called *incremental analysis*, analyzes differential revenues and costs in order to determine the differential impact on income of two alternative courses of action.

Differential revenue is the amount of increase or decrease in revenue that is expected from a course of action compared to an alternative. **Differential cost** is the amount of increase or decrease in cost that is expected from a course of action as compared to an alternative. **Differential income (loss)** is the difference between the differential revenue and differential costs. Differential income indicates that a decision is expected to increase income, while a differential loss indicates the decision is expected to decrease income.

To illustrate, the differential analysis as of July 11, 2014, for Bryant Restaurants is shown in Exhibit 1.

EXHIBIT 1

Differential Analysis—Bryant Restaurants

Differential Analysis
Tables (Alternative 1) or Salad Bar (Alternative 2)
July 11, 2014

	Tables (Alternative 1)	Salad Bar (Alternative 2)	Differential Effect on Income (Alternative 2)
Revenues	$100,000	$120,000	$20,000
Costs	−60,000	−65,000	−5,000
Income (loss)	$ 40,000	$ 55,000	$15,000

The differential analysis is prepared in three columns, where positive amounts indicate the effect is to increase income and negative amounts indicate the effect is to decrease income. The first column is the revenues, costs, and income for maintaining floor space for tables (Alternative 1). The second column is the revenues, costs, and income for using that floor space for a salad bar (Alternative 2). The third column is the difference between the revenue, costs, and income of one alternative over the other.

In Exhibit 1, the salad bar is being considered over retaining the existing tables. Thus, Column 3 in Exhibit 1 is expressed in terms of Alternative 2 (salad bar) over Alternative 1 (tables).

In Exhibit 1, the differential revenue of a salad bar over tables is $20,000 ($120,000 − $100,000). Since the increased revenue would increase income, it is entered as a positive $20,000 in the Differential Effect on Income column. The differential cost of a salad bar over tables is $5,000 ($65,000 − $60,000). Since the increased costs will decrease income, it is entered as a negative $5,000 in the Differential Effect on Income column.

The differential income (loss) of a salad bar over tables of $15,000 is determined by subtracting the differential costs from the differential revenues in the Differential Effect on Income column. Thus, installing a salad bar increases income by $15,000.

The preceding differential revenue, costs, and income can also be determined using the following formulas:

Differential Revenue = Revenue (Alt. 2) − Revenue (Alt. 1)
Differential Revenue = $120,000 − $100,000 = $20,000

Differential Costs = Costs (Alt. 2) − Costs (Alt. 1)
Differential Costs = −$65,000 − (−$60,000) = −$5,000

Differential Income (Loss) = Income (Alt. 2) − Income (Alt. 1)
Differential Income (Loss) = $55,000 − $40,000 = $15,000

Step 4. Based upon the differential analysis report shown in Exhibit 1, Bryant Restaurants should decide to replace some of its tables with a salad bar. Doing so will increase its income by $15,000.

Step 5. Over time, Bryant Restaurants' decision should be reviewed based upon actual revenues and costs. If the actual revenues and costs differ significantly from those gathered in Step 3, another differential analysis might be necessary to verify that the correct decision was made.

In this chapter, differential analysis is illustrated for the following common decisions:

1. Leasing or selling equipment
2. Discontinuing an unprofitable segment
3. Manufacturing or purchasing a needed part
4. Replacing fixed assets
5. Selling a product or processing further
6. Accepting additional business at a special price

Lease or Sell

Management may lease or sell a piece of equipment that is no longer needed. This may occur when a company changes its manufacturing process and can no longer use the equipment in the manufacturing process. In making a decision, differential analysis can be used.

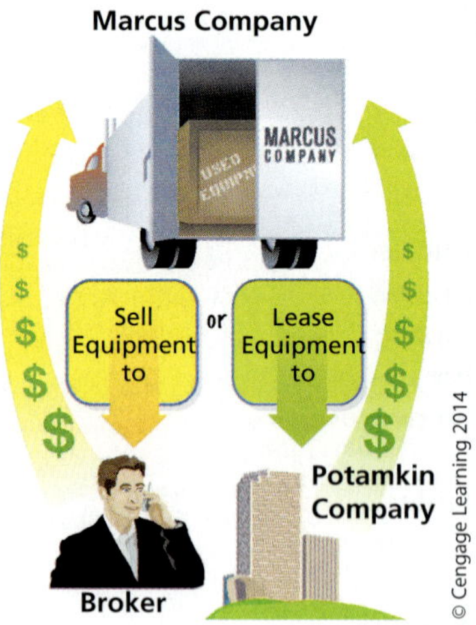

To illustrate, assume that on June 22, 2014, Marcus Company is considering leasing or disposing of the following equipment:

Cost of equipment	$200,000
Less accumulated depreciation	120,000
Book value	$ 80,000
Lease (Alternative 1):	
Total revenue for five-year lease	$160,000
Total estimated repair, insurance, and property tax expenses during life of lease	35,000
Residual value at end of fifth year of lease	0
Sell (Alternative 2):	
Sales price	$100,000
Commission on sales	6%

Exhibit 2 shows the differential analysis of whether to lease (Alternative 1) or sell (Alternative 2) the equipment.

EXHIBIT 2

Differential Analysis—Lease or Sell Equipment

Differential Analysis
Lease Equipment (Alternative 1) or Sell Equipment (Alternative 2)
June 22, 2014

	Lease Equipment (Alternative 1)	Sell Equipment (Alternative 2)	Differential Effect on Income (Alternative 2)
Revenues	$160,000	$100,000	–$60,000
Costs	–35,000	–6,000	29,000
Income (loss)	$125,000	$ 94,000	–$31,000

If the equipment is sold, differential revenues will decrease by $60,000, differential costs will decrease by $29,000, and the differential effect on income is a decrease of $31,000. Thus, the decision should be to lease the equipment.

Exhibit 2 includes only the differential revenues and differential costs associated with the lease-or-sell decision. The $80,000 book value ($200,000 – $120,000) of the equipment is a *sunk* cost and is not considered in the differential analysis. **Sunk costs** are costs that have been incurred in the past, cannot be recouped, and are not relevant to future decisions. That is, the $80,000 is not affected regardless of which decision is made. For example, if the $80,000 were included in Exhibit 2, the costs for each alternative would both increase by $80,000, but the differential effect on income of –$31,000 would remain unchanged.

Have you ever walked out on a bad movie? The cost of the ticket is a sunk cost and, thus, irrelevant to the decision to walk out early.

To simplify, the following factors were not considered in Exhibit 2:

1. Differential revenue from investing funds
2. Differential income tax

Differential revenue, such as interest revenue, could arise from investing the cash created by the two alternatives. Differential income tax could also arise from differences in income. These factors are discussed in Chapter 25.

Example Exercise 24-1 Lease or Sell

OBJ 1

Casper Company owns office space with a cost of $100,000 and accumulated depreciation of $30,000 that can be sold for $150,000, less a 6% broker commission. Alternatively, the office space can be leased by Casper Company for 10 years for a total of $170,000, at the end of which there is no residual value. In addition, repair, insurance, and property tax that would be incurred by Casper Company on the rented office space would total $24,000 over the 10 years. Prepare a differential analysis on May 30, 2014, as to whether Casper Company should lease (Alternative 1) or sell (Alternative 2) the office space.

Follow My Example 24-1

Differential Analysis
Lease Office Space (Alternative 1) or Sell Office Space (Alternative 2)
May 30, 2014

	Lease Office Space (Alternative 1)	Sell Office Space (Alternative 2)	Differential Effect on Income (Alternative 2)
Revenues	$170,000	$150,000	–$20,000
Costs	–24,000	–9,000*	15,000
Income (loss)	$146,000	$141,000	–$ 5,000

*$150,000 × 6%

Casper Company should lease the office space.

Practice Exercises: **PE 24-1A, PE 24-1B**

Discontinue a Segment or Product

A product, department, branch, territory, or other segment of a business may be generating losses. As a result, management may consider discontinuing (eliminating) the product or segment. In such cases, it may be erroneously assumed that the total company income will increase by eliminating the operating loss.

Discontinuing the product or segment usually eliminates all of the product's or segment's variable costs. Such costs include direct materials, direct labor, variable factory overhead, and sales commissions. However, fixed costs such as depreciation, insurance, and property taxes may not be eliminated. Thus, it is possible for total company income to decrease rather than increase if the unprofitable product or segment is discontinued.

To illustrate, the income statement for Battle Creek Cereal Co. is shown in Exhibit 3. As shown in Exhibit 3, Bran Flakes incurred an operating loss of $11,000. Because Bran Flakes has incurred annual losses for several years, management is considering discontinuing it.

EXHIBIT 3

Income (Loss) by Product

Battle Creek Cereal Co.
Condensed Income Statement
For the Year Ended August 31, 2014

	Corn Flakes	Toasted Oats	Bran Flakes	Total Company
Sales	$500,000	$400,000	$100,000	$1,000,000
Cost of goods sold:				
Variable costs	$220,000	$200,000	$ 60,000	$ 480,000
Fixed costs	120,000	80,000	20,000	220,000
Total cost of goods sold	$340,000	$280,000	$ 80,000	$ 700,000
Gross profit	$160,000	$120,000	$ 20,000	$ 300,000
Operating expenses:				
Variable expenses	$ 95,000	$ 60,000	$ 25,000	$ 180,000
Fixed expenses	25,000	20,000	6,000	51,000
Total operating expenses	$120,000	$ 80,000	$ 31,000	$ 231,000
Income (loss) from operations	$ 40,000	$ 40,000	$ (11,000)	$ 69,000

If Bran Flakes is discontinued, what would be the total annual operating income of Battle Creek Cereal? The first impression is that total annual operating income would be $80,000, as shown below.

	Corn Flakes	Toasted Oats	Total Company
Income from operations	$40,000	$40,000	$80,000

However, the differential analysis dated September 29, 2014, in Exhibit 4 indicates that discontinuing Bran Flakes (Alternative 2) actually decreases operating income by $15,000. This is because discontinuing Bran Flakes has no effect on fixed costs and expenses. This is confirmed by the income statement analysis in Exhibit 5, which indicates that income from operations would decrease from $69,000 to $54,000 if Bran Flakes were discontinued.

Exhibits 4 and 5 consider only the short-term (one-year) effects of discontinuing Bran Flakes. When discontinuing a product or segment, long-term effects should also be considered. For example, discontinuing Bran Flakes could decrease sales of other products. This might be the case if customers upset with the discontinuance of Bran Flakes quit buying other products from the company. Finally, employee morale and productivity might suffer if employees have to be laid off or relocated.

EXHIBIT 4

Differential Analysis—Continue or Discontinue Bran Flakes

Differential Analysis
Continue Bran Flakes (Alternative 1) or Discontinue Bran Flakes (Alternative 2)
September 29, 2014

	Continue Bran Flakes (Alternative 1)	Discontinue Bran Flakes (Alternative 2)	Differential Effect on Income (Alternative 2)
Revenues	$100,000	$ 0	–$100,000
Costs:			
Variable	$ 85,000	$ 0	$ 85,000
Fixed	–26,000	–26,000	0
Total costs	–$111,000	–$26,000	$ 85,000
Income (loss)	–$ 11,000	–$26,000	–$ 15,000

EXHIBIT 5

Income Statement Analysis

Proposal to Discontinue Bran Flakes
September 29, 2014

	Bran Flakes, Toasted Oats, and Corn Flakes	Discontinue Bran Flakes*	Toasted Oats and Corn Flakes
Sales	$1,000,000	$100,000	$900,000
Cost of goods sold:			
Variable costs	$ 480,000	$ 60,000	$420,000
Fixed costs	220,000	0	220,000
Total cost of goods sold	$ 700,000	$ 60,000	$640,000
Gross profit	$ 300,000	$ 40,000	$260,000
Operating expenses:			
Variable expenses	$ 180,000	$ 25,000	$155,000
Fixed expenses	51,000	0	51,000
Total operating expenses	$ 231,000	$ 25,000	$206,000
Income (loss) from operations	**$ 69,000**	**$ 15,000**	**$ 54,000**

*Fixed costs are assumed to remain unchanged with the discontinuance of Bran Flakes.

Example Exercise 24-2 Discontinue a Segment

OBJ 1

Product K has revenue of $65,000, variable cost of goods sold of $50,000, variable selling expenses of $12,000, and fixed costs of $25,000, creating a loss from operations of $22,000. Prepare a differential analysis dated February 22, 2014, to determine if Product K should be continued (Alternative 1) or discontinued (Alternative 2), assuming fixed costs are unaffected by the decision.

Follow My Example 24-2

Differential Analysis
Continue K (Alternative 1) or Discontinue K (Alternative 2)
February 22, 2014

	Continue Product K (Alternative 1)	Discontinue Product K (Alternative 2)	Differential Effect on Income (Alternative 2)
Revenues	$65,000	$ 0	–$65,000
Costs:			
Variable	–$62,000*	$ 0	$62,000
Fixed	–25,000	–25,000	0
Total costs	–$87,000	–$25,000	$62,000
Income (loss)	–$22,000	–$25,000	–$ 3,000

*$50,000 + $12,000

Product K should be continued.

Practice Exercises: **PE 24-2A, PE 24-2B**

Make or Buy

Companies often manufacture products made up of components that are assembled into a final product. For example, an automobile manufacturer assembles tires, radios, motors, interior seats, transmissions, and other parts into a finished automobile. In such cases, the manufacturer must decide whether to make a part or purchase it from a supplier.

Differential analysis can be used to decide whether to make or buy a part. The analysis is similar whether management is considering making a part that is currently being purchased or purchasing a part that is currently being made.

To illustrate, assume that an automobile manufacturer has been purchasing instrument panels for $240 a unit. The factory is currently operating at 80% of capacity, and no major increase in production is expected in the near future. The cost per unit of manufacturing an instrument panel internally is estimated on February 15, 2014, as follows:

Direct materials	$ 80
Direct labor	80
Variable factory overhead	52
Fixed factory overhead	68
Total cost per unit	$280

If the make price of $280 is simply compared with the buy price of $240, the decision is to buy the instrument panel. However, if unused capacity could be used in manufacturing the part, there would be no increase in the total fixed factory overhead costs. Thus, only the variable factory overhead costs would be incurred.

The differential analysis for this make (Alternative 1) or buy (Alternative 2) decision is shown in Exhibit 6. The fixed factory overhead cannot be eliminated by purchasing the panels. Thus, both alternatives include the fixed factory overhead. The differential analysis indicates there is a loss of $28 per unit from buying the instrument panels. Thus, the instrument panels should be manufactured.

EXHIBIT 6

Differential Analysis—Make or Buy Instrument Panels

Differential Analysis
Make Panels (Alternative 1) or Buy Panels (Alternative 2)
February 15, 2014

	Make Panels (Alternative 1)	Buy Panels (Alternative 2)	Differential Effect on Income (Alternative 2)
Unit costs:			
Purchase price	$ 0	–$240	–$240
Direct materials	–80	0	80
Direct labor	–80	0	80
Variable factory overhead	–52	0	52
Fixed factory overhead	–68	–68	0
Income (loss)	–$280	–$308	–$ 28

Other factors should also be considered in the analysis. For example, productive capacity used to make the instrument panel would not be available for other production. The decision may also affect the future business relationship with the instrument panel supplier. For example, if the supplier provides other parts, the company's decision to make instrument panels might jeopardize the timely delivery of other parts.

Example Exercise 24-3 Make or Buy OBJ 1

A company manufactures a subcomponent of an assembly for $80 per unit, including fixed costs of $25 per unit. A proposal is offered to purchase the subcomponent from an outside source for $60 per unit, plus $5 per unit freight. Prepare a differential analysis dated November 2, 2014, to determine whether the company should make (Alternative 1) or buy (Alternative 2) the subcomponent, assuming fixed costs are unaffected by the decision.

(Continued)

Follow My Example 24-3

Differential Analysis
Make Subcomponent (Alternative 1) or Buy Subcomponent (Alternative 2)
November 2, 2014

	Make Subcomponent (Alternative 1)	Buy Subcomponent (Alternative 2)	Differential Effect on Income (Alternative 2)
Unit costs:			
Purchase price	$ 0	−$60	−$60
Freight	0	−5	−5
Variable costs ($80 − $25)	−55	0	55
Fixed factory overhead	−25	−25	0
Income (loss)	−$80	−$90	−$10

The company should make the subcomponent.

Practice Exercises: **PE 24-3A, PE 24-3B**

Replace Equipment

The usefulness of a fixed asset may decrease before it is worn out. For example, old equipment may no longer be as efficient as new equipment.

Differential analysis can be used for decisions to replace fixed assets such as equipment and machinery. The analysis normally focuses on the costs of continuing to use the old equipment versus replacing the equipment. The book value of the old equipment is a sunk cost and thus is irrelevant.

To illustrate, assume that on November 28, 2014, a business is considering replacing the following machine:

Old Machine	
Book value	$100,000
Estimated annual variable manufacturing costs	225,000
Estimated selling price	25,000
Estimated remaining useful life	5 years
New Machine	
Cost of new machine	$250,000
Estimated annual variable manufacturing costs	150,000
Estimated residual value	0
Estimated useful life	5 years

The differential analysis for whether to continue with the old machine (Alternative 1) or replace the old machine with a new machine (Alternative 2) is shown in Exhibit 7.

EXHIBIT 7

Differential Analysis—Continue with or Replace Old Equipment

Differential Analysis
Continue with Old Machine (Alternative 1) or Replace Old Machine (Alternative 2)
November 28, 2014

	Continue with Old Machine (Alternative 1)	Replace Old Machine (Alternative 2)	Differential Effect on Income (Alternative 2)
Revenues:			
Proceeds from sale of old machine	$ 0	$ 25,000	$ 25,000
Costs:			
Purchase price	$ 0	−$ 250,000	−$250,000
Annual variable costs (5 years)	−1,125,000	−750,000	375,000
Total costs	−$1,125,000	−$1,000,000	$125,000
Income (loss)	−$1,125,000	−$ 975,000	$150,000

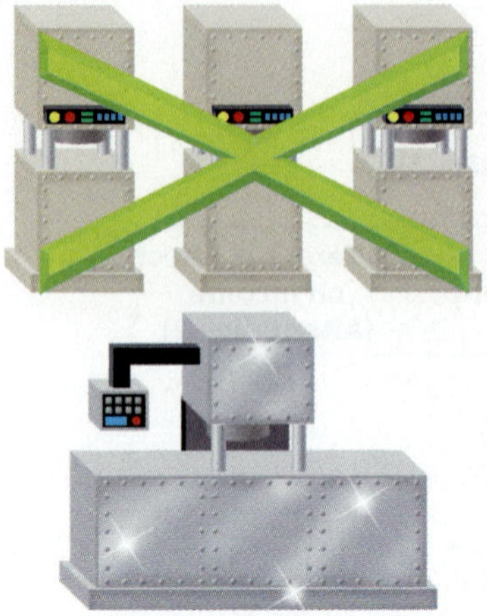

Differential effect on income, $30,000 per year

As shown in Exhibit 7, there is five-year differential effect on income of $150,000 (or $30,000 per year) from replacing the machine. Thus, the decision should be to purchase the new machine and sell the old machine.

Other factors are often important in equipment replacement decisions. For example, differences between the remaining useful life of the old equipment and the estimated life of the new equipment could exist. In addition, the new equipment might improve the overall quality of the product and, thus, increase sales.

The time value of money and other uses for the cash needed to purchase the new equipment could also affect the decision to replace equipment.[1] The revenue that is forgone from an alternative use of an asset, such as cash, is called an **opportunity cost**. Although the opportunity cost is not recorded in the accounting records, it is useful in analyzing alternative courses of action.

Example Exercise 24-4 Replace Equipment

OBJ 1

A machine with a book value of $32,000 has an estimated four-year life. A proposal is offered to sell the old machine for $10,000 and replace it with a new machine at a cost of $45,000. The new machine has a four-year life with no residual value. The new machine would reduce annual direct labor costs from $33,000 to $22,000. Prepare a differential analysis dated October 7, 2014, on whether to continue with the old machine (Alternative 1) or replace the old machine (Alternative 2).

Follow My Example 24-4

Differential Analysis
Continue with Old Machine (Alternative 1) or Replace Old Machine (Alternative 2)
October 7, 2014

	Continue with Old Machine (Alternative 1)	Replace Old Machine (Alternative 2)	Differential Effect on Income (Alternative 2)
Revenues:			
Proceeds from sale of old machine	$ 0	$ 10,000	$10,000
Costs:			
Purchase price	$ 0	–$ 45,000	–$45,000
Direct labor (4 years)	–132,000*	–88,000**	44,000
Total costs	–$132,000	–$133,000	–$ 1,000
Total income (loss)	–$132,000	–$123,000	$ 9,000

*$33,000 × 4 years
**$22,000 × 4 years

The old machine should be sold and replaced with the new machine.

Practice Exercises: **PE 24-4A, PE 24-4B**

Process or Sell

During manufacturing, a product normally progresses through various stages or processes. In some cases, a product can be sold at an intermediate stage of production, or it can be processed further and then sold.

Differential analysis can be used to decide whether to sell a product at an intermediate stage or to process it further. In doing so, the differential revenues and costs from further processing are compared. The costs of producing the intermediate product do not change, regardless of whether the intermediate product is sold or processed further.

1 The time value of money in purchasing equipment (capital assets) is discussed in Chapter 25.

To illustrate, assume that a business produces kerosene as follows:

Kerosene:	
Batch size	4,000 gallons
Cost of producing kerosene	$2,400 per batch
Selling price	$2.50 per gallon

The kerosene can be processed further to yield gasoline as follows:

Gasoline:	
Input batch size	4,000 gallons
Less evaporation (20%)	800 (4,000 × 20%)
Output batch size	3,200 gallons
Cost of producing gasoline	$3,050 per batch
Selling price	$3.50 per gallon

Exhibit 8 shows the differential analysis dated October 1, 2014, for whether to sell kerosene (Alternative 1) or process it further into gasoline (Alternative 2).

EXHIBIT 8

Differential Analysis—Sell Kerosene or Process Further into Gasoline

Differential Analysis
Sell Kerosene (Alternative 1) or Process Further into Gasoline (Alternative 2)
October 1, 2014

	Sell Kerosene (Alternative 1)	Process Further into Gasoline (Alternative 2)	Differential Effect on Income (Alternative 2)
Revenues	$10,000*	$11,200**	$1,200
Costs	−2,400	−3,050	−650
Income (loss)	$ 7,600	$ 8,150	$ 550

*4,000 gallons × $2.50
**(4,000 gallons – 800 gallons) × $3.50

As shown in Exhibit 8, there is additional income of $550 per batch from further processing the kerosene into gasoline. Therefore, the decision should be to process the kerosene further into gasoline.

Example Exercise 24-5 Process or Sell

OBJ 1

Product T is produced for $2.50 per gallon. Product T can be sold without additional processing for $3.50 per gallon, or processed further into Product V at an additional total cost of $0.70 per gallon. Product V can be sold for $4.00 per gallon. Prepare a differential analysis dated April 8, 2014, on whether to sell Product T (Alternative 1) or process it further into Product V (Alternative 2).

Follow My Example 24-5

Differential Analysis
Sell Product T (Alternative 1) or Process Further into Product V (Alternative 2)
April 8, 2014

	Sell Product T (Alternative 1)	Process Further into Product V (Alternative 2)	Differential Effect on Income (Alternative 2)
Revenues, per unit	$3.50	$4.00	$0.50
Costs, per unit	−2.50	−3.20*	−0.70
Income (loss), per unit	$1.00	$0.80	−$0.20

*$2.50 + $0.70

The decision should be to sell Product T.

Practice Exercises: **PE 24-5A, PE 24-5B**

Accept Business at a Special Price

A company may be offered the opportunity to sell its products at prices other than normal prices. For example, an exporter may offer to sell a company's products overseas at special discount prices.

Differential analysis can be used to decide whether to accept additional business at a special price. The differential revenue from accepting the additional business is compared to the differential costs of producing and delivering the product to the customer.

The differential costs of accepting additional business depend on whether the company is operating at full capacity.

1. If the company is *operating at full capacity,* any additional production increases fixed and variable manufacturing costs. Selling and administrative expenses may also increase because of the additional business.
2. If the company is *operating below full capacity,* any additional production does not increase fixed manufacturing costs. In this case, the differential costs of the additional production are the variable manufacturing costs. Selling and administrative expenses may also increase because of the additional business.

To illustrate, assume that B-Ball Inc. manufactures basketballs as follows:

Monthly productive capacity	12,500 basketballs
Current monthly sales	10,000 basketballs
Normal (domestic) selling price	$30.00 per basketball
Manufacturing costs:	
Variable costs	$12.50 per basketball
Fixed costs	7.50
Total	$20.00 per basketball

On March 10, 2014, B-Ball Inc. received an offer from an exporter for 5,000 basketballs at $18 each. Production can be spread over three months without interfering with normal production or incurring overtime costs. Pricing policies in the domestic market will not be affected.

Comparing the special offer sales price of $18 with the manufacturing cost of $20 per basketball indicates that the offer should be rejected. However, as shown in Exhibit 9, a differential analysis on whether to reject the order (Alternative 1) or accept the order (Alternative 2) shows that the special order should be accepted. This is because the fixed costs are not affected by the decision, and are thus omitted from the analysis.

EXHIBIT 9

Differential Analysis—Accept Business at a Special Price

Differential Analysis
Reject Order (Alternative 1) or Accept Order (Alternative 2)
March 10, 2014

	Reject Order (Alternative 1)	Accept Order (Alternative 2)	Differential Effect on Income (Alternative 2)
Revenues	$0	$90,000*	$90,000
Costs:			
Variable manufacturing costs	0	−62,500**	−62,500
Income (loss)	$0	$27,500	$27,500

*5,000 units × $18
**5,000 units × $12.50 variable cost per unit

Proposals to sell products at special prices often require additional considerations. For example, special prices in one geographic area may result in price reductions in other areas, with the result that total company sales revenues decrease. Manufacturers must also conform to the Robinson-Patman Act, which prohibits price discrimination within the United States unless price differences can be justified by different costs.

Business Connection

NAME YOUR OWN PRICE

Priceline.com Inc. was founded in the late 1990s and has become a successful survivor of the Internet revolution. Priceline developed the "name your price®" bidding format, which can provide price discounts of up to 60% for travel services. How does it work? For hotel services, Priceline has arrangements with hotels to provide discounted rooms. These rooms are sold to customers based on a name-your-own-price bid. Customers must identify a zone (approximate location for the hotel), quality level, and dates, and then submit a price bid for a hotel. If you place a bid that is rejected, you can try again after 24 hours. If your bid is accepted, you are committed to pay for the hotel that has been selected according to your criteria. Why do hotels provide rooms at such a large discount? If the hotel has unused rooms, the variable cost of an incremental guest is low relative to the fixed cost of the room. Thus, during low occupancy times, any price above the variable cost of providing the room can add to the profitability of the hotel.

Example Exercise 24-6 Accept Business at Special Price

OBJ 1

Product D is normally sold for $4.40 per unit. A special price of $3.60 is offered for the export market. The variable production cost is $3.00 per unit. An additional export tariff of 10% of revenue must be paid for all export products. Assume there is sufficient capacity for the special order. Prepare a differential analysis dated January 14, 2014, on whether to reject (Alternative 1) or accept (Alternative 2) the special order.

Follow My Example 24-6

Differential Analysis
Reject Order (Alternative 1) or Accept Order (Alternative 2)
January 14, 2014

	Reject Order (Alternative 1)	Accept Order (Alternative 2)	Differential Effect on Income (Alternative 2)
Per unit:			
Revenues	$0	$3.60	$3.60
Costs:			
Variable manufacturing costs	$0	–$3.00	–$3.00
Export tariff	0	–0.36*	–0.36
Total costs	$0	–$3.36	–$3.36
Income (loss)	$0	$0.24	$0.24

*$3.60 × 10%

The special order should be accepted.

Practice Exercises: **PE 24-6A, PE 24-6B**

OBJ 2 Determine the selling price of a product, using the product cost concept.

Setting Normal Product Selling Prices

The *normal* selling price is the target selling price to be achieved in the long term. The normal selling price must be set high enough to cover all costs and expenses (fixed and variable) and provide a reasonable profit. Otherwise, the business will not survive.

In contrast, in deciding whether to accept additional business at a special price, only differential costs are considered. Any price above the differential costs will increase profits in the short term. However, in the long term, products are sold at normal prices rather than special prices.

Hotels and motels use the demand-based concept in setting room rates. Room rates are set low during off-season travel periods (low demand) and high for peak-season travel periods (high demand) such as holidays.

Managers can use one of two market methods to determine selling price:

1. Demand-based concept
2. Competition-based concept

The demand-based concept sets the price according to the demand for the product. If there is high demand for the product, then the price is set high. Likewise, if there is a low demand for the product, then the price is set low.

The competition-based concept sets the price according to the price offered by competitors. For example, if a competitor reduces the price, then management adjusts the price to meet the competition. The market-based pricing approaches are discussed in greater detail in marketing courses.

Managers can also use one of three cost-plus methods to determine the selling price:

1. Product cost concept
2. Total cost concept
3. Variable cost concept

The product cost concept is illustrated in this section. The total cost and variable cost concepts are illustrated in the appendix to this chapter.

Integrity, Objectivity, and Ethics in Business

PRICE FIXING

Federal law prevents companies competing in similar markets from sharing cost and price information, or what is commonly termed "price fixing." For example, the Federal Trade Commission (FTC) brought a suit against U-Haul for releasing company-wide memorandums to its managers telling them to encourage competitors to match U-Haul price increases. Commenting on the case, the chairman of the FTC stated, "It's a bedrock principle that you can't conspire with your competitors to fix prices, and shouldn't even try."

Source: Edward Wyatt, "U-Haul to Settle with Trade Agency in Case on Truck Rental Price-Fixing," *The New York Times*, June 10, 2010, p. B3.

Product Cost Concept

Cost-plus methods determine the normal selling price by estimating a cost amount per unit and adding a markup, as shown below.

Normal Selling Price = Cost Amount per Unit + Markup

Management determines the markup based on the desired profit for the product. The markup should be sufficient to earn the desired profit plus cover any costs and expenses that are not included in the cost amount.

Under the **product cost concept**, only the costs of manufacturing the product, termed the *product costs,* are included in the cost amount per unit to which the markup is added. Estimated selling expenses, administrative expenses, and desired profit are included in the markup. The markup per unit is then computed and added to the product cost per unit to determine the normal selling price.

The product cost concept is applied using the following steps:

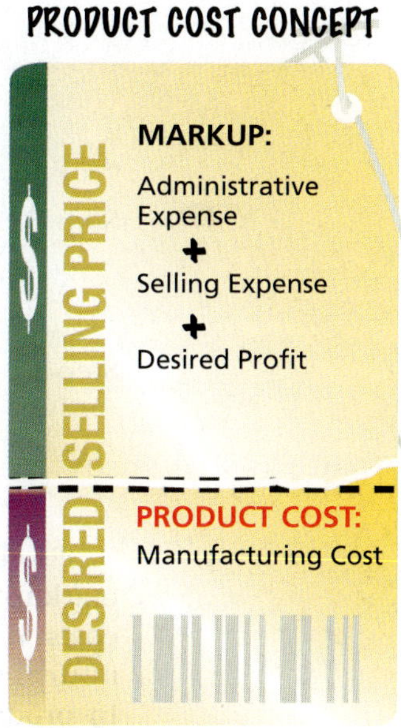

Step 1. Estimate the total product costs as follows:

Product costs:	
Direct materials	$XXX
Direct labor	XXX
Factory overhead	XXX
Total product cost	$XXX

Step 2. Estimate the total selling and administrative expenses.

Step 3. Divide the total product cost by the number of units expected to be produced and sold to determine the total product cost per unit, as shown below.

$$\text{Product Cost per Unit} = \frac{\text{Total Product Cost}}{\text{Estimated Units Produced and Sold}}$$

Step 4. Compute the markup percentage as follows:

$$\text{Markup Percentage} = \frac{\text{Desired Profit} + \text{Total Selling and Administrative Expenses}}{\text{Total Product Cost}}$$

The numerator of the markup percentage is the desired profit plus the total selling and administrative expenses. These expenses must be included in the markup percentage, since they are not included in the cost amount to which the markup is added.

The desired profit is normally computed based on a rate of return on assets as follows:

$$\text{Desired Profit} = \text{Desired Rate of Return} \times \text{Total Assets}$$

Step 5. Determine the markup per unit by multiplying the markup percentage times the product cost per unit as follows:

$$\text{Markup per Unit} = \text{Markup Percentage} \times \text{Product Cost per Unit}$$

Step 6. Determine the normal selling price by adding the markup per unit to the product cost per unit as follows:

Product cost per unit	$XXX
Markup per unit	XXX
Normal selling price per unit	$XXX

To illustrate, assume the following data for 100,000 calculators that Digital Solutions Inc. expects to produce and sell during the current year:

Manufacturing costs:	
Direct materials ($3.00 × 100,000)	$ 300,000
Direct labor ($10.00 × 100,000)	1,000,000
Factory overhead	200,000
Total manufacturing costs	$1,500,000
Selling and administrative expenses	170,000
Total cost	$1,670,000
Total assets	$800,000
Desired rate of return	20%

The normal selling price of $18.30 is determined under the product cost concept as follows:

Step 1. Total product cost: $1,500,000

Step 2. Total selling and administrative expenses: $170,000

Step 3. Total product cost per unit: $15.00

$$\text{Total Cost per Unit} = \frac{\text{Total Product Cost}}{\text{Estimated Units Produced and Sold}} = \frac{\$1{,}500{,}000}{100{,}000 \text{ units}} = \$15.00 \text{ per unit}$$

Step 4. Markup percentage: 22%

$$\text{Desired Profit} = \text{Desired Rate of Return} \times \text{Total Assets} = 20\% \times \$800{,}000 = \$160{,}000$$

$$\text{Markup Percentage} = \frac{\text{Desired Profit} + \text{Total Selling and Administrative Expenses}}{\text{Total Product Cost}}$$

$$\text{Markup Percentage} = \frac{\$160{,}000 + \$170{,}000}{\$1{,}500{,}000} = \frac{\$330{,}000}{\$1{,}500{,}000} = 22\%$$

Step 5. Markup per unit: $3.30

Markup per Unit = Markup Percentage × Product Cost per Unit
Markup per Unit = 22% × $15.00 = $3.30 per unit

Step 6. Normal selling price: $18.30

Total product cost per unit	$15.00
Markup per unit	3.30
Normal selling price per unit	$18.30

Product cost estimates, rather than actual costs, may be used in computing the markup. Management should be careful, however, when using estimated or standard costs in applying the cost-plus approach. Specifically, estimates should be based on normal (attainable) operating levels and not theoretical (ideal) levels of performance. In product pricing, the use of estimates based on ideal operating performance could lead to setting product prices too low.

Example Exercise 24-7 Product Cost Markup Percentage

OBJ 2

Apex Corporation produces and sells Product Z at a total cost of $30 per unit, of which $20 is product cost and $10 is selling and administrative expenses. In addition, the total cost of $30 is made up of $18 variable cost and $12 fixed cost. The desired profit is $3 per unit. Determine the markup percentage on product cost.

Follow My Example 24-7

Markup percentage on product cost: $\frac{\$3 + \$10}{\$20} = 65.0\%$

Practice Exercises: **PE 24-7A, PE 24-7B**

Business Connection

iPHONE PRODUCT COST

Market research firm iSuppli opened up an Apple iPhone 4S® to estimate its total variable manufacturing cost. After listing and analyzing all of the components, it determined that the iPhone has a total variable production cost of $196. This is about 30% of the wholesale price, which is estimated to be in line with other Apple products. The direct labor was estimated to be only $8 of the $196, while the remaining $188 was for direct materials. Much of the $188 in materials costs went to components to enhance functionality and make the product easy to use. Approximately $37 of the iPhone's material cost is devoted to powering the touch screen interface. Memory represents the second largest cost component ($28.30), while the wireless components and camera added $23.54 and $17.60 to the material cost, respectively. These parts came from across the globe from such companies as LG Display, Qualcomm, and Hynix Semiconductor. As illustrated with the iPhone, sophisticated products require extensive collaboration across many different companies to provide exciting product features at a reasonable cost.

Source: Arik Hesseldahl, "New iPhone 4S Cracked Open," *The Wall Street Journal*, October 20, 2011, pp. B1, B5.

Target Costing

Target costing is a method of setting prices that combines market-based pricing with a cost-reduction emphasis. Under target costing, a future selling price is anticipated, using the demand-based or the competition-based concepts. The target cost is then determined by subtracting a desired profit from the expected selling price, as shown below.

Target Cost = Expected Selling Price – Desired Profit

Target costing tries to reduce costs as shown in Exhibit 10. The bar at the left in Exhibit 10 shows the actual cost and profit that can be earned during the current period. The bar at the right shows that the market price is expected to decline in the future. The target cost is estimated as the difference between the expected market price and the desired profit.

The target cost is normally less than the current cost. Thus, managers must try to reduce costs from the design and manufacture of the product. The planned cost reduction is sometimes referred to as the cost "drift." Costs can be reduced in a variety of ways such as the following:

1. Simplifying the design
2. Reducing the cost of direct materials
3. Reducing the direct labor costs
4. Eliminating waste

Target costing is especially useful in highly competitive markets such as the market for personal computers. Such markets require continual product cost reductions to remain competitive.

EXHIBIT 10

Target Cost Concept

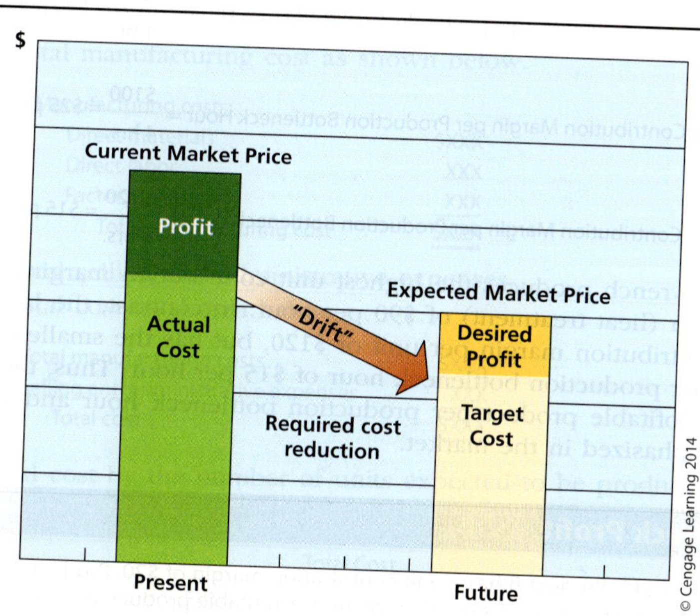

Production Bottlenecks

OBJ 3 Compute the relative profitability of products in bottleneck production processes.

A **production bottleneck** (or *constraint*) is a point in the manufacturing process where the demand for the company's product exceeds the ability to produce the product. The **theory of constraints (TOC)** is a manufacturing strategy that focuses on reducing the influence of bottlenecks on production processes.

When a company has a production bottleneck in its production process, it should attempt to maximize its profits, subject to the production bottleneck. In doing so, the unit contribution margin of each product per production bottleneck constraint is used.

To illustrate, assume that PrideCraft Tool Company makes three types of wrenches: small, medium, and large. All three products are processed through a heat treatment

a. Determine the amount of desired profit from the production and sale of 800 handbags.
b. Determine the product cost per unit for the production of 800 handbags.
c. Determine the product cost markup percentage for handbags.
d. Determine the selling price of handbags.

EX 24-17 Product cost concept of product costing **OBJ. 2**

✔ d. $325

Smart Stream Inc. uses the product cost concept of applying the cost-plus approach to product pricing. The costs of producing and selling 10,000 cellular phones are as follows:

Variable costs:		Fixed costs:	
Direct materials	$150 per unit	Factory overhead	$350,000
Direct labor	25	Selling and admin. exp.	140,000
Factory overhead	40		
Selling and admin. exp.	25		
Total	$240 per unit		

Smart Stream desires a profit equal to a 30% rate of return on invested assets of $1,200,000.

a. Determine the amount of desired profit from the production and sale of 10,000 cellular phones.
b. Determine the product cost and the cost amount per unit for the production of 10,000 cellular phones.
c. Determine the product cost markup percentage for cellular phones.
d. Determine the selling price of cellular phones.

EX 24-18 Target costing **OBJ. 2**

Toyota Motor Corporation uses target costing. Assume that Toyota marketing personnel estimate that the competitive selling price for the Camry in the upcoming model year will need to be $28,000. Assume further that the Camry's total unit cost for the upcoming model year is estimated to be $23,200 and that Toyota requires a 20% profit margin on selling price (which is equivalent to a 25% markup on total cost).

a. What price will Toyota establish for the Camry for the upcoming model year?
b. What impact will target costing have on Toyota, given the assumed information?

EX 24-19 Target costing **OBJ. 2**

✔ b. $30

Instant Image Inc. manufactures color laser printers. Model J20 presently sells for $460 and has a product cost of $230, as follows:

Direct materials	$175
Direct labor	40
Factory overhead	15
Total	$230

It is estimated that the competitive selling price for color laser printers of this type will drop to $400 next year. Instant Image has established a target cost to maintain its historical markup percentage on product cost. Engineers have provided the following cost reduction ideas:

1. Purchase a plastic printer cover with snap-on assembly, rather than with screws. This will reduce the amount of direct labor by 15 minutes per unit.
2. Add an inspection step that will add six minutes per unit of direct labor but reduce the materials cost by $20 per unit.
3. Decrease the cycle time of the injection-molding machine from four minutes to three minutes per part. Forty percent of the direct labor and 48% of the factory overhead are related to running injection-molding machines.

The direct labor rate is $30 per hour.

a. Determine the target cost for Model J20, assuming that the historical markup on product cost and selling price is maintained.

b. Determine the required cost reduction.

c. Evaluate the three engineering improvements together to determine if the required cost reduction (drift) can be achieved.

EX 24-20 Product decisions under bottlenecked operations **OBJ. 3**

Mill Metals Inc. has three grades of metal product, Type 5, Type 10, and Type 20. Financial data for the three grades are as follows:

	Type 5	Type 10	Type 20
Revenues	$43,000	$49,000	$56,500
Variable cost	$34,000	$28,000	$26,500
Fixed cost	8,000	8,000	8,000
Total cost	$42,000	$36,000	$34,500
Income from operations	$ 1,000	$13,000	$22,000
Number of units	÷ 5,000	÷ 5,000	÷ 5,000
Income from operations per unit	$ 0.20	$ 2.60	$ 4.40

Mill's operations require all three grades to be melted in a furnace before being formed. The furnace runs 24 hours a day, 7 days a week, and is a production bottleneck. The furnace hours required per unit of each product are as follows:

Type 5:	6 hours
Type 10:	6 hours
Type 20:	12 hours

The Marketing Department is considering a new marketing and sales campaign.

Which product should be emphasized in the marketing and sales campaign in order to maximize profitability?

EX 24-21 Product decisions under bottlenecked operations **OBJ. 3**

✔ a. Total income from operations, $269,000

Youngstown Glass Company manufactures three types of safety plate glass: large, medium, and small. All three products have high demand. Thus, Youngstown Glass is able to sell all the safety glass that it can make. The production process includes an autoclave operation, which is a pressurized heat treatment. The autoclave is a production bottleneck. Total fixed costs are $85,000 for the company as a whole. In addition, the following information is available about the three products:

	Large	Medium	Small
Unit selling price	$184	$160	$100
Unit variable cost	130	120	76
Unit contribution margin	$ 54	$ 40	$ 24
Autoclave hours per unit	3	2	1
Total process hours per unit	5	4	2
Budgeted units of production	3,000	3,000	3,000

a. Determine the contribution margin by glass type and the total company income from operations for the budgeted units of production.

b. Prepare an analysis showing which product is the most profitable per bottleneck hour.

Appendix

EX 24-22 Total cost concept of product pricing

✔ b. 12.46%

Based on the data presented in Exercise 24-17, assume that Smart Stream Inc. uses the total cost concept of applying the cost-plus approach to product pricing.

a. Determine the total costs and the total cost amount per unit for the production and sale of 10,000 cellular phones.

b. Determine the total cost markup percentage (rounded to two decimal places) for cellular phones.

c. Determine the selling price of cellular phones. Round to the nearest dollar.

Appendix

EX 24-23 Variable cost concept of product pricing

✔ b. 35.42%

Based on the data presented in Exercise 24-17, assume that Smart Stream Inc. uses the variable cost concept of applying the cost-plus approach to product pricing.

a. Determine the variable costs and the variable cost amount per unit for the production and sale of 10,000 cellular phones.

b. Determine the variable cost markup percentage (rounded to two decimal places) for cellular phones.

c. Determine the selling price of cellular phones. Round to the nearest dollar.

Problems Series A

PR 24-1A Differential analysis involving opportunity costs **OBJ. 1**

SPREADSHEET

On October 1, White Way Stores Inc. is considering leasing a building and purchasing the necessary equipment to operate a retail store. Alternatively, the company could use the funds to invest in $180,000 of 6% U.S. Treasury bonds that mature in 16 years. The bonds could be purchased at face value. The following data have been assembled:

Cost of store equipment	$180,000
Life of store equipment	16 years
Estimated residual value of store equipment	$15,000
Yearly costs to operate the store, excluding depreciation of store equipment	$58,000
Yearly expected revenues—years 1–8	$85,000
Yearly expected revenues—years 9–16	$73,000

Instructions

1. Prepare a differential analysis as of October 1, 2014, presenting the proposed operation of the store for the 16 years (Alternative 1) as compared with investing in U.S. Treasury bonds (Alternative 2).
2. Based on the results disclosed by the differential analysis, should the proposal be accepted?
3. If the proposal is accepted, what would be the total estimated income from operations of the store for the 16 years?

PR 24-2A Differential analysis for machine replacement proposal **OBJ. 1**

SPREADSHEET

Universal Graphic Printing Company is considering replacing a machine that has been used in its factory for four years. Relevant data associated with the operations of the old machine and the new machine, neither of which has any estimated residual value, are as follows:

Old Machine	
Cost of machine, 10-year life	$75,300
Annual depreciation (straight-line)	7,530
Annual manufacturing costs, excluding depreciation	21,300
Annual nonmanufacturing operating expenses	5,200
Annual revenue	67,500
Current estimated selling price of machine	26,800

New Machine	
Cost of machine, six-year life	$111,000
Annual depreciation (straight-line)	18,500
Estimated annual manufacturing costs, excluding depreciation	6,400

Annual nonmanufacturing operating expenses and revenue are not expected to be affected by purchase of the new machine.

Instructions

1. Prepare a differential analysis as of April 30, 2014, comparing operations using the present machine (Alternative 1) with operations using the new machine (Alternative 2). The analysis should indicate the total differential income that would result over the six-year period if the new machine is acquired.
2. List other factors that should be considered before a final decision is reached.

PR 24-3A Differential analysis for sales promotion proposal **OBJ. 1**

✔ 1. Differential revenue, −$112,000

SPREADSHEET

Essence of Esther Cosmetics Company is planning a one-month campaign for September to promote sales of one of its two cosmetics products. A total of $150,000 has been budgeted for advertising, contests, redeemable coupons, and other promotional activities. The following data have been assembled for their possible usefulness in deciding which of the products to select for the campaign:

	Moisturizer	Perfume
Unit selling price	$48	$52
Unit production costs:		
Direct materials	$ 8	$13
Direct labor	3	4
Variable factory overhead	2	4
Fixed factory overhead	6	4
Total unit production costs	$19	$25
Unit variable selling expenses	14	13
Unit fixed selling expenses	10	5
Total unit costs	$43	$43
Operating income per unit	$ 5	$ 9

No increase in facilities would be necessary to produce and sell the increased output. It is anticipated that 24,000 additional units of moisturizer or 20,000 additional units of perfume could be sold without changing the unit selling price of either product.

Instructions

1. Prepare a differential analysis as of August 21, 2014, to determine whether to promote moisturizer (Alternative 1) or perfume (Alternative 2).
2. The sales manager had tentatively decided to promote perfume, estimating that operating income would be increased by $30,000 ($9 operating income per unit for 20,000 units, less promotion expenses of $150,000). The manager also believed that the selection of moisturizer would reduce operating income by $30,000 ($5 operating income per unit for 24,000 units, less promotion expenses of $150,000). State briefly your reasons for supporting or opposing the tentative decision.

PR 24-4A Differential analysis for further processing **OBJ. 1**

✔ 1. Raw sugar income, $23,800

The management of Dominican Sugar Company is considering whether to process further raw sugar into refined sugar. Refined sugar can be sold for $2.20 per pound, and raw sugar can be sold without further processing for $1.40 per pound. Raw sugar is produced in batches of 42,000 pounds by processing 100,000 pounds of sugar cane, which costs $0.35 per pound of cane. Refined sugar will require additional processing costs of $0.50 per pound of raw sugar, and 1.25 pounds of raw sugar will produce 1 pound of refined sugar.

Instructions

1. Prepare a differential analysis as of March 24, 2014, to determine whether to sell raw sugar (Alternative 1) or process further into refined sugar (Alternative 2).
2. Briefly report your recommendations.

PR 24-5A Product pricing using the cost-plus approach concepts; differential analysis for accepting additional business **OBJ. 1,2, and Appendix**

✔ 2. b. Markup percentage, 44%

Crystal Displays Inc. recently began production of a new product, flat panel displays, which required the investment of $1,500,000 in assets. The costs of producing and selling 5,000 units of flat panel displays are estimated as follows:

Variable costs per unit:		Fixed costs:	
Direct materials	$120	Factory overhead	$250,000
Direct labor	30	Selling and administrative expenses	150,000
Factory overhead	50		
Selling and administrative expenses	35		
Total	$235		

Crystal Displays Inc. is currently considering establishing a selling price for flat panel displays. The president of Crystal Displays has decided to use the cost-plus approach to product pricing and has indicated that the displays must earn a 15% rate of return on invested assets.

Instructions

1. Determine the amount of desired profit from the production and sale of flat panel displays.
2. Assuming that the product cost concept is used, determine (a) the cost amount per unit, (b) the markup percentage, and (c) the selling price of flat panel displays.
3. **Appendix** Assuming that the total cost concept is used, determine (a) the cost amount per unit, (b) the markup percentage (rounded to two decimal places), and (c) the selling price of flat panel displays (rounded to nearest whole dollar).
4. **Appendix** Assuming that the variable cost concept is used, determine (a) the cost amount per unit, (b) the markup percentage (rounded to two decimal places), and (c) the selling price of flat panel displays (rounded to nearest whole dollar).
5. Comment on any additional considerations that could influence establishing the selling price for flat panel displays.
6. Assume that as of August 1, 2014, 3,000 units of flat panel displays have been produced and sold during the current year. Analysis of the domestic market indicates that 2,000 additional units are expected to be sold during the remainder of the year at the normal product price determined under the product cost concept. On August 3, Crystal Displays Inc. received an offer from Maple Leaf Visual Inc. for 800 units of flat panel displays at $225 each. Maple Leaf Visual Inc. will market the units in Canada under its own brand name, and no variable selling and administrative expenses associated with the sale will be incurred by Crystal Displays Inc. The additional business is not expected to affect the domestic sales of flat panel displays, and the additional units could be produced using existing factory, selling, and administrative capacity.
   a. Prepare a differential analysis of the proposed sale to Maple Leaf Visual Inc.
   b. Based on the differential analysis in part (a), should the proposal be accepted?

PR 24-6A Product pricing and profit analysis with bottleneck operations **OBJ. 3**

✔ 1. High Grade, $10

SPREADSHEET

Hercules Steel Company produces three grades of steel: high, good, and regular grade. Each of these products (grades) has high demand in the market, and Hercules is able to sell as much as it can produce of all three. The furnace operation is a bottleneck in the process and is running at 100% of capacity. Hercules wants to improve steel operation profitability. The variable conversion cost is $15 per process hour. The fixed cost is $200,000. In addition, the cost analyst was able to determine the following information about the three products:

	High Grade	Good Grade	Regular Grade
Budgeted units produced	5,000	5,000	5,000
Total process hours per unit	12	11	10
Furnace hours per unit	4	3	2.5
Unit selling price	$280	$270	$250
Direct materials cost per unit	$90	$84	$80

The furnace operation is part of the total process for each of these three products. Thus, for example, 4.0 of the 12.0 hours required to process High Grade steel are associated with the furnace.

Instructions

1. Determine the unit contribution margin for each product.
2. Provide an analysis to determine the relative product profitability, assuming that the furnace is a bottleneck.

Problems Series B

PR 24-1B Differential analysis involving opportunity costs — OBJ. 1

SPREADSHEET

On July 1, Coastal Distribution Company is considering leasing a building and buying the necessary equipment to operate a public warehouse. Alternatively, the company could use the funds to invest in $740,000 of 5% U.S. Treasury bonds that mature in 14 years. The bonds could be purchased at face value. The following data have been assembled:

Cost of equipment	$740,000
Life of equipment	14 years
Estimated residual value of equipment	$75,000
Yearly costs to operate the warehouse, excluding depreciation of equipment	$175,000
Yearly expected revenues—years 1–7	$280,000
Yearly expected revenues—years 8–14	$240,000

Instructions

1. Prepare a differential analysis as of July 1, 2014, presenting the proposed operation of the warehouse for the 14 years (Alternative 1) as compared with investing in U.S. Treasury bonds (Alternative 2).
2. Based on the results disclosed by the differential analysis, should the proposal be accepted?
3. If the proposal is accepted, what is the total estimated income from operations of the warehouse for the 14 years?

PR 24-2B Differential analysis for machine replacement proposal — OBJ. 1

SPREADSHEET

Flint Tooling Company is considering replacing a machine that has been used in its factory for two years. Relevant data associated with the operations of the old machine and the new machine, neither of which has any estimated residual value, are as follows:

Old Machine	
Cost of machine, eight-year life	$38,000
Annual depreciation (straight-line)	4,750
Annual manufacturing costs, excluding depreciation	12,400
Annual nonmanufacturing operating expenses	2,700
Annual revenue	32,400
Current estimated selling price of the machine	12,900

New Machine	
Cost of machine, six-year life	$57,000
Annual depreciation (straight-line)	9,500
Estimated annual manufacturing costs, exclusive of depreciation	3,400

Annual nonmanufacturing operating expenses and revenue are not expected to be affected by purchase of the new machine.

Instructions

1. Prepare a differential analysis as of November 8, 2014, comparing operations using the present machine (Alternative 1) with operations using the new machine (Alternative 2). The analysis should indicate the differential income that would result over the six-year period if the new machine is acquired.
2. List other factors that should be considered before a final decision is reached.

PR 24-3B Differential analysis for sales promotion proposal **OBJ. 1**

✔ 1. Differential revenue, $105,000

SPREADSHEET

Sole Mates Inc. is planning a one-month campaign for July to promote sales of one of its two shoe products. A total of $100,000 has been budgeted for advertising, contests, redeemable coupons, and other promotional activities. The following data have been assembled for their possible usefulness in deciding which of the products to select for the campaign.

	Tennis Shoe	Walking Shoe
Unit selling price	$ 85	$100
Unit production costs:		
Direct materials	$ 19	$ 32
Direct labor	8	12
Variable factory overhead	7	5
Fixed factory overhead	16	11
Total unit production costs	$ 50	$ 60
Unit variable selling expenses	6	10
Unit fixed selling expenses	20	15
Total unit costs	$ 76	$ 85
Operating income per unit	$ 9	$ 15

No increase in facilities would be necessary to produce and sell the increased output. It is anticipated that 7,000 additional units of tennis shoes or 7,000 additional units of walking shoes could be sold without changing the unit selling price of either product.

Instructions

1. Prepare a differential analysis as of June 19, 2014, to determine whether to promote tennis shoes (Alternative 1) or walking shoes (Alternative 2).
2. The sales manager had tentatively decided to promote walking shoes, estimating that operating income would be increased by $5,000 ($15 operating income per unit for 7,000 units, less promotion expenses of $100,000). The manager also believed that the selection of tennis shoes would reduce operating income by $37,000 ($9 operating income per unit for 7,000 units, less promotion expenses of $100,000). State briefly your reasons for supporting or opposing the tentative decision.

PR 24-4B Differential analysis for further processing **OBJ. 1**

✔ 1. Ingot income, $35,500

The management of International Aluminum Co. is considering whether to process aluminum ingot further into rolled aluminum. Rolled aluminum can be sold for $2,200 per ton, and ingot can be sold without further processing for $1,100 per ton. Ingot is produced in batches of 80 tons by smelting 500 tons of bauxite, which costs $105 per ton of bauxite. Rolled aluminum will require additional processing costs of $620 per ton of ingot, and 1.25 tons of ingot will produce 1 ton of rolled aluminum (due to trim losses).

Instructions

1. Prepare a differential analysis as of February 5, 2014, to determine whether to sell aluminum ingot (Alternative 1) or process further into rolled aluminum (Alternative 2).
2. Briefly report your recommendations.

PR 24-5B Product pricing using the cost-plus approach concepts; differential analysis for accepting additional business **OBJ. 1,2, and Appendix**

✔ 2. b. Markup percentage, 30%

Night Glow Inc. recently began production of a new product, the halogen light, which required the investment of $600,000 in assets. The costs of producing and selling 10,000 halogen lights are estimated as follows:

Variable costs per unit:		Fixed costs:	
Direct materials	$32	Factory overhead	$180,000
Direct labor	12	Selling and administrative expenses	80,000
Factory overhead	8		
Selling and administrative expenses	7		
Total	$59		

Night Glow Inc. is currently considering establishing a selling price for the halogen light. The president of Night Glow Inc. has decided to use the cost-plus approach to product pricing and has indicated that the halogen light must earn a 10% rate of return on invested assets.

Instructions

1. Determine the amount of desired profit from the production and sale of the halogen light.
2. Assuming that the product cost concept is used, determine (a) the cost amount per unit, (b) the markup percentage, and (c) the selling price of the halogen light.
3. **Appendix** Assuming that the total cost concept is used, determine (a) the cost amount per unit, (b) the markup percentage (rounded to two decimal places), and (c) the selling price of the halogen light (rounded to the nearest whole dollar).
4. **Appendix** Assuming that the variable cost concept is used, determine (a) the cost amount per unit, (b) the markup percentage (rounded to two decimal places), and (c) the selling price of the halogen light (rounded to nearest whole dollar).
5. Comment on any additional considerations that could influence establishing the selling price for the halogen light.
6. Assume that as of September 1, 2014, 7,000 units of halogen light have been produced and sold during the current year. Analysis of the domestic market indicates that 3,000 additional units of the halogen light are expected to be sold during the remainder of the year at the normal product price determined under the product cost concept. On September 5, Night Glow Inc. received an offer from Tokyo Lighting Inc. for 1,600 units of the halogen light at $57 each. Tokyo Lighting Inc. will market the units in Japan under its own brand name, and no variable selling and administrative expenses associated with the sale will be incurred by Night Glow Inc. The additional business is not expected to affect the domestic sales of the halogen light, and the additional units could be produced using existing productive, selling, and administrative capacity.
   a. Prepare a differential analysis of the proposed sale to Tokyo Lighting Inc.
   b. Based on the differential analysis in part (a), should the proposal be accepted?

PR 24-6B Product pricing and profit analysis with bottleneck operations **OBJ. 3**

✔ 1. Ethylene, $15

SPREADSHEET

Wilmington Chemical Company produces three products: ethylene, butane, and ester. Each of these products has high demand in the market, and Wilmington Chemical is able to sell as much as it can produce of all three. The reaction operation is a bottleneck in the process and is running at 100% of capacity. Wilmington wants to improve chemical operation profitability. The variable conversion cost is $10 per process hour. The fixed cost is $400,000. In addition, the cost analyst was able to determine the following information about the three products:

	Ethylene	Butane	Ester
Budgeted units produced	9,000	9,000	9,000
Total process hours per unit	4.0	4.0	3.0
Reactor hours per unit	1.5	1.0	0.5
Unit selling price	$170	$155	$130
Direct materials cost per unit	$115	$88	$85

The reaction operation is part of the total process for each of these three products. Thus, for example, 1.5 of the 4.0 hours required to process ethylene is associated with the reactor.

Instructions

1. Determine the unit contribution margin for each product.
2. Provide an analysis to determine the relative product profitabilities, assuming that the reactor is a bottleneck.

Cases & Projects

CP 24-1 Ethics and professional conduct in business

Aaron McKinney is a cost accountant for Majik Systems Inc. Martin Dodd, vice president of marketing, has asked Aaron to meet with representatives of Majik Systems' major competitor to discuss product cost data. Martin indicates that the sharing of these data will enable Majik Systems to determine a fair and equitable price for its products.

Would it be ethical for Aaron to attend the meeting and share the relevant cost data?

CP 24-2 Decision on accepting additional business

A manager of Varden Sporting Goods Company is considering accepting an order from an overseas customer. This customer has requested an order for 20,000 dozen golf balls at a price of $22 per dozen. The variable cost to manufacture a dozen golf balls is $18 per dozen. The full cost is $25 per dozen. Varden has a normal selling price of $35 per dozen. Varden's plant has just enough excess capacity on the second shift to make the overseas order.

What are some considerations in accepting or rejecting this order?

CP 24-3 Accept business at a special price

Internet Project

If you are not familiar with Priceline.com Inc., go to its Web site. Assume that an individual "names a price" of $85 on Priceline.com for a room in Seattle, Washington, on April 22. Assume that April 22 is a Saturday, with low expected room demand in Seattle at a Marriott International, Inc., hotel, so there is excess room capacity. The fully allocated cost per room per day is assumed from hotel records as follows:

Housekeeping labor cost*	$ 38
Hotel depreciation expense	43
Cost of room supplies (soap, paper, etc.)	8
Laundry labor and material cost*	10
Cost of desk staff	6
Utility cost (mostly air conditioning)	5
Total cost per room per day	$110

*Both housekeeping and laundry staff include many part-time workers, so that the workload is variable to demand.

Should Marriott accept the customer bid for a night in Seattle on April 22 at a price of $85?

CP 24-4 Cost-plus and target costing concepts

The following conversation took place between Juanita Jackson, vice president of marketing, and Les Miles, controller of Diamond Computer Company:

Juanita: I am really excited about our new computer coming out. I think it will be a real market success.

Les: I'm really glad you think so. I know that our success will be determined by our price. If our price is too high, our competitors will be the ones with the market success.

Juanita: Don't worry about it. We'll just mark our product cost up by 25% and it will all work out. I know we'll make money at those markups. By the way, what does the estimated product cost look like?

Les: Well, there's the rub. The product cost looks as if it's going to come in at around $1,200. With a 25% markup, that will give us a selling price of $1,500.

Juanita: I see your concern. That's a little high. Our research indicates that computer prices are dropping and that this type of computer should be selling for around $1,250 when we release it to the market.

Les: I'm not sure what to do.

Juanita: Let me see if I can help. How much of the $1,200 is fixed cost?

Les: About $200.

Juanita: There you go. The fixed cost is sunk. We don't need to consider it in our pricing decision. If we reduce the product cost by $200, the new price with a 25% markup would be right at $1,250. Boy, I was really worried for a minute there. I knew something wasn't right.

a. If you were Les, how would you respond to Juanita's solution to the pricing problem?
b. How might target costing be used to help solve this pricing dilemma?

CP 24-5 Pricing decisions and markup on variable costs

Internet Project

Group Project

Many businesses are offering their products and services over the Internet. Some of these companies and their Internet addresses are listed below.

Company Name	Internet Address (URL)	Product
Delta Air Lines	http://www.delta.com	Airline tickets
Amazon.com	http://www.amazon.com	Books
Dell Inc.	http://www.dell.com	Personal computers

a. In groups of three, assign each person in your group to one of the Internet sites listed above. For each site, determine the following:
   1. A product (or service) description.
   2. A product price.
   3. A list of costs that are required to produce and sell the product selected in part (1) as listed in the annual report on SEC Form 10-K.
   4. Whether the costs identified in part (3) are fixed costs or variable costs.

b. Which of the three products do you believe has the largest markup on variable cost?

	Present Value of $1 (Exhibit 1)
Present value of $1 for 1 year @12%	0.893
Present value of $1 for 2 years @12%	0.797
Present value of $1 for 3 years @12%	0.712
Present value of $1 for 4 years @12%	0.636
Present value of $1 for 5 years @12%	0.567
Present value of an annuity of $1 for 5 years (from Exhibit 2)	3.605

Multiplying $100 by 3.605 yields the same amount ($360.50) as follows:

Present Value		Amount to Be Received Annually for 5 Years		Present Value of an Annuity of $1 to Be Received for 5 Years (Exhibit 2)
$360.50	=	$100	×	3.605

This is the same amount ($360.50) that was determined in the preceding illustration by five successive multiplications.

EXHIBIT 2

Partial Present Value of an Annuity Table

Present Value of an Annuity of $1 at Compound Interest

Year	6%	10%	12%	15%	20%
1	0.943	0.909	0.893	0.870	0.833
2	1.833	1.736	1.690	1.626	1.528
3	2.673	2.487	2.402	2.283	2.106
4	3.465	3.170	3.037	2.855	2.589
5	4.212	3.791	3.605	3.353	2.991
6	4.917	4.355	4.111	3.785	3.326
7	5.582	4.868	4.564	4.160	3.605
8	6.210	5.335	4.968	4.487	3.837
9	6.802	5.759	5.328	4.772	4.031
10	7.360	6.145	5.650	5.019	4.192

Net Present Value Method

The **net present value method** compares the amount to be invested with the present value of the net cash inflows. It is sometimes called the *discounted cash flow method.*

The interest rate (return) used in net present value analysis is the company's minimum desired rate of return. This rate, sometimes termed the *hurdle rate*, is based on such factors as the purpose of the investment and the cost of obtaining funds for the investment. If the present value of the cash inflows equals or exceeds the amount to be invested, the proposal is desirable.

To illustrate, assume the following data for a proposed investment in new equipment:

Note:
The net present value method compares an investment's initial cash outflow with the present value of its cash inflows.

Cost of new equipment	$200,000
Expected useful life	5 years
Minimum desired rate of return	10%
Expected cash flows to be received each year:	
Year 1	$ 70,000
Year 2	60,000
Year 3	50,000
Year 4	40,000
Year 5	40,000
Total expected cash flows	$260,000

The present value of the net cash flow for each year is computed by multiplying the net cash flow for the year by the present value factor of $1 for that year as shown below.

Year	Present Value of $1 at 10%	Net Cash Flow	Present Value of Net Cash Flow
1	0.909	$ 70,000	$ 63,630
2	0.826	60,000	49,560
3	0.751	50,000	37,550
4	0.683	40,000	27,320
5	0.621	40,000	24,840
Total		$260,000	$202,900
Less amount to be invested			200,000
Net present value			$ 2,900

The preceding computations are also graphically illustrated below.

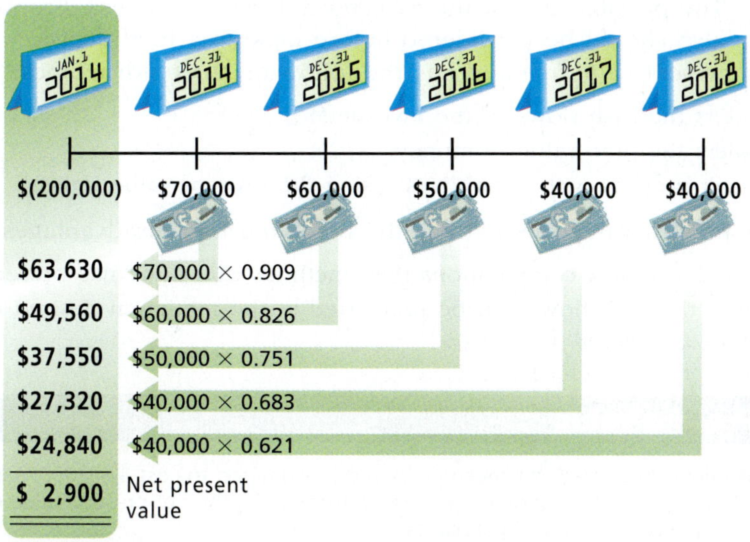

The net present value of $2,900 indicates that the purchase of the new equipment is expected to recover the investment and provide more than the minimum rate of return of 10%. Thus, the purchase of the new equipment is desirable.

When capital investment funds are limited and the proposals involve different investments, a ranking of the proposals can be prepared by using a present value index. The **present value index** is computed as follows:

$$\text{Present Value Index} = \frac{\text{Total Present Value of Net Cash Flow}}{\text{Amount to Be Invested}}$$

The present value index for the investment in the preceding illustration is 1.0145, as computed below.

$$\text{Present Value Index} = \frac{\text{Total Present Value of Net Cash Flow}}{\text{Amount to Be Invested}}$$

$$\text{Present Value Index} = \frac{\$202{,}900}{\$200{,}000} = 1.0145$$

Assume that a company is considering three proposals. The net present value and the present value index for each proposal are as follows:

	Proposal A	Proposal B	Proposal C
Total present value of net cash flow	$107,000	$86,400	$86,400
Less amount to be invested	100,000	80,000	90,000
Net present value	$ 7,000	$ 6,400	$ (3,600)
Present value index:			
Proposal A ($107,000/$100,000)	1.07		
Proposal B ($86,400/$80,000)		1.08	
Proposal C ($86,400/$90,000)			0.96

A project will have a present value index greater than 1 when the net present value is positive. This is the case for Proposals A and B. When the net present value is negative, the present value index will be less than 1, as is the case for Proposal C.

Although Proposal A has the largest net present value, the present value indices indicate that it is not as desirable as Proposal B. That is, Proposal B returns $1.08 present value per dollar invested, whereas Proposal A returns only $1.07. Proposal B requires an investment of $80,000, compared to an investment of $100,000 for Proposal A. The possible use of the $20,000 difference between Proposals A and B investments also should be considered before making a final decision.

The use of spreadsheet software such as Microsoft Excel can simplify present value computations.

The net present value method has the following three advantages:

1. It considers the cash flows of the investment.
2. It considers the time value of money.
3. It can rank projects with equal lives, using the present value index.

The net present value method has the following two disadvantages:

1. It has more complex computations than methods that don't use present value.
2. It assumes the cash flows can be reinvested at the minimum desired rate of return, which may not be valid.

Example Exercise 25-3 Net Present Value OBJ 3

A project has estimated annual net cash flows of $50,000 for seven years and is estimated to cost $240,000. Assume a minimum acceptable rate of return of 12%. Using Exhibit 2 on page 1168, determine (a) the net present value of the project and (b) the present value index, rounded to two decimal places.

Follow My Example 25-3

a. ($11,800) [($50,000 × 4.564) – $240,000]
b. 0.95 ($228,200/$240,000)

Practice Exercises: **PE 25-3A, PE 25-3B**

Internal Rate of Return Method

The **internal rate of return (IRR) method** uses present value concepts to compute the rate of return from a capital investment proposal based on its expected net cash flows. This method, sometimes called the *time-adjusted rate of return method*, starts with the proposal's net cash flows and works backward to estimate the proposal's expected rate of return.

To illustrate, assume that management is evaluating the following proposal to purchase new equipment:

Cost of new equipment	$33,530
Yearly expected cash flows to be received	$10,000
Expected life	5 years
Minimum desired rate of return	12%

The present value of the net cash flows, using the present value of an annuity table in Exhibit 2 on page 1168, is $2,520, as shown in Exhibit 3.

EXHIBIT 3

Net Present Value Analysis at 12%

Annual net cash flow (at the end of each of five years)	$10,000
Present value of an annuity of $1 at 12% for five years (Exhibit 2)	× 3.605
Present value of annual net cash flows	$36,050
Less amount to be invested	33,530
Net present value	$ 2,520

In Exhibit 3, the $36,050 present value of the cash inflows, based on a 12% rate of return, is greater than the $33,530 to be invested. Thus, the internal rate of return must be greater than 12%. Through trial and error, the rate of return equating the $33,530 cost of the investment with the present value of the net cash flows can be determined to be 15%, as shown below.

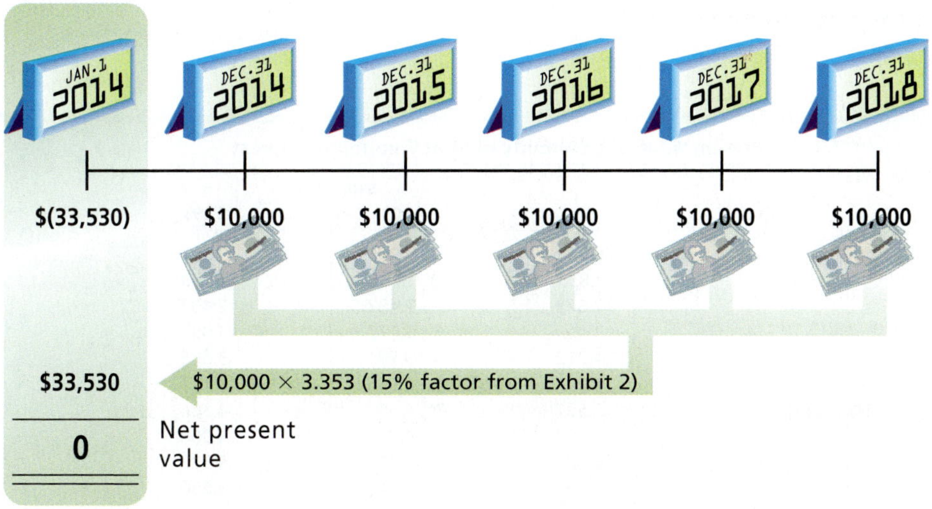

When equal annual net cash flows are expected from a proposal, as in the above example, the internal rate of return can be determined as follows:[4]

Step 1. Determine a present value factor for an annuity of $1 as follows:

$$\text{Present Value Factor for an Annuity of \$1} = \frac{\text{Amount to Be Invested}}{\text{Equal Annual Net Cash Flows}}$$

Step 2. Locate the present value factor determined in Step 1 in the present value of an annuity of $1 table (Exhibit 2 on page 1168) as follows:
  a. Locate the number of years of expected useful life of the investment in the Year column.
  b. Proceed horizontally across the table until you find the present value factor computed in Step 1.

Step 3. Identify the internal rate of return by the heading of the column in which the present value factor in Step 2 is located.

4 To simplify, equal annual net cash flows are assumed. If the net cash flows are not equal, spreadsheet software can be used to determine the rate of return.

To illustrate, assume that management is evaluating the following proposal to purchase new equipment:

Cost of new equipment	$97,360
Yearly expected cash flows to be received	$20,000
Expected useful life	7 years

Step 1: The present value factor for an annuity of $1 is 4.868, as shown below.

$$\text{Present Value Factor for an Annuity of \$1} = \frac{\text{Amount to Be Invested}}{\text{Equal Annual Net Cash Flows}}$$

$$\text{Present Value Factor for an Annuity of \$1} = \frac{\$97{,}360}{\$20{,}000} = 4.868$$

Using the partial present value of an annuity of $1 table shown below and a period of seven years, the factor 4.868 is related to 10%. Thus, the internal rate of return for this proposal is 10%.

Present Value of an Annuity of $1 at Compound Interest

	Year	6%		10% (Step 3)	12%
	1	0.943		0.909	0.893
	2	1.833		1.736	1.690
	3	2.673		2.487	2.402
	4	3.465		3.170	3.037
	5	4.212		3.791	3.605
	6	4.917	**Step 2(b)**	4.355	4.111
Step 2(a)	7	5.582	→	4.868	4.564
	8	6.210		5.335	4.968
	9	6.802		5.759	5.328
	10	7.360		6.145	5.650

Step 1: Determine present value factor for an annuity of $1 $= \frac{\$97{,}360}{\$20{,}000} = 4.868$

If the minimum acceptable rate of return is 10%, then the proposal is considered acceptable. Several proposals can be ranked by their internal rates of return. The proposal with the highest rate is the most desirable.

The internal rate of return method has the following three advantages:

1. It considers the cash flows of the investment.
2. It considers the time value of money.
3. It ranks proposals based upon the cash flows over their complete useful life, even if the project lives are not the same.

The internal rate of return method has the following two disadvantages:

1. It has complex computations, requiring a computer if the periodic cash flows are not equal.
2. It assumes the cash received from a proposal can be reinvested at the internal rate of return, which may not be valid.

Example Exercise 25-4 Internal Rate of Return OBJ 3

A project is estimated to cost $208,175 and provide annual net cash flows of $55,000 for six years. Determine the internal rate of return for this project, using Exhibit 2 on page 1168.

Follow My Example 25-4

15% [($208,175/$55,000) = 3.785, the present value of an annuity factor for six periods at 15%, from Exhibit 2]

Practice Exercises: **PE 25-4A, PE 25-4B**

Business Connection

PANERA BREAD STORE RATE OF RETURN

Panera Bread owns, operates, and franchises bakery-cafes throughout the United States. A recent annual report to the Securities and Exchange Commission (SEC Form 10-K) disclosed the following information about an average company-owned store:

Operating profit	$376,000
Depreciation	86,000
Investment	880,000

Assume that the operating profit and depreciation will remain unchanged for the next 15 years. Assume operating profit plus depreciation approximates annual net cash flows, and that the investment residual value will be zero. The average rate of return and internal rate of return can then be estimated. The average rate of return on a company-owned store is:

$$\frac{\$376{,}000}{\$880{,}000/2} = 85.5\%$$

The internal rate of return is calculated by first determining the present value of an annuity of $1:

$$\text{Present Value of an Annuity of \$1} = \frac{\$880{,}000}{\$376{,}000 + \$86{,}000} = 1.90$$

For a period of three years, this factor implies an internal rate of return over 20% (from Exhibit 2). However, if we more realistically assumed these cash flows for 15 years, Panera's company-owned stores generate an estimated internal rate of return of approximately 52% (from a spreadsheet calculation). Clearly, both investment evaluation methods indicate a highly successful business.

© Jeff Greenberg/Alamy

Factors That Complicate Capital Investment Analysis

OBJ 4 List and describe factors that complicate capital investment analysis.

Four widely used methods of evaluating capital investment proposals have been described and illustrated in this chapter. In practice, additional factors such as the following may impact capital investment decisions:

1. Income tax
2. Proposals with unequal lives
3. Leasing versus purchasing
4. Uncertainty
5. Changes in price levels
6. Qualitative factors

Income Tax

The impact of income taxes on capital investment decisions can be material. For example, in determining depreciation for federal income tax purposes, useful lives that are much shorter than the actual useful lives are often used. Also, depreciation for tax purposes often differs from depreciation for financial statement purposes. As a result, the timing of the cash flows for income taxes can have a significant impact on capital investment analysis.[5]

Unequal Proposal Lives

The prior capital investment illustrations assumed that the alternative proposals had the same useful lives. In practice, however, proposals often have different lives.

To illustrate, assume that a company is considering purchasing a new truck or a new computer network. The data for each proposal are shown below.

	Truck	Computer Network
Cost	$100,000	$100,000
Minimum desired rate of return	10%	10%
Expected useful life	8 years	5 years
Yearly expected cash flows to be received:		
Year 1	$ 30,000	$ 30,000
Year 2	30,000	30,000
Year 3	25,000	30,000
Year 4	20,000	30,000
Year 5	15,000	35,000
Year 6	15,000	0
Year 7	10,000	0
Year 8	10,000	0
Total	$155,000	$155,000

The expected cash flows and net present value for each proposal are shown in Exhibit 4. Because of the unequal useful lives, however, the net present values in Exhibit 4 are not comparable.

To make the proposals comparable, the useful lives are adjusted to end at the same time. In this illustration, this is done by assuming that the truck will be sold at the end of five years. The selling price (residual value) of the truck at the end of five years is estimated and included in the cash inflows. Both proposals will then cover five years; thus, the net present value analyses will be comparable.

To illustrate, assume that the truck's estimated selling price (residual value) at the end of Year 5 is $40,000. Exhibit 5 shows the truck's revised present value analysis assuming a five-year life.

As shown in Exhibit 5, the net present value for the truck exceeds the net present value for the computer network by $1,835 ($18,640 – $16,805). Thus, the truck is the more attractive of the two proposals.

Example Exercise 25-5 Net Present Value—Unequal Lives

OBJ 4

Project 1 requires an original investment of $50,000. The project will yield cash flows of $12,000 per year for seven years. Project 2 has a calculated net present value of $8,900 over a five-year life. Project 1 could be sold at the end of five years for a price of $30,000. (a) Determine the net present value of Project 1 over a five-year life, with residual value, assuming a minimum rate of return of 12%. (b) Which project provides the greatest net present value?

Follow My Example 25-5

Project 1

a. Present value of $12,000 per year at 12% for 5 years	$43,260	[$12,000 × 3.605 (Exhibit 2, 12%, 5 years)]
Present value of $30,000 at 12% at the end of 5 years	17,010	[$30,000 × 0.567 (Exhibit 1, 12%, 5 years)]
Total present value of Project 1	$60,270	
Total cost of Project 1	50,000	
Net present value of Project 1	$10,270	

b. Project 1—$10,270 is greater than the net present value of Project 2, $8,900.

Practice Exercises: **PE 25-5A, PE 25-5B**

5 The impact of taxes on capital investment analysis is covered in advanced accounting textbooks.

EXHIBIT 4 **Net Present Value Analysis—Unequal Lives of Proposals**

	A	B	C	D
1			Truck	
2	Year	Present	Net	Present
3		Value of	Cash	Value of
4		$1 at 10%	Flow	Net Cash Flow
5	1	0.909	$ 30,000	$ 27,270
6	2	0.826	30,000	24,780
7	3	0.751	25,000	18,775
8	4	0.683	20,000	13,660
9	5	0.621	15,000	9,315
10	6	0.564	15,000	8,460
11	7	0.513	10,000	5,130
12	8	0.467	10,000	4,670
13	Total		$155,000	$112,060
14				
15	Less amount to be invested			100,000
16	Net present value			$ 12,060

	A	B	C	D
1			Computer Network	
2	Year	Present	Net	Present
3		Value of	Cash	Value of
4		$1 at 10%	Flow	Net Cash Flow
5	1	0.909	$ 30,000	$ 27,270
6	2	0.826	30,000	24,780
7	3	0.751	30,000	22,530
8	4	0.683	30,000	20,490
9	5	0.621	35,000	21,735
10	Total		$155,000	$116,805
11				
12	Less amount to be invested			100,000
13	Net present value			$ 16,805

Cannot be compared (unequal lives)

Compared (equal lives)

EXHIBIT 5 **Net Present Value Analysis—Equalized Lives of Proposals**

	A	B	C	D
1			Truck—Revised to 5-Year Life	
2	Year	Present	Net	Present
3		Value of	Cash	Value of
4		$1 at 10%	Flow	Net Cash Flow
5	1	0.909	$ 30,000	$ 27,270
6	2	0.826	30,000	24,780
7	3	0.751	25,000	18,775
8	4	0.683	20,000	13,660
9	5	0.621	15,000	9,315
10	5 (Residual			
11	value)	0.621	40,000	24,840
12	Total		$160,000	$118,640
13				
14	Less amount to be invested			100,000
15	Net present value			$ 18,640

Truck Net Present Value Greater than Computer Network Net Present Value by $1,835

Lease versus Capital Investment

Leasing fixed assets is common in many industries. For example, hospitals often lease medical equipment. Some advantages of leasing a fixed asset include the following:

1. The company has use of the fixed asset without spending large amounts of cash to purchase the asset.
2. The company eliminates the risk of owning an obsolete asset.
3. The company may deduct the annual lease payments for income tax purposes.

OBJ 5

Diagram the capital rationing process.

Key Points Capital rationing refers to the process by which management allocates available investment funds among competing capital investment proposals. A diagram of the capital rationing process appears in Exhibit 6.

Learning Outcomes	Example Exercises	Practice Exercises
• Define *capital rationing*.		
• Diagram the capital rationing process.		

Key Terms

annuity (1167)
average rate of return (1163)
capital investment analysis (1162)
capital rationing (1177)
cash payback period (1164)
currency exchange rate (1176)
inflation (1176)
internal rate of return (IRR) method (1170)
net present value method (1168)
present value concept (1166)
present value index (1169)
present value of an annuity (1167)
time value of money concept (1162)

Illustrative Problem

The capital investment committee of Hopewell Company is currently considering two investments. The estimated income from operations and net cash flows expected from each investment are as follows:

	Truck		Equipment	
Year	**Income from Operations**	**Net Cash Flow**	**Income from Operations**	**Net Cash Flow**
1	$ 6,000	$ 22,000	$13,000	$ 29,000
2	9,000	25,000	10,000	26,000
3	10,000	26,000	8,000	24,000
4	8,000	24,000	8,000	24,000
5	11,000	27,000	3,000	19,000
	$44,000	$124,000	$42,000	$122,000

Each investment requires $80,000. Straight-line depreciation will be used, and no residual value is expected. The committee has selected a rate of 15% for purposes of the net present value analysis.

Instructions

1. Compute the following:
   a. The average rate of return for each investment.
   b. The net present value for each investment. Use the present value of $1 table appearing in this chapter (Exhibit 1).
2. Why is the net present value of the equipment greater than the truck, even though its average rate of return is less?
3. Prepare a summary for the capital investment committee, advising it on the relative merits of the two investments.

Solution

1. a. Average rate of return for the truck:

$$\frac{\$44{,}000 \div 5}{(\$80{,}000 + \$0) \div 2} = 22\%$$

Average rate of return for the equipment:

$$\frac{\$42{,}000 \div 5}{(\$80{,}000 + \$0) \div 2} = 21\%$$

b. Net present value analysis:

Year	Present Value of $1 at 15%	Net Cash Flow: Truck	Net Cash Flow: Equipment	Present Value of Net Cash Flow: Truck	Present Value of Net Cash Flow: Equipment
1	0.870	$ 22,000	$ 29,000	$19,140	$25,230
2	0.756	25,000	26,000	18,900	19,656
3	0.658	26,000	24,000	17,108	15,792
4	0.572	24,000	24,000	13,728	13,728
5	0.497	27,000	19,000	13,419	9,443
Total		$124,000	$122,000	$82,295	$83,849
Less amount to be invested				80,000	80,000
Net present value				$ 2,295	$ 3,849

2. The equipment has a lower average rate of return than the truck because the equipment's total income from operations for the five years is $42,000, which is $2,000 less than the truck's. Even so, the net present value of the equipment is greater than that of the truck, because the equipment has higher cash flows in the early years.
3. Both investments exceed the selected rate established for the net present value analysis. The truck has a higher average rate of return, but the equipment offers a larger net present value. Thus, if only one of the two investments can be accepted, the equipment would be the more attractive.

Discussion Questions

1. What are the principal objections to the use of the average rate of return method in evaluating capital investment proposals?
2. Discuss the principal limitations of the cash payback method for evaluating capital investment proposals.
3. Why would the average rate of return differ from the internal rate of return on the same project?
4. Your boss has suggested that a one-year payback period is the same as a 100% average rate of return. Do you agree?
5. Why would the cash payback method understate the attractiveness of a project with a large residual value?
6. Why would the use of the cash payback period for analyzing the financial performance of theatrical releases from a motion picture production studio be supported over the net present value method?
7. A net present value analysis used to evaluate a proposed equipment acquisition indicated a $7,900 net present value. What is the meaning of the $7,900 as it relates to the desirability of the proposal?
8. Two projects have an identical net present value of $9,000. Are both projects equal in desirability?
9. What are the major disadvantages of the use of the net present value method of analyzing capital investment proposals?
10. What are the major disadvantages of the use of the internal rate of return method of analyzing capital investment proposals?
11. What are the major advantages of leasing a fixed asset rather than purchasing it?
12. Give an example of a qualitative factor that should be considered in a capital investment analysis related to acquiring automated factory equipment.

Practice Exercises

Example Exercises

EE 25-1 *p. 1164*

PE 25-1A Average rate of return **OBJ. 2**

Determine the average rate of return for a project that is estimated to yield total income of $148,500 over five years, has a cost of $300,000, and has a $30,000 residual value.

EE 25-1 *p. 1164*

PE 25-1B Average rate of return **OBJ. 2**

Determine the average rate of return for a project that is estimated to yield total income of $36,000 over three years, has a cost of $70,000, and has a $10,000 residual value.

EE 25-2 *p. 1165*

PE 25-2A Cash payback period **OBJ. 2**

A project has estimated annual net cash flows of $135,800. It is estimated to cost $787,640. Determine the cash payback period. Round to one decimal place.

EE 25-2 *p. 1165*

PE 25-2B Cash payback period **OBJ. 2**

A project has estimated annual net cash flows of $9,300. It is estimated to cost $41,850. Determine the cash payback period. Round to one decimal place.

Example Exercises

EE 25-3 *p. 1170*

PE 25-3A Net present value **OBJ. 3**

A project has estimated annual net cash flows of $12,200 for five years and is estimated to cost $39,800. Assume a minimum acceptable rate of return of 12%. Using Exhibit 2, determine (1) the net present value of the project and (2) the present value index, rounded to two decimal places.

EE 25-3 *p. 1170*

PE 25-3B Net present value **OBJ. 3**

A project has estimated annual net cash flows of $96,200 for four years and is estimated to cost $315,500. Assume a minimum acceptable rate of return of 10%. Using Exhibit 2, determine (1) the net present value of the project and (2) the present value index, rounded to two decimal places.

EE 25-4 *p. 1173*

PE 25-4A Internal rate of return **OBJ. 3**

A project is estimated to cost $74,035 and provide annual net cash flows of $17,000 for six years. Determine the internal rate of return for this project, using Exhibit 2.

EE 25-4 *p. 1173*

PE 25-4B Internal rate of return **OBJ. 3**

A project is estimated to cost $362,672 and provide annual net cash flows of $76,000 for nine years. Determine the internal rate of return for this project, using Exhibit 2.

EE 25-5 *p. 1174*

PE 25-5A Net present value—unequal lives **OBJ. 4**

Project A requires an original investment of $22,500. The project will yield cash flows of $5,000 per year for nine years. Project B has a calculated net present value of $3,500 over a six-year life. Project A could be sold at the end of six years for a price of $12,000. (a) Determine the net present value of Project A over a six-year life, with residual value, assuming a minimum rate of return of 12%. (b) Which project provides the greatest net present value?

EE 25-5 *p. 1174*

PE 25-5B Net present value—unequal lives **OBJ. 4**

Project 1 requires an original investment of $55,000. The project will yield cash flows of $15,000 per year for seven years. Project 2 has a calculated net present value of $5,000 over a four-year life. Project 1 could be sold at the end of four years for a price of $38,000. (a) Determine the net present value of Project 1 over a four-year life, with residual value, assuming a minimum rate of return of 20%. (b) Which project provides the greatest net present value?

Exercises

EX 25-1 Average rate of return **OBJ. 2**

✔ Testing equipment, 6%

The following data are accumulated by Bio Metrics Inc. in evaluating two competing capital investment proposals:

	Testing Equipment	Vehicle
Amount of investment	$104,000	$32,000
Useful life	6 years	8 years
Estimated residual value	0	0
Estimated total income over the useful life	$18,720	$15,360

Determine the expected average rate of return for each proposal.

EX 25-2 Average rate of return—cost savings **OBJ. 2**

Midwest Fabricators Inc. is considering an investment in equipment that will replace direct labor. The equipment has a cost of $132,000 with a $16,000 residual value and a 10-year life. The equipment will replace one employee who has an average wage of $34,000 per year. In addition, the equipment will have operating and energy costs of $5,380 per year.

Determine the average rate of return on the equipment, giving effect to straight-line depreciation on the investment.

EX 25-3 Average rate of return—new product **OBJ. 2**

✔ Average annual income, $240,000

Ray Zor Inc. is considering an investment in new equipment that will be used to manufacture a smartphone. The phone is expected to generate additional annual sales of 4,000 units at $410 per unit. The equipment has a cost of $525,000, residual value of $75,000, and an eight-year life. The equipment can only be used to manufacture the phone. The cost to manufacture the phone is shown below.

Cost per unit:	
Direct labor	$ 30
Direct materials	280
Factory overhead (including depreciation)	40
Total cost per unit	$350

Determine the average rate of return on the equipment.

EX 25-4 Calculate cash flows **OBJ. 2**

Year 1: ($47,200)

Cornucopia Inc. is planning to invest in new manufacturing equipment to make a new garden tool. The new garden tool is expected to generate additional annual sales of 4,000 units at $68 each. The new manufacturing equipment will cost $107,000 and is expected to have a 10-year life and $13,000 residual value. Selling expenses related to the new product are expected to be 5% of sales revenue. The cost to manufacture the product includes the following on a per-unit basis:

Direct labor	$ 9.00
Direct materials	36.00
Fixed factory overhead—depreciation	2.35
Variable factory overhead	4.65
Total	$52.00

Determine the net cash flows for the first year of the project, Years 2–9, and for the last year of the project.

EX 25-5 Cash payback period **OBJ. 2**

✔ Location 1: 5 years

Nations Trust is evaluating two capital investment proposals for a drive-up ATM kiosk, each requiring an investment of $380,000 and each with an eight-year life and expected total net cash flows of $608,000. Location 1 is expected to provide equal annual net cash flows of $76,000, and Location 2 is expected to have the following unequal annual net cash flows:

Year 1	$120,000	Year 5	$57,000
Year 2	90,000	Year 6	57,000
Year 3	90,000	Year 7	57,000
Year 4	80,000	Year 8	57,000

Determine the cash payback period for both location proposals.

EX 25-6 Cash payback method **OBJ. 2**

SPREADSHEET

Lily Products Company is considering an investment in one of two new product lines. The investment required for either product line is $540,000. The net cash flows associated with each product are as follows:

Year	Liquid Soap	Body Lotion
1	$170,000	$ 90,000
2	150,000	90,000
3	120,000	90,000
4	100,000	90,000
5	70,000	90,000
6	40,000	90,000
7	40,000	90,000
8	30,000	90,000
Total	$720,000	$720,000

a. Recommend a product offering to Lily Products Company, based on the cash payback period for each product line.

b. Why is one product line preferred over the other, even though they both have the same total net cash flows through eight periods?

EX 25-7 Net present value method **OBJ. 3**

✔ a. NPV, $7,158

The following data are accumulated by Bannister Company in evaluating the purchase of $48,500 of equipment, having a four-year useful life:

	Net Income	Net Cash Flow
Year 1	$ 6,875	$19,000
Year 2	10,875	23,000
Year 3	7,875	20,000
Year 4	2,875	15,000

a. Assuming that the desired rate of return is 15%, determine the net present value for the proposal. Use the table of the present value of $1 appearing in Exhibit 1 of this chapter.

b. Would management be likely to look with favor on the proposal? Explain.

EX 25-8 Net present value method **OBJ. 3**

✔ a. 2014, $13,000

AM Express Inc. is considering the purchase of an additional delivery vehicle for $55,000 on January 1, 2014. The truck is expected to have a five-year life with an expected residual value of $15,000 at the end of five years. The expected additional revenues from the added delivery capacity are anticipated to be $58,000 per year for each of the next five years. A driver will cost $42,000 in 2014, with an expected annual salary increase of $1,000 for each year thereafter. The annual operating costs for the truck are estimated to be $3,000 per year.

a. Determine the expected annual net cash flows from the delivery truck investment for 2014–2018.

b. Calculate the net present value of the investment, assuming that the minimum desired rate of return is 12%. Use the present value of $1 table appearing in Exhibit 1 of this chapter.

c. Is the additional truck a good investment based on your analysis?

EX 25-9 Net present value method—annuity **OBJ. 3**

✔ a. $19 million

Keystone Hotels is considering the construction of a new hotel for $120 million. The expected life of the hotel is 30 years, with no residual value. The hotel is expected to earn revenues of $47 million per year. Total expenses, including depreciation, are expected to be $32 million per year. Keystone management has set a minimum acceptable rate of return of 14%.

a. Determine the equal annual net cash flows from operating the hotel.

b. Calculate the net present value of the new hotel, using the present value of an annuity of $1 table found in Appendix A. Round to the nearest million dollars.

c. Does your analysis support construction of the new hotel?

EX 25-10 Net present value method—annuity **OBJ. 3**

✔ a. $46,000

Briggs Excavation Company is planning an investment of $132,000 for a bulldozer. The bulldozer is expected to operate for 1,500 hours per year for five years. Customers will be charged $110 per hour for bulldozer work. The bulldozer operator costs $28 per hour in wages and benefits. The bulldozer is expected to require annual maintenance costing $8,000. The bulldozer uses fuel that is expected to cost $46 per hour of bulldozer operation.

a. Determine the equal annual net cash flows from operating the bulldozer.

b. Determine the net present value of the investment, assuming that the desired rate of return is 10%. Use the present value of an annuity of $1 table in the chapter (Exhibit 2). Round to the nearest dollar.

c. Should Briggs invest in the bulldozer, based on this analysis?

d. Determine the number of operating hours such that the present value of cash flows equals the amount to be invested.

EX 25-11 Net present value method **OBJ. 3**

✔ a. $157,600,000

Carnival Corporation has recently placed into service some of the largest cruise ships in the world. One of these ships, the *Carnival Breeze*, can hold up to 3,600 passengers, and it can cost $750 million to build. Assume the following additional information:

- There will be 330 cruise days per year operated at a full capacity of 3,600 passengers.
- The variable expenses per passenger are estimated to be $140 per cruise day.
- The revenue per passenger is expected to be $340 per cruise day.
- The fixed expenses for running the ship, other than depreciation, are estimated to be $80,000,000 per year.
- The ship has a service life of 10 years, with a residual value of $140,000,000 at the end of 10 years.

a. Determine the annual net cash flow from operating the cruise ship.

b. Determine the net present value of this investment, assuming a 12% minimum rate of return. Use the present value tables provided in the chapter in determining your answer.

EX 25-12 Present value index **OBJ. 3**

✔ Lee's Summit, 0.96

Double K Doughnuts has computed the net present value for capital expenditure at two locations. Relevant data related to the computation are as follows:

	Blue Springs	Lee's Summit
Total present value of net cash flow	$540,750	$484,800
Less amount to be invested	525,000	505,000
Net present value	$ 15,750	$ (20,200)

a. Determine the present value index for each proposal.

b. Which location does your analysis support?

EX 25-13 Net present value method and present value index — OBJ. 3

✔ b. Packing machine, 1.55

Diamond & Turf Inc. is considering an investment in one of two machines. The sewing machine will increase productivity from sewing 150 baseballs per hour to sewing 290 per hour. The contribution margin per unit is $0.32 per baseball. Assume that any increased production of baseballs can be sold. The second machine is an automatic packing machine for the golf ball line. The packing machine will reduce packing labor cost. The labor cost saved is equivalent to $21 per hour. The sewing machine will cost $260,000, have an eight-year life, and will operate for 1,800 hours per year. The packing machine will cost $85,000, have an eight-year life, and will operate for 1,400 hours per year. Diamond & Turf seeks a minimum rate of return of 15% on its investments.

a. Determine the net present value for the two machines. Use the present value of an annuity of $1 table in the chapter (Exhibit 2). Round to the nearest dollar.

b. Determine the present value index for the two machines. Round to two decimal places.

c. If Diamond & Turf has sufficient funds for only one of the machines and qualitative factors are equal between the two machines, in which machine should it invest?

EX 25-14 Average rate of return, cash payback period, net present value method — OBJ. 2, 3

✔ b. 6 years

Great Plains Railroad Inc. is considering acquiring equipment at a cost of $450,000. The equipment has an estimated life of 10 years and no residual value. It is expected to provide yearly net cash flows of $75,000. The company's minimum desired rate of return for net present value analysis is 10%.

Compute the following:

a. The average rate of return, giving effect to straight-line depreciation on the investment. Round whole percent to one decimal place.

b. The cash payback period.

c. The net present value. Use the present value of an annuity of $1 table appearing in this chapter (Exhibit 2). Round to the nearest dollar.

EX 25-15 Cash payback period, net present value analysis, and qualitative considerations — OBJ. 2, 3, 4

✔ a. 4 years

The plant manager of Taiwan Electronics Company is considering the purchase of new automated assembly equipment. The new equipment will cost $1,400,000. The manager believes that the new investment will result in direct labor savings of $350,000 per year for 10 years.

a. What is the payback period on this project?

b. What is the net present value, assuming a 10% rate of return? Use the present value of an annuity of $1 table in Exhibit 2.

c. What else should the manager consider in the analysis?

EX 25-16 Internal rate of return method — OBJ. 3

✔ a. 4.111

The internal rate of return method is used by Merit Construction Co. in analyzing a capital expenditure proposal that involves an investment of $82,220 and annual net cash flows of $20,000 for each of the six years of its useful life.

a. Determine a present value factor for an annuity of $1, which can be used in determining the internal rate of return.

b. Using the factor determined in part (a) and the present value of an annuity of $1 table appearing in this chapter (Exhibit 2), determine the internal rate of return for the proposal.

EX 25-17 Internal rate of return method **OBJ. 3, 4**

The Canyons Resort, a Utah ski resort, recently announced a $415 million expansion of lodging properties, lifts, and terrain. Assume that this investment is estimated to produce $99 million in equal annual cash flows for each of the first 10 years of the project life.

a. Determine the expected internal rate of return of this project for 10 years, using the present value of an annuity of $1 table found in Exhibit 2.

b. What are some uncertainties that could reduce the internal rate of return of this project?

EX 25-18 Internal rate of return method—two projects **OBJ. 3**

✔ **a. Delivery truck, 15%**

Munch N' Crunch Snack Company is considering two possible investments: a delivery truck or a bagging machine. The delivery truck would cost $43,056 and could be used to deliver an additional 95,000 bags of pretzels per year. Each bag of pretzels can be sold for a contribution margin of $0.45. The delivery truck operating expenses, excluding depreciation, are $1.35 per mile for 24,000 miles per year. The bagging machine would replace an old bagging machine, and its net investment cost would be $61,614. The new machine would require three fewer hours of direct labor per day. Direct labor is $18 per hour. There are 250 operating days in the year. Both the truck and the bagging machine are estimated to have seven-year lives. The minimum rate of return is 13%. However, Munch N' Crunch has funds to invest in only one of the projects.

a. Compute the internal rate of return for each investment. Use the present value of an annuity of $1 table appearing in this chapter (Exhibit 2).

b. Provide a memo to management, with a recommendation.

EX 25-19 Net present value method and internal rate of return method **OBJ. 3**

✔ **a. ($12,845)**

Buckeye Healthcare Corp. is proposing to spend $186,725 on an eight-year project that has estimated net cash flows of $35,000 for each of the eight years.

a. Compute the net present value, using a rate of return of 12%. Use the present value of an annuity of $1 table in the chapter (Exhibit 2).

b. Based on the analysis prepared in part (a), is the rate of return (1) more than 12%, (2) 12%, or (3) less than 12%? Explain.

c. Determine the internal rate of return by computing a present value factor for an annuity of $1 and using the present value of an annuity of $1 table presented in the text (Exhibit 2).

EX 25-20 Identify error in capital investment analysis calculations **OBJ. 3**

Artscape Inc. is considering the purchase of automated machinery that is expected to have a useful life of five years and no residual value. The average rate of return on the average investment has been computed to be 20%, and the cash payback period was computed to be 5.5 years.

Do you see any reason to question the validity of the data presented? Explain.

EX 25-21 Net present value—unequal lives **OBJ. 3, 4**

✔ **Net present value, Processing mill, $196,220**

SPREADSHEET

Bunker Hill Mining Company has two competing proposals: a processing mill and an electric shovel. Both pieces of equipment have an initial investment of $750,000. The net cash flows estimated for the two proposals are as follows:

	Net Cash Flow	
Year	**Processing Mill**	**Electric Shovel**
1	$310,000	$330,000
2	260,000	325,000
3	260,000	325,000
4	260,000	320,000
5	180,000	
6	130,000	
7	120,000	
8	120,000	

The estimated residual value of the processing mill at the end of Year 4 is $280,000.

Determine which equipment should be favored, comparing the net present values of the two proposals and assuming a minimum rate of return of 15%. Use the present value tables presented in this chapter (Exhibits 1 and 2).

EX 25-22 Net present value—unequal lives **OBJ. 3, 4**

Daisy's Creamery Inc. is considering one of two investment options. Option 1 is a $75,000 investment in new blending equipment that is expected to produce equal annual cash flows of $19,000 for each of seven years. Option 2 is a $90,000 investment in a new computer system that is expected to produce equal annual cash flows of $27,000 for each of five years. The residual value of the blending equipment at the end of the fifth year is estimated to be $15,000. The computer system has no expected residual value at the end of the fifth year.

Assume there is sufficient capital to fund only one of the projects. Determine which project should be selected, comparing the (a) net present values and (b) present value indices of the two projects. Assume a minimum rate of return of 10%. Round the present value index to two decimal places. Use the present value tables presented in this chapter (Exhibits 1 and 2).

Problems Series A

PR 25-1A Average rate of return method, net present value method, and analysis **OBJ. 2, 3**

✔ 1. a. 17.5%

SPREADSHEET

The capital investment committee of Touch of Eden Landscaping Company is considering two capital investments. The estimated income from operations and net cash flows from each investment are as follows:

	Greenhouse		Front End Loader	
Year	Income from Operations	Net Cash Flow	Income from Operations	Net Cash Flow
1	$22,000	$ 38,000	$ 7,000	$ 23,000
2	12,000	28,000	7,000	23,000
3	9,000	25,000	7,000	23,000
4	(4,000)	12,000	7,000	23,000
5	(4,000)	12,000	7,000	23,000
	$35,000	$115,000	$35,000	$115,000

Each project requires an investment of $80,000. Straight-line depreciation will be used, and no residual value is expected. The committee has selected a rate of 12% for purposes of the net present value analysis.

Instructions

1. Compute the following:
   a. The average rate of return for each investment. Round to one decimal place.
   b. The net present value for each investment. Use the present value of $1 table appearing in this chapter (Exhibit 1).
2. Prepare a brief report for the capital investment committee, advising it on the relative merits of the two investments.

PR 25-2A Cash payback period, net present value method, and analysis **OBJ. 2, 3**

✔ 1. b. Plant expansion, $57,010

SPREADSHEET

Celebration Apparel Inc. is considering two investment projects. The estimated net cash flows from each project are as follows:

Learning Objectives

After studying this chapter, you should be able to: *Example Exercises*

OBJ	Objective	Example Exercises
1	Identify three methods used for allocating factory overhead costs to products.	
	Product Costing Allocation Methods	
2	Use a single plantwide factory overhead rate for product costing.	
	Single Plantwide Factory Overhead Rate Method	EE 26-1
3	Use multiple production department factory overhead rates for product costing.	
	Multiple Production Department Factory Overhead Rate Method	
	Department Overhead Rates and Allocation	EE 26-2
	Distortion of Product Costs	EE 26-2
4	Use activity-based costing for product costing.	
	Activity-Based Costing Method	
	Activity Rates and Allocation	EE 26-3
	Distortion in Product Costs	EE 26-3
	Dangers of Product Cost Distortion	EE 26-3
5	Use activity-based costing to allocate selling and administrative expenses to products.	
	Activity-Based Costing for Selling and Administrative Expenses	EE 26-4
6	Use activity-based costing in a service business.	
	Activity-Based Costing in Service Businesses	EE 26-5

At a Glance 26 Page 1218

OBJ 1 Identify three methods used for allocating factory overhead costs to products.

Product Costing Allocation Methods

Determining the cost of a product is termed **product costing**. Product costs consist of direct materials, direct labor, and factory overhead. The direct materials and direct labor are direct costs that can be traced to the product. However, factory overhead includes indirect costs that must be allocated to the product.

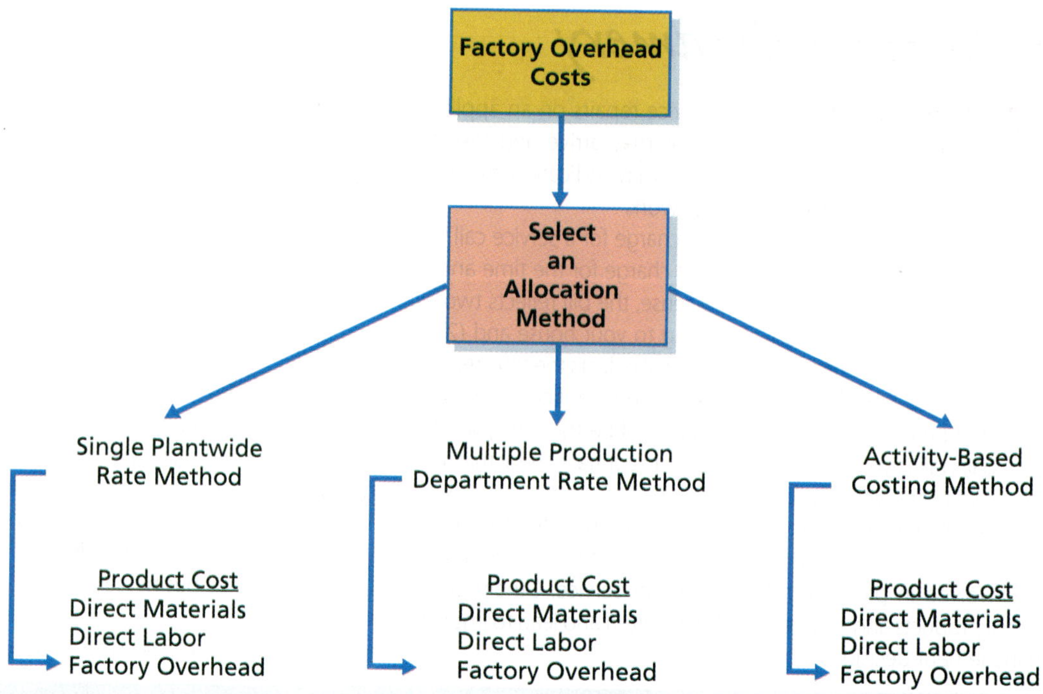

In Chapter 17, the allocation of factory overhead using a predetermined factory overhead rate was illustrated. The most common methods of allocating factory overhead using predetermined factory overhead rates are:

1. Single plantwide factory overhead rate method
2. Multiple production department factory overhead rate method
3. Activity-based costing method

The choice of allocation method is important to managers because the allocation affects the product cost, as shown in the illustration at the bottom of the previous page. Managers are concerned about the accuracy of product costs, which are used for decisions such as determining product mix, establishing product price, and determining whether to discontinue a product line.

Single Plantwide Factory Overhead Rate Method

OBJ 2 Use a single plantwide factory overhead rate for product costing.

A company may use a predetermined factory overhead rate to allocate factory overhead costs to products. Under the **single plantwide factory overhead rate method**, factory overhead costs are allocated to products using only one rate.

To illustrate, assume the following data for Ruiz Company, which manufactures snowmobiles and riding mowers in a single factory.

Total budgeted factory overhead costs for the year	$1,600,000
Total budgeted direct labor hours (as computed below)	20,000 hours

	Snowmobiles	Riding Mowers	Total
Planned production for the year...........	1,000 units	1,000 units	
Direct labor hours per unit	× 10 hours	× 10 hours	
Budgeted direct labor hours	10,000 hours	10,000 hours	20,000 hours

Under the single plantwide factory overhead rate method, the $1,600,000 budgeted factory overhead is applied to all products by using one rate. This rate is computed as follows:

$$\text{Single Plantwide Factory Overhead Rate} = \frac{\text{Total Budgeted Factory Overhead}}{\text{Total Budgeted Plantwide Allocation Base}}$$

The budgeted allocation base is a measure of operating activity in the factory. Common allocation bases would include direct labor hours, direct labor dollars, and machine hours. Ruiz Company allocates factory overhead using budgeted direct labor hours as the plantwide allocation base. Thus, Ruiz's single plantwide factory overhead rate is $80 per direct labor hour, computed as follows:

$$\text{Single Plantwide Factory Overhead Rate} = \frac{\$1{,}600{,}000}{20{,}000 \text{ direct labor hours}}$$

$$\text{Single Plantwide Factory Overhead Rate} = \$80 \text{ per direct labor hour}$$

Ruiz uses the plantwide rate of $80 per direct labor hour to allocate factory overhead to snowmobiles and riding mowers as shown below.

	Single Plantwide Factory Overhead Rate	×	Direct Labor Hours per Unit	=	Factory Overhead Cost per Unit
Snowmobile	$80 per direct labor hour	×	10 direct labor hours	=	$800
Riding mower	$80 per direct labor hour	×	10 direct labor hours	=	$800

As shown above, the factory overhead allocated to each product is $800. This is because each product uses the same number of direct labor hours.

In some cases, selling and administrative expenses may be more related to *customer* behaviors than to differences in products. That is, some customers may demand more service and selling activities than other customers. In such cases, activity-based costing would allocate selling and administrative expenses to customers.

Example Exercise 26-4 Activity-Based Costing: Selling and Administrative Expenses

OBJ 5

Converse Company manufactures and sells LCD display products. Converse uses activity-based costing to determine the cost of the customer return processing and the shipping activity. The customer return processing activity has an activity rate of $90 per return, and the shipping activity has an activity rate of $15 per shipment. Converse shipped 4,000 units of LCD Model A1 in 2,200 shipments (some shipments are more than one unit). There were 200 returns. Determine the (a) total and (b) per-unit customer return processing and shipping activity cost for Model A1.

Follow My Example 26-4

a. Return activity: 200 returns × $90 per return =	$18,000
Shipping activity: 2,200 shipments × $15 per shipment =	33,000
Total activity cost	$51,000
b. $12.75 per unit ($51,000/4,000 units)	

Practice Exercises: **PE 26-4A, PE 26-4B**

OBJ 6 Use activity-based costing in a service business.

Activity-Based Costing in Service Businesses

Service companies need to determine the cost of their services so that they can make pricing, promoting, and other decisions. The use of single and multiple department overhead rate methods may lead to distortions similar to those of manufacturing firms. Thus, many service companies use activity-based costing for determining the cost of services.

To illustrate, assume that Hopewell Hospital uses activity-based costing to allocate hospital overhead to patients. Hopewell Hospital applies activity-based costing by

1. Identifying activities.
2. Determining activity rates for each activity.
3. Allocating overhead costs to patients based upon activity-base usage.

Hopewell Hospital has identified the following activities:

1. Admission
2. Radiological testing
3. Operating room
4. Pathological testing
5. Dietary and laundry

Each activity has an estimated patient activity-base usage. Based on the budgeted costs for each activity and related estimated activity-base usage, the activity rates shown in Exhibit 12 were developed.

To illustrate, assume the following data for radiological testing:

Budgeted costs	$960,000
Total estimated activity-base usage	3,000 images

The activity rate of $320 per radiological image is computed as:

$$\text{Activity Rate} = \frac{\text{Budgeted Activity Cost}}{\text{Total Activity-Base Usage}}$$

$$\text{Radiological Testing Activity Rate} = \frac{\text{Budgeted Radiological Testing}}{\text{Total Estimated Images}}$$

$$= \frac{\$960{,}000}{3{,}000 \text{ images}} = \$320 \text{ per image}$$

EXHIBIT 12 **Activity-Based Costing Method—Hopewell Hospital**

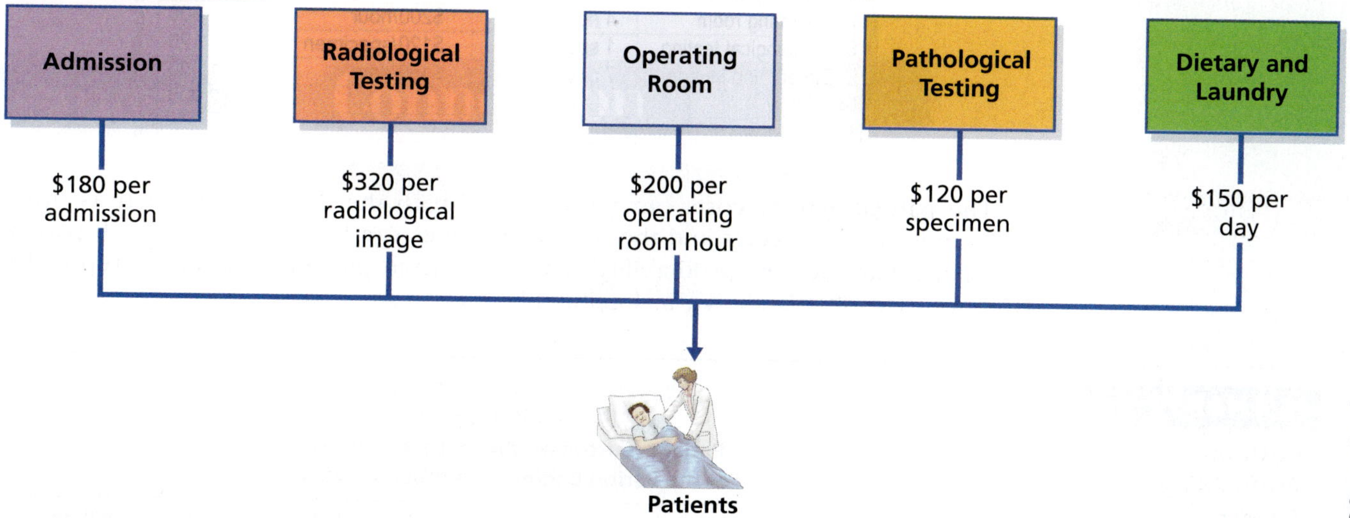

The activity rates for the other activities are determined in a similar manner. These activity rates along with the patient activity-base usage are used to allocate costs to patients as follows:

$$\text{Activity Cost Allocated to Patient} = \text{Patient Activity-Base Usage} \times \text{Activity Rate}$$

To illustrate, assume that Mia Wilson was a patient of the hospital. The hospital overhead services (activities) performed for Mia Wilson are shown below.

	Patient (Mia Wilson) Activity-Base Usage
Admission	1 admission
Radiological testing	2 images
Operating room	4 hours
Pathological testing	1 specimen
Dietary and laundry	7 days

Business Connection

UNIVERSITY AND COMMUNITY PARTNERSHIP—LEARNING YOUR ABC'S

Students at Harvard's Kennedy School of Government joined with the city of Somerville, Massachusetts, in building an activity-based cost system for the city. The students volunteered several hours a week in four-person teams, interviewing city officials within 18 departments. The students were able to determine activity costs, such as the cost to fill a pothole, processing a building permit, or responding to a four-alarm fire. Their study was used by the city in forming the city budget. As stated by some of the students participating on this project: "It makes sense to use the resources of the university for community building. . . . Real-world experience is a tremendous thing to have in your back pocket. We learned from the mayor and the fire chief, who are seasoned professionals in their own right."

Source: *Kennedy School Bulletin*, Spring 2005, "Easy as A-B-C: Students Take on the Somerville Budget Overhaul."

At a Glance 26

OBJ 1 Identify three methods used for allocating factory costs to products.

Key Points Three cost allocation methods used for determining product costs are the (1) single plantwide factory overhead rate method, (2) multiple production department rate method, and (3) activity-based costing method.

Learning Outcome	Example Exercises	Practice Exercises
• List the three methods for allocating factory overhead costs to products.		

OBJ 2 Use a single plantwide factory overhead rate for product costing.

Key Points A single plantwide factory overhead rate can be used to allocate all plant overhead to all products. The single plantwide factory overhead rate is simple to apply, but can lead to product cost distortions.

Learning Outcomes	Example Exercises	Practice Exercises
• Compute the single plantwide factory overhead rate and use it to allocate factory overhead costs to products.	EE26-1	PE26-1A, 26-1B
• Identify the conditions that favor the use of a single plantwide factory overhead rate for allocating factory overhead costs to products.		

OBJ 3 Use multiple production department factory overhead rates for product costing.

Key Points Product costing using multiple production department factory overhead rates requires identifying the factory overhead by each production department. Using these rates can result in greater accuracy than using single plantwide factory overhead rates when:
1. There are significant differences in the factory overhead rates across different production departments.
2. The products require different ratios of allocation-base usage in each production department.

Learning Outcomes	Example Exercises	Practice Exercises
• Compute multiple production department overhead rates and use these rates to allocate factory overhead costs to products.	EE26-2	PE26-2A, 26-2B
• Identify and describe the two conditions that favor the use of multiple production department factory overhead rates for allocating factory overhead costs to products as compared to the single plantwide factory overhead rate method.		

OBJ 4 Use activity-based costing for product costing.

Key Points Activity-based costing requires factory overhead to be budgeted to activities. The budgeted activity costs are allocated to products by multiplying activity rates by the activity-base quantity consumed for each product. Activity-based costing is more accurate when products consume activities in proportions unrelated to plantwide or departmental allocation bases.

Learning Outcomes	Example Exercises	Practice Exercises
• Compute activity rates and use these rates to allocate factory overhead costs to products.	EE26-3	PE26-3A, 26-3B
• Identify the conditions that favor the use of activity-based rates for allocating factory overhead costs to products, as compared to the other two methods of cost allocation.		
• Compare the three factory overhead allocation methods and describe the causes of cost allocation distortion.		

OBJ 5 Use activity-based costing to allocate selling and administrative expenses to products.

Key Points Selling and administrative expenses can be allocated to products for management profit reporting, using activity-based costing. Activity-based costing would be preferred when the products use selling and administrative activities in ratios that are unrelated to their sales volumes.

Learning Outcomes	Example Exercises	Practice Exercises
• Compute selling and administrative activity rates and use these rates to allocate selling and administrative expenses to either a product or customer.	EE26-4	PE26-4A, 26-4B
• Identify the conditions that would favor the use of activity-based costing for allocating selling and administrative expenses.		

OBJ 6 Use activity-based costing in a service business.

Key Points Activity-based costing may be applied in service settings to determine the cost of individual service offerings. Service costs are determined by multiplying activity rates by the amount of activity-base quantities consumed by the customer using the service offering.

Learning Outcomes	Example Exercises	Practice Exercises
• Compute activity rates for service offerings and use these rates to allocate indirect costs to either a service product line or a customer.	EE26-5	PE26-5A, 26-5B
• Prepare a customer profitability report using the cost of activities.		
• Describe how activity-based cost information can be used in a service business for improved decision making.		

Key Terms

activities (1207)
activity base (1209)
activity rates (1208)
activity-based costing (ABC) method (1207)
engineering change order (ECO) (1208)
multiple production department factory overhead rate method (1203)
product costing (1200)
production department factory overhead rate (1204)
setup (1208)
single plantwide factory overhead rate method (1201)

Illustrative Problem

Hammer Company plans to use activity-based costing to determine its product costs. It presently uses a single plantwide factory overhead rate for allocating factory overhead to products, based on direct labor hours. The total factory overhead cost is as follows:

Department	Factory Overhead
Production Support	$1,225,000
Production (factory overhead only)	175,000
Total cost	$1,400,000

The company determined that it performed four major activities in the Production Support Department. These activities, along with their budgeted activity costs, are as follows:

Production Support Activities	Budgeted Activity Cost
Setup	$ 428,750
Production control	245,000
Quality control	183,750
Materials management	367,500
Total	$1,225,000

Hammer Company estimated the following activity-base usage and units produced for each of its three products:

Products	Number of Units	Direct Labor Hrs.	Setups	Production Orders	Inspections	Material Requisitions
TV	10,000	25,000	80	80	35	320
Computer	2,000	10,000	40	40	40	400
Cell phone	50,000	140,000	5	5	0	30
Total cost	62,000	175,000	125	125	75	750

Instructions

1. Determine the factory overhead cost per unit for the TV, computer, and cell phone under the single plantwide factory overhead rate method. Use direct labor hours as the activity base.
2. Determine the factory overhead cost per unit for the TV, computer, and cell phone under activity-based costing. Round to whole cents.
3. Which method provides more accurate product costing? Why?

Solution

1. Single Plantwide Factory Overhead Rate $= \dfrac{\$1{,}400{,}000}{175{,}000 \text{ direct labor hours}}$

$= \$8$ per direct labor hour

Factory overhead cost per unit:

	TV	Computer	Cell Phone
Number of direct labor hours	25,000	10,000	140,000
Single plantwide factory overhead rate	× $8/dlh	× $8/dlh	× $8/dlh
Total factory overhead	$200,000	$ 80,000	$ 1,120,000
Number of units	÷ 10,000	÷ 2,000	÷ 50,000
Factory overhead cost per unit	$ 20.00	$ 40.00	$ 22.40

2. Under activity-based costing, an activity rate must be determined for each activity pool:

Activity	Budgeted Activity Cost	÷	Total Activity-Base Usage	=	Activity Rate
Setup	$428,750	÷	125 setups	=	$3,430 per setup
Production control	$245,000	÷	125 production orders	=	$1,960 per production order
Quality control	$183,750	÷	75 inspections	=	$2,450 per inspection
Materials management	$367,500	÷	750 requisitions	=	$490 per requisition
Production	$175,000	÷	175,000 direct labor hours	=	$1 per direct labor hour

These activity rates can be used to determine the activity-based factory overhead cost per unit as follows:

TV

Activity	Activity-Base Usage	×	Activity Rate	=	Activity Cost
Setup	80 setups	×	$3,430	=	$274,400
Production control	80 production orders	×	$1,960	=	156,800
Quality control	35 inspections	×	$2,450	=	85,750
Materials management	320 requisitions	×	$490	=	156,800
Production	25,000 direct labor hrs.	×	$1	=	25,000
Total factory overhead					$698,750
Unit volume					÷ 10,000
Factory overhead cost per unit					$ 69.88

Computer

Activity	Activity-Base Usage	×	Activity Rate	=	Activity Cost
Setup	40 setups	×	$3,430	=	$137,200
Production control	40 production orders	×	$1,960	=	78,400
Quality control	40 inspections	×	$2,450	=	98,000
Materials management	400 requisitions	×	$490	=	196,000
Production	10,000 direct labor hrs.	×	$1	=	10,000
Total factory overhead					$519,600
Unit volume					÷ 2,000
Factory overhead cost per unit					$ 259.80

Cell phone

Activity	Activity-Base Usage	×	Activity Rate	=	Activity Cost
Setup	5 setups	×	$3,430	=	$ 17,150
Production control	5 production orders	×	$1,960	=	9,800
Quality control	0 inspections	×	$2,450	=	0
Materials management	30 requisitions	×	$490	=	14,700
Production	140,000 direct labor hrs.	×	$1	=	140,000
Total factory overhead					$181,650
Unit volume					÷ 50,000
Factory overhead cost per unit					$ 3.63

3. Activity-based costing is more accurate, compared to the single plantwide factory overhead rate method. Activity-based costing properly shows that the cell phone is actually less expensive to make, while the other two products are more expensive to make. The reason is that the single plantwide factory overhead rate method fails to account for activity costs correctly. The setup, production control, quality-control, and materials management activities are all performed on products in amounts that are proportionately different than their volumes. For example, the computer requires many of these activities relative to its actual unit volume. The computer requires 40 setups over a volume of 2,000 units (average production run size = 50 units), while the cell phone has only 5 setups over 50,000 units (average production run size = 10,000 units). Thus, the computer requires greater support costs relative to the cell phone.

The cell phone requires minimum activity support because it is scheduled in large batches and requires no inspections (has high quality) and few requisitions. The other two products exhibit the opposite characteristics.

Discussion Questions

1. Why would management be concerned about the accuracy of product costs?
2. Why would a manufacturing company with multiple production departments still prefer to use a single plantwide overhead rate?
3. How do the multiple production department and the single plantwide factory overhead rate methods differ?
4. Under what two conditions would the multiple production department factory overhead rate method provide more accurate product costs than the single plantwide factory overhead rate method?
5. How does activity-based costing differ from the multiple production department factory overhead rate method?
6. Shipping, selling, marketing, sales order processing, return processing, and advertising activities can be related to products by using activity-based costing. Would allocating these activities to products for financial statement reporting be acceptable according to GAAP?
7. What would happen to net income if the activities noted in Discussion Question 6 were allocated to products for financial statement reporting and the inventory increased?
8. Under what circumstances might the activity-based costing method provide more accurate product costs than the multiple production department factory overhead rate method?
9. When might activity-based costing be preferred over using a relative amount of product sales in allocating selling and administrative expenses to products?
10. How can activity-based costing be used in service companies?

Practice Exercises

Example Exercises

EE 26-1 *p. 1202* **PE 26-1A Single plantwide overhead rate** **OBJ. 2**

The total factory overhead for Klein Calvin Inc. is budgeted for the year at $225,000. Klein Calvin manufactures two types of men's pants: jeans and khakis. The jeans and khakis each require 0.15 direct labor hour for manufacture. Each product is budgeted for 15,000 units of production for the year. Determine (a) the total number of budgeted direct labor hours for the year, (b) the single plantwide factory overhead rate, and (c) the factory overhead allocated per unit for each product using the single plantwide factory overhead rate.

EE 26-1 *p. 1202* **PE 26-1B Single plantwide overhead rate** **OBJ. 2**

The total factory overhead for Bardot Marine Company is budgeted for the year at $600,000. Bardot Marine manufactures two types of boats: speedboats and bass boats. The speedboat and bass boat each require 12 direct labor hours for manufacture. Each product is budgeted for 250 units of production for the year. Determine (a) the total number of budgeted direct labor hours for the year, (b) the single plantwide factory overhead rate, and (c) the factory overhead allocated per unit for each product using the single plantwide factory overhead rate.

EE 26-2 *p. 1207* **PE 26-2A Multiple production department overhead rates** **OBJ. 3**

The total factory overhead for Klein Calvin is budgeted for the year at $225,000, divided into two departments: Cutting, $72,000, and Sewing, $153,000. Klein Calvin manufactures two types of men's pants: jeans and khakis. The jeans require 0.05 direct labor hour in Cutting and 0.10 direct labor hour in Sewing. The khakis require 0.10 direct labor hour in Cutting and 0.05 direct labor hour in Sewing. Each product is budgeted for 15,000 units of production for the year. Determine (a) the total number of budgeted direct labor hours for the year in each department, (b) the departmental factory overhead rates for both departments, and (c) the factory overhead allocated per unit for each product using the department factory overhead allocation rates.

EE 26-2 *p. 1207* **PE 26-2B Multiple production department overhead rates** **OBJ. 3**

The total factory overhead for Bardot Marine Company is budgeted for the year at $600,000 divided into two departments: Fabrication, $420,000, and Assembly, $180,000. Bardot Marine manufactures two types of boats: speedboats and bass boats. The speedboats require 8 direct labor hours in Fabrication and 4 direct labor hours in Assembly. The bass boats require 4 direct labor hours in Fabrication and 8 direct labor hours in Assembly. Each product is budgeted for 250 units of production for the year. Determine (a) the total number of budgeted direct labor hours for the year in each department, (b) the departmental factory overhead rates for both departments, and (c) the factory overhead allocated per unit for each product using the department factory overhead allocation rates.

EE 26-3 *p. 1212* **PE 26-3A Activity-based costing: factory overhead costs** **OBJ. 4**

The total factory overhead for Klein Calvin is budgeted for the year at $225,000, divided into four activities: cutting, $22,500; sewing, $45,000; setup, $100,000; and inspection, $57,500. Klein Calvin manufactures two types of men's pants: jeans and khakis. The activity-base usage quantities for each product by each activity are as follows:

Example Exercises

	Cutting	Sewing	Setup	Inspection
Jeans	750 dlh	1,500 dlh	1,600 setups	4,000 inspections
Khakis	1,500	750	400	1,750
	2,250 dlh	2,250 dlh	2,000 setups	5,750 inspections

Each product is budgeted for 15,000 units of production for the year. Determine (a) the activity rates for each activity and (b) the activity-based factory overhead per unit for each product.

EE 26-3 *p. 1212* **PE 26-3B Activity-based costing: factory overhead costs** **OBJ. 4**

The total factory overhead for Bardot Marine Company is budgeted for the year at $600,000, divided into four activities: fabrication, $204,000; assembly, $105,000; setup, $156,000; and inspection, $135,000. Bardot Marine manufactures two types of boats: speedboats and bass boats. The activity-base usage quantities for each product by each activity are as follows:

	Fabrication	Assembly	Setup	Inspection
Speedboat	2,000 dlh	1,000 dlh	300 setups	1,100 inspections
Bass boat	1,000	2,000	100	400
	3,000 dlh	3,000 dlh	400 setups	1,500 inspections

Each product is budgeted for 250 units of production for the year. Determine (a) the activity rates for each activity and (b) the activity-based factory overhead per unit for each product.

EE 26-4 *p. 1214* **PE 26-4A Activity-based costing: selling and administrative expenses** **OBJ. 5**

Fancy Feet Company manufactures and sells shoes. Fancy Feet uses activity-based costing to determine the cost of the sales order processing and the shipping activity. The sales order processing activity has an activity rate of $12 per sales order, and the shipping activity has an activity rate of $20 per shipment. Fancy Feet sold 27,500 units of walking shoes, which consisted of 5,000 orders and 1,400 shipments. Determine (a) the total and (b) the per-unit sales order processing and shipping activity cost for walking shoes.

EE 26-4 *p. 1214* **PE 26-4B Activity-based costing: selling and administrative expenses** **OBJ. 5**

Jungle Junior Company manufactures and sells outdoor play equipment. Jungle Junior uses activity-based costing to determine the cost of the sales order processing and the customer return activity. The sales order processing activity has an activity rate of $20 per sales order, and the customer return activity has an activity rate of $100 per return. Jungle Junior sold 2,500 swing sets, which consisted of 750 orders and 80 returns. Determine (a) the total and (b) the per-unit sales order processing and customer return activity cost for swing sets.

EE 26-5 *p. 1217* **PE 26-5A Activity-based costing: service business** **OBJ. 6**

Draper Bank uses activity-based costing to determine the cost of servicing customers. There are three activity pools: teller transaction processing, check processing, and ATM transaction processing. The activity rates associated with each activity pool are $3.50 per teller transaction, $0.12 per canceled check, and $0.10 per ATM transaction. Corner Cleaners Inc. had 12 teller transactions, 100 canceled checks, and 20 ATM transactions during the month. Determine the total monthly activity-based cost for Corner Cleaners Inc. during the month.

EE 26-5 *p. 1217* **PE 26-5B Activity-based costing: service business** **OBJ. 6**

Sterling Hotel uses activity-based costing to determine the cost of servicing customers. There are three activity pools: guest check-in, room cleaning, and meal service. The activity rates associated with each activity pool are $8.00 per guest check-in, $25.00 per room cleaning, and $4.00 per served meal (not including food). Ginny Campbell visited the hotel for a 3-night stay. Campbell had three meals in the hotel during her visit. Determine the total activity-based cost for Campbell's visit.

Exercises

EX 26-1 Single plantwide factory overhead rate **OBJ. 2**

Jesse James Metal Inc.'s Fabrication Department incurred $420,000 of factory overhead cost in producing gears and sprockets. The two products consumed a total of 6,000 direct machine hours. Of that amount, sprockets consumed 3,200 direct machine hours.

Determine the total amount of factory overhead that should be allocated to sprockets using machine hours as the allocation base.

EX 26-2 Single plantwide factory overhead rate **OBJ. 2**

✔ a. $50 per direct labor hour

Armstrong Band Instruments Inc. makes three musical instruments: trumpets, tubas, and trombones. The budgeted factory overhead cost is $145,500. Factory overhead is allocated to the three products on the basis of direct labor hours. The products have the following budgeted production volume and direct labor hours per unit:

	Budgeted Production Volume	Direct Labor Hours per Unit
Trumpets	1,600 units	0.6
Tubas	500	1.5
Trombones	1,000	1.2

a. Determine the single plantwide factory overhead rate.
b. Use the factory overhead rate in (a) to determine the amount of total and per-unit factory overhead allocated to each of the three products.

EX 26-3 Single plantwide factory overhead rate **OBJ. 2**

✔ a. $70 per processing hour

Savory Snack Food Company manufactures three types of snack foods: tortilla chips, potato chips, and pretzels. The company has budgeted the following costs for the upcoming period:

Factory depreciation	$ 21,120
Indirect labor	52,800
Factory electricity	5,280
Indirect materials	18,800
Selling expenses	22,000
Administrative expenses	12,000
Total costs	$132,000

Factory overhead is allocated to the three products on the basis of processing hours. The products had the following production budget and processing hours per case:

	Budgeted Volume (Cases)	Processing Hours per Case
Tortilla chips	3,000	0.16
Potato chips	5,250	0.12
Pretzels	1,450	0.20
Total	9,700	

a. Determine the single plantwide factory overhead rate.
b. Use the factory overhead rate in (a) to determine the amount of total and per-case factory overhead allocated to each of the three products under generally accepted accounting principles.

EX 26-4 Product costs and product profitability reports, using a single plantwide factory overhead rate

OBJ. 2

✔ c. Pistons gross profit, $108,000

SPREADSHEET

Orange County Engine Parts Inc. (OCEP) produces three products—pistons, valves, and cams—for the heavy equipment industry. OCEP has a very simple production process and product line and uses a single plantwide factory overhead rate to allocate overhead to the three products. The factory overhead rate is based on direct labor hours. Information about the three products for 2014 is as follows:

	Budgeted Volume (Units)	Direct Labor Hours per Unit	Price per Unit	Direct Materials per Unit
Pistons	7,200	0.20	$50	$25
Valves	28,800	0.15	10	4
Cams	1,200	0.32	70	29

The estimated direct labor rate is $20 per direct labor hour. Beginning and ending inventories are negligible and are, thus, assumed to be zero. The budgeted factory overhead for OCEP is $184,320.

a. Determine the plantwide factory overhead rate.
b. Determine the factory overhead and direct labor cost per unit for each product.
c. Use the information above to construct a budgeted gross profit report by product line for the year ended December 31, 2014. Include the gross profit as a percent of sales in the last line of your report, rounded to one decimal place.
d. What does the report in (c) indicate to you?

EX 26-5 Multiple production department factory overhead rate method

OBJ. 3

✔ b. Small glove, $17.80 per unit

SPREADSHEET

Sports Glove Company produces three types of high performance sports gloves: small, medium, and large. A glove pattern is first stenciled onto leather in the Pattern Department. The stenciled patterns are then sent to the Cut and Sew Department, where the final glove is cut and sewed together. Sports Glove uses the multiple production department factory overhead rate method of allocating factory overhead costs. Its factory overhead costs were budgeted as follows:

Pattern Department overhead	$204,000
Cut and Sew Department overhead	303,600
Total	$507,600

The direct labor estimated for each production department was as follows:

Pattern Department	2,400 direct labor hours
Cut and Sew Department	2,760
Total	5,160 direct labor hours

Direct labor hours are used to allocate the production department overhead to the products. The direct labor hours per unit for each product for each production department were obtained from the engineering records as follows:

Production Departments	Small Glove	Medium Glove	Large Glove
Pattern Department	0.08	0.10	0.12
Cut and Sew Department	0.10	0.12	0.14
Direct labor hours per unit	0.18	0.22	0.26

a. Determine the two production department factory overhead rates.
b. Use the two production department factory overhead rates to determine the factory overhead per unit for each product.

EX 26-6 Single plantwide and multiple production department factory overhead rate methods and product cost distortion **OBJ. 2, 3**

✔ **b. Portable computer, $630 per unit**

Mango Computer Company manufactures a desktop and portable computer through two production departments, Assembly and Testing. Presently, the company uses a single plantwide factory overhead rate for allocating factory overhead to the two products. However, management is considering using the multiple production department factory overhead rate method. The following factory overhead was budgeted for Mango:

Assembly Department	$187,500
Testing Department	600,000
Total	$787,500

Direct machine hours were estimated as follows:

Assembly Department	2,500 hours
Testing Department	5,000
Total	7,500 hours

In addition, the direct machine hours (dmh) used to produce a unit of each product in each department were determined from engineering records, as follows:

	Desktop	Portable
Assembly Department	1.0 dmh	2.0 dmh
Testing Department	2.0	4.0
Total machine hours per unit	3.0 dmh	6.0 dmh

a. Determine the per-unit factory overhead allocated to the desktop and portable computers under the single plantwide factory overhead rate method, using direct machine hours as the allocation base.
b. Determine the per-unit factory overhead allocated to the desktop and portable computers under the multiple production department factory overhead rate method, using direct machine hours as the allocation base for each department.
c. Recommend to management a product costing approach, based on your analyses in (a) and (b). Support your recommendation.

EX 26-7 Single plantwide and multiple production department factory overhead rate methods and product cost distortion **OBJ. 2, 3**

✔ **b. Diesel engine, $420 per unit**

The management of Cobalt Engines Inc. manufactures gasoline and diesel engines through two production departments, Fabrication and Assembly. Management needs accurate product cost information in order to guide product strategy. Presently, the company uses a single plantwide factory overhead rate for allocating factory overhead to the two products. However, management is considering the multiple production department factory overhead rate method. The following factory overhead was budgeted for Cobalt:

Fabrication Department factory overhead	$630,000
Assembly Department factory overhead	252,000
Total	$882,000

Direct labor hours were estimated as follows:

Fabrication Department	4,200 hours
Assembly Department	4,200
Total	8,400 hours

In addition, the direct labor hours (dlh) used to produce a unit of each product in each department were determined from engineering records, as follows:

Production Departments	Gasoline Engine	Diesel Engine
Fabrication Department	1.0 dlh	2.4 dlh
Assembly Department	2.4	1.0
Direct labor hours per unit	3.4 dlh	3.4 dlh

a. Determine the per-unit factory overhead allocated to the gasoline and diesel engines under the single plantwide factory overhead rate method, using direct labor hours as the activity base.
b. Determine the per-unit factory overhead allocated to the gasoline and diesel engines under the multiple production department factory overhead rate method, using direct labor hours as the activity base for each department.
c. Recommend to management a product costing approach, based on your analyses in (a) and (b). Support your recommendation.

EX 26-8 Identifying activity bases in an activity-based cost system **OBJ. 4**

Select Foods Inc. uses activity-based costing to determine product costs. For each activity listed in the left column, match an appropriate activity base from the right column. You may use items in the activity-base list more than once or not at all.

Activity	Activity Base
Accounting reports	Engineering change orders
Customer return processing	Kilowatt hours used
Electric power	Number of accounting reports
Human resources	Number of customers
Inventory control	Number of customer orders
Invoice and collecting	Number of customer returns
Machine depreciation	Number of employees
Materials handling	Number of inspections
Order shipping	Number of inventory transactions
Payroll	Number of machine hours
Production control	Number of material moves
Production setup	Number of payroll checks processed
Purchasing	Number of production orders
Quality control	Number of purchase orders
Sales order processing	Number of sales orders
	Number of setups

EX 26-9 Product costs using activity rates **OBJ. 4**

✔ b. $50,600

Elegant Occasions Inc. sells china and flatware over the Internet. For the next period, the budgeted cost of the sales order processing activity is $115,500 and 5,250 sales orders are estimated to be processed.

a. Determine the activity rate of the sales order processing activity.
b. Determine the amount of sales order processing cost that Elegant Occasions would receive if it had 2,300 sales orders.

EX 26-10 Product costs using activity rates **OBJ. 4**

✔ Treadmill activity cost per unit, $230

SPREADSHEET

Cardio Care Inc. manufactures stationary bicycles and treadmills. The products are produced in its Fabrication and Assembly production departments. In addition to production activities, several other activities are required to produce the two products. These activities and their associated activity rates are as follows:

Activity	Activity Rate
Fabrication	$32 per machine hour
Assembly	$12 per direct labor hour
Setup	$60 per setup
Inspecting	$30 per inspection
Production scheduling	$13 per production order
Purchasing	$11 per purchase order

The activity-base usage quantities and units produced for each product were as follows:

Activity Base	Stationary Bicycle	Treadmill
Machine hours	1,600	1,000
Direct labor hours	420	134
Setups	46	12
Inspections	300	280
Production orders	35	30
Purchase orders	325	262
Units produced	600	200

Use the activity rate and usage information to calculate the total activity cost and activity cost per unit for each product.

EX 26-11 Activity rates and product costs using activity-based costing

OBJ. 4

✔ b. Dining room lighting fixtures, $40 per unit

SPREADSHEET

Contemporary Lighting Inc. manufactures entry and dining room lighting fixtures. Five activities are used in manufacturing the fixtures. These activities and their associated budgeted activity costs and activity bases are as follows:

Activity	Budgeted Activity Cost	Activity Base
Casting	$136,800	Machine hours
Assembly	71,100	Direct labor hours
Inspecting	23,680	Number of inspections
Setup	43,800	Number of setups
Materials handling	46,350	Number of loads

Corporate records were obtained to estimate the amount of activity to be used by the two products. The estimated activity-base usage quantities and units produced are provided in the table below.

Activity Base	Entry	Dining	Total
Machine hours	3,120	1,440	4,560
Direct labor hours	1,200	2,750	3,950
Number of inspections	1,080	400	1,480
Number of setups	220	72	292
Number of loads	730	300	1,030
Units produced	9,015	3,085	12,100

a. Determine the activity rate for each activity.
b. Use the activity rates in (a) to determine the total and per-unit activity costs associated with each product.

EX 26-12 Activity cost pools, activity rates, and product costs using activity-based costing

OBJ. 4

✔ b. Ovens, $60 per unit

SPREADSHEET

Kitchen Mate Inc. is estimating the activity cost associated with producing ovens and refrigerators. The indirect labor can be traced into four separate activity pools, based on time records provided by the employees. The budgeted activity cost and activity-base information are provided as follows:

Activity	Activity Pool Cost	Activity Base
Procurement	$150,800	Number of purchase orders
Scheduling	10,750	Number of production orders
Materials handling	29,050	Number of moves
Product development	21,900	Number of engineering changes
Total cost	$212,500	

The estimated activity-base usage and unit information for Kitchen Mate's two product lines was determined from corporate records as follows:

	Number of Purchase Orders	Number of Production Orders	Number of Moves	Number of Engineering Changes	Units
Ovens	800	280	480	154	2,200
Refrigerators	500	150	350	65	1,750
Totals	1,300	430	830	219	3,950

a. Determine the activity rate for each activity cost pool.
b. Determine the activity-based cost per unit of each product.

EX 26-13 Activity-based costing and product cost distortion **OBJ. 2, 4**

✔ c. Cell phones, $1.68 per unit

SPREADSHEET

Digital Storage Concept Inc. is considering a change to activity-based product costing. The company produces two products, cell phones and tablet PCs, in a single production department. The production department is estimated to require 3,750 direct labor hours. The total indirect labor is budgeted to be $375,000.

Time records from indirect labor employees revealed that they spent 40% of their time setting up production runs and 60% of their time supporting actual production.

The following information about cell phones and tablet PCs was determined from the corporate records:

	Number of Setups	Direct Labor Hours	Units
Cell phones	600	1,875	93,750
Tablet PCs	1,400	1,875	93,750
Total	2,000	3,750	187,500

a. Determine the indirect labor cost per unit allocated to cell phones and tablet PCs under a single plantwide factory overhead rate system using the direct labor hours as the allocation base.
b. Determine the budgeted activity costs and activity rates for the indirect labor under activity-based costing. Assume two activities—one for setup and the other for production support.
c. Determine the activity cost per unit for indirect labor allocated to each product under activity-based costing.
d. Why are the per-unit allocated costs in (a) different from the per-unit activity cost assigned to the products in (c)?

EX 26-14 Multiple production department factory overhead rate method **OBJ. 3**

✔ b. Blender, $18.20 per unit

SPREADSHEET

Four Finger Appliance Company manufactures small kitchen appliances. The product line consists of blenders and toaster ovens. Four Finger Appliance presently uses the multiple production department factory overhead rate method. The factory overhead is as follows:

Assembly Department	$186,000
Test and Pack Department	120,000
Total	$306,000

The direct labor information for the production of 7,500 units of each product is as follows:

	Assembly Department	Test and Pack Department
Blender	750 dlh	2,250 dlh
Toaster oven	2,250	750
Total	3,000 dlh	3,000 dlh

Four Finger Appliance used direct labor hours to allocate production department factory overhead to products.

a. Determine the two production department factory overhead rates.
b. Determine the total factory overhead and the factory overhead per unit allocated to each product.

EX 26-15 Activity-based costing and product cost distortion OBJ. 4

✔ b. Blender, $23.60 per unit

SPREADSHEET

The management of Four Finger Appliance Company in Exercise 26-14 has asked you to use activity-based costing to allocate factory overhead costs to the two products. You have determined that $81,000 of factory overhead from each of the production departments can be associated with setup activity ($162,000 in total). Company records indicate that blenders required 135 setups, while the toaster ovens required only 45 setups. Each product has a production volume of 7,500 units.

a. Determine the three activity rates (assembly, test and pack, and setup).
b. Determine the total factory overhead and factory overhead per unit allocated to each product using the activity rates in (a).

EX 26-16 Single plantwide rate and activity-based costing OBJ. 2, 4

✔ a. Low, Col. C, 93.5%

SPREADSHEET

Whirlpool Corporation conducted an activity-based costing study of its Evansville, Indiana, plant in order to identify its most profitable products. Assume that we select three representative refrigerators (out of 333): one low-, one medium-, and one high-volume refrigerator. Additionally, we assume the following activity-base information for each of the three refrigerators:

Three Representative Refrigerators	Number of Machine Hours	Number of Setups	Number of Sales Orders	Number of Units
Refrigerator—Low Volume	24	14	38	160
Refrigerator—Medium Volume	225	13	88	1,500
Refrigerator—High Volume	900	9	120	6,000

Prior to conducting the study, the factory overhead allocation was based on a single machine hour rate. The machine hour rate was $200 per hour. After conducting the activity-based costing study, assume that three activities were used to allocate the factory overhead. The new activity rate information is assumed to be as follows:

	Machining Activity	Setup Activity	Sales Order Processing Activity
Activity rate	$160	$240	$55

a. Complete the following table, using the single machine hour rate to determine the per-unit factory overhead for each refrigerator (Column A) and the three activity-based rates to determine the activity-based factory overhead per unit (Column B). Finally, compute the percent change in per-unit allocation from the single to activity-based rate methods (Column C). Round per-unit overhead to nearest cent and whole percents to one decimal place.

Product Volume Class	Column A Single Rate Overhead Allocation per Unit	Column B ABC Overhead Allocation per Unit	Column C Percent Change in Allocation (Col. B – Col. A)/Col. A
Low			
Medium			
High			

b. Why is the traditional overhead rate per machine hour greater under the single rate method than under the activity-based method?
c. Interpret Column C in your table from part (a).

The activity usage information associated with the two patients is as follows:

	Patient Blair	Patient Thatcher
Number of days	4 days	7 days
Number of images	2 images	4 images
Number of physician orders	4 orders	5 orders
Number of tests	3 tests	6 tests
Number of operating room hours	2 hours	6 hours

a. Determine the activity cost associated with each patient.
b. Why is the total activity cost different for the two patients?

✔ a. Auto, Income from operations, $820,380

SPREADSHEET

EX 26-21 Activity-based costing in an insurance company **OBJ. 5, 6**

Safety First Insurance Company carries three major lines of insurance: auto, workers' compensation, and homeowners. The company has prepared the following report for 2015:

Safety First Insurance Company
Product Profitability Report
For the Year Ended December 31, 2015

	Auto	Workers' Compensation	Homeowners
Premium revenue	$5,750,000	$6,240,000	$8,160,000
Less estimated claims	4,312,500	4,680,000	6,120,000
Underwriting income	$1,437,500	$1,560,000	$2,040,000
Underwriting income as a percent of premium revenue	25%	25%	25%

Management is concerned that the administrative expenses may make some of the insurance lines unprofitable. However, the administrative expenses have not been allocated to the insurance lines. The controller has suggested that the administrative expenses could be assigned to the insurance lines using activity-based costing. The administrative expenses are comprised of five activities. The activities and their rates are as follows:

	Activity Rates
New policy processing	$120 per new policy
Cancellation processing	$175 per cancellation
Claim audits	$320 per claim audit
Claim disbursements processing	$104 per disbursement
Premium collection processing	$24 per premium collected

Activity-base usage data for each line of insurance was retrieved from the corporate records and is shown below.

	Auto	Workers' Compensation	Homeowners
Number of new policies	1,320	1,500	4,080
Number of canceled policies	480	240	2,160
Number of audited claims	385	120	960
Number of claim disbursements	480	216	840
Number of premiums collected	8,400	1,800	15,000

a. Complete the product profitability report through the administrative activities. Determine the income from operations as a percent of premium revenue, rounded to the nearest whole percent.
b. Interpret the report.

Problems Series A

PR 26-1A Single plantwide factory overhead rate

OBJ. 2

✔ **1. b. $48 per machine hour**

Orange County Chrome Company manufactures three chrome-plated products—automobile bumpers, valve covers, and wheels. These products are manufactured in two production departments (Stamping and Plating). The factory overhead for Orange County Chrome is $220,800.

The three products consume both machine hours and direct labor hours in the two production departments as follows:

	Direct Labor Hours	Machine Hours
Stamping Department		
Automobile bumpers	560	800
Valve covers	300	560
Wheels	340	600
	1,200	1,960
Plating Department		
Automobile bumpers	170	1,170
Valve covers	180	710
Wheels	175	760
	525	2,640
Total	1,725	4,600

Instructions

1. Determine the single plantwide factory overhead rate, using each of the following allocation bases: (a) direct labor hours and (b) machine hours.
2. Determine the product factory overhead costs, using (a) the direct labor hour plantwide factory overhead rate and (b) the machine hour plantwide factory overhead rate.

PR 26-2A Multiple production department factor overhead rates

OBJ. 3

✔ **2. Wheels, $63,040**

The management of Orange County Chrome Company, described in Problem 26-1A, now plans to use the multiple production department factory overhead rate method. The total factory overhead associated with each department is as follows:

Stamping Department	$115,200
Plating Department	105,600
Total	$220,800

Instructions

1. Determine the multiple production department factory overhead rates, using direct labor hours for the Stamping Department and machine hours for the Plating Department.
2. Determine the product factory overhead costs, using the multiple production department rates in (1).

PR 26-3A Activity-based and department rate product costing and product cost distortions

OBJ. 3, 4

✔ **2. Snowboards, $390,000 and $65**

SPREADSHEET

Black and Blue Sports Inc. manufactures two products: snowboards and skis. The factory overhead incurred is as follows:

Indirect labor	$507,000
Cutting Department	156,000
Finishing Department	192,000
Total	$855,000

The activity base associated with the two production departments is direct labor hours. The indirect labor can be assigned to two different activities as follows:

Activity	Budgeted Activity Cost	Activity Base
Production control	$237,000	Number of production runs
Materials handling	270,000	Number of moves
Total	$507,000	

The activity-base usage quantities and units produced for the two products are shown below.

	Number of Production Runs	Number of Moves	Direct Labor Hours—Cutting	Direct Labor Hours—Finishing	Units Produced
Snowboards	430	5,000	4,000	2,000	6,000
Skis	70	2,500	2,000	4,000	6,000
Total	500	7,500	6,000	6,000	12,000

Instructions

1. Determine the factory overhead rates under the multiple production department rate method. Assume that indirect labor is associated with the production departments, so that the total factory overhead is $315,000 and $540,000 for the Cutting and Finishing departments, respectively.
2. Determine the total and per-unit factory overhead costs allocated to each product, using the multiple production department overhead rates in (1).
3. Determine the activity rates, assuming that the indirect labor is associated with activities rather than with the production departments.
4. Determine the total and per-unit cost assigned to each product under activity-based costing.
5. Explain the difference in the per-unit overhead allocated to each product under the multiple production department factory overhead rate and activity-based costing methods.

PR 26-4A Activity-based product costing

OBJ. 4

✔ 2. Newsprint total activity cost, $317,700

SPREADSHEET

Teldar Paper Company manufactures three products (computer paper, newsprint, and specialty paper) in a continuous production process. Senior management has asked the controller to conduct an activity-based costing study. The controller identified the amount of factory overhead required by the critical activities of the organization as follows:

Activity	Activity Cost Pool
Production	$ 640,000
Setup	211,200
Moving	35,100
Shipping	131,625
Product engineering	161,500
Total	$1,179,425

The activity bases identified for each activity are as follows:

Activity	Activity Base
Production	Machine hours
Setup	Number of setups
Moving	Number of moves
Shipping	Number of customer orders
Product engineering	Number of test runs

The activity-base usage quantities and units produced for the three products were determined from corporate records and are as follows:

	Machine Hours	Number of Setups	Number of Moves	Number of Customer Orders	Number of Test Runs	Units
Computer paper	1,400	180	400	660	120	1,750
Newsprint	1,600	75	165	210	40	2,000
Specialty paper	1,000	405	605	885	220	1,250
Total	4,000	660	1,170	1,755	380	5,000

Each product requires 0.8 machine hour per unit.

Instructions

1. Determine the activity rate for each activity.
2. Determine the total and per-unit activity cost for all three products.
3. Why aren't the activity unit costs equal across all three products since they require the same machine time per unit?

PR 26-5A Allocating selling and administrative expenses using activity-based costing

OBJ. 5

✔ **3. Break-a-Leg Hospital loss from operations, ($7,350)**

SPREADSHEET

Cold Zone Mechancial Inc. manufactures cooling units for commercial buildings. The price and cost of goods sold for each unit are as follows:

Price	$63,500 per unit
Cost of goods sold	36,000
Gross profit	$27,500 per unit

In addition, the company incurs selling and administrative expenses of $240,940. The company wishes to assign these costs to its three major customers, Good Knowledge University, Hot Shotz Arena, and Break-a-Leg Hospital. These expenses are related to three major nonmanufacturing activities: customer service, project bidding, and engineering support. The engineering support is in the form of engineering changes that are placed by the customer to change the design of a product. The budgeted activity costs and activity bases associated with these activities are:

Activity	Budgeted Activity Cost	Activity Base
Customer service	$ 85,800	Number of service requests
Project bidding	63,640	Number of bids
Engineering support	91,500	Number of customer design changes
Total costs	$240,940	

Activity-base usage and unit volume information for the three customers is as follows:

	Good Knowledge University	Hot Shotz Arena	Break-a-Leg Hospital	Total
Number of service requests	50	44	170	264
Number of bids	31	15	40	86
Number of customer design changes	38	25	120	183
Unit volume	19	12	5	36

Instructions

1. Determine the activity rates for each of the three nonmanufacturing activity pools.
2. Determine the activity costs allocated to the three customers, using the activity rates in (1).

(Continued)

3. Construct customer profitability reports for the three customers, dated for the year ended December 31, 2014, using the activity costs in (2). The reports should disclose the gross profit and income from operations associated with each customer.
4. Provide recommendations to management, based on the profitability reports in (3).

PR 26-6A Product costing and decision analysis for a hospital — OBJ. 6

✔ 3. Procedure B excess, $597,700

SPREADSHEET

Pleasant Stay Medical Inc. wishes to determine its product costs. Pleasant Stay offers a variety of medical procedures (operations) that are considered its "products." The overhead has been separated into three major activities. The annual estimated activity costs and activity bases are provided below.

Activity	Budgeted Activity Cost	Activity Base
Scheduling and admitting	$ 432,000	Number of patients
Housekeeping	4,212,000	Number of patient days
Nursing	5,376,000	Weighted care unit
Total costs	$10,020,000	

Total "patient days" are determined by multiplying the number of patients by the average length of stay in the hospital. A weighted care unit (wcu) is a measure of nursing effort used to care for patients. There were 192,000 weighted care units estimated for the year. In addition, Pleasant Stay estimated 6,000 patients and 27,000 patient days for the year. (The average patient is expected to have a a little more than a four-day stay in the hospital.)

During a portion of the year, Pleasant Stay collected patient information for three selected procedures, as shown below.

	Activity-Base Usage
Procedure A	
Number of patients	280
Average length of stay	× 6 days
Patient days	1,680
Weighted care units	19,200
Procedure B	
Number of patients	650
Average length of stay	× 5 days
Patient days	3,250
Weighted care units	6,000
Procedure C	
Number of patients	1,200
Average length of stay	× 4 days
Patient days	4,800
Weighted care units	24,000

Private insurance reimburses the hospital for these activities at a fixed daily rate of $406 per patient day for all three procedures.

Instructions

1. Determine the activity rates.
2. Determine the activity cost for each procedure.
3. Determine the excess or deficiency of reimbursements to activity cost.
4. Interpret your results.

Problems Series B

PR 26-1B Single plantwide factory overhead rate

OBJ. 2

✔ 1. b. $111 per machine hour

Spotted Cow Dairy Company manufactures three products—whole milk, skim milk, and cream—in two production departments, Blending and Packing. The factory overhead for Spotted Cow Dairy is $299,700.

The three products consume both machine hours and direct labor hours in the two production departments as follows:

	Direct Labor Hours	Machine Hours
Blending Department		
Whole milk	260	650
Skim milk	245	710
Cream	215	260
	720	1,620
Packing Department		
Whole milk	470	500
Skim milk	300	415
Cream	130	165
	900	1,080
Total	1,620	2,700

Instructions

1. Determine the single plantwide factory overhead rate, using each of the following allocation bases: (a) direct labor hours and (b) machine hours.
2. Determine the product factory overhead costs, using (a) the direct labor hour plantwide factory overhead rate and (b) the machine hour plantwide factory overhead rate.

PR 26-2B Multiple production department factory overhead rates

OBJ. 3

✔ 2. Cream, $46,150

The management of Spotted Cow Dairy Company, described in Problem 26-1B, now plans to use the multiple production department factory overhead rate method. The total factory overhead associated with each department is as follows:

Blending Department	$178,200
Packing Department	121,500
Total	$299,700

Instructions

1. Determine the multiple production department factory overhead rates, using machine hours for the Blending Department and direct labor hours for the Packing Department.
2. Determine the product factory overhead costs, using the multiple production department rates in (1).

PR 26-3B Activity-based department rate product costing and product cost distortions

OBJ. 3, 4

✔ 4. Loudspeakers, $465,430 and $66.49

SPREADSHEET

Big Sound Inc. manufactures two products: receivers and loudspeakers. The factory overhead incurred is as follows:

Indirect labor	$400,400
Subassembly Department	198,800
Final Assembly Department	114,800
Total	$714,000

(Continued)

The activity base associated with the two production departments is direct labor hours. The indirect labor can be assigned to two different activities as follows:

Activity	Budgeted Activity Cost	Activity Base
Setup	$138,600	Number of setups
Quality control	261,800	Number of inspections
Total	$400,400	

The activity-base usage quantities and units produced for the two products are shown below.

	Number of Setups	Number of Inspections	Direct Labor Hours—Subassembly	Direct Labor Hours—Final Assembly	Units Produced
Receivers	80	450	875	525	7,000
Loudspeakers	320	1,750	525	875	7,000
Total	400	2,200	1,400	1,400	14,000

Instructions

1. Determine the factory overhead rates under the multiple production department rate method. Assume that indirect labor is associated with the production departments, so that the total factory overhead is $420,000 and $294,000 for the Subassembly and Final Assembly departments, respectively.
2. Determine the total and per-unit factory overhead costs allocated to each product, using the multiple production department overhead rates in (1).
3. Determine the activity rates, assuming that the indirect labor is associated with activities rather than with the production departments.
4. Determine the total and per-unit cost assigned to each product under activity-based costing.
5. Explain the difference in the per-unit overhead allocated to each product under the multiple production department factory overhead rate and activity-based costing methods.

PR 26-4B Activity-based product costing

OBJ. 4

✔ 2. Brown sugar total activity cost, $293,600

SPREADSHEET

Sweet Sugar Company manufactures three products (white sugar, brown sugar, and powdered sugar) in a continuous production process. Senior management has asked the controller to conduct an activity-based costing study. The controller identified the amount of factory overhead required by the critical activities of the organization as follows:

Activity	Budgeted Activity Cost
Production	$500,000
Setup	144,000
Inspection	44,000
Shipping	115,000
Customer service	84,000
Total	$887,000

The activity bases identified for each activity are as follows:

Activity	Activity Base
Production	Machine hours
Setup	Number of setups
Inspection	Number of inspections
Shipping	Number of customer orders
Customer service	Number of customer service requests

The activity-base usage quantities and units produced for the three products were determined from corporate records and are as follows:

	Machine Hours	Number of Setups	Number of Inspections	Number of Customer Orders	Customer Service Requests	Units
White sugar	5,000	85	220	1,150	60	10,000
Brown sugar	2,500	170	330	2,600	350	5,000
Powdered sugar	2,500	195	550	2,000	190	5,000
Total	10,000	450	1,100	5,750	600	20,000

Each product requires 0.5 machine hour per unit.

Instructions

1. Determine the activity rate for each activity.
2. Determine the total and per-unit activity cost for all three products. Round to the nearest cent.
3. Why aren't the activity unit costs equal across all three products since they require the same machine time per unit?

PR 26-5B Allocating selling and administrative expenses using activity-based costing

OBJ. 5

✔ 3. Supply Universe, income from operations, $283,820

SPREADSHEET

Shrute Inc. manufactures office copiers, which are sold to retailers. The price and cost of goods sold for each copier are as follows:

Price	$1,110 per unit
Cost of goods sold	682
Gross profit	$ 428 per unit

In addition, the company incurs selling and administrative expenses of $414,030. The company wishes to assign these costs to its three major retail customers, The Warehouse, Kosmo Co., and Supply Universe. These expenses are related to its three major nonmanufacturing activities: customer service, sales order processing, and advertising support. The advertising support is in the form of advertisements that are placed by Shrute Inc. to support the retailer's sale of Shrute copiers to consumers. The budgeted activity costs and activity bases associated with these activities are:

Activity	Budgeted Activity Cost	Activity Base
Customer service	$ 76,860	Number of service requests
Sales order processing	25,920	Number of sales orders
Advertising support	311,250	Number of ads placed
Total activity cost	$414,030	

Activity-base usage and unit volume information for the three customers is as follows:

	The Warehouse	Kosmo Co.	Supply Universe	Total
Number of service requests	62	340	25	427
Number of sales orders	300	640	140	1,080
Number of ads placed	25	180	44	249
Unit volume	810	810	810	2,430

Instructions

1. Determine the activity rates for each of the three nonmanufacturing activities.
2. Determine the activity costs allocated to the three customers, using the activity rates in (1).
3. Construct customer profitability reports for the three customers, dated for the year ended December 31, 2014, using the activity costs in (2). The reports should disclose the gross profit and income from operations associated with each customer.
4. Provide recommendations to management, based on the profitability reports in (3).

PR 26-6B Product costing and decision analysis for a passenger airline — OBJ. 6

✔ 3. Flight 102 income from operations, $4,415

SPREADSHEET

Blue Star Airline provides passenger airline service, using small jets. The airline connects four major cities: Charlotte, Pittsburgh, Detroit, and San Francisco. The company expects to fly 170,000 miles during a month. The following costs are budgeted for a month:

Fuel	$2,120,000
Ground personnel	788,500
Crew salaries	850,000
Depreciation	430,000
Total costs	$4,188,500

Blue Star management wishes to assign these costs to individual flights in order to gauge the profitability of its service offerings. The following activity bases were identified with the budgeted costs:

Airline Cost	Activity Base
Fuel, crew, and depreciation costs	Number of miles flown
Ground personnel	Number of arrivals and departures at an airport

The size of the company's ground operation in each city is determined by the size of the workforce. The following monthly data are available from corporate records for each terminal operation:

Terminal City	Ground Personnel Cost	Number of Arrivals/Departures
Charlotte	$256,000	320
Pittsburgh	97,500	130
Detroit	129,000	150
San Francisco	306,000	340
Total	$788,500	940

Three recent representative flights have been selected for the profitability study. Their characteristics are as follows:

	Description	Miles Flown	Number of Passengers	Ticket Price per Passenger
Flight 101	Charlotte to San Francisco	2,000	80	$695.00
Flight 102	Detroit to Charlotte	800	50	441.50
Flight 103	Charlotte to Pittsburgh	400	20	382.00

Instructions

1. Determine the fuel, crew, and depreciation cost per mile flown.
2. Determine the cost per arrival or departure by terminal city.
3. Use the information in (1) and (2) to construct a profitability report for the three flights. Each flight has a single arrival and departure to its origin and destination city pairs.
4. Evaluate flight profitability by determining the break-even number of passengers required for each flight assuming all the costs of a flight are fixed. Round to the nearest whole number.

Cases & Projects

CP 26-1 Ethics and professional conduct in business

The controller of Tri Con Global Systems Inc. devised a new costing system based on tracing the cost of activities to products. The controller was able to measure post-manufacturing activities, such as selling, promotional, and distribution activities, and allocate these activities to products in order to have a more complete view of the company's product costs. This effort produced better strategic information about the relative profitability of product lines. In addition, the controller used the same product cost information for inventory valuation on the financial statements. Surprisingly, the controller discovered that the company's reported net income was larger under this scheme than under the traditional costing approach.

Why was the net income larger, and how would you react to the controller's action?

CP 26-2 Identifying product cost distortion

Beachside Beverages Company manufactures soft drinks. Information about two products is as follows:

	Volume	Sales Price per Case	Gross Profit per Case
Storm Soda	800,000 cases	$30	$12
Fizz Wiz	10,000 cases	30	12

It is known that both products have the same direct materials and direct labor costs per case. Beachside Beverages allocates factory overhead to products by using a single plantwide factory overhead rate, based on direct labor cost. Additional information about the two products is as follows:

Storm Soda Requires minor process preparation and sterilization prior to processing. The ingredients are acquired locally. The formulation is simple, and it is easy to maintain quality. Lastly, the product is sold in large bulk (full truckload) orders.

Fizz Wiz: Requires extensive process preparation and sterilization prior to processing. The ingredients are from Jamaica, requiring complex import controls. The formulation is complex, and it is thus difficult to maintain quality. Lastly, the product is sold in small (less than full truckload) orders.

Explain the product profitability report in light of the additional data.

CP 26-3 Activity-based costing

Wells Fargo Insurance Services (WFIS) is an insurance brokerage company that classified insurance products as either "easy" or "difficult." Easy and difficult products were defined as follows:

Easy: Electronic claims, few inquiries, mature product

Difficult: Paper claims, complex claims to process, many inquiries, a new product with complex options

The company originally allocated processing and service expenses on the basis of revenue. Under this traditional allocation approach, the product profitability report revealed the following:

	Easy Product	Difficult Product	Total
Revenue	$600	$400	$1,000
Processing and service expenses	420	280	700
Income from operations	$180	$120	$ 300
Operating income margin	30%	30%	30%

WFIS decided to use activity-based costing to allocate the processing and service expenses. The following activity-based costing analysis of the same data illustrates a much different profit picture for the two types of products.

	Easy Product	Difficult Product	Total
Revenue	$600	$ 400	$1,000
Processing and service expenses	183	517	700
Income from operations	$417	$(117)	$ 300
Operating income margin	70%	(29%)	30%

Explain why the activity-based profitability report reveals different information from the traditional sales allocation report.

Source: Dan Patras and Kevin Clancy, "ABC in the Service Industry: Product Line Profitability at Acordia, Inc." As Easy as ABC Newsletter, Issue 12, Spring 1993.

Learning Objectives

After studying this chapter, you should be able to: | *Example Exercises*

Objective	Example Exercises
OBJ 1 Describe just-in-time manufacturing practices.	
Just-in-Time Practices	
Reducing Inventory	
Reducing Lead Times	
Reducing Setup Time	EE 27-1
Emphasizing Product-Oriented Layout	EE 27-2
Emphasizing Employee Involvement	EE 27-2
Emphasizing Pull Manufacturing	EE 27-2
Emphasizing Zero Defects	EE 27-2
Emphasizing Supply Chain Management	EE 27-2
OBJ 2 Apply just-in-time practices to a nonmanufacturing setting.	
Just-in-Time for Nonmanufacturing Processes	
OBJ 3 Describe the implications of just-in-time manufacturing on cost accounting and performance measurement.	
Accounting for Just-in-Time Manufacturing	
Fewer Transactions	EE 27-3
Combined Accounts	EE 27-3
Nonfinancial Performance Measures	
Direct Tracing of Overhead	
OBJ 4 Describe and illustrate activity analysis for improving operations.	
Activity Analysis	
Costs of Quality	
Quality Activity Analysis	EE 27-4
Value-Added Activity Analysis	
Process Activity Analysis	EE 27-5

At a Glance 27 Page 1263

OBJ 1 Describe just-in-time manufacturing practices.

Just-in-Time Practices

The objective of most manufacturers is to produce products with high quality, low cost, and instant availability. In attempting to achieve this objective, many manufacturers have implemented just-in-time processing. **Just-in-time processing (JIT)**, sometimes called *lean manufacturing,* is a philosophy that focuses on reducing time and cost, and eliminating poor quality.

Exhibit 1 lists just-in-time manufacturing and the traditional manufacturing practices. Each of the just-in-time practices is discussed in this section.

EXHIBIT 1

Operating Principles of Just-in-Time versus Traditional Manufacturing

Issue	Just-in-Time Manufacturing	Traditional Manufacturing
Inventory	Reduces inventory.	Increases inventory to protect against process problems.
Lead time	Reduces lead time.	Increases lead time to protect against uncertainty.
Setup time	Reduces setup time.	Disregards setup time as an improvement priority.
Production layout	Emphasizes product-oriented layout.	Emphasizes process-oriented layout.
Role of the employee	Emphasizes team-oriented employee involvement.	Emphasizes work of individuals, following manager instructions.
Production scheduling policy	Emphasizes pull manufacturing.	Emphasizes push manufacturing.
Quality	Emphasizes zero defects.	Tolerates defects.
Suppliers and customers	Emphasizes supply chain management.	Treats suppliers and customers as "arm's-length," independent entities.

Reducing Inventory

Just-in-time (JIT) manufacturing views inventory as wasteful and unnecessary. As a result, JIT emphasizes reducing or eliminating inventory.

Under traditional manufacturing, inventory often hides underlying production problems. For example, if machine breakdowns occur, work in process inventories can be used to keep production running in other departments while the machines are being repaired. Likewise, inventories can be used to hide problems caused by a shortage of trained employees, unreliable suppliers, or poor quality.

In contrast, just-in-time manufacturing attempts to solve and remove production problems. In this way, raw materials, work in process, and finished goods inventories are reduced or eliminated.

The role of inventory in manufacturing can be illustrated using a river. Inventory is the water in a river. The rocks at the bottom of the river are production problems. When the water level (inventory) is high, the rocks (production problems) at the bottom of the river are hidden. As the water level (inventory) drops, the rocks (production problems) become visible, one by one. JIT manufacturing reduces the water level (inventory), exposes the rocks (production problems), and removes the rocks so that the river can flow smoothly.

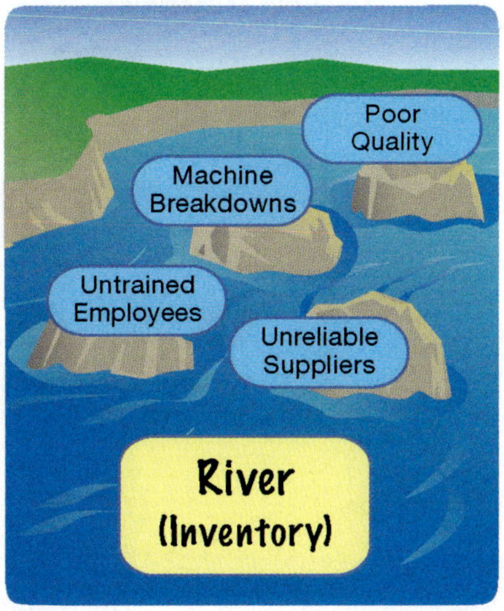

Integrity, Objectivity, and Ethics in Business

THE INVENTORY SHIFT

Some managers take a shortcut to reducing inventory by shifting inventory to their suppliers. With this tactic, the hard work of improving processes is avoided. Enlightened managers realize that such tactics often have short-lived savings. Suppliers will eventually increase their prices to compensate for the additional inventory holding costs, thus resulting in no savings. Therefore, shifting a problem doesn't eliminate a problem.

Reducing Lead Times

Lead time, sometimes called *throughput time*, measures the time interval between a product entering production (is started) and when it is completed (finished). That is, lead time measures how long it takes to manufacture a product. For example, if a product enters production at 1:00 P.M. and is completed at 5:00 P.M., the lead time is four hours.

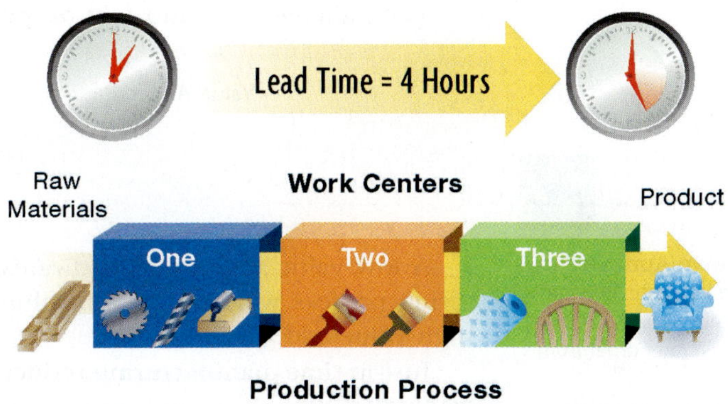

The lead time can be classified as one of the following:

1. **Value-added lead time**, which is the time spent in converting raw materials into a finished unit of product
2. **Non-value-added lead time**, which is the time spent while the unit of product is waiting to enter the next production process or is moved from one process to another

Exhibit 2 illustrates value-added and non-value-added lead time. The time spent drilling and packing the unit of product is value-added time. The time spent waiting to enter the next process or the time spent moving the unit of product from one process to another is non-value-added time.

EXHIBIT 2 **Components of Lead Time**

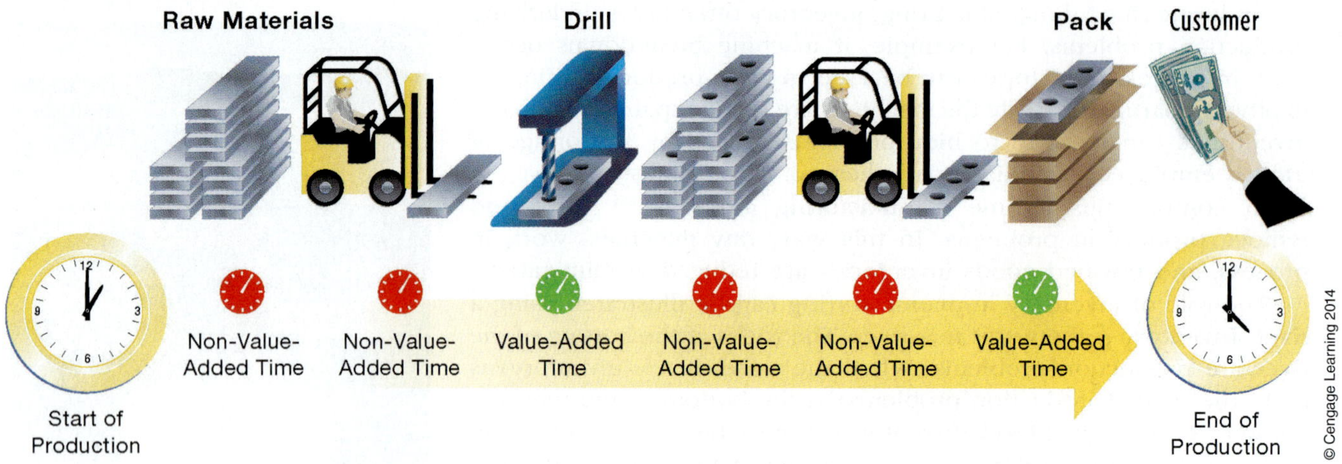

The **value-added ratio** is computed as follows:

$$\text{Value-Added Ratio} = \frac{\text{Value-Added Lead Time}}{\text{Total Lead Time}}$$

To illustrate, assume that the lead time to manufacture a unit of product is as follows:

Move raw materials to machining	5 minutes
Machining	**35**
Move time to assembly	10
Assembly	**20**
Move time to packing	15
Wait time for packing	30
Packing	**10**
Total lead time	125 minutes

The value-added ratio for the preceding product is 52%, as computed below.

$$\text{Value-Added Ratio} = \frac{\text{Value-Added Lead Time}}{\text{Total Lead Time}}$$

$$= \frac{(35 + 20 + 10)\text{ minutes}}{125\text{ minutes}} = \frac{65\text{ minutes}}{125\text{ minutes}} = 52\%$$

Crown Audio reduced the lead time between receiving and delivering a customer order from 30 days to 12 hours by using just-in-time principles.

A low value-added ratio indicates a poor manufacturing process. A good manufacturing process will reduce non-value-added lead time to a minimum and thus have a high value-added ratio.

Just-in-time manufacturing reduces or eliminates non-value-added time. In contrast, traditional manufacturing processes may have a value-added ratio as small as 5%.

Reducing Setup Time

A *setup* is the effort spent preparing an operation or process for a production run. If setups are long and costly, the batch size (number of units) for the related production run is normally large. Large batch sizes allow setup costs to be spread over more units and, thus, reduce the cost per unit. However, large batch sizes increase inventory and lead time.

Exhibit 3 shows the relationship between setup times and lead time.

EXHIBIT 3 **Relationship between Setup Times and Lead Time**

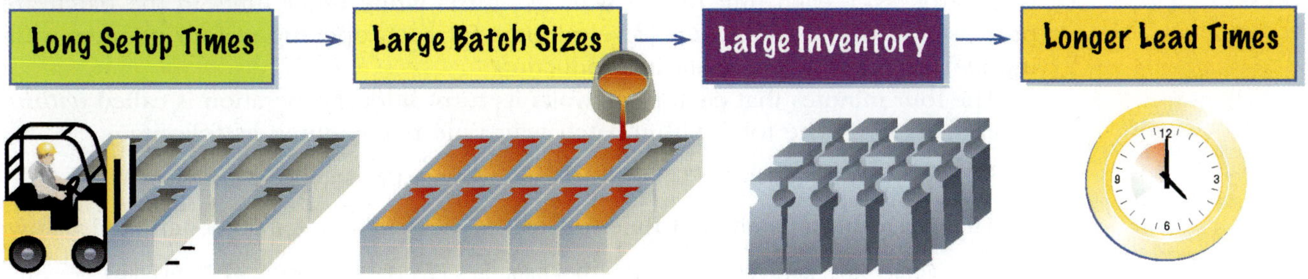

To illustrate, assume that a product can be manufactured in Process X or Process Y as follows:

	Process X	Process Y
Operation A	1 minute	1 minute
Operation B	1	1
Operation C	1	1
Total	3 minutes	3 minutes
Batch size	1 unit	5 units

Exhibit 4 shows that the lead time for Process X is three minutes. In contrast, the lead time for Process Y is 15 minutes.

EXHIBIT 4 **Impact of Batch Sizes on Lead Times**

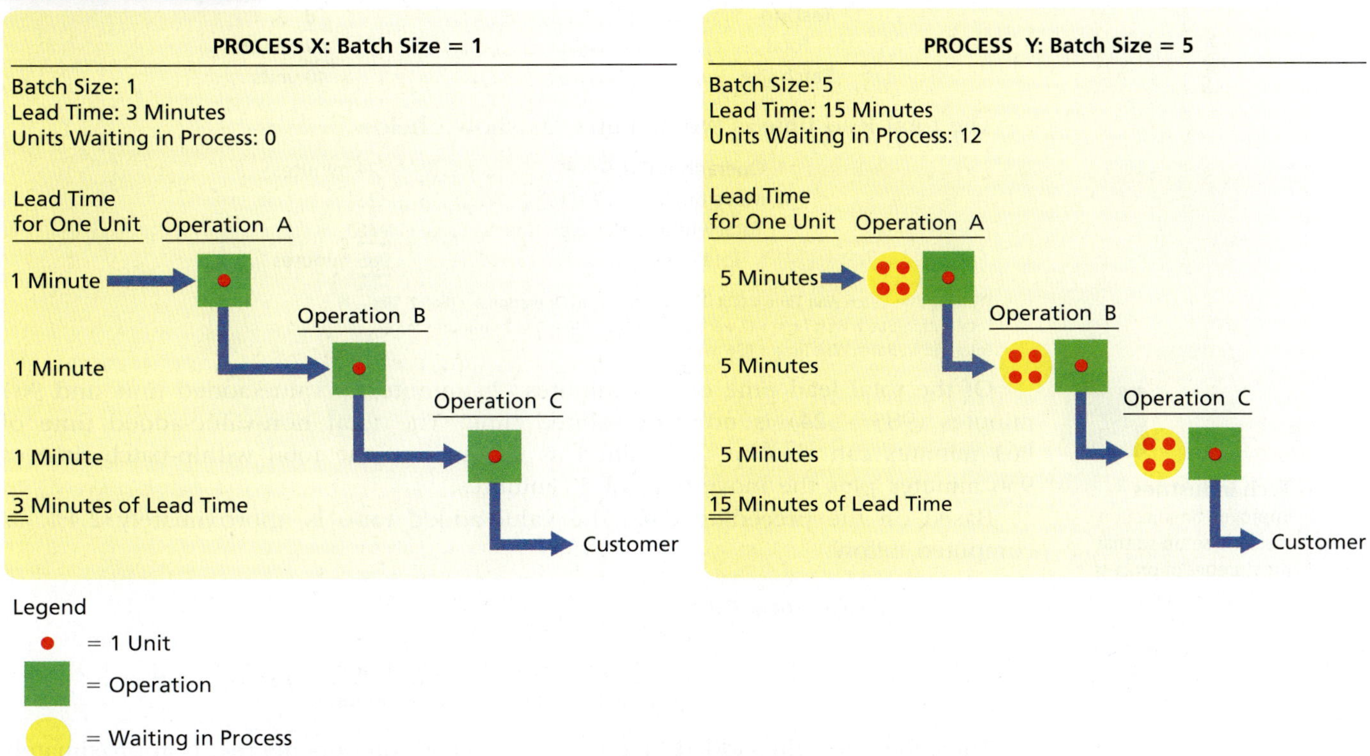

The lead time for Process Y is longer because while three units are being produced in Operations A, B, and C, 12 other units are waiting to be processed. That is, in Process Y each unit has to wait its "turn" while other units in the batch are processed. Thus, it takes a unit five minutes for each operation—four minutes waiting its "turn" and one minute in production.

The four minutes that each part "waits its turn" at each operation is called *within-batch wait time*. The total within-batch wait time is computed as follows:

$$\text{Total Within-Batch Wait Time} = (\text{Total Time to Perform Operations}) \times (\text{Batch Size} - 1)$$

The total within-batch wait time for Process Y is 12 minutes, as computed below.

$$\text{Total Within-Batch Wait Time} = (1 + 1 + 1) \text{ minutes} \times (5 - 1) = 3 \text{ minutes} \times 4 = 12 \text{ minutes}$$

The value-added ratio for Process Y is 20%, as computed below.

$$\text{Value-Added Ratio} = \frac{\text{Value-Added Lead Time}}{\text{Total Lead Time}}$$

$$= \frac{(1 + 1 + 1) \text{ minutes}}{(3 + 12) \text{ minutes}} = \frac{3 \text{ minutes}}{15 \text{ minutes}} = 20\%$$

Thus, 80% (100% – 20%) of the lead time in Process Y is non-value-added time.

Just-in-time manufacturing emphasizes decreasing setup times in order to reduce the batch size. By reducing batch sizes, work in process and wait time are decreased, thus reducing total lead time and increasing the value-added ratio.

To illustrate, assume that Automotive Components Inc. manufactures engine starters as follows:

Operations	**Processing Time per Unit**
Move raw materials to Machining	5 minutes
Machining	**7**
Move time to Assembly	10
Assembly	**9**
Move time to Testing	10
Testing	**8**
Total	49 minutes
Batch size	40 units

The total lead time is 985 minutes, as shown below.

Operations (7 + 9 + 8)	24 minutes
Move time (5 + 10 + 10)	25
Total within-batch wait time	936*
Total time	985 minutes

*Total Within-Batch Wait Time = (Total Time to Perform Operations) × (Batch Size – 1)
Total Within-Batch Wait Time = (7 + 9 + 8) minutes × (40 – 1) = 24 minutes × 39
Total Within-Batch Wait Time = 936 minutes

Tech Industries improved an injection machine setup so that the number of process steps was reduced from 84 to 19 and the setup time was reduced from five hours to one hour.

Of the total lead time of 985 minutes, 24 minutes is value-added time and 961 minutes (985 – 24) is non-value-added time. The total non-value-added time of 961 minutes can also be determined as the sum of the total within-batch time of 936 minutes plus the move time of 25 minutes.

Based on the preceding data, the value-added ratio is approximately 2.4%, as computed below.

$$\text{Value-Added Ratio} = \frac{\text{Value-Added Lead Time}}{\text{Total Lead Time}}$$

$$= \frac{(7 + 9 + 8) \text{ minutes}}{985 \text{ minutes}} = \frac{24 \text{ minutes}}{985 \text{ minutes}} = 2.4\% \text{ (rounded)}$$

Thus, the non-value-added time for Automotive Components Inc. is approximately 97.6% (100% – 2.4%).

Automotive Components can increase its value-added ratio by reducing setups so that the batch size is one unit, termed *one-piece flow*. Automotive Components could also move the Machining, Assembly, and Testing operations closer to each other so that the move time could be reduced. With these changes, Automotive Components' value-added ratio would increase.

Business Connection

P&G'S "PIT STOPS"

What do Procter & Gamble and Formula One racing have in common? The answer begins with P&G's Packing Department, which is where detergents and other products are filled on a "pack line." Containers move down the pack line and are filled with products from a packing machine. When it was time to change from a 36-oz. to a 54-oz. *Tide* box, for example, the changeover involved stopping the line, adjusting guide rails, retrieving items from the tool room, placing items back in the tool room, changing and cleaning the pack heads, and performing routine maintenance. Changing the pack line could be a very difficult process and typically took up to several hours.

Management realized that it was important to reduce this time significantly in order to become more flexible and cost efficient in packing products. Where could they learn how to do setups faster? They turned to Formula One racing, reasoning that a pit stop was much like a setup. As a result, P&G videotaped actual Formula One pit stops. These videos were used to form the following principles for conducting a fast setup:

- Position the tools near their point of use on the line prior to stopping the line, to reduce time going back and forth to the tool room.
- Arrange the tools in the exact order of work, so that no time is wasted looking for a tool.
- Have each employee perform a very specific task during the setup.
- Design the workflow so that employees don't interfere with each other.
- Have each employee in position at the moment the line is stopped.
- Train each employee, and practice, practice, practice.
- Put a stop watch on the setup process.
- Plot improvements over time on a visible chart.

As a result of these changes, P&G was able to reduce pack-line setup time from several hours to 20 minutes. This decrease allowed the company to reduce lead time and to improve the cost performance of the Packing Department.

Example Exercise 27-1 Lead Time

OBJ 1

The Helping Hands glove company manufactures gloves in the cutting and assembly process. Gloves are manufactured in 50-glove batch sizes. The cutting time is 4 minutes per glove. The assembly time is 6 minutes per glove. It takes 12 minutes to move a batch of gloves from cutting to assembly.

a. Compute the value-added, non-value-added, and total lead time of this process.
b. Compute the value-added ratio. Round to one decimal.

Follow My Example 27-1

a.

Value-added lead time:	10 min.	= (4 min. + 6 min.)
Non-value-added lead time:		
Total within-batch wait time	490	= (4 + 6) minutes × (50 – 1)
Move time	12	
Total lead time	512 min.	

b. Value-added ratio: $\frac{10\text{ min.}}{512\text{ min.}}$ = 2% (rounded)

Practice Exercises: **PE 27-1A, PE 27-1B**

Emphasizing Product-Oriented Layout

Manufacturing processes can be organized around a product, which is called a **product-oriented layout** (or *product cells*). Alternatively, manufacturing processes can be organized around a process, which is called a **process-oriented layout**.

Just-in-time normally organizes manufacturing around products rather than processes. Organizing work around products reduces:

1. Moving materials and products between processes
2. Work in process inventory
3. Lead time
4. Production costs

In addition, a product-oriented layout improves coordination among operations.

Emphasizing Employee Involvement

Employee involvement is a management approach that grants employees the responsibility and authority to make decisions about operations. Employee involvement is often applied in a just-in-time operation by organizing employees into *product cells*. Within each product cell, employees are organized as teams where the employees are *cross-trained* to perform any operation within the product cell.

To illustrate, employees learn how to operate several different machines within their product cell. In addition, team members are trained to perform functions traditionally performed by centralized service departments. For example, product cell employees may perform their own equipment maintenance, quality control, and housekeeping.

Emphasizing Pull Manufacturing

Pull manufacturing (or *make to order*) is an important just-in-time practice. In pull manufacturing, products are manufactured only as they are needed by the customer. Products can be thought of as being pulled through the manufacturing process. In other words, the status of the next operation determines when products are moved or produced. If the next operation is busy, production stops so that work in process does not pile up in front of the busy operation. When the next operation is ready, the product is moved to that operation.

A system used in pull manufacturing is *kanban*, which is Japanese for "cards." Electronic cards or containers signal production quantities to be filled by the preceding operation. The cards link the customer's order for a product back through each stage of production. In other words, when a consumer orders a product, a kanban card triggers the manufacture of the product.

In contrast, the traditional approach to manufacturing is based on estimated customer demand. This principle is called **push manufacturing** (or make to stock). In push manufacturing, products are manufactured according to a production schedule that is based upon estimated sales. The schedule "pushes" product into inventory before customer orders are received. As a result, push manufacturers normally have more inventory than pull manufacturers.

Emphasizing Zero Defects

Just-in-time manufacturing attempts to eliminate poor quality. Poor quality creates:

1. Scrap
2. Rework, which is fixing product made wrong the first time
3. Disruption in the production process
4. Dissatisfied customers
5. Warranty costs and expenses

One way to improve product quality and manufacturing processes is Six Sigma. **Six Sigma** was developed by Motorola Corporation and consists of five steps: define, measure, analyze, improve, and control (DMAIC).[1] Since its development, Six Sigma has been adopted by thousands of organizations worldwide.

1 The term "six sigma" refers to a statistical property where a process has less than 3.4 defects per one million items.

Emphasizing Supply Chain Management

Supply chain management coordinates and controls the flow of materials, services, information, and finances with suppliers, manufacturers, and customers. Supply chain management partners with suppliers using long-term agreements. These agreements ensure that products are delivered with the right quality, at the right cost, at the right time.

To enhance the interchange of information between suppliers and customers, supply chain management often uses:

1. **Electronic data interchange** (EDI), which uses computers to electronically communicate orders, relay information, and make or receive payments from one organization to another
2. **Radio frequency identification devices** (RFID), which are electronic tags (chips) placed on or embedded within products that can be read by radio waves that allow instant monitoring of product location
3. **Enterprise resource planning** (ERP) systems, which are used to plan and control internal and supply chain operations

Business Connection

JUST-IN-TIME IN ACTION

- Yamaha manufactures musical instruments such as trumpets, horns, saxophones, clarinets, and flutes using **product-oriented layouts**.
- Sony uses **employee involvement** to organize employees into small four-person teams to completely assemble a camcorder, doing everything from soldering to testing. This team-based approach reduces assembly time from 70 minutes to 15 minutes per camcorder.
- Kenney Manufacturing Company, a manufacturer of window shades, estimated that 50% of its window shade process was non-value-added. By using **pull manufacturing** and changing the line layout, it was able to reduce inventory by 82% and lead time by 84%.
- Motorola has claimed over $17 billion in savings from **Six Sigma**.
- Hyundia/Kia Motors Group will use 20 million RFID tags annually to track automotive parts from its suppliers, providing greater **supply chain** transparency and flexibility.

Example Exercise 27-2 Just-in-Time Features

OBJ 1

Which of the following are features of a just-in-time manufacturing system?

a. Reduced space
b. Larger inventory
c. Longer lead times
d. Reduced setups

Follow My Example 27-2

a. Reduced space
d. Reduced setups

Practice Exercises: **PE 27-2A, PE 27-2B**

Just-in-Time for Nonmanufacturing Processes

OBJ 2 Apply just-in-time practices to a non-manufacturing setting.

Just-in-time practices may also be applied to service businesses or administrative processes. Examples of service businesses that use just-in-time practices include hospitals, banks, insurance companies, and hotels. Examples of administrative processes that use just-in-time practices include processing of insurance applications, product designs, and sales orders. In the case of a service business, the "product" is normally the customer or patient. In the case of administrative processes, the "product" is normally information.

For example, a traditional accounting department can deliver month-end financial statements using a sequential, process-oriented layout. Using JIT principles, the lead time for producing financial statements can be reduced significantly by employing a product-oriented layout. In this case, the "products" are the individual inputs to financial statement consolidation from the payroll, accounts payable, and accounts receivable functions. A product layout may allow these inputs to be processed in parallel, rather than sequentially, thus reducing non-value-added lead time.

OBJ 3 Describe the implications of just-in-time manufacturing on cost accounting and performance measurement.

Accounting for Just-in-Time Manufacturing

In just-in-time manufacturing, the accounting system has the following characteristics:

1. *Fewer transactions.* There are fewer transactions to record, thus simplifying the accounting system.
2. *Combined accounts.* All in-process work is combined with raw materials to form a new account, **Raw and In Process (RIP) Inventory**. Direct labor is also combined with other costs to form a new account titled **Conversion Costs**.
3. *Nonfinancial performance measures.* Nonfinancial performance measures are emphasized.
4. *Direct tracing of overhead.* Indirect labor is directly assigned to product cells; thus, less factory overhead is allocated to products.

Fewer Transactions

The traditional process cost accounting system accumulates product costs by department. These costs are transferred from department to department as the product is manufactured. Thus, materials are recorded into and out of work in process inventories as the product moves through the factory.

The recording of product costs by departments facilitates the control of costs. However, this requires that many transactions and costs be recorded and reported. This adds cost and complexity to the cost accounting system.

In just-in-time manufacturing, there is less need for cost control. This is because lower inventory levels make problems more visible. That is, managers don't need accounting reports to indicate problems because any problems become immediately known.

The accounting system for just-in-time manufacturing is simplified by eliminating the accumulation and transfer of product costs by departments. Instead, costs are transferred from combined material and conversion cost accounts directly to finished goods inventory. Costs are not transferred through intermediate departmental work in process accounts. Such just-in-time accounting is called **backflush accounting**.

Combined Accounts

Materials are received directly by the product cells and enter immediately into production. Thus, there is no central materials inventory location (warehouse) or a materials account. Instead, just-in-time debits all materials and conversion costs to an account titled *Raw and In Process Inventory*. Doing so combines materials and work in process costs into one account.

Just-in-time manufacturing often does not use a separate direct labor cost classification. This is because the employees in product cells perform many tasks. Some of these tasks could be classified as direct, such as performing operations, and some as indirect, such as performing repairs. Thus, labor cost (direct and indirect) is combined with other product cell overhead costs and recorded in an account titled *Conversion Costs*.

To illustrate, assume the following data for Anderson Metal Fabricators, a manufacturer of metal covers for electronic test equipment:

Budgeted conversion cost	$2,400,000
Planned hours of production	1,920 hours

The cell conversion cost rate is determined as follows:

$$\text{Cell Conversion Cost Rate} = \frac{\text{Budgeted Conversion Cost}}{\text{Planned Hours of Production}}$$

$$= \frac{\$2{,}400{,}000}{1{,}920 \text{ hours}} = \$1{,}250 \text{ per hour}$$

The cell conversion rate is similar to a predetermined factory overhead rate, except that it includes all conversion costs in the numerator.

Assume that Anderson Metal's cover product cell is expected to require 0.02 hour of manufacturing time per unit. Thus, the conversion cost for the cover is $25 per unit, as shown below.

Conversion Cost for Cover = Manufacturing Time × Cell Conversion Cost Rate
Conversion Cost for Cover = 0.02 hour × $1,250 = $25 per unit

The recording of selected just-in-time transactions for Anderson Metal Fabricators for April is illustrated below.

Transaction	Journal Entry			Comment

1. Steel coil is purchased for producing 8,000 covers. The purchase cost was $120,000, or $15 per unit.	Raw and In Process Inventory
	  Accounts Payable
	   To record materials purchases.
		120,000	
			120,000
				Note that the materials purchased are debited to the combined account, Raw and In Process Inventory. A separate materials account is not used, because materials are received directly in the product cells, rather than in an inventory location.

2. Conversion costs are applied to 8,000 covers at a rate of $25 per cover.	Raw and In Process Inventory
	  Conversion Costs
	   To record applied conversion costs of the medium-cover line.
		200,000	
			200,000
				The raw and in process inventory account is used to accumulate the applied cell conversion costs during the period. The credit to Conversion Costs is similar to the treatment of applied factory overhead.

3. All 8,000 covers were completed in the cell. The raw and in process inventory account is reduced by the $15 per unit materials cost and the $25 per unit conversion cost.	Finished Goods Inventory
	  Raw and In Process Inventory
	   To transfer the cost of completed units to finished goods.
		320,000	
			320,000
				Materials ($15 × 8,000 units) $120,000
				Conversion ($25 × 8,000 units) 200,000
				Total $320,000
				
				After the cost of the completed units is transferred from the raw and in process inventory account, the account's balance is zero. There are no units left in process within the cell.[2] This is a backflush transaction.

4. Of the 8,000 units completed, 7,800 were sold and shipped to customers at $70 per unit, leaving 200 finished units in stock. Thus, the finished goods inventory account has a balance of $8,000 (200 × $40).	Accounts Receivable
	  Sales
	   To record sales.
	
	Cost of Goods Sold
	  Finished Goods
	   To record cost of goods sold.
		546,000
		
		312,000
			
			546,000
			
			312,000
				Units sold 7,800
				Conversion and materials cost per unit × $40
				Transferred to Cost of Goods Sold $312,000

2 The actual conversion cost per unit may be different from the budgeted conversion cost per unit due to cell inefficiency, improvements in processing methods, or excess scrap. These deviations from the budgeted cost can be accounted for as cost variances, as illustrated in more advanced texts.

Example Exercise 27-3 Just-in-Time Journal Entries

OBJ 3

The budgeted conversion costs for a just-in-time cell are $142,500 for 1,900 production hours. Each unit produced by the cell requires 10 minutes of cell process time. During the month, 1,050 units are manufactured in the cell. The estimated materials cost is $46 per unit. Provide the following journal entries:

a. Materials are purchased to produce 1,100 units.
b. Conversion costs are applied to 1,050 units of production.
c. 1,030 units are completed and placed into finished goods.

Follow My Example 27-3

a.	Raw and In Process Inventory	50,600*	
	Accounts Payable		50,600
	*$46 per unit × 1,100 units		
b.	Raw and In Process Inventory	13,125*	
	Conversion Costs		13,125
	*[($142,500/1,900 hours) × (10 min./60 min.)] = $12.50 per unit; $12.50 × 1,050 units = $13,125		
c.	Finished Goods Inventory	60,255*	
	Raw and In Process Inventory		60,255
	*($46.00 + $12.50) × 1,030 units		

Practice Exercises: **PE 27-3A, PE 27-3B**

Nonfinancial Performance Measures

Just-in-time manufacturing normally uses nonfinancial measures to help guide short-term operating performance. A **nonfinancial measure** is operating information not stated in dollar terms. Examples of nonfinancial measures of performance include:

1. Lead time
2. Value-added ratio
3. Setup time
4. Number of production line stops
5. Number of units scrapped
6. Deviations from scheduled production
7. Number of failed inspections

Most companies use a combination of financial and nonfinancial operating measures, which are often referred to as *key performance indicators* (or *KPIs*). Nonfinancial measures are often available more quickly than financial measures. Thus, nonfinancial measures are often used for day-to-day operating decisions that require quick or instant feedback. In contrast, traditional financial accounting measures are often used for longer-term operating decisions.

Direct Tracing of Overhead

In just-in-time manufacturing, many indirect tasks are assigned to a product cell. For example, maintenance department personnel may be assigned to a product cell and cross-trained to perform other operations. Thus, the salary of this person can be traced directly to the product cell.

In traditional manufacturing, maintenance personnel are part of the maintenance department. The cost of the maintenance department is then allocated to products based on service charges. Such allocations are not necessary when maintenance personnel are assigned directly to a product cell and, thus, to the product.

Activity Analysis

OBJ 4 Describe and illustrate activity analysis for improving operations.

In the previous chapter, we discussed activity-based costing for product costing. Activities can also be used to support operational improvement using activity analysis. **Activity analysis** determines the cost of activities. An activity analysis can be used to determine the cost of:

1. Quality
2. Value-added activities
3. Processes

Costs of Quality

Competition encourages businesses to emphasize high-quality products, services, and processes. In doing so, businesses incur **costs of quality**, which can be classified as follows:

1. **Prevention costs**, which are costs of preventing defects before or during the manufacture of the product or delivery of services

   Examples: Costs of engineering good product design, controlling vendor quality, training equipment operators, maintaining equipment
2. **Appraisal costs**, which are costs of activities that detect, measure, evaluate, and inspect products and processes to ensure that they meet customer needs

   Examples: Costs of inspecting and testing products
3. **Internal failure costs**, which are costs associated with defects discovered before the product is delivered to the consumer

   Examples: Cost of scrap and rework
4. **External failure costs**, which are costs incurred after defective products have been delivered to consumers

   Examples: Cost of recalls and warranty work

Prevention and appraisal costs can be thought of as costs of controlling quality *before* any products are known to be defective. Internal and external failure costs can be thought of as the cost of controlling quality *after* products have become defective. Internal and external failure costs also can be thought of as the costs of "failing to control quality" through prevention and appraisal efforts.

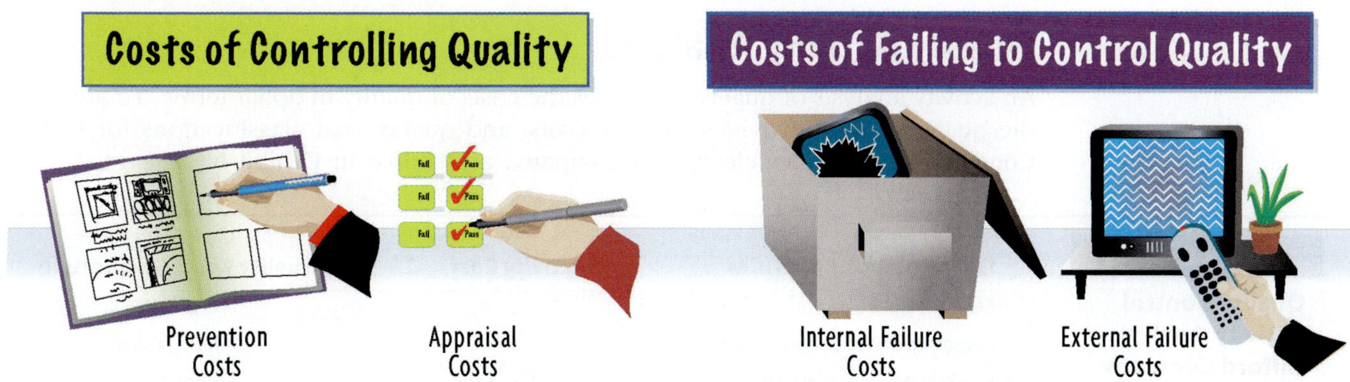

Prevention and appraisal costs are incurred *before* the product is manufactured or delivered to the customer. Prevention costs are incurred in an attempt to permanently improve product quality. In contrast, appraisal costs are incurred in an attempt to limit the amount of defective products that "slip out the door."

Internal and external failure costs are incurred *after* the defective products have been discovered. In addition to costs of scrap and rework, internal failure costs may be incurred for lost equipment time because of rework and the costs of carrying additional inventory used for reworking. In addition to costs of recall and warranty work, external failure costs include the loss of customer goodwill. Although the loss of customer goodwill is difficult to measure, it may be the largest and most important quality control cost.

It is said that every dissatisfied customer tells at least ten people about an unhappy experience with a product.

The relationship between the costs of quality is shown in Exhibit 5. The graph in Exhibit 5 indicates that as prevention and appraisal costs (blue line) increase, the percent of good units increases. In contrast, as internal and external failure costs (green line) decrease, the percent of good units increases. Total quality cost (red line) is the sum of the prevention/appraisal costs and internal/external failure costs.

EXHIBIT 5

The Relationship between the Costs of Quality

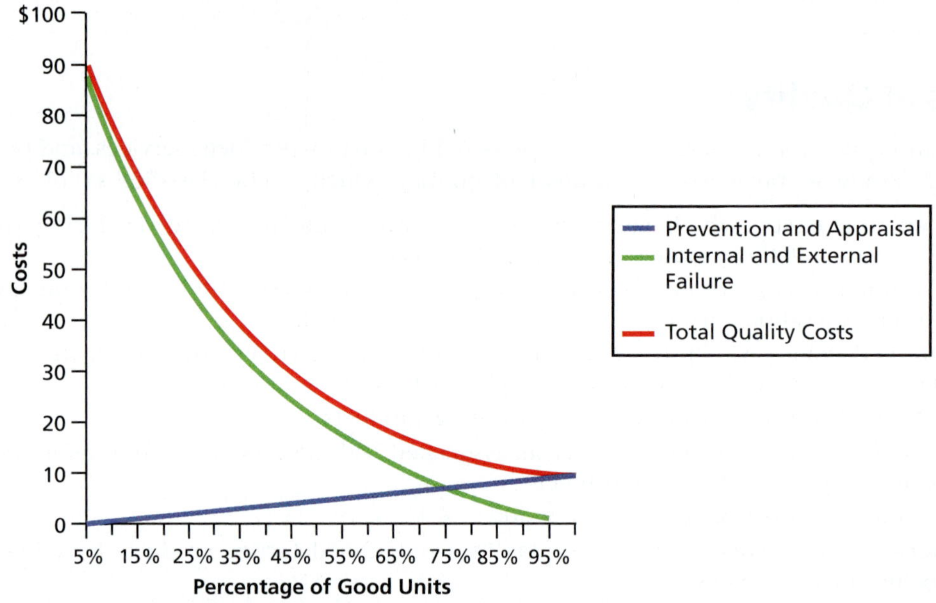

The optimal level of quality (percent of good units) is the one that minimizes the total quality costs. At this point, prevention and appraisal costs are balanced against internal and external failure costs. Exhibit 5 indicates that the optimal level of quality occurs at (or near) 100% quality. This is because prevention and appraisal costs grow moderately as quality increases. However, the costs of internal and external failure drop dramatically as quality increases.

Quality Activity Analysis

An activity analysis of quality quantifies the costs of quality in dollar terms. To illustrate, the quality control activities, activity costs, and quality cost classifications for Gifford Company, a consumer electronics company, are shown in Exhibit 6.

EXHIBIT 6

Quality Control Activity Analysis—Gifford Company

Quality Control Activities	Activity Cost	Quality Cost Classification
Design engineering	$ 55,000	Prevention
Disposing of rejected materials	160,000	Internal Failure
Finished goods inspection	140,000	Appraisal
Materials inspection	70,000	Appraisal
Preventive maintenance	80,000	Prevention
Processing returned materials	150,000	External Failure
Disposing of scrap	195,000	Internal Failure
Assessing vendor quality	45,000	Prevention
Rework	380,000	Internal Failure
Warranty work	225,000	External Failure
Total activity cost	$1,500,000	

Pareto Chart of Quality Costs One method of reporting quality cost information is using a Pareto chart. A **Pareto chart** is a bar chart that shows the totals of an attribute for a number of categories. The categories are ranked and shown left to right, so that the largest total attribute is on the left and the smallest total is on the right.

To illustrate, Exhibit 7 is a Pareto chart for the quality control activities in Exhibit 6.

EXHIBIT 7

Pareto Chart of Quality Costs

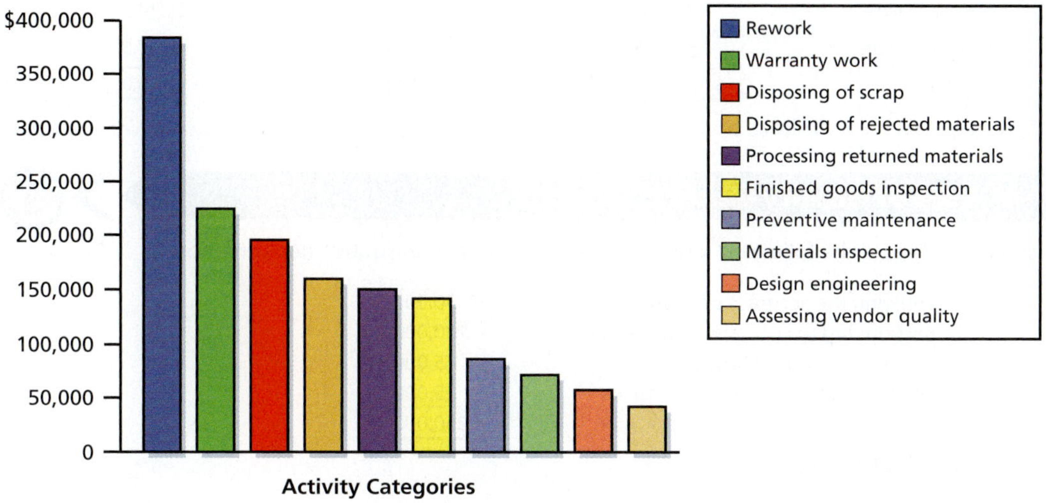

In Exhibit 7, the vertical axis is dollars, which represents quality control costs. The horizontal axis represents activity categories, which are the ten quality control cost activities. The ten quality control cost categories are ranked from the one with the largest total on the left to the one with the smallest total on the right. Thus, the largest bar on the left is rework costs ($380,000), the second bar is warranty work ($225,000), and so on.

The Pareto chart gives managers a quick visual tool for identifying the most important quality control cost categories. Exhibit 7 indicates that Gifford Company should focus efforts on reducing rework and warranty costs.

Cost of Quality Report The costs of quality also can be summarized in a cost of quality report. A **cost of quality report** normally reports the:

1. Total activity cost for each quality cost classification
2. Percent of total quality costs associated with each classification
3. Percent of each quality cost classification to sales

Exhibit 8 is a cost of quality report for Gifford Company, based on assumed sales of $5,000,000. Exhibit 8 indicates that only 12% of the total quality cost is the cost of preventing quality problems, while 14% is the cost of appraisal activities. Thus, prevention and appraisal costs make up only 26% of the total quality control costs. In contrast, 74% (49% + 25%) of the quality control costs are incurred for internal (49%) and external failure (25%) costs. In addition, internal and external failure costs are 22.2% (14.7% + 7.5%) of sales.

Exhibit 8 implies that Gifford Company is not spending enough on prevention and appraisal activities. By spending more on prevention and appraisal, internal and external failure costs will decrease, as was shown in Exhibit 5.

EXHIBIT 8

Cost of Quality Report—Gifford Company

Gifford Company
Cost of Quality Report

Quality Cost Classification	Quality Cost	Percent of Total Quality Cost	Percent of Total Sales
Prevention	$ 180,000	12%	3.6%
Appraisal	210,000	14	4.2
Internal failure	735,000	49	14.7
External failure	375,000	25	7.5
Total	$1,500,000	100%	30.0%

Example Exercise 27-4 Cost of Quality Report

OBJ 4

A quality control activity analysis indicated the following four activity costs of an administrative department:

Verifying the accuracy of a form	$ 50,000
Responding to customer complaints	100,000
Correcting errors in forms	75,000
Redesigning forms to reduce errors	25,000
Total	$250,000

Sales are $2,000,000. Prepare a cost of quality report.

Follow My Example 27-4

Cost of Quality Report

Quality Cost Classification	Quality Cost	Percent of Total Quality Cost	Percent of Total Sales
Prevention	$ 25,000	10%	1.25%
Appraisal	50,000	20	2.50
Internal failure	75,000	30	3.75
External failure	100,000	40	5.00
Total	$250,000	100%	12.50%

Practice Exercises: **PE 27-4A, PE 27-4B**

Value-Added Activity Analysis

In the preceding section, the quality control activities of Gifford Company were classified as prevention, appraisal, internal failure, and external failure activities. Activities also may be classified as:

1. Value-added
2. Non-value-added

A **value-added activity** is one that is necessary to meet customer requirements. A **non-value-added activity** is *not* required by the customer but occurs because of mistakes, errors, omissions, and process failures.

To illustrate, Exhibit 9 shows the value-added and non-value-added classification for the quality control activities for Gifford Company.[3] This exhibit also reveals that internal and external failure costs are classified as non-value-added. In contrast, prevention and appraisal costs are classified as value-added.[4]

3 We use the quality control activities for illustrating the value-added and non-value-added activities in this section. However, a value-added/non-value-added activity analysis can be done for any activity in a business, not just quality control activities.

4 Some believe that appraisal costs are non-value-added. They argue that if the product had been made correctly, then no inspection would be required. We take a less strict view and assume that appraisal costs are value-added.

EXHIBIT 9

Value-Added/ Non-Value-Added Quality Control Activities

Quality Control Activities	Activity Cost	Classification
Design engineering	$ 55,000	Value-added
Disposing of rejected materials	160,000	Non-value-added
Finished goods inspection	140,000	Value-added
Materials inspection	70,000	Value-added
Preventive maintenance	80,000	Value-added
Processing returned materials	150,000	Non-value-added
Disposing of scrap	195,000	Non-value-added
Assessing vendor quality	45,000	Value-added
Rework	380,000	Non-value-added
Warranty work	225,000	Non-value-added
Total activity cost	$1,500,000	

A summary of the value-added and non-value-added activities is shown below. The summary expresses value-added and non-value-added costs as a percent of total costs.

Classification	Amount	Percent
Value-added	$ 390,000	26%
Non-value-added	1,110,000	74
Total	$1,500,000	100%

The preceding summary indicates that 74% of Gifford Company's quality control activities are non-value-added. This should motivate Gifford Company to make improvements to reduce non-value-added activities.

Process Activity Analysis

Activity analysis can be used to evaluate business processes. A **process** is a series of activities that converts an input into an output. In other words, a process is a set of activities linked together by inputs and outputs. Common business processes include:

1. Procurement
2. Product development
3. Manufacturing
4. Distribution
5. Sales order fulfillment

Exhibit 10 shows a sales order fulfillment process for Masters Company. This process converts a customer order (the input) into a product received by the customer (the output).

EXHIBIT 10 **Frozen Delight's Cost Flows**

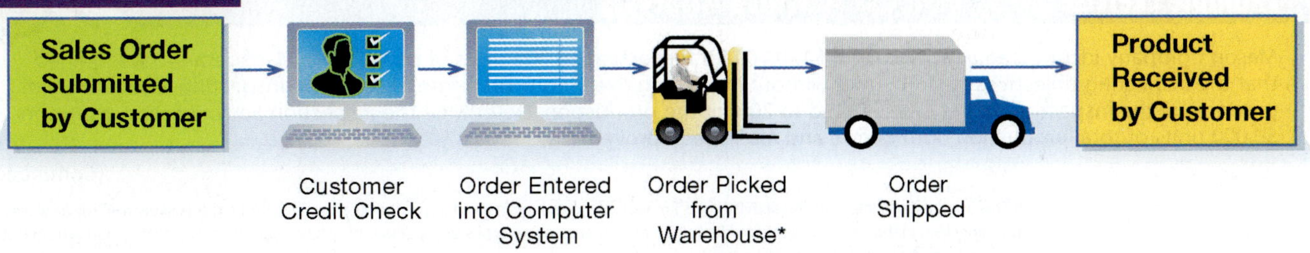

*Operators driving forklifts receive a list of orders, drive to stacking locations within the warehouse, pick the orders, and then transport them back to an area to prepare for shipment.

Exhibit 10 indicates that Masters Company's sales order fulfillment process has the following four activities:

1. Customer credit check
2. Order entered into computer system
3. Order picked from warehouse
4. Order shipped

A process activity analysis can be used to determine the cost of the preceding activities. To illustrate, assume that a process activity analysis determines that the cost of the four activities is as follows:

Sales Order Fulfillment Activities	Activity Cost	Percent of Total Process Cost
Customer credit check	$14,400	18%
Order entered into computer system	9,600	12
Order picked from warehouse	36,000	45
Order shipped	20,000	25
Total sales order fulfillment process cost	$80,000	100%

If 10,000 sales orders are filled during the current period, the per-unit process cost is $8 per order ($80,000/10,000 orders).

Management can use process activity analysis to improve a process. To illustrate, assume that Masters Company sets a cost improvement target of $6 per order. A $2 reduction per order ($8 – $6) requires improving efficiency or eliminating unnecessary activities.

Masters Company determines that only *new* customers need to have a credit check. If this change is made, it is estimated that only 25% of sales orders would require credit checks. In addition, by revising the warehouse product layout, it is estimated that the cost of picking orders can be reduced by 35%.

Assuming that 10,000 orders will be filled, the cost savings from these two improvements are as follows:

Sales Order Fulfillment Activities	Activity Cost Prior to Improvement	Activity Cost After Improvement	Activity Cost Savings
Customer credit check	$14,400	$ 3,600*	$10,800
Order entered in computer system	9,600	9,600	0
Order picked from warehouse	36,000	23,400**	12,600
Order shipped	20,000	20,000	0
Total sales order fulfillment process cost	$80,000	$56,600	$23,400
Cost per order (total cost divided by 10,000 orders)	$8.00	$5.66	

*$14,400 × 25%

**$36,000 – ($36,000 × 35%)

As shown above, the activity changes generate a savings of $23,400.[5] In addition, the cost per order is reduced to $5.66, which is less than the $6.00 per order targeted cost.[6]

Example Exercise 27-5 Process Activity Analysis

OBJ 5

Mason Company incurred an activity cost of $120,000 for inspecting 50,000 units of production. Management determined that the inspecting objectives could be met without inspecting every unit. Therefore, rather than inspecting 50,000 units of production, the inspection activity was limited to 20% of the production. Determine the inspection activity cost per unit on 50,000 units of total production both before and after the improvement.

(Continued)

5 This analysis assumes that the activity costs are variable to the inputs and outputs of the process. While this is likely true for processes primarily using labor, such as a sales order fulfillment process, other types of processes may have significant fixed costs that would not change with changes of inputs and outputs.

6 Process activity analysis also can be integrated into a company's budgeting system using flexible budgets. Process activity analysis used in this way is discussed in advanced texts.

Follow My Example 27-5

Inspection activity before improvement: $120,000/50,000 units = $2.40 per unit
Inspection activity after improvement:

Revised inspection cost	(20% × 50,000 units) × $2.40 per unit = $24,000
Revised inspection cost per unit	$24,000/50,000 units = $0.48 per unit

Practice Exercises: **PE 27-5A, PE 27-5B**

At a Glance 27

OBJ 1 Describe just-in-time (JIT) manufacturing practices.

Key Points Just-in-time emphasizes reduced lead time, a product-oriented production layout, a team-oriented work environment, setup time reduction, pull manufacturing, high quality, and supplier and customer partnering in order to improve the supply chain.

Learning Outcomes	Example Exercises	Practice Exercises
• Describe the relationships among setup time, batch size, inventory, and lead time.		
• Compute lead time and the value-added ratio.	EE27-1	PE27-1A, 27-1B
• Identify the characteristics of a just-in-time manufacturing environment and compare it to traditional approaches.	EE27-2	PE27-2A, 27-2B

OBJ 2 Apply just-in-time practices to a nonmanufacturing setting.

Key Points Just-in-time principles can be used in service businesses and administrative processes. In such processes, just-in-time principles are used to process information, such as an engineering design, or people, such as a patient.

Learning Outcome	Example Exercises	Practice Exercises
• Illustrate the use of just-in-time principles in a nonmanufacturing setting, such as an accounting report.		

OBJ 3 Describe the implications of just-in-time manufacturing on cost accounting and performance measurement.

Key Points Under just-in-time, the cost accounting system will have fewer transactions, will combine the materials and work in process accounts, and will account for direct labor as a part of cell conversion cost. Just-in-time will use nonfinancial reporting measures and result in more direct tracing of factory overhead to product cells.

Learning Outcomes	Example Exercises	Practice Exercises
• Identify the implications of the just-in-time philosophy for cost accounting.		
• Prepare just-in-time journal entries for material purchases, application of cell conversion cost, and transfer of cell costs to finished goods.	EE27-3	PE27-3A, 27-3B
• Describe nonfinancial performance measures.		

OBJ 4 Describe and illustrate activity analysis for improving operations.

Key Points Companies use activity analysis to identify the costs of quality, which include prevention, appraisal, internal failure, and external failure costs. The quality cost activities may be reported on a Pareto chart or quality cost report. An alternative method for categorizing activities is by value-added and non-value-added classifications. An activity analysis also can be used to improve the cost of processes.

Learning Outcomes	Example Exercises	Practice Exercises
• Define the costs of quality.		
• Define and prepare a Pareto chart.		
• Prepare a cost of quality report.	EE27-4	PE27-4A, 27-4B
• Identify value-added and non-value-added activity costs.		
• Use process activity analysis to measure process improvement.	EE27-5	PE27-5A, 27-5B

Key Terms

activity analysis (1257)
appraisal costs (1257)
backflush accounting (1254)
conversion costs (1254)
cost of quality report (1259)
costs of quality (1257)
electronic data interchange (EDI) (1253)
employee involvement (1252)
enterprise resource planning (ERP) (1253)
external failure costs (1257)
internal failure costs (1257)
just-in-time (JIT) processing (1246)
lead time (1247)
nonfinancial measure (1256)
non-value-added activity (1260)
non-value-added lead time (1247)
Pareto chart (1259)
prevention costs (1257)
process (1261)
process-oriented layout (1251)
product-oriented layout (1251)
pull manufacturing (1252)
push manufacturing (1252)
radio frequency identification devices (RFID) (1253)
Raw and In Process (RIP) Inventory (1254)
Six Sigma (1252)
supply chain management (1253)
value-added activity (1260)
value-added lead time (1247)
value-added ratio (1248)

Illustrative Problem

Krisco Company operates under the just-in-time philosophy. As such, it has a production cell for its microwave ovens. The conversion cost for 2,400 hours of production is budgeted for the year at $4,800,000.

During January, 2,000 microwave ovens were started and completed. Each oven requires six minutes of cell processing time. The materials cost for each oven is $100.

Instructions

1. Determine the budgeted cell conversion cost per hour.
2. Determine the manufacturing cost per unit.
3. Journalize the entry to record the costs charged to the production cell in January.
4. Journalize the entry to record the costs transferred to finished goods.

Solution

1. Budgeted Cell Conversion Cost Rate = $\frac{\$4,800,000}{2,400 \text{ hours}}$ = $2,000 per cell hour

2.

Materials	$100 per unit
Conversion cost [($2,000 per hour/60 min.) × 6 min.]	200
Total	$300 per unit

3.	Raw and In Process Inventory	200,000	
	Accounts Payable		200,000
	To record materials costs.		
	(2,000 units × $100 per unit)		
	Raw and In Process Inventory	400,000	
	Conversion Costs		400,000
	To record conversion costs.		
	(2,000 units × $200 per unit)		
4.	Finished Goods (2,000 × $300 per unit)	600,000	
	Raw and In Process Inventory		600,000
	To record finished production.		

Discussion Questions

1. What is the benefit of just-in-time processing?
2. What are some examples of non-value-added lead time?
3. Why is a product-oriented layout preferred by just-in-time manufacturers over a process-oriented layout?
4. How is setup time related to lead time?
5. Why do just-in-time manufacturers favor pull or "make to order" manufacturing?
6. Why would a just-in-time manufacturer strive to produce zero defects?
7. How is supply chain management different from traditional supplier and customer relationships?
8. Why does accounting in a just-in-time environment result in fewer transactions?
9. Why do just-in-time manufacturers use a "raw and in process inventory" account, rather than separately reporting materials and work in process?
10. Why is the direct labor cost category eliminated in many just-in-time environments?
11. How does a Pareto chart assist management?
12. What is the benefit of identifying non-value-added activities?
13. What ways can the cost of a process be improved?

Practice Exercises

Example Exercises

EE 27-1 *p. 1251*

PE 27-1A Lead time

OBJ. 1

The Snow Glide Ski Company manufactures skis in the finishing and assembly process. Skis are manufactured in 40-ski batch sizes. The finishing time is 16 minutes per ski. The assembly time is 12 minutes per ski. It takes 15 minutes to move a batch of skis from finishing to assembly.

a. Compute the value-added, non-value-added, and total lead time of this process.

b. Compute the value-added ratio. Round to one decimal.

EE 27-1 *p. 1251*

PE 27-1B Lead time

OBJ. 1

The Texas Jean Company manufactures jeans in the cutting and sewing process. Jeans are manufactured in 100-jean batch sizes. The cutting time is 11 minutes per jean. The sewing time is 8 minutes per jean. It takes 15 minutes to move a batch of jeans from cutting to sewing.

a. Compute the value-added, non-value-added, and total lead time of this process.

b. Compute the value-added ratio. Round to one decimal.

Example Exercises

EE 27-2 p. 1253

PE 27-2A Just-in-time features **OBJ. 1**

Which of the following are features of a just-in-time manufacturing system?

a. Centralized maintenance areas

b. Smaller batch sizes

c. Employee involvement

d. Less wasted movement of material and people

EE 27-2 p. 1253

PE 27-2B Just-in-time features **OBJ. 1**

Which of the following are features of a just-in-time manufacturing system?

a. Production pace matches demand

b. Centralized work in process inventory locations

c. Push scheduling

d. Receive raw materials directly to manufacturing cells

EE 27-3 p. 1256

PE 27-3A Just-in-time journal entries **OBJ. 3**

The annual budgeted conversion costs for a just-in-time cell are $819,000 for 1,950 production hours. Each unit produced by the cell requires 16 minutes of cell process time. During the month, 630 units are manufactured in the cell. The estimated materials costs are $270 per unit. Provide the following journal entries:

a. Materials are purchased to produce 650 units.

b. Conversion costs are applied to 630 units of production.

c. 625 units are completed and placed into finished goods.

EE 27-3 p. 1256

PE 27-3B Just-in-time journal entries **OBJ. 3**

The annual budgeted conversion costs for a just-in-time cell are $144,000 for 1,800 production hours. Each unit produced by the cell requires 9 minutes of cell process time. During the month, 1,000 units are manufactured in the cell. The estimated materials costs are $65 per unit. Provide the following journal entries:

a. Materials are purchased to produce 1,050 units.

b. Conversion costs are applied to 1,000 units of production.

c. 980 units are completed and placed into finished goods.

EE 27-4 p. 1260

PE 27-4A Cost of quality report **OBJ. 4**

A quality control activity analysis indicated the following four activity costs of a manufacturing department:

Rework	$ 28,000
Inspecting incoming raw materials	30,000
Warranty work	16,000
Process improvement effort	126,000
Total	$200,000

Sales are $1,000,000. Prepare a cost of quality report.

EE 27-4 p. 1260

PE 27-4B Cost of quality report **OBJ. 4**

A quality control activity analysis indicated the following four activity costs of a hotel:

Inspecting cleanliness of rooms	$ 108,000
Processing lost customer reservations	450,000
Rework incorrectly prepared room service meal	54,000
Employee training	288,000
Total	$900,000

Sales are $3,000,000. Prepare a cost of quality report.

Example Exercises

EE 27-5 *p. 1262*

PE 27-5A Process activity analysis **OBJ. 5**

Garnett Company incurred an activity cost of $360,000 for inspecting 60,000 units of production. Management determined that the inspecting objectives could be met without inspecting every unit. Therefore, rather than inspecting 60,000 units of production, the inspection activity was limited to 30% of the production. Determine the inspection activity cost per unit on 60,000 units of total production both before and after the improvement.

EE 27-5 *p. 1262*

PE 27-5B Process activity analysis **OBJ. 5**

Boswell Company incurred an activity cost of $68,000 for inspecting 16,000 units of production. Management determined that the inspecting objectives could be met without inspecting every unit. Therefore, rather than inspecting 16,000 units of production, the inspection activity was limited to a random selection of 3,200 units out of the 16,000 units of production. Determine the inspection activity cost per unit on 16,000 units of total production both before and after the improvement.

Exercises

EX 27-1 Just-in-time principles **OBJ. 1**

The chief executive officer (CEO) of Platnum Inc. has just returned from a management seminar describing the benefits of the just-in-time philosophy. The CEO issued the following statement after returning from the conference:

This company will become a just-in-time manufacturing company. Presently, we have too much inventory. To become just-in-time, we need to eliminate the excess inventory. Therefore, I want all employees to begin reducing inventories until we are just-in-time. Thank you for your cooperation.

How would you respond to the CEO's statement?

EX 27-2 Just-in-time as a strategy **OBJ. 1**

The American textile industry has moved much of its operations offshore in the pursuit of lower labor costs. Textile imports have risen from 2% of all textile production in 1962 to over 70% in 2012. Offshore manufacturers make long runs of standard mass-market apparel items. These are then brought to the United States in container ships, requiring significant time between original order and delivery. As a result, retail customers must accurately forecast market demands for imported apparel items.

Assuming that you work for a U.S.-based textile company, how would you recommend responding to the low-cost imports?

EX 27-3 Just-in-time principles **OBJ. 1**

Active Apparel Company manufactures various styles of men's casual wear. Shirts are cut and assembled by a workforce that is paid by piece rate. This means that they are paid according to the amount of work completed during a period of time. To illustrate, if the piece rate is $0.15 per sleeve assembled, and the worker assembles 700 sleeves during the day, then the worker would be paid $105 (700 × $0.15) for the day's work.

The company is considering adopting a just-in-time manufacturing philosophy by organizing work cells around various types of products and employing pull manufacturing. However, no change is expected in the compensation policy. On this point, the manufacturing manager stated the following:

"Piecework compensation provides an incentive to work fast. Without it, the workers will just goof off and expect a full day's pay. We can't pay straight hourly wages—at least not in this industry."

How would you respond to the manufacturing manager's comments?

The following summary events took place in the Lion Model cell during May:

a. Electronic parts were purchased to produce 10,700 Lion Model assemblies in May.
b. Conversion costs were applied for 10,500 units of production in May.
c. 10,200 units were completed and transferred to finished goods in May.
d. 10,000 units were shipped to customers at a price of $500 per unit.

Instructions

1. Determine the budgeted cell conversion cost per hour.
2. Determine the budgeted cell conversion cost per unit.
3. Journalize the summary transactions (a) through (d).
4. Determine the ending balance in Raw and In Process Inventory and Finished Goods Inventory.
5. How does the accounting in a JIT environment differ from traditional accounting?

PR 27-4B Pareto chart and cost of quality report—manufacturing company **OBJ. 4**

✔ 3. Non-value-added, 35%

The president of Mission Inc. has been concerned about the growth in costs over the last several years. The president asked the controller to perform an activity analysis to gain a better insight into these costs. The activity analysis revealed the following:

Activities	Activity Cost
Correcting invoice errors	$ 7,500
Disposing of incoming materials with poor quality	15,000
Disposing of scrap	27,500
Expediting late production	22,500
Final inspection	20,000
Inspecting incoming materials	5,000
Inspecting work in process	25,000
Preventive machine maintenance	15,000
Producing product	97,500
Responding to customer quality complaints	15,000
Total	$250,000

The production process is complicated by quality problems, requiring the production manager to expedite production and dispose of scrap.

Instructions

1. Prepare a Pareto chart of the company activities.
2. Use the activity cost information to determine the percentages of total costs that are prevention, appraisal, internal failure, external failure, and not costs of quality (producing product).
3. Determine the percentages of total costs that are value- and non-value-added.
4. Interpret the information.

Cases & Projects

CP 27-1 Ethics and professional conduct in business

In August, Lannister Company introduced a new performance measurement system in manufacturing operations. One of the new performance measures was lead time. The lead time was determined by tagging a random sample of items with a log sheet throughout the month. This log sheet recorded the time that the item started and the time that it ended production, as well as all steps in between. The controller collected the log sheets and calculated the average lead time of the tagged products. This number was reported to central management and was used to evaluate the performance of the plant manager. The plant was under extreme pressure to reduce lead time because of poor lead time results reported in September.

The following memo was intercepted by the controller.

> Date: October 1
> To: Hourly Employees
> From: Plant Manager
>
> During last month, you noticed that some of the products were tagged with a log sheet. This sheet records the time that a product enters production and the time that it leaves production. The difference between these two times is termed the "lead time." Our plant is evaluated on improving lead time. From now on, I ask all of you to keep an eye out for the tagged items. When you receive a tagged item, it is to receive special attention. Work on that item first, and then immediately move it to the next operation. Under no circumstances should tagged items wait on any other work that you have. Naturally, report accurate information. I insist that you record the correct times on the log sheet as the product goes through your operations.

How should the controller respond to this discovery?

CP 27-2 Just-in-time principles

Reliant Products Inc. manufactures electric space heaters. While the CEO, Lynn Jennings, is visiting the production facility, the following conversation takes place with the plant manager, Aaron Clark:

Lynn: As I walk around the facility, I can't help noticing all the materials inventories. What's going on?

Aaron: I have found our suppliers to be very unreliable in meeting their delivery commitments. Thus, I keep a lot of materials on hand so as to not risk running out and shutting down production.

Lynn: Not only do I see a lot of materials inventory, but there also seems to be a lot of finished goods inventory on hand. Why is this?

Aaron: As you know, I am evaluated on maintaining a low cost per unit. The one way that I am able to reduce my unit costs is by producing as many space heaters as possible. This allows me to spread my fixed costs over a larger base. When orders are down, the excess production builds up as inventory, as we are seeing now. But don't worry—I'm really keeping our unit costs down this way.

Lynn: I'm not so sure. It seems that this inventory must cost us something.

Aaron: Not really. I'll eventually use the materials and we'll eventually sell the finished goods. By keeping the plant busy, I'm using our plant assets wisely. This is reflected in the low unit costs that I'm able to maintain.

If you were Lynn Jennings, how would you respond to Aaron Clark? What recommendations would you provide Aaron Clark?

CP 27-3 Just-in-time principles

Maxxim Inc. prepared the following performance graphs for the prior year:

Total Manufacturing Lead Time

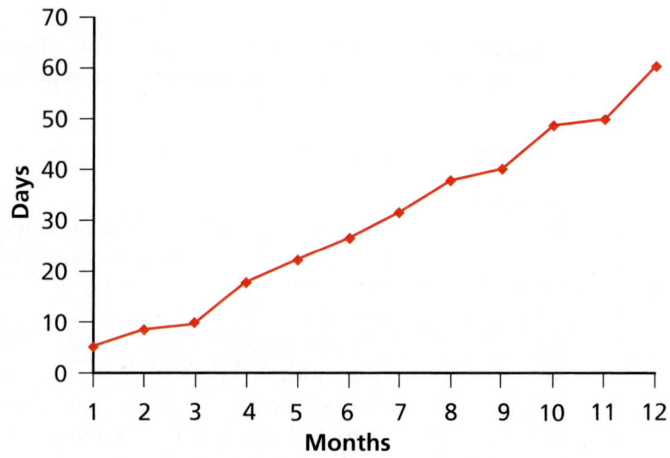

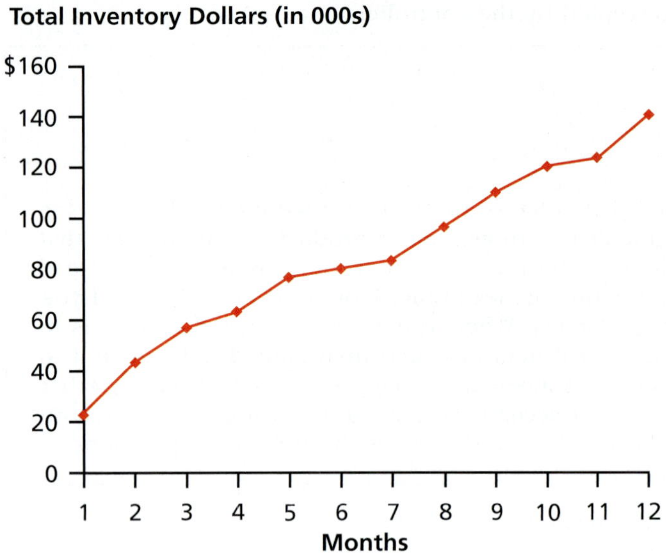

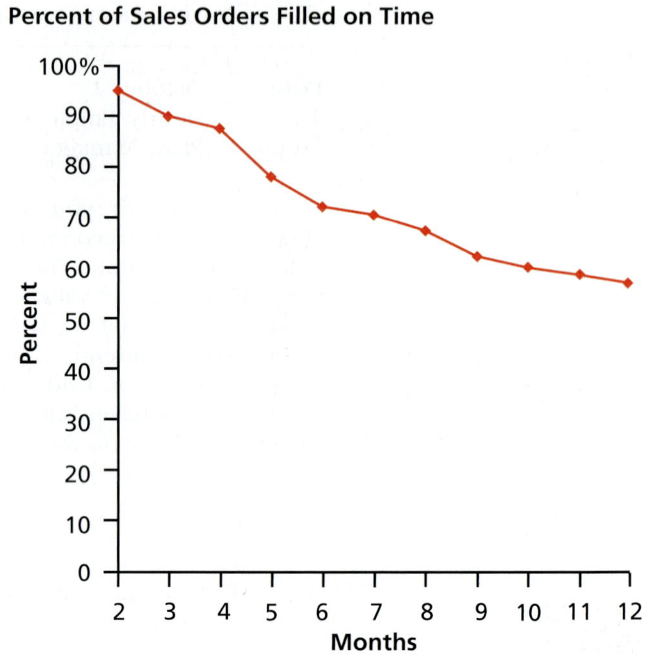

What do these appear to indicate?

CP 27-4 Value-added and non-value-added activity costs

Pryor Company prepared the following factory overhead report from its general ledger:

Indirect labor	$250,000
Fringe benefits	30,000
Supplies	70,000
Depreciation	50,000
Total	$400,000

The management of Pryor Company was dissatisfied with this report and asked the controller to prepare an activity analysis of the same information. This activity analysis was as follows:

Processing sales orders	$ 68,000	17%
Disposing of scrap	96,000	24
Expediting work orders	80,000	20
Producing parts	44,000	11
Resolving supplier quality problems	56,000	14
Reissuing corrected purchase orders	40,000	10
Expediting customer orders	16,000	4
Total	$400,000	100%

Interpret the activity analysis by identifying value-added and non-value-added activity costs. How does the activity cost report differ from the general ledger report?

CP 27-5 Lead time

Group Project

In groups of two to four people, visit a sit-down restaurant and do a lead time study. If more than one group chooses to visit the same restaurant, choose different times for your visits. Note the time when you walk in the door of the restaurant and the time when you walk out the door after you have eaten. The difference between these two times is the total lead time of your restaurant experience. While in the restaurant, determine the time spent on non-value-added time, such as wait time, and the time spent on value-added eating time. Note the various activities and the time required to perform each activity during your visit to the restaurant. Compare your analyses, identifying possible reasons for differences in the times recorded by groups that visited the same restaurant.

Appendices

Appendix A

Interest Tables

Present Value of $1 at Compound Interest Due in *n* Periods

Periods	4.0%	4.5%	5%	5.5%	6%	6.5%	7%
1	0.96154	0.95694	0.95238	0.94787	0.94340	0.93897	0.93458
2	0.92456	0.91573	0.90703	0.89845	0.89000	0.88166	0.87344
3	0.88900	0.87630	0.86384	0.85161	0.83962	0.82785	0.81630
4	0.85480	0.83856	0.82270	0.80722	0.79209	0.77732	0.76290
5	0.82193	0.80245	0.78353	0.76513	0.74726	0.72988	0.71299
6	0.79031	0.76790	0.74622	0.72525	0.70496	0.68533	0.66634
7	0.75992	0.73483	0.71068	0.68744	0.66506	0.64351	0.62275
8	0.73069	0.70319	0.67684	0.65160	0.62741	0.60423	0.58201
9	0.70259	0.67290	0.64461	0.61763	0.59190	0.56735	0.54393
10	0.67556	0.64393	0.61391	0.58543	0.55839	0.53273	0.50835
11	0.64958	0.61620	0.58468	0.55491	0.52679	0.50021	0.47509
12	0.62460	0.58966	0.55684	0.52598	0.49697	0.46968	0.44401
13	0.60057	0.56427	0.53032	0.49856	0.46884	0.44102	0.41496
14	0.57748	0.53997	0.50507	0.47257	0.44230	0.41410	0.38782
15	0.55526	0.51672	0.48102	0.44793	0.41727	0.38883	0.36245
16	0.53391	0.49447	0.45811	0.42458	0.39365	0.36510	0.33873
17	0.51337	0.47318	0.43630	0.40245	0.37136	0.34281	0.31657
18	0.49363	0.45280	0.41552	0.38147	0.35034	0.32189	0.29586
19	0.47464	0.43330	0.39573	0.36158	0.33051	0.30224	0.27651
20	0.45639	0.41464	0.37689	0.34273	0.31180	0.28380	0.25842
21	0.43883	0.39679	0.35894	0.32486	0.29416	0.26648	0.24151
22	0.42196	0.37970	0.34185	0.30793	0.27751	0.25021	0.22571
23	0.40573	0.36335	0.32557	0.29187	0.26180	0.23494	0.21095
24	0.39012	0.34770	0.31007	0.27666	0.24698	0.22060	0.19715
25	0.37512	0.33273	0.29530	0.26223	0.23300	0.20714	0.18425
26	0.36069	0.31840	0.28124	0.24856	0.21981	0.19450	0.17220
27	0.34682	0.30469	0.26785	0.23560	0.20737	0.18263	0.16093
28	0.33348	0.29157	0.25509	0.22332	0.19563	0.17148	0.15040
29	0.32065	0.27902	0.24295	0.21168	0.18456	0.16101	0.14056
30	0.30832	0.26700	0.23138	0.20064	0.17411	0.15119	0.13137
31	0.29646	0.25550	0.22036	0.19018	0.16425	0.14196	0.12277
32	0.28506	0.24450	0.20987	0.18027	0.15496	0.13329	0.11474
33	0.27409	0.23397	0.19987	0.17087	0.14619	0.12516	0.10723
34	0.26355	0.22390	0.19035	0.16196	0.13791	0.11752	0.10022
35	0.25342	0.21425	0.18129	0.15352	0.13011	0.11035	0.09366
40	0.20829	0.17193	0.14205	0.11746	0.09722	0.08054	0.06678
45	0.17120	0.13796	0.11130	0.08988	0.07265	0.05879	0.04761
50	0.14071	0.11071	0.08720	0.06877	0.05429	0.04291	0.03395

Present Value of $1 at Compound Interest Due in *n* Periods

Periods	8%	9%	10%	11%	12%	13%	14%
1	0.92593	0.91743	0.90909	0.90090	0.89286	0.88496	0.87719
2	0.85734	0.84168	0.82645	0.81162	0.79719	0.78315	0.76947
3	0.79383	0.77218	0.75131	0.73119	0.71178	0.69305	0.67497
4	0.73503	0.70843	0.68301	0.65873	0.63552	0.61332	0.59208
5	0.68058	0.64993	0.62092	0.59345	0.56743	0.54276	0.51937
6	0.63017	0.59627	0.56447	0.53464	0.50663	0.48032	0.45559
7	0.58349	0.54703	0.51316	0.48166	0.45235	0.42506	0.39964
8	0.54027	0.50187	0.46651	0.43393	0.40388	0.37616	0.35056
9	0.50025	0.46043	0.42410	0.39092	0.36061	0.33288	0.30751
10	0.46319	0.42241	0.38554	0.35218	0.32197	0.29459	0.26974
11	0.42888	0.38753	0.35049	0.31728	0.28748	0.26070	0.23662
12	0.39711	0.35553	0.31863	0.28584	0.25668	0.23071	0.20756
13	0.36770	0.32618	0.28966	0.25751	0.22917	0.20416	0.18207
14	0.34046	0.29925	0.26333	0.23199	0.20462	0.18068	0.15971
15	0.31524	0.27454	0.23939	0.20900	0.18270	0.15989	0.14010
16	0.29189	0.25187	0.21763	0.18829	0.16312	0.14150	0.12289
17	0.27027	0.23107	0.19784	0.16963	0.14564	0.12522	0.10780
18	0.25025	0.21199	0.17986	0.15282	0.13004	0.11081	0.09456
19	0.23171	0.19449	0.16351	0.13768	0.11611	0.09806	0.08295
20	0.21455	0.17843	0.14864	0.12403	0.10367	0.08678	0.07276
21	0.19866	0.16370	0.13513	0.11174	0.09256	0.07680	0.06383
22	0.18394	0.15018	0.12285	0.10067	0.08264	0.06796	0.05599
23	0.17032	0.13778	0.11168	0.09069	0.07379	0.06014	0.04911
24	0.15770	0.12640	0.10153	0.08170	0.06588	0.05323	0.04308
25	0.14602	0.11597	0.09230	0.07361	0.05882	0.04710	0.03779
26	0.13520	0.10639	0.08391	0.06631	0.05252	0.04168	0.03315
27	0.12519	0.09761	0.07628	0.05974	0.04689	0.03689	0.02908
28	0.11591	0.08955	0.06934	0.05382	0.04187	0.03264	0.02551
29	0.10733	0.08215	0.06304	0.04849	0.03738	0.02889	0.02237
30	0.09938	0.07537	0.05731	0.04368	0.03338	0.02557	0.01963
31	0.09202	0.06915	0.05210	0.03935	0.02980	0.02262	0.01722
32	0.08520	0.06344	0.04736	0.03545	0.02661	0.02002	0.01510
33	0.07889	0.05820	0.04306	0.03194	0.02376	0.01772	0.01325
34	0.07305	0.05339	0.03914	0.02878	0.02121	0.01568	0.01162
35	0.06763	0.04899	0.03558	0.02592	0.01894	0.01388	0.01019
40	0.04603	0.03184	0.02209	0.01538	0.01075	0.00753	0.00529
45	0.03133	0.02069	0.01372	0.00913	0.00610	0.00409	0.00275
50	0.02132	0.01345	0.00852	0.00542	0.00346	0.00222	0.00143

Present Value of Ordinary Annuity of $1 per Period

Periods	4.0%	4.5%	5%	5.5%	6%	6.5%	7%
1	0.96154	0.95694	0.95238	0.94787	0.94340	0.93897	0.93458
2	1.88609	1.87267	1.85941	1.84632	1.83339	1.82063	1.80802
3	2.77509	2.74896	2.72325	2.69793	2.67301	2.64848	2.62432
4	3.62990	3.58753	3.54595	3.50515	3.46511	3.42580	3.38721
5	4.45182	4.38998	4.32948	4.27028	4.21236	4.15568	4.10020
6	5.24214	5.15787	5.07569	4.99553	4.91732	4.84101	4.76654
7	6.00205	5.89270	5.78637	5.68297	5.58238	5.48452	5.38929
8	6.73274	6.59589	6.46321	6.33457	6.20979	6.08875	5.97130
9	7.43533	7.26879	7.10782	6.95220	6.80169	6.65610	6.51523
10	8.11090	7.91272	7.72173	7.53763	7.36009	7.18883	7.02358
11	8.76048	8.52892	8.30641	8.09254	7.88687	7.68904	7.49867
12	9.38507	9.11858	8.86325	8.61852	8.38384	8.15873	7.94269
13	9.98565	9.68285	9.39357	9.11708	8.85268	8.59974	8.35765
14	10.56312	10.22283	9.89864	9.58965	9.29498	9.01384	8.74547
15	11.11839	10.73955	10.37966	10.03758	9.71225	9.40267	9.10791
16	11.65230	11.23402	10.83777	10.46216	10.10590	9.76776	9.44665
17	12.16567	11.70719	11.27407	10.86461	10.47726	10.11058	9.76322
18	12.65930	12.15999	11.68959	11.24607	10.82760	10.43247	10.05909
19	13.13394	12.59329	12.08532	11.60765	11.15812	10.73471	10.33560
20	13.59033	13.00794	12.46221	11.95038	11.46992	11.01851	10.59401
21	14.02916	13.40472	12.82115	12.27524	11.76408	11.28498	10.83553
22	14.45112	13.78442	13.16300	12.58317	12.04158	11.53520	11.06124
23	14.85684	14.14777	13.48857	12.87504	12.30338	11.77014	11.27219
24	15.24696	14.49548	13.79864	13.15170	12.55036	11.99074	11.46933
25	15.62208	14.82821	14.09394	13.41393	12.78336	12.19788	11.65358
26	15.98277	15.14661	14.37519	13.66250	13.00317	12.39237	11.82578
27	16.32959	15.45130	14.64303	13.89810	13.21053	12.57500	11.98671
28	16.66306	15.74287	14.89813	14.12142	13.40616	12.74648	12.13711
29	16.98371	16.02189	15.14107	14.33310	13.59072	12.90749	12.27767
30	17.29203	16.28889	15.37245	14.53375	13.76483	13.05868	12.40904
31	17.58849	16.54439	15.59281	14.72393	13.92909	13.20063	12.53181
32	17.87355	16.78889	15.80268	14.90420	14.08404	13.33393	12.64656
33	18.14765	17.02286	16.00255	15.07507	14.23023	13.45909	12.75379
34	18.41120	17.24676	16.19290	15.23703	14.36814	13.57661	12.85401
35	18.66461	17.46101	16.37419	15.39055	14.49825	13.68696	12.94767
40	19.79277	18.40158	17.15909	16.04612	15.04630	14.14553	13.33171
45	20.72004	19.15635	17.77407	16.54773	15.45583	14.48023	13.60552
50	21.48218	19.76201	18.25593	16.93152	15.76186	14.72452	13.80075

Present Value of Ordinary Annuity of $1 per Period

Periods	8%	9%	10%	11%	12%	13%	14%
1	0.92593	0.91743	0.90909	0.90090	0.89286	0.88496	0.87719
2	1.78326	1.75911	1.73554	1.71252	1.69005	1.66810	1.64666
3	2.57710	2.53129	2.48685	2.44371	2.40183	2.36115	2.32163
4	3.31213	3.23972	3.16987	3.10245	3.03735	2.97447	2.91371
5	3.99271	3.88965	3.79079	3.69590	3.60478	3.51723	3.43308
6	4.62288	4.48592	4.35526	4.23054	4.11141	3.99755	3.88867
7	5.20637	5.03295	4.86842	4.71220	4.56376	4.42261	4.28830
8	5.74664	5.53482	5.33493	5.14612	4.96764	4.79677	4.63886
9	6.24689	5.99525	5.75902	5.53705	5.32825	5.13166	4.94637
10	6.71008	6.41766	6.14457	5.88923	5.65022	5.42624	5.21612
11	7.13896	6.80519	6.49506	6.20652	5.93770	5.68694	5.45273
12	7.53608	7.16073	6.81369	6.49236	6.19437	5.91765	5.66029
13	7.90378	7.48690	7.10336	6.74987	6.42355	6.12181	5.84236
14	8.22424	7.78615	7.36669	6.96187	6.62817	6.30249	6.00207
15	8.55948	8.06069	7.60608	7.19087	6.81086	6.46238	6.14217
16	8.85137	8.31256	7.82371	7.37916	6.97399	6.60388	6.26506
17	9.12164	8.54363	8.02155	7.54879	7.11963	6.72909	6.37286
18	9.37189	8.75563	8.20141	7.70162	7.24967	6.83991	6.46742
19	9.60360	8.95011	8.36492	7.83929	7.36578	6.93797	6.55037
20	9.81815	9.12855	8.51356	7.96333	7.46944	7.02475	6.62313
21	10.01680	9.29224	8.64869	8.07507	7.56200	7.10155	6.68696
22	10.20074	9.44243	8.77154	8.17574	7.64465	7.16951	6.74294
23	10.37106	9.58021	8.88322	8.26643	7.71843	7.22966	6.79206
24	10.52876	9.70661	8.98474	8.34814	7.78432	7.28288	6.83514
25	10.67478	9.82258	9.07704	8.42174	7.84314	7.32998	6.87293
26	10.80998	9.92897	9.16095	8.48806	7.89566	7.37167	6.90608
27	10.93516	10.02658	9.23722	8.54780	7.94255	7.40856	6.93515
28	11.05108	10.11613	9.30657	8.60162	7.98442	7.44120	6.96066
29	11.15841	10.19828	9.36961	8.65011	8.02181	7.47009	6.98304
30	11.25778	10.27365	9.42691	8.69379	8.05518	7.49565	7.00266
31	11.34980	10.34280	9.47901	8.73315	8.08499	7.51828	7.01988
32	11.43500	10.40624	9.52638	8.76860	8.11159	7.53830	7.03498
33	11.51389	10.46444	9.56943	8.80054	8.13535	7.55602	7.04823
34	11.58693	10.51784	9.60857	8.82932	8.15656	7.57170	7.05985
35	11.65457	10.56682	9.64416	8.85524	8.17550	7.58557	7.07005
40	11.92461	10.75736	9.77905	8.95105	8.24378	7.63438	7.10504
45	12.10840	10.88120	9.86281	9.00791	8.28252	7.66086	7.12322
50	12.23348	10.96168	9.91481	9.04165	8.30450	7.67524	7.13266

Present Value of Ordinary Annuity of $1 per Period

Appendix B

NIKE INC

FORM 10-K
(Annual Report)

Filed 07/22/11 for the Period Ending 05/31/11

Address	ONE BOWERMAN DR BEAVERTON, OR 97005-6453
Telephone	5036713173
CIK	0000320187
Symbol	NKE
SIC Code	3021 - Rubber and Plastics Footwear
Industry	Footwear
Sector	Consumer Cyclical
Fiscal Year	05/31

Source: Nike, Inc. Annual Report pursuant to Section 13 or 15(b) of the Securities Exchange Act of 1934. For the fiscal year ended May 31, 2011. United States Securities and Exchange Commission, Washington D.C. 20549.

Table of Contents

Management's Annual Report on Internal Control Over Financial Reporting

Management is responsible for establishing and maintaining adequate internal control over financial reporting, as such term is defined in Rule 13a-15(f) and Rule 15d-15(f) of the Securities Exchange Act of 1934, as amended. Internal control over financial reporting is a process designed to provide reasonable assurance regarding the reliability of financial reporting and the preparation of the financial statements for external purposes in accordance with generally accepted accounting principles in the United States of America. Internal control over financial reporting includes those policies and procedures that: (i) pertain to the maintenance of records that, in reasonable detail, accurately and fairly reflect the transactions and dispositions of assets of the company; (ii) provide reasonable assurance that transactions are recorded as necessary to permit preparation of financial statements in accordance with generally accepted accounting principles, and that receipts and expenditures of the company are being made only in accordance with authorizations of our management and directors; and (iii) provide reasonable assurance regarding prevention or timely detection of unauthorized acquisition, use or disposition of assets of the company that could have a material effect on the financial statements.

While "reasonable assurance" is a high level of assurance, it does not mean absolute assurance. Because of its inherent limitations, internal control over financial reporting may not prevent or detect every misstatement and instance of fraud. Controls are susceptible to manipulation, especially in instances of fraud caused by the collusion of two or more people, including our senior management. Also, projections of any evaluation of effectiveness to future periods are subject to the risk that controls may become inadequate because of changes in conditions, or that the degree of compliance with the policies or procedures may deteriorate.

Under the supervision and with the participation of our Chief Executive Officer and Chief Financial Officer, our management conducted an evaluation of the effectiveness of our internal control over financial reporting based upon the framework in *Internal Control — Integrated Framework* issued by the Committee of Sponsoring Organizations of the Treadway Commission (COSO). Based on the results of our evaluation, our management concluded that our internal control over financial reporting was effective as of May 31, 2011.

PricewaterhouseCoopers LLP, an independent registered public accounting firm, has audited (1) the consolidated financial statements and (2) the effectiveness of our internal control over financial reporting as of May 31, 2011, as stated in their report herein.

Mark G. Parker
Chief Executive Officer and President

Donald W. Blair
Chief Financial Officer

Table of Contents

REPORT OF INDEPENDENT REGISTERED PUBLIC ACCOUNTING FIRM

To the Board of Directors and
Shareholders of NIKE, Inc.:

In our opinion, the consolidated financial statements listed in the index appearing under Item 15(a)(1) present fairly, in all material respects, the financial position of NIKE, Inc. and its subsidiaries at May 31, 2011 and 2010, and the results of their operations and their cash flows for each of the three years in the period ended May 31, 2011 in conformity with accounting principles generally accepted in the United States of America. In addition, in our opinion, the financial statement schedule listed in the appendix appearing under Item 15(a)(2) presents fairly, in all material respects, the information set forth therein when read in conjunction with the related consolidated financial statements. Also in our opinion, the Company maintained, in all material respects, effective internal control over financial reporting as of May 31, 2011, based on criteria established in *Internal Control — Integrated Framework* issued by the Committee of Sponsoring Organizations of the Treadway Commission (COSO). The Company's management is responsible for these financial statements and financial statement schedule, for maintaining effective internal control over financial reporting and for its assessment of the effectiveness of internal control over financial reporting, included in Management's Annual Report on Internal Control Over Financial Reporting appearing under Item 8. Our responsibility is to express opinions on these financial statements, on the financial statement schedule, and on the Company's internal control over financial reporting based on our integrated audits. We conducted our audits in accordance with the standards of the Public Company Accounting Oversight Board (United States). Those standards require that we plan and perform the audits to obtain reasonable assurance about whether the financial statements are free of material misstatement and whether effective internal control over financial reporting was maintained in all material respects. Our audits of the financial statements included examining, on a test basis, evidence supporting the amounts and disclosures in the financial statements, assessing the accounting principles used and significant estimates made by management, and evaluating the overall financial statement presentation. Our audit of internal control over financial reporting included obtaining an understanding of internal control over financial reporting, assessing the risk that a material weakness exists, and testing and evaluating the design and operating effectiveness of internal control based on the assessed risk. Our audits also included performing such other procedures as we considered necessary in the circumstances. We believe that our audits provide a reasonable basis for our opinions.

A company's internal control over financial reporting is a process designed to provide reasonable assurance regarding the reliability of financial reporting and the preparation of financial statements for external purposes in accordance with generally accepted accounting principles. A company's internal control over financial reporting includes those policies and procedures that (i) pertain to the maintenance of records that, in reasonable detail, accurately and fairly reflect the transactions and dispositions of the assets of the company; (ii) provide reasonable assurance that transactions are recorded as necessary to permit preparation of financial statements in accordance with generally accepted accounting principles, and that receipts and expenditures of the company are being made only in accordance with authorizations of management and directors of the company; and (iii) provide reasonable assurance regarding prevention or timely detection of unauthorized acquisition, use, or disposition of the company's assets that could have a material effect on the financial statements.

Because of its inherent limitations, internal control over financial reporting may not prevent or detect misstatements. Also, projections of any evaluation of effectiveness to future periods are subject to the risk that controls may become inadequate because of changes in conditions, or that the degree of compliance with the policies or procedures may deteriorate.

/s/ P RICEWATERHOUSE C OOPERS LLP

Portland, Oregon
July 22, 2011

NIKE, INC.
CONSOLIDATED STATEMENTS OF INCOME

	Year Ended May 31, 2011	2010	2009
	(In millions, except per share data)		
Revenues	$20,862	$19,014	$19,176
Cost of sales	11,354	10,214	10,572
Gross margin	9,508	8,800	8,604
Demand creation expense	2,448	2,356	2,352
Operating overhead expense	4,245	3,970	3,798
Total selling and administrative expense	6,693	6,326	6,150
Restructuring charges (Note 16)	—	—	195
Goodwill impairment (Note 4)	—	—	199
Intangible and other asset impairment (Note 4)	—	—	202
Interest expense (income), net (Notes 6, 7 and 8)	4	6	(10)
Other (income), net (Note 17)	(33)	(49)	(89)
Income before income taxes	2,844	2,517	1,957
Income taxes (Note 9)	711	610	470
Net income	$ 2,133	$ 1,907	$ 1,487
Basic earnings per common share (Notes 1 and 12)	$ 4.48	$ 3.93	$ 3.07
Diluted earnings per common share (Notes 1 and 12)	$ 4.39	$ 3.86	$ 3.03
Dividends declared per common share	$ 1.20	$ 1.06	$ 0.98

The accompanying notes to consolidated financial statements are an integral part of this statement.

Table of Contents

NIKE, INC.

CONSOLIDATED BALANCE SHEETS

	May 31, 2011	May 31, 2010
	(In millions)	
ASSETS		
Current assets:		
Cash and equivalents	$ 1,955	$ 3,079
Short-term investments (Note 6)	2,583	2,067
Accounts receivable, net (Note 1)	3,138	2,650
Inventories (Notes 1 and 2)	2,715	2,041
Deferred income taxes (Note 9)	312	249
Prepaid expenses and other current assets	594	873
Total current assets	11,297	10,959
Property, plant and equipment, net (Note 3)	2,115	1,932
Identifiable intangible assets, net (Note 4)	487	467
Goodwill (Note 4)	205	188
Deferred income taxes and other assets (Notes 9 and 17)	894	873
Total assets	$14,998	$14,419
LIABILITIES AND SHAREHOLDERS' EQUITY		
Current liabilities:		
Current portion of long-term debt (Note 8)	$ 200	$ 7
Notes payable (Note 7)	187	139
Accounts payable (Note 7)	1,469	1,255
Accrued liabilities (Notes 5 and 17)	1,985	1,904
Income taxes payable (Note 9)	117	59
Total current liabilities	3,958	3,364
Long-term debt (Note 8)	276	446
Deferred income taxes and other liabilities (Notes 9 and 17)	921	855
Commitments and contingencies (Note 15)	—	—
Redeemable Preferred Stock (Note 10)	—	—
Shareholders' equity:		
Common stock at stated value (Note 11):		
Class A convertible — 90 and 90 shares outstanding	—	—
Class B — 378 and 394 shares outstanding	3	3
Capital in excess of stated value	3,944	3,441
Accumulated other comprehensive income (Note 14)	95	215
Retained earnings	5,801	6,095
Total shareholders' equity	9,843	9,754
Total liabilities and shareholders' equity	$14,998	$14,419

The accompanying notes to consolidated financial statements are an integral part of this statement.

Table of Contents

NIKE, INC.
CONSOLIDATED STATEMENTS OF CASH FLOWS

	Year Ended May 31,		
	2011	2010	2009
		(In millions)	
Cash provided by operations:			
Net income	$ 2,133	$ 1,907	$ 1,487
Income charges (credits) not affecting cash:			
Depreciation	335	324	335
Deferred income taxes	(76)	8	(294)
Stock-based compensation (Note 11)	105	159	171
Impairment of goodwill, intangibles and other assets (Note 4)	—	—	401
Amortization and other	23	72	48
Changes in certain working capital components and other assets and liabilities excluding the impact of acquisition and divestitures:			
(Increase) decrease in accounts receivable	(273)	182	(238)
(Increase) decrease in inventories	(551)	285	32
(Increase) decrease in prepaid expenses and other current assets	(35)	(70)	14
Increase (decrease) in accounts payable, accrued liabilities and income taxes payable	151	297	(220)
Cash provided by operations	1,812	3,164	1,736
Cash used by investing activities:			
Purchases of short-term investments	(7,616)	(3,724)	(2,909)
Maturities of short-term investments	4,313	2,334	1,280
Sales of short-term investments	2,766	453	1,110
Additions to property, plant and equipment	(432)	(335)	(456)
Disposals of property, plant and equipment	1	10	33
Increase in other assets, net of other liabilities	(30)	(11)	(47)
Settlement of net investment hedges	(23)	5	191
Cash used by investing activities	(1,021)	(1,268)	(798)
Cash used by financing activities:			
Reductions in long-term debt, including current portion	(8)	(32)	(7)
Increase (decrease) in notes payable	41	(205)	177
Proceeds from exercise of stock options and other stock issuances	345	364	187
Excess tax benefits from share-based payment arrangements	64	58	25
Repurchase of common stock	(1,859)	(741)	(649)
Dividends — common and preferred	(555)	(505)	(467)
Cash used by financing activities	(1,972)	(1,061)	(734)
Effect of exchange rate changes	57	(47)	(47)
Net (decrease) increase in cash and equivalents	(1,124)	788	157
Cash and equivalents, beginning of year	3,079	2,291	2,134
Cash and equivalents, end of year	$ 1,955	$ 3,079	$ 2,291
Supplemental disclosure of cash flow information:			
Cash paid during the year for:			
Interest, net of capitalized interest	$ 32	$ 48	$ 47
Income taxes	736	537	765
Dividends declared and not paid	145	131	121

The accompanying notes to consolidated financial statements are an integral part of this statement.

Table of Contents

NIKE, INC.
CONSOLIDATED STATEMENTS OF SHAREHOLDERS' EQUITY

	Common Stock Class A Shares	Common Stock Class A Amount	Common Stock Class B Shares	Common Stock Class B Amount	Capital in Excess of Stated Value	Accumulated Other Comprehensive Income	Retained Earnings	Total
	(In millions, except per share data)							
Balance at May 31, 2008	**97**	**$ —**	**394**	**$ 3**	**$ 2,498**	**$ 251**	**$ 5,073**	**$ 7,825**
Stock options exercised			4		167			167
Conversion to Class B Common Stock	(2)		2					—
Repurchase of Class B Common Stock			(11)		(6)		(633)	(639)
Dividends on Common stock ($0.98 per share)							(475)	(475)
Issuance of shares to employees			1		45			45
Stock-based compensation (Note 11):					171			171
Forfeiture of shares from employees			—		(4)		(1)	(5)
Comprehensive income:								
Net income							1,487	1,487
Other comprehensive income:								
Foreign currency translation and other (net of tax benefit of $178)						(335)		(335)
Net gain on cash flow hedges (net of tax expense of $168)						454		454
Net gain on net investment hedges (net of tax expense of $55)						106		106
Reclassification to net income of previously deferred net gains related to hedge derivatives (net of tax expense of $40)						(108)		(108)
Total comprehensive income						117	1,487	1,604
Balance at May 31, 2009	**95**	**$ —**	**390**	**$ 3**	**$ 2,871**	**$ 368**	**$ 5,451**	**$ 8,693**
Stock options exercised			9		380			380
Conversion to Class B Common Stock	(5)		5					—
Repurchase of Class B Common Stock			(11)		(7)		(747)	(754)
Dividends on Common stock ($1.06 per share)							(515)	(515)
Issuance of shares to employees			1		40			40
Stock-based compensation (Note 11):					159			159
Forfeiture of shares from employees			—		(2)		(1)	(3)
Comprehensive income:								
Net income							1,907	1,907
Other comprehensive income (Notes 14 and 17):								
Foreign currency translation and other (net of tax benefit of $72)						(159)		(159)
Net gain on cash flow hedges (net of tax expense of $28)						87		87
Net gain on net investment hedges (net of tax expense of $21)						45		45
Reclassification to net income of previously deferred net gains related to hedge derivatives (net of tax expense of $42)						(122)		(122)
Reclassification of ineffective hedge gains to net income (net of tax expense of $1)						(4)		(4)
Total comprehensive income						(153)	1,907	1,754
Balance at May 31, 2010	**90**	**$ —**	**394**	**$ 3**	**$ 3,441**	**$ 215**	**$ 6,095**	**$ 9,754**
Stock options exercised			7		368			368
Repurchase of Class B Common Stock			(24)		(14)		(1,857)	(1,871)
Dividends on Common stock ($1.20 per share)							(569)	(569)
Issuance of shares to employees			1		49			49
Stock-based compensation (Note 11):					105			105
Forfeiture of shares from employees			—		(5)		(1)	(6)
Comprehensive income:								
Net income							2,133	2,133
Other comprehensive income (Notes 14 and 17):								
Foreign currency translation and other (net of tax expense of $121)						263		263
Net loss on cash flow hedges (net of tax benefit of $66)						(242)		(242)
Net loss on net investment hedges (net of tax benefit of $28)						(57)		(57)
Reclassification to net income of previously deferred net gains related to hedge derivatives (net of tax expense of $24)						(84)		(84)
Total comprehensive income						(120)	2,133	2,013
Balance at May 31, 2011	**90**	**$ —**	**378**	**$ 3**	**$ 3,944**	**$ 95**	**$ 5,801**	**$ 9,843**

The accompanying notes to consolidated financial statements are an integral part of this statement.

Table of Contents

NIKE, INC.
NOTES TO CONSOLIDATED FINANCIAL STATEMENTS

Note 1 — Summary of Significant Accounting Policies

Description of Business

NIKE, Inc. is a worldwide leader in the design, marketing and distribution of athletic and sports-inspired footwear, apparel, equipment and accessories. Wholly-owned NIKE subsidiaries include Cole Haan, which designs, markets and distributes dress and casual shoes, handbags, accessories and coats; Converse Inc., which designs, markets and distributes athletic and casual footwear, apparel and accessories; Hurley International LLC, which designs, markets and distributes action sports and youth lifestyle footwear, apparel and accessories; and Umbro International Limited, which designs, distributes and licenses athletic and casual footwear, apparel and equipment, primarily for the sport of soccer.

Basis of Consolidation

The consolidated financial statements include the accounts of NIKE, Inc. and its subsidiaries (the "Company"). All significant intercompany transactions and balances have been eliminated.

Recognition of Revenues

Wholesale revenues are recognized when title passes and the risks and rewards of ownership have passed to the customer, based on the terms of sale. This occurs upon shipment or upon receipt by the customer depending on the country of the sale and the agreement with the customer. Retail store revenues are recorded at the time of sale. Provisions for sales discounts, returns and miscellaneous claims from customers are made at the time of sale. As of May 31, 2011 and 2010, the Company's reserve balances for sales discounts, returns and miscellaneous claims were $423 million and $371 million, respectively.

Shipping and Handling Costs

Shipping and handling costs are expensed as incurred and included in cost of sales.

Demand Creation Expense

Demand creation expense consists of advertising and promotion costs, including costs of endorsement contracts, television, digital and print advertising, brand events, and retail brand presentation. Advertising production costs are expensed the first time an advertisement is run. Advertising placement costs are expensed in the month the advertising appears, while costs related to brand events are expensed when the event occurs. Costs related to retail brand presentation are expensed when the presentation is completed and delivered. A significant amount of the Company's promotional expenses result from payments under endorsement contracts. Accounting for endorsement payments is based upon specific contract provisions. Generally, endorsement payments are expensed on a straight-line basis over the term of the contract after giving recognition to periodic performance compliance provisions of the contracts. Prepayments made under contracts are included in prepaid expenses or other assets depending on the period to which the prepayment applies.

Through cooperative advertising programs, the Company reimburses retail customers for certain costs of advertising the Company's products. The Company records these costs in selling and administrative expense at the point in time when it is obligated to its customers for the costs, which is when the related revenues are recognized. This obligation may arise prior to the related advertisement being run.

Total advertising and promotion expenses were $2,448 million, $2,356 million, and $2,352 million for the years ended May 31, 2011, 2010 and 2009, respectively. Prepaid advertising and promotion expenses recorded in prepaid expenses and other assets totaled $291 million and $261 million at May 31, 2011 and 2010, respectively.

Table of Contents

NIKE, INC.

NOTES TO CONSOLIDATED FINANCIAL STATEMENTS — (Continued)

Cash and Equivalents

Cash and equivalents represent cash and short-term, highly liquid investments with maturities of three months or less at date of purchase. The carrying amounts reflected in the consolidated balance sheet for cash and equivalents approximate fair value.

Short-Term Investments

Short-term investments consist of highly liquid investments, including commercial paper, U.S. treasury, U.S. agency, and corporate debt securities, with maturities over three months from the date of purchase. Debt securities that the Company has the ability and positive intent to hold to maturity are carried at amortized cost. At May 31, 2011 and 2010, the Company did not hold any short-term investments that were classified as trading or held-to-maturity.

At May 31, 2011 and 2010, short-term investments consisted of available-for-sale securities. Available-for-sale securities are recorded at fair value with unrealized gains and losses reported, net of tax, in other comprehensive income, unless unrealized losses are determined to be other than temporary. The Company considers all available-for-sale securities, including those with maturity dates beyond 12 months, as available to support current operational liquidity needs and therefore classifies all securities with maturity dates beyond three months at the date of purchase as current assets within short-term investments on the consolidated balance sheet.

See Note 6 — Fair Value Measurements for more information on the Company's short term investments.

Allowance for Uncollectible Accounts Receivable

Accounts receivable consists primarily of amounts receivable from customers. We make ongoing estimates relating to the collectability of our accounts receivable and maintain an allowance for estimated losses resulting from the inability of our customers to make required payments. In determining the amount of the allowance, we consider our historical level of credit losses and make judgments about the creditworthiness of significant customers based on ongoing credit evaluations. Accounts receivable with anticipated collection dates greater than 12 months from the balance sheet date and related allowances are considered non-current and recorded in other assets. The allowance for uncollectible accounts receivable was $124 million and $117 million at May 31, 2011 and 2010, respectively, of which $50 million and $43 million was classified as long-term and recorded in other assets.

Inventory Valuation

Inventories are stated at lower of cost or market and valued on a first-in, first-out ("FIFO") or moving average cost basis.

Property, Plant and Equipment and Depreciation

Property, plant and equipment are recorded at cost. Depreciation for financial reporting purposes is determined on a straight-line basis for buildings and leasehold improvements over 2 to 40 years and for machinery and equipment over 2 to 15 years. Computer software (including, in some cases, the cost of internal labor) is depreciated on a straight-line basis over 3 to 10 years.

Impairment of Long-Lived Assets

The Company reviews the carrying value of long-lived assets or asset groups to be used in operations whenever events or changes in circumstances indicate that the carrying amount of the assets might not be recoverable. Factors that would necessitate an impairment assessment include a significant adverse change in the

Table of Contents

NIKE, INC.

NOTES TO CONSOLIDATED FINANCIAL STATEMENTS — (Continued)

extent or manner in which an asset is used, a significant adverse change in legal factors or the business climate that could affect the value of the asset, or a significant decline in the observable market value of an asset, among others. If such facts indicate a potential impairment, the Company would assess the recoverability of an asset group by determining if the carrying value of the asset group exceeds the sum of the projected undiscounted cash flows expected to result from the use and eventual disposition of the assets over the remaining economic life of the primary asset in the asset group. If the recoverability test indicates that the carrying value of the asset group is not recoverable, the Company will estimate the fair value of the asset group using appropriate valuation methodologies which would typically include an estimate of discounted cash flows. Any impairment would be measured as the difference between the asset groups carrying amount and its estimated fair value.

Identifiable Intangible Assets and Goodwill

The Company performs annual impairment tests on goodwill and intangible assets with indefinite lives in the fourth quarter of each fiscal year, or when events occur or circumstances change that would, more likely than not, reduce the fair value of a reporting unit or an intangible asset with an indefinite life below its carrying value. Events or changes in circumstances that may trigger interim impairment reviews include significant changes in business climate, operating results, planned investments in the reporting unit, or an expectation that the carrying amount may not be recoverable, among other factors. The impairment test requires the Company to estimate the fair value of its reporting units. If the carrying value of a reporting unit exceeds its fair value, the goodwill of that reporting unit is potentially impaired and the Company proceeds to step two of the impairment analysis. In step two of the analysis, the Company measures and records an impairment loss equal to the excess of the carrying value of the reporting unit's goodwill over its implied fair value should such a circumstance arise.

The Company generally bases its measurement of fair value of a reporting unit on a blended analysis of the present value of future discounted cash flows and the market valuation approach. The discounted cash flows model indicates the fair value of the reporting unit based on the present value of the cash flows that the Company expects the reporting unit to generate in the future. The Company's significant estimates in the discounted cash flows model include: its weighted average cost of capital; long-term rate of growth and profitability of the reporting unit's business; and working capital effects. The market valuation approach indicates the fair value of the business based on a comparison of the reporting unit to comparable publicly traded companies in similar lines of business. Significant estimates in the market valuation approach model include identifying similar companies with comparable business factors such as size, growth, profitability, risk and return on investment, and assessing comparable revenue and operating income multiples in estimating the fair value of the reporting unit.

The Company believes the weighted use of discounted cash flows and the market valuation approach is the best method for determining the fair value of its reporting units because these are the most common valuation methodologies used within its industry; and the blended use of both models compensates for the inherent risks associated with either model if used on a stand-alone basis.

Indefinite-lived intangible assets primarily consist of acquired trade names and trademarks. In measuring the fair value for these intangible assets, the Company utilizes the relief-from-royalty method. This method assumes that trade names and trademarks have value to the extent that their owner is relieved of the obligation to pay royalties for the benefits received from them. This method requires the Company to estimate the future revenue for the related brands, the appropriate royalty rate and the weighted average cost of capital.

Foreign Currency Translation and Foreign Currency Transactions

Adjustments resulting from translating foreign functional currency financial statements into U.S. dollars are included in the foreign currency translation adjustment, a component of accumulated other comprehensive income in shareholders' equity.

Table of Contents

NIKE, INC.
NOTES TO CONSOLIDATED FINANCIAL STATEMENTS — (Continued)

The Company's global subsidiaries have various assets and liabilities, primarily receivables and payables, that are denominated in currencies other than their functional currency. These balance sheet items are subject to remeasurement, the impact of which is recorded in other (income), net, within our consolidated statement of income.

Accounting for Derivatives and Hedging Activities

The Company uses derivative financial instruments to limit exposure to changes in foreign currency exchange rates and interest rates. All derivatives are recorded at fair value on the balance sheet and changes in the fair value of derivative financial instruments are either recognized in other comprehensive income (a component of shareholders' equity), debt or net income depending on the nature of the underlying exposure, whether the derivative is formally designated as a hedge, and, if designated, the extent to which the hedge is effective. The Company classifies the cash flows at settlement from derivatives in the same category as the cash flows from the related hedged items. For undesignated hedges and designated cash flow hedges, this is within the cash provided by operations component of the consolidated statements of cash flows. For designated net investment hedges, this is generally within the cash used by investing activities component of the cash flow statement. As our fair value hedges are receive-fixed, pay-variable interest rate swaps, the cash flows associated with these derivative instruments are periodic interest payments while the swaps are outstanding, which are reflected in net income within the cash provided by operations component of the cash flow statement.

See Note 17 — Risk Management and Derivatives for more information on the Company's risk management program and derivatives.

Stock-Based Compensation

The Company estimates the fair value of options and stock appreciation rights granted under the NIKE, Inc. 1990 Stock Incentive Plan (the "1990 Plan") and employees' purchase rights under the Employee Stock Purchase Plans ("ESPPs") using the Black-Scholes option pricing model. The Company recognizes this fair value, net of estimated forfeitures, as selling and administrative expense in the consolidated statements of income over the vesting period using the straight-line method.

See Note 11 — Common Stock and Stock-Based Compensation for more information on the Company's stock programs.

Income Taxes

The Company accounts for income taxes using the asset and liability method. This approach requires the recognition of deferred tax assets and liabilities for the expected future tax consequences of temporary differences between the carrying amounts and the tax basis of assets and liabilities. United States income taxes are provided currently on financial statement earnings of non-U.S. subsidiaries that are expected to be repatriated. The Company determines annually the amount of undistributed non-U.S. earnings to invest indefinitely in its non-U.S. operations. The Company recognizes interest and penalties related to income tax matters in income tax expense.

See Note 9 — Income Taxes for further discussion.

Earnings Per Share

Basic earnings per common share is calculated by dividing net income by the weighted average number of common shares outstanding during the year. Diluted earnings per common share is calculated by adjusting weighted average outstanding shares, assuming conversion of all potentially dilutive stock options and awards.

NIKE, INC.

NOTES TO CONSOLIDATED FINANCIAL STATEMENTS — (Continued)

plans available to U.S.-based employees. The Company matches a portion of employee contributions. Company contributions to the savings plans were $39 million, $34 million, and $38 million for the years ended May 31, 2011, 2010, and 2009, respectively, and are included in selling and administrative expense.

The Company also has a Long-Term Incentive Plan ("LTIP") that was adopted by the Board of Directors and approved by shareholders in September 1997 and later amended in fiscal 2007. The Company recognized $31 million, $24 million, and $18 million of selling and administrative expense related to cash awards under the LTIP during the years ended May 31, 2011, 2010, and 2009, respectively.

The Company has pension plans in various countries worldwide. The pension plans are only available to local employees and are generally government mandated. The liability related to the unfunded pension liabilities of the plans was $93 million and $113 million at May 31, 2011 and 2010, respectively, which was primarily classified as long-term in other liabilities.

Note 14 — Accumulated Other Comprehensive Income

The components of accumulated other comprehensive income, net of tax, are as follows:

	May 31, 2011	May 31, 2010
	(In millions)	
Cumulative translation adjustment and other	$ 168	$ (95)
Net deferred gain on net investment hedge derivatives	50	107
Net deferred (loss) gain on cash flow hedge derivatives	(123)	203
	$ 95	$215

Note 15 — Commitments and Contingencies

The Company leases space for certain of its offices, warehouses and retail stores under leases expiring from 1 to 24 years after May 31, 2011. Rent expense was $446 million, $416 million, and $397 million for the years ended May 31, 2011, 2010 and 2009, respectively. Amounts of minimum future annual rental commitments under non-cancelable operating leases in each of the five years ending May 31, 2012 through 2016 are $374 million, $310 million, $253 million, $198 million, $174 million, respectively, and $535 million in later years.

As of May 31, 2011 and 2010, the Company had letters of credit outstanding totaling $99 million and $101 million, respectively. These letters of credit were generally issued for the purchase of inventory.

In connection with various contracts and agreements, the Company provides routine indemnifications relating to the enforceability of intellectual property rights, coverage for legal issues that arise and other items where the Company is acting as the guarantor. Currently, the Company has several such agreements in place. However, based on the Company's historical experience and the estimated probability of future loss, the Company has determined that the fair value of such indemnifications is not material to the Company's financial position or results of operations.

In the ordinary course of its business, the Company is involved in various legal proceedings involving contractual and employment relationships, product liability claims, trademark rights, and a variety of other matters. The Company does not believe there are any pending legal proceedings that will have a material impact on the Company's financial position or results of operations.

NIKE, INC.

NOTES TO CONSOLIDATED FINANCIAL STATEMENTS — (Continued)

Note 16 — Restructuring Charges

During fiscal 2009, the Company took necessary steps to streamline its management structure, enhance consumer focus, drive innovation more quickly to market and establish a more scalable, long-term cost structure. As a result, the Company reduced its global workforce by approximately 5% and incurred pre-tax restructuring charges of $195 million, primarily consisting of severance costs related to the workforce reduction. As nearly all of the restructuring activities were completed in fiscal 2009, the Company did not recognize additional costs relating to these actions. The restructuring charge is reflected in the corporate expense line in the segment presentation of earnings before interest and taxes in Note 18 — Operating Segments and Related Information. The restructuring accrual included in accrued liabilities in the consolidated balance sheet was $3 million and $8 million as of May 31, 2011 and 2010, respectively.

Note 17 — Risk Management and Derivatives

The Company is exposed to global market risks, including the effect of changes in foreign currency exchange rates and interest rates, and uses derivatives to manage financial exposures that occur in the normal course of business. The Company does not hold or issue derivatives for trading purposes.

The Company formally documents all relationships between formally designated hedging instruments and hedged items, as well as its risk management objective and strategy for undertaking hedge transactions. This process includes linking all derivatives to either specific firm commitments or forecasted transactions. The Company also enters into foreign exchange forwards to mitigate the change in fair value of specific assets and liabilities on the balance sheet, which are not designated as hedging instruments under the accounting standards for derivatives and hedging. Accordingly, changes in the fair value of these non-designated instruments of recorded balance sheet positions are recognized immediately in other (income), net, on the income statement together with the transaction gain or loss from the hedged balance sheet position. The Company classifies the cash flows at settlement from these undesignated instruments in the same category as the cash flows from the related hedged items, generally within the cash provided by operations component of the cash flow statement.

The majority of derivatives outstanding as of May 31, 2011 are designated as cash flow, fair value or net investment hedges. All derivatives are recognized on the balance sheet at their fair value and classified based on the instrument's maturity date. The total notional amount of outstanding derivatives as of May 31, 2011 was $7 billion, which is primarily comprised of cash flow hedges for Euro/U.S. Dollar, British Pound/Euro, and Japanese Yen/U.S. Dollar currency pairs.

Table of Contents

NIKE, INC.
NOTES TO CONSOLIDATED FINANCIAL STATEMENTS — (Continued)

The following table presents the fair values of derivative instruments included within the consolidated balance sheet as of May 31, 2011 and 2010:

	Asset Derivatives			Liability Derivatives		
	Balance Sheet Location	May 31, 2011	May 31, 2010	Balance Sheet Location	May 31, 2011	May 31, 2010
		(in millions)				
Derivatives formally designated as hedging instruments:						
Foreign exchange forwards and options	Prepaid expenses and other current assets	$ 22	$ 316	Accrued liabilities	$ 170	$ 25
Foreign exchange forwards and options	Deferred income taxes and other long-term assets	7	—	Deferred income taxes and other long-term liabilities	10	—
Interest rate swap contracts	Deferred income taxes and other long-term assets	15	15	Deferred income taxes and other long-term liabilities	—	—
Total derivatives formally designated as hedging instruments		44	331		180	25
Derivatives not designated as hedging instruments:						
Foreign exchange forwards and options	Prepaid expenses and other current assets	$ 9	$ 104	Accrued liabilities	$ 16	$ 139
Foreign exchange forwards and options	Deferred income taxes and other long-term assets	—	—	Deferred income taxes and other long-term liabilities	1	1
Total derivatives not designated as hedging instruments		9	104		17	140
Total derivatives		$ 53	$ 435		$ 197	$ 165

The following tables present the amounts affecting the consolidated statements of income for years ended May 31, 2011, 2010 and 2009:

Derivatives formally designated	Amount of Gain (Loss) Recognized in Other Comprehensive Income on Derivatives (1) — Year Ended May 31, 2011	2010	2009	Location of Gain (Loss) Reclassified From Accumulated Other Comprehensive Income Into Income (1)	Amount of Gain (Loss) Reclassified From Accumulated Other Comprehensive Income into Income (1) — Year Ended May 31, 2011	2010	2009
			(in millions)				
Derivatives designated as cash flow hedges:							
Foreign exchange forwards and options	$ (87)	$ (30)	$ 106	Revenue	$ (30)	$ 51	$ 93
Foreign exchange forwards and options	(152)	89	350	Cost of sales	103	60	(14)
Foreign exchange forwards and options	(4)	5	—	Selling and administrative expense	1	1	1
Foreign exchange forwards and options	(65)	51	165	Other (income), net	34	56	68
Total designated cash flow hedges	$ (308)	$ 115	$ 621		$ 108	$ 168	$ 148
Derivatives designated as net investment hedges:							
Foreign exchange forwards and options	$ (85)	$ 66	$ 161	Other (income), net	$ —	$ —	$ —

(1) For the year ended May 31, 2011 and 2009, the Company recorded an immaterial amount of ineffectiveness from cash flow hedges in other (income), net. For the year ended May 31, 2010, $5 million of ineffectiveness from cash flow hedges was recorded in other (income), net.

Table of Contents

NIKE, INC.
NOTES TO CONSOLIDATED FINANCIAL STATEMENTS — (Continued)

	Amount of Gain (Loss) recognized in Income on Derivatives Year Ended May 31,			Location of Gain (Loss) Recognized in Income on Derivatives
	2011	2010 (in millions)	2009	
Derivatives designated as fair value hedges:				
Interest rate swaps [(1)]	$ 6	$ 7	$ 2	Interest expense (income), net
Derivatives not designated as hedging instruments:				
Foreign exchange forwards and options	$(30)	$(91)	$(83)	Other (income), net

(1) All interest rate swap agreements meet the shortcut method requirements under the accounting standards for derivatives and hedging. Accordingly, changes in the fair values of the interest rate swap agreements are exactly offset by changes in the fair value of the underlying long-term debt. Refer to section "Fair Value Hedges" for additional detail.

Refer to Note 5 — Accrued Liabilities for derivative instruments recorded in accrued liabilities, Note 6 —Fair Value Measurements for a description of how the above financial instruments are valued, Note 14 — Accumulated Other Comprehensive Income and the consolidated statements of shareholders' equity for additional information on changes in other comprehensive income for the years ended May 31, 2011, 2010 and 2009.

Cash Flow Hedges

The purpose of the Company's foreign currency hedging activities is to protect the Company from the risk that the eventual cash flows resulting from transactions in foreign currencies, including revenues, product costs, selling and administrative expense, investments in U.S. dollar-denominated available-for-sale debt securities and intercompany transactions, including intercompany borrowings, will be adversely affected by changes in exchange rates. It is the Company's policy to utilize derivatives to reduce foreign exchange risks where internal netting strategies cannot be effectively employed. Hedged transactions are denominated primarily in Euros, British Pounds and Japanese Yen. The Company hedges up to 100% of anticipated exposures typically 12 months in advance, but has hedged as much as 34 months in advance.

All changes in fair values of outstanding cash flow hedge derivatives, except the ineffective portion, are recorded in other comprehensive income until net income is affected by the variability of cash flows of the hedged transaction. In most cases, amounts recorded in other comprehensive income will be released to net income some time after the maturity of the related derivative. The consolidated statement of income classification of effective hedge results is the same as that of the underlying exposure. Results of hedges of revenue and product costs are recorded in revenue and cost of sales, respectively, when the underlying hedged transaction affects net income. Results of hedges of selling and administrative expense are recorded together with those costs when the related expense is recorded. Results of hedges of forecasted purchases of U.S. dollar-denominated available-for-sale securities are recorded in other (income), net when the securities are sold. Results of hedges of forecasted intercompany transactions are recorded in other (income), net when the transaction occurs. The Company classifies the cash flows at settlement from these designated cash flow hedge derivatives in the same category as the cash flows from the related hedged items, generally within the cash provided by operations component of the cash flow statement.

Premiums paid on options are initially recorded as deferred charges. The Company assesses the effectiveness of options based on the total cash flows method and records total changes in the options' fair value to other comprehensive income to the degree they are effective.

Table of Contents

NIKE, INC.

NOTES TO CONSOLIDATED FINANCIAL STATEMENTS — (Continued)

As of May 31, 2011, $120 million of deferred net losses (net of tax) on both outstanding and matured derivatives accumulated in other comprehensive income are expected to be reclassified to net income during the next 12 months as a result of underlying hedged transactions also being recorded in net income. Actual amounts ultimately reclassified to net income are dependent on the exchange rates in effect when derivative contracts that are currently outstanding mature. As of May 31, 2011, the maximum term over which the Company is hedging exposures to the variability of cash flows for its forecasted and recorded transactions is 15 months.

The Company formally assesses both at a hedge's inception and on an ongoing basis, whether the derivatives that are used in the hedging transaction have been highly effective in offsetting changes in the cash flows of hedged items and whether those derivatives may be expected to remain highly effective in future periods. Effectiveness for cash flow hedges is assessed based on forward rates. When it is determined that a derivative is not, or has ceased to be, highly effective as a hedge, the Company discontinues hedge accounting.

The Company discontinues hedge accounting prospectively when (1) it determines that the derivative is no longer highly effective in offsetting changes in the cash flows of a hedged item (including hedged items such as firm commitments or forecasted transactions); (2) the derivative expires or is sold, terminated, or exercised; (3) it is no longer probable that the forecasted transaction will occur; or (4) management determines that designating the derivative as a hedging instrument is no longer appropriate.

When the Company discontinues hedge accounting because it is no longer probable that the forecasted transaction will occur in the originally expected period, but is expected to occur within an additional two-month period of time thereafter, the gain or loss on the derivative remains in accumulated other comprehensive income and is reclassified to net income when the forecasted transaction affects net income. However, if it is probable that a forecasted transaction will not occur by the end of the originally specified time period or within an additional two-month period of time thereafter, the gains and losses that were accumulated in other comprehensive income will be recognized immediately in net income. In all situations in which hedge accounting is discontinued and the derivative remains outstanding, the Company will carry the derivative at its fair value on the balance sheet, recognizing future changes in the fair value in other (income), net. For the year ended May 31, 2011 an immaterial amount of ineffectiveness was recorded to other (income), net. For the years ended May 31, 2010 and 2009, the Company recorded in other (income), net $5 million gain and an immaterial amount of ineffectiveness from cash flow hedges, respectively.

Fair Value Hedges

The Company is also exposed to the risk of changes in the fair value of certain fixed-rate debt attributable to changes in interest rates. Derivatives currently used by the Company to hedge this risk are receive-fixed, pay-variable interest rate swaps. As of May 31, 2011, all interest rate swap agreements are designated as fair value hedges of the related long-term debt and meet the shortcut method requirements under the accounting standards for derivatives and hedging. Accordingly, changes in the fair values of the interest rate swap agreements are exactly offset by changes in the fair value of the underlying long-term debt. The cash flows associated with the Company's fair value hedges are periodic interest payments while the swaps are outstanding, which are reflected in net income within the cash provided by operations component of the cash flow statement. No ineffectiveness has been recorded to net income related to interest rate swaps designated as fair value hedges for the years ended May 31, 2011, 2010, and 2009.

In fiscal 2003, the Company entered into a receive-floating, pay-fixed interest rate swap agreement related to a Japanese Yen denominated intercompany loan with one of the Company's Japanese subsidiaries. This interest rate swap was not designated as a hedge under the accounting standards for derivatives and hedging.

NIKE, INC.

NOTES TO CONSOLIDATED FINANCIAL STATEMENTS — (Continued)

Accordingly, changes in the fair value of the swap were recorded to net income each period through maturity as a component of interest expense (income), net. Both the intercompany loan and the related interest rate swap matured during the year ended May 31, 2009.

Net Investment Hedges

The Company also hedges the risk of variability in foreign-currency-denominated net investments in wholly-owned international operations. All changes in fair value of the derivatives designated as net investment hedges, except ineffective portions, are reported in the cumulative translation adjustment component of other comprehensive income along with the foreign currency translation adjustments on those investments. The Company classifies the cash flows at settlement of its net investment hedges within the cash used by investing component of the cash flow statement. The Company assesses hedge effectiveness based on changes in forward rates. The Company recorded no ineffectiveness from its net investment hedges for the years ended May 31, 2011, 2010, and 2009.

Credit Risk

The Company is exposed to credit-related losses in the event of non-performance by counterparties to hedging instruments. The counterparties to all derivative transactions are major financial institutions with investment grade credit ratings. However, this does not eliminate the Company's exposure to credit risk with these institutions. This credit risk is limited to the unrealized gains in such contracts should any of these counterparties fail to perform as contracted. To manage this risk, the Company has established strict counterparty credit guidelines that are continually monitored and reported to senior management according to prescribed guidelines. The Company also utilizes a portfolio of financial institutions either headquartered or operating in the same countries the Company conducts its business.

The Company's derivative contracts contain credit risk related contingent features aiming to protect against significant deterioration in counterparties' creditworthiness and their ultimate ability to settle outstanding derivative contracts in the normal course of business. The Company's bilateral credit related contingent features require the owing entity, either the Company or the derivative counterparty, to post collateral should the fair value of outstanding derivatives per counterparty be greater than $50 million. Additionally, a certain level of decline in credit rating of either the Company or the counterparty could trigger collateral requirements. As of May 31, 2011, the Company was in compliance with all such credit risk related contingent features. The aggregate fair value of derivative instruments with credit risk related contingent features that are in a net liability position at May 31, 2011 was $160 million. The Company, or any counterparty, were not required to post any collateral as a result of these contingent features. As a result of the above considerations, the Company considers the impact of the risk of counterparty default to be immaterial.

Note 18 — Operating Segments and Related Information

Operating Segments. The Company's operating segments are evidence of the structure of the Company's internal organization. The major segments are defined by geographic regions for operations participating in NIKE Brand sales activity excluding NIKE Golf. Each NIKE Brand geographic segment operates predominantly in one industry: the design, development, marketing and selling of athletic footwear, apparel, and equipment. In fiscal 2009, the Company initiated a reorganization of the NIKE Brand into a new model consisting of six geographies. Effective June 1, 2009, the Company's new reportable operating segments for the NIKE Brand are: North America, Western Europe, Central and Eastern Europe, Greater China, Japan, and Emerging Markets. Previously, NIKE Brand operations were organized into the following four geographic regions: U.S., Europe, Middle East and Africa (collectively, "EMEA"), Asia Pacific, and Americas. The Company's NIKE Brand Direct to Consumer operations are managed within each geographic segment.

Appendix C

International Financial Reporting Standards (IFRS)

The Need for Global Accounting Standards

As discussed in Chapter 1, the Financial Accounting Standards Board (FASB) establishes generally accepted accounting principles (GAAP) for public companies in the United States. Of course, there is a world beyond the borders of the United States. In recent years, the removal of trade barriers and the growth in cross-border equity and debt issuances have led to a dramatic increase in international commerce. As a result, companies are often reporting financial results to users outside of the United States.

Historically, accounting standards have varied considerably across countries. These variances have been driven by cultural, legal, and political differences, and resulted in financial statements that were not easily comparable and difficult to interpret. These differences caused problems for companies in Europe and Asia, where local economies have become increasingly tied to international commerce.

During the last decade, however, a common set of International Financial Reporting Standards (IFRS) has emerged to reduce cross-country differences in accounting standards, primarily in countries outside of North America. While much of the world has migrated to IFRS, the United States has not. Because of the size of the United States and its significant role in world commerce, however, U.S. GAAP still has a global impact. As a result, there are currently two major accounting standard-setting efforts in the world, U.S. GAAP and IFRS. These two sets of accounting standards add cost and complexity for companies doing business and obtaining financing internationally.

Overview of IFRS

International Financial Reporting Standards have emerged during the last 10 years to meet the financial reporting needs of an increasingly global business environment.

What Is IFRS? International Financial Reporting Standards are a set of global accounting standards developed by an international standard-setting body called the International Accounting Standards Board (IASB). Like the Financial Accounting Standards Board, the IASB is an independent entity that establishes accounting rules. Unlike the FASB, the IASB does not establish accounting rules for any specific country. Rather, it develops accounting rules that can be used by a variety of countries, with the goal of developing a single set of global accounting standards.

Who Uses IFRS? IFRS applies to companies that issue publicly traded debt or equity securities, called **public companies**, in countries that have adopted IFRS as their accounting standards. Since 2005, all 27 countries in the European Union (EU) have been required to prepare financial statements using IFRS. In addition, over 100 other countries have adopted IFRS for public companies (see Exhibit 1). In other major economies, Japan is considering mandatory adoption by 2016, India allows limited use of IFRS, and China is converging its standards with IFRS over time. In addition, the G20 (Group of 20) leadership has called for uniform global accounting standards.

EXHIBIT 1

IFRS Adopters

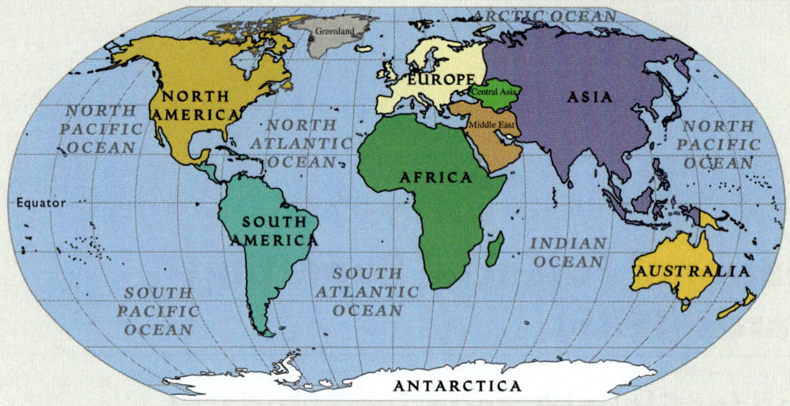

Abu Dhabi-UAE	Hong Kong	Norway
Argentina	Hungary	Panama
Austria	Iceland	Peru
Australia	Iraq	Poland
Belgium	Ireland	Portugal
Bosnia	Israel	Qatar
Brazil	Italy	Romania
Bulgaria	Jamaica	Russia
Canada	Jordan	Serbia
Chile	Kenya	Slovak Republic
Costa Rica	Kuwait	Slovenia
Croatia	Latvia	South Africa
Czech Republic	Lebanon	South Korea
Denmark	Liechtenstein	Spain
Dubai-UAE	Lithuania	Sweden
Ecuador	Luxembourg	Turkey
Egypt	Libya	United Kingdom
Estonia	Mexico	Zambia
Finland	Mongolia	
France	Netherlands	
Germany	New Zealand	
Greece	Nicaragua	
Guatemala	Nigeria	

Source: Deloitte, Touche Tohmatsu Limited, http://www.iasplus.com/en/resources/use-of-ifrs.

U.S. GAAP and IFRS: The Road Forward

The United States has not formally adopted IFRS for U.S. companies. The wide acceptance being gained by IFRS around the world, however, has placed considerable pressure on the United States to align U.S. GAAP with IFRS. There are two possible paths that the United States could take to achieve this: (1) adoption of IFRS by the U.S. Securities and Exchange Commission or (2) convergence of U.S. GAAP and IFRS. These two options are briefly discussed below.

Adoption of IFRS by the SEC The U.S. Securities and Exchange Commission (SEC) is the U.S. governmental agency that has authority over the accounting and financial disclosures for U.S. public companies. Only the SEC has the authority to adopt IFRS for U.S. public companies. In 2008, the SEC presented a "roadmap" to adopting IFRS, which outlined a timetable along with a set of "milestones" that needed to be met before the SEC would be willing to adopt IFRS. In 2010, the SEC reiterated the milestones outlined in the roadmap. According to the work plan, the SEC plans on deciding whether to incorporate IFRS into U.S. GAAP for public companies. The SEC published a Final Report on the issues surrounding IFRS adoption in 2012[1]. A final decision on IFRS adoption by the SEC is anticipated by 2013.

If the SEC adopts IFRS for U.S. GAAP, it has determined that the FASB would retain a "critical and substantive role in achieving the goal of global accounting standards." This suggests that the FASB will not necessarily be eliminated. More likely, the FASB would provide input to the IASB so that U.S. accounting perspectives are considered.

Convergence of U.S. GAAP and IFRS If the SEC does not adopt IFRS, an alternative approach would be for the FASB and IASB to converge U.S. GAAP and IFRS. This would involve aligning IFRS and U.S. GAAP one topic at a time, slowly merging IFRS and U.S. GAAP into two broadly uniform sets of accounting standards. To this end, the FASB and IASB have agreed to work together on a number of difficult and high-profile accounting issues. These issues frame a large portion of the disagreement between the two sets of standards and, if accomplished, will significantly reduce the differences between U.S. GAAP and IFRS. The projects selected for the convergence effort represent some of the more technical topics in accounting and are covered in intermediate and advanced accounting courses. The FASB and IASB have set 2013 as the target for establishing final standards.

One of the major limitations of convergence is that both the FASB and IASB continue to operate as the accounting standard-setting bodies for their respective jurisdictions. As such, convergence would not result in a single set of global accounting standards. Only those standards that go through the joint FASB–IASB standard-setting process would be released as uniform. Standards that do not go through a joint standard-setting process may create inconsistencies between U.S. GAAP and IFRS. Thus, convergence does not guarantee complete uniformity between U.S. GAAP and IFRS. A brief summary of the major U.S. decisions related to IFRS are outlined in the table below.

The Road to IFRS

2002	IASB and FASB jointly agree to work toward making IFRS and U.S. GAAP compatible.
2005	EU adopts IFRS for all companies engaged in international markets.
	SEC and European Commission jointly agree to work toward a "Roadmap for Convergence."
2007	SEC allows foreign (non-U.S.) companies to use IFRS financial statements to meet U.S. filing requirements.
2008	SEC issues proposed "Roadmap" with timeline and key milestones for adopting IFRS.
2010	SEC reiterates milestones in the proposed "Roadmap."
2013	Target date for FASB and IASB convergence on major standard-setting projects.
	Target date for SEC's tentative decision regarding IFRS adoption.
2015	Earliest date the SEC would require IFRS for U.S. public companies.

Differences Between U.S. GAAP and IFRS

U.S. GAAP and IFRS differ both in their approach to standard setting, as well as their financial statement presentation and recording of transactions.

Rules-Based vs. Principles Approach to Standard Setting U.S. GAAP is considered to be a "rules-based" approach to accounting standard setting. The accounting standards provide detailed and specific rules on the accounting for business transactions. There are few exceptions or varying interpretations of the accounting for a business event. This structure is consistent with the U.S. legal and regulatory system, reflecting the social and economic values of the United States.

[1] Work Plan for the Consideration of Incorporating International Financial Accounting Standards into the Financial Reporting System for U.S. Issuers: Final Staff Report, U.S. Securities Exchange Commission, July 13, 2012.

In contrast, IFRS is designed to meet the needs of many countries. Differences in legal, political, and economic systems create different needs for and uses of financial information in different countries. For example, Germany needs a financial reporting system that reflects the central role of banks in its financial system, while the Netherlands needs a financial reporting system that reflects the significant role of outside equity in its financial system.

To accommodate economic, legal, and social diversity, IFRS must be broad enough to capture these differences, while still presenting comparable financial statements. Under IFRS, there is greater opportunity for different interpretations of the accounting treatment of a business event across different business entities. To support this, IFRS often has more extensive disclosures that support alternative assumptions. Thus, IFRS provides more latitude for professional judgment than typically found in comparable U.S. GAAP. Many countries find this feature attractive in reducing regulatory costs associated with using and auditing financial reports. This "principles-based" approach presents one of the most significant challenges to adopting IFRS in the United States.

Technical Differences Between IFRS and U.S. GAAP Although U.S. GAAP is similar to IFRS, differences arise in the presentation format, balance sheet valuations, and technical accounting procedures. The Mornin' Joe International financial statements presented on pages 632–639 highlight the financial statement format, presentation, and recording differences between U.S. GAAP and IFRS. In addition, the International Connection boxes in Chapters 1, 4, 6, 9, 11, and 14 discuss some of the significant differences between U.S. GAAP and IFRS. A more comprehensive summary of the key differences between U.S. GAAP and IFRS that are relevant to an introductory accounting course is provided in the table on the following pages. As standards continue to evolve, this table will be updated periodically online. Visit this book's student Web site at www.cengagebrain.com.

Discussion Questions

1. Briefly discuss why global accounting standards are needed in today's business environment.
2. What are International Financial Reporting Standards? Who uses these accounting standards?
3. What body is responsible for setting International Financial Reporting Standards?
4. Briefly discuss the differences between (a) convergence of U.S. GAAP with IFRS and (b) adoption of IFRS by the U.S. Securities and Exchange Commission.
5. Briefly discuss the difference between (a) a "rules-based" approach to accounting standard setting and (b) a "principles-based" approach to accounting standard setting.
6. How is property, plant, and equipment measured on the balance sheet under IFRS? How does this differ from the way property, plant, and equipment is measured on the balance sheet under U.S. GAAP?
7. What inventory costing methods are allowed under IFRS? How does this differ from the treatment under U.S. GAAP?

Comparison of Accounting for Selected Items Under U.S. GAAP and IFRS

	U.S. GAAP	IFRS	Text Reference
General:			
Financial statement titles	Balance Sheet Statement of Stockholders' Equity Statement of Cash Flows	Statement of Financial Position Statement of Changes in Equity Statement of Cash Flows	General
Financial periods presented	Public companies must present two years of comparative information for income statement, statement of stockholders' equity, and statement of cash flows	One year of comparative information must be presented	General
Conceptual basis for standard setting	"Rules-based" approach	"Principles-based" approach	General
Internal control requirements	Sarbanes-Oxley Act (SOX) Section 404		Ch 7; LO 1
Balance Sheet:	***Balance Sheet***	***Statement of Financial Position***	
Terminology differences	"Payable" "Stockholders' Equity" "Net Income (Loss)"	"Provision" "Capital and Reserves" "Profit or (Loss)"	Ch 10 Ch 10 General
Inventory—LIFO	LIFO allowed	LIFO prohibited	Ch 6; LO 3, 4, 5
Inventory—valuation	Market is defined as "replacement value" Reversal of lower-of-cost-or-market write-downs not allowed	Market is defined as "fair value" Reversal of write-downs allowed	Ch 6; LO 6 Ch 6; LO 6
Long-lived assets	May NOT be revalued to fair value	May be revalued to fair value on a regular basis	Ch 9; LO 1

(Continued)

Comparison of Accounting for Selected Items Under U.S. GAAP and IFRS *(Continued)*

	U.S. GAAP	IFRS	Text Reference
Land held for investment	Treated as held for use or sale, and recorded at historical cost	May be accounted for on a historical cost basis or on a fair value basis with changes in fair value recognized through profit and loss	Ch 9; LO 1
Property, plant, & equipment—valuation	Historical cost If impaired, impairment loss may NOT be reversed in future periods	May select between historical cost or revalued amount (a form of fair value) If impaired, impairment loss may be reversed in future periods	Ch 9; LO 1
Cost of major overhaul (Capital and revenue expenditures)	Different treatment for ordinary repairs and maintenance, asset improvement, extraordinary repairs	Typically included as part of the cost of the asset if future economic benefit is probable and can be reliably measured	Ch 9; LO 1
Intangible assets—valuation	Acquisition cost, unless impaired	Fair value permitted if the intangible asset trades in an active market	Ch 9; LO 5
Intangible assets—impairment loss reversal	Prohibited	Prohibited for goodwill, but allowed for other intangible assets	Ch 9; LO 5
Deferred tax liability	The amount due within one year classified as current	Always noncurrent	Appendix C
Income Statement:	***Income Statement***	***Statement of Comprehensive Income***	
Revenue recognition	Detailed guidance depending on the transaction	Broad guidance	Ch 3; LO 1
Classification of expenses on income statement	Public companies must present expenses on the income statement by function (e.g., cost of goods sold, selling, administrative)	Expenses may be presented based either by function (e.g., cost of goods sold, selling) or by the nature of expense (e.g., wages expense, interest expense)	Ch 5; LO 1
Research and development costs	Expensed as incurred	Research costs expensed Development costs capitalized once technical and economic feasibility attained	Ch 9; LO 5
Extraordinary items	Allowed for items that are both unusual in nature and infrequent in occurrence	Prohibited	Ch 15; Appendix

(Continued)

Comparison of Accounting for Selected Items Under U.S. GAAP and IFRS *(Concluded)*

	U.S. GAAP	IFRS	Text Reference
Statement of Cash Flows:	***Statement of Cash Flows***	***Statement of Cash Flows***	
Classification of interest paid or received	Treated as an operating activity	Interest paid may be treated as either an operating or a financing activity, interest received may be treated as an operating or investing activity	Ch 14; LO 3
Classification of dividend paid or received	Dividend paid treated as a financing activity, dividend received treated as an operating activity	Dividend paid may be treated as either an operating or a financing activity, dividend received may be treated as an operating or investing activity	Ch 14; LO 3

Glossary

A

absorption costing The reporting of the costs of manufactured products, normally direct materials, direct labor, and factory overhead, as product costs in financial statements. (906, 934)

accelerated depreciation method A depreciation method that provides for a higher depreciation amount in the first year of the asset's use, followed by a gradually declining amount of depreciation. (415)

account An accounting form that is used to record the increases and decreases in each accounting equation element. (52)

account form The form of balance sheet that resembles the basic format of the accounting equation, with assets on the left side and the liabilities and stockholders' equity sections on the right side. (18, 231)

account payable The liability created by a purchase on account. (11)

account receivable A claim against the customer created by selling merchandise or services on credit. (12, 65, 362)

accounting An information system that provides reports to users about the economic activities and condition of a business. (3)

accounting cycle The process that begins with analyzing and journalizing transactions and ends with the post-closing trial balance. (162)

accounting equation Assets = Liabilities + Stockholders' Equity. (9)

accounting period concept The accounting concept that divides the economic life of the business into time periods and requires that revenues and expenses be reported in the proper period. (104)

accounts payable subsidiary ledger The subsidiary ledger containing the individual creditor accounts in alphabetical order. (214)

accounts receivable analysis A company's ability to collect its accounts receivable. (706)

accounts receivable subsidiary ledger The subsidiary ledger containing the individual customer accounts in alphabetical order. (214)

accounts receivable turnover The relationship between sales and accounts receivable, computed by dividing the sales by the average accounts receivable; measures how frequently during the year the accounts receivable are being converted to cash. (377, 706)

accrual basis of accounting Under this basis of accounting, revenues and expenses are reported in the income statement in the period in which they are earned or incurred. (104)

accrued expenses Unrecorded expenses that have been incurred and for which cash has yet to be paid. (108)

accrued revenues Unrecorded revenues that have been earned and for which cash has yet to be received. (107)

Accumulated Depreciation The contra asset account that is credited when recording the depreciation of a fixed asset. (117)

accumulated other comprehensive income The cumulative effects of other comprehensive income items reported separately in the Stockholders' Equity section of the balance sheet. (603)

activities The types of work, or actions, involved in a manufacturing process or service activity. (1207)

activity analysis The study of employee effort and other business records to determine the cost of activities. (1257)

activity base (activity driver or allocation base) A measure of activity that is related to changes in cost and is used in analyzing and classifying cost behavior. Activity bases are also used in the denominator in calculating the predetermined factory overhead rate to assign overhead costs to cost objects. (798, 884, 1209)

activity rate The budgeted activity cost divided by total activity-base usage. (1208)

activity-based costing (ABC) A cost allocation method that identifies activities causing the incurrence of costs and allocates these costs to products (or other cost objects), based on activity drivers (bases). (799, 1207)

adjusted trial balance The trial balance prepared after all the adjusting entries have been posted. (123)

adjusting entries The journal entries that bring the accounts up to date at the end of the accounting period. (105)

adjusting process The analysis and updating of accounts at the end of the period before the financial statements are prepared. (105)

administrative expenses (general expenses) Expenses incurred in the administration or general operations of the business. (230)

aging the receivables The process of analyzing the accounts receivable and classifying them according to various age groupings, with the due date being the base point for determining age. (369)

Allowance for Doubtful Accounts The contra asset account for accounts receivable. (365)

allowance method The method of accounting for uncollectible accounts that provides an expense for uncollectible receivables in advance of their write-off. (363)

amortization The periodic transfer of the cost of an intangible asset to expense. (422)

annuity A series of equal net cash flows at fixed time intervals. (1167)

appraisal costs Costs to detect, measure, evaluate, and audit products and process to ensure that they conform to customer requirements and performance standards. (1257)

assets The resources owned by a business. (8, 54)

available-for-sale securities Debt and equity securities that are neither held for trading, held to maturity, or held for strategic reasons. (595)

average rate of return A method of evaluating capital investment proposals that focuses on the expected profitability of the investment; sometimes called the accounting rate of return. (1163)

B

backflush accounting Simplification of the accounting system by eliminating accumulation and transfer of costs as products move through production. (1254)

bad debt expense The operating expense incurred because of the failure to collect receivables. (363)

balance of the account The excess of the debits of an asset account over its credits. (53)

balance sheet A list of the assets, liabilities, and stockholders' equity as of a specific date, usually at the close of the last day of a month or a year. (15)

balanced scorecard A performance evaluation approach that incorporates multiple performance dimensions by combining financial and nonfinancial measures. (1088)

bank reconciliation The analysis that details the items responsible for the difference between the cash balance reported in the bank statement and the balance of the cash account in the ledger. (331)

bank statement A summary of all transactions mailed to the depositor or made available online by the bank each month. (328)

bond A form of an interest-bearing note used by corporations to borrow on a long-term basis. (542)

bond indenture The contract between a corporation issuing bonds and the bondholders. (544)

book value The cost of a fixed asset minus accumulated depreciation on the asset. (415)

book value of the asset (net book value) The difference between the cost of a fixed asset and its accumulated depreciation. (118)

boot The amount a buyer owes a seller when a fixed asset is traded in on a similar asset. (428)

break-even point The level of business operations at which revenues and expenses are equal. (892)

budget An accounting device used to plan and control resources of operational departments and divisions. (982)

budget performance report A report that summarizes actual costs, standard costs, and the differences for the units produced. (1033)

budgetary slack Excess resources set within a budget to provide for uncertain events. (984)

budgeted variable factory overhead The standard variable overhead for the actual units produced. (1042)

business An organization in which basic resources (inputs), such as materials and labor, are assembled and processed to provide goods or services (outputs) to customers. (2)

business combination A business making an investment in another business by acquiring a controlling share, greater than 50%, of the outstanding voting stock of another corporation by paying cash or exchanging stock. (592)

business entity concept A concept of accounting that limits the economic data in the accounting system to data related directly to the activities of the business. (7)

business transaction An economic event or condition that directly changes an entity's financial condition or its results of operations. (9)

C

capital expenditures The costs of acquiring fixed assets, adding to a fixed asset, improving a fixed asset, or extending a fixed asset's useful life. (409)

capital expenditures budget The budget summarizing future plans for acquiring fixed assets such as plant facilities and equipment. (1001)

capital investment analysis (capital budgeting) The process by which management plans, evaluates, and controls long-term capital investments involving property, plant, and equipment. (1162)

capital lease A lease that includes one or more provisions that result in treating the leased asset as a purchased asset in the accounts. (410)

capital rationing The decision process by which management allocates funds among competing capital investment proposals. (1177)

capital stock The portion of a corporation's stockholders' equity contributed by investors (owners) in exchange for shares of stock. (10)

carrying amount The balance of the bonds payable account (face amount of the bonds) less any unamortized discount or plus any unamortized premium. (551)

cash Coins, currency (paper money), checks, money orders, and money on deposit that is available for unrestricted withdrawal from banks and other financial institutions. (325)

cash basis of accounting Under this basis of accounting, revenues and expenses are reported on the income statement in the period in which cash is received or paid. (104)

cash budget A budget of estimated cash receipts and payments for a period of time. (998)

cash dividend A cash distribution of earnings by a corporation to its shareholders. (505)

cash equivalents Highly liquid investments that are usually reported with cash on the balance sheet. (336)

cash flow per share Normally computed as cash flow from operations per share. (645)

cash flows from financing activities The section of the statement of cash flows that reports cash flows from transactions affecting the equity and debt of the business. (643)

cash flows from investing activities The section of the statement of cash flows that reports cash flows from transactions affecting investments in noncurrent assets. (642)

cash flows from operating activities The section of the statement of cash flows that reports the cash transactions affecting the determination of net income. (642)

cash payback period The expected period of time that will elapse between the date of an investment and the complete recovery in cash of the amount invested. (1164)

cash short and over account An account which has recorded errors in cash sales or errors in making change causing the amount of actual cash on hand to differ from the beginning amount of cash plus the cash sales for the day. (326)

Certified Public Accountant (CPA) Public accountants who have met a state's education, experience, and examination requirements. (6)

chart of accounts A list of the accounts in the ledger. (54)

clearing account Another name for the income summary account because it has the effect of clearing the revenue and expense accounts of their balances. (157)

closing entries The entries that transfer the temporary account balances of the revenue, expense, and drawing accounts to permanent accounts at the end of the accounting period. (157)

closing process The transfer process of converting temporary account balances to zero by transferring the revenue and expense account balances to Income Summary, transferring the income summary account balance to the retained earnings account, and transferring the dividends account to the retained earnings account. (157)

closing the books The process of transferring temporary accounts balances to permanent accounts at the end of the accounting period. (157)

common stock The stock outstanding when a corporation has issued only one class of stock; each share of common stock has equal rights. (501)

common-sized statement A financial statement in which all items are expressed only in relative terms as percentages, without dollar amounts shown. (702)

compensating balance A requirement by some banks requiring depositors to maintain minimum cash balances in their bank accounts. (337)

comprehensive income All changes in stockholders' equity during a period, except those resulting from dividends and stockholders' investments. (602)

consigned inventory Merchandise that is shipped by manufacturers to retailers who act as the manufacturer's selling agent. (286)

consignee The name for the retailer in a consigned inventory arrangement. (286)

consignor The name for the manufacturer in a consigned inventory arrangement. (286)

consolidated financial statements Financial statements resulting from combining parent and subsidiary statements. (592)

contingent liabilities Liabilities that may arise from past transactions if certain events occur in the future. (467)

continuous budgeting A method of budgeting that maintains a 12-month projection into the future. (984)

continuous process improvement A management approach that is part of the overall total quality management philosophy. The approach requires all employees to constantly improve processes of which they are a part or for which they have managerial responsibility. (757)

contra accounts (contra asset accounts) An account offset against another account. (117)

contract rate (coupon rate) The periodic interest to be paid on the bond that is identified in the bond indenture; expressed as a percentage of the face amount of the bond. (545)

contribution margin Sales less variable costs and variable selling and administrative expenses. (890, 935)

contribution margin analysis The systematic examination of the differences between planned and actual contribution margins. (949)

contribution margin ratio The percentage of each sales dollar that is available to cover the fixed costs and to provide income from operations. (890)

control environment The overall attitude of management and employees about the importance of controls. (321)

controllable costs Costs that can be influenced (increased or decreased) by management at that level of management. (944)

controllable expenses Costs that can be influenced (controlled) by the decisions of profit center managers. (1080)

controllable revenues Revenues earned by the profit center. (1080)

controllable variance The difference between the actual variable factory overhead cost and the budgeted variable factory overhead for actual production. (1042)

controller The chief management accountant of a division or other segment of a business. (756)

controlling A phase in the management process that consists of monitoring the operating results of implemented plans and comparing the actual results with the expected results. (757)

controlling account The account in the general ledger that summarizes the balances of the accounts in a subsidiary ledger. (214)

conversion costs The combination of direct labor and factory overhead costs. (762, 1254)

copyright An exclusive right to publish and sell a literary, artistic, or musical composition. (423)

corporation A business organized under state or federal statutes as a separate legal taxable entity. (7)

correcting journal entry An entry that is prepared when an error has already been journalized and posted. (72)

cost A payment of cash (or a commitment to pay cash in the future) for the purpose of generating revenues. (759)

cost accounting systems Systems that measure, record, and report product costs. (792)

cost allocation The process of assigning indirect cost to a cost object, such as a job. (798)

cost behavior The manner in which a cost changes in relation to its activity base (driver). (884)

cost center A decentralized unit in which the department or division manager has responsibility for the control of costs incurred and the authority to make decisions that affect these costs. (1078)

cost concept A concept of accounting that records the amounts initially in the accounting records at their cost or purchase price. (8)

cost method A method of accounting for equity investments representing less than 20% of the outstanding shares of the investee. The purchase is at original cost, and any gains or losses upon sale are recognized by the difference between the sale proceeds and the original cost. (589)

cost object The object or segment of operations to which costs are related for management's use, such as a product or department. (759)

cost of finished goods available The beginning finished goods inventory added to the cost of goods manufactured during the period. (766)

cost of goods manufactured The total cost of making products that are available for sale during the period. (766)

cost of goods sold The cost of finished goods available for sale minus the ending finished goods inventory. (766)

cost of goods sold budget A budget of the estimated direct materials, direct labor, and factory overhead consumed by sold products. (995)

cost of merchandise sold The cost that is reported as an expense when merchandise is sold; determined by subtracting the ending merchandise inventory from the cost of merchandise available for sale. (212, 765)

cost of production report A report prepared periodically by a processing department, summarizing (1) the units for which the department is accountable and the disposition of those units and (2) the costs incurred by the department and the allocation of those costs between completed (transferred out) and partially completed units. (838)

cost of quality report A report summarizing the costs, percent of total, and percent of sales by appraisal, prevention, internal failure, and external failure cost of quality categories. (1259)

cost per equivalent unit The rate used to allocate costs between completed and partially completed production. (845)

cost price approach An approach to transfer pricing that uses cost as the basis for setting the transfer price. (1093)

cost variance The difference between actual cost and standard cost. (1033)

costs of quality The cost associated with controlling quality (prevention and appraisal) and failing to control quality (internal and external failure). (1257)

cost-volume-profit analysis The systematic examination of the relationships among selling prices, volume of sales and production, costs, expenses, and profits. (890)

cost-volume-profit chart A chart used to assist management in understanding the relationships among sales, costs, and operating profit or loss; sometimes called a break-even chart. (897)

credit Amount entered on the right side of an account. (53)

credit memorandum (credit memo) A form used by a seller to inform the buyer of the amount the seller authorizes to credit to the buyer's account receivable. (221)

credit period The amount of time the buyer is allowed in which to pay the seller. (215)

credit terms Terms for payment on account by the buyer to the seller. (215)

cumulative preferred stock Stock that has a right to receive regular dividends that were not declared (paid) in prior years. (501)

currency exchange rate The rate at which currency in another country can be exchanged for local currency. (1176)

current assets Cash and other assets that are expected to be converted to cash or sold or used up usually within one year or less, through the normal operations of the business. (155)

current liabilities Liabilities that will be due within a short time (usually one year or less) and that are to be paid out of current assets. (155)

current position analysis A company's ability to pay its current liabilities. (469, 704)

current ratio A financial ratio that is computed by dividing current assets by current liabilities. (175, 704)

currently attainable standards Standards that represent levels of operation that can be attained with reasonable effort; sometimes called normal standards. (1031)

D

debit Amount entered on the left side of an account. (53)

debit memorandum (debit memo) A form used by a buyer to inform the seller of the amount the buyer proposes to debit to the account payable due the seller. (217)

debt securities Notes and bond investments that provide interest revenue over a fixed maturity. (585)

decision making A component inherent in the other management processes of planning, directing, controlling, and improving. (757)

defined benefit plan A pension plan that promises employees a fixed annual pension benefit at retirement, normally based on years of service, age, and past compensation levels. (465)

defined contribution plan A pension plan that requires a fixed amount of money to be invested on the employee's behalf during the employee's working years. (465)

depletion The process of transferring the cost of natural resources to an expense account. (421)

depreciate To lose usefulness as all fixed assets except land do. (117)

depreciation The systematic periodic transfer of the cost of a fixed asset to an expense account during its expected useful life. (117, 411)

depreciation expense The portion of the cost of a fixed asset that is recorded as an expense each year of its useful life. (117)

differential analysis The area of accounting concerned with the effect of alternative courses of action on revenues and costs. (1118)

differential cost The amount of increase or decrease in cost expected from a particular course of action compared with an alternative. (1119)

differential income (loss) The difference between the differential revenue and the differential costs. (1119)

differential revenue The amount of increase or decrease in revenue expected from a particular course of action as compared with an alternative. (1119)

direct costs Costs that can be traced directly to a cost object. (759)

direct labor cost The wages of factory workers who are directly involved in converting materials into a finished product. (761)

direct labor cost budget Budget that estimates direct labor hours and related costs needed to support budgeted production. (993)

direct labor rate variance The cost associated with the difference between the standard rate and the actual rate paid for direct labor used in producing a commodity. (1038)

direct labor time variance The cost associated with the difference between the standard hours and the actual hours of direct labor spent producing a commodity. (1039)

direct materials cost The cost of materials that are an integral part of the finished product. (760)

direct materials price variance The cost associated with the difference between the standard price and the actual price of direct materials used in producing a commodity. (1036)

direct materials purchases budget A budget that estimates the quantities of direct materials to be purchased to support budgeted production and desired inventory levels. (992)

direct materials quantity variance The cost associated with the difference between the standard quantity and the actual quantity of direct materials used in producing a commodity. (1036)

direct method A method of reporting the cash flows from operating activities as the difference between the operating cash receipts and the operating cash payments. (643)

direct write-off method The method of accounting for uncollectible receivables that recognizes the expense only when an account is determined to be worthless. (363)

directing The process by which managers, given their assigned level of responsibilities, run day-to-day operations. (757)

discount The interest deducted from the maturity value of a note or the excess of the face amount of bonds over their selling price. (502, 545)

dishonored note receivable A note that the maker fails to pay on the due date. (375)

dividend yield A ratio, computed by dividing the dividends per share of common stock by the market price per share of common stock, that indicates the rate of return to stockholders in terms of cash dividend distributions. (601, 717)

dividends Distributions of a corporation's earnings to stockholders. (13, 54, 584)

dividends per share Measures the extent to which earnings are being distributed to common shareholders. (716)

double-declining-balance method A method of depreciation that provides periodic depreciation expense based on the declining book value of a fixed asset over its estimated life. (415)

double-entry accounting system A system based on the accounting equation that requires every business transaction to be recorded in at least two accounts, and total debits to be equal to total credits. (55)

DuPont formula An expanded expression of return on investment determined by multiplying the profit margin by the investment turnover. (1084)

E

earnings The amount by which revenues exceed expenses. (15)

earnings per common share (EPS) Net income per share of common stock outstanding during a period. (516, 543)

earnings per share (EPS) on common stock The profitability ratio of net income available to common shareholders to the number of common shares outstanding. (626, 715)

effective interest rate method The method of amortizing discounts and premiums that provides for a constant rate of interest on the carrying amount of the bonds at the beginning of each period; often called simply the "interest method." (548)

effective rate of interest The market rate of interest at the time bonds are issued. (545)

electronic data interchange (EDI) An information technology that allows different business organizations to use computers to communicate orders, relay information, and make or receive payments. (1253)

electronic funds transfer (EFT) A system in which computers rather than paper (money, checks, etc.) are used to effect cash transactions. (327)

elements of internal control The control environment, risk assessment, control activities, information and communication, and monitoring. (320)

employee fraud The intentional act of deceiving an employer for personal gain. (320)

employee involvement A philosophy that grants employees the responsibility and authority to make their own decisions about their operations. (1252)

employee's earnings record A detailed record of each employee's earnings. (460)

engineering change order (ECO) The document that initiates changing a product or process. (1208)

enterprise resource planning (ERP) An integrated business and information system used by companies to plan and control both internal and supply chain operations. (1253)

equity method A method of accounting for an investment in common stock by which the investment account is adjusted for the investor's share of periodic net income and cash dividends of the investee; method used for investments of between 20% and 50% of the investee's outstanding stock. (590)

equity securities The common and preferred stock that represent ownership in a company and do not have a fixed maturity date. (585)

equivalent units of production The portion of whole units that are complete with respect to materials or conversion (direct labor and factory overhead) costs. (841)

ethics Moral principles that guide the conduct of individuals. (4)

expenses Assets used up or services consumed in the process of generating revenues. (12, 55)

external failure costs The costs incurred after defective units or services have been delivered to consumers. (1257)

extraordinary item An event or a transaction that is both (1) unusual in nature and (2) infrequent in occurrence. (721)

F

face amount An amount at which bonds sell if the market rate equals the contract rate. (545)

factory burden Another term for manufacturing overhead or factory overhead. (761)

factory overhead cost All of the costs of producing a product except for direct materials and direct labor. (761)

factory overhead cost budget Budget that estimates the cost for each item of factory overhead needed to support budgeted production. (995)

factory overhead cost variance report Reports budgeted and actual costs for variable and fixed factory overhead along with the related controllable and volume variances. (1045)

fair value The price that would be received for selling an asset or paying off a liability, often the market price for an equity or debt security. (593)

favorable cost variance A variance that occurs when the actual cost is less than standard cost. (1033)

feedback Measures provided to operational employees or managers on the performance of subunits of the organization. These measures are used by employees to adjust a process or a behavior to achieve goals. See management by exception. (757)

fees earned Revenue from providing services. (11)

FICA tax Federal Insurance Contributions Act tax used to finance federal programs for retiree, survivor, and disability benefits (social security) and health insurance for senior citizens (Medicare). (456)

financial accounting The branch of accounting that is concerned with recording transactions using generally accepted accounting principles (GAAP) for a business or other economic unit and with a periodic preparation of various statements from such records. (4, 755)

Financial Accounting Standards Board (FASB) The authoritative body that has the primary responsibility for developing accounting principles. (6)

financial statements Financial reports that summarize the effects of events on a business. (14)

finished goods inventory The direct materials costs, direct labor costs, and factory overhead costs of finished products that have not been sold. (764)

finished goods ledger The subsidiary ledger that contains the individual accounts for each kind of commodity or product produced. (803)

first-in, first-out (FIFO) method The method of inventory costing based on the assumption that the costs of merchandise sold should be charged against revenue in the order in which the costs were incurred. (272, 840)

fiscal year The annual accounting period adopted by a business. (173)

fixed asset turnover ratio The number of dollars of sales that are generated from each dollar of average fixed assets during the year, computed by dividing the net sales by the average net fixed assets. (426)

fixed assets (plant assets) Long-term or relatively permanent tangible assets such as equipment, machinery, buildings, and land that are used in the normal business operations and that depreciate over time (with the exception of land). (117, 155, 406)

fixed costs Costs that tend to remain the same in amount, regardless of variations in the level of activity. (886)

flexible budget A budget that shows expected results of a responsibility center for several activity levels. (986)

FOB (free on board) destination Freight terms in which the seller pays the freight costs from the shipping point to the buyer's final destination. (223)

FOB (free on board) shipping point Freight terms in which the buyer pays the freight costs from the shipping point to the final destination. (222)

free cash flow The amount of operating cash flow remaining after purchasing the plant, property, and equipment (PP&E) necessary to maintain current productive capacity. (661)

fringe benefits Benefits provided to employees in addition to wages and salaries. (464)

G

general ledger The primary ledger, when used in conjunction with subsidiary ledgers, that contains all of the balance sheet and income statement accounts. (214)

general-purpose financial statements A type of financial accounting report that is distributed to external users. The term "general-purpose" refers to the wide range of decision-making needs that these reports are designed to serve. (4)

generally accepted accounting principles (GAAP) Generally accepted guidelines for the preparation of financial statements. (6)

goal conflict A condition that occurs when individual objectives conflict with organizational objectives. (984)

goodwill An intangible asset that is created from such favorable factors as location, product quality, reputation, and managerial skill. (423)

gross pay The total earnings of an employee for a payroll period. (454)

gross profit Sales minus the cost of merchandise sold. (212)

gross profit method A method of estimating inventory cost that is based on the relationship of gross profit to sales. (292)

H

held-to-maturity securities Investments in bonds or other debt securities that a company intends to hold until their maturity date. (597)

high-low method A technique that uses the highest and lowest total costs as a basis for estimating the variable cost per unit and the fixed cost component of a mixed cost. (887)

horizontal analysis Financial analysis that compares an item in a current statement with the same item in prior statements. (73, 698)

I

ideal standards Standards that can be achieved only under perfect operating conditions, such as no idle time, no machine breakdowns, and no materials spoilage; also called theoretical standards. (1031)

in arrears Cumulative preferred stock dividends that have not been paid in prior years are said to be in arrears. (501)

income from operations (operating income) Gross profit less operating expenses, which are normally classified as either selling or administrative expenses. (229)

income statement A summary of the revenue and expenses for a specific period of time, such as a month or a year. (15)

Income Summary A temporary account (only used during the closing process) to which the revenue and expense account balances are transferred at the end of a period. (157)

indirect costs Costs that cannot be traced directly to a cost object. (759)

indirect method A method of reporting the cash flows from operating activities as the net income from operations adjusted for all deferrals of past cash receipts and payments and all accruals of expected future cash receipts and payments. (644)

inflation A period when prices in general are rising and the purchasing power of money is declining. (1176)

installment note A debt that requires the borrower to make equal periodic payments to the lender for the term of the note. (552)

intangible assets Long-term assets that are useful in the operations of a business, are not held for sale, and are without physical qualities. (422)

interest revenue Money received for interest. (11)

internal controls The policies and procedures used to safeguard assets, ensure accurate business information, and ensure compliance with laws and regulations. (318, 360)

internal failure costs The costs associated with defects that are discovered by the organization before the product or service is delivered to the consumer. (1257)

internal rate of return (IRR) method A method of analysis of proposed capital investments that uses present value concepts to compute the rate of return from the net cash flows expected from the investment. (1170)

International Accounting Standards Board (IASB) An organization that issues *International Financial Reporting Standards* for many countries outside the United States. (7)

inventory analysis A company's ability to manage its inventory effectively. (707)

inventory shrinkage (inventory shortage) The amount by which the merchandise for sale, as indicated by the balance of the merchandise inventory account, is larger than the total amount of merchandise counted during the physical inventory. (232)

inventory subsidiary ledger A ledger containing individual accounts with a common characteristic. (5)

inventory turnover The relationship between the cost of goods sold and the amount of inventory carried during the period, computed by dividing the cost of goods sold by the average inventory. (288, 708)

investee The company whose stock is purchased by the investor. (588)

investment center A decentralized unit in which the manager has the responsibility and authority to make decisions that affect not only costs and revenues but also the fixed assets invested in the center. (1083)

investment turnover A component of the rate of return on investment, computed as the ratio of sales to invested assets. (1084)

investments The balance sheet caption used to report temporary investments in debt and equity securities; their primary objective is to earn interest revenue, receive dividends, and realize gains from market price increases. (585)

investor The company investing in another company's stock. (588)

invoice The bill that the seller sends to the buyer. (215, 257)

J

job cost sheet An account in the work in process subsidiary ledger in which the costs charged to a particular job order are recorded. (795)

job order cost system A type of cost accounting system that provides product costs for each quantity of product that is manufactured. (792)

journal The initial record in which the effects of transactions are recorded. (57)

journal entry The form of recording a transaction in the journal. (58)

journalizing The process of recording a transaction in the journal. (58)

just-in-time (JIT) processing A processing approach that focuses on eliminating time, cost, and poor quality within manufacturing and nonmanufacturing processes. (854, 1246)

L

last-in, first-out (LIFO) inventory cost flow method A method of inventory costing based on the assumption that the most recent merchandise inventory costs should be charged against revenue. (272)

lead time The elapsed time between starting a unit of product into the beginning of a process and its completion. (1247)

ledger A group of accounts for a business. (54)

leverage Using debt to increase the return on an investment. (713)

liabilities The rights of creditors that represent debts of the business. (8, 54)

limited liability company (LLC) A business form consisting of one or more persons or entities filing an operating agreement with a state to conduct business with limited liability to the owners, yet treated as a partnership for tax purposes. (7, 540)

line department A unit that is directly involved in providing goods or services to the customers of the company. (756)

liquidity The ability to convert assets into cash. (174, 703)

long-term liabilities Liabilities that usually will not be due for more than one year. (155)

lower-of-cost-or-market (LCM) method A method of valuing inventory that reports the inventory at the lower of its cost or current market value (replacement cost). (283)

M

management (managerial) accounting The branch of accounting that uses both historical and estimated data in providing information that management uses in conducting daily operations, in planning future operations, and in developing overall business strategies. (3, 755)

management by exception The philosophy of managing which involves monitoring the operating results of implemented plans and comparing the expected results with the actual results. This feedback allows management to isolate significant variations for further investigation and possible remedial action. (757)

management process The five basic management functions of (1) planning, (2) directing, (3) controlling, (4) improving, and (5) decision making. (756)

Management's Discussion and Analysis (MD&A) An annual report disclosure that provides management's analysis of current operations and its plans for the future. (719)

manufacturing business A type of business that changes basic inputs into products that are sold to customers. (3)

manufacturing cells A grouping of processes (work centers) where employees are cross-trained to perform more than one function. (855)

manufacturing margin The variable cost of goods sold deducted from sales. (935)

manufacturing overhead Costs, other than direct materials and direct labor costs, that are incurred in the manufacturing process. (761)

margin of safety Indicates the possible decrease in sales that may occur before an operating loss results. (905)

market price approach An approach to transfer pricing that uses the price at which the product or service transferred could be sold to outside buyers. (1090)

market rate of interest The rate determined from sales and purchases of similar bonds. (545)

market segment A portion of business that can be assigned to a manager for profit responsibility. (944)

master budget The comprehensive budget plan linking all the individual budgets related to sales, cost of goods sold, operating expenses, projects, capital expenditures, and cash. (989)

matching concept (matching principle) A concept of accounting in which expenses are matched with the revenue generated during a period by those expenses. (15, 104)

materials inventory The cost of materials that have not yet entered into the manufacturing process. (764)

materials ledger The subsidiary ledger containing the individual accounts for each type of material. (793)

materials requisition The form or electronic transmission used by a manufacturing department to authorize materials issuances from the storeroom. (795)

maturity value The amount that is due at the maturity or due date of a note. (374)

merchandise available for sale The cost of merchandise available for sale to customers calculated by adding the beginning merchandise inventory to net purchases. (765)

merchandise inventory Merchandise on hand (not sold) at the end of an accounting period. (212)

merchandising business A type of business that purchases products from other businesses and sells them to customers. (3)

mixed costs Costs with both variable and fixed characteristics; sometimes called semivariable or semifixed costs. (887)

mortgage notes An installment note secured by a pledge of the borrower's assets. (552)

multiple production department factory overhead rate method A method that allocated factory overhead to product by using factory overhead rates for each production department. (1203)

multiple-step income statement A form of income statement that contains several sections, subsections, and subtotals. (229)

N

natural business year A fiscal year that ends when business activities have reached the lowest point in an annual operating cycle. (174)

negotiated price approach An approach to transfer pricing that allows managers of decentralized units to agree (negotiate) among themselves on a transfer price. (1091)

net income or net profit The amount by which revenues exceed expenses. (15)

net loss The amount by which expenses exceed revenues. (15)

net pay Gross pay less payroll deductions; the amount the employer is obligated to pay the employee. (454)

net present value method A method of analysis that compares the amount to be invested with the present value of the net cash in flows expected from the investments; sometimes called the discounted cash flow method. (1168)

net realizable value The estimated selling price of an item of inventory less any direct costs of disposal, such as sales commissions. (284, 365)

net sales Revenue received for merchandise sold to customers less any sales returns and allowances and sales discounts. (229)

noncontrollable costs Costs that cannot be influenced (increased, decreased, or eliminated) by someone such as a manager or factory worker. (944)

nonfinancial performance measure A performance measure expressed in a measure other than dollars. (1050, 1256)

non-value-added activity The cost of activities that are perceived as unnecessary from the customer's perspective and are thus candidates for elimination. (1260)

non-value-added lead time The time that units wait in inventories, move unnecessarily, and wait during machine breakdowns. (1247)

normal balance of an account Either a debit or a credit balance depending on whether increases in the account are recorded as debits or credits. (56)

notes receivable A customer's written promise to pay an amount and possibly interest at an agreed-upon rate. (155, 362)

number of days' sales in inventory Measures the length of time it takes to acquire, sell, and replace inventory, computed by dividing the average inventory by the average daily cost of goods sold. (289, 708)

number of days' sales in receivables An estimate of the length of time the accounts receivable have been outstanding, computed by dividing the average accounts receivable by the average daily sales. (377, 707)

number of times interest charges are earned A ratio that measures creditor margin of safety for interest payments, calculated as income before interest and taxes divided by interest expense. (555, 710)

O

objectives (goals) Developed in the planning stage, these reflect the direction and desired outcomes of certain courses of action. (757)

objectivity concept A concept of accounting that requires the amounts recorded in the accounting records to be based on objective evidence. (8)

operating lease A lease that does not meet the criteria for capital leases and thus is accounted for as an operating expense. (411)

operating leverage A measure of the relative mix of a business's variable costs and fixed costs, computed as contribution margin divided by operating income. (903)

operational planning The development of short-term actions for managing the day-to-day operations of the company. (757)

opportunity cost The amount of revenue that is forgone from an alternative use of an asset, such as cash. (1126)

other comprehensive income Specified items that are reported separately from net income, including foreign currency items, pension liability adjustments, and unrealized gains and losses on investments. (602)

other expense An expense that cannot be traced directly to the normal operations of the business. (230)

other income Revenue from sources other than the primary operating activity of a business. (230)

outstanding stock The stock in the hands of stockholders. (500)

overapplied factory overhead The amount of factory overhead applied in excess of the actual factory overhead costs incurred for production during a period; this credit balance also is called overabsorbed factory overhead. (800)

owner's equity The owner's right to the assets of the business for a proprietorship, partnership, or limited liability company. (9, 54)

P

par The monetary amount printed on a stock certificate. (500)

parent company The corporation owning all or a majority of the voting stock of the other corporation. (592)

Pareto chart A bar chart that shows the totals of a particular attribute for a number of categories, ranked left to right from the largest to smallest totals. (1259)

partnership An unincorporated business form consisting of two or more persons conducting business as co-owners for profit. (7)

patents Exclusive rights to produce and sell goods with one or more unique features. (422)

payroll The total amount paid to employees for a certain period. (453)

payroll register A multicolumn report used to assemble and summarize payroll data at the end of each payroll period. (458)

pension A cash payment to retired employees. (465)

period costs Those costs that are used up in generating revenue during the current period and that are not involved in manufacturing a product, such as selling, general, and administrative expenses. (762)

periodic inventory system The inventory system in which the inventory records do not show the amount available for sale or sold during the period. (214)

perpetual inventory system The inventory system in which each purchase and sale of merchandise is recorded in an inventory account. (214)

petty cash fund A special cash fund to pay relatively small amounts. (335)

physical inventory A detailed listing of merchandise on hand. (214, 271)

planning A phase of the management process whereby objectives are outlined and courses of action are determined. (757)

posting The process of transferring the debits and credits from the journal entries to the accounts. (61)

predetermined factory overhead rate The rate used to apply factory overhead costs to the goods manufactured. The rate is determined by dividing the estimated total factory overhead costs by the estimated activity base at the beginning of the fiscal period. (798)

preferred stock A class of stock with preferential rights over common stock. (501)

premium The excess of the issue price of a stock over its par value or the excess of the issue price of bonds over their face amount. (502, 545)

prepaid expenses Items such as supplies that will be used in the business in the future. (11, 105)

present value concept Cash to be received (or paid) in the future is not the equivalent of the same amount of money received at an earlier date. (1166)

present value index An index computed by dividing the total present value of the net cash flow to be received from a proposed capital investment by the amount to be invested. (1169)

present value of an annuity The sum of the present values of each cash flow; the amount of cash needed today to yield a series of equal net cash flows at fixed time intervals in the future. (1167)

prevention costs Costs incurred to prevent defects from occurring during the design and delivery of products or services. (1257)

price-earnings (P/E) ratio The ratio of the market price per share of common stock, at a specific date, to the annual earnings per share. (716)

prime costs The combination of direct materials and direct labor costs. (762)

prior period adjustments Corrections of material errors related to a prior period or periods, excluded from the determination of net income. (513)

private accounting The field of accounting whereby accountants are employed by a business firm or a not-for-profit organization. (4)

process A sequence of activities linked together by inputs and outputs to perform a particular task. (1050, 1261)

process-oriented layout Organizing work in a plant or administrative function around processes (tasks). (1251)

process cost system A type of cost accounting system that provides product costs for each manufacturing department or process. (792, 834)

process manufacturer A manufacturer that produces products that are indistinguishable from each other using a continuous production process (such as oil refineries, paper producers, and chemical/food processors). (834)

product cost concept A concept used in applying the cost-plus approach to product pricing in which only the costs of manufacturing the product, termed the product cost, are included in the cost amount to which the markup is added. (1130)

product costing Determining the cost of a product. (1200)

product costs The three components of manufacturing cost: direct materials, direct labor, and factory overhead costs. (762)

production bottleneck (constraint) A condition that occurs when product demand exceeds production capacity. (1133)

production budget A budget of estimated unit production to meet budgeted sales and desired inventory levels. (991)

production department factory overhead rates Rates determined by dividing the budgeted production department factory overhead by the budgeted allocation base for each department. (1204)

product-oriented layout Organizing work in a plant or administrative function around products; sometimes referred to as product cells. (1251)

profit The difference between the amounts received from customers for goods or services provided and the amounts paid for the inputs used to provide the goods or services. (2)

profit center A decentralized unit in which the manager has the responsibility and the authority to make decisions that affect both costs and revenues (and thus profits). (1080)

profit margin A component of the rate of return on investment, computed as the ratio of income from operations to sales. (1084)

profit-volume chart A chart that plots only the difference between total sales and total costs (or profits), used to assist management in understanding the relationship between profit and volume. (899)

profitability The ability of a firm to earn income. (703)

proprietorship A business owned by one individual. (7)

public accounting The field of accounting where accountants and their staff provide services on a fee basis. (6)

pull manufacturing A just-in-time method wherein customer orders trigger the release of finished goods, which triggers production, which triggers release of materials from suppliers. (1252)

purchase order The purchase order authorizes the purchase of the inventory from an approved vendor. (270)

purchases discounts Discounts taken by the buyer for early payment of an invoice. (216)

purchases journal The journal in which all items purchased on account are recorded. (214)

purchases returns and allowances From the buyer's perspective, returned merchandise or an adjustment for defective merchandise. (217)

push manufacturing Materials are released into production and work in process is released into finished goods in anticipation of future sales. (1252)

Q

quantity factor The effect of a difference in the number of units sold, assuming no change in unit sales price or unit cost. (949)

quick assets Cash and other current assets that can be quickly converted to cash, such as marketable securities and receivables. (470, 705)

quick ratio A financial ratio that measures the ability to pay current liabilities with quick assets (cash, marketable securities, accounts receivable). (470, 705)

R

radio frequency identification devices (RFID) Electronic tags (chips) placed on or embedded within products that can be read by radio waves that allow instant monitoring or production location. (1253)

rate earned on common stockholders' equity A measure of profitability computed by dividing net income, reduced by preferred dividend requirements, by average common stockholders' equity. (713)

rate earned on stockholders' equity A measure of profitability computed by dividing net income by average total stockholders' equity. (713)

rate earned on total assets A measure of the profitability of assets, without regard to the equity of creditors and stockholders in the assets. (712)

rate of return on investment (ROI) A measure of managerial efficiency in the use of investments in assets, computed as income from operations divided by invested assets. (1116)

ratio of cash to monthly cash expenses Ratio that helps assess how long a company can continue to operate without additional financing or without generating positive cash flows from operations. (337)

ratio of fixed assets to long-term liabilities A leverage ratio that measures the margin of safety of long-term creditors, calculated as the net fixed assets divided by the long-term liabilities. (709)

ratio of liabilities to stockholders' equity A comprehensive leverage ratio that measures the relationship of the claims of creditors to stockholders' equity. (21, 709)

ratio of net sales to assets Ratio that measures how effectively a company uses its assets to generate sales, computed as net sales divided by average total assets. (234, 711)

Raw and In Process (RIP) Inventory The capitalized cost of direct materials purchases, labor, and overhead charged to the production cell. (1254)

real (permanent) accounts Term for balance sheet accounts because they are relatively permanent and are carried forward from year to year. (156)

receivables All money claims against other entities, including people, companies, and other organizations. (362)

receiving report The form or electronic transmission used by the receiving personnel to indicate that materials have been received and inspected. (271, 795)

relevant range The range of activity over which changes in cost are of interest to management. (884)

rent revenue Money received for rent. (11)

report form The form of balance sheet presented in a downward sequence with the liabilities and stockholders' equity sections below the assets section. (231)

residual income The excess of income from operations over a minimum acceptable income from operations. (1087)

residual value The estimated value of a fixed asset at the end of its useful life. (411)

responsibility accounting The process of measuring and reporting operating data by responsibility center. (1077)

responsibility center An organizational unit for which a manager is assigned the authority and responsibility for achieving the center's budgeted goals. (983)

restrictions (appropriations) Amounts of retained earnings that have been limited for use as dividends. (513)

retail inventory method A method of estimating inventory cost that is based on the relationship of cost to retail price. (291)

retained earnings The stockholders' equity created from business operations through revenue and expense transactions; net income retained in a corporation. (13)

retained earnings statement A summary of the changes in the retained earnings in a corporation for a specific period of time, such as a month or a year. (15)

revenue expenditures Costs that benefit only the current period or costs incurred for normal maintenance and repairs of fixed assets. (409)

revenue recognition concept The accounting concept that supports reporting revenues when the services are provided to customers. (104)

revenues Increases in stockholders' equity as a result of selling services or products to customers. (11, 54)

rules of debit and credit In the double-entry accounting system, specific rules for recording debits and credits based on the type of account. (55)

S

sales The total amount charged customers for merchandise sold, including cash sales and sales on account. (11, 212)

sales budget One of the major elements of the income statement budget that indicates the quantity of estimated sales and the expected unit selling price. (990)

sales discounts From the seller's perspective, discounts that a seller may offer the buyer for early payment. (220)

sales mix The relative distribution of sales among the various products sold by a company; sometimes referred to as product mix. (902, 946)

sales returns and allowances From the seller's perspective, returned merchandise or an adjustment for defective or damaged merchandise. (220)

Sarbanes-Oxley Act of 2002 An act passed by Congress to restore public confidence and trust in the financial statements of companies. (318)

Securities and Exchange Commission (SEC) An agency of the U.S. government that has authority over the accounting and financial disclosures for companies whose shares of ownership (stock) are traded and sold to the public. (6)

selling expenses Expenses that are incurred directly in the selling of merchandise. (230)

service business A business providing services rather than products to customers. (2)

service department charges The costs of services provided by an internal service department and allocated to profit centers based on the usage of the service by each profit center. (1080)

setup An overhead activity that consists of changing tooling in machines in preparation for making a new product. (1208)

single-step income statement A form of income statement in which the total of all expenses is deducted in one step from the total of all revenues. (230)

single plantwide factory overhead rate method A method that allocates all factory overhead to products by using a single factory overhead rate. (1201)

six sigma A quality improvement process developed by Motorola Corporation consisting of five steps: define, measure, analyze, improve, and control (DMAIC). (1252)

slide An error in which the entire number is moved one or more spaces to the right or the left, such as writing $542.00 as $54.20 or $5,420.00. (71)

solvency The ability of a firm to pay its debts as they come due. (174, 703)

special journals Journals designed to be used for recording similar types of transactions. (214)

special-purpose funds Cash funds used for a special business need. (336)

specific identification inventory cost flow method Inventory method in which the unit sold is identified with a specific purchase. (272)

staff department A unit that provides services, assistance, and advice to the departments with line or other staff responsibilities. (756)

standard cost A detailed estimate of what a product should cost. (1030)

standard cost systems Accounting systems that use standards for each element of manufacturing cost entering into the finished product. (1030)

standards Performance goals, often relating to how much a product should cost. (1030)

statement of cash flows A summary of the cash receipts and cash payments for a specific period of time, such as a month or a year. (15, 642)

statement of cost of goods manufactured The statement that summarizes the cost of goods manufactured during the period. (766)

statement of stockholders' equity A summary of the changes in the stockholders' equity in a corporation that have occurred during a specific period of time, prepared when a corporation has changes in stock and paid-in capital accounts. (513)

static budget A budget that shows the expected results of a responsibility center for only one activity level. (985)

stock Shares of ownership of a corporation. (498)

stock dividend A distribution of shares of stock to its stockholders. (507)

stock split A reduction in the par or stated value of a common stock and the issuance of a proportionate number of additional shares. (515)

stockholders The owners of a corporation; shareholders who own the stock. (498)

stockholders' equity The stockholders' right to the assets of the business, represented by the balance of the capital stock and retained earnings accounts. (9, 54)

straight-line method A method of depreciation that provides for equal periodic depreciation expense over the estimated life of a fixed asset. (413)

strategic planning The development of a long-range course of action to achieve business goals. (757)

strategies The means by which business goals and objectives will be achieved. (757)

subsidiary company The corporation that is controlled by a parent company. (592)

subsidiary inventory ledger The subsidiary ledger containing individual accounts for items of inventory. (271)

subsidiary ledger A ledger containing individual accounts with a common characteristic. (214)

sunk cost A cost that has been incurred in the past, cannot be recouped, and is not affected by subsequent decisions. (1121)

supply chain management The coordination and control of materials, services, information, and finances as they move in a process from supplier, through the manufacturer, wholesaler, and retailer to the consumer. (1253)

T

T account The simplest form of an account. (52)

target costing A method of setting prices that combines market-based pricing with a cost-reduction emphasis. The target cost is determined by subtracting a desired profit from the expected selling price, determined from demand-based or competition-based concepts. (1133)

temporary (nominal) accounts Accounts that report amounts for only one period. (156)

theory of constraints (TOC) A manufacturing strategy that focuses on reducing the influence of bottlenecks (constraints) on production processes. (1133)

time tickets The form on which the amount of time spent by each employee and the labor cost incurred for each individual job are recorded. (796)

time value of money concept The concept that recognizes a dollar today is worth more than a dollar tomorrow because today's dollar can be invested. (1162)

total cost concept A concept used in applying the cost-plus approach to product pricing in which all the costs of manufacturing the product plus the selling and administrative expenses are included in the cost amount to which the markup is added. (1135)

total manufacturing cost variance The difference between total standard costs and total actual costs for the units produced. (1034)

trade discounts Discounts from the list prices in published catalogs or special discounts offered to certain classes of buyers. (228)

trade-in allowance The amount a seller allows a buyer for a fixed asset that is traded in for a similar asset. (428)

trademark A name, term, or symbol used to identify a business and its products. (423)

trading securities Debt and equity securities that are purchased to earn short-term profits from changes in their market prices. (593)

transfer price The price charged one decentralized unit by another for the goods or services provided. (1089)

transposition An error in which the order of the digits is changed, such as writing $542 as $452 or $524. (71)

treasury stock Stock that a corporation has issued and then reacquired. (509)

trial balance A summary listing of the titles and balances of accounts in the ledger. (70)

U

unadjusted trial balance A summary listing of the titles and balances of accounts in the ledger prior to the posting of adjusting entries. (70)

underapplied factory overhead The amount of actual factory overhead in excess of the factory overhead applied to production during a period; this debit balance also is called underabsorbed factory overhead. (800)

unearned revenue The liability created by receiving revenue in advance. (63, 106)

unfavorable cost variance A variance that occurs when the actual cost exceeds the standard cost. (1033)

unit contribution margin The dollars available from each unit of sales to cover fixed costs and provide operating profits. (891)

unit of measure concept A concept of accounting requiring that economic data be recorded in dollars. (8)

units-of-output method A method of depreciation that provides for depreciation expense based on the expected productive capacity of a fixed asset. (414)

unit price (cost) factor The effect of a difference in unit sales price or unit cost on the number of units sold. (950)

unrealized gain or loss Changes in the fair value of the portfolio (group) of trading securities for a period. (593)

V

value-added activity The cost of activities that are needed to meet customer requirements. (1260)

value-added lead time The time required to manufacture a unit of product or other output. (1247)

value-added ratio The ratio of the value-added lead time to the total lead time. (1248)

B

G

H

I

J

K

L

M

N

O

P

Q

R

S

T

U

V

W

Y

Z

Company Index